PARTYKNIFE

Birds, LLC
Austin, Minneapolis, New York, Raleigh
www.birdsllc.com

Cover art by Matt Bollinger
Interior designed by Michael Newton

Library of Congress Cataloging-in-Publication Data:
Magers, Dan
Partyknife/Dan Magers
Library of Congress Control Number: 2011938985

First Edition, 2012.
ISBN-13: 9780982617779
Printed in the USA

Side A.

(All poems composed by D. Magers)

Side B.

(All poems composed by D. Magers)

A.

Cecilia's here, smart person among smart people.

She's a pulsing brain.

Smart people just want to talk about how smart Cecilia is.
I'm doing it right now.

I was invited to Richard Tuttle's house,

and I thought I'd go there and see a piece of paper on the floor,
and they'd be like, "Don't touch that,
that's called *The Volition of Myth.*"

I'm Lost in the Jungle of My Soul.

Now My Band Will Fuck You.

Meaning contains a glancing similarity
to what is happening to me.

I love my liberal friends. I am a liberal.

The Marlboro Man in his prime
given free cigarettes, so why not smoke them?

Just keep making your clown music for retards.
Your hard-earned success flowers only jealousy.

Today, I implicated three friends in reveries
of fanciful rage. You're the friend that gets me
seventy-five percent.

We got addicted to snorting 9/11 dust
and listened to the feel good hits of Generation X.

The races are really getting together in this PowerPoint presentation.

I'm so lonely I could die.

A hot body and a face that looks like intestines.
Feel it in the thickness! Give me full umlaut.

Their response was unanimous:
Frábær mynd!
Glæsileg mynd, mjög falleg!

You appear as the ache in my body.

Retell it funny. Then remember it as funny,

Violet red, violet wet,

a sharp release, and daylights are forever
granulated, a shade of sun for every day.
Each one is music, entered and forgotten,

and the person you were is a joke to you.

At karaoke, I ruined 'Don't Stop Believing' for everyone.

Someone is having a lot of trouble
in the bathroom—gasps and groans,

and whoever's in there is morphing "Thriller"-style.

Another inelegant night last night. Nice and stoned
back at the lab with Dr. Rob.

His mix tapes suck.
Putting together at random would have more effect.
Mixing tapes at random,
then chunks of songs at random.

I release them under the name Girl Talk.

Looking at my face without mirrors
just blew my mind.

Some serious dudes place amps
in full-circle manner of Stonehenge.

The amps are the band. The dudes are the roadies.

Noise through another
all layered and decayed.

We tried to achieve hypnosis
and one of us levitated.

If you're doing it with that girl right now
then this message means jackshit, but probably
you're not–probably she's like, "Where's the beer?"
and you're like, "I don't got any,"

but we've got the beer right here.

People are bored and look at their holes.
My eyes watch anything. Anything is endless.

Tell everyone your business. Be comforted by examples of great and doomed men.
That's where emotions come from.

ALL THE BANDS ARE ABOUT HOW NEUROTIC WE ARE.

AND NOT HAVING FUN.
WHICH IS WHAT THE EIGHTIES WERE ABOUT.

Without more than ever. We didn't like it.

We're like,
"It didn't sound too good to us,"

we wanted it so bad.

In the falafel place with Tamaki to meet
all her immature friends stacked in
the NYU dorm.

Tamaki introduces me as her brother and then grabs my junk.

I have no idea what these kids are talking about.
Lacan and baby food.

Girls that could fit in the crook of my arm. They take me
to their dorm, and I buy them two backpacks of beer,

and the boys and me play Wisest Wizard.

You drink a can of Natty Ice,
then tape each one you finish to the bottom of the last.

I got to Level Seven with the one called Jonathan.
We face off with Boss Jameson,
and I show him who the wizard is.

I'm the Jesus of making out with girls drunk.

Networking is the gift that giveth back;
Dr. Rob was there and obliterated.

I want forty minutes of hot shimmering.
Walls are humming electricity.

This is the last time I will carry around this knife,
because when am I really going to use it?

Behold their pro-choice purple day music:

Artist Gregory T___. He seems like a nice guy.
Don't really know him that well. He is a crazy dude
who wakes up in the ocean and talks like this.

I want to make love to your praise for me.

Yet oh yet the stars that shine around the earth.

IN THE MANNER LOSERESQUE

The poster looks like the artist had never seen a baby or a woman.

He really knew about hair though.

Private life is constructed,
but some constructed things are nice,
like houses. You build a table to make it easier
to eat off.

Engineering your problems into a monument
so immense and indelible
that modification means blowing up,

making your way through the crowds disappearing
into you.

A pamphlet called "What Kills You Must Be Really Beautiful"
posits an absolute belief in your instincts.

To marry the severity of the world and the lightness of the light.

At the party, she holds high the mandolin
to escape the harm we are doing.

TOTAL SUMMER VIBE

When you said Pratt party, I heard frat party.

The punk kid in the punk house laughs at the paint he wipes on my new shirt,
but I am an insane god.

My intern broke up with her boyfriend for me.
I did not ask for this. When she spoke
I saw your face.

Misheard lyrics of my favorite songs inextricably linked
to my love and that time.

Yeah, I love it the best.

Fetishize the moment into a lifetime.

Subscription probe - please ignore.

There's something about 4am that robs legitimacy of every effort.

Check out that coat! I need me that coat!
That coat just says FUCK YOU WHITE PEOPLE!

Dancing girls dance away from me.

The genius's greater perversity is what I pin my hopes to.
Taking my place among other left-handed men:
Babe Ruth, Lou Gehrig, Richard Nixon, Randy "Macho Man" Savage.
I touch my tie.

Adderall is doing such amazing work in me,
I have little time to figure it out.

Then I realized they were slumming
and were not my friends.

Some kids have paranormal abilities,
and the TV producers bring them all together
to explore the pet afterlife.

ALL TASTES ARE IN NATURE

With Tamaki on the third floor, and her ex-boyfriend below,
and suddenly we are having sex
and can hear the bed creaking above the flames

prepped on the wall, gesso-white,
and her moaning makes the bed break
through the floor,
crushing him in his bed below.

Sometimes I think that I'm doing all this cross training
so I can do more cocaine.

On the treadmill, running-from-the-cops speed,
and I hold it there for two straight minutes.

Cecilia goes outside to smoke.
I go outside to support Cecilia's smoking.
Her nerves are split ends.

Everything that feels good is good.

Everything is plugged in at top volume,
and I'm shaking like a junkie.

Please come get me. I can't mobilize.
Also prepare to rrrrummmbllleee....

Maybe bring a sweater too.

I ejaculate into a sock and give it to Chinese people to wash.

They are my equal. I am their better.

I am an expert in my field, and I receive the perfect pay for my expertise.

I don't care if you earn it. I just want to be with you.
And I don't want the things you have,
I just want your accomplishments.

I want to look at myself in five years
and be gratified.

Now you know the perversity of the situation.

I farted until the television came on.

Frank O'Hara with a Blackberry.

Either he would have loved it
or rejected it, being an anachronism of the '40s.

So we should say that if Frank O'Hara were *born
into our time*, he likely would have loved the Blackberry,
and not just simply *transported from his own time*,
going through all the levels and cycles of death.

Recaps mixed with pornography. I trust
Yahweh with delicate issues.

Yahweh and I are engaged to be married.

Tamaki asks me to talk dirty to her without being degrading,
but I don't know the difference.

The colors of her mouth in white daydream shades
are various views of Midori Mako so fond
of sight.

The playlist is completely random,
but I say to understand me,
you must figure out the sequence.

I stare at the painting
like I give a shit. Following the lead of the master,
he painted the pears with a hue
resembling the color of Paris that fall.

You're just jealous because I'm friends with John Cale,
and he likes to hear about the girls I fuck.

I want men to not only like my lyrics,
but to like me personally.

It is not enough for them to want to buy me a beer.

They must respect me as a guitarist, wish to hear
and respond favorably to my work.

With women, additionally, I would like them
to think I am sexually attractive,
though not necessarily want to date me.

There goes a man with a powerful head of hair.

I don't want it, but I follow that hair intensely.
It is the difference between beholding the Burning Bush
and being CONSUMED by it.

Well, anyway, happy belated birthday.

I wanted to be high, but now I'm trapped in my life,
withdrawing cash from the cash machine,
where the cash is infinite,

like the soul is good and floats above the ether.

What did Tamaki do to me that made me so jealous
of her dancing with other dudes?

Pretty girls surround me at parties,
chatting me up, but they won't go home with me.

They want my essence, not my substance.

I stumbled upstairs to bed,
and I could hear my friends downstairs
talking shit behind my back.

And coming down to confront them,
I peed on the floor and said,
you're going to die up there.

I beat *Halo* with my project management skills.

If stupidity is to lust, then intelligence
is to what?

I wasted the whole month on emotional feelings.

Flip the controller across the body. Flip the controller across the bed.

Ethnic wars proliferated through
Call of Duty. Emote your way
to more immortal levels of the game.

You make having a
girlfriend
sound
like torture.

Elliot is stapling away in the cubicle next to mine.
In lock step does he collate.

Not since I have become an adult
have I sat next to someone for so many consecutive days.

I think he can hear my thoughts.

In the era of panic attacks, I might have given a fuck.

Dr. Rob takes a pull and tells me that Trans Am is like Gary Numan
riding a hell beast, and I tell him that in every era

desire is introduced into popular consciousness first,
and sex is always introduced last,
and in every decade it is revealed a little further.

$0 + 0 = 20$ tonight.
There are some people who work themselves to death.
I just want to die last.

Dr. Rob asks me to visit his open house
to pretend I want to sublet his apartment.

One room is a closet where the Dr. sleeps.
The other room he sublets to rich foreign kids
enrolled in MBA programs.

Look at this water pressure! I'll pay anything! I say.

These are hallways? I'll pay anything!

Tamaki isn't returning my calls right now.

I hoard boundless energy into this exact spot.
I made the mistake of telling Mom about her.

I saved her last voicemail:
I did some stuff with construction paper,
talked to my roommate, and ate some bread.

Love is a prelude to an afterthought.

Forever is a feeling. A god revealed in revenge.

When I fuck her,
it's like I'm fucking everyone who rejected me.

Where twinkling is nothing
and rolling with The Hated Few, Druid,
Polar Sun, Unicorn Power, and The Tibetan Noise Ensemble.

Red on cotton violence.
The point is being ready to die a thousand times.

No one likes a little dude girl.

One small step for man. One giant leap for all his friends.

I pretend that she's eighteen, and I'm her dad,
and it's her birthday, and we are in
the Japanese suicide forest.

Yahweh took away my stutter. And heaven
is fuck-like in its intensity.

I disrobe and piss before I eat. I am free and light.

My fat is warm and surrounds me like a mother.

I see into the deep soul of space around me
and direct my path with glimmers every new hour;
the reward is overwhelming.

My passion is pursued in filling it,
wriggling, as if immersed,
and when the elder dies, we will have electricity.

The dance clubs are burning up their young.

I want to think about what you think
my problems are.

Anal slave love parade
where nothing is personal.

Coors 40,
I bought you at seven-nineteen
and at nine thirty-one you were gone,
but your ghost lives on inside of me,
infusing all my actions
with what you always dreamed for me to accomplish,

which will be directed by Hong Kong Phenom
Whak-Sleep Wake.

Crawling over the luminous veil, trying to cry,
we are almost dead. Then we kept dying.

NO MAKEUP

A city with the population of Morrissey albums sold.

You lowered yourself to my pleasure.

An album is a heartbeat
obliterated in repetition.

The stillness shines against dark hair.

The future is so sophisticated
one wants to Google the features of her face,

and in the future, every woman will find,
eight years ago, your friends were confused

and going through sexual situations,
or shitting on a coke mirror at a party.

Your tattoos suck.

We are a generation of women who won't take no for an answer.

She was too girly sweet.

Do you ever see TV dots?
Well, did you used to do a lot of acid?

They're these green and red and blue-colored lights

that cover my friends and bedroom like wallpaper.
I call them TV dots.

I am so glad you found me.

We are a generation of men
who won't take no for an answer.

The stories you made up
shape my mind.

You called me when you fucked your boyfriend.

And I was very listening. I was very high.

Rarely do I indulge in the Fallacy
of the Bygone Era,
but I must now purify.

We are so close to not giving a fuck.

Then rolling
yr nuts off
meeee too
hopefully 1 of these sperms
will get lucky
people arnt having
kids as early
its taking longer
to actualize
im pretty much there
i deserve a kid
gratis.

An earlier version of this poem misspelled the name of Tamaki Katori.

Hot dogs are my children.

Taking-Off-My-Clothes-to-Eat-My-Food Relaxed,
I attend to each one like little Buddhas,

then do the blood sacrifice. I am by myself again.

Lifetime Original Movies recreate the neighborhoods
of the audience they want, and all who aspire
to that,

a naturalistic, uncluttered realism
that, in the best instances,
descends into hysteria
and moral panic.

We were not fuck buddies.
We were not even buddies.

We were just fucks.

KISH
KASH
KATORI!

Are the Black Panthers after you again
so you had to go and delete your profile?

The car demolished the driver inside. Handsome and weird,
the man had mystique.

A great player is sometimes a decoy.

A manager, a master of letting shit happen.

I think that people who think about themselves will go to Hell.

For some, it is their Hell magnified,
how Tamaki thinks about me on her ride home is Hell on Earth
because it is me thinking that.

That there is perfect beauty
reveals the fact that you can never get it right again.

A book about the history of breakfast.
A strategy for placing flowers on the cigarette box,
because apparently everyone draws now.

THERE'S A LECTURE AT JAPAN SOCIETY ABOUT ROBOTS,
AND THEY'RE GOING TO HAVE SOME OF THE HUMANOID BOTS
THERE!!!

I'm bleeding from the nose. I'm not broken.

Give mushrooms to art students
and record their movements and conversations.

Tamaki Katori,
                    beautiful to the point of cruelty,

maybe you can save my life,
and we can have cake and babies.

I banged my head pretty bad again. The mood was gleeful haywire.

We're all hurting, but none of us feel pain.

A velvet blazer is what we'll be wearing to the apocalypse.
We encounter the edge as soft beings.

What is a love that lasts forever?

And when does *I'm doing it for experience*
become the experience itself?

I take all of it, and I really can't have any of it.

From nothing to something to nothing is a soul.
And everything else is matter.

We partied during the war years, and his face melted off.

That's "Cash Money," by Cash Money Millionaires.

What can I give you today
that you don't already have?

I give advice for you to follow,
for when I am the first to go,
you'll know I knew better.

Miracle of sound into music, music to memory,
but why would I want to bring
more people into this hell?

I saw my reflection in someone's trash.
I turn it into onomatopoeia that everyone loves.

Fall is dreamy.

I don't know how to be someone you miss.

I'll smoke your pot, but don't tell me
pot is better than beer.

Beer is better than you and Cecilia combined.

There are five words here
stars are streaming out of,

lightly dusted with the New York sensibility
of 2003, before the beginning of
the complete regret of memory.

I am a scholar of that feeling.

This book is dedicated to all of us who believe
in the wonders of human ingenuity and robot servitude
for the betterment of human life.

B.

PARTYKNIFE, OHIO TOUR

I, Codeine, at your barbeque, drank eight or ten beers
and then ate five ice cream sandwiches.

Surrounded by death notes, notebooks.

Cecilia, will you tell me how darling you are?

Some people have the stomach for it.

Right now I have to pee. We are not in crisis mode yet,
but it infuses my every thought.

I am a slave to my appetites.

I wanted to drown in a vision. I wanted to be talked about a lot.

I say it, and she makes a song out of it.
Ordinary objects imbued with meaning. Guitar riffs.

And then the toaster tells me WALK ON IN DARKNESS:
ALL THE FOUNDATIONS OF THE EARTH ARE OUT OF COURSE.

I just say it's awesome.

And then my friends say it's awesome
and we start the School of Awesome.

My wisdom has made me a sage among my peers.

Cecilia can do anything. Anything is I.
Just a limitless vertical.

Some people go out every night and it's fine.

Courting my obsolescence,
it's just noise I never gave my heart.

Sometimes I take a hit and look at the bathroom fan above
and think that it is a strong brown god,

and that I worship him by exhaling smoke at him;
the longer I hold it in and stare,
the better do I worship him.

I could stand to be hurt.

In my literary daydreams,
all the bar scenes take place at KGB,
but I fucking hate that place.

Then you leaned back and laughed and said,
"Did you think it would be so fucking easy?"

And then you said it was,

real life real love,
always just this once.

The idea of smoking pot to regulate my life is unraveling,
so I need to make necessary improvements.

I am a nationally-known public speaker.

Sexy like a Muppet,
guzzling Diet Cokes like I was Bill Clinton,

my blankness is the blankness of Reagan.

Then I become hungry like a fat person.

In preparation for Fucktime,
I threw my bedding in the dryer
that was defective and everything burned.

Dr. Rob said it smelled like skin.
You know what it was?

It was the beginning of tomorrow.

And today is all your life will ever be.

Cecilia, the hours in the last four years
would equal a Saturday night of parties I saw you at.

Hours together convulsing in your life
as you age through, handling your beer.

Reacquainting repeats from a demo tape
to marketing.

The apparition appears every four months,
and does your drugs,
and remains the background noise
of about thirty people
I call friends.

Occasionally the center of attention
brings into focus a girl who loves erasing.

Feel the feeling. Then see it clearly.

There were three writers at a Christmas party
in Brooklyn, and they were talking about
another writer.

That writer was me.

The point of a chest tattoo is that you can take your shirt off
no matter how out of shape you are.

The merlot was passed around until I was
Jesus Christ, King of the Zombies.

And at once he uttered the human feeling
that cannot be willed, and he said

that when I become his age I would feel it,
and I just didn't.

I'M WITH THE BAND

Let's call this city a room. Whatever we want, we walk to it.

You're kind of my hero, getting fired for liking music so much.

Sleeping on a floor that isn't yours,

disciplining the body with what it doesn't want.

You're kind of my idea of a woman in passion,
carried away into a bed that isn't yours.

Passion's without reason.
We are friends.

Whatever I want, I talk about

on couches of people who know you through your work.

"Are You Ready for the Sex Girls" is a song beyond irony.

If you play it, you will ruin the party.

Passing around a pipe from the future,
Cecilia's friends emerge languid and mid-tempo.

What is a love that lasts forever?

I want to hear the contents of what your friends say about me,
but not what they feel.

I know this is difficult to talk about,
and that it operates outside of articulation,

but "Are You Ready for the Sex Girls" will make you so lonely.

Maybe if I masturbate again, I'll know what to do.

A style is just a life.

Desire is just putting nouns before abstractions,
giving ardor its bright plume.

There are two types of people. Those who drink
and those who do not drink.

Bringing all my friends back to my bed,
friends of friends.

Your shoulders curved thereafter for me the power of that desire.

There is a momentary chord that makes the impossible worthwhile.

Useless and something else.

There are two types of people.
Those who would kill themselves and those who would pussy out.

Yearning has its own limitations to thank. What I can't give
with such extravagance.

Checking every LES building's door
to smuggle in for some rooftop drinking.

Rob, will you be my dad?

I've *lived* in New Orleans, I've KNOWN vampires.

If I leapt back, do you think I could fly?

New Year's Eve fireworks…an uphill run along the campus,
the dorm way out above, the frozen lake below.

Hip-checking girls along 3rd Avenue,

and I laughed at your rape jokes until I got the hiccups;
asked by paramedics what my name is

in a bagel place, tiny as shit, busy as fuck.

SUICIDE GIRLS

If it feels good, it probably has a name.

Working that mood for years now,
a faded, older guy in passion.

Two ladies writhe around in my desire.
It feels good. It has a name.
There is a rainbow. I want to throw myself through it.

The guy will always get the girl.
This unicorn shirt will outlast the irony.

When my mother dies, I will drape her in this unicorn shirt.

And I cried, "I DON'T WANT
TO BE ALONE!" and I
rubbed my back and began the sweat quest.

They even let fat people into this party.

I'm a walking panic attack, but I think I've figured out why.

I attract fun and amusing experiences.

My childish sense of humor is attractive and contagious.

When I'm high, I succeed beyond my wildest expectations.

Emotionally available partners line up for my spirit.
My phone is ringing off the hook.

I share my friends with other people,
and they let me help with their sexy problems.

A shade deeper than you think you can control.

I have nothing to say to you. You are just me.

The gorgeous is bullshit and the salvation I slave before.

On stage,
I cannot hit all the guitar notes,
but I can vomit up a pint of chicken blood.

At the lake, some music summarized the different parts of my life into one feeling...

Cecilia joined a dance cult with all her talented friends.

Your group shed me like skin,
a living and feeling membrane.

I don't even know why I resuscitated, it was so good...

And someday I'll be murdered by my Filipina love bride,
who escapes with tens of dollars.

Why would I want that time returned,
except to do it over? Never regret.

There was a girl dressed as Angela Chase
sitting on the couch, looking broody. I was in
such a great costume.

The sign on the door said, WARNING! THIS IS A MAKEOUT PARTY.
Then in an ambulance, which seemed obvious,

and before that staggering around, I remember that

there is one less of us.

The blue light of my phone
in those places I was
unconscious in.

No matter how drunk I was,
I was afraid to talk to Angela Chase.

Crying is just nature's way of saying you're wrong.

JUICE CLEANSE

I had an anxiety attack during the three-way.
I see through all appearance and know abundance.

All of this is the weakest shit ever. Fat falls off me
so fast that everyone looks. What lastly
were they looking for—

Chaka Khan or Jacques Lacan?
Heidegger or Rah Digga? Remember her?

I attract romance in the most magical and unexpected ways.
I am silly at heart and it shows.
I drink large amounts of thirst-quenching water every day.

My wallet is bulging with money.
I rub elbows with wondrous people.

Dr. Rob's project to gather friends on Brighton Beach
on the cold sand to sing Nirvana songs
became just hanging out.

Here my friends are
scraped out for kindling for this bonfire.

Tamaki shimmers here like a random piece of trance.

What she is doing, my sleep is bigger than.

I GOT A '90s BONER!!!!!!!!!!!!!
and then I realize Rob is dangerously drunk,

and Tamaki moves to him like a magnet.

I worship him, but that is my fault.
In the tent it sounds like he is killing her.

MIND QUEEF, A ONE-ACT PLAY BY HITLER

Technically, the dumpster in back is part of the Whitney.

I love, and just push my heart out.

I can't be psyched to play *Guitar Hero*,
because it reminds me that I can't play real guitar.

A manner of fashion that could transcend ten months
and become the fashion forever.

I am quiet and also very boring.

The idea, the list, the spiritual realm—a litany, a soul sick
list plus
transcendent, gravity plus parallel
plus journaling plus lament.

Also Zem is NOT San Francisco's eco-fashion guru;
she is San Francisco's eco-lifestyle guru.

This is important.

MERCY FUCK

I've seen everything that's funny on the Internet.
Rockstar of masturbation and hot dog violence.

I serve everything I get.
What comes in is entered out of pity.

Oh my god, it's happening!

Talking about the history of black metal,
I realized I know nothing about black metal
and had a panic attack.

I tried to mouth off to some people,
and they just took it.

What a wimpy birthday.

Even though I'm hanging out with white people,
it's turning out pretty well.

Why would I pee on the bath mat? The toilet is right there.

I tried to start a rumor that Cecilia's career will stall
because she is epileptic
and has seizures in discos.

It's as if the wind just dies away,
but this is not the masochistic work of man. It is nature within man.

Eventually she transforms into a tree, and it is beautiful.

It heals.
That's the power of skin.

And when I die, I'll just be dead.

There is something beautiful and touching about talentless people making art.

Kneeling at the altar of the merely beautiful.

We understand that you like the feedback,
but we want to sound like Kiss.

I'm done. What a creative boy.

What a creative man.

Let's just lie out on the bed.
Look at all the pulpiness of paper.

I have no money. ababcdcdefefgg.
I hate my job. abbacddcefgefg.

All my friends are alcoholics.
123456, 615243, 631452 and on and on.

Incapable of writing five bad songs in a row,
you can certainly write four.

The stars are geometric—utopian
and fascist.
                Rob's shirt was tighter than the color
I fantasized about. I held your breath.

(The straining rain inside her room completes
right at the end of her virginity).

I am Curious Blue, I am Curious Red
I'm in love with you; you love him instead.

Those years! I spent them talking you down from the ledge
of being depressed. And now you're not depressed.

WE WERE D00D BROS

Rob and I each chugged a 40 on the couch
to see who could go the longest without peeing.

There was an imbalance of metabolism and body weight,
but the point wasn't a contest of discipline. The point was pain.

We had a lot of time back then. We could fill it up with what we wanted.

I think of it now, and then it exists on the Internet.

Having never thought of it before,
and there it is on hipsterrunoff.com.

When I learned I can never articulate how I feel,
and that people present themselves
in the exact way I want to be,

that's what I taught the world about shame.

I was a Teenage Blowjob Machine EP.

Rob was birthed full-grown
from some clenched fist.

Tell your friends my mouth is like an orgasm.

Say hi to forever.

We breast feed from GROoPIES. The astronaut.
Rob, ride the air-guitar. RIDE THAT PONY TO THE SKY!

Partyknife/Bitch Blade Split 7 inch.

Dr. Rob faked his death on the message board,
but sometimes logs on as sweatyjames:

TOO SHY TO F#CK WITH TINY D$CK?!?!

That's the mutability that crowns the powerful.

Black dudes always know when you're high.

I just discovered I was a Verificationist in college.
I didn't know a name existed for what I felt.

Verification overlaid with a deeply sublimated monotheism
is what I took for completion.

Awash in Tamaki's beauty,
I am the Burger King of crying right now.

Soul, I said, please let me be done with this thought,
and like voodoo it became part of myself.

My mix tapes mostly touch only me.
Catharsis becomes just someone
who cries a lot.

Final Encounter of the Legend Tour,
everything follows the wind.

I'M NOT AFRAID OF BEING PULLED INTO A GREAT CULTURAL MOVEMENT

Neo-decadence reigned in that time,
in a manner just close enough to what he wanted
that it disgusted him. And completely disillusioned,
Dr. Rob, to such a degree lashed out
against the people who were his brothers.

To this he gave his name.

It's basically just some well-edited videos
featuring outrageously hot girls speaking French
hanging out
AND GETTING FUCKED!

Delighting in your thinness
when you were brightness
and a mask of pain.

The world will teach you what I think.

Exclamation points, no matter how many,
cannot say what all caps articulates from my soul.

Weeks too late to dump the Christmas tree to the curb,
shamed by critical hipster girls in my mind,
we cut it up—Mafia-style—and put it in three trash bags on the street.

Your comment that my bag is faggy is not so interesting
except it's my worst fear you would think it so.

Our money is made of blue jeans,
the coolest fabric we wear.

I don't want to be remembered
except as what the worst person thought of me then.

A perfect time before it was gone
stands for what I am now and later.

How you want to be remembered faded like me.

Crushing and snorting Paxil. Burning our sinuses,
three of us screaming freeform.

Or stealing my roommate's Vicodin, New Year's Eve,
fireworks at the lake. Something in me heaven desires,

and I can never have that back. It hurts so much,

Cecilia and Rob just leaving me there.

Only some of this will affect you. I never wanted to be anything.

I want their voices again,
but that will be over in a few minutes,
weightless before disappearing through the ice.

If only my friends knew what it takes
out of me to love them.

My whole body scraped out,
coming back completely new.

The Gary Kasparov flying penis debacle is fully subtitled for the first time.

Strong characters overcome their history.

Rob, you must have five songs to cry to….

Dr. Rob is not a real Dr.,

flagging down random cars in Bed-Stuy.

Two of mine are from the golden era of rock and roll…
running from the lake…Rob and Cecilia….

Currently, I'm trying to see through paper
(last week, I saw through some tin foil).

Spiritual progression,
more audio-driven,
fragile bones of hearing,

honed into a megaphone, you said.

And I yelled completely.

The Dr. makes one note banged over and over,
completely disproportionate to your physical comfort.

For my older self to no longer understand new music
would be for my younger self
the ultimate sin.

I will lose everything.

Talking to Cecilia, you must have five songs.

Listening to some music. Hearing some friends.

I'm going to go ahead and stop talking to you.

I had three right then.

Do not contact me; do not call this number again.

Enjoy the wonderful cake you destroyed.

IN MY DAY PEOPLE WOULD LISTEN TO MUSIC ON CDs

Hey man, that's a really cool album.
—It is?!

Then my twenty-year-old self steps from behind
the shadows and says what a jaded piece of shit.

I want the first time every time.

Like serial-killer normal,
the dream of a perfect reception,

the dream of never going out of style.

In a half-remembered blur of wanting to get it over with,
I died in my arms tonight.

Sometimes I like to massage the keyboard as;ldfjsl;dfsodugashg
  that was weird
  sorry

PARTY SUMMER '98

Piano smash!   THREE SMASHING GARB!
seventeen now! crack Pearl Jam
cover band!

Party!   Alright! Lawns, stereo,

attention made lips red. More dials!
MORE BATHROOM! Yr not going to yak are you!?

Concussions leave band mates in a murky world.

Cecilia, recite the names of pets you owned, feel
better soon. Smiles and violets.

Then nineteen minutes before the police invasion,
some teenage stoner beholds the *Knight Rider* tapes.

And that's how GPS was invented.

A green number 6 billiard ball,
perfectly halved that I found on the street.
A toy robot inexplicably with your name on its chest.

These wonderful things I give to Cecilia.

Stayed up most of the night listening to your songs
and writing all about them in a letter to you,

back to where we are almost making it
in blooming red,

in blush and sex

an intense order of meaningful moments of my life….

People are lonely and bored, and need to see
a version of themselves with more possibilities,
possibly going platinum.

A gift is not a gift unless you miss it.

The girl who Dr. Rob thought was a hippie
wasn't—we turned to ask Chavez—
and then she was GONE.

I told you about the ghost hippie.

Tamaki and Ron Forty grasped the twirling dancer,
and they all plunged from the roof.

I'm such a mess right now
touch to move her
she is going to sleep.

I'll never forget that night we spent,
but for you it was one eventful evening
among many. Love picks you up, and then you fly.

There are so many Wii characters of people I don't see anymore.

My dream
of the reality show where strippers lead me through
the locker room for an interview.

I had my wish
before the stripper dream, which makes me think
of logical connections there.

A fantasy of infinite impact.
It builds and

pierces light inside of you,
and that point is turned sideways into a horizon.

And when you die
you will go to a place of your choosing.
Whatever you wanted most in life will be yours.

After you took it, when did you realize you were really relaxed?

Right now I'm having breakfast ii,
imagining how relaxed you are.

My dream is to drive a 1978 Lincoln Continental
off Niagara Falls and scream
WHATDOYOUTHINKOFTHAT!

Drunk in Chinatown, I left my copy of
the Anne Carson book *Balls Are Beef Hilarious*
in a Vietnamese Restaurant. But I don't know which one!
Was it Pho Bang or Pho?

Everything I hated has become my life now.

By which I mean how happy I am.

IBIZA DAWN CHILL MIX 9

Let's take the night to its logical terminus.

No one wants to be like you.

For awhile, every commercial film in the United States
ended to the patter of Peter Gabriel's "Solsbury Hill,"
hoariest of boomer songs.

All of that is over now.

We were all in it trying to be famous, but what we ended with
were good friends and great memories,

and isn't that what it's always about,

legs squeaking against vinyl

in the summer time
in the parking lot.

Cecilia, thank you for making out with me.

The snowflakes hold the air
once I see the frozen lake. A song–

a girl goes back in time to save her friend.

I can't wait to meet you there.

Experimentation becomes so serious,
and panic is the monster you sent me, consumed
in happiness. A song would save my life.

About a girl who goes back in time.

Lucid dreams and near-death experiences
become so serious. A night
I wanted changed will have forgotten
how to, leaving only that I wanted something else.

A song would save my life.

Welling up in my hands are emotions,
and I awakened in her wake,
and I almost saw heaven then.

The other productive thing I did was eat Thai food.
My boss had to take the day off when his retainer fell out.

The free clinic girl turned to me glistening,
Don't you sometimes feel that this is just a dream?

Stars to Earth and currents passing....

This feels so good. Slap me if I fall asleep,
she says you've been sleeping this whole time.

Like a teenager again.

Dust motes exploding off her hair.

And I woke up in a wheel chair.

NOTES

Page 31 – last line of the poem is from *The Exorcist.*

Page 52 – "Walk on in darkness: all the foundations of the earth are out of course" is from Psalm 82:5, King James Version.

Page 69 – lines 7-9 are from an Amazon review of Zachary Schomberg's *Scary, No Scary* by "John S. Williams".

Page 71 – first two lines adapted from Arion Berger's March 2, 2000 review of The Cure album *Bloodflowers* for *Rolling Stone.*

Page 74 – line 13 is the name of Leslie Cheung's 1989 "retirement" tour. Line 14 is from the title of his posthumous album.

Page 78 – line 1 is from a note about the "Gary Kasparov and the Flying Penis" video on YouTube.

Additionally, lines and sentences from several poems are affirmations from www.drstandley.com. Specifically, page 27, line 8; page 28, last two sentences; page 62, lines 3-7 (sometimes wildly adapted); page 65, lines 2 and 8-12 (sometimes wildly adapted).

ACKNOWLEDGEMENTS

For their friendship and support, thanks to Lara Belonogoff, Nova Bradfield, Seth Bressack, Ian Dreiblatt, Farrah Field, Doug Hahn, Mike Harris, Joseph Housley, Eleanor Jaekel, Steven Karl, Amy Lawless, Marc Mascarello, Vedrana Misic, Gina Myers, Kelly Nichols, Carol Rhyu, Steve Roberts, Jackson Scarlett (who came up with this book's title), Rich Scheiwe, Alex Smith, Paige Taggart, Danielle Trent, Jared White, and Hitomi Yoshio. Special thanks to Matt Bollinger for his amazing cover and devoted friendship all these years.

Thanks to the Birds, LLC crew for making this book what it turned out to be: Justin Marks, Chris Tonelli, Dan Boehl, Matt Rasmussen, Michael Newton, and especially my editor Sampson Starkweather, who made the manuscript ten times better than it should have been, and for his dedicated encouragement, coaching, and friendship.

Thanks to Farrah, Jared, Steven, Ian, Rich, Kaveh Bassiri, and Christie Ann Reynolds who read earlier versions of this manuscript with an encouraging and critical eye. And additionally to Lauren Ireland, Molly Dorozenski and Steve Roberts for helpful comments on earlier versions of many of these poems. Thanks to Adam Robinson, Blake Butler, Ben Fama, and Francesca Chabrier for early encouragement on this book.

And of course for love and support from Mom, Dad, George, Eric, and Clare.

Many of the poems on Side A were originally published, sometimes in different form, as an online chapbook called *White-Collar Worker: I am a Destiny*, from H_NGM_N B__KS. Thanks to Nate Pritts for his enthusiasm and for publishing it. Poems were also first published in the following journals:

Supermachine: "Black dudes always know when you're high."; "There is something beautiful and touching about talentless people making art."; "Tamaki asks me to talk dirty to her without being degrading." Many thanks to Ben Fama.

Keyhole Magazine: "He's not actually a person..."; "Dr. Rob asks me to visit his open house..."; "That there is perfect beauty..." Many thanks to Gabe Durham.

Forklift, Ohio: "Some serious dudes place amps..."; "I'm the Jesus of making out with girls drunk." Many thanks to Matt Hart and Brett Price.

Sixth Finch: "People are bored and look at their holes." Originally published as "In Praise of Angst." Many thanks to Rob MacDonald.

Dan Magers is co-founder and co-editor of *Sink Review*, an online poetry journal as well as founder and editor of Immaculate Disciples Press, a handmade chapbook press focused on poetry and visual arts collaborations. He grew up in Kansas City, Missouri and now lives in Brooklyn, New York.

Magers scribes as if poet-ghost adrift thru dressing rooms backstage taking notes, capturing the moment in all its lovely eros and happiness and cause for alarm. Writing poems like these is just as good as starting a band when poems like songs flood the brain. I like your smile.

    —Thurston Moore

"I wanted to be high, but now I'm trapped in my life." Frustrated by the limits of his world, *Partyknife*'s youthful speaker wears a mask of aloofness that incompletely conceals his yearning. His poems strain to hold his exuberance, and his studied detachment belies his racing heart. "Everything I hated has become my life now. By which I mean how happy I am." These poems are angry, insistent, and wildly in love with life.

    —Sarah Manguso

I know in blurbs you're supposed to name things more explicitly than *This book slays*, but hey, listen, THIS BOOK FUCKING SLAYS. With this maniacally deadpan *Partyknife*, Dan Magers has hacked out the machine-logic of aging in a kind of air where electronic lighting fills our body at the same speed as death metal or beer; where just saying it can make "0 + 0 = 20 tonight," and where it's only an opening idea that reveals how, "Technically, the dumpster in back is part of the Whitney." Can I compare Dan Magers to a chopped n screwed iWittgenstein for a second, only hilarious, and that we wished went on forever? Sure I can. Now we can be anything.

    —Blake Butler

Triggering "Conversion"

Although this conversion procedure is mandatory, not discretionary,[451] conversion does not occur automatically.[452] The court retains the discretion to ignore any extra-pleading materials that the parties have submitted, and instead to resolve the motion solely on the basis of the pleading itself, in which case no conversion is necessary.[453] In fact, even when the court fails to expressly exclude the extra-pleading materials,[454] a conversion may not be necessary if the materials were, in fact, ignored by the court or otherwise irrelevant to the court's resolution of the motion.[455]

Type of Required Notice of "Conversion"

The required notice of conversion may be either actual or constructive.[456] Actual, formal notice might not be necessary if the non-moving party should have reasonably anticipated the conversion, was not taken by surprise, and was not deprived a reasonable opportunity to respond to the extra-pleading materials.[457] Thus, a court's neglect in providing this formal notice may be excused, for example, where the moving party dual-labeled its motion to dismiss as a motion for summary judgment "in the alternative,"[458] where the non-movants had submitted extra-pleading materials of their own,[459] or where the non-movants failed to show that factual materials existed which controvert the moving party's contentions.[460]

Exceptions to the "Conversion" Requirement

Various exceptions to the conversion procedure have been recognized. First, no conversion is required when the court considers exhibits attached to the complaint (unless their authenticity is questioned);[461] documents that the complaint incorporates by reference or are otherwise integral to the claim (provided they are undisputed);[462] information subject to judicial notice;[463] matters of public record (including orders and other materials in the record of the case);[464] and concessions by plaintiffs made in their response to the motion.[465]

---

[451] See Nakahata v. New York-Presbyterian Healthcare Sys., Inc., 723 F.3d 192, 203 (2d Cir. 2013).

[452] See Sorace v. U.S., 788 F.3d 758, 767 (8th Cir. 2015).

[453] See Sorace v. U.S., 788 F.3d 758, 767 (8th Cir. 2015).

[454] There is a division among the Circuits as to when the conversion obligation is triggered. There are three approaches. Some courts require conversion anytime extrinsic evidence is not expressly excluded, others require conversion only if the court "considers" the extrinsic evidence, and still others require conversion only if, after considering the extrinsic evidence, the court chooses to "rely" on it. See Max Arnold & Sons, LLC v. W.L. Hailey & Co., Inc., 452 F.3d 494, 502–03 (6th Cir. 2006) (collecting cases, and electing first approach).

[455] See Gorog v. Best Buy Co., 760 F.3d 787, 790 (8th Cir. 2014); In re Mortg. Elec. Registration Sys., Inc., 754 F.3d 772, 781 (9th Cir. 2014).

[456] See Barron ex rel. D.B. v. South Dakota Bd. of Regents, 655 F.3d 787, 791–92 (8th Cir. 2011).

[457] See Foley v. Wells Fargo Bank, N.A., 772 F.3d 63, 72 (1st Cir. 2014).

[458] See Hearing v. Minnesota Life Ins. Co., 793 F.3d 888, 892 (8th Cir. 2015).

[459] See Hearing v. Minnesota Life Ins. Co., 793 F.3d 888, 892 (8th Cir. 2015).

[460] See U.S. v. Rogers Cartage Co., 794 F.3d 854, 860 (7th Cir. 2015).

[461] See Free Speech v. Federal Election Com'n, 720 F.3d 788, 792 (10th Cir. 2013). See also Occupy Columbia v. Haley, 738 F.3d 107, 116–17 (4th Cir. 2013) (surveying Circuit split on whether affidavits attached as exhibits may be considered).

[462] See Zak v. Chelsea Therapeutics Int'l, Ltd., 780 F.3d 597, 606–07 (4th Cir. 2015).

[463] See Zak v. Chelsea Therapeutics Int'l, Ltd., 780 F.3d 597, 607 (4th Cir. 2015).

[464] See Massey v. Ojaniit, 759 F.3d 343, 352–53 (4th Cir. 2014).

[465] See Newman v. Krintzman, 723 F.3d 308, 309 (1st Cir. 2013).

Note, however, that parties cannot escape this conversion rule simply by attaching to their answer whatever extrinsic materials might be helpful to their later motion.[466]

Second, no conversion is usually required if only a portion of a document is attached as an exhibit to the complaint, and the moving party submits remaining portions with the motion.[467]

Third, a party may waive any objection to a failure to properly convert by failing to timely contest it.[468]

Fourth, even if not waived, a failure to properly convert may be deemed harmless if the non-moving party had an adequate opportunity to respond and was not otherwise prejudiced.[469]

Notifying *Pro Se* Litigants of Conversion

Because they are unlikely to appreciate the consequence of a conversion to summary judgment procedures, *pro se* litigants will ordinarily be entitled to unequivocal notice of that conversion and its meaning.[470]

RULE 12(e)—MOTION FOR MORE DEFINITE STATEMENT

CORE CONCEPT

If a pleading is so vague or ambiguous that a responsive pleading cannot be prepared, the responding party need not counter-plead, but may instead move the court for an order directing the pleader to serve a more definite statement.

APPLICATIONS

Distinct from Rule 12(b)(6) Motions

Motions to dismiss and motions for more definite statements are not interchangeable. A motion to dismiss under Rule 12(b)(6) attacks a pleading for failing to allege a cognizable claim eligible for some type of relief. In contrast, a Rule 12(e) motion for more definite statements attacks pleadings that might well state cognizable legal claims, but are so unintelligibly unclear in their present form that drafting a response to them is impossible.[471] Where the defending party is unable to frame a fair response to a pleading because the pleading's meaning is unclear, the proper remedy is ordinarily not a motion to dismiss but instead a motion for a more definite statement.[472]

- *Mislabeled Motions:* A motion to dismiss under Rule 12(b)(6) that, more correctly, is a motion for a more definite statement may be so converted by the court in its discretion.[473]

- *Filing Both Motions:* A party may file a motion to dismiss and a motion for more definite statement at the same time. In an appropriate case, the court may

---

[466] *See Horsley v. Feldt,* 304 F.3d 1125, 1134–35 (11th Cir. 2002) ("Otherwise, the conversion clause of Rule 12(c) would be too easily circumvented and disputed documents attached to an answer would have to be taken as true at the pleadings stage. The written instrument provision of Rule 10(c) does not require that.").

[467] *See Cooper v. Pickett,* 137 F.3d 616, 622–23 (9th Cir. 1997).

[468] *See Berera v. Mesa Med. Group, PLLC,* 779 F.3d 352, 358 n.7 (6th Cir. 2015).

[469] *See Russell v. Harman Int'l Indus., Inc.,* 773 F.3d 253, 255 (D.C.Cir. 2014).

[470] *See Parada v. Banco Industrial De Venezuela, C.A.,* 753 F.3d 62, 68 (2d Cir. 2014).

[471] *See Allstate Indem. Co. v. Dixon,* 304 F.R.D. 580, 582 (W.D.Mo. 2015).

[472] *See American Nurses' Ass'n v. State of Ill.,* 783 F.2d 716, 725 (7th Cir. 1986).

[473] *See Luna-Reyes v. RFI Const., LLC,* 57 F.Supp.3d 495, 504 (M.D.N.C. 2014).

consider the motion for more definite statement first and hold the motion to dismiss in abeyance.[474]

Disfavored Motion

The Rules require the pleader to serve only a short, plain statement showing an entitlement to relief.[475] Due to these liberal pleading requirements in federal court, motions for a more definite statement are disfavored and granted only sparingly.[476] They are not a substitute for discovery,[477] and ordinarily will not be granted where the level and nature of the detail sought is a proper role for discovery.[478]

Legal Test

Motions for a more definite statement will ordinarily only be granted where the pleading is "unintelligible": so hopelessly vague and ambiguous that a defendant cannot fairly be expected to frame a response or denial, at least not without risking prejudice.[479] Such motions are particularly ill-suited to situations where the information sought is already within the defendant's knowledge, and the motion merely seeks the formality of the recital of known facts.[480] Nevertheless, courts continue to grant these motions, even though disfavored, where the federal "notice pleading" standards are not met.[481] Just as Rule 12(e) motions are not legitimate substitutes for discovery, discovery is not a fair substitute for proper pleading.[482] Both the court and the litigants are entitled to know, at the pleading stage, who is being sued, why, and for what.[483] Courts have also used Rule 12(e) for various other purposes:

- *Special Pleading Obligations:* To seek facts that must be specially pleaded, such as fraud, mistake, denial of performance or occurrence, and special damages.[484]

- *Threshold Defenses:* To seek (in certain particular situations only) facts necessary to determine whether threshold defenses exist, such as statute of limitations

---

[474] *See Thomas v. Independence Tp.*, 463 F.3d 285, 301 (3d Cir. 2006).

[475] *See* Rule 8(a)(2).

[476] *See Allstate Indem. Co. v. Dixon*, 304 F.R.D. 580, 582 (W.D.Mo. 2015).

[477] *See Allstate Indem. Co. v. Dixon*, 304 F.R.D. 580, 582 (W.D.Mo. 2015).

[478] *See Sanchez v. City of Fresno*, 914 F.Supp.2d 1079, 1121–22 (E.D.Cal. 2012); *Tempur-Pedic Int'l Inc. v. Angel Beds LLC*, 902 F.Supp.2d 958, 971 (S.D.Tex. 2012).

[479] *See Allstate Indem. Co. v. Dixon*, 304 F.R.D. 580, 582 (W.D.Mo. 2015).

[480] *See Babcock & Wilcox Co. v. McGriff, Seibels & Williams, Inc.*, 235 F.R.D. 632, 633 (E.D. La. 2006).

[481] *See Swierkiewicz v. Sorema N. A*, 534 U.S. 506, 512, 122 S.Ct. 992, 998, 152 L.Ed.2d 1 (2002) (noting that if pleading "fails to specify the allegations in a manner that provides sufficient notice", defendant can move for more definite statement before responding).

[482] *Cf. Eisenach v. Miller-Dwan Medical Center*, 162 F.R.D. 346, 348 (D. Minn. 1995) ("any current view that the deficiencies in pleading may be cured through liberalized discovery is at increasingly mounting odds with the public's dissatisfaction with exorbitantly expansive discovery, and the impact that the public outcry has had upon our discovery Rules").

[483] *See Fant v. City of Ferguson*, 107 F. Supp. 3d 1016, 1027 (E.D. Mo. 2015). *See generally McHenry v. Renne*, 84 F.3d 1172, 1179–80 (9th Cir. 1996) (writing that "[p]rolix, confusing complaints such as the ones plaintiffs filed in this case impose unfair burdens on litigants and judges. As a practical matter, the judge and opposing counsel, in order to perform their responsibilities, cannot use a complaint such as the one plaintiffs filed, and must prepare outlines to determine who is being sued for what. Defendants are then put at risk that their outline differs from the judge's, that plaintiffs will surprise them with something new at trial which they reasonably did not understand to be in the case at all, and that res judicata effects of settlement or judgment will be different from what they reasonably expected. . . . The judge wastes half a day in chambers preparing the 'short and plain statement' which Rule 8 obligated plaintiffs to submit. He then must manage the litigation without knowing what claims are made against whom. This leads to discovery disputes and lengthy trials, prejudicing litigants in other case who follow the rules, as well as defendants in the case in which the prolix pleading is filed.").

[484] *See* Rule 9. *See also Wagner v. First Horizon Pharmaceutical Corp.*, 464 F.3d 1273, 1280 (11th Cir. 2006).

(when claim arose) or statute of frauds (whether contract was written or oral, term for performance).[485]

- *Rule 10 Violations:* To seek a repleading of a complaint or claim that is confusingly consolidated in a single count (when multiple counts would be proper), fails to properly paragraph, or otherwise violates the presentation dictates of Rule 10.[486]

- *Changing Circumstances:* To update facts when changed circumstances or the passage of time makes the lawsuit's viability clouded.[487]

- *RICO Case Statements:* To compel the filing of "RICO Case Statements", required in many judicial districts to flesh out the factual predicates and legal theory underlying federal civil racketeering claims.[488]

Burden of Proof

The burden lies with the moving party to demonstrate that the challenged pleading is too vague or ambiguous to permit a response. The moving party must identify the deficiencies in the pleading, list the details sought to be provided, and assert an inability to frame a response.[489]

Timing

Obviously, a motion for more definite statement must be filed before the party serves a response to the pleading claimed to be too vague or ambiguous.[490] Additionally, the moving party should appreciate the significance of moving for Rule 12(e) relief—once a Rule 12 motion is made, any waivable defense that should have been joined in that Rule 12 motion may be lost.[491] To abate the harshness of this result, the court may permit the moving party to withdraw the Rule 12(e) motion so as to permit a larger Rule 12 filing.[492]

Applies Only to Pleadings

By its terms, Rule 12(e) is available to compel more definite statements only in pleadings. It cannot be used to require added detail in motions.[493]

---

[485] *See Thomas v. Independence Tp.*, 463 F.3d 285, 289 (3d Cir. 2006) (noting motion's usefulness in immunity cases).

[486] *See Davis v. Coca-Cola Bottling Co. Consol.*, 516 F.3d 955, 983–84 (11th Cir. 2008).

[487] *See Thorp v. District of Columbia*, 309 F.R.D. 88, 90–91 (D.D.C. 2015).

[488] *See Northland Ins. Co. v. Shell Oil Co.*, 930 F.Supp. 1069, 1074 (D.N.J. 1996). Where claims are asserted under the federal Racketeer Influenced and Corrupt Organizations Act ("RICO"), 18 U.S.C.A. §§ 1961 to 68, many judicial districts now require, by Standing Order, chambers policy, or otherwise, that the pleader answer a series of questions that supplement the RICO allegations of the complaint. *See, e.g., National Organization for Women, Inc. v. Scheidler,* 510 U.S. 249, 249, 114 S.Ct. 798, 800, 127 L.Ed.2d 99 (1994) (noting local rule in force in Northern District of Illinois). This pleading obligation is especially important where the facts noted in the RICO Case Statement are deemed to be pleading averments, properly considered in ruling upon a motion to dismiss. *See Glessner v. Kenny,* 952 F.2d 702, 712 (3d Cir. 1991) (collecting cases so holding).

[489] *See Alford v. Chevron U.S.A. Inc.*, 13 F.Supp.2d 581, 590 (E.D. La. 2014).

[490] *See Marx v. Gumbinner*, 855 F.2d 783, 792 (11th Cir. 1988). *See generally Santana Products, Inc. v. Sylvester & Associates, Ltd.,* 121 F.Supp.2d 729, 738 (E.D. N.Y. 1999) (because Rule 12(e) motions must be presented before filing a responsive pleading, defendants' decision to file an answer precluded relief under motion).

[491] *See Rules 12(g) & 12(h). See also Caldwell-Baker Co. v. Southern Illinois Railcar Co.*, 225 F.Supp.2d 1243, 1259 (D. Kan. 2002) (noting substantial number of courts that had ruled that a party moving for more definite statement may not later assert by motion another Rule 12(b) defense that was then available).

[492] *See Caldwell-Baker Co. v. Southern Illinois Railcar Co.*, 225 F.Supp.2d 1243, 1259 (D. Kan. 2002) (holding that party's withdrawal of Rule 12(e) motion abated possible waiver of motion to dismiss for lack of personal jurisdiction).

[493] *See Brown v. F.B.I.*, 793 F.Supp.2d 368, 382 (D.D.C. 2011).

Use by Claimants

When an answer pleads an unintelligible defense, some courts permit claimants to invoke Rule 12(e) to force a repleading of that defense.[494] Other courts reject that use, reasoning that, because claimants are usually not required to counter-plead to an answer, Rule 12(e)—by its terms—is inapplicable.[495]

Sua Sponte Motions

The district court may, on its own initiative, strike a deficient pleading and direct the pleader to file a more definite statement.[496] This *sua sponte* option is especially valuable to resolve "shotgun pleading" deficiencies,[497] or when a motion to dismiss is pending but the more appropriate relief is repleading with a more definite statement.[498]

Discretion of Trial Court

The decision to grant or deny a motion for a more definite statement is committed to the district court's sound discretion.[499]

Tolling Effect

While the motion is pending, the party's time for serving a responsive pleading is tolled. Once the court rules on the motion, a new (but shortened) response time begins. If the motion is granted, the party must serve a responsive pleading within 14 days after the more definite statement is served or within such other time as the court may direct. If the motion is denied, the party must serve a responsive pleading within 14 days of the court's order.

Remedy

To comply with a Rule 12(e) order for a more definite statement, the pleader must amend the pleading to add sufficient detail to satisfy the court and to meet the adversary's objections.[500] If the pleader fails to serve the more definite statement, or fails to do so within the designated time period, the court may strike the pleading or make such other order as it deems just.[501]

RULE 12(f)—MOTION TO STRIKE

CORE CONCEPT

On its own initiative or upon motion, the court may strike from a pleading any insufficient defense or any redundant, immaterial, impertinent, or scandalous matter.

APPLICATIONS

Purpose

Both insufficient defenses and redundant, immaterial, impertinent, or scandalous matter are properly stricken from a pleading in order to avoid the time, effort, and expense

---

[494] *See Exhibit Icons, LLC v. XP Cos., LLC*, 609 F.Supp.2d 1282, 1300 (S.D. Fla. 2009).

[495] *See* Rule 12(e) (permitting motions for more definite statements only for those pleadings "to which a responsive pleading is allowed"). *See also Armstrong v. Snyder*, 103 F.R.D. 96, 100 (E.D.Wis. 1984) ("where a responsive pleading is not required or permitted, a motion under Rule 12(e) for a more definite statement is inappropriate").

[496] *See Miccosukee Tribe of Indians of Fla. v. United States,*716 F.3d 535, 557 (11th Cir. 2013).

[497] *See Weiland v. Palm Beach Cty. Sheriff's Office*, 792 F.3d 1313, 1321 n.10 (11th Cir. 2015).

[498] *See Thomas v. Independence Tp.*, 463 F.3d 285, 289 (3d Cir. 2006).

[499] *See Cooper v. Harvey*, 108 F. Supp. 3d 463, 468–69 (N.D. Tex. 2015).

[500] *See Chennareddy v. Dodaro*, 282 F.R.D. 9, 14 (D.D.C. 2012); *Sefton v. Jew*, 204 F.R.D. 104, 106 (W.D. Tex. 2000).

[501] *See Chennareddy v. Dodaro*, 282 F.R.D. 9, 14 (D.D.C. 2012); *Sefton v. Jew*, 204 F.R.D. 104, 106 (W.D. Tex. 2000).

necessary to litigate spurious issues.[502] Such motions may be granted when necessary to clean up the pleadings, streamline the litigation, or sidestep unnecessary efforts on immaterial issues.[503] But this remedy is considered a "drastic" one,[504] and is never permitted for idle ends. The motion generally cannot be used to purposelessly cull pleadings of "inappropriately hyperbolic allegations, ill-conceived attempts at levity, and other similar manifestations of bad judgment in drafting".[505]

General Test

Motions to strike are disfavored by the courts,[506] and especially so when they delay the litigation with little corresponding benefit.[507] In considering a motion to strike, courts will generally apply the same test used to determine a Rule 12(b)(6) motion[508]—the courts will deem as admitted all of the nonmoving party's well-pleaded facts, draw all reasonable inferences in the pleader's favor, and resolve all doubts in favor of denying the motion to strike.[509] But the court will not accept as true the non-moving party's conclusions of law.[510] If disputed questions of fact or law remain as to the challenged material or defense, the motion to strike must be denied.[511] Likewise, if any doubt remains as to the potential later relevance of the contested allegations, the motion will be denied.[512]

Burden of Proof

The burden lies with the party moving to strike.[513] Given the disfavored nature of the relief, the burden on the moving party is "formidable".[514] The moving party must state the basis for the motion with particularity and identify specifically the relief sought.[515] The moving party must generally make at least two showings: first, the challenged allegations must be clearly unrelated to the pleader's claims,[516] *and,* second, the moving party must be prejudiced by permitting those allegations to remain in the pleading.[517] This prejudice requirement remains controversial among the courts. Rule 12(f) does not, by its terms, require any showing of prejudice, and for this reason some courts have refused to impose that obligation on the movant.[518] A great many other courts, however, test for prejudice, citing the disfavor with which Rule 12(f) relief is viewed as support.[519] If considered in ruling

---

[502] *See Operating Eng'rs Local 324 Health Care Plan v. G & W Const. Co.,* 783 F.3d 1045, 1050 (6th Cir. 2015).

[503] *See Ford-Greene v. NHS, Inc.,* 106 F. Supp. 3d 590, 615 (E.D.Pa. 2015).

[504] *See Stanbury Law Firm v. I.R.S.,* 221 F.3d 1059, 1063 (8th Cir. 2000).

[505] *See Saylavee LLC v. Hockler,* 228 F.R.D. 425, 426 (D. Conn. 2005).

[506] *See Operating Eng'rs Local 324 Health Care Plan v. G & W Const. Co.,* 783 F.3d 1045, 1050 (6th Cir. 2015).

[507] *See Manning v. Boston Med. Ctr. Corp.,* 725 F.3d 34, 59 (1st Cir. 2013); *Newborn Bros. Co. v. Albion Eng'g Co.,* 299 F.R.D. 90, 94 (D.N.J. 2014).

[508] *See Johnson Outdoors Inc. v. Navico, Inc.,* 774 F.Supp.2d 1191, 1195 (M.D.Ala. 2011); *Starnes Family Office, LLC v. McCullar,* 765 F.Supp.2d 1036, 1047 (W.D.Tenn. 2011).

[509] *See Petrie v. Electronic Game Card, Inc.,* 761 F.3d 959 965 (9th Cir. 2014); *Senju Pharm. Co. v. Apotex, Inc.,* 921 F.Supp.2d 297, 301 (D.Del. 2013).

[510] *See Dodson v. Strategic Restaurants Acquisition Co. II, LLC,* 289 F.R.D. 595, 603 (E.D.Cal. 2013); *United States v. Rohm and Haas Co.,* 939 F.Supp. 1142, 1151 (D.N.J. 1996).

[511] *See Hemlock Semiconductor Corp. v. Deutsche Solar GmbH,* 116 F. Supp. 3d 818, 822–23 (E.D.Mich. 2015).

[512] *See Encore Bank, N.A. v. Bank of America, N.A.,* 918 F.Supp.2d 633, 642 (S.D.Tex. 2013); *Beatie & Osborn LLP v. Patriot Scientific Corp.,* 431 F.Supp.2d 367, 398 (S.D. N.Y. 2006).

[513] *See Lutzeier v. Citigroup Inc.,* 305 F.R.D. 107, 110–11 (E.D.Mo. 2015).

[514] *See Gates v. District of Columbia,* 66 F.Supp.3d 1, 27 (D.D.C. 2014).

[515] *See Anderson v. Davis Polk & Wardwell LLP,* 850 F.Supp.2d 392, 409 (S.D.N.Y. 2012).

[516] *See Mori v. Allegheny County,* 51 F.Supp.3d 558, 570 n.6 (W.D.Pa. 2014).

[517] *See Harris v. Chipotle Mexican Grill, Inc.,* 303 F.R.D. 625, 628 (E.D.Cal. 2014).

[518] *See Lane v. Page,* 272 F.R.D. 581, 598–600 (D.N.M. 2011) (discussing controversy, listing cases, and refusing to require showing of prejudice).

[519] *See, e.g., Nguyen v. CTS Elecs. Mfg. Solutions Inc.,* 301 F.R.D. 337, 344 (N.D. Cal. 2014).

on the motion, the requisite prejudice will exist when the contested allegation would confuse the issues or, by its length and complexity, would place an undue burden on the respondent, inject the possibility of unnecessarily extensive and burdensome discovery, improperly increase the time, expense, and complexity of the trial, or otherwise unduly burden the moving party.[520]

Test for Striking Defenses

A motion to strike is the claimant's parallel to a Rule 12(b)(6) motion to dismiss. The court may strike any defense that is legally insufficient either as a matter of pleading or as a matter of law. Defenses that are insufficiently pleaded are those that fail to impart the level of notice required by Rules 8 and 9[521] (note, the courts are divided whether affirmative defenses must satisfy the *Twombly* "plausibility" standard;[522] some impose the *Twombly* standard[523] and some do not[524]). Defenses that are insufficient as a matter of law are those that might confuse the issues in the lawsuit[525] and could not succeed under any circumstances[526] (that is, no evidence in support of that defense would be admissible at trial).[527] The objective of such strikes is to eliminate irrelevant and frivolous defenses, the trial of which would otherwise unnecessarily waste time and money.[528] Thus, to strike a defense, the moving party must generally show (a) there is no question of fact or law which might allow the challenged defense to succeed, (b) it appears to a certainty that the defense will fail regardless of what evidence is marshalled to support it, and (c) prejudice if the defense remains in the case.[529] In conducting this analysis, the court will construe the pleadings liberally in the favor of the defendant (the non-moving party).[530] However, the court is not obligated to accept naked, conclusory defenses, and inadequately pleaded defenses may be stricken.[531] Ordinarily, if the motion has merit, the court will strike the insufficient defense in its entirety, and will not attempt to carve the defense in portions.[532] Moreover, if the defense is stricken, the pleader will generally be granted leave to file an amended answer unless the amendment would be futile.[533]

- *Strikes Involving Inference-Drawing:* Defenses will not be stricken on a motion to strike if the court would be required to draw factual inferences or decide disputed questions of fact in a manner that favors the moving party.[534]

---

[520] *See Lutzeier v. Citigroup Inc.*, 305 F.R.D. 107, 111 (E.D.Mo. 2015).

[521] *See Haley Paint Co. v. E.I. Du Pont De Nemours & Co.*, 279 F.R.D. 331, 335–36 (D.Md. 2012).

[522] *See* William M. Janssen, *The Odd State of* Twiqbal *Plausibility in Pleading Affirmative Defenses*, 70 Wash. & Lee L. Rev. 1573 (2013) (surveying national case law, finding substantial majority of courts reject *Twiqbal* for testing affirmative defenses). For a discussion of the *Twombly* standard, *see supra* Authors' Commentary to Rule 8(a) (**"Element 2: Short and Plain Statement of Claim"**) *and* Authors' Commentary to Rule 12(b)(6) (**"Rule 12(b)(6) After *Bell Atlantic v. Twombly"*).

[523] *See Hernandez v. County of Monterey*, 306 F.R.D. 279, 283 (N.D.Cal. 2015).

[524] *See Sibley v. Choice Hotels Int'l, Inc.*, 304 F.R.D. 125, 132–33 (E.D.N.Y. 2015).

[525] *See Waste Mgmt. Holdings, Inc. v. Gilmore*, 252 F.3d 316, 347 (4th Cir. 2001); *United States v. Honeywell Int'l, Inc.*, 841 F.Supp.2d 112, 113 (D.D.C. 2012).

[526] *See Operating Eng'rs Local 324 Health Care Plan v. G & W Const. Co.*, 783 F.3d 1045, 1050 (6th Cir. 2015).

[527] *See Openshaw v. Cohen, Klingenstein & Marks, Inc.*, 320 F.Supp.2d 357, 364 (D. Md. 2004).

[528] *See E.E.O.C. v. Bay Ridge Toyota, Inc.*, 327 F.Supp.2d 167, 170 (E.D. N.Y. 2004).

[529] *See Sibley v. Choice Hotels Int'l, Inc.*, 304 F.R.D. 125, 132 (E.D.N.Y. 2015).

[530] *See E.E.O.C. v. Product Fabricators, Inc.*, 873 F.Supp.2d 1093, 1097 (D.Minn. 2012).

[531] *See Fesnak & Assocs., LLP v. U.S. Bank Nat'l Ass'n*, 722 F.Supp.2d 496, 502 (D.Del. 2010).

[532] *See Stowe Woodward, L.L.C. v. Sensor Products, Inc.*, 230 F.R.D. 463, 468–69 (W.D. Va. 2005).

[533] *See Vogel v. Huntington Oaks Del. Partners, LLC*, 291 F.R.D. 438, 439–40 (C.D.Cal. 2013).

[534] *See Augustus v. Board of Public Instruction of Escambia County, Fla.*, 306 F.2d 862, 868 (5th Cir. 1962); *Newborn Bros. Co. v. Albion Eng'g Co.*, 299 F.R.D. 90, 93–94 (D.N.J. 2014).

- *Strikes Involving Substantial and Disputed Questions:* Motions to strike are generally not intended to resolve substantial and disputed questions of law: legal issues on which courts are divided, confused or unsettled legal areas, or issues involving close or new questions of law.[535]

- *Strikes Involving Admissibility:* Motions to strike are ordinarily improper tools for making anticipatory evidentiary and admissibility judgments.[536]

- *Strikes Before Discovery:* Although motions to strike must generally be filed before a responsive pleading is served, some courts have noted their reluctance to strike defenses where there has been "no significant discovery".[537]

Test for Striking Redundant, Immaterial, Impertinent, or Scandalous Matter

Absent a "strong reason for so doing", courts will generally "not tamper with pleadings".[538] The court will not strike such matter unless it bears no possible relation to the parties' dispute, or could confuse the issues.[539] Moreover, mere redundancy, immateriality, impertinence, or scandalousness is not sufficient to justify striking an allegation—the allegation must also be shown to be prejudicial to the moving party.[540] If any doubt exists whether the contested matter should be stricken, the motion should be denied.[541] Consequently, to prevail on such a motion, the moving party must establish that: (1) no evidence in support of the contested allegations would be admissible at trial; (2) the allegations have no bearing on the relevant issues in the case; and (3) denying the strike would prejudice the moving party.[542] The court will also be disinclined to strike matter where the case will be tried without a jury.

If granted, the court's order will typically describe in detail the precise matter that must be stricken.[543]

- *Redundant Matter:* A redundant allegation is a needless repetition of other averments.[544]

- *Immaterial Matter:* Immaterial allegations are those that either bear no essential or important relationship to the pleader's claim for relief or contain a statement of

---

[535] *See Karpov v. Karpov*, 307 F.R.D. 345, 348 (D.Del. 2015). *See also Canadian St. Regis Band of Mohawk Indians ex rel. Francis v. New York*, 278 F.Supp.2d 313, 324 (N.D. N.Y. 2003) (noting that, otherwise, courts would risk "offering an advisory opinion on an abstract and hypothetical set of facts").

[536] *See Aoki v. Benihana, Inc.*, 839 F.Supp.2d 759, 764 (D.Del. 2012).

[537] *See Canadian St. Regis Band of Mohawk Indians ex rel. Francis v. New York,* 278 F.Supp.2d 313, 324–25 (N.D. N.Y. 2003).

[538] *See McCrae Associates, LLC v. Universal Capital Management, Inc.*, 554 F.Supp.2d 249, 254 (D. Conn. 2008).

[539] *See Lipsky v. Commonwealth United Corp.*, 551 F.2d 887, 893 (2d Cir.1976) *See also Salahuddin v. Cuomo,* 861 F.2d 40, 42 (2d Cir. 1988) (Rule 12(f) reserved for instances where the pleading "is so confused, ambiguous, vague, or otherwise unintelligible that its true substance, if any, is well disguised");

[540] *See Greenwich Ins. Co. v. Rodgers*, 729 F.Supp.2d 1158, 1162 (C.D.Cal. 2010).

[541] *See Southwestern Bell Telephone, L.P. v. Missouri Public Service Com'n*, 461 F.Supp.2d 1055, 1064 (E.D. Mo. 2006), *aff'd*, 530 F.3d 676 (8th Cir. 2008).

[542] *See Tucker v. American Int'l. Group, Inc.*, 936 F.Supp.2d 1, 16–17 (D.Conn. 2013).

[543] *See Salahuddin v. Cuomo*, 861 F.2d 40, 43 (2d Cir. 1988) (noting that court would strike only so much of pleading as is redundant or immaterial).

[544] *See Lutzeier v. Citigroup Inc.*, 305 F.R.D. 107, 110 n.4 (E.D.Mo. 2015). *See also Sorosky v. Burroughs Corp.*, 826 F.2d 794, 802 (9th Cir. 1987) (where no arguments were presented in support of theory, it was vulnerable to dismissal as redundant). *But cf. Dethmers Mfg. Co., Inc. v. Automatic Equipment Mfg. Co.*, 23 F.Supp.2d 974, 1008–09 (N.D. Iowa 1998) (mere duplicative remedies do not necessarily make claims "redundant" if those claims require proof of different elements, but claim that simply recasts same elements under the guise of different theory may be stricken as redundant).

unnecessary particulars.[545] Allegations are immaterial if no evidence to support them would be admissible at trial.[546]

- *Impertinent Matter:* An impertinent allegation is an averment that does not pertain to, or is unnecessary to, the issues in dispute.[547] If the pleader would not be permitted to offer evidence at trial in support of the allegation, the allegation is likely impertinent.[548]

- *Scandalous Matter:* Scandalous matter does not merely offend someone's sensibilities; it must improperly cast a person or entity in a derogatory light.[549] Moreover, such matter will not be stricken if it describes acts or events relevant to the parties' dispute, unless the descriptions contain unnecessary detail.[550]

Striking Prayers for Relief

The courts are unclear whether Rule 12(f) motions are properly used to strike prayers seeking relief that are precluded as a matter of law. Some courts hold such use improper (reasoning that Rule 12(b)(6) or Rule 12(c) motions are the appropriate vehicles for such a remedy).[551]

Striking Improper Jury Demands

Rule 12(f) is a proper vehicle for striking an improper demand for trial by jury.[552]

Striking Class Action Allegations

Rule 12(f) is theoretically available to strike class action allegations, but only in the rare instance where it is obvious from the pleadings that class treatment would not be proper.[553]

Striking Portions of Judicial Opinion

Rule 12(f) cannot ordinarily be invoked to strike a portion of a court's judicial decision.[554]

---

[545] *See Petrie v. Electronic Game Card, Inc.*, 761 F.3d 959, 967 (9th Cir. 2014).

[546] *See Holmes v. Fischer*, 764 F.Supp.2d 523, 532 (W.D.N.Y. 2011).

[547] *See Whittlestone, Inc. v. Handicraft Co.*, 618 F.3d 970, 974 (9th Cir. 2010).

[548] *See Fantasy, Inc. v. Fogerty*, 984 F.2d 1524, 1527 (9th Cir. 1993), *rev'd on other grounds*, 510 U.S. 517, 114 S.Ct. 1023, 127 L.Ed.2d 455 (1994); *Holmes v. Fischer*, 764 F.Supp.2d 523, 532 (W.D.N.Y. 2011).

[549] *See Cortina v. Goya Foods, Inc.*, 94 F. Supp. 3d 1174, 1182 (S.D.Cal. 2015). *See, e.g., Alvarado-Morales v. Digital Equipment Corp.*, 843 F.2d 613, 617–18 (1st Cir. 1988) (striking as "scandalous" references to "concentration camp", "brainwash", and "torture" which impugned the characters of the defendant); *Right haven LLC v. Democratic Underground, LLC*, 791 F.Supp.2d 968, 977 (D.Nev. 2011) (casts person in "cruelly derogatory light"); *Florance v. Buchmeyer*, 500 F.Supp.2d 618, 645 (N.D. Tex. 2007) ("unnecessarily reflect[ ] on the moral character of an individual or state[ ] anything in repulsive language that detracts from the dignity of the court"); *Global View Ltd. Venture Capital v. Great Central Basin Exploration, L.L.C.*, 288 F.Supp.2d 473, 481 (S.D. N.Y. 2003) (it "amounts to nothing more than name calling, and does not contribute to [the] . . . substantive claims").

[550] *See United States v. Coney*, 689 F.3d 365, 379–80 (5th Cir. 2012) (mere risk of offending someone's sensibilities does not justify a strike if pleadings are directly relevant and minimally supported); *Talbot v. Robert Matthews Distributing Co.*, 961 F.2d 654, 664–65 (7th Cir. 1992) (matter is "scandalous" if it bears no possible relation to the controversy).

[551] *See Whittlestone, Inc. v. Handicraft Co.*, 618 F.3d 970, 974 (9th Cir. 2010).

[552] *See Starnes Family Office, LLC v. McCullar*, 765 F.Supp.2d 1036, 1055 (W.D.Tenn. 2011).

[553] *See Manning v. Boston Med. Ctr. Corp.*, 725 F.3d 34, 59 (1st Cir. 2013).

[554] *See Act Now to Stop War and End Racism Coalition v. District of Columbia*, 286 F.R.D. 117, 125 & 132 (D.D.C. 2012).

Striking Documents Other than Pleadings

As defined in Rule 12(f), motions to strike are directed to "pleadings" only. Consequently, these motions are technically not available to strike material contained in motions, briefs, memoranda, or affidavits.[555] Some courts, however, have permitted Rule 12(f) motions to strike affidavits and other materials that support pleadings,[556] and, in certain cases, expert reports.[557] Of those courts, some reason that Rule 12(f) offers the "only viable method" for challenging the materiality and pertinence of the documents under attack.[558] Others treat this technically improper use of Rule 12(f) as an "invitation" to adjudicate the admissibility of the contested materials.[559] Not all courts, however, will accept these uses of the motion.[560] Note, however, that local rules may permit courts to "strike" a document that violates a properly promulgated local requirement (such as no surreply briefs without prior approval).[561]

Timing

A motion to strike must be made before a responsive pleading is served or, if no responsive pleading is required, within 21 days after service of the preceding pleading.[562] In view of the court's authority to strike on its own initiative, this 21-day period is often not applied strictly when the proposal to strike has merit.[563]

Discretion of Trial Court

The decision to grant or deny a motion to strike is vested in the trial judge's sound discretion.[564]

Sua Sponte Strikes

At any time, the court may, on its own initiative, strike matter from a pleading.[565] Thus, the court may properly consider a party's untimely motion or "suggestion" under Rule 12(f) to strike matter from the pleading.[566]

Extrinsic Materials

Generally, the court will not consider extrinsic materials on a motion to strike.[567] Instead, the grounds supporting the motion to strike must be readily apparent from the face of the pleadings at issue, from materials incorporated within them by reference, or matters

---

[555] *See Pilgrim v. Trustees of Tufts College,* 118 F.3d 864, 868 (1st Cir.1997) (not for motion papers or supporting affidavits); *Mallory v. City of Riverside,* 35 F.Supp.3d 910, 940 (S.D. Ohio 2014) (not for reply briefs); *Gaylor v. Greenbriar of Dahlonega Shopping Ctr., Inc.,* 975 F.Supp.2d 1374, 1381 (N.D. Ga. 2013) (not for affidavits) *Hagen v. Siouxland Obstetrics & Gynecology, P.C.,* 934 F.Supp.2d 1026, 1042–43 (N.D. Iowa 2013) (not for appendix and facts statement); *Albertson v. Fremont County,* 834 F.Supp.2d 1117, 1123 n.3 (D.Idaho 2011) (not for exhibits to motion response); *MJ Harbor Hotel, LLC v. McCormick & Schmick Restaurant Corp.,* 599 F.Supp.2d 612, 623 (D.Md. 2009) (not for expert report or testimony); *Dragon v. I.C. System, Inc.,* 241 F.R.D. 424, 425–26 (D. Conn. 2007) (not for summary judgment statements).

[556] *See Henok v. Chase Home Finance, LLC,* 925 F.Supp.2d 46, 53 n.2 (D.D.C. 2013).

[557] *See Barnes v. District of Columbia,* 289 F.R.D. 1, 6 (D.D.C. 2012).

[558] *See Wane v. Loan Corp.,* 926 F.Supp.2d 1312, 1317 (M.D.Fla. 2013).

[559] *See Natural Resources Defense Council v. Kempthorne,* 539 F.Supp.2d 1155, 1161–61 (E.D. Cal. 2008).

[560] *See Johnson v. Gestamp Alabama, LLC,* 946 F.Supp.2d 1180, 1192 (N.D.Ala. 2013) (discussing differing views, and rejecting use of motion to strike).

[561] *See Estate of Anderson v. Denny's Inc.,* 291 F.R.D. 622, 631 (D.N.M. 2013).

[562] *See United States v. $38,000.00 Dollars in U.S. Currency,* 816 F.2d 1538, 1547 (11th Cir. 1987).

[563] *See Phoenix Ins. Co. v. Small,* 307 F.R.D. 426, 434 (E.D.Pa. 2015).

[564] *See Delta Consulting Group, Inc. v. R. Randle Const., Inc.,* 554 F.3d 1133, 1141 (7th Cir. 2009).

[565] *See Delta Consulting Group, Inc. v. R. Randle Const., Inc.,* 554 F.3d 1133, 1141 (7th Cir. 2009).

[566] *See United States v. Lot 65 Pine Meadow,* 976 F.2d 1155, 1157 (8th Cir. 1992).

[567] *See Karpov v. Karpov,* 307 F.R.D. 345, 347 (D.Del. 2015).

of which the court may take judicial notice.[568] If the court does consider extrinsic materials, the motion to strike must ordinarily be converted into a motion for summary judgment.[569]

Converting Mislabeled Rule 12(f) Motions

The appropriate vehicle for testing the factual sufficiency of a pleading is usually not a motion to strike, but a Rule 12(b)(6) motion to dismiss or a Rule 12(c) motion for judgment on the pleadings.[570] Ordinarily, a mislabeled motion to strike that challenges factual sufficiency will simply be treated as a motion to dismiss.[571]

Prejudice on Dismissal

Where an allegation or defense is stricken as technically deficient, the dismissal is generally without prejudice to refile with a technically correct pleading.[572]

RULE 12(g)—JOINING MOTIONS

CORE CONCEPT

A defending party may file a pre-answer motion (which usually postpones the obligation to file an answer) in order to assert defenses and objections listed in Rule 12. If a defending party elects to do so, that party must then include all of its Rule 12 defenses and objections then available in a single, omnibus motion. Rule 12(g) must be read in conjunction with Rule 12(h), concerning waiver of certain defenses.

APPLICATIONS

Rule and Its Consequences

Any Rule 12 motion may be joined with any other Rule 12 motion.[573] The consequences of making a Rule 12 motion are four-fold. *First,* a party is generally permitted to make only one Rule 12 motion; thus, a party who intends to have the court resolve *any* Rule 12 defense or objection at the pre-answer motion stage must also simultaneously present to the court *every* other Rule 12 defense or objection the party intends to raise.[574] *Second,* including all such Rule 12 defenses and objections together at once causes no forfeiture of those that are inconsistent with one another.[575] *Third,* omitting from any Rule 12 pre-answer motion an objection to personal jurisdiction, venue, process, or service of process likely waives that objection.[576] *Fourth,* omitting other, non-waivable Rule 12 defenses and objections still likely waives the party's right to have those matters considered at the pre-answer stage, thus relegating the party to having to wait until later in the case to assert them.[577] The intent behind these consequences is to avoid piecemeal litigating tactics, where defendants seek dismissal on one ground, lose there, and then seek dismissal anew on a different ground.[578]

---

[568] *See Petrie v. Electronic Game Card, Inc.,* 761 F.3d 959, 966 (9th Cir. 2014).

[569] *See Liberty Mut. Ins. Co. v. Precision Valve Corp.,* 402 F.Supp.2d 481, 484 (S.D. N.Y. 2005).

[570] *See Williams v. County of Alameda,* 26 F.Supp.3d 925 (N.D. Cal. 2014).

[571] *See Williams v. County of Alameda,* 26 F.Supp.3d 925 (N.D. Cal. 2014).

[572] *See Amini Innovation Corp. v. McFerran Home Furnishings, Inc.,* 301 F.R.D. 487, 490 (C.D. Cal. 2014).

[573] *See* Rule 12(g)(1).

[574] *See* Rule 12(g)(2). *See McCurdy v. American Bd. of Plastic Surgery,* 157 F.3d 191, 194 (3d Cir. 1998).

[575] *See Mattiaccio v. DHA Group, Inc.,* 20 F.Supp.2d 220, 226 (D.D.C. 2014). *See also Duro Textiles, LLC v. Sunbelt Corp.,* 12 F.Supp.2d 221, 224 (D. Mass. 2014) (improper to "reserve" on raising defenses in fear that the mere raising of them will forfeit others).

[576] *See* Rule 12(h)(1). *See also infra* Authors' Commentary to Rule 12(h)(1) ("Basic Rule: Waived Defenses and Objections").

[577] *See Jaffer v. Standard Chartered Bank,* 301 F.R.D. 256, 259 (N.D. Tex. 2014).

[578] *See Ennenga v. Starns,* 677 F.3d 766, 773 (7th Cir. 2012).

Exception—Prohibition Applies Only to Defenses "Then Available"

A party is required to assert in an omnibus motion only those defenses and objections "then available" to that party.[579] For example, a party is obviously not obliged to assert an objection to timely service while the time permitted for timely service has not yet expired.[580] Thus, new defenses and objections may be later asserted if they are triggered by an amended pleading or a more definite statement,[581] by a change in the law occurring while the motion is pending,[582] or by other interim developments.[583] But parties must act promptly. An unnecessarily lengthy delay in asserting a latent Rule 12 objection may, itself, be deemed a waiver.[584]

Exception—Amended Complaints

Because an amended complaint supersedes its predecessor, some courts permit the filing of new Rule 12 motions against the amended complaint, even though those grounds were or could have been asserted against the original pleading.[585] Other courts reject this approach.[586]

Exception—Prior Motions to Stay/Dismiss/Abstain

Some courts have ruled that this preclusion of successive Rule 12 motions to dismiss will not apply where the preceding motion to dismiss or to stay was based on an alleged lack of federal jurisdiction under some abstention principle.[587]

Exception—No Unnecessary Delay

Even where other exceptions do not apply, the prohibition on successive Rule 12 motions is not absolute. Some courts have permitted a second motion where it would not result in unnecessary delay, expense, or inconvenience and would promote a more expeditious resolution of the case.[588]

Exception—Objections to Subject Matter Jurisdiction

Objections to subject matter jurisdiction concern the court's authority to hear and decide the case. Consequently, such objections cannot generally be lost through waiver.[589]

"Amending" a Rule 12 Motion

To avoid waiving Rule 12 defenses that were omitted inadvertently from a Rule 12 motion, parties may seek leave of court to "amend" or supplement their Rule 12 motions to include the omitted defenses or objections.[590] In considering such amendments, the court may examine whether the amendment request was filed before the Rule 12 motion was heard, the time interval between the original Rule 12 motion and the attempted correction,

---

[579] *See Gilmore v. Palestinian Interim Self-Gov't Auth.*, 8 F.Supp.2d 9, 12 (D.D.C. 2014).

[580] *See Teamsters Local 639Employers, Health Trust v. Hileman*, 988 F.Supp.2d 18, 25 (D.D.C. 2013).

[581] *See McCurdy v. American Bd. of Plastic Surgery*, 157 F.3d 191, 196 (3d Cir. 1998).

[582] *See Holzsager v. Valley Hospital*, 646 F.2d 792, 796 (2d Cir. 1981) (courts will not demand clairvoyance from litigants; parties not deemed to have waived defenses or objections not then known to them); *Engel v. CBS, Inc.*, 886 F.Supp. 728, 728–730 (C.D. Cal. 1995) (holding that Rule 12(g) will not fault defendants for failing to press a defense they did not then know was available to them).

[583] *See Allstate Ins. Co. v. Elzanaty*, 929 F.Supp.2d 199, 214 (E.D.N.Y. 2013).

[584] *See Gilmore v. Palestinian Interim Self-Gov't Auth.*, 8 F.Supp.2d 9, 12 (D.D.C. 2014).

[585] *See In re WellPoint, Inc. Out-of-Network UCR Rates Litig.*, 903 F.Supp.2d 880, 893–94 (C.D.Cal. 2012).

[586] *See Rowley v. McMillan*, 502 F.2d 1326, 1332–33 (4th Cir. 1974).

[587] *See Aetna Life Ins. Co. v. Alla Medical Services, Inc.*, 855 F.2d 1470, 1475 (9th Cir. 1988).

[588] *See Hobart Corp. v. Dayton Power & Light Co.*, 997 F.Supp.2d 835, 851, n.5 (S.D. Ohio 2014).

[589] *See Rule 12(h)(3).*

[590] *See Chatman-Bey v. Thornburgh*, 864 F.2d 804, 813 (D.C. Cir. 1988).

the moving party's good faith, and the likelihood that the omission was intentional and tactical, or merely inadvertent.[591]

Applies Only to Same Moving Party

The consolidation obligation is only triggered when the same party attempts to make a later Rule 12 motion. Thus, a Rule 12 filing by one co-defendant does not foreclose a later Rule 12 filing by a different co-defendant,[592] even when they share the same counsel.[593] Similarly, a law enforcement officer who moves to dismiss claims filed against him in his official capacity is likely not foreclosed from later asserting Rule 12 defendants to claims filed against him in his individual capacity.[594]

Applies to All Rule 12 Motions

This omnibus "consolidation" requirement applies to all Rule 12 motions, including the Rule 12(b) defenses as well as Rule 12(e) motions for more definite statements and Rule 12(f) motions to strike.[595] Thus, for example, a motion seeking only a more definite statement will likely have the effect of waiving challenges to personal jurisdiction, venue, process, and service.

Applies Only to Rule 12 Motions

This "consolidation" provision applies only to Rule 12 motions and only to defenses that may be asserted under Rule 12. It does not apply to motions allowed under other Rules or laws,[596] nor does it apply to affirmative defenses (which remain preserved, even after a Rule 12 motion, if timely asserted in the responsive pleading).[597]

Successive Rule 12(b)(6) Motions to Dismiss

The *defense* of failure-to-state-a-claim is not waived if omitted from a pre-answer Rule 12 motion; to the contrary, that *defense* may be raised in a later pleading, a Rule 12(c) motion for judgment on the pleadings, or at trial. [598] Less clear, however, is whether that *defense* can be raised in a second or subsequent *pre-answer* motion, or must it wait until later. Some courts have interpreted this Rule to tolerate multiple, successive pre-answer Rule 12(b)(6) motions (at least absent prejudice or adverse impact on judicial economy).[599] Other courts have reached the opposite conclusion, reading the Rule to preclude the filing of successive pre-answer motions (at least where they raise arguments that could have been asserted earlier).[600] Those same courts may impose this prohibition as well to Rule 12(b)(6) motions filed against amended complaints that raise grounds that could have been pressed against

---

[591] *See Thomas v. Bank,* 2009 WL 481349, at *1 (M.D.Ga. Feb. 25, 2009) (denying amendment sought tactically). *See also Maxtena, Inc. v. Marks,* 2012 WL 113386, at *11 (D.Md. Jan. 12, 2012) (rejecting, seemingly categorically, such amendments as "an end run around both Rule 12(g)(2) and settled law).

[592] *See Muhammed v. Bernstein,* 2013 WL 3177864, at *4 (D.Md. June 21, 2013) (co-defendant have no obligation to file joint Rule 12 motions).

[593] *See Schnabel v. Lui,* 302 F.3d 1023, 1034 (9th Cir. 2002).

[594] *See King v. Taylor,* 694 F.3d 650, 656–57 (6th Cir. 2012).

[595] *See Gables Ins. Recovery v. United Healthcare Ins. Co.,* 39 F.Supp.3d 1377, 1390, n.10 (S.D. Fla. 2013).

[596] *See, e.g., Conrad v. Phone Directories Co.,* 585 F.3d 1376, 1383 n.2 (10th Cir. 2009) (not to motion to compel arbitration under FAA); *Yavuz v. 61 MM, Ltd.,* 576 F.3d 1166, 1173 (10th Cir. 2009) (not to forum non conveniens motions).

[597] *See Parker v. United States,*110 F.3d 678, 682 (9th Cir. 1997).

[598] *See* Rule 12(g)(2). *See also Ennenga v. Starns,* 677 F.3d 766, 773 (7th Cir. 2012) (confirming that Rule 12(g) does not preclude a new Rule 12(b)(6) argument made in a later motion).

[599] *See Allstate Ins. Co. v. Elzanaty,* 929 F.Supp.2d 199, 214 (E.D.N.Y. 2013). *See generally Styles v. Triple Crown Publ'ns, LLC,* 2012 WL 1964443, at *3 (D.Md. May 30, 2012) (collecting cases).

[600] *See McClain v. Citizen's Bank, N.A.,* 57 F.Supp.3d 438, 443 (E.D.Pa. 2014).

the original complaint.[601] Still other courts sidestep this knotty debate entirely, ruling that even if successful motions are technically improper, the result is harmless error.[602]

Later Rule 12(c) Motion on Same Grounds

A party enjoys the right to press a failure to state a claim defense in a post-answer Rule 12(c) motion for judgment on the pleadings.[603] Most courts construe this right broadly, permitting its use even where the party could have, or actually did, press this same defense in its earlier pre-answer motion.[604] Other courts question whether such a use comports with Rule 12(g)'s "consolidation" policy.[605]

RULE 12(h)—WAIVING AND PRESERVING CERTAIN DEFENSES

CORE CONCEPT

Rule 12(h) sets forth the defenses and objections that are waived if not timely asserted, and lists the defenses and objections that are not waivable.

APPLICATIONS

Basic Rule: Waived Defenses and Objections

Defenses and objections to personal jurisdiction (Rule 12(b)(2)), improper venue (Rule 12(b)(3)), insufficient process (Rule 12(b)(4)), and insufficient service (Rule 12(b)(5)), are waived [606] unless they are *either*:

- *Asserted by Motion:* In an omnibus Rule 12(b) motion, if one is filed, *or*

- *Asserted by Responsive Pleading:* If an omnibus Rule 12(b) motion is not filed.

Purpose

Judicial economy underlies this waiver provision. Automatic waiver is designed to prevent the delaying effect of the piecemeal assertion of Rule 12 objections and defenses through multiple motions, and to permit the early dismissal of inappropriate claims before the court devotes unnecessary time and resources to adjudication.[607]

Waiver Is Mandatory, Not Discretionary

The waiver provision of Rule 12(h) imposes a mandatory, not discretionary, obligation upon the district court.[608]

---

[601] *See Albany Ins. Co. v. Almacenadora Somex, S.A.,* 5 F.3d 907, 909 (5th Cir. 1993). *See also Pruco Life Ins. Co. v. Wilmington Trust Co.,* 616 F.Supp.2d 210, 214–16 (D.R.I. 2009) ("in law, as in life, do-overs are a rare commodity, and Rule 12 does not provide one here").

[602] *See Albers v. Bd. of Cty. Com'rs of Jefferson Cty.,* 771 F.3d 697, 703–04 (10th Cir. 2014).

[603] *See* Rule 12(g)(2) (failure to state claim is exception to bar on later motions); Rule 12(h)(2)(B) (permitting failure to state a claim to be raised on later Rule 12(c) motion).

[604] *See Abecassis v. Wyatt,* 7 F.Supp.3d 668 670 (S.D. Tex. 2014).

[605] *See Sprint Telephony PCS, L.P. v. County of San Diego,* 311 F.Supp.2d 898, 904–05 (S.D. Cal. 2004).

[606] *See, e.g., Wachovia Bank v. Schmidt,* 546 U.S. 303, 316, 126 S.Ct. 941, 950, 163 L.Ed.2d 797 (2006) (venue waived if not timely raised); *Ennenga v. Starns,* 677 F.3d 766, 773 (7th Cir. 2012) (untimely raised personal jurisdiction, venue, process, or service objections are waived).

[607] *See Ennenga v. Starns,* 677 F.3d 766, 773 (7th Cir. 2012).

[608] *See Pusey v. Dallas Corp.,* 938 F.2d 498, 501 n.4 (4th Cir.1991) (trial court *prohibited* from dismissing on basis of waived defense).

Waiver by Improper Assertion

A Rule 12(h) waivable defense may be lost by asserting it too obscurely or indirectly,[609] by asserting it incompletely,[610] or by asserting it too late in the applicable pleading or motion process.[611]

Waiver by Pre-Answer Summary Judgment Omission

A party cannot escape waiver by jumping ahead of the answer/pre-answer motion to dismiss stage and filing an early motion for summary judgment. Defenses (like personal jurisdiction) that could have, but were not, raised in such a summary judgment motion likely result in waiver as well.[612]

Waiver by Implication

By the very act of suing, a plaintiff impliedly waives any personal jurisdiction and venue objections.[613] Defendants, too, by their conduct, may impliedly waive objections to personal jurisdiction, venue, insufficient process, or insufficient service of process, even though those defenses were set forth in a timely motion to dismiss or in a responsive pleading. For example, a defendant who timely objects to personal jurisdiction, but then fails to timely bring the defense to the court for a ruling, choosing instead to participate actively in the litigation as though jurisdiction, venue, and proper service existed, may be deemed to have waived the jurisdictional objection.[614]

- *Waiver and Asserting Affirmative Claims:* Although some contrary authority persists,[615] the developing trend seems to suggest that a party does *not* waive a properly, timely asserted objection to jurisdiction by pressing an affirmative claim for relief,[616] or by filing ancillary motions (*e.g.*, for stay or injunction pending appeal) premised on the asserted jurisdictional defense.[617] This trend construes such affirmative claims for relief as simply contingent on the court's denial of the party's jurisdictional objections.[618]

---

[609] *See, e.g., Hemispherx Biopharma, Inc. v. Johannesburg Consol. Invs.,* 553 F.3d 1351, 1360–61 (11th Cir. 2008) (personal jurisdiction challenge does not imply a companion (but unasserted) service challenge).

[610] *See Crispin-Taveras v. Municipality of Carolina,* 647 F.3d 1, 7 (1st Cir. 2011) (objection to manner of service waived when party earlier objected only to service timeliness).

[611] *See Ramer v. United States,*620 F.Supp.2d 90, 102 (D.D.C. 2009) (defense waived when asserted in motion reply brief, not opening brief).

[612] *See Casares v. Agri-Placements Int'l, Inc.,* 12 F.Supp.2d 956, 966 (S.D. Tex. 2014).

[613] *See Adam v. Saenger,* 303 U.S. 59, 67–68, 58 S.Ct. 454, 458, 82 L. Ed. 649 (1938).

[614] *See King v. Taylor,* 694 F.3d 650, 658–61 (6th Cir. 2012). *See generally Fabara v. GoFit, LLC,* 308 F.R.D. 380, 390 (D.N.M. 2015) (collecting cases on waiver by delay in assertion of defense).

[615] *See Frank's Casing Crew & Rental Tools, Inc. v. PMR Technologies, Ltd.,* 292 F.3d 1363, 1372 (Fed. Cir. 2002) (holding that non-resident defendant in patent noninfringement declaratory judgment action waived personal jurisdiction objection when it filed class action counterclaim asserting unrelated infringements of patent by others).

[616] *See Hillis v. Heineman,* 626 F.3d 1014, 1017–19 (9th Cir. 2010) (filing of counterclaim and third-party complaint did not waive properly pleaded venue or personal jurisdiction defense); *Bayou Steel Corp. v. M/V Amstelvoorn,* 809 F.2d 1147, 1149 (5th Cir.1987) (discussing divergent views, but holding that filing of counterclaim, crossclaim, or third-party claim does not waive properly preserved objection to personal jurisdiction).

[617] *See PaineWebber Inc. v. Chase Manhattan Private Bank (Switzerland),* 260 F.3d 453, 461 (5th Cir. 2001) (defendant who timely and properly asserted personal jurisdiction objection by motion, and engaged in no counterclaim or third-party practice, did not waive defense by filing motion for stay and injunction pending appeal premised on the jurisdictional defense).

[618] *See Bayou Steel Corp. v. M/V Amstelvoorn,* 809 F.2d 1147, 1149 (5th Cir. 1987).

Avoiding Waiver by Answering Only (No Motion)

Notwithstanding a language anomaly in Rule 12,[619] parties have the option of asserting their defenses *either* by motion *or* in their responsive pleading.[620] Thus, unless a waiver by implication later occurs (see above), parties who elect not to file a Rule 12 motion at all still dutifully preserve their defenses and objections by asserting them in their responsive pleading,[621] and may thereafter challenge them on a Rule 12(c) motion for judgment on the pleadings.[622]

Avoiding Waiver Through Amendment

A party's failure to assert a timely defense or objection can be cured if the court grants the delinquent party leave to amend the pleading or the Rule 12 motion.[623] Before granting such a waiver-rescuing amendment, the court may examine the timeliness of the amendment request (*e.g.,* if filed before the motion was heard), the time interval between the original filing and the attempted correction, the movant's good faith, and the likelihood the omission was inadvertent rather than intentional and tactical.[624]

Preserved Defenses and Objections

Defenses and objections to a failure to state a claim upon which relief can be granted (Rule 12(b)(6)), failure to join an indispensable party (Rule 12(b)(7)), and failure to state a legal defense (Rule 12(f)) are waived *only* if not asserted before the close of trial.[625] These defenses, though generally preserved throughout the lawsuit, may not be raised for the first time in post-trial motions or on appeal.[626]

- *Only One Pre-Answer Rule 12(b)(6) Motion:* Some (but not all) courts have ruled that successive, pre-answer Rule 12(b)(6) motions are prohibited by Rule 12(g)'s requirement that all Rule 12 defenses (including failure to state a claim) be raised in a single, omnibus, pre-answer motion-if the party chooses to file a motion at all.[627]

- *Non-Waiver Applies to "Indispensable" Parties Only:* Rule 12(h) preserves only the defense of dismissal for failing to join an "indispensable" party. Where a party is necessary for proper adjudication under Rule 19, but can be joined as a party in the lawsuit, a motion for joinder may not be made if omitted from an omnibus Rule 12 motion or, alternatively, from the responsive pleading.[628]

- *Preserved in Multi-Case Litigations:* A defendant sued in multiple lawsuits does not waive Rule 12(b) defenses in later cases by having failed to assert similar defenses in earlier cases.[629]

Objections to Subject Matter Jurisdiction

Because objections to the court's subject matter jurisdiction concern the court's authority to hear and decide the parties' dispute, no one can waive such an objection, be

---

[619] *See Pope v. Elabo GmbH,* 588 F.Supp.2d 1008, 1012–13 (D.Minn. 2008) (noting anomaly).

[620] *See* Rule 12(h)(1)(B).

[621] *See Argentine Republic v. National Grid Plc,* 637 F.3d 365, 367 (D.C.Cir. 2011).

[622] *See Adami v. Cardo Windows, Inc.,* 299 F.R.D. 68, 88 (D.N.J. 2014).

[623] *See* Rule 12(h)(1)(B)(ii); Rule 15. *See also Gray v. Snow King Resort, Inc.,* 889 F.Supp. 1473, 1475 (D. Wyo. 1995).

[624] *See Nycal Corp. v. Inoco PLC,* 949 F.Supp. 1115, 1119–20 (S.D. N.Y. 1997) (denying amendment sought tactically).

[625] *See Arbaugh v. Y&H Corp.,* 546 U.S. 500, 507, 126 S.Ct. 1235, 1236, 163 L.Ed.2d 1097 (2006).

[626] *Brown v. Trustees of Boston University,* 891 F.2d 337, 357 (1st Cir. 1989).

[627] *See supra* Authors' Commentary to Rule 12(g) (**"Successive Rule 12 Motions to Dismiss"**).

[628] *See Citibank, N.A. v. Oxford Properties & Finance Ltd.,* 688 F.2d 1259, 1262–63 (9th Cir. 1982).

[629] *See In re Cathode Ray Tube (CRT) Antitrust Litig.,* 27 F.Supp.3d 1002, 1009 (N.D. Cal. 2014).

estopped from raising the objection, or cure such a problem by consenting to jurisdiction where none exists.[630]

- *Asserted at Any Time:* Objections to subject matter jurisdiction may be made in the omnibus Rule 12 motion, in the responsive pleading, in subsequent pretrial motions, in a motion for relief from final judgment, or on appeal.[631] There is some authority that this liberality might not be unbounded; one court has ruled that the objection must be made while the case is still pending (*e.g.,* before trial, at trial, or on appeal); it cannot be raised for the first time as a collateral attack on the earlier judgment.[632]

- *"Suggestions":* Although a motion to dismiss for lack of subject matter jurisdiction is technically untimely if filed after the pleadings are closed, the courts will typically treat such a belated motion as a "suggestion" to the court that it lacks subject matter jurisdiction, and will then proceed to consider it on its merits.[633]

- *Raised by Court:* The trial court or the court of appeals may raise an objection to subject matter jurisdiction on its own initiative.[634]

Waiting for Default, Then Collaterally Attacking

Although the Rules require defendants to raise their objections to process, service, and personal jurisdiction in either an omnibus Rule 12 motion or the answer (if no motion is filed), these defenses are not necessarily lost where the defendants neither appear nor defend, but default.[635] In that instance, the constitutional protections of due process should permit those defendants to raise those objections in opposition to the motion for default [636] or collaterally.[637] But defendants act at their peril if they actually receive notice of the pending lawsuit and choose to ignore it, in reliance on their own, untested belief that process, service, or personal jurisdiction was faulty. Minimally, they must guess correctly. If they've guessed wrong, they likely forfeit their right to defend on the merits.[638] Conversely, if they timely raise these objections (and thus avoid a default), they have assented to the forum's jurisdiction to determine its own jurisdiction, and are thereby barred from attacking collaterally and, instead, must take any resulting jurisdictional grievance up on a direct appeal.[639]

---

[630] *See* Rule 12(b)(1)'s *Wachovia Bank v. Schmidt,* 546 U.S. 303, 316, 126 S.Ct. 941, 950, 163 L.Ed.2d 797 (2006) (subject matter jurisdiction must be considered by court, even if parties do not raise it).

[631] *See Arbaugh v. Y&H Corp.,* 546 U.S. 500, 506, 126 S.Ct. 1235, 1236, 163 L.Ed.2d 1097 (2006).

[632] *See City of South Pasadena v. Mineta,* 284 F.3d 1154, 1156–57 (9th Cir. 2002).

[633] *See S.J. v. Hamilton County, Ohio,* 374 F.3d 416, 418 n.1 (6th Cir. 2004).

[634] *See Wachovia Bank v. Schmidt,* 546 U.S. 303, 316, 126 S.Ct. 941, 163 L.Ed.2d 797 (2006); *Insurance Corp. of Ireland, Ltd. v. Compagnie des Bauxites de Guinee,* 456 U.S. 694, 704, 102 S.Ct. 2099, 2105, 72 L.Ed.2d 492 (1982). *See also Aljabri v. Holder,* 745 F.3d 816, 818 (7th Cir. 2014) (courts have "obligation" to raise issue independently).

[635] *See Wong v. PartyGaming Ltd.,* 589 F.3d 821, 826 n.3 (6th Cir. 2009) (party does not waive Rule 12(b) defense simply by failing to respond timely).

[636] *See Stinecipher v. United States,*239 F.R.D. 282, 283 (D.D.C. 2006) (unless proper service is satisfied, court lacks power to assert personal jurisdiction). *See also Trustees of the St. Paul Elec. Const. Industry Fringe Benefit Funds v. Martens Elec. Co.,* 485 F.Supp.2d 1063, 1065 (D. Minn. 2007) (noting that defendants who are not properly served are protected against default).

[637] *See Insurance Corp. of Ireland, Ltd. v. Compagnie des Bauxites de Guinee,* 456 U.S. 694, 706, 102 S.Ct. 2099, 72 L.Ed.2d 492, 34 Fed.R.Serv.2d 1 (1982) ("A defendant is always free to ignore the judicial proceedings, risk a default judgment, and then challenge that judgment on jurisdictional grounds in a collateral proceeding."); *Baldwin v. Iowa State Traveling Men's Ass'n,* 283 U.S. 522, 525, 51 S.Ct. 517, 75 L.Ed. 1244 (1931) (defendant objecting to personal jurisdiction has "the election not to appear at all," and then to attack collaterally).

[638] *See* Rule 12(h)(1) (if court *has* jurisdiction, failure to properly assert process, service, and personal jurisdiction defense waives them); Rule 8(b)(6) (any allegation not timely denied is admitted, if response was required).

[639] *See Philos Techs., Inc. v. Philos & D, Inc.,* 645 F.3d 851, 856 (7th Cir. 2011).

- *Actual Notice:* Defendants who seek to object on service grounds, but who received actual notice of the lawsuit, may be found to have waived their service objections [640] or to have had those objections otherwise materially compromised.[641]

- *Appearing to Defend Default:* Appearing to participate in proceedings following entry of default will likely waive service and personal jurisdiction objections, unless, upon appearing, the defaulting party promptly asserts them.[642]

- *Appearing and Abandoning:* Likewise, those objections may also be waived if the defendant begins to assert them and then abandons them.[643]

- *Burden of Proof:* In a direct challenge, the party invoking the court's jurisdiction bears the burden of proving it; in a collateral challenge, the party contesting the original court's jurisdiction has the burden of disproving it.[644]

RULE 12(i)—HEARING BEFORE TRIAL

CORE CONCEPT

Unless the court orders that such motions are deferred until trial, the court may, *sua sponte* or upon a party's request, schedule Rule 12(b) and Rule 12(c) motions for a pretrial hearing and resolution.

APPLICATIONS

Impact of 2007 "Restyling" Amendments

Rule 12(i) was repositioned in 2007. The current content of Rule 12(i) was formerly found in Rule 12(d). In researching Rule 12(i), practitioners should be mindful of this change.

Rule 12(b) Defenses Asserted by Motion

When a Rule 12(b) defense or objection is asserted on a Rule 12(b) or Rule 12(c) motion, the moving papers themselves should include a "notice of hearing" or similar references following the practice dictated by the specific judicial district's local rules. As a matter of usual practice, the court will ordinarily resolve Rule 12(b) and Rule 12(c) motions by issuing a pretrial Memorandum and Order.

Rule 12(b) Defenses Asserted by Responsive Pleading

When a Rule 12(b) defense or objection is asserted only in the responsive pleading (*i.e.,* where no pre-answer Rule 12(b) motion for dismissal is filed), a Rule 12(i) application for

---

[640] *See Corestates Leasing, Inc. v. Wright-Way Exp., Inc.,* 190 F.R.D. 356, 358 (E.D. Pa. 2000); *see also O'Meara v. Waters,* 464 F.Supp.2d 474, 476 (D. Md. 2006) (if defendants receive actual notice, failure to comply strictly with Rule 4 might be excused and service deemed valid). *See also* 5A Charles Alan Wright & Arthur R. Miller, Federal Practice & Procedure § 1391, at 755 to 56 (1990) ("But when the party has received actual notice of the suit there is no due process problem in requiring him to object to the ineffective service within the period prescribed by Rule 12(h)(1) and the defense is one that he certainly can waive if he wishes to do so. This is because the defendant has failed to do what the rule says he must do if he is to avoid a waiver.").

[641] *See Burda Media, Inc. v. Viertel,* 417 F.3d 292, 299 (2d Cir.2005) (ruling that where defaulting defendant had actual knowledge of proceeding, but delayed challenging allegedly improper service of process, that defendant will, in subsequent motion to vacate default, bear burden of proving that contested service did not occur).

[642] *See Democratic Republic of Congo v. FG Hemisphere Associates, LLC,* 508 F.3d 1062, 1064–65 (D.C. Cir. 2007).

[643] *See City of New York v. Mickalis Pawn Shop, LLC,* 645 F.3d 114, 134–36 (2d Cir. 2011).

[644] *See Philos Techs., Inc. v. Philos & D, Inc.,* 645 F.3d 851, 856–57 (7th Cir. 2011).

preliminary hearing is necessary to obtain a pretrial determination from the court on those defenses and objections.[645]

When Pretrial Determinations Are Proper

Even in the presence of a genuine factual dispute, the court may nevertheless decide, *pretrial,* challenges affecting subject matter jurisdiction, personal jurisdiction, standing, venue, and certain threshold defenses (like preclusion).[646] Such hearings have also proved useful in assessing pleadings against the *Twombly* standard.[647] In deciding whether these types of issues should be determined preliminarily (or should, instead, await resolution at trial), the court weighs the need to test these defenses and the litigants' interest in having the objections resolved promptly, against the expense and delay of a preliminary hearing, the court's difficulty in deciding the issues preliminarily, and the likelihood that the issues will become so interconnected with the merits that deferring them until trial would be preferable.[648]

On Motion or *Sua Sponte*

A hearing may be ordered upon a party's request or by the court *sua sponte.*[649]

When Pretrial Determinations Are Properly Deferred

This Rule confirms that a district court's *pretrial* review and disposition of Rule 12(b) defenses and Rule 12(c) motions is discretionary, not mandatory. In appropriate cases, involving peculiarly complicated factual and legal issues, or where further factual development is necessary, the court may defer resolving Rule 12(b) defenses until time of trial.[650]

Oral Argument and Hearing

The moving party is generally not *entitled* to oral argument or an evidentiary hearing on the motion; instead, the right of "hearing" is ordinarily satisfied upon permitting a party the opportunity to, in some manner, present its views and arguments to the court.[651] Moreover, the court enjoys discretion on what type of hearing to allow: a hearing only on briefs, an oral argument,[652] or a full evidentiary hearing.[653]

---

[645] *See Rivera-Gomez v. de Castro,* 900 F.2d 1, 2 (1st Cir. 1990) (noting that Rule is "perhaps too infrequently invoked and too often overlooked"; it can, in appropriate instances, "be an excellent device for conserving time, expenses, and scarce judicial resources by targeting early resolution of threshold issues").

[646] *See Cameron v. Children's Hosp. Medical Center,* 131 F.3d 1167, 1170 (6th Cir. 1997).

[647] *See Kregler v. City of New York,* 646 F.Supp.2d 570, 572 (S.D.N.Y. 2009), *vacated on other grounds,* 2010 WL 1740806 (2d Cir. May 3, 2010).

[648] *See Cameron v. Children's Hosp. Medical Center,* 131 F.3d 1167, 1170–71 (6th Cir. 1997).

[649] *See Beltre v. Lititz Healthcare Staffing Solutions LLC,* 757 F.Supp.2d 373, 376 (S.D.N.Y. 2010).

[650] *See North Carolina State Conference of NAACP v. McCrory,* 997 F.Supp.2d 322 (M.D.N.C. 2014); *Nissim Corp. v. ClearPlay, Inc.,* 351 F.Supp.2d 1343, 1346 (S.D. Fla. 2004).

[651] *See Greene v. WCI Holdings Corp.,* 136 F.3d 313, 316 (2d Cir. 1998).

[652] *See Obert v. Republic Western Ins. Co.,* 398 F.3d 138, 143 (1st Cir. 2005).

[653] *See Kregler v. City of New York,* 646 F.Supp.2d 570, 578 (S.D.N.Y. 2009), *vacated on other grounds,* 2010 WL 1740806 (2d Cir. May 3, 2010).

ADDITIONAL RESEARCH REFERENCES

C.J.S., Federal Civil Procedure § 302, §§ 376 to 409 et seq., §§ 413 to 440 et seq., §§ 796 et seq., §§ 842 et seq.

West's Key Number Digest, Federal Civil Procedure ⊶734 to 735, ⊶941 to 1020, ⊶1041 to 1068, ⊶1101 to 1150, ⊶1721 to 1843

RULE 13

COUNTERCLAIM AND CROSSCLAIM

(a) Compulsory Counterclaim.

    (1) *In General.* A pleading must state as a counterclaim any claim that—at the time of its service—the pleader has against an opposing party if the claim:

        (A) arises out of the transaction or occurrence that is the subject matter of the opposing party's claim; and

        (B) does not require adding another party over whom the court cannot acquire jurisdiction.

    (2) *Exceptions.* The pleader need not state the claim if:

        (A) when the action was commenced, the claim was the subject of another pending action; or

        (B) the opposing party sued on its claim by attachment or other process that did not establish personal jurisdiction over the pleader on that claim, and the pleader does not assert any counterclaim under this rule

(b) Permissive Counterclaim. A pleading may state as a counterclaim against an opposing party any claim that is not compulsory.

(c) Relief Sought in a Counterclaim. A counterclaim need not diminish or defeat the recovery sought by the opposing party. It may request relief that exceeds in amount or differs in kind from the relief sought by the opposing party.

(d) Counterclaim Against the United States. These rules do not expand the right to assert a counterclaim-or to claim a credit-against the United States or a United States officer or agency.

(e) Counterclaim Maturing or Acquired After Pleading. The court may permit a party to file a supplemental pleading asserting a counterclaim that matured or was acquired by the party after serving an earlier pleading.

(f) [Abrogated]

(g) Crossclaim Against a Coparty. A pleading may state as a crossclaim any claim by one party against a coparty if the claim arises out of the transaction or occurrence that is the subject matter of the original action or of a counterclaim, or if the claim relates to any property that is the subject matter of the original action. The crossclaim may include a claim that the coparty is or may

be liable to the crossclaimant for all or part of a claim asserted in the action against the cross-claimant.

(h) Joining Additional Parties. Rules 19 and 20 govern the addition of a person as a party to a counterclaim or crossclaim.

(i) Separate Trials; Separate Judgments. If the court orders separate trials under Rule 42(b), it may enter judgment on a counterclaim or cross-claim under Rule 54(b) when it has jurisdiction to do so, even if the opposing party's claims have been dismissed or otherwise resolved.

[Amended effective March 19, 1948; July 1, 1963; July 1, 1966; August 1, 1987; April 30, 2007, effective December 1, 2007; March 26, 2009, effective December 1, 2009.]

AUTHORS' COMMENTARY ON RULE 13

PURPOSE AND SCOPE

Rule 13 authorizes persons who are already parties to an action to assert counterclaims against an opposing party. The Rule distinguishes between counterclaims that must be raised in pending litigation and counterclaims that may either be raised in the pending litigation or retained for subsequent litigation. Rule 13 also controls the circumstances in which cross-claims against co-parties—*i.e.*, against persons who are aligned on the same side of the case—may be asserted in a pending action.

RULE 13(a)—COMPULSORY COUNTERCLAIM

CORE CONCEPT

Subject to some exceptions discussed below, compulsory counterclaims are those counterclaims arising from the same transaction or occurrence that gave rise to the plaintiff's complaint. Such counterclaims are so closely related to claims already raised by a plaintiff that it would be inefficient to litigate them in separate actions. Consequently, compulsory counterclaims generally must be asserted in the pending litigation or they are waived.

APPLICATIONS

Procedure

Compulsory counterclaims are asserted by pleading them in the answer to a complaint or other claim—a defendant might file an answer that includes counterclaims against the plaintiff.[1]

Same Transaction or Occurrence

Counterclaims are generally deemed compulsory if they arise out of the same transaction or occurrence that is the subject of the opposing party's claim. Courts generally agree that this standard for identifying compulsory counterclaims should be construed liberally to further the goal of judicial economy.[2] However, courts differ in the way they actually apply the standard to specific facts. One application holds that the standard should be based on four inquiries: (1) whether the issues of law and fact in the various claims are

---

[1]   *See, e.g., Shelter Mut. Ins. Co. v. Public Water Supply Dist. No. 7 of Jefferson County, Mo.*, 747 F.2d 1195 (8th Cir. 1984).

[2]   *See, e.g., Transamerica Occidental Life Ins. Co. v. Aviation Office of America, Inc.*, 292 F.3d 384, 390 (3d Cir. 2002) ("[T]he objective of Rule 13(a) is to promote judicial economy, so the term 'transaction or occurrence' is construed generously to further this purpose.").

essentially the same; (2) whether, in the absence of the compulsory counterclaim rule, res judicata would bar a subsequent suit on the counterclaim; (3) whether the same evidence could be used to support or refute the claim and counterclaim; and (4) whether a logical relationship exists between the claim and counterclaim.[3] This approach does not require that all the questions be answered affirmatively before a counterclaim may be deemed compulsory.[4] Other courts are even more liberal in the way they apply the "same transaction or occurrence" standard, sometimes finding a compulsory counterclaim when there is any significant logical relationship between the plaintiff's claim and the counterclaim.[5]

Other, less broad, applications of the standard may require substantial overlap in all elements of the claims before a counterclaim is deemed compulsory.[6]

Exceptions to "Same Transaction" Standard

There are a number of circumstances in which a counterclaim need not be asserted even though it shares the same transaction or occurrence as a claim filed by an opposing party.

(1)   *Immature Claims:* A counterclaim that does not mature until after the party has served a pleading is not a compulsory counterclaim, even if it arises from the same transaction or occurrence as a claim filed by an opposing party.[7] Rule 13(e) provides that such a claim may be asserted as a permissive counterclaim by filing a supplemental pleading, as provided by Rule 15(d), or it may be retained for future litigation, at the discretion of the party who holds the claim.

(2)   *Rule 13(a) Inapplicable Until Service of Pleading:* Even if a counterclaim arises from the same transaction or occurrence as a plaintiff's claim, Rule 13(a) provides that it does not become a compulsory counterclaim until the time when the party holding the counterclaim is required to file a responsive pleading.[8] Thus, if a defendant initially filed a motion to dismiss under Rule 12(b) prior to answering the complaint and the court granted the motion to dismiss, the defendant never had an obligation to file a responsive pleading. In that circumstance, any claim the defendant had against the plaintiff would not be deemed a compulsory counterclaim, and would be preserved for assertion in subsequent litigation. Similarly, if a plaintiff and defendant settle the plaintiff's claim before expiration of the time in which the defendant must answer, any counterclaim the defendant might have is not compulsory.[9]

---

[3]   *See, e.g., Q Intern. Courier Inc. v. Smoak,* 441 F.3d 214, 219 (4th Cir. 2006) (citing line of cases using this approach).

[4]   *See, e.g., Painter v. Harvey,* 863 F.2d 329, 331 (4th Cir. 1988) (inquiries are not a "litmus test"; better analogy is to a "guideline").

[5]   *See, e.g., In re Eldercare Properties, Ltd.,* 568 F.3d 506, 519 (5th Cir. 2009) (requiring only a logical relationship between claim and counterclaim).

[6]   *See, e.g., In re Harchar,* 694 F.3d 639, 649 (6th Cir. 2012) (due process claim did not arise from same transaction or occurrence as IRS proof of claim; "because the IRS's and Harchar's claims are 'not connected in time, require 'consideration of different law and evidence,' and because Harchar's due process claim would not be barred by 'res judicata,' the claims did not arise out of the same transaction or occurrence").

[7]   *See, e.g., Allan Block Corp. v. County Materials Corp.,* 512 F.3d 912, 920 (7th Cir. 2008) ("Rule 13(a) does not require the defendant to file as a compulsory counterclaim a claim that hasn't accrued yet . . . either because it has not yet come into being or, though it has, the plaintiff could not have discovered it.").

[8]   *Cf., e.g., Tyler v. DH Capital Management, Inc.,* 736 F.3d 455, 459 (6th Cir. 2013) ("Where the adverse party has no opportunity to file a pleading, it has no opportunity to assert its counterclaim, and thus its claim will not be barred.").

[9]   *See, e.g., Bluegrass Hosiery, Inc. v. Speizman Industries, Inc.,* 214 F.3d 770 (6th Cir. 2000).

(3) *Lack of Jurisdiction over Third Parties:* If a counterclaim requires joinder of some additional person not subject to the court's jurisdiction, the counterclaim will not be deemed compulsory, irrespective of the amount of overlap it shares with the plaintiff's claim.[10]

(4) *Pending Lawsuits:* A counterclaim is not compulsory within the meaning of Rule 13(a) if it has already been sued upon in other litigation. Thus, if one person filed suit in a state court, and the opponent of that claim then sued in federal court, the original state claim would not be a compulsory counterclaim in federal court because it is already the subject of pending litigation.[11]

(5) *Quasi In Rem/In Rem Jurisdiction:* Where the plaintiff's complaint rests on the court's *quasi in rem* or *in rem* jurisdiction, a counterclaim will not be compulsory so long as the defendant refrains from raising any counterclaims under Rule 13.[12] If, however, the defendant raises any Rule 13 counterclaim, then all other counterclaims that fall within the same transaction or occurrence as the plaintiff's claim—and not exempted by other exceptions, discussed above—are compulsory counterclaims and must be asserted.

(6) *Injunction/Declaratory Judgment Actions:* In some circumstances, defendants who have been sued only on equity claims may not be required to assert claims for money damages as counterclaims.[13]

Subject Matter Jurisdiction

Compulsory counterclaims must satisfy subject matter jurisdiction. They do so by satisfying the requirements of either federal question jurisdiction or diversity jurisdiction, or by qualifying for supplemental jurisdiction. Because compulsory counterclaims must arise from the same transaction or occurrence as the plaintiff's claim, counterclaims that do not qualify for federal question jurisdiction or diversity jurisdiction nevertheless usually meet the requirements for supplemental jurisdiction.[14] The party asserting a counterclaim must include allegations demonstrating that the requirement of subject matter jurisdiction is met.[15]

Personal Jurisdiction over Plaintiffs

Assertion of a compulsory counterclaim usually involves very few problems with personal jurisdiction over the plaintiff. By instituting an action, a plaintiff is held to have consented to the court's jurisdiction to adjudicate related claims,[16] and by definition, a compulsory counterclaim is closely related to the plaintiff's claim.

---

[10] *See, e.g., Landmark Bank v. Machera,* 736 F.Supp. 375, 379 (D. Mass. 1990) ("Rule 13(a) specifically precludes compulsory counterclaims that require for adjudication the presence of third parties over whom 'the court cannot acquire jurisdiction.'").

[11] *See, e.g., Canon Latin America, Inc. v. Lantech (CR), S.A.,* 508 F.3d 597, 602 (11th Cir. 2007) (claim which was the subject of a Costa Rican suit pending when district court suit filed was not a compulsory counterclaim).

[12] *Baker v. Gold Seal Liquors, Inc.,* 417 U.S. 467, 469, 94 S.Ct. 2504, 2506, 41 L.Ed.2d 243 (1974) ("The claim is not compulsory . . . if the opposing party brought his suit by attachment or other process not resulting in personal jurisdiction but only in rem or quasi in rem jurisdiction.").

[13] *See, e.g., Allan Block Corp. v. County Materials Corp.,* 512 F.3d 912, 916 (7th Cir. 2008) (declaratory judgment exception to res judicata is consistent with Rule 13 as rule is "in effect a procedural implementation of" the doctrine of res judicata).

[14] *Baker v. Gold Seal Liquors, Inc.,* 417 U.S. 467, 94 S.Ct. 2504, 41 L.Ed.2d 243 (1974).

[15] *McNutt v. General Motors Acceptance Corp. of Indiana,* 298 U.S. 178, 189, 56 S.Ct. 780, 785, 80 L. Ed. 1135 (1936) ("[P]rerequisites to the exercise of jurisdiction . . . are conditions which must be met by the party who seeks the exercise of jurisdiction in his favor. He must allege in his pleading the facts essential to show jurisdiction.").

[16] *Adam v. Saenger,* 303 U.S. 59, 58 S.Ct. 454, 82 L. Ed. 649 (1938).

Venue

Most courts hold that compulsory counterclaims need not satisfy venue requirements.[17]

Failure to Assert a Compulsory Counterclaim

Defendants who do not assert compulsory counterclaims are usually barred from raising the claims in subsequent litigation.[18]

Amendment to Add Counterclaim

If a defendant inadvertently omits a counterclaim, Rule 15(a) permits a party to amend a pleading once as of right within certain designated time frames. Thus, a party who failed to include a compulsory counterclaim within an initial answer might be able to use Rule 15(a) to amend the answer of right or, if the time in which to amend of right has already passed, to seek leave of opposing counsel or leave of court to amend.

Exception: Class Actions

The normal requirement that a compulsory counterclaim must be timely raised is generally inapplicable to claims held by class action defendants.[19]

Mislabelled Counterclaims

Parties sometimes mistakenly identify counterclaims as cross-claims, and *vice versa*. They may also mislabel a counterclaim as a defense. Courts usually attach no significance to such errors, unless somehow they unfairly prejudice an opposing party.[20]

Statutes of Limitations

Courts are divided as to the effect that a complaint has on statutes of limitations applicable to compulsory counterclaims. Most agree that if the counterclaim was still timely at the time the complaint was filed, the limitation period on the counterclaim is tolled by the filing of the complaint.[21]

RULE 13(b)—PERMISSIVE COUNTERCLAIM

CORE CONCEPT

Permissive counterclaims are all counterclaims that are not compulsory, including counterclaims arising out of the same transaction or occurrence as the opposing party's claims, but which fall within one or more of the exceptions to Rule 13(a) compulsory counterclaims, discussed above. Permissive counterclaims may be filed in the pending action, but they may also be asserted in a separate action.

---

[17] *See, e.g., Schoot v. United States,* 664 F.Supp. 293, 295 (N.D. Ill. 1987) ("[I]n the case of compulsory counterclaims, the venue statutes have been construed to apply only to the original claim, and not to the compulsory counterclaims.").

[18] *Baker v. Gold Seal Liquors, Inc.,* 417 U.S. 467, 469, 94 S.Ct. 2504, 41 L.Ed.2d 243 (1974) ("A counterclaim which is compulsory but is not brought is thereafter barred.").

[19] *See, e.g., Allapattah Services, Inc. v. Exxon Corp.,* 333 F.3d 1248 (11th Cir. 2003), aff'd, 545 U.S. 546, 125 S.Ct. 2611, 162 L.Ed.2d 502 (2005) (normal practice is to wait until liability is established and individual class members file damage claims; at that point setoffs and counterclaims can properly be adjudicated on an individual basis).

[20] *Reiter v. Cooper,* 507 U.S. 258, 262, 113 S.Ct. 1213, 1217, 122 L.Ed.2d 604 (1993) (holding that counterclaim mislabelled as defense should simply be treated as counterclaim).

[21] *See, e.g., Kirkpatrick v. Lenoir County Bd. of Educ.,* 216 F.3d 380, 388 (4th Cir. 2000) ("Because [plaintiffs] timely filed [their] actions, [defendant's] counterclaim relates back to the date of the original filing. Therefore, the counterclaim was timely regardless of whether the statute of limitations governing the matter was thirty days or three years.").

APPLICATIONS

Procedure

Permissive counterclaims are filed in answers to complaints or other claims—a defendant might file an answer that includes counterclaims against the plaintiff.[22]

Different Transaction or Occurrence

The standard for measuring whether a permissive counterclaim arises from a transaction or occurrence dissimilar from that underlying the complaint is the mirror image of the same transaction or occurrence test of compulsory counterclaims discussed above.

Subject Matter Jurisdiction

Permissive counterclaims must satisfy requirements for subject matter jurisdiction, like all other claims. Unlike compulsory counterclaims, however, supplemental jurisdiction is less likely to apply many permissive counterclaims because they generally do not arise out of the same case or controversy as the claims already in the case (or they would be compulsory).[23] Conversely, permissive counterclaims that arise from the same transaction or occurrence but which are not for some reason compulsory are likely to qualify for supplemental jurisdiction.[24]

It should be noted that the party asserting a permissive counterclaim must include an allegation of facts demonstrating that the requirement of subject matter jurisdiction is met.[25]

Personal Jurisdiction: Waiver of Defense

The objection to personal jurisdiction is waived where a defendant seeks affirmative relief in the form of a permissive counterclaim. This may be true even where those defenses were set forth in a timely motion to dismiss or in a responsive pleading.[26]

Venue

It is unclear whether permissive counterclaims must satisfy venue requirements.[27]

Failure to Assert a Permissive Counterclaim

No sanction attaches if a party holding a permissive counterclaim chooses not to assert it in pending litigation. The claim is not treated as barred, and may be asserted at a later date.[28]

Mislabelled Counterclaims

Parties sometimes mistakenly identify counterclaims as cross-claims, and *vice versa*. They may also mislabel a counterclaim as a defense. Courts usually attach no significance to such errors, unless somehow they unfairly prejudice an opposing party.[29]

---

[22] *See, e.g., Shelter Mut. Ins. Co. v. Public Water Supply Dist. No. 7 of Jefferson County, Mo.*, 747 F.2d 1195 (8th Cir. 1984).

[23] *See, e.g., Oak Park Trust and Sav. Bank v. Therkildsen*, 209 F.3d 648, 651 (7th Cir. 2000).

[24] *See, e.g., Leipzig v. AIG Life Ins. Co.*, 362 F.3d 406, 410 (7th Cir. 2004).

[25] *McNutt v. General Motors Acceptance Corp. of Indiana*, 298 U.S. 178, 189, 56 S.Ct. 780, 785, 80 L. Ed. 1135 (1936).

[26] *See* Author's Commentary to Rule 12(h), *supra*, "Implied Waiver."

[27] *See, e.g., Hansen v. Shearson/American Exp., Inc.*, 116 F.R.D. 246, 251 (E.D. Pa. 1987).

[28] *See, e.g., U.S. Philips Corp. v. Sears Roebuck & Co.*, 55 F.3d 592, 599 (Fed. Cir. 1995).

[29] *Reiter v. Cooper*, 507 U.S. 258, 262, 113 S.Ct. 1213, 1217, 122 L.Ed.2d 604 (1993).

Statutes of Limitations

An opposing party's decision to file a claim does not toll the time in which a permissive counterclaim not arising from the same transaction or occurrence must be filed.[30]

Counterclaims Maturing After Pleading

Rule 13(b) should be read in conjunction with Rule 13(e), which provides that counterclaims maturing or acquired after pleading are permissive counterclaims that may be filed in the pending action, subject to the court's discretion.

Separate Trials

Permissive counterclaims not arising from the same transaction or occurrence as the opposing party's claim may present substantial potential for confusing the trier of fact or delaying adjudication of the original claims. Thus, Rule 13(i) authorizes the court to order separate proceedings.

RULE 13(c)—RELIEF SOUGHT IN A COUNTERCLAIM

CORE CONCEPT

Rule 13(c) provides that: (1) counterclaims may be for any amount, irrespective of whether the amount sought in the counterclaim exceeds the amount sought in the other party's claim; and (2) counterclaims may seek kinds of relief not sought in the opposing party's claim. For example, if the opposing party's claim sought money damages only, the counterclaim could seek either money damages, equitable relief, or both money damages and equitable relief.

RULE 13(d)—COUNTERCLAIM AGAINST THE UNITED STATES

CORE CONCEPT

As a general rule, the United States and its officers and agencies are immune from suits in federal courts unless the United States waives that sovereign immunity. Rule 13(d) expressly provides that the counterclaim provisions of Rule 13(a) and (b) do not alter the law of sovereign immunity.[31]

APPLICATIONS

Waiver of Immunity

A decision by the United States to sue on a claim generally does not constitute a waiver of sovereign immunity as to counterclaims for amounts above those sums for which the United States is suing. This result applies even if the counterclaims arise from the same transaction or occurrence as the complaint brought by the United States.[32] By contrast, a State which voluntarily joins litigation waives sovereign immunity for all compulsory counterclaims.[33]

Setoffs

Some courts have permitted counterclaims against the United States where the claim and counterclaim arise from the same transaction or occurrence and the money sought is a setoff against the government's claim that will only reduce the government's recovery.[34]

---

[30] *See, e.g., Employers Ins. of Wausau v. United States,* 764 F.2d 1572, 1576 (Fed. Cir. 1985).

[31] *See, e.g., In re Armstrong,* 206 F.3d 465, 473 (5th Cir. 2000).

[32] *See, e.g., United States v. Johnson,* 853 F.2d 619, 621 (8th Cir. 1988).

[33] *Gardner v. New Jersey,* 329 U.S. 565, 574, 67 S.Ct. 467, 91 L.Ed. 504 (1947).

[34] *See, e.g., United States v. Forma,* 42 F.3d 759, 765 (2d Cir. 1994).

RULE 13(e)—COUNTERCLAIM MATURING OR ACQUIRED AFTER PLEADING

CORE CONCEPT

Rule 13(e) provides that if counterclaims mature or are acquired after a party has pleaded, the party may choose to assert them in a supplemental pleading, subject to the court's discretion.

APPLICATIONS

Procedure

A party seeking to assert a Rule 13(e) counterclaim must file a motion and supporting materials explaining the circumstances in which the counterclaim matured or was acquired.[35]

Party's Discretion

Rule 13(e) is permissive in nature, even if the counterclaim arises from the same transaction or occurrence as the opposing party's claim. Thus, a party holding a counterclaim of the kind controlled by Rule 13(e) may assert it, subject to the court's permission, but is under no obligation to do so.[36]

Judicial Discretion

If a party seeks to raise a Rule 13(e) counterclaim, the court retains discretion to refuse to hear the counterclaim in the pending action.[37] Generally, courts permit Rule 13(e) counterclaims where they will not confuse the trier of fact or where they will not unfairly prejudice other parties, particularly through excessively delaying the litigation.[38] Additionally, Rule 13(e) counterclaims that arise out of the same transaction or occurrence as the opposing party's claim are more likely to be heard in the pending litigation.

Jurisdiction

Rule 13(e) counterclaims must meet one of the bases of subject matter jurisdiction, such as federal question jurisdiction, diversity jurisdiction, or supplemental jurisdiction. If the Rule 13(e) counterclaim arises out of the same transaction or occurrence as the original claim, then it will likely satisfy supplemental jurisdiction. If not, the counterclaim will need an independent basis of jurisdiction.

Venue

There is no venue requirement for Rule 13(e) counterclaims.

RULE 13(f)—(ABROGATED)

RULE 13(g)—CROSSCLAIM AGAINST CO-PARTY

CORE CONCEPT

Rule 13(g) permits persons who are already parties to a suit to bring related claims against persons on the same side of the litigation.

---

[35] *See, e.g., All West Pet Supply Co. v. Hill's Pet Products Div., Colgate-Palmolive Co.,* 152 F.R.D. 202, 204 (D. Kan. 1993) (court has discretion to permit or reject supplemental counterclaim).

[36] *Stone v. Department of Aviation,* 453 F.3d 1271 (10th Cir.2006) (where plaintiff had not received his right-to-sue letter at time of initial filing, the claim had not matured and was not a compulsory counterclaim).

[37] *See, e.g., id.*

[38] *See, e.g., id.* (noting that in absence of factors indicating unfair prejudice to opponent, policy of liberally granting leave to file supplemental claims also applies to Rule 13(e) counterclaims).

APPLICATIONS

Procedure

Crossclaims are typically raised in a responsive pleading—a defendant might file an answer that includes crossclaims against a co-defendant.

Crossclaims Are Always Permissive

Unlike compulsory counterclaims, all crossclaims are permissive, and may therefore be asserted in the pending litigation or in a separate action.[39]

Same Transaction or Occurrence

To assert crossclaims, a party must assert at least one claim that arises out of the same transaction or occurrence as the original action, or that relates to the same property that is in dispute in the original action.[40] In this important sense, crossclaims, though permissive, are fundamentally different from permissive counterclaims, which often arise from a transaction or occurrence that is different from the original action. The standard of same transaction or occurrence varies from court to court. The most liberal interpretation requires a logical relation between the cross-claim and the original action.[41] Other courts look to the degree of overlap between the evidence to be used in the crossclaim and the evidence relevant to the original action.[42]

Additional Claims

Once a party has asserted one crossclaim that qualifies as under Rule 13(g)—it is transactionally related—the party may assert any other claims it has against the crossclaim defendant, even if entirely unrelated, under Rule 18(a).

Crossclaims Against Nonparties

Rule 13(g) provides that crossclaims may be brought only if at least one crossclaim defendant is a person already party to the action.[43] However, if a single crossclaim defendant is a party to the original action, additional persons may also be sued on the crossclaim, as provided by Rule 13(h) (discussed below).

Comparison with Impleader

A key difference between Rule 13(g) and Rule 14 impleader is that Rule 13(g) requires that at least one crossclaim defendant be a party. Rule 14, by contrast, provides a means of joining persons who were not previously parties to a pending suit.[44] Additionally, Rule 14 requires a claim asserting that the third-party defendant is liable, in whole or in part, for the liabilities asserted against the third-party plaintiff (sometimes called "derivative liability"). Rule 13(g) requires that the crossclaim arise out of the same transaction or occurrence, which may or may not be derivative.

Subject Matter Jurisdiction

Crossclaims must meet the standards of either federal question jurisdiction, diversity jurisdiction, or supplemental jurisdiction. Moreover, the party asserting a crossclaim must

---

[39] *See, e.g., United States v. Confederate Acres Sanitary Sewage and Drainage System, Inc.*, 935 F.2d 796, 799 (6th Cir. 1991) (Rule 13(g) makes crossclaims permissive).

[40] *See, e.g., Federal Land Bank of St. Louis v. Cupples Bro.*, 116 F.R.D. 63, 65 (E.D. Ark. 1987).

[41] *See, e.g., Seattle Audubon Soc. v. Lyons*, 871 F.Supp. 1286, 1290 (W.D. Wash. 1994) (treating same transaction or occurrence as synonymous with "logical relationship" test).

[42] *See, e.g., Danner v. Anskis*, 256 F.2d 123 (3d Cir.1958).

[43] *See, e.g., In re Oil Spill by Amoco Cadiz off Coast of France on March 16, 1978*, 699 F.2d 909, 913 (7th Cir. 1983) ("[A] Rule 13(g) cross-claim will lie only against an existing defendant.").

[44] *See, e.g., Ambraco, Inc. v. Bossclip B.V.*, 570 F.3d 233, 242 (5th Cir. 2009).

include an allegation of facts demonstrating that the requirement of subject matter jurisdiction is met.[45] However, subject matter jurisdiction is usually not a problem with crossclaims; because Rule 13(g) requires that crossclaims arise out of the same transaction or occurrence as the original action, crossclaims usually will satisfy the requirements of supplemental jurisdiction.[46] Additional claims joined pursuant to Rule 18(a) may not, though.

Personal Jurisdiction

Crossclaims must meet the requirements of personal jurisdiction. If the court in the original action has already acquired jurisdiction over the parties, it will normally also have jurisdiction over crossclaim defendants. If, however, jurisdiction is defective in the original action, it is possible that the crossclaim will suffer from similar jurisdictional defects.

Venue

Crossclaims need not satisfy venue requirements.[47]

Mislabelled Crossclaims

Parties sometimes mistakenly identify crossclaims as counterclaims, and *vice versa*. Courts usually attach no significance to such errors, unless somehow they unfairly prejudice an opposing party.[48]

Statutes of Limitations: "Relation Back"

Crossclaims seeking "affirmative and independent relief" do not relate back to the original complaint. By contrast, crossclaims "in the nature of recoupment, indemnity, or contribution" will typically enjoy the benefit of relation back to the date of the filing of the original action.[49]

RULE 13(h)—JOINING ADDITIONAL PARTIES

CORE CONCEPT

Many times a counterclaim or crossclaim will require, for the just adjudication of the case, the joinder of persons who are not yet parties. Rule 13(h) expressly authorizes the use of Rules 19 and 20, governing joinder of persons, to achieve that end.

APPLICATIONS

Procedure

Although the law is not entirely settled, it appears that when counterclaimants or crossclaimants seek to join additional parties under Rule 13(h), they may simply make appropriate service on the parties to be joined and provide notice to those already parties. There appears to be no need to file a motion requesting leave to join the parties.[50]

Prerequisite of One Party

Rule 13(a), (b), and (g) provide that counterclaims and crossclaims cannot be sued upon unless at least one person being sued is already a party to the action. However, once one

---

[45] *McNutt v. General Motors Acceptance Corp. of Indiana,* 298 U.S. 178, 189, 56 S.Ct. 780, 785, 80 L. Ed. 1135 (1936).

[46] *See, e.g., Ryan ex rel. Ryan v. Schneider Nat. Carriers, Inc.,* 263 F.3d 816, 819 (8th Cir. 2001).

[47] *See, e.g., Bredberg v. Long,* 778 F.2d 1285, 1288 (8th Cir. 1985) (if venue is proper on original claims, there may be no venue objection to crossclaims).

[48] *See, e.g., Schwab v. Erie Lackawanna R. Co.,* 438 F.2d 62, 64 (3d Cir. 1971) (mislabelling need not be fatal).

[49] *See, e.g., Kansa Reinsurance Co., Ltd. v. Congressional Mortg. Corp. of Texas,* 20 F.3d 1362, 1367–68 (5th Cir. 1994).

[50] *See, e.g., Northfield Ins. Co. v. Bender Shipbuilding & Repair Co., Inc.,* 122 F.R.D. 30 (S.D. Ala. 1988).

such person is sued on a counterclaim or crossclaim, Rule 13(h) permits joinder of other persons on that counterclaim or crossclaim, subject to the authority of Rules 19 and 20.[51]

Subject Matter Jurisdiction

Rule 13(h) claims must satisfy either original or supplemental jurisdiction.[52] Since Rule 13(h) contemplates the addition of parties under Rules 19 and 20, be sure to consider the exception to supplemental jurisdiction under 28 U.S.C.A. § 1367(b).

Personal Jurisdiction

Additional parties may be joined under Rule 13(h) only if they are subject to the jurisdiction of the court.[53]

Venue

Venue requirements do not apply to counterclaims or crossclaims in which Rule 13(h) joinder is sought.[54]

RULE 13(i)—SEPARATE TRIALS; SEPARATE JUDGMENTS

CORE CONCEPT

Because additional claims added to a case through Rule 13(a), (b), and (g) have substantial potential for confusing the trier of fact or delaying adjudication of the original claims, Rule 13(i) authorizes the court to hold separate hearings, as provided by Rule 42(b), and/or enter separate judgments, as provided by Rule 54(b).

APPLICATIONS

Judicial Discretion

Courts have substantial discretion to order separate trials and enter separate judgments, and the decision to process claims separately is not normally disturbed on appeal.[55]

ADDITIONAL RESEARCH REFERENCES

Wright & Miller, *Federal Practice and Procedure* §§ 1401 to 37

C.J.S., Federal Civil Procedure §§ 309 to 319 et seq.

West's Key Number Digest, Federal Civil Procedure ⊶771 to 786

---

[51] *See, e.g., Asset Allocation and Management Co. v. Western Employers Ins. Co.,* 892 F.2d 566, 574 (7th Cir. 1989) (noting interplay of Rules 13(h) and 20).

[52] *But see, Rayman v. Peoples Sav. Corp.,* 735 F.Supp. 842, 854 (N.D. Ill. 1990) (compulsory counterclaims or crossclaims will usually satisfy supplemental jurisdiction).

[53] *See, e.g., Cordner v. Metropolitan Life Ins. Co.,* 234 F.Supp. 765, 769 (S.D. N.Y. 1964).

[54] *See, e.g., Lesnik v. Public Industrials Corporation,* 144 F.2d 968, 977 (C.C.A. 2d Cir. 1944).

[55] *See, e.g., McLaughlin v. State Farm Mut. Auto. Ins. Co.,* 30 F.3d 861, 870 (7th Cir. 1994).

RULE 14

THIRD-PARTY PRACTICE

(a) When a Defending Party May Bring in a Third Party.

(1) *Timing of the Summons and Complaint.* A defending party may, as third-party plaintiff, serve a summons and complaint on a nonparty who is or may be liable to it for all or part of the claim against it. But the third-party plaintiff must, by motion, obtain the court's leave if it files the third-party complaint more than 14 days after serving its original answer.

(2) *Third-Party Defendant's Claims and Defenses.* The person served with the summons and third-party complaint-the "third-party defendant":

    (A) must assert any defense against the third-party plaintiff's claim under Rule 12;

    (B) must assert any counterclaim against the third-party plaintiff under Rule 13(a), and may assert any counterclaim against the third-party plaintiff under Rule 13(b) or any crossclaim against another third-party defendant under Rule 13(g);

    (C) may assert against the plaintiff any defense that the third-party plaintiff has to the plaintiff's claim; and

    (D) may also assert against the plaintiff any claim arising out of the transaction or occurrence that is the subject matter of the plaintiff's claim against the third-party plaintiff.

(3) *Plaintiff's Claims Against a Third-Party Defendant.* The plaintiff may assert against the third-party defendant any claim arising out of the transaction or occurrence that is the subject matter of the plaintiff's claim against the third-party plaintiff. The third-party defendant must then assert any defense under Rule 12 and any counterclaim under Rule 13(a), and may assert any counterclaim under Rule 13(b) or any crossclaim under Rule 13(g).

(4) *Motion to Strike, Sever, or Try Separately.* Any party may move to strike the third-party claim, to sever it, or to try it separately.

(5) *Third-Party Defendant's Claim Against a Nonparty.* A third-party defendant may proceed under this rule against a nonparty who is or may be liable to the third-party defendant for all or part of any claim against it.

(6) *Third-Party Complaint In Rem.* If it is within the admiralty or maritime jurisdiction, a third-party complaint may be in rem. In that event, a

353

reference in this rule to the "summons" includes the warrant of arrest, and a reference to the defendant or third-party plaintiff includes, when appropriate, a person who asserts a right under Supplemental Rule C(6)(a)(i) in the property arrested.

(b) When a Plaintiff May Bring in a Third Party. When a claim is asserted against a plaintiff, the plaintiff may bring in a third party if this rule would allow a defendant to do so.

(c) Admiralty or Maritime Claim.

(1) *Scope of Impleader.* If a plaintiff asserts an admiralty or maritime claim under Rule 9(h), the defendant or a person who asserts a right under Supplemental Rule C(6)(a)(i) may, as a third-party plaintiff, bring in a third-party defendant who may be wholly or partly liable—either to the plaintiff or to the third-party plaintiff-for remedy over, contribution, or otherwise on account of the same transaction, occurrence, or series of transactions or occurrences.

(2) *Defending Against a Demand for Judgment for the Plaintiff.* The third-party plaintiff may demand judgment in the plaintiff's favor against the third-party defendant. In that event, the third-party defendant must defend under Rule 12 against the plaintiff's claim as well as the third-party plaintiff's claim; and the action proceeds as if the plaintiff had sued both the third-party defendant and the third-party plaintiff.

[Amended effective March 19, 1948; July 1, 1963; July 1, 1966; August 1, 1987; April 17, 2000, effective December 1, 2000; April 12, 2006, effective December 1, 2006; April 30, 2007, effective December 1, 2007; March 26, 2009, effective December 1, 2009.]

AUTHORS' COMMENTARY ON RULE 14

PURPOSE AND SCOPE

Rule 14 permits parties who are defending against claims to join other persons, not yet parties, who may be obligated to reimburse the party defending the claim for some or all of that party's liability. The decision to seek joinder, or to hold the claim for assertion in later litigation, belongs to the party defending on the claim: Rule 14 contains no requirement similar to Rule 13(a), which makes compulsory the assertion of certain counterclaims. Third-party practice is commonly employed when an alleged tortfeasor seeks contribution from others who may also be liable but whom the plaintiff has not sued. The Rule also describes the rights of persons who are joined as third-party defendants to claim and defend against the original plaintiffs and defendants, as well as to join still other persons who may be liable to the third parties.

Nomenclature: The labels necessitated by Rule 14 are superficially complex, but follow a consistent pattern. A party who seeks to join another person under Rule 14 is called a third-party plaintiff. The person joined is called a third-party defendant. Thus, if a defendant in a pending action sought to join someone not yet a party under Rule 14, the defendant would carry the additional title of third-party plaintiff, and the person joined would be a third-party defendant. If the third-party defendant sought, in turn, to join someone else, the person joined would be a fourth-party defendant, and the third-party defendant would carry the additional title of fourth-party plaintiff.

RULE 14(a)—A DEFENDING PARTY MAY BRING IN A THIRD PARTY

CORE CONCEPT

Rule 14(a) describes the power of defendants to implead third parties. The Rule also describes the defenses available to third-party defendants, as well as the circumstances in which third-party defendants may claim against plaintiffs and defendants. Finally, Rule 14(a) authorizes third-party defendants to implead potential fourth-party defendants who may be liable for some or all of any claim the third-party defendants might have to pay.

APPLICATIONS

Purpose

The purpose of Rule 14 is to permit additional parties whose rights may be affected by the decision in the original action to be joined so as to expedite the final determination of the rights and liabilities of all the interested parties in one suit.[1]

Third-Party Plaintiff's Discretion

Where applicable, a party's right to implead under Rule 14 is optional; there is no obligation to implead third parties.[2]

Who May Be Impleaded

Only persons not already parties may be impleaded.[3] This provision of Rule 14 stands in contrast to provisions of Rule 13 governing counterclaims and crossclaims, in which at least one of the persons sued on a counterclaim or crossclaim must already be a party to the case.

Procedure

A third-party defendant is joined upon service of a proper summons and third-party complaint.[4] Rule 4(k) permits service on a third-party defendant found within 100 miles of the place from where the summons issued, without regard to whether such service takes place within another state.[5] This is a small but sometimes crucial expansion of personal jurisdiction in the context of Rule 14.

Time; Leave of Court

Rule 14(a) permits service of a third-party complaint "at any time." However, a party may file a third-party complaint without obtaining leave of court only in the 14-day period following that party's service of an answer to a claim, or by a different deadline set by court order.[6] Thereafter, a third-party complaint may be filed only upon motion, served on all parties, and after obtaining leave of court.[7] Generally, courts permit assertion of impleader claims unless they are raised so late in a pending suit that they unreasonably prejudice persons who are already parties.[8]

---

[1]   *American Zurich Ins. Co. v. Cooper Tire & Rubber Co.*, 512 F.3d 800, 805 (6th Cir. 2008).

[2]   *See, e.g., Fernandez v. Corporacion Insular De Seguros*, 79 F.3d 207 (1st Cir.1996).

[3]   *See, e.g., Cutting Underwater Technologies USA, Inc. v. Eni U.S. Operating Co.*, 671 F.3d 512, 514, n.2 (5th Cir. 2012) (claim asserted against nonparties were third-party claims and not counterclaims).

[4]   *See, e.g., Jackson v. Southeastern Pennsylvania Transp. Authority*, 727 F.Supp. 965, 966 (E.D. Pa. 1990).

[5]   Fed.R.Civ.P. 4(k).

[6]   *See, e.g., Smith v. Local 819 I.B.T. Pension Plan*, 291 F.3d 236 (2d Cir. 2002).

[7]   *See, e.g., Raytheon Aircraft Credit Corp. v. Pal Air Intern., Inc.*, 923 F.Supp. 1408 (D. Kan. 1996).

[8]   *See, e.g., State of N.Y. v. Solvent Chemical Co., Inc.*, 875 F.Supp. 1015 (W.D.N.Y. 1995) (impleader allowed more than 10 years after original complaint was filed).

Derivative Liability

Rule 14(a) explicitly provides that a third-party complaint must include a claim asserting that a third-party defendant is or may be liable for all or part of the claim asserted against the third-party plaintiff (sometimes called "derivative liability"). Rule 14(a) provides no authorization to assert claims against third-party plaintiffs that are unrelated to claims already pending.[9]

Affirmative Relief

Although Rule 14(a)'s literal language might seem to limit third-party practice to claims for reimbursement or compensation, once a party is properly impleaded under Rule 14, Rule 18(a) authorizes the joinder or addition of any other claims, related or not, derivative or not, that the third-party plaintiff has against the third-party defendant.[10]

Defenses Available

Third-party defendants are entitled to raise their own defenses against the third-party plaintiff.[11] Third-party defendants may also assert defenses that the third-party plaintiff may have against the original claim.[12]

Counterclaims by Third-Party Defendants

Third-party defendants may file counterclaims against third-party plaintiffs,[13] consistent with the requirements of Rule 13. The requirements of Rule 13(a) apply, and compulsory counterclaims are waived if not filed in the pending action.

Crossclaims by Third-Party Defendants

If more than one third-party defendant has been impleaded, the third-party defendants may file crossclaims against one another, subject to the requirements of Rule 13(g).

Third-Party Defendants' Claims Against Plaintiffs

Rule 14(a) permits a third-party defendant to make claims against an original plaintiff that arise out of the same transaction or occurrence as the claims originally filed by the plaintiff. Such claims are permissive, in that they may either be raised or retained for subsequent litigation. Note, however, that if an original plaintiff has already asserted a claim against the third-party defendant in the litigation (as discussed in the next bullet), the third-party defendant's claims against the plaintiff may be compulsory counterclaims subject to Rule 13(a). In such a circumstance, a third-party defendant's claims against a plaintiff are not permissive. Once a third-party defendant has asserted one qualified claim under Rule 14(a), it may assert additional claims, related or unrelated, under Rule 18(a).

Plaintiffs' Claims Against Third-Party Defendants

Rule 14(a) also permits plaintiffs to assert a claim against persons joined as third-party defendants, provided that the claim arises out of the same transaction or occurrence as the original claims against the defendants.[14] The language of Rule 14(a) makes clear that assertion of such claims is discretionary, and a plaintiff may choose to retain the claims for subsequent litigation.[15] Once a plaintiff has asserted one qualified claim under Rule 14(a), it may assert additional claims, related or unrelated, under Rule 18(a). All such claims by

---

[9] *See, e.g., American Zurich Ins. Co. v. Cooper Tire & Rubber Co.,* 512 F.3d 800, 805 (6th Cir. 2008).

[10] *See, e.g., F.D.I.C. v. Bathgate,* 27 F.3d 850, 872 (3d Cir. 1994).

[11] *See, e.g., Coons v. Industrial Knife Co.,* 620 F.3d 38, 43 (1st Cir. 2010).

[12] Fed.R.Civ.P. 14(a).

[13] *Cf. Thomas v. Barton Lodge II, Ltd.,* 174 F.3d 636 (5th Cir.1999).

[14] *U.S. ex rel. S. Prawer and Co. v. Fleet Bank of Maine,* 24 F.3d 320, 328 (1st Cir. 1994).

[15] *See, e.g., Atchison, Topeka and Santa Fe Ry. Co. v. Hercules Inc.,* 146 F.3d 1071, 1073 (9th Cir. 1998).

the original plaintiff potentially implicate the exception to supplemental jurisdiction in 28 U.S.C.A. § 1367(b).

Third-Party Defendants' Counterclaims Against Plaintiffs

If a plaintiff sues a third-party defendant, any counterclaims the third-party defendant may have are governed by Rule 13.

Third-Party Defendants' Crossclaims upon Suit by Plaintiffs

Just as Rule 14(a) permits third-party defendants to crossclaim against one another after being joined by a third-party plaintiff, the Rule also permits third-party defendants to crossclaim against one another if one or more third-party defendants is sued by a plaintiff. Rule 14(a) expressly provides that such crossclaims are regulated by Rule 13.

Severance; Separate Trials

Third-party practice has obvious potential for complexity and for confusing a trier of fact. Rule 14(a) therefore provides that any party to the litigation may move to strike or sever the claims. Courts have substantial discretion when deciding such motions.[16]

Fourth-Party Practice

Rule 14(a) grants third-party defendants the same power to implead as is enjoyed by the defendants. Thus, third-party defendants may join persons not yet parties who may be liable to the third-party defendants for part or all of the liability the third-party defendants may have to the parties asserting claims against them.

Rights of Fourth-Party Defendants

Although not explicitly addressed in Rule 14(a), fourth-party defendants enjoy all the rights the Rule provides to third-party defendants, including availability of defenses, counterclaims, cross-claims, and impleader of additional persons.[17]

Subject Matter Jurisdiction

Every third-party claim must satisfy either original or supplemental jurisdiction. Because third-party claims are generally closely related to the original claims between the plaintiff and defendant, subject matter jurisdiction can usually be obtained under supplemental jurisdiction.[18] However, keep in mind the exception to supplemental jurisdiction in 28 U.S.C.A. § 1367(b) when a plaintiff is asserting a claim against an impleaded party.[19]

Personal Jurisdiction; Service of Process

Every third-party claim must also satisfy requirements of jurisdiction over persons and things.[20] For service of process on parties joined under Rule 14, a special provision in Rule 4(k)(1)(B) provides a sometimes useful extension of normal limits on service, permitting service on a third-party defendant found within 100 miles of the place from where the summons was issued, without regard to whether such service takes place within another state.[21]

---

[16]   *See, e.g., First Nat. Bank of Nocona v. Duncan Sav. and Loan Ass'n,* 957 F.2d 775, 777 (10th Cir. 1992).

[17]   *See, e.g., Garnay, Inc. v. M/V Lindo Maersk,* 816 F.Supp. 888 (S.D.N.Y. 1993).

[18]   *See, e.g., Grimes v. Mazda North American Operations,* 355 F.3d 566, 572 (6th Cir. 2004).

[19]   *See, e.g., State Nat. Ins. Co. Inc. v. Yates,* 391 F.3d 577, 579 (5th Cir. 2004).

[20]   *See, e.g., Rodd v. Region Const. Co.,* 783 F.2d 89 (7th Cir. 1986).

[21]   *See, e.g., ESAB Group, Inc. v. Centricut, Inc.,* 126 F.3d 617, 622 (4th Cir. 1997).

Venue

Requirements of venue do not apply to claims asserted under Rule 14.[22]

RULE 14(b)—WHEN A PLAINTIFF MAY BRING IN A THIRD PARTY

CORE CONCEPT

Rule 14(b) provides that if a plaintiff is the subject of a counterclaim, the plaintiff may join third parties who may be liable for part or all of that claim, in the same manner that Rule 14(a) authorizes defendants to join third parties.

APPLICATIONS

When Available

A plaintiff may not join persons under Rule 14 until a counterclaim or other claim has been asserted against the plaintiff. If a claim has been asserted against a plaintiff, that plaintiff may bring third-party claims in the same manner as a defendant under Rule 14(a).[23]

Subject Matter Jurisdiction; Restraints on Supplemental Jurisdiction

Like all other claims, claims by plaintiffs under Rule 14(b) must qualify for original or supplemental jurisdiction. However, keep in mind that the exception to supplemental jurisdiction in 28 U.S.C.A. § 1367(b) is potentially implicated when plaintiffs bring such claims. *See* § 2.13.

Personal Jurisdiction

A plaintiff's third-party claims must satisfy requirements of jurisdiction over persons and things. *See* §§ 2.2 to 2.9.

RULE 14(c)—ADMIRALTY OR MARITIME CLAIM

CORE CONCEPT

When the original cause of action arises under the court's admiralty jurisdiction, the defendant may join third persons by alleging either that: they are liable to reimburse the defendant for some or all of the defendant's liability, or that the third persons are liable directly to the plaintiff. This expands the general practice of impleader under Rule 14(a), where a defendant may implead only to establish that the person joined is liable to the defendant, and may not implead by alleging that the person to be joined is liable directly to the plaintiff.[24] The practical result of this feature of Rule 14(c) is that the third person becomes a co-defendant in the original action, rather than a third-party defendant.[25]

APPLICATIONS

Demand for Judgment

In order to designate an impleaded third-party defendant as a defendant to the plaintiff's original complaint, the literal language of Rule 14(c) appears to require that the third-party complaint "demand judgment against the third-party defendant in favor of the plaintiff." While there is some authority indicating that the third-party complaint must specifically demand judgment in that precise way, the greater weight of authority is that the requirement of Rule 14(c) should be liberally construed. Thus, clear language intending to

---

22   *See, e.g., Gundle Lining Const. Corp. v. Adams County Asphalt, Inc.,* 85 F.3d 201 (5th Cir. 1996).

23   *See, e.g., Chase Manhattan Bank, N.A. v. Aldridge,* 906 F.Supp. 866, 867 (S.D.N.Y. 1995).

24   *See, e.g., Spring City Corp. v. American Bldgs. Co.,* 193 F.3d 165, 169 (3d Cir. 1999).

25   *See, e.g., Mike Hooks Dredging Co., Inc. v. Marquette Transp. Gulf-Inland, L.L.C.,* 716 F.3d 886 (5th Cir. 2013).

implead third-party defendants as co-defendants to the original complaint satisfies the requirement of Rule 14(c).[26]

Applicability of Rule 14(a)

Beyond the special provision of Rule 14(c) that may make the third party a co-defendant, Rule 14(c) impleader actions generally proceed as though controlled by relevant provisions of Rule 14(a).[27]

Subject Matter Jurisdiction

Persons impleaded under Rule 14(c) will generally be subject to the admiralty jurisdiction of the court.[28]

Personal Jurisdiction

Persons impleaded under Rule 14(c) must be within either the personal jurisdiction, *quasi in rem* jurisdiction, or *in rem* jurisdiction of the court. Because *in rem* jurisdiction is generally available in admiralty practice, however, jurisdictional requirements may usually be satisfied without difficulty.

Venue

Venue requirements do not generally apply to claims asserted under Rule 14.[29]

ADDITIONAL RESEARCH REFERENCES

Wright & Miller, *Federal Practice and Procedure* §§ 1441 to 65

C.J.S., Federal Civil Procedure §§ 117 to 126 et seq., § 318

West's Key Number Digest, Federal Civil Procedure ⊶281 to 297

---

[26] *See, e.g., Royal Ins. Co. of America v. Southwest Marine,* 194 F.3d 1009, 1018 (9th Cir. 1999).

[27] *See, e.g., Rosario v. American Export-Isbrandtsen Lines, Inc.,* 531 F.2d 1227, 1231–32 (3d Cir. 1976).

[28] *See, e.g., Harrison v. Glendel Drilling Co.,* 679 F.Supp. 1413, 1417 (W.D. La. 1988).

[29] *See, e.g., Gundle Lining Const. Corp. v. Adams County Asphalt, Inc.,* 85 F.3d 201 (5th Cir. 1996).

RULE 15

AMENDED AND SUPPLEMENTAL PLEADINGS

(a) Amendments Before Trial.

(1) *Amending as a Matter of Course.* A party may amend its pleading once as a matter of course within:

(A) 21 days after serving it, or

(B) if the pleading is one to which a responsive pleading is required, 21 days after service of a responsive pleading or 21 days after service of a motion under Rule 12(b), (e), or (f), whichever is earlier.

(2) *Other Amendments.* In all other cases, a party may amend its pleading only with the opposing party's written consent or the court's leave. The court should freely give leave when justice so requires.

(3) *Time to Respond.* Unless the court orders otherwise, any required response to an amended pleading must be made within the time remaining to respond to the original pleading or within 14 days after service of the amended pleading, whichever is later.

(b) Amendments During and After Trial.

(1) *Based on an Objection at Trial.* If, at trial, a party objects that evidence is not within the issues raised in the pleadings, the court may permit the pleadings to be amended. The court should freely permit an amendment when doing so will aid in presenting the merits and the objecting party fails to satisfy the court that the evidence would prejudice that party's action or defense on the merits. The court may grant a continuance to enable the objecting party to meet the evidence.

(2) *For Issues Tried by Consent.* When an issue not raised by the pleadings is tried by the parties' express or implied consent, it must be treated in all respects as if raised in the pleadings. A party may move—at any time, even after judgment—to amend the pleadings to conform them to the evidence and to raise an unpleaded issue. But failure to amend does not affect the result of the trial of that issue.

(c) Relation Back of Amendments.

(1) *When an Amendment Relates Back.* An amendment to a pleading relates back to the date of the original pleading when:

(A) the law that provides the applicable statute of limitations allows relation back;

    (B) the amendment asserts a claim or defense that arose out of the conduct, transaction, or occurrence set out—or attempted to be set out—in the original pleading; or

    (C) the amendment changes the party or the naming of the party against whom a claim is asserted, if Rule 15(c)(1)(B) is satisfied and if, within the period provided by Rule 4(m) for serving the summons and complaint, the party to be brought in by amendment:

        (i) received such notice of the action that it will not be prejudiced in defending on the merits; and

        (ii) knew or should have known that the action would have been brought against it, but for a mistake concerning the proper party's identity.

  (2) *Notice to the United States.* When the United States or a United States officer or agency is added as a defendant by amendment, the notice requirements of Rule 15(c)(1)(C)(i) and (ii) are satisfied if, during the stated period, process was delivered or mailed to the United States attorney or the United States attorney's designee, to the Attorney General of the United States, or to the officer or agency.

(d) Supplemental Pleadings. On motion and reasonable notice, the court may, on just terms, permit a party to serve a supplemental pleading setting out any transaction, occurrence, or event that happened after the date of the pleading to be supplemented. The court may permit supplementation even though the original pleading is defective in stating a claim or defense. The court may order that the opposing party plead to the supplemental pleading within a specified time.

[Amended January 21, 1963, effective July 1, 1963; February 28, 1966, effective July 1, 1966; March 2, 1987, effective August 1, 1987; April 30, 1991, effective December 1, 1991; amended by Pub.L. 102–198, § 11, December 9, 1991, 105 Stat. 1626; amended April 22, 1993, effective December 1, 1993; April 30, 2007, effective December 1, 2007; March 26, 2009, effective December 1, 2009.]

AUTHORS' COMMENTARY ON RULE 15

PURPOSE AND SCOPE

    Rule 15 governs the circumstances in which parties are permitted to amend their pleadings. The Rule also provides the circumstances in which parties will be allowed to file new supplemental pleadings describing events that have occurred since the original pleadings were filed. Finally, it establishes the requirements for an amended pleading to "relate back" to the original pleading, such that, for purposes of the statute of limitations, the amended pleading will be deemed to have been filed as of the date of the original pleading.

RULE 15(a)—AMENDMENTS BEFORE TRIAL

CORE CONCEPT

Rule 15(a) provides an automatic right to amend a pleading a single time within 21 days after serving it. Additionally, if the pleading is one that requires a responsive pleading, the pleading may be amended of right once within 21 days after service of either a responsive pleading or a motion under Rule 12(b), (e), or (f), whichever is earlier.[1]

If a party's right to amend has lapsed, Rule 15(a)(2) provides a potential opportunity to obtain *leave* to amend from either the opposing party or the court.

♦   **NOTE:** On some occasions an amended pleading may be feasible under Rule 15(a), but the effects of the pleading will be restricted by Rule 15(c). Rule 15(c) determines whether an amended pleading will be treated as though it was filed on the date of the original pleading or on the date of filing. When the timing of a pleading asserting a claim is at issue, attorneys should consult both Rule 15(a) and Rule 15(c).

APPLICATIONS

Amendment of Right

A party may amend a pleading without leave of court or consent of opposing parties once, under either of two circumstances. First, a pleading may be amended of right if the amendment is filed within 21 days after serving it.[2] Additionally, if the pleading to be amended requires a responsive pleading, it may be amended of right within 21 days of service of a responsive pleading or 21 days after service of a motion under Rule 12(b), (e), or (f) (whichever is earlier).

No *Sua Sponte* Authority to Amend

Only parties may amend a pleading. While the court has authority to accept or refuse an amendment in many circumstances, the court has no authority to enter an amendment *sua sponte*.[3]

Leave of Court

If a proposed amendment cannot be filed as of right, and the opposing party will not consent, a party may file a motion seeking leave to amend. In that circumstance, permission to amend rests within the discretion of the court. However, Rule 15(a) directs the court to grant leave to amend "when justice so requires," and in practice the burden is usually on the party opposing the amendment to demonstrate why the amendment should not be permitted.[4] Moreover, at least some courts hold that where a complaint's deficiency could be cured by an amendment, leave to amend must be given.[5]

Requirement to Submit Proposed Amendment

A party filing a motion for leave to amend must submit a proposed amendment to the court.[6]

---

[1]   *Vanguard Outdoor, LLC v. City of Los Angeles,* 648 F.3d 737 (9th Cir. 2011).

[2]   *Mayle v. Felix,* 545 U.S. 644, 125 S.Ct. 2562, 2569, 162 L.Ed.2d 582 (2005).

[3]   *See e.g., Miccosukee Tribe of Indians of Florida v. United States,* 716 F.3d 535, 559 (11th Cir. 2013) (reason is that if court itself amended pleading, it would create impression that court was advocating for a particular party).

[4]   *Foman v. Davis,* 371 U.S. 178, 83 S.Ct. 227, 9 L.Ed.2d 222 (1962).

[5]   *Shane v. Fauver,* 213 F.3d 113 (3d Cir. 2000).

[6]   *See, e.g., Spadafore v. Gardner,* 330 F.3d 849, 853 (6th Cir. 2003) (otherwise court is unable to determine whether to grant leave to amend); *Gilmour v. Gates, McDonald and Co.,* 382 F.3d 1312, 1315 (11th Cir. 2004).

Request in Brief Insufficient

The motion to amend should be in a formal motion; arguments in a brief in support of a motion for summary judgment will not be treated as a request to amend a pleading.[7]

Standard of Discretion

Generally, leave to amend is liberally granted.[8] In particular, if leave to amend is denied, it will often occur because an amendment would create unfair prejudice to another party.[9] Prejudice is most commonly found when there has been substantial unjustified delay in moving to amend that creates an unfair disadvantage for an opposing party.[10] By contrast, no unfair prejudice exists simply because a party has to defend against new or better pleaded claims.[11] However, while Rule 15(a) imposes no time limits on motions for leave to amend pleadings, substantial unexplained and unjustified delays in seeking leave to amend generally reduce the prospects for obtaining leave to amend.[12]

A court's normally liberal approach to granting leave to amend may be circumscribed if the pleading has already been the subject of previous amendments.[13]

Futility

When a party has no right to amend and must obtain leave of court to do so, a court may deny leave if the amendment would be futile, *e.g.,* would still fail to state a claim.[14] However, if a party still has a right to amend, it is unclear whether the court can reject the amendment because it would be futile.[15]

Cases Removed from State Court

Section 1447(e) of Title 28 of the United States Code provides that if, after a case is removed, a plaintiff seeks to amend the complaint to join non-diverse defendants whose joinder would destroy diversity, the district may permit or deny joinder. If the court denies joinder, the court continues to have jurisdiction over the case. However, if the court permits joinder, diversity jurisdiction no longer exists and (in the absence of some other basis for subject matter jurisdiction) the court must then remand the case to state court.

That situation gets more complicated if, after removal but before a responsive pleading has been filed, a plaintiff exercises the right to amend a pleading and joins a non-diverse defendant under Rule 15(a) without needing leave of court. If Rule 15(a) could be used in that manner, it would undermine the district court's discretion under § 1447(e) to retain the removed case by denying joinder. Courts have resolved this conflict by concluding that the courts have authority to deny joinder under Rule 15(a), notwithstanding the plaintiff's apparent right under that Rule.[16]

Rights of Joined Parties

If a party is served with an amended pleading permitted under Rule 15, that party normally enjoys a minimum of 14 days from the date of service of the amended pleading to

---

[7]   *See, e.g., Anderson v. Donahoe,* 699 F.3d 989, 998 (7th Cir. 2012).

[8]   *See, e.g., Jackson v. Rockford Housing Authority,* 213 F.3d 389 (7th Cir.2000).

[9]   *See, e.g., Eminence Capital, LLC v. Aspeon, Inc.,* 316 F.3d 1048, 1052 (9th Cir. 2003) (consideration of prejudice to the opposing party carries the greatest weight.).

[10] *See, e.g., Jin v. Metropolitan Life Ins. Co.,* 295 F.3d 335 (2d Cir. 2002).

[11] *See, e.g., Popp Telcom v. American Sharecom, Inc.,* 210 F.3d 928, 943 (8th Cir. 2000).

[12] *Krupski v. Costa Crociere, S.p.A.,* 560 U.S. 536, 130 S.Ct. 2485, 177 L.Ed.2d 48 (2010).

[13] *See, e.g., Ascon Properties, Inc. v. Mobil Oil Co.,* 866 F.2d 1149, 1160 (9th Cir. 1989).

[14] *See, e.g., In re NVE Corp. Securities Litigation,* 527 F.3d 749, 752 (8th Cir. 2008).

[15] *See, e.g., Williams v. Board of Regents of University System of Georgia,* 441 F.3d 1287, 1296 (11th Cir. 2006).

[16] *See, e.g., Mayes v. Rapoport,* 198 F.3d 457, 461 (4th Cir. 1999).

respond to it.[17] Rule 15(a) expressly provides the district court with authority to modify that time limit.

Termination of Right to Amend

Many courts hold that once the court has entered final judgment, a party's ability to amend of right terminates.[18] Thus if the court grants a motion to dismiss and enters judgment, the dismissed party's right to amend expires.[19]

Multiple Opposing Parties

If some opposing parties have already filed responsive pleadings and others have not, courts generally hold that the original pleading may be amended as of right, at least as to those parties that have not yet pleaded.[20]

Relation to Joinder Rules

When a party seeks to amend a complaint under Rule 15(a) to join additional claims or parties, the joinder will not be permitted simply because the requirements of Rule 15 have been met. In addition, the applicable joinder rules must also be satisfied.[21]

Relation to Rule 41(a)

When a plaintiff seeks to dismiss all of its claims, the proper procedure is dismissal under Rule 41(a).[22] If a plaintiff seeks to dismiss some, but not all, claims, the courts are divided as to whether the proper procedure is amendment under Rule 15(a) or dismissal under Rule 41(a).[23]

Relation with Rule 81(c)

If a case is removed from state court, it is possible that a party will be ordered under Rule 81(c) to file a repleading that conforms to federal practice. Generally, such a mandated repleading will not deprive a party of a one-time right to amend that may be available under Rule 15(a).[24]

Adverse Party's Consent

If a party's proposed amendment falls outside the time limits described above, the opposing party may consent to the amendment. When their duties to their own clients are not at issue, attorneys often cooperate in such matters as a matter of professional courtesy, and because they recognize that refusing to consent may lead to an expensive motion with the same outcome. If the opposing party consents to an amendment, there is no need to obtain court approval.[25] Rule 15(a) requires that consent of other parties be in writing,[26] which is usually filed with the court in the form of a praecipe.

---

[17]   *Nelson v. Adams USA, Inc.,* 529 U.S. 460, 465, 120 S.Ct. 1579, 1584, 146 L.Ed.2d 530 (2000).

[18]   *See, e.g., Jacobs v. Tempur-Pedic International, Inc.,* 626 F.3d 1327,1344 (11th Cir. 2010).

[19]   *See, e.g., Gates v. Syrian Arab Republic,* 646 F.3d 1 (D.C. Cir. 2011).

[20]   *See, e.g., Williams v. Board of Regents of University System of Georgia,* 441 F.3d 1287, 1296 (11th Cir. 2006).

[21]   *See, e.g., Hinson v. Norwest Financial South Carolina, Inc.,* 239 F.3d 611, 618 (4th Cir. 2001). *But see Bibbs v. Early,* 541 F.3d 267, 275 n.39 (5th Cir. 2008) (if a party seeks to amend a pleading to drop or add parties, Rule 15 takes precedence over Rule 21).

[22]   *See, e.g., Sneller v. City of Bainbridge Island,* 606 F.3d 636, 639 (9th Cir. 2010).

[23]   *See, e.g., Bowers v. National Collegiate Athletic Ass'n,* 346 F.3d 402, 413 (3d Cir. 2003) (Rule 41); *Campbell v. Altec Industries, Inc.,* 605 F.3d 839 (11th Cir. 2010) (Rule 15).

[24]   *See, e.g., Kuehl v. F.D.I.C.,* 8 F.3d 905, 907 (1st Cir. 1993) (but where party engages in dilatory conduct in meeting Rule 81(c) requirements, Rule 15(a) right to amend may be treated as exhausted).

[25]   *See, e.g., American States Ins. Co. v. Dastar Corp.,* 318 F.3d 881, 888 (9th Cir. 2003).

[26]   *See, e.g., Minter v. Prime Equipment Co.,* 451 F.3d 1196, 1204 (10th Cir. 2006).

Rule 16 and Case Management

While, as a general rule, leave to amend is granted freely in the interest of justice, the likelihood of obtaining permission to amend diminishes drastically if the court has entered a scheduling order with a deadline for amending pleadings and that deadline has passed. In that situation, the "good cause" standard for changing a deadline in a Rule 16 order controls, not the liberal amendment standard under Rule 15.[27]

Effect of Amendment

Once an amendment is properly filed, it displaces the earlier pleading which it amends.[28]

Responding to Amended Pleadings

If the pleading amended is one to which a responsive pleading is appropriate, the opposing party will have either the time remaining before a response to the unamended version was due or fourteen days—whichever is longer—in which to respond.[29] However, the court has authority to alter those time limits.

Relationship to Rule 15(b)

Technically, a motion for leave of court to amend a pleading may be made at any time under Rule 15(a). However, if a suit has advanced to trial or post-trial motions, Rule 15(b), pertaining to amendments to conform to the evidence, is probably a more appropriate vehicle. The difference between Rule 15(a) and (b) is not a bright line, and generally courts are liberal in granting permission for substantive amendments under either provision provided that no unfair prejudice thereby accrues to other parties.[30]

RULE 15(b)—AMENDMENTS DURING AND AFTER TRIAL

CORE CONCEPT

Rule 15(b) permits amendments to pleadings in two circumstances. The first situation arises when an issue not raised in the original pleadings is tried without objection. The second occurs when an issue not raised in the pleadings is objected to, but the proposed amendment will either not create unfair prejudice or such prejudice can be cured.

APPLICATIONS

Timing; Relationship to Rule 15(a)

Motions to amend under Rule 15(b) may theoretically be made at any time. The language of the Rule, however, speaks to matters raised at trial, suggesting that the Rule should not generally be used at early stages of litigation.[31] Instead, early in the litigation it is more appropriate to seek to amend a pleading under the authority of Rule 15(a). Generally speaking, motions to amend under Rule 15(b) are made at trial or in the immediate aftermath of a trial.[32]

---

[27] *See, e.g., Byrd v. Guess,* 137 F.3d 1126, 1131–32 (9th Cir. 1998).

[28] *See, e.g., In re Wireless Telephone Federal Cost Recovery Fees Litigation,* 396 F.3d 922, 928 (8th Cir. 2005).

[29] *See, e.g., General Mills, Inc. v. Kraft Foods Global, Inc.,* 495 F.3d 1378, 1379 (Fed. Cir. 2007).

[30] *See, e.g., U.S. for Use and Benefit of Seminole Sheet Metal Co. v. SCI, Inc.,* 828 F.2d 671 (11th Cir. 1987).

[31] *See, e.g., Cook v. City of Bella Villa,* 582 F.3d 840, 852 (8th Cir. 2009); *Gold v. Local 7 United Food and Commercial Workers Union,* 159 F.3d 1307, 1309 (10th Cir. 1998). *But see Desertrain v. City of Los Angeles,* 754 F.3d 1147, 1154 (9th Cir. 2014) (amendment under Rule 15(b) permissible in motion for summary judgment); *Ahmad v. Furlong,* 435 F.3d 1196, 1203 (10th Cir. 2006) (noting extensive split of authority as to whether Rule 15(b) should be applied to issues raised in a motion for summary judgment on the eve of trial).

[32] *See, e.g., United States v. 5443 Suffield Terrace,* 607 F.3d 504 (7th Cir. 2010).

Relationship to Rule 15(c)

If a new claim is asserted through a pleading amended pursuant to Rule 15(b), there may still be questions about the timeliness of the claim. While Rule 15(b) may permit the amended pleading, Rule 15(c) controls whether the amended pleading is deemed to have been filed on the date of the original pleading or the date of the amendment. The distinction is significant when questions of statutes of limitations are raised.

Counterclaims

Rule 15(b) may be employed to assert a counterclaim where evidence on the counterclaim was heard at trial.[33]

Failure to Object

An opposing party's consent to a Rule 15(b) amendment may be express or implied.[34] Thus, the court may find that parties who fail to object to the introduction of evidence relating to matters not within the four corners of the original pleadings have impliedly consented to adjudication of those matters and will deem the pleadings accordingly amended.[35]

Failure to File an Amended Pleading; Motions to Amend

Rule 15(b) expressly provides that if parties are found to have consented to litigation of issues outside the original pleadings, there is no requirement that a formal amended pleading be filed.[36]

However, if an opposing party makes a proper objection to evidence going to a new claim, the party seeking relief under Rule 15(b) must make an appropriate motion to amend.[37]

Amendments over Objections to Evidence

If a party objects to the use of evidence on the ground that it does not address issues raised in the original pleadings, the court may allow amendments that encompass such evidence.[38] Such amendments may be permitted on either of two grounds: the absence of unfair prejudice to the objecting party[61] or the ability of the court to cure such prejudice.[39]

Grounds for Denying Rule 15(b) Amendments

Courts deny Rule 15(b) amendments on any of four grounds: bad faith; undue delay; unfair prejudice to an opponent; or futility of a proposed amendment.[40] If an issue is tried with the express or implied consent of the parties, however, the district court must accept the amended pleading. In such circumstances, the court has no discretion, and acceptance of the amendment is mandatory.[41]

---

[33]   *See, e.g., In re Meyertech Corp.,* 831 F.2d 410, 421 (3d Cir. 1987).

[34]   *See, e.g., U.S. ex rel. Modern Elec., Inc. v. Ideal Electronic Sec. Co., Inc.,* 81 F.3d 240 (D.C. Cir. 1996).

[35]   *See, e.g., Eich v. Board of Regents for Cent. Missouri State University,* 350 F.3d 752, 762 (8th Cir. 2003).

[36]   *See, e.g., People for Ethical Treatment of Animals v. Doughney,* 263 F.3d 359, 367 (4th Cir. 2001).

[37]   *See, e.g., Green Country Food Market, Inc. v. Bottling Group, LLC,* 371 F.3d 1275, 1281 (10th Cir. 2004).

[38]   *Cf. Moncrief v. Williston Basin Interstate Pipeline Co.,* 174 F.3d 1150 (10th Cir.1999) (party seeking amendment must make motion to amend, court cannot amend *sua sponte*).

[61]   *See, e.g., New York State Elec. & Gas Corp. v. Secretary of Labor,* 88 F.3d 98 (2d Cir. 1996).

[39]   *See, e.g., Green Country Food Market, Inc. v. Bottling Group, LLC,* 371 F.3d 1275, 1280 (10th Cir. 2004).

[40]   *See, e.g., FilmTec Corp. v. Hydranautics,* 67 F.3d 931, 935 (Fed. Cir. 1995).

[41]   *See, e.g., Wallin v. Fuller,* 476 F.2d 1204, 1210 (5th Cir. 1973).

Unfair Prejudice

Determinations of unfair prejudice are highly fact specific. The most likely circumstance in which such prejudice will be found occurs when the objecting party is surprised by the evidence and has no reasonable opportunity to meet it.[42]

Curing Unfair Prejudice

If the source of unfair prejudice is surprise, courts may attempt to cure the problem by using their authority under Rule 15(b) to grant a continuance so that the objecting party can prepare for the new evidence.[43] Such an order may include reopening opportunities for discovery.

Relation to Rule 16

As discussed under Rule 16, the court's final pretrial order supplants the pleadings and controls the issues to be tried. The provisions of Rule 15(b) authorize amendment to include issues outside the final pretrial order as well as issues outside the pleadings.[44]

Relation to Rule 56

Rule 15(b) questions usually arise in situations where a case has gone to trial and a dispute has arisen as to whether an issue or claim has been "tried by express or implied consent." Whether the principles underlying Rule 15(b) apply to cases decided on summary judgment appears to be an open question.[45]

Relation to Rule 60

Rule 60 governs motions to vacate judgments. A pleading may be amended under Rule 15 if a motion to vacate a judgment has been granted.[46]

RULE 15(c)—RELATION BACK OF AMENDMENTS

CORE CONCEPT

Rule 15(c) governs the circumstances in which an amended pleading will be treated as though it was filed on the date of the original pleading. This determination is highly relevant to the applicability of statutes of limitations to claims raised or parties joined in amended pleadings.

APPLICATIONS

Amendment Adding New Claim

When an amended pleading adds a new claim among the existing parties, it will relate back to the original pleading when the claim or defense in the amended pleading arises from the same transaction or occurrence as that set forth—or attempted to be set forth—in the original pleading.

Same Transaction or Occurrence: Courts look to the degree of overlap of evidence between the occurrences raised in the amended pleading and the original pleading to determine whether they arise out of the same transaction or occurrence.[47] This standard is measured by the facts pleaded; it does not depend on the legal theory offered. Thus, an

---

[42] *See, e.g., Walton v. Nalco Chemical Co.,* 272 F.3d 13, 20 (1st Cir. 2001).

[43] *See, e.g., Menendez v. Perishable Distributors, Inc.,* 763 F.2d 1374, 1379 (11th Cir. 1985).

[44] *See, e.g., Clark v. Martinez,* 295 F.3d 809 (8th Cir.2002).

[45] *See, e.g., Independent Petroleum Ass'n of America v. Babbitt,* 235 F.3d 588, 596 (D.C. Cir. 2001).

[46] *Cf., e.g., Morse v. McWhorter,* 290 F.3d 795, 799 (6th Cir. 2002).

[47] *Mayle v. Felix,* 545 U.S. 644, 125 S.Ct. 2562, 2569–75, 162 L.Ed.2d 582 (2005).

amendment may relate back notwithstanding that the proffered amendment offers a new legal theory.[48]

Amendment Adding a New Party

When an amended pleading adds a new party, it will relate back to the original pleading if: (1) the claim against the new party arises from the same transaction or occurrence set forth in, or attempted to be set forth in, the original pleading; and (2) within the 90-day period after filing of the original pleading that Rule 4(m) provides for service of process, the new party named in the amended pleading both received sufficient notice of the pendency of the action so as not to be prejudiced in preparing a defense, and knew or should have known that but for a mistake of identity the party would have been named in the original pleading. The first element—same transaction or occurrence—is the requirement relating to amendments adding a new claim. The other element has two parts—fair notice and awareness of a mistake in identity—that are explained immediately below. In determining whether relation back should be permitted, a district court may consider extrinsic evidence, and is not confined to examination of the pleadings themselves.[49]

(1) *Notice:* The notice must, in the particular circumstances of the case, ensure that the party joined is not unfairly prejudiced by an amended pleading that relates back to an earlier date.[50] In general, notice may be actual or constructive.[51] If a party to be joined in an amended complaint learned of the suit within the 90-day period provided by Rule 4(m) for service of the original complaint,[52] and that party's opportunity to prepare a defense was not hindered by the time lag between the original pleading and the amended pleading, the requirement of notice generally would be satisfied.[53] For example, corporations in a parent-subsidiary relationship with an entity sued in the original complaint would probably be held to have notice of the original action.[54]

(2) *Knowledge of Mistaken Identity:* Before an amended pleading joining a new party may relate back, the proponent of the pleading must also establish that within the 90-day period provided by Rule 4(m), the person to be joined knew, or should have known, that the person would have been sued in the original pleading but for a mistake in identity.[55] It is unclear whether the mistake may be one of either fact or law.[56] Thus, if a subsidiary corporation was sued when the claim should have been against its parent, and was served within the period provided by Rule 4(m), the parent might be charged with timely knowledge of the fact that the proper defendant should have been the parent.[57] With natural persons, the requirement may be satisfied when the name of the proper defendant is similar to the name of the person originally designated as a defendant, *and* the proper defendant knew of the mistake within the time limit established by Rule 4(m).[58]

---

[48] *See, e.g., Maegdlin v. International Ass'n of Machinists and Aerospace Workers, Dist. 949*, 309 F.3d 1051, 1053 (8th Cir. 2002).

[49] *See, e.g., Wilkins v. Montgomery*, 751 F.3d 214, 225 (4th Cir. 2014).

[50] *See, e.g., Glover v. F.D.I.C.*, 698 F.3d 139, 146 (3d Cir. 2012).

[51] *See, e.g., Force v. City of Memphis*, 101 F.3d 702, 884 (6th Cir. 1996).

[52] *See, e.g., Jones v. Bernanke*, 557 F.3d 670, 675 (D.C. Cir. 2009).

[53] *See, e.g., Singletary v. Pennsylvania Dept. of Corrections*, 266 F.3d 186, 189 (3d Cir. 2001).

[54] *See, e.g., Andrews v. Lakeshore Rehabilitation Hosp.*, 140 F.3d 1405, 1408 (11th Cir. 1998).

[55] *Krupski v. Costa Crociere, S.p.A.*, 560 U.S. 538, 130 S.Ct. 2485, 177 L.Ed.2d 48 (2010) (issue is whether defendant understood or should have understood that it was the proper defendant).

[56] *Compare, e.g., Woods v. Indiana University-Purdue University at Indianapolis*, 996 F.2d 880, 887 (7th Cir. 1993) (indicating that mistake may be of fact or law), *with Rendall-Speranza v. Nassim*, 107 F.3d 913, 918 (D.C. Cir. 1997) (amendment permitted, if at all, only for mistake of fact).

[57] *Krupski v. Costa Crociere, S.p.A.*, 560 U.S. 538, 130 S.Ct. 2485, 177 L.Ed.2d 48 (2010).

[58] *See, e.g., Brown v. Shaner*, 172 F.3d 927, 933 (6th Cir. 1999).

Amendment Changing the Name of a Party

An amendment changing the name of a party will relate back to the original pleading under the same circumstances as an amendment adding a new party, discussed immediately above.[59]

Relation Back Authorized by Statute of Limitations

Relation back is also authorized when the applicable statute of limitations provides for relation back.[60] Rule 15(c)(1)(A) defers to a statute of limitations only if the statute is more generous on relation back. Rule 15(c)(1)(A) does not apply if the statute is more restrictive. In that circumstance the provisions of Rule 15(c)(1)(B) or (C) would determine whether an amended pleading would relate back.[61]

Right to Amend Independent

Rule 15(c) deals only with whether an amendment will be treated as though it was filed at an earlier date rather than the actual date of filing—whether the amendment relates back to the date the original pleading was filed. The determination of the right to amend is controlled by Rules 15(a) and (b).

Right to Amend Not Restricted to "Pleadings"

Although Rule 15(c) itself refers only to amendments of pleadings, it is also appropriately applied to amendments of some other documents filed in district court.[62] However, Rule 15(c) does not apply to permit relation back of an untimely notice of appeal.[63]

Amendments Adding New Plaintiffs

In general, late-added plaintiffs cannot obtain the benefit of relation back to the date of the complaint by the original plaintiffs.[64] Exceptions to this prohibition on relation back by new plaintiffs arise when new plaintiffs share a great deal of overlapping interest with original plaintiffs or to correct a misnomer or misidentification.[65]

Undue Delay and Relation Back

Under Rule 15(a), a court may properly deny leave to amend a pleading when a party has delayed excessively and without good cause in seeking leave.[66] However, undue delay plays no role in an evaluation of relation back under Rule 15(c).[67]

Relation to Laches

Laches is a case law doctrine that may be raised by a defendant where the plaintiff unreasonably delays in bringing a lawsuit, and thereby unfairly harms the defendant. Rule 15(c) governs the timing of an amended pleading for purposes of a statute of limitations.

---

[59] Fed.R.Civ.P. 15(c)(1)(C).

[60] Fed.R.Civ.P. 15(c)(1)(A).

[61] *See, e.g., Morel v. Daimler-Chrysler AG,* 565 F.3d 20, 26 (1st Cir. 2009).

[62] *Scarborough v. Principi,* 541 U.S. 401, 416–18, 124 S.Ct. 1856, 1867–68, 158 L.Ed.2d 674 (2004) (applying Rule 15(c) to application for award of attorney fees).

[63] *See, e.g., Cruz v. International Collection Corp.,* 673 F.3d 991, 1002 (9th Cir. 2012).

[64] *See, e.g., Asher v. Unarco Material Handling, Inc.,* 596 F.3d 313, 318 (6th Cir. 2010).

[65] *See, e.g., Young v. Lepone,* 305 F.3d 1, 14 (1st Cir. 2002) (relation back of new plaintiffs' claims "theoretically available," but there must be an identity of interest with claims of original plaintiffs).

[66] *See* Authors' Commentary on Rule 15(a).

[67] *Krupski v. Costa Crociere, S.p.A.* 560 U.S. 538, 130 S.Ct. 2485, 177 L.Ed.2d 48 (2010).

Rule 15 "has no controlling force where . . . a defendant's remedy is provided by the equitable doctrine of laches.[68]

Comparison to Rule 17

Rule 17(a), governing requirements to prosecute a case in the name of the real party in interest, expressly provides that joinder or substitution of the real party in interest automatically relates back to the original filing date, apparently without regard to the requirements of Rule 15. Although the matter is not free of doubt, it appears that in such circumstances Rule 17(a), and not Rule 15, should control.[69]

"John Doe" Pleadings

Some courts hold that an amendment that substitutes the actual defendant for a "John Doe" designation cannot relate back because the plaintiff was unaware of the defendant's identity, not mistaken.[70]

Relation Back Against the United States

When the United States is a defendant, the requirements of timely notice of the action and knowledge of a mistake in identity, discussed above, are satisfied if the original pleading was served on the United States Attorney (or designee), the Attorney General, or an agency or officer who would have been a proper defendant if named in the original complaint.[71] This express provision cuts through much of what might otherwise have been substantial technical obstacles to use of relation back against the United States.[72] However, even when the United States is a defendant, the amended pleading must still arise out of the same transaction or occurrence as the original pleading, and service of the original pleading upon the federal officers identified above must occur within the 90-day period provided by Rule 4(m).

RULE 15(d)—SUPPLEMENTAL PLEADINGS

CORE CONCEPT

Rule 15(d) governs circumstances in which parties are permitted to supplement previous pleadings to encompass events that have occurred since the earlier pleadings were filed.

APPLICATIONS

Leave of Court

There is no unqualified right to file a supplemental pleading.[73] Authority to file a supplemental pleading is obtained by filing a motion.[74] Courts grant such leave when the supplemental pleadings will not unfairly prejudice other parties.[75]

---

[68] *Brzozowski v. Correctional Physician Services, Inc.*, 360 F.3d 173, 182 (3d Cir. 2004).

[69] *See, e.g., Scheufler v. General Host Corp.*, 126 F.3d 1261, 1271 (10th Cir. 1997) (applying relation-back provisions of Rule 17(a)).

[70] *See, e.g., Hogan v. Fischer*, 738 F.3d 509, 518–20 (2d Cir. 2013).

[71] *See, e.g., Roman v. Townsend*, 224 F.3d 24, 28 (1st Cir. 2000).

[72] *See, e.g., Delgado-Brunet v. Clark*, 93 F.3d 339, 344 (7th Cir. 1996).

[73] *Zenith Radio Corp. v. Hazeltine Research, Inc.*, 401 U.S. 321, 91 S.Ct. 795, 28 L.Ed.2d 77 (1971).

[74] *See, e.g., Bornholdt v. Brady*, 869 F.2d 57, 68 (2d Cir. 1989) (Rule 15(d) requires a motion).

[75] *See, e.g., Quaratino v. Tiffany & Co.*, 71 F.3d 58, 66 (2d Cir. 1995).

Party's Discretion

Supplemental pleadings are optional. Thus, if a party acquires a claim as a result of facts arising after the original pleading was filed, and the requirements of Rule 15(d) are satisfied, there is an opportunity, but not a duty, to file a supplemental claim.[76]

Same Transaction or Occurrence

If the issues addressed in a proposed supplemental pleading are related to the transaction or occurrence that gave rise to the original pleadings, and no other considerations of fairness weigh against hearing the supplemental pleading, courts generally permit the supplemental pleading.[77] A supplemental pleading may be permitted even if it arises from a separate transaction, but totally unrelated supplemental pleadings are disfavored.

Same Standard as Rule 15(a)

Judicial decisions to grant or deny Rule 15(d) motions to supplement pleadings are generally based on the same factors of fairness courts weigh when considering motions to amend pleadings under Rule 15(a).[78]

Time to File

Rule 15(d) contains no restriction on the time in which a supplemental pleading may be filed. However, the court may consider inappropriate delay in attempting to assert supplemental claims as grounds for refusing to grant permission to file the supplemental pleading.[79]

Developments After the Initial Pleading

Supplemental pleadings are restricted to events occurring since initiation of the suit.[80] If the issues raised predate the original pleadings, an amended, not supplemental, pleading is the appropriate mechanism for raising them[81]

Intervening Judicial Decisions

Intervening judicial decisions that change the applicable law are not the sort of "occurrences or events" that might implicate Rule 15(d).[82]

Relationship to Original Pleadings

Unlike amended pleadings, supplemental pleadings do not displace the original pleadings. Thus, there is no necessity to incorporate portions of the original pleadings in a supplemental pleading simply to preserve the original pleadings.

Mislabelled Pleadings

If a party inadvertently mislabels a supplemental pleading as an amended pleading, the court will disregard the error if it does not unfairly prejudice an opposing party.[83]

---

[76] *See, e.g., Lundquist v. Rice Memorial Hosp.,* 238 F.3d 975, 977 (8th Cir. 2001).

[77] *City of Hawthorne v. Wright,* 493 U.S. 813, 110 S.Ct. 61, 107 L.Ed.2d 28 (1989).

[78] *See, e.g., Glatt v. Chicago Park Dist.,* 87 F.3d 190 (7th Cir. 1996).

[79] *See, e.g., Quaratino v. Tiffany & Co.,* 71 F.3d 58, 66 (2d Cir. 1995).

[80] *See Haggard v. Bank of the Ozarks, Inc.,* 668 F.3d 196, 202 (5th Cir. 2012).

[81] *See, e.g., Flaherty v. Lang,* 199 F.3d 607, 613 (2d Cir. 1999).

[82] *See, e.g., United States v. Hicks,* 283 F.3d 380, 385 (D.C. Cir. 2002).

[83] *See, e.g., Cabrera v. City of Huntington Park,* 159 F.3d 374, 382 (9th Cir. 1998).

Defective Original Pleadings

Rule 15(d) explicitly provides that defects in the original pleadings have no effect on a party's ability to file a supplemental pleading. Thus, even an uncorrectable defect in the original pleading, requiring dismissal of the counts that pleading contains, does not necessarily bar filing of a supplemental pleading, if the supplemental pleading itself is free from substantial defects.

Responses to Supplemental Pleadings

Rule 15(d) does not create either a right or duty to respond to a supplemental pleading. Instead, the Rule vests the court with authority to order a response when appropriate in the circumstances of a case. Typically, an opportunity to respond will be permitted when the supplemental pleading asserts a new cause of action.

Relation Back of Supplemental Pleadings

Because supplemental pleadings address only events that have occurred since the original pleadings were filed, no question normally arises as to whether supplemental pleadings relate back to the date the original pleadings were filed.[84] However, where relation back is important to the supplemental pleadings, courts tend to apply the standards of Rule 15(c) to determine whether relation back should be permitted.[85]

ADDITIONAL RESEARCH REFERENCES

Wright & Miller, *Federal Practice and Procedure* §§ 1471 to 1510

C.J.S., Federal Civil Procedure §§ 322 to 356 et seq.

West's Key Number Digest, Federal Civil Procedure ↪821 to 853, ↪861 to 852

---

[84] *But see Innovative Therapies, Inc. v. Kinetic Concepts, Inc.,* 599 F.3d 1377, 1384 (Fed. Cir. 2010).

[85] *See, e.g., F.D.I.C. v. Knostman,* 966 F.2d 1133, 1138 (7th Cir. 1992) (using standards of Rule 15(c)).

RULE 16

PRETRIAL CONFERENCES; SCHEDULING; MANAGEMENT

(a) Purposes of a Pretrial Conference. In any action, the court may order the attorneys and any unrepresented parties to appear for one or more pretrial conferences for such purposes as:

(1) expediting disposition of the action;

(2) establishing early and continuing control so that the case will not be protracted because of lack of management;

(3) discouraging wasteful pretrial activities;

(4) improving the quality of the trial through more thorough preparation; and

(5) facilitating settlement.

(b) Scheduling.

(1) *Scheduling Order.* Except in categories of actions exempted by local rule, the district judge—or a magistrate judge when authorized by local rule—must issue a scheduling order:

    (A) after receiving the parties' report under Rule 26(f); or

    (B) after consulting with the parties' attorneys and any unrepresented parties at a scheduling conference.

(2) *Time to Issue.* The judge must issue the scheduling order as soon as practicable, but unless the judge finds good cause for delay, the judge must issue it within the earlier of 90 days after any defendant has been served with the complaint or 60 days after any defendant has appeared.

(3) *Contents of the Order.*

    (A) *Required Contents.* The scheduling order must limit the time to join other parties, amend the pleadings, complete discovery, and file motions.

    (B) *Permitted Contents.* The scheduling order may:

        (i) modify the timing of disclosures under Rules 26(a) and 26(e)(1);

        (ii) modify the extent of discovery;

        (iii) provide for disclosure, discovery, or preservation of electronically stored information;

(iv) include any agreements the parties reach for asserting claims of privilege or of protection as trial-preparation material after information is produced, including agreements reached under Federal Rule of Evidence 502;

(v) direct that before moving for an order relating to discovery, the movant must request a conference with the court;

(vi) set dates for pretrial conferences and for trial; and

(vii) include other appropriate matters.

(4) *Modifying a Schedule.* A schedule may be modified only for good cause and with the judge's consent.

(c) Attendance and Matters for Consideration at a Pretrial Conference.

(1) *Attendance.* A represented party must authorize at least one of its attorneys to make stipulations and admissions about all matters that can reasonably be anticipated for discussion at a pretrial conference. If appropriate, the court may require that a party or its representative be present or reasonably available by other means to consider possible settlement.

(2) *Matters for Consideration.* At any pretrial conference, the court may consider and take appropriate action on the following matters:

(A) formulating and simplifying the issues, and eliminating frivolous claims or defenses;

(B) amending the pleadings if necessary or desirable;

(C) obtaining admissions and stipulations about facts and documents to avoid unnecessary proof, and ruling in advance on the admissibility of evidence;

(D) avoiding unnecessary proof and cumulative evidence, and limiting the use of testimony under Federal Rule of Evidence 702;

(E) determining the appropriateness and timing of summary adjudication under Rule 56;

(F) controlling and scheduling discovery, including orders affecting disclosures and discovery under Rule 26 and Rules 29 through 37;

(G) identifying witnesses and documents, scheduling the filing and exchange of any pretrial briefs, and setting dates for further conferences and for trial;

(H) referring matters to a magistrate judge or a master;

(I)   settling the case and using special procedures to assist in resolving the dispute when authorized by statute or local rule;

(J)   determining the form and content of the pretrial order;

(K) disposing of pending motions;

(L)   adopting special procedures for managing potentially difficult or protracted actions that may involve complex issues, multiple parties, difficult legal questions, or unusual proof problems;

(M) ordering a separate trial under Rule 42(b) of a claim, counterclaim, crossclaim, third-party claim, or particular issue;

(N) ordering the presentation of evidence early in the trial on a manageable issue that might, on the evidence, be the basis for a judgment as a matter of law under Rule 50(a) or a judgment on partial findings under Rule 52(c);

(O) establishing a reasonable limit on the time allowed to present evidence; and

(P)   facilitating in other ways the just, speedy, and inexpensive disposition of the action.

(d) Pretrial Orders. After any conference under this rule, the court should issue an order reciting the action taken. This order controls the course of the action unless the court modifies it.

(e) Final Pretrial Conference and Orders. The court may hold a final pretrial conference to formulate a trial plan, including a plan to facilitate the admission of evidence. The conference must be held as close to the start of trial as is reasonable, and must be attended by at least one attorney who will conduct the trial for each party and by any unrepresented party. The court may modify the order issued after a final pretrial conference only to prevent manifest injustice.

(f) Sanctions.

(1) *In General.* On motion or on its own, the court may issue any just orders, including those authorized by Rule 37(b)(2)(A)(ii)—(vii), if a party or its attorney:

(A) fails to appear at a scheduling or other pretrial conference;

(B) is substantially unprepared to participate-or does not participate in good faith-in the conference; or

(C) fails to obey a scheduling or other pretrial order.

(2) *Imposing Fees and Costs.* Instead of or in addition to any other sanction, the court must order the party, its attorney, or both to pay the reasonable expenses—including attorney's fees—incurred because of any noncompliance with this rule, unless the noncompliance was substantially justified or other circumstances make an award of expenses unjust.

[Amended April 28, 1983, effective August 1, 1983; March 2, 1987, effective August 1, 1987; April 22, 1993, effective December 1, 1993; April 12, 2006, effective December 1, 2006; April 30, 2007, effective December 1, 2007; April 29, 2015, effective December 1, 2015.]

AUTHORS' COMMENTARY ON RULE 16

PURPOSE AND SCOPE

Rule 16 authorizes the district court to convene pretrial conferences for a variety of purposes. While the court has discretion to hold such pretrial conferences, Rule 16 *requires* the court to issue a scheduling order setting procedures for discovery and trial, unless the case falls into a category which the court, by local rule, has exempted from the requirement for a scheduling order. Further, if a pretrial conference is held, Rule 16 also requires the court to issue a pretrial order after such a pretrial conference detailing the action at the conference and establishing the course of action to be followed. Such orders are binding unless subsequently modified by the court.

RULE 16(a)—PRETRIAL CONFERENCES

CORE CONCEPT

Rule 16(a) outlines the parameters and objectives for the court's pretrial conferences with the parties. When preparing for a pretrial conference, the litigants should consult both Rule 16(c) and the local rules concerning the subjects to be discussed at a pretrial conference.

APPLICATIONS

Pretrial Conferences

(1) *Initial or First Conference:* The court may convene the first pretrial conference as soon as all of the parties have been served with the complaint. Typically, the court will delay the pretrial conference until after an answer is filed or preliminary motions to dismiss are resolved. The first pretrial conference permits the parties to familiarize the court with the issues in the case and to propose a discovery schedule. After the conference, the court will issue an order detailing the decisions reached and action taken. Typically, the initial conference will address issues of scope and timing of discovery, deadlines for amending the pleadings and impleading new parties, the timing for filing of motions, alternative dispute resolution, and settlement.

(2) *Subsequent and Final Pretrial Conferences:* Ordinarily, the court holds a final pretrial conference after the close of discovery, after ruling on dispositive pretrial motions, and after the filing of the pretrial narrative statements.[1] At this conference, the court sets a trial date, seeks to further clarify the issues, discusses any extraneous matters, sets a schedule for any remaining motions, and encourages settlement discussions.[2]

---

[1]   *But see Mizwicki v. Helwig,* 196 F.3d 828, 833 (7th Cir. 1999) (there is no requirement that the court conduct a final pretrial conference).

[2]   *Cf. Colon-Cabrera v. Esso Standard Oil Co. (Puerto Rico),* 723 F.3d 82, 89–90 (1st Cir. 2013) (acknowledging district court's authority to participate in settlement discussions).

(3)   *Other Pretrial Conferences:* The court may hold as many pretrial conferences as it deems necessary.

Pretrial Orders

The court is required to issue a pretrial order detailing the action taken at any pretrial conference conducted pursuant to Rule 16, as provided by Rule 16(e).

Who Must Attend

Rule 16(a) authorizes the court to order attorneys and unrepresented parties to attend pretrial conferences,[3] and makes no reference to represented parties. Courts have held that represented parties (in contrast to their attorneys) may also be directed to attend.[4] Additionally, at least one court has held that the judge must also attend, and cannot delegate that function to a law clerk.[5]

Motion for Pretrial Conference

Generally, the court will set the time for pretrial conferences. However, the parties may seek a pretrial conference either by informal request or by motion.[6]

RULE 16(b)—SCHEDULING

CORE CONCEPT

After receiving the discovery report required under Rule 26(f) or after conducting a scheduling conference under Rule 16(a), the court must issue a scheduling order setting timetables for pretrial matters. This scheduling order must be issued within 60 days after the appearance of a defendant and within 90 days of the service of the complaint.[7] The district judge may prepare the scheduling order or may refer this task to a magistrate judge.

APPLICATIONS

Mandatory Topics

Rule 16(b) requires the court's order to include time limits for: joining parties;[8] amending pleadings;[9] filing motions;[10] and completing discovery.[11]

Optional Topics

At the court's discretion, the scheduling order may also include: modifications of time limits for disclosures under Rule 26(a) and (e)(1) and of the extent of discovery; the disclosure, discovery, or preservation of electronic data;[12] provisions for recalling privileged documents inadvertently produced;[13] a requirement that parties request a conference with

---

[3]   *Royal Palace Hotel Associates, Inc. v. International Resort Classics, Inc.,* 178 F.R.D. 595, 597 (M.D. Fla. 1998) (local rule requiring attendance of lead trial counsel is enforceable).

[4]   *See, e.g., Matter of Sargeant Farms, Inc.,* 224 B.R. 842, 845 (M.D. Fla. 1998).

[5]   *Connolly v. National School Bus Service, Inc.,* 177 F.3d 593 (7th Cir. 1999).

[6]   *See, e.g., Garcia-Perez v. Hospital Metropolitano,* 597 F.3d 6, 9 (1st Cir. 2010).

[7]   *O'Connell v. Hyatt Hotels of Puerto Rico,* 357 F.3d 152, 154 (1st Cir. 2004).

[8]   *Johnson v. Mammoth Recreations, Inc.,* 975 F.2d 604, 608 (9th Cir. 1992).

[9]   *See, e.g., AmerisourceBergen Corp. v. Dialysist West, Inc.,* 445 F.3d 1132, 1141 (9th Cir. 2006).

[10]   *Rosario-Diaz v. Gonzalez,* 140 F.3d 312 (1st Cir.1998).

[11]   *Suntrust Bank v. Blue Water Fiber, L.P.,* 210 F.R.D. 196, 199 (E.D. Mich. 2002).

[12]   *See* the discussion in the commentary to Rule 26 for a discussion of the aspects of the discovery of electronic data that the parties may want to discuss in the Rule 16 conference and include in the Rule 26(f) report.

[13]   *See* the discussion in the commentary to Rule 26(b)(5) and the advisory committee note to the 2006 Amendment to Rule 26(b)(5) for discussions of the methods for recalling produced privileged information.

the court before filing a discovery motion; dates for pretrial conferences and for trial; and other matters the court deems appropriate.[14]

Modification of Scheduling Order Deadlines

For good cause shown,[15] the court may grant a motion modifying or enlarging the deadlines in the scheduling order.[16] Good cause is shown when the schedule cannot reasonably be met despite the diligence of the party seeking the extension.[17]

Relation to Rule 15

Rule 15 governs amended and supplemental pleadings. If a party seeks to amend a pleading before the district court enters a Rule 16(b) scheduling order or before the time limit of a scheduling order expires, the proposed amended pleading will be evaluated under the liberal amendment standard of Rule 15(a). Once the deadline in the court's scheduling order has passed, the "good cause" standard of Rule 16(b) for modifying the scheduling order controls, not the liberal amendment standard of Rule 15(a).[18]

Rule 15(b) has a different relationship with Rule 16(b) than Rule 15(a). Rule 15(b) generally governs amendments of pleadings that arise during the course of a trial.[19] Thus, almost by definition, a pleading amended pursuant to Rule 15(b) will be amended well after the expiration of the time limit in the court's scheduling order. If Rule 15(b) is to have any meaning, therefore, it must govern amendments occurring at or after trial, notwithstanding the expiration of time limits for amendments in the court's scheduling order.[20]

RULE 16(c)—ATTENDANCE AND MATTERS FOR CONSIDERATION AT PRETRIAL CONFERENCES

CORE CONCEPT

Rule 16(c) contains a list of topics that the court may consider at Rule 16 conferences. Rule 16(c) also allows for the consideration of any other matters that may facilitate the "just, speedy, and inexpensive disposition of the action."

APPLICATIONS

Topics for Conferences

During a pretrial conference, the court may seek to define and simplify the contested facts, theories, and issues,[21] eliminate frivolous claims or defenses,[22] determine whether an amendment of the pleadings is necessary,[23] address disclosure and discovery issues,[24] seek the admission or denial of facts or documents, make advance rulings on the admissibility of

---

[14] *Does I thru XXIII v. Advanced Textile Corp.*, 214 F.3d 1058, 1068 (9th Cir. 2000) (the court may use its powers under Rule 16 to address a party's need for anonymity).

[15] *Hussain v. Nicholson*, 435 F.3d 359, 368 (D.C. Cir. 2006) (attorney error generally does not constitute good cause, but may in extreme circumstances).

[16] *See, e.g., O'Connell v. Hyatt Hotels of Puerto Rico*, 357 F.3d 152, 154 (1st Cir. 2004).

[17] Advisory committee notes to Rule 16 (1983 amendments).

[18] *See, e.g., Pressure Products Medical Supplies, Inc. v. Greatbatch, Ltd.*, 599 F.3d 1308, 1315 (Fed. Cir. 2010).

[19] Fed.R.Civ.P. 15(b).

[20] *See, e.g., Clark v. Martinez*, 295 F.3d 809, 815 (8th Cir. 2002).

[21] *See, e.g., Lassiter v. City of Philadelphia*, 716 F.3d 53, 55 (3d Cir. 2013) (statute of limitations).

[22] *See, e.g., MacArthur v. San Juan County*, 495 F.3d 1157, 1161–62 (10th Cir. 2007).

[23] *See, e.g., Lassiter v. City of Philadelphia*, 716 F.3d 53, 55 (3d Cir. 2013).

[24] *See, e.g., Arias v. DynCorp*, 752 F.3d 1011, 1014 (D.C. Cir. 2014).

evidence[25] and the appropriateness of expert witnesses,[26] require parties to file lists identifying witnesses[27] and documents, entertain requests to limit witnesses,[28] govern the order of proof at trial,[29] and discuss pretrial narrative statements, pending motions, stipulations limiting the issues for trial,[30] and scheduling matters. The court may consider stays, consolidations, or separate trials.[31] The court may also require parties to schedule presentation of evidence so that, if judgment as a matter of law or judgment on partial findings is appropriate, the court may reach those questions early in the trial. The court will also likely pursue the potential for settlement.[32]

Authority of Representatives

An attorney or party representative with the authority to enter stipulations and make admissions must be present at Rule 16 conferences. Rule 16(c) authorizes the court, if appropriate, to allow that an attorney or party representative with that authority to be present or available by other means, such as by telephone.

Memorializing Pretrial Conference

A court reporter generally will be present at pretrial conferences. In unusual circumstances and at the discretion of the court, parties may bring their own stenographers if the court does not order a court reporter.

Settlement

It has been held that the court may order parties to attend a conference where settlement will be discussed[33] but may not coerce parties into settlement.[34]

Rulings on Motions

At the pretrial conference, the court may rule on discovery motions, jurisdictional challenges, Rule 12(b) defenses, other Rule 12 motions, motions for summary judgment,[35] or motions in limine.[36]

Binding Effect of Statements at Pretrial Conference

A party is held at trial to admissions and stipulations made at a pretrial conference. However, the court may permit a party in certain circumstances to withdraw its stipulations.

---

[25] *Skydive Arizona, Inc. v. Quattrocchi,* 673 F.3d 1105, 1113 (9th Cir. 2012).

[26] *See, e.g., Avila v. Willits Environmental Remediation Trust,* 633 F.3d 828, 833–34 (9th Cir. 2011).

[27] *Hollander v. Sandoz Pharmaceuticals Corp.,* 289 F.3d 1193 (10th Cir. 2002).

[28] *Planned Parenthood of Cent. New Jersey v. Verniero,* 22 F.Supp.2d 331, 339 (D.N.J. 1998).

[29] *Dick v. Department of Veterans Affairs,* 290 F.3d 1356 (Fed. Cir. 2002).

[30] *In re Air Crash Over Taiwan Straits on May 25, 2002,* 331 F.Supp.2d 1176, 1194 (C.D. Cal. 2004) (discussing the split in authority over whether a court can require a party to stipulate as to uncontested facts).

[31] *See, e.g., Center for Biological Diversity, Inc. v. BP America Production Co.,* 704 F.3d 413, 432 (5th Cir. 2013).

[32] *F.T.C. v. Freecom Communications, Inc.,* 401 F.3d 1192, 1208 (10th Cir. 2005).

[33] *In re Patenaude,* 210 F.3d 135, 144 (3d Cir. 2000).

[34] *Goss Graphics Systems, Inc. v. DEV Industries, Inc.,* 267 F.3d 624, 627 (7th Cir. 2001).

[35] *Pine Ridge Coal Co. v. Local 8377, United Min e Workers of America,* 187 F.3d 415, 419 (4th Cir. 1999).

[36] *Tucker v. Ohtsu Tire & Rubber Co., Ltd.,* 49 F.Supp.2d 456, 462–63 (D. Md. 1999).

RULE 16(d)—PRETRIAL ORDERS

CORE CONCEPT

The court must issue a pretrial order memorializing the action taken at any pretrial conference.[37] A pretrial order may include amendments to the pleadings,[38] stipulations, a statement of the issues for trial, the defenses available, the date for the filing of pretrial narrative statements, evidentiary or witness lists, and the date set for trial. The court may order a party to draft the order on the court's behalf. The court may impose sanctions under Rule 16(f) for a party's failure to comply with the order.

RULE 16(e)—FINAL PRETRIAL CONFERENCE AND ORDERS

CORE CONCEPT

The court will usually conduct the final pretrial conference after the pretrial narrative statements have been filed and as close to trial as possible.[39] At the final pretrial conference, the court will make a schedule for any remaining motions and set a trial date.[40] An attorney who will conduct the trial or an unrepresented party must attend the conference with the authority to enter stipulations and make admissions.[41]

APPLICATIONS

Pretrial Memorandum or Narrative Statement

(1) *Time:* The court will usually provide a date on which the parties must file a pretrial memorandum or pretrial narrative statement. The court usually orders the plaintiff's pretrial narrative statement to be filed first and the defendant's pretrial narrative statement several weeks after the filing of the plaintiff's statement.

(2) *Contents:* Local rule or court order will typically define the information parties are required to include in their pretrial narrative statements. Ordinarily, the parties must state their legal theories or defenses, provide a list of witnesses and documents to be presented at trial, detail the intended use of expert witnesses, and describe any exceptional legal or evidentiary questions that will be asserted at trial.

Final Pretrial Order

The court will incorporate the information provided by the parties in their pretrial narrative statements and other submissions into its final pretrial order. Once a pretrial order has been entered,[42] it supersedes all pleadings and controls the subsequent course of the case.[43]

Modification of Final Pretrial Order

In contrast to other Rule 16 orders which may be modified for good cause, the final pretrial order may be modified only to prevent manifest injustice.[44]

---

[37] *Athridge v. Rivas,* 141 F.3d 357, 362 (D.C. Cir. 1998).

[38] *Deere v. Goodyear Tire and Rubber Co.,* 175 F.R.D. 157, 164–65 (N.D. N.Y. 1997).

[39] *See Matter of Rhone-Poulenc Rorer Pharmaceuticals, Inc.,* 138 F.3d 695, 697 (7th Cir. 1998).

[40] *See, e.g., Dream Games of Arizona, Inc. v. PC Onsite,* 561 F.3d 983, 996 (9th Cir. 2009).

[41] *But cf., eg., Briscoe v. Klaus,* 538 F.3d 252, 260 (3d Cir. 2008) (pro se litigant with no history of dilatoriness should not be disciplined for violation of Rule 16(e) without first having opportunity to be heard).

[42] *Wall v. County of Orange,* 364 F.3d 1107, 1111 (9th Cir. 2004) (a pretrial order that was lodged but not entered is not controlling).

[43] *Rockwell Intern. Corp. v. United States,*549 U.S. 457, 127 S.Ct. 1397, 167 L.Ed.2d 190 (2007).

[44] *Galdamez v. Potter,* 415 F.3d 1015, 1020 (9th Cir. 2005).

Objection to Final Pretrial Order and Preservation of Right to Appeal

In order to preserve a party's rights on appeal, a party should object to the final pretrial order at the time it is issued or at the commencement of trial by asserting a motion to amend the order.

Appeal of Pretrial Order

Prior to the entry of judgment, a party has no right to a direct appeal from the final pretrial order.[45]

RULE 16(f)—SANCTIONS

CORE CONCEPT

Upon motion or on the court's own initiative, the court will impose sanctions to force parties to comply with scheduling and pretrial orders and to compensate parties for expenses caused by an opposing party's noncompliance.[46] Sanctions may also attach to incorrect or incomplete pretrial statements,[47] or the failure to participate in a settlement conference in good faith.[48]

APPLICATIONS

Sanctions Imposed on Party's Motion

A party may file a motion for sanctions when a party or a party's attorney does not obey a scheduling[49] or pretrial order, when a party does not appear at a pretrial conference,[50] when a party is unprepared at a pretrial conference, or when a party does not act in good faith at a pretrial conference. The motion should be asserted as soon as possible after the sanctionable activity. Unless made during a hearing or trial, a party must file a written motion stating the reasons for the sanctions with particularity and the relief or order sought.

Sanctions Imposed *Sua Sponte*

When the court seeks to impose sanctions on its own initiative, the court must first provide notice and an opportunity to be heard to the sanctionable party.[51]

Bad Faith Not Required

The court has discretion to impose sanctions even in the absence of bad faith.[52] The court will not impose sanctions when the party can substantially justify its violation[53] or where the award of expenses would be unjust.

Nature of Sanctions

Sanctions may be assessed to punish for improper conduct,[54] for purposes of deterrence, or to compensate the party injured by the improper conduct.[55] The court will design a

---

[45] *Bradley v. Milliken*, 468 F.2d 902 (6th Cir. 1972).

[46] *Garlepied v. Main*, 2001 WL 305264 (E.D. La. 2001).

[47] *Bronk v. Ineichen*, 54 F.3d 425, 10 A.D.D. 143 (7th Cir. 1995) (excluding testimony of witness not named in pretrial statement).

[48] *Smith v. Northwest Financial Acceptance, Inc.*, 129 F.3d 1408, 1419 (10th Cir. 1997).

[49] *Lucas Automotive Engineering, Inc. v. Bridgestone/Firestone, Inc.*, 275 F.3d 762 (9th Cir. 2001).

[50] *Templet v. HydroChem Inc.*, 367 F.3d 473, 481 (5th Cir. 2004).

[51] *Ford v. Alfaro*, 785 F.2d 835 (9th Cir. 1986); *Newton v. A.C. & S., Inc.*, 918 F.2d 1121 (3d Cir. 1990).

[52] *Rice v. Barnes*, 201 F.R.D. 549, 551 (M.D. Ala. 2001).

[53] *Firefighter's Institute for Racial Equality ex rel. Anderson v. City of St. Louis*, 220 F.3d 898, 902 (8th Cir. 2000).

[54] *United States v. Samaniego*, 345 F.3d 1280, 1284 (11th Cir. 2003).

[55] *See Media Duplication Services, Ltd. v. HDG Software, Inc.*, 928 F.2d 1228, 1242 (1st Cir. 1991) (deterrence).

sanction that appropriately matches the violation.[56] The court can impose any sanctions it deems appropriate,[57] including but not limited to the following:[58]

(1) *Discovery Sanctions:* Rule 16(f) incorporates the discovery sanctions found in Rule 37(b)(2)(B), (C), and (D), such as refusing to allow a party to support or oppose designated claims or defenses,[59] striking pleadings or parts thereof, precluding witnesses not properly disclosed,[60] or treating the conduct as contempt of court.[61]

(2) *Reasonable Expenses:* The court must require the sanctioned person to pay reasonable expenses,[62] including costs and attorney's fees caused by noncompliance with Rule 16, unless the court finds that the noncompliance was "substantially justified" or that an award of expenses would be "unjust."[63] These expenses may be the only sanctions ordered or may be in addition to another sanction.

(3) *Court Costs:* The court may impose court costs on a party who causes court expense by the sanctionable activities.

(4) *Dismissal:* The court may even dismiss a case[64] or enter default judgment[65] for failure to obey pretrial orders.[66] However, a trial court must apply lesser sanctions than dismissal except in an extreme situation where there is a clear record of delay or disobedience.[67] Some pertinent factors considered by the courts are the severity of the violation, the legitimacy of the party's excuse, repetition of violations, the deliberateness of the misconduct, mitigating excuses, prejudice to the court or opponent, and the adequacy of lesser sanctions.[68]

Who May Be Sanctioned

The court may impose sanctions against the party and/or any attorney of the party.[69] Where a represented party has no knowledge of the sanctionable activity, the court may order sanctions against the attorney alone and preclude reimbursement from the client.

Procedural and Substantive Errors

When a party commits a procedural error, courts generally will not impose sanctions that compromise the merits of the case.[70] Instead the court should impose costs and fees.[71]

---

[56] *Republic of Philippines v. Westinghouse Elec. Corp.*, 43 F.3d 65 (3d Cir. 1994); *Smith v. Rowe*, 761 F.2d 360 (7th Cir. 1985).

[57] *Young v. Gordon*, 330 F.3d 76 (1st Cir. 2003); *Arnold v. Krause, Inc.*, 233 F.R.D. 126, 129 (W.D. N.Y. 2005).

[58] *Nick v. Morgan's Foods, Inc.*, 270 F.3d 590, 595–96 (8th Cir. 2001).

[59] *Velez v. Awning Windows, Inc.*, 375 F.3d 35, 42 (1st Cir. 2004).

[60] *Potomac Elec. Power Co. v. Electric Motor Supply, Inc.*, 190 F.R.D. 372 (D. Md. 1999).

[61] *Trilogy Communications, Inc. v. Times Fiber Communications, Inc.*, 109 F.3d 739, 745 (Fed. Cir. 1997).

[62] *See, e.g., Tracinda Corp. v. DaimlerChrysler AG*, 502 F.3d 212, 214 (3d Cir. 2007).

[63] *Richardson v. Nassau County*, 184 F.R.D. 497 (E.D. N.Y. 1999).

[64] *See, e.g., Nascimento v. Dummer*, 508 F.3d 905, 909 (9th Cir. 2007).

[65] *DIRECTV, Inc. v. Huynh*, 318 F.Supp.2d 1122 (M.D. Ala. 2004).

[66] *Bay Fireworks, Inc. v. Frenkel & Co., Inc.*, 359 F.Supp.2d 257, 262 (E.D.N.Y. 2005).

[67] *Tower Ventures, Inc. v. City of Westfield*, 296 F.3d 43, 45–46 (1st Cir. 2002).

[68] *Gripe v. City of Enid, Okl.*, 312 F.3d 1184, 1188 (10th Cir. 2002).

[69] *Nick v. Morgan's Foods, Inc.*, 270 F.3d 590, 597 (8th Cir. 2001).

[70] *Rice v. City of Chicago*, 333 F.3d 780, 786 (7th Cir. 2003) (a judge should consider punishing the lawyer through sanctions rather than the plaintiff through dismissal of the suit).

[71] *Sanders v. Union Pacific R. Co.*, 154 F.3d 1037, 1042 (9th Cir. 1998) (imposing monetary sanctions on attorney can appropriately punish the one responsible for the harm).

When a party commits a substantive error, the court may impose sanctions which compromise the merits of a party's case.[72]

Appeal

An order imposing sanctions for failing to obey a Rule 16 scheduling or pretrial order is appealable only after final judgment has been entered in the underlying action.[73]

ADDITIONAL RESEARCH REFERENCES

Wright & Miller, *Federal Practice and Procedure* §§ 1521 to 1540

C.J.S., Federal Civil Procedure §§ 905 to 914

West's Key Number Digest, Federal Civil Procedure ⌐1921 to 1943

---

[72] *See, e.g., Lucien v. Breweur, 9* F.3d 26, 29 (7th Cir. 1993) (willful failure to attend final pretrial conference can be cause for dismissal with prejudice).

[73] *Cato v. Fresno City,* 220 F.3d 1073, 1074 (9th Cir. 2000).

IV. PARTIES

RULE 17

PLAINTIFF AND DEFENDANT; CAPACITY; PUBLIC OFFICERS

(a) Real Party in Interest.

(1) *Designation in General.* An action must be prosecuted in the name of the real party in interest. The following may sue in their own names without joining the person for whose benefit the action is brought:

(A) an executor;

(B) an administrator;

(C) a guardian;

(D) a bailee;

(E) a trustee of an express trust;

(F) a party with whom or in whose name a contract has been made for another's benefit; and

(G) a party authorized by statute.

(2) *Action in the Name of the United States for Another's Use or Benefit.* When a federal statute so provides, an action for another's use or benefit must be brought in the name of the United States.

(3) *Joinder of the Real Party in Interest.* The court may not dismiss an action for failure to prosecute in the name of the real party in interest until, after an objection, a reasonable time has been allowed for the real party in interest to ratify, join, or be substituted into the action. After ratification, joinder, or substitution, the action proceeds as if it had been originally commenced by the real party in interest.

(b) Capacity to Sue or Be Sued. Capacity to sue or be sued is determined as follows:

(1) for an individual who is not acting in a representative capacity, by the law of the individual's domicile;

(2) for a corporation, by the law under which it was organized; and

(3) for all other parties, by the law of the state where the court is located, except that:

(A) a partnership or other unincorporated association with no such capacity under that state's law may sue or be sued in its common

name to enforce a substantive right existing under the United States Constitution or laws; and

(B) 28 U.S.C. §§ 754 and 959(a) govern the capacity of a receiver appointed by a United States court to sue or be sued in a United States court.

(c) Minor or Incompetent Person.

(1) *With a Representative.* The following representatives may sue or defend on behalf of a minor or an incompetent person:

(A) a general guardian;

(B) a committee;

(C) a conservator; or

(D) a like fiduciary.

(2) *Without a Representative.* A minor or an incompetent person who does not have a duly appointed representative may sue by a next friend or by a guardian ad litem. The court must appoint a guardian ad litem—or issue another appropriate order—to protect a minor or incompetent person who is unrepresented in an action.

(d) Public Officer's Title and Name. A public officer who sues or is sued in an official capacity may be designated by official title rather than by name, but the court may order that the officer's name be added.

[Amended effective March 19, 1948; October 20, 1949; July 1, 1966; August 1, 1987; August 1, 1988; November 18, 1988; April 30, 2007, effective December 1, 2007.]

AUTHORS' COMMENTARY ON RULE 17
PURPOSE AND SCOPE

Rule 17 controls the determination of who may prosecute or defend an action in federal court. The standards are mandatory, but they can usually be satisfied without fundamentally altering the litigation.

RULE 17(a)—REAL PARTY IN INTEREST

CORE CONCEPT

The only parties on whose behalf suits may be initiated are those persons whose interests will be materially affected by the outcome.[1] Such persons should be the named plaintiffs, with certain exceptions. This requirement is imposed on plaintiffs so that defendants will only have to face one suit over the same interest.[2]

---

[1]   *See, e.g., United HealthCare Corp. v. American Trade Ins. Co., Ltd.,* 88 F.3d 563, 569 (8th Cir. 1996).

[2]   *See, e.g., Curtis Lumber Co. v. Louisiana Pacific Corp.,* 618 F.3d 762, 771 (8th Cir. 2010) (purpose of Rule 17(a) is to ensure that defendant will obtain benefit of res judicata).

APPLICATIONS

Naming the Interested Party

Subject to exceptions discussed below, the suit must be commenced not only on behalf of the real party in interest but also in the name of the real party in interest.[3] Thus, the real party in interest generally must be named in the caption.[4]

Relation to Rules 5.2 and 10

Rule 10 governs the form in which a pleading must be presented to the court. It requires that a complaint include the names of all the plaintiffs.[5] Rule 5.2 authorizes the court to redact certain information or place it under seal.[6] In limited circumstances Rule 5.2 may be used to modify the application of Rule 10(a). Rule 17(a)'s requirement that a real party in interest prosecute a lawsuit has little or no relation to this interplay of Rules 5.2 and 10. Instead, Rule 17 only ensures that a lawsuit is not prosecuted by someone who has no real interest in the case, without regard to the formalities of a lawsuit's captioning.[7]

No Mandatory Joinder of All Plaintiffs: Rule 19

The plaintiff (or claimant) must generally be a real party in interest. However, there is no need to join all other persons who are real parties in interest.[8] It may still be true, however, that Rule 19 would require such nonparties' participation.[9]

Rule 17(a) and Defendants

Rule 17(a) governs circumstances in which plaintiffs (or persons asserting claims) must be added. It does not address whether defendants must be joined—see Rule 19 addressing required parties.[10]

Standing vs. Real Party in Interest

While the requirements of standing and Rule 17(a) may differ in some respects,[11] it is clear that both share the requirement that the plaintiff has a personal interest in the case.[12]

Raising a Rule 17 Defense

The manner in which a party may invoke Rule 17(a) is not clear.[13] Some courts indicate that the appropriate way to raise Rule 17 is through the answer,[14] while other authority indicates it might be the appropriate subject of a motion.[15]

---

[3]   *But cf. Sealed Plaintiff v. Sealed Defendant,* 537 F.3d 185, 191 n.3 (2d Cir. 2008).

[4]   *Lincoln Property Co. v. Roche,* 546 U.S. 81, 126 S.Ct. 606, 163 L.Ed.2d 415 (2005).

[5]   Fed.R.Civ.P. 10(a).

[6]   Fed.R.Civ.P. 5.2(e) and (f).

[7]   *See, e.g., Sealed Plaintiff v. Sealed Defendant,* 537 F.3d 185, 191 n.3 (2d Cir. 2008).

[8]   *See, e.g., HB General Corp. v. Manchester Partners, L.P.,* 95 F.3d 1185, 1196 (3d Cir. 1996).

[9]   *See, e.g., Tifford v. Tandem Energy Corp.,* 562 F.3d 699, 707 (5th Cir. 2009). *See also* Authors' Commentary on Rule 19.

[10]   *Lincoln Property Co. v. Roche,* 546 U.S. 81, 90, 126 S.Ct. 606, 614, 163 L.Ed.2d 415 (2005).

[11]   *See, e.g., Rawoof v. Texor Petroleum Co.,* 521 F.3d 750, 756 (7th Cir. 2008).

[12]   *See, e.g., APCC Services, Inc. v. Sprint Communications Co.,* 418 F.3d 1238 (D.C. Cir. 2005).

[13]   *See, e.g., Whelan v. Abell,* 953 F.2d 663, 672 n.7 (D.C. Cir. 1992) ("We note that the question of how a Rule 17(a) defense is raised (as a 12(b)(6) motion or as a Rule 8(c) affirmative defense) remains unsettled.").

[14]   *See, e.g., Weissman v. Weener,* 12 F.3d 84, 85 (7th Cir. 1993).

[15]   *See, e.g., In re Signal Intern., LLC,* 579 F.3d 478, 490 n.8 (5th Cir. 2009).

Invoking Rule 17(a) *Sua Sponte*

Most courts hold that the district court, as well as the parties, may raise a Rule 17(a) issue.[16]

Timing; Waiver

Rule 17(a) does not provide a time limit for asserting a Rule 17 defense. However, if the defense is not asserted with reasonable promptness, it is waived.[17]

Exceptions to Naming Interested Party

Rule 17(a) explicitly exempts the following categories of persons from the general principle that the named party be the real party in interest: executors, administrators, guardians, bailees, trustees,[18] persons who have made contracts on behalf of third parties,[19] and circumstances where a statute authorizes suit in the name of a representative party.[20]

Diversity Jurisdiction

In the circumstances where Rule 17(a) allows a representative to sue on behalf of the real parties in interest, discussed above, it is important to determine whether diversity jurisdiction will depend on the citizenship of the representative or the real parties in interest. This requires context-specific research.[21]

Suits in the Name of the United States

If a statute allows the United States to sue on behalf of a real party in interest, Rule 17(a) also permits the United States to be the named plaintiff.

Intervenors Under Rule 24

If a person seeks to intervene in an action under Rule 24 in order to assert a claim, that potential party must meet the requirements of Rule 17(a).[22]

Relation to Rule 25

Rule 17 applies to transfers of interest prior to initiation of the suit, while Rule 25(c) controls transfers occurring after the suit is filed.[23]

Remedy

The preferred remedy is to provide an opportunity to amend so that the action can be prosecuted by the real party in interest.[24] Dismissal is a disfavored remedy for violation of the requirement to name the real party in interest.[25] Before a court grants a motion to dismiss, it must allow a real party in interest a reasonable opportunity to join the action, or,

---

[16]   *See, e.g., Weissman v. Weener,* 12 F.3d 84 (7th Cir. 1993).

[17]   *See, e.g., School Board of Avoyelles Parish v. Department of Interior,* 647 F.3d 570, 577–78 (5th Cir. 2011).

[18]   *See, e.g., Lenon v. St. Paul Mercury Ins. Co.,* 136 F.3d 1365, 1370 n.2 (10th Cir. 1998).

[19]   *See, e.g., Local 538 United Broth. of Carpenters and Joiners of America v. U.S. Fidelity and Guar. Co.,* 70 F.3d 741, 743 (2d Cir. 1995).

[20]   *See, e.g., U.S. ex rel. Long v. SCS Business & Technical Institute, Inc.,* 173 F.3d 870 (D.C. Cir. 1999) (in *qui tam* action under False Claims Act, 31 U.S.C.A. § 3730(b) provides that both the United States and the relator are real parties in interest).

[21]   *See, e.g., Americold Realty Trust v. Conagra Foods, Inc.,* ___ U.S. ___, 136 S.Ct. 1012, 1015–17 (2016) (nature of the action determines whether diversity jurisdiction turns on citizenship of trustee or trust members).

[22]   *See, e.g., Ross v. Marshall,* 426 F.3d 745, 757 (5th Cir. 2005).

[23]   *See, e.g., F.D.I.C. v. Deglau,* 207 F.3d 153, 159 (3d Cir. 2000).

[24]   *See, e.g., Dunmore v. United States,* 358 F.3d 1107, 1112 (9th Cir. 2004).

[25]   *See, e.g., Intown Properties Management, Inc. v. Wheaton Van Lines, Inc.,* 271 F.3d 164, 170 (4th Cir. 2001).

if permitted as an exception to Rule 17(a), to ratify continuation of the action in the name of the original plaintiff.

RULE 17(b)—CAPACITY TO SUE OR BE SUED

CORE CONCEPT

Rule 17(b) chooses the law that will govern the capacity of a person to prosecute or defend a suit.

APPLICATIONS

Natural Persons

For individuals, the law which determines their capacity to sue or be sued is the law of their domicile.[26] Domicile is generally defined as the jurisdiction where a person has established a physical presence and has the intent to remain for an indefinite period.[27]

Natural Persons as Representatives of Others

For natural persons suing on behalf of another, such as guardians or executors of estates, the law which determines their capacity to sue or be sued is the law of the state in which the court sits.[28]

Corporations

The capacity of a corporation to sue or be sued is governed by the law of the jurisdiction in which the corporation is incorporated.[29]

Unincorporated Associations

The capacity of an unincorporated association to sue or be sued is governed by the law of the state where the court is located.[30] However, if that state law does not provide such capacity for the association, then Rule 17(b) establishes the capacity when the cause of action is based on the Constitution or a federal statute.[31]

Receivers

The capacity of receivers appointed by a federal court to litigate in a federal court is governed by 28 U.S.C.A. §§ 754 (appointment of receivers in different federal judicial districts) and 959(a) (suits against receivers).

Capacity for All Other Parties

For circumstances not addressed by the specific provisions in Rule 17(b), the law governing capacity is that of the state in which the court sits.[32]

Capacity Distinguished from Real Party in Interest

Capacity and real party in interest advance two different concepts. Capacity addresses the capability of the type of party to participate in litigation. For example, individuals may, because they are individuals, have capacity to sue or be sued. Capacity alone, however, does not permit those individuals to bring a particular claim. Unless they also have a material interest in the outcome of a cause of action, they may not bring a suit because they are not

---

[26] *See, e.g., Johns v. County of San Diego,* 114 F.3d 874 (9th Cir.1997).

[27] *See, e.g., Stifel v. Hopkins,* 477 F.2d 1116, 1120 (6th Cir. 1973).

[28] *See, e.g., Maroni v. Pemi-Baker Regional School Dist.,* 346 F.3d 247, 249 n.2 (1st Cir. 2003).

[29] *See, e.g., Citizens Elec. Corp. v. Bituminous Fire & Marine Ins. Co.,* 68 F.3d 1016, 1019 (7th Cir. 1995).

[30] *See, e.g., Lundquist v. University of South Dakota Sanford School of Medicine,* 705 F.3d 378, 380 (8th Cir. 2013).

[31] *See, e.g., Curley v. Brignoli, Curley & Roberts Associates,* 915 F.2d 81, 87 (2d Cir. 1990).

[32] *See, e.g., Kauffman v. Anglo-American School of Sofia,* 28 F.3d 1223, 1225 (D.C. Cir. 1994).

also the real parties in interest.[33] Thus, to bring a suit, a party must have both "capacity," under the applicable law chosen by Rule 17(b), and a real stake in the outcome, as defined by Rule 17(a). To be sued, a defendant need only satisfy the law of capacity selected by Rule 17(b).

RULE 17(c)—MINOR OR INCOMPETENT PERSONS

CORE CONCEPT

Rule 17(c) controls the manner in which infants and other persons unable to represent their own interests will be represented in federal court.[34] The provisions apply irrespective of whether the infant or incompetent person is participating as a plaintiff or defendant.

APPLICATIONS

Infants and Incompetents Already Represented

Where persons unable to protect their own interests already have others charged with the duty to care for them outside of litigation, such as guardians, such guardians have authority to sue on behalf of the persons in their care.[35]

Infants and Incompetents Not Already Represented

Where persons unable to protect their own interests are not already within the legal care of others, they may be represented in litigation by persons chosen to protect their interests. The court has power to appoint such guardians *ad litem* (persons who will represent the interest of others in litigation),[36] and to make other orders consistent with the best interests of infants and incompetents in litigation.[37]

Determination of Incompetence

There is no prerequisite that a state authority determine incompetence before a district court appoints a guardian *ad litem*.[38] However, if it has been determined that an unrepresented party is incompetent, the district court has an affirmative duty to appoint a guardian *ad litem* or to take other appropriate action.[39] In the absence of actual documentation or testimony by a mental health professional, a court of record, or a relevant public agency, the district court has no duty to make a *sua sponte* inquiry into a party's lack of mental capacity.[40] On the other hand, if a district court receives "verifiable evidence of incompetence" it is required to make a *sua sponte* inquiry.[41]

---

[33] *See, e.g., Lans v. Digital Equipment Corp.,* 252 F.3d 1320 (Fed. Cir. 2001).

[34] *See, e.g., Baloco ex rel. Tapia v. Drummond Co.,* 640 F.3d 1338, 1350 (11th Cir. 2011) (minor may sue or be sued only through a representative).

[35] *See, e.g., Fernandez-Vargas v. Pfizer,* 522 F.3d 55, 67 (1st Cir. 2008) (where no wrongdoing or conflict of interest is present, parent will often be suitable representative of minor).

[36] *See, e.g., Gibbs ex rel. Gibbs v. Carnival Cruise Lines,* 314 F.3d 125, 135–36 (3d Cir. 2002) (where infant is unrepresented, Rule 17(c) authorizes court to appoint guardian ad litem).

[37] *See, e.g., Berrios v. New York City Housing Authority,* 564 F.3d 130, 134 (2d Cir. 2009) ("[A]s to a claim on behalf of an unrepresented minor or incompetent person, the court is not to reach the merits without appointing a suitable representative.").

[38] *See, e.g., Fonner v. Fairfax County, VA,* 415 F.3d 325 (4th Cir. 2005).

[39] *See, e.g., Ferrelli v. River Manor Health Care Center,* 323 F.3d 196, 202 (2d Cir. 2003).

[40] *See, e.g., Ferrelli v. River Manor Health Care Center,* 323 F.3d 196, 202 (2d Cir. 2003) ("bizarre behavior" by itself does not require examination of competence).

[41] *See, e.g., Powell v. Symons,* 680 F.3d 301, 307 (3d Cir. 2012).

Authority of Representative

When a representative is appointed under Rule 17(c), that person has most of the authority that a competent client would have. However, Rule 17(c) does not by itself give the appointed person the right to serve as legal counsel for the infant or incompetent person.[42]

Other Orders

The district court may issue other orders necessary to protect infants and incompetents.[43] This authority includes the power to determine rates of compensation for guardians *ad litem* and to determine which party shall bear the cost of such expenses.[44]

RULE 17(d)—PUBLIC OFFICER'S TITLE AND NAME

CORE CONCEPT

Rule 17(d) allows suit by or against a public officer under either that person's official title or personal name. The court, however, may add the individual's name in cases where the official title alone has been used. The primary advantage of suing a public officer by title, rather than individual name, is that departure of the person from office thereby does not require a substitution of names under Rule 25.

ADDITIONAL RESEARCH REFERENCES

Wright & Miller, *Federal Practice and Procedure* §§ 1541 to 73

C.J.S., Federal Civil Procedure §§ 46 to 62 et seq.

West's Key Number Digest, Federal Civil Procedure ➥111, ➥131 to 149

---

[42] *See, e.g., Tindall v. Poultney High School Dist.,* 414 F.3d 281 (2d Cir. 2005) (right to proceed *pro se* does not apply to non-attorney parents who are guardians ad litem of minor children); *Cavanaugh ex rel. Cavanaugh v. Cardinal Local School Dist.,* 409 F.3d 753, 755 (6th Cir. 2005).

[43] *See, e.g., Robidowc v. Rosengren,* 638 F.3d 1177,1181 (9th Cir. 2011) (judicial inquiry under Rule 17(c) focuses on fairness of net recovery to minors, not to amounts allocated to adults or attorneys).

[44] *Gaddis v. United States,*381 F.3d 444, 453 (5th Cir. 2004) (en banc) (court may apportion guardian ad litem fees as court costs).

RULE 18

JOINDER OF CLAIMS

(a) In General. A party asserting a claim, counterclaim, crossclaim, or third-party claim may join, as independent or alternative claims, as many claims as it has against an opposing party.

(b) Joinder of Contingent Claims. A party may join two claims even though one of them is contingent on the disposition of the other; but the court may grant relief only in accordance with the parties' relative substantive rights. In particular, a plaintiff may state a claim for money and a claim to set aside a conveyance that is fraudulent as to that plaintiff, without first obtaining a judgment for the money.

[Amended effective July 1, 1966; August 1, 1987; April 30, 2007, effective December 1, 2007.]

AUTHORS' COMMENTARY ON RULE 18

PURPOSE AND SCOPE

Rule 18 permits claimants to bring all claims they may have against persons already parties to a case, notwithstanding the fact that the claims may be unrelated to one another.

CORE CONCEPT

Rule 18(a) abolishes prohibitions against bringing unrelated claims against the same defendant in a single action. The origin of the claims, whether equitable, legal, or originating in admiralty, is irrelevant to the right to plead claims in a single action.[1]

APPLICATIONS

Parties Who May Join Claims

The right to join claims is available to any claimant who is a party to the case, irrespective of whether the claims filed will be counterclaims, crossclaims, third-party claims, or original claims filed by the plaintiff.[2]

Rule 18(a) Is Permissive, Not Compulsory

A party choosing not to bring unrelated claims is free to file them in separate actions.[3]

♦ **NOTE:** Notwithstanding the permissive nature of Rule 18(a), there may be problems in subsequent litigation if the claims not filed in the initial litigation were related to the claims actually raised. In that circumstance, suits filed later may be subject to the bar of res judicata or collateral estoppel.

Separate Trials

Notwithstanding the liberal nature of this joinder provision, the trial court may still exercise its discretion to order separate trials on different claims pursuant to Rule 42(b).[4]

---

[1]   *See, e.g., Vodusek v. Bayliner Marine Corp.,* 71 F.3d 148, 154 (4th Cir. 1995) (Rule 18 permits "joinder of claims at law, in equity, and in admiralty").

[2]   *See, e.g., First Nat. Bank of Cincinnati v. Pepper,* 454 F.2d 626, 635 (2d Cir. 1972).

[3]   *See, e.g., Perkins v. Board of Trustees of University of Illinois,* 116 F.3d 235 (7th Cir. 1997).

[4]   *See, e.g., Parmer v. National Cash Register Co.,* 503 F.2d 275, 277 (6th Cir. 1974).

Relation to Rule 14

Rule 14 provides that, in order to implead a nonparty, a defendant must assert a claim contending that the third-party defendant is liable, in whole or in part, for the claim asserted against the defendant/third-party plaintiff. Once the third-party plaintiff has asserted one such claim, Rule 18 authorizes joinder of any other claims the third-party plaintiff has against the third-party defendant, regardless of whether they qualify under Rule 14 or are even related to other claims in the action.[5]

Relation to Rule 13(g)

Rule 13(g) provides that a party may assert a crossclaim against a coparty that arises out of the same transaction or occurrence that is the subject matter of the claims asserted against that party. Once a party has asserted one such crossclaim, Rule 18 authorizes joinder of any other claims the party has against the crossclaim defendant, regardless of whether they qualify under Rule 13(g) or are even related to other claims in the action.

Jurisdiction and Venue

Joinder under Rule 18(a) is subject to requirements of jurisdiction and venue. Thus, Rule 18(a) permits joinder of claims only where the claims independently satisfy such requirements.[6] For a further discussion of jurisdiction and venue, *see* §§ 2.1 to 2.14.

Joinder of Parties

Rule 18(a) authorizes only joinder of claims, not the addition of parties.[7] If joining a particular claim also requires joining additional parties, such parties may be added only as permitted under other applicable Rules.[8]

RULE 18(b)—JOINDER OF CONTINGENT CLAIMS

CORE CONCEPT

A claimant may join two claims in a single action even if the outcome of the second claim is contingent on the outcome of the first claim. For example, a plaintiff may sue on a personal injury and add a count accusing the defendant of fraudulently transferring assets to the defendant's spouse as a means of frustrating enforcement of a judgment the plaintiff might obtain.

ADDITIONAL RESEARCH REFERENCES

Wright & Miller, *Federal Practice and Procedure* §§ 1581 to 94

C.J.S., Federal Civil Procedure §§ 40 to 41, § 301

Fraudulent Conveyances § 331, § 494

West's Key Number Digest, Federal Civil Procedure ⇨81 to 87

---

[5]   *See, e.g., Lehman v. Revolution Portfolio L.L.C.,* 166 F.3d 389, 394 (1st Cir. 1999).

[6]   *See, e.g., King Fisher Marine Service, Inc. v. 21st Phoenix Corp.,* 893 F.2d 1155, 1158 (10th Cir. 1990).

[7]   *See, e.g., Bradbury Co., Inc. v. Teissier-duCros,* 231 F.R.D. 413, 415 (D. Kan. 2005).

[8]   *See e.g.,* Rule 20, concerning joinder of parties. *See also Wheeler v. Wexford Health Sources, Inc.,* 689 F.3d 680, 683 (7th Cir. 2012).

Joi
court m
19(b) to

R

CORE CONCEP

Rule 19(b) g
who cannot be j
substantial discre
the litigation with

♦ **NOTE:**
dismiss it.[20]
ways to reac
more favora
particularly

APPLICATION!

Relation to

If
such ca

Who May R

Tł
issues ≀

Relative W

Tł
one mi
must be
it is po
import;

Factors

(1
whethe
withou
the pot

19 *See, e.g., Ba*
20 *Republic of .*
21 *See, e.g., Sn*
22 *See, e.g., Mc*
23 *See, e.g., De*
24 *See, e.g., Un*
25 *See, e.g., Ga*
26 *Cf. HB Gen*
partnership itself n
27 *See, e.g., Es*
proceeding in case ⫠
persons in state cou

Joinder of Parties !

The court n

(1) The cc
be granted to th

(2) The c⫠
practically or le
controlled by th
order the joinde
fund before it
adequately repı

(3) Wher
court may orde
example, if a te
can arise if the
person. In that
landlord will be

Procedure

Only a pa
19 joinder mo
events, use of
affected by a c
12(b)(7), gove:
determine wh⫠
19. Typically,
dismiss; (2) re
the person cr⫠
grant the mot

Service on Nonp

If the cou
that service ł
Rule 4(k), peı
regard to noı

3 *See, e.g., Disabled*
4 *Samantar v. Yousi*
5 *See, e.g., In re Tor*
6 *See, e.g., Salt Rive*
7 *See, e.g., Helzberg*
Cir.1977).
8 *Republic of Philiµ*
9 *See, e.g., HS Reso*
10 *See, e.g., PaineW⫠*
11 Fed.R.Civ.P. 4(k)

RULE 19

REQUIRED JOINDER OF PARTIES

(a) Persons Required to Be Joined if Feasible.

(1) *Required Party.* A person who is subject to service of process and whose joinder will not deprive the court of subject-matter jurisdiction must be joined as a party if:

(A) in that person's absence, the court cannot accord complete relief among existing parties; or

(B) that person claims an interest relating to the subject of the action and is so situated that disposing of the action in the person's absence may:

(i) as a practical matter impair or impede the person's ability to protect the interest; or

(ii) leave an existing party subject to a substantial risk of incurring double, multiple, or otherwise inconsistent obligations because of the interest.

(2) *Joinder by Court Order.* If a person has not been joined as required, the court must order that the person be made a party. A person who refuses to join as a plaintiff may be made either a defendant or, in a proper case, an involuntary plaintiff.

(3) *Venue.* If a joined party objects to venue and the joinder would make venue improper, the court must dismiss that party.

(b) When Joinder Is Not Feasible. If a person who is required to be joined if feasible cannot be joined, the court must determine whether, in equity and good conscience, the action should proceed among the existing parties or should be dismissed. The factors for the court to consider include:

(1) the extent to which a judgment rendered in the person's absence might prejudice that person or the existing parties;

(2) the extent to which any prejudice could be lessened or avoided by:

(A) protective provisions in the judgment;

(B) shaping the relief; or

(C) other measures;

(3) whether a judgment rendered in the person's absence would be adequate; and

Fragments (leftmost page, Rule 19)

(4) whether th
dismissed f

(c) Pleading the
a party must s

(1) the name,
but is not j

(2) the reason

(d) Exception fo

[Amended effective July 1,

Rule 19(a) descri
the case. If such a per
jurisdiction and venue
the court should dism
arises when a defend
plaintiff failed to join

CORE CONCEPT

When feasible,
likelihood that the
nonparties themselve

APPLICATIONS

Analytical Sec

Use of
must deter
the court c
on the oth
of Rule 19
second qu
greater le
joined, the
party. Ho
proceed to
Using Ru
without th
administe

[1] *See, e.g., Hamr*
absent persons, as well
or other practical impa

[2] *Northern Arap*

Fragments (second page)

Prerequi

prere
in co

Time

motic
party
plead
motic

Joinder

joind

Relation

inter
from
that
pract

Joinder

juris
perso
could
juris
How
diver
19(b)

[12] *Compare,*
a party will be joi
Peabody Western
against third per

[13] *See, e.g.,*
30, 43 (1st Cir. 2

[14] *See, e.g.,*
prejudiced by jud

[15] *Independ*
(1926). *But see,*
owner to refuse t
473 F.2d 959, 96

[16] *See, e.g.,*
Cir. 2007).

[17] *Koster v.*

[18] *See Rave*
who is dispensab

Full page (rightmost, Rule 19)

joined may be harmed if the suit proceeds to judgment and exhausts a fund from which compensation might otherwise have been anticipated.[28] Finally, if there is a risk of collateral estoppel for the absent person, that factor weighs in favor of dismissing the action.[29] By contrast, if a potential party shows no interest in a case, its interests probably are not significantly affected by the outcome of the case.[30]

If the interest at risk is that of the absent party, and that interest is adequately represented by someone already in the case, it is possible that a court will consider the risk of impairment to be nullified.[31] However, courts are cautious in reaching the conclusion that an interest is adequately represented by existing parties.[32]

(2) *Avoiding Adverse Consequences:* The court will determine if means are available to the court for minimizing potential damage to the interests that are at risk without the participation of the person at issue. For example, if a tenant sought injunctive relief against a landlord but did not include another person also claiming to have rights as a tenant, and the tenant agreed to a damage remedy rather than an injunction, the risk to the landlord of mutually inconsistent injunctions is minimized, and the case may be allowed to proceed.[33]

(3) *Adequacy of a Judgment:* This consideration addresses "adequacy" primarily from the point of view of the public interest in efficient and final disposition of legal disputes. Thus a judgment in a person's absence that will leave related claims by or against that person undecided may be deemed an "inadequate" judgment.[34]

(4) *Availability of Another Forum:* The court will examine whether another forum is available in which the claimant may sue existing defendants as well as the person who cannot be joined.[35] When another forum is not available to the claimant, the court in most cases will proceed with the action.[36]

Public Interest Exception

In some cases where a public right is to be litigated, but some persons cannot be joined, courts have fashioned a "public interest exception" to Rule 19. When applicable, this exception means that such absent persons are not deemed crucial, without regard to whatever a Rule 19 analysis might have concluded.[37]

Relation to Rule 14

If an absent person whose joinder is important can be added by impleader under Rule 14, dismissal under Rule 19(b) is not available.[38]

[28] *See, e.g., In re Torcise,* 116 F.3d 860, 865 (11th Cir. 1997).

[29] *See, e.g., Schulman v. J.P. Morgan Inv. Management, Inc.,* 35 F.3d 799, 806 (3d Cir. 1994).

[30] *See, e.g., Gardiner v. Virgin Islands Water & Power Authority,* 145 F.3d 635 (3d Cir.1998).

[31] *See, e.g., Hooper v. Wolfe,* 396 F.3d 744, 749 (6th Cir. 2005).

[32] *See, e.g., Tell v. Trustees of Dartmouth College,* 145 F.3d 417 (1st Cir. 1998).

[33] *See, e.g., Smith v. United Brotherhood of Carpenters & Joiners of America,* 685 F.2d 164, 166 (6th Cir. 1982).

[34] *Republic of Philippines v. Pimentel,* 553 U.S. 851, 128 S.Ct. 2180, 2193, 171 L.Ed.2d 131 (2008).

[35] *See Laker Airways, Inc. v. British Airways, PLC,* 182 F.3d 843, 849 (11th Cir. 1999).

[36] *See Dawavendewa v. Salt River Project Agr. Imp. and Power Dist.,* 276 F.3d 1150, 1161 (9th Cir. 2002).

[37] *See, e.g., Kickapoo Tribe of Indians of Kickapoo Reservation in Kansas v. Babbitt,* 43 F.3d 1491, 1500 (D.C. Cir. 1995).

[38] *See, e.g., EEOC v. Peabody Western Coal Co.,* 610 F.3d 1070 (9th Cir. 2010).

Comparison with Rule 20

Rule 20 governs circumstances in which a plaintiff has ***authority*** to join other persons as parties when they share an interest in a lawsuit.[39] Rule 19, by contrast, ***requires*** joinder when a person's presence is central to the administration of justice in the case.

Removed Cases

In circumstances where a lawsuit was removed from state court, the inability of a district court to join a person crucial to the case due to, *e.g.*, a jurisdictional defect may not inevitably force the court to choose between dismissal and continuation of the case without the absent person. Instead, the court has statutory discretion to permit joinder, followed by remand to the state court.[40]

Effect of Dismissal: Relation to Rule 41(b)

Rule 41 governs the effects of dismissals. In cases that have been dismissed for failure to join a party under Rule 19, the dismissal is without prejudice to refiling unless the order of dismissal provides otherwise.[41]

RULE 19(c)—PLEADING THE REASONS FOR NONJOINDER

CORE CONCEPT

Rule 19(c) places an affirmative duty on parties seeking relief to identify in their pleadings potentially interested persons who have not been joined. A court may use such information to notify these persons, so that they may join on their own initiative.

APPLICATIONS

Motions to Dismiss

The defendant may use the names provided by the plaintiff as a basis for a motion to dismiss the action for failure to join necessary parties under Rule 12(b)(7). In addition, defendants may make similar use of any such knowledge they possess independently of the pleadings.

RULE 19(d)—EXCEPTION FOR CLASS ACTIONS

CORE CONCEPT

When Rule 19 and Rule 23, governing class actions, both apply to a case, and they are in conflict, Rule 23 controls.

ADDITIONAL RESEARCH REFERENCES

Wright & Miller, *Federal Practice and Procedure* §§ 1601 to 26

C.J.S., Federal Civil Procedure §§ 95 to 112 et seq.

West's Key Number Digest, Federal Civil Procedure ⊷201 to 233

---

[39] Fed.R.Civ.P. 20(a).

[40] 28 U.S.C. § 1447(e). *See, e.g., Bailey v. Bayer CropScience L.P.*, 563 F.3d 302, 308 (8th Cir. 2009).

[41] Fed.R.Civ.P. 41(b). *See also U.S. ex rel. May v. Purdue Pharma, L.P.*, 737 F.3d 908, 914 (4th Cir. 2013).

of an opponent. In general, however, the rule's language is construed to be broad enough to permit separation when injustice would occur.[13] Moreover, the court has discretion to order separate proceedings of any claim in the interest of justice or convenience under Rules 21 and 42(b).

ADDITIONAL RESEARCH REFERENCES

Wright & Miller, *Federal Practice and Procedure* §§ 1651 to 60

C.J.S., Federal Civil Procedure §§ 94 to 116

C.J.S., Federal Civil Procedure § 318, § 917, § 918

West's Key Number Digest, Federal Civil Procedure ⊶241 to 267

must be inte

transactions

law or fact.[1]

APPLICATI

Joinder

exi

pla

ma

Same T

in

tr

wl

re

tr

a

Duty

F

F

Com

Perr

Der

[1] S

[2] S

[3] M

[4] S

[5] S

[6] S

option, d

[7]

defenda

---

[13] *See, e.g., Coleman v. Quaker Oats Co.,* 232 F.3d 1271, 1296 (9th Cir. 2000) (separate trials appropriate where having all ten plaintiffs, alleging age discrimination, testify in one trial might cause confusion and prejudice).

RULE 21

MISJOINDER AND NONJOINDER OF PARTIES

Misjoinder of parties is not a ground for dismissing an action. On motion or on its own, the court may at any time, on just terms, add or drop a party. The court may also sever any claim against a party.

[April 30, 2007, effective December 1, 2007.]

AUTHORS' COMMENTARY ON RULE 21

PURPOSE AND SCOPE

Rule 21 contains the remedy for misjoinder or nonjoinder that violates other Rules governing multiparty litigation. It clarifies that dismissal is not a ground for misjoinder of parties. It also provides the court with discretion to sever claims against a party for separate trials, or to order separate trials for joined parties, even if the joinder was otherwise appropriate.

APPLICATIONS

What Constitutes Misjoinder

Joinder may be improper for a variety of reasons, including joinder that does not meet the requirements of the joinder rules, such as Rule 20(a) or Rule 14,[1] and situations in which joinder of parties produces defects in jurisdiction or venue.[2]

Consequence of Misjoinder

The consequence of misjoinder depends on the nature of the misjoinder. If the joinder does not comply with the rules governing joinder of parties, the court will order the inappropriately joined party dismissed, so that the remainder of the action may continue.[3] If the joinder of the party produces defects in jurisdiction or venue, then proper remedy depends on whether the party is an indispensable party under Rule 19. If so, then the court will likely dismiss the entire action. If not, the court is more likely to dismiss the party who produces the defect.[4]

Failure to Join

If a party should have been joined but was not, the court will simply order joinder of the missing party.[5]

Relation to Rule 15

If parties seek to add a party under Rule 21, courts generally use the standard of Rule 15, governing amendments to pleadings, to determine whether to allow the addition.[6]

---

[1] *See, e.g., Acevedo v. Allsup's Convenience Stores, Inc.,* 600 F.3d 516, 521 (5th Cir. 2010) ("Since Rule 21 does not provide any standards by which district courts can determine if parties are misjoined, courts have looked to Rule 20 for guidance.").

[2] *See, e.g., Whitaker v. American Telecasting, Inc.,* 261 F.3d 196, 206–07 (2d Cir. 2001) (approving use of Rule 21 to dismiss non-diverse defendant who had no real connection to litigation).

[3] *Newman-Green, Inc. v. Alfonzo-Larrain,* 490 U.S. 826, 832, 109 S.Ct. 2218, 2222, 104 L.Ed.2d 893 (1989).

[4] *See, e.g., Ravenswood Inv. Co. v. Avalon Correctional Services,* 651 F.3d 1219, 1225 (10th Cir. 2011) (court may dismiss a dispensable nondiverse party to cure a jurisdictional defect even after judgment entered).

[5] *See, e.g., Teamsters Local Union No. 116 v. Fargo-Moorhead Auto. Dealers Ass'n,* 620 F.2d 204 (8th Cir. 1980).

[6] *See, e.g., Galustian v. Peter,* 591 F.3d 724, 730 (4th Cir. 2010) (acknowledging that some courts do not use Rule 15(a)).

Relation to Rule 25

Rule 25 governs substitution of parties in circumstances like death or incapacity of a party. Rule 21 governs substitution in situations not covered by Rule 25.[7]

Relation to Rule 42(b)

When a claim is severed under Rule 21, it ceases to be part of the same suit.[8] By contrast, if an issue is separated under Rule 42(b), it will be tried separately but remain part of the same lawsuit. The most important result of this distinction is that severed proceedings under Rule 21 become final as each proceeding goes to judgment, and may be appealed individually. Separate trials under Rule 42(b), by contrast, are typically *not* ready for appeal until all claims and issues are decided.[9]

Timing

The court may order dismissal or the addition of a party at any time in the action, subject only to the need to protect all parties from unfair prejudice.[10]

Motion

Adding or dropping a party may be done upon motion of someone already a party, or upon the court's own initiative.[11]

Preserving Diversity Jurisdiction

Even where a party is appropriately joined, circumstances can arise where the court can apply Rule 21 to drop a party, such as when a court dismisses a nondiverse party in order to obtain diversity jurisdiction over the remaining parties.[12]

Severance of Claims or Parties

Even if parties or claims have been appropriately joined, the court may nonetheless use Rule 21 to order separate trials in the interest of justice.[13]

Transfer and Severance

District courts have broad authority to transfer litigation to another district court.[14] In a circumstance where only part of an action should be transferred, Rule 21 complements § 1404 by authorizing severance of the case so that portions eligible for transfer may be transferred.[15]

ADDITIONAL RESEARCH REFERENCES

Wright & Miller, *Federal Practice and Procedure* §§ 1681 to 89

C.J.S., Federal Civil Procedure §§ 117 to 126 et seq., §§ 171 to 177 et seq., §§ 318, §§ 343, §§ 803 to 809

West's Key Number Digest, Federal Civil Procedure ⚭87, ⚭384 to 386, ⚭387 to 388

[7] *Mathis v. Bess*, 761 F.Supp. 1023, 1026 (S.D. N.Y. 1991).

[8] *See, e.g., Rice v. Sunrise Express, Inc.*, 209 F.3d 1008, 1013 (7th Cir. 2000).

[9] *See, e.g., Acevedo-Garcia v. Monroig*, 351 F.3d 547, 559–60 (1st Cir. 2003).

[10] *Newman-Green, Inc. v. Alfonzo-Larrain*, 490 U.S. 826, 832, 109 S.Ct. 2218, 2223, 104 L.Ed.2d 893 (1989).

[11] *See, e.g., Delgado v. Plaza Las Americas, Inc.*, 139 F.3d 1 (1st Cir.1998) (court may raise nonjoinder *sua sponte*).

[12] *See, e.g., Newman-Green, Inc. v. Alfonzo-Larrain*, 490 U.S. 826, 832–33, 109 S.Ct. 2218, 2222–23, 104 L.Ed.2d 893 (1989).

[13] *See, e.g., Rice v. Sunrise Express, Inc.*, 209 F.3d 1008, 1016 (7th Cir. 2000).

[14] 28 U.S.C. § 1404(a).

[15] *See, e.g., In re Nintendo of America, Inc.*, 756 F.3d 1363 (Fed. Cir. 2014).

RULE 22

INTERPLEADER

(a) Grounds.

(1) *By a Plaintiff.* Persons with claims that may expose a plaintiff to double or multiple liability may be joined as defendants and required to interplead. Joinder for interpleader is proper even though:

    (A) the claims of the several claimants, or the titles on which their claims depend, lack a common origin or are adverse and independent rather than identical; or

    (B) the plaintiff denies liability in whole or in part to any or all of the claimants.

(2) *By a Defendant.* A defendant exposed to similar liability may seek interpleader through a crossclaim or counterclaim.

(b) Relation to Other Rules and Statutes.
This rule supplements—and does not limit—the joinder of parties allowed by Rule 20. The remedy this rule provides is in addition to—and does not supersede or limit—the remedy provided by 28 U.S.C. §§ 1335, 1397, and 2361. An action under those statutes must be conducted under these rules.

[Amended effective October 20, 1949; August 1, 1987; April 30, 2007, effective December 1, 2007.]

AUTHORS' COMMENTARY ON RULE 22

PURPOSE AND SCOPE

Rule 22 permits a person who holds an asset to join or interplead all of the parties with potential claims to the asset so that the court can determine the validity and priority of the claims.

RULE 22(a)—GROUNDS

CORE CONCEPT

Interpleader complements liberal joinder of parties under Rule 20 by allowing an asset holder to join multiple, mutually inconsistent claims of various parties, and thereby determine rights in the asset (the "stake") in a single proceeding.

♦   **NOTE:** Rule 22 interpleader is not the only kind of federal interpleader available. Statutory interpleader, found at 28 U.S.C.A. §§ 1335, 1397, and 2361, discussed below, is another important source of interpleader authority. Although the two kinds of interpleader may often be employed in the same action, the differing characteristics of the two interpleaders sometimes make one more desirable, or available when the other is unavailable. Thus, both versions should be considered when contemplating an interpleader action.

APPLICATIONS

Claims Against the Stake

    The only requirement under Rule 22 is that the interpleader plaintiff plead that the competing claims are at least partly inconsistent with one another, *e.g.,* where the claims

against a fund exceed the value of the fund.[1] Interpleader actions need not be based on identical competing claims, or claims with a common origin, nor must the claims be totally incompatible with one another.

Requirement of Good Faith

Irrespective of whether a stakeholder is seeking relief under Rule 22 or statutory interpleader, the stakeholder must have a "good faith" belief in the existence of colorable competing claims against the stake.[2]

Plaintiff as Claimant

Although the interpleader plaintiff does not need to have a claim to or interest in the stake, it may assert such a claim. For example where a limited insurance fund is subject to claims exceeding the value of the fund, the insurance company may initiate the interpleader action and then contend that none of the claims against the insurance fund has merit.[3]

Defendants May Employ Interpleader

Sometimes a stakeholder will already have been sued by a claimant, but other claimants are not parties to the action. In such circumstances the stakeholder is entitled to initiate the interpleader action through a counterclaim or crossclaim, and then join the other claimants in the action.[4]

Subject Matter Jurisdiction

Rule 22 does not create subject matter jurisdiction in interpleader actions. Federal subject matter jurisdiction is still required.[5] If the underlying cause of action is a federal question, subject matter jurisdiction for an interpleader is usually satisfied without difficulty. More commonly, however, the interpleader will arise from a state cause of action, and then the standard requirements for diversity jurisdiction must also be satisfied. The citizenship of the stakeholder must be diverse from that of the claimants,[6] and the amount in controversy must exceed $75,000. The claimants need not be diverse among themselves.[7]

Statutory interpleader under 28 U.S.C.A. § 1335, discussed below, creates different conditions for subject matter jurisdiction.[8]

Personal Jurisdiction

Interpleader actions are actions against individuals, not against the asset, and so must satisfy requirements of personal jurisdiction. This means that service of process on claimants must satisfy Rule 4 service requirements as well as constitutional Due Process protections discussed in sections 2.3–2.7.[9]

---

[1]   *See, e.g., Rhoades v. Casey,* 196 F.3d 592, 600 (5th Cir. 1999) ("there must be a single, identifiable, fund.").

[2]   *See, e.g., Michelman v. Lincoln National Life Insurance Co.,* 685 F.3d 887, 894 (9th Cir. 2012).

[3]   *Cf. Nationwide Mut. Fire Ins. Co. v. Eason,* 736 F.2d 130, 133 (4th Cir. 1984).

[4]   *Grubbs v. General Elec. Credit Corp.,* 405 U.S. 699, 92 S.Ct. 1344, 31 L.Ed.2d 612 (1972).

[5]   *See, e.g., Arnold v. KJD Real Estate, LLC,* 752 F.3d 700, 704 (7th Cir. 2014).

[6]   *See, e.g., Lee v. West Coast Life Insurance Co.,* 688 F.3d 1004, 1008 (9th Cir. 2012).

[7]   *See, e.g., Hussain v. Boston Old Colony Ins. Co.,* 311 F.3d 623, 635 n.46 (5th Cir. 2002).

[8]   *See Arnold v. KJD Real Estate, LLC,* 752 F.3d 700, 704 (7th Cir. 2014).

[9]   *See, e.g., Metropolitan Life Ins. Co. v. Chase,* 294 F.2d 500, 502 (3d Cir. 1961) (interpleader under Rule 22 requires personal jurisdiction over the claimants).

RULE 23

CLASS ACTIONS

(a) Prerequisites. One or more members of a class may sue or be sued as representative parties on behalf of all members only if:

(1) the class is so numerous that joinder of all members is impracticable;

(2) there are questions of law or fact common to the class;

(3) the claims or defenses of the representative parties are typical of the claims or defenses of the class; and

(4) the representative parties will fairly and adequately protect the interests of the class.

(b) Types of Class Actions. A class action may be maintained if Rule 23(a) is satisfied and if:

(1) prosecuting separate actions by or against individual class members would create a risk of:

　(A) inconsistent or varying adjudications with respect to individual class members that would establish incompatible standards of conduct for the party opposing the class; or

　(B) adjudications with respect to individual class members that, as a practical matter, would be dispositive of the interests of the other members not parties to the individual adjudications or would substantially impair or impede their ability to protect their interests;

(2) the party opposing the class has acted or refused to act on grounds that apply generally to the class, so that final injunctive relief or corresponding declaratory relief is appropriate respecting the class as a whole; or

(3) the court finds that the questions of law or fact common to class members predominate over any questions affecting only individual members, and that a class action is superior to other available methods for fairly and efficiently adjudicating the controversy. The matters pertinent to these findings include:

　(A) the class members' interests in individually controlling the prosecution or defense of separate actions;

　(B) the extent and nature of any litigation concerning the controversy already begun by or against class members;

　(C) the desirability or undesirability of concentrating the litigation of the claims in the particular forum; and

      (D) the likely difficulties in managing a class action.

(c) Certification Order; Notice to Class Members; Judgment; Issues Classes; Subclasses.

  (1) *Certification Order.*

    (A) *Time to Issue.* At an early practicable time after a person sues or is sued as a class representative, the court must determine by order whether to certify the action as a class action.

    (B) *Defining the Class; Appointing Class Counsel.* An order that certifies a class action must define the class and the class claims, issues, or defenses, and must appoint class counsel under Rule 23(g).

    (C) *Altering or Amending the Order.* An order that grants or denies class certification may be altered or amended before final judgment.

  (2) *Notice.*

    (A) *For (b)(1) or (b)(2) Classes.* For any class certified under Rule 23(b)(1) or (b)(2), the court may direct appropriate notice to the class.

    (B) *For (b)(3) Classes.* For any class certified under Rule 23(b)(3), the court must direct to class members the best notice that is practicable under the circumstances, including individual notice to all members who can be identified through reasonable effort. The notice must clearly and concisely state in plain, easily understood language:

      (i)   the nature of the action;

      (ii)   the definition of the class certified;

      (iii)   the class claims, issues, or defenses;

      (iv)   that a class member may enter an appearance through an attorney if the member so desires;

      (v)   that the court will exclude from the class any member who requests exclusion;

      (vi)   the time and manner for requesting exclusion; and

      (vii)   the binding effect of a class judgment on members under Rule 23(c)(3).

  (3) *Judgment.* Whether or not favorable to the class, the judgment in a class action must:

    (A) for any class certified under Rule 23(b)(1) or (b)(2), include and describe those whom the court finds to be class members; and

    (B) for any class certified under Rule 23(b)(3), include and specify or describe those to whom the Rule 23(c)(2) notice was directed, who have not requested exclusion, and whom the court finds to be class members.

  (4) *Particular Issues.* When appropriate, an action may be brought or maintained as a class action with respect to particular issues.

  (5) *Subclasses.* When appropriate, a class may be divided into subclasses that are each treated as a class under this rule.

(d) Conducting the Action.

  (1) *In General.* In conducting an action under this rule, the court may issue orders that:

    (A) determine the course of proceedings or prescribe measures to prevent undue repetition or complication in presenting evidence or argument;

    (B) require—to protect class members and fairly conduct the action—giving appropriate notice to some or all class members of:

      (i) any step in the action;

      (ii) the proposed extent of the judgment; or

      (iii) the members' opportunity to signify whether they consider the representation fair and adequate, to intervene and present claims or defenses, or to otherwise come into the action;

    (C) impose conditions on the representative parties or on intervenors;

    (D) require that the pleadings be amended to eliminate allegations about representation of absent persons and that the action proceed accordingly; or

    (E) deal with similar procedural matters.

  (2) *Combining and Amending Orders.* An order under Rule 23(d)(1) may be altered or amended from time to time and may be combined with an order under Rule 16.

(e) Settlement, Voluntary Dismissal, or Compromise. The claims, issues, or defenses of a certified class may be settled, voluntarily dismissed, or compromised only with the court's approval. The following procedures apply to a proposed settlement, voluntary dismissal, or compromise:

  (1) The court must direct notice in a reasonable manner to all class members who would be bound by the proposal.

  (2) If the proposal would bind class members, the court may approve it only after a hearing and on finding that it is fair, reasonable, and adequate.

(3) The parties seeking approval must file a statement identifying any agreement made in connection with the proposal.

(4) If the class action was previously certified under Rule 23(b)(3), the court may refuse to approve a settlement unless it affords a new opportunity to request exclusion to individual class members who had an earlier opportunity to request exclusion but did not do so.

(5) Any class member may object to the proposal if it requires court approval under this subdivision (e); the objection may be withdrawn only with the court's approval.

(f) Appeals. A court of appeals may permit an appeal from an order granting or denying class-action certification under this rule if a petition for permission to appeal is filed with the circuit clerk within 14 days after the order is entered. An appeal does not stay proceedings in the district court unless the district judge or the court of appeals so orders.

(g) Class Counsel.

(1) *Appointing Class Counsel.* Unless a statute provides otherwise, a court that certifies a class must appoint class counsel. In appointing class counsel, the court:

(A) must consider:

(i) the work counsel has done in identifying or investigating potential claims in the action;

(ii) counsel's experience in handling class actions, other complex litigation, and the types of claims asserted in the action;

(iii) counsel's knowledge of the applicable law; and

(iv) the resources that counsel will commit to representing the class;

(B) may consider any other matter pertinent to counsel's ability to fairly and adequately represent the interests of the class;

(C) may order potential class counsel to provide information on any subject pertinent to the appointment and to propose terms for attorney's fees and nontaxable costs;

(D) may include in the appointing order provisions about the award of attorney's fees or nontaxable costs under Rule 23(h); and

(E) may make further orders in connection with the appointment.

(2) *Standard for Appointing Class Counsel.* When one applicant seeks appointment as class counsel, the court may appoint that applicant only if the applicant is adequate under Rule 23(g)(1) and (4). If more than one

adequate applicant seeks appointment, the court must appoint the applicant best able to represent the interests of the class.

(3) *Interim Counsel.* The court may designate interim counsel to act on behalf of a putative class before determining whether to certify the action as a class action.

(4) *Duty of Class Counsel.* Class counsel must fairly and adequately represent the interests of the class.

(h) Attorney's Fees and Nontaxable Costs. In a certified class action, the court may award reasonable attorney's fees and nontaxable costs that are authorized by law or by the parties' agreement. The following procedures apply:

(1) A claim for an award must be made by motion under Rule 54(d)(2), subject to the provisions of this subdivision (h), at a time the court sets. Notice of the motion must be served on all parties and, for motions by class counsel, directed to class members in a reasonable manner.

(2) A class member, or a party from whom payment is sought, may object to the motion.

(3) The court may hold a hearing and must find the facts and state its legal conclusions under Rule 52(a).

(4) The court may refer issues related to the amount of the award to a special master or a magistrate judge, as provided in Rule 54(d)(2)(D).

[Amended effective July 1, 1966; August 1, 1987; April 24, 1998, effective December 1, 1998; March 27, 2003, effective December 1, 2003; April 30, 2007, effective December 1, 2007; March 26, 2009, effective December 1, 2009.]

AUTHORS' COMMENTARY ON RULE 23

PURPOSE AND SCOPE

Rule 23 provides a means of joining parties in a class action in situations where the number of parties is sufficiently large that it is impractical or inefficient for the parties to pursue their claims individually or through more conventional methods of joinder. Class actions are distinct from typical joinder situations in both the number of litigants involved and in the manner in which most class members participate in the case; the class of litigants is represented both by counsel and by "class representatives," *i.e.*, active members of the class who make many decisions for the entire class. Because there is potential for enriching the representatives at the expense of the class members who are not representatives and who therefore do not participate fully in many decisions, the court is charged with the obligation to monitor carefully important steps in the litigation process, such as approval of class litigation at the onset and potential settlements at the end. Class actions also present special problems of case management for the courts, so the trial judge has substantial additional authority to supervise progress in the case.

RULE 23(a)—PREREQUISITES

CORE CONCEPT

The specialized purpose of class actions—handling large numbers of litigants through class representatives—makes necessary a series of requirements intended to ensure that the opportunity to bring a class action is not misused or abused.[1] Rule 23(a) sets forth four requirements, all of which must be satisfied before the court will certify a class action.[2]

♦ **NOTE:** In addition to the requirements of case law and Rule 23(a), a court will not certify a class action unless it fits within one of the categories of class action in Rule 23(b) as well.[3] Class actions must also meet the requirements of personal jurisdiction, federal subject matter jurisdiction, and venue, although these requirements apply somewhat differently to class actions. Additionally, even if a proposed class meets all the requirements mentioned above, the district court may still decide not to certify the class action.

APPLICATIONS

Rule 23(a) Requirements for a Class

Every class action in federal court must meet the four prerequisites set forth in Rule 23(a), discussed below, and then also fall into one of the four categories of class action set forth in Rule 23(b).

(1) *Numerosity:* Rule 23(a)(1) requires that the class membership be so large that the alternative of joinder is "impracticable".[4] There is no threshold number of class members guaranteed to satisfy the numerosity requirement.[5] A class comprised of many hundreds or thousands of members will almost surely meet this test.[6] Classes of ten litigants or less will almost certainly not meet this test,[7] and will instead be consigned to joinder of parties under Rule 20. When the number of members falls between twenty-five and one hundred, the probability of meeting the numerosity requirement varies from one judicial district to another.[8]

While the numerosity requirement is very fact specific, the requirement of impracticability of joinder must be affirmatively and specifically addressed in the certification motion.[9] It is not necessary that joinder of all parties is impossible, only that difficulty or inconvenience of joining all parties make a class action appropriate.[10]

---

[1]   *Taylor v. Sturgell,* 128 S.Ct. 2161, 171 L.Ed.2d 155 (U.S. 2008) (procedural safeguards of Rule 23 have overriding purpose of safeguarding interests of passive class members).

[2]   *Wal-Mart Stores, Inc. v. Dukes,* 559 U.S. 393, 131 S.Ct. 2541, 176 L.Ed.2d 311 (2011).

[3]   *Wal-Mart Stores, Inc. v. Dukes,* 559 U.S. 393, 131 S.Ct. 2541, 176 L.Ed.2d 311 (2011); *Shady Grove Orthopedic Associates, P.A. v. Allstate Insurance Co.,* 559 U.S. 393, 130 S.Ct. 1431, 1437, 176 L.Ed.2d 311 (2010).

[4]   *See, e.g., Central States Southeast and Southwest Areas Health and Welfare Fund v. Merck-Medco Managed Care, L.L.C.,* 504 F.3d 229, 244–45 (2d Cir. 2007) ("The numerosity requirement . . . does not mandate that joinder of all parties be impossible—only that the difficulty or inconvenience of joining all members of the class make use of the class action appropriate.").

[5]   *See, e.g., Trevizo v. Adams,* 455 F.3d 1155 (10th Cir.2006).

[6]   *See, e.g., Bacon v. Honda of America Mfg., Inc.,* 370 F.3d 565, 570 (6th Cir. 2004) ("sheer number of potential litigants in a class, especially if it is more than several hundred, can be the only factor needed to satisfy Rule 23(a)(1).").

[7]   *General Tel. Co. of the Northwest, Inc. v. Equal Employment Opportunity Commission,* 446 U.S. 318, 330, 100 S.Ct. 1698, 1706, 64 L.Ed.2d 319 (1980) (classes of 15 members will often be too small).

[8]   *See, e.g., Stewart v. Abraham,* 275 F.3d 220, 226–27 (3d Cir. 2001) (more than 40 is generally sufficient).

[9]   *Golden v. City of Columbus,* 404 F.3d 950, 965 (6th Cir. 2005).

[10]   *See, e.g., Novella v. Westchester County,* 661 F.3d 128, 143 (2d Cir. 2011).

(2) *Commonality:* Rule 23(a)(2) requires the existence of common questions of law or fact among the class members before the case will be certified as a class action.[11] To satisfy this requirement, the common questions need not predominate. Failure to meet the commonality requirement of Rule 23(a)(2) is, by itself, sufficient ground to deny certification.[12] Moreover, mere allegations that class members have suffered common injuries does not satisfy the commonality requirement. Instead, Rule 23(a)(2) requires not only common allegations but also that class litigation will resolve at least one issue common to the class.[13]

♦   **NOTE:** Although Rule 23(a) may be satisfied even if the common questions of law or fact do not predominate in the case, a class seeking certification under Rule 23(b)(3) must nevertheless include common questions of law or fact that *do* predominate over other questions. The interplay between Rule 23(a) and Rule 23(b) is discussed further below.

(3) *Typicality:* Rule 23(a)(3) requires that the claims of class representatives be typical of the class as a whole, not merely some portion of the class.[14] Generally the class representatives need not have claims identical in all respects with those of other members of the class.[15] Substantial commonality appears to be sufficient, even if differences among the claims, such as different issues of damages, also exist.[16] This requirement is intended to ensure that class representatives will represent the best interests of class members who are not playing an active part in managing the litigation. It also overlaps considerably with the case law requirement that class representatives be members of the class.[17]

(4) *Representatives Must Fairly Protect the Class:* Because class actions vest authority over the interests of passive members of the class in the hands of class activists, Rule 23(a)(4) requires the court to ensure that class representatives will include individuals who will meet those responsibilities fully and capably.[18] However, this "adequacy" requirement does not necessarily mean that all class representatives must be adequate. In a situation where there is more than one named representative, the requirement may be satisfied when only one representative is adequate.[19]

There is no "bright line" establishing when Rule 23(a)(4) is satisfied.[20] Nevertheless, courts tend to be particularly sensitive to this requirement.[21] Potential conflicts of interest may disqualify applicants,[22] as can a suggestion that the proposed class representative lacks

---

[11] *Wal-Mart Stores, Inc. v. Dukes,* 559 U.S. 393, 131 S.Ct. 2541, 180 L.Ed.2d 374 (2011) (single common question of law or fact may satisfy Rule 23(a)(2)).

[12] *Wal-Mart Stores, Inc. v. Dukes,* 559 U.S. 393, 131 S.Ct. 2541, 180 L.Ed.2d 374 (2011).

[13] *Wal-Mart Stores, Inc. v. Dukes,* 559 U.S. 393, 131 S.Ct. 2541, 2551, 180 L.Ed.2d 274 (2011).

[14] *See, e.g., Rector v. City and County of Denver,* 348 F.3d 935, 950 (10th Cir. 2003).

[15] *See, e.g., Lightbourn v. County of El Paso, Tex.,* 118 F.3d 421, 426, 22 A.D.D. 618 (5th Cir. 1997) ("The test for typicality, like the test for commonality, is not demanding.").

[16] *See, e.g., Ball v. Union Carbide Corp.,* 376 F.3d 554 (6th Cir.2004).

[17] *See, e.g., Robinson v. Sheriff of Cook County,* 167 F.3d 1155, 1157 (7th Cir. 1999).

[18] *See, e.g., Radcliffe v. Experian Information Solutions, Inc.,* 715 F.3d 1157, 1166 (9th Cir. 2013) (representation is inadequate where settlement will bestow $5,000 on each representative while absent class members will receive at little as $26).

[19] *See, e.g., Rodriguez v. West Publishing Corp.,* 563 F.3d 948, 961 (9th Cir. 2009).

[20] *But cf. Denney v. Deutsche Bank AG,* 443 F.3d 253, 268 (2d Cir. 2006) ("Adequacy is twofold: the proposed class representative must have an interest in vigorously pursuing the claims of the class, and must have no interests antagonistic to the interests of other class members.").

[21] *See, e.g., Stirman v. Exxon Corp.,* 280 F.3d 554, 563 (5th Cir. 2002) (error not to examine adequacy of class representatives as well as counsel).

[22] *Ortiz v. Fibreboard Corp.,* 527 U.S. 815, 119 S.Ct. 2295, 144 L.Ed.2d 715 (1999) (class comprised of holders of both present and future tort claims should be divided into subclasses with different counsel for each subclass).

integrity.[23] If, in the course of litigation, the trial court finds that class representatives previously approved have become inadequate, the court retains authority to order appointment of new representatives.[24]

Diversity Jurisdiction

In most class actions, federal subject matter jurisdiction based on diversity of citizenship is governed by 28 U.S.C.A. § 1332(d). Subject to a few exceptions, § 1332(d)(2) provides that the amount in controversy requirement for class actions is a sum that exceeds $5,000,000, exclusive of interest and costs. Section 1332(d)(6) allows aggregation of the class claims to satisfy this requirement, in contrast to the non-class context in which aggregation of claims by multiple plaintiffs is greatly limited.[25]

Section 1332(d)(2) contains relaxed standards for diversity of citizenship as well, permitting the diversity of citizenship requirement to be met in any of three ways: (A) a single member of the class may be a citizen of an American state that is different from the citizenship of any defendant; (B) a single member of the class may be a citizen or subject of a foreign state and any defendant is a citizen of an American state; or (C) a single member of a class may be a citizen of an American state and any defendant is either a foreign state or a citizen or subject of a foreign state.[26] This standard is sometimes referred to as "minimal diversity," in contrast to "complete diversity" for non-class actions.[27]

Section 1332(d) also contains exceptions to the special jurisdictional standards for class actions. Together, however, these exceptions probably constitute a relatively small proportion of the total number of class actions that are now otherwise jurisdictionally eligible to be filed in federal district court. The first exception arises when more than one-third, but less than two-thirds, of the class members as well as the primary defendants are citizens of the same state in which the action was originally filed. In that circumstance, § 1332(d) affords the district court discretion to decline to exercise its jurisdiction, in the interest of justice and considering the totality of the circumstances, after considering six factors: whether the claims involve matters of national or interstate interest; whether the claims will be subject to the law of the forum state or the laws of other states; whether the original pleading in the class action was pleaded in a manner intended to avoid federal jurisdiction; whether the action was filed in a forum with a "distinct" nexus with the class, the alleged wrong, or the defendants; whether the forum is the place of citizenship of a disproportionate number of class members, and the remaining class members are dispersed among a substantial number of other states; and whether, during the previous three years, other class actions asserting similar claims were filed on behalf of the same persons.[28]

Another exception requires the district court to decline jurisdiction if the following elements are met: 1) more than two-thirds of the class members are citizens of the forum state; and 2) the primary defendants are citizens of the forum state or: 1) at least one significant defendant is a citizen of the forum state; 2) principal injuries giving rise to the cause of action occurred in the forum state; and 3) during the previous three years, no similar class action involving essentially the same parties has been filed.[29]

---

[23] *See, e.g., Savino v. Computer Credit, Inc.,* 164 F.3d 81, 87 (2d Cir. 1998).

[24] *See, e.g., Binta B. ex rel. S.A. v. Gordon,* 710 F.3d 608, 618 (6th Cir. 2013).

[25] *See Frazier v. Pioneer Americas LLC,* 455 F.3d 542 (5th Cir. 2006) ("Unlike § 1332(a), [§ 1332(d)(6)] explicitly allows aggregation of each class member's claim.").

[26] 28 U.S.C.A. § 1332(d)(2)(A) to (C).

[27] *See, e.g., Evans v. Walter Industries, Inc.,* 449 F.3d 1159, 1163 (11th Cir. 2006).

[28] 28 U.S.C.A. § 1332(d)(3).

[29] 28 U.S.C.A. § 1332(d)(4).

Additionally, the more generous jurisdictional standards of § 1332(d) do not apply if the primary defendants are states, state agencies, or state officials, or if the membership of the proposed class is less than one hundred.[30] Finally, these new jurisdictional standards do not apply to three distinct categories of class actions: lawsuits arising under designated federal securities laws; lawsuits relating to the internal affairs of corporations arising under the laws of the states where such corporations are incorporated; and lawsuits relating to the rights, duties, and obligations pursuant to a security as defined by federal law.[31]

For purposes of § 1332(d), the citizenship of an unincorporated association is the same as for a corporation—it will be deemed a citizen of the state in which its principal place of business is located as well as the state in which it was organized.[32]

Where § 1332(d) does not apply, diversity of citizenship is satisfied if the class representatives are diverse from the party opposing the class[33] and the normal standard for amount in controversy requirement is satisfied.

Supplemental Jurisdiction

Under the aggregation provisions of § 1332(d), class action plaintiffs have significantly less need for supplemental jurisdiction. Under the normal diversity jurisdiction rules, only one class member need meet the amount in controversy requirement—supplemental jurisdiction will exist over claims below the requirement if the other elements of § 1367 are satisfied.[34]

Federal Question Jurisdiction

Federal courts have subject matter jurisdiction over class actions involving federal questions in the same manner as conventional litigation.

Personal Jurisdiction

Jurisdiction over a defendant in a class action is obtained in the same manner, and subject to the same requirements, as jurisdiction over any defendant in conventional litigation. The same is true for personal jurisdiction over a class of defendants, *i.e.*, each individual must be subject to the jurisdiction of the court before that individual is subject to the judgment.

Venue

Venue in class actions does not generally differ from venue in conventional litigation, with one potential exception. If venue is based on the residence of the class, the residences of the class representatives are examined, not those of the entire class.[35]

Removal

Removal of a class action is governed by 28 U.S.C.A. § 1453. It generally provides that removal of class actions is similar to removal of other claims, as provided in § 1446, with a few exceptions. First, the one year limitation on removal based on after-acquired diversity jurisdiction does not apply. Second, the limitation on removal by a defendant who is a resident of the forum state does not apply. Finally, the requirement that all parties join in

---

[30] 28 U.S.C.A. § 1332(d)(5).

[31] 28 U.S.C.A. § 1332(d)(9).

[32] 28 U.S.C.A. § 1332(d)(10).

[33] *Supreme Tribe of Ben Hur v. Cauble,* 255 U.S. 356, 41 S.Ct. 338, 65 L.Ed. 673 (1921) (overruled in part on other grounds by, *Toucey v. New York Life Ins. Co.,* 314 U.S. 118, 62 S.Ct. 139, 86 L.Ed. 100 (1941)).

[34] *Exxon Mobil Corp. v. Allapattah Services, Inc.,* 545 U.S. 546, 125 S.Ct. 2611, 2621–25, 162 L.Ed.2d 502 (2005).

[35] *See, e.g., Appleton Elec. Co. v. Advance-United Expressways,* 494 F.2d 126, 140 (7th Cir. 1974).

or consent to the removal does not apply. If a case was properly removed but class certification is later denied, the district court retains jurisdiction over the case.[36]

Defendant Classes

Most class action cases are suits in which the class members are the plaintiffs. However, it is possible that the class members may be the defendants.[37] In that unusual circumstance, the provisions of Rule 23 apply in much the same fashion as they apply to plaintiff classes, with only a few differences. One difference is that members of a defendant class are entitled to constitutional protections of notice, in addition to the protections provided by Rule 23. This difference tends to have little practical impact, however, because class representatives are obligated to protect the interests of passive class members, including appropriate notice, as provided in Rule 23(c). A more significant potential distinction between a plaintiff class and a defendant class is heightened concern to ensure that the representatives of a defendant class adequately represent the interests of the class. The concern is greater with defendant classes because, at least initially, the representatives of a defendant class are chosen by the plaintiff who is suing the class.[38]

Certification and the Merits

The question whether a district court may properly consider the merits of the case when deciding a certification motion has long been unresolved.[39] The analysis necessary for certification may often properly overlap with assessment of the merits of the plaintiffs' claim.[40] However, dismissal of a case without deciding a motion for certification is authorized if, for example, the plaintiff cannot state a cognizable claim or satisfy jurisdiction.[41]

Burden of Proof

The party who seeks certification has the burden of proving by a preponderance of the evidence that the requirements for class certification are satisfied.[42]

Pro Se Classes

A *pro se* plaintiff cannot represent a class.[43]

Defining the Class

A prerequisite to class certification is the existence of a class that can be defined with reasonable particularity.[44]

---

[36] *See, e.g., United Steel, Paper & Forestry, Rubber, Manufacturing, Energy, Allied Industrial & Service Workers International Union v. Shell Oil Co.,* 602 F.3d 1087, 1091 (9th Cir. 2010).

[37] *See, e.g., Consolidated Rail Corp. v. Town of Hyde Park,* 47 F.3d 473 (2d Cir. 1995).

[38] *See, e.g., Ameritech Ben. Plan Committee v. Communication Workers of America,* 220 F.3d 814, 819 (7th Cir. 2000).

[39] *Compare Eisen v. Carlisle and Jacquelin,* 417 U.S. 156, 177, 94 S.Ct. 2140, 40 L.Ed.2d 732 (1974) ("We find nothing in either the language or history of Rule 23 that gives a court any authority to conduct a preliminary inquiry into the merits of a suit in order to determine whether it may be maintained as a class action.") *with General Telephone Co. of Southwest v. Falcon,* 457 U.S. 147, 160, 102 S.Ct. 2364, 72 L.Ed.2d 740 (1982) ("[S]ometimes it may be necessary for the court to probe behind the pleadings before coming to rest on the certification question.").

[40] *Comcast Corp. v. Behrend,* ___ U.S. ___, 133 S.Ct. 1426, 185 L.Ed.2d 515 (2013) (error to restrict argument against certification on basis that such argument might overlap with merits); *Amgen Inc. v. Connecticut Retirement Plans Trust Funds,* ___ U.S. ___, 133 S.Ct. 1184, 1194–95, 185 L.Ed.2d 308 (2013) (inquiry into merits permitted, but only to extent that merits are also relevant to issue of class certification); *Wal-Mart Stores, Inc. v. Dukes,* 564 U.S. 338, 131 S.Ct. 2541, 180 L.Ed.2d 374 (2011) (overlap between certification and merits "cannot be helped").

[41] *See, e.g., Boulware v. Crossland Mortg. Corp.,* 291 F.3d 261, 268 n.4 (4th Cir. 2002).

[42] *See, e.g., Novella v. Westchester County,* 661 F.3d 128, 149 (2d Cir. 2011).

[43] *See, e.g., Fymbo v. State Farm Fire and Casualty Co.,* 213 F.3d 1320, 1321 (10th Cir. 2000).

[44] *See, e.g., Young v. Nationwide Mutual Insurance Co.,* 693 F.3d 532, 538 (6th Cir. 2012) (class certification will fail if proposed class is "amorphous" or "imprecise").

Class Representatives Must Be Class Members

At least initially, the class representatives must be members of the class.[45] The purpose of this requirement is part of the courts' determination that class representatives will reflect the interests of the class. If a class representative was once a member but ceases to be a member of the class, the proper remedy is to select a new, suitable member of the class as a replacement representative.[46]

"Implicit" or "Implied" Classes

Rule 23 establishes a rigorous procedure to be followed before a case will be certified as a class action. However, it is possible (though unusual) that in some circuits, classwide relief may be obtained notwithstanding the fact that the district court failed to follow the Rule 23 process for class certification.[47] Other courts have been reluctant to embrace this approach.[48]

Contractual Waivers

In general, a contractual provision precluding class arbitration or class litigation is enforceable, notwithstanding state law to the contrary.[49]

Other State Bars to Federal Class Actions

Rule 23's procedures regarding class actions are procedural law, not substantive law, and thus apply in diversity cases even if a state law would bar class action treatment under the circumstances of the case.[50]

Choice of Law

In class actions based on state law, the court can only apply the law of a jurisdiction that has a sufficient relationship with an individual litigant. Thus individual litigants from states other than the forum may be entitled to have the law of some other state applied to their claims. In a class action, therefore, it is possible that the court may have to apply the laws of a variety of states to different class members.[51]

Relation to Rule 68

Rule 68 governs offers of judgment. Circuit courts have identified at least two points of overlap between Rule 23 and Rule 68.

The first problem arises when a defendant makes an offer of judgment for the full amount of the claims of the named representatives, trying to moot their claims. Courts recognize this potential problem, and have held that a Rule 68 offer of judgment to an individual plaintiff cannot be used to render a putative class action moot.[52]

---

[45] *East Texas Motor Freight System Inc. v. Rodriguez,* 431 U.S. 395, 403, 97 S.Ct. 1891, 1896, 52 L.Ed.2d 453 (1977).

[46] *See, e.g., Holmes v. Pension Plan of Bethlehem Steel Corp.,* 213 F.3d 124, 135–36 (3d Cir. 2000) (if class representative has "live claim" at time of motion for class certification, "neither a pending motion nor a certified class action need be dismissed if his individual claim subsequently becomes moot"; but if claim became moot prior to motion for class certification, motion will be denied and case will be dismissed).

[47] *See, e.g., Doe, 1–13 ex rel. Doe Sr. 1–13 v. Bush,* 261 F.3d 1037, 1050 (11th Cir. 2001).

[48] *See, e.g., Partington v. American Intern. Specialty Lines Ins. Co.,* 443 F.3d 334, 341 (4th Cir. 2006).

[49] *AT&T Mobility LLC v. Concepcion,* 363 U.S. 333, 131 S.Ct. 1740, 179 L.Ed.2d 742 (2011) (Federal Arbitration Act overrides state law nullifying arbitration clause that contains waiver of class actions).

[50] *Shady Grove Orthopedic Associates, P.A. v. Allstate Insurance Co.,* 559 U.S. 393, 402, 130 S.Ct. 1431, 176 L.Ed.2d 311 (2010).

[51] *Phillips Petroleum Co. v. Shutts,* 472 U.S. 797, 105 S.Ct. 2965, 86 L.Ed.2d 628 (1985).

[52] *See, e.g., Lucero v. Bureau of Collection Recovery, Inc.,* 639 F.3d 1239, 1249 (10th Cir. 2011).

The second problem arises because Rule 68 provides that if a proper offer of judgment is made and accepted, the court has no discretion in the matter and must enter judgment.[53] Rule 23, by contrast, affords the court substantial authority to review and approve (or veto) a proposed settlement of a class action. Courts have resolved this apparent conflict by treating the authority of a district court under Rule 23 as an exception to the general requirement of Rule 68.[54]

Securities Litigation

When a class action falls within the scope of the Private Securities Litigation Reform Act of 1995,[55] the court must appoint as lead plaintiff the "most adequate plaintiff." Such a person is identified as that member of the class who is most capable of representing the class. This requirement, however, has been held not to require that the chosen person possess unique advantages of experience, expertise, wealth, or intellect.[56]

Statutes of Limitation: Equitable Tolling

In a case based on federal question jurisdiction, institution of the class action tolls applicable statutes of limitations for the class.[57] The statute remains in suspension unless and until the district court denies certification.[58] If the statute resumes running, it does so from the point at which it was tolled.[59] Further, if the class was certified under Rule 23(b)(3) and some members of the class exercise their right to opt out of the class under Rule 23(c)(2), the statute remains tolled as to those individuals until they exercise the right to opt out.[60] This protection applies even to members of the class who were unaware of the pendency of the class litigation.[61]

This doctrine of equitable tolling applies to class actions arising from state law claims only when state law also provides for equitable tolling.

RULE 23(b)—TYPES OF CLASS ACTIONS

CORE CONCEPT

In addition to the four prerequisites for every class action in Rule 23(a), a class must fit within at least one of the categories of class described in Rule 23(b).[62]

♦ **NOTE:** Although a class may be certified if it fits within only one of the Rule 23(b) categories, there are sometimes advantages to fitting within more than one of the categories.

APPLICATIONS

Category 1: Risk of Incompatible Duties for Class Opponent

A class will be certified if the opposing party will otherwise be at risk of being subjected to incompatible duties.[63] For example, a class of employees could sue an employer who, in

---

[53] Fed.R.Civ.P. 68. *See, e.g., Webb v. James,* 147 F.3d 617, 621 (7th Cir. 1998).

[54] *See, e.g., Ramming v. Natural Gas Pipeline Co. of America,* 390 F.3d 366, 371 (5th Cir. 2004).

[55] 15 U.S.C.A. § 78u–4(a)(3)(B).

[56] *Berger v. Compaq Computer Corp.,* 279 F.3d 313 (5th Cir.2002).

[57] *American Pipe & Const. Co. v. Utah,* 414 U.S. 538, 550–51, 94 S.Ct. 756, 764–65, 38 L.Ed.2d 713 (1974).

[58] *See, e.g., Taylor v. United Parcel Service, Inc.,* 554 F.3d 510, 519 (5th Cir. 2008).

[59] *American Pipe & Const. Co. v. Utah,* 414 U.S. 538, 542–43, 94 S.Ct. 756, 760–61, 38 L.Ed.2d 713 (1974).

[60] *American Pipe & Const. Co. v. Utah,* 414 U.S. 538, 550–51, 94 S.Ct. 756, 38 L.Ed.2d 713 (1974).

[61] *American Pipe & Const. Co. v. Utah,* 414 U.S. 538, 551, 94 S.Ct. 756, 38 L.Ed.2d 713 (1974).

[62] *See, e.g., Puffer v. Allstate Insurance Co.,* 675 F.3d 709, 716 (7th Cir. 2012).

[63] *Cf. In re Integra Realty Resources, Inc.,* 354 F.3d 1246, 1263–64 (10th Cir. 2004).

the absence of a class action, might have owed benefit obligations to the class that were inconsistent with the employer's obligations to other employees.[64]

Category 2: Risk of Practical Impairment of Nonparties' Interests

A class will be certified if piecemeal litigation involving individual class members may, as a practical matter, produce injustice for class members who are not parties to the individual litigation.[65] One of the most common applications of this category of class occurs when numerous claimants may seek relief from a limited fund and, in the absence of class certification, individual lawsuits might deplete the fund before all worthy claimants had a chance to obtain some share of the fund.[66] However, to obtain certification in such circumstances, the "limited" fund must be "limited by more than the agreement of the parties."[67]

"Incompatible Duties" Contrasted with "Risk of Practical Impairment"

Rule 23(b)(1)(A), establishing the "incompatible duties" standard, protects the opponent of the class from the possibility of inconsistent obligations. Rule 23(b)(1)(B), protecting against the risk of impairment, protects the individual members, who otherwise will not be able to share recovery in limited resources in a proportional manner, fair to all.[68]

Category 3: Classes Seeking Injunctive or Declaratory Relief

Rule 23(b)(2) permits certification of class actions where the primary relief sought is injunctive or declaratory in nature.[69] There are two elements to satisfy before a class may be certified under Rule 23(b)(2): the class must share a general claim against the non-class party;[70] and the class must seek either final injunctive or declaratory relief.[71] Race and gender discrimination class actions, seeking an alteration in the future behavior of the opponent of the class, are typical of the class actions certified under Rule 23(b)(2).[72]

Obtaining Damages in Injunctive Relief Class Actions

Certification of a class under Rule 23(b)(2) requires that the relief sought in the case is primarily declaratory or injunctive in nature. It may not always be disabling to attach a plea for damages to a Rule 23(b)(2) certification, but seeking damages in a Rule 23(b)(2) case could damage the prospects for certification under that provision.[73]

---

[64] *Mungin v. Florida East Coast Ry. Co.*, 318 F.Supp. 720 (M.D. Fla. 1970).

[65] *Flanagan v. McDonnell Douglas Corp.*, 425 U.S. 911, 96 S.Ct. 1506, 47 L.Ed.2d 761 (1976) (class certification appropriate to ensure "equitable distribution of the refund program").

[66] *See, e.g., Trautz v. Weisman*, 846 F.Supp. 1160, 4 A.D.D. 955 (S.D. N.Y. 1994).

[67] *Ortiz v. Fibreboard Corp.*, 527 U.S. 815, 119 S.Ct. 2295, 144 L.Ed.2d 715 (1999).

[68] *Ortiz v. Fibreboard Corp.*, 527 U.S. 815, 834, 119 S.Ct. 2295, 144 L.Ed.2d 715 (1999).

[69] *Wal-Mart Stores, Inc. v. Dukes*, 564 U.S. 338, 131 S.Ct. 2541, 180 L.Ed.2d 374 (2011) (Rule 23(b)(2) addresses only injunctive relief, not other equitable relief such as back pay).

[70] *See, e.g., Gates v. Rohm & Haas Co.*, 655 F.3d 255, 264 (3d Cir. 2011) (differing circumstances of individuals may affect cohesiveness of class and thereby cause denial of certification).

[71] *Wal-Mart Stores, Inc. v. Dukes*, 564 U.S. 338, 131 S.Ct. 2541, 180 L.Ed.2d 374 (2011).

[72] *See, e.g., Vallario v. Vandehey*, 554 F.3d 1259, 1269 (10th Cir. 2009).

[73] *Wal-Mart Stores, Inc. v. Dukes*, 564 U.S. 338, 131 S.Ct. 2541, 180 L.Ed.2d 374 (2011) (absence of procedural protections of notice and right to opt out that are found in Rule 23(b)(3) are reasons to curtail use of Rule 23(b)(2) in cases involving monetary claims).

Supervisory Problems in Injunctive Relief Class Actions

Certification under Rule 23(b)(2) may be denied because the injunctive relief necessary would place an undue administrative burden on the court.[74]

Category 4: Predominance of Common Legal or Factual Questions

A class may be certified if questions of law or fact common to the members of the class predominate over other questions. Rule 23(b)(3) certification is often a last resort for litigants who cannot be certified under any other portion of Rule 23(b).[75] Two special requirements exist for Rule 23(b)(3) classes. Both must be satisfied to achieve certification under Rule 23(b)(3).

Predominance

First among these is the requirement that common questions *predominate* over individual interests.[76] Resolution of the "predominance" analysis rests heavily on the facts of particular cases.[77] Individual damages issues are a potential complication when the district court addresses the question of predominance, but the court has some flexibility in considering ways to address this point.[78] The party seeking certification must prove that the predominance requirement is met.[79]

Superior Means

The second requirement for certification under Rule 23(b)(3) is a finding that a class action is the superior means of adjudicating the controversy.[80] In reaching the "superiority" determination, a court is required to make four findings described below. While the court is required to make findings on the four points listed, there is no requirement that all four findings must be resolved in favor of certification. Instead, the court has discretion to weigh its findings in determining whether class certification is the superior method of litigating the controversy. The court may also address other issues that, in particular cases, are relevant to determining whether certification of a class action is the best way to process a case.[81]

(1) *Rule 23(b)(3)(A)—Individual Interests in Separate Actions:* The court will evaluate the desire, if any, of individual litigants to pursue their own separate actions, and the net balance of interests between such individuals and the class as a whole.[82] Because individual litigants who feel the need to control their own cases may exercise their right under Rule 23(c) to "opt out" of a Rule 23(b)(3) class, it is usually possible to certify the class and still

---

[74] *See, e.g., Kartman v. State Farm Mutual Automobile Insurance Co.,* 634 F.3d 883, 893 (7th Cir. 2011) (denying certification where injunctive relief would be "administratively challenging" requiring a judge "to write an insurance-adjustment code").

[75] *See, e.g., DeBoer v. Mellon Mortg. Co.,* 64 F.3d 1171, 1175 (8th Cir. 1995) (where certification is appropriate under either Rule 23(b)(1) or (2), certification under Rule 23(b)(3) is inappropriate).

[76] *Amgen Inc. v. Connecticut Retirement Plans and Trust Funds,* ___ U.S. ___, 133 S.Ct. 1184, 185 L.Ed.2d 308 (2013) (if an issue's resolution will cause class to win or lose case, Rule 23(b)(3) predominance test is satisfied); *Amchem Products, Inc. v. Windsor,* 521 U.S. 591, 623, 117 S.Ct. 2231, 2250, 138 L.Ed.2d 689 (1997).

[77] *See also Tardiff v. Knox County,* 365 F.3d 1, 4 (1st Cir. 2004).

[78] *See, e.g., Carnegie v. Household International, Inc.,* 376 F.3d 656, 661 (7th Cir. 2004).

[79] *Comcast Corp v. Behrend,* ___ U.S. ___, 133 S.Ct. 1426, 185 L.Ed.2d 515 (2013); *Wal-Mart Stores, Inc. v. Dukes,* 564 U.S. 338, 350, 131 S.Ct. 2541, 2551–52, 180 L.Ed.2d 374 (2011). But *cf. Halliburton Co. v. Erica P. John Fund, Inc.,* ___ U.S. ___, 134 S.Ct. 2398, 189 L.Ed.2d 339 (2014) (requirement in stock fraud class actions that every plaintiff prove direct reliance on defendant's misrepresentation would make certification under Rule 23(b)(3) practically impossible).

[80] *See, e.g., Gregory v. Finova Capital Corp.,* 442 F.3d 188, 191 n.3 (4th Cir. 2006).

[81] *See, e.g., Castano v. American Tobacco Co.,* 84 F.3d 734 (5th Cir. 1996) (court may consider whether class action will preserve judicial resources).

[82] *See, e.g., Zinser v. Accufix Research Institute, Inc.,* 253 F.3d 1180 (9th Cir. 2001) ("Where damages suffered by each putative class member are not large, this factor weighs in favor of certifying a class action").

accommodate most of the needs of such individuals. Harmonizing individual interests with class certification would be more difficult if it was likely that so many individuals would opt out that the class no longer represented the bulk of its potential members. In that circumstance, the evidence of such strong interest in individual litigation would argue strongly against certifying a Rule 23(b)(3) class.

(2) *Rule 23(b)(3)(B)—Pending Litigation:* The court will also consider the effects of any other pending litigation on the proposed class action. If individual class members have already begun to pursue their own cases, it may be difficult to justify certification of a Rule 23(b)(3) class on grounds of judicial economy.[83] Indeed, it is possible that such pending litigation will reach judgment before the class action, and many of the contested issues in the class action might then be resolved through application of principles of *stare decisis* or collateral estoppel.

(3) *Rule 23(b)(3)(C)—Geography:* If the case is being heard in an area of the country where the class or the evidence is concentrated, this may be an argument for continuing in the chosen forum.[84]

(4) *Rule 23(b)(3)(D)—Difficulties in Managing a Class Action:* Courts can refuse to certify if too many administrative difficulties exist in class actions. In exercising this discretion, courts consider a wide variety of factors affecting ease of administration of a case. Examples of problems in managing a class include internal disputes within a class, problems of notification of class members,[85] and the impact that state law variations can have on management in a multi-state case.[86]

Affirmative Defenses

A defendant's affirmative defenses against claims by individual class members will not, of themselves, require a finding that common issues do not predominate.[87]

RULE 23(c)—CERTIFICATION ORDER; NOTICE TO CLASS MEMBERS; JUDGMENT; ISSUES CLASSES; SUBCLASSES

CORE CONCEPT

Rule 23(c) establishes the procedure and timing of motions to certify and the process to be followed once a class is certified.

APPLICATIONS

Certification by Motion or Court Initiative

A party may seek certification by motion. If the class representatives do not make a motion to certify, the court may make the certification decision on its own initiative. The lack of a motion to certify cannot be the basis for denial of class certification.[88]

---

[83] *See, e.g., City of Inglewood v. City of Los Angeles,* 451 F.2d 948, 952 n.4 (9th Cir. 1971).

[84] *See, e.g., Zinser v. Accufix Research Institute, Inc.,* 253 F.3d 1180 (9th Cir. 2001) (where potential plaintiffs, witnesses and evidence are spread across country, it is undesirable to concentrate litigation in instant forum unless plaintiff can demonstrate adequate justification).

[85] *See, e.g., Zinser v. Accufix Research Institute, Inc.,* 253 F.3d 1180 (9th Cir. 2001).

[86] *See, e.g., Castano v. American Tobacco Co.,* 84 F.3d 734 (5th Cir. 1996).

[87] *See, e.g., Smilow v. Southwestern Bell Mobile Systems, Inc.,* 323 F.3d 32, 39–40 (1st Cir. 2003).

[88] *See, e.g., Trevizo v. Adams,* 455 F.3d 1155 (10th Cir.2006) ("Rule 23(c)(1) places the onus on the court to make a determination irrespective of whether the parties have requested class action status.").

Presumptions

For purposes of ruling on a certification motion, the district court will normally treat the factual allegations contained in the complaint as true.[89] However, if an expert's evidence is necessary for certification, a district court must first rule on the expert's qualifications or evidence before ruling on class certification.[90]

"Implied" Classes

A court's failure to make a formal certification ruling does not mean the case cannot proceed as a class action. If the elements required for class certification are satisfied and the parties proceed as if it were a class, an "implied" class may exist notwithstanding a lack of formal certification by the district court.[91]

Timing

Rule 23(c) provides no rigid timetable for resolving the certification issue, but courts are directed to make the decision "at an early practicable time."[92]

Preemptive Motion to Deny Certification

The opponent of a class may move to deny certification, even if the proponent of the class has not yet sought certification.[93]

Conditional Certification

In the past, Rule 23(c)(1) permitted the court to make certification conditional upon later developments in the case. Following the 2003 amendment to Rule 23(c)(1), conditional certification is no longer authorized, and courts are encouraged to withhold certification until the requirements of Rule 23 are met.[94]

Defining Claims, Issues, or Defenses

If a class is certified, Rule 23(c)(1)(B) directs the district court to define the class, *i.e.,* to include in the certification order a clear and complete summary of the claims, issues, and defenses subject to class treatment.[95] The definition should describe the class in a way that makes clear the scope of the litigation and the breadth of the *res judicata* effect.[96]

Amending a Certification Order

A district court may alter or amend its original certification order at any time prior to final judgment on the merits.[97]

---

[89] *See, e.g., Vallario v. Vandehey,* 554 F.3d 1259, 1265 (10th Cir. 2009).

[90] *See, e.g., American Honda Motor Co. v. Allen,* 600 F.3d 813, 816 (7th Cir. 2010) (per curiam) (court must perform full analysis required by *Daubert*).

[91] *See, e.g., Navarro-Ayala v. Hernandez-Colon,* 951 F.2d 1325, 1333 (1st Cir. 1991).

[92] *See, e.g., Kerkhof v. MCI WorldCom, Inc.,* 282 F.3d 44, 55 (1st Cir. 2002) (post-judgment certification should usually be discouraged).

[93] *See, e.g., Kasalo v. Harris & Harris, Ltd.,* 656 F.3d 557, 563 (7th Cir. 2011).

[94] *See, e.g., Hohider v. United Parcel Service, Inc.,* 574 F.3d 169, 202 (3d Cir. 2009) (while district court retains authority to alter or amend its order, it must initially make a "definitive determination" that requirements of Rule 23 are met; court may no longer make a "conditional" certification and then await events).

[95] *See, e.g., Lewis v. City of Chicago,* 702 F.3d 958, 962 (7th Cir. 2012).

[96] *Spano v. Boeing Co.,* 633 F.3d 574, 584 (7th Cir. 2011).

[97] *See, e.g., White v. National Football League,* 756 F.3d 585, 594 (8th Cir. 2014) (court may decertify class *sua sponte*, even at the appellate level).

Notice

Rule 23(c)(2) establishes various notice options and/or requirements for class actions. For classes certified pursuant to Rule 23(b)(1) or (2), Rule 23(c)(2)(A) authorizes, but does not require, the district court to order notice to class members.[98] This authority supplements the court's already existing power under Rule 23(d)(2) to issue notice to class members.[99] Courts will be cautious in their use of notice to Rule 23(b)(1) and (2) classes so as not to burden the class representatives with unnecessary costs of notice.[100]

Rule 23(c)(2) also provides that individual members of Rule 23(b)(3) classes must receive the "best notice practicable," which will often be mail service on all class members whose identities and addresses are known.[101] The reason for this provision arises from the special nature of Rule 23(b)(3) suits, in which common questions must predominate and the class suit must be superior to alternative methods of adjudication. Such suits tend to involve the least homogeneous classes. Lack of homogeneity increases the risk that informal notice of the class action may not flow freely within the class, and thus makes notice more important.

Elements of Notice to Rule 23(b)(3) Classes

Rule 23(c)(2) specifies that notification will include the following pieces of information: (1) the nature of the action; (2) the definition of the class certified; (3) the class claims, issues, or defenses; (4) the right of individual members of the class to appear through counsel; (5) the right to opt out of the class and not be bound by any judgment;[102] (6) the time and manner of opting out; and (7) the binding effect of a class judgment on members of the class who do not opt out.[103]

Opting Out of Rule 23(b)(1) and (b)(2) Classes

The opt-out provision of Rule 23(c)(2) literally applies to Rule 23(b)(3) classes only. However, a district court has discretion to permit opting out of Rule 23(b)(1) and (b)(2) classes.[104]

Expense of Notice

The financial burden of notification in Rule 23(b)(3) cases is generally borne by the class representatives.[105] Thus, in some cases class representatives should be selected with an eye to their financial resources as well as their dedication to the litigation. When the burden of Rule 23(b)(3) notification is onerous, the possibility of certification under another portion of Rule 23(b) should be explored.

No Requirement to "Opt In"

There is no provision in Rule 23(c) requiring class members to "opt in" or be excluded from a class.[106] Rule 23(c) contains only an "opt out" provision.

---

[98] *See, e.g., Randall v. Rolls-Royce Corp.,* 637 F.3d 818, 820 (7th Cir. 2011).

[99] *See* Rule 23(c)(2) advisory committee notes to 2003 amendments. *See also Eubanks v. Billington,* 110 F.3d 87, 96 (D.C. Cir. 1997).

[100] *See* Rule 23(c)(2) advisory committee notes to 2003 amendments.

[101] *See generally Schwarzschild v. Tse,* 69 F.3d 293, 295 (9th Cir. 1995) (in general, Rule 23(c)(2) requires notice to class members before merits are adjudicated).

[102] *See, e.g., Abbott Laboratories v. CVS Pharmacy, Inc.,* 290 F.3d 854, 859 (7th Cir. 2002).

[103] *See generally Eisen v. Carlisle and Jacquelin,* 417 U.S. 156, 94 S.Ct. 2140, 40 L.Ed.2d 732 (1974).

[104] *See, e.g., McReynolds v. Richards-Cantave,* 588 F.3d 790, 800 (2d Cir. 2009).

[105] *Oppenheimer Fund, Inc. v. Sanders,* 437 U.S. 340, 356–59, 98 S.Ct. 2380, 2392–93, 57 L.Ed.2d 253 (1978) (but if defendant could perform task more efficiently, burden may be shifted to defendant).

[106] *Phillips Petroleum Co. v. Shutts,* 472 U.S. 797, 105 S.Ct. 2965, 86 L.Ed.2d 628 (1985).

Parties Bound by Judgment

Class actions certified under either Rule 23(b)(1) or (b)(2) have binding effect on whomever the court finds to be within the membership of the class.[107] Rule 23(b)(3) actions bind class members who did not opt out and whom the court defines as members.[108] If a class action is not certified, its result is not binding on nonparties.[109]

Subclasses

Rule 23(c)(4) authorizes the court to create classes only as to particular issues.[110] Rule 23(c)(5) authorizes the court to create subclasses within an action.[111] If subclasses are certified, each subclass is treated as an independent class for purposes of the action.

The circumstances in which the court is most likely to create subclasses occur when the class members share a cause of action against a class opponent, but also experience differing interests among themselves.[112] The most common use of subclasses is to help simplify the manageability of the primary class action. Occasionally, however, subclasses can help the overarching class meet the certification requirements of Rule 23. Moreover, even if a global class cannot be certified, some plaintiffs have attempted to replace the global class with multiple subclasses that may be certifiable by themselves.[113]

Classes for Settlement

Courts are authorized to certify classes created for purposes of settlement only. When a court considers certification of a settlement class, it must first ensure that all the relevant elements of Rule 23 are met.[114]

If a court considers certification of a settlement class, it may notify class members of the possibility of class certification at the time the court notifies class members of the proposed settlement.[115] Persons who wish to contest settlements in class actions may seek to intervene.[116]

RULE 23(d)—CONDUCTING THE ACTION

CORE CONCEPT

Rule 23(d) provides the court explicit authority to craft orders governing class actions. Central to class actions is a need to protect the interests of parties who are less active than persons engaged in more conventional litigation. At the same time, the potential administrative complexity of class actions

---

[107] *Taylor v. Sturgell,* 128 S.Ct. 2161, 171 L.Ed.2d 155 (U.S. 2008).

[108] *Eisen v. Carlisle and Jacquelin,* 417 U.S. 156, 94 S.Ct. 2140, 40 L.Ed.2d 732 (1974).

[109] *Smith v. Bayer Corp.,* 564 U.S. 299, 131 S.Ct. 2368, 2380, 180 L.Ed.2d 341 (2011).

[110] *See, e.g., Castano v. American Tobacco Co.,* 84 F.3d 734, 745 n.21 (5th Cir. 1996).

[111] *In re Visa Check MasterMoney Antitrust Litigation,* 280 F.3d 124, 141 (2d Cir. 2001).

[112] *Ortiz v. Fibreboard Corp.,* 527 U.S. 815, 119 S.Ct. 2295, 144 L.Ed.2d 715 (1999) (class comprised holders of both present and future claims "requires subdivision into homogenous subclasses").

[113] *Compare, e.g., Klay v. Humana, Inc.,* 382 F.3d 1241, 1261–62 (11th Cir. 2004 (subclasses may be used this way) *with Sprague v. General Motors Corp.,* 133 F.3d 388, 396–99 & n.9 (6th Cir. 1998) (en banc) (if global class is uncertifiable, subclasses are unavailable). The authors of this text are grateful to Professor Scott Dodson, who appears to be the first commentator to identify this issue and who generously provided us with both his research and suggested language for this point. *See* Scott Dodson, *Subclassing,* 27 Cardozo L. Rev. 2351 (2006).

[114] *Ortiz v. Fibreboard Corp.,* 527 U.S. 815, 119 S.Ct. 2295, 144 L.Ed.2d 715 (1999); *Amchem Products, Inc. v. Windsor,* 521 U.S. 591, 117 S.Ct. 2231, 138 L.Ed.2d 689 (1997).

[115] *See, e.g., In re General Motors Corp. Pick-Up Truck Fuel Tank Products Liability Litigation,* 55 F.3d 768 (3d Cir. 1995).

[116] *See, e.g., Crawford v. Equifax Payment Services, Inc.,* 201 F.3d 877, 881 (7th Cir. 2000).

requires that the court have tools immediately at hand to ensure that the litigation remains manageable.

APPLICATIONS

Undue Repetition of Evidence

The court has broad discretion to issue orders prescribing measures designed to limit cumulative or repetitive evidence.

Additional Notice to Class Members

The court may order additional notice to class members to ensure fair treatment of passive members of the class.[117] The court's authority under this provision is very broad, and encompasses discretion to order notice to the class of almost any important event in the litigation.[118] The court may use its power in a variety of circumstances, including: notice to a class of pending litigation; discussion of proposed judgments; identification of class representatives to the whole class; and informing the class of key decision points in the suit so the class can participate in decisions, or evaluate opportunities to seek to participate more actively as class representatives.

Supervision of Class Representatives and Intervenors

The court may issue orders imposing conditions on class representatives and intervenors to advance both fair representation for the class and expeditious processing of the entire case.[119]

Removing Class Allegations

The court may enter an order that the pleadings be amended to remove allegations concerning class representation. This provision is typically employed when the court has already refused to certify the case as a class action. It may also be used if the court originally certified a class, but later altered its decision and refused certification. In either circumstance, a suit denied class certification may still proceed as conventional litigation, assuming that the requirements of such litigation are satisfied.

Other Procedural Matters

The court has authority to issue other orders to process a class action expeditiously and fairly.[120]

Alteration of Prior Rulings

Rule 23(d)(2) authorizes alteration or amendment of any order previously issued under Rule 23(d)(1). Thus, the court enjoys almost complete flexibility to adjust class litigation as events may require. In particular, courts are prepared to change earlier orders appointing class representatives if events show that the representatives are not protecting adequately the interests of the whole class.

Combining Orders

An order under Rule 23(d)(1) may be combined with a pretrial order issued under Rule 16. However, when orders under Rules 16 and 23(d)(2) are combined, a request to amend

---

[117] *See, e.g., Southern Ute Indian Tribe v. Amoco Production Co.,* 2 F.3d 1023 (10th Cir.1993) (using Rule 23(d) to order representatives of defendant class—not plaintiff—to notify passive members of defendant class of pending litigation).

[118] *See, e.g., Jefferson v. Ingersoll Intern. Inc.,* 195 F.3d 894, 898 (7th Cir. 1999).

[119] *But see Cobell v. Kempthorne,* 455 F.3d 317, 323 (D.C. Cir. 2006) (Rule 23(d)(3) cannot be used to impose a condition on non-class defendant).

[120] *See, e.g., Molski v. Gleich,* 318 F.3d 937, 947 (9th Cir. 2003).

the class action aspects of the order are subject to the less exacting standard in Rule 23(d)(2), not the good cause standard in Rule 16.[121]

RULE 23(e)—SETTLEMENT, VOLUNTARY DISMISSAL, OR COMPROMISE

CORE CONCEPT

Rule 23(e) requires court approval of voluntary dismissal or compromise, and requires that proposals to settle the case be submitted to the entire class for approval. This requirement of court supervision recognizes the fact that class actions are especially vulnerable to the possibility that the class representatives or the class attorneys may be placed in circumstances where their personal interests conflict with the interests of passive class members. The risk of inappropriate collaboration between class representatives or class counsel and the class opponent is probably greatest when questions of settlement or voluntary dismissal are at issue.[122] Rule 23(e) attempts to suppress the possibility of such collaboration by imposing a series of obligations on both the court and the parties seeking approval of the proposed settlement.

APPLICATIONS

Authority to Settle: Judicial Approval

Class representatives have authority to settle claims, issues, or defenses as appropriate.[123] However, the district court must approve or veto settlement, and must solicit the views of class members before making its decision. Additionally, in many circumstances a district court's approval of a settlement is subject to challenge on appeal by non-named class members.[124]

Protection of Class Opponents

The duty of the district court under Rule 23(e) to protect the interests of class members does not extend to parties (usually defendants) who are not members of the class.[125]

Comparison with Conventional Litigation

Rule 23(e) is an exception to the standard practice that parties may normally settle their disputes without the approval of the court.[126]

All Class Actions

Rule 23(e) applies to all actions certified under any portion of Rule 23(b).[127]

Effect on Individual Claims

The power of the court to approve or reject settlements of class litigation does not extend to individual claims which members of the class may possess separate from the class claims.[128]

---

[121] Rule 23 advisory committee notes to 2007 amendments.

[122] *See, e.g., In re Vitamins Antitrust Class Actions,* 215 F.3d 26 (D.C. Cir.2000).

[123] *See* Rule 23(e)(1)(A) advisory committee notes to 2003 amendments.

[124] *Devin v. Scardelletti,* 536 U.S. 1, 14, 122 S.Ct. 2005, 153 L.Ed.2d 27 (2002) (non-named member of mandatory class under Rule 23(b)(1) who makes timely objection to settlement may appeal without intervening first).

[125] *See, e.g., In re Deepwater Horizon,* 739 F.3d 790, 820 (5th Cir. 2014).

[126] *See, e.g., In re Cendant Corp. Litigation,* 264 F.3d 201, 231 (3d Cir. 2001).

[127] *See, e.g., Grimes v. Vitalink Communications Corp.,* 17 F.3d 1553, 1557 (3d Cir. 1994) (duty to monitor fairness of settlement is "particularly acute" in Rule 23(b)(1) and (2) class actions, because members of those classes cannot opt out of the class litigation).

[128] *See* Rule 23(e)(1)(A) advisory committee notes to 2003 amendments.

Hearing and Findings re Settlement

The district court must hold a hearing and make findings before approving a class settlement or voluntary dismissal.[129] The findings must include a determination that the proposed course of resolution for the class action is "fair, reasonable, and adequate."[130]

Notice of Proposed Settlement or Voluntary Dismissal

The court must direct notice to all class members who will be bound by the settlement or voluntary dismissal. Within the limits of due process, courts may treat the requirements of Rule 23(e) as satisfied by less notice than, for example, the requirement of first-class mail that may accompany notice obligations under Rule 23(c)(2) (governing notice in Rule 23(b)(3) "predominance of common questions" classes).[131]

Disclosure of Side Agreements

The proponents of a proposed settlement or voluntary dismissal must disclose any agreements that have been made that relate to the proposal.[132]

Standard for Approving Settlement

Courts evaluating the fairness of a proposed settlement consider a number of factors, including: (1) possibility of fraud; (2) complexity and expense; (3) amount of discovery undertaken; (4) likelihood of success; (5) views of lawyers on both sides; (6) views of class members; and (7) the public interest.[133] The power to approve settlement of a class action lies within the court's discretion, and such decisions are rarely disturbed on appeal.[134] However, some important considerations may restrict judicial discretion. First, while the court is authorized to determine whether the settlement is fair to passive members of the class, the court must still give substantial deference to a consensus of class members on the wisdom of the settlement.[135] Disregarding such a consensus is not automatically abuse of discretion, but is likely to enhance the chances that the trial court's decision will be overturned on appeal. Second, while the court must pass on the fairness of the proposal, it may not rewrite the settlement to make it conform to the court's view of a satisfactory settlement.[136] Third, the court's duty is primarily to the members of the class.[137] If persons have previously opted out of the class, the court has no power or duty to use the settlement process to address their interests.[138] Fourth, at least in class actions affected by fee shifting provisions in civil rights cases, the court has the authority and duty to review waivers of attorney's fees that are part of a proposed settlement.[139] Finally, the court's authority to certify a class created for purposes of settlement and to approve the proposed settlement is subject to a determination that the proposed class meets the requirements of Rule 23(a) and (b).[140]

---

[129] *See, e.g., In re Syncor ERISA Litigation,* 516 F.3d 1095, 1097 (9th Cir. 2008).

[130] *See, e.g., International Union, United Auto., Aerospace, and Agr. Implement Workers of America v. General Motors Corp.,* 497 F.3d 615, 629 (6th Cir. 2007).

[131] *See, e.g., Denney v. Deutsche Bank AG,* 443 F.3d 253, 271 (2d Cir. 2006).

[132] *See* Rule 23(e)(2) advisory committee notes to 2003 amendments.

[133] *See, e.g., Poplar Creek Development Co. v. Chesapeake Applachia, L.L.C.,* 636 F.3d 235, 244 (6th Cir. 2011).

[134] *See, e.g., Durkin v. Shea & Gould,* 92 F.3d 1510, 1512 (9th Cir. 1996).

[135] *See, e.g., County of Suffolk v. Alcorn,* 266 F.3d 131, 135 (2d Cir. 2001).

[136] *Evans v. Jeff D.,* 475 U.S. 717, 726, 106 S.Ct. 1531, 1537, 89 L.Ed.2d 747 (1986).

[137] *See, e.g., In re Cendant Corp. Litigation,* 264 F.3d 286, 295 (3d Cir. 2001) (district court has no duty to assess fairness of settlement to corporate opponent of class).

[138] *See, e.g., In re Vitamins Antitrust Class Actions,* 215 F.3d 26 (D.C. Cir.2000).

[139] *Evans v. Jeff D.,* 475 U.S. 717, 728, 106 S.Ct. 1531, 1538, 89 L.Ed.2d 747 (1986).

[140] *Amchem Products, Inc. v. Windsor,* 521 U.S. 591, 117 S.Ct. 2231, 138 L.Ed.2d 689 (1997).

Protection Against Geographic Discrimination

The court may not approve a settlement in which some members of the class receive greater amounts of value than others based "solely" on their closer geographic ties to the location of the court hearing the case.[141]

Additional Opportunity to Opt Out of Class

Members of classes previously certified under Rule 23(b)(3) are entitled to an additional opportunity to opt out of a proposed settlement or voluntary dismissal.[142] The notification obligations attendant on this opportunity will be the same as those required for initial certification of a Rule 23(b)(3) class under Rule 23(c)(2)(B).

Special Provisions for "Coupon" Settlements

Congress has enacted a number of provisions that are effective in class actions in which some or all members of the class will receive their award in the form of coupons. In such cases, the court must hold a hearing and determine, in a written finding, that the settlement is fair, reasonable, and adequate to class members. The court has authority, upon motion of one of the parties, to obtain expert testimony on the issue of the actual value to class members of the coupons that are redeemed.[143]

When the attorney will receive a contingency fee based on the value of the coupons, the fee shall be based on the value to class members of the coupons that are actually redeemed.[144] The effect of this provision is to reduce at least somewhat any apparent disparities between the award of contingency fees to class counsel and the nominal value of coupons to class members. Additionally, if a proposed settlement will provide the class with coupons, but the attorney's fee is not measured solely as a contingency award, the additional portion of the attorney's fee shall be based on the reasonable amount of time the lawyer expended on the case.[145]

Finally, the court may require that a portion of the value of unclaimed coupons be distributed to charitable or governmental organizations, as the parties choose. Such a distribution, however, cannot be used to calculate attorney's fees.[146]

Class Settlements and *Cy Pres*

Cy Pres is a doctrine that originated in the context of charitable trusts and distributions. Historically, it has been applied when the terms of a charitable gift cannot be fulfilled. In that situation, rather than treating the gift as having failed, courts sometimes apply *cy pres* to re-direct the gift to a deserving third party to achieve a purpose similar to the original intent of the gift.

In the context of class action settlements, *cy pres* has sometimes been applied to re-distribute excess settlement funds when, *e.g.*, the identity of class members is unknown or some other reason prevents distribution to class members.[147]

---

[141] 28 U.S.C.A. § 1714.

[142] *See, e.g., Moulton v. United States Steel Corp.*, 581 F.3d 344, 354 (6th Cir. 2009).

[143] 28 U.S.C.A. § 1712(d).

[144] 28 U.S.C.A. § 1712(a).

[145] 28 U.S.C.A. § 1712(b)(1).

[146] 28 U.S.C.A. § 1712(e).

[147] *See, e.g., In re Baby Products Antitrust Litigation*, 708 F.3d 163, 172 (3d Cir. 2013) (*cy pres* provision approved by parties does not necessarily invalidate settlement).

Objections to Settlement

Any member of a class has standing to object to a proposed settlement or voluntary dismissal of a kind that requires judicial approval under Rule 23(e).[148] Once such an objection has been made, it can be withdrawn only with the court's approval.[149]

Notice of Settlement to Government Officials

Within ten days of the filing of a proposed settlement with the district court, each defendant participating in the proposed settlement must serve notice of the proposed settlement, to include the following documents on both the appropriate federal official and the appropriate state official in each state in which any class member resides: (1) the complaint, amended complaint (if any), and material filed with such pleadings (unless such documents are available electronically, in which case an appropriate explanation of access to the documents will suffice); (2) notice of any scheduled hearing in the case; (3) notice of any proposed or final notification to class members of their right to seek exclusion from the case, or a statement that no such right exists, as well as a copy of the proposed settlement; (4) a copy of the final settlement; (5) a copy of any contemporaneous agreement reached between class counsel and defendant's counsel; (6) any final judgment or notice of dismissal; (7) if feasible, names of the class members residing in each state and an estimate of the proportion of the settlement likely to be distributed in each state, or if that information is not reasonably available, a reasonable estimate of such information; and (8) any written judicial opinions relating to items three through six.[150]

For purposes of this provision, the appropriate federal official is the Attorney General of the United States. The appropriate state official is that person with primary regulatory authority over the business in which the defendant engages. If there is no such person, the appropriate state official is the state attorney general. If the defendant is a federal or state depositary institution, a foreign bank, or a subsidiary of any such institution, the appropriate federal official is not the Attorney General, but the person who has primary federal regulatory authority over such an entity. The appropriate state official also becomes the corresponding state official with similar regulatory authority when a defendant is a state financial institution.[151]

Presumably so that appropriate federal or state officials may participate in the settlement process, a final order approving a settlement may not issue until at least 90 days after the latest date of notification to federal or state officials.[152] If a class member is able to establish that proper notice was not provided to the officials, the class member has the option to refuse to comply with the settlement agreement.[153]

RULE 23(f)—APPEALS

CORE CONCEPT

Rule 23(f) creates the possibility that a district court's decision granting or denying class certification could be appealed on an interlocutory basis, without waiting until the end of the litigation in the district court to learn whether the decision to certify (or not) would be upheld.

---

[148] *In re Rite Aid Corp. Securities Litigation*, 396 F.3d 294, 299 (3d Cir. 2005).

[149] *See* Rule 23(e)(5) advisory committee notes to 2003 amendments.

[150] 28 U.S.C.A. § 1715(b).

[151] 28 U.S.C.A. § 1715(a).

[152] 28 U.S.C.A. § 1715(d).

[153] 28 U.S.C.A. 1715(e).

APPLICATIONS

Appellate Discretion

Appellate courts have discretion to permit or deny an appeal granting or denying class certification.[154] In general, interlocutory review should not be a commonplace event.[155] Nevertheless, several situations arise where a circuit court is more likely than not to permit interlocutory appellate review of a class certification decision. First, if a denial of class certification would probably preclude any realistic chance that individual claims could be prosecuted and the district court's decision was questionable, circuits are inclined to grant review.[156] Second, if a district court's grant of class certification puts substantial pressure on a defendant to settle without regard to the merits of a case and the certification grant was questionable, review is appropriate.[157] Third, circuits generally agree that review is appropriate if it will help develop law regarding class actions.[158]

Another possibility for obtaining interlocutory review arises if a party can demonstrate that the district court's certification decision is clear error. In that circumstance, some circuits have held that review should normally occur without regard to whether other factors, such as those discussed immediately above, are present.[159]

Time

By its terms, Rule 23(f) requires that any application for such an appeal be made to the circuit court within 14 days after the district court has entered its order granting or denying class certification.[160] The computation of time for Rule 23(f) is governed by Rule 6(a).[161] Filing a motion for reconsideration within 14 days of the district court's entry of its order tolls the running of the Rule 23(f) time limit.[162]

Raising Other Issues on Appeal

Rule 23(f) authorizes appeal of class certification only. In general, other issues will not be considered when the basis for appeal is Rule 23(f).[163] Two exceptions to that practice are standing and subject matter jurisdiction, which appellate courts are willing to consider on an appeal under Rule 23(f).[164]

---

[154] *See, e.g., Gutierrez v. Johnson & Johnson,* 523 F.3d 187, 192 (3d Cir. 2008).

[155] *See, e.g., In re Lorazepam & Clorazepate Antitrust Litigation,* 289 F.3d 98, 105 (D.C. Cir. 2002).

[156] *See, e.g., Sumitomo Copper Litigation v. Credit Lyonnais Rouse, Ltd.,* 262 F.3d 134, 140 (2d Cir. 2001) (review likely if certification denial is death knell for case, and certification decision was questionable).

[157] *See, e.g., Tardiff v. Knox County,* 365 F.3d 1, 3 (1st Cir. 2004) ("One reason for review is a threat of liability so large as to place on the defendant an 'irresistible pressure to settle.' ").

[158] *See, e.g., Carnegie v. Household Intern., Inc.,* 376 F.3d 656 (7th Cir. 2004).

[159] *See, e.g., Prado-Steiman ex rel. Prado v. Bush,* 221 F.3d 1266, 1275 (11th Cir. 2000).

[160] *See, e.g., Gutierrez v. Johnson & Johnson,* 523 F.3d 187, 192 (3d Cir. 2008) ("This 14-day limit . . . is strict and mandatory.").

[161] *See, e.g., In re Veneman,* 309 F.3d 789, 793 (D.C. Cir. 2002).

[162] *See, e.g., Shin v. Cobb County Bd. of Educ.,* 248 F.3d 1061, 1064–65 (11th Cir. 2001). *But cf. Gary v. Sheahan,* 188 F.3d 891, 893 (7th Cir. 1999) (late or successive motions to reconsider the district court's certification decision do not toll the time limits of Rule 23(f)).

[163] *See, e.g., Asher v. Baxter Intern. Inc.,* 505 F.3d 736, 738 (7th Cir. 2007) ("Rule 23(f) does not allow interlocutory appeals from orders designating (or not designating) lead plaintiffs.").

[164] *See, e.g., Rivera v. Wyeth-Ayerst Laboratories,* 283 F.3d 315, 319 (5th Cir. 2002) ("[S]tanding may—indeed must—be addressed even under the limits of a Rule 23(f) appeal.")

Stay of District Court Proceedings

If the circuit court allows an appeal under Rule 23(f), the appeal does not automatically stay proceedings in the district court.[165] Instead, a party seeking such a stay must apply to either the district court or the court of appeals.

RULE 23(g)—CLASS COUNSEL

CORE CONCEPT

Rule 23(g) governs the manner in which a court will supervise the appointment of counsel to represent the class.

APPLICATIONS

Prerequisite: Certification of a Class

A decision to appoint class counsel should not occur until the court first certifies a class.[166]

Applicable Standards

Rule 23(g) identifies four factors the court must evaluate in appointing class counsel: the work an attorney has already done on the case; the attorney's experience in other class actions and complex litigation;[167] the attorney's familiarity with law applicable to the case; and the attorney's resources.[168]

At the end of its evaluation, the court should be able to satisfy itself that the potential class counsel will "fairly and adequately represent the interests of the class."[169] In this process the court may consider the costs and fees a proposed attorney expects to get from the case.[170] Ultimately, the court has a duty to select from among the potential attorneys the lawyer(s) who will best represent the class."[171]

RULE 23(h)—ATTORNEY'S FEES AND NONTAXABLE COSTS

CORE CONCEPT

Rule 23(h) establishes a procedure by which an attorney's fee application may be made and objections to that application may be heard.

APPLICATIONS

Methods of Calculation

Measurement of the appropriate amount of a fee is usually been determined through one of two methods. If a fund is available, courts award the lawyers a percentage of the fund.[172] In circumstances where the court believes another approach was appropriate or

---

[165] *See, e.g., Prado-Steiman ex rel. Prado v. Bush,* 221 F.3d 1266, 1273 (11th Cir. 2000) (in most cases, discovery will continue notwithstanding the pendency of an appeal of the class certification order.).

[166] *See, e.g., Sheinberg v. Sorensen,* 606 F.3d 130, 132 (3d Cir. 2010).

[167] Fed.R.Civ.P. 23(g). *See also Sheinberg v. Sorensen,* 606 F.3d 130, 132 (3d Cir. 2010).

[168] Fed.R.Civ.P. 23(g)(1)(C) and (E).

[169] Fed.R.Civ.P. 23(g)(4). *See, e.g., Eubank v. Pella Corp.,* 753 F.3d 718, 724 (7th Cir. 2014).

[170] Fed.R.Civ.P. 23(g)(1)(C) to (D).

[171] Fed.R.Civ.P. 23(g)(2). *But cf. Martin v. Blessing,* ___ U.S. ___, 134 S.Ct. 402, 187 L.Ed.2d 446 (2013) (district court's broad discretion to evaluate matters pertinent to certification do not extend to consideration of race and gender of class counsel).

[172] *Blum v. Stenson,* 465 U.S. 886, 900, 104 S.Ct. 1541, 1550 n.16, 79 L.Ed.2d 891 (1984).

where no fund was available, *e.g.,* where the class sought injunctive relief, courts typically measure the appropriate fee through a "lodestar" approach.[173] This calculation begins by determining appropriate hourly rates for individual lawyers, which are then multiplied by the number of hours actually and reasonably expended on the project. Finally, factors such as difficulty of the case, quality of legal work, risk of failure, etc., may be used in some cases to modify the result (up or down) reached by the simple multiplication of hours and rates.[174] While the lodestar method has been used in many class actions, the use of so-called "risk multipliers" has *not* been available in class actions where a fee is imposed based on a fee shifting statute. In such cases, district courts have made their lodestar calculation based only on the reasonable hourly rate multiplied by the reasonable number of hours devoted to the case.[175]

Motion Required

An application for attorney's fees must be made by motion, subject to Rule 54(d) (governing taxation of costs).[176]

Notice

The motion for fees must be served on all parties. If the motion is made by class counsel, as it typically will be, it must also be directed to class members in a reasonable manner.[177]

Objections, Hearing, and Findings

Both class members and the party who may have to pay the fees have standing to object to the motion. The court has discretion—not an obligation—to hold a hearing on the motion. The court must make findings of fact and conclusions of law in a manner consistent with the requirements of Rule 52(a) (governing the court's duty in such matters when issues are tried to the court).

If the court approves a lump-sum attorney's fee, it may be appropriate to permit attorneys to divide the fee among themselves by agreement.[178]

Special Masters and Magistrate Judges

The district court may refer matters relating to fees to special masters or magistrate judges.[179]

Independent Assessment

A court's duty to assess the reasonableness of an award of fees is an independent obligation, even where parties have reached agreement on a dollar amount.[180]

Protection Against Loss by Class Members

The court has authority to approve a proposed settlement involving a payment by members of the class to class counsel that would result in a net loss to the class members. However, that authority is restricted to cases in which the court, by a written finding, concludes that nonmonetary benefits to the class "substantially" outweigh the monetary loss.[181]

---

[173] *See, e.g.,* 28 U.S.C.A. § 1712(b).

[174] *See, e.g., Gunter v. Ridgewood Energy Corp.,* 223 F.3d 190, 195 n.1 (3d Cir. 2000).

[175] *City of Burlington v. Dague,* 505 U.S. 557, 565–66, 112 S.Ct. 2638, 2642–43, 120 L.Ed.2d 449 (1992).

[176] *See, e.g., Feldman v. Olin Corp.,* 673 F.3d 515, 517 (7th Cir. 2012).

[177] *In re Delphi Corp. Securities, Derivative & "ERISA" Litigation,* 248 F.R.D. 483, 506 (E.D. Mich. 2008).

[178] *See, e.g., In re High Sulfur Content Gasoline Products Liability Litigation,* 517 F.3d 220, 234 (5th Cir. 2008).

[179] *See, e.g., In re Volkswagen and Audi Warranty Extension Litigation,* 692 F.3d 4, 10 n.3 (1st Cir. 2012).

[180] *See, e.g., In re Bluetooth Headset Products Liability Litigation,* 654 F.3d 935, 943 (9th Cir. 2011).

[181] 28 U.S.C.A. § 1713.

ADDITIONAL RESEARCH REFERENCES

Wright & Miller, *Federal Practice and Procedure* §§ 1751 to 1805

C.J.S., Federal Civil Procedure §§ 63 to 92, § 170

West's Key Number Digest, Federal Civil Procedure ⟜161 to 189

RULE 23.1

DERIVATIVE ACTIONS BY SHAREHOLDERS

(a) Prerequisites. This rule applies when one or more shareholders or members of a corporation or an unincorporated association bring a derivative action to enforce a right that the corporation or association may properly assert but has failed to enforce. The derivative action may not be maintained if it appears that the plaintiff does not fairly and adequately represent the interests of shareholders or members who are similarly situated in enforcing the right of the corporation or association.

(b) Pleading Requirements. The complaint must be verified and must:

(1) allege that the plaintiff was a shareholder or member at the time of the transaction complained of, or that the plaintiffs share or membership later devolved on it by operation of law;

(2) allege that the action is not a collusive one to confer jurisdiction that the court would otherwise lack; and

(3) state with particularity:

   (A) any effort by the plaintiff to obtain the desired action from the directors or comparable authority and, if necessary, from the shareholders or members; and

   (B) the reasons for not obtaining the action or not making the effort.

(c) Settlement, Dismissal, and Compromise. A derivative action may be settled, voluntarily dismissed, or compromised only with the court's approval. Notice of a proposed settlement, voluntary dismissal, or compromise must be given to shareholders or members in the manner that the court orders.

[Added effective July 1, 1966; amended effective August 1, 1987; April 30, 2007, effective December 1, 2007.]

AUTHORS' COMMENTARY ON RULE 23.1

PURPOSE AND SCOPE

In a shareholder derivative suit, a shareholder sues on behalf of a corporation and/or its shareholders by alleging that the officers and directors who control the corporation will not institute the suit. In fact, often the officers and directors are themselves defendants in the derivative suit. The utility of shareholder derivative suits is balanced by the risk that this type of litigation can be used to harass corporate officers and directors into settlements favorable to the plaintiffs, at the expense of degrading corporate assets that are the common property of all shareholders. Through a series of procedural requirements not normally imposed on other kinds of litigation, Rule 23.1 attempts to preserve the social value of derivative suits, while reducing the risk of inappropriate harassment. Some of these requirements bear substantial similarity to elements of Rule 23, governing class actions.

RULE 23.1(a)—DERIVATIVE ACTION

CORE CONCEPT

Rule 23.1(a) provides that shareholders or members of a corporation may bring, on the corporation's behalf, an action that the corporation has not asserted. Only persons who will fairly and adequately represent the interests of other shareholders or members, and who will represent the interests of other similarly situated shareholders or members, may enforce the corporation's rights.

APPLICATIONS

Applicability

To implicate Rule 23.1, a plaintiff must be a "shareholder" or "member" seeking to enforce a right of a corporation or unincorporated association.[1] Other types of derivative claims need not meet the standards of Rule 23.1.[2]

Subject Matter Jurisdiction

If the cause of action is based exclusively on state law, the requirements of diversity jurisdiction must be satisfied. Because the corporation is normally treated as an indispensable party needed for just adjudication, alignment of the corporate entity as a plaintiff or defendant can have significant consequences for cases based on diversity jurisdiction. Although there is no absolute rule governing this issue, it is likely that the court will not align the corporation in a way that defeats diversity jurisdiction. But courts still retain discretion in this area, and have on occasion aligned the corporation in a way that defeats diversity.[3]

Personal Jurisdiction

Personal jurisdiction over defendants who are natural persons is obtained in derivative suits in the same manner as in other litigation. For corporations aligned as defendants, however, Congress has enacted a special service of process provision, which allows plaintiffs in shareholder derivative suits to serve process on such corporate defendants "in any district where [they are] organized or licensed to do business or . . . doing business."[4]

Venue

A special venue statute for derivative suits provides that the plaintiff may sue in any judicial district where the corporation might have sued the same defendants.[5] As a practical matter, this means shareholder derivative claims will typically implicate the general venue requirements for diversity suits and many claims based on federal questions.

---

[1] *See* Rule 23.1(b)(1). *See generally Lefkovitz v. Wagner,* 395 F.3d 773, 776 (7th Cir. 2005) ("Although most derivative suits are brought on behalf of corporations, a derivative suit can be brought on behalf of a partnership or other unincorporated form.").

[2] *See Daily Income Fund, Inc. v. Fox,* 464 U.S. 523, 528, 104 S.Ct. 831, 834, 78 L.Ed.2d 645 (1984) (Rule 23.1 applies only when "a shareholder claims a right that could have been, but was not, 'asserted' by the corporation.").

[3] *See, e.g., Liddy v. Urbanek,* 707 F.2d 1222, 1224 (11th Cir. 1983) ("[F]inal alignment of the parties should reflect the actual antagonisms between the plaintiffs, the corporation, and the directors; held, corporation should be joined where appropriate, even when joinder will destroy diversity); *Frank v. Hadesman & Frank, Inc.,* 83 F.3d 158 (7th Cir.1996) (in derivative suit, corporation is aligned as plaintiff if shareholders have suffered harm in common; citing state law; dismissing because corporation is not diverse from defendant).

[4] *See* 28 U.S.C.A. § 1695.

[5] *See* 28 U.S.C.A. § 1401.

RULE 23.1(b)—PLEADING REQUIREMENTS

CORE CONCEPT

Special pleading requirements govern shareholder derivative actions, and complaints must be verified.

APPLICATIONS

Verification of Complaint

Unlike the general practice in federal civil procedure, complaints that initiate shareholders' derivative actions must be sworn to and notarized. This verification requirement is often not applied in a way that prohibits a layperson from relying on competent information in bringing a derivative suit.[6] Thus, a shareholder who has undertaken a reasonable investigation, in person or through the advice of qualified persons, into the allegations in the complaint, should be able to satisfy the verification requirement without undue difficulty.[7]

Pleading Standing: Continuous Ownership Requirement

A shareholders' derivative complaint must state that the action is initiated on behalf of a person:

(1) who was a shareholder at the time the cause of action arose, or who became a shareholder by operation of law from someone who had been a shareholder at that time; *and*

(2) who remained a shareholder at the time the suit was filed.[8]

If the plaintiff is divested of ownership while the suit is pending, the suit will usually be dismissed.[9] In diversity suits, these standing requirements will apparently apply even if state law might be less strict, though the matter is not entirely free from doubt.[10]

Pleading Absence of Collusion

The plaintiff must affirm that a shareholder derivative suit based on diversity jurisdiction was not brought to manufacture federal court jurisdiction on behalf of the corporation. The possibility of manipulation may arise from a determination of the corporation's status as a plaintiff or defendant. In most cases it is probable that the

---

[6] *See Surowitz v. Hilton Hotels Corp.,* 383 U.S. 363, 86 S.Ct. 845, 15 L.Ed.2d 807 (1966).

[7] *See, e.g., Lewis v. Curtis,* 671 F.2d 779, 788 (3d Cir. 1982) (reliance on Wall Street Journal article satisfies requirement).

[8] *See, e.g., In re Bank of New York Derivative Litig.,* 320 F.3d 291, 298 (2d Cir. 2003) (requiring plaintiff to own stock *"throughout* the course of the activities that constitute the *primary basis* of the complaint;" rejecting use of continuing wrong doctrine to expand definition of transaction; holding that plaintiff need not have owned stock during "the entire course of all relevants," but plaintiff must have owned stock "before the case of the allegedly wrongful conduct transpired"); *Rosenbaum v. MacAllister,* 64 F.3d 1439, 1443 (10th Cir. 1995) (explaining requirements of contemporaneous ownership and continuing ownership).

[9] *See, e.g., Johnson v. United States,* 317 F.3d 1331, 1333–34 (Fed. Cir. 2003) (plaintiff who loses shareholder status through bankruptcy proceeding while lawsuit was pending loses standing upon cancellation of shares); *Schilling v. Belcher,* 582 F.2d 995, 999 (5th Cir. 1978) ("It is generally held that the ownership requirement continues throughout the life of the suit and that the action will abate if the plaintiff ceases to be a shareholder before the litigation ends.").

[10] *See, e.g., Kona Enters., Inc. v. Estate of Bishop,* 179 F.3d 767, 769 (9th Cir. 1999) (holding that standing requirement of Rule 23.1 "is procedural in nature and thus applicable in diversity actions"). *But see Fagin v. Gilmartin,* 432 F.3d 276, 285 (3d Cir. 2005) ("The question of whether the plaintiff is a 'shareholder' is determined by state law."); *Batchelder v. Kawamoto,* 147 F.3d 915, 917–18 (9th Cir. 1998) (where choice of law clause provided that Japanese law governed rights of interest holders, neither Rule 23.1 nor state law applied).

corporation on whose behalf the derivative lawsuit was filed will be aligned as a plaintiff.[11] If a corporate plaintiff is not diverse from all of the defendants, there is obviously a jurisdictional problem.[12] The solution lies in realignment of the corporation from plaintiff to defendant—a solution permissible when the court finds that the corporation is controlled by persons antagonistic to the interests of the stockholder plaintiffs.[13] Antagonism of this nature may be found where the corporate managers are simply opposed to the lawsuit.[14] In such circumstances, if the court realigns the corporation as a defendant, the problem with diversity jurisdiction may be resolved.

Pleading Demand or Demand Futility

Before filing the claim, a shareholder's derivative plaintiff must first make a demand on the corporate officers to pursue the lawsuit themselves ("demand"), or demonstrate why it is clear on the facts that such a demand ought to be excused ("futility").[15] The facts of this demand[16] or the facts demonstrating its futility[17] must be pleaded with particularity. The standard by which the facts are evaluated is a matter of state law.[18] Consequently, the plaintiff must allege in the complaint, with particularity, the following facts:

(1)   the efforts plaintiff made, if any, to encourage those who control the corporation—shareholders, officers and/or directors—to take action; *and*

(2)   the reasons why the efforts were unsuccessful, or reasons why no effort was made.[19]

This enhanced pleading obligation requires the plaintiff to provide more factual detail than might be ordinarily required in federal practice. However, the requirement is usually

---

[11]   *Koster v. Lumbermens Mutual Casualty Co.,* 330 U.S. 518, 522–23, 67 S.Ct. 828, 91 L.Ed. 1067 (1947) (derivative lawsuit does not belong to individual plaintiffs but to corporation, which is "the real party in interest").

[12]   *See* 28 U.S.C. § 1332.

[13]   *See Smith v. Sperling,* 354 U.S. 91, 95–96 n.3, 77 S.Ct. 1112, 1 L.Ed.2d 1205 (1957) ("The ultimate interest of the corporation made defendant may be the same as that of the stockholder made plaintiff, but the corporation may be under a control antagonistic to him, and made to act in a way detrimental to his rights."). *See, e.g., In re Digimarc Corp. Derivative Litig.,* 549 F.3d 1223, 1234 (9th Cir. 2008) (exception applies "when a corporation's officers or directors are 'antagonistic' to those of the shareholder plaintiff(s)").

[14]   *See Swanson v. Traer,* 354 U.S. 114, 116, 77 S.Ct. 1116, 1 L.Ed.2d 1221 (1957). *Cf. In re Digimarc Corp. Derivative Litig.,* 549 F.3d 1223, 1235 (9th Cir. 2008) (antagonism determined on face of pleadings and nature of dispute; noting that some other courts find antagonism where complaint alleges that defendants who control corporation are engaged in fraud or malfeasance).

[15]   *See, e.g., Santomenno ex rel. John Hancock Trust v. John Hancock Life Ins. Co.,* 677 F.3d 178, 184 (3d Cir. 2012) (demand requirement applies to all claims that corporation could have brought on its own behalf). *But cf. Daily Income Fund, Inc. v. Fox,* 464 U.S. 523, 528, 104 S.Ct. 831, 78 L.Ed.2d 645 (1984) (Rule 23.1 demand requirement applicable only to corporation or other association eligible to enforce rights in their own name, not to, e.g., funds that may not sue in their own name).

[16]   *See, e.g., Potter v. Hughes,* 546 F.3d 1051, 1055 (9th Cir. 2008) (finding of proper demand is prerequisite to determination of subject matter jurisdiction).

[17]   *See McCall v. Scott,* 239 F.3d 808, 816 (6th Cir. 2001) (demand may be excused "because either the directors were incapable of making an impartial decision, or the directors wrongfully refused a demand to sue"). *See also Westmoreland County Employee Retirement Sys. v. Parkinson,* 727 F.3d 719, 722 (7th Cir. 2013) (adequacy of Rule 23.1 pleading (*i.e.,* degree of required detail) measured by federal law).

[18]   *See Kamen v. Kemper Financial Services, Inc.,* 500 U.S. 90, 111 S.Ct. 1711, 114 L.Ed.2d 152 (1991) (Rule 23.1 controls adequacy of pleadings. State law controls substantive standard). *See, e.g., In re Ferro Corp. Derivative Litig.,* 511 F.3d 611, 617 (6th Cir. 2008) ("Even when the derivative claims are brought under federal law, we apply the substantive law of the state of incorporation . . . to determine whether Plaintiffs' failure to make a demand is excused.").

[19]   *See, e.g., Gomes v. American Century Cos., Inc.,* 710 F.3d 811, 815 (8th Cir. 2013) (noting both particularity requirement and, alternatively, reason for not trying to induce directors to bring action); *Stepak v. Addison,* 20 F.3d 398, 402 (11th Cir. 1994); (Rule 23.1 imposes "more stringent pleading requirements" than Rules 8 and 12(b)(6)).

satisfied without difficulty by simply explaining the facts behind the allegation.[20] Plaintiffs, though, are not ordinarily entitled to discovery to establish the particular facts underlying an allegation of futility.[21]

Special Litigation Committees

When officers of a business entity are faced with a Rule 23.1 demand to pursue a lawsuit, a typical response has been to appoint a special litigation committee to investigate the matter. In that circumstance courts will usually grant a request to stay proceedings in the derivative action until the committee can complete its work and make a report recommending a course of action, (*e.g.,* terminate the litigation, take it over, or authorize the original plaintiff to continue it). The court has authority to accept or reject the recommendation.[22]

Adequacy of Representation

The plaintiff in a shareholder derivative suit must be a person who will adequately represent the best interests of those—the corporation and other shareholders—on whose behalf the suit is prosecuted.[23]

RULE 23.1(c)—SETTLEMENT, DISMISSAL, AND COMPROMISE

CORE CONCEPT

Any settlement of a derivative action is subject to the court's approval, following appropriate notice.

APPLICATIONS

Settlement Subject to Court Approval

Derivative suits may not be dismissed or settled without prior judicial approval.[24] The district court enjoys broad discretion to evaluate a proposed settlement.[25] In determining whether to approve a settlement, the court may consider the reaction of persons, such as other shareholders, who will be affected by the outcome of the case.[26] In theory, the court should not re-write a proposed settlement, but should limit itself to approving or

---

[20] *See, e.g., In re Abbott Labs. Derivative Shareholders Litig.,* 325 F.3d 795, 804 (7th Cir. 2003) (holding requirement satisfied when "[a]lthough plaintiffs have a conclusory paragraph in their claim of demand futility, they have also incorporated all of the detailed factual allegations")

[21] *See, e.g., In re Merck & Co., Inc. Securities, Derivative & ERISA Litig.,* 493 F.3d 393 (3d Cir. 2007) (if discovery was allowed, "shareholder plaintiffs [would] have incentive to make baseless allegations and then engage in discovery fishing expeditions").

[22] *See, e.g., Strougo on Behalf of Brazil Fund, Inc. v. Padegs,* 986 F.Supp. 812, 814 (S.D. N.Y. 1997) (explaining process and noting courts' awareness of special litigation committee's potential bias toward protecting corporate board and officers).

[23] *But see Powers v. Eichen,* 229 F.3d 1249, 1254 (9th Cir. 2000) (concluding that Rule 23.1 does not offer as much protection as Rule 23; "Unlike . . . Rule 23, in shareholder derivative suits under Rule 23.1, a preliminary affirmative determination that the named plaintiffs will fairly and adequately represent the interests of the other class members is not a prerequisite to the maintenance of the action.").

[24] *See Burks v. Lasker,* 441 U.S. 471, 485 n.16, 99 S.Ct. 1831, 60 L.Ed.2d 404 (1979) (provision applies "only to voluntary settlements between derivative plaintiffs and defendants. [Rule 23.1 provision does] not apply where the plaintiffs' action is involuntarily dismissed by a court."). *But cf. In re Sonus Networks, Inc, Shareholder Derivative Litig.,* 499 F.3d 47, 65 (1st Cir. 2007) (noting *Burks,* but also noting that "some involuntary dismissals have been held to be the functional equivalent of a voluntary dismissal and thus are subject to the notice-before-dismissal requirement.").

[25] *See, e.g., McDannold v. Star Bank, N.A.,* 261 F.3d 478, 488 (6th Cir. 2001).

[26] *See, e.g., Bell Atlantic Corp. v. Bolger,* 2 F.3d 1304 (3d Cir.1993).

disapproving the proposal.[27] In practice, courts have substantial ability to influence the contents of a settlement by indicating what the court deems a satisfactory compromise. In any event, persons who wish to oppose a proposed settlement or appeal a settlement must first intervene in the case.[28]

Notice of Settlement

The court must order notice of voluntary dismissals or proposed settlements to interested persons.[29] Subject to the constraints of due process, the court enjoys substantial discretion, within the circumstances of the particular case, to determine the manner in which notification will occur,[30] though such notices are often less demanding than those issued in class actions.[31]

Bond Requirements

Many states require that plaintiffs in derivative lawsuits post bonds, from which the defendants will be compensated for litigation expenses if the defendants prevail. Rule 23.1 contains no such requirement. In diversity lawsuits, however, it is settled that federal courts will enforce requirements established under state law.[32]

Numerosity Requirements

Rule 23.1 does not require that the plaintiff represent any number of similarly situated persons. Thus, it will often be to the advantage of a shareholder who is one among a small group of similarly situated people to file a derivative action, rather than try to file a class action, which requires a greater number of plaintiffs.

ADDITIONAL RESEARCH REFERENCES

Wright & Miller, *Federal Practice and Procedure* §§ 1821 to 41

C.J.S., Corporations §§ 397 to 413

Corporations and Business Organizations ⊶2020 to 2065, ⊶2020 to 2115, ⊶2120 to 2165, ⊶2170 to 2212, ⊶2220 to 2244

---

[27] *See, e.g., United Founders Life Ins. Co. v. Consumers Nat'l Life Ins. Co.,* 447 F.2d 647, 655 (7th Cir. 1971) ("The business judgment of the court is not to be substituted for that of the parties.").

[28] *See, e.g., Robert F. Booth Trust v. Crowley,* 687 F.3d 314, 318 (7th Cir. 2012) (intervention should be granted freely).

[29] *See, e.g., Robert F. Booth Trust v. Crowley,* 687 F.3d 314, 318 (7th Cir. 2012) (settlement requires notice followed by judicial approval).

[30] *See Kyriazi v. Western Elec. Co.,* 647 F.2d 388, 395 (3d Cir. 1981) (manner of notification within court's discretion, provided notice satisfies dues process).

[31] *See, e.g., In re UnitedHealth Group Shareholder Derivative Litigation,* 631 F.3d 913, 917 (8th Cir. 2011) (noting that notice requirements for class actions are usually more extensive than notice requirements under Rule 23.1(c)).

[32] *See Cohen v. Beneficial Indus. Loan Corp.,* 337 U.S. 541, 69 S.Ct. 1221, 93 L. Ed. 1528 (1949) (state bond requirement applicable to diversity suit).

RULE 23.2

ACTIONS RELATING TO UNINCORPORATED ASSOCIATIONS

This rule applies to an action brought by or against the members of an unincorporated association as a class by naming certain members as representative parties. The action may be maintained only if it appears that those parties will fairly and adequately protect the interests of the association and its members. In conducting the action, the court may issue any appropriate orders corresponding with those in Rule 23(d), and the procedure for settlement, voluntary dismissal, or compromise must correspond with the procedure in Rule 23(e).

[Added effective July 1, 1966; April 30, 2007, effective December 1, 2007.]

AUTHORS' COMMENTARY ON RULE 23.2

PURPOSE AND SCOPE

Rule 23.2 extends some of the procedural protections of class actions under Rule 23 and shareholder derivative suits under Rule 23.1 to members of *unincorporated* associations who are sued through representatives, or on whose behalf representatives have initiated suit. Each of these three rules address situations where persons will be affected by the outcome of suits without necessarily having an opportunity to participate fully in litigation. Rule 23.2 is devoted to ensuring that representatives of the *unincorporated* association's membership adequately represent the interest of the entire membership.

APPLICATIONS

No New Substantive Right-to-Sue Created

This Rule does not *create* a right for representatives of an unincorporated association to sue or be sued. Rather, it governs such a suit when the applicable state or federal law provides a cause of action by or against the unincorporated association, but does not permit a suit by or against the association as an entity.[1]

Requirement of Membership in Unincorporated Association

Before a plaintiff may represent the interests of an unincorporated association, the plaintiff must prove that an association exists and the plaintiff is a member. The legal existence of an unincorporated association is controlled by the law of the forum state.[2]

Fair and Adequate Representation

The court's first concern is to ascertain whether the interests of the proposed representatives of the unincorporated association conflict with those of the association itself or its membership. However, the case law is divided as to whether an association's

---

[1] *See, e.g., Northbrook Excess & Surplus Ins. Co. v. Medical Malpractice Joint Underwriting Ass'n of Mass.,* 900 F.2d 476, 477 (1st Cir. 1990). *Cf. Benn v. Seventh-Day Adventist Church,* 304 F.Supp.2d 716, 723 (D. Md. 2004) (most courts hold that where state law permits suit by unincorporated association as an entity, "Rule 23.2 is unavailable.").

[2] *See* Fed.R.Civ.P. 17(b).

representatives must meet the standards developed for adequate class representation in class actions.[3]

Orders Regulating Proceedings

Rule 23.2 explicitly incorporates Rule 23(d), governing the court's power to issue orders in the course of class action litigation. Because the court's authority under Rule 23(d) is broad, the effect of this incorporation is to give the trial court wide discretion to issue orders ensuring both the efficient processing of the case and substantial protection for passive members of the unincorporated association.

Approval of Settlement

Rule 23.2 also explicitly incorporates Rule 23(e), which provides a court substantial authority to approve or disapprove settlements in class actions. As a practical matter, the effect is to require not only consultation of Rule 23(e), but also strong consideration of the possibility of inviting the trial judge to participate in settlement discussions whenever the discussions have advanced sufficiently to make participation practicable.

Numerosity

Rule 23.2 contains no requirement that the membership of the unincorporated association rise above some minimum number.[4]

Citizenship for Diversity Jurisdiction

Where an unincorporated association may sue or be sued through representatives, an established practice is to determine diversity by examining the citizenship of the representatives.[5] Thus, an unincorporated association often can create diversity jurisdiction by selecting a representative who is a citizen of a different state from the defendants (provided that the amount in controversy exceeds $75,000, exclusive of interest and costs).

Amount in Controversy

The prevailing practice in federal district courts is to determine the amount in controversy by examining the individual claims of the membership of the unincorporated association. This approach creates a substantial hurdle to achieving diversity jurisdiction. Thus, if an unincorporated association has a claim for $1,000,000, the claim would appear to exceed the more-than-$75,000 requirement by a safe margin. If, however, the association has 10,000 members, and each member has an equal share in the aggregate claim of $1,000,000, the value of the suit to each member is only $100—well short of the threshold for diversity jurisdiction.

ADDITIONAL RESEARCH REFERENCES

Wright & Miller, Federal Practice and Procedure § 1861

C.J.S., Associations § 8, §§ 40 to 48, §§ 51 to 53; Federal Civil Procedure §§ 76 to 93

West's Key Number Digest, Associations ↦20(1); Federal Civil Procedure ↦186.5

---

[3]   *Compare Gravenstein v. Campion,* 96 F.R.D. 137,140 (D. Alaska 1982) (Rule 23 requirements applied to Rule 23.2 lawsuit) *with Curley v. Brignoli, Curley & Roberts Assocs.,* 915 F.2d 81, 86 (2d Cir. 1990) (requirements of Rule 23(a) do not apply to cases proceeding under Rule 23.2).

[4]   *See, e.g., Curley v. Brignoli, Curley & Roberts Assocs.,* 915 F.2d 81, 86 (2d Cir. 1990) (numerosity and other prerequisites of Rule 23(a) inapplicable in Rule 23.2 case).

[5]   *See, e.g., Aetna Cas. & Sur. Co. v. Iso-Tex, Inc.,* 75 F.3d 216, 218 (5th Cir. 1996) (diversity tested by looking to citizenship of named representatives).

RULE 24

INTERVENTION

(a) Intervention of Right. On timely motion, the court must permit anyone to intervene who:

(1) is given an unconditional right to intervene by a federal statute; or

(2) claims an interest relating to the property or transaction that is the subject of the action, and is so situated that disposing of the action may as a practical matter impair or impede the movant's ability to protect its interest, unless existing parties adequately represent that interest.

(b) Permissive Intervention.

(1) *In General.* On timely motion, the court may permit anyone to intervene who:

(A) is given a conditional right to intervene by a federal statute; or

(B) has a claim or defense that shares with the main action a common question of law or fact.

(2) *By a Government Officer or Agency.* On timely motion, the court may permit a federal or state governmental officer or agency to intervene if a party's claim or defense is based on:

(A) a statute or executive order administered by the officer or agency; or

(B) any regulation, order, requirement, or agreement issued or made under the statute or executive order.

(3) *Delay or Prejudice.* In exercising its discretion, the court must consider whether the intervention will unduly delay or prejudice the adjudication of the original parties' rights.

(c) Notice and Pleading Required. A motion to intervene must be served on the parties as provided in Rule 5. The motion must state the grounds for intervention and be accompanied by a pleading that sets out the claim or defense for which intervention is sought.

[Amended effective March 19, 1948; October 20, 1949; July 1, 1963; July 1, 1966; August 1, 1987; December 1, 1991; April 12, 2006, effective December 1, 2006; April 30, 2007, effective December 1, 2007.]

AUTHORS' COMMENTARY ON RULE 24

PURPOSE AND SCOPE

Rule 24 governs situations in which persons not already parties may intervene in existing litigation to which the nonparty was not previously invited. Rule 24 attempts to balance the interest of the person seeking intervention with the burdens such intervention may impose on parties to pending suits. The Rule divides intervenors into two basic groups: those seeking intervention as of right and those who seek the court's leave to intervene permissively. The court enjoys substantial

discretion when deciding whether to permit intervention under either group. There remain, however, important distinctions in the factors courts consider in exercising discretion. Finally, while cases granting applications to intervene often declare that intervention provisions are to be construed liberally,[1] the application of Rule 24 to particular motions is not always as generous as such general statements might suggest.

RULE 24(a)—INTERVENTION OF RIGHT

CORE CONCEPT

A party may intervene as of right under two circumstances: where a federal statute confers an unconditional right to intervene; and where the intervenor, in a timely manner, shows a legally protectable interest that is not adequately represented by the existing parties and which, unless intervention is granted, could be impaired or impeded.[2]

APPLICATIONS

Intervenor's Choice

There is no obligation to intervene. If the requirements of intervention are met, the decision to intervene rests with the potential intervenor.[3]

Intervention by Unconditional Statutory Right

The first basis for intervention of right—Rule 24(a)(1)—depends on the applicability of some federal statute that confers on the prospective intervenor an unconditional right to intervene in pending litigation. If applicants satisfy this statutory intervention right, they need not also show an interest-impairment based right under Rule 24(a)(2); the two bases operate independently.[4] But statutory intervention rights are construed narrowly.[5] As a practical result, persons seeking to intervene under Rule 24(a) are often well-served arguing for intervention under the interest-impairment test of Rule 24(a)(2)—even in circumstances where they believe they might qualify for intervention as a statutory right under Rule 24(a)(1).[6]

Intervention by Showing Interest Is Impaired or Impeded

The right to intervene under Rule 24(a)(2) exists only when the court holds that a person seeking intervention has established three elements: (1) an interest in the subject matter of the pending litigation; (2) a substantial risk that the litigation will, as a practical matter, impair or impede that interest; and (3) the existing litigants do not adequately represent that interest. By the terms of the Rule, a final element—timeliness—must also be

---

[1] *See, e.g., South Dakota ex rel Barnett v. U.S. Dep't of Interior,* 317 F.3d 783, 785 (8th Cir. 2003) (" . . . Rule 24 should be liberally construed with all doubts resolved in favor of the proposed intervenor.").

[2] *See Deutsche Bank Nat'l Trust Co. v. F.D.I.C.,* 717 F.3d 189, 192 (D.C. Cir. 2013).

[3] *See Martin v. Wilks,* 490 U.S. 755, 109 S.Ct. 2180 (1989) (Rule 24 does not require intervention; it is permissive, not mandatory; drawing contrast with Rule 19). *See also Kourtis v. Cameron,* 419 F.3d 989 (9th Cir.2005) ("There is no duty of mandatory intervention imposed upon nonparties, and the decision not to intervene thus does not expose a nonparty to the earlier proceedings' preclusive effects.").

[4] *See Ruiz v. Estelle,* 161 F.3d 814, 828 (5th Cir. 1998) ("Under Rule 24(a) (1), intervenors need not even prove a 'sufficient' interest relating to the subject matter of the controversy, since *Congress* has already declared that interest sufficient by granting the statutory right to intervene." However, statutory intervention is still subject to a determination of timeliness, over which the district court enjoys substantial discretion).

[5] *See, e.g., Phar-Mor, Inc. v. Coopers & Lybrand,* 22 F.3d 1228, 1232 (3d Cir. 1994) ("[C]ourts have construed Rule 24(a)(1) narrowly; these courts have been reluctant to interpret statutes to grant an unconditional right to intervene to private parties."). *Cf. Schultz v. United States,* 594 F.3d 1120, 1123 (9th Cir. 2010) (where Mandatory Victims Restitution Act provided for exclusive remedy, no intervention as of right would be allowed).

[6] *Cf. Yorkshire v. U.S. I.R.S.,* 26 F.3d 942, 944 (9th Cir. 1994) (Rule 24(a)(2) "is construed broadly in favor of the applicants").

shown.[7] Each of these elements must be satisfied before an applicant may exercise a right to intervene under Rule 24(a)(2).[8] Not all courts give the three factors equal weight, however.[9]

Once intervention is granted the intervening party must continue to meet these requirements throughout the duration of the litigation, or be subject to being dismissed from the case.[10]

Showing #1—Interest in the Subject Matter

The type of "interest" that will satisfy Rule 24(a)(2) is difficult to define and always fact-dependent.[11] A person who has an interest that by itself could be a case or controversy will meet the requirement of Rule 24(a)(2).[12] However, it is not always necessary that the intervenor possess the right to bring the cause of action independently.[13] An economic interest in the subject matter of the litigation may satisfy this element of the Rule;[14] however, a property interest is also not always essential.[15] A substantial privacy interest has also been found sufficient.[16] Also, if the intervening party will be legally bound by the

---

[7]   *See, e.g., League of United Latin Am. Citizens, Dist. 19 v. City of Boerne,* 659 F.3d 421, 433 (5th Cir. 2011).

[8]   *See, e.g., Arakaki v. Cayetano,* 324 F.3d 1078, 1083 (9th Cir. 2003) (requirement is that all four elements must be satisfied). *But cf. Ross v. Marshall,* 426 F.3d 745, 753 (5th Cir. 2005) (acknowledging that all elements must be met, but examination should be flexible and non-technical; "Intervention should generally be allowed where 'no one would be hurt and greater justice could be attained.' ").

[9]   *See WildEarth Guardians v. Nat'l Park Serv.,* 604 F.3d 1192, 1199–1200 (10th Cir. 2010) (impairment of interest and inadequate representation were both minimal burdens).

[10]   *See Coalition to Defend Affirmative Action v. Regents of Univ. of Mich.,* 652 F.3d 607, 633 (6th Cir. 2011) (dismissing party after he entered stipulation with defendant effectively aligning their interests and making his "presence in the litigation . . . a mere makeweight"; collecting cases).

[11]   *See, e.g., Utahns for Better Transp. v. U.S. Dep't of Transp.,* 295 F.3d 1111 (10th Cir. 2002) ("The sufficiency of an applicant's interest is a highly fact-specific determination." Also noting that "[t]here is some value in having the parties before the court so that they will be bound by the result."); *Daggett v. Comm'n on Gov'tl Ethics & Election Practices,* 172 F.3d 104, 110 (1st Cir. 1999) (noting that narrow reading of interest is disfavored, "although clear outer boundaries have yet to be developed").

[12]   *See, e.g., Aurora Loan Servs., Inc. v. Craddieth,* 442 F.3d 1018, 1022 (7th Cir. 2006) ("[T]he applicant's interest must be one on which an independent federal suit could be based, consistent with Article III's requirement that only a case or controversy can be litigated in a federal court at any stage of the proceeding.").

[13]   *See, e.g., United States v. Philip Morris USA Inc.,* 566 F.3d 1095, 1145 (D.C. Cir. 2009) (public health organizations which could not have instituted RICO suit were nevertheless entitled to intervene in government's RICO prosecution); *Solid Waste Agency of Northern Cook County v. U.S. Army Corps of Engineers,* 101 F.3d 503, 507 (7th Cir. 1996) ("The strongest case for intervention is not where the aspirant for intervention could file an independent suit, but where the intervenor-aspirant has no claim against the defendant yet a legally protected interest that could be impaired by the suit.").

[14]   *See, e.g., Flying J, Inc. v. Van Hollen,* 578 F.3d 569, 572 (7th Cir. 2009) (gasoline retailers who sought to intervene in suit to invalidate state law setting minimum price for gasoline had sufficient interest to intervene as of right as they would be "directly rather than remotely harmed by the invalidation of the statute", losing business to more efficient competitors); *Fund For Animals, Inc. v. Norton,* 322 F.3d 728, 733 (D.C. Cir. 2003) (interest of foreign government agency in protecting flow of tourist dollars meets interest requirement of Rule 24(a)); *Utahns for Better Transp. v. U.S. Dep't of Transp.,* 295 F.3d 1111 (10th Cir. 2002) ("The threat of economic injury from the outcome of the litigation undoubtedly gives a petitioner the requisite interest."). *But see Deutsche Bank Nat'l Trust Co. v. F.D.I.C.,* 717 F.3d 189, 195 (D.C. Cir. 2013) ("other circuits have generally concluded that a party may not intervene in support of a defendant solely to protect judgment funds that the party wishes to recover itself").

[15]   *See, e.g., WildEarth Guardians v. National Park Service,* 604 F.3d 1192, 1198–1201 (10th Cir. 2010) (hunting and conservation organization allowed to intervene as of right in suit brought by environmental organization challenging National Park Service's proposal to cull elk population; group's interest in culling of elk was sufficient interest to intervene, and impairment of interest and inadequate representation were both minimal burdens); *United States v. Carpenter,* 526 F.3d 1237, 1241 (9th Cir. 2008) (environmental groups' interest in seeing wilderness area preserved was sufficient to allow them to intervene in Quiet Title Act action even though they did not have a property interest).

[16]   *See Doe v. Oberweis Dairy,* 456 F.3d 704, 718 (7th Cir. 2006) (mother and sister of plaintiff asserting Title VII sexual harassment were entitled to intervene to contest trial court's grant of employer's motion for access to the plaintiff's psychiatric records, where mother and sister were present and participated in some of the sessions). *Cf. In re Request*

judgment in the pending litigation, an "interest" exists that satisfies Rule 24(a)(2).[17] A desire to add to the factual record[18] or advance a general ideological viewpoint have[19] been found insufficient.[20] The cases confirm that the concept of "interest" is a somewhat unpredictable, fact-bound inquiry.[21]

Showing #2—Impairing (or Impeding) of That Interest

An applicant's interest may be impaired or impeded by an actual legal impairment, such as a risk that principles of stare decisis may apply.[22] At the same time, other practical consequences of litigation may also satisfy the "impairment" element. For example, even though a party may not, through res judicata or collateral estoppel, be bound by the judgment, a substantial risk of practical impairments can sometimes constitute sufficient risk of "impairment" to a party seeking to intervene.[23] A certainty that the interest will be impaired or impeded is generally unnecessary.[24]

Showing #3—Adequate Representation by Existing Parties

Even if the person seeking intervention demonstrates that the elements of "interest" and "impairment" are satisfied, intervention under Rule 24(a)(2) will be denied if the interest

---

from United Kingdom Pursuant to Treaty Between Gov't of U.S. and Gov't of United . . . , 685 F.3d 1, 22 (1st Cir. 2012) (academic researchers did not have a legally-significant protectable interest to intervene in criminal proceeding attempting to subpoena information from their institution despite intention of donator that information be kept confidential).

[17] *See, e.g., Stauffer v. Brooks Bros., Inc.,* 619 F.3d 1321, 1329 (Fed. Cir. 2010) (intervention allowed where res judicata would prevent government from recovering fine for violation of patent); *City of Emeryville v. Robinson,* 621 F.3d 1251 (9th Cir. 2010) (property owners in CERCLA case had sufficient interest to intervene when facing imminent extinction of their state law rights of contribution for site clean-up costs, even though the interest was contingent upon the outcome of the litigation).

[18] *See Brandt v. Gooding,* 636 F.3d 124, 131 (4th Cir. 2011) (upheld denial of intervention as of right to attorney who sought to intervene in former client's habeas proceeding; attorney "sought 'to add to the factual record' . . . this interest failed 'to satisfy the requirements for intervention of right or permissive intervention' ").

[19] *See Coalition to Defend Affirmative Action v. Granholm,* 501 F.3d 775, 781–83 (6th Cir. 2007) (finding that organizations that favored constitutional amendment had a "general ideological interest" and not a "substantial legal interest" and therefore could not intervene as of right in action challenging validity of amendment).

[20] *See Brandt v. Gooding,* 636 F.3d 124, 131 (4th Cir. 2011) (upheld denial of intervention as of right to attorney who sought to intervene in former client's habeas proceeding; attorney "sought 'to add to the factual record' . . . this interest failed 'to satisfy the requirements for intervention of right or permissive intervention' ").

[21] *See, e.g., League of United Latin Am. Citizens, Dist. 19 v. City of Boerne,* 659 F.3d 421, 434–35 (5th Cir. 2011) (voter had sufficient interest to intervene where outcome impacted his right to vote and he had no other procedural vehicle to protect his interest); *Perry v. Schwarzenegger,* 630 F.3d 898, 903–04 (9th Cir. 2011) (intervention in suit challenging constitutionality of law prohibiting same-sex marriages denied; deputy county clerk's desire to avoid "legal uncertainty and confusion" not a "significant protectable interest"); *Bridgeport Guardians, Inc. v. Delmonte,* 602 F.3d 469, 474 (2d Cir. 2010) (White and Hispanic police officers allowed to intervene as of right in city challenge to 1982 order intended to remedy civil rights violations against minorities when officers claimed proposed settlement permitted illegal race-norming of tests required for promotions; intervenors had sufficient interest in their employers' employment practices); *Roeder v. Islamic Republic of Iran,* 333 F.3d 228, 233 (D.C. Cir. 2003) (interest in protecting diplomatic agreement with foreign sovereign that might be affected by litigation gave United States interest that met intervention requirement); *In re Grand Jury Subpoena,* 274 F.3d 563, 570 (1st Cir. 2001) (appropriate intervention by attorney and corporate officers to attempt to quash grand jury subpoena; "[c]olorable claims of attorney-client and work product privilege qualify as sufficient interests to ground intervention as of right").

[22] *See, e.g., Sierra Club v. Espy,* 18 F.3d 1202, 1207 (5th Cir. 1994) (stare decisis effect of decision is sufficient potential impairment to satisfy requirements of Rule 24(a)(2)).

[23] *See, e.g., City of Chicago v. Federal Emergency Mgmt. Agency,* 660 F.3d 980, 986 (7th Cir. 2011) (ability of would-be intervenor to litigate claim in future not automatic bar to intervention); *Utah Ass'n of Counties v. Clinton,* 255 F.3d 1246, 1253 (10th Cir. 2001) (question of impairment cannot be separated from question of existence of interest; moreover, " 'the court is not limited to consequences of a strictly legal nature' ").

[24] *See United States v. City of Los Angeles,* 288 F.3d 391, 401 (9th Cir. 2002) (potential impairment is sufficient; no requirement that outcome will necessarily impair interest).

at risk is represented adequately by persons already parties to the action.[25] The intervenor bears this burden, but is minimal.[26] Typically, a potential intervenor will not have great difficulty establishing a lack of adequate representation by existing parties,[27] unless the intervenor and an existing party share identical objectives.[28] Lack of adequate representation is most easily demonstrated if the interest is not currently represented at all, or if the persons already parties have positions clearly adverse to those of the intervention applicant.[29] However, a difference in tactics does not of itself necessarily indicate a lack of adequate representation.[30] Adequate representation is generally presumed where a state represents its citizens, citizens seek to intervene as of right, and the state shares the same interest as the citizens.[31] There must continue to be a lack of adequate representation by

---

[25] *See, e.g., Daggett v. Comm'n on Gov'tl Ethics & Election Practices,* 172 F.3d 104, 111 (1st Cir. 1999) (rebuttable presumption that government's defense of validity of statute adequately represents interests of citizens who support statute); *Clark v. Putnam County,* 168 F.3d 458, 461 (11th Cir. 1999) ("weak" presumption of adequate representation when "existing party seeks the same objectives as the would-be intervenor").

[26] *See Trbovch v. United Mine Workers of Am.,* 404 U.S. 528, 538 n.10, 92 S.Ct. 630, 636, 30 L.Ed.2d 686 (1972) ("The requirement of the Rule is satisfied if the applicant shows that representation of his interest 'may be' inadequate; and the burden of making that showing should be treated as minimal.").

[27] *See, e.g., Perry v. Brown,* 671 F.3d 1052, 1068 (9th Cir. 2012) (proponents of state constitutional amendment outlawing gay marriage allowed to intervene in suit challenging constitutionality of amendment where existing defendants refused to argue for amendment's constitutionality); *Citizens for Balanced Use v. Montana Wilderness Ass'n,* 647 F.3d 893, 899 (9th Cir. 2011) (U.S. Forest Service did not adequately represent interests of conservation groups in action challenging order limiting motorized vehicles in wilderness study area; Service acted under compulsion of district court decision gained by previous litigation and Service was appealing that prior decision; appeal "demonstrates the fundamentally differing points of view between applicants and the Forest Service on the litigation as a whole). *But see Southern Utah Wilderness Alliance v. Kempthorne,* 525 F.3d 966, 970 (10th Cir. 2008) (denied intervention of lessees in suit brought by environmental organizations challenging Bureau of Land Management's (BLM) sale of oil and gas leases on public land, ruling that BLM adequately represented lessees' interest, and any damage to them was speculative).

[28] *See, e.g., Wisconsin Educ. Ass'n Council v. Walker,* 705 F.3d 640, 659 (7th Cir. 2013) (where objectives match there is a rebuttable presumption of adequate representation); *Wolfsen Land & Cattle Co. v. Pacific Coast Federation of Fishermen's Associations,* 695 F.3d 1310, 1315 (D.C. Cir. 2012) (association of fishermen not entitled to intervene in suit by downstream property owners suing to stop release of damn water; government and fishermen had same interest in restoring fish populations in dry riverbed).

[29] *See, e.g., City of Chicago v. Federal Emergency Mgmt. Agency,* 660 F.3d 980, 986–87 (7th Cir. 2011) (intervention of right appropriate when original party does not advance ground that would confer a tangible benefit on intervenor); *Twelve John Does v. District of Columbia,* 117 F.3d 571 (D.C. Cir. 1997) (existing representation is generally adequate where there is no conflicting interest between representative and would-be intervenor and where representative has ability to litigate the issues with vigor). *But see Jordan v. Michigan Conference of Teamsters Welfare Fund,* 207 F.3d 854, 863 (6th Cir. 2000) (movant's burden is only to show that representation "may be" inadequate, not that representation "will in fact be inadequate".

[30] *See Wisconsin Educ. Ass'n Council v. Walker,* 705 F.3d 640, 659 (7th Cir. 2013) ("post-hoc quibbles with the state's litigation strategy" not sufficient for intervention). *See, e.g., United States v. City of Miami,* 278 F.3d 1174, 1179 (11th Cir. 2002) (police associations concerned with advancement of blacks and women is adequately represented by government interest in ending discrimination for all minorities); *B.H. v. McDonald,* 49 F.3d 294 (7th Cir.1995) (party's preference to in-chamber conferences as opposed to open court hearings does not constitute inadequate representation). *But see B. Fernandez & Hnos., Inc. v. Kellogg USA, Inc.,* 440 F.3d 541, 546 (1st Cir. 2006) (presumption of adequate representation not established solely by fact that existing party and intervenor are subsidiaries of same parent); *Utahns for Better Transp. v. U.S. Dep't of Transp.,* 295 F.3d 1111 (10th Cir. 2002) (burden of showing inadequacy of representation is minimal; relying on government creates potential conflict between government's duty to protect public interest and private interests of private intervention petitioners; also, private parties have expertise that government lacks; finally, government's silence on its intent to protect private parties is "deafening").

[31] *See e.g., Stuart v. Huff,* 706 F.3d 345, 351–54 (4th Cir. 2013) (must be a very strong showing of inadequacy in government representation; finding that attorney general adequately represented interests of group of pro-life doctors, former abortion patients, and pregnancy counseling centers to insure women were informed before undergoing an abortion; where would be intervenors shared the same objective as government, difference of opinion as to legal tactics did not warrant intervention); *Department of Fair Employment & Housing v. Lucent Techs., Inc.,* 642 F.3d 728, 740 (9th Cir. 2011) ("In the absence of a very compelling showing to the contrary, it will be presumed that a state adequately represents its citizens when the applicant shares the same interest."). *Compare Benjamin ex rel. Yock v. Department of Public Welfare of Pa.,* 701 F.3d 938, 958 (3d Cir. 2012) ("when an agency's views are necessarily colored by its view of the

other parties throughout the litigation or the intervenor risks being dismissed from the case.[32]

Timing

Applicants must also meet a "timeliness" requirement to intervene.[33] However, unlike timing elements in some other Federal Rules, the actual time limits are not set out in Rule 24(a).[34] Generally, courts weigh four factors[35] in determining timeliness: (1) length of delay in seeking intervention;[36] (2) prejudicial impact of such delay on existing parties;[37] (3) prejudice to intervenor if intervention is denied; and (4) other factors affecting fairness in an individual case.[38] Requests for intervention made post-judgment or post-settlement are less likely to be granted.[39] The timeliness of a motion to intervene is frequently measured from the time the applicant should have known his interest was not adequately represented.[40] In this timing analysis, courts frequently distinguish intervention during a district court case from intervention on appeal.[41] An initial decision to reject intervention on

---

public welfare rather than the more parochial views of a proposed intervenor whose interest is personal to it, the burden is comparatively light;" citations omitted).

[32] *See Coalition to Defend Affirmative Action v. Regents of Univ. of Mich.*, 652 F.3d 607, 633 (6th Cir. 2011) (dismissing intervening party after he entered stipulation with defendant effectively aligning their interests; "courts must be able to ensure that parties maintain a live interest in a case," citing authority).

[33] *See, e.g., Associated Builders & Contractors, Inc. v. Herman*, 166 F.3d 1248, 1257 (D.C. Cir. 1999) ("If the motion was not timely, there is no need for the court to address the other factors that enter into an intervention analysis.").

[34] *See, e.g., Heaton v. Monogram Credit Card Bank of Georgia*, 297 F.3d 416 (5th Cir.2002) ("There are no absolute measures of timeliness; it is determined from all the circumstances."); *United States v. State of Wash.*, 86 F.3d 1499, 1503 (9th Cir. 1996) ("[A]ny substantial lapse of time weighs heavily against intervention."); *Atlantic Mut. Ins. Co. v. Northwest Airlines, Inc.*, 24 F.3d 958, 961 (7th Cir. 1994) (timeliness means intervenor applicant must "act with dispatch").

[35] Although substantially the same, the factors are sometimes stated differently. *See e.g., In re Uponor, Inc., F1807 Plumbing Fittings Products Liability Litig.*, 716 F.3d 1057 (8th Cir. 2013) ((1) the extent the litigation has progressed at the time of the motion to intervene; (2) the prospective intervenor's knowledge of the litigation; (3) the reason for the delay in seeking intervention; and (4) whether the delay in seeking intervention may prejudice the existing parties"; *Benjamin ex rel. Yock v. Department of Public Welfare of Pa.*, 701 F.3d 938, 949–57 (3d Cir. 2012) ((1) the stage of the proceeding; (2) the prejudice that delay may cause the parties; and (3) the reason for the delay") (citations omitted); *Geiger v. Foley Hoag LLP Retirement Plan*, 521 F.3d 60, 65 (1st Cir. 2008) (factors are (1) progress of case; (2) length of time intervenor knew her interest was imperiled; (3) foreseeable prejudice to existing parties if intervention is granted, or to intervenor if it is denied; and (4) any idiosyncratic circumstances that weigh for or against intervention).

[36] *See, e.g., United States v. Ritchie Special Credit Investments, Ltd.*, 620 F.3d 824, 831 (8th Cir. 2010) (intervention untimely where there was six-month delay between the entry of injunction freezing assets and filing of motion to intervene by secured creditor); *Zbaraz v. Madigan*, 572 F.3d 370 (7th Cir. 2009) (holding motion to intervene untimely where court had denied two motions to reconsider, defendants has filed notice of appeal, and nearly twenty-five years after initiation of litigation).

[37] *Cf. Effjohn Int'l Cruise Holdings, Inc. v. A&L Sales, Inc.*, 346 F.3d 552, 561 (5th Cir. 2003) (noting prejudice factor, but explaining, "[t]he inquiry for this factor is whether other parties were prejudiced *by the delay*, not whether they would be prejudiced *by the addition of the claim* (obviously, in the sense that they may obtain less, existing parties are always prejudiced by new claims) [emphasis in original]").

[38] *See, e.g., Alt v. EPA*, 758 F.3d 588, 591 (4th Cir. 2014) (consolidating factors into three: (1) progress already made in suit; (2) prejudice that delay caused by intervention may impose on other parties; (3) reason for delay in moving to intervene); *American Civil Liberties Union of Minn. v. Tarek ibn Ziyad Academy*, 643 F.3d 1088 (8th Cir. 2011) (motion filed fourteen months after original suit untimely; no adequate explanation offered for lengthy delay which would prejudice existing parties).

[39] *See, e.g., Bond v. Utreras*, 585 F.3d 1061, 1071 (7th Cir. 2009) ("intervention postjudgment—which necessarily disturbs the final adjudication of the parties' rights—should generally be disfavored."); *R & G Mortg. Corp. v. Federal Home Loan Mortg. Corp.*, 584 F.3d 1, 10 (1st Cir. 2009) ("Requests for post-settlement intervention are rarely granted.").

[40] *See, e.g., Chamness v. Bowen*, 722 F.3d 1110 (9th Cir. 2013) (viewed from date person should have been aware interests not adequately protected by parties, not date person learned of litigation); *Benjamin ex rel. Yock v. Department of Public Welfare of Pa.*, 701 F.3d 938, 950 (3d Cir. 2012) (delay measured from the time the proposed intervenor knows or should have known of the alleged risks to his or her rights).

[41] *See Negron-Almeda v. Santiago*, 528 F.3d 15, 22 (1st Cir. 2008) (where "the proposed intervention post-dates the entry of judgment, timeliness is a crucial element in the Rule 24(a)(2) calculus"); *Elliott Indus. Limited P'ship v. BP Am.*

grounds of lack of timeliness is rarely disturbed on appeal.[42] This is probably the most important kind of discretion courts possess when considering applications to intervene under Rule 24(a).

- *"Collateral Purpose" Exception:* Some courts modify the timeliness requirement of Rule 24(a) when the purpose of the intervention application is only to, for example, modify an existing protective order.[43] This view has not been adopted in all circuits.[44]

Burden of Proof

While an applicant seeking to intervene as of right has the burden to show that requirements for intervention are met, those requirements are broadly interpreted in favor of intervention.[45]

Judicial Discretion

The grant or denial of a motion to intervene as of right is generally reviewed under the abuse-of-discretion standard.[46] This appellate deference is appropriate given the "dynamics that develop in the trial court and that the court is accordingly in the best position to evaluate."[47]

Conditional Intervention

If a court permits intervention as of right, it may impose conditions on such intervention.[48]

Subject Matter Jurisdiction

When a person seeks to intervene as of right, subject matter jurisdiction may be established either through an independent basis of jurisdiction (such as diversity of citizenship[49] or federal question jurisdiction[50]) or through supplemental jurisdiction.[51] However, in diversity cases where the intervening person is not diverse, the availability of supplemental jurisdiction depends on whether the would-be intervenor will be aligned as a plaintiff or a defendant. If the intervenor will be a plaintiff, it is probable that the intervenor

---

Prod'n Co., 407 F.3d 1091, 1103 (10th Cir.2005) ("[I]ntervention on appeal will be permitted 'only in exceptional case for imperative reasons.'").

[42] *See, e.g., Negron-Almeda v. Santiago,* 528 F.3d 15, 21 (1st Cir. 2008) (applying abuse of discretion standard to district court's ruling regarding timeliness of motion for intervention as of right, holding "abuse of discretion is a relatively deferential standard of review" but not a "rubber stamp"). *Caterino v. Barry,* 922 F.2d 37, 40 (1st Cir. 1990) (trial court entitled to "substantive deference" on timeliness).

[43] *See, e.g., United Nuclear Corp. v. Cranford Ins. Co.,* 905 F.2d 1424, 1427 (10th Cir. 1990).

[44] *See, e.g., Empire Blue Cross & Blue Shield v. Janet Greeson's A Place For Us, Inc.,* 62 F.3d 1217, 1221 (9th Cir. 1995); *Banco Popular de Puerto Rico v. Greenblatt,* 964 F.2d 1227, 1230–34 (1st Cir. 1992).

[45] *See Citizens for Balanced Use v. Montana Wilderness Ass'n,* 647 F.3d 893 897 (9th Cir. 2011). *See also United States v. Ritchie Special Credit Investments, Ltd.,* 620 F.3d 824, 831 (8th Cir. 2010) (construes the intervention rule liberally and resolves any doubts in favor of the proposed intervenors).

[46] *See, e.g., Ungar v. Arafat,* 634 F.3d 46 (1st Cir. 2011).

[47] *See Stuart v. Huff,* 706 F.3d 345, 350 (4th Cir. 2013).

[48] *See, e.g., United States v. City of Detroit,* 712 F.3d 925, 931 (6th Cir. 2013) ("But courts are not faced with an all-or-nothing choice between grant or denial: Rule 24 also provides for limited-in-scope intervention;" citing advisory committee's note and cases permitting conditional or limited intervention); *Colony Ins. Co. v. Burke,* 698 F.3d 1222, 1239 (10th Cir. 2012) ("even an intervenor of right . . . does not have an unlimited right to participate in every aspect of the litigation").

[49] 28 U.S.C.A. § 1332.

[50] 28 U.S.C.A. § 1331.

[51] 28 U.S.C.A. § 1367.

will not be able to employ supplemental jurisdiction.[52] If, on the other hand, the intervenor will be aligned as a defendant, supplemental jurisdiction will normally be available.[53] Moreover, where a non-diverse party who is not indispensable under Rule 19 seeks to intervene, diversity jurisdiction is not necessarily defeated.[54]

Where the original basis for jurisdiction in the underlying case is a federal question, supplemental jurisdiction is routinely available without regard to the intervenor's status as a plaintiff or defendant.[55]

Ordinarily, an intervenor's arrival into a lawsuit cannot rescue an absence of subject matter jurisdiction.[56] Where, however, the intervention is sought early in the action (and before the defendants have acted), a court might treat the pleading of the intervenor as a separate action even if the underlying claim is jurisdictionally deficient.[57]

Standing Requirement and Interventors

The courts are divided on whether the intervenor, like a party, must satisfy the requirement of independent standing.[58] In considering the issue, one Circuit concluded that neglecting to require standing by intervenors would make intervention of right too easy and thus "clutter too many lawsuits with too many parties."[59]

---

[52] 28 U.S.C.A. § 1367(b) (in cases where original basis of jurisdiction is diversity and person intervening under Rule 24 will be aligned as a plaintiff, supplemental jurisdiction is not available). *See Exxon Mobil Corp. v. Allapattah Servs., Inc.,* 545 U.S. 546, 125 S.Ct. 2611, 2621, 162 L.Ed.2d 502 (2005) ("Section 1367(b) withholds supplemental jurisdiction over the claims of plaintiffs who seek to intervene pursuant to Rule 24."). *But cf. Aurora Loan Servs., Inc. v. Craddieth,* 442 F.3d 1018, 1025 (7th Cir. 2006) (in diversity cases supplemental jurisdiction normally not available to intervenor plaintiffs; but prohibition on use of supplemental jurisdiction inapplicable where a person is "forced to intervene to protect an interest that arose during the course of a federal litigation in which he had no stake at the outset").

[53] *See Exxon Mobil Corp. v. Allapattah Servs., Inc.,* 545 U.S. 546, 125 S.Ct. 2611, 2621, 162 L.Ed.2d 502 (2005) (noting that 28 U.S.C.A. § 1367(b) does not prohibit use of supplemental jurisdiction in such circumstances).

[54] *In re Olympic Mills Corp.,* 477 F.3d 1, 12 (1st Cir. 2007) (in bankruptcy case, court reviewed case law and concluded "the weight of authority holds that claims launched by necessary but dispensable, nondiverse defendant-intervenors do not defeat the original jurisdiction (diversity) that obtained at the commencement of the action").

[55] *See, e.g., Grace United Methodist Church v. City of Cheyenne,* 451 F.3d 643, 672–73 (10th Cir. 2006) (for intervention of right in case originally based on federal question jurisdiction, supplemental jurisdiction is sufficient and no independent basis of jurisdiction is require).

[56] *See e.g., Police & Fire Retirement Sys. of City of Detroit v. IndyMac MBS, Inc.,* 721 F.3d 95 (2d Cir. 2013) (stating rule and holding that where no named plaintiff in the suit had constitutional standing to bring asserted claims intervention not proper); *Disability Advocates, Inc. v. New York Coalition for Quality Assisted Living, Inc.,* 675 F.3d 149, 160–161 (2d Cir. 2012) (intervention denied six years into litigation and after five week hearing where court found original plaintiffs lacked standing).

[57] *See, e.g., Miller & Miller Auctioneers, Inc. v. G.W. Murphy Indus., Inc.,* 472 F.2d 893, 895–96 (10th Cir. 1973) (upheld interpleader where intervenor had separate and independent basis for jurisdiction despite lack of jurisdiction for underlying case); *Hackner v. Guar. Trust Co.,* 117 F.2d 95, 98 (2d Cir. 1941) (Amendment to Complaint adding plaintiff filed twenty-two days after initial complaint and before any action by the defendants).

[58] *See, e.g., Deutsche Bank Nat'l Trust Co. v. F.D.I.C.,* 717 F.3d 189 (D.C. Cir. 2013) (discussing split among circuits and concluding that the D.C. Circuit requires that intervenors have Article III standing); *American Auto. Ins. Co. v. Murray,* 658 F.3d 311, 318 n.4 (3d Cir. 2011) (neither this Court nor the Supreme Court has determined whether a potential intervenor must have Article III standing); *Diamond v. Charles,* 476 U.S. 54, 68–69, 106 S.Ct. 1697, 90 L.Ed.2d 48 (1986) (leaving undecided the question whether every intervenor must demonstrate standing in addition to the requirements of Rule 24).

[59] *See City of Chicago v. Federal Emergency Mgmt. Agency,* 660 F.3d 980, 984–85 (7th Cir. 2011).

Personal Jurisdiction

When a person attempts to intervene, that person submits to the jurisdiction of the court.[60] However, where the would-be intervenor simultaneously objects to personal jurisdiction, the court may rule that such consent is absent.[61]

Class Actions

A class member seeking intervention as of right must satisfy the same requirements as other intervenors.[62] It is settled that if a non-named class member objects in a timely manner to a proposed settlement, that member need not intervene in order to appeal the settlement.[63] In a class action lawsuit, the timeliness clock does not start running until the putative intervenor knows that the class representative will not represent his interest.[64]

Amicus Curiae Are Not Intervenors

Courts do not equate amicus status with the rights and responsibilities of a party joined through intervention.[65]

RULE 24(b)—PERMISSIVE INTERVENTION

CORE CONCEPT

An applicant who lacks an enforceable right to intervene (under Rule 24(a)) may request the court to allow an intervention permissively. This process applies a substantially more relaxed approach to motions to intervene,[66] and does not obligate the applicant to demonstrate the sort of interest required for intervention of right. Instead, a court may grant permissive intervention when it has an independent ground for jurisdiction and the intervention is either conditionally authorized by statute or is timely sought by motion and raises a common question of law or fact.[67] The court's discretion to grant or reject such intervention applications is broader than with intervention of right.[68]

---

[60] *See, e.g., County Sec. Agency v. Ohio Dept. of Commerce,* 296 F.3d 477 (6th Cir. 2002) (refusing to permit reservation of objections to jurisdiction made by petitioning intervenor; "a motion to intervene is fundamentally incompatible with an objection to personal jurisdiction").

[61] *See S.E.C. v. Ross,* 504 F.3d 1130, 1149–50 (9th Cir. 2007) (reviews cases and acknowledges that courts have generally concluded that a party who intervenes consents to jurisdiction as a matter of law, but declines to find such consent where intervenor objected to court's exercise of personal jurisdiction, sufficiency of process, and venue).

[62] *See In re Pet Foods Products Liability Litig.,* 629 F.3d 333, 349 (3d Cir. 2010).

[63] *See Devlin v. Scardelletti,* 536 U.S. 1, 122 S.Ct. 2005, 153 L.Ed.2d 27 (2002) (held, such a party easily satisfies standing requirement, and right to appeal is not restricted to named parties).

[64] *See, e.g., In re Lease Oil Antitrust Litig.,* 570 F.3d 244, 248 (5th Cir. 2009). *See also Sierra Club v. Espy,* 18 F.3d 1202, 1206 (5th Cir. 1994) (noting alacrity with which would-be intervenor acted when it became aware that its interest would no longer be protected by original parties).

[65] *See, e.g., United States v. City of Los Angeles,* 288 F.3d 391, 400 (9th Cir. 2002) ("[A]micus status is insufficient to protect the [petitioner for intervention's] rights because such status does not allow the [petitioner] to raise issues or arguments formally and gives it no right of appeal."); *Coalition of Arizona/New Mexico Counties for Stable Economic Growth v. Department of Interior,* 100 F.3d 837, 844 (10th Cir. 1996) ("[T]he right to file a brief as amicus curiae is no substitute for the right to intervene as a party in the action under Rule 24(a)(2)."). Courts sometimes agree to consider the filings of a failed intervenor as they would the filings of amicus curiae. *See, e.g., Coalition to Defend Affirmative Action v. Regents of Univ. of Mich.,* 652 F.3d 607, 633 (6th Cir. 2011) (while party was rejected as intervenor, judges "nonetheless have considered his filings as we would those of amicus curiae").

[66] *Cf. Grochocinski v. Mayer Brown Rowe & Maw, LLP.,* 719 F.3d 785, 798, n.9 (7th Cir. 2013) (if intervention of right fails, permissive intervention may still be possible).

[67] *See Blum v. Merrill Lynch Pierce Fenner & Smith Inc.,* 712 F.3d 1349, 1353 (9th Cir. 2013).

[68] *See United States v. Albert Inv. Co., Inc.,* 585 F.3d 1386, 1390 (10th Cir. 2009).

APPLICATIONS

Permissive Intervention by Conditional Statutory Right

Fewer cases deal with permissive statutory intervention. Such statutes often afford the court authority to allow intervention by some public official, such as the Attorney General.[69] Although the paucity of case law makes conclusions difficult, the inclination of courts to construe narrowly statutes that clearly contemplate intervention as of right may suggest that courts will be inclined to construe the uncertain statutes as authorizing permissive statutory intervention under Rule 24(b)(1) rather than statutory intervention as of right under Rule 24(a)(1).

Permissive Intervention by Showing a Common Question of Law or Fact

More often, permissive intervention is granted where the person seeking it demonstrates a common question of law or fact between that person's claim or defense and the pending litigation.[70]

Standing for Non-Statutory Permissive Intervention

Although a person seeking intervention under Rule 24(b)(2) need not demonstrate an "interest" within the kinds contemplated by Rule 24(a)(2), the person seeking permissive intervention may be required to have a sufficient stake in the litigation to satisfy ordinary requirements for standing.[71] Whether standing is required for permissive intervention may depend on the type of case and the status of the case at the time.[72]

Independent Basis for Subject Matter Jurisdiction

Persons attempting to intervene under Rule 24(b)(2) must establish an independent basis for subject matter jurisdiction. Supplemental jurisdiction is not available to would-be permissive intervenors.[73]

Timing

Applications to intervene under Rule 24(b) must be "timely". The determination of what constitutes a timely application rests within the court's discretion in the context of the facts in a particular case.[74] Because Rule 24(b) intervention questions do not typically affect the interests of nonparties as importantly as Rule 24(a) intervention of right cases, courts tend

---

[69] *See, e.g.,* 42 U.S.C.A. § 2000a–3(a).

[70] *See, e.g., Kootenai Tribe of Idaho v. Veneman,* 313 F.3d 1094, 1108 (9th Cir. 2002) (standard for permissive intervention under Rule 24(b) is common question of law or fact, not more rigorous standard of interest that may be impaired).

[71] *See, e.g., United States v. Napper,* 887 F.2d 1528, 1532 (11th Cir. 1989) (standing is required for both intervenors of right and permissive intervenors). *See also Defenders of Wildlife v. Perciasepe,* 714 F.3d 1317, 1327 (D.C. Cir. 2013) (issue of whether standing required for permissive intervention is an open question in D.C. Circuit). *Cf. City of Herriman v. Bell,* 590 F.3d 1176, 1184 (10th Cir. 2010) (while would-be intervenor need not have standing in the Tenth Circuit, the claimant must "have a claim or defense that shares at least some aspect with a claim or defense presented", and the City of Herriman, as a political subdivision, lacked authority to bring equal protection challenge against another political subdivision and therefore could not intervene in equal protection suit brought by voters).

[72] *See Bond v. Utreras,* 585 F.3d 1061, 1069–70 (7th Cir. 2009) (setting aside parties to the pending litigation, questions of whether a permissive intervenor must establish standing to challenge a protective order in an ongoing case, but holding that an intervenor must establish standing to challenge a protective order after the case has been dismissed).

[73] *See, e.g., E.E.O.C. v. National Children's Ctr., Inc.,* 146 F.3d 1042, 1046 (D.C. Cir. 1998) ("Permissive intervention . . . has always required an independent basis for jurisdiction.").

[74] *See, e.g., Blum v. Merrill Lynch Pierce Fenner & Smith Inc.,* 712 F.3d 1349, 1353 (9th Cir. 2013) (motion to intervene to modify protective order in long concluded litigation not untimely; collecting cases); *Fox v. Tyson Foods, Inc.,* 519 F.3d 1298, 1304–1305 (11th Cir. 2008) (district court did not clearly abuse discretion in denying permissive intervention of 161 petitioners where action had been filed several years earlier and employer would need at least one additional year to depose the petitioners).

to hold motions for permissive intervention to a more rigorous standard of timeliness than would be applied to motions for intervention of right.[75]

Delay or Prejudice

Permissive intervention may be denied if it would unduly delay or prejudice the pending litigation. That might occur if the complexity added by an intervenor would prolong the litigation excessively.[76] Similarly, inappropriate prejudice to existing parties might occur if the presence of the intervenor might shift the focus of the litigation from the pending issues to those newly introduced by the intervenor.[77] Rule 24(b)(3) has been interpreted to suggest "that intervention postjudgment—which necessarily disturbs the final adjudication of the parties' rights—should generally be disfavored."[78] To the extent that the intervenor's claim is duplicative or weak on its merits, the court will be inclined to give greater weight to concerns about delay or prejudice.[79]

Discretion

The standard of review for permissive intervention is clear abuse of discretion.[80] The district court must, of course, apply the correct legal standard to be entitled to this deference.[81] A district court's decision to deny permissive intervention is rarely overturned on appeal.[82]

---

[75] *See, e.g., Banco Popular de Puerto Rico v. Greenblatt,* 964 F.2d 1227, 1230 (1st Cir. 1992) (timeliness standard more strict for Rule 24(a) than Rule 24(b)). *Cf. R & G Mortg. Corp. v. Federal Home Loan Mortg. Corp.,* 584 F.3d 1, 11 (1st Cir. 2009) (when intervenor seeks both as of right and permissive intervention, a finding of untimeliness with respect to the former normally applies to the latter).

[76] *See, e.g., McHenry v. C.I.R.,* 677 F.3d 214, 216 (4th Cir. 2012) (permissive intervention by the Government of the United States Virgin Islands denied where it would "introduce redundancy into the proceedings"; Virgin Islands sought to intervene in tax case claiming interpretation of law could discourage entrepreneurs from coming to the Virgin Islands); *Massachusetts v. Microsoft Corp.,* 373 F.3d 1199 (D.C. Cir.2004) (prejudice evaluation "captures all the possible drawbacks of piling on parties," including extra cost and increased risk of error).

[77] *See Alaniz v. Tillie Lewis Foods,* 572 F.2d 657, 659 (9th Cir. 1978), (per curiam).

[78] *See Bond v. Utreras,* 585 F.3d 1061, 1071 (7th Cir. 2009); *Farmland Dairies v. Commissioner of New York State Dep't of Agriculture & Markets,* 847 F.2d 1038, 1044 (2d Cir. 1988) (post-judgment intervention is disfavored). *See also Beaver v. Alaniz,* 439 U.S. 837, 99 S.Ct. 123, 58 L.Ed.2d 134 (1978) (post-resolution intervention often unfairly hard on existing parties).
But see Blum v. Merrill Lynch Pierce Fenner & Smith Inc., 712 F.3d 1349, 1354 (9th Cir. 2013) (no prejudice where action between original litigants had been settled).

[79] *See, e.g., Massachusetts v. Microsoft Corp.,* 373 F.3d 1199 (D.C. Cir.2004) (but in instant case intervention is appropriate because concerns about delay or prejudice are minimal).

[80] *See, e.g., Blum v. Merrill Lynch Pierce Fenner & Smith Inc.,* 712 F.3d 1349, 1352 (9th Cir. 2013).

[81] *See Coffey v. C.I.R.,* 663 F.3d 947, 951 (8th Cir. 2011) (reversed denial of permissive intervention where district court considered, whether the proposed intervenor's participation was "necessary to advocate for an unaddressed issue" rather than the correct standard, "whether the intervention will cause 'undue delay' or 'prejudice the adjudication of the original parties' rights', citing Rule 24 (b)(3)); *Freedom from Religion Found., Inc. v. Geithner,* 644 F.3d 836 (9th Cir. 2011) (reversed denial of permissive intervention where district court rejected the motion opining that intervention would destroy diversity jurisdiction; the jurisdiction in question was actually based on a federal question).

[82] *See, e.g., Northland Family Planning Clinic, Inc. v. Cox,* 487 F.3d 323, 346 (6th Cir. 2007) (denial of permissive intervention is reversed only for clear abuse of discretion by trial judge); *Purcell v. BankAtlantic Fin. Corp.,* 85 F.3d 1508, 1513 (11th Cir. 1996) (Rule 24(b) intervention is "wholly discretionary" even where the requirements of Rule 24(b) are satisfied); *Shea v. Angulo,* 19 F.3d 343, 346 (7th Cir. 1994) (reversal of district court's decision denying permissive intervention " 'is a very rare bird indeed, so seldom seen as to be unique.' ").

Permissive Intervention for Public Officials

Permissive intervention is authorized for officers or agencies if the pending litigation raises questions of law administered by the officer or agency, or questions of regulations issued by the officer or agency.[83]

Conditional Permissive Intervention

If permissive intervention is granted, the court has substantial authority to impose conditions on the intervention.[84]

RULE 24(c)—NOTICE AND PLEADING REQUIRED

CORE CONCEPT

Intervention motions must be served on the existing litigants, state the grounds for intervention, and be accompanied by the prospective intervenor's pleading.

APPLICATIONS

Service of Process

The motion to intervene should be filed with the court and served on all persons as provided in Rule 5.[85]

Service of Proposed Pleading

Accompanying the as-filed and as-served motion must be a proposed pleading by the intervenor that sets out the claim or defense for which intervention is being sought.[86]

Failure to Meet Motion, Pleading, and Service Requirements

Courts are divided on the consequences of an applicant's failure to meet the motion, service, and pleading requirements for intervention. A majority holds that failure to comply with these requirements should not alone disqualify the attempt to intervene,[87] while a minority would be more rigorous.[88]

---

[83] *See, e.g., Harris v. Amoco Prod'n Co.,* 768 F.2d 669, 680 (5th Cir. 1985) (citing federal law authorizing permissive intervention for federal agency).

[84] *See, e.g., Beauregard, Inc. v. Sword Servs. L.L.C.,* 107 F.3d 351, 352 (5th Cir. 1997) ("It is undisputed that virtually any condition may be attached to a grant of permissive intervention."); *Vassalle v. Midland Funding LLC,* 708 F.3d 747, 759 (6th Cir. 2013) (upheld intervention to present objections to proposed settlement, discovery by intervenor not permitted).

[85] *See, e.g., In re Chinese Manufactured Drywall Products Liability Litig.,* 753 F.3d 576, 593 (5th Cir. 2014) (noting application of Rule 5).

[86] *See, e.g., Bridges v. Dep't of Maryland State Police,* 441 F.3d 197, 208 (4th Cir. 2006) (pleading gives existing parties notice of claim or defense for which intervention is sought); *Retired Chicago Police Ass'n v. City of Chicago,* 7 F.3d 584, 595 (7th Cir. 1993) (for purposes of Rule 24(c), intervenor should provide an original pleading, not merely an adoption by reference of prior pleadings; Rule 10(c), permitting adoption by reference in other situations, does not apply to pleadings required under Rule 24(c)).

[87] *See, e.g., Westchester Fire Ins. Co. v. Mendez,* 585 F.3d 1183, 1189 (9th Cir. 2009) (allowed intervention despite failure to file a pleading, holding that interest did not disappear because of a "procedural misstep"); *United States v. Metropolitan St. Louis Sewer District,* 569 F.3d 829, 834 (8th Cir. 2009) ("statement of interest" provided sufficient notice and thereby satisfied requirement); *Providence Baptist Church v. Hillandale Comm., Ltd.,* 425 F.3d 309, 314 (6th Cir. 2005) (abuse of discretion to reject motion to intervene for failure to include pleading).

[88] *See, e.g., King v. University Healthcare Sys., L.C.,* 645 F.3d 713, 727 (5th Cir. 2011) (would-be intervenor/law firm attempted to attach judgment to former client through "a largely unexplained motion asking us to enforce a statutory privilege in its favor;" court denied motion to amend and to intervene); *Hollywood Mobile Estates Ltd. v. Seminole Tribe of Florida,* 641 F.3d 1259 (11th Cir. 2011) (would-be intervenor failed to attach copy of pleading to motion and so did not establish constitutional standing; motion to amend complaint denied as "futile" after conclusion that intervenors did not have standing in any case); *Public Serv. Co. of New Hampshire v. Patch,* 136 F.3d 197, 205 n.6 (1st Cir. 1998) (failure to include pleading "ordinarily would warrant dismissal" of motion, but such result unnecessary in instant case because lower court rejected motion on other grounds).

ADDITIONAL RESEARCH REFERENCES

Wright & Miller, *Federal Practice and Procedure* §§ 1900 to 23

C.J.S., Federal Civil Procedure §§ 128 to 155

West's Key Number Digest, Federal Civil Procedure ⊶311 to 345

RULE 25

SUBSTITUTION OF PARTIES

(a) Death.

    (1) *Substitution if the Claim Is Not Extinguished.* If a party dies and the claim is not extinguished, the court may order substitution of the proper party. A motion for substitution may be made by any party or by the decedent's successor or representative. If the motion is not made within 90 days after service of a statement noting the death, the action by or against the decedent must be dismissed.

    (2) *Continuation Among the Remaining Parties.* After a party's death, if the right sought to be enforced survives only to or against the remaining parties, the action does not abate, but proceeds in favor of or against the remaining parties. The death should be noted on the record.

    (3) *Service.* A motion to substitute, together with a notice of hearing, must be served on the parties as provided in Rule 5 and on nonparties as provided in Rule 4. A statement noting death must be served in the same manner. Service may be made in any judicial district.

(b) Incompetency. If a party becomes incompetent, the court may, on motion, permit the action to be continued by or against the party's representative. The motion must be served as provided in Rule 25(a)(3).

(c) Transfer of Interest. If an interest is transferred, the action may be continued by or against the original party unless the court, on motion, orders the transferee to be substituted in the action or joined with the original party. The motion must be served as provided in Rule 25(a)(3).

(d) Public Officers; Death or Separation from Office. An action does not abate when a public officer who is a party in an official capacity dies, resigns, or otherwise ceases to hold office while the action is pending. The officer's successor is automatically substituted as a party. Later proceedings should be in the substituted party's name, but any misnomer not affecting the parties' substantial rights must be disregarded. The court may order substitution at any time, but the absence of such an order does not affect the substitution.

[Amended effective October 20, 1949; July 19, 1961; July 1, 1963; August 1, 1987; April 30, 2007, effective December 1, 2007.]

AUTHORS' COMMENTARY ON RULE 25

PURPOSE AND SCOPE

Rule 25 prescribes the process for substituting parties in a pending lawsuit following a party's death, incompetency, transfer of interest, or departure from public office.

RULE 25(a)—DEATH

CORE CONCEPT

A successor can be substituted for a party who dies, provided the applicable substantive law permits the claim in litigation to survive.

APPLICATIONS

When Substitution Is Permitted

A threshold prerequisite for substitution requires that the claim in litigation must be capable of surviving the death of the party, a matter which is resolved by deferring to the controlling federal or state law.[1] If, under that controlling law, the claim does not survive the death of a party, there can be no substitution.[2]

- *Multi-Party Litigations:* In multi-party litigation, the controlling substantive law might extinguish the deceased party's claim, yet still permit the right at issue to be enforced by (or against) the remaining parties. In such instances, the lawsuit does not abate, but proceeds with the remaining parties alone. The death should, however, be noted in the case record.

Procedure for Substitution—Suggestion of Death

The fact that a party has died is brought to the court's attention by a written "suggestion of death," filed and served on all parties pursuant to Rule 5.[3] Nonparty representatives of the deceased should be served pursuant to Rule 4.[4]

Procedure for Substitution—Motion for Substitution

Next,[5] any party, or persons affiliated with the deceased party, will make a motion for substitution.[6] The motion (along with a notice of hearing) must be filed and served on all parties in accordance with Rule 5 and on any nonparties in accordance with Rule 4.[7] Service may be made in any federal judicial district.[8] Until a motion for substitution has been made and granted, the court has no authority to proceed with the deceased party's case.[9]

---

[1]   *See Figueroa v. Secretary of Health & Human Servs.,* 715 F.3d 1314, 1321 (Fed. Cir. 2013).

[2]   *See, e.g., Asklar v. Honeywell, Inc.,* 95 F.R.D. 419, 422 (D. Conn. 1982) (substantive law determines whether case may proceed after death of party).

[3]   *See Grandbouche v. Lovell,* 913 F.2d 835, 836 (10th Cir. 1990).

[4]   *See Barlow v. Ground,* 39 F.3d 231, 233 (9th Cir. 1994) (requiring service on nonparty representatives of estate under Rule 4).

[5]   It is not essential that the service of a motion for substitution always await the filing of the formal suggestion of death. *See Dolgow v. Anderson,* 45 F.R.D. 470, 471 (E.D.N.Y. 1968).

[6]   *See, e.g., In re Baycol Prods. Litig.,* 616 F.3d 778, 785 (8th Cir. 2010) ("successor" can include persons, apart from administrator or executor of estate, who may move for substitution; persons eligible for status of successor include: primary distributee of estate that has been distributed; named executor of estate, "even if the will is not probated;" "primary beneficiary of an unprobated intestate, which need not be probated;" acknowledging that state law governs who may be a successor); *Atkins v. City of Chicago,* 547 F.3d 869, 872 (7th Cir. 2008) (attorney for deceased party may not file motion on his own behalf or on behalf of deceased client, but may file motion if estate is not represented by executor or administrator); *Unicorn Tales, Inc. v. Banerjee,* 138 F.3d 467 (2d Cir.1998) (suggestion can be made by widow who is not a party, and need not be made by formally appointed representative of estate).

[7]   *See Rule 25(a)(3). See also Giles v. Campbell,* 698 F.3d 153, 158 (3d Cir. 2012).

[8]   *See Rule 25(a)(3).*

[9]   *See, e.g., Campbell v. State of Iowa, Third Judicial District Dep't of Correctional Servs.,* 702 F.3d 1140, 1141–42 (8th Cir. 2013) (court may not proceed until proper party is substituted for deceased person).

Procedure for Substitution—Time for Making

Motions for substitution must be made within 90 days after the "suggestion of death" is served.[10] Although a party may have been deceased for a substantial period before a formal "suggestion of death" is made, the 90-day limitation is not usually triggered until the that filing occurs.[11] If, however, the movant delays more than 90 days after the "suggestion of death" is made, the action by or against the deceased "must" be dismissed.[12] Notwithstanding this apparently mandatory language, however, courts have exercised discretion to extend the time in which a party may move for substitution.[13]

Hearing

If there is a dispute as to the appropriateness of the proposed substituted party, the court has a duty to resolve the issue and may hold a hearing before ruling on the motion.[14] The notice of hearing should be filed and served on all parties in the manner provided by Rule 5.

Status of Successor

A party who replaces a deceased party receives the status the deceased party possessed at the time of death. For example, if the deceased party had already consented to trial by a magistrate judge, the successor is bound by that consent.[15]

RULE 25(b)—INCOMPETENCY

CORE CONCEPT

On motion, a successor can also be substituted for a party who becomes incompetent in the course of litigation.

APPLICATIONS

Survival of the Action

Incompetency will not extinguish a cause of action.

Procedure for Substitution—Motion for Substitution

The incompetent party's representation must file a motion with the court for substitution.[16] The motion (along with a notice of hearing) must be filed and served on all

---

[10] *See* Rule 25(a)(1).

[11] *See generally* 7C CHARLES ALAN WRIGHT, ARTHUR R. MILLER, & MARY KAY KANE, FEDERAL PRACTICE AND PROCEDURE § 1955 (2007) ("It is no longer the date of death that starts the time for substitution running, as it has been under the former rule. Instead, the time does not run until the death is noted on the record by service of a statement of the fact of death, and there is no particular time period within which that statement must be made after the death occurs.") (footnotes omitted). *But see Miles, Inc. v. Scripps Clinic and Research Foundation,* 810 F.Supp. 1091, 1102 (S.D. Cal. 1993) (party who delays unreasonably in filing suggestion of death may be denied permission to substitute a party).

[12] *See* Rule 25(a)(3).

[13] *See, e.g., Atkins v. City of Chicago,* 547 F.3d 869, 872 (7th Cir. 2008) (time does not start to run until all parties and interested nonparties have been served); *Continental Bank, N.A. v. Meyer,* 10 F.3d 1293, 1297 (7th Cir. 1993) (extensions of 90-day time period may be granted liberally). *But see Kaubisch v. Weber,* 408 F.3d 540, 543 (8th Cir. 2005) (acknowledging district court's discretion; but "the misapplication or misreading of the plain language of Rule 25 does not establish excusable neglect").

[14] *See, e.g., Escareno v. Noltina Crucible & Refractory Corp.,* 139 F.3d 1456 (11th Cir.1998) (court has duty to determine whether substitute party-here an administrator of estate-was properly appointed; issue in instant case was whether probate court had jurisdiction to appoint administrator).

[15] *See, e.g., Brook, Weiner, Sered, Kreger & Weinberg v. Coreq, Inc.,* 53 F.3d 851, 852 (7th Cir. 1995) ("A successor takes over without any other change in the status of the case," and therefore decedent's consent to trial by magistrate judge binds successor).

[16] *See* Rule 25(b).

parties in accordance with Rule 5 and on any nonparties in accordance with Rule 4, and service may be made in any federal judicial district.[17]

Procedure for Substitution—Timing

The Rule contains no express reference to time limitations for motions to substitute incompetent parties, though some courts have imposed a "reasonable" time filing obligation.[18]

RULE 25(c)—TRANSFER OF INTEREST

CORE CONCEPT

When the holder of an interest in litigation transfers that interest to another, the lawsuit may be continued by (or against) that original party. However, the transferee may, upon motion, seek permission to join in the lawsuit or to substitute in place of the original party.

APPLICATIONS

Option to Substitute Parties

The new holder of the interest is not required to be substituted for the transferor-party.[19] Instead, the action to continue in the name of the transferor unless the court chooses to order the joinder or substitution of the transferee.[20] Thus, the case may go to judgment without any substitution of parties having occurred, and the absence of a formal substitution will have no consequence.[21] If it is appropriate in the circumstances of the particular case, both the transferor and transferee will be bound by the court's judgment.[22]

When the Transferee Is Bound

For Rule 25(c) to bind a transferee to the same obligations that burdened the transferor, an "interest" must be transferred between the parties.[23] The Rule does not define an interest, but it appears settled that the mere purchase of assets by a successor entity does not usually bind the successor to the obligations of the transferor.[24]

---

[17] *See* Rule 25(b) (adopting by reference Rule 25(a)(3)).

[18] *See Kuelbs v. Hill,* 615 F.3d 1037, 1042 (8th Cir. 2010) (if party becomes incompetent during pendency of case, Rule 25(b) motion for substitution must take place in reasonable period of time; otherwise action may be dismissed under Rule 17(a)).

[19] *See, e.g., F.D.I.C. v. SLE, Inc.,* 722 F.3d 264 (5th Cir. 2013) (Rule 25(c) does not require transferee to be substituted in place of original party); *In re Bernal,* 207 F.3d 595, 598 (9th Cir. 2000) (Rule 25(c) requires no action by anyone after a transfer of interest; judgment binds successor in interest even if successor is not named).

[20] *See, e.g., Burka v. Aetna Life Ins. Co.,* 87 F.3d 478 (D.C. Cir. 1996) (noting that Rule 25(c) affords option of replacing one party with another, or joining a person with original party).

[21] *See, e.g., Arnold Graphics Indus., Inc. v. Indep't Agent Ctr., Inc.,* 775 F.2d 38, 40 (2d Cir. 1985) (enforcing judgment against successor corporation where substitution was made only after judgment).

[22] *See, e.g., Luxliner P.L. Export, Co. v. RDI/Luxliner, Inc.,* 13 F.3d 69, 71 (3d Cir. 1993) (even if no substitution is sought, judgment against original defendant can bind successor). *But cf. Organic Cow, LLC v. Center for New England Dairy Compact Research,* 335 F.3d 66, 72 (2d Cir. 2003) ("Where . . . a government entity terminates with no provision for naming a successor and with no appropriate governmental body to stand in its shoes for purposes of litigation . . . there can be no substitution of parties under Rule 25.").

[23] *See, e.g., Sullivan v. Running Waters Irrigation, Inc.,* 739 F.3d 354, 357 (7th Cir. 2014).

[24] *See, e.g., Sullivan v. Running Waters Irrigation, Inc.,* 739 F.3d 354, 357–58 (7th Cir. 2014). *But see Upholsterers' International Union Pension Fund v. Artistic Furniture of Pontiac,* 920 F.2d 1323, 1327–29 (7th Cir. 1990) (in ERISA action to recover delinquent pension fund obligation, purchase of assets is transfer of interest under Rule 25(c) that creates binding obligations in transferee entity).

Procedure for Substitution—Motion for Substitution

A transferee who seeks to join or substitute must file a motion with the court.[25] The motion (along with a notice of hearing) must be filed and served on all parties in accordance with Rule 5 and on any nonparties in accordance with Rule 4, and service may be made in any federal judicial district.[26]

Procedure for Substitution—Timing

The Rule contains no express reference to time limitations for motions by transferees to join or substitute.

Subject Matter Jurisdiction

Joinder of a nondiverse transferee under Rule 25(c) does not usually destroy diversity jurisdiction.[18] However, if the nondiverse transferee was someone who would have been indispensable under Rule 19 at the time the case was filed, joinder will destroy diversity jurisdiction.[19]

Personal Jurisdiction

When successors in interest are joined under Rule 25(c), they are subject to the personal jurisdiction of the court simply because they are successors in interest, "without regard to whether they had any other minimum contacts."[27]

Evidentiary Hearing

Although it will often be true that a court will conduct an evidentiary hearing, there is no express requirement that the district court conduct on prior to resolving a Rule 25(c) motion.[28]

Status of Successor

A party who enters a case as the legal successor of a corporation receives the status which the predecessor corporation possessed at the time the successor entered the case. For example, if the predecessor corporation had already consented to trial by a magistrate judge, the successor is bound by that consent.[29]

Relation to Rule 17

Rule 25(c) governs transfers of interest during the pendency of a case. Rule 17(a), by contrast, governs situations in which an interest is transferred before the suit is filed.[30]

---

[25] *See* Rule 25(c).

[26] *See* Rule 25(c) (adopting by reference Rule 25(a)(3)).

[18] *See Freeport-McMoRan, Inc. v. K N Energy, Inc.,* 498 U.S. 426, 428, 111 S.Ct. 858, 859, 112 L.Ed.2d 951 (1991) (per curiam) (any other result would impede "normal business transactions during the pendency of what might be lengthy litigation").

[19] *See Freeport-McMoRan, Inc. v. K N Energy, Inc.,* 498 U.S. 426, 111 S.Ct. 858, 112 L.Ed.2d 951 (1991) (per curiam).

[27] *See LiButti v. United States,*178 F.3d 114 (2d Cir. 1999) (collecting other case authority).

[28] *See, e.g., Sullivan v. Running Waters Irrigation, Inc.,* 739 F.3d 354, 359–60 (7th Cir. 2014) (particularly true where party did not request hearing or demonstrate need for hearing).

[29] *See, e.g., Andrews v. Lakeshore Rehabilitation Hosp.,* 140 F.3d 1405, 1408 (11th Cir. 1998) (where transfer of interest occurs prior to trial, Rule 25(c) is not applicable and therefore "does not save plaintiffs amendments from the statute of limitations"); *Brook, Weiner, Sered, Kreger & Weinberg v. Coreq, Inc.,* 53 F.3d 851, 852 (7th Cir. 1995) ("A successor takes over without any other change in the status of the case," and therefore a successor to a corporation is bound by the corporation's previous consent to trial by a magistrate judge).

[30] *See, e.g., F.D.I.C. v. Deglau,* 207 F.3d 153, 159 (3d Cir. 2000) (Rule 17 governs transfers prior to filing of lawsuit; after lawsuit begins, Rule 25 governs).

Extinguishing Corporate Causes of Action

Rule 25(c) is subordinate to substantive law on the issue of survival of a cause of action after corporate reorganizations. Thus, if substantive law directs that dissolution of a corporation also extinguishes the corporation's causes of action, Rule 25(c) will not save the cause of action.[20]

RULE 25(d)—PUBLIC OFFICERS; DEATH OR SEPARATION FROM OFFICE

CORE CONCEPT

When a public officer sues or is sued in an official capacity, but then ceases to hold that public office (through death, resignation, or otherwise), the departing officer's successor is substituted automatically into the lawsuit and the case continues.

APPLICATIONS

Applies in Official Capacity Lawsuits Only

This automatic substitution procedure applies only when public officers are named as parties in their official capacities. It does not control substitution where those persons (who happen to be public officers) are suing or being sued personally.[31]

Procedure for Substitution—No Motion Necessary

Because the substitution of public officers occurs automatically, there is no need to file or serve any motion for substitution.[32]

Procedure for Substitution—Timing

Likewise, because the Rule directs that substitution occur "automatically", there is no need for any time requirement.

Order of Substitution

The court has discretion to issue a formal order that a new public officer be substituted for a predecessor, but need not do so. However the court decides does not alter the fact that the automatic substitution has already occurred.[33]

---

[20] *See, e.g., Citibank v. Grupo Cupey, Inc.,* 382 F.3d 29, 32–33 (1st Cir. 2004) ("Rule 25 does not substantively determine what actions survive the transfer of an interest."); *ELCA Enters., Inc. v. Sisco Equipment Rental & Sales, Inc.,* 53 F.3d 186, 190 (8th Cir. 1995) ("Rule 25 does not substantively determine what actions survive the transfer of an interest; rather, it provides substitution procedures for an action that does survive."). *See also Organic Cow, LLC v. Center for New England Dairy Compact Research,* 335 F.3d 66 (2d Cir. 2003) (when mandate of commission created by Congress to administer dairy compact expired without renewal, private entity could not be substituted under Rule 25(c) because private entity had no authority to perform role of commission).

[31] *See, e.g., Society of Separationists v. Pleasant Grove City,* 416 F.3d 1239 (10th Cir.2005) (absence of claims against defendants personally makes substitution of successors proper, because suit was brought against elected officials in their official capacity); *Bunn v. Conley,* 309 F.3d 1002, 1009 (7th Cir. 2002) (*Bivens* claim is suit against government officer in individual (not official) capacity; thus newly appointed officer cannot be substituted for officer originally sued in individual capacity).

[32] *See Cheney v. U.S. Dist. Court for Dist. of Columbia,* 541 U.S. 913, 916, 124 S.Ct. 1391, 1395, 158 L.Ed.2d 225 (2004) (substitution is automatic). *See, e.g., King v. McMillan,* 594 F.3d 301, 308 (4th Cir. 2010) (state law cannot cut off substitution under Rule 25(d)); *Negron Gaztambide v. Hernandez Torres,* 145 F.3d 410 (1st Cir. 1998) (per curiam) (new officeholders are substituted automatically for their predecessors and automatically have same standing to litigate case).

[33] *See, e.g., Shakman v. Democratic Org. of Cook County,* 919 F.2d 455, 456 (7th Cir. 1990) (challenger who wins election against official defendant "automatically became a party to . . . consent decree").

Substitutions in the Caption of the Case

Proceedings subsequent to the substitution shall be in the name of the substituted party. However, this directive is usually no more than a formality, for no consequence attaches to the erroneous use of the name of the departing party—unless such error somehow has an adverse effect on the case.[34]

Effect of Automatic Substitution—Survival of the Action

An action by or against a public officer does not abate when the incumbent officer leaves his or her post.[35]

Events Prior to Substitution: Stipulations, Admissions, etc.

Substitution of an official for a predecessor in office ordinarily binds the successor to the results of previous events in the case as surely as if no substitution had been made.[36]

ADDITIONAL RESEARCH REFERENCES

Wright & Miller, *Federal Practice and Procedure* §§ 1951 to 62

C.J.S., Federal Civil Procedure §§ 156 to 168 et seq.

West's Key Number Digest, Federal Civil Procedure ⊷351 to 366, ⊷391

---

[34] *See, e.g., Cable v. Ivy Tech State College,* 200 F.3d 467, 475 (7th Cir. 1999) (Rule 17(d) "expressly directs that any misnomer of the parties that does not affect their substantive rights shall be disregarded even without a motion or order for substitution"); *Presbytery of New Jersey of Orthodox Presbyterian Church v. Florio,* 40 F.3d 1454, 1458 (3d Cir. 1994) (failure to amend caption to reflect election of new governor/defendant does not affect case).

[35] *See, e.g., Saldana-Sanchez v. Lopez-Gerena,* 256 F.3d 1, 10 (1st Cir. 2001) ("As Fed. R. Civ. P. 25(d)(1) makes clear, the substitution of a public official by his or her successor in an official capacity suit does not affect the underlying action.").

[36] *See, e.g., Morales Feliciano v. Rullan,* 303 F.3d 1, 7–8 (1st Cir. 2002) (holding that substituted party cannot repudiate stipulations to which predecessor agreed).

RULE 26

DUTY TO DISCLOSE; GENERAL PROVISIONS GOVERNING DISCOVERY

(a) Required Disclosures.

(1) *Initial Disclosure.*

(A) *In General.* Except as exempted by Rule 26(a)(1)(B) or as otherwise stipulated or ordered by the court, a party must, without awaiting a discovery request, provide to the other parties:

(i) the name and, if known, the address and telephone number of each individual likely to have discoverable information—along with the subjects of that information—that the disclosing party may use to support its claims or defenses, unless the use would be solely for impeachment;

(ii) a copy—or a description by category and location—of all documents, electronically stored information, and tangible things that the disclosing party has in its possession, custody, or control and may use to support its claims or defenses, unless the use would be solely for impeachment;

(iii) a computation of each category of damages claimed by the disclosing party—who must also make available for inspection and copying as under Rule 34 the documents or other evidentiary material, unless privileged or protected from disclosure, on which each computation is based, including materials bearing on the nature and extent of injuries suffered; and

(iv) for inspection and copying as under Rule 34, any insurance agreement under which an insurance business may be liable to satisfy all or part of a possible judgment in the action or to indemnify or reimburse for payments made to satisfy the judgment.

(B) *Proceedings Exempt from Initial Disclosure.* The following proceedings are exempt from initial disclosure:

(i) an action for review on an administrative record;

(ii) a forfeiture action in rem arising from a federal statute;

(iii) a petition for habeas corpus or any other proceeding to challenge a criminal conviction or sentence;

(iv) an action brought without an attorney by a person in the custody of the United States, a state, or a state subdivision;

(v) an action to enforce or quash an administrative summons or subpoena;

(vi) an action by the United States to recover benefit payments;

(vii) an action by the United States to collect on a student loan guaranteed by the United States;

(viii) a proceeding ancillary to a proceeding in another court; and

(ix) an action to enforce an arbitration award.

(C) *Time for Initial Disclosures—In General.* A party must make the initial disclosures at or within 14 days after the parties' Rule 26(f) conference unless a different time is set by stipulation or court order, or unless a party objects during the conference that initial disclosures are not appropriate in this action and states the objection in the proposed discovery plan. In ruling on the objection, the court must determine what disclosures, if any, are to be made and must set the time for disclosure.

(D) *Time for Initial Disclosures—For Parties Served or Joined Later.* A party that is first served or otherwise joined after the Rule 26(f) conference must make the initial disclosures within 30 days after being served or joined, unless a different time is set by stipulation or court order.

(E) *Basis for Initial Disclosure; Unacceptable Excuses.* A party must make its initial disclosures based on the information then reasonably available to it. A party is not excused from making its disclosures because it has not fully investigated the case or because it challenges the sufficiency of another party's disclosures or because another party has not made its disclosures.

(2) *Disclosure of Expert Testimony.*

(A) *In General.* In addition to the disclosures required by Rule 26(a)(1), a party must disclose to the other parties the identity of any witness it may use at trial to present evidence under Federal Rule of Evidence 702, 703, or 705.

(B) *Witnesses Who Must Provide a Written Report.* Unless otherwise stipulated or ordered by the court, this disclosure must be accompanied by a written report—prepared and signed by the witness—if the witness is one retained or specially employed to provide expert testimony in the case or one whose duties as the

party's employee regularly involve giving expert testimony. The report must contain:

   (i) a complete statement of all opinions the witness will express and the basis and reasons for them;

  (ii) the facts or data considered by the witness in forming them;

 (iii) any exhibits that will be used to summarize or support them;

 (iv) the witness's qualifications, including a list of all publications authored in the previous 10 years;

  (v) a list of all other cases in which, during the previous 4 years, the witness testified as an expert at trial or by deposition; and

 (vi) a statement of the compensation to be paid for the study and testimony in the case.

(C) *Witnesses Who Do Not Provide a Written Report.* Unless otherwise stipulated or ordered by the court, if the witness is not required to provide a written report, this disclosure must state:

  (i) the subject matter on which the witness is expected to present evidence under Federal Rule of Evidence 702, 703, or 705; and

  (ii) a summary of the facts and opinions to which the witness is expected to testify.

(D) *Time to Disclose Expert Testimony.* A party must make these disclosures at the times and in the sequence that the court orders. Absent a stipulation or a court order, the disclosures must be made:

  (i) at least 90 days before the date set for trial or for the case to be ready for trial; or

  (ii) if the evidence is intended solely to contradict or rebut evidence on the same subject matter identified by another party under Rule 26(a)(2)(B) or (C), within 30 days after the other party's disclosure.

(E) *Supplementing the Disclosure.* The parties must supplement these disclosures when required under Rule 26(e).

(3) *Pretrial Disclosures.*

(A) *In General.* In addition to the disclosures required by Rule 26(a)(1) and (2), a party must provide to the other parties and promptly file the following information about the evidence that it may present at trial other than solely for impeachment:

    (i) the name and, if not previously provided, the address and telephone number of each witness—separately identifying those the party expects to present and those it may call if the need arises;

    (ii) the designation of those witnesses whose testimony the party expects to present by deposition and, if not taken stenographically, a transcript of the pertinent parts of the deposition; and

    (iii) an identification of each document or other exhibit, including summaries of other evidence—separately identifying those items the party expects to offer and those it may offer if the need arises.

(B) *Time for Pretrial Disclosures; Objections.* Unless the court orders otherwise, these disclosures must be made at least 30 days before trial. Within 14 days after they are made, unless the court sets a different time, a party may serve and promptly file a list of the following objections: any objections to the use under Rule 32(a) of a deposition designated by another party under Rule 26(a)(3)(A)(ii); and any objection, together with the grounds for it, that may be made to the admissibility of materials identified under Rule 26(a)(3)(A)(iii). An objection not so made—except for one under Federal Rule of Evidence 402 or 403—is waived unless excused by the court for good cause.

(4) *Form of Disclosures.* Unless the court orders otherwise, all disclosures under Rule 26(a) must be in writing, signed, and served.

(b) Discovery Scope and Limits.

(1) *Scope in General.* Unless otherwise limited by court order, the scope of discovery is as follows: Parties may obtain discovery regarding any nonprivileged matter that is relevant to any party's claim or defense and proportional to the needs of the case, considering the importance of the issues at stake in the action, the amount in controversy, the parties' relative access to relevant information, the parties' resources, the importance of the discovery in resolving the issues, and whether the burden or expense of the proposed discovery outweighs its likely benefit. Information within this scope of discovery need not be admissible in evidence to be discoverable.

(2) *Limitations on Frequency and Extent.*

    (A) *When Permitted.* By order, the court may alter the limits in these rules on the number of depositions and interrogatories or on the

length of depositions under Rule 30. By order or local rule, the court may also limit the number of requests under Rule 36.

(B) *Specific Limitations on Electronically Stored Information.* A party need not provide discovery of electronically stored information from sources that the party identifies as not reasonably accessible because of undue burden or cost. On motion to compel discovery or for a protective order, the party from whom discovery is sought must show that the information is not reasonably accessible because of undue burden or cost. If that showing is made, the court may nonetheless order discovery from such sources if the requesting party shows good cause, considering the limitations of Rule 26(b)(2)(C). The court may specify conditions for the discovery.

(C) *When Required.* On motion or on its own, the court must limit the frequency or extent of discovery otherwise allowed by these rules or by local rule if it determines that:

(i)   the discovery sought is unreasonably cumulative or duplicative, or can be obtained from some other source that is more convenient, less burdensome, or less expensive;

(ii) the party seeking discovery has had ample opportunity to obtain the information by discovery in the action; or

(iii) the proposed discovery is outside the scope permitted by Rule 26(b)(1).

(3) *Trial Preparation: Materials.*

(A) *Documents and Tangible Things.* Ordinarily, a party may not discover documents and tangible things that are prepared in anticipation of litigation or for trial by or for another party or its representative (including the other party's attorney, consultant, surety, indemnitor, insurer, or agent). But, subject to Rule 26(b)(4), those materials may be discovered if:

(i)   they are otherwise discoverable under Rule 26(b)(1); and

(ii) the party shows that it has substantial need for the materials to prepare its case and cannot, without undue hardship, obtain their substantial equivalent by other means.

(B) *Protection Against Disclosure.* If the court orders discovery of those materials, it must protect against disclosure of the mental impressions, conclusions, opinions, or legal theories of a party's attorney or other representative concerning the litigation.

479

(C) *Previous Statement.* Any party or other person may, on request and without the required showing, obtain the person's own previous statement about the action or its subject matter. If the request is refused, the person may move for a court order, and Rule 37(a)(5) applies to the award of expenses. A previous statement is either:

    (i) a written statement that the person has signed or otherwise adopted or approved; or

    (ii) a contemporaneous stenographic, mechanical, electrical, or other recording—or a transcription of it—that recites substantially verbatim the person's oral statement.

(4) *Trial Preparation: Experts.*

    (A) *Deposition of an Expert Who May Testify.* A party may depose any person who has been identified as an expert whose opinions may be presented at trial. If Rule 26(a)(2)(B) requires a report from the expert, the deposition may be conducted only after the report is provided.

    (B) *Trial-Preparation Protection for Draft Reports or Disclosures.* Rules 26(b)(3)(A) and (B) protect drafts of any report or disclosure required under Rule 26(a)(2), regardless of the form in which the draft is recorded.

    (C) *Trial-Preparation Protection for Communications Between a Party's Attorney and Expert Witnesses.* Rules 26(b)(3)(A) and (B) protect communications between the party's attorney and any witness required to provide a report under Rule 26(a)(2)(B), regardless of the form of the communications, except to the extent that the communications:

        (i) relate to compensation for the expert's study or testimony;

        (ii) identify facts or data that the party's attorney provided and that the expert considered in forming the opinions to be expressed; or

        (iii) identify assumptions that the party's attorney provided and that the expert relied on in forming the opinions to be expressed.

    (D) *Expert Employed Only for Trial Preparation.* Ordinarily, a party may not, by interrogatories or deposition, discover facts known or opinions held by an expert who has been retained or specially employed by another party in anticipation of litigation or to prepare for trial and who is not expected to be called as a witness at trial. But a party may do so only:

        (i) as provided in Rule 35(b); or

          (ii) on showing exceptional circumstances under which it is impracticable for the party to obtain facts or opinions on the same subject by other means.

    (E) *Payment.* Unless manifest injustice would result, the court must require that the party seeking discovery:

          (i) pay the expert a reasonable fee for time spent in responding to discovery under Rule 26(b)(4)(A) or (D); and

          (ii) for discovery under (D), also pay the other party a fair portion of the fees and expenses it reasonably incurred in obtaining the expert's facts and opinions.

  (5) *Claiming Privilege or Protecting Trial-Preparation Materials.*

    (A) *Information Withheld.* When a party withholds information otherwise discoverable by claiming that the information is privileged or subject to protection as trial-preparation material, the party must:

          (i) expressly make the claim; and

          (ii) describe the nature of the documents, communications, or tangible things not produced or disclosed—and do so in a manner that, without revealing information itself privileged or protected, will enable other parties to assess the claim.

    (B) *Information Produced.* If information produced in discovery is subject to a claim of privilege or of protection as trial-preparation material, the party making the claim may notify any party that received the information of the claim and the basis for it. After being notified, a party must promptly return, sequester, or destroy the specified information and any copies it has; must not use or disclose the information until the claim is resolved; must take reasonable steps to retrieve the information if the party disclosed it before being notified; and may promptly present the information to the court under seal for a determination of the claim. The producing party must preserve the information until the claim is resolved.

(c) Protective Orders.

  (1) *In General.* A party or any person from whom discovery is sought may move for a protective order in the court where the action is pending—or as an alternative on matters relating to a deposition, in the court for the district where the deposition will be taken. The motion must include a certification that the movant has in good faith conferred or attempted to confer with other affected parties in an effort to resolve the dispute without court action. The court may, for good cause, issue an order to

protect a party or person from annoyance, embarrassment, oppression, or undue burden or expense, including one or more of the following:

(A) forbidding the disclosure or discovery;

(B) specifying terms, including time and place or the allocation of expenses, for the disclosure or discovery;

(C) prescribing a discovery method other than the one selected by the party seeking discovery;

(D) forbidding inquiry into certain matters, or limiting the scope of disclosure or discovery to certain matters;

(E) designating the persons who may be present while the discovery is conducted;

(F) requiring that a deposition be sealed and opened only on court order;

(G) requiring that a trade secret or other confidential research, development, or commercial information not be revealed or be revealed only in a specified way; and

(H) requiring that the parties simultaneously file specified documents or information in sealed envelopes, to be opened as the court directs.

(2) *Ordering Discovery.* If a motion for a protective order is wholly or partly denied, the court may, on just terms, order that any party or person provide or permit discovery.

(3) *Awarding Expenses.* Rule 37(a)(5) applies to the award of expenses.

(d) Timing and Sequence of Discovery.

(1) *Timing.* A party may not seek discovery from any source before the parties have conferred as required by Rule 26(f), except in a proceeding exempted from initial disclosure under Rule 26(a)(1)(B), or when authorized by these rules, by stipulation, or by court order.

(2) *Early Rule 34 Requests.*

(A) *Time to Deliver.* More than 21 days after the summons and complaint are served on a party, a request under Rule 34 may be delivered:

(i) to that party by any other party, and

(ii) by that party to any plaintiff or to any other party that has been served.

(B) *When Considered Served.* The request is considered to have been served at the first Rule 26(f) conference.

(3) *Sequence.* Unless the parties stipulate or the court orders otherwise for the parties' and witnesses' convenience and in the interests of justice:

(A) methods of discovery may be used in any sequence; and

(B) discovery by one party does not require any other party to delay its discovery.

(e) Supplementing Disclosures and Responses.

(1) *In General.* A party who has made a disclosure under Rule 26(a)—or who has responded to an interrogatory, request for production, or request for admission—must supplement or correct its disclosure or response:

(A) in a timely manner if the party learns that in some material respect the disclosure or response is incomplete or incorrect, and if the additional or corrective information has not otherwise been made known to the other parties during the discovery process or in writing; or

(B) as ordered by the court.

(2) *Expert Witness.* For an expert whose report must be disclosed under Rule 26(a)(2)(B), the party's duty to supplement extends both to information included in the report and to information given during the expert's deposition. Any additions or changes to this information must be disclosed by the time the party's pretrial disclosures under Rule 26(a)(3) are due.

(f) Conference of the Parties; Planning for Discovery.

(1) *Conference Timing.* Except in a proceeding exempted from initial disclosure under Rule 26(a)(1)(B) or when the court orders otherwise, the parties must confer as soon as practicable—and in any event at least 21 days before a scheduling conference is to be held or a scheduling order is due under Rule 16(b).

(2) *Conference Content; Parties' Responsibilities.* In conferring, the parties must consider the nature and basis of their claims and defenses and the possibilities for promptly settling or resolving the case; make or arrange for the disclosures required by Rule 26(a)(1); discuss any issues about preserving discoverable information; and develop a proposed discovery plan. The attorneys of record and all unrepresented parties that have appeared in the case are jointly responsible for arranging the conference, for attempting in good faith to agree on the proposed discovery plan, and for submitting to the court within 14 days after the conference a written report outlining the plan. The court may order the parties or attorneys to attend the conference in person.

(3) *Discovery Plan.* A discovery plan must state the parties' views and proposals on:

    (A) what changes should be made in the timing, form, or requirement for disclosures under Rule 26(a), including a statement of when initial disclosures were made or will be made;

    (B) the subjects on which discovery may be needed, when discovery should be completed, and whether discovery should be conducted in phases or be limited to or focused on particular issues;

    (C) any issues about disclosure, discovery, or preservation of electronically stored information, including the form or forms in which it should be produced;

    (D) any issues about claims of privilege or of protection as trial-preparation materials, including—if the parties agree on a procedure to assert these claims after production—whether to ask the court to include their agreement in an order under Federal Rule of Evidence 502;

    (E) what changes should be made in the limitations on discovery imposed under these rules or by local rule, and what other limitations should be imposed; and

    (F) any other orders that the court should issue under Rule 26(c) or under Rule 16(b) and (c).

(4) *Expedited Schedule.* If necessary to comply with its expedited schedule for Rule 16(b) conferences, a court may by local rule:

    (A) require the parties' conference to occur less than 21 days before the scheduling conference is held or a scheduling order is due under Rule 16(b); and

    (B) require the written report outlining the discovery plan to be filed less than 14 days after the parties' conference, or excuse the parties from submitting a written report and permit them to report orally on their discovery plan at the Rule 16(b) conference.

(g) Signing Disclosures and Discovery Requests, Responses, and Objections.

(1) *Signature Required; Effect of Signature.* Every disclosure under Rule 26(a)(1) or (a)(3) and every discovery request, response, or objection must be signed by at least one attorney of record in the attorney's own name— or by the party personally, if unrepresented—and must state the signer's address, e-mail address, and telephone number. By signing, an attorney

or party certifies that to the best of the person's knowledge, information, and belief formed after a reasonable inquiry:

    (A) with respect to a disclosure, it is complete and correct as of the time it is made; and

    (B) with respect to a discovery request, response, or objection, it is:

        (i) consistent with these rules and warranted by existing law or by a nonfrivolous argument for extending, modifying, or reversing existing law, or for establishing new law;

        (ii) not interposed for any improper purpose, such as to harass, cause unnecessary delay, or needlessly increase the cost of litigation; and

        (iii) neither unreasonable nor unduly burdensome or expensive, considering the needs of the case, prior discovery in the case, the amount in controversy, and the importance of the issues at stake in the action.

  (2) *Failure to Sign.* Other parties have no duty to act on an unsigned disclosure, request, response, or objection until it is signed, and the court must strike it unless a signature is promptly supplied after the omission is called to the attorney's or party's attention.

  (3) *Sanction for Improper Certification.* If a certification violates this rule without substantial justification, the court, on motion or on its own, must impose an appropriate sanction on the signer, the party on whose behalf the signer was acting, or both. The sanction may include an order to pay the reasonable expenses, including attorney's fees, caused by the violation.

[Amended December 27, 1946, effective March 19, 1948; January 21, 1963, effective July 1, 1963; February 28, 1966, effective July 1, 1966; March 30, 1970, effective July 1, 1970; April 29, 1980, effective August 1, 1980; April 28, 1983, effective August 1, 1983; March 2, 1987, effective August 1, 1987; April 22, 1993, effective December 1, 1993; April 17, 2000, effective December 1, 2000; April 12, 2006, effective December 1, 2006; April 30, 2007, effective December 1, 2007; April 28, 2010, effective December 1, 2010; April 29, 2015, effective December 1, 2015.]

AUTHORS' COMMENTARY ON RULE 26

PURPOSE AND SCOPE

Rule 26 contains the general provisions governing discovery. It sets forth the general discovery procedures, controls the scope of inquiry allowed, provides for protective orders, and imposes a duty to supplement discovery responses. The general provisions in Rule 26 apply to the specific discovery devices in Rules 27 through 37.

    ♦   **NOTE:** Rule 26 and the other discovery rules were substantially revised in 1970, 1993, 2000, 2006, 2007, 2010, and 2015. Therefore, great care should be exercised when citing or relying on decisions pertaining to Rule 26.

RULE 26(a)—REQUIRED DISCLOSURES

CORE CONCEPT

Rule 26(a) requires that parties disclose certain information automatically, without the need for discovery requests, at three points during the litigation. First, all parties must make broad initial disclosures at or shortly after they conduct the discovery meeting under Rule 26(f). Second, all parties must make disclosures about expert testimony 90 days before trial. Third, all parties must make the pretrial disclosures 30 days before trial. These disclosure deadlines are often modified by court order. Rule 26(a) also establishes the exclusive list of available discovery methods to supplement the automatic disclosures. In general, the only discovery devices that parties may use are: depositions upon oral examination (Rules 30, 27, 28, and 32); depositions upon written questions (Rules 31, 27, 28, and 32); written interrogatories (Rule 33); production of documents and things and entry onto land for inspection (Rule 34); physical and mental inspections (Rule 35); and requests for admission (Rule 36).

RULE 26(a)(1)—INITIAL DISCLOSURE

CORE CONCEPT

At the commencement of discovery, each party must disclose the identity of individuals with discoverable information that the party may use to support its claims or defenses, a description of documents that the party may use to support its claims or defenses by category and location, a computation of each category of damages, and insurance information.

APPLICATIONS

Time for Initial Disclosure

Parties must make their initial disclosures at or within 14 days after the discovery meeting required by Rule 26(f), unless a different time is set by court order or stipulation.[1] Thus, Rule 26 establishes the following typical sequence for the early discovery events: first, the court may schedule an initial scheduling conference and must issue an initial scheduling order; second, the parties conduct a discovery meeting at least 21 days before the court's initial scheduling conference or the due date for the scheduling order; third, the parties make their voluntary disclosures; fourth, in cases where the court conducts an initial scheduling conference, the parties meet with the judge to set the timetable for the balance of the discovery events; and finally, the court issues its initial scheduling order. Parties joined or served after the Rule 26(f) conference must make the initial disclosures within 30 days after being joined or served, unless a different time is set by stipulation or court order.

Service and Filing

Initial disclosures are served on the other parties, but not filed unless they are used in the proceedings or the court orders filing.[2]

Content of Initial Disclosure

Rule 26(a)(1) requires automatic initial disclosure of four categories of information:

(A) *Potential Witnesses:* Parties must disclose the name, and if known the address and telephone number,[3] of each individual likely to have discoverable information that

---

[1] *Novak v. Board of Trustees of Southern Illinois University,* 777 F.3d 966, 972 (7th Cir. 2015) (disclosure by court set deadline).

[2] *See Fed.R.Civ.P. 5(d)(1); Laslovich v. State Farm Fire and Cas. Co.,* 307 F.R.D. 533, 537 (D. Mont. 2015).

[3] *Tamas v. Family Video Movie Club, Inc.,* 304 F.R.D. 543, 545 (N.D. Ill. 2015) (address).

the disclosing party may use to support its claims or defenses.[4] Parties must also identify the subjects of such information.[5]

(B) *Documents:* Parties must provide a copy of, or a description by category and location of, all documents, electronically stored information, and tangible things[6] that the disclosing party may use to support its claims or defenses.[7] Except in cases with very few documents, parties will often disclose categories and locations rather than producing all the documents.[8] Parties must provide or describe all disclosable documents in their possession, custody, or control.[9]

(C) *Damages Computations:* Each party must provide a computation of any category of damages claimed by that party.[10] Each party must also produce the non-privileged documents supporting the computation, including documents bearing on the nature and extent of injuries suffered.[11]

(D) *Insurance:* Each party must provide all insurance policies that may provide coverage for part or all of any judgment that might be entered in the action.[12]

Only Information to Support Claims or Defenses

Rule 26(a)(1) requires disclosure only of information and documents that the disclosing party may use to support its claims or defenses.[13] This provision dovetails with the exclusionary sanction of Rule 37(c)(1), so that a party may not use information or documents not disclosed initially or by supplement.[14] To obtain information or documents that do not support a party's claims or defenses, opposing parties must serve affirmative discovery like interrogatories or document requests.[15]

Impeachment

Information and documents that a party may use solely for impeachment need not be disclosed.[16]

Electronic Data

Rule 26(a)(1)(A)(ii) specifically requires the disclosure of the "electronically stored information"[17] that it may use to support its claims or defenses. If electronic data is very costly or burdensome to disclose, a party may invoke the procedure under Rule 26(b)(2) (under which a party may notify the other parties that it is not collecting and disclosing

---

[4] *Cummings v. General Motors Corp.,* 365 F.3d 944, 954 (10th Cir. 2004) (a party is not obligated to disclose witnesses or documents, whether favorable or unfavorable, that it does not intend to use).

[5] *Harriman v. Hancock County,* 627 F.3d 22, 29 (1st Cir. 2010).

[6] *U.S. United Ocean Services, LLC v. Powerhouse Diesel Services, Inc.,* 932 F.Supp.2d 717 (E.D.La. 2013) (requiring disclosure of a boat).

[7] *Karpenski v. American General Life Companies, LLC,* 999 F.Supp.2d 1235, 1241 (W.D.Wash. 2014).

[8] *See Nieves v. OPA, Inc.,* 948 F.Supp.2d 887 (N.D.Ill. 2013).

[9] *See* Rule 34(a) for an explanation of the scope of documents within a party's possession, custody, or control. *See also Ogden v. Bumble Bee Foods, LLC,* 292 F.R.D. 620 (N.D.Cal. 2013).

[10] *Carmody v. Kansas City Bd. of Police Com'rs,* 713 F.3d 401, 404–05 (8th Cir. 2013).

[11] *R & R Sails, Inc. v. Ins. Co. of Pennsylvania,* 673 F.3d 1240, 1246 (9th Cir. 2012) (party must make the documents supporting the computation available for inspection).

[12] *Wickens v. Shell Oil Co.,* 620 F.3d 747, 759 (7th Cir. 2010).

[13] *Reinsdorf v. Skechers U.S.A., Inc.,* 296 F.R.D. 604, 619 (C.D.Cal. 2013).

[14] The 2000 Amendment to the advisory committee note to Rule 26(a)(1).

[15] *Allen v. Mill-Tel, Inc.,* 283 F.R.D. 631 (D.Kan. 2012).

[16] *Standley v. Edmonds-Leach,* 783 F.3d 1276, 1284 (D.C. Cir. 2015) (witness used for corroboration and impeachment not used "solely for impeachment").

[17] The advisory committee notes to the 2006 Amendments indicate that the term "electronically stored information" is consistent with the prior case law requiring the production of electronic documents and "data compilations."

certain electronic data, and then either party may ask the court to determine whether the data need be disclosed).

Excluded Proceedings

Rule 26(a)(1)(B) excludes 8 categories of proceedings from the initial disclosures:

(1) appeals from administrative proceedings;

(2) a forfeiture action *in rem* arising from a federal statute;

(3) petitions for habeas corpus or like challenges to criminal convictions or sentences;

(4) *pro se* prisoner actions;

(5) actions to enforce or quash an administrative summons or subpoena;

(6) actions by the United States to recover benefit payments;

(7) actions by the United States to collect on student loans guaranteed by the United States;

(8) proceedings ancillary to proceedings in other courts; and

(9) actions to enforce arbitration awards.

Disclose Information "Reasonably Available"

The parties must make their initial disclosures based on the information then "reasonably available."[18] A party may not avoid the initial disclosure requirements by claiming that its investigation is not yet complete.[19]

Failure to Disclose

Failure to make the initial disclosures required by Rule 26(a)(1) results in the exclusion of the undisclosed witness or information,[20] unless the party failing to make the disclosure can demonstrate that the failure was harmless or there was substantial justification.[21] Generally, providing the identity of a witness or producing the documents in discovery will not excuse failure to disclose under Rule 26(a)(1), because that does not put the other party on notice that the producing party may use that witness or those documents to support its claims or defenses.[22]

Other Party's Failure to Disclose

A party may not refuse to make the Rule 26(a) disclosures because another party has also failed to do so.[23] Likewise, a party believing that another party's disclosure was not sufficient must nonetheless make its own disclosures.[24]

---

[18] *San Francisco Baykeeper v. West Bay Sanitary Dist.,* 791 F.Supp.2d 719 (N.D.Cal. 2011) (defining "reasonably available").

[19] *Wallace v. U.S.A.A. Life Gen. Agency, Inc.,* 862 F.Supp.2d 1062 (D.Nev. 2012).

[20] *Wilson v. AM General Corp.,* 167 F.3d 1114 (7th Cir.1999) (rejecting claim that the witnesses were impeachment witnesses and excluding their testimony).

[21] *Russell v. Absolute Collection Services, Inc.,* 763 F.3d 385, 396 (4th Cir. 2014) (court has broad discretion in determining sanctions).

[22] *See Wallace v. U.S.A.A. Life Gen. Agency, Inc.,* 862 F.Supp.2d 1062 (D.Nev. 2012).

[23] *See Jacobsen v. Deseret Book Co.,* 287 F.3d 936, 954 (10th Cir. 2002).

[24] Rule 26(a)(1)(E).

Disclosures Automatic

The initial disclosures are automatically required, without any need for a request or demand.[25]

Stipulations Not to Disclose

The parties may stipulate to the elimination or modification of the initial disclosures, unless precluded from doing so by local rule or court order.

Form of Disclosures

The initial disclosures should be in writing, signed, and served on other parties unless otherwise directed by local rule or court order.[26] The signature constitutes a certification that the disclosure is complete and accurate under Rule 26(g)(1).[27]

Objections to Making the Disclosures

A party believing that Rule 26(a)(1) initial disclosures are "not appropriate in the circumstances of the action" may object during the Rule 26(f) discovery conference. If not resolved, the objection should be stated in the Rule 26(f) discovery plan filed with the court. Disclosures are not required thereafter except as ordered by the court.[28] In ruling on the objection, the court must determine what disclosures, if any, will be made and set the time for such disclosures.

New or Late Served Parties

Parties that have not been joined or served at the time of the initial disclosures or the Rule 26(f) discovery conference must make initial disclosures 30 days from when they are served or joined, unless modified by stipulation or order. The scope of such parties' disclosures will be similar to the original parties' with respect to any stipulations or court orders.[29]

Duty to Supplement

Rule 26(e) requires a party to supplement its Rule 26(a)(1) disclosure if it learns that the information was incomplete or incorrect.[30]

RULE 26(a)(2)—DISCLOSURE OF EXPERT TESTIMONY

CORE CONCEPT

Each party must disclose the identity of its testifying expert witnesses and produce an expert report for certain categories of testifying experts.

APPLICATIONS

Which Experts

Each party must disclose the identity of any person who "may be used at trial to present evidence" under the Federal Rules of Evidence governing expert testimony.[31] Parties need

---

[25]   *See Ball v. LeBlanc*, 300 F.R.D. 270, 287 (M.D. La. 2013).

[26]   *See S.E.C. v. TheStreet.Com*, 273 F.3d 222, 233 (2d Cir. 2001) (initial disclosures under Rule 26(a)(1) are not filed unless ordered by the court or used in a subsequent stage of the proceedings).

[27]   *Moore v. Publicis Groupe*, 287 F.R.D. 182, 188 (S.D.N.Y. 2012).

[28]   The 2000 Amendment to the advisory committee note to Rule 26(a)(1).

[29]   The advisory committee note to the 2000 Amendment to Rule 26(a)(1).

[30]   *See Pina v. Children's Place*, 740 F.3d 785 (1st Cir. 2014).

[31]   *Tribble v. Evangelides*, 670 F.3d 753, 758 (7th Cir. 2012).

not disclose experts who will not testify at trial but who serve some other function, such as providing an affidavit in connection with a motion.[32]

Time for Expert Disclosure

The time for expert disclosures can be set by the court or stipulated by the parties.[33] In the absence of a court order or stipulation, the expert disclosures must be made 90 days before the trial date.[34] If the expert testimony is purely to contradict or rebut testimony disclosed by another party, then the disclosure must be made within 30 days after the disclosure by the other party.[35] Leave may be obtained to disclose an expert report for a rebuttal expert witness after the time for expert disclosures under Rule 26(a)(2).[36]

Service and Filing

Expert disclosures are served on the other parties, but not filed unless they are used in the proceedings or the court orders filing.

Rebuttal and Impeachment Testimony

Parties must disclose rebuttal expert testimony. The court usually sets the time for disclosure of rebuttal testimony, which is often 30 days after disclosure of the testimony it is rebutting.[37] Rebuttal testimony must explain, repel, counteract, or disprove evidence of the adverse party; courts will not allow parties to use rebuttal expert testimony to advance new arguments or new evidence.[38] The courts are divided about whether expert impeachment evidence must be disclosed.[39]

Content of Disclosure

The disclosure must contain the identity of any witness who may provide expert testimony under the Federal Rules of Evidence governing expert testimony.[40] For witnesses who were retained or specially employed to provide expert testimony, the disclosure must include an expert report.[41] For all other experts, the disclosure must contain:

- the subject matter on which the expert is expected to present evidence; and

- a summary of the facts and opinions to which the witness is expected to testify.[42]

---

[32] *Moore v. Napolitano,* 926 F.Supp.2d 8 (D.D.C. 2013).

[33] *Wilkins v. Montgomery,* 751 F.3d 214, 221 (4th Cir. 2014).

[34] *Lutz v. Glendale Union High School,* 403 F.3d 1061, 1071 (9th Cir. 2005) (the 90-day period applies only in the absence of a court established deadline).

[35] *United States v. $231,930.00 in U.S. Currency,* 614 F.3d 837, 841 (8th Cir. 2010) (discussing the difference between rebuttal and impeachment testimony).

[36] *See Wegener v. Johnson,* 527 F.3d 687, 692 (8th Cir. 2008) (the court has discretion to exclude the untimely report when allowing it would require another continuance of the trial).

[37] *See Bradshaw v. FFE Transp. Services, Inc.,* 715 F.3d 1104 (8th Cir. 2013).

[38] *Blake v. Securitas Sec. Services, Inc.,* 962 F.R.D. 141 (D.D.C. 2013).

[39] *See United States v. $231,930.00 in U.S. Currency,* 614 F.3d 837, 841 (8th Cir. 2010) (impeachment evidence need not be disclosed); *Wegener v. Johnson,* 527 F.3d 687, 690–91 (8th Cir. 2008) (impeachment evidence must be disclosed).

[40] *Hamburger v. State Farm Mut. Auto. Ins. Co.,* 361 F.3d 875, 883 n.4 (5th Cir. 2004).

[41] *E.E.O.C. v. AutoZone, Inc.,* 707 F.3d 824, 833 (7th Cir. 2013).

[42] *M.B. v. CSX Transp., Inc.,* 299 F.R.D. 341 (N.D.N.Y. 2014).

Expert Report

Each expert report must be in writing and signed by the expert,[43] and must contain: a complete statement of all the expert's opinions and the basis and reasons therefor;[44] the facts or data considered by the expert,[45] including documents provided by counsel;[46] any exhibits to be used as support for or as a summary of the opinions;[47] the qualifications of the expert and all publications authored by the expert in the past 10 years; the expert's compensation for the review and testimony; and a list of all other cases in which the expert has testified at trial or at deposition in the past 4 years.[48] The report itself should contain all the required information with considerable detail,[49] and may not satisfy Rule 26(a)(2)(B) by incorporating other material.[50]

Failure to Disclose Report

The failure to disclose a report meeting the requirements of Rule 26(a)(2)(B) may preclude the party from introducing the testimony as evidence on a motion, at a hearing, or at trial, either altogether [51] or as to specific opinions not disclosed in the report.[52] Such sanctions are "automatic and mandatory"[53] unless the party failing to disclose can show the failure was justified or harmless.[54] A party who believes that an opposing party has disclosed an inadequate expert report should file a motion to compel a more complete report or a motion to exclude the expert promptly, as waiting until trial to raise the issue may result in waiver.[55] The courts are divided as to whether disclosure of the expert opinions or required information in deposition is a substitute for inclusion in the expert disclosure.[56]

Stipulations Not to Disclose Expert Reports

The parties may stipulate to the elimination or modification of the expert report disclosures, unless precluded from doing so by local rule or court order.

---

[43] *United States v. Kalymon,* 541 F.3d 624, 638 (6th Cir. 2008) (the attorney may provide assistance to the expert, or even draft the report, so long as it contains the expert's opinions).

[44] *R.C. Olmstead, Inc., v. CU Interface, LLC,* 606 F.3d 262 (6th Cir. 2010) (report should contain enough detail such that the party does not have to depose the expert to avoid ambush).

[45] *Republic of Ecuador v. Hinchee,* 741 F.3d 1185, 1195 (11th Cir. 2013) ("the term 'facts or data' should 'be interpreted broadly to require disclosure of any material considered by the expert, from whatever source, that contains factual ingredients.' ").

[46] *Fidelity Nat. Title Ins. Co. of New York v. Intercounty Nat. Title Ins. Co.,* 412 F.3d 745 (7th Cir.2005) (party must disclose all documents "considered" by the expert, without regard to the expert's document retention policy).

[47] *Bradshaw v. FFE Transp. Services, Inc.,* 715 F.3d 1104 (8th Cir. 2013).

[48] *Coleman v. Dydula,* 190 F.R.D. 316, 318 (W.D. N.Y. 1999) (the list of cases should, at a minimum, include the name of the court where the testimony occurred, the names of the parties, the case number, and whether the testimony was given at a deposition or trial).

[49] *Walter Intern. Prods., Inc. v. Salinas,* 650 F.3d 1402, 1410 (11th Cir. 2011) (short letter deemed inadequate).

[50] *Ingram v. Novartis Pharms. Corp.,* 888 F.R.D. 1241 (W.D.Okla. 2012) (references to other reports and testimony improper).

[51] *Wilkins v. Montgomery,* 751 F.3d 214, 221 (4th Cir. 2014).

[52] *Boston Gas Co. v. Century Indem. Co.,* 529 F.3d 8 (1st Cir. 2008).

[53] *But see S.E.C. v. Jasper,* 678 F.3d 1116, 1124 (9th Cir. 2012) (no error in admitting document prepared by undisclosed expert where the opposing party did not object under Rule 26(a)(2)).

[54] *Goodman v. Staples The Office Superstore, LLC,* 644 F.3d 817 (9th Cir. 2011) (treating physician who did not prepare an expert report allowed to testify because rule was murky as to treating physicians).

[55] *Rodrick v. Wal-Mart Stores East, L.P.,* 666 F.3d 1093, 1096 (8th Cir. 2012).

[56] *See Walter Intern. Prods., Inc. v. Salinas,* 650 F.3d 1402, 1410 (11th Cir. 2011) (a report is necessary to effectively take an expert deposition); *Smith v. Tenet Healthsystem SL, Inc.,* 436 F.3d 879, 889 (8th Cir. 2006) (expert could rely on x-rays disclosed at the deposition because failure to disclose in the report was harmless); *In re Sulfuric Acid Antitrust Litigation,* 432 F.Supp.2d 794 (N.D. Ill. 2006) (asking about additional opinions at deposition may open the door for admission of those opinions at trial).

Testimony Is Measure, Not Witness Qualification

The expert disclosures are required if the testimony is expert in nature, not factual; expert disclosures are not required if an expert is being called to give percipient factual testimony.[57]

Experts Employed by a Party

A party must produce an expert report for an employee only if the employee's duties regularly involve giving expert testimony or the employee was specially employed to provide expert testimony.[58] This requirement will only apply, however, if the employee is giving expert testimony.[59] Likewise, an individual party who intends to present expert testimony must list him or herself as an expert and disclose the information required by Rule 26(a)(2)(C), but need not produce an expert report.[60]

Treating Physicians

An expert report is generally not required for a treating physician to testify regarding the treatment if the party has not retained the physician as an expert,[61] although a number of courts require an expert report when the treating physician will offer testimony beyond the scope of the treatment rendered.[62] However, parties must disclose the subject matter and a summary of the facts and opinions as to which a treating physician is expected to testify under F.R.E. 702 (pertaining to expert testimony).[63] It is unsettled whether a treating physician's testimony about the treatment constitutes F.R.E. 702 expert testimony or percipient fact testimony.[64] A physician conducting an Independent Medical Examination will generally be considered an expert for purposes of Rule 26(a)(2),[65] but the obligation to produce a report for a physician conducting an examination under Rule 35 is governed by Rule 35, not by Rule 26(a)(2).[66] When the attorney has referred the client to the physician, the physician is more likely to be treated as a specially retained expert.[67]

Disclosures Automatic

The expert disclosures are automatically required, without any need for a request or demand.

Form of Disclosures

The expert disclosures should be in writing, signed, and served on other parties, unless otherwise directed by local rule or court order.[68] The signature constitutes a certification that the disclosure is complete and accurate under Rule 26(g)(1).

---

[57] *Ryan Development Co., L.C. v. Indiana Lumbermens Mut. Ins. Co.,* 711 F.3d 1165, 1170–71 (10th Cir. 2013) (accountants permitted to testify as percipient witnesses).

[58] *Tokai Corp. v. Easton Enterprises, Inc.,* 632 F.3d 1358, 1364–65 (Fed.Cir. 2011) (party seeking to use an employee expert bears the burden of showing that the expert is specially employed or regularly testifies).

[59] *Watson v. United States,* 485 F.3d 1100 (10th Cir. 2007) (employee allowed to give expert testimony without expert report because he did not regularly give expert testimony).

[60] *U.S. ex rel. Jones v. Brigham & Women's Hosp.,* 678 F.3d 72, 90 (1st Cir. 2012).

[61] *See E.E.O.C. v. AutoZone, Inc.,* 707 F.3d 824, 833 (7th Cir. 2013).

[62] *See Bradshaw v. FFE Transp. Services, Inc.,* 715 F.3d 1104 (8th Cir. 2013).

[63] *See Derosa v. Blood Systems, Inc.,* 298 F.R.D. 661 (D.Nev. 2014).

[64] *See, Goodman v. Staples The Office Superstore, LLC,* 644 F.3d 817, (9th Cir. 2011) (discussing the split in authority).

[65] *Whitney v. United States,* 251 F.R.D. 1 (D.D.C. 2008).

[66] *Diaz v. Con-Way Truckload, Inc.,* 279 F.R.D. 412, 418 (S.D.Tex. 2012).

[67] *Perkins v. United States,* 626 F.Supp.2d 587 (E.D.Va. 2009).

[68] *See S.E.C. v. TheStreet.Com,* 273 F.3d 222, 233 (2d Cir. 2001) (initial disclosures under Rule 26(a)(2) are not filed unless ordered by the court or used in a subsequent stage of the proceedings).

Sanctions for Improper Disclosures

Sanctions for an insufficient disclosure are governed by the sanctions provisions in Rule 37(c)(1).

Duty to Supplement

Rule 26(e) requires a party to supplement its expert disclosures if the party learns that the information disclosed was incomplete or incorrect.[69] Supplemental expert information should be disclosed by the time the pretrial disclosures are made under Rule 26(a)(3), 30 days before trial unless otherwise set by the court.[70]

RULE 26(a)(3)—PRETRIAL DISCLOSURES

CORE CONCEPT

Prior to trial, each party must disclose the witnesses that they may call at trial, the deposition testimony that they may offer at trial, and the exhibits that they may offer at trial.

APPLICATIONS

Time for Pretrial Disclosure

The time for pretrial disclosures is often set by the court. In the absence of a court order, the expert disclosures must be made 30 days before the trial date.[71] Parties will not be required to respond to discovery requests seeking the information covered by Rule 26(a)(3) at an earlier stage in the litigation.[72]

Service and Filing

Pretrial disclosures are served on the other parties, but not filed unless they are used in the proceedings or the court orders filing.

Content of Pretrial Disclosure

Rule 26(a)(3) requires a pretrial disclosure of the following information:

(A) *Witnesses:* Each party must disclose the name and, unless already disclosed, the address and phone number of each witness that they may call at trial.[73] The disclosure should indicate those witnesses the party expects to testify and those the party may call if needed.[74]

(B) *Depositions:* Each party must designate the testimony that the party intends to introduce in the form of a deposition. If the deposition was recorded other than stenographically, then the party must provide a transcript of the pertinent parts of the testimony.[75]

(C) *Exhibits:* Each party must identify all exhibits, including demonstrative or summary exhibits. The disclosure should indicate those exhibits that the party expects to introduce and those that the party may introduce if needed.

---

[69] *David E. Watson, P.C. v. United States,* 668 F.3d 1008, 1014 (8th Cir. 2012).

[70] *U.S. S.E.C. v. Maxxon, Inc.,* 465 F.3d 1174, 1182 (10th Cir.2006).

[71] *Trafton v. Sunbury Primary Care, P.A.,* 689 F.Supp.2d 198 (D.Me. 2010).

[72] *Banks v. Office of Senate Sergeant-at-Arms,* 222 F.R.D. 7, 15 (D.D.C. 2004).

[73] *See Wilson v. Superclub Ibiza, LLC,* 279 F.Supp.2d 176 (D.D.C. 2013) (exclusion of witness not warranted for failure to disclose address).

[74] *But see Walter Intern. Prods. Inc. v. Salinas,* 650 F.3d 1402, 1415 (11th Cir. 2011) (court may require the parties to submit a list of witnesses they will actually call, not those that they "may" call).

[75] *Tilton v. Capital Cities/ABC, Inc.,* 115 F.3d 1471, 1478 (10th Cir. 1997).

Impeachment

The pretrial disclosure is not required to include documents or testimony to be introduced solely for impeachment.[76]

Failure to Disclose

Any witnesses, depositions, or exhibits not properly disclosed under Rule 26(a)(3) will be excluded from use at trial unless the failure was substantially justified or harmless.[77]

Objections to Deposition Testimony or Exhibits

Any objection to the use of a deposition or exhibit must be served and filed within 14 days of the disclosure of the intent to use the deposition or exhibit. The statement of the objection should specify the grounds for the objection. Failure to disclose such an objection is a waiver of the objection,[78] except for objections to relevancy under Rules 402 and 403 of the Federal Rules of Evidence. Note that an objection to the disclosure is not the same as objecting to the evidence not properly disclosed; a party must still object when the deposition or exhibit is offered at trial.[79]

Disclosures Automatic

The pretrial disclosures are automatically required, without any need for a request or demand.

Form of Disclosures

The pretrial disclosures should be in writing, signed, served on other parties, and filed with the court, unless otherwise directed by local rule or court order. The signature constitutes a certification that the disclosure is complete and accurate under Rule 26(g)(1).

RULE 26(a)(4)—FORM OF DISCLOSURES

CORE CONCEPT

The automatic disclosures under Rule 26(a) should be in writing, signed, and served on other parties, unless otherwise directed by local rule or court order. Only the pretrial disclosure under Rule 26(a)(3) must be filed. The signature constitutes a certification that the disclosure is complete and accurate under Rule 26(g)(1).

RULE 26(b)(1)—DISCOVERY SCOPE AND LIMITS— SCOPE IN GENERAL

CORE CONCEPT

In general, any matter that is relevant to the claim or defense of any party in the pending action and is proportional to the needs of the case is discoverable unless it is privileged.[80] Discovery is more limited with respect to trial preparation materials, non-testifying expert witnesses, and physical or mental examinations.

---

[76] *Sanchez v. City of Chicago,* 700 F.3d 919, 930 (7th Cir. 2012).

[77] *Diaz-Garcia v. Surillo-Ruiz,* 98 F.Supp.3d 396, 401–02 (D. Puerto Rico 2015).

[78] *Martin v. Harris,* 560 F.3d 210, 219 (4th Cir. 2009).

[79] The advisory committee note to the 1993 Amendment to Rule 26.

[80] *Gov't of Ghana v. ProEnergy Servs., LLC,* 677 F.3d 340, 342 (8th Cir. 2012).

APPLICATIONS

Covered Actions

The discovery rules apply to all civil actions in federal court, except for the narrow exceptions listed in Rule 81 (such as certain admiralty matters and matters in arbitration pursuant to federal statute). The Rules apply in bankruptcy proceedings, patent actions, and civil contempt proceedings. They apply in habeas corpus actions if the court grants leave to conduct discovery.

"Relevant" Defined

The term "relevant" is not defined by the Rules, but is extremely broad.[81] Courts have defined "relevant" to encompass "any matter that bears on, or that reasonably could lead to other matters that could bear on, any issue that is or may be in the case."[82] Courts also have defined "relevant" as "germane."[83]

Relevant to Any Party's Claim or Defense

A party may discover any matter that is relevant to any claim or defense that is pleaded in the case, regardless of which party raises the claim or defense. Discovery is not permitted to develop potential additional claims or defenses.[84] Discovery is permitted with respect to claims that have been challenged by a motion to dismiss or motion for summary judgment. However, if a claim has been dismissed, further discovery that is relevant only to that claim will not be allowed.[85]

Relevant vs. Admissible

Evidence need not be admissible to be relevant, and thus discoverable.[86] Conversely, admissible evidence is almost always discoverable.[87]

Proportionality

Discovery must be "proportional to the needs of the case"—essentially the expected benefits of the discovery must be in line with the cost and burden of the discovery and the value of the case. Rule 26(b)(1) contains a list of factors for evaluating proportionality: the importance of the issues at stake in the action, the amount in controversy, the parties' relative access to relevant information, the parties' resources, the importance of the discovery in resolving the issues, and whether the burden or expense of the proposed discovery outweighs its likely benefit.

Limitations on Discovery

The broad scope of discovery under Rule 26(b)(1) must be read in conjunction with the two limitations in Rule 26(b)(2) relating to discovery that is cumulative or unduly burdensome.[88]

---

[81]   *United Oil Co., Inc. v. Parts Associates, Inc.,* 227 F.R.D. 404 (D. Md. 2005).

[82]   *Oil, Chem. & Atomic Workers Local Union No. 6–418, AFL-CIO v. N.L.R.B.,* 711 F.2d 348, 360 (D.C. Cir. 1983).

[83]   *Oppenheimer Fund, Inc. v. Sanders,* 437 U.S. 340, 351, 98 S.Ct. 2380, 2389–90, 57 L.Ed.2d 253 (1978).

[84]   The advisory committee note to the 2000 Amendment to Rule 26(b)(1).

[85]   *Oppenheimer Fund, Inc. v. Sanders,* 437 U.S. 340, 351, 98 S.Ct. 2380, 2389–90, 57 L.Ed.2d 253 (1978).

[86]   *Seattle Times Co. v. Rhinehart,* 467 U.S. 20, 104 S.Ct. 2199, 81 L.Ed.2d 17 (1984).

[87]   *Terwilliger v. York Intern. Corp.,* 176 F.R.D. 214, 218 (W.D. Va. 1997).

[88]   *In re Cooper Tire & Rubber Co.,* 568 F.3d 1180 (10th Cir. 2009).

Duty to Preserve

It is well recognized that parties and attorneys have a duty to preserve relevant evidence once litigation has commenced or is reasonably anticipated. Some courts find this duty arises in part under Rule 26(b)(1).[89]

Jurisdictional Issues

Discovery is allowed with respect to jurisdictional issues.[90] Thus, parties may conduct discovery pertaining to other parties' citizenship, the amount in controversy, or a party's contacts with the forum state.

Location of Evidence

Parties may take discovery about the location and existence of documents and other evidence[91] and about the identity and location of persons having knowledge of discoverable matters.[92]

Matters Known to Others

A party must provide information and documents it possesses, regardless of who else possesses that information. Thus, it generally is not proper to object on the basis that the party already has the information it is requesting or that information is in the public record[93] or is otherwise available to the party[94] (although the court might curtail such requests as unduly burdensome in some circumstances).

Impeachment

Discovery is generally allowed of matters that would be used to impeach other parties' witnesses.[95] Thus, one normally may ask whether the responding party has any criminal convictions and may inquire as to prior statements.[96] It is less clear whether one may inquire as to what other parties will use for impeachment.

Discovery of Attorneys

Attorneys with discoverable facts not covered by attorney-client privilege or work product protection are subject to discovery despite being retained by one of the parties to represent it in the litigation.[97]

Privileges

Privileged matters are protected from discovery.[98] Privileges in federal court depend upon whether the action involves a state law issue or a federal cause of action. If a state's substantive laws are being applied, that state's laws of privilege also apply,[99] except as to the trial preparation materials (work product) protection, which is governed by Rule 26(b)(3)

---

[89]   *See Yelton v. PHI, Inc.,* 279 F.R.D. 377, 384 (E.D.La. 2011).

[90]   *Oppenheimer Fund, Inc. v. Sanders,* 437 U.S. 340, 351, 98 S.Ct. 2380, 57 L.Ed.2d 253 (1978).

[91]   *Dauska v. Green Bay Packaging Inc.,* 291 F.R.D. 251 (E.D.Wis. 2013).

[92]   *Brooks v. Kerry,* 37 F.Supp.2d 187, 202–03 (D.D.C. 2014).

[93]   *Mid-Atlantic Recycling Technologies, Inc. v. City of Vineland,* 222 F.R.D. 81 (D.N.J. 2004).

[94]   *Abrahamsen v. Trans-State Exp., Inc.,* 92 F.3d 425, 428 (6th Cir. 1996).

[95]   *Hickman v. Taylor,* 329 U.S. 495, 511, 67 S.Ct. 385, 394, 91 L. Ed. 451 (1947).

[96]   *See Curro v. Watson,* 884 F.Supp. 708 (E.D. N.Y. 1995), aff'd, 100 F.3d 942 (2d Cir. 1996) (limiting impeachment discovery to areas related to expected testimony).

[97]   *United Phosphorus, Ltd. v. Midland Fumigant, Inc.,* 164 F.R.D. 245 (D. Kan. 1995).

[98]   *Perry v. Schwarzenegger,* 591 F.3d 1126, 1140 (9th Cir. 2009) (communications protected by the First Amendment are privileged).

[99]   *Brown v. Waco Fire & Cas. Co.,* 73 F.R.D. 297 (S.D. Miss. 1976).

and federal common law.[100] If the action is governed by federal law, then Rule 501 of the Federal Rules of Evidence applies. Essentially, Rule 501 instructs the federal courts to develop a body of federal common law privileges. When a deposition is taken in a state other than the state in which the action is pending, the privilege analysis becomes very complicated, and depends upon each state's choice of law provisions.

Raising Claim of Privilege

The normal manner for raising a privilege is by objecting to a particular request or inquiry. For example, at a deposition, a party may orally raise an objection to an individual question, then refuse to provide the privileged information (by counsel instructing the witness not to answer). In response to interrogatories, document requests, or requests for admission, a party may make a written objection to individual questions or requests and withhold the privileged information. The objection must include sufficient information so that the court and opposing counsel can assess the applicability of the privilege.[101]

Who May Assert

Usually, a privilege may only be asserted by the person holding the privilege. Certainly, a party may not assert a privilege of a nonparty witness or another party. When an attorney is deposed it is unclear who may assert the privilege—the privilege technically belongs to the client, but courts allow the attorney to assert the privilege if asked about an attorney-client communication.[102]

Waiver of Privilege

Privileges generally are waived by voluntary disclosure,[103] either during discovery or elsewhere.[104] Thus, caution should be exercised in discussing or responding to discovery requests pertaining to privileged matters.

Documents Containing Privileged and Non-Privileged Matters

If part of a document contains privileged matters and part does not, a party must provide the non-privileged matter, but may redact the privileged matter.

Privileged Matters to Be Introduced at Trial

A majority of courts hold that a party cannot assert a privilege at the discovery stage, then introduce the privileged matter at trial.[105] Consequently, any matter intended to be introduced at trial should be produced during discovery if requested.

Particular Privileges

A detailed analysis of every potential privilege is beyond the scope of this book. The following is an overview of the most commonly asserted privileges:

- *Attorney-Client:* The attorney-client privilege applies to all confidential communications between a client and the client's attorney that occur in connection with legal representation or in the process of obtaining legal representation.[106] It applies to communications to an in-house attorney if the attorney is providing legal

---

[100] *Tompkins v. R.J. Reynolds Tobacco Co.,* 92 F.Supp.2d 70 (N.D. N.Y. 2000).

[101] Rule 26(b)(5); *Burns v. Imagine Films Entertainment, Inc.,* 164 F.R.D. 589 (W.D. N.Y. 1996).

[102] *See Martin Marietta Materials, Inc. v. Bedford Reinforced Plastics, Inc.,* 227 F.R.D. 382, 390 (W.D. Pa. 2005) (privilege belongs to the client, not to the attorney).

[103] *Appleton Papers, Inc. v. E.P.A.,* 702 F.3d 1018, 1024 (7th Cir. 2012).

[104] *See In re Lott,* 424 F.3d 446, 452 (6th Cir. 2005) (attorney-client privilege is waived when the legal advice is placed at issue).

[105] *Doe v. Eli Lilly & Co., Inc.,* 99 F.R.D. 126, 127 (D.D.C. 1983).

[106] *Diversified Industries, Inc. v. Meredith,* 572 F.2d 596, 612 (8th Cir. 1977).

services. The privilege does not protect communications between one party and the attorney for another party. It does not protect documents or other physical evidence provided to the attorney (other than written communications to the attorney), the underlying facts,[107] information or evidence gathered by the attorney from other sources, or notes and memoranda prepared by the attorney (but see the discussion of attorney-work product under Rule 26(b)(3)).

- *Self-Incrimination:* The Fifth Amendment to the United States Constitution provides all persons (whether or not parties to a litigation) with a privilege against testifying in a manner that would tend to incriminate them.[108] The privilege applies at depositions,[109] interrogatories, requests for admission, and production of documents,[110] as well as at trial. Corporations may not assert the privilege, but corporate representatives may assert it if their testimony would incriminate them personally, regardless of whether they are testifying in their individual or representative capacities.[111] There can be no penalties or sanctions for properly exercising the Fifth Amendment privilege.

- *Governmental Privileges:* The United States has some extra privileges:

  o *Governmental Informer Privilege:* The United States has a qualified privilege to refuse to reveal the identity of an informer.[112] The privilege belongs to the government, and protects only the identity of the informer, not the information provided by the informer.

  o *Government's Privilege for Military or State Secrets:* The United States has a qualified privilege for matters that involve military or state secrets.[113]

  o *Government's Statutory Privilege:* Some statutes require governmental agencies and other entities to file certain documents or reports, and designate the submissions as confidential. A common example is income tax returns. Under the regulation,[114] the United States receives and keeps tax returns, but is not required to produce them to private litigants.

  o *Executive Privilege:* The Executive branch of the United States government has a general qualified privilege, grounded in the need for the executive branch to gather information.[115]

- *Other Privileges:* In some states, communications with spouses, physicians, clergy, journalists,[116] accountants, and social workers are privileged.

---

[107] *Martin Marietta Materials, Inc. v. Bedford Reinforced Plastics, Inc.,* 227 F.R.D. 382, 392 (W.D. Pa. 2005).

[108] *De Vita v. Sills,* 422 F.2d 1172 (3d Cir.1970).

[109] *In re Folding Carton Antitrust Litigation,* 609 F.2d 867 (7th Cir. 1979).

[110] *Gordon v. Federal Deposit Ins. Corp.,* 427 F.2d 578, 580 (D.C. Cir. 1970).

[111] *United States v. Kordel,* 397 U.S. 1, 8, 90 S.Ct. 763, 767, 25 L.Ed.2d 1 (1970).

[112] *Roviaro v. United States,* 353 U.S. 53, 59, 77 S.Ct. 623, 627, 1 L.Ed.2d 639 (1957).

[113] *See General Dynamics Corp. v. United States,* 563 U.S. 478, 131 S.Ct. 1900, 1905, 179 L.Ed.2d 957 (2011).

[114] 26 C.F.R. § 301.6103(a–1)(c).

[115] *United States v. Nixon,* 418 U.S. 683, 94 S.Ct. 3090, 41 L.Ed.2d 1039 (1974).

[116] *In re Madden,* 151 F.3d 125, 128 (3d Cir. 1998) (recognizing qualified journalists' privilege).

Burden of Proof

The party raising a privilege has the burden of establishing the existence of the privilege.[117] Case law varies as to which party has the burden of proving relevance or non-relevance.[118]

RULE 26(b)(2)—LIMITATIONS ON FREQUENCY AND EXTENT

CORE CONCEPT

Rule 26(b)(2) requires the court, "on motion or on its own,"[119] to limit discovery if the discovery is unreasonably cumulative or duplicative or the discovery is obtainable from another source more conveniently. The court must also limit discovery if the party seeking the discovery has had "ample opportunity" to obtain the information during prior discovery. Rule 26(b)(2)(B) also establishes a procedure for limiting the need to search for and produce electronic data if it would be unreasonably burdensome or costly to do so.

APPLICATIONS

Objections to Specific Requests

One method of asserting the limitations in Rule 26(b)(2) is by making an objection to a discovery request, such as objecting to an interrogatory or request for production as cumulative or overly burdensome.

Motion for Protective Order

A party seeking to limit another party's use of certain discovery procedures should make a motion for a protective order under Rule 26(c).

Required Limitations

The court must limit discovery in 3 circumstances:

(i)   if the discovery is unreasonably cumulative or duplicative, or can be obtained from another source that is more convenient, less burdensome, or less expensive;[120]

(ii)   if the party seeking the discovery has already had ample opportunity to obtain the information in discovery;[121] or

(iii) if the discovery is outside the scope permitted by Rule 26(b)(1), *i.e.*, is not relevant to a party's claim or defense and is not proportional.

Limits Established by Other Rules

Other Rules place limits on discovery, such as the duration of depositions and the number of interrogatories and depositions, which may be altered by court order.[122] These limits may also be altered by stipulation under Rule 29.

---

[117] *Republic of Ecuador v. Hinchee*, 741 F.3d 1185, 1189 (11th Cir. 2013).

[118] *Moss v. Blue Cross and Blue Shield of Kansas, Inc.*, 241 F.R.D. 683 (D. Kan. 2007) (when the discovery sought appears relevant, the party opposing production has the burden to establish lack of relevance; when the discovery does not appear relevant, the party seeking production has the burden to demonstrate relevance).

[119] *Shukh v. Seagate Technology, LLC*, 295 F.R.D. 228, 237 (D.Minn. 2013).

[120] *See Garcia v. Tyson Foods, Inc.*, 770 F.3d 1300, 1309 (10th Cir. 2014).

[121] *Jackson v. Federal Exp.*, 766 F.3d 189, 199 (2d Cir. 2014).

[122] *Scott v. City of Sioux City, Iowa*, 298 F.R.D. 400, 401–02 (N.D. Iowa 2014).

Electronic Data

Rule 26(b)(2)(B) limits discovery of electronically stored information from sources that are not "reasonably accessible" because of undue burden or cost, and establishes a procedure for invoking the limitation.[123] The party invoking the protection must identify the sources of information that it is neither searching nor producing with sufficient particularity that the requesting party can evaluate the burden and cost of producing the information.[124] If the requesting party still believes that the information should be produced, the parties must confer to see if they can resolve the issue without court intervention.[125] If an informal conference does not resolve the issue, the requesting party may file a motion to compel[126] or the responding party may file a motion for a protective order. In either type of motion, the responding party bears the burden of showing that the information is not reasonably accessible, in terms of undue burden or cost. Even following such a showing, the court may require production of the information upon good cause shown.[127] Relevant factors include the specificity of the request, the information that is or should be available from other sources, predictions of the importance of the information, the importance of the issues at stake, and the parties' resources.[128]

RULE 26(b)(3)—TRIAL PREPARATION: MATERIALS

CORE CONCEPT

Rule 26(b)(3) provides limited protection to otherwise discoverable[129] trial preparation materials.[130] Such materials must be produced in discovery *only* when the information contained there is not reasonably available from any other source. The protection for "trial preparation materials" in Rule 26(b)(3) is essentially the codification of the "work product" doctrine first announced by the Supreme Court in *Hickman v. Taylor*,[131] and this section will use both terms.

APPLICATIONS

Documents Only (and Intangible Mental Impressions)

The trial preparation materials protection applies only to documents.[132] However, some courts allow a party to assert the work product protection at a deposition when questions go to the party's trial strategy, counsel's mental impressions, or "intangible work product."[133] It does not apply to facts known or gathered relating to the litigation, which generally are

---

[123] *W Holding Co., Inc. v. Chartis Ins. Co. of Puerto Rico,* 293 F.R.D. 68 (D.Puerto Rico 2013) (cost alone is not sufficient).

[124] The 2006 Amendment to the advisory committee note to Rule 26(b)(2).

[125] The 2006 Amendment to the advisory committee note to Rule 26(b)(2).

[126] *Knickerbocker v. Corinthian Colleges,* 298 F.R.D. 670, n.6 (W.D.Wa. 2014).

[127] *Rodriguez-Torres v. Government Development Bank of Puerto Rico,* 265 F.R.D. 40, 44 (D.Puerto Rico 2010).

[128] *Disability Rights Council of Greater Washington v. Washington Metropolitan Transit Authority,* 242 F.R.D. 139 (D.D.C. 2007).

[129] *Stoffels v. SBC Communications, Inc.,* 263 F.R.D. 406, 411–12 (W.D.Tex. 2009) (first step is to determine if materials are attorney-client communications, because work product protection only applies to documents that are otherwise discoverable).

[130] *See In re Perrigo Co.,* 128 F.3d 430, 437 (6th Cir. 1997) (noting that the work product doctrine creates a qualified immunity rather than a privilege).

[131] 329 U.S. 495, 67 S.Ct. 385, 91 L.Ed. 451 (1947).

[132] *In re Professionals Direct Ins. Co.,* 578 F.3d 432, 438 (6th Cir. 2009).

[133] *Bear Republic Brewing Co. v. Central City Brewing Co.,* 275 F.R.D. 43 (D.Mass. 2011) (work product doctrine may be asserted at the deposition of a party's investigator).

discoverable,[134] although it may apply to documents that summarize the facts.[135] It is unsettled whether the trial preparation materials protection applies to compilations of documents, such as documents selected for deposition preparation.[136] The protection has been held not to apply to electronic images of documents created for use in the litigation.[137]

Prepared in Anticipation of Litigation

The trial preparation materials protection applies only to documents prepared in anticipation of litigation.[138] Most courts apply the protection to documents prepared when litigation is expected but has not yet been commenced;[139] the timing of the preparation of the documents is not critical, as long as they were primarily concerned with the litigation.[140] Conversely, the protection does not apply to documents prepared in the regular course of business while litigation is pending.[141] The trend seems to be to apply the protection to documents prepared in anticipation of any litigation, not just the pending action.[142]

Prepared by Parties and Their Agents

The trial preparation materials protection applies to documents prepared by parties[143] and their agents.[144] Thus, the trial preparation materials protection applies to reports prepared by investigators on behalf of a party.[145] Unlike the attorney-client privilege, the trial preparation materials protection does not require any involvement by an attorney, so long as the document is prepared by a party or a party's agent in anticipation of litigation.[146]

Prepared by Experts

Generally, the discoverability of documents prepared by experts or of communications with experts is governed by Rule 26(b)(4)—titled Trial Preparation; Experts—not by the general trial preparation materials protections under Rule 26(b)(3).[147]

Who May Assert

The trial preparation material protection may be invoked by the party or the party's attorney.[148]

---

[134] *See In re Cendant Corp. Securities Litigation,* 343 F.3d 658, 662 (3d Cir. 2003).

[135] *US Airline Pilots Ass'n v. Pension Ben. Guar. Corp.,* 274 F.R.D. 28 (D.D.C. 2011).

[136] *See In re Grand Jury Subpoenas Dated March 19, 2002 and August 2, 2002,* 318 F.3d 379, 385 (2d Cir. 2003).

[137] *Hines v. Widnall,* 183 F.R.D. 596 (N.D. Fla. 1998).

[138] *F.T.C. v. Boehringer Ingelheim Pharmaceuticals, Inc.,* 778 F.3d 142, 149 (D.C. Cir. 2015) (employing a "because of" test).

[139] *E.E.O.C. v. Lutheran Social Services,* 186 F.3d 959 (D.C. Cir. 1999).

[140] *In re Professionals Direct Ins. Co.,* 578 F.3d 432, 439 (6th Cir. 2009) (the party must demonstrate that litigation was the "driving force" behind the preparation of the document).

[141] *Simon v. G.D. Searle & Co.,* 816 F.2d 397, 401 (8th Cir. 1987).

[142] *See F.T.C. v. Grolier, Inc.,* 462 U.S. 19, 26, 103 S.Ct. 2209, 76 L.Ed.2d 387 (1983).

[143] *Serrano v. Chesapeake Appalachia, LLC,* 298 F.R.D. 271, 277 (W.D. Pa. 2014) (a nonparty may not assert the trial preparation materials protection, but may be able to assert the common law work product doctrine).

[144] *McKinley v. Board of Governors of Federal Reserve System,* 647 F.3d 331 (D.C.Cir. 2011) (consultant deemed to be party's agent).

[145] *See In re Grand Jury Subpoena (Mark Torf/Torf Environmental Management),* 357 F.3d 900, 907 (9th Cir. 2004) (the work product doctrine applies to documents created by investigators working for attorneys, provided the documents were created in anticipation of litigation).

[146] *Kandel v. Brother Intern. Corp.,* 683 F.Supp.2d 1076, 1084 (C.D.Cal. 2010).

[147] *Republic of Ecuador v. Mackay,* 742 F.3d 860, 865–71 (9th Cir. 2014).

[148] *Hobley v. Burge,* 433 F.3d 946, 949 (7th Cir. 2006).

Obtaining Trial Preparation Materials

Trial preparation materials are discoverable if the attorney makes a sufficient showing that there is no reasonable alternative source for the same or substantially equivalent information,[149] and that the attorney has a *substantial* need for the information.[150] For example, a party may obtain a written statement in opposing counsel's files if the witness is no longer available.[151] Similarly, there may be no substitute for photographs taken shortly after an incident.[152]

Mental and Legal Impressions

The mental impressions and legal evaluations of an attorney, investigator, or claims agent (sometimes referred to as "core" or "opinion" work product) enjoy an almost absolute privilege from disclosure.[153] Thus, an attorney may redact statements reflecting mental and legal impressions from trial preparation materials that must be disclosed under Rule 26(b)(3).[154] Note, however, that the protections in Rule 26(b)(3) do not apply to interrogatories, which may require the respondent to make legal conclusions requiring the application of law to facts (in other words, the responding attorney may not interpose an objection on the basis that such a legal conclusion is the attorney's work product).

Statement of a Party

A party may always obtain a copy of the party's own statement.[155] A party may similarly obtain a copy of a statement by the party's agent or representative.[156] To obtain a copy of a party's statement, the party does not need to use the document request procedures in Rule 34, but instead may simply make a request under Rule 26(b)(3).[157] A statement can either be a written statement that the party has signed or otherwise adopted or approved, or a contemporaneous verbatim recording of the party's oral statement.

Statement of a Witness

A nonparty witness has a right to a copy of the witness's own statement.[158] If a party refuses to provide a witness with a copy of the witness's statement, the witness may move to compel and for sanctions under Rule 37(a)(4). Parties, in contrast, do not have an absolute right to a copy of a nonparty witness's statement.[159] A party can attempt to get a copy of a witness's statement directly from the witness or by making the showing of necessity required to obtain trial preparation materials.[160]

---

[149] *Appleton Papers, Inc. v. E.P.A.,* 702 F.3d 1018, 1023 (7th Cir. 2012).

[150] *Republic of Ecuador v. Mackay,* 742 F.3d 860, 866 (9th Cir. 2014).

[151] *McCoo v. Denny's Inc.,* 192 F.R.D. 675 (D. Kan. 2000) (statements from witnesses who failed to appear for their depositions must be produced).

[152] *See Sorrels v. NCL (Bahamas) Ltd.,* 291 F.R.D. 682, 683 (S.D. Fla. 2013).

[153] *Appleton Papers, Inc. v. E.P.A.,* 702 F.3d 1018, 1023–24 (7th Cir. 2012).

[154] *See In re EchoStar Communications Corp.,* 448 F.3d 1294 (Fed. Cir. 2006).

[155] *Corley v. Rosewood Care Center, Inc.,* 142 F.3d 1041, 1052 (7th Cir. 1998).

[156] *Woodard v. Nabors Offshore Corp.,* 2001 WL 13339 (E.D. La. 2001).

[157] *Manske v. UPS Cartage Services, Inc.,* 789 F.Supp.2d 213 (D.Me. 2011) (discussing the timing for production of a statement under Rule 26(b)(3)).

[158] *Thomas v. Old Town Dental Group, P.A.,* 300 F.R.D. 585 (S.D.Fla. 2014).

[159] *Ott v. City of Milwaukee,* 291 F.R.D. 151 (E.D.Wis. 2013) (disclosure of witness statements is particularly discouraged).

[160] *Garcia v. City of El Centro,* 214 F.R.D. 587, 594–95 (S.D. Cal. 2003) (there is a split as to whether the mere passage of time creates a substantial need for a witness statement).

Controlling Law

Unlike most privileges, the trial preparation materials doctrine is controlled by federal common law, even in diversity cases.[161]

Burden of Proof

The party asserting the trial preparation materials doctrine has the burden of demonstrating that the subject documents are trial preparation materials.[162] The party seeking the opponent's trial preparation materials then has the burden of showing the necessity of obtaining the trial preparation materials.[163]

Waiver

Evaluating waiver of the trial preparation materials doctrine entails an evaluation of F.R.E. 502 as well as Rule 26(b)(3).[164] Generally, disclosure of documents to an adverse party, or in a manner such that an adverse party may see the documents,[165] constitutes a waiver of the trial preparation materials protection with respect to those documents.[166] Disclosure of documents to someone not adverse,[167] such as a co-defendant or a consultant,[168] may not constitute a waiver of the trial preparation materials protection.[169] Note that this differs from most privileges, which are waived by disclosure to anyone, not just parties.[170] Note also that some courts hold that, in contrast to the attorney-client privilege, waiver of the trial preparation materials protection applies only to the documents disclosed, not to the entire subject matter.[171] The courts are divided as to which party has the burden of proving waiver.[172]

Recalling Trial Preparation Materials

Rule 26(b)(5)(B) establishes a procedure to recall attorney trial preparation materials that has already been produced, which is described below.

Discovery Stage Only

Trial preparation materials may be withheld as privileged during discovery, then used at trial. Note the contrast with most other privileges, which cannot be asserted during discovery then waived at trial.

---

[161] *Black & Veatch Corp. v. Aspen Ins. (UK) Ltd.*, 297 F.R.D. 611, 615, n.21 (D. Kan. 2014).

[162] *Biegas v. Quickway Carriers, Inc.*, 573 F.3d 365, 381 (6th Cir. 2009) (conclusory affidavit not sufficient to carry burden of proof).

[163] *Costello v. Poisella*, 291 F.R.D. 224 (N.D.Ill. 2013).

[164] *See Appleton Papers, Inc. v. E.P.A.*, 702 F.3d 1018, 1026 (7th Cir. 2012).

[165] *Goodrich Corp. v. U.S. E.P.A.*, 593 F.Supp.2d 184, 190–92 (D.D.C. 2009) (disclosure to a 3rd party who discloses to the opposing party deemed a waiver).

[166] *Menasha Corp. v. U.S. Dept. of Justice*, 707 F.3d 846, 847 (7th Cir. 2013).

[167] *Menasha Corp. v. U.S. Dept. of Justice*, 707 F.3d 846 (7th Cir. 2013) (different branches of the U.S. government not considered adverse parties, even though often at odds).

[168] *Appleton Papers, Inc. v. E.P.A.*, 702 F.3d 1018, 1021–22 (7th Cir. 2012) (disclosure to a non-testifying expert does not cause waiver).

[169] *Trustees of Elec. Workers Local No. 26 Pension Trust Fund v. Trust Fund Advisors, Inc.*, 266 F.R.D. 1, 14 (D.D.C. 2010).

[170] *See In re Columbia/HCA Healthcare Corp. Billing Practices Litigation*, 293 F.3d 289, 314 (6th Cir. 2002) (disclosure to third parties does not waive the work product protection).

[171] *See, e.g., Appleton Papers, Inc. v. E.P.A.*, 702 F.3d 1018, 1025–26 (7th Cir. 2012).

[172] *See Schaeffler v. United States*, 22 F.Supp.2d 319, 335 (S.D.N.Y. 2014) (party making work product claim has the burden of proving non-waiver).

RULE 26(b)(4)—TRIAL PREPARATION: EXPERTS

CORE CONCEPT

Parties may depose expert witnesses who may testify at trial. Draft expert reports and most communications with experts are protected as trial preparation materials. Only very limited discovery is permitted with respect to non-testifying experts.

APPLICATIONS

Depositions of Experts

Parties may take the deposition of any expert witness that may testify at trial.[173]

Time for Expert Depositions

If an expert report is to be disclosed for an expert witness, then the deposition of that witness may not occur before the report is disclosed.

Experts Specially Retained but Not Expected to Testify

A party may not obtain discovery pertaining to experts who are not expected to testify, including their identity,[174] unless the party makes a showing of exceptional circumstances rendering it impracticable to obtain facts or opinions on the same subject by other means.[175] Such further discovery might be allowed when the particular consulting expert was the only expert to examine evidence that is no longer available (such as a blood sample).[176] Some courts hold that a non-testifying expert loses the protections from discovery if the expert consults with the testifying experts.[177]

Discovery of Treating Physician

There is a split of authority as to whether a treating physician is a fact witness or an expert witness for purposes of the provisions of Rule 26(b)(4).[178]

Experts Informally Consulted

No discovery is permitted of experts informally consulted but not retained.[179]

Experts Generally Retained

Full discovery is permitted regarding an expert who is a full-time employee of a party, or who was retained generally, rather than in connection with pending or anticipated litigation.[180] No expert fees are awarded in connection with such discovery.

Experts Who Witnessed or Participated in Events

Discovery pertaining to an expert who acquired her knowledge through witnessing or participating in the events that form the basis for the complaint is not covered by Rule 26(b)(4), which is limited to information acquired or developed in anticipation of litigation.[181]

---

[173] *R.C. Olmstead, Inc., v. CU Interface, LLC*, 606 F.3d 262 (6th Cir. 2010).

[174] *Williams v. Bridgeport Music, Inc.*, 300 F.R.D. 120 (S.D.N.Y. 2014).

[175] *Republic of Ecuador v. Mackay*, 742 F.3d 860, 866 (9th Cir. 2014).

[176] *See, e.g., Spearman Industries, Inc. v. St. Paul Fire and Marine Ins. Co.*, 128 F.Supp.2d 1148 (N.D. Ill. 2001) (describing circumstances where a party might obtain discovery from a non-testifying expert).

[177] *See In re Chevron Corp.*, 633 F.3d 153, 164, n.17 (3d Cir. 2011).

[178] *See, e.g., Patterson v. Avis Rent A Car Systems, Inc.*, 48 F.Supp.3d 532, 533 (S.D.N.Y. 2014) (treating physician entitled to fees for attending deposition); *Demar v. United States,*199 F.R.D. 617 (N.D. Ill. 2001) (treating physician not entitled to expert fees from the party noticing the physician's deposition).

[179] *Eisai Co., Ltd. v. Teva Pharmaceuticals USA, Inc.*, 247 F.R.D. 440, 442 (D.N.J. 2007).

[180] *Dunn v. Sears, Roebuck & Co.*, 639 F.2d 1171, 1174 (5th Cir. 1981).

[181] *Battle ex rel. Battle v. Memorial Hosp. at Gulfport*, 228 F.3d 544, 551 (5th Cir. 2000).

Thus, full fact discovery is allowed regarding such experts, and no expert fees are awarded.[182]

Party Who Is an Expert

A party cannot avoid discovery or obtain expert fees by claiming to be an expert witness.[183]

Drafts of Expert Reports and Disclosures

Drafts of expert reports are not discoverable.[184]

Communications with Experts

Communications between counsel and experts who are required to provide an expert report (*i.e.*, those retained or specially employed to testify) are protected as trial preparation materials unless they pertain to: (i) compensation for the expert; (ii) the facts or data that counsel provided and the expert considered in forming the opinions to be expressed; or (iii) the assumptions that counsel provided and the expert relied on in forming the opinions to be expressed.[185] Communications with experts who are not required to provide expert reports (*i.e.*, treating physicians and other experts not retained or specially employed) are not protected under Rule 26(b)(4)—but they may be protected under other doctrines or privileges.[186] Rule 26(b)(4) only references communications between experts and counsel, and most courts have declined to apply the protection to communications between experts and non-lawyers.[187]

Duty of Attorney to Review Expert's File

Some courts hold that the attorney has a duty to review the expert's files to determine which communications and documents should be disclosed.[188]

Ex Parte Communications with Experts

A party should not have *ex parte* communications with an expert for another party.[189]

Testifying Expert Fees

The court must impose on the party seeking discovery of a testifying expert the reasonable expert fees incurred in responding to the discovery[190] unless manifest injustice would result.[191] For a deposition, the fee normally includes compensation for time testifying and may or may not include preparation time.[192] However, if the expert charges more than a "reasonable" fee, the party retaining that expert must pay the amount over and above the

---

[182] *Paquin v. Federal Nat. Mortg. Ass'n,* 119 F.3d 23, 33 (D.C. Cir. 1997) (denying payment of fees for alleged experts with personal knowledge).

[183] *See Krepps v. NIIT (USA), Inc.,* 297 F.R.D. 579, 580–81 (N.D. Ill. 2013).

[184] *Republic of Ecuador v. Mackay,* 742 F.3d 860, 866 (9th Cir. 2014).

[185] *Republic of Ecuador v. Mackay,* 742 F.3d 860, 866 (9th Cir. 2014).

[186] Advisory committee notes to the 2010 Amendments to Rule 26(b)(4)(C).

[187] *See, e.g., Republic of Ecuador v. Hinchee,* 741 F.3d 1185, 1189 (11th Cir. 2013).

[188] *See Gerke v. Travelers Cas. Ins. Co. of America,* 289 F.R.D. 316, 322 (D.Or. 2013).

[189] *See Sanderson v. Boddie-Noell Enterprises, Inc.,* 227 F.R.D. 448 (E.D. Va. 2005).

[190] *Stanley v. Cottrell, Inc.,* 784 F.3d 454, 464 (8th Cir. 2015).

[191] *Nilssen v. Osram Sylvania, Inc.,* 528 F.3d 1352 (Fed.Cir. 2008) (injustice is not limited to indigence, and can be based on the conduct of the party seeking fees; the decision not to award fees is reviewed for abuse of discretion).

[192] *Knight v. Kirby Inland Marine Inc.,* 482 F.3d 347, 356 (5th Cir. 2007) (fees for testimony are mandatory, but fees for other discovery are within the court's discretion).

"reasonable" rate for that witness' deposition.[193] Courts are split as to whether and when treating physicians are entitled to an expert witness fee.[194]

Non-Testifying Expert Fees

If discovery is obtained from non-testifying experts, the court must also require the party to pay a fair share of the expenses the experts incurred to form their opinions, in addition to the experts' fees for the time testifying or responding to the discovery.[195]

RULE 26(b)(5)—CLAIMING PRIVILEGE OR PROTECTING TRIAL-PREPARATION MATERIALS

CORE CONCEPT

A party who withholds information based on a claim of privilege or trial preparation materials protection must state the claim expressly and describe the nature of the documents or information so withheld in a manner that will enable other parties to assess the claim of privilege or protection. If privileged information is inadvertently produced in discovery, the producing party may notify the parties that received the information. The receiving parties must then either return the information or present the information to the court.

APPLICATIONS

Manner of Asserting Privilege

Many courts require a party asserting a privilege to produce a privilege log describing the documents withheld.[196] The Rules do not specify the time for production of a privilege log, and the case law varies.[197] Some courts hold that the log must be produced immediately[198] and some allow a "reasonable" time. Privileges may be waived broadly for failure to produce a privilege log[199] or to produce a sufficiently detailed log,[200] or specifically for any documents omitted from the privilege log.[201] The courts are divided as to how to handle email (and particularly email chains) on a privilege log.[202] Parties may not be required to log communications with counsel after the litigation has commenced, and counsel often agree not to log such communications.[203] Some courts hold that a party does not need to log expert materials shielded from discovery under Rule 26(b)(4), such as draft reports.[204]

---

[193] *Fiber Optic Designs, Inc. v. New England Pottery, LLC,* 262 F.R.D. 586, 590–91 (D.Colo. 2009) (declining to impose surcharge by expert agency).

[194] *See Wirtz v. Kansas Farm Bureau Services, Inc.,* 355 F.Supp.2d 1190, 1212–13 (D. Kan. 2005).

[195] *Guarantee Trust Life Ins. Co. v. American Medical and Life Ins. Co.,* 291 F.R.D. 234, 238 (N.D. Ill. 2013).

[196] *Perry v. Schwarzenegger,* 591 F.3d 1126, 1133, n.1 (9th Cir. 2009) (privilege log is required and does not impose an unconstitutional burden). *But see Burlington Northern & Santa Fe Ry. Co. v. U.S. Dist. Court for Dist. of Mont.,* 408 F.3d 1142, 1147 (9th Cir. 2005) (rejecting a *per se* rule that failure to provide a timely privilege log is a waiver of the privilege).

[197] *Banks v. Office of the Senate Sergeant-at-Arms and Doorkeeper,* 226 F.R.D. 113 (D.D.C. 2005).

[198] *See, e.g., S.E.C. v. v. Yorkville Advisors, LLC,* 300 F.R.D. 152 (S.D.N.Y. 2014).

[199] *Tom v. S.B., Inc.,* 280 F.R.D. 603, 614 (D.N.M. 2012).

[200] *S.E.C. v. v. Yorkville Advisors, LLC,* 300 F.R.D. 152 (S.D.N.Y. 2014); *but see Progressive Cas. Ins. Co. v. F.D.I.C.,* 298 F.R.D. 417, 421 (N.D. Iowa 2014) (in the absence of bad faith, waiver is not an appropriate remedy for technical shortcomings of the log).

[201] *Robinson v. Texas Auto. Dealers Ass'n,* 214 F.R.D. 432, 456 (E.D. Tex. 2003).

[202] *Muro v. Target Corp.,* 250 F.R.D. 350 (N.D. Ill. 2007).

[203] *Grider v. Keystone Health Plan Central, Inc.,* 580 F.3d 119, 140, n.22 (3d Cir. 2009).

[204] *See Williams v. Bridgeport Music, Inc.,* 300 F.R.D. 120 (S.D.N.Y. 2014).

Failure to State Claim of Privilege with Sufficient Specificity

If a party withholds information without properly disclosing the basis, the party may have waived the privilege,[205] and may be subject to sanctions under Rule 37(b)(2).[206]

Challenging Privilege Assertions

A party may challenge the privilege assertion for documents listed on a privilege log by filing a motion to compel, which places the burden on the party asserting the privilege to establish an evidentiary basis, by affidavit, deposition transcript, or other evidence, for each element of the privilege.[207]

Recalling Privileged Information

Rule 26(b)(5)(B) establishes a procedure to recall privileged information that has already been produced.[208] A party believing that it has produced privileged information may provide a notification to the parties who have received the information. The notification should be in writing (unless circumstances do not allow, such as in a deposition) and should be sufficiently detailed to allow the receiving parties to evaluate the claim of privilege.[209] After receiving such a notification, the receiving parties must return, sequester, or destroy the specified information and all copies (including taking reasonable steps to retrieve any information that the receiving party had already disclosed to other persons).[210] If they do not agree with the privilege assertion, they can present the information to the court under seal for a determination of the privilege claim. During the court's review of the privilege claim, the receiving parties are prohibited from using the information and the producing party must preserve it. Alternatively, the parties can propose their own procedures for privileged information that has been produced or disclosed.

Waiver of the Privilege for Recalled Information

Rule 26(b)(5)(B) does not address whether the privilege or protection is preserved or waived for information that was disclosed and then recalled. There is substantial case law addressing this topic that is unaffected by the procedures in Rule 26(b)(5)(B).[211]

RULE 26(c)—PROTECTIVE ORDERS

CORE CONCEPT

The court may enter orders designed to protect the parties and witnesses during the discovery process.

---

[205] *Hobley v. Burge*, 433 F.3d 946, 951 (7th Cir. 2006); *ePlus Inc. v. Lawson Software, Inc.*, 280 F.R.D. 247, 252 (E.D.Va. 2012) (failure to disclose author and recipients results in waiver).

[206] *Westfield Ins. Co. v. Carpenter Reclamation, Inc.*, 301 F.R.D. 235, 247 (S.D.W. Va. 2014).

[207] *See N.L.R.B. v. Interbake Foods, LLC*, 637 F.3d 492, 501 (4th Cir. 2011).

[208] *See Stewart Title Guar. Co. v. Owlett & Lewis, P.C.*, 297 F.R.D. 232, 240 (M.D. Pa. 2013).

[209] The 2006 Amendment to the advisory committee note to Rule 26(b)(5)(B).

[210] *See Edelen v. Campbell Soup Co.*, 265 F.R.D. 676, 698 (N.D.Ga. 2010).

[211] The 2006 Amendment to the advisory committee note to Rule 26(b)(2).

APPLICATIONS

Motion

Protective orders are obtained by motion filed in the district where the action is pending.[212] In the case of a deposition that is to occur in a different district, a motion may also be filed where the deposition is to occur.[213]

Certificate of Conference

A motion for protective order must include a certification that the movant has in good faith conferred or attempted to confer with the other party in an effort to resolve the dispute without court action.[214] Courts will frequently deny motions for protective orders that do not include the meet and confer certificate.[215]

Timing

There is no set period for filing a motion for a protective order.[216] Normally, the motion must be filed before the discovery is to occur, unless there is no opportunity to do so.[217]

Who May File

A motion may be made by a party or by a witness from whom discovery is sought.[218] The motion must be brought by the individual whose interests are affected. Thus, a party may not move for a protective order to protect the interests of another, but may move to protect the party's own interests when discovery is sought from another.[219]

Purpose of Protective Order

Rule 26(c) specifically instructs the court to limit the frequency or extent of discovery if justice so requires to protect a party or witness from annoyance, embarrassment,[220] oppression,[221] or undue burden[222] or expense.[223] Protective orders are also frequently used to enforce Rule 26(b)(2)(C), which instructs the court to limit the frequency or extent of discovery if: (i) the discovery sought is unreasonably cumulative or is obtainable from a more convenient or less burdensome or expensive source; (ii) the party seeking the discovery has had ample opportunity to obtain the information; or (iii) the discovery is outside the scope of discovery set forth in Rule 26(b)(1).

---

[212] *Victor Stanley, Inc. v. Creative Pipe, Inc.,* 250 F.R.D. 251 (D.Md. 2008).

[213] *In re Sealed Case,* 141 F.3d 337 (D.C. Cir. 1998) (nonparty witness has a right to have a motion for protective order heard in the district where the deposition is to occur).

[214] *Gov't of Ghana . ProEnergy Services, LLC,* 677 F.3d 340, 342 (8th Cir. 2012).

[215] *See Government of Ghana v. ProEnergy Services, LLC,* 677 F.3d 340, 342 (8th Cir. 2012).

[216] *United States v. Smith,* 985 F.Supp.2d 506 (S.D.N.Y. 2013) (discussing waiver).

[217] *Mims v. Central Mfrs. Mut. Ins. Co.,* 178 F.2d 56 (5th Cir.1949).

[218] *Silkwood v. Kerr-McGee Corp.,* 563 F.2d 433 (10th Cir.1977).

[219] *See Sun Capital Partners, Inc. v. Twin City Fire Ins. Co.,* 303 F.R.D. 673, 678 (S.D. Fla. 2014) (motion for protective order re subpoena issued to nonparty).

[220] *Seattle Times Co. v. Rhinehart,* 467 U.S. 20, 35 n.21, 104 S.Ct. 2199, 81 L.Ed.2d 17 (1984) (the rule serves in part to protect parties' privacy interests).

[221] *Nieves v. OPA, Inc.,* 948 F.Supp.2d 887 (N.D.Ill. 2013).

[222] *Jackson v. Allstate Ins. Co.,* 785 F.3d 1193, 1202 (8th Cir. 2015).

[223] *Stagman v. Ryan,* 176 F.3d 986 (7th Cir. 1999).

Good Cause

Protective orders are entered for "good cause."[224] The court has almost complete discretion in determining what constitutes good cause.[225] In general, the court will balance the need of the party seeking the discovery against the burden on the party responding.[226]

Burden of Proof

The party seeking the protective order has the burden of showing that good cause exists by stating particular and specific facts.[227]

Depositions

Motions for protective orders are most common in connection with depositions, because such motions are the only mechanism for challenging a deposition in advance of its occurrence.[228] With interrogatories, document requests, and requests for admission, a party can make objections to individual requests without providing a substantive response. The onus then shifts to the party seeking the discovery to move to compel an answer under Rule 37(a).

Types of Protective Order

Rule 26(c) lists eight kinds of protective orders, which are discussed immediately below. The list is not exclusive, however, and the court may make any type of protective order required by justice.[229] The specifically enumerated categories are:

(1) *Order That Disclosure or Discovery Not Be Had:* the court may order that the automatic disclosure or requested discovery not occur.[230]

(2) *Specified Terms and Conditions:* The court can impose terms and conditions on the automatic disclosure or the taking of discovery.[231] The court may designate the time and location of a deposition,[232] or the time to respond to interrogatories, document requests, requests for admission, or other discovery activities.[233] The court may order the party seeking discovery to pay the responding party's resulting expenses or may allocate the costs or responding among the parties.[234] The court may set deadlines for the completion of various phases of discovery or order that discovery be conducted in a particular sequence.[235] The court may issue a stay of discovery.[236] The court may also modify any of the terms and conditions in subsequent orders.[237]

---

[224] *Apple Inc. v. Samsung Electronics Co., Ltd.,* 727 F.3d 1214, 1222 (Fed. Cir. 2013).

[225] *Seattle Times Co. v. Rhinehart,* 467 U.S. 20, 104 S.Ct. 2199, 81 L.Ed.2d 17 (1984).

[226] *In re Sealed Case (Medical Records),* 381 F.3d 1205, 1215–16 (D.C. Cir. 2004).

[227] *Gulf Oil Co. v. Bernard,* 452 U.S. 89, 102, 101 S.Ct. 2193, 2201, 68 L.Ed.2d 693 (1981).

[228] *See United States v. One Gulfstream G-V Jet Aircraft Displaying Tail Number VPCES,* 304 F.R.D. 10, 12–13 (D.D.C. 2014) (motion for protective order re deposition location).

[229] *Chicago Mercantile Exch., Inc. v. Tech. Research Grp., LLC,* 276 F.R.D. 237, 239 (N.D.Ill. 2011).

[230] *CineTel Films, Inc. v. Does 1–1,052,* 853 F.Supp.2d 545 (D.Md. 2012).

[231] *Duling v. Gristede's Operating Corp.,* 266 F.R.D. 66, 71 (S.D.N.Y. 2010).

[232] *Paleteria La Michoacana, Inc. v. Productos Lacteos Tocumbo S.A. de C.V.,* 292 F.R.D. 19 (D.D.C. 2013).

[233] *Manske v. UPS Cartage Services, Inc.,* 789 F.Supp.2d 213 (D.Me. 2011).

[234] Prior to the 2015 amendments, courts inferred the right to allocate costs, but the 2015 amendments made that authority explicit.

[235] *Builders Ass'n of Greater Chicago v. City of Chicago,* 170 F.R.D. 435, 437 (N.D. Ill. 1996) (order setting the sequence of discovery appropriate when a potentially dispositive threshold issue has been raised).

[236] *Hong Leong Finance Ltd. (Singapore) v. Pinnacle Performance Ltd.,* 297 F.R.D. 69 (S.D.N.Y. 2013).

[237] *Martin v. Reynolds Metals Corp.,* 297 F.2d 49 (9th Cir.1961).

(3) *Method of Discovery:* The court may restrict discovery to a particular method (such as no depositions or depositions only upon written questions). The general principle is that the parties may select their own discovery methods without unnecessary interference from the court.[238] Thus, most motions to restrict the discovery methods are denied unless the moving party shows special circumstances.[239]

(4) *Limit of Scope or Time:* The court may limit the scope of the automatic disclosures or discovery to specific areas of inquiry or to a specific time period.[240] The court may also limit discovery to a critical or threshold issue.[241] For example, if a jurisdictional dispute exists, the court may restrict discovery to the jurisdictional issues, then permit broad discovery if jurisdiction is found to exist.[242] Similarly, if liability and damages are to be tried separately, the court may restrict discovery to liability issues until the first phase of the case is complete.

(5) *Persons Present:* The court may exclude the public, the press, other witnesses, or other nonparties from a deposition or access to documents produced in discovery.[243] The court generally will not exclude the parties or their attorneys.

(6) *Sealed Transcript:* The court may order a deposition transcript sealed, and thus not part of the public record.[244] Similar orders have been entered with respect to interrogatory answers or documents to be produced,[245] although such orders are not expressly authorized by 26(c)(1)(F).[246] Once a sealing order has been entered, parties are prohibited from disclosing to third persons information obtained pursuant to the court order.

(7) *Confidential Information:* The court may enter an order restricting disclosure of private personal information,[247] trade secrets, and confidential research, development, or commercial information[248] obtained during discovery.[249] There is no absolute privilege or protection with respect to such matters.[250] The normal procedure is for the parties to negotiate an agreement as to the handling of confidential information, which is often memorialized in a stipulated confidentiality order signed by the court—this procedure gives the court the ability to enforce the parties' agreement. If the parties cannot agree to a confidentiality stipulation, the responding party can move for a protective order or the party

---

[238] *National Life Ins. Co. v. Hartford Acc. and Indem. Co.,* 615 F.2d 595 (3d Cir. 1980).

[239] *Nguyen v. Excel Corp.,* 197 F.3d 200, 208–09 (5th Cir. 1999) (for "good cause shown," court may order discovery taken by a method other than that selected by the party seeking the discovery).

[240] *See Liese v. Indian River County Hosp. Dist.,* 701 F.3d 334, 335 (11th Cir. 2012).

[241] *Vivid Technologies, Inc. v. American Science & Engineering, Inc.,* 200 F.3d 795, 804 (Fed. Cir. 1999) (staying discovery on all other issues until critical issue is resolved).

[242] *Orchid Biosciences, Inc. v. St. Louis University,* 198 F.R.D. 670 (S.D. Cal. 2001).

[243] *Phillips ex rel. Estates of Byrd v. General Motors Corp.,* 307 F.3d 1206 (9th Cir. 2002) (the public generally, and the press in particular, are presumptively entitled to access documents produced in discovery, and good cause must be demonstrated to limit such access).

[244] *Pintos v. Pacific Creditors Ass'n,* 565 F.3d 1106, 1115 (9th Cir. 2009) (once documents have been attached to a dispositive motion and become part of the public record, having them sealed involves a heightened burden).

[245] *Apple Inc. v. Samsung Electronics Co., Ltd.,* 727 F.3d 1214, 1222 (Fed. Cir. 2013).

[246] *Morgan v. U.S. Dept. of Justice,* 923 F.2d 195 (D.C. Cir. 1991).

[247] *DaCosta v. City of Danbury,* 298 F.R.D. 37, 41 (D. Conn. 2014).

[248] *R.C. Olmstead, Inc., v. CU Interface, LLC,* 606 F.3d 262 (6th Cir. 2010) (court may decide whether trade secrets are relevant and whether the need for discovery outweighs the harm of production).

[249] *Seattle Times Co. v. Rhinehart,* 467 U.S. 20, 104 S.Ct. 2199, 81 L.Ed.2d 17 (1984).

[250] *Federal Open Market Committee of Federal Reserve System v. Merrill,* 443 U.S. 340, 99 S.Ct. 2800, 61 L.Ed.2d 587 (1979).

seeking the discovery can move to compel under Rule 37(a). The party seeking the discovery will have the burden of showing that the information is relevant and needed.[251] In most cases, the discovery will be allowed, but under restricted conditions regarding further disclosure. The court can fashion any order it sees fit, limiting how the information may be used, who may see it, etc.[252] The court can also designate an impartial third person to examine the confidential information.

(8) *Simultaneous Exchange:* The court may order the parties to simultaneously file designated documents or information in sealed envelopes, to be opened as directed by the court. This procedure is most common in patent cases, where it can be an advantage to know an opponent's claims.

Order Compelling Discovery

If the court denies a motion for a protective order, it may at the same time issue an order compelling the discovery. Such an order can facilitate obtaining sanctions under Rule 37.

Discovery While Motion for Protective Order Pending

Technically, a motion for protective order does not automatically stay the discovery that is the subject of the motion.[253] Thus, for example, a motion for protective order to prevent a deposition should not be filed on the day of the deposition, unless it was not practical to file it sooner. However, some local rules provide for an automatic stay of the subject discovery.[254]

Discovery Public When Filed

In general, discovery produced by private litigants is private until it is filed, at which point it becomes public.[255]

Expenses and Attorney's Fees

The court must require the party losing a motion for protective order to pay the expenses the opposing party incurred in connection with the motion, including reasonable attorney's fees, unless the losing party's position was "substantially justified," or other circumstances make such an award unjust.[256] The court will not award expenses to a moving party who failed to meet and confer before filing the motion.[257]

Motion to Vacate or Modify Protective Order

If circumstances change, a party may move to vacate or modify a protective order.[258]

Appeal of Discovery Order by Party

Discovery orders are normally interlocutory, not final, and thus not appealable until the end of the lawsuit.[259] A discovery order will be final if the underlying motion was the entire proceeding, such as with an order granting or denying a deposition to perpetuate testimony under Rule 27, an order denying discovery in aid of execution, an order granting

---

[251] *In re Cooper Tire & Rubber Co.,* 568 F.3d 1180 (10th Cir. 2009) (the burden then shifts to the party seeking the information to show that it is relevant and necessary).

[252] *See Paycom Payroll, LLC v. Richison,* 758 F.3d 1198, 1202–03 (10th Cir. 2014) (attorney's eyes only).

[253] *Creative Solutions Group, Inc. v. Pentzer Corp.,* 199 F.R.D. 443, 444 (D. Mass. 2001) (motion to stay discovery does not stay discovery).

[254] *Ecrix Corp. v. Exabyte Corp.,* 191 F.R.D. 611, 617 (D. Colo. 2000).

[255] *Bond v. Utreras,* 585 F.3d 1061, 1065–66 (7th Cir. 2009) (older cases allowing access were based on the prior version of Rule 5(d), which generally required discovery documents to be filed).

[256] *Josendis v. Wall to Wall Residence Repairs, Inc.,* 662 F.3d 1292, 1313 (11th Cir. 2011).

[257] *Bark v. Northrop,* 2 F.Supp.3d 1147 (D. Oregon 2014).

[258] *F.T.C. v. AbbVie Products LLC,* 713 F.3d 54, 66 (11th Cir. 2013) (burden is on the party seeking modification).

[259] *Cipollone v. Liggett Group, Inc.,* 785 F.2d 1108, 1116 (3d Cir. 1986).

Rule 26

learns was incorrect or incomplete and the information has not otherwise been made known to the other parties;[277] and

   (3)   *Court Order:* The duty to supplement may also arise by court order.[278]

After Acquired Information

The duty to supplement is triggered by information or documents acquired after serving the original disclosure or response—it is not an excuse that the disclosure or response was accurate when made.[279]

Timing of Supplemental Responses

No specific time periods are established for the duty to supplement.[280] Instead, supplements are to be made "in a timely manner."[281] The duty to supplement does not end when discovery ends.[282] Supplements made after the close of discovery, however, may not satisfy the Rules, particularly when the party had the documents or information in its possession, custody, or control prior to the close of discovery.[283]

No Request to Supplement Needed

The obligations to supplement are self-effectuating; there is no need to serve a request to supplement or motion to compel.[284] Nonetheless, a party will sometimes serve a request to supplement if it is concerned that another party has new information that it has not yet disclosed or produced.

Supplementing Expert Discovery

The obligations to supplement described above apply to both expert reports[285] and depositions of such experts.[286] Supplemental expert information should be disclosed by the time the pretrial disclosures are made, 30 days before trial unless otherwise set by the court.[287] A party may not use the supplementing procedure to submit an amended or rebuttal report not based on new information.[288]

Information Already Provided

A party need not supplement a disclosure or discovery response if the other parties have already received the additional or corrective information during the discovery process or in writing.[289]

---

[277] *Woods v. DeAngelo Marine Exhaust, Inc.*, 692 F.3d 1272, 1278–83 (Fed. Cir. 2012).

[278] *Chevron Corp. v. Salazar*, 275 F.R.D. 437, 449 (S.D.N.Y. 2011).

[279] *See Woods v. DeAngelo Marine Exhaust, Inc.*, 692 F.3d 1272, 1278–83 (Fed. Cir. 2012).

[280] *See Jama v. City and County of Denver*, 304 F.Supp.2d 289, 299–300 (D. Col. 2014).

[281] *Allstate Interiors & Exteriors, Inc. v. Stonestreet Const., LLC*, 730 F.3d 67, 75–6 (1st Cir. 2013).

[282] *Hernandez v. Polanco Enterprises, Inc.*, 19 F.Supp.2d 918, 933 (N.D. Cal. 2013).

[283] *In re Delta/AirTran Baggage Fee Antitrust Litig.*, 846 F.Supp.2d 1335, 1355 (N.D.Ga. 2012).

[284] *See Midwestern Pet Foods, Inc. v. Societe des Produits Nestle S.A.*, 685 F.3d 1046, 1056–57 (Fed. Cir. 2012).

[285] *See Brainard v. American Skandia Life Assur. Corp.*, 432 F.3d 655, 664 (6th Cir. 2005).

[286] *Osunde v. Lewis*, 281 F.R.D. 250, 257 (D.Md. 2012).

[287] *ZF Meritor, LLC v. Eaton Corp.*, 696 F.3d 254, 297 (3d Cir. 2012).

[288] *See, E.E.O.C. v. Freeman*, 778 F.3d 463, 467, n.7 (4th Cir. 2015).

[289] *Pina v. Children's Place*, 740 F.3d 785, 793 (1st Cir. 2014).

No Other Duty

The duties described in Rule 26(e) are the only duties to supplement.[290] Thus, an instruction in a set of interrogatories that the interrogatories are continuing or purporting to impose a duty to supplement is ineffective.

Sanctions

Failure to supplement a disclosure or discovery response is the equivalent of providing incorrect information in the initial disclosure or response. The court may exclude evidence[291] or claims,[292] may order a continuance and further discovery, or take any other action it deems appropriate[293] (*see* Rule 37 for a more detailed analysis of the available sanctions).

RULE 26(f)—CONFERENCE OF THE PARTIES; PLANNING FOR DISCOVERY

CORE CONCEPT

The parties must confer and develop a proposed discovery plan to be submitted to the court in writing addressing the discovery schedule and any modifications to the limits or scope of discovery.

APPLICATIONS

Time for Conference

The parties must confer "as soon as practicable and in any event at least 21 days before a scheduling conference is held or a scheduling order is due under Rule 16(b)."[294] The timing of the discovery conference may be modified by local rule or court order.

In-Person Attendance

The rules do not require that the Rule 26(f) conference be conducted in person, and the parties may participate by telephone.[295] However, the court can order the parties to participate in person.

Agenda for Discovery Conference

At the discovery conference, the parties must discuss the nature and basis of their claims and defenses[296] and the possibilities of prompt settlement or resolution of the case.[297] They must also make or arrange for the initial automatic disclosures required by Rule 26(a)(1), discuss orders that the court should enter[298] and issues relating to preserving discoverable information,[299] and develop a proposed discovery plan, as described below. The

---

[290] *Alvariza v. Home Depot,* 240 F.R.D. 586, 590 (D. Colo. 2007), aff'd, 241 F.R.D. 663 (D. Colo. 2007) (no duty to supplement documents informally produced by agreement).

[291] *Woods v. DeAngelo Marine Exhaust, Inc.,* 692 F.3d 1272, 1279–83 (Fed. Cir. 2012).

[292] *United States v. Philip Morris USA, Inc.,* 219 F.R.D. 198, 200–01 (D.D.C. 2004).

[293] *Townsend v. Daniel, Mann, Johnson & Mendenhall,* 196 F.3d 1140, 1151 (10th Cir. 1999) (no sanction warranted where conduct not culpable and no harm to defendant).

[294] *See Apple Inc. v. Samsung Electronics Co., Ltd.,* 768 F.Supp.2d 1040, 1044 (N.D.Cal. 2011);.

[295] The advisory committee note to the 2000 Amendment to Rule 26(f) expresses a preference for in-person meetings, but recognizes that the distances some counsel would have to travel and the resulting expenses may outweigh the benefits of an in-person meeting.

[296] *King v. Taylor,* 694 F.3d 650, 660, n.6 (6th Cir. 2012).

[297] *See U.S. ex rel. FLFMC, LLC v. TFH Publ'ns., Inc.,* 855 F.Supp.2d 300 (D.N.J. 2012) (discussion of alternative dispute resolution required by local rules).

[298] *Mallinckrodt, Inc. v. Masimo Corp.,* 254 F.Supp.2d 1140, 1157 (C.D. Cal. 2003).

[299] Although not specifically so limited, the 2006 Amendment to Rule 26(f) added information preservation to the agenda for the Rule 26 conference to address issues related to the preservation of electronically stored information.

parties may also attempt to reach a consensus as to the disputed facts alleged in the pleadings with particularity for purpose of the disclosures under Rule 26(a).

Content of Discovery Plan

The discovery plan should indicate the parties' positions or proposals concerning:

(1) *Automatic Disclosures:* Any changes to the timing, form, or requirement for disclosures under Rule 26(a).[300] The plan must explicitly state when the initial disclosures were or are to be made;

(2) *Discovery Scope and Schedule:* The likely subjects of discovery, the completion date for discovery, and any discovery that should be conducted in phases or limited to or focused on particular issues;[301]

(3) *Electronic Information:* Issues relating to the disclosure, production, or preservation of electronically stored information, including the sources of such data, the form in which it should be produced (i.e., in paper or electronic form, and if electronic, how it will be made available), and the costs of such production;[302]

(4) *Privilege Issues:* Issues relating to claims of privilege or work product protection, including any procedures to be used in the event of the inadvertent production of privileged information (to the extent that they differ from the procedures in Rule 26(b)(2)(B));[303]

(5) *Discovery Limits:* Any changes to the discovery limits established by the Rules or by local rule, plus any additional limits; and

(6) *Other Orders:* Any other case management or protective orders proposed to the court for consideration at the court's scheduling conference.

Submission of Plan

The parties should submit to the court a written report outlining the plan within 14 days of the discovery meeting.[304] The court may order that the discovery plan be submitted at a different time or that the plan be submitted at the Rule 16 conference with the court. Many local rules contain a sample report.

Good Faith Participation

Rule 26(f) places a joint obligation on the attorneys (and on unrepresented parties) to schedule the discovery conference and to attempt in good faith to agree on a proposed discovery plan and a report outlining the plan.[305]

Excluded Proceedings

A discovery conference and discovery plan are not required in proceedings listed in Rule 26(a)(1)(B) as exempted from initial disclosures.[306] Additionally, the parties may be excused from the discovery conference and plan requirements by court order.

---

[300] *In re Bristol-Myers Squibb Securities Litigation,* 205 F.R.D. 437, 440–41 (D.N.J. 2002) (the discovery conference should include a discussion of what documents are available in electronic format, and the format to be used for disclosures and production of such documents).

[301] *Fiber Optic Designs, Inc. v. New England Pottery, LLC,* 262 F.R.D. 586, 599 (D.Colo. 2009).

[302] *Rodriguez-Torres v. Government Development Bank of Puerto Rico,* 704 F.Supp.2d 81 (D.Puerto Rico 2010).

[303] See the 2006 Amendment to the advisory committee note to Rule 26(f) for a discussion of possible agreements regarding inadvertently produced privileged material, such as the "quick peek" procedure and the "clawback" procedure.

[304] *Siems v. City of Minneapolis,* 560 F.3d 824, 825, n.2 (8th Cir. 2009).

[305] *See Siems v. City of Minneapolis*, 560 F.3d 824, 826–27 (8th Cir. 2009) (dismissal based, in part, on failure to participate in the Rule 26(f) conference).

[306] *See, e.g., Orbe v. True,* 201 F.Supp.2d 671 (E.D. Va. 2002) (habeas corpus proceedings exempt from Rule 26(f)).

RULE 26(g)—SIGNING DISCLOSURES AND DISCOVERY REQUESTS, RESPONSES, AND OBJECTIONS

CORE CONCEPT

Every disclosure, request for discovery, and response or objection must be signed by at least one attorney of record. The signature constitutes a certification that to the best of the signer's knowledge, information, and belief, the document is complete and correct, and is being served for proper purposes within the Rules.

APPLICATIONS

Signature

Every disclosure, discovery request, response, or objection must be signed by at least one attorney of record (or by the party, if unrepresented).[307] The document must also state the address, e-mail address, and telephone number of the signer.

Certification for Rule 26(a) Disclosures

For the initial disclosures and the pretrial disclosures, the signature constitutes a certification to the best of the signer's knowledge, information, and belief formed after "reasonable inquiry" that the disclosure is complete and correct.[308]

Certification for Other Discovery Documents

For discovery requests, responses, and objections, the signature constitutes a certification to the best of the signer's knowledge, information, and belief formed after "reasonable inquiry"[309] that:

(A) The document is consistent with the Rules and existing law, or with a nonfrivolous argument for extension, modification, or reversal of existing law, or for establishing new law;[310]

(B) The document is not imposed for any improper purpose, such as to harass, delay, or cause needless expense for an opponent;[311] and

(C) The discovery is not unreasonably or unduly burdensome or expensive, given the nature of the case, the discovery already conducted, the amount in controversy, and the importance of the issues at stake in the litigation.[312]

Duty of Inquiry

The signer of a discovery document is under an obligation to make a reasonable inquiry into the issues covered by the certification before signing the document.[313]

---

[307] *U.S. v. Real Property Known As 200 Acres of Land Near FM 2686 Rio Grande City, Tex.,* 773 F.3d 654, 661 (5th Cir. 2014) (objection not signed).

[308] *Johnson v. BAE Systems, Inc.,* 4 F.Supp.2d 62 (D.D.C. 2013).

[309] *Guantanamera Cigar Co. v. Corporacion Habanos, S.A.,* 263 F.R.D. 1, 5 (D.D.C. 2009).

[310] *Victor Stanley, Inc. v. Creative Pipe, Inc.,* 250 F.R.D. 251 (D.Md. 2008) (filing a discovery response asserting a privilege without a factual basis to support each element of each privilege is sanctionable).

[311] *United States v. Kouri-Perez,* 187 F.3d 1, 6 (1st Cir. 1999).

[312] *See Legault v. Zambarano,* 105 F.3d 24, 27 (1st Cir. 1997).

[313] *Green Leaf Nursery v. E.I. DuPont De Nemours and Co.,* 341 F.3d 1292, 1305 (11th Cir. 2003) (the signature certifies that the lawyer has made a reasonable effort to assure that the client has provided all the information and documents available to him that are responsive to the discovery demand).

Unsigned Discovery Documents

If without substantial justification a discovery disclosure, request, response, or objection is unsigned, other parties should advise the party making the disclosure, request, response, or objection. If counsel for that party fails to sign the document promptly, the unsigned document will be stricken, no party will be obligated to respond to the unsigned document,[314] and the attorney serving the unsigned discovery document may be subject to sanctions.[315]

Unrepresented Parties

An unrepresented party should sign disclosures, discovery requests, responses, and objections and should list the party's address.

Sanctions

If without a substantial justification[316] a certification is made in violation of Rule 26(g), the court must impose an appropriate sanction[317] on the party, the attorney, or both.[318] The sanction may include expenses incurred because of the violation, including attorney's fees,[319] and may also include substantive sanctions like dismissal.[320]

ADDITIONAL RESEARCH REFERENCES

Wright & Miller, *Federal Practice and Procedure* §§ 2001 to 2052

C.J.S., Federal Civil Procedure §§ 526 to 535

West's Key Number Digest, Federal Civil Procedure ⊷1261 to 1278

---

[314] *Johnson v. BAE Systems, Inc.*, 4 F.Supp.2d 62 (D.D.C. 2013).

[315] *Walls v. Paulson*, 250 F.R.D. 48 (D.D.C. 2008).

[316] *Grider v. Keystone Health Plan Central, Inc.*, 580 F.3d 119, 139–40 (3d Cir. 2009) (sanctions vacated because the court did not expressly consider whether the violators had substantial justification).

[317] *Mancia v. Mayflower Textile Servs. Co.*, 253 F.R.D. 354, 358 (D.Md. 2008) (Rule 26(g) is designed to curb discovery abuses).

[318] *Rojas v. Town of Cicero, Ill.*, 775 F.3d 906, 909 (7th Cir. 2015) (award of sanction is mandatory—court's discretion is limited to selecting an appropriate sanction).

[319] *In re Delta AirTran Baggage Fee Antitrust Litig.*, 846 F.Supp.2d 1335, 1349–50 (N.D.Ga. 2012).

[320] *Zalaski v. City of Hartford*, 723 F.3d 382, 395 (2d Cir. 2013).

RULE 27

DEPOSITIONS TO PERPETUATE TESTIMONY

(a) Before an Action Is Filed.

(1) *Petition.* A person who wants to perpetuate testimony about any matter cognizable in a United States court may file a verified petition in the district court for the district where any expected adverse party resides. The petition must ask for an order authorizing the petitioner to depose the named persons in order to perpetuate their testimony. The petition must be titled in the petitioner's name and must show:

(A) that the petitioner expects to be a party to an action cognizable in a United States court but cannot presently bring it or cause it to be brought;

(B) the subject matter of the expected action and the petitioner's interest;

(C) the facts that the petitioner wants to establish by the proposed testimony and the reasons to perpetuate it;

(D) the names or a description of the persons whom the petitioner expects to be adverse parties and their addresses, so far as known; and

(E) the name, address, and expected substance of the testimony of each deponent.

(2) *Notice and Service.* At least 21 days before the hearing date, the petitioner must serve each expected adverse party with a copy of the petition and a notice stating the time and place of the hearing. The notice may be served either inside or outside the district or state in the manner provided in Rule 4. If that service cannot be made with reasonable diligence on an expected adverse party, the court may order service by publication or otherwise. The court must appoint an attorney to represent persons not served in the manner provided in Rule 4 and to cross-examine the deponent if an unserved person is not otherwise represented. If any expected adverse party is a minor or is incompetent, Rule 17(c) applies.

(3) *Order and Examination.* If satisfied that perpetuating the testimony may prevent a failure or delay of justice, the court must issue an order that designates or describes the persons whose depositions may be taken, specifies the subject matter of the examinations, and states whether the depositions will be taken orally or by written interrogatories. The depositions may then be taken under these rules, and the court may issue orders like those authorized by Rules 34 and 35. A reference in these

rules to the court where an action is pending means, for purposes of this rule, the court where the petition for the deposition was filed.

(4) *Using the Deposition.* A deposition to perpetuate testimony may be used under Rule 32(a) in any later-filed district-court action involving the same subject matter if the deposition either was taken under these rules or, although not so taken, would be admissible in evidence in the courts of the state where it was taken.

(b) Pending Appeal.

(1) *In General.* The court where a judgment has been rendered may, if an appeal has been taken or may still be taken, permit a party to depose witnesses to perpetuate their testimony for use in the event of further proceedings in that court.

(2) *Motion.* The party who wants to perpetuate testimony may move for leave to take the depositions, on the same notice and service as if the action were pending in the district court. The motion must show:

(A) the name, address, and expected substance of the testimony of each deponent; and

(B) the reasons for perpetuating the testimony.

(3) *Court Order.* If the court finds that perpetuating the testimony may prevent a failure or delay of justice, the court may permit the depositions to be taken and may issue orders like those authorized by Rules 34 and 35. The depositions may be taken and used as any other deposition taken in a pending district-court action.

(c) Perpetuation by an Action. This rule does not limit a court's power to entertain an action to perpetuate testimony.

[Amended effective March 19, 1948; October 20, 1949; July 1, 1971; August 1, 1987; April 25, 2005, effective December 1, 2005; April 30, 2007, effective December 1, 2007; March 26, 2009, effective December 1, 2009.]

AUTHORS' COMMENTARY ON RULE 27

PURPOSE AND SCOPE

Sometimes it will be important to preserve or perpetuate testimony before an action is commenced or during the appeal of an action. Rule 27 provides one mechanism for perpetuating such testimony by taking a deposition.

RULE 27(a)—BEFORE AN ACTION IS FILED

CORE CONCEPT

Rule 27 is most commonly used to perpetuate testimony when there is a danger that important testimony will be lost, but for some reason a civil action cannot yet be commenced.

APPLICATIONS

Verified Petition

A request for a deposition under Rule 27 must be by *verified* petition (*i.e.,* a petition accompanied by a statement signed by the petitioner that the factual averments are accurate).[1]

Contents of Petition

A Rule 27 petition must contain the following:

(1) A statement that the petitioner expects to be a party to an action in federal court,[2] but is presently unable to bring the action;

(2) A description of the subject matter of the anticipated action and the petitioner's relationship to the action;

(3) The facts that the petitioner intends to establish by the testimony, and the petitioner's need for perpetuating it;[3]

(4) The identities and addresses[4] of the persons expected to be adverse parties in the action; and

(5) The identity of the deponent(s) and a detailed description of the substance of their testimony.[5]

The petition must also include a proposed order describing the procedure and scope of the deposition.

Preservation of Evidence

On its face, Rule 27 only authorizes depositions, not document requests.[6] However, some courts will allow Rule 27 petitions to preserve evidence that might be lost.[7]

Certainty of Litigation Unnecessary

A party need not demonstrate that litigation is absolutely certain in order to file a motion to perpetuate; instead, the party must be found to be acting in anticipation of litigation.[8]

Need to Perpetuate

It is not necessary to show that the deponents are on their death beds. Rather, one must show that there is a danger of the testimony or evidence being lost,[9] such as when

---

[1] *In re Chester County Elec., Inc.,* 208 F.R.D. 545, 546–47 (E.D. Pa. 2002).

[2] *See Advanced Orthopedic Designs, L.L.C. v. Shinseki,* 886 F.Supp.2d 546, 554 (W.D.Tex. 2012).

[3] *In re Yamaha Motor Corp., U.S.A.,* 251 F.R.D. 97, 99 (N.D.N.Y. 2008).

[4] *Norex Petroleum Ltd. v. Access Industries, Inc.,* 620 F.Supp.2d 587 (S.D.N.Y. 2009) (petition defective because it did not include the witness's address).

[5] *Penn Mut. Life Ins. Co. v. United States,*68 F.3d 1371, 1374 (D.C. Cir. 1995) (instructing the district court on remand of a Rule 27 ruling to require a "narrowly tailored showing of the substance" of the testimony).

[6] *United States v. Van Rossem,* 180 F.R.D. 245, 247 (W.D.N.Y. 1998).

[7] *Application of Deiulemar Compagnia Di Navigazione S.p.A. v. M/V Allegra,* 198 F.3d 473, 478 (4th Cir. 1999) (inspection of ship engine repairs).

[8] *Calderon v. U.S. Dist. Court for Northern Dist. of California,* 144 F.3d 618 (9th Cir. 1998).

[9] *Calderon v. U.S. Dist. Court for Northern Dist. of California,* 144 F.3d 618 (9th Cir. 1998).

circumstances indicate that memories may fade.[10] In making this determination, the deponent's age alone can present a sufficient risk the deponent will be unable to testify.[11]

Pre-Litigation Only

Once litigation has been commenced, Rule 27(a) may no longer be used to perpetuate testimony, and Rules 26 and 30 take over.[12]

Inability to Bring Suit

One requirement for petitions to perpetuate testimony under Rule 27(a) is that the movant not be able to bring a lawsuit.[13] One basis for such inability is a lack of sufficient information to draft the complaint under the constraints of Rule 11.[14] However, Rule 27 may not be used to uncover or discover testimony necessary to file suit,[15] and applies only where known testimony is to be preserved.[16]

Place of Filing

The petition may be filed in the district in which any of the adverse parties reside. If *all* adverse parties are both not American citizens and not residing in the United States, the petition may be filed in any district.

Hearing

The court must hold a hearing on a Rule 27 petition.[17]

Notice and Service

At least 21 days prior to the hearing, the petitioner must send notice and a copy of the petition to all expected adverse parties.[18] The notice may be served in the manner provided under Rule 4. If personal service cannot be made, the court can order service by publication or otherwise.

Standard for Ruling

The court will order the deposition if it is satisfied that the perpetuation of the testimony may prevent a future failure or delay of justice.[19]

Conduct of the Deposition

The court must designate the deponent(s), the subject matter of the examination, and whether the deposition will be oral or written.[20] The deposition is then taken in accordance with the court order and Rules pertaining to depositions (*see* Rule 30 and Rule 31).

Scope of Deposition

The scope of a deposition under Rule 27 is often narrower than a typical discovery deposition, and generally will be governed by the court's order.[21] In general, courts have

---

[10] *State of Arizona v. State of California,* 292 U.S. 341, 54 S.Ct. 735, 78 L. Ed. 1298 (1934).

[11] *Penn Mut. Life Ins. Co. v. United States,*68 F.3d 1371, 1375 (D.C. Cir. 1995).

[12] *19th Street Baptist Church v. St. Peters Episcopal Church,* 190 F.R.D. 345, 348 (E.D. Pa. 2000).

[13] *In re Enable Commerce, Inc.,* 256 F.R.D. 527, 532 (N.D.Tex. 2009).

[14] *Petition of Alpha Industries, Inc.,* 159 F.R.D. 456 (S.D. N.Y. 1995).

[15] *Application of Deiulemar Compagnia Di Navigazione S.p.A. v. M/V Allegra,* 198 F.3d 473, 485 (4th Cir. 1999).

[16] *In re Ramirez,* 241 F.R.D. 595 (W.D.Tex. 2006).

[17] *In re I-35W Bridge Collapse Site Inspection,* 243 F.R.D. 349, 351 (D. Minn. 2007).

[18] *In re Petition of Allegretti,* 229 F.R.D. 93, 96 (S.D. N.Y. 2005).

[19] *In re Charter Communications, Inc., Subpoena Enforcement Matter,* 393 F.3d 771, 784 (8th Cir. 2005).

[20] *Martin v. Reynolds Metals Corp.,* 297 F.2d 49, 55 (9th Cir. 1961).

[21] *State of Nev. v. O'Leary,* 63 F.3d 932, 936 (9th Cir. 1995).

required that the evidence to be preserved be material and competent, not merely discoverable under general discovery provisions.[22]

Use of the Transcript

A deposition taken pursuant to Rule 27 may be used in any subsequent action in federal court involving the subject matter identified in the petition under the general terms and conditions governing use of depositions in Rule 32(a).

Subject Matter Jurisdiction

A proceeding to perpetuate testimony is not a separate civil action, and does not require its own basis for jurisdiction.[23] However, the petition must demonstrate that the anticipated legal action will proceed in federal court.[24]

Appeals

A grant or denial of a Rule 27 petition is appealable as a final order.[25]

RULE 27(b)—PENDING APPEAL

CORE CONCEPT

Rule 27 may be used while a case is on appeal, or while the period to appeal is running, to preserve testimony in the event that further proceedings are needed.[26] A request for a deposition pending an appeal is made by motion (not petition) to the district court where the action proceeded.[27] The motion must include the names and addresses of the deponents, the substance of their testimony, and the reasons for perpetuating their testimony.[28] Otherwise, a motion pursuant to Rule 27(b) is subject to the notice, service, and other requirements and conditions for a petition under Rule 27(a) described above.

RULE 27(c)—PERPETUATION BY AN ACTION

CORE CONCEPT

Rule 27 is not the exclusive method of perpetuating testimony.[29] Thus, for example, a deposition that would be admissible in a subsequent proceeding in state court will also be admissible in federal court, even though the offering party may not have complied with Rule 27. Likewise, a party may preserve testimony under a method authorized by statute.

ADDITIONAL RESEARCH REFERENCES

Wright & Miller, *Federal Practice and Procedure* §§ 2071 to 2076.

Lisnek & Kaufman, Depositions: Procedure, Strategy and Technique

---

[22]   *In re Hopson Marine Transp., Inc.,* 168 F.R.D. 560, 565 (E.D. La. 1996).

[23]   *Socha v. Pollard,* 621 F.3d 667, 671 (7th Cir. 2010).

[24]   *Advanced Orthopedic Designs, L.L.C. v. Shinseki,* 886 F.Supp.2d 546, 554 (W.D.Tex. 2012).

[25]   *Martin v. Reynolds Metals Corp.,* 297 F.2d 49 (9th Cir.1961).

[26]   *See Schreier v. Weight Watchers Northeast Region, Inc.,* 872 F.Supp. 1 (E.D. N.Y. 1994), aff'd, 57 F.3d 1064 (2d Cir. 1995).

[27]   *United States v. Van Rossem,* 180 F.R.D. 245, 247 (W.D. N.Y. 1998) (motion to compel Rule 27 discovery denied because need to perpetuate testimony was not demonstrated).

[28]   *Foy v. Dicks,* 1996 WL 745501 (E.D. Pa. 1996) (petitioners' Rule 27 motion denied for failure to assert reasons why perpetuation of evidence was necessary).

[29]   *See Nissei Sangyo America, Ltd. v. United States,* 31 F.3d 435 (7th Cir. 1994) (action to perpetuate foreign bank records).

C.J.S., Federal Civil Procedure §§ 544 to 547

West's Key Number Digest, Federal Civil Procedure ⊶1291 to 1299

RULE 28

PERSONS BEFORE WHOM DEPOSITIONS
MAY BE TAKEN

(a) Within the United States.

(1) *In General.* Within the United States or a territory or insular possession subject to United States jurisdiction, a deposition must be taken before:

    (A) an officer authorized to administer oaths either by federal law or by the law in the place of examination; or

    (B) a person appointed by the court where the action is pending to administer oaths and take testimony.

(2) *Definition of "Officer."* The term "officer" in Rules 30, 31, and 32 includes a person appointed by the court under this rule or designated by the parties under Rule 29(a).

(b) In a Foreign Country.

(1) *In General.* A deposition may be taken in a foreign country:

    (A) under an applicable treaty or convention;

    (B) under a letter of request, whether or not captioned a "letter rogatory";

    (C) on notice, before a person authorized to administer oaths either by federal law or by the law in the place of examination; or

    (D) before a person commissioned by the court to administer any necessary oath and take testimony.

(2) *Issuing a Letter of Request or a Commission.* A letter of request, a commission, or both may be issued:

    (A) on appropriate terms after an application and notice of it; and

    (B) without a showing that taking the deposition in another manner is impracticable or inconvenient.

(3) *Form of a Request, Notice, or Commission.* When a letter of request or any other device is used according to a treaty or convention, it must be captioned in the form prescribed by that treaty or convention. A letter of request may be addressed "To the Appropriate Authority in [name of country]." A deposition notice or a commission must designate by name or descriptive title the person before whom the deposition is to be taken.

(4) *Letter of Request—Admitting Evidence.* Evidence obtained in response to a letter of request need not be excluded merely because it is not a verbatim transcript, because the testimony was not taken under oath, or

because of any similar departure from the requirements for depositions taken within the United States.

(c) Disqualification. A deposition must not be taken before a person who is any party's relative, employee, or attorney; who is related to or employed by any party's attorney; or who is financially interested in the action.

[Amended December 27, 1946, effective March 19, 1948; January 21, 1963, effective July 1, 1963; April 29, 1980, effective August 1, 1980; March 2, 1987, effective August 1, 1987; April 22, 1993, effective December 1, 1993; April 30, 2007, effective December 1, 2007.]

AUTHORS' COMMENTARY ON RULE 28

PURPOSE AND SCOPE

Rule 28 specifies the type of person who must be present at a deposition to administer the oath and to record the testimony.

RULE 28(a)—WITHIN THE UNITED STATES

CORE CONCEPT

In the United States, or a territory or insular possession, depositions may be taken before an officer authorized to administer oaths under federal or state law.[1] Typically, a stenographer is such an officer. A deposition may also be taken before someone appointed by the court, or before a person designated by the parties pursuant to Rule 29.[2]

RULE 28(b)—IN A FOREIGN COUNTRY

CORE CONCEPT

The procedures for taking depositions in a foreign country depend upon the particular country. Some countries have treaties with the United States that facilitate such depositions. Other countries strictly prohibit such depositions altogether.

♦ **NOTE:** In some countries, the taking of evidence under unauthorized procedures may subject the interrogator to severe—even criminal—sanctions. Before taking such evidence, a practitioner should consult the Hague Convention and all treaty supplements.

APPLICATIONS

Alternatives

Depending upon the laws of the foreign country, a deposition in a foreign country may be taken:

(1) Pursuant to any applicable treaty or convention (such as the Hague Convention);[3]

(2) Pursuant to a letter request (or letter rogatory), which is a formal communication between the court in which an action is proceeding and another court requesting that the testimony of a foreign witness be taken under the direction of the foreign court;[4]

---

[1]   *Hudson v. Spellman High Voltage,* 178 F.R.D. 29, 32 (E.D. N.Y. 1998).

[2]   *Popular Imports, Inc. v. Wong's Intern., Inc.,* 166 F.R.D. 276, 279–80 (E.D. N.Y. 1996).

[3]   *International Ins. Co. v. Caja Nacional De Ahoroo Y Seguro,* 2004 WL 555618 (N.D. Ill. 2004).

[4]   *See Murata Mfg. Co., Ltd. v. Bel Fuse, Inc.,* 242 F.R.D. 470 (N.D. Ill. 2007).

(3) Upon a notice of deposition by any person authorized to administer oaths either by the laws of the foreign country or the United States; or

(4) Before persons commissioned by the court, who will have power to administer an oath and hear testimony by virtue of their oaths.

Method Optional

A party seeking to depose a witness in a foreign country may use any of the methods listed in Rule 28(b) allowed by the foreign country's laws, and may combine two or more methods.

Issuance of Letter Requests

All courts of the United States are authorized to issue letter requests or letters rogatory,[5] which are typically channeled through the United States Department of State.

Testimony Pursuant to a Letter Request

The evidence taken pursuant to a letter request varies according to the foreign country's laws. Sometimes the foreign judge examines the witness, then makes a written summary of the testimony, which is acknowledged as correct by the witness. The United States court will then decide what weight to give the testimony depending upon the method of recording.

Compelling Attendance of Witness

If the witness is a party, then the witness is subject to the United States court's sanctions if the witness fails to appear as noticed. If the nonparty witness is a United States citizen, then the witness still may be subject to the United States court's subpoena power. However, if the nonparty witness is an alien, then the party will have to rely on a letter request.

RULE 28(c)—DISQUALIFICATION

CORE CONCEPT

The officer at a deposition may not be a relative, employee, or attorney of any of the parties,[6] or an employee or relative of an attorney for a party, or anyone with a financial interest in the action.[7]

APPLICATIONS

Objections

Objections to the officer must be raised before the deposition starts, or as soon thereafter as the interest of the officer becomes known or should have become known with due diligence. Otherwise, the objection is waived.[8]

ADDITIONAL RESEARCH REFERENCES

Wright & Miller, *Federal Practice and Procedure* §§ 2081 to 2084

C.J.S., Federal Civil Procedure § 593

West's Key Number Digest, Federal Civil Procedure ⊶1371

---

[5]   *See United States v. Reagan*, 453 F.2d 165 (6th Cir. 1971).

[6]   *See Schoolcraft v. City of New York*, 296 F.R.D. 231, 239 (S.D.N.Y. 2013) (plaintiff's attorney may not operate the videocamera).

[7]   *Ott v. Stipe Law Firm*, 169 F.R.D. 380, 381 (E.D. Okla. 1996) (plaintiff is not permitted to administer oath).

[8]   *See* Rule 32(d)(2).

RULE 29

STIPULATIONS ABOUT DISCOVERY PROCEDURE

Unless the court orders otherwise, the parties may stipulate that:

(a) a deposition may be taken before any person, at any time or place, on any notice, and in the manner specified—in which event it may be used in the same way as any other deposition; and

(b) other procedures governing or limiting discovery be modified—but a stipulation extending the time for any form of discovery must have court approval if it would interfere with the time set for completing discovery, for hearing a motion, or for trial.

[Amended March 30, 1970, effective July 1, 1970; April 22, 1993, effective December 1, 1993; April 30, 2007, effective December 1, 2007.]

AUTHORS' COMMENTARY ON RULE 29

PURPOSE AND SCOPE

For their convenience, the parties may stipulate to modified procedures for taking depositions and for other discovery methods as long as the stipulation does not interfere with a hearing or trial date or the discovery deadline.

APPLICATIONS

Procedures

Stipulations under Rule 29 are self-effectuating, and do not need to be filed with the court.[1] Stipulations may be written or oral.[2]

Depositions

The parties may designate the person before whom a deposition will occur, and the time, location, notice requirements, and method of taking the deposition.[3] Thereafter, a deposition taken in accordance with the stipulation may be used as if taken in accordance with the provisions governing depositions in Rules 30 and 31.[4]

Other Discovery Methods/Court Approval

The parties may also stipulate to any other discovery method,[5] except that the parties need court approval to modify the time to respond to interrogatories, document requests, and requests for admission set forth in Rules 33, 34, and 36 if the extension would interfere with the court's discovery deadline or with a hearing or trial date.[6]

---

[1]   *In re DFI Proceeds, Inc.,* B.R. 914, 916 (Bankr.N.D.Ind. 2011).

[2]   *I/P Engine, Inc. v. AOL, Inc.,* 441 283 F.R.D. 322, 324, n.3 (E.D.Va. 2012).

[3]   *Reder Enterprises, Inc. v. Loomis, Fargo & Co. Corp.,* 490 F.Supp.2d 111 (D. Mass. 2007) (parties may stipulate that depositions be taken "at any . . . place").

[4]   *See In re Angst,* 428 B.R. 776 (Bankr.N.D.Ohio 2010).

[5]   *See Erie Ins. Property & Cas. Co. v. Johnson,* 272 F.R.D. 177, 182 (S.D.W.Va. 2010) (extension of time to respond to disclosures or discovery).

[6]   *See Laborers' Pension Fund v. Blackmore Sewer Const., Inc.,* 298 F.3d 600, 605–06 (7th Cir. 2002).

Court Override

The court can order that parties perform under the Rules as written, vitiating any stipulations.[7]

ADDITIONAL RESEARCH REFERENCES

Wright & Miller, *Federal Practice and Procedure* §§ 2091 to 2092

C.J.S., Federal Civil Procedure § 566

West's Key Number Digest, Federal Civil Procedure ⊶1326

---

[7]   *In re Westinghouse Elec. Corp. Uranium Contracts Litig.,* 570 F.2d 899, 902 (10th Cir.1978).

RULE 30

DEPOSITIONS BY ORAL EXAMINATION

(a) When a Deposition May Be Taken.

(1) *Without Leave.* A party may, by oral questions, depose any person, including a party, without leave of court except as provided in Rule 30(a)(2). The deponent's attendance may be compelled by subpoena under Rule 45.

(2) *With Leave.* A party must obtain leave of court, and the court must grant leave to the extent consistent with Rule 26(b)(1) and (2):

    (A) if the parties have not stipulated to the deposition and:

        (i) the deposition would result in more than 10 depositions being taken under this rule or Rule 31 by the plaintiffs, or by the defendants, or by the third-party defendants;

        (ii) the deponent has already been deposed in the case; or

        (iii) the party seeks to take the deposition before the time specified in Rule 26(d), unless the party certifies in the notice, with supporting facts, that the deponent is expected to leave the United States and be unavailable for examination in this country after that time; or

    (B) if the deponent is confined in prison.

(b) Notice of the Deposition; Other Formal Requirements.

(1) *Notice in General.* A party who wants to depose a person by oral questions must give reasonable written notice to every other party. The notice must state the time and place of the deposition and, if known, the deponent's name and address. If the name is unknown, the notice must provide a general description sufficient to identify the person or the particular class or group to which the person belongs.

(2) *Producing Documents.* If a subpoena duces tecum is to be served on the deponent, the materials designated for production, as set out in the subpoena, must be listed in the notice or in an attachment. The notice to a party deponent may be accompanied by a request under Rule 34 to produce documents and tangible things at the deposition.

(3) *Method of Recording.*

    (A) *Method Stated in the Notice.* The party who notices the deposition must state in the notice the method for recording the testimony. Unless the court orders otherwise, testimony may be recorded by

audio, audiovisual, or stenographic means. The noticing party bears the recording costs. Any party may arrange to transcribe a deposition.

(B) *Additional Method.* With prior notice to the deponent and other parties, any party may designate another method for recording the testimony in addition to that specified in the original notice. That party bears the expense of the additional record or transcript unless the court orders otherwise.

(4) *By Remote Means.* The parties may stipulate—or the court may on motion order—that a deposition be taken by telephone or other remote means. For the purpose of this rule and Rules 28(a), 37(a)(2), and 37(b)(1), the deposition takes place where the deponent answers the questions.

(5) *Officer's Duties.*

(A) *Before the Deposition.* Unless the parties stipulate otherwise, a deposition must be conducted before an officer appointed or designated under Rule 28. The officer must begin the deposition with an on-the-record statement that includes:

(i)   the officer's name and business address;

(ii) the date, time, and place of the deposition;

(iii) the deponent's name;

(iv) the officer's administration of the oath or affirmation to the deponent; and

(v)   the identity of all persons present.

(B) *Conducting the Deposition; Avoiding Distortion.* If the deposition is recorded nonstenographically, the officer must repeat the items in Rule 30(b)(5)(A)(i)—(iii) at the beginning of each unit of the recording medium. The deponent's and attorneys' appearance or demeanor must not be distorted through recording techniques.

(C) *After the Deposition.* At the end of a deposition, the officer must state on the record that the deposition is complete and must set out any stipulations made by the attorneys about custody of the transcript or recording and of the exhibits, or about any other pertinent matters.

(6) *Notice or Subpoena Directed to an Organization.* In its notice or subpoena, a party may name as the deponent a public or private corporation, a partnership, an association, a governmental agency, or other entity and must describe with reasonable particularity the matters for examination. The named organization must then designate one or

more officers, directors, or managing agents, or designate other persons who consent to testify on its behalf; and it may set out the matters on which each person designated will testify. A subpoena must advise a nonparty organization of its duty to make this designation. The persons designated must testify about information known or reasonably available to the organization. This paragraph (6) does not preclude a deposition by any other procedure allowed by these rules.

(c) Examination and Cross-Examination; Record of the Examination; Objections; Written Questions.

(1) *Examination and Cross-Examination.* The examination and cross-examination of a deponent proceed as they would at trial under the Federal Rules of Evidence, except Rules 103 and 615. After putting the deponent under oath or affirmation, the officer must record the testimony by the method designated under Rule 30(b)(3)(A). The testimony must be recorded by the officer personally or by a person acting in the presence and under the direction of the officer.

(2) *Objections.* An objection at the time of the examination—whether to evidence, to a party's conduct, to the officer's qualifications, to the manner of taking the deposition, or to any other aspect of the deposition—must be noted on the record, but the examination still proceeds; the testimony is taken subject to any objection. An objection must be stated concisely in a nonargumentative and nonsuggestive manner. A person may instruct a deponent not to answer only when necessary to preserve a privilege, to enforce a limitation ordered by the court, or to present a motion under Rule 30(d)(3).

(3) *Participating Through Written Questions.* Instead of participating in the oral examination, a party may serve written questions in a sealed envelope on the party noticing the deposition, who must deliver them to the officer. The officer must ask the deponent those questions and record the answers verbatim.

(d) Duration; Sanction; Motion to Terminate or Limit.

(1) *Duration.* Unless otherwise stipulated or ordered by the court, a deposition is limited to 1 day of 7 hours. The court must allow additional time consistent with Rule 26(b)(1) and (2) if needed to fairly examine the deponent or if the deponent, another person, or any other circumstance impedes or delays the examination.

(2) *Sanction.* The court may impose an appropriate sanction—including the reasonable expenses and attorney's fees incurred by any party—on a

person who impedes, delays, or frustrates the fair examination of the deponent.

  (3) *Motion to Terminate or Limit.*

    (A) *Grounds.* At any time during a deposition, the deponent or a party may move to terminate or limit it on the ground that it is being conducted in bad faith or in a manner that unreasonably annoys, embarrasses, or oppresses the deponent or party. The motion may be filed in the court where the action is pending or the deposition is being taken. If the objecting deponent or party so demands, the deposition must be suspended for the time necessary to obtain an order.

    (B) *Order.* The court may order that the deposition be terminated or may limit its scope and manner as provided in Rule 26(c). If terminated, the deposition may be resumed only by order of the court where the action is pending.

    (C) *Award of Expenses.* Rule 37(a)(5) applies to the award of expenses.

(e) Review by the Witness; Changes.

  (1) *Review; Statement of Changes.* On request by the deponent or a party before the deposition is completed, the deponent must be allowed 30 days after being notified by the officer that the transcript or recording is available in which:

    (A) to review the transcript or recording; and

    (B) if there are changes in form or substance, to sign a statement listing the changes and the reasons for making them.

  (2) *Changes Indicated in the Officer's Certificate.* The officer must note in the certificate prescribed by Rule 30(f)(1) whether a review was requested and, if so, must attach any changes the deponent makes during the 30-day period.

(f) Certification and Delivery; Exhibits; Copies of the Transcript or Recording; Filing.

  (1) *Certification and Delivery.* The officer must certify in writing that the witness was duly sworn and that the deposition accurately records the witness's testimony. The certificate must accompany the record of the deposition. Unless the court orders otherwise, the officer must seal the deposition in an envelope or package bearing the title of the action and marked "Deposition of [witness's name]" and must promptly send it to the attorney who arranged for the transcript or recording. The attorney

must store it under conditions that will protect it against loss, destruction, tampering, or deterioration.

(2) *Documents and Tangible Things.*

    (A) *Originals and Copies.* Documents and tangible things produced for inspection during a deposition must, on a party's request, be marked for identification and attached to the deposition. Any party may inspect and copy them. But if the person who produced them wants to keep the originals, the person may:

        (i) offer copies to be marked, attached to the deposition, and then used as originals—after giving all parties a fair opportunity to verify the copies by comparing them with the originals; or

        (ii) give all parties a fair opportunity to inspect and copy the originals after they are marked-in which event the originals may be used as if attached to the deposition.

    (B) *Order Regarding the Originals.* Any party may move for an order that the originals be attached to the deposition pending final disposition of the case.

(3) *Copies of the Transcript or Recording.* Unless otherwise stipulated or ordered by the court, the officer must retain the stenographic notes of a deposition taken stenographically or a copy of the recording of a deposition taken by another method. When paid reasonable charges, the officer must furnish a copy of the transcript or recording to any party or the deponent.

(4) *Notice of Filing.* A party who files the deposition must promptly notify all other parties of the filing.

(g) Failure to Attend a Deposition or Serve a Subpoena; Expenses. A party who, expecting a deposition to be taken, attends in person or by an attorney may recover reasonable expenses for attending, including attorney's fees, if the noticing party failed to:

(1) attend and proceed with the deposition; or

(2) serve a subpoena on a nonparty deponent, who consequently did not attend.

[Amended January 21, 1963, effective July 1, 1963; March 30, 1970, effective July 1, 1970; March 1, 1971, effective July 1, 1971; November 20, 1972, effective July 1, 1975; April 29, 1980, effective August 1, 1980; March 2, 1987, effective August 1, 1987; April 22, 1993, effective December 1, 1993; April 17, 2000, effective December 1, 2000; April 30, 2007, effective December 1, 2007; April 29, 2015, effective December 1, 2015.]

AUTHORS' COMMENTARY ON RULE 30
PURPOSE AND SCOPE

Rule 30 sets forth the procedures for the taking of depositions by oral examination. Rule 30 must be considered in conjunction with the other discovery rules, and in particular Rule 26 governing the scope of discovery.

♦ **NOTE:** Rule 30 was substantially revised in 1993, 2000, and 2007, and great care should be exercised when citing decisions pertaining to Rule 30.

RULE 30(a)—WHEN A DEPOSITION MAY BE TAKEN

CORE CONCEPT

In general, a party may take the deposition of up to 10 witnesses, party or otherwise, at any time after the parties have conducted the discovery conference under Rule 26(f).

APPLICATIONS

Persons Subject to Deposition

Rule 30 authorizes any party to take the deposition of any person, party or not.[1] A party may even take the party's own deposition if, for example, the party will be unable to attend trial. One may also take the deposition of attorneys, including the attorneys for parties,[2] although the attorney-client privilege may shield most of an attorney's information. Depositions are also permitted of public officials, the United States, individual states, and other governmental subdivisions.[3]

Number of Depositions

The plaintiffs as a group are limited to 10 depositions total, by written and/or oral examination, as are the defendants and third-party defendants.[4] Subpoenas to produce documents do not count towards the 10 deposition limit.[5] It is not clear whether expert depositions count toward the limit.[6] This number may be increased or decreased by stipulation or by order of court.[7] In ruling on a motion to expand the number of depositions, the court will consider not only the necessity of the additional depositions, but also the necessity of the depositions already conducted.[8]

Counting Depositions of Rule 30(b)(6) Representatives

A notice to take the deposition of a corporate representative under Rule 30(b)(6) will count as one deposition toward the 10 deposition limit, regardless of the number of representatives designated to appear and testify.[9] The application of the limitation on repeat depositions of the same individual to Rule 30(b)(6) depositions are less clear. Some courts have held that it is impermissible to issue a second Rule 30(b)(6) notice without leave of

---

[1]   *CSC Holdings, Inc. v. Redisi,* 309 F.3d 988, 993 (7th Cir. 2002) (a party has a general right to compel any person to appear at a deposition).

[2]   *Shelton v. American Motors Corp.,* 805 F.2d 1323 (8th Cir.1986).

[3]   *United States v. Procter & Gamble Co.,* 356 U.S. 677, 78 S.Ct. 983, 2 L.Ed.2d 1077 (1958).

[4]   *O'Leary v. Accretive Health, Inc.,* 657 F.3d 625, 636 (7th Cir. 2011).

[5]   *Andamiro U.S.A. v. Konami Amusement of America, Inc.,* 2001 WL 535667 (C.D. Cal. 2001).

[6]   *Express One Intern., Inc. v. Sochata,* 2001 WL 363073 (N.D. Tex. 2001).

[7]   *O'Leary v. Accretive Health, Inc.,* 657 F.3d 625, 636 (7th Cir. 2011).

[8]   *Madison v. Jack Link Associates Stage Lighting & Productions, Inc.,* 297 F.R.D. 532, 535 (S.D. Fla. 2013).

[9]   *MMG Ins. Co. v. Samsung Electronics America, Inc.,* 293 F.R.D. 58 (D.N.H. 2013).

court.[10] Other courts have held that leave of court is not required to take the deposition of a witness as a Rule 30(b)(6) representative even if the witness has already been deposed in his or her individual capacity.[11]

Repeat Depositions

Leave of court or a stipulation of the parties is required to depose someone a second time. Leave of court is not required to reconvene and continue a deposition that was suspended or not completed the first day.[12] This restriction arguably applies to depositions of a corporate representative under Rule 30(b)(6).[13] Leave shall be granted subject to the principles in Rule 26(b)(1) and (2), such as when the sought-after information could not have been obtained in the first deposition.[14]

When Depositions May Be Conducted

Depositions generally may be taken at any time after the Rule 26(f) discovery conference and before the cut-off date for discovery established by the court. Leave of court is generally required to depose someone outside these time limits.[15] Additionally, in proceedings listed in Rule 26(a)(1)(B) as exempt from initial disclosures, there is no preliminary waiting period for depositions.

Post-Judgment Depositions

A judgment creditor is entitled to take depositions of the judgment debtor to inquire into the assets necessary to satisfy the judgment.[16]

Deponent in Prison

Leave of court must be obtained in order to take the deposition of a person confined in prison.[17]

RULE 30(b)(1)—NOTICE OF THE DEPOSITION; OTHER FORMAL REQUIREMENTS: NOTICE IN GENERAL

CORE CONCEPT

A party desiring to take a deposition must serve a written notice upon all other parties identifying the deponent and time and location of the deposition.[18] Depositions are only admissible against parties properly noticed or actually represented at the deposition.

---

[10] *See Ameristar Jet Charter, Inc. v. Signal Composites, Inc.*, 244 F.3d 189 (1st Cir. 2001).

[11] *See Beaulieu v. Board of Trustees of University of West Fla.*, 2007 WL 4468704 (N.D.Fla. 2007).

[12] *Paige v. Consumer Programs, Inc.*, 248 F.R.D. 272, 275 (C.D. Cal. 2008) (when the party appears but the deposition does not occur, the party may be re-noticed without violating the rule against second depositions).

[13] *See Ameristar Jet Charter, Inc. v. Signal Composites, Inc.*, 244 F.3d 189 (1st Cir.2001).

[14] *Collins v. International Dairy Queen*, 189 F.R.D. 496, 498 (M.D. Ga. 1999).

[15] *Simon v. Republic of Hungary*, 37 F.Supp.2d 381 (D.D.C. 2014).

[16] *Credit Lyonnais, S.A. v. SGC Intern., Inc.*, 160 F.3d 428, 430 (8th Cir. 1998).

[17] *Smith v. Florida Dept. of Corrections*, 713 F.3d 1059, 1062, n.3 (11th Cir. 2013).

[18] *Pegoraro v. Marrero*, 281 F.R.D. 122, 128 (S.D.N.Y. 2012) (court cannot compel witnesses to attend deposition without proof of a proper deposition notice).

APPLICATIONS

Content of Notice

The notice must state the time and place of the deposition,[19] and the manner of recording the deposition.[20] It must also state the name and address of the deponent, if known, or a general description sufficient to identify the deponent. The deposition notice does not need to describe the topics to be covered in the deposition.[21] If a subpoena *duces tecum* (seeking documents) is to be served under Rule 45, then the notice must include a description of the documents sought.[22]

Filing of Notice

The notice need not be filed.

Deposition of a Party

A deposition notice compels parties to attend a deposition, without the need for a subpoena.[23] A corporate party is required to produce directors, officers, and managing agents [24] pursuant to a notice of deposition; a subpoena is required for other employees.[25]

Deposition of a Nonparty

A notice of deposition is not binding on a nonparty. Instead, a subpoena must be issued pursuant to Rule 45 to force a nonparty to attend a deposition.[26] However, the party taking the deposition must still serve a deposition notice upon the other parties.[27]

Failure to Notify

If a party does not receive a notice of a deposition and does not appear or is not represented at the deposition, the testimony cannot be used against that party, even if the party had actual knowledge of the deposition.[28]

Timing of Notice

Rule 30(b)(1) states that a party must give "reasonable" notice.[29] There is no bright line as to what is reasonable notice, and the determination is extremely fact-specific.[30] If the parties cannot agree on a mutually acceptable date, then the reasonableness of the notice may be challenged by a motion for a protective order under Rule 26(c).

---

[19] *Shockey v. Huhtamaki, Inc.*, 280 F.R.D. 598, 600 (D.Kan. 2012).

[20] *Schoolcraft v. City of New York*, 296 F.R.D. 231, 239 (S.D.N.Y. 2013).

[21] *Whitehead v. Hidden Tavern, Inc.*, 765 F.Supp.2d 878, 881 (W.D. Tex. 2011) (only depositions of organizations under Rule 30(b)(6) require a list of topics).

[22] *Orleman v. Jumpking, Inc.*, 2000 WL 1114849 (D. Kan. 2000) (description of documents to be produced must be attached to or included in the notice).

[23] *Calderon v. Experian Information Solutions, Inc.*, 287 F.R.D. 629, 631 (D.Idaho 2012), aff'd, 290 F.R.D. 508 (D. Idaho 2013).

[24] *Murata Mfg. Co., Ltd. v. Bel Fuse, Inc.*, 242 F.R.D. 470 (N.D. Ill. 2007) (managing agents generally are current employees with control or authority over day-to-day business decisions).

[25] *Calderon v. Experian Information Solutions, Inc.*, 287 F.R.D. 629, 631 (D.Idaho 2012), aff'd, 290 F.R.D. 508 (D. Idaho 2013).

[26] *Lefkoe v. Jos. A. Bank Clothiers, Inc.*, 577 F.3d 240, 246 (4th Cir. 2009).

[27] *Lefkoe v. Jos. A. Bank Clothiers, Inc.*, 577 F.3d 240, 246 (4th Cir. 2009).

[28] *Nuskey v. Lambright*, 251 F.R.D. 3, 12 (D.D.C. 2008).

[29] *Kolon Industries Inc. v. E.I. DuPont de Nemours & Co.*, 748 F.3d 160, 173 (4th Cir. 2014).

[30] *Kolon Industries Inc. v. E.I. DuPont de Nemours & Co.*, 748 F.3d 160, 173 (4th Cir. 2014) (5 days' notice not reasonable).

One Notice Sufficient for All Parties

Each party does not have to serve its own notice in order to examine the witness; all parties are entitled to conduct examination once a deposition has been noticed.[31]

Sanctions for Failure to Appear

The sanctions for failure to appear at a deposition depend upon whether the witness is a party. Nonparty witnesses may be held in contempt of court for failure to obey a subpoena. Party witnesses are subject to the sanctions described in Rule 37(d).

Place of Examination

For a party deponent, one may select any location for the deposition, subject to the party's right to move for a protective order (but see the general rules below).[32] For a nonparty witness, the witness must travel up to 100 miles from the place where the witness resides, is employed, or regularly transacts business.[33]

General Rules for Deposition Location

The court has discretion to control the location of a deposition.[34] In general, however, plaintiffs will be required to travel to the district where the suit is pending for their depositions,[35] whereas defendants can have their depositions taken where they work or live.[36] Also, in general, the deposition of a corporation occurs at its principal place of business.[37] These general principles are, of course, subject to extenuating circumstances, such as a plaintiff who is too sick to travel.

Motion for Protective Order

If a notice of deposition is facially valid, then the witness must attend or file a motion for a protective order pursuant to Rule 26(c).[38] The motion must be made before the time scheduled for the deposition, and must show good cause for the requested protection. The motion must be accompanied by a certification that the parties met prior to the filing of the motion and attempted to resolve their dispute without intervention by the court.[39]

RULE 30(b)(2)—PRODUCING DOCUMENTS

CORE CONCEPT

A witness may be compelled to bring documents to a deposition by including a description of the documents in the notice of deposition (for a party witness) or by issuing a subpoena *duces tecum* under Rule 45(a)(1)(A)(iii) and including a description in the notice (for a nonparty witness).[40] However, if the witness is a party, then the witness must be accorded 30 days to interpose objections to the

---

[31]   *FCC v. Mizuho Medy Co. Ltd.*, 257 F.R.D. 679, 681–82 (S.D.Cal. 2009).

[32]   *United States v. One Gulfstream G-V Jet Aircraft Displaying Tail Number VPCES, Its Tools and Appurtenances*, 304 F.R.D. 10 (D.D.C. 2014).

[33]   *See* Rule 45(c)(1).

[34]   *In re Standard Metals Corp.*, 817 F.2d 625, 628 (10th Cir. 1987).

[35]   *Shockey v. Huhtamaki, Inc.*, 280 F.R.D. 598, 600 (D.Kan. 2012).

[36]   *Rapoca Energy Company, L.P. v. Amci Export Corp.*, 199 F.R.D. 191, 193 (W.D. Va. 2001).

[37]   *United States v. One Gulfstream G-V Jet Aircraft Displaying Tail Number VPCES, Its Tools and Appurtenances*, 304 F.R.D. 10 (D.D.C. 2014).

[38]   *Collins v. Wayland*, 139 F.2d 677 (C.C.A. 9th Cir. 1944).

[39]   *F.C.C. v. Mizuho Medy Co. Ltd.*, 257 F.R.D. 679, 681 (S.D. Cal. 2009).

[40]   *Lee v. U.S. Dept. of Justice*, 287 F.Supp.2d 15, 22 (D.D.C. 2003), aff'd, 413 F.3d 53 (D.C. Cir. 2005).

document request [41] (the rationale being that one should not be able to circumvent the 30-day period in the document request rule by issuing a notice of deposition).[42]

RULE 30(b)(3)—METHOD OF RECORDING

CORE CONCEPT

The notice of deposition must specify the method for recording the deposition testimony.[43]

APPLICATIONS

Methods Available

The party taking the deposition may have it recorded by audio, audiovisual, or stenographic means, unless the court orders otherwise.[44] Other parties may arrange for additional methods of recording.

Cost of Recording

The party taking the deposition bears the cost of the party's chosen method(s) of recording.[45]

Transcript

Any party may, at its own expense, arrange for a transcript to be made of a deposition recorded by nonstenographic means.[46]

Additional Methods of Recording

Any party may arrange for a method of recording a deposition in addition to that specified in the notice of deposition.[47] The party desiring such additional method of recording must send prior notice to all other parties and to the deponent,[48] and will bear the expense of the additional recording unless otherwise ordered by the court.[49] Some courts allow an attorney to record or videotape a deposition for his or her own use, but such a recording would not be admissible.[50]

Use of Nonstenographic Depositions

In order to use a nonstenographically recorded deposition at trial or in connection with a dispositive motion, a party must submit a transcript of the portions to be introduced for the court's use.[51]

---

[41] *Dowling v. Cleveland Clinic Foundation,* 593 F.3d 472, 479 (6th Cir. 2010).

[42] *See Canal Barge Co. v. Commonwealth Edison Co.,* 2001 WL 817853 (N.D. Ill. 2001) (discussing the relationship between document requests under Rule 34 and requests to bring documents to depositions).

[43] *Pioneer Drive, LLC v. Nissan Diesel America, Inc.,* 262 F.R.D. 552, 555, n.2 (D.Mont. 2009).

[44] *Planned Parenthood of Columbia / Willamette, Inc. v. American Coalition of Life Activists,* 290 F.3d 1058 (9th Cir. 2002) ("nonstenographic" means audio or audiovisual).

[45] *Morrison v. Reichhold Chemicals, Inc.,* 97 F.3d 460, 464 (11th Cir. 1996).

[46] *Hudson v. Spellman High Voltage,* 178 F.R.D. 29 (E.D. N.Y. 1998).

[47] *Pioneer Drive, LLC v. Nissan Diesel America, Inc.,* 262 F.R.D. 552, 555 (D.Mont. 2009).

[48] *Ogden v. Keystone Residence,* 226 F.Supp.2d 588, 605 (M.D. Pa. 2002).

[49] *See Craftsmen Limousine, Inc. v. Ford Motor Co.,* 579 F.3d 894, 897 (8th Cir. 2009) (discussing when the expenses of a videotaped deposition can be recovered as costs).

[50] *See Schoolcraft v. City of New York,* 296 F.R.D. 231, 240 (S.D.N.Y. 2013).

[51] Rule 26(a)(3)(A)(ii) and Rule 32(c). *But see Hudson v. Spellman High Voltage,* 178 F.R.D. 29 (E.D. N.Y. 1998) ("there is no requirement that a party taking a deposition by nonstenographic means provide a written transcript of the entire deposition to other parties.").

Objections

Objections to the manner of recording of a deposition should be raised prior to the commencement of the deposition via a motion for protective order under Rule 26(c) or at the commencement of the deposition under Rule 30(c).[52]

RULE 30(b)(4)—BY REMOTE MEANS

CORE CONCEPT

The parties may stipulate, or move the court for an order, that a deposition be taken by telephone, videoconference, or other remote means.[53] Generally, leave to take depositions by remote means will be granted liberally.[54] Such depositions are deemed to occur in the district where the deponent is located when answering the questions,[55] and the court reporter should be in the presence of the witness, not the attorneys.[56]

Although motions to take depositions remotely are typically filed by the noticing party seeking to avoid traveling to the witness, they can also be filed by the receiving party seeking to avoid traveling to the location of the deposition.[57] The provisions for remote depositions apply to depositions of party representatives under Rule 30(b)(6) as well as to depositions of specific individuals.[58]

RULE 30(b)(5)—OFFICER'S DUTIES

CORE CONCEPT

At the beginning of a deposition, the officer shall place on the record administrative details identifying and describing the deposition. During the deposition, the demeanor of the witnesses shall not be distorted in the recording.

APPLICATIONS

Statement at Deposition Beginning

The officer recording the deposition shall begin the record with a statement that includes:

A) the officer's name and business address;

B) the date, time, and place of deposition;

C) the name of the deponent;

D) the administration of the oath or affirmation to the deponent; and

E) an identification of all persons present.

If the deposition is recorded other than stenographically, then each separate tape or unit of recording must begin with the officer's name and business address, the date, time and place of the deposition, and the deponent's name.

---

[52] *Fanelli v. Centenary College*, 211 F.R.D. 268 (D.N.J. 2002) (anxiety over videotaping not good cause sufficient to warrant a protective order).

[53] *United States v. One Gulfstream G-V Jet Aircraft Displaying Tail Number VPCES, Its Tools and Appurtenances*, 304 F.R.D. 10 (D.D.C. 2014) (final determination is within the court's discretion).

[54] *United States v. One Gulfstream G-V Jet Aircraft Displaying Tail Number VPCES, Its Tools and Appurtenances*, 304 F.R.D. 10 (D.D.C. 2014) (expressing a preference for a videoconference deposition over a telephonic deposition).

[55] *Hudson v. Spellman High Voltage*, 178 F.R.D. 29, 32 (E.D. N.Y. 1998).

[56] *Aquino v. Automotive Service Industry Ass'n*, 93 F.Supp.2d 922 (N.D. Ill. 2000).

[57] *S.E.C. v. Razmilovic*, 738 F.3d 14, 21 (2d Cir. 2013).

[58] *See Estate of Gerasimenko v. Cape Wind Trading Co.*, 272 F.R.D. 385, 390 (S.D.N.Y. 2011).

Statement at Deposition End

The officer recording the deposition shall close the record by stating that the deposition is complete and setting forth any administrative stipulations regarding the deposition.

Witness Demeanor

The recording device should accurately and neutrally depict the witness's demeanor and appearance.[59]

RULE 30(b)(6)—NOTICE OR SUBPOENA DIRECTED TO AN ORGANIZATION

CORE CONCEPT

Rule 30(b)(6) allows a party to notice the deposition of a corporation, partnership,[60] association, governmental agency,[61] or other entity [62] and to specify the areas of inquiry. The named organization must then designate one or more representatives to testify as to the areas of inquiry.

APPLICATIONS

Content of Notice

The notice (and the subpoena, for a nonparty) must state that the corporation has the duty to designate a representative, and must specify the areas of inquiry with reasonable particularity.[63] Notices that list too many topics or are otherwise too burdensome may not be enforceable.[64]

Notice vs. Subpoena

If the corporation or organization is a party, a notice of deposition is all that is needed. If the organization is not a party, then the requesting party must serve a subpoena on the organization and a notice of deposition on all parties.[65] The distance limitations and other protections of Rule 45 pertain to subpoenas to take the deposition of a designated representative.[66]

Objections to the Notice

The Rules do not establish a procedure for objecting to a Rule 30(b)(6) deposition notice. While parties sometimes serve formal objections to the notice, the objections do not relieve the party of the obligation to produce a witness or to respond to questions under topics to which the party has objected.[67] Rather, the safer procedure (assuming discussions with opposing counsel do not result in agreement) is to move for a protective order under Rule 26(c) if you believe the Rule 30(b)(6) notice is problematic.

---

[59] *Pioneer Drive, LLC v. Nissan Diesel America, Inc.*, 262 F.R.D. 552, 555 (D.Mont. 2009) (deposition cannot be recorded in such a way that the appearance and demeanor of the deponent or attorneys are distorted).

[60] *Starlight Intern. Inc. v. Herlihy*, 186 F.R.D. 626, 638 (D. Kan. 1999) (Rule 30(b)(6) applies to partnerships and joint ventures).

[61] *Watts v. S.E.C.*, 482 F.3d 501, 505 (D.C. Cir. 2007).

[62] Advisory committee notes to the 2007 Amendments (the phrase "other entity" is intended to capture any type of organization not specifically listed, such as limited liability companies).

[63] *Whitehead v. Hidden Tavern, Inc.*, 765 F.Supp.2d 878 (W.D.Tex. 2011).

[64] *See Edelen v. Campbell Soup Co.*, 265 F.R.D. 676 (N.D.Ga. 2010) (40 pages and 120 topics was too burdensome).

[65] *See Mattel, Inc. v. Walking Mountain Productions*, 353 F.3d 792, 797 (9th Cir. 2003).

[66] *Wultz v. Bank of China Ltd.*, 293 F.R.D. 677, 679–81 (S.D.N.Y. 2013).

[67] *See Lykins v. CertainTeed Corp.*, 2012 WL 3542016 (D. Kan. 2012).

Selection of Representatives

The representative does not have to be an officer or director of the organization, and in fact does not even need to be employed by the organization.[68] Instead, the company has a duty to make a conscientious, good-faith effort to designate a knowledgeable representative.[69] Regardless of the status of the representative, however, the representative's testimony will be admissible against the organization and the organization must prepare the representative to testify as to the organization's collective knowledge and information.[70] If no single individual can provide the corporation's testimony as to all the designated topics, the corporation must name more than one representative.[71] Sometimes, corporate counsel is selected as the corporate representative.[72]

Deposition of Particular Officer

To depose a specific officer, director, or managing agent, there is no need to use Rule 30(b)(6); a notice of deposition may be sent indicating that the individual's testimony is sought in the individual's official capacity.[73] The corporation is then subject to sanctions if the named representative fails to appear.[74]

Deposition of Party Employee

One cannot compel the attendance at a deposition of an employee who is not an officer, director, or managing agent of the organization merely by sending a notice.[75] Such an employee may be served with a subpoena,[76] and the employee is then subject to sanctions if the employee fails to appear. The corporation is not bound by the statements of such employees.[77]

Sanctions Against Organization

If the designated officer, director, or managing agent fails to appear for a deposition, the corporation or organization is subject to sanctions.[78] Likewise, if a corporation provides witnesses who cannot answer questions listed in the notice of deposition, then the corporation has failed to comply with its obligations under the rule and may be subject to sanctions.[79] The organization can also be sanctioned for failing to designate representatives.[80]

---

[68] *See Ecclesiastes 9:10–11–12, Inc. v. LMC Holding Co.*, 497 F.3d 1135, 1146–47 (10th Cir. 2007).

[69] *Ecclesiastes 9:10–11–12, Inc. v. LMC Holding Co.*, 497 F.3d 1135, 1146–47 (10th Cir. 2007) (organization must designate representatives, and cannot use lack of knowledgeable employees as an excuse).

[70] *Wultz v. Bank of China Ltd.*, 298 F.R.D. 91, 99 (S.D.N.Y. 2014).

[71] *QBE Ins. Corp. v. Jorda Enters., Inc.*, 277 F.R.D. 676 (S.D.Fla. 2012).

[72] *See In re Pioneer Hi-Bred Intern., Inc.*, 238 F.3d 1370, 1376 (Fed. Cir. 2001) (addressing the attorney-client privilege issues when counsel is designated as the corporate representative).

[73] *Cummings v. General Motors Corp.*, 365 F.3d 944, 953 (10th Cir. 2004).

[74] *Bon Air Hotel, Inc. v. Time, Inc.*, 376 F.2d 118 (5th Cir. 1967).

[75] *See Calderon v. Experian Information Solutions, Inc.*, 290 F.R.D. 508 (D.Idaho 2013) (examining whether agents of a sister corporation were subject to a notice).

[76] *Calderon v. Experian Information Solutions, Inc.*, 290 F.R.D. 508 (D.Idaho 2013).

[77] *Burns Bros. v. the B & 0 No. 177*, 21 F.R.D. 142 (E.D. N.Y. 1957).

[78] *John Wiley & Sons, Inc. v. Book Dog Books, LLC*, 298 F.R.D. 145, 148 (S.D.N.Y. 2014).

[79] *Baker v. St. Paul Travelers Ins. Co.*, 670 F.3d 119, 124 (1st Cir. 2012).

[80] *Ecclesiastes 9:10–11–12, Inc. v. LMC Holding Co.*, 497 F.3d 1135 (10th Cir. 2007) (case dismissed after plaintiff delayed making designation, then the logical representative died).

Scope of Testimony

The corporation or organization must select an individual or individuals who can testify to the areas specified in the notice.[81] The individual(s) must testify to all matters known or reasonably available to the corporation,[82] which may necessitate gathering documents and interviewing witnesses and having the individual(s) review and become familiar with the documents and information.[83] Thus, the individual will often testify to matters outside the individual's personal knowledge.[84] The courts are divided as to whether the examination of the representative is limited to the areas of inquiry identified in the notice of deposition.[85]

Contentions, Legal Positions, and Theories

The courts are divided as to whether topics for a Rule 30(b)(6) deposition may include the party's contentions or facts supporting those contentions.[86] Many courts are reluctant to allow depositions of opposing counsel, and will closely examine notices under Rule 30(b)(6) that are "back door" attempts to depose opposing counsel.[87]

Duty to Prepare

The organization has a duty to gather the information and prepare the representative(s) so that the representatives can give complete, knowledgeable, and binding testimony.[88] Failure to adequately prepare the representative can result in sanctions.[89]

Effect of Testimony

Testimony by a Rule 30(b)(6) representative has the effect of an evidentiary admission, not a judicial admission, and thus may be controverted or explained by the party.[90] However, courts will sometimes prevent a party from contradicting its designee to defeat summary judgment, under the "sham affidavit rule."[91] The organization may be prohibited from using theories or information not disclosed during the Rule 30(b)(6) deposition unless the information was unavailable at the time of the deposition.[92]

---

[81]   *Poole ex rel. Elliott v. Textron, Inc.,* 192 F.R.D. 494 (D. Md. 2000) (a corporation should make a "diligent inquiry" to determine the individual(s) best suited to testify).

[82]   *Crawford v. George & Lynch, Inc.,* 19 F.Supp.3d 546 (D. Del. 2013) (parties have the same duty to gather information under Rule 30(b)(6) as they do for any other form of discovery).

[83]   *Poole ex rel. Elliott v. Textron, Inc.,* 192 F.R.D. 494 (D. Md. 2000).

[84]   *Pina v. Children's Place,* 740 F.3d 785, 793, n.7 (1st Cir. 2014).

[85]   *Crawford v. George & Lynch, Inc.,* 19 F.Supp.2d 546 (D. Del. 2013).

[86]   *See Brazos River Authority v. GE Ionics, Inc.,* 469 F.3d 416, 432 (5th Cir. 2006) (representative must testify to organization's subjective beliefs and opinions); *HSK v. Provident Live & Accident Ins. Co..* 128 F.Supp.3d 874, 881 (representative's legal conclusions not binding).

[87]   *See E.E.O.C. v. Pointe at Kirby Gate, LLC,* 290 F.R.D. 89, 90 (W.D.Tenn. 2003).

[88]   *Brazos River Authority v. GE Ionics, Inc.,* 469 F.3d 416, 433 (5th Cir. 2006).

[89]   *Black Horse Lane Assoc., L.P. v. Dow Chemical Corp.,* 228 F.3d 275, 301–05 (3d Cir. 2000).

[90]   *Southern Wine and Spirits of America, Inc. v. Division of Alcohol and Tobacco Control,* 731 F.3d 799, 811 (8th Cir. 2013) (representative's legal conclusions are not binding on the party).

[91]   *Cooper v. United Air Lines, Inc.,* 82 F.Supp.3d 1084, 1096 (N.D. Cal. 2015) (sham affidavit rule only applies to clear conflict between testimony and affidavit).

[92]   *QBE Ins. Corp. v. Jorda Enters., Inc.,* 277 F.R.D. 676 (S.D.Fla. 2012).

RULE 30(c)—EXAMINATION AND CROSS-EXAMINATION; RECORD OF THE EXAMINATION; OBJECTIONS; WRITTEN QUESTIONS

CORE CONCEPT

In general, the examination of witnesses at a deposition proceeds much like at trial, except that most objections are reserved until the testimony is offered into evidence. Objections to questions must be stated in a non-suggestive and nonargumentative manner.

APPLICATIONS

Oath or Affirmation

The officer before whom the deposition is to be taken (usually the stenographer) will put the witness under oath or affirmation at the beginning of the deposition.

Recording

The officer will arrange to have the testimony recorded, either stenographically or otherwise (as discussed above under Rule 30(b)(3)).

Examination

Examination proceeds as at trial,[93] with direct examination and cross-examination,[94] except that examination proceeds irrespective of objections.[95] Unlike trial, cross-examination is not limited to matters raised on direct, although the admission at trial of the deposition transcript may be limited on that basis.

Witness's Rights

At a deposition, witnesses have the same rights as at trial, and may refresh their recollection with former testimony.[96] The extent to which a witness has the right to confer with counsel during a deposition is unsettled.[97]

Refusal to Answer Question

If a witness refuses to answer a question, the examining party may suspend the proceedings to seek an order under Rule 37(a) compelling an answer or may reserve the right to move for an order to compel and proceed to other areas.

Objections to Questions

Some objections to questions must be raised at the time of the deposition or they are waived, others are reserved until trial. The way to determine whether an objection must be made is to determine whether the examiner could rephrase the question to cure the objection.[98] Thus, parties must object to leading questions in order to give the examiner an opportunity to ask the question in a non-leading fashion. Conversely, parties do not need to raise objections such as relevancy or competency that cannot be cured.

---

[93] *Brincko v. Rio Props., Inc.,* 278 F.R.D. 576, 579 (D. Nev. 2011).

[94] *Sperling v. City of Kennesaw Dept.,* 202 F.R.D. 325, 329 (N.D. Ga. 2001) (adverse party entitled to review and use writing used by witness to refresh recollection).

[95] *Rangel v. Gonzalez Mascorro,* 274 F.R.D. 585 (S.D.Tex. 2011).

[96] *See Magee v. Paul Revere Life Ins. Co.,* 172 F.R.D. 627, 637 (E.D. N.Y. 1997) (deponent repeatedly consulted his notes to refresh his memory at the deposition).

[97] *See, e.g., In re Stratosphere Corp. Securities Litigation,* 182 F.R.D. 614, 620 (D. Nev. 1998) (witness not permitted to confer while a question is pending).

[98] *Quiksilver, Inc. v. Kymsta Corp.,* 247 F.R.D. 579, 582 (C.D. Cal. 2007) (objections waived as to errors that could be obviated, removed, or cured).

Stating Objections

Objections must be stated in a non-suggestive manner.[99] Attorneys should not use an objection to instruct the witnesses how to answer (or not answer) a question.[100] However, the specific nature of the objection should be stated so that the court later can rule on the objection (*e.g.,* "objection, leading" or "objection, lack of foundation").[101]

Instruction Not to Answer

Directions to a witness not to answer a question are only allowed in three narrow circumstances:[102] to claim a privilege (*i.e.,* attorney-client communication);[103] to enforce a court directive limiting the scope or length of the deposition;[104] or to suspend the deposition for purposes of a motion under Rule 30(d)(3) relating to improper harassing conduct.[105] Thus, it is inappropriate for counsel to instruct a witness not to answer a question on the basis of relevance,[106] on the basis that the question has been asked and answered,[107] is harassing,[108] or is outside the areas of inquiry identified in the notice of deposition for a Rule 30(b)(6) deposition of a party representative.[109]

Documents Reviewed by the Witness

One common topic at depositions is which documents the witness reviewed in preparation for the deposition. Some courts consider the attorney's selection of the important documents for review to be attorney work product.[110] Others apply FRE 612, which requires disclosure of documents used to refresh the witness's recollection.[111]

All Objections on the Record

All objections to the qualifications of the officer, to the manner of recording, to questions, or to any other procedure must be raised at the deposition and noted by the officer or they are waived.[112]

Objections to Exhibits

Exhibits that have been objected to are taken and appended to the transcript subject to a subsequent ruling on the objection.

Procedure After Objections

After an objection to the officer recording the deposition, the manner of taking the deposition, the evidence, the conduct of a party, the nature of a question, or any other aspect

---

[99] *Banks v. Office of the Senate Sergeant-At-Arms,* 241 F.R.D. 370 (D.D.C. 2007).

[100] *Board of Trustees of Leland Stanford Junior University v. Tyco Intern. Ltd.,* 253 F.R.D. 524 (C.D.Cal. 2008); *Calzaturficio S.C.A.R.P.A. s.p.a. v. Fabiano Shoe Co., Inc.,* 201 F.R.D. 33 (D. Mass. 2001).

[101] *Moloney v. United States,*204 F.R.D. 16, 20–21 (D. Mass. 2001) (certain privileges were waived because the objection did not identify those privileges).

[102] *Baker v. St. Paul Travelers Ins. Co.,* 670 F.3d 119, 123 (1st Cir. 2012).

[103] *Stewart Title Guar. Co. v. Owlett & Lewis, P.C.,* 297 F.R.D. 232, 241–42 (M.D. Pa. 2013).

[104] *Baker v. St. Paul Travelers Ins. Co.,* 670 F.3d 119, 123 (1st Cir. 2012).

[105] *See Biovail Laboratories, Inc. v. Anchen Pharmaceuticals, Inc.,* 233 F.R.D. 648, 653 (C.D. Cal. 2006) (Rule 30(d)(4) is the only authority allowing the interruption of a deposition).

[106] *Resolution Trust Corp. v. Dabney,* 73 F.3d 262, 266 (10th Cir. 1995).

[107] *Brincko v. Rio Props.,* Inc., 278 F.R.D. 576, 581 (D.Nev. 2011).

[108] *Redwood v. Dobson,* 476 F.3d 462, 467–68 (7th Cir. 2007).

[109] *See E.E.O.C. v. Freeman,* 288 F.R.D. 92, 97–99 (D.Md. 2012).

[110] *See Sporck v. Peil,* 759 F.2d 312, 315 (3d Cir. 1985).

[111] *See Northern Natural Gas Co. v. Approximately 9117.53 acres in Pratt, Kingman, and Reno Counties, Kan.,* 289 F.R.D. 644 (D.Kan. 2013).

[112] *Pioneer Drive, LLC v. Nissan Diesel America, Inc.,* 262 F.R.D. 552, 556 (D.Mont. 2009).

of the deposition, the deposition should continue subject to the objection.[113] The court then rules on any objections at the time the testimony is offered into evidence or otherwise proffered to the court.[114]

Written Questions

Instead of attending a deposition in person, a party can send written questions to the party taking the deposition, who will then ask the questions to the deponent on the record.[115] This procedure is rarely used.

Attendance by Other Persons

Other witnesses are not automatically excluded from observing a deposition absent a court order under Rule 30(d) and Rule 26(c)(1)(E).[116] Disputes regarding who may be present during a deposition are resolved by motion for protective order under Rule 26(c).[117]

RULE 30(d)—DURATION; SANCTION; MOTION TO TERMINATE OR LIMIT

CORE CONCEPT

Rule 30(d) provides for a 7-hour time limit on depositions, which may be extended by court order. Rule 30(d) also provides protection from unreasonable or vexatious examination during a deposition.

APPLICATIONS

Duration of Depositions

Rule 30(d)(1) sets a time limit for depositions of 1 day of 7 hours. The time period includes only time spent examining the witness; lunch and other breaks are not counted.[118] The parties can extend or eliminate the time limitation by stipulation,[119] or can file a motion to extend the time limit (discussed below).

Motion to Extend Time

A party may file a motion to extend the 1-day 7-hour limitation for specified depositions or for the case in general.[120] The court must allow additional time if needed for a "fair examination" of the witness or if the examination has been impeded or delayed by another person or by circumstances.[121] Examples of situations in which an extended deposition would be warranted include: witnesses who need interpreters; examinations covering long periods of time or numerous and/or lengthy documents (although the Advisory Committee suggests that a prerequisite might be sending the documents to the witness to review prior to the deposition); instances where documents were requested but not produced prior to the deposition; multi-party cases (if the parties have taken measures to avoid duplicative questioning); depositions in which the lawyer for the witness also wants to ask questions;

---

[113] *Schoolcraft v. City of New York*, 296 F.R.D. 231, 240 (S.D.N.Y. 2013).

[114] *See Betker v. City of Milwaukee*, 800 F.Supp.2d 1002 (E.D. Wis. 2014).

[115] *See United States v. One Gulfstream G-V Jet Aircraft Displaying Tail Number VPCES, Its Tools and Appurtenances*, 304 F.R.D. 10 (D.D.C. 2014).

[116] *In re Terra Intern., Inc.*, 134 F.3d 302, 305–06 (5th Cir. 1998) (party moving to exclude other witnesses must show good cause why such witnesses should not attend).

[117] *See D.A. v. Meridian Joint School Dist. No. 2*, 289 F.R.D. 614 (D.Idaho 2013) (allowing the witness's psychologist to be present).

[118] The advisory committee note to the 2000 Amendment to Rule 30(d).

[119] *Vazquez-Rijos v. Anhang*, 654 F.3d 122, 130 (1st Cir. 2011).

[120] *See JTR Enterprises, LLC v. An Unknown Quantity of Colombian Emeralds, Amethysts and Quartz Crystals*, 297 F.R.D. 522, 531–32 (S.D. Fla. 2013).

[121] *George v. City of Buffalo*, 789 F.Supp.2d 417 (W.D.N.Y. 2011).

depositions of expert witnesses; depositions interrupted by power outage, health emergency, or other like event; and depositions in which improper objections or other conduct by other attorneys or the witness has impeded the examination.[122] The court need not order an extended deposition if the extended deposition would be cumulative or unreasonably burdensome, as provided by Rule 26(b)(2).[123] The burden will be on the party moving for an extension to show good cause why the extension is warranted.[124]

Motion to Terminate or Limit Deposition

A party may move to limit the time of or terminate a deposition. In order to prevail on a motion to terminate or limit an examination, the moving party must demonstrate that the examination was being conducted in bad faith or in an unreasonably annoying, embarrassing, or oppressive manner.[125] The court can then order the deposition concluded or can limit the time and/or scope of the deposition,[126] and may impose upon the losing party or attorney an appropriate sanction, including the reasonable costs and attorney's fees incurred by any parties as a result.[127]

Designated Representatives

If a corporation or entity designates more than 1 representative in response to a deposition notice under Rule 30(b)(6), the 1-day 7-hour limitation will apply separately to each representative.[128]

Sanctions for Impediment or Delay

Parties or witnesses should not engage in conduct that unreasonably impedes, delays, or otherwise frustrates a deposition.[129] When such conduct occurs, the court may impose the costs of such conduct, including attorney's fees, on the party or attorney[130] engaging in the obstructive behavior.[131] Nonparty witnesses are also subject to such sanctions.

Which Court for Motion to Terminate

A motion to terminate or limit the deposition may be filed either in the court where the case is pending or in the district where the deposition is occurring.

Suspension of Deposition

A party desiring to make a motion to terminate or limit the deposition may suspend the deposition for the period of time necessary to make the motion.[132]

Expenses of Motion to Terminate

In ruling on a motion to terminate or limit the deposition, the court must consider awarding expenses to the prevailing party, in accordance with Rule 37(a)(3).[133]

---

[122] *Kleppinger v. Texas Dept. of Transp.*, 283 F.R.D. 330 (S.D.Tex. 2012).

[123] *George v. City of Buffalo*, 789 F.Supp.2d 417 (W.D.N.Y. 2011).

[124] *Kleppinger v. Texas Dept. of Transp.*, 283 F.R.D. 330 (S.D.Tex. 2012).

[125] *Garland v. Torre*, 259 F.2d 545 (2d Cir. 1958).

[126] *Brincko v. Rio Props., Inc.*, 278 F.R.D. 576, 581 (D.Nev. 2011).

[127] *Horton v. Maersk Line, Ltd.*, 294 F.R.D. 690, 696–98 (S.D. Ga. 2013).

[128] The advisory committee note to the 2000 Amendment to Rule 30(d)(2).

[129] *Baker v. St. Paul Travelers Ins. Co.*, 670 F.3d 119, 123 (1st Cir. 2012).

[130] *GMAC Bank v. HTFC Corp.*, 252 F.R.D. 253 (E.D.Pa. 2008) (attorney sanctioned for sitting idly by while the client engaged in abusive conduct).

[131] *Pioneer Drive, LLC v. Nissan Diesel America, Inc.*, 262 F.R.D. 552, 556 (D.Mont. 2009) (sanctions imposed for improperly halting deposition).

[132] *McClelland v. Blazin'Wings, Inc.*, 675 F.Supp.2d 1074, 1081 (D.Colo. 2009).

[133] *Brincko v. Rio Props., Inc.*, 278 F.R.D. 576, 581 (D.Nev. 2011).

Resuming Terminated Deposition

Once a deposition has been terminated by the court upon a Rule 30(d)(3) motion, it cannot be resumed or re-noticed without leave of court.

Parallel to Protective Order

A party may seek the same types of protection for a deposition under Rule 30(d) that are available under a protective order under Rule 26(c).[134] A motion for a protective order under Rule 26(c) provides similar protection before a deposition begins, at which point Rule 30(d) takes over.

RULE 30(e)—REVIEW BY THE WITNESS; CHANGES

CORE CONCEPT

The opportunity to review and correct the transcript is available upon timely request.

APPLICATIONS

Request to Review

To obtain an opportunity to review and correct the transcript, the deponent or a party must make a request prior to the completion of the deposition.[135] Typically, the court reporter will ask at the end of a deposition whether the witness wishes to read and sign the transcript or waive signature.

Submission of Changes

If a review is requested, the court reporter will make the deposition transcript available to the witness, typically by sending a copy to the witness to review.[136] The witness must submit an errata statement describing any changes within 30 days of notification that the transcript is available.[137] The statement should state the reasons for the changes[138] and be signed by the witness. The time for submission of changes may be extended by the court upon motion.[139] Any changes that are submitted are attached to the transcript.

Changes in Form

Changes in form, such as typographic errors, are entered into the transcript with an explanation as to the reason for the change.

Changes in Substance

The courts vary as to whether and when they will allow a witness to make changes in the substance of the testimony,[140] which are also entered into the transcript with an explanation as to the reason for the change.[141] With changes in substance, the deposition

---

[134] *In re CFS-Related Securities Fraud Litigation,* 256 F.Supp.2d 1227, 1240 (N.D. Okla. 2003) (a deposition transcript may be placed under seal under Rule 30(d)).

[135] *Hambleton Bros. Lumber Co. v. Balkin Enterprises, Inc.,* 397 F.3d 1217, 1226 (9th Cir. 2005).

[136] *Parkland Venture, LLC v. City of Muskego,* 270 F.R.D. 439, 441 (E.D.Wis. 2010) (court reporter not required to send a copy to the witness, can make the copy available at the reporter's office).

[137] *Monge v. RG Petro-Machinery (Group) Co. Ltd.,* 701 F.3d 598, 612 (10th Cir. 2012).

[138] *E.E.O.C. v. Skanska USA Bldg., Inc.,* 278 F.R.D. 407, 409–10 (W.D.Tenn. 2012).

[139] *Statzer v. Town of Lebanaon, VA,* 2001 WL 604160 (W.D. Va. 2001).

[140] *See Pina v. Children's Place,* 740 F.3d 785, 792 (1st Cir. 2014) (Rule 30(e) authorizes changes in form or substance); *Gonzalez v. Fresenius Medical Care North America,* 689 F.3d 470, 480 (5th Cir. 2012) (substantive changes drafted by counsel not proper).

[141] *Norelus v. Denny's, Inc.,* 628 F.3d 1270, 1295 (11th Cir. 2010).

can be reconvened.[142] A deponent who changes the answers may be impeached with the former answers.[143] Some courts do not allow substantive changes when they view the changes as an attempt to create issues of fact to prevent summary judgment, sometimes referred to as the "sham affidavit" rule.[144]

Failure to Submit Changes

A witness who fails to submit any changes or return the signed errata sheet within the time period allowed waives the right to make corrections to the transcript.[145]

RULE 30(f)—CERTIFICATION AND DELIVERY; EXHIBITS; COPIES OF THE TRANSCRIPT OR RECORDING; FILING

CORE CONCEPT

The officer must certify that the witness was duly sworn and that the deposition transcript was a true record of the testimony given by the deponent.

APPLICATIONS

Certificate

The officer shall prepare a written certificate to accompany the record of the deposition.[146] The certificate should indicate that the witness was sworn, that the deposition is a true and accurate record of the testimony, and whether review of the record was requested.[147]

Uncertified Transcript

A deposition transcript that is not properly certified is inadmissible.[148]

Filing of Transcript

Ordinarily, deposition transcripts should not be filed. However, under Rule 5(d), once a deposition is used in a proceeding, the attorney must file it.

Original Transcript

The stenographer should supply the original transcript and certification to the party noticing the deposition in a sealed envelope, which should be preserved for use at trial.[149]

Copies of the Transcript

Any party or the deponent can obtain a copy of the recording of the deposition for a reasonable charge.[150] If the deposition was recorded stenographically and has not been

---

[142] *See Pina v. Children's Place,* 740 F.3d 785, 791 (1st Cir. 2014).

[143] *Podell v. Citicorp Diners Club, Inc.,* 112 F.3d 98 (2d Cir.1997) (the changes made do not replace the deponent's original answers; the original information remains part of the record and may be introduced at trial).

[144] *Karpenski v. American General Life Companies, LLC,* 999 F.Supp.2d 1218 (W.D. Wash. 2014).

[145] *Karpenski v. American General Life Companies, LLC,* 999 F.Supp.2d 1218 (W.D. Wash. 2014) (missing by a day or 2 might not warrant waiver).

[146] *Orr v. Bank of America, NT & SA,* 285 F.3d 764, 774 (9th Cir. 2002) (an affidavit of counsel is not sufficient to authenticate a deposition transcript).

[147] *Del Toro-Pacheco v. Pereira-Castillo,* 662 F.Supp.2d 202, 211 (D.Puerto Rico 2009).

[148] *Berbick v. Precinct 42,* 977 F.Supp.2d 268, 273–74 (S.D.N.Y. 2013) (excerpt of deposition was properly considered in the context of a motion for summary judgment even though signature was not included).

[149] *Barton v. City and County of Denver,* 432 F.Supp.2d 1178, 1199 n.6 (D. Colo. 2006), aff'd, 2007 WL 3104909 (10th Cir. 2007).

[150] *Rivera v. DiSabato,* 962 F.Supp. 38, 39–40 (D.N.J. 1997).

transcribed, then the party seeking the transcript will normally have to pay the transcription costs, unless the court orders otherwise.

Exhibits

Upon the request of a party, a document produced at a deposition (or any other document) may be marked for identification and annexed to the deposition transcript. A copy of a document may be substituted for the original. If documents are produced at a deposition, any party has a right to inspect and copy them.

Retaining Recording

The officer should retain a copy of the transcript or recording of the deposition.

RULE 30(g)—FAILURE TO ATTEND A DEPOSITION OR SERVE SUBPOENA; EXPENSES

CORE CONCEPT

The court may award expenses, including attorney's fees, to a party that appears for a deposition that does not occur because either: (1) the party noticing the deposition does not attend;[151] or (2) the party fails to subpoena a witness and that witness does not appear. In both cases, the party noticing the deposition may be ordered to pay the expenses of other parties incurred as a result of appearing for the deposition.

ADDITIONAL RESEARCH REFERENCES

Wright & Miller, *Federal Practice and Procedure* §§ 2101 to 2120

C.J.S., Federal Civil Procedure §§ 548 to 583 et seq., 600 to 644 et seq.

West's Key Number Digest, Federal Civil Procedure ☞1311 to 1456

---

[151] *Albee v. Continental Tire North America, Inc.,* 780 F.Supp.2d 1005 (E.D.Cal. 2011) (awarding fees based on the cancellation of a deposition the night before, when the witness had already prepared and traveled).

RULE 31

DEPOSITIONS BY WRITTEN QUESTIONS

(a) When a Deposition May Be Taken.

(1) *Without Leave.* A party may, by written questions, depose any person, including a party, without leave of court except as provided in Rule 31(a)(2). The deponent's attendance may be compelled by subpoena under Rule 45.

(2) *With Leave.* A party must obtain leave of court, and the court must grant leave to the extent consistent with Rule 26(b)(1) and (2):

    (A) if the parties have not stipulated to the deposition and:

        (i) the deposition would result in more than 10 depositions being taken under this rule or Rule 30 by the plaintiffs, or by the defendants, or by the third-party defendants;

        (ii) the deponent has already been deposed in the case; or (iii) the party seeks to take a deposition before the time specified in Rule 26(d); or

    (B) if the deponent is confined in prison.

(3) *Service; Required Notice.* A party who wants to depose a person by written questions must serve them on every other party, with a notice stating, if known, the deponent's name and address. If the name is unknown, the notice must provide a general description sufficient to identify the person or the particular class or group to which the person belongs. The notice must also state the name or descriptive title and the address of the officer before whom the deposition will be taken.

(4) *Questions Directed to an Organization.* A public or private corporation, a partnership, an association, or a governmental agency may be deposed by written questions in accordance with Rule 30(b)(6).

(5) *Questions from Other Parties.* Any questions to the deponent from other parties must be served on all parties as follows: cross-questions, within 14 days after being served with the notice and direct questions; redirect questions, within 7 days after being served with cross-questions; and recross-questions, within 7 days after being served with redirect questions. The court may, for good cause, extend or shorten these times.

(b) Delivery to the Officer; Officer's Duties.
The party who noticed the deposition must deliver to the officer a copy of all the questions served and of the notice. The officer must promptly proceed in the manner provided in Rule 30(c), (e), and (f) to:

(1) take the deponent's testimony in response to the questions;

(2) prepare and certify the deposition; and

(3) send it to the party, attaching a copy of the questions and of the notice.

(c) Notice of Completion or Filing.

(1) *Completion.* The party who noticed the deposition must notify all other parties when it is completed.

(2) *Filing.* A party who files the deposition must promptly notify all other parties of the filing.

[Amended March 30, 1970, effective July 1, 1970; March 2, 1987, effective August 1, 1987; April 22, 1993, effective December 1, 1993; April 30, 2007, effective December 1, 2007; April 29, 2015, effective December 1, 2015.]

AUTHORS' COMMENTARY ON RULE 31

PURPOSE AND SCOPE

Rule 31 contains the procedures for taking depositions through written questions.

RULE 31(a)—WHEN A DEPOSITION MAY BE TAKEN

CORE CONCEPT

Any party may take depositions by serving written questions, which are asked by the deposition officer (typically, the stenographer) and answered orally by the witness. Depositions by written question are rarely used, and their only advantage seems to be that they may be less expensive than depositions by oral question.[1]

APPLICATIONS

Notice

A party seeking to take a deposition by written questions must serve a notice on all other parties stating the name and address of the deponent, if known, or a general description sufficient to identify the deponent and providing the name or title and address of the stenographer or officer before whom the deposition will be taken.[2]

Timing of Notice

The notice of written deposition may be served at any time after the parties have conducted the discovery conference under Rule 26(f), or earlier with leave of court. In proceedings listed in Rule 26(a)(1)(B) as exempt from initial disclosures, there is no preliminary waiting period for written depositions. The latest time to conduct a deposition upon written questions will be governed by the court's scheduling order.[3]

---

[1] *See Brown v. Carr,* 236 F.R.D. 311 (S.D. Tex. 2006) ("If plaintiff is unable to afford to take depositions via telephone, then he may take depositions upon written questions.").

[2] *Rahn v. Hawkins,* 464 F.3d 813, 821–22 (8th Cir. 2006).

[3] *See Summerville v. Local 77,* 369 F.Supp.2d 648, 651 (M.D. N.C. 2005), aff'd, 142 Fed. Appx. 762 (4th Cir. 2005) (written deposition questions are treated like other written discovery, and must be served such that the responses are due before the close of written discovery).

Subpoenas vs. Deposition Notices

Subpoenas must be used to compel the attendance of nonparty witnesses. Party witnesses and representatives of corporations are compelled to attend by virtue of the deposition notice alone.

Service of Direct-Examination

The written deposition questions for direct examination are served upon all parties with the notice.[4]

Cross, Redirect, and Recross

Within 14 days of service of the notice and direct examination questions, any other party may serve cross-examination questions. The noticing party may then serve redirect examination questions within 7 days, and the other party may serve recross examination questions within 7 more days. The court may shorten or lengthen these time periods upon motion and for cause shown. All questions should be served on all parties.

Number of Depositions

The plaintiffs as a group are limited to 10 depositions total, by written and/or oral examination, as are the defendants and the third-party defendants. This number may be increased by stipulation or by leave of court.

Scope of Questions

The scope of the written deposition questions is the same as oral questions, and is controlled by Rule 26.

Persons Subject

Both parties and nonparties are subject to written depositions.[5]

Corporate Representative

A party may require a corporation or organization to designate a representative to respond to the questions, as described in detail under Rule 30(b)(6).

Repeat Depositions

Leave of court is required to depose someone a second time.[6]

Deponent in Prison

If the deponent is in prison, leave of court is required to take a written deposition.[7]

Objections

Objections to the form of a written question (*e.g.,* because it is leading) must be served in writing upon the party serving the question within the time for serving succeeding questions and within 7 days of the last questions authorized.[8]

---

[4]   *In re Lenders Mortg. Services, Inc.,* 224 B.R. 707, 710 (Bankr. E.D. Mo. 1997).

[5]   *New Hampshire Motor Transport Ass'n v. Rowe,* 324 F.Supp.2d 231, 237 (D. Me. 2004) (written deposition questions, in contrast to interrogatories, can be served on nonparties).

[6]   *Rahn v. Hawkins,* 464 F.3d 813, 821–22 (8th Cir. 2006).

[7]   *Whitehurst v. United States,* 231 F.R.D. 500. 501 (S.D. Tex. 2005).

[8]   *See* Rule 32(d)(3)(C); *Whitehurst v. United States,* 231 F.R.D. 500, 501 (S.D. Tex. 2005).

RULE 31(b)—DELIVERY TO THE OFFICER; OFFICER'S DUTIES

CORE CONCEPT

Once all the questions have been served, the party initiating the deposition provides all the questions to the deposition officer. The officer then promptly takes the deposition by reading the questions and recording the answers.[9] A transcript is then prepared and submitted to the witness as provided in Rule 30 governing oral depositions.

RULE 31(c)—NOTICE OF COMPLETION OR FILING

CORE CONCEPT

When the deposition has been completed, the party who noticed the deposition must provide notice to all other parties. Local rules usually determine whether the officer files a sealed transcript with the court. If so, the party noticing the deposition must promptly give notice of the filing of the transcript to all other parties.

ADDITIONAL RESEARCH REFERENCES

Wright & Miller, *Federal Practice and Procedure* §§ 2131 to 2133

C.J.S., Federal Civil Procedure §§ 591 to 592

West's Key Number Digest, Federal Civil Procedure ⊶1369 to 1370

---

[9]   *See Sherrod v. Breitbart,* 304 F.R.D. 73, 76, n.3 (D.D.C. 2014) (the witness must be present and testifies live, not by written responses).

RULE 32

USING DEPOSITIONS IN
COURT PROCEEDINGS

(a) Using Depositions.

(1) *In General.* At a hearing or trial, all or part of a deposition may be used against a party on these conditions:

(A) the party was present or represented at the taking of the deposition or had reasonable notice of it;

(B) it is used to the extent it would be admissible under the Federal Rules of Evidence if the deponent were present and testifying; and

(C) the use is allowed by Rule 32(a)(2) through (8).

(2) *Impeachment and Other Uses.* Any party may use a deposition to contradict or impeach the testimony given by the deponent as a witness, or for any other purpose allowed by the Federal Rules of Evidence.

(3) *Deposition of Party, Agent, or Designee.* An adverse party may use for any purpose the deposition of a party or anyone who, when deposed, was the party's officer, director, managing agent, or designee under Rule 30(b)(6) or 31(a)(4).

(4) *Unavailable Witness.* A party may use for any purpose the deposition of a witness, whether or not a party, if the court finds:

(A) that the witness is dead;

(B) that the witness is more than 100 miles from the place of hearing or trial or is outside the United States, unless it appears that the witness's absence was procured by the party offering the deposition;

(C) that the witness cannot attend or testify because of age, illness, infirmity, or imprisonment;

(D) that the party offering the deposition could not procure the witness's attendance by subpoena; or

(E) on motion and notice, that exceptional circumstances make it desirable—in the interest of justice and with due regard to the importance of live testimony in open court—to permit the deposition to be used.

(5) *Limitations on Use.*

(A) *Deposition Taken on Short Notice.* A deposition must not be used against a party who, having received less than 14 days' notice of the

557

deposition, promptly moved for a protective order under Rule 26(c)(1)(B) requesting that it not be taken or be taken at a different time or place—and this motion was still pending when the deposition was taken.

(B) *Unavailable Deponent; Party Could Not Obtain an Attorney.* A deposition taken without leave of court under the unavailability provision of Rule 30(a)(2)(A)(iii) must not be used against a party who shows that, when served with the notice, it could not, despite diligent efforts, obtain an attorney to represent it at the deposition.

(6) *Using Part of a Deposition.* If a party offers in evidence only part of a deposition, an adverse party may require the offeror to introduce other parts that in fairness should be considered with the part introduced, and any party may itself introduce any other parts.

(7) *Substituting a Party.* Substituting a party under Rule 25 does not affect the right to use a deposition previously taken.

(8) *Deposition Taken in an Earlier Action.* A deposition lawfully taken and, if required, filed in any federal- or state-court action may be used in a later action involving the same subject matter between the same parties, or their representatives or successors in interest, to the same extent as if taken in the later action. A deposition previously taken may also be used as allowed by the Federal Rules of Evidence.

(b) Objections to Admissibility. Subject to Rules 28(b) and 32(d)(3), an objection may be made at a hearing or trial to the admission of any deposition testimony that would be inadmissible if the witness were present and testifying.

(c) Form of Presentation. Unless the court orders otherwise, a party must provide a transcript of any deposition testimony the party offers, but may provide the court with the testimony in nontranscript form as well. On any party's request, deposition testimony offered in a jury trial for any purpose other than impeachment must be presented in nontranscript form, if available, unless the court for good cause orders otherwise.

(d) Waiver of Objections.

(1) *To the Notice.* An objection to an error or irregularity in a deposition notice is waived unless promptly served in writing on the party giving the notice.

(2) *To the Officer's Qualification.* An objection based on disqualification of the officer before whom a deposition is to be taken is waived if not made:

(A) before the deposition begins; or

    (B) promptly after the basis for disqualification becomes known or, with reasonable diligence, could have been known.

  (3) *To the Taking of the Deposition.*

    (A) *Objection to Competence, Relevance, or Materiality.* An objection to a deponent's competence—or to the competence, relevance, or materiality of testimony—is not waived by a failure to make the objection before or during the deposition, unless the ground for it might have been corrected at that time.

    (B) *Objection to an Error or Irregularity.* An objection to an error or irregularity at an oral examination is waived if:

      (i) it relates to the manner of taking the deposition, the form of a question or answer, the oath or affirmation, a party's conduct, or other matters that might have been corrected at that time; and

      (ii) it is not timely made during the deposition.

    (C) *Objection to a Written Question.* An objection to the form of a written question under Rule 31 is waived if not served in writing on the party submitting the question within the time for serving responsive questions or, if the question is a recross-question, within 7 days after being served with it.

  (4) *To Completing and Returning the Deposition.* An objection to how the officer transcribed the testimony—or prepared, signed, certified, sealed, endorsed, sent, or otherwise dealt with the deposition—is waived unless a motion to suppress is made promptly after the error or irregularity becomes known or, with reasonable diligence, could have been known.

[Amended March 30, 1970, effective July 1, 1970; November 20, 1972, effective July 1, 1975; April 29, 1980, effective August 1, 1980; March 2, 1987, effective August 1, 1987; April 22, 1993, effective December 1, 1993; April 30, 2007, effective December 1, 2007; March 26, 2009, effective December 1, 2009.]

AUTHORS' COMMENTARY ON RULE 32

PURPOSE AND SCOPE

Rule 32 specifies the circumstances in which a deposition is admissible at trial. Any analysis, however, must always include reference to the applicable rules of evidence.

RULE 32(a)—USING DEPOSITIONS

CORE CONCEPT

Rule 32 establishes a three-part test for admissibility of deposition testimony that the party seeking to introduce the testimony must satisfy:[1]

---

[1]   *Howard v. Gray*, 291 F.R.D. 6 (D.D.C. 2013) (burden is on the party seeking to introduce the testimony).

1. The party against whom the testimony is offered was present at, represented at, or had reasonable notice of, the deposition;

2. The testimony is otherwise admissible under the Federal Rules of Evidence; and

3. The testimony is admissible under the provisions in Rule 34(a)(2)-(8), which allows testimony for impeachment, testimony of an adverse party, and testimony of an unavailable witness.[2]

APPLICATIONS

Impeachment

A deposition may be used to impeach or contradict a witness. A party may use a deposition to impeach the party's own witness, if permitted by the applicable rules of evidence.

Deposition of Adverse Party or Rule 30(b)(6) Designee

The deposition of an adverse party may be used for any purpose (*i.e.*, as substantive evidence or for impeachment).[3] This principle applies to a party organization's officers, directors, and managing agents,[4] and to representatives designated under Rule 30(b)(6).[5]

Unavailable Nonparty Witness

The deposition of a witness may be used as substantive, non-impeachment evidence only under certain circumstances (but see Rules 801(d) and 801(d)(2) of the Federal Rules of Evidence relating to hearsay). The general requirement is that the witness be unavailable at the time of trial.[6] More specifically, the party seeking to introduce the testimony must establish the existence of one of the following five conditions:

(A) The witness is dead.[7] However, if the witness dies during the taking of the deposition, so that one party does not have a full opportunity to examine the witness, then the Court has discretion as to whether to admit the testimony;

(B) The witness is more than 100 miles from the courthouse (measured "as the crow flies")[8] or outside the United States, unless it appears that the party offering the testimony procured the absence of the witness;[9]

(C) The deponent is unable to attend trial because of age,[10] sickness,[11] infirmity, or imprisonment;[12]

---

[2]   *MMG Ins. Co. v. Samsung Electronics America, Inc.*, 293 F.Supp.2d 58 (D.N.H. 2013).

[3]   *Creative Consumer Concepts, Inc. v. Kreisler*, 563 F.3d 1070, 1080 (10th Cir. 2009) (no need to show that the witness is unavailable when introducing the testimony of a party opponent).

[4]   *Shanklin v. Norfolk Southern Ry. Co.*, 369 F.3d 978 (6th Cir.2004).

[5]   *Estate of Thompson v. Kawasaki Heavy Industries, Ltd.*, 291 F.R.D. 297 (N.D.Iowa 2013).

[6]   *Estate of Thompson v. Kawasaki Heavy Industries, Ltd.*, 291 F.R.D. 297 (N.D.Iowa 2013) (availability is evaluated at the time of the testimony).

[7]   *See Dellwood Farms, Inc. v. Cargill, Inc.*, 128 F.3d 1122, 1128 (7th Cir. 1997).

[8]   *Chrysler Intern. Corp. v. Chemaly*, 280 F.3d 1358, 1359 (11th Cir. 2002).

[9]   *Garcia-Martinez v. City and County of Denver*, 392 F.3d 1187, 1191–92 (10th Cir. 2004).

[10]   *United States v. Firishchak*, 468 F.3d 1015, 1023 (7th Cir. 2006).

[11]   *Smith v. Pfizer Inc.*, 688 F.Supp.2d 735 (M.D.Tenn. 2010).

[12]   *Delgado v. Pawtucket Police Dept.*, 668 F.3d 42, 46 (1st Cir. 2012) (it is not enough to show the witness is in prison, the party must show that the witness is unavailable because of imprisonment).

(D)   The party offering the deposition was unable to procure the deponent's attendance at trial by subpoena;[13] or

(E)   Exceptional other circumstances.[14] In order to take advantage of the catchall in Rule 32(a)(4)(E), a party must give notice to the other party of its intent.[15] Note, however, that the general policy favoring live testimony leads to a restrictive reading of this "catchall" clause.[16]

Must Comply with Rules of Evidence

Once the criteria in Rule 32 for use of a deposition have been satisfied, the deposition must still be admissible under the rules of evidence.[17] The rules of evidence are applied as though the deponent were present and testifying.[18] Thus, the effect of Rule 32 is to negate the hearsay objection.[19] Furthermore, as with any evidence, the admission of deposition testimony is subject to the Court's discretion.[20]

Use of Part of a Deposition

If a party introduces only part of a deposition, any adverse party may require the offering party to introduce additional parts necessary to clarify the offered text.[21] Such adverse parties have the right to have the additional text introduced immediately following the admission of the offered testimony.[22] The admission of the additional parts is still subject to evidentiary objections.[23]

Deposition Taken in Another Matter

A deposition from another matter may be used if the witness is unavailable and if the party against whom the testimony is offered (or the party's predecessor in interest)[24] had an opportunity and similar motive to examine the witness at the deposition.[25]

Who May Use

Deposition transcripts may be used by any party, regardless of who noticed the deposition.[26]

---

[13] *Thomas v. Cook County Sheriff's Dept.*, 604 F.3d 293, 308 (7th Cir. 2009) (knowledge of the witness's location is not dispositive if the party has exercised reasonable efforts to obtain the witness's attendance).

[14] *See Battle ex rel. Battle v. Memorial Hosp. at Gulfport*, 228 F.3d 544, 554 (5th Cir. 2000) (videotaped deposition of physician allowed).

[15] *In re Hayes Lemmerz Intern., Inc.*, 340 B.R. 461, 468 (Bankr. D. Del. 2006).

[16] *Griman v. Makousky*, 76 F.3d 151, 153 (7th Cir. 1996).

[17] *See Reeg v. Shaughnessy*, 570 F.2d 309 (10th Cir.1978).

[18] *Sara Lee Corp. v. Kraft Foods Inc.*, 276 F.R.D. 500, 502–03 (N.D.Ill. 2011).

[19] *Ueland v. United States,*291 F.2d 993 (7th Cir. 2002).

[20] *Coletti v. Cudd Pressure Control*, 165 F.3d 767, 773 (10th Cir. 1999) (upholding trial court's refusal to admit deposition testimony as substantive evidence).

[21] *Lentomyynti Oy v. Medivac, Inc.*, 997 F.2d 364 (7th Cir.1993).

[22] *Westinghouse Elec. Corp. v. Wray Equipment Corp.*, 286 F.2d 491, 494 (1st Cir. 1961).

[23] *See Heary Bros. Lightning Protection Co., Inc. v. Lightning Protection Institute*, 287 F.Supp.2d 1038, 1065 n.10 (D. Ariz. 2003), aff'd in part, rev'd in part, 262 Fed. Appx. 815 (9th Cir. 2008).

[24] *Barraford v. T & N Ltd.*, 988 F.Supp.2d 81 (D. Mass. 2013).

[25] *See* Fed.R.Evid. 804(b)(1); *Alexander v. Casino Queen, Inc.*, 739 F.3d 972, 978 (7th Cir. 2014).

[26] *Savoie v. Lafourche Boat Rentals, Inc.*, 627 F.2d 722 (5th Cir. 1980).

Use of One's Own Deposition

Parties may notice their own deposition for use at trial if they know they will be "unavailable" under the provisions of Rule 32(a)(4).[27] The court will evaluate whether the party truly was unavailable.[28]

Against Whom/Reasonable Notice

The deposition may be used against any party who was present or represented at, or had reasonable notice of, the deposition.[29] A deposition cannot be used against a party who demonstrates that it was unable to obtain counsel to represent it at the deposition despite the exercise of diligence. Likewise, the deposition cannot be used against a party who received less than 14 days' notice and who had filed a motion for a protective order that was pending at the time of the deposition.[30]

Discovery Depositions vs. Depositions for Use at Trial

Rule 32 does not draw any distinctions between depositions taken for discovery purposes and those taken "for use at trial."[31]

Motion for Summary Judgment

Deposition transcripts may be used in support of or in opposition to motions for summary judgment.[32] Indeed, some courts treat deposition testimony as equivalent to an affidavit in the context of a summary judgment motion, and allow use of deposition testimony even if all of the criteria of Rule 32 are not satisfied.[33] The use of depositions in connection with summary judgment is governed by Rule 56(c).

RULE 32(b)—OBJECTIONS TO ADMISSIBILITY

CORE CONCEPT

Objections to the admissibility of a deposition under Rule 32 must be made at the time the testimony is offered at trial or the objections are waived.

APPLICATIONS

Rules of Evidence

A deposition admissible under Rule 32 must also be admissible under the rules of evidence.[34] Evidentiary rulings are made as though the deponent were present and testifying.

RULE 32(c)—FORM OF PRESENTATION

CORE CONCEPT

Deposition testimony may be offered in stenographic or nonstenographic form. In jury trials, any party may require that the nonstenographic form be used if available.

---

[27] *Richmond v. Brooks,* 227 F.2d 490 (2d Cir.1955).

[28] *Vevelstad v. Flynn,* 16 Alaska 83, 230 F.2d 695 (9th Cir. 1956).

[29] *Creative Consumer Concepts, Inc. v. Kreisler,* 563 F.3d 1070, 1080 (10th Cir. 2009).

[30] *U.S. S.E.C. v. Talbot,* 430 F.Supp.2d 1029 (C.D. Cal. 2006), rev'd on other grounds, 530 F.3d 1085 (9th Cir. 2008).

[31] *Manley v. AmBase Corp.,* 337 F.3d 237, 247 (2d Cir. 2003).

[32] *Carmen v. San Francisco Unified School Dist.,* 237 F.3d 1026, 1028 (9th Cir. 2001).

[33] *Alexander v. Casino Queen, Inc.,* 739 F.3d 972, 978 (7th Cir. 2014) (Rule 32 is primarily a limitation on the use of deposition testimony *at trial*).

[34] *Marshall v. Planz,* 145 F.Supp.2d 1258 (M.D. Ala. 2001).

APPLICATIONS

Nonstenographic Forms

A party expecting to use a nonstenographic form of deposition at trial must provide other parties with a transcript in advance of trial under Rule 26(a)(3)(A)(ii). When nonstenographic forms of testimony are offered, the offering party shall also provide the court a transcript.[35] Rule 32 does not authorize the submission of deposition summaries in lieu of the transcript.[36]

Jury Trials

In a jury trial, any party may require that depositions be offered in nonstenographic form if available unless the deposition is being used for impeachment or the court orders otherwise for good cause shown.

RULE 32(d)—WAIVER OF OBJECTIONS

CORE CONCEPT

Objections to the procedures at a deposition must be asserted as soon as practicable or they are waived.

APPLICATIONS

Defects in Notice

Objections to the notice must be made in writing to the party issuing the notice,[37] unless there was no opportunity to object.[38]

Disqualification of Officer

Objections to the qualifications of the officer (e.g., stenographer), which are set forth in Rule 28, must be made before the start of the deposition or they are waived.

Objections to Testimony

Objections that can be cured by rephrasing the question, such as leading question objections, must be raised at the deposition or they are waived.[39] All other objections, such as relevance,[40] capacity, etc., are reserved until the testimony is offered at trial.[41]

Objections as to Oath

Objections as to the manner of the oath or affirmation administered must be made at the time of the deposition or they are waived.[42]

---

[35] *Tilton v. Capital Cities/ABC, Inc.*, 115 F.3d 1471, 1479 (10th Cir. 1997) (a party intending to use a videotape deposition must provide a transcript).

[36] *Planned Parenthood of Columbia/Willamette, Inc. v. American Coalition of Life Activists*, 290 F.3d 1058, 1117 (9th Cir. 2002).

[37] *State Farm Mut. Auto. Ins. Co. v. Dowdy ex rel. Dowdy*, 445 F.Supp.2d 1289, 1293 (N.D. Okla. 2006).

[38] *Oates v. S. J. Groves & Sons Co.*, 248 F.2d 388 (6th Cir. 1957).

[39] *SkinMedica, Inc. v. Histogen Inc.*, 727 F.3d 1187, 1213 (Fed. Cir. 2013).

[40] *Rangel v. Gonzalez Mascorro*, 274 F.R.D. 585 (S.D.Tex. 2011).

[41] *State Farm Mut. Auto. Ins. Co. v. Dowdy ex rel. Dowdy*, 445 F.Supp.2d 1289, 1293 (N.D. Okla. 2006) (such objections should not be made at the deposition).

[42] *Cabello v. Fernandez-Larios*, 402 F.3d 1148, 1160 (11th Cir. 2005).

Objections to Written Deposition Questions

Objections to the form of a written question *(e.g., because it is leading)* must be served in writing upon the party propounding the question within the time for serving succeeding questions and within 7 days of the last questions authorized.

Objections as to Manner of Transcription

Objections as to the manner of transcription or as to the procedures used in correcting and signing the transcript must be made in the form of a motion to suppress, which must be made with "reasonable promptness" after the defect is discovered or should have been discovered with due diligence.[43]

ADDITIONAL RESEARCH REFERENCES

Wright & Miller, *Federal Practice and Procedure* §§ 2142 to 2157

C.J.S., Federal Civil Procedure §§ 544 to 568, 633 to 638 et seq.

West's Key Number Digest, Federal Civil Procedure ↦ 1297, 1298, 1334, 1432 to 1440

---

[43]   *Trade Development Bank v. Continental Ins. Co.,* 469 F.2d 35 (2d Cir. 1972).

RULE 33

INTERROGATORIES TO PARTIES

(a) In General.

    (1) *Number.* Unless otherwise stipulated or ordered by the court, a party may serve on any other party no more than 25 written interrogatories, including all discrete subparts. Leave to serve additional interrogatories may be granted to the extent consistent with Rule 26(b)(1) and (2).

    (2) *Scope.* An interrogatory may relate to any matter that may be inquired into under Rule 26(b). An interrogatory is not objectionable merely because it asks for an opinion or contention that relates to fact or the application of law to fact, but the court may order that the interrogatory need not be answered until designated discovery is complete, or until a pretrial conference or some other time.

(b) Answers and Objections.

    (1) *Responding Party.* The interrogatories must be answered:

        (A) by the party to whom they are directed; or

        (B) if that party is a public or private corporation, a partnership, an association, or a governmental agency, by any officer or agent, who must furnish the information available to the party.

    (2) *Time to Respond.* The responding party must serve its answers and any objections within 30 days after being served with the interrogatories. A shorter or longer time may be stipulated to under Rule 29 or be ordered by the court.

    (3) *Answering Each Interrogatory.* Each interrogatory must, to the extent it is not objected to, be answered separately and fully in writing under oath.

    (4) *Objections.* The grounds for objecting to an interrogatory must be stated with specificity. Any ground not stated in a timely objection is waived unless the court, for good cause, excuses the failure.

    (5) *Signature.* The person who makes the answers must sign them, and the attorney who objects must sign any objections.

(c) Use. An answer to an interrogatory may be used to the extent allowed by the Federal Rules of Evidence.

(d) Option to Produce Business Records. If the answer to an interrogatory may be determined by examining, auditing, compiling, abstracting, or summarizing a party's business records (including electronically stored

information), and if the burden of deriving or ascertaining the answer will be substantially the same for either party, the responding party may answer by:

(1) specifying the records that must be reviewed, in sufficient detail to enable the interrogating party to locate and identify them as readily as the responding party could; and

(2) giving the interrogating party a reasonable opportunity to examine and audit the records and to make copies, compilations, abstracts, or summaries.

[Amended December 27, 1946, effective March 19, 1948; March 30, 1970, effective July 1, 1970; April 29, 1980, effective August 1, 1980; April 22, 1993, effective December 1, 1993; April 12, 2006, effective December 1, 2006; April 30, 2007, effective December 1, 2007; April 29, 2015, effective December 1, 2015.]

AUTHORS' COMMENTARY ON RULE 33

PURPOSE AND SCOPE

Rule 33 sets forth the procedures for using interrogatories. It must be read in conjunction with Rule 26, which establishes the scope of all the discovery rules.

♦ **NOTE:** Rule 33 was substantially revised in 1970, 1993, 2006, and 2007, and great care should be exercised when citing decisions pertaining to Rule 33.

RULE 33(a)—IN GENERAL

CORE CONCEPT

Any party may serve up to 25 interrogatories or questions on any other party. The scope of interrogatories is the broad discovery available under Rule 26.

APPLICATIONS

Who May Serve

Any party may serve interrogatories.

Who May Be Served

Interrogatories are limited to parties to the action,[1] although the party need not be an adverse party. The interrogatories must be addressed to the party. Thus, if the party is a corporation, interrogatories should be addressed to the corporation, not to a corporate officer or the attorney.[2] In a class action, the courts are split as to whether only the named representatives can be served.[3]

Time for Service

Interrogatories can be served after the parties have conducted the discovery conference under Rule 26(f),[4] or earlier with leave of court. In proceedings listed in Rule 26(a)(1)(B) as exempt from initial disclosures, there is no preliminary waiting period for interrogatories.

---

[1]   *United States v. Lot 41, Berryhill Farm Estates,* 128 F.3d 1386, 1397 (10th Cir. 1997).

[2]   *Holland v. Minneapolis-Honeywell Regulator Co.,* 28 F.R.D. 595 (D. D.C. 1961).

[3]   *Brennan v. Midwestern United Life Ins. Co.,* 450 F.2d 999 (7th Cir. 1971) (unnamed members of class required to respond); *Wainwright v. Kraftco Corp.,* 54 F.R.D. 532 (N.D. Ga. 1972) (unnamed members of class not required to respond).

[4]   *Krause v. Buffalo and Erie County Workforce Development Consortium, Inc.,* 425 F.Supp.2d 352 (W.D. N.Y. 2006).

The Rules do not set an outer limit on how late in the case interrogatories may be served, but many local rules or case management orders will set such a limit. Usually, when such a limit exists, interrogatories must be served so that the answers are due before the close of discovery.[5]

Number

Each party may serve up to 25 interrogatories on each other party.[6] Additional interrogatories may be served pursuant to a court order or stipulation.[7] Note that parties may coordinate to maximize their allowable interrogatories, such that in a case with multiple plaintiffs, for example, they may divide up topics, effectively expanding the number of interrogatories that may be served on each defendant. If an interrogatory has subparts, each subpart may count as a separate interrogatory if it is really a discrete question.[8]

Scope of Questions

The scope of interrogatories is controlled by Rule 26(b).[9] The information sought must be relevant to the claims or defenses in the case and proportional to the needs of the case, but need not be admissible evidence. Privileged information is not discoverable, and discovery is limited with respect to expert witnesses and trial preparation materials as discussed in Rule 26(b).

Opinions or Contentions

An interrogatory is not objectionable because it seeks an opinion or contention that relates to fact or the application of law to fact.[10] However, the court may order that a contention interrogatory not be answered until discovery is complete or until after the pretrial conference is held.[11] An interrogatory that asks for a pure legal conclusion, without application to the facts, is improper.[12]

Form

Parties have a great deal of latitude in framing interrogatories, as long as the responding party can reasonably determine the information to include in the answer. Only rarely will a question be so ambiguous that it does not require an answer, although the responding party can limit the scope of its answer.

Proceedings Where Interrogatories Available

Rule 33 applies to all civil actions in district court, including post-judgment proceedings (*i.e.*, interrogatories in aid of execution). Rule 33 does not apply to habeas proceedings.[13]

---

[5]   *Thomas v. Pacificorp*, 324 F.3d 1176 (10th Cir. 2003).

[6]   *Chudasama v. Mazda Motor Corp.*, 123 F.3d 1353, 1357 (11th Cir. 1997).

[7]   *Rates Technology, Inc. v. Mediatrix Telecom, Inc.*, 688 F.3d 742, 748 (Fed.Cir. 2012).

[8]   *Erfindergemeinschaft Uropep GbR v. Eli Lilly and Company*, ___ F.R.D. ___, ___, 2016 WL 2807640, *2 (E.D. Tex. 2016).

[9]   *Barnes v. District of Columbia*, 289 F.R.D. 1, 5 (D.D.C. 2012).

[10]   *In re Rail Freight Fuel Surcharge Antitrust Litig.*, 281 F.R.D. 1, 4 (D.D.C. 2011) (work product doctrine is not a valid objection to contention interrogatory).

[11]   *See Bortex Industry Co. Ltd. v. Fiber Optic Designs, Inc.*, 296 F.R.D. 373, 377, n.5 (E.D. Pa. 2013) ("Courts have considerable discretion in allowing delayed responses to contention interrogatories.").

[12]   *Gingerich v. City of Elkhart Probation Dept.*, 273 F.R.D. 532 (N.D.Ind. 2011).

[13]   *Harris v. Nelson*, 394 U.S. 286, 293–94, 89 S.Ct. 1082, 1087, 22 L.Ed.2d 281 (1969).

RULE 33(b)—ANSWERS AND OBJECTIONS

CORE CONCEPT

The responding party must answer interrogatories separately and in writing within 30 days after service. Objections must be stated with specificity, and objections are waived if not made timely. The responding party must sign the answers and the attorney must sign any objections.

APPLICATIONS

Answers

Each interrogatory must be answered separately and fully [14] in writing,[15] unless an objection is interposed in lieu of an answer.[16] The answer must include all information within the party's possession, custody, or control or known by the party's agents.[17] This includes *facts* in an attorney's possession and information supplied to the party by others.[18] At the same time, a party does not have to obtain publically available information not in its possession, custody, or control.[19] If no such information is available, the answer may so state.[20] If only some information is available, that information must be provided, and may be prefaced with a statement placing the answer in context. Generally, incorporating the pleadings or other discovery will not be sufficient, although the answer to one interrogatory may incorporate information provided in another.[21] The responding party must serve the answers on all other parties.

Time to Answer

Answers and objections are due within 30 days of service unless the parties or the court stipulate to a different amount of time.[22] Failure to serve a response in a timely manner (*i.e.*, within 30 days of service) may constitute a waiver of all objections.[23] The time to answer may be extended by order of court or written agreement under Rule 29.[24]

Who Answers

The party must answer the interrogatories, not the party's attorney (although it is common practice for the attorney to draft the answers).[25] The attorney interposes the objections. If the party is a corporation or organization, an officer or agent will answer for the corporation.[26] In this case, the attorney may answer the interrogatories as agent for the corporation.[27] The answering officer or agent need not have first-hand knowledge of the information being provided.[28] However, the responding agent's answers must provide the

---

[14]   *See Barnes v. District of Columbia*, 289 F.R.D. 1, 6 (D.D.C. 2012).

[15]   *Wsol v. Fiduciary Management Associates, Inc.*, 2000 WL 748143 (N.D. Ill. 2000) (oral answers are not permitted).

[16]   *Vazquez-Fernandez v. Cambridge College, Inc.*, 269 F.R.D. 150, 154 (D.Puerto Rico 2010).

[17]   *Costa v. Kerzner Intern. Resorts, Inc.*, 277 F.R.D. 468, 472–73 (S.D.Fla. 2011) (information held by affiliated corporation within the control of a party).

[18]   *Hickman v. Taylor,* 329 U.S. 495, 504, 67 S.Ct. 385, 390, 91 L. Ed. 451 (1947).

[19]   *Huthnance v. District of Columbia*, 255 F.R.D. 285, 292 (D.D.C. 2008).

[20]   *Hansel v. Shell Oil Corp.*, 169 F.R.D. 303, 305 (E.D. Pa. 1996) (answer should set forth the efforts used to attempt to obtain the requested information).

[21]   *Vazquez-Fernandez v. Cambridge College, Inc.*, 269 F.R.D. 150, 156 (D.Puerto Rico 2010).

[22]   *See Verkuilen v. South Shore Bldg. and Mortg. Co.*, 122 F.3d 410, 411 (7th Cir. 1997).

[23]   *See Mulero-Abreu v. Puerto Rico Police Dept.*, 675 F.3d 88, 90 (1st Cir. 2012).

[24]   *See Underdog Trucking, L.L.C. v. Verizon Services Corp.*, 273 F.R.D. 372 (S.D.N.Y. 2011).

[25]   *Huthnance v. District of Columbia*, 255 F.R.D. 297, 300 (D.D.C. 2008).

[26]   *General Dynamics Corp. v. Selb Mfg. Co.*, 481 F.2d 1204 (8th Cir. 1973).

[27]   *Wilson v. Volkswagen of America, Inc.*, 561 F.2d 494, 508 (4th Cir. 1977).

[28]   *Jiminez-Carillo v. Autopart Intern., Inc.*, 285 F.R.D. 668, 670 (S.D.Fla. 2012).

composite knowledge available to the party.[29] If the party is an infant, the infant's attorney or next friend may answer.[30]

Verification

When the party is an individual, the party, not the attorney,[31] must sign a verification or affidavit as to the accuracy of the answers.[32] This is one of the few exceptions to the general principle under the Federal Rules of Civil Procedure that the attorney may sign all pleadings and papers. A representative of a corporate party may verify interrogatory answers without personal knowledge of every response by furnishing the information available to the corporation.[33] The courts are divided as to whether an attorney can verify interrogatory answers for a corporation.[34]

Objections

If the responding party believes that a particular interrogatory is outside the scope of discovery or otherwise improper, the party may object to the question in lieu of answering it or in conjunction with an answer that takes the objection into account.[35] The objection must be made in writing, must state the grounds of the objection with specificity,[36] and must be signed by the attorney for the responding party.[37] Some common objections are:

- *Overly broad, unduly vague, and ambiguous:* When a question is written so broadly that it extends to information not relevant to the claims or defenses in the matter (such as a question not limited in time to the events relevant to the complaint), the question may be overly broad.[38] When a question is susceptible to numerous meanings, it may be unduly vague and ambiguous. In general, these objections are probably not justification for refusing to answer a question altogether, but the responding party can raise the objection, then expressly limit the scope of the response.

- *Burdensome and oppressive:* In general, the responding party must produce the information available without undue effort or expense. Thus, questions that require extensive research, compilation of data, or evaluation of data may be objectionable.[39] The responding party is not required to prepare the adverse party's case. Likewise, an interrogatory that seeks a high level of detail may be

---

[29] *Jiminez-Carillo v. Autopart Intern., Inc.,* 285 F.R.D. 668, 670 (S.D.Fla. 2012).

[30] *Hall v. Hague,* 34 F.R.D. 449 (D. Md. 1964).

[31] *Saria v. Massachusetts Mut. Life Ins. Co.,* 228 F.R.D. 536, 538–39 (S.D. W. Va. 2005) (verification by the attorney renders the attorney a witness).

[32] *In re World Trade Center Lower Manhattan Disaster Site Litigation,* 758 F.3d 202 (2d Cir. 2014) (dismissing claims for repeated failure to verify interrogatory answers); *In re World Trade Center Disaster Site Litigation,* 722 F.3d 483, 485 (2d Cir. 2013) (if the signature is not under oath, it does not satisfy Rule 33(b)).

[33] *Shepherd v. American Broadcasting Companies, Inc.,* 62 F.3d 1469, 1482 (D.C. Cir. 1995).

[34] *Compare Sorrell v. District of Columbia,* 252 F.R.D. 37, 43 (D.D.C. 2008) (paralegal signature not permitted) *with Rea v. Wichita Mortg. Corp.,* 747 F.2d 567, 574, n.6 (10th Cir. 1984) (attorney signature allowed).

[35] *But see Gassaway v. Jarden Corp.,* 292 F.R.D. 676, 681–82 (D. Kan. 2013) (holding that a party who objects to and answers an interrogatory waives the objections. Note, however, that this appears to be an outlier position).

[36] *See Mulero-Abreu v. Puerto Rico Police Dept.,* 675 F.3d 88, 93 (1st Cir. 2012) (blanket objection improper).

[37] *Moreno Rivera v. DHL Global Forwarding,* 272 F.R.D. 50, 55 (D.Puerto Rico 2011).

[38] *Jewish Hospital Ass'n of Louisville, Ky. v. Struck Const. Co., Inc.,* 77 F.R.D. 59 (W.D. Ky. 1978).

[39] *IBP, Inc. v. Mercantile Bank of Topeka,* 179 F.R.D. 316, 321 (D. Kan. 1998) (interrogatory asking for every fact and application of law to fact supporting claim held burdensome).

overly burdensome.[40] The reasonableness of an interrogatory is within the court's discretion.

- *Privileged information:* Questions that seek information protected by the attorney-client privilege or by another privilege are objectionable. When privileged information is withheld, the responding party must explicitly state the objection and describe the nature of the information not provided sufficiently to enable other parties to assess the applicability of the privilege. Care should be exercised in responding to such interrogatories, because the privilege may be waived by revealing part or all of the privileged communication.

- *Attorney work product:* Rule 26(b)(3) provides a qualified protection for documents prepared in anticipation of litigation.[41]

- *Non-discoverable expert information:* Rule 26(b)(4) limits the scope of discovery directed towards experts. It generally requires the responding party to provide an expert report for each expert it may call as a witness, and thereafter allows other parties to depose such experts. Further discovery with respect to such witnesses is available only upon motion. Rule 26(b)(4)(B) does not allow any discovery with respect to experts not intended to be called as witnesses, absent "exceptional circumstances."[42]

- *Not proportional to the needs of the case:* A party may object that an interrogatory seeks information that is not proportional to the needs of the case, in light of the factors listed in Rule 26(b)(1).

Failure to Object Is Waiver

All grounds for objection must be specifically stated in a timely response or they are waived, unless excused by the court for good cause shown.[43]

Objection to Part of Interrogatory

If only part of an interrogatory is objectionable, the responding party must answer the interrogatory to the extent that it is not objectionable.[44] Thus, if an interrogatory is overly broad, the responding party should provide information responsive to the interrogatory as if narrowed so as not to be overly broad.[45] A number of courts have held that the common practice of objecting, then answering "subject to and without waiving" the objections is improper and waives the objections unless the response describes in particularity the information not being provided. [46]

Motion for a Protective Order

As an alternative to making objections to individual questions, the responding party may make a motion for a protective order under Rule 26(c). A motion for a protective order is appropriate when most or all of a set of interrogatories is too burdensome or cumulative. The burden is on the moving party to show good cause for the protective order.[47] The motion

---

[40] *See Ritchie Risk-Linked Strategies Trading (Ireland), Ltd. v. Coventry First LLC,* 273 F.R.D. 367 (S.D.N.Y. 2010) (requests for every fact, piece of evidence, and witness supporting the party's position is overly broad and unduly burdensome).

[41] *See* Rule 26(b)(3) (in-depth discussion of discovery of work product).

[42] *See* Rule 26(b)(4) (in-depth discussion of discovery directed toward experts).

[43] *Black Hills Molding, Inc. v. Brandom Holdings, LLC,* 295 F.R.D. 403, 411–12 (D.S.D. 2013).

[44] *Khadim v. Lab. Corp. of Am.,* 838 F.Supp.2d 448, 465 (W.D.Va. 2011).

[45] *See Walls v. International Paper Co.,* 192 F.R.D. 294 (D. Kan. 2000).

[46] *See Heller v. City of Dallas,* 303 F.R.D. 466, 488–90 (N.D. Tex. 2014).

[47] *BPP Retail Properties, LLC v. North American Roofing Services, Inc.,* 300 F.R.D. 59 (D.P.R. 2014).

must be accompanied by a certification that the parties met prior to the filing of the motion and attempted to resolve their dispute without intervention by the court.

Motion to Compel

If the responding party fails to answer sufficiently or objects to an interrogatory, the propounding party may file a motion to compel under Rule 37(a).[48] The court will award the prevailing party its reasonable expenses, including attorney's fees, incurred in connection with the motion to compel, unless the conduct of the losing party was justified (*i.e.,* not frivolous). The motion must be accompanied by a certification that the moving party met and conferred with the opposing party before seeking relief from the court. In a motion to compel, the burden is on the moving party to demonstrate that the responses were incomplete,[49] and the burden is on the responding party (the non-moving party) to convince the court that the interrogatories were objectionable.[50]

Discretion of Court

The district court has extremely broad discretion in ruling on objections to interrogatories.[51] The court will balance the need and the burden, but will generally require an answer unless the administration of justice would be impeded.

Appeals

The court's rulings on objections to interrogatories are not final orders, and cannot be appealed until the conclusion of the case.

Sanctions for Failure to Answer

If a party files no response to an interrogatory (as opposed to an insufficient response as discussed above), the court may impose the sanctions specified in Rule 37(b)(2), such as deeming certain facts established or refusing to allow the party to oppose or support certain claims.[52]

Sanctions for Untrue Answers

If an answer is untrue, either at the time it was made or subsequently, and is not supplemented, the court may exclude certain testimony or make whatever order justice requires.[53]

Duty to Supplement

A party must supplement its response to an interrogatory if the party learns that the response is in some material respect incomplete or incorrect and if the additional or corrective information has not been provided to the other parties in writing or at a deposition.[54] Supplemental responses must be verified just like original responses.[55]

---

[48] *PCS Phosphate Co., Inc. v. Norfolk Southern Corp.,* 238 F.R.D. 555, 559 (E.D. N.C. 2006).

[49] *Haynes v. Navy Federal Credit Union,* 286 F.R.D. 33, 37 (D.D.C. 2012).

[50] *See Donahay v. Palm Beach Tours & Transp., Inc.,* 242 F.R.D. 685 (S.D. Fla. 2007).

[51] *Mack v. Great Atlantic and Pacific Tea Co., Inc.,* 871 F.2d 179, 186 (1st Cir. 1989).

[52] *See* Rule 37(d).

[53] *Garcia v. Berkshire Life Ins. Co. of America,* 569 F.3d 1174, 1180 (10th Cir. 2009) (dismissing the case based on fabrications).

[54] *See Covad Communications Co. v. Revonet, Inc.,* 258 F.R.D. 17 (D.D.C. 2009) (because the responding party has a continuing duty to supplement, the party may state that it is unable to provide the information requested but will supplement its answers as information becomes available).

[55] *Knights Armament Co. v. Optical Systems Technology, Inc.,* 254 F.R.D. 463, 466 (M.D.Fla. 2008).

Requests for Documents

Interrogatories may not be used to obtain documents.[56] Rather, a document request must be made under Rule 34. However, interrogatories may inquire about the existence of documents and the facts contained therein. Furthermore, documents may, under certain circumstances, be produced in lieu of answering an interrogatory, as discussed below under Rule 33(d).

RULE 33(c)—USE

CORE CONCEPT

Interrogatory answers are not binding admissions, but generally may be used as though statements made in court by the party.

APPLICATIONS

Use of Interrogatory Answers at Trial

Answers to interrogatories are treated like any other evidence, and may be offered[57] and admitted into evidence as allowed by the Federal Rules of Evidence.[58] Interrogatory answers are generally not hearsay with respect to the party making the answer because they are party admissions.[59] However, they may be hearsay if offered against another party. Interrogatory answers may be objected to on any other grounds, such as relevance. If only part of an answer is read, the responding party may require that other parts of the answer be admitted at the same time in order to clarify the portion offered.[60]

Answers Not Binding

Answers to interrogatories are not binding admissions, and a party is not bound by its answers.[61] Thus, a party can supplement or amend its answers, and is obligated to do so under certain circumstances discussed above. Even absent an amendment, a party may take a different position at trial unless it would prejudice another party.[62] Opposing parties may then impeach by questioning the reason for the changed answer.

Use of Interrogatory Answers in a Summary Judgment Motion

Interrogatory answers may be used in support of or in opposition to a motion for summary judgment, as provided in Rule 56(c).[63]

RULE 33(d)—OPTION TO PRODUCE BUSINESS RECORDS

CORE CONCEPT

A party may produce business records in lieu of answering an interrogatory when the burden of extracting the requested information would be substantially equal for either party.

---

[56] *Alltmont v. United States,* 177 F.2d 971 (3d Cir. 1949).

[57] *Cimino v. Raymark Industries, Inc.,* 151 F.3d 297, 309 (5th Cir. 1998) (interrogatory answers are not part of the record unless formally offered into evidence).

[58] *AMCO Ins. Co. v. Inspired Techs., Inc.,* 648 F.3d 875, 881 (8th Cir. 2011).

[59] *Underberg v. United States,* 362 F.Supp.2d 1278, 1283 (D.N.M. 2005).

[60] *Grace & Co. v. City of Los Angeles,* 278 F.2d 771 (9th Cir.1960).

[61] *Bradley v. Allstate Ins. Co.,* 620 F.3d 509, 527, n.21 (5th Cir. 2010).

[62] *Sunshine Heifers, LLC v. Moohaven Dairy, LLC,* 13 F.Supp.3d 770 (E.D. Mich. 2014).

[63] *Bradley v. Allstate Ins. Co.,* 620 F.3d 509, 527, n.21 (5th Cir. 2010).

APPLICATIONS

Business Records Only

Only business records of the responding party may be used in lieu of interrogatory answers.[64] Thus, one cannot produce pleadings[65] or deposition transcripts[66] or refer to the administrative record[67] instead of answering an interrogatory.

Documents Must Contain Information

In order to respond to an interrogatory by producing business records, a party must state that the documents contain the requested information.[68] It is not sufficient to state that the documents *may* contain the information.[69]

Identify Specific Documents

A party responding to an interrogatory by producing business records must provide sufficient detail so that the propounding party can identify which individual documents contain the information requested.[70]

Equal Burden

In order to respond to interrogatories by producing business records, the burden of deriving or ascertaining the answer must be substantially equal for the requesting party and the producing party.[71] If the sufficiency of the response is challenged, the producing party will bear the burden of making this showing.[72]

Contention Interrogatories

A number of courts have held that a party may not refer to documents in lieu of responding to contention interrogatories, as the responding party's contentions are not likely to be found in business records.[73]

Privileged Documents

A party cannot elect to produce business records and then withhold the documents as privileged in order to prevent a party from deriving an answer.[74]

Expense of Compiling Records

Under proper circumstances, the court will, upon motion for a protective order, require the propounding party to pay the cost of compiling the records.[75]

---

[64] *Covad Communications Co. v. Revonet, Inc.*, 258 F.R.D. 17, 20 (D.D.C. 2009) (responding party may not refer to the opposing party's records).

[65] *Melius v. National Indian Gaming Com'n*, 2000 WL 1174994 (D.D.C. 2000).

[66] *Starlight Intern., Inc. v. Herlihy*, 190 F.R.D. 587 (D. Kan. 1999).

[67] *Mullins v. Prudential Ins. Co. of America*, 267 F.R.D. 504, 514 (W.D.Ky. 2010) (Rule 33(d) is not a procedural device for avoiding the duty to provide the information).

[68] *See Nature's Plus Nordic A/S v. Natural Organics, Inc.*, 274 F.R.D. 437 (E.D.N.Y. 2011) (documents in foreign language do not contain the information as contemplated by Rule 32(d)).

[69] *Daiflon, Inc. v. Allied Chemical Corp.*, 534 F.2d 221 (10th Cir. 1976).

[70] *Alexsam, Inc. v. IDT Corp.*, 715 F.3d 1336 (Fed.Cir. 2013).

[71] *Nature's Plus Nordic A/S v. Natural Organics, Inc.*, 274 F.R.D. 437 (E.D.N.Y. 2011) (burden of obtaining responsive information from documents in foreign language not equal).

[72] *U.S. S.E.C. v. Elfindepan, S.A.*, 206 F.R.D. 574, 577 (M.D. N.C. 2002).

[73] *United States ex rel. Landis v. Tailwind Sports Corp.*, ___ F.Supp.3d ___, ___, 2016 WL 2944648, *3 (D.D.C. 2016).

[74] *Westfield Ins. Co. v. Carpenter Reclamation, Inc.*, 301 F.R.D. 235 (S.D.W. Va. 2014).

[75] *See* Rule 26(c) (detail on costs).

Motion to Compel

If the propounding party believes that its burden to find the answers from the records is substantially greater than that of the responding party, the propounding party can file a motion to compel an answer.[76]

ADDITIONAL RESEARCH REFERENCES

Wright & Miller, *Federal Practice and Procedure* §§ 2161 to 2182

C.J.S., Federal Civil Procedure §§ 645 to 695 et seq.

West's Key Number Digest, Federal Civil Procedure ↦1471 to 1542

---

[76]   *See Maxtena, Inc. v. Marks,* 289 F.R.D. 427 (D.Md. 2012).

RULE 34

PRODUCING DOCUMENTS, ELECTRONICALLY STORED INFORMATION, AND TANGIBLE THINGS, OR ENTERING ONTO LAND, FOR INSPECTION AND OTHER PURPOSES

(a) In General. A party may serve on any other party a request within the scope of Rule 26(b):

(1) to produce and permit the requesting party or its representative to inspect, copy, test, or sample the following items in the responding party's possession, custody, or control:

(A) any designated documents or electronically stored information—including writings, drawings, graphs, charts, photographs, sound recordings, images, and other data or data compilations—stored in any medium from which information can be obtained either directly or, if necessary, after translation by the responding party into a reasonably usable form; or

(B) any designated tangible things; or

(2) to permit entry onto designated land or other property possessed or controlled by the responding party, so that the requesting party may inspect, measure, survey, photograph, test, or sample the property or any designated object or operation on it.

(b) Procedure.

(1) *Contents of the Request.* The request:

(A) must describe with reasonable particularity each item or category of items to be inspected;

(B) must specify a reasonable time, place, and manner for the inspection and for performing the related acts; and

(C) may specify the form or forms in which electronically stored information is to be produced.

(2) *Responses and Objections.*

(A) *Time to Respond.* The party to whom the request is directed must respond in writing within 30 days after being served or—if the request was delivered under Rule 26(d)(2)—within 30 days after the parties' first Rule 26(f) conference. A shorter or longer time may be stipulated to under Rule 29 or be ordered by the court.

(B) *Responding to Each Item.* For each item or category, the response must either state that inspection and related activities will be permitted as requested or state with specificity the grounds for objecting to the request, including the reasons. The responding party may state that it will produce copies of documents or of electronically stored information instead of permitting inspection. The production must then be completed no later than the time for inspection specified in the request or another reasonable time specified in the response.

(C) *Objections.* An objection must state whether any responsive materials are being withheld on the basis of that objection. An objection to part of a request must specify the part and permit inspection of the rest.

(D) *Responding to a Request for Production of Electronically Stored Information.* The response may state an objection to a requested form for producing electronically stored information. If the responding party objects to a requested form—or if no form was specified in the request—the party must state the form or forms it intends to use.

(E) *Producing the Documents or Electronically Stored Information.* Unless otherwise stipulated or ordered by the court, these procedures apply to producing documents or electronically stored information:

  (i)   A party must produce documents as they are kept in the usual course of business or must organize and label them to correspond to the categories in the request;

  (ii) If a request does not specify a form for producing electronically stored information, a party must produce it in a form or forms in which it is ordinarily maintained or in a reasonably usable form or forms; and

  (iii) A party need not produce the same electronically stored information in more than one form.

(c) Nonparties. As provided in Rule 45, a nonparty may be compelled to produce documents and tangible things or to permit an inspection.

[Amended December 27, 1946, effective March 19, 1948; March 30, 1970, effective July 1, 1970; April 29, 1980, effective August 1, 1980; March 2, 1987, effective August 1, 1987; April 30, 1991, effective December 1, 1991; April 22, 1993, effective December 1, 1993; April 12, 2006, effective December 1, 2006; April 30, 2007, effective December 1, 2007; April 29, 2015, effective December 1, 2015.]

AUTHORS' COMMENTARY ON RULE 34

PURPOSE AND SCOPE

Rule 34 sets forth the procedures for obtaining access to documents and things within the control of other parties, and for gaining entry upon other parties' land for inspection. It must be read in conjunction with Rule 26, which establishes the scope of all discovery rules.

♦ **NOTE:** Rule 34 was substantially revised in 1970, 1991, 1993, 2006, 2007, and 2015, and great care should be exercised when citing decisions pertaining to Rule 34.

RULE 34(a)—IN GENERAL

CORE CONCEPT

The scope of document requests and other discovery under Rule 34 is the broad discovery available under Rule 26.[1] Generally, any non-privileged document that is relevant to any party's claim or defense is discoverable unless it was prepared in anticipation of litigation, pertains to expert witnesses, or would be disproportionate to the needs of the case or unreasonably burdensome to produce.

APPLICATIONS

Documents

"Documents" is broadly defined to include all forms of recorded information. Rule 34(a) specifically lists writings, drawings, graphs, charts, photographs, phonorecords, and other data compilations.[2]

Electronic Data

Rule 34(a) specifically includes "electronically stored information" or "ESI" among the categories of documents and things that must be produced.[3] ESI is intended to be a broad and flexible term encompassing email and information "stored in any medium."[4] ESI must be produced in the form in which it is ordinarily maintained or, if necessary, translated into a reasonably usable form.[5] For more information about the discovery of ESI, see the Sedona Principles: Best Practices, Recommendations & Principles for Addressing Electronic Document Production, Second Edition,[6] upon which the courts have come to rely.[7]

Metadata

One particular form of electronically stored information that has drawn considerable attention in litigation is metadata (data about data), which describes the data that many programs store about the documents created in the program, such as the identity of the author, when the document was created, the identity of those editing the document, and when those edits occurred.[8] Metadata raises a host of issues (including preservation or

---

[1] *Trask v. Olin Corp.*, 298 F.R.D. 244, 259 (W.D. Pa. 2014).

[2] *Anderson Living Trust v. WPX Energy Production, LLC,* 298 F.R.D. 514, 521 (D.N.M. 2014) ("other data compilations" was added in 1970 to expressly include electronically stored information).

[3] *Anderson Living Trust v. WPX Energy Production, LLC,* 298 F.R.D. 514, 523 (D.N.M. 2014).

[4] *See Columbia Pictures, Inc. v. Bunnell,* 245 F.R.D. 443, 446–47 (C.D. Cal. 2007) (Rule 34(a)(1) is expansive and includes any type of information that is stored electronically, including information in RAM).

[5] *United States v. Capitol Supply, Inc.,* 27 F.Supp.3d 91 (D.D.C. 2014).

[6] Available at http://www.thesedonaconference.org/content/miscFiles/TSC_PRINCP_2nd_ed_607.pdf.

[7] *See, e.g., John B. v. Goetz,* 531 F.3d 448, 460 (6th Cir. 2008).

[8] *CBT Flint Partners, LLC v. Return Path, Inc.,* 737 F.3d 1320, 1328, n.2 (Fed. Cir. 2013); The Sedona Principles: Best Practices, Recommendations & Principles for Addressing Electronic Document Production, Second Edition 11, 28

destruction of metadata and potential attorney-client privilege issues),[9] and should be discussed during the Rule 26(f) conference. A party seeking metadata should specifically request it.[10]

No Duty to Create Documents

Generally, a party is not required to create documents meeting the document requests, only to produce documents already in existence.[11]

Tangible Things

Rule 34 allows a party to inspect and copy, test, or sample tangible things relevant to the action (*e.g.*, the allegedly defective product in a product liability case).[12]

Property

A party has the right to enter onto another party's land and inspect, measure, survey, photograph, test, or sample property or a designated object or operation thereon if relevant to the pending action.[13] The persons conducting the inspections are not permitted to question the representatives of the party whose property is being inspected.[14]

Parties Only

Only parties are obligated to respond to document requests.[15] "Party" is sometimes liberally construed, such as to include experts,[16] insurance companies,[17] and garnishees.[18] Documents may be obtained from nonparties by a subpoena under Rule 45.[19]

Documents Within Party's Possession, Custody, or Control

A party must produce all discoverable documents or things responsive to a request that are in the party's possession, custody, or control.[20] Control means the legal right to obtain the documents on demand.[21] Documents held by the party's attorney,[22] expert,[23] insurance

---

(The Sedona Conference Working Group Series, 2007), available at http://www.thesedonaconference.org/content/misc Files/TSC_PRINCP_2nd_ed_607.pdf.

[9]   *See, e.g., Southern New England Telephone Co. v. Global NAPs, Inc.,* 251 F.R.D. 82, 89 (D.Conn. 2008).

[10]   *See, e.g., Covad Communications Co. v. Revonet, Inc.,* 267 F.R.D. 14 (D.D.C. 2010) (native format, with metadata, is not the only acceptable form of production).

[11]   *Harris v. Advance America Cash Advance Centers, Inc.,* 288 F.R.D. 170, 172 (S.D.Ohio 2012); but *see Harris v. Athol-Royalston Regional School District Committee,* 200 F.R.D. 18 (D. Mass. 2001) (party required to create a handwriting exemplar for examination by the opposing party's expert).

[12]   *Ramos v. Carter Exp. Inc.,* 292 F.R.D. 406, 408 (S.D. Tex. 2013).

[13]   *Albany Bank & Trust Co. v. Exxon Mobil Corp.,* 310 F.3d 969, 974 (7th Cir. 2002).

[14]   *United States v. Territory of the Virgin Islands,* 280 F.R.D. 232, 236–37 (D.Virgin Islands 2012).

[15]   *See Hobley v. Burge,* 433 F.3d 946, 949 (7th Cir. 2006).

[16]   *Alper v. United States,*190 F.R.D. 281, 283 (D. Mass. 2000) (document request to the party's expert is deemed a document request to the party).

[17]   *See, e.g., Parrett v. Ford Motor Co.,* 47 F.R.D. 22, 24 (W.D. Mo. 1968).

[18]   *See, e.g., Conversion Chemical Corp. v. Dr.-Ing. Max Schloetter Fabrik Fur Galvanotechnik,* 49 F.R.D. 126 (D. Conn. 1969).

[19]   *Hobley v. Burge,* 433 F.3d 946, 949 (7th Cir. 2006) (Rule 45 subpoena is the only way to get documents from a nonparty).

[20]   *Kissinger v. Reporters Committee for Freedom of the Press,* 445 U.S. 136, 166, 100 S.Ct. 960, 976, 63 L.Ed.2d 267 (1980).

[21]   *Thermal Design, Inc. v. Am. Soc'y of Heating Refrigerating and Air–Conditioning Eng'rs, Inc.,* 755 F.3d 832 (7th Cir. 2014).

[22]   *Hobley v. Burge,* 433 F.3d 946, 949–50 (7th Cir. 2006) (documents held by former attorney are not within the party's control).

[23]   *Alper v. United States,*190 F.R.D. 281, 283 (D. Mass. 2000) (documents held by the party's expert are within the party's control).

company,[24] accountant,[25] spouse,[26] contractor,[27] officer,[28] or agent[29] are deemed to be within the party's control. Likewise, documents held by a subsidiary, affiliated corporation,[30] or branch office in another state may be within a party's control.[31] Documents owned by a third person but possessed by a party are within the party's custody.[32] Electronic documents on the server of a third party provider, such as text messages or emails, are within the control of the party.[33] The courts are divided as to whether a party will be deemed to have possession, custody, or control of documents which the party may release by authorization, such as medical records.[34]

Duty to Search for Documents

A responding party must make a reasonable search of all sources reasonably likely to contain responsive documents.[35]

Documents Available from Another Source

The fact that documents are available from another source, such as public records, is not, by itself, a valid basis for objecting or refusing to produce such documents if they are within the possession, custody, or control of the responding party.[36] Depending on the circumstances, however, the availability of alternative sources for the requested documents may support an objection on the basis of undue burden.[37] A party that does not have the requested records in its possession, custody, or control will not be required to obtain those documents from public sources or third parties.[38]

Proceedings Where Requests Available

Document requests are available in all civil actions in federal court, subject to certain narrow exceptions listed in Rule 81. Document requests are available in bankruptcy proceedings.

---

[24] *Henderson v. Zurn Industries, Inc.,* 131 F.R.D. 560, 567 (S.D. Ind. 1990). *But see Japan Halon Co., Ltd. v. Great Lakes Chemical Corp.,* 155 F.R.D. 626 (N.D. Ind. 1993) (subsidiary not required to obtain documents from parent in another country).

[25] *Wardrip v. Hart,* 934 F.Supp. 1282, 1286, 18 A.D.D. 447 (D. Kan. 1996) (financial records of defendant in possession of defendant's accountant are in defendant's control).

[26] *Monroe's Estate v. Bottle Rock Power Corp.,* 2004 WL 737463 (E.D. La. 2004).

[27] *Mercy Catholic Medical Center v. Thompson,* 380 F.3d 142, 160 (3d Cir. 2004).

[28] *Flagg v. City of Detroit,* 252 F.R.D. 346, 353 (E.D.Mich. 2008).

[29] *American Rock Salt Co., LLC v. Norfolk Southern Corp.,* 228 F.R.D. 426, 457 (W.D. N.Y. 2004).

[30] *Shcherbakovskiy v. Da Capo Al Fine, Ltd.,* 490 F.3d 130, 138 (2d Cir. 2007) (documents held by a corporation held to be in the control of a board member).

[31] *Goodman v. Praxair Services, Inc.,* 632 F.Supp.2d 494, 513 (D.Md. 2009).

[32] *Societe Internationale Pour Participations Industrielles Et Commerciales, S. A. v. Rogers,* 357 U.S. 197, 78 S.Ct. 1087, 2 L.Ed.2d 1255 (1958).

[33] *Flagg v. City of Detroit,* 252 F.R.D. 346, 352–53 (E.D.Mich. 2008) (text messages are within the party's control).

[34] *Compare In re Parker,* 488 B.R. 794 (N.D.Ga. 2013) (requiring the plaintiff to sign an authorization for obtaining tax documents), *with Vazquez-Fernandez v. Cambridge College, Inc.,* 269 F.R.D. 150, 165 (D.Puerto Rico 2010) (party not required to sign release for bank records).

[35] *Tucker v. Am. Intern. Grp., Inc.,* 281 F.R.D. 85, 90–91 (D.Conn. 2012) (responding party makes the search; requesting party has no right to search responding party's documents).

[36] *Sabouri v. Ohio Bureau of Employment Services,* 2000 WL 1620915 (S.D. Ohio 2000) (party required to produce a pleading that could also be obtained from the courthouse). *But see Bleecker v. Standard Fire Ins. Co.,* 130 F.Supp.2d 726 (E.D. N.C. 2000) (discovery is not required when documents are readily obtainable by the party seeking a motion to compel).

[37] *See Tequila Centinela, S.A. de C.V. v. Bacardi & Co. Ltd.,* 242 F.R.D. 1 (D.D.C. 2007).

[38] *Shcherbakovskiy v. Da Capo Al Fine, Ltd.,* 490 F.3d 130, 138 (2d Cir. 2007).

Procedure to Perpetuate Testimony

A party may file a motion to obtain documents in connection with an action to perpetuate testimony under Rule 27.

Procedures in Aid of Execution

Document requests may be served following the entry of judgment, as part of procedures in aid of execution.

Motion for a Protective Order

As an alternative to making objections to individual document requests, the responding party may make a motion for a protective order under Rule 26(c).[39] A motion for a protective order is appropriate when most or all of a set of document requests is too burdensome or cumulative. The burden is on the moving party to show hardship or injustice. The motion must be accompanied by a certification that the parties met prior to the filing of the motion and attempted to resolve their dispute without intervention by the court.

Contractual Agreements

Parties sometimes have previously entered into agreements defining a right to inspect designated documents (such as an agreement restricting one party's right to inspect another party's financial records for one year). Such agreements may be upheld by the court, if reasonable.

RULE 34(b)—PROCEDURE

CORE CONCEPT

Any party may serve document requests on any other party, who must respond in writing within 30 days.

APPLICATIONS

Who May Serve

Any party may serve document requests.

Who May Be Served

Document requests are limited to parties to the action, although the party need not be an adverse party (documents are obtained from nonparties by a subpoena under Rule 45). The document requests must be addressed to the party. Thus, if the party is a corporation, document requests should be addressed to the corporation, not to a corporate officer or the attorney. In a class action, the courts are split as to whether only the named representatives can be served.[40] Copies of the document requests should be served upon all parties.

Time for Service

Starting 21 days after a defendant has been served with the summons and complaint, Rule 34 requests may be served on that party or by that party on a plaintiff or any other defendant who has also been served. The Rules do not set an outer limit on how late in the case document requests may be served, but many local rules or case management orders will

---

[39] *Simms v. Center for Correctional Health and Policy Studies,* 272 F.R.D. 36, 40 (D.D.C. 2011) (motion for protective order to shift costs of production).

[40] *Compare Brennan v. Midwestern United Life Ins. Co.,* 450 F.2d 999 (7th Cir. 1971) (unnamed members of class required to respond), *with Wainwright v. Kraftco Corp.,* 54 F.R.D. 532 (N.D. Ga. 1972) (unnamed members of class not required to respond).

set such a limit. Usually, when such a limit exists, document requests must be served so that the response is due before the close of discovery.[41]

Number

The Rule contains no limitation on the number of document requests.[42] Some districts have local rules limiting the number of document requests.[43]

Designation of Documents in Request

Documents to be produced must be designated with "reasonable particularity."[44] Rule 34(b) permits requests for categories of documents as long as the category is described with reasonable particularity.[45] Essentially, the test is whether the responding party can determine what documents to produce.

Form of Requests

A request for inspection should be a formal document[46] setting forth the items or categories of items[47] to be inspected with "reasonable particularity."[48] Some courts allow informal requests to be enforced under appropriate circumstances.[49] What constitutes "reasonable particularity" depends on the circumstances. The request should also specify a reasonable time, place, and manner for the inspection.[50] The time designated should be after the time to respond has elapsed (30 days). As an alternative, the serving party may designate "a time and location convenient to the parties," then reach an agreement with opposing counsel. If the request seeks electronic data, the request may, but is not required to, specify the form in which electronic data is to be produced.

Response

A party served with a document request must serve a written response[51] or move for a protective order under Rule 26(c). Otherwise, the party will be subject to the sanctions in Rule 37(d). The response should fairly respond to each request.[52] It may state that the request will be complied with in the manner requested.[53] It may also state that the request will be complied with, but at some other time or place, or in some other manner. It is common to state in the response that responsive documents will be produced at a mutually convenient time and location.[54] The response may also raise objections to some or all of the requests.[55] If the request does not specify the form for production of electronic data, or if the responding

---

[41]   *Thomas v. Pacificorp,* 324 F.3d 1176, 1179 (10th Cir. 2003).

[42]   *Bourguignon v. Spielvogel,* 2004 WL 743668 (D. Conn. 2004).

[43]   *See Lurensky v. Wellinghoff,* 258 F.R.D. 27 (D.D.C. 2009).

[44]   *Hager v. Graham,* 267 F.R.D. 486 (N.D.W.Va. 2010); *Hager v. Graham,* 267 F.R.D. 486 (N.D.W.Va. 2010).

[45]   *Goosman v. A. Duie Pyle, Inc.,* 320 F.2d 45 (4th Cir.1963).

[46]   *Suid v. Cigna Corp.,* 203 F.R.D. 227, 229–29 (D.V.I. 2001) (letters between counsel are not document requests under Rule 34).

[47]   *Dauska v. Green Bay Packaging Inc.,* 291 F.R.D. 251 (E.D.Wis. 2013).

[48]   *Regan-Touhy v. Walgreen Co.,* 526 F.3d 641, 649–50 (10th Cir. 2008) (all-encompassing requests are not sufficiently particular).

[49]   *See Trask v. Olin Corp.,* 298 F.R.D. 244, 259–60 (W.D. Pa. 2014) (discussing the split of authority on this issue).

[50]   *Mezu v. Morgan State University,* 775 F.Supp.2d 801 (D.Md. 2011).

[51]   *Starcher v. Correctional Medical Systems, Inc.,* 144 F.3d 418, 420–21 (6th Cir. 1998), aff'd, 527 U.S. 198, 119 S.Ct. 1915, 144 L.Ed.2d 184 (1999).

[52]   *Mulero-Abreu v. Puerto Rico Police Dept.,* 675 F.3d 88, 93 (1st Cir. 2012).

[53]   *Renfrow v. Redwood Fire and Cas. Ins. Co.,* 288 F.R.D. 514, 521 (D.Nev. 2013).

[54]   *But see Mezu v. Morgan State University,* 269 F.R.D. 565, 574 (D.Md. 2010) (it is improper to state that documents will be produced at some unspecified time).

[55]   *Renfrow v. Redwood Fire and Cas. Ins. Co.,* 288 F.R.D. 514, 521 (D.Nev. 2013).

party has objected to the form specified in the request, then the response must specify the form in which electronic data will be produced. Finally, the response may advise that the party has no such documents in its possession, custody, or control.[56] The response is generally not required to be verified or under oath, in contrast to interrogatory answers.[57]

Time to Answer

A written response is due within 30 days of service, except that, for document requests served before the parties' Rule 26(f) conference, the responses are due 30 days after the Rule 26(f) conference.[58] The time to answer may be extended by written agreement under Rule 29.[59] If the responding party intends to object to some of the document requests, the stipulation should specify that the time is extended to answer and file objections.[60] The period for responding may also be shortened or lengthened by the court, typically upon motion by one of the parties.[61]

Service of Response

The response must be served upon all parties.

Objections

If the responding party determines that a particular document request is outside the scope of discovery or otherwise problematic, the party may object to the request in lieu of or in addition to making the documents available for inspection.[62] The objection must be made in writing, must state the grounds of the objection with specificity,[63] and must be signed by the attorney for the responding party.[64] Some common objections are:

- *Overly broad, unduly vague, and/or ambiguous:* When a document request is written so broadly that it extends to documents not relevant to the claims or defenses in the matter (such as a request not limited in time to the events relevant to the complaint), the request may be overly broad.[65] When a request is susceptible to numerous meanings, it may be unduly vague and ambiguous. In general, these objections are probably not justification for refusing to provide documents altogether, but the responding party can raise the objection, then expressly limit the scope of the response.

- *Burdensome and oppressive:* In general, the responding party must produce the documents available without undue effort or expense. Thus, requests that require extensive research, compilation, or evaluation of documents may be objectionable.[66] The responding party is not required to prepare the adverse party's case. The reasonableness of a request is within the court's discretion.

---

[56] *See Fishel v. BASF Group,* 175 F.R.D. 525, 531 (S.D. Iowa 1997) ("Even if there are no such documents, plaintiff is entitled to a response as required by Fed.R.Civ.P. 34(b) and the Court will so order.").

[57] *Napolitano v. Synthes USA, LLC,* 297 F.R.D. 194, 200 (D. Conn. 2014).

[58] Rule 34(b)(2)(A).

[59] *Tropix, Inc. v. Lyon & Lyon,* 169 F.R.D. 3 (D. Mass. 1996).

[60] *Coregis Ins. Co. v. Baratta & Fenerty, Ltd.,* 187 F.R.D. 528, 530 (E.D. Pa. 1999).

[61] *Ellsworth Associates, Inc. v. United States,* 917 F.Supp. 841, 844 (D.D.C. 1996) (motion for expedited discovery is particularly appropriate with a claim for injunctive relief).

[62] *Lurensky v. Wellinghoff,* 258 F.R.D. 27 (D.D.C. 2009) (objections must be to specific requests—general objection that the requests are burdensome is insufficient).

[63] *United States v. Philip Morris Inc.,* 347 F.3d 951, 954 (D.C. Cir. 2003).

[64] *Frontier-Kemper Constructors, Inc. v. Elk Run Coal Co., Inc.,* 246 F.R.D. 522, 527–28 (S.D. W. Va. 2007).

[65] *Westhemeco Ltd. v. New Hampshire Ins. Co.,* 82 F.R.D. 702 (S.D. N.Y. 1979).

[66] *Chambers (Robert) v. Capital Cities/ABC, Burke (Daniel), Callahan (Robert),* 154 F.R.D. 63 (S.D. N.Y. 1994).

- *Privileged information:* Requests that seek documents protected by the attorney-client privilege or by another privilege are objectionable.[67] When privileged documents are withheld, the responding party must explicitly state the objection and describe the nature of the documents not produced sufficiently to enable other parties to assess the applicability of the privilege.[68] A log of the documents withheld on the basis of privilege should be provided to the requesting party, either at the time of the responses or at a mutually agreeable time.[69] Care should be exercised in responding to such requests, because the privilege may be waived by revealing part or all of the privileged documents.

- *Attorney work product:* Rule 26(b)(3) provides that trial preparation materials may be discovered only upon a showing that the party is unable to obtain the equivalent information through other means without undue hardship.[70]

- *Non-discoverable expert information:* Rule 26(b)(4) limits the scope of discovery directed towards experts. It generally requires the responding party to provide an expert report for each expert the party may call as a witness, and thereafter allows other parties to depose such experts. Further discovery with respect to such witnesses is available only upon motion. Rule 26(b)(4)(B) does not allow any discovery with respect to experts not intended to be called as witnesses, absent "exceptional circumstances."[71]

- *Not proportional to the needs of the case:* A party may object that a document request seeks information that is not proportional to the needs of the case, in light of the factors listed in Rule 26(b)(1).

- *Form of Electronic Data:* If the requesting party specifies a form for the production of electronic data that the responding party believes is burdensome or otherwise objectionable, Rule 34(b) specifically provides for objections to the request.

Statement Regarding Objections and Withheld Documents

A party making an objection to a Rule 34 request must state whether any responsive materials are being withheld on the basis of that objection. The responding party does not need to make a detailed log of each document withheld, and only needs to alert other parties to the fact that documents have been withheld, so they can make a more informed decision as to whether to challenge the objection. An objection that explains the scope of the response will be deemed to satisfy this requirement. For example, if the response objects that the request is overly broad in terms of the time covered by the request, then states that the responding party will produce all responsive documents within the last five years, other parties will be on notice that the responding party has withheld documents more than five years old.

Failure to Object Is Waiver

In contrast to Rule 33 governing interrogatories, Rule 34 does not contain an explicit provision stating that failure to serve timely objections results in a waiver of those

---

[67] *Tequila Centinela, S.A. de C.V. v. Bacardi & Co. Ltd.,* 242 F.R.D. 1 (D.D.C. 2007).

[68] *United States v. Philip Morris Inc.,* 347 F.3d 951, 954 (D.C. Cir. 2003).

[69] *Burlington Northern & Santa Fe Ry. Co. v. U.S. Dist. Court for Dist. of Mont.,* 408 F.3d 1142, 1147 (9th Cir. 2005) (failure to produce a privilege log within 30 days is not a per se waiver of the privilege).

[70] *See* Rule 26(b)(3) (discovery of work product).

[71] *See* Rule 26(b)(4) (in-depth discussion of discovery directed toward experts).

objections. Some courts hold that such waiver is implied.[72] The court can excuse the waiver for good cause shown.[73]

Objection to Part of Request

If any part of a request is objectionable, the responding party must specify the objectionable part and respond to the remaining parts.[74] A number of courts have held that the common practice of objecting, then answering "subject to and without waiving" the objections is improper and waives the objections unless the response describes in particularity the documents not being provided. [75]

Production of Documents

The responding party has the option of allowing the serving party to inspect, copy, test, or sample the documents or of providing copies of the responsive documents. If the responding party chooses to allow the requesting party to inspect the documents, the responding party may allow access to the documents as they are normally kept (*i.e.*, "There is our file room.").[76] If the responding party provides copies of or access to selected responsive documents, the party must organize and label them to correspond to the categories requested.[77] Some courts do not require a party to organize and label ESI, recognizing that parties use electronic searching techniques for ESI.[78] The requesting party may insist on inspecting an original when a copy would not reflect the colors or signature on the original.[79]

Time for Production

The responding party must produce the responsive documents at the time specified in the request or at another "reasonable time" specified in the response. Neither the Rule nor the advisory committee notes give any guidance as to what would be considered a reasonable time.

Use of Documents at Trial

Documents produced in response to document requests are treated like any other evidence, and are admissible as allowed by the rules of evidence and subject to any applicable objections.

Cost of Gathering and Copying

In general, the producing party bears the cost of searching for and gathering responsive documents. If the responding party makes documents available for inspection, the requesting party must pay for copies of the documents it chooses to have copied. The rules are silent about who pays for copies if the responding party chooses to produce copies of the responsive documents instead of making them available for inspection, and the courts have not yet addressed this issue. The court has the authority to shift some or all of the costs of collecting and producing documents to the requesting party.[80] Cost shifting has become increasingly common with ESI.[81]

---

[72] *See Mills v. Iowa,* 285 F.R.D. 411, 413 (S.D.Iowa 2012).

[73] *United Auto. Ins. Co. v. Veluchamy,* 747 F.Supp.2d 1021, 1027 (N.D.Ill. 2010).

[74] *Wultz v. Bank of China Ltd.,* 910 F.Supp.2d 548 (S.D.N.Y. 2012).

[75] *See Heller v. City of Dallas,* 303 F.R.D. 466, 488–90 (N.D. Tex. 2014).

[76] *Mezu v. Morgan State University,* 775 F.Supp.2d 801 (D.Md. 2011).

[77] *Go v. Rockefeller Univ.,* 280 F.R.D. 165, 169 (S.D.N.Y. 2012).

[78] *See Anderson Living Trust v. WPX Energy Production, LLC,* 298 F.R.D. 514, 515–27 (D.N.M. 2014).

[79] *Robinson-Reeder v. American Council on Educ.,* 262 F.R.D. 41, 45 (D.D.C. 2009).

[80] *See U.S. ex rel. Carter v. Bridgepoint Educ., Inc.,* 305 F.R.D. 225, 237–40 (S.D. Cal. 2015).

[81] *See U.S. ex rel. Carter v. Bridgepoint Educ., Inc.,* 305 F.R.D. 225, 240 (S.D. Cal. 2015).

Production of Electronic Data

Rule 34(b) allows, but does not require, the requesting party to specify the form in which it is requesting electronic data.[82] If the requesting party wants the electronic data in a particular format (such as one that is compatible with a particular software application or one that includes metadata), the requesting party should so specify in the request.[83] The responding party can then produce it in that form or object and specify the form in which it will produce the electronic data.[84] If the requesting party does not specify the form, then the responding party must produce it in the form in which it is ordinarily maintained or in a form that is reasonably usable.[85] Unless the responding party is producing the data in the form specified by the requesting party, the responding party must specify the form it intends to use for production in its written response to the document request.[86] If the responding party objects to the form stated by the requesting party, or if the requesting party is not satisfied with the form specified by the responding party, then the parties must meet and confer under Rule 37(a)(2)(B).[87] Under any of these scenarios, a party need not produce electronic data in more than one form.[88] Sometimes, the requesting party will seek to have the producing party's servers or hard drives imaged so that the requesting party can conduct its own searches or forensic analysis, but the courts will require imaging only when the specific situation warrants.[89] The preservation and production of electronically stored information raises a host of issues, many of which are discussed in the Sedona Principles: Best Practices, Recommendations & Principles for Addressing Electronic Document Production.[90]

Procedures for Inspection, Testing, or Sampling

Procedures for inspections, testing, or sampling, such as who will be present and protocols for the testing or sampling, are set by agreement of the parties or by the court on motion for a protective order or motion to compel.[91] Requests to perform destructive testing or invasive sampling are more likely to draw objection or require court intervention.[92]

Motion to Compel

If the responding party fails to respond to a document request or to allow an inspection, or objects to a document request, the propounding party may file a motion to compel under Rule 37(a), after conducting the required meet and confer with opposing counsel.[93] In a

---

[82] *Star Direct Telecom, Inc. v. Global Crossing Bandwidth, Inc.,* 272 F.R.D. 350, 359 (W.D.N.Y. 2011).

[83] *See Autotech Technologies Ltd. Partnership v. Automationdirect.com, Inc.,* 248 F.R.D. 556, 558–59 (N.D. Ill. 2008) (requesting party did not specify metadata, and therefore cannot complain when it did not receive the electronic files in a format that preserved metadata).

[84] *Ford Motor Co. v. Edgewood Properties, Inc.,* 257 F.R.D. 418 (D.N.J. 2009).

[85] *CBT Flint Partners, LLC v. Return Path, Inc.,* 737 F.3d 1320, 1331 (Fed. Cir. 2013) (encrypted data must be decrypted).

[86] The 2006 Amendment to the advisory committee note to Rule 34(b).

[87] *Ford Motor Co. v. Edgewood Properties, Inc.,* 257 F.R.D. 418 (D.N.J. 2009).

[88] *Automated Merchandising Sys. Inc. v. Crane Co.,* 279 F.R.D. 366, 373 (N.D.W.Va. 2011).

[89] *See, e.g., John B. v. Goetz,* 531 F.3d 448, 460 (6th Cir. 2008) (referring to the advisory committee's warning not to turn every case into a forensic exercise).

[90] The Sedona Principles: Best Practices, Recommendations & Principles for Addressing Electronic Document Production, Second Edition 11, 28 (The Sedona Conference Working Group Series, 2007), available at http://www.the sedonaconference.org/content/miscFiles/TSC_PRINCP_2nd_ed_607.pdf.

[91] *See Ramos v. Carter Exp. Inc.,* 292 F.R.D. 406, 408–11 (S.D. Tex. 2013).

[92] *See Ramos v. Carter Exp. Inc.,* 292 F.R.D. 406, 408–11 (S.D. Tex. 2013).

[93] *Molski v. Franklin,* 222 F.R.D. 433, 435 (S.D. Cal. 2004).

motion to compel, the burden is on the responding party (the non-moving party) to convince the court that a document request is objectionable.[94]

Discretion of Court

The district court has extremely broad discretion in ruling on objections to document requests.[95] The court will balance the need for the documents and the burden of producing them, but will generally require production unless the administration of justice would be impeded. The court may allow inspection under limited conditions, and may restrict further disclosure of sensitive documents. The court may also privately inspect the documents before ruling.

Appeals

The court's rulings on objections to document requests are not final orders, and cannot be appealed until the conclusion of the case.

Sanctions for Failure to Respond

If a party files no response to a set of document requests, the court may impose sanctions under Rule 37(b)(2), such as deeming certain facts established or refusing to allow the party to oppose or support certain claims.[96] The court may also deem objections to the document requests waived by the failure to file a timely response.[97] Furthermore, the court must award reasonable expenses, including attorney's fees, caused by the responding party's failure to answer, unless the court finds that the failure to answer was justified.

RULE 34(c)—NONPARTIES

CORE CONCEPT

Although document requests or requests for inspection cannot be served on a nonparty, documents or inspections can be obtained from a nonparty by a subpoena under Rule 45.[98] Furthermore, Rule 34 does not preclude an independent action for production of documents or things or for permission to enter onto land (but such actions may be unnecessary under the expanded subpoena powers in Rule 45).[99]

ADDITIONAL RESEARCH REFERENCES

Wright & Miller, *Federal Practice and Procedure* §§ 2201 to 2218

C.J.S., Federal Civil Procedure §§ 696 to 740 et seq.

West's Key Number Digest, Federal Civil Procedure ⊶1551 to 1640

---

[94] *Gorrell v. Sneath*, 292 F.R.D. 629 (E.D.Cal. 2013).

[95] *McConnell v. Canadian Pac. Realty Co.*, 280 F.R.D. 188, 192 (M.D.Pa. 2011) (discretion extends to magistrate judges).

[96] *See* Rule 37(d); *Land Ocean Logistics, Inc. v. Aqua Gulf Corp.*, 181 F.R.D. 229, 235 (W.D. N.Y. 1998) (preclusion of evidence is a harsh sanction reserved for exceptional cases).

[97] *Scaturro v. Warren and Sweat Mfg. Co., Inc.*, 160 F.R.D. 44 (M.D. Pa. 1995).

[98] *Hobley v. Burge*, 433 F.3d 946, 949 (7th Cir. 2006).

[99] *See Darbeau v. Library of Congress*, 453 F.Supp.2d 168, 171 (D.D.C. 2006).

RULE 35

PHYSICAL AND MENTAL EXAMINATIONS

(a) Order for an Examination.

(1) *In General.* The court where the action is pending may order a party whose mental or physical condition—including blood group—is in controversy to submit to a physical or mental examination by a suitably licensed or certified examiner. The court has the same authority to order a party to produce for examination a person who is in its custody or under its legal control.

(2) *Motion and Notice; Contents of the Order.* The order:

(A) may be made only on motion for good cause and on notice to all parties and the person to be examined; and

(B) must specify the time, place, manner, conditions, and scope of the examination, as well as the person or persons who will perform it.

(b) Examiner's Report.

(1) *Request by the Party or Person Examined.* The party who moved for the examination must, on request, deliver to the requester a copy of the examiner's report, together with like reports of all earlier examinations of the same condition. The request may be made by the party against whom the examination order was issued or by the person examined.

(2) *Contents.* The examiner's report must be in writing and must set out in detail the examiner's findings, including diagnoses, conclusions, and the results of any tests.

(3) *Request by the Moving Party.* After delivering the reports, the party who moved for the examination may request—and is entitled to receive—from the party against whom the examination order was issued like reports of all earlier or later examinations of the same condition. But those reports need not be delivered by the party with custody or control of the person examined if the party shows that it could not obtain them.

(4) *Waiver of Privilege.* By requesting and obtaining the examiner's report, or by deposing the examiner, the party examined waives any privilege it may have—in that action or any other action involving the same controversy—concerning testimony about all examinations of the same condition.

(5) *Failure to Deliver a Report.* The court on motion may order—on just terms—that a party deliver the report of an examination. If the report is not provided, the court may exclude the examiner's testimony at trial.

(6) *Scope.* This subdivision (b) applies also to an examination made by the parties' agreement, unless the agreement states otherwise. This subdivision does not preclude obtaining an examiner's report or deposing an examiner under other rules.

[Amended effective July 1, 1970; August 1, 1987; November 18, 1988; December 1, 1991; April 30, 2007, effective December 1, 2007.]

AUTHORS' COMMENTARY ON RULE 35

PURPOSE AND SCOPE

Rule 35 requires a party to submit to a mental or physical examination when the party's mental or physical condition is at issue in the action. In contrast to most other discovery procedures, mental or physical examinations are available only by stipulation or motion for "good cause."

RULE 35(a)—ORDER FOR AN EXAMINATION

CORE CONCEPT

Examination is compulsory only if ordered by the court. A court will order examination for good cause shown, which will generally exist in every case in which the plaintiff is claiming personal injuries.

APPLICATIONS

Motion

A request for examination must be made by motion, with a proposed order attached, served upon the person to be examined and all parties.[1] The motion should specify the time, place, manner, conditions, and scope of the examination and the person or persons by whom it is to be made, as well as the grounds supporting the motion.[2] Typically, however, examination is arranged by consent.

Order

If the court grants a motion for a Rule 35 examination, it must issue an order that specifies the examiner and the time, place, manner, conditions, and scope of the examination.[3] These topics are discussed individually below. The order may also include protective measures deemed appropriate by the court.[4]

Condition at Issue

Examinations for a particular condition are allowed only when that condition is in controversy.[5] The plaintiff's condition is typically placed at issue by the claims in the complaint, but can also be placed at issue by a defense.[6]

---

[1]   *Gavin v. Hilton Worldwide, Inc.*, 291 F.R.D. 161 (N.D.Cal. 2013).

[2]   *See Ornelas v. Southern Tire Mart, LLC*, 292 F.R.D. 388 (S.D.Tex. 2013) (movant required to supplement motion with types of test to be conducted).

[3]   *Schaeffer v. Sequoyah Trading & Transp.*, 273 F.R.D. 662 (D.Kan. 2011).

[4]   *Schaeffer v. Sequoyah Trading & Transp.*, 273 F.R.D. 662 (D.Kan. 2011) (ordering videotaping of the examination).

[5]   *Green v. Branson*, 108 F.3d 1296, 1304 (10th Cir. 1997) (denying motion by the plaintiff to have himself examined where purpose was for the plaintiff, a prisoner, to obtain treatment).

[6]   *See Flores-Febus v. MVM, Inc.*, 299 F.R.D. 338 (D. Puerto Rico 2014).

Good Cause

The court will order an examination "for good cause shown."[7] The burden of demonstrating good cause rests with the moving party.[8] The requirement of good cause is not a formality; the court must genuinely balance the need for the information with the right to privacy and safety of the party.[9] In a tort action where the plaintiff seeks to recover for personal injuries, good cause will almost always be found to exist.[10] It becomes less clear when the party has not put the party's own mental or physical condition at issue.[11]

Time for Filing Motion

There is no time limit on the filing of a motion for an examination, although the court can take the timing of the motion into account in considering the motion.[12]

Who Conducts Exam

Rule 35 states that the examination may be conducted by any suitably licensed or certified examiner or examiners.[13] It does not address the selection of a particular examiner. In general, the court will allow the movant to select the examiner unless the person to be examined raises a valid objection.[14] The court may reject a particular examiner upon a showing of bias[15] or, under certain circumstances, if the examiner is a different gender from the person to be examined. Some local rules have provisions regarding the selection of a neutral examiner.[16] The court order must designate the examiner and may be invalid if it fails to do so.

Testimony of Examiner

The party conducting the examination may call the examiner to testify as an expert witness (assuming the criteria for expert testimony are satisfied). The courts are split as to whether the party who was examined may call the examiner as an expert.[17]

Scope of Examination

The type of exams allowable depends on the circumstances of the case. Exams can include blood tests, x-rays,[18] electrocardiograms, fingerprint analysis,[19] and other safe,

---

[7] *Schlagenhauf v. Holder,* 379 U.S. 104, 85 S.Ct. 234, 13 L.Ed.2d 152 (1964) (describing "good cause" as a determination that must be made on a case-by-case basis).

[8] *Ornelas v. Southern Tire Mart, LLC,* 292 F.R.D. 388 (S.D.Tex. 2013).

[9] *Schlagenhauf v. Holder,* 379 U.S. 104, 118, 85 S.Ct. 234, 242, 13 L.Ed.2d 152 (1964).

[10] *See Chaney v. Venture Transport, Inc.,* 2004 WL 445134 (E.D. La. 2004).

[11] *See Ornelas v. Southern Tire Mart, LLC,* 292 F.R.D. 388 (S.D.Tex. 2013).

[12] *Diaz v. Con-Way Truckload, Inc.,* 279 F.R.D. 412, 416–21 (S.D.Tex. 2012) (discussing the role of the deadline for expert reports in evaluating a Rule 35 motion).

[13] *Merritt v. Stolt Offshore, Inc.,* 2004 WL 224578 (E.D. La. 2004) (holding that the court may order more than one examiner, but noting that some states hold differently).

[14] *Douponce v. Drake,* 183 F.R.D. 565, 566 (D. Colo. 1998) (allowing the defendant's selected examiner despite allegations of bias).

[15] *See O'Sullivan v. Rivera,* 229 F.R.D. 184 (D.N.M. 2004) (the fact that the expert regularly testifies for defendants does not disqualify the expert under Rule 35).

[16] *But see Hunt v. R & B Falcon Drilling USA, Inc.,* 2000 WL 1838327 (E.D. La. 2000) (a motion for a court-appointed examiner is more properly brought under Federal Rule of Evidence 706).

[17] *Lehan v. Ambassador Programs, Inc.,* 190 F.R.D. 670 (E.D. Wash. 2000) (discussing the various positions taken by the courts on this issue).

[18] *Tarte v. United States,* 249 F.R.D. 856 (S.D.Fla. 2008) (x-rays and MRIs are routine procedures).

[19] *Harris v. Athol-Royalston Regional School Dist. Committee,* 206 F.R.D. 30, 32–33 (D. Mass. 2002) (fingerprint samples may be obtained under either Rule 34 or Rule 35).

medically accepted tests indicated by the condition at issue.[20] Vocational exams are also permissible under Rule 35.[21] The burden on the movant to show good cause will be greater if the tests are more invasive, painful, or burdensome, or if repeated examinations are sought. However, a party that objects to a particular test as too painful or invasive may be precluded from offering evidence of the type that would result from the test. The courts are divided as to whether the motion must identify each test to be administered.[22]

Mental Examinations

Psychiatric examinations are allowable if a person's mental condition is at issue.[23] The examination may be conducted by a psychiatrist or psychologist. Many courts are reluctant to order a mental examination based solely on a "garden variety" emotional distress allegation.[24]

Safety of Tests

In order to oppose a mental or physical exam on the grounds that the exam is unsafe, a party must demonstrate that the proposed test is potentially dangerous. Thereafter, the burden shifts to the party requesting the examination to show that it is both necessary and safe.[25]

Number of Examinations

If multiple conditions of the plaintiff are at issue, the court can order multiple examinations.[26] When permanent injuries are claimed or under other appropriate circumstances, the court may allow a second examination just before trial.[27] A stronger showing of necessity is usually required for a second examination.[28]

Time and Location

The court will designate the time and location of the examination in the order. Usually, the plaintiff will be required to travel to the district where the action is pending to be examined.[29]

Cost of Examination

The moving party must pay the medical or professional expenses of the examination. The person to be examined is not compensated, however, for transportation costs[30] and lost time.

---

[20] *See Jefferys v. LRP Publications, Inc.,* 184 F.R.D. 262, 263 (E.D. Pa. 1999) (allowing interview by vocational expert).

[21] *See Ornelas v. Southern Tire Mart, LLC,* 292 F.R.D. 388 (S.D.Tex. 2013).

[22] *Hirschheimer v. Associated Metals & Minerals Corp.,* 7 Nat'l Disability Law Rep. P 318, 1995 WL 736901 (S.D. N.Y. 1995); *contra Ragge v. MCA/Universal Studios,* 165 F.R.D. 605, 609 (C.D. Cal. 1995).

[23] *Flores-Febus v. MVM, Inc.,* 299 F.R.D. 338 (D. Puerto Rico 2014).

[24] *See Flores-Febus v. MVM, Inc.,* 299 F.R.D. 338 (D. Puerto Rico 2014).

[25] *Pena v. Troup,* 163 F.R.D. 352, 353–54 (D. Colo. 1995).

[26] *See Ornelas v. Southern Tire Mart, LLC,* 292 F.R.D. 388 (S.D.Tex. 2013).

[27] *See Galieti v. State Farm Mut. Auto. Ins. Co.,* 154 F.R.D. 262 (D. Colo. 1994).

[28] *Furlong v. Circle Line Statue of Liberty Ferry, Inc.,* 902 F.Supp. 65 (S.D. N.Y. 1995).

[29] *Ornelas v. Southern Tire Mart, LLC,* 292 F.R.D. 388 (S.D.Tex. 2013).

[30] *McCloskey v. United Parcel Service General Services Co.,* 171 F.R.D. 268, 270 (D. Or. 1997).

Who Is Present at Examination

The court has discretion to determine who may be present at the examination.[31] Some courts allow persons being examined by a doctor to bring their own physicians, others do not.[32] It is also unsettled as to whether attorneys have a right to be present.[33]

Audio and Video Recording

The court may, in its discretion, allow the Rule 35 examination to be videotaped, but many courts do not allow audio and/or video recording of the examination absent "special circumstances."[34]

Persons Subject to Examination

Only parties are subject to Rule 35 examination.[35] Additionally, a person who is within the control of a party may be subject to examination. Thus, a parent suing on behalf of an injured child may have to produce the child for examination.[36] This principle has also been extended to a spouse when one spouse is suing for injuries to the other.[37] In such case, the party has a duty to make a good faith effort to obtain the person's presence.[38]

Sanctions

If a party fails to comply with the order, most of the sanctions in Rule 37(b)(2) are available, such as deeming certain facts established or refusing to allow the violator to oppose or support certain claims. However, contempt sanctions are not available for failure to submit to the examination.[39] If a person within the control of a party is to be examined, no sanctions apply to that person because he is not a party. The party's duty is to make a good faith effort to obtain the person's presence, and the party will be subject to the sanctions if the party fails to make the requisite good faith effort.[40]

Actions Applicable

Examinations are available in all civil actions in federal court,[41] subject to certain narrow exceptions in Rule 81. The court may also order an examination in connection with a deposition to perpetuate testimony under Rule 27.[42]

---

[31] *See Tarte v. United States,*249 F.R.D. 856 (S.D.Fla. 2008) (presence of 3rd party or recording device are within the court's discretion).

[32] *See Ornelas v. Southern Tire Mart, LLC,* 292 F.R.D. 388 (S.D.Tex. 2013) (requiring special circumstances for a 3rd party to be present).

[33] *See Ornelas v. Southern Tire Mart, LLC,* 292 F.R.D. 388 (S.D.Tex. 2013) (requiring special circumstances for counsel to be present).

[34] *Ornelas v. Southern Tire Mart, LLC,* 292 F.R.D. 388 (S.D.Tex. 2013).

[35] *Schlagenhauf v. Holder,* 379 U.S. 104, 85 S.Ct. 234, 13 L.Ed.2d 152 (1964).

[36] The advisory committee note to the 1970 amendment of Rule 35(a); *but see Caban ex rel. Crespo v. 600 E. 21st Street Co.,* 200 F.R.D. 176 (E.D. N.Y. 2001) (a guardian suing on behalf of a child is not the party or within the control of the party, and thus is not subject to examination under Rule 35).

[37] *In re Certain Asbestos Cases,* 112 F.R.D. 427, 434 (N.D. Tex. 1986).

[38] The advisory committee note to the 1970 amendment of Rule 35(a).

[39] *Sibbach v. Wilson & Co.,* 312 U.S. 1, 312 U.S. 655, 61 S.Ct. 422, 85 L. Ed. 479 (1941).

[40] The advisory committee note to the 1970 amendment of Rule 35(a).

[41] *Caban ex rel. Crespo v. 600 E. 21st Street Co.,* 200 F.R.D. 176 (E.D. N.Y. 2001) (Rule 35 governs in diversity cases even in the face of conflicting state rules regarding examinations of parties).

[42] *See* Rules 27(a)(3) and 27(b).

Appeal

The courts are split as to whether an order directing or refusing an examination is interlocutory, and thus generally not appealable until the end of the action, or may be appealed immediately as a collateral order.[43]

RULE 35(b)—EXAMINER'S REPORT

CORE CONCEPT

Upon request by the party or person examined, the party moving for the examination must provide a copy of a detailed written report by the examiner, together with any reports of earlier examinations for the same condition. Following the delivery of such a copy, the examined party must provide copies of reports of the results of any other examinations for the same condition, whether conducted before or after the Rule 35 examination.

APPLICATIONS

Examination by Agreement

The report exchanging provisions apply to examinations by agreement unless the agreement expressly provides otherwise.

Effect of Report

Testimony by the examiner will be limited to the opinions disclosed in the report.[44]

Waiver of Privilege

A request for a report under Rule 35 acts as a waiver of the doctor-patient or psychologist-patient privilege for other examinations for the same condition.[45] Thus, the examined party may not refuse to produce other reports on the basis of privilege once the party has requested a copy of the report of the Rule 35 examination. Note that the Rule 35 waiver may be avoided by attempting to obtain the reports via another discovery rule or another procedural device.

Other Discovery Procedures

The parties may use other discovery procedures in lieu of or in addition to the report exchange procedures in Rule 35, such as document requests or depositions of the examiner.[46]

Failure to Exchange

If either party fails to provide covered reports, the court can order production.

Failure to Draft Report

If the examiner fails to prepare or provide a report, the court may exclude the examiner's testimony.

Extraneous Material

If the report contains extraneous or unreasonably prejudicial material, the court can order those portions excised.

---

[43] *See Goodman v. Harris County,* 443 F.3d 464, 467–68 (5th Cir. 2006) (applying the factors for appeal of a collateral order to a Rule 35 order).

[44] *Licciardi v. TIG Ins. Group,* 140 F.3d 357 (1st Cir. 1998) (testimony beyond the scope of the report excluded).

[45] *Cunningham v. Connecticut Mut. Life Ins.,* 845 F.Supp. 1403 (S.D. Cal. 1994).

[46] *Tarte v. United States,* 249 F.R.D. 856 (S.D.Fla. 2008).

ADDITIONAL RESEARCH REFERENCES

Wright & Miller, *Federal Practice and Procedure* §§ 2231 to 2239

C.J.S., Federal Civil Procedure §§ 752 to 755

West's Key Number Digest, Federal Civil Procedure ⊶1651 to 1664

RULE 36

REQUESTS FOR ADMISSION

(a) Scope and Procedure.

(1) *Scope.* A party may serve on any other party a written request to admit, for purposes of the pending action only, the truth of any matters within the scope of Rule 26(b)(1) relating to:

    (A) Facts, The Application Of Law To Fact, Or Opinions about either; and

    (B) the genuineness of any described documents.

(2) *Form; Copy of a Document.* Each matter must be separately stated. A request to admit the genuineness of a document must be accompanied by a copy of the document unless it is, or has been, otherwise furnished or made available for inspection and copying.

(3) *Time to Respond; Effect of Not Responding.* A matter is admitted unless, within 30 days after being served, the party to whom the request is directed serves on the requesting party a written answer or objection addressed to the matter and signed by the party or its attorney. A shorter or longer time for responding may be stipulated to under Rule 29 or be ordered by the court.

(4) *Answer.* If a matter is not admitted, the answer must specifically deny it or state in detail why the answering party cannot truthfully admit or deny it. A denial must fairly respond to the substance of the matter; and when good faith requires that a party qualify an answer or deny only a part of a matter, the answer must specify the part admitted and qualify or deny the rest. The answering party may assert lack of knowledge or information as a reason for failing to admit or deny only if the party states that it has made reasonable inquiry and that the information it knows or can readily obtain is insufficient to enable it to admit or deny.

(5) *Objections.* The grounds for objecting to a request must be stated. A party must not object solely on the ground that the request presents a genuine issue for trial.

(6) *Motion Regarding the Sufficiency of an Answer or Objection.* The requesting party may move to determine the sufficiency of an answer or objection. Unless the court finds an objection justified, it must order that an answer be served. On finding that an answer does not comply with this rule, the court may order either that the matter is admitted or that an amended answer be served. The court may defer its final decision until a pretrial conference or a specified time before trial. Rule 37(a)(5) applies to an award of expenses.

(b) Effect of an Admission; Withdrawing or Amending It. A matter admitted under this rule is conclusively established unless the court, on motion, permits the admission to be withdrawn or amended. Subject to Rule 16(e), the court may permit withdrawal or amendment if it would promote the presentation of the merits of the action and if the court is not persuaded that it would prejudice the requesting party in maintaining or defending the action on the merits. An admission under this rule is not an admission for any other purpose and cannot be used against the party in any other proceeding.

[Amended December 27, 1946, effective March 19, 1948; March 30, 1970, effective July 1, 1970; March 2, 1987, effective August 1, 1987; April 22, 1993, effective December 1, 1993; April 30, 2007, effective December 1, 2007.]

AUTHORS' COMMENTARY ON RULE 36

PURPOSE AND SCOPE

Rule 36 allows each party to require other parties to admit each relevant fact not in controversy, thereby eliminating the need to produce witnesses and evidence in support of these facts. It must be read in conjunction with Rule 26, which establishes the scope of all discovery rules.

RULE 36(a)—SCOPE AND PROCEDURE

CORE CONCEPT

Rule 36 establishes a procedure whereby one party serves requests for admission on another party, who must investigate and either admit, deny with specificity, justify an inability to admit or deny, or object to each requested admission.

APPLICATIONS

Who May Serve

Any party may serve requests for admission.

Who May Be Served

Requests for admission are limited to parties to the action, although the party need not be an adverse party.

Time for Service

Requests for admission can be served after the parties have conducted the discovery conference under Rule 26(f).[1] In proceedings listed in Rule 26(a)(1)(B) as exempt from initial disclosures, there is no preliminary waiting period for requests for admission. The Rules do not set an outer limit on how late in the case requests for admission may be served, and courts are split as to whether requests for admission are discovery devices subject to a general discovery cutoff.[2] However, many local rules or case management orders will set a limit for requests for admission. Usually, when such a time limit exists, requests for admission must be served so that the response is due before the specified deadline.[3]

---

[1]   *DIRECTV, Inc. v. DeVries*, 302 F.Supp.2d 837, 838 (W.D. Mich. 2004).

[2]   *See Freeman v. City of Detroit*, 274 F.R.D. 610 (E.D.Mich. 2011) (discussing the split).

[3]   *Laborers' Pension Fund v. Blackmore Sewer Const., Inc.*, 298 F.3d 600, 605 (7th Cir. 2002).

Contents of Request

Each fact or matter for which admission is requested should be set forth in a separate paragraph.[4] All facts that are part of the request should be set forth in the request; it is improper to incorporate facts by reference to other text. Requests for admission must be simple, direct, and concise so they may be admitted or denied with little or no explanation or qualification.[5]

Scope and Topics

The scope of requests for admission is the broad discovery available under Rule 26.[6] Within that scope, Rule 36 authorizes requests for admission in two categories:

- *Facts, the Application of Law to Fact, or Opinions About Either:* Requests for admission may pertain to any issue in the case, including the ultimate facts at issue,[7] the application of law to fact,[8] or jurisdictional issues, but may not seek an admission as to a pure conclusion of law.[9] The purpose of requests for admission, however, is to narrow the issues for trial, not to lead to the discovery of admissible evidence.[10]

- *Authenticity of Documents:* A request may ask that the genuineness or authenticity of a document be admitted. If so, a copy of the document should be attached, unless it has already been provided.

Number

Rule 36 contains no limitation on the number of requests for admission. Some districts have local rules limiting the number of requests.

Who Must Receive Copies

All parties must be served with a copy of the requests for admissions.

Time to Answer

A written response is due within 30 days of service.[11] The time to answer may be extended by written agreement under Rule 29.[12] Additionally, the court has discretion to lengthen or shorten the time in which a party must respond.[13]

Service of Response

Copies of the response should be served on the propounding party and all other parties, unless the court has ordered otherwise.

---

[4]   *See Helget v. City of Hays, Kan.,* 300 F.R.D. 496 (D. Kan. 2014) (where request contains multiple compound facts, responding party may deny if any of the facts are not true).

[5]   *United Coal v. Powell Construction,* 839 F.2d 958, 967–68 (3d Cir. 1988).

[6]   *Johnson v. Royal Coal Co.,* 326 F.3d 421, 424 n.2 (4th Cir. 2003).

[7]   *In re Carney,* 258 F.3d 415, 419 (5th Cir. 2001).

[8]   *Quasius v. Schwan Food Co.,* 596 F.3d 947, 950 (8th Cir. 2010).

[9]   *P.L.U.S. Brokerage, Inc. v. Jong Eun Kim,* 908 F.Supp.2d 711 (D.Md. 2012).

[10] *Napolitano v. Synthes USA, LLC,* 297 F.R.D. 194, 198 (D. Conn. 2014).

[11] *Edeh v. Equifax Information Services, LLC,* 295 F.R.D. 219, 228 (D. Minn. 2013).

[12] *Edeh v. Equifax Information Services, LLC,* 295 F.R.D. 219, 228 (D. Minn. 2013).

[13] *Manatt v. Union Pacific R. Co.,* 122 F.3d 514, 517 (8th Cir. 1997).

Form of Response

The response should be in writing and signed by the attorney, or by the party if unrepresented.[14] It should be a single document organized in numbered paragraphs to correspond to the requests.

Responses

The responding party essentially has four possible responses to a request for admission. The party can admit the request (in part or in full), deny the request (in part or in full), set forth reasons why the party cannot admit or deny the request, or object to the request (by a specific objection or by a motion for a protective order).

Duty to Supplement

Rule 26(e) imposes a duty to supplement a denial or statement of inability to admit or deny if the party learns that the original response is in some material respect incomplete or incorrect, and if the additional or corrective information has not been provided to the other parties in writing or at a deposition.[15]

Denials

A denial must specifically address the substance of the requested admission.[16] The denial may be as simple as the single word "denied,"[17] or may be a longer sentence, but may not sidestep the request or be evasive.[18] If the propounding party feels that the denial is not sufficiently specific, the party can move the court to determine the sufficiency of the denial. If the court deems the denial not sufficiently specific, it can deem the denial an admission or order a more specific answer.

Partial Denials

If the responding party believes that part of a requested admission is accurate and part is not, the proper response is to admit the accurate portion and deny the balance.[19]

Inability to Admit or Deny

If the responding party is genuinely unable to admit or deny the requested admission, the party can so state, but must describe in detail why after reasonable inquiry the party cannot admit or deny.[20] A general statement that the responding party has insufficient information to respond will be treated as an insufficient answer, and upon motion the court will treat the answer as an admission or will order a further answer.[21] However, some courts hold that a statement that the responding party has made reasonable inquiry is sufficient, without detail about the nature of the inquiry.[22]

---

[14] The advisory committee note to Rule 36(a).

[15] *See House v. Giant of Maryland LLC,* 232 F.R.D. 257, 259 (E.D. Va. 2005).

[16] *Helget v. City of Hays, Kan.,* 300 F.R.D. 496 (D. Kan. 2014) (improper to change the wording in the request).

[17] *Caruso v. Coleman Co.,* 1995 WL 347003 (E.D. Pa. 1995).

[18] *Asea, Inc. v. Southern Pac. Transp. Co.,* 669 F.2d 1242, 1245 (9th Cir. 1981) (evasive denial may be deemed an admission).

[19] *ATD Corp. v. Lydall, Inc.,* 159 F.3d 534, 549 (Fed. Cir. 1998).

[20] *S.E.C. v. Goldstone,* 300 F.R.D. 505 (D.N.M. 2014).

[21] *Erie Ins. Property & Cas. Co. v. Johnson,* 272 F.R.D. 177, 184 (S.D.W. Va. 2010).

[22] *See S.E.C. v. Goldstone,* 300 F.R.D. 505 (D.N.M. 2014).

Objections

Objections must be made in writing within the time allowed for answering.[23] Typical grounds for objections to requests for admission are:

- *Privilege:* If a response requires the disclosure of privileged matters, it is objectionable.[24] *See* Rule 26 (discussing commonly asserted privileges).

- *Vague or Ambiguous:* A request may be objectionable if it is so vague or ambiguous that the responding party cannot answer it.[25]

Improper Objections

A party cannot refuse to answer a request on the basis that the serving party already knows the answer, that the request calls for an opinion or contention, that the subject matter is within the other party's own knowledge, that it invades the province of the jury, that it addresses a subject for expert testimony, that it presents a genuine issue for trial,[26] that the document at issue speaks for itself, that the responding party is not the custodian of the document, or that it is more properly directed to another party.[27] Likewise, it is irrelevant who has the ultimate burden of proof with respect to the matter for which admission is requested. An improper objection is not the same as an admission, and the proper response to an improper objection is to file a motion to compel a further response.[28]

Opinions and Conclusions

Rule 36 explicitly states that a request for admission is not objectionable because it involves an opinion or contention that relates to fact or the application of law to fact.[29] Rule 36 does not authorize a request that requires a pure legal conclusion, without application to the facts.[30]

Motion for a Protective Order

As an alternative to making objections to individual requests for admission, the responding party may make a motion for a protective order under Rule 26(c). A motion for a protective order is appropriate when most or all of a set of requests is objectionable. The motion must be accompanied by a certification that the parties met prior to the filing of the motion and attempted to resolve their dispute without intervention of the court.

Failure to Respond

Failure to respond in a timely fashion is deemed an admission.[31] The court has discretion to allow a party to submit responses after the allowed time for a response.[32]

---

[23] *P.L.U.S. Brokerage, Inc. v. Jong Eun Kim,* 908 F.Supp.2d 711 (D.Md. 2012) (failure to assert objections waives the objections).

[24] *United States v. One Tract of Real Property Together With all Bldgs., Improvements, Appurtenances and Fixtures,* 95 F.3d 422, 428 (6th Cir. 1996).

[25] *See Erie Ins. Property & Cas. Co. v. Johnson,* 272 F.R.D. 177, 185 (S.D.W.Va. 2010).

[26] *Sommerfield v. City of Chicago,* 251 F.R.D. 353, 356 (N.D.Ill. 2008).

[27] *Harris v. Koenig,* 271 F.R.D. 356, 374 (D.D.C. 2010).

[28] *Butler v. Oak Creek-Franklin School Dist.,* 172 F.Supp.2d 1102, 1122 (E.D. Wis. 2001).

[29] *Marchand v. Mercy Medical Center,* 22 F.3d 933 (9th Cir.1994).

[30] *Tobkin v. The Florida Bar,* 509 B.R. 731, 734 (S.D. Fla. 2014).

[31] *In re Taylor,* 655 F.3d 274, 280 (3d Cir. 2011).

[32] *United States v. Petroff-Kline,* 557 F.3d 285, 293–93 (6th Cir. 2009) (responses 3 days late deemed timely).

Motion to Determine Sufficiency

If a party believes that a response is insufficient or that an objection is improper, the party can move the court to determine the sufficiency of the answer or objection.[33] Note that "insufficient" refers to the specificity of the response, not whether the response is correct or in good faith.[34] The burden will be on the party raising an objection to show that the objection was proper.[35] If the court determines that the answer was insufficient, it can deem the answer an admission or can order a more complete answer.[36] The court may also defer ruling until later in the pretrial proceedings.[37]

Expenses of Motion to Determine Sufficiency

The party losing a motion to determine the sufficiency of a response pays the other party's expenses, including a reasonable attorney's fee, incurred in connection with the motion, pursuant to Rule 37(a)(5).[38]

Sanctions

The sanctions available depend upon the conduct of the responding party. The sanction for failure to respond is that the requests are deemed admitted.[39] The sanction for improperly denying a request is that the responding party will be required to pay the costs of the other party incurred in proving the matter, including attorney's fees, under Rule 37(c).[40] The sanction for an insufficient answer or improper objection is that the response may be deemed an admission, plus the responding party will be liable for the other party's expenses in bringing the motion, including a reasonable attorney's fee. Sanctions can be awarded against the party under Rule 37(c) and/or against the attorney under Rule 26(g).[41]

Appeals

The court's rulings on the sufficiency of and objections to requests for admissions are not final orders, and cannot be appealed until the conclusion of the case.

RULE 36(b)—EFFECT OF AN ADMISSION; WITHDRAWING OR AMENDING IT

CORE CONCEPT

An admission is deemed conclusively established unless the court permits withdrawal or amendment of the admission.

---

[33] *Praetorian Ins. Co. v. Site Inspection, LLC,* 604 F.3d 509 (8th Cir. 2010).

[34] *Foretich v. Chung,* 151 F.R.D. 3 (D.D.C. 1993).

[35] *Moses v. Halstead,* 236 F.R.D. 667, 680 (D. Kan. 2006).

[36] *Lynn v. Monarch Recovery Management, Inc.,* 285 F.R.D. 350, 363 (D.Md. 2012).

[37] The advisory committee note to Rule 36(a).

[38] *Epling v. UCB Films, Inc.,* 2000 WL 1466216 (D. Kan. 2000).

[39] *Microsoft Corp. v. EEE Business Inc.,* 555 F.Supp.2d 1051, 1058 (N.D.Cal. 2008).

[40] *Lynn v. Monarch Recovery Mgmt., Inc.,* 285 F.Supp.2d 350 (D.Md. 2012).

[41] *Johnson Intern. Co. v. Jackson Nat. Life Ins. Co.,* 19 F.3d 431 (8th Cir. 1994).

APPLICATIONS

Proceedings Covered

An admission is only binding within the action in which the request was served.[42] An admission may be introduced at trial or in the context of a motion, such as a motion for summary judgment.[43]

Evidentiary Objections

Admissions are still subject to evidentiary objections at trial, such as hearsay.[44] However, adverse parties can use the exception to the hearsay rule for admissions of party opponents.[45]

Party Making Admission

The party making the admission may not introduce it at trial.[46]

Coparties Not Bound

An admission will only be binding on the admitting party and will not be binding on any coparties.[47]

Withdrawal

A party may move to withdraw or amend an admission.[48] The court may allow withdrawal or amendment when it will aid in the resolution of the matter on the merits and when the party who obtained the admission will not be prejudiced by the amendment or withdrawal.[49] Notably absent from this test is any mention of the responding party's conduct or reason for seeking the amendment or withdrawal.[50] Amendment or withdrawal will not be allowed where prejudice will result to the opponent from reliance on the admission.[51] The court has broad discretion in ruling on motions to withdraw or amend admissions.[52] Some local rules require parties to meet and confer before filing a motion to withdraw or amend admissions.[53]

Binding Nature of Formal Admissions

A matter formally admitted under Rule 36 is conclusively established and may not be contradicted.[54] In contrast, an informal, extrajudicial admission is evidence, but not conclusive.[55] Likewise, a statement at a deposition or in an interrogatory answer may be controverted or explained away at trial.[56]

---

[42]   *American Civil Liberties Union v. The Florida Bar,* 999 F.2d 1486 (11th Cir. 1993).

[43]   *Quasius v. Schwan Food Co.,* 596 F.3d 947, 950–51 (8th Cir. 2010).

[44]   *Walsh v. McCain Foods Ltd.,* 81 F.3d 722, 726 (7th Cir. 1996).

[45]   *Walsh v. McCain Foods Ltd.,* 81 F.3d 722, 726 (7th Cir. 1996).

[46]   *In re Air Crash,* 982 F.Supp. 1060, 1067 (D.S.C. 1996).

[47]   *Becerra v. Asher,* 921 F.Supp. 1538, 1544 (S.D. Tex. 1996), aff'd, 105 F.3d 1042 (5th Cir. 1997).

[48]   *Quasius v. Schwan Food Co.,* 596 F.3d 947, 951–52 (8th Cir. 2010) (request to withdraw must be by motion).

[49]   *Raiser v. Utah County,* 409 F.3d 1243, 1246 (10th Cir. 2005) (inconvenience does not constitute prejudice).

[50]   *See River Light V, L.P. v. Lin & J Intern., Inc.,* 299 F.R.D. 61 (S.D.N.Y. 2014) ("Rule 36(b) does not include an "excusable neglect" requirement.").

[51]   *Sonoda v. Cabrera,* 255 F.3d 1035, 1039 (9th Cir. 2001) (prejudice refers to the difficulty the non-moving party will have in proving its case, such as by the unavailability of witnesses related to the delay).

[52]   *Conlon v. United States,* 474 F.3d 616, 621 (9th Cir. 2007) (Rule 36(b) is permissive, not mandatory).

[53]   *See, e.g., Edeh v. Equifax Information Services, LLC,* 295 F.R.D. 219, 224 (D. Minn. 2013).

[54]   *Checkpoint Systems, Inc. v. All-Tag Sec. S.A.,* 711 F.3d 1341, 1347 (Fed.Cir. 2013).

[55]   *Murrey v. United States,* 73 F.3d 1448, 1455 (7th Cir. 1996).

[56]   *Berkowitz v. Berkowitz,* 817 F.3d 809, 812 (1st Cir. 2016).

Proof of Admission by Failure to Answer

In order to use the failure to answer as an admission, the offering party must prove service of the requests and the failure to answer.[57]

ADDITIONAL RESEARCH REFERENCES

Wright & Miller, *Federal Practice and Procedure* §§ 2251 to 2265

C.J.S., Federal Civil Procedure §§ 756 to 774 et seq.

West's Key Number Digest, Federal Civil Procedure ⊶ 1671 to 1686

---

[57]   *Gilbert v. General Motors Corporation,* 133 F.2d 997 (C.C.A. 2d Cir. 1943).

RULE 37

FAILURE TO MAKE DISCLOSURES OR TO COOPERATE IN DISCOVERY; SANCTIONS

(a) Motion for an Order Compelling Disclosure or Discovery.

(1) *In General.* On notice to other parties and all affected persons, a party may move for an order compelling disclosure or discovery. The motion must include a certification that the movant has in good faith conferred or attempted to confer with the person or party failing to make disclosure or discovery in an effort to obtain it without court action.

(2) *Appropriate Court.* A motion for an order to a party must be made in the court where the action is pending. A motion for an order to a nonparty must be made in the court where the discovery is or will be taken.

(3) *Specific Motions.*

(A) *To Compel Disclosure.* If a party fails to make a disclosure required by Rule 26(a), any other party may move to compel disclosure and for appropriate sanctions.

(B) *To Compel a Discovery Response.* A party seeking discovery may move for an order compelling an answer, designation, production, or inspection. This motion may be made if:

(i) a deponent fails to answer a question asked under Rule 30 or 31;

(ii) a corporation or other entity fails to make a designation under Rule 30(b)(6) or 31(a)(4);

(iii) a party fails to answer an interrogatory submitted under Rule 33; or

(iv) a party fails to produce documents or fails to respond that inspection will be permitted—or fails to permit inspection—as requested under Rule 34.

(C) *Related to a Deposition.* When taking an oral deposition, the party asking a question may complete or adjourn the examination before moving for an order.

(4) *Evasive or Incomplete Disclosure, Answer, or Response.* For purposes of this subdivision (a), an evasive or incomplete disclosure, answer, or response must be treated as a failure to disclose, answer, or respond.

(5) *Payment of Expenses; Protective Orders.*

(A) *If the Motion Is Granted (or Disclosure or Discovery Is Provided After Filing).* If the motion is granted—or if the disclosure or requested

603

discovery is provided after the motion was filed—the court must, after giving an opportunity to be heard, require the party or deponent whose conduct necessitated the motion, the party or attorney advising that conduct, or both to pay the movant's reasonable expenses incurred in making the motion, including attorney's fees. But the court must not order this payment if:

(i) the movant filed the motion before attempting in good faith to obtain the disclosure or discovery without court action;

(ii) the opposing party's nondisclosure, response, or objection was substantially justified; or

(iii) other circumstances make an award of expenses unjust.

(B) *If the Motion Is Denied.* If the motion is denied, the court may issue any protective order authorized under Rule 26(c) and must, after giving an opportunity to be heard, require the movant, the attorney filing the motion, or both to pay the party or deponent who opposed the motion its reasonable expenses incurred in opposing the motion, including attorney's fees. But the court must not order this payment if the motion was substantially justified or other circumstances make an award of expenses unjust.

(C) *If the Motion Is Granted in Part and Denied in Part.* If the motion is granted in part and denied in part, the court may issue any protective order authorized under Rule 26(c) and may, after giving an opportunity to be heard, apportion the reasonable expenses for the motion.

(b) Failure to Comply with a Court Order.

(1) *Sanctions in the District Where the Deposition Is Taken.* If the court where the discovery is taken orders a deponent to be sworn or to answer a question and the deponent fails to obey, the failure may be treated as contempt of court. If a deposition-related motion is transferred to the court where the action is pending, and that court orders a deponent to be sworn or to answer a question and the deponent fails to obey, the failure may be treated as contempt of either the court where the discovery is taken or the court where the action is pending.

(2) *Sanctions Sought in the District Where the Action Is Pending.*

(A) *For Not Obeying a Discovery Order.* If a party or a party's officer, director, or managing agent—or a witness designated under Rule 30(b)(6) or 31(a)(4)—fails to obey an order to provide or permit discovery, including an order under Rule 26(f), 35, or 37(a), the court

where the action is pending may issue further just orders. They may include the following:

(i)   directing that the matters embraced in the order or other designated facts be taken as established for purposes of the action, as the prevailing party claims;

(ii) prohibiting the disobedient party from supporting or opposing designated claims or defenses, or from introducing designated matters in evidence;

(iii) striking pleadings in whole or in part;

(iv) staying further proceedings until the order is obeyed;

(v) dismissing the action or proceeding in whole or in part;

(vi) rendering a default judgment against the disobedient party; or

(vii) treating as contempt of court the failure to obey any order except an order to submit to a physical or mental examination.

(B) *For Not Producing a Person for Examination.* If a party fails to comply with an order under Rule 35(a) requiring it to produce another person for examination, the court may issue any of the orders listed in Rule 37(b)(2)(A)(i)(vi), unless the disobedient party shows that it cannot produce the other person.

(C) *Payment of Expenses.* Instead of or in addition to the orders above, the court must order the disobedient party, the attorney advising that party, or both to pay the reasonable expenses, including attorney's fees, caused by the failure, unless the failure was substantially justified or other circumstances make an award of expenses unjust.

(c) Failure to Disclose, to Supplement an Earlier Response, or to Admit.

(1) *Failure to Disclose or Supplement.* If a party fails to provide information or identify a witness as required by Rule 26(a) or (e), the party is not allowed to use that information or witness to supply evidence on a motion, at a hearing, or at a trial, unless the failure was substantially justified or is harmless. In addition to or instead of this sanction, the court, on motion and after giving an opportunity to be heard:

(A) may order payment of the reasonable expenses, including attorney's fees, caused by the failure;

(B) may inform the jury of the party's failure; and

(C) may impose other appropriate sanctions, including any of the orders listed in Rule 37(b)(2)(A)(i)-(vi).

(2) *Failure to Admit.* If a party fails to admit what is requested under Rule 36 and if the requesting party later proves a document to be genuine or the matter true, the requesting party may move that the party who failed to admit pay the reasonable expenses, including attorney's fees, incurred in making that proof. The court must so order unless:

(A) the request was held objectionable under Rule 36(a);

(B) the admission sought was of no substantial importance;

(C) the party failing to admit had a reasonable ground to believe that it might prevail on the matter; or

(D) there was other good reason for the failure to admit.

(d) Party's Failure to Attend Its Own Deposition, Serve Answers to Interrogatories, or Respond to a Request for Inspection.

(1) *In General.*

(A) *Motion; Grounds for Sanctions.* The court where the action is pending may, on motion, order sanctions if:

(i) a party or a party's officer, director, or managing agent—or a person designated under Rule 30(b)(6) or 31(a)(4)—fails, after being served with proper notice, to appear for that person's deposition; or

(ii) a party, after being properly served with interrogatories under Rule 33 or a request for inspection under Rule 34, fails to serve its answers, objections, or written response.

(B) *Certification.* A motion for sanctions for failing to answer or respond must include a certification that the movant has in good faith conferred or attempted to confer with the party failing to act in an effort to obtain the answer or response without court action.

(2) *Unacceptable Excuse for Failing to Act.* A failure described in Rule 37(d)(1)(A) is not excused on the ground that the discovery sought was objectionable, unless the party failing to act has a pending motion for a protective order under Rule 26(c).

(3) *Types of Sanctions.* Sanctions may include any of the orders listed in Rule 37(b)(2)(A)(i)—(vi). Instead of or in addition to these sanctions, the court must require the party failing to act, the attorney advising that party, or both to pay the reasonable expenses, including attorney's fees, caused by the failure, unless the failure was substantially justified or other circumstances make an award of expenses unjust.

(e) Failure to Preserve Electronically Stored Information. If electronically stored information that should have been preserved in the anticipation or conduct of litigation is lost because a party failed to take reasonable steps to preserve it, and it cannot be restored or replaced through additional discovery, the court:

    (1) upon finding prejudice to another party from loss of the information, may order measures no greater than necessary to cure the prejudice; or

    (2) only upon finding that the party acted with the intent to deprive another party of the information's use in the litigation may:

        (A) presume that the lost information was unfavorable to the party;

        (B) instruct the jury that it may or must presume the information was unfavorable to the party; or

        (C) dismiss the action or enter a default judgment.

(f) Failure to Participate in Framing a Discovery Plan. If a party or its attorney fails to participate in good faith in developing and submitting a proposed discovery plan as required by Rule 26(f), the court may, after giving an opportunity to be heard, require that party or attorney to pay to any other party the reasonable expenses, including attorney's fees, caused by the failure.

[Amended December 29, 1948, effective October 20, 1949; March 30, 1970, effective July 1, 1970; April 29, 1980, effective August 1, 1980; amended by Pub.L. 96–481, Title II, § 205(a), October 21, 1980, 94 Stat. 2330, effective October 1, 1981; amended March 2, 1987, effective August 1, 1987; April 22, 1993, effective December 1, 1993; April 17, 2000, effective December 1, 2000; April 12, 2006, effective December 1, 2006; April 30, 2007, effective December 1, 2007; April 16, 2013, effective December 1, 2013; April 29, 2015, effective December 1, 2015.]

AUTHORS' COMMENTARY ON RULE 37

PURPOSE AND SCOPE

Rule 37 contains the mechanisms for enforcing the provisions of the other discovery rules by imposing sanctions on parties who violate the Rules. In general, obtaining sanctions is a two-step process in which a party must first obtain an order compelling discovery under Rule 37(a), then move for sanctions under Rule 37(b) for failure to comply with the order. If, however, the responding party totally fails to respond to an entire discovery request, the sanctions may be available immediately.

While Rule 37 provides the mechanism in the Rules for enforcing the parties' discovery obligations, a court may also use its inherent power to control cases on its docket.[1]

♦ **NOTE:** Rule 37 was revised in 1993, 2000, 2006, and 2007, and 2015, and care should be exercised when citing case law pertaining to Rule 37.

---

[1] *Haeger v. Goodyear Tire & Rubber Co.*, 813 F.3d 1233, 1244–45 (9th Cir. 2015).

RULE 37(a)—MOTION FOR AN ORDER COMPELLING DISCLOSURE OR DISCOVERY

CORE CONCEPT

If an opponent fails to make the automatic disclosures required by Rule 26(a), fails to respond to discovery served pursuant to the discovery rules, or makes an improper or incomplete disclosure or discovery response, the first step—after trying to resolve the dispute informally—is to make a motion for an order compelling the discovery sought.

APPLICATIONS

Basis for Motion to Compel

A motion to compel may be filed if another party has failed to make any of the disclosures required under Rule 26(a). A motion to compel may be filed after a discovery request has been properly served and the opposing party has failed to respond or failed to respond properly.[2] A motion to compel may also be filed when the moving party disagrees with the objections interposed by the other party and wants to compel more complete answers.[3] A motion to compel may be filed after a witness improperly refuses to answer a deposition question.[4]

Procedures

Motions to compel are served on all parties and filed with the court. There is no set time limit for filing a motion to compel, and the court will consider delay in filing the motion and the procedural posture of the case in deciding whether a motion to compel is timely.[5] The courts differ on which party has the burden of proof in a motion to compel.[6]

Meet and Confer Certification

The motion to compel must be accompanied by a certification that the movant has in good faith conferred or attempted to confer with the other party or person in an effort to resolve the dispute without court action.[7]

Which Court

The proper court in which to file a motion to compel depends on the location and status of the person that is the subject of the motion. If the individual or entity is a party, then a motion to compel must be filed in the court where the action is pending.[8] If the motion to compel pertains to a nonparty witness pursuant to a subpoena for deposition or to produce documents, then a motion to compel should be filed in the district where performance was to occur.[9] That court can adjudicate the motion or transfer it to the court where the action is pending.[10]

---

[2]   *Ward v. Am. Pizza Co.,* 279 F.R.D. 451, 454 (S.D.Ohio 2012) (party may not move to compel production of documents in the absence of a formal document request).

[3]   *See Silicon Knights, Inc. v. Epic Games, Inc.,* 917 F.Supp.2d 503 (E.D.N.C. 2012).

[4]   *See Bell v. Vill. of Streamwood,* 806 F.Supp.2d 1052, 1058 (N.D. Ill. 2011).

[5]   *PCS Phosphate Co., Inc. v. Norfolk Southern Corp.,* 238 F.R.D. 555, 558 (E.D. N.C. 2006) (close of discovery often considered deadline for motions to compel where no deadline expressly set).

[6]   *See Abt v. Jewell,* 303 F.R.D. 166 (D.D.C. 2014) (party seeking to compel discovery has the burden of proving that the prior response was inadequate); *But see Myhre v. Seventh-Day Adventist Church Reform Movement Am. Union Int'l Missionary Soc'y,* 298 F.R.D. 633 (S.D. Cal. 2014) (party opposing discovery bears burden of resisting disclosure).

[7]   *Rivera-Almodovar v. Instituto Socioeconomico Comunitario, Inc.,* 730 F.3d 23, 27–28 (1st Cir. 2013).

[8]   *U.S. ex rel. Pogue v. Diabetes Treatment Centers of America, Inc.,* 444 F.3d 462, 468 (6th Cir. 2006).

[9]   Rule 45(d)(2)(B)(i); *Gordon v. Borigini,* 297 F.R.D. 1, 2 (D.D.C. 2013).

[10]   Rule 45(f).

Expenses

In general, the victorious party in a motion to compel is entitled to recover its expenses in preparing the motion, including reasonable attorney's fees,[11] from the losing party, its attorney, or both.[12] The movant is also entitled to expenses if the respondent provides a disclosure or discovery response after the motion was filed.[13] The award of expenses by the court is mandatory[14] unless the movant failed to confer with the respondent in good faith prior to filing the motion[15] or the losing party demonstrates that its conduct was "substantially justified,"[16] or if other circumstances render an award of expenses "unjust."[17] The award of sanctions does not depend on a finding of bad faith or willful misconduct by the sanctioned party.[18]

- *Substantially Justified:* Good faith generally does not equate to substantial justification; the losing party must demonstrate some unsettled issue of law or like circumstance.[19]

- *Opportunity to be Heard:* The court must provide the non-moving party with an opportunity to be heard, either orally or in writing.[20]

- *Who Pays Expenses:* The court may impose the expenses on the party, the attorney, or both.[21]

- *Motion Granted in Part:* If a motion to compel is granted in part and denied in part, the court may apportion the expenses as it sees fit.[22]

- *Nonparties:* The expense provisions apply only to certain motions involving nonparties. Fees will be awarded in connection with a nonparty making a motion to obtain a copy of the nonparty's statement. A nonparty may be required to pay expenses incurred because of the nonparty's failure to attend a deposition if a court order had already been entered compelling the nonparty's attendance.

- *Motion to Compel:* The expense provisions of Rule 37(a) apply to motions to compel granted in conjunction with the denial of a motion for protective order under Rule 26(c).[23]

---

[11]   *Josendis v. Wall to Wall Residence Repairs, Inc.,* 662 F.3d 1292, 1313–14 (11th Cir. 2011).

[12]   *Josendis v. Wall to Wall Residence Repairs, Inc.,* 662 F.3d 1292, 1313 (11th Cir. 2011).

[13]   *Lynn v. Monarch Recovery Management, Inc.,* 285 F.R.D. 350, 366 (D.Md. 2012).

[14]   *Bravia Capital Partners, Inc. v. Fike,* 296 F.R.D. 136 (S.D.N.Y. 2013).

[15]   *Arnold v. ADT Sec. Services, Inc.,* 627 F.3d 716, 720 (8th Cir. 2010).

[16]   *Josendis v. Wall to Wall Residence Repairs, Inc.,* 662 F.3d 1292, 1314 (11th Cir. 2011) (objections are substantially justified when reasonable people could differ as to the appropriateness of the contested action).

[17]   *Arnold v. ADT Sec. Services, Inc.,* 627 F.3d 716, 721 (8th Cir. 2010); *Rickels v. City of South Bend, Ind.,* 33 F.3d 785 (7th Cir.1994).

[18]   *Underdog Trucking, L.L.C. v. Verizon Services Corp.,* 273 F.R.D. 372 (S.D.N.Y. 2011).

[19]   *Pierce v. Underwood,* 487 U.S. 552, 565, 108 S.Ct. 2541, 2550, 101 L.Ed.2d 490 (1988) (motion is substantially justified if it raises an issue about which there is a genuine dispute, or if reasonable people could differ as to the appropriateness of the contested action).

[20]   *Kister v. District of Columbia,* 229 F.R.D. 326, 329 n.2 (D.D.C. 2005) (written submissions provide an opportunity to be heard).

[21]   *A. Farber & Partners, Inc. v. Garber,* 237 F.R.D. 250, 257 (C.D. Cal. 2006) (fees awarded jointly against party and attorney).

[22]   *Josendis v. Wall to Wall Residence Repairs, Inc.,* 662 F.3d 1292, 1313–14 (11th Cir. 2011).

[23]   *Josendis v. Wall to Wall Residence Repairs, Inc.,* 662 F.3d 1292, 1313 (11th Cir. 2011).

- *Fees from United States:* Attorney's fees can be awarded against the United States.[24]

- *Appeal of Fee Award:* An award of attorney's fees under Rule 37(a)(5) is not a final, appealable order.[25]

Evasive or Incomplete Answer

An evasive or incomplete answer or disclosure is treated as a failure to answer or disclose.[26]

Motion Denied

If the court denies a motion to compel, it can at the same time enter a protective order under Rule 26(c).[27] The court will award expenses to the party who obtained the protective order.[28]

RULE 37(b)—FAILURE TO COMPLY WITH A COURT ORDER

CORE CONCEPT

The sanctions listed in Rule 37(b) become available if a party or deponent fails to obey a court order compelling discovery under Rule 37(a) or if the party fails altogether to perform certain discovery obligations as described in Rules 37(c) and (d). The court has broad discretion to impose one or more of the listed sanctions or any other sanction it deems appropriate.

APPLICATIONS

Order Prerequisite

Rule 37(b) does not authorize sanctions unless the court has already issued an order to provide or permit discovery with which a party or deponent has failed to comply.[29] The order may be pursuant to a motion to compel under Rule 37(a), an order issued in a conference under Rule 16,[30] or an order requiring an examination under Rule 35.[31] Some courts authorize sanctions under Rule 37(b) for violations of protective orders issued under Rule 26(c).[32] Note, however, that Rules 37(c) and 37(d) authorize the court to impose the sanctions listed under Rule 37(b) for conduct other than failure to comply with an order, as discussed below.

Exception to Order Prerequisite

Courts occasionally use Rule 37(b) to impose sanctions for egregious conduct in the absence of a violation of an order compelling discovery.[33]

---

[24] *United States v. Horn,* 29 F.3d 754 (1st Cir. 1994) (fees may be assessed against the United States as a sanction).

[25] *Cunningham v. Hamilton County, Ohio,* 527 U.S. 198, 200, 119 S.Ct. 1915, 1917, 144 L.Ed.2d 184 (1999).

[26] *International Broth. of Elec. Workers, Local Union No. 545 v. Hope Elec. Corp.,* 380 F.3d 1084, 1105 (8th Cir. 2004).

[27] Rule 36(a)(5).

[28] *Rodriquez v. Parsons Infrastructure & Technology Group, Inc.,* 271 F.R.D. 620, 622–23 (S.D.Ind. 2010).

[29] *Holmes v. Trinity Health,* 729 F.3d 817, 821 (8th Cir. 2013).

[30] *But See Holmes v. Trinity Health,* 729 F.3d 817, 820–21 (8th Cir. 2013) (preliminary scheduling order not sufficient to support Rule 37(b) sanctions).

[31] *Smith & Fuller, P.A. v. Cooper Tire & Rubber Co.,* 685 F.3d 486, 488–90 (5th Cir. 2012).

[32] *See Smith & Fuller, P.A. v. Cooper Tire & Rubber Co.,* 685 F.3d 486, 489 (5th Cir. 2012) (discussing the split of authority on this issue).

[33] *Melendez-Garcia v. Sanchez,* 629 F.3d 25, 33, n.5 (1st Cir. 2010) (discussing case law allowing sanctions without an order to compel for serious disregard of discovery obligations).

Sanctions by Court Where Action Pending

Rule 37(b)(2) lists specific categories of sanctions that the court where the action is pending may impose on a party (or an officer, director, or managing agent of a party)[34] who fails to obey an order to permit or provide discovery. The court has broad discretion to impose any sanction or combination of sanctions[35] it deems appropriate,[36] including the following listed sanctions:

- *Deem Facts Established:* The court may deem as established the facts that the moving party was seeking to establish.[37]

- *Prohibit Evidence:* The court may refuse to allow the disobedient party to introduce certain matters into evidence, or to support or oppose certain claims.[38]

- *Strike Pleadings:* The court may strike any pleading or portion of a pleading.[39]

- *Issue Stay:* The court may stay further proceedings until the order is obeyed.[40]

- *Dispositive Ruling:* In extreme situations, the court may dismiss an action or portions of the action.[41] The court may also enter judgment against the disobedient party.[42]

- *Contempt:* The court may treat the failure to obey its order as a contempt of court,[43] with the exception of a failure to submit to a mental or physical examination (which is punishable by other sanctions, but not as contempt).[44]

List Not Exclusive

The court is not limited to the sanctions listed in Rule 37(b)(2), and may make any order that is "just."[45] In practice, however, courts generally have imposed only those sanctions listed.

Sanctions by Court Where Deposition to Occur

If a nonparty witness fails to comply with an order to appear and be sworn in for a deposition or an order to answer a question at a deposition, the court issuing the order— typically the court where the deposition was to occur—may treat the failure as a contempt of court under Rule 37(b)(1).[46] If a motion was filed in the court where the discovery was to occur and that court transferred the motion to the court where the action was pending, then either court may impose contempt sanction for failure to obey the order.[47]

---

[34] *U.S. ex rel. Pogue v. Diabetes Treatment Centers of America, Inc.,* 444 F.3d 462, 468 (6th Cir. 2006).

[35] *Davis v. District of Columbia Child and Family Services Agency,* 304 F.R.D. 51 (D.D.C. 2014) (court may impose multiple sanctions).

[36] *Klein-Becker USA, LLC v. Englert,* 711 F.3d 1153, 1159 (10th Cir. 2013).

[37] *Insurance Corp. of Ireland, Ltd. v. Compagnie des Bauxites de Guinee,* 456 U.S. 694, 102 S.Ct. 2099, 72 L.Ed.2d 492 (1982) (deeming personal jurisdiction established as a discovery sanction).

[38] *E.E.O.C. v. CRST Van Expedited, Inc.,* 679 F.3d 657, 692 (8th Cir. 2012).

[39] *See St. Louis Produce Market v. Hughes,* 735 F.3d 829, 832–33 (8th Cir. 2013).

[40] Rule 37(b)(2)(A)(iv).

[41] *Moore v. CITGO Refining and Chemicals Co.,* L.P., 735 F.3d 309, 316 (5th Cir. 2013).

[42] *Dreith v. Nu Image, Inc.,* 648 F.3d 779, 786–87 (9th Cir. 2011) (default judgment).

[43] *Serra Chevrolet, Inc. v. General Motors Corp.,* 446 F.3d 1137 (11th Cir. 2006).

[44] Rule 37(b)(2)(A)(vii).

[45] *S.E.C. v. Razmilovic,* 738 F.3d 14, 25 (2d Cir. 2013).

[46] *See* Rules 45(d)(2)(B)(i) and Rule 45(f).

[47] Rule 37(b)(1).

Magistrate Judges

Magistrate Judges can impose sanctions under Rule 37(b).[48]

Notice and Opportunity to Be Heard

Before imposing discovery sanctions, the court should provide the offending party with notice and an opportunity to be heard.[49]

Failure to Produce Another for Examination

If a party fails to comply with an order to produce another person for a mental or physical examination, the party is subject to the same sanctions that would apply if the party failed to appear, unless the party can show that the party was unable to produce the individual.[50]

Preservation Order

The importance of discovery of electronically stored information has led parties to seek orders requiring opposing parties to preserve evidence.[51] If a party violates a preservation order by failing to preserve ESI, sanctions are available under Rule 37(e), which controls sanctions for spoliation of ESI. If a party violates a preservation order by failing to preserve evidence other than ESI, sanctions are available under Rule 37(b).[52] Courts also may impose Rule 37 sanctions for spoliation of evidence in the absence of an order to preserve.[53]

Multiple Sanctions

The court may impose any combination of sanctions it deems appropriate.[54]

Expenses

The court will also require the party not complying with the court order and/or the party's attorney[55] to pay all expenses, including reasonable attorney's fees,[56] incurred by the moving party as a result of the failure to comply.[57] This includes expenses incurred in the motion for sanctions, but not expenses incurred in obtaining the order compelling the discovery (although those expenses may be recoverable under Rule 37(a) as discussed above). The court must award such expenses unless it finds that the failure was "substantially justified" or that other circumstances exist that would make the award "unjust."[58]

Failure to Comply by Corporate Representative

The court may also impose sanctions on a party that is a corporation or organization if its officer, director, managing agent, or designated representative fails to obey an order.[59]

---

[48]   *See Moore v. Napolitano,* 723 F.Supp.2d 167, 171–72 (D.D.C. 2010).

[49]   *See McLaughlin v. Phelan Hallinan & Schmieg, LLP,* 756 F.3d 240 (3d Cir. 2014).

[50]   *Societe Internationale Pour Participations Industrielles Et Commerciales, S. A. v. Rogers,* 357 U.S. 197, 78 S.Ct. 1087, 2 L.Ed.2d 1255 (1958).

[51]   *See Moore v. CITGO Refining and Chemicals Co., L.P.,* 735 F.3d 309, 314 (5th Cir. 2013).

[52]   *See Moore v. CITGO Refining and Chemicals Co., L.P.,* 735 F.3d 309, 316 (5th Cir. 2013) (dismissing case for failure to preserve critical notes).

[53]   *See, e.g., Taylor v. City of New York,* 293 F.R.D. 601, 609 (S.D.N.Y. 2013).

[54]   *See O'Neill v. AGWI Lines,* 74 F.3d 93 (5th Cir.1996) (dismissing the action and imposing attorney's fees).

[55]   *Rates Technology, Inc. v. Mediatrix Telecom, Inc.,* 688 F.3d 742, 748 (Fed.Cir. 2012).

[56]   *Davis v. District of Columbia Child and Family Services Agency,* 789 F.R.D. 65 (D.D.C. 2014) (lodestar method is common approach to determining reasonable fees).

[57]   *McLaughlin v. Phelan Hallinan & Schmieg, LLP,* 756 F.3d 240 (3d Cir. 2014).

[58]   *McLaughlin v. Phelan Hallinan & Schmieg, LLP,* 756 F.3d 240 (3d Cir. 2014).

[59]   *Bon Air Hotel, Inc. v. Time, Inc.,* 376 F.2d 118 (5th Cir. 1967).

The party noticing the deposition will have the burden of showing that the person had the necessary relationship to the corporation.

Waiver of Sanctions

A party might be deemed to have waived its rights to sanctions by not strictly enforcing the order, such as by failing to make attempts to schedule a physical examination[60] or by failing to bring a motion for sanctions in a reasonable period of time.[61]

Appeals

Sanctions orders are normally interlocutory orders not immediately appealable, but sometimes may be appealed under the collateral order doctrine.[62]

RULE 37(c)—FAILURE TO DISCLOSE, TO SUPPLEMENT AN EARLIER RESPONSE, OR TO ADMIT

CORE CONCEPT

If a party improperly fails to make the automatic disclosures under Rule 26(a) or makes false or misleading disclosures, or if a party fails to supplement a prior discovery response as required by Rule 26(e)(1), the party generally will not be permitted to use the information or documents not properly provided, and may be subject to a variety of additional sanctions. If a party improperly fails to admit a matter, Rule 37(c) imposes on that party the cost to the other party in proving the matter.

APPLICATIONS

Failure to Disclose

If a party fails to make the automatic disclosures under Rule 26(a)[63] in a timely manner[64] or makes false or misleading disclosures, the party will not be permitted to use at trial or in a motion[65] the documents, information,[66] expert testimony,[67] or witnesses[68] not properly disclosed,[69] unless the failure was "substantial justified"[70] or harmless.[71] The exclusion of evidence or witnesses not properly disclosed is automatic, and there is no need to file a motion for sanctions.[72]

---

[60] *Hinson v. Michigan Mut. Liability Co.,* 275 F.2d 537 (5th Cir. 1960).

[61] *U.S. Fidelity & Guar. Co. v. Baker Material Handling Corp.,* 62 F.3d 24, 29 (1st Cir. 1995).

[62] *U.S. ex rel. Pogue v. Diabetes Treatment Centers of America, Inc.,* 444 F.3d 462, 472 (6th Cir. 2006).

[63] *Alvariza v. Home Depot,* 240 F.R.D. 586, 590 (D. Colo. 2007), aff'd, 241 F.R.D. 663 (D. Colo. 2007) (Rule 37(c) sanctions do not apply to informal agreements to disclose, only to the formal Rule 26(a) disclosure process).

[64] *Trost v. Trek Bicycle Corp.,* 162 F.3d 1004, 1008 (8th Cir. 1998) (failure to disclose in a timely manner is equivalent to failure to disclose).

[65] *Glowczenski v. Taser Intern., Inc.,* 928 F.Supp.2d 564 (E.D.N.Y. 2013).

[66] *E.E.O.C. v. Serv. Temps Inc.,* 679 F.3d 323, 334 (5th Cir. 2012) (exclusion of damages information not disclosed).

[67] *Wilkins v. Montgomery,* 751 F.3d 214, 220–23 (4th Cir. 2014).

[68] *Doe v. Young,* 664 F.3d 727, 734 (8th Cir. 2011).

[69] *Elion v. Jackson,* 544 F.Supp.2d 1, 5 (D.D.C. 2008) (exclusion is self-executing sanction, and the motive or reason for failure is irrelevant).

[70] *Grider v. Keystone Health Plan Central, Inc.,* 580 F.3d 119, 141 (3d Cir. 2009) (sanctions vacated because the court did not expressly evaluate substantial justification).

[71] *Rembrandt Vision Technologies, L.P. v. Johnson & Johnson Vision Care, Inc.,* 725 F.3d 1377, 1381 (Fed. Cir. 2013) (burden is on party seeking to avoid sanctions to show substantial justification or harmlessness).

[72] *Wilkins v. Montgomery,* 751 F.3d 214, 221 (4th Cir. 2014); *but see Malik v. Falcon Holdings, LLC,* 675 F.3d 646, 649 (7th Cir. 2012) (defendant could not wait until discovery closed to raise its contention that the damages disclosure was inadequate).

Failure to Supplement

If a party fails to supplement its automatic disclosures or to supplement a prior discovery response as required under Rule 26(e)(1), the party will not be permitted to use at trial the documents, information, opinions,[73] or witnesses not properly disclosed,[74] unless the party had "substantial justification" or the failure was harmless.[75]

When Exclusion Is a Dispositive Sanction

When exclusion of information or documents is effectively dispositive of a claim, the court may scrutinize the sanction more closely.[76]

Additional Sanctions

In addition to or in lieu of[77] precluding the evidence, upon motion and after an opportunity to be heard,[78] the court may impose additional sanctions, including:

- payment of reasonable expenses, including attorney's and/or expert fees, caused by the failure;[79]

- reopening discovery;[80]

- informing the jury of the failure to make the disclosure;[81]

- deeming certain matters established;

- precluding the non-disclosing party from supporting or opposing designated claims or defenses;[82]

- striking pleadings or portions of pleadings;[83]

- staying the action pending proper disclosure; or

- dismissing or entering judgment as to part or all of the action.[84]

The court has broad discretion in awarding sanctions under Rule 37(c).[85]

Sanctions Apply at Trial, Hearing, or Motion

The information or witnesses not properly disclosed are most commonly excluded from trial, but also may be excluded from a hearing or motion for summary judgment.[86]

---

[73] *Air Turbine Technology, Inc. v. Atlas Copco AB,* 410 F.3d 701, 711–12 (Fed. Cir. 2005).

[74] *Edwards v. National Vision, Inc.,* 946 F.Supp.2d 1153 (N.D.Ala. 2013).

[75] *Harriman v. Hancock County,* 627 F.3d 22, 29 (1st Cir. 2010) (although sanctions can vary depending on the circumstances, the required sanction in the ordinary case is mandatory preclusion).

[76] *R & R Sails, Inc. v. Ins. Co. of Pennsylvania,* 673 F.3d 1240, 1247–48 (9th Cir. 2012).

[77] *Genereux v. Raytheon Co.,* 754 F.3d 51 (1st Cir. 2014).

[78] *Paladin Associates, Inc. v. Montana Power Co.,* 328 F.3d 1145, 1164–65 (9th Cir. 2003) (the opportunity to submit briefs was an opportunity to be heard).

[79] *Hicks v. Avery Drei, LLC,* 654 F.3d 739, 745 (7th Cir. 2011).

[80] *Webster v. Dollar General, Inc.,* 314 F.R.D. 367, 371 (D.N.J. 2016).

[81] *Hicks v. Avery Drei, LLC,* 654 F.3d 739, 745 (7th Cir. 2011).

[82] *Patterson v. State Auto. Mut. Ins. Co.,* 105 F.3d 1251, 1252 (8th Cir. 1997) (expert's testimony about his unannounced second visit to site was precluded due to prejudice on opposing party).

[83] *Second Chance Body Armor, Inc. v. American Body Armor, Inc.,* 177 F.R.D. 633, 637 (N.D. Ill. 1998).

[84] *Vallejo v. Santini-Padilla,* 607 F.3d 1, 6 (1st Cir. 2010).

[85] *Gagnon v. Teledyne Princeton, Inc.,* 437 F.3d 188, 191 (1st Cir. 2006).

[86] *Gagnon v. Teledyne Princeton, Inc.,* 437 F.3d 188, 199 (1st Cir. 2006) (motion for summary judgment based on lack of any expert testimony following exclusion based on untimely expert disclosure).

Failure to Admit

If a party fails to admit a matter that another party subsequently proves,[87] the other party can move for its reasonable expenses, including reasonable attorney's fees, incurred in proving the matter.[88] The court must[89] then award expenses unless one of the following four conditions exists:

(1)   The request was objectionable;[90]

(2)   The admission sought was of no substantial importance, such as when the proof of the matter was trivial;[91]

(3)   The party refusing to admit had reasonable grounds to believe that it would be successful on the matter;[92] or

(4)   Other good reasons exist for the failure to admit, such as a genuine inability to determine the truth of the matter.[93]

Party Only

Expenses and fees under Rule 37(c) may be awarded against the party only, not against the attorney, in contrast to other provisions of Rule 37.[94]

Improper Statement of Inability to Admit

The sanctions in Rule 37(c) apply to an improper statement of inability to admit or deny, as well as to an improper denial.

Explanation of Sanctions

The court order must state the basis for its decision to impose sanctions so that the sanctioned party may obtain meaningful appellate review.[95]

RULE 37(d)—PARTY'S FAILURE TO ATTEND ITS OWN DEPOSITION, SERVE ANSWERS TO INTERROGATORIES, OR RESPOND TO A REQUEST FOR INSPECTION

CORE CONCEPT

Rule 37(d) provides that upon motion sanctions are immediately available against a party who completely fails to participate in the discovery process.

---

[87]   *Joseph v. Fratar,* 197 F.R.D. 20 (D. Mass. 2000) (motion for expenses for improper failure to admit may not be made until after trial).

[88]   *Bradshaw v. Thompson,* 454 F.2d 75 (6th Cir. 1972).

[89]   *Sparks v. Reneau Pub. Inc.,* 245 F.R.D. 583, 588 (E.D. Tex. 2007) (court has no discretion; it *shall* award fees unless one of the exceptions exists).

[90]   *Russo v. Baxter Healthcare Corp.,* 51 F.Supp.2d 70, 78 (D.R.I. 1999).

[91]   *Read-Rite Corp. v. Burlington Air Express, Inc.,* 183 F.R.D. 545, 547 (N.D. Cal. 1998).

[92]   *Mutual Service Ins. Co. v. Frit Industries, Inc.,* 358 F.3d 1312, 1326 (11th Cir. 2004) (the true test is not whether a party prevailed at trial, but whether it acted reasonably in believing that it might prevail).

[93]   *Maynard v. Nygren,* 332 F.3d 462, 470 (7th Cir. 2003) (attorneys can be sanctioned for failure-to-disclose violations under Rule 26(g)(3)).

[94]   *Grider v. Keystone Health Plan Central, Inc.,* 580 F.3d 119, 141 (3d Cir. 2009).

[95]   *Mutual Service Ins. Co. v. Frit Industries, Inc.,* 358 F.3d 1312, 1326 (11th Cir. 2004) ("[I]n cases invoking the sanction power of Rule 37 the district court must 'clearly state its reasons so that meaningful review may be had on appeal.' "); *but see Umbenhower v. Copart, Inc.,* 222 F.R.D. 672, 675 (D. Kan. 2004) (court need not make explicit findings regarding substantial justification or harmlessness).

APPLICATIONS

When Available

Sanctions under Rule 37(d) are available when a party fails to appear for the party's deposition after being served with proper notice,[96] fails to answer or object to properly-served interrogatories,[97] or fails to serve a written response to a properly-served request to inspect documents or things.[98] Thus, a court order is not a prerequisite to sanctions under Rule 37(d).[99] Rule 37(d) does not specify when the motion for sanctions must be filed, but some courts have held that the motion must be filed without "unreasonable delay,"[100] or before the entry of judgment.[101]

Parties Only

Rule 37(d) applies only to parties; a nonparty's failure to attend a deposition does not result in automatic sanctions under Rule 37(d).[102]

Party's Representative's Failure

A corporation or organization that is a party is subject to the sanctions in Rule 37(d) if its officer, director, managing agent, or person designated to testify under Rule 30(b)(6) fails to appear for a deposition after being properly noticed.[103] Likewise, if a party refuses to designate a representative, the party will be subject to sanctions under Rule 37(d).[104] In extreme cases, a party who produces an unprepared or inappropriate representative may also be subject to sanctions under Rule 37(d).[105]

Certification of Conference

A motion for sanctions under Rule 37(d) for failure to respond to interrogatories or requests for inspection must include a certification that the movant has in good faith conferred or attempted to confer with the other party or person in an effort to obtain a response without court action.[106] Note that this requirement does not apply to the failure to appear for a deposition.[107]

Sanctions

Rule 37(d) states that the court may impose whatever sanctions are "just,"[108] including those listed in Rule 37(b)(2)(A),[109] which are essentially the sanctions discussed above except

---

[96] *Wolters Kluwer Financial Services, Inc. v. Scivantage,* 564 F.3d 110, 118 (2d Cir. 2009).

[97] *Roney v. Starwood Hotels & Resorts Worldwide, Inc.,* 236 F.R.D. 346 (E.D. Mich. 2006).

[98] *Alvariza v. Home Depot,* 240 F.R.D. 586, 590 (D. Colo. 2007), aff'd, 241 F.R.D. 663 (D. Colo. 2007) (Rule 37(c) sanctions do not apply to informal agreements to provide documents, only to properly served Rule 34 document requests).

[99] *Guidry v. Continental Oil Co.,* 640 F.2d 523, 533 (5th Cir. 1981).

[100] *See Lancaster v. Independent School Dist. No. 5,* 149 F.3d 1228, 1237 (10th Cir. 1998).

[101] *See Mercy v. Suffolk County, New York,* 748 F.2d 52, 55–56 (2d Cir. 1984).

[102] *Kamps v. Fried, Frank, Harris, Shriver & Jacobson L.L.P.,* 274 F.R.D. 115 (S.D.N.Y. 2011).

[103] *Ecclesiastes 9:10–11–12, Inc. v. LMC Holding Co.,* 497 F.3d 1135, 1147 (10th Cir. 2007) (corporation required to produce its directors, officers, and managing agents).

[104] *Ferko v. National Ass'n for Stock Car Auto Racing, Inc.,* 218 F.R.D. 125, 133 (E.D. Tex. 2003).

[105] *See Baker v. St. Paul Travelers Ins. Co.,* 670 F.3d 119, 124 (1st Cir. 2012).

[106] *Guy v. Vilsack,* 293 F.R.D. 8, 12 (D.D.C. 2013).

[107] *Grand Oaks, Inc. v. Anderson,* 175 F.R.D. 247, 250 (N.D. Miss. 1997); *but see Simms v. Center for Correctional Health and Policy Studies,* 272 F.R.D. 36, 39 (D.D.C. 2011) (requiring a certification of conference even for failure to attend a deposition).

[108] *In re Hutter,* 207 B.R. 981, 986 (Bankr. D. Conn. 1997), aff'd, 2001 WL 34778750 (D. Conn. 2001).

[109] *Laukus v. Rio Brands, Inc.,* 292 F.R.D. 485 (N.D.Ohio 2013).

for contempt of court sanctions.[110] The court has broad discretion in deciding what sanction to impose.[111] The court can consider all the circumstances, such as whether the failure was accidental or in bad faith in determining the sanctions to impose.[112]

Expenses

The court must require that the party failing to participate in discovery and/or the party's attorney pay the resulting expenses of the other party,[113] including reasonable attorney's fees.[114] The court must award such expenses unless it finds that the failure was "substantially justified"[115] or that other circumstances exist that would make the award "unjust."[116] The award of expenses can be in addition to or instead of other sanctions.

Improper Grounds for Failure to Perform Discovery Obligations

It is not a defense to a motion for sanctions under Rule 37(d) to argue that the discovery request was objectionable.[117] Likewise, a party may not refuse to respond to discovery requests or appear for a deposition because the opposing party has committed discovery violations.[118] Informal notification that a party will not appear for a deposition, particularly when given shortly before the deposition, will not excuse failure to attend.[119] The proper response to an objectionable discovery request is to serve a response interposing the objections or file a motion for a protective order under Rule 26(c), not to ignore the discovery request.[120]

Court Order

Although a court order is not a prerequisite to a motion for sanctions under Rule 37(d), the motion may still be brought if the party failing to participate in discovery had been ordered to participate.[121]

Refusal to Be Sworn In

A party appearing at the designated time but who refuses to be sworn in is not generally subject to Rule 37(d) sanctions.[122]

Refusal to Answer Specific Questions

A party who appears and is sworn in, but who then refuses to answer a specific question or questions is not subject to sanctions under Rule 37(d).[123] The proper procedure is for the party taking the deposition to move to compel answers under Rule 37(a), then move for

---

[110] *See Bishop v. First Mississippi Financial Group, Inc.,* 221 F.R.D. 461 (S.D. Miss. 2004) (dismissal for failure to appear at depositions and respond to motions).

[111] *Black Horse Lane Assoc., L.P. v. Dow Chemical Corp.,* 228 F.3d 275, 301 (3d Cir. 2000).

[112] *In re Sumitomo Copper Litigation,* 204 F.R.D. 58, 60–61 (S.D. N.Y. 2001) (case dismissed based on willful failure to appear at deposition).

[113] *John Wiley & Sons, Inc. v. Book Dog Books, LLC,* 298 F.R.D. 145, 149–52 (S.D.N.Y. 2014) (awarding hotel and travel costs and court reporter fees).

[114] *Hyde & Drath v. Baker,* 24 F.3d 1162 (9th Cir.1994).

[115] *Telluride Management Solutions, Inc. v. Telluride Inv. Group,* 55 F.3d 463 (9th Cir. 1995) (good faith but incorrect belief that the action had been dismissed was not sufficient to excuse absence from a deposition).

[116] *Miller v. International Paper Co.,* 408 F.2d 283, 292–94 (5th Cir. 1969).

[117] *International Broth. of Elec. Workers, Local Union No. 545 v. Hope Elec. Corp.,* 380 F.3d 1084, 1106 (8th Cir. 2004).

[118] *John Wiley & Sons, Inc. v. Book Dog Books, LLC,* 298 F.R.D. 145, 148–49 (S.D.N.Y. 2014).

[119] *John Wiley & Sons, Inc. v. Book Dog Books, LLC,* 298 F.R.D. 145, 149 (S.D.N.Y. 2014).

[120] *Kamps v. Fried, Frank, Harris, Shriver & Jacobson L.L.P.,* 274 F.R.D. 115 (S.D.N.Y. 2011).

[121] *See Independent Productions Corp. v. Loew's Inc.,* 283 F.2d 730 (2d Cir. 1960).

[122] *Aziz v. Wright,* 34 F.3d 587 (8th Cir. 1994).

[123] *See Baker v. St. Paul Travelers Ins. Co.,* 670 F.3d 119, 123 (1st Cir. 2012).

sanctions under Rule 37(b) if the party still refuses to answer.[124] The same result is reached with respect to evasive or incomplete answers. However, if the party refuses to answer all or substantially all of the questions, Rule 37(d) will apply.[125]

Continuation of Deposition

Courts differ as to whether Rule 37(d) sanctions apply to a party who fails to appear for the continuation of a deposition.[126]

Incomplete Response to Interrogatories or Document Requests

Rule 37(d) only applies if the party fails altogether to serve a response to interrogatories or document requests. If the party serves an incomplete or evasive response, the proper procedure is a motion to compel under Rule 37(a), then a motion for sanctions under Rule 37(b) if the party does not comply with the court order.[127] Some courts allow sanctions under Rule 37(d) when the response to the discovery requests is so deficient as to be tantamount to no response at all.[128]

Compliance After Motion

Once a motion for sanctions has been filed, the nonparticipating party cannot avoid sanctions by responding to the discovery request. However, the court can consider that conduct in deciding what sanctions to impose.[129]

RULE 37(e)—FAILURE TO PRESERVE ELECTRONICALLY STORED INFORMATION

CORE CONCEPT

Rule 37(e) contains the provisions for sanctioning a party who fails to preserve ESI. It does not authorize any sanctions unless there was a duty to preserve the lost information, the information was lost because a party failed to take reasonable steps to preserve it, and the information cannot be restored or replaced through additional discovery. If the court finds prejudice to another party from the loss of the information, it may impose only measures no greater than necessary to cure the prejudice. If the court finds that the spoliating party acted with the intent to deprive another party of the information's use in the litigation, the court may impose the more severe sanctions of presuming that the information was unfavorable to the spoliating party, instructing the jury that it may or must presume that the information was unfavorable to the spoliating party, dismissing the action, or entering a default judgment.

APPLICATIONS

Prerequisites for Sanctions

Rule 37(e) authorizes sanctions for failure to preserve ESI only if three prerequisites are met:

(1) There must have been a duty to preserve the ESI. Rule 37 does not create a duty to preserve; that duty is found in common law or statutes and typically arises when litigation has been commenced or is reasonably anticipated and the ESI is reasonably

---

[124] *Independent Productions Corp. v. Loew's Inc.*, 283 F.2d 730 (2d Cir. 1960).

[125] *GMAC Bank v. HTFC Corp.*, 248 F.R.D. 182, 185 (E.D. Pa. 2008) (sanctions are available under Rule 37(d) if the deponent's conduct is so egregious that it impedes, delays, or frustrates the fair examination).

[126] *Miller v. International Paper Co.*, 408 F.2d 283, 292–294 (5th Cir. 1969) (no sanctions if continuation date not set forth in a deposition notice).

[127] *Fjelstad v. American Honda Motor Co., Inc.*, 762 F.2d 1334 (9th Cir. 1985).

[128] *See Melendez-Garcia v. Sanchez*, 629 F.3d 25, 33, n.5 (1st Cir. 2010).

[129] *Antico v. Honda of Camden*, 85 F.R.D. 34, 36 (E.D. Pa. 1979).

likely to be relevant to a party's claim or defense. Additionally, the court may create or enhance the duty by issuing a preservation order;

(2) The ESI was lost because a party failed to take reasonable steps to preserve it. ESI lost despite reasonable measures to preserve it, such as through the routine operation of a computer system or as a result of damage to a computer system, will not support sanctions. The loss must have occurred after the duty to preserve the ESI arose; and

(3) The ESI cannot be restored or replaced through additional discovery. ESI often exists in multiple locations, so loss from one location will not support sanctions if the ESI also exists in another location. ESI that might have been deemed inaccessible, such as ESI located on backup tapes—might become discoverable if the accessible versions have been lost.

Sanctions for Prejudice to Another Party

If the court finds the above prerequisites satisfied and finds prejudice to another party from the loss of the information, the court may impose sanctions, but may only impose measures no greater than necessary to cure the prejudice. The rule does not assign the burden of proving prejudice to either party, and it will be up to the court's discretion to assess prejudice. The court also has wide discretion in fashioning an appropriate sanction to cure the prejudice, and the measures need not cure every conceivable prejudicial effect. The measures may not include the more severe sanctions in Rule 37(e)(2), however. Examples of appropriate sanctions include forbidding the spoliating party from introducing certain evidence at trial, permitting parties to present evidence and arguments to the jury about the loss of the ESI, and giving instructions to the jury to assist it in evaluating such evidence and argument.

Sanctions for Intent to Affect the Litigation

If the court finds the above prerequisites satisfied and finds that the party acted with the intent to deprive another party of the information's use in the litigation, the court may impose more severe sanctions. In a bench trial, the court may presume that the lost ESI was unfavorable to the party failing to preserve it. In a jury trial, the court may make an adverse inference instruction to the jury that it may or must presume the information was unfavorable to the party failing to preserve it. The court may also impose dispositive sanctions, dismissing the action or entering default judgment for the plaintiff. The court does not need to find prejudice to another party to impose the sanctions in Rule 37(e)(2).

Proportionality

Throughout the ESI spoliation analysis, the courts will include proportionality in their analysis. For example, in determining whether a party failed to take reasonable steps to preserve ESI, the court will consider the cost of the steps, the value of the case, and the proportionality factors.

Other Authority for Sanctions

Rule 37(e) is the court's only sanctioning authority for spoliation of ESI, and forecloses reliance on the court's inherent authority or state law as authority for such sanctions. It does

not affect spoliation of evidence other than ESI or the viability of an independent tort claim for spoliation if state law applies and authorizes the claim.

RULE 37(f)—FAILURE TO PARTICIPATE IN FRAMING A DISCOVERY PLAN

CORE CONCEPT

If a party fails to participate in developing a proposed discovery plan as required by Rule 26(f), the court may, after opportunity for a hearing, require the party failing to participate to pay the expenses of the other party, including reasonable attorney's fees, caused by the failure.

ADDITIONAL RESEARCH REFERENCES

Wright & Miller, *Federal Practice and Procedure* §§ 2281 to 2293

C.J.S., Federal Civil Procedure §§ 535 to 547, 640 to 644, 694, 695, 748 to 774

West's Key Number Digest, Federal Civil Procedure ⊶1278, 1299, 1451 to 1456, 1537 to 1542, 1636 to 1640, 1663 to 1664, 1685

VI. TRIALS

RULE 38

RIGHT TO A JURY TRIAL; DEMAND

(a) Right Preserved. The right of trial by jury as declared by the Seventh Amendment to the Constitution—or as provided by a federal statute—is preserved to the parties inviolate.

(b) Demand. On any issue triable of right by a jury, a party may demand a jury trial by:

(1) serving the other parties with a written demand—which may be included in a pleading—no later than 14 days after the last pleading directed to the issue is served; and

(2) filing the demand in accordance with Rule 5(d).

(c) Specifying Issues. In its demand, a party may specify the issues that it wishes to have tried by a jury; otherwise, it is considered to have demanded a jury trial on all the issues so triable. If the party has demanded a jury trial on only some issues, any other party may—within 14 days after being served with the demand or within a shorter time ordered by the court—serve a demand for a jury trial on any other or all factual issues triable by jury.

(d) Waiver; Withdrawal. A party waives a jury trial unless its demand is properly served and filed. A proper demand may be withdrawn only if the parties consent.

(e) Admiralty and Maritime Claims. These rules do not create a right to a jury trial on issues in a claim that is an admiralty or maritime claim under Rule 9(h).

[Amended February 28, 1966, effective July 1, 1966; March 2, 1987, effective August 1, 1987; April 22, 1993, effective December 1, 1993; April 30, 2007, effective December 1, 2007; March 26, 2009, effective December 1, 2009.]

AUTHORS' COMMENTARY ON RULE 38

PURPOSE AND SCOPE

Rule 38 governs the parties' right to a trial by jury and how the parties exercise their right to such a trial. Rule 38 essentially serves two functions: (1) Rules 38(a) and 38(e) describe the issues for which the parties have a right to a jury trial; and (2) Rules 38(b), 38(c), and 38(d) control the procedural aspects of making a jury trial demand and the consequences of failing to do so.

♦ **NOTE:** The right to a jury trial is waived unless a jury trial demand is served within 14 days of the answer or last pleading.

RULE 38(a)—RIGHT PRESERVED

CORE CONCEPT

Rule 38 essentially codifies the Constitution's Seventh Amendment, which provides that the parties have a right to trial by jury for all suits at common law with more than $20 in controversy.[1]

APPLICATIONS

Law vs. Equity

Under Rule 38, the parties have a right to a jury in all actions that historically would have been tried at law, such as actions for damages, but no right to a jury in actions that historically would have been tried in the courts of equity, such as actions for specific performance[2] or injunctive relief.[3]

Jury Right Provided by Statute

The right to a jury trial may also be provided by statute.[4]

Counterclaims

The right to a jury trial extends to counterclaims (permissive or compulsory), even if the complaint only contains equitable claims.[5]

Declaratory Judgment Actions

The right to a jury trial is preserved in declaratory judgment actions. If the issues would have been triable by a jury had something other than declaratory relief been sought, a right to a jury trial exists in a declaratory judgment action.[6]

Individual Issues

The right to a jury trial is evaluated claim by claim, not for the entire case.[7] If one claim triable at law is present in the case, then the parties have a right to a jury trial on that claim; whether the primary or principal claim is legal or equitable is immaterial.[8]

Statutory Claims

Because statutory claims did not generally exist in 1791 at the time of the Seventh Amendment, the Supreme Court developed a two-pronged analysis to evaluate the right to a jury trial for such claims. The court will try to determine the cause of action in existence in 1791 most analogous to the statutory claim, and will consider whether the relief sought is more akin to a legal or equitable remedy, with the latter factor having a greater impact on the outcome.[9]

---

[1]   *Jones v. United Parcel Serv., Inc.,* 674 F.3d 1187, 1203 (10th Cir. 2012).

[2]   *See Tull v. United States,* 481 U.S. 412, 417, 107 S.Ct. 1831, 1835, 95 L.Ed.2d 365 (1987); *Parklane Hosiery Co., Inc. v. Shore,* 439 U.S. 322, 99 S.Ct. 645, 58 L.Ed.2d 552 (1979).

[3]   *United States v. Porath,* 764 F.Supp.2d 883 (E.D.Mich. 2011) (to assess eligibility for a jury trial, court must determine whether the matter would have been brought in a court of law or equity in 18th century England).

[4]   *In re Oil Spill by the Oil Rig Deepwater Horizon in the Gulf of Mexico,* 98 F.Supp.3d 872, 878 (E.D. La. 2015).

[5]   *See Beacon Theatres, Inc. v. Westover,* 359 U.S. 500 (1959).

[6]   *See Simler v. Conner,* 372 U.S. 221, 83 S.Ct. 609, 9 L.Ed.2d 691 (1963); *Beacon Theatres, Inc. v. Westover,* 359 U.S. 500, 79 S.Ct. 948, 3 L.Ed.2d 988 (1959).

[7]   *Bleecker v. Standard Fire Ins. Co.,* 130 F.Supp.2d 726, 737 (E.D. N.C. 2000).

[8]   *Beacon Theatres, Inc. v. Westover,* 359 U.S. 500, 79 S.Ct. 948, 3 L.Ed.2d 988 (1959).

[9]   *Chauffeurs, Teamsters and Helpers, Local No. 391 v. Terry,* 494 U.S. 558, 110 S.Ct. 1339 (1990).

Policy Favors Jury Trials

There is a strong policy in favor of jury trials, so courts will tend to allow jury trials if it is unclear whether an issue historically would have been triable at law.[10]

Governing Law

Federal law generally governs whether an issue is legal or equitable, not state law.[11] The determination of whether a party has a right to a jury trial is a legal determination subject to de novo review.[12]

Right Depends on Facts

The court bases its rulings on the issues raised by the *facts* alleged in the pleadings, not on the labels used by the parties.[13]

Jury Issues First

When there are jury and nonjury issues or claims present, typically the jury first determines the jury trial issues, then the court resolves any remaining issues. Any factual findings made by the jury are then binding on the court when trying the nonjury issues. The court may also conduct completely separate trials of jury and nonjury issues.[14] In any event, the court should endeavor not to let the right to a jury trial on legal issues be lost through a prior determination of the equitable issues.[15]

Procedural Posture

The procedural device by which the parties arrive at court is irrelevant; legal issues are tried by jury even if the claims are brought under the historically equitable joinder provisions such as class actions, derivative actions, and intervention.[16]

RULE 38(b)—DEMAND

CORE CONCEPT

Any party may make a jury trial demand. The demand then applies to all parties for the duration of the case.

APPLICATIONS

Form of Demand

The jury trial demand should be in writing,[17] and can be part of pleading[18] or a separate signed document.[19] Rule 38 does not require any particular language or placement, so long as the intent to demand a jury is clear.[20] To avoid timing problems, it is advisable to include the jury demand on the complaint or answer. Note that it is probably not sufficient to

---

[10] *Beacon Theatres, Inc. v. Westover*, 359 U.S. 500, 79 S.Ct. 948, 3 L.Ed.2d 988 (1959).

[11] *Simler v. Conner*, 372 U.S. 221, 83 S.Ct. 609, 9 L.Ed.2d 691 (1963).

[12] *Indiana Lumbermens Mut. Ins. Co. v. Timberland Pallet and Lumber Co., Inc.*, 195 F.3d 368, 374 (8th Cir. 1999).

[13] *Dairy Queen, Inc. v. Wood*, 369 U.S. 469, 82 S.Ct. 894, 8 L.Ed.2d 44 (1962).

[14] *Beacon Theatres, Inc. v. Westover*, 359 U.S. 500, 79 S.Ct. 948, 3 L.Ed.2d 988 (1959).

[15] *Beacon Theatres, Inc. v. Westover*, 359 U.S. 500, 79 S.Ct. 948, 3 L.Ed.2d 988 (1959).

[16] *Ross v. Bernhard*, 396 U.S. 531, 90 S.Ct. 733, 24 L.Ed.2d 729 (1970).

[17] *Solis v. County of Los Angeles*, 514 F.3d 946, 954 n.ll (9th Cir. 2008).

[18] *Solis v. County of Los Angeles*, 514 F.3d 946, 953 (9th Cir. 2008) (the demand may be endorsed on a pleading).

[19] *Davis v. Nationwide Mut. Fire Ins. Co.*, 783 F.Supp.2d 825 (E.D.Va. 2011) (jury demand in brief that was filed and served effective).

[20] *Lutz v. Glendale Union High School*, 403 F.3d 1061, 1063 (9th Cir. 2005) (local rule requiring a particular placement is unenforceable, test is whether a careful reader would understand that a jury trial had been demanded).

indicate a jury trial on the civil coversheet or legal backer.[21] Likewise, a jury trial demand in a motion is probably not effective.[22]

Timing of Service and Filing

A party wishing a jury trial for an issue must *serve* a jury trial demand within 14 days after service of the last pleading raising or responding to that issue.[23] Normally, the last pleading is the answer to the pleading raising the issue.[24] The party must also *file* the jury trial demand within a reasonable time, as provided in Rule 5(d).[25] If a jury trial demand is served after the 14th day, the court has discretion to consider the demand.[26]

Other Parties

Once one party has made a jury demand, the other parties may rely on that demand and do not need to file jury demands of their own.[27] A party may not rely on the designation on the docket, however, only upon a proper demand by another party.[28]

Amendments

An amended or supplemental pleading does not restart the jury trial demand clock for issues raised in the original pleading.[29] The focus is the issue, not the remedy.[30] Therefore, if the original complaint seeks specific performance of a breached contract and the amended complaint adds a damages claim arising out of the same breach, under the majority approach, the parties do not have the right to demand a jury trial 14 days after service of the amended complaint.[31]

Removal

The removing party may make a jury trial demand within 14 days of filing the removal petition.[32] Others may make demands within 14 days of service of the petition.[33] If a pleading is filed after the petition, then all parties have 14 days from service of the pleading.[34] If, prior to removal, a party has made a jury demand in accordance with state procedures or has made a jury demand that would satisfy federal requirements,[35] or if state procedures do not require an express demand, then no jury demand is necessary following removal.[36]

---

[21] *Johnson v. Dalton,* 57 F.Supp.2d 958, 959 (C.D. Cal. 1999). *But see Wright v. Lewis,* 76 F.3d 57, 59 (2d Cir. 1996) (a jury trial demand on a civil cover sheet can satisfy Rule 38(b) if the cover sheet is served).

[22] *Bogosian v. Woloohojian Realty Corp.,* 323 F.3d 55, 62 (1st Cir. 2003).

[23] *Marshall v. Knight,* 445 F.3d 965, 970 n.5 (7th Cir. 2006) (jury demand may be made not later than 10 days after *service).*

[24] *See United States v. California Mobile Home Park Management Co.,* 107 F.3d 1374, 1378, 20 A.D.D. 658 (9th Cir. 1997) ("last pleading" is the answer to the intervenor's complaint, rather than the answer to the original complaint filed).

[25] *Solis v. County of Los Angeles,* 514 F.3d 946, 954 n.ll (9th Cir. 2008).

[26] *Zivkovic v. Southern California Edison Co.,* 302 F.3d 1080 (9th Cir. 2002) (the district court's discretion is narrow and does not permit a court to grant relief when the failure to make a timely demand results from an oversight or inadvertence, such as a good faith mistake with respect to the deadline for demanding a jury trial).

[27] *California Scents v. Surco Products, Inc.,* 406 F.3d 1102, 1106 (9th Cir. 2005).

[28] *KnightBrook Ins. Co. v. Payless Car Rental System, Inc.,* 43 F.Supp.3d 965, 983–84 (D. Ariz. 2014).

[29] *Mega Life and Health Ins. Co. v. Pieniozek,* 585 F.3d 1399, 1404 (11th Cir. 2009).

[30] *See Ramirez-Suarez v. Foot Locker Inc.,* 609 F.Supp.2d 181, 184 (D.Puerto Rico 2009).

[31] *See, e.g., California Scents v. Surco Products, Inc.,* 406 F.3d 1102, 1106 (9th Cir. 2005).

[32] *Wilhelm v. Wilhelm,* 662 F.Supp.2d 424, 426 (D.Md. 2009).

[33] *Wilhelm v. Wilhelm,* 662 F.Supp.2d 424, 426 (D.Md. 2009).

[34] *See* Rule 81(c); *Lutz v. Glendale Union High School,* 403 F.3d 1061, 1063 (9th Cir. 2005).

[35] *Lutz v. Glendale Union High School,* 403 F.3d 1061, 1063 (9th Cir. 2005).

[36] Rule 81(c); *Wilhelm v. Wilhelm,* 662 F.Supp.2d 424, 426 (D. Md. 2009).

Objections to Jury Trial Demand

A party objecting to a jury trial demand may challenge it by filing a motion to strike. The Rules do not specify a time limit for moving to strike a jury trial demand.[37]

Appeals

A party who believes that the court has incorrectly denied its right to a jury trial may either seek a Writ of Mandamus or take an appeal after final judgment.[38]

RULE 38(c)—SPECIFYING ISSUES

CORE CONCEPT

A party may limit a jury trial demand to specific issues.[39] Other parties then have 14 days to make a jury trial demand for remaining issues.

APPLICATIONS

Demand Not Specifying Issues

A demand that does not specify individual issues is deemed a demand for a jury trial on all issues that are properly triable to a jury.[40]

RULE 38(d)—WAIVER; WITHDRAWAL

CORE CONCEPT

Failure to serve and file a timely jury trial demand is a waiver of the right, even if the failure was inadvertent.[41]

APPLICATIONS

Waiver by Agreement

Parties may agree—as part of a contract, for example—to waive their right to a jury trial.

Participation in Bench Trial

A party waives the right to a jury trial if the party participates in a nonjury trial without objecting.[42]

Withdrawal of Demand

Once a jury trial demand has been made, it cannot be withdrawn except with the consent of all parties.[43] Note, however, that if the case develops such that the right to a jury trial no longer exists, the court can designate the case as nonjury without the consent of the parties.[44]

---

[37] *Jones-Hailey v. Corporation of Tennessee Valley Authority,* 660 F.Supp. 551, 553 (E.D. Tenn. 1987) (motion to strike jury trial demand allowed one month before trial because Rule 38 contains no time limit).

[38] *Dairy Queen, Inc. v. Wood,* 369 U.S. 469, 82 S.Ct. 894, 8 L.Ed.2d 44 (1962).

[39] *Athridge v. Iglesias,* 2003 WL 23100036 (D.D.C. 2003).

[40] *See Allison v. Citgo Petroleum Corp.,* 151 F.3d 402 (5th Cir. 1998).

[41] *Solis v. County of Los Angeles,* 514 F.3d 946, 955 (9th Cir. 2008) (local rule cannot create additional requirements resulting in waivers).

[42] *United States v. Resnick,* 594 F.3d 562, 569 (7th Cir. 2010).

[43] *Lamex Foods, Inc. v. Audeliz Lebron Corp.,* 646 F.3d 100, 106 (1st Cir. 2011).

[44] *Kramer v. Bane of America Securities, LLC,* 355 F.3d 961, 968 (7th Cir. 2004).

RULE 38(e)—ADMIRALTY AND MARITIME CLAIMS

CORE CONCEPT

Rule 38 does not create a right to a jury trial for admiralty or maritime claims.[45] However, jury trials in an admiralty claim are not forbidden.[46]

ADDITIONAL RESEARCH REFERENCES

Wright & Miller, *Federal Practice and Procedure* §§ 2301 to 2322

C.J.S., Admiralty §§ 216 to 218; Federal Civil Procedure §§ 943 to 950; Juries §§ 9, 11, 84 to 113 et seq.

West's Key Number Digest, Admiralty ⊶880; Jury ⊶9 to 37

---

[45] *See Fitzgerald v. U.S. Lines Co.,* 374 U.S. 16, 83 S.Ct. 1646, 10 L.Ed.2d 720 (1963).
[46] *See Luera v. M/V Alberta,* 635 F.3d 181, 194 (5th Cir. 2011).

RULE 39

TRIAL BY JURY OR BY THE COURT

(a) When a Demand Is Made. When a jury trial has been demanded under Rule 38, the action must be designated on the docket as a jury action. The trial on all issues so demanded must be by jury unless:

(1) the parties or their attorneys file a stipulation to a nonjury trial or so stipulate on the record; or

(2) the court, on motion or on its own, finds that on some or all of those issues there is no federal right to a jury trial.

(b) When No Demand Is Made. Issues on which a jury trial is not properly demanded are to be tried by the court. But the court may, on motion, order a jury trial on any issue for which a jury might have been demanded.

(c) Advisory Jury; Jury Trial by Consent. In an action not triable of right by a jury, the court, on motion or on its own:

(1) may try any issue with an advisory jury; or

(2) may, with the parties' consent, try any issue by a jury whose verdict has the same effect as if a jury trial had been a matter of right, unless the action is against the United States and a federal statute provides for a nonjury trial.

[Amended April 30, 2007, effective December 1, 2007.]

AUTHORS' COMMENTARY ON RULE 39

PURPOSE AND SCOPE

Rule 39 describes the mechanisms for allocating issues for trial by jury or nonjury. Rule 39 also covers advisory juries.

RULE 39(a)—WHEN A DEMAND IS MADE

CORE CONCEPT

Once a jury trial has been demanded for a claim, the docket will be so designated and the claim will be tried to a jury unless the parties stipulate otherwise or the court determines that no right to a jury trial exists.[1]

---

[1]   *Solis v. County of Los Angeles,* 514 F.3d 946, 954 (9th Cir. 2008).

APPLICATIONS

Stipulations

The parties may stipulate to a nonjury trial, even if a timely jury trial demand has been filed.[2] The parties may also stipulate to trial by the court of specific issues.[3] Such a stipulation should be clear and unambiguous,[4] and must be made either:

- in writing and filed with the court;[5] or

- orally in open court and entered in the record.[6]

Striking Improper Jury Demand

When a party has filed a jury trial demand for an equity claim, the court should order a nonjury trial, either *sua sponte*[7] or upon motion.[8]

Jury Verdict Binding

If a trial occurs before a jury following a jury trial demand, the verdict is binding and may not be treated as advisory.[9]

Contractual Waiver

The courts are split as to whether they will enforce contractual agreements agreeing to waive the right to a jury trial.[10]

Waiver by Participation in Bench Trial

Participating in a bench trial without objection may constitute a waiver of the right to a jury trial, even if a timely demand has been filed.[11]

Interlocutory Appeal

If the district court improperly denies a party the right to a jury trial, the party may attempt to challenge that ruling immediately by writ of mandamus under the All Writs Act.[12]

RULE 39(b)—WHEN NO DEMAND IS MADE

CORE CONCEPT

Claims for which no party has filed a jury trial demand are tried by the court.[13]

---

[2]   *Clark v. Runyon,* 218 F.3d 915, 917–18 (8th Cir. 2000).

[3]   *Gaworski v. ITT Commercial Finance Corp.,* 17 F.3d 1104 (8th Cir. 1994).

[4]   *Hupp v. Siroflex of America, Inc.,* 159 F.R.D. 29 (S.D. Tex. 1994) (failure to object is not a stipulation).

[5]   *Solis v. County of Los Angeles,* 514 F.3d 946, 955 (9th Cir. 2008).

[6]   *Solis v. County of Los Angeles,* 514 F.3d 946,955 (9th Cir. 2008).

[7]   *Tegal Corp. v. Tokyo Electron America, Inc.,* 257 F.3d 1331, 1341 (Fed. Cir. 2001).

[8]   *Tracinda Corp. v. DaimlerChrysler AG,* 502 F.3d 212, 226–27 (3d Cir. 2007) (motion to strike can be filed at any time, even on the eve of trial).

[9]   *Smith Flooring, Inc. v. Pennsylvania Lumbermens Mut. Ins. Co.,* 713 F.3d 933, 939 (8th Cir. 2013).

[10]   *Hulsey v. West,* 966 F.2d 579, 581 (10th Cir.1992).

[11]   *Solis v. County of Los Angeles,* 514 F.3d 946, 955–56 (9th Cir. 2008) (waiver only applies when the party is trying to get a second bite at the apple).

[12]   *In re County of Orange,* 784 F.3d 520, 525–26 (9th Cir. 2015).

[13]   *Sikes v. United States,*987 F.Supp.2d 1355, n.5 (S.D. Ga. 2013).

APPLICATIONS

No Jury Without Demand or Motion

The court may not empanel a jury without a demand or motion,[14] except in an advisory capacity.[15]

Motion for Jury Trial

When a jury demand is omitted or filed out-of-time, the court, upon motion[16] and in its discretion, may order a jury trial of claims for which a jury trial could properly have been made.[17] Courts are split on the standard for granting such motions.[18]

RULE 39(c)—ADVISORY JURY; JURY TRIAL BY CONSENT

CORE CONCEPT

The judge may empanel an advisory jury if the case will not be tried to a binding jury.

APPLICATIONS

Verdict Non-Binding

The judge is the ultimate trier of fact with an advisory jury,[19] and has complete discretion to adopt or reject the verdict of the advisory jury.[20]

Findings of Fact and Conclusions of Law

The court must make its own findings of fact and conclusions of law in cases tried with an advisory jury.[21]

Broad Discretion to Empanel Advisory Jury

The court has broad discretion as to whether to empanel an advisory jury even if the parties do not consent.[22]

Binding Jury with Consent

If no claims at law are present, the judge still may empanel a normal, binding jury with the consent (either express or by failure to object) of *all* parties.[23] Consent of the parties does not require the judge to empanel a jury, it merely gives the court the discretion to do so.[24] An exception to this rule is that certain statutes prohibit jury trials in specified actions against the United States.[25]

---

[14] *Sartin v. Cliff's Drilling Co.,* 2004 WL 551209 (E.D. La. 2004) (Rule 39(b) requires a motion by a party; the court may not employ Rule 39(b) of its own initiative).

[15] *Swofford v. B & W, Inc.,* 336 F.2d 406, 409 (5th Cir. 1964).

[16] *Ramirez-Suarez v. Foot Locker Inc.,* 609 F.Supp.2d 181, 185 (D.Puerto Rico 2009) ("on motion" requirement was inserted to prevent district courts from ordering a jury trial *sua sponte* when the parties agreed to a bench trial).

[17] *U.S. S.E.C. v. Infinity Group Co.,* 212 F.3d 180 (3d Cir. 2000).

[18] *See Pacific Fisheries Corp. v. HIH Cas. & General Ins., Ltd.,* 239 F.3d 1000, 1002 (9th Cir. 2001) (discretion to grant an untimely jury trial is narrow, and does not permit a court to grant relief when the failure to make a timely demand results from an oversight or inadvertence).

[19] *The City of New York v. Mickalis Pawn Shop, LLC,* 645 F.3d 114 (2d Cir. 2011) (judge sits as the finder of fact).

[20] *Schaffart v. ONEOK, Inc.,* 686 F.3d 461, 475 (8th Cir. 2012).

[21] Rule 52(a); *Kinetic Concepts, Inc. v. Smith & Nephew, Inc.,* 688 F.3d 1342, 1357 (Fed. Cir. 2012).

[22] *Mala v. Crown Bay Marina, Inc.,* 704 F.3d 239, 249 (3d Cir. 2013).

[23] *See Holland v. Gee,* 677 F.3d 1047, 1064, n.8 (11th Cir. 2012).

[24] *Ed Peters Jewelry Co., Inc. v. C & J Jewelry Co., Inc.,* 215 F.3d 182 (1st Cir.2000).

[25] *See Palischak v. Allied Signal Aerospace Co.,* 893 F.Supp. 341, 342 (D.N.J. 1995).

Mixed Jury and Nonjury Issues

In a case in which a jury trial has been demanded as to some of the claims (or if the right to a jury trial exists as to only some of the claims), the court may consider the nonjury claims as being submitted to the jury on an advisory basis.[26]

Advisory Jury with Legal Claims

Rule 39(c) states that a judge may empanel an advisory jury "[i]n an action not triable of right by a jury. . . . "[27] Some courts construe this language broadly to include any action for which the right has not been exercised.[28]

ADDITIONAL RESEARCH REFERENCES

Wright & Miller, *Federal Practice and Procedure* §§ 2323 to 2350

C.J.S., Federal Civil Procedure §§ 933, 946, 1028 to 1030; Juries §§ 11, 91 to 98

West's Key Number Digest, Federal Civil Procedure ➼1991, 2251, 2252; Jury, ➼25(1), 28(6)

---

[26]   *AMW Materials Testing, Inc. v. Town of Babylon*, 584 F.3d 436, 441 (2d Cir. 2009).

[27]   *See Ernster v. Luxco, Inc.,* 596 F.3d 1000, 1006, n.5 (8th Cir. 2010).

[28]   *See Affordable Communities of Missouri v. EF & A Capital Corp.*, 295 F.R.D. 389, 391 (E.D. Mo. 2013).

RULE 40

SCHEDULING CASES FOR TRIAL

Each court must provide by rule for scheduling trials. The court must give priority to actions entitled to priority by a federal statute.

[Amended April 30, 2007, effective December 1, 2007.]

AUTHORS' COMMENTARY ON RULE 40

PURPOSE AND SCOPE

Rule 40 allows individual district courts to formulate their own rules for placing cases on the trial calendar.

APPLICATIONS

Broad Discretion

Individual judges have broad discretion in enforcing the district court's rules regarding assignment of cases. They may give precedence to cases of public importance or cases in which delay will cause hardship.[1]

Precedence by Statute

Some statutes provide for precedence for actions brought under the statute's provisions.

Motion for Continuance

The trial judge has great discretion in ruling on motions for continuance.[2]

ADDITIONAL RESEARCH REFERENCES

Wright & Miller, *Federal Practice and Procedure* §§ 2351 to 2352

C.J.S., Federal Civil Procedure § 934

West's Key Number Digest, Federal Civil Procedure ⊶1993 to 1994

---

[1] *See Clinton v. Jones,* 520 U.S. 681, 707–708, 117 S.Ct. 1636, 1650–51, 137 L.Ed.2d 945 (1997) (the court abused its discretion in deferring trial until after president left office).

[2] *Clinton v. Jones,* 520 U.S. 681, 706–707, 117 S.Ct. 1636, 1650–51, 137 L.Ed.2d 945 (1997).

RULE 41

DISMISSAL OF ACTIONS

(a) Voluntary Dismissal.

    (1) *By the Plaintiff.*

        (A) *Without a Court Order.* Subject to Rules 23(e), 23.1(c), 23.2, and 66 and any applicable federal statute, the plaintiff may dismiss an action without a court order by filing:

            (i) a notice of dismissal before the opposing party serves either an answer or a motion for summary judgment; or

            (ii) a stipulation of dismissal signed by all parties who have appeared.

        (B) *Effect.* Unless the notice or stipulation states otherwise, the dismissal is without prejudice. But if the plaintiff previously dismissed any federal-or state-court action based on or including the same claim, a notice of dismissal operates as an adjudication on the merits.

    (2) *By Court Order; Effect.* Except as provided in Rule 41(a)(1), an action may be dismissed at the plaintiff's request only by court order, on terms that the court considers proper. If a defendant has pleaded a counterclaim before being served with the plaintiff's motion to dismiss, the action may be dismissed over the defendant's objection only if the counterclaim can remain pending for independent adjudication. Unless the order states otherwise, a dismissal under this paragraph (2) is without prejudice.

(b) Involuntary Dismissal; Effect. If the plaintiff fails to prosecute or to comply with these rules or a court order, a defendant may move to dismiss the action or any claim against it. Unless the dismissal order states otherwise, a dismissal under this subdivision (b) and any dismissal not under this rule—except one for lack of jurisdiction, improper venue, or failure to join a party under Rule 19—operates as an adjudication on the merits.

(c) Dismissing a Counterclaim, Crossclaim, or Third-Party Claim. This rule applies to a dismissal of any counterclaim, crossclaim, or third-party claim. A claimant's voluntary dismissal under Rule 41(a)(1)(A)(i) must be made:

    (1) before a responsive pleading is served; or

    (2) if there is no responsive pleading, before evidence is introduced at a hearing or trial.

(d) Costs of a Previously Dismissed Action. If a plaintiff who previously dismissed an action in any court files an action based on or including the same claim against the same defendant, the court:

(1) may order the plaintiff to pay all or part of the costs of that previous action; and

(2) may stay the proceedings until the plaintiff has complied.

[Amended effective March 19, 1948; July 1, 1963; July 1, 1966; July 1, 1968; August 1, 1987; December 1, 1991; April 30, 2007, effective December 1, 2007.]

AUTHORS' COMMENTARY ON RULE 41

PURPOSE AND SCOPE

Rule 41 controls the procedural aspects and effects of dismissals. It addresses both voluntary and involuntary dismissals, as well as the plaintiff's ability to initiate another action based on the same cause of action.

♦   **NOTE:** The second voluntary dismissal by the plaintiff acts as an adjudication on the merits and will bar subsequent actions based on the same claims.

RULE 41(a)(1)—VOLUNTARY DISMISSAL; BY THE PLAINTIFF

CORE CONCEPT

The plaintiff may dismiss an action without consent of the court either by stipulation of all parties or unilaterally if the defendant has not yet filed an answer or motion for summary judgment.

APPLICATIONS

Notice of Dismissal

Dismissal under Rule 41(a)(1) is achieved by filing a *notice* of dismissal, no motion or court order is required.[1] The notice is effective when filed,[2] but must be served on all parties pursuant to Rule 5(a).

Timing of Notice

Unless stipulated to by all parties, a plaintiff may file a notice of dismissal under Rule 41(a)(1) only if the defendant has not yet served an answer or motion for summary judgment.[3] Otherwise, a plaintiff must file a motion under Rule 41(a)(2).[4]

---

[1]   *Michigan Surgery Inv., LLC v. Arman,* 627 F.3d 572, 575 (6th Cir. 2010).

[2]   *Anago Franchising, Inc. v. Shaz, LLC,* 677 F.3d 1272, 1277 (11th Cir. 2012) (once the notice of dismissal is filed, the district court loses jurisdiction over the action).

[3]   *RFR Industries, Inc. v. Century Steps, Inc.,* 477 F.3d 1348, 1351–52 (Fed. Cir. 2007) (answer that had been filed and faxed but not properly served did not preclude a voluntary dismissal).

[4]   *GF Gaming Corp. v. City of Black Hawk, Colo.,* 405 F.3d 876, 887–88 (10th Cir. 2005).

Notice Must Be Unconditional

A notice of dismissal must be unconditional[5] and unequivocal[6] in both dismissals by notice and by stipulation, although the parties may privately impose conditions (such as the payment of a sum of money) on their participation in a stipulation for dismissal.

Stipulation by All Parties

A stipulation for dismissal must be signed by all parties who have appeared in the action or it is not effective.[7]

Effect of Voluntary Dismissal

A voluntary dismissal leaves the situation as if the lawsuit had never been filed, unless the dismissal is specified as with prejudice.[8] A voluntary dismissal that is specified as with prejudice is given the same res judicata effect as any other judgment.[9] In general, a dismissal under Rule 41(a) deprives the court of any further jurisdiction.[10] If parties want the court to retain jurisdiction (such as to enforce a settlement agreement), they need to ask the court to enter an order to that effect before the dismissal is filed.[11] Most courts hold that a Rule 41(a)(1) dismissal constitutes a judgment for purposes of a motion for relief from a judgment under Rule 60.[12]

Absolute Right

Generally, the right to voluntarily dismiss an action is considered absolute, not requiring assent by the court or opposing parties.[13] Likewise, the court cannot impose conditions in connection with a voluntary dismissal[14] (although it can do so in connection with a motion for voluntary dismissal under Rule 41(a)(2)).

Prejudice; Two Dismissal Rule

Dismissals by stipulation are presumed without prejudice unless they specify otherwise.[15] Dismissals unilaterally by the plaintiff are governed by the Two Dismissal Rule: the first voluntary dismissal of a given claim is without prejudice; the second dismissal acts as a final adjudication on the merits and will preclude a third action based on the same claim.[16]

---

[5]   *Scam Instrument Corp. v. Control Data Corp.*, 458 F.2d 885 (7th Cir. 1972).

[6]   *Carter v. Beverly Hills Sav. and Loan Ass'n,* 884 F.2d 1186 (9th Cir. 1989).

[7]   *See Garber v. Chicago Mercantile Exchange,* 570 F.3d 1361, 1365 (Fed.Cir. 2009).

[8]   *Nelson v. Napolitano,* 657 F.3d 586, 587 (7th Cir. 2011).

[9]   *Norfolk Southern Corp. v. Chevron, U.S.A., Inc.,* 371 F.3d 1285 (11th Cir.2004); *but see Headwaters Inc. v. U.S. Forest Service,* 399 F.3d 1047 (9th Cir. 2005) (although dismissals under Rule 41 are commonly denominated adjudications "on the merits," only a judgment that actually passes directly on the substance of a particular claim before the court triggers the doctrine of *res judicata* or claim preclusion).

[10]   *Nelson v. Napolitano,* 657 F.3d 586, 588–89 (7th Cir. 2011) (although the court generally loses jurisdiction, it retains the supervisory power to consider collateral matters).

[11]   *Anago Franchising, Inc. v. Shaz, LLC,* 677 F.3d 1272, 1280 (11th Cir. 2012).

[12]   *White v. National Football League,* 756 F.3d 585 (8th Cir. 2014).

[13]   *Wolters Kluwer Financial Services, Inc. v. Scivantage,* 564 F.3d 110, 114 (2d Cir. 2009) (the plaintiff has an "unfettered right" to voluntary dismissal, even where the reason is to flee the jurisdiction or the judge).

[14]   *Commercial Space Management Co., Inc. v. Boeing Co., Inc.,* 193 F.3d 1074, 1076 (9th Cir. 1999).

[15]   *Youssef v. Tishman Const. Corp.,* 744 F.3d 821, 823 (2d Cir. 2014) (court has no discretion to treat a Rule 41(a)(1) dismissal by notice as with prejudice).

[16]   *Anderson v. Aon Corp.,* 614 F.3d 361, 365 (7th Cir. 2010); *Murray v. Conseco, Inc.,* 467 F.3d 602, 605 (7th Cir. 2006) (dismissal for lack of subject matter does not implicate the Two Dismissal Rule).

Two Dismissal Rule for Actions in State Court

The Two Dismissal Rule applies to actions filed in state court on the first occasion. However, if the second action is filed and dismissed in state court, it will not trigger the Two Dismissal Rule[17] unless the state has a similar rule.[18] Once an action is barred in federal court by the Two Dismissal Rule, it will also be barred in state court.

Statute of Limitations

An action dismissed without prejudice does not toll the statute of limitations.[19]

Rules and Statutes Requiring Court Approval of Dismissals

Rule 41 is expressly subject to the provisions of Rule 23(e) (requiring court approval for the dismissal of a class action)[20] and Rule 66 (governing cases in which a receiver has been appointed). Rule 41 also may not apply in other statutorily controlled areas, such as *qui tam* actions,[21] actions under the Fair Labor Standards Act,[22] and shareholders' derivative actions.[23] Rule 41 does apply to appeals of certain proceedings, such as an appeal of a decision by the Board of Veterans' Appeals.[24]

Removal

Rule 41 applies with equal force to cases removed from state court.[25]

Dismissal Following Rule 12 Motions

In general, a motion to dismiss pursuant to Rule 12(b) for failure to state a claim or for lack of jurisdiction or venue does not terminate the plaintiff's unilateral right to dismiss.[26] An exception may arise if the court has held extensive hearings on the motion,[27] or converted the motion to dismiss into a motion for summary judgment.[28]

Dismissal of Part of Action

Courts differ as to the proper procedural mechanism for voluntarily dismissing part of an action. Some courts allow voluntary dismissal of part of an action by notice pursuant to Rule 41.[29] Some courts require a motion to amend pursuant to Rule 15(a).[30] A third party plaintiff may voluntarily dismiss the third party complaint under Rule 41(a)(1).[31]

---

[17] *Rader v. Baltimore & O. R. Co.*, 108 F.2d 980 (C.C.A. 7th Cir. 1940).

[18] *Manning v. South Carolina Dept. of Highway and Public Transp.*, 914 F.2d 44 (4th Cir.1990).

[19] *Beck v. Caterpillar Inc.*, 50 F.3d 405 (7th Cir.1995).

[20] *Crawford v. F. Hoffman-La Roche Ltd.*, 267 F.3d 760, 764 (8th Cir. 2001).

[21] *See Youssef v. Tishman Const. Corp.*, 744 F.3d 821, 825–26 (2d Cir. 2014).

[22] *Socias v. Vornado Realty L.P.*, 297 F.R.D. 38, 39–41 (E.D.N.Y. 2014) (requiring a fairness hearing before allowing a Rule 41 dismissal).

[23] *Baker v. America's Mortg. Servicing, Inc.*, 58 F.3d 321 (7th Cir. 1995).

[24] *Graves v. Principi*, 294 F.3d 1350 (Fed. Cir. 2002).

[25] *Grivas v. Parmelee Transp. Co.*, 207 F.2d 334 (7th Cir. 1953).

[26] *Manze v. State Farm Ins. Co.*, 817 F.2d 1062, 1066 (3d Cir. 1987).

[27] *Harvey Aluminum, Inc. v. American Cyanamid Co.*, 203 F.2d 105 (2d Cir. 1953).

[28] *In re Bath and Kitchen Fixtures Antitrust Litigation*, 535 F.3d 161, 166 (3d Cir. 2008) (motion to dismiss including new factual material does not cut off the right to voluntary dismissal until it is actually converted into a motion for summary judgment).

[29] *See Bowers v. National Collegiate Athletic Ass'n*, 346 F.3d 402, 413 (3d Cir. 2003).

[30] *See Campbell v. Altec Industries, Inc.*, 605 F.3d 839 (11th Cir. 2010).

[31] *Century Mfg. Co., Inc. v. Central Transport Intern., Inc.*, 209 F.R.D. 647 (D. Mass. 2002).

Costs and Fees

Following a voluntary dismissal under Rule 41, the district court retains jurisdiction over the matter to award costs.[32] The defendant is not considered the prevailing party following a voluntary dismissal pursuant to Rule 41(a)(1) for purposes of statutes governing the award of attorney's fees to the prevailing party.[33]

Appeals

The first voluntary dismissal under Rule 41(a)(1) is normally not considered a final order and thus not appealable.[34] The second dismissal, however, is a final, appealable order.[35]

RULE 41(a)(2)—BY COURT ORDER; EFFECT

CORE CONCEPT

Except as provided in Rule 41(a)(1) above (dismissal by stipulation or before an answer or motion for summary judgment has been filed), dismissal of an action must be by court order.[36]

APPLICATIONS

Prejudice

A voluntary dismissal by order of court can be with or without prejudice.[37] A court order granting voluntary dismissal is presumed to be without prejudice unless it explicitly specifies otherwise.[38]

Discretion of Court

The decision whether to grant or deny the plaintiff's motion for voluntary dismissal is within the sound discretion of the court,[39] although some courts hold that the court has no discretion to deny a motion to dismiss *with prejudice* (reasoning that it is unfair to force an unwilling plaintiff to go to trial).[40] A court should grant a Rule 41(a)(2) motion for voluntary dismissal unless a defendant can show that it will suffer some plain legal prejudice as a result.[41] In general, courts are more likely to grant motions for voluntary dismissal at earlier stages of the litigation.[42]

Conditions

The court may include terms and conditions in its order granting voluntary dismissal in order to prevent prejudice to the defendant.[43] These conditions may be proposed by the

---

[32] *Sequa Corp. v. Cooper,* 245 F.3d 1036, 1037 (8th Cir. 2001).

[33] *See RFR Industries, Inc. v. Century Steps, Inc.,* 477 F.3d 1348, 1351–52 (Fed. Cir. 2007) (the defendant is not the prevailing party for purposes of 35 U.S.C. § 285).

[34] *Versa Products, Inc. v. Home Depot, USA, Inc.,* 387 F.3d 1325 (11th Cir. 2004); *but see Youssef v. Tishman Const. Corp.,* 744 F.3d 821, 824 (2d Cir. 2014) (plaintiff may appeal Rule 41(a)(1) dismissal if the court deems the dismissal with prejudice).

[35] *Muzikowski v. Paramount Pictures Corp.,* 322 F.3d 918, 923–24 (7th Cir. 2003).

[36] *Youssef v. Tishman Const. Corp.,* 744 F.3d 821, 823 (2d Cir. 2014).

[37] *See, e.g., Minnesota Mining And Mfg. Co. v. Barr Laboratories, Inc.,* 289 F.3d 775, 779 (Fed. Cir. 2002).

[38] *Wells Fargo Bank, N.A. v. Younan Properties, Inc.,* 737 F.3d 465, 468 (7th Cir. 2013).

[39] *Goodwin v. Reynolds,* 757 F.3d 1216 (11th Cir. 2014); *Donner v. Alcoa, Inc.,* 709 F.3d 694, 697 (8th Cir. 2013).

[40] *Smoot v. Fox,* 340 F.2d 301 (6th Cir. 1964).

[41] *WPP Luxembourg Gamma Three Sarl v. Spot Runner, Inc.,* 655 F.3d 1039, 1058, n.6 (9th Cir. 2011).

[42] *See Thatcher v. Hanover Ins. Grp., Inc.,* 659 F.3d 1212, 1214 (8th Cir. 2011).

[43] *Bridgeport Music, Inc. v. Universal-MCA Music Pub., Inc.,* 583 F.3d 948, 953 (6th Cir. 2009).

parties or *sua sponte* by the court.[44] Examples of such conditions include the payment of costs[45] and/or attorney's fees,[46] the production of specified documents,[47] making the dismissal with prejudice,[48] and an agreement not to assert specified claims in another action. If the plaintiff is unhappy with the conditions imposed by the court, the plaintiff may decline the dismissal.[49]

Defendant as Prevailing Party

For purposes of statutes that award costs or fees to the prevailing party, a defendant can be deemed the prevailing party following a dismissal under Rule 41(a)(2).[50]

Counterclaims

If the defendant has filed a counterclaim, then the plaintiff cannot dismiss the action against the defendant's objections unless the counterclaim can remain pending for adjudication.[51] The defendant may dismiss its counterclaim in the same manner that Rule 41 provides for dismissal of the plaintiff's claims.[52]

Dismissal of Part of Action

The plaintiff may dismiss some, but not all, of the defendants.[53] Courts differ as to the proper procedural mechanism for voluntarily dismissing part of an action.[54] Some courts allow voluntary dismissal by court order pursuant to Rule 41(a)(2).[55] Some courts require a motion to amend pursuant to Rule 15(a).[56]

Enforcement of Settlement Agreement

Normally, a federal court does not retain jurisdiction over an action to enforce the terms of a settlement and stipulated dismissal.[57] In order to vest the district court with such jurisdiction, parties often include in their motion for voluntary dismissal or in their attached proposed order a provision that the court will continue to have jurisdiction to enforce the parties' settlement agreement.

---

[44] *Brown v. Baeke,* 413 F.3d 1121, 1123 (10th Cir. 2005) (some conditions proposed by the plaintiff, and others added by the court).

[45] *Chavez v. Illinois State Police,* 251 F.3d 612 (7th Cir.2001).

[46] *Steinert v. Winn Group, Inc.,* 440 F.3d 1214, 1222 (10th Cir. 2006) (when dismissal is *without* prejudice, attorney's fees should only be awarded in extreme circumstances).

[47] *In re Vitamins Antitrust Litigation,* 198 F.R.D. 296 (D.D.C. 2000) (dismissal conditioned on the plaintiff responding to outstanding document requests and interrogatories).

[48] *Michigan Surgery Inv., LLC v. Arman,* 627 F.3d 572, 575 (6th Cir. 2010) (must give the plaintiff notice and an opportunity to withdraw the motion before making dismissal with prejudice).

[49] *Michigan Surgery Inv., LLC v. Arman,* 627 F.3d 572, 575 (6th Cir. 2010).

[50] *Riviera Distributors, Inc. v. Jones,* 517 F.3d 926, 928 (7th Cir. 2008).

[51] *See Walter Kidde Portable Equipment, Inc. v. Universal Sec. Instruments, Inc.,* 479 F.3d 1330, 1336 (Fed. Cir. 2007).

[52] *eCash Technologies, Inc. v. Guagliardo,* 127 F.Supp.2d 1069, 1081–82 (C.D. Cal. 2000), aff'd, 35 Fed. Appx. 498 (9th Cir. 2002).

[53] *Protocomm Corp. v. Novell, Inc.,* 171 F.Supp.2d 459, 471 (E.D. Pa. 2001) (dismissal of some defendants is permissible even in the presence of crossclaims).

[54] *See Jet, Inc. v. Sewage Aeration Systems,* 223 F.3d 1360, 1364 (Fed. Cir. 2000) (Rule 41(a)(2) and Rule 15(a) are functionally interchangeable).

[55] *See Transwitch Corp. v. Galazar Networks, Inc.,* 377 F.Supp.2d 284 (D. Mass. 2005) (allowing motion for voluntary dismissal of all claims and substitution of new claims under Rule 41).

[56] *See Campbell v. Altec Industries, Inc.,* 635 F.3d 1212 (11th Cir. 2010).

[57] *Solv-Ex Corp. v. Quillen,* 186 F.R.D. 313, 315 (S.D. N.Y. 1999).

Circumvention of Rules or Prior Rulings

A court may not allow dismissal without prejudice to circumvent limitations in the Rules, to avoid the effects of prior rulings, or to obtain a more advantageous forum.[58] So, for example, a party may not use Rule 41(a)(2) to cure an untimely jury demand (by dismissal, then refiling a new complaint with a jury demand).[59]

Appeal

The plaintiff normally cannot appeal the granting or denial of a motion for voluntary dismissal.[60] However, mandamus will lie if the motion was to dismiss with prejudice.[61] The plaintiff may be able to appeal the granting of its own motion to dismiss if the court imposes conditions on the dismissal that prejudice the plaintiff and to which the plaintiff has not acquiesced [62] or if the purpose of the dismissal was to expedite appeal of rulings that effectively ended the case.[63] The defendant may appeal an order granting a motion for voluntary dismissal.[64]

RULE 41(b)—INVOLUNTARY DISMISSAL; EFFECT

CORE CONCEPT

Rule 41(b) governs two types of involuntary dismissals: dismissal for failure to prosecute; and dismissal for failure to comply with other Rules or with a court order.

APPLICATIONS

Disfavored

Involuntary dismissal is within the discretion of the court, but is disfavored and is granted sparingly.[65]

Failure to Prosecute

The court may dismiss for failure to prosecute *sua sponte* or upon motion.[66] Local Rules frequently specify the conditions for dismissal for failure to prosecute (for example, lack of activity for a period of one year).[67]

Failure to Comply with Order

The court may dismiss an action based on the plaintiff's failure to comply with a court order *sua sponte* or upon motion.[68]

Failure to Comply with Rules

The court may dismiss an action for failure to comply with the Rules. For example, the plaintiff may risk involuntary dismissal by persistently refusing to file a pretrial statement.

---

[58] *Donner v. Alcoa, Inc.*, 709 F.3d 694, 697 (8th Cir. 2013).

[59] *Russ v. Standard Ins. Co.*, 120 F.3d 988, 990 (9th Cir. 1997).

[60] *Ali v. Federal Ins. Co.*, 719 F.3d 83 (2d Cir. 2013).

[61] *In re Intern. Business Machines Corp.*, 687 F.2d 591 (2d Cir. 1982).

[62] *See Versa Products, Inc. v. Home Depot, USA, Inc.*, 387 F.3d 1325 (11th Cir. 2004).

[63] *Ali v. Federal Ins. Co.*, 719 F.3d 83 (2d Cir. 2013).

[64] *Pontenberg v. Boston Scientific Corp.*, 252 F.3d 1253 (11th Cir.2001) (order granting dismissal is reviewed under the abuse of discretion standard).

[65] *Salata v. Weyerhaeuser Co.*, 757 F.3d 695 (7th Cir. 2014).

[66] *Salata v. Weyerhaeuser Co.*, 757 F.3d 695 (7th Cir. 2014) (case dismissed when plaintiff failed to appear for court dates and respond to discovery).

[67] *See Wagner v. Ashcroft*, 214 F.R.D. 78 (N.D.N.Y. 2003).

[68] *Slack v. McDaniel*, 529 U.S. 473, 120 S.Ct. 1595, 146 L.Ed.2d 542 (2000).

In contrast, if a party fails to comply with the discovery rules, sanctions are appropriate under the discovery rules, not Rule 41.[69] To determine whether Rule 41 dismissal is an appropriate sanction for violation of a particular Rule, also review the author commentary and case law discussing that Rule.

With Prejudice

Involuntary dismissals are presumed to be with prejudice unless the court specifies otherwise.[70]

Appeal/Relief from Order

The plaintiff may appeal an involuntary dismissal as a final order.[71] The plaintiff may also seek relief from the order under Rule 60.[72]

RULE 41(c)—DISMISSING A COUNTERCLAIM, CROSSCLAIM, OR THIRD-PARTY CLAIM

CORE CONCEPT

The provisions of Rule 41 apply to counterclaims, crossclaims, and third-party claims with equal force.[73]

RULE 41(d)—COSTS OF A PREVIOUSLY DISMISSED ACTION

CORE CONCEPT

If a plaintiff who has already *voluntarily* dismissed an action commences another action on the same claim, the court, in its discretion, can stay the second action until the plaintiff[74] pays such costs of the first action as the court deems appropriate.[75] The courts are split as to whether an award of costs under Rule 41(d) may include attorney's fees.[76]

ADDITIONAL RESEARCH REFERENCES

Wright & Miller, *Federal Practice and Procedure* §§ 2361 to 2376

C.J.S., Federal Civil Procedure §§ 486, 775 to 819 et seq., 839 to 869 et seq.

West's Key Number Digest, Federal Civil Procedure ⊶1691 to 1715, 1721 to 1729, 1741, 1758 to 1765, 1821 to 1842

---

[69] *Reyes v. Dart*, 801 F.3d 879, 881 (7th Cir. 2015).

[70] *Rollins v. Wackenhut Services, Inc.*, 703 F.3d 122, 131 (D.C. Cir. 2012).

[71] *Lal v. California*, 610 F.3d 518, 523 (9th Cir. 2010).

[72] *Okafor v. Statebridge Company LLC*, 311 F.R.D. 24, 25 (D. Mass. 2015).

[73] *Orca Yachts, L.L.C. v. Mollicam, Inc.*, 287 F.3d 316, 319 (4th Cir. 2002).

[74] *Duffy v. Ford Motor Co.*, 218 F.3d 623, 636 (6th Cir. 2000) (Rule 41(d) discusses the imposition of costs upon the plaintiffs, not counsel).

[75] *Pontenberg v. Boston Scientific Corp.*, 252 F.3d 1253 (11th Cir. 2001).

[76] *See Rogers v. Wal-Mart Stores, Inc.*, 230 F.3d 868, 875 (6th Cir. 2000) (noting the split and determining that fees are not available in the 6th Circuit).

RULE 42

CONSOLIDATION; SEPARATE TRIALS

(a) Consolidation. If actions before the court involve a common question of law or fact, the court may:

    (1) join for hearing or trial any or all matters at issue in the actions;

    (2) consolidate the actions; or

    (3) issue any other orders to avoid unnecessary cost or delay.

(b) Separate Trials. For convenience, to avoid prejudice, or to expedite and economize, the court may order a separate trial of one or more separate issues, claims, crossclaims, counterclaims, or third-party claims. When ordering a separate trial, the court must preserve any federal right to a jury trial.

[Amended effective July 1, 1966; April 30, 2007, effective December 1, 2007.]

AUTHORS' COMMENTARY ON RULE 42

PURPOSE AND SCOPE

Rule 42 allows the court to control the manner in which the cases on its docket are tried; the court may consolidate several actions into a single proceeding or may conduct separate trials of various issues within a single action.

RULE 42(a)—CONSOLIDATION

CORE CONCEPT

When multiple actions pending before one court[1] share common issues of law or fact, the court can consolidate the actions, either completely or for limited proceedings or stages.

APPLICATIONS

Court's Discretion

In deciding whether to consolidate actions, the court should balance the savings to the judicial system against the possible inconvenience, delay, or prejudice to the parties.[2] The court has broad discretion in this balancing process,[3] and does not need the parties' consent.[4] The party seeking consolidation bears the burden of persuading the court that consolidation is appropriate.[5]

---

   [1] *Mourik Intern. B.V. v. Reactor Services Intern., Inc.,* 182 F.Supp.2d 599, 602 (S.D. Tex. 2002) (the cases must be properly pending before the court to be consolidated; an improperly removed case could not be consolidated).

   [2] *Arnold v. Eastern Air Lines, Inc.,* 681 F.2d 186, 193 (4th Cir. 1982).

   [3] *Blue Cross Blue Shield of Massachusetts, Inc. v. BCS Ins. Co.,* 671 F.3d 635, 640 (7th Cir. 2011).

   [4] *Connecticut General Life Ins. Co. v. Sun Life Assur. Co. of Canada,* 210 F.3d 771 (7th Cir. 2000).

   [5] *Anderson Living Trust v. WPX Energy Production, LLC,* 297 F.R.D. 622, 630 (D.N.M. 2014).

Common Issues Necessary

Although the court has broad discretion, it may not consolidate actions that do not share common issues of law or fact.[6] It may consolidate actions that do not have the same parties, however.[7]

Limited Consolidation

The court may consolidate actions for all purposes, for pretrial proceedings only, or for specified hearings or issues.[8]

Actions in Different Districts

Actions in different districts may not be consolidated. However, if actions are pending in different districts that ought to be consolidated, the actions may be transferred to a single district, then consolidated, as provided in the Multidistrict Litigation, or MDL, procedures.[9]

Actions Remain Separate

In general, consolidated actions retain their separate identity.[10] Thus, the pleadings will remain separate and the court will enter separate judgments in each action.[11] However, the court can merge the cases or order that briefs and rulings apply to all consolidated cases.[12]

Conflicts of Interest

Consolidation may be improper if it aligns parties who have conflicting interests.[13]

Arbitration

Many courts do not permit consolidation of arbitrations unless there is an express provision in the arbitration agreements providing for consolidation.[14]

Procedures

Consolidation is achieved by motion of any party or by the court *sua sponte*.[15] Local rules may determine to which judge a motion to consolidate should be presented if the matters are pending before different judges.[16] In appropriate circumstances, the court may appoint one counsel as lead or liaison counsel.[17]

---

[6] *Malcolm v. National Gypsum Co.*, 995 F.2d 346 (2d Cir.1993).

[7] *National Ass'n of Mortg. Brokers v. Board of Governors of Federal Reserve System*, 773 F.Supp.2d 151 (D.D.C. 2011).

[8] *Cleveland v. City of Montgomery*, 300 F.R.D. 578 (M.D. Ala. 2014) (request to participate in an oral argument).

[9] *In re Korean Air Lines Co., Ltd.*, 642 F.3d 685, 699–700 (9th Cir. 2011).

[10] *Horizon Asset Management Inc. v. H & R Block, Inc.*, 580 F.3d 755, 769 (8th Cir. 2009).

[11] *Horizon Asset Management Inc. v. H & R Block, Inc.*, 580 F.3d 755, 769 (8th Cir. 2009) (plaintiffs are entitled to a decision on the merits of their claims even though their case has been consolidated).

[12] *In re Air Crash at Lexington, KY, AUGUST 27, 2006*, 251 F.R.D. 258, 260–61 (E.D. Ky. 2008).

[13] *Dupont v. Southern Pac. Co.*, 366 F.2d 193 (5th Cir. 1966); *Atkinson v. Roth*, 297 F.2d 570 (3d Cir.1961).

[14] *Champ v. Siegel Trading Co., Inc.*, 55 F.3d 269, 274 (7th Cir. 1995); *but see Office & Professional Employees Intern. Union, AFL-CIO v. Sea-Land Service, Inc.*, 210 F.3d 117, 123 (2d Cir. 2000) (developing common law of labor contracts empowered district court to consolidate two arbitration proceedings without consideration of whether such consolidation was authorized by Fed.R.Civ.P. 42(a)).

[15] *National Ass'n of Mortg. Brokers v. Board of Governors of Federal Reserve System*, 773 F.Supp.2d 151 (D.D.C. 2011).

[16] *Stewart v. O'Neill*, 225 F.Supp.2d 16, 21 (D.D.C. 2002) (local rule providing that the motion to consolidate should be presented in the matter first filed).

[17] *See, e.g., Outten v. Wilmington Trust Corp.*, 281 F.R.D. 193 (D. Del. 2012).

Appeals

An order granting or denying a motion for consolidation is not appealable as a final judgment,[18] although mandamus may be available under extreme circumstances.[19]

RULE 42(b)—SEPARATE TRIALS

CORE CONCEPT

The court may conduct separate trials of any claim or issue.[20]

APPLICATIONS

Court's Discretion

In deciding whether to order separate trials, the court should balance the savings to the judicial system against the possible inconvenience, delay, or prejudice to the parties.[21] The court has broad discretion in this balancing process.[22]

Burden of Proof

The burden is on the moving party to demonstrate that bifurcation is justified even in cases where bifurcation is not uncommon.[23]

Single Action

A separation under Rule 42 separates aspects of the action for trial, but the aspects remain part of a single action, and result in a single judgment.[24] This contrasts with claims that are severed pursuant to Rule 21.[25]

Liability and Damages

The most common instance of separate trials is when the court first conducts a trial as to liability, then as to damages if necessary.[26]

Separate Trials for Each Defendant

The court may order separate trials for each defendant, particularly if one is in bankruptcy, as long as the defendants are not indispensable parties.[27]

Procedure

The court may order separate trials *sua sponte* or by motion of any party.[28]

---

[18] *National Ass'n for Advancement of Colored People of Louisiana v. Michot,* 480 F.2d 547, 548 (5th Cir. 1973).

[19] *In re Repetitive Stress Injury Litigation,* 11 F.3d 368 (2d Cir.1993).

[20] *Bridgeport Music, Inc. v. Justin Combs Pub.,* 507 F.3d 470, 481 (6th Cir. 2007).

[21] *Athridge v. Aetna Cas. and Sur. Co.,* 604 F.3d 625 (D.C. Cir. 2010).

[22] *U.S. ex rel. Bahrani v. ConAgra, Inc.,* 624 F.3d 1275, 1283 (10th Cir. 2010).

[23] *See Doe No. 1 v. Knights of Columbus,* 930 F.Supp.2d 337 (D. Conn. 2013).

[24] *White v. ABCO Engineering Corp.,* 199 F.3d 140, 145 (3d Cir. 1999).

[25] *Rice v. Sunrise Express, Inc.,* 209 F.3d 1008, 1014–16 (7th Cir. 2000).

[26] *See Gafford v. General Elec. Co.,* 997 F.2d 150 (6th Cir. 1993).

[27] *Hecht v. City of New York,* 217 F.R.D. 148, 150 (S.D.N.Y. 2003).

[28] *Coffeyville Resources Refining & Marketing, LLC v. Illinois Union Ins. Co.,* 979 F.Supp.2d 1199, 1206 (D. Kan. 2013).

Jury Trials

The procedures for separate trials do not affect the parties' rights to a jury trial.[29] Separate trials may be conducted before one jury or different juries.[30] If there are jury and non-jury claims present, the jury claims may have to be tried first, so that the court does not make factual findings that should properly have been made by the jury.[31]

Appeals

An order granting or denying a motion for bifurcation is not appealable as a final judgment, although mandamus may be available under extreme circumstances.[32]

ADDITIONAL RESEARCH REFERENCES

Wright & Miller, *Federal Practice and Procedure* §§ 2381 to 2392

C.J.S., Federal Civil Procedure §§ 611, 916 to 918

West's Key Number Digest, Federal Civil Procedure ⊶8, 1953 to 1965

---

[29] *Shum v. Intel Corp.,* 499 F.3d 1272, 1276 (Fed. Cir. 2007) (trial court must ensure that the litigant's constitutional right to a jury is preserved).

[30] *See Reid v. General Motors Corp.,* 240 F.R.D. 260, 263 (E.D. Tex. 2007) (separate juries should not be allowed to pass on overlapping issues of fact because of the risk of inconsistent verdicts).

[31] *See Dairy Queen, Inc. v. Wood,* 369 U.S. 469, 479, 82 S.Ct. 894, 8 L.Ed.2d 44 (1962); *Beacon Theatres, Inc. v. Westover,* 359 U.S. 500, 79 S.Ct. 948, 3 L.Ed.2d 988 (1959).

[32] *See In re Repetitive Stress Injury Litigation,* 11 F.3d 368 (2d Cir. 1993).

RULE 43

TAKING TESTIMONY

(a) In Open Court. At trial, the witnesses' testimony must be taken in open court unless a federal statute, the Federal Rules of Evidence, these rules, or other rules adopted by the Supreme Court provide otherwise. For good cause in compelling circumstances and with appropriate safeguards, the court may permit testimony in open court by contemporaneous transmission from a different location.

(b) Affirmation Instead of an Oath. When these rules require an oath, a solemn affirmation suffices.

(c) Evidence on a Motion. When a motion relies on facts outside the record, the court may hear the matter on affidavits or may hear it wholly or partly on oral testimony or on depositions.

(d) Interpreter. The court may appoint an interpreter of its choosing; fix reasonable compensation to be paid from funds provided by law or by one or more parties; and tax the compensation as costs.

[Amended effective July 1, 1966; July 1, 1975; August 1, 1987, December 1, 1996; April 30, 2007, effective December 1, 2007.]

AUTHORS' COMMENTARY ON RULE 43

PURPOSE AND SCOPE

Rule 43, formerly entitled "Evidence" was largely supplanted by the Federal Rules of Evidence. The remaining provisions establish a preference for live testimony in open court, allow witnesses to take an affirmation or an oath, and address the manner in which evidence is presented in support of motions, and the use of interpreters.

RULE 43(a)—IN OPEN COURT

CORE CONCEPT

There is a preference in federal court for testimony taken in open court. All testimony shall be in that form unless otherwise authorized by the Federal Rules of Evidence,[1] federal statute, or stipulation by the parties.[2]

---

[1]   *Kuntz v. Sea Eagle Diving Adventures Corp.*, 199 F.R.D. 665, 667 (D. Haw. 2001) (Federal Rules of Evidence authorize the submission of testimony by affidavit).

[2]   *Charlton Memorial Hosp. v. Sullivan*, 816 F.Supp. 50 (D. Mass. 1993).

APPLICATIONS

Live Testimony

The Rules place a strong emphasis on live testimony taken in open court.[3] Rule 43(a) reflects the permissible use of other forms of communication, such as writing or sign language, if the witness cannot speak.[4]

Remote Testimony

Rule 43(a) allows the transmitting of testimony from a different location.[5] However, the Rules continue to emphasize live testimony in court, and transmitted testimony is permitted only for good cause shown in compelling circumstances.[6] In cases where remote testimony is to be used, the court must employ appropriate safeguards to protect the procedure and the parties' interests.[7] Transmitted testimony might be allowed when unexpected circumstances, such as an accident or illness, render a witness unable to appear in court.[8]

RULE 43(b)—AFFIRMATION INSTEAD OF AN OATH

CORE CONCEPT

A party who, for religious reasons or otherwise, chooses not to take an oath, may make a "solemn affirmation" instead.[9]

RULE 43(c)—EVIDENCE ON A MOTION

CORE CONCEPT

A party may submit affidavits and documentary evidence in support of or in opposition to a motion; an evidentiary hearing is not required.[10] The court, in its discretion, may order oral evidence taken[11] or may request deposition transcripts when a motion is based on facts not of record.[12] The court may also consider a motion solely on the parties' written submissions.[13]

RULE 43(d)—INTERPRETER

CORE CONCEPT

The court may, in its discretion, appoint an interpreter,[14] who then should take an oath or affirmation that the translation will be accurate. If an interpreter is appointed, the court may

---

[3]   *Palmer v. Valdez,* 560 F.3d 965, 969, n.4 (9th Cir. 2009).

[4]   The advisory committee note to the 1996 Amendment to Rule 43.

[5]   *Parkhurst v. Belt,* 567 F.3d 995 (8th Cir. 2009) (testimony by closed circuit television allowed).

[6]   *See Eller v. Trans Union, LLC,* 739 F.3d 467, 478 (10th Cir. 2013) (inconvenience is not good cause); *El-Hadad v. United Arab Emirates,* 496 F.3d 658, 668–69 (D.C. Cir. 2007) (good cause demonstrated when witness could not get a visa to enter the United States).

[7]   *Parkhurst v. Belt,* 567 F.3d 995 (8th Cir. 2009); *F.T.C. v. Swedish Match North America, Inc.,* 197 F.R.D. 1 (D.D.C. 2000) (in assessing the safeguards of remote testimony, the courts focus on whether the testimony was made in open court, under oath, and whether the opportunity for cross examination was available).

[8]   The advisory committee note to the 1996 Amendment to Rule 43.

[9]   *Doe v. Phillips,* 81 F.3d 1204 (2d Cir. 1996).

[10]   *Archdiocese of Milwaukee v. Doe,* 743 F.3d 1101, 1109 (7th Cir. 2014).

[11]   *Archdiocese of Milwaukee v. Doe,* 743 F.3d 1101, 1109 (7th Cir. 2014) (oral testimony is not favored in summary judgment motions because of the temptation to make credibility determinations).

[12]   *Smith v. Oakland County Circuit Court,* 344 F.Supp.2d 1030, 1051 (E.D. Mich. 2004).

[13]   *Sunseri v. Macro Cellular Partners,* 412 F.3d 1247, 1248 (11th Cir. 2005).

[14]   *Pedraza v. Phoenix,* 1994 WL 177285 (S.D.N.Y. 1994) (no right to a court-ordered translation of pre-trial motions).

determine the interpreter's fees. The court may order that one party pay the fees, and may award the fees as costs after the conclusion of the trial.

ADDITIONAL RESEARCH REFERENCES

Wright & Miller, *Federal Practice and Procedure* §§ 2401 to 2417

C.J.S., Courts § 1–110; Federal Civil Procedure §§ 368, 373, 935; Witnesses §§ 320 to 326

West's Key Number Digest, Courts ⊷56; Federal Civil Procedure ⊷2011; West's Key Number Digest, Witnesses ⊷227, 228, 230

RULE 44

PROVING AN OFFICIAL RECORD

(a) Means of Proving.

(1) *Domestic Record.* Each of the following evidences an official record—or an entry in it—that is otherwise admissible and is kept within the United States, any state, district, or commonwealth, or any territory subject to the administrative or judicial jurisdiction of the United States:

(A) an official publication of the record; or

(B) a copy attested by the officer with legal custody of the record—or by the officer's deputy—and accompanied by a certificate that the officer has custody. The certificate must be made under seal:

(i) by a judge of a court of record in the district or political subdivision where the record is kept; or

(ii) by any public officer with a seal of office and with official duties in the district or political subdivision where the record is kept.

(2) *Foreign Record.*

(A) *In General.* Each of the following evidences a foreign official record—or an entry in it—that is otherwise admissible:

(i) an official publication of the record; or

(ii) the record—or a copy—that is attested by an authorized person and is accompanied either by a final certification of genuineness or by a certification under a treaty or convention to which the United States and the country where the record is located are parties.

(B) *Final Certification of Genuineness.* A final certification must certify the genuineness of the signature and official position of the attester or of any foreign official whose certificate of genuineness relates to the attestation or is in a chain of certificates of genuineness relating to the attestation. A final certification may be made by a secretary of a United States embassy or legation; by a consul general, vice consul, or consular agent of the United States; or by a diplomatic or consular official of the foreign country assigned or accredited to the United States.

(C) *Other Means of Proof.* If all parties have had a reasonable opportunity to investigate a foreign record's authenticity and accuracy, the court may, for good cause, either:

    (i) admit an attested copy without final certification; or

    (ii) permit the record to be evidenced by an attested summary with or without a final certification.

(b) Lack of a Record. A written statement that a diligent search of designated records revealed no record or entry of a specified tenor is admissible as evidence that the records contain no such record or entry. For domestic records, the statement must be authenticated under Rule 44(a)(1). For foreign records, the statement must comply with (a)(2)(C)(ii).

(c) Other Proof. A party may prove an official record—or an entry or lack of an entry in it—by any other method authorized by law.

[Amended effective July 1, 1966; August 1, 1987; December 1, 1991; April 30, 2007, effective December 1, 2007.]

AUTHORS' COMMENTARY ON RULE 44

PURPOSE AND SCOPE

Rule 44 describes methods for authenticating official records of the United States or foreign governments. It also provides methods to demonstrate the absence of a particular official document or record.

RULE 44(a)(1)—MEANS OF PROVING; DOMESTIC RECORD

CORE CONCEPT

An official record kept within the United States is authenticated if it is an official publication or if it is a copy of an official record which is attested to by the legal custodian and accompanied by a certificate made by a judge or public officer with a seal of office.

APPLICATIONS

Official Record

"Official record" is not a defined term, but includes such documents as weather bureau records, records of conviction, tax returns, marriage and birth certificates, and selective service files. "Official" does not mean "public"; the public need not have access to "official records."

No Summaries

The Rule applies only to the record itself, not to summaries of the contents of the record.

Authentication Only

Rule 44 only *authenticates* records. It does not render the records admissible or immune from other objections, such as relevance or hearsay (but see the exception to the hearsay rule for official records).[1]

Official Publication

When a document has been printed by government authority, its authenticity is established.

---

[1] *Moreno v. Macaluso,* 844 F.Supp. 736 (M.D. Fla. 1994).

Documents Kept in the United States

Rule 44 applies to all official federal, state, or local records physically maintained within the United States or within territories subject to United States jurisdiction, not just to United States official records. Thus, it includes foreign government records maintained in the United States.

Attested Copy

A copy of an official record may be attested to by the officer having legal custody of the record or by the officer's deputy.[2]

Certificate

The attested copy must be accompanied by a certificate that the attesting individual has custody of the record.[3] The certificate must be made by a judge in the district or political subdivision in which the document is kept, or by a public official with duties in the district or political subdivision in which the document is kept, provided that the official has a seal of office and authenticates the certificate with that seal.[4]

RULE 44(a)(2)—MEANS OF PROVING; FOREIGN RECORD

CORE CONCEPT

A foreign official record may be authenticated in essentially the same manner as a domestic record (described immediately above), with some minor variations.

APPLICATIONS

Official Publication

As with a domestic official record, official publications of foreign official records are self-authenticating.[5]

Attested Copy with Certificate

A foreign official record may be attested to by any person authorized by the laws of that country to attest records if the signature is certified by a secretary of embassy or legation, consul general, consul, vice consul or consular agent of the United States, or a diplomatic or consular official of the foreign country assigned or accredited to the United States.[6] The certification will not be necessary if the United States and the foreign country are signatories to a treaty providing for proof of foreign records without a certification and the foreign record is submitted in accordance with the treaty.[7] In particular, see the Hague Public Documents Convention,[8] and the Convention Abolishing the Requirement of Legalization for Foreign Public Documents.[9]

---

[2] *United States v. Estrada-Eliverio*, 583 F.3d 669, 672 (9th Cir. 2009).

[3] *United States v. Estrada-Eliverio*, 583 F.3d 669, 672 (9th Cir. 2009).

[4] *Espinoza v. I.N.S.*, 45 F.3d 308 (9th Cir. 1995).

[5] *Construction Drilling, Inc. v. Chusid*, 63 F.Supp.2d 509 (D.N.J. 1999).

[6] *Starski v. Kirzhnev*, 682 F.3d 51, 53 (1st Cir. 2012).

[7] *Corovic v. Mukasey*, 519 F.3d 90, 93 n.2 (2d Cir. 2008) (verification by apostille); *United States v. Pintado-Isiordia*, 448 F.3d 1155, 1157 (9th Cir. 2006) (Mexican birth certificate self-authenticating).

[8] Reprinted in *Martindale Hubbell*, International Law Digests. *See also Jiang v. Gonzales*, 474 F.3d 25, 29 n.4 (1st Cir. 2007).

[9] The Convention Abolishing the Requirement of Legalization for Foreign Public Documents may be found on WESTLAW.

Attested Copy Without Certificate

The court has discretion to admit an attested copy of a foreign official record without a certificate if all parties have had a reasonable opportunity to investigate the authenticity and accuracy of the record, or for good cause.[10]

RULE 44(b)—LACK OF A RECORD

CORE CONCEPT

One may prove the absence of a particular record with a written statement that after diligent search, no record or entry of the specified nature exists. The statement must be authenticated in the same manner as for an official record.

RULE 44(c)—OTHER PROOF

CORE CONCEPT

The methods in Rule 44 are not exclusive.[11] Quite often, an official will testify as to the authenticity of an official record. Similarly, certain documents are self-authenticating under Rules 901 and 902 of the Federal Rules of Evidence.[12] Additionally Rule 902 allows the court to relax the Rule 44 authentication requirements if the party so requesting shows that it was unable to satisfy the Rule's requirements for authentication despite reasonable efforts.[13]

ADDITIONAL RESEARCH REFERENCES

Wright & Miller, *Federal Practice and Procedure* §§ 2431 to 2437

C.J.S., Evidence §§ 634 et seq.

West's Key Number Digest, Evidence ⊶366

---

[10] *Vatyan v. Mukasey,* 508 F.3d 1179, 1184 (9th Cir. 2007) (exception is only when it is shown that the party is unable to satisfy the basic requirements despite reasonable efforts).

[11] *United States v. Lopez,* 747 F.3d 1141, 1150, n.5 (9th Cir. 2014) (record authenticated under FRE 901).

[12] *See United States v. Lopez,* 747 F.3d 1141, 1150, n.5 (9th Cir. 2014).

[13] *Starski v. Kirzhnev,* 682 F.3d 51, 54 (1st Cir. 2012).

RULE 44.1

DETERMINING FOREIGN LAW

A party who intends to raise an issue about a foreign country's law must give notice by a pleading or other writing. In determining foreign law, the court may consider any relevant material or source, including testimony, whether or not submitted by a party or admissible under the Federal Rules of Evidence. The court's determination must be treated as a ruling on a question of law.

[Added effective July 1, 1966; amended effective July 1, 1975; August 1, 1987; April 30, 2007, effective December 1, 2007.]

AUTHORS' COMMENTARY ON RULE 44.1

PURPOSE AND SCOPE

Rule 44.1 contains the provisions for raising and determining issues concerning the law of a foreign country. A party must give notice of its intent to raise an issue of foreign law. Thereafter, the judge will determine the applicable law of the foreign country.

APPLICATIONS

Notice of Foreign Law Issue

A party must give written notice to the court and all other parties of its intent to raise an issue concerning foreign law.[1] The notice should specify the issues or claims purportedly governed by foreign law, but need not state the specific provisions of the foreign law. Failure to provide the required notice of intent to raise an issue concerning foreign law can result in a waiver of the right to raise the issue.[2]

Form of Notice

The notice may be included in a pleading or may be a separate document.[3]

Timing for Notice

Rule 44.1 does not set a specific time for filing the notice. If the notice is a separate document, it should be served as soon as possible to give a reasonable opportunity to all parties to prepare.[4] If not already raised, issues of foreign law are sometimes raised at the pretrial conference.[5]

Party Giving Notice

Notice is normally given by the party whose claim or defense is based on foreign law, but may be raised by any party. If one party has given notice, other parties can rely on that notice and do not need to provide their own notices.[6] If parties believe that a different foreign law applies from the law raised by another party, they should issue separate notices.

---

[1] *In re Griffin Trading Co.*, 683 F.3d 819, 822 (7th Cir. 2012) (notice only need be reasonable to avoid unfair surprise).

[2] *In re Magnetic Audiotape Antitrust Litigation*, 334 F.3d 204 (2d Cir.2003).

[3] *In re Griffin Trading Co.*, 683 F.3d 819, 822 (7th Cir. 2012) (notice in the complaint is sufficient).

[4] *See APL Co. Pte. Ltd. v. UK Aerosols Ltd.*, 582 F.3d 947, 955 (9th Cir. 2009).

[5] *Mutual Service Ins. Co. v. Frit Industries, Inc.*, 358 F.3d 1312, 1321 (11th Cir. 2004) (notice at pretrial conference held reasonable); *but see Whirlpool Financial Corp. v. Sevaux*, 96 F.3d 216, 221 (7th Cir. 1996) (choice-of-law issue is waived if party brings it up after summary judgment is rendered).

[6] *In re Griffin Trading Co.*, 683 F.3d 819, 823 (7th Cir. 2012).

Court Determines Foreign Law

The determination of foreign law is a matter of law, not a matter of fact, and is therefore made by the court.[7]

Materials Used by the Court

The court may consider any relevant material or source to determine foreign law,[8] regardless of whether it is admissible.[9] Common methods of proving foreign law are through expert testimony,[10] affidavits from lawyers practicing in the foreign country,[11] and treatises.[12] The court may also do its own research[13] or seek the aid of an expert witness to help in the interpretation of foreign law,[14] but is under no obligation to do so.[15]

Burden of Proof

The party seeking application of foreign law has the burden of proving the applicability and content of the foreign law.[16] In the absence of proof of foreign law, the court may presume that the foreign law would be the same as local law.[17]

Summary Judgment

As an issue of law, a determination of foreign law is appropriate for summary judgment.[18]

Choice of Law

In diversity cases, the state conflict of law rules will determine which jurisdiction's laws apply. Rule 44.1 is implicated only after the court has determined that a foreign country's laws apply.

Appellate Review

A ruling as to foreign law is interlocutory, and cannot be immediately appealed.

ADDITIONAL RESEARCH REFERENCES

Wright & Miller, *Federal Practice and Procedure* §§ 2441 to 2447

C.J.S., Evidence §§ 12 to 26

West's Key Number Digest, Action ⊸ 17

---

[7]   *Iracheta v. Holder*, 730 F.3d 419, 423 (5th Cir. 2013).

[8]   *McGee v. Arkel Intern.*, LLC, 671 F.3d 539, 546 (5th Cir. 2012).

[9]   *Tobar v. United States,* 731 F.3d 938, 942 (9th Cir. 2013).

[10]   *See Tobar v. United States,* 731 F.3d 938, 942 (9th Cir. 2013) (allowing expert affidavits).

[11]   *EduMoz, LLC v. Republic of Mozambique,* 968 F.Supp.2d 1041, 1053–54 (C.D. Cal. 2013).

[12]   *See Access Telecom, Inc. v. MCI Telecommunications Corp.,* 197 F.3d 694, 713 (5th Cir. 1999).

[13]   *McGee v. Arkel Intern.*, LLC, 671 F.3d 539, 546 (5th Cir. 2012).

[14]   *In re Agent Orange Product Liability Litigation,* 373 F.Supp.2d 7, 18 (E.D.N.Y. 2005), aff'd, 517 F.3d 104 (2d Cir. 2008) (court has broad discretion to rely on expert testimony to interpret foreign law).

[15]   *Bodum USA, Inc. v. La Cafetiere, Inc.,* 621 F.3d 624, 628 (7th Cir. 2010).

[16]   *Bel–Ray Co., Inc. v. Chemrite Ltd.,* 181 F.3d 435, 440 (3d Cir.1999).

[17]   *Ferrostaal, Inc. v. M/V Sea Phoenix,* 447 F.3d 212, 216 (3d Cir. 2006).

[18]   *McKesson HBOC, Inc. v. Islamic Republic of Iran,* 271 F.3d 1101, 1108 (D.C. Cir. 2001).

RULE 45

SUBPOENA

(a) In General.

(1) *Form and Contents.*

    (A) *Requirements—In General.* Every subpoena must:

        (i) state the court from which it issued;

        (ii) state the title of the action and its civil-action number;

        (iii) command each person to whom it is directed to do the following at a specified time and place: attend and testify; produce designated documents, electronically stored information, or tangible things in that person's possession, custody, or control; or permit the inspection of premises; and

        (iv) set out the text of Rule 45(d) and (e).

    (B) *Command to Attend a Deposition—Notice of the Recording Method.* A subpoena commanding attendance at a deposition must state the method for recording the testimony.

    (C) *Combining or Separating a Command to Produce or to Permit Inspection; Specifying the Form for Electronically Stored Information.* A command to produce documents, electronically stored information, or tangible things or to permit the inspection of premises may be included in a subpoena commanding attendance at a deposition, hearing, or trial, or may be set out in a separate subpoena. A subpoena may specify the form or forms in which electronically stored information is to be produced.

    (D) *Command to Produce; Included Obligations.* A command in a subpoena to produce documents, electronically stored information, or tangible things requires the responding person to permit inspection, copying, testing, or sampling of the materials.

(2) *Issuing Court.* A subpoena must issue from the court where the action is pending.

(3) *Issued by Whom.* The clerk must issue a subpoena, signed but otherwise in blank, to a party who requests it. That party must complete it before service. An attorney also may issue and sign a subpoena if the attorney is authorized to practice in the issuing court.

(4) *Notice to Other Parties Before Service.* If the subpoena commands the production of documents, electronically stored information, or tangible

things or the inspection of premises before trial, then before it is served on the person to whom it is directed, a notice and a copy of the subpoena must be served on each party.

(b) Service.

(1) *By Whom and How; Tendering Fees.* Any person who is at least 18 years old and not a party may serve a subpoena. Serving a subpoena requires delivering a copy to the named person and, if the subpoena requires that person's attendance, tendering the fees for 1 day's attendance and the mileage allowed by law. Fees and mileage need not be tendered when the subpoena issues on behalf of the United States or any of its officers or agencies.

(2) *Service in the United States.* A subpoena may be served at any place within the United States.

(3) *Service in a Foreign Country.* 28 U.S.C. § 1783 governs issuing and serving a subpoena directed to a United States national or resident who is in a foreign country.

(4) *Proof of Service.* Proving service, when necessary, requires filing with the issuing court a statement showing the date and manner of service and the names of the persons served. The statement must be certified by the server.

(c) Place of Compliance.

(1) *For a Trial, Hearing, or Deposition.* A subpoena may command a person to attend a trial, hearing, or deposition only as follows:

(A) within 100 miles of where the person resides, is employed, or regularly transacts business in person; or

(B) within the state where the person resides, is employed, or regularly transacts business in person, if the person

(i) is a party or a party's officer; or

(ii) is commanded to attend a trial and would not incur substantial expense.

(2) *For Other Discovery.* A subpoena may command:

(A) production of documents, electronically stored information, or tangible things at a place within 100 miles of where the person resides, is employed, or regularly transacts business in person; and

(B) inspection of premises at the premises to be inspected.

(d) Protecting a Person Subject to a Subpoena; Enforcement.

(1) *Avoiding Undue Burden or Expense; Sanctions.* A party or attorney responsible for issuing and serving a subpoena must take reasonable steps to avoid imposing undue burden or expense on a person subject to the subpoena. The court for the district where compliance is required must enforce this duty and impose an appropriate sanction—which may include lost earnings and reasonable attorney's fees—on a party or attorney who fails to comply.

(2) *Command to Produce Materials or Permit Inspection.*

(A) *Appearance Not Required.* A person commanded to produce documents, electronically stored information, or tangible things, or to permit the inspection of premises, need not appear in person at the place of production or inspection unless also commanded to appear for a deposition, hearing, or trial.

(B) *Objections.* A person commanded to produce documents or tangible things or to permit inspection may serve on the party or attorney designated in the subpoena a written objection to inspecting, copying, testing, or sampling any or all of the materials or to inspecting the premises—or to producing electronically stored information in the form or forms requested. The objection must be served before the earlier of the time specified for compliance or 14 days after the subpoena is served. If an objection is made, the following rules apply:

(i) At any time, on notice to the commanded person, the serving party may move the court for the district where compliance is required for an order compelling production or inspection.

(ii) These acts may be required only as directed in the order, and the order must protect a person who is neither a party nor a party's officer from significant expense resulting from compliance.

(3) *Quashing or Modifying a Subpoena.*

(A) *When Required.* On timely motion, the court for the district where compliance is required must quash or modify a subpoena that:

(i)   fails to allow a reasonable time to comply;

(ii) requires a person to comply beyond the geographical limits specified in Rule 45(c);

(iii) requires disclosure of privileged or other protected matter, if no exception or waiver applies; or

(iv) subjects a person to undue burden.

(B) *When Permitted.* To protect a person subject to or affected by a subpoena, the court for the district where compliance is required may, on motion, quash or modify the subpoena if it requires:

(i) disclosing a trade secret or other confidential research, development, or commercial information; or

(ii) disclosing an unretained expert's opinion or information that does not describe specific occurrences in dispute and results from the expert's study that was not requested by a party.

(C) *Specifying Conditions as an Alternative.* In the circumstances described in Rule 45(d)(3)(B), the court may, instead of quashing or modifying a subpoena, order appearance or production under specified conditions if the serving party:

(i) shows a substantial need for the testimony or material that cannot be otherwise met without undue hardship; and

(ii) ensures that the subpoenaed person will be reasonably compensated.

(e) Duties in Responding to a Subpoena.

(1) *Producing Documents or Electronically Stored Information.* These procedures apply to producing documents or electronically stored information:

(A) *Documents.* A person responding to a subpoena to produce documents must produce them as they are kept in the ordinary course of business or must organize and label them to correspond to the categories in the demand.

(B) *Form for Producing Electronically Stored Information Not Specified.* If a subpoena does not specify a form for producing electronically stored information, the person responding must produce it in a form or forms in which it is ordinarily maintained or in a reasonably usable form or forms.

(C) *Electronically Stored Information Produced in Only One Form.* The person responding need not produce the same electronically stored information in more than one form.

(D) *Inaccessible Electronically Stored Information.* The person responding need not provide discovery of electronically stored information from sources that the person identifies as not reasonably accessible because of undue burden or cost. On motion to compel discovery or for a protective order, the person responding must show that the information is not reasonably accessible because of undue

burden or cost. If that showing is made, the court may nonetheless order discovery from such sources if the requesting party shows good cause, considering the limitations of Rule 26(b)(2)(C). The court may specify conditions for the discovery.

(2) *Claiming Privilege or Protection.*

(A) *Information Withheld.* A person withholding subpoenaed information under a claim that it is privileged or subject to protection as trial-preparation material must:

(i) expressly make the claim; and

(ii) describe the nature of the withheld documents, communications, or tangible things in a manner that, without revealing information itself privileged or protected, will enable the parties to assess the claim.

(B) *Information Produced.* If information produced in response to a subpoena is subject to a claim of privilege or of protection as trial-preparation material, the person making the claim may notify any party that received the information of the claim and the basis for it. After being notified, a party must promptly return, sequester, or destroy the specified information and any copies it has; must not use or disclose the information until the claim is resolved; must take reasonable steps to retrieve the information if the party disclosed it before being notified; and may promptly present the information under seal to the court for the district where compliance is required for a determination of the claim. The person who produced the information must preserve the information until the claim is resolved.

(f) Transferring a Subpoena-Related Motion. When the court where compliance is required did not issue the subpoena, it may transfer a motion under this rule to the issuing court if the person subject to the subpoena consents or if the court finds exceptional circumstances. Then, if the attorney for a person subject to a subpoena is authorized to practice in the court where the motion was made, the attorney may file papers and appear on the motion as an officer of the issuing court. To enforce its order, the issuing court may transfer the order to the court where the motion was made.

(g) Contempt. The court for the district where compliance is required—and also, after a motion is transferred, the issuing court—may hold in contempt a person who, having been served, fails without adequate excuse to obey the subpoena or an order related to it.

[Amended December 27, 1946, effective March 19, 1948; December 29, 1948, effective October 20, 1949; March 30, 1970, effective July 1, 1970; April 29, 1980, effective August 1, 1980; April 29, 1985, effective August 1, 1985; March 2, 1987, effective August 1, 1987; April 30, 1991, effective December 1, 1991; April 25, 2005, effective December 1, 2005; April 12, 2006, effective December 1, 2006; April 30, 2007, effective December 1, 2007; April 16, 2013, effective December 1, 2013.]

AUTHORS' COMMENTARY ON RULE 45

PURPOSE AND SCOPE

Rule 45 governs subpoenas, which are the mechanism for obtaining discovery and testimony from **nonparties.** It addresses subpoenas *ad testificandum,* pertaining to testimony, and subpoenas *duces tecum,* pertaining to documents.

RULE 45(a)—IN GENERAL

CORE CONCEPT

Parties to legal proceedings have the power to issue a subpoena compelling a nonparty to appear and testify at a designated time and location, produce documents or things, or permit the inspection of premises.

APPLICATIONS

Issued by Clerk

A subpoena may be issued by the clerk of court.[1] The clerk will issue subpoenas with the name of the recipient left blank, to be filled in by the party.[2]

Issued by Attorney

A subpoena may also be issued by an attorney, acting as an officer of the court.[3] To be effective, the subpoena must be signed by the issuing attorney.[4] An attorney may issue a subpoena on behalf of any court before which the attorney is authorized to practice. This applies equally to attorneys admitted *pro hac vice* (for one matter only).

Which Court

All subpoenas are issued from the court where the action is pending.[5]

Contents

Every subpoena should:

(1)   state the name of the court issuing the subpoena;[6]

(2)   contain the caption and civil action number of the case;[7]

(3)   command the recipient to appear and give testimony, to produce for inspection the documents, electronically stored information, or things described in the subpoena

---

[1]   *U.S. S.E.C. v. Hyatt,* 621 F.3d 687, 693 (7th Cir. 2010).

[2]   *U.S. S.E.C. v. Hyatt,* 621 F.3d 687, 693 (7th Cir. 2010).

[3]   *U.S. S.E.C. v. Hyatt,* 621 F.3d 687, 693 (7th Cir. 2010).

[4]   *Atlantic Inv. Management, LLC v. Millennium Fund I, Ltd.,* 212 F.R.D. 395, 397 (N.D. Ill. 2002) (lack of signature waived by conduct of recipient).

[5]   *Martensen v. Koch,* 301 F.R.D. 562 (D. Colo. 2014).

[6]   *Morris v. Sequa Corp.,* 275 F.R.D. 562, 565 (N.D. Ala. 2011).

[7]   *United States v. Patiwana,* 267 F.Supp.2d 301 (E.D.N.Y. 2003) (enforcing subpoena despite failure to include a civil action number).

or in an attachment thereto,[8] or to permit inspection of premises, at a designated time and location;[9] and

(4)   recite the language in subsections (c) and (d) of Rule 45.[10]

♦ **NOTE:** Blank subpoenas generally are available at the clerk's office and will include the requisite language.

Scope

The scope of documents or information that can be obtained by subpoena is the same as the scope of discovery generally under Rule 26.[11]

Multiple Commands

A subpoena to produce documents or to inspect premises may be issued separately or joined with a command to appear to testify.

Number

There is no limit on the number of subpoenas in a civil action.

Time

Subpoenas for trial testimony may be served at any time. The majority of the courts treat subpoenas to testify at depositions or for production of documents as discovery activities that must be issued prior to the discovery deadline.[12]

Documents

Witnesses may be compelled to produce documents in their possession, custody, or control.[13] See the coverage of Rule 34(a) for a discussion of the meaning of "possession, custody, or control." A subpoena for documents—a subpoena *duces tecum*—may, but does not need to, accompany a subpoena to testify.[14]

Electronic Data

Rule 45 allows a party to request by subpoena to inspect, copy, sample, or test electronically stored information or ESI. The provisions regarding subpoenas for ESI are set forth in Rule 45(e) below.

Property

A subpoena may be used to obtain inspection, testing, or sampling of the real or personal property of a nonparty.[15]

Asserting Privileges

The recipient of a subpoena *duces tecum* may refuse to produce privileged documents.[16] If the issuing party contests the asserted privilege, that party can move to compel production

---

[8]   *Orleman v. Jumpking, Inc.,* 2000 WL 1114849 (D. Kan. 2000).

[9]   *Kinetic Concepts, Inc. v. Convatec Inc.,* 268 F.R.D. 226 (M.D.N.C. 2010).

[10]   *Bertrand v. Cordiner Enters., Inc.,* 2011 WL 3036128 (V.I. Super. 2011) (subpoena enforced despite omission of language from Rule 45(c) and (d) based on absence of real prejudice).

[11]   *In re Denture Cream Products Liability Litigation,* 292 F.R.D. 120, 123 (D.D.C. 2013).

[12]   *See Buhrmaster v. Overnite Transp. Co.,* 61 F.3d 461, 464 (6th Cir. 1995).

[13]   *Hay Group, Inc. v. E.B.S. Acquisition Corp.,* 360 F.3d 404, 408 (3d Cir. 2004).

[14]   *El Encanto, Inc. v. Hatch Chile Company, Inc.,* ___ F.3d ___, ___, 2016 WL 3361487, *3 (10th Cir. 2016).

[15]   *Fitzpatrick v. Arco Marine, Inc.,* 199 F.R.D. 663, 664 (C.D. Cal. 2001) (allowing inspection of a nonparty's ship).

[16]   *See In re Teligent, Inc.,* 459 B.R. 190, 199–200 (S.D.N.Y. 2011).

of the document and can request that the court conduct an *in camera* inspection of such documents.

Parties

A subpoena is not necessary to take the deposition of a party or an officer, director, or managing agent of a party,[17] or to compel a party to produce documents;[18] a notice of deposition pursuant to Rules 30(b) and 31(a) or a document request under Rule 34 is sufficient.[19] A subpoena is necessary for all other employees of corporations.[20] Subpoenas may be used to require parties to appear and testify at hearings or trial.[21] The courts are divided as to whether a party may issue a subpoena to another party for discovery purposes.[22]

Corporations

In deposing a corporation, one may describe the information sought in the subpoena and require the corporation to designate a representative qualified to testify about the designated issues.[23]

United States or States

As a general rule, agencies and representatives of the United States or a State must comply with subpoenas.[24]

RULE 45(b)—SERVICE

CORE CONCEPT

Subpoenas may be served by any nonparty not under the age of 18.

APPLICATIONS

Personal Service

The courts are divided as to whether service of a subpoena must be personal, in-hand service, or can be accomplished by delivery to the recipient's residence or place of business.[25]

Proof of Service

If necessary, service can be proved by filing a statement of the date and manner of service, certified by the person making service, with the clerk of the court issuing the subpoena.

---

[17] *E.I. DuPont de Nemours and Co. v. Kolon Industries, Inc.*, 268 F.R.D. 45 (E.D. Va. 2010) (the law is not well defined as to who is considered a managing agent).

[18] *Dixon v. Ford Motor Credit Co.*, 2000 WL 1182274 (E.D. La. 2000) (Rule 34, not Rule 45, provides the proper way for a party to obtain documents from another party).

[19] *COMSAT Corp. v. National Science Foundation*, 190 F.3d 269, 278 (4th Cir. 1999).

[20] *Memory Bowl v. North Pointe Ins. Co.*, 280 F.R.D. 181, 187 (D.N.J. 2012).

[21] *See Chao v. Tyson Foods, Inc.*, 255 F.R.D. 556, 557–58 (N.D. Ala. 2009).

[22] *See U.S. v. 2121 Celeste Road SW, Albuquerque, N.M.*, 307 F.R.D. 572, 588–89 (D.N. Mex. 2015) (discussing the split).

[23] *Price Waterhouse LLP v. First American Corp.*, 182 F.R.D. 56, 61 (S.D.N.Y. 1998).

[24] *Ott v. City of Milwaukee*, 682 F.3d 552, 557 (7th Cir. 2012) (state agencies are persons subject to subpoena).

[25] *See Ott v. City of Milwaukee*, 682 F.3d 552, 557 (7th Cir. 2012) (personal service not required).

Deadline for Subpoenas

Rule 45 does not establish any cutoff or deadline for serving subpoenas. However, a subpoena for a deposition or for the production of documents may be governed by the discovery deadline.[26]

Not on Lawyer

Service upon the witness's lawyer is not sufficient.

Corporations

Service on the agent of a corporation is sufficient to obtain service on the corporation.[27]

Expenses

If the recipient's attendance is commanded, service must be accompanied by the tender of the fees and expenses for a 1-day appearance, unless the issuing party is the United States or officer or agency thereof.[28] There is no requirement to tender witness fees and expenses when the subpoena is only for the production of documents, and no witness is commanded to appear.[29] The amount of fees and expenses is controlled by 28 U.S.C.A. § 1821.[30]

Place of Service

A subpoena may be served at any place within the United States.

Foreign Countries

Under certain circumstances, a witness subject to the jurisdiction of the court may be in a foreign country. The procedure for issuing a subpoena to such a witness is governed by 28 U.S.C.A. § 1783 (The Walsh Act), which provides for the issuance of such a subpoena if the court finds that the witness's testimony or documents are "necessary in the interest of justice," and it is not possible to obtain the testimony or documents by other means. The person serving such a subpoena must advance the recipient estimated travel expenses.

♦   NOTE: The Walsh Act, 28 U.S.C.A. § 1783, only governs issuing a subpoena to a trial witness. Rule 30 discusses when foreign witnesses may be deposed.

Service on Other Parties

If the subpoena is for a deposition, a notice of deposition and the subpoena must be served on all parties pursuant to Rule 30 or 31. If the subpoena requires the production of documents or inspection of premises, notice must be served upon all parties prior to service on the recipient so that they may assert any privileges or objections and may obtain the same or additional documents.[31]

Arbitrations

The federal courts can enforce subpoenas issued by arbitrators under the provisions of the Federal Arbitration Act, 9 U.S.C. §§ 1 *et seq.*[32]

---

[26]   *See Alper v. United States,*190 F.R.D. 281, 283 (D. Mass. 2000).

[27]   *In re Motorsports Merchandise Antitrust Litigation*, 186 F.R.D. 344 (W.D. Va. 1999) (look to Rule 4 to determine proper service on a corporation).

[28]   *In re Hunt*, 238 F.3d 1098, 1100 (9th Cir. 2001) (subpoena quashed because service not accompanied by witness fee and mileage).

[29]   *U.S. E.E.O.C. v. Laidlaw Waste, Inc.*, 934 F.Supp. 286, 290 n.6 (N.D. Ill. 1996).

[30]   28 U.S.C.A. § 1821 is reprinted in this book. *See also Fisher v. Ford Motor Co.*, 178 F.R.D. 195 (N.D. Ohio 1998).

[31]   *Josendis v. Wall to Wall Residence Repairs, Inc.*, 662 F.3d 1292, 1303, n.17 (11th Cir. 2011).

[32]   *Festus & Helen Stacy Foundation, Inc. v. Merrill Lynch, Pierce Fenner, & Smith Inc.*, 432 F.Supp.2d 1375, 1377–78 (N.D. Ga. 2006).

RULE 45(c)—PLACE OF COMPLIANCE

CORE CONCEPT

The recipient of a subpoena generally will not be required to travel more than 100 miles from where the recipient resides, works, or regularly transacts business to perform the functions required by the subpoena *(e.g.,* testify and/or produce documents). A recipient may be required to travel anywhere within the state where the person resides, works, or regularly transacts business if the person is a party, an officer of a party, or is commanded to testify at trial.

APPLICATIONS

Deposition or Hearing

A subpoena to testify at a deposition or hearing may require the recipient to travel at most 100 miles from where the recipient resides, is employed, or regularly transacts business in person.[33] If the recipient is a party or officer of a party, the recipient may be required to travel anywhere with the state where the recipient resides, is employed, or regularly transacts business in person.

Trial

A subpoena to testify at trial may require the recipient to travel at most 100 miles from where the recipient resides, is employed, or regularly transacts business in person, or anywhere within the state where the recipient resides, is employed, or regularly transacts business in person if the recipient is a party or officer of a party or would not incur substantial expense to comply. If a recipient would otherwise incur substantial expense to travel within the state but more than 100 miles, the issuing party can reimburse the recipient for the travel expenses, thereby requiring the recipient to travel within the state.[34]

Production of Documents, ESI, and Tangible Things

A subpoena to produce documents, ESI, or tangible things may require the recipient to travel at most 100 miles from where the recipient resides, is employed, or regularly transacts business in person. ESI is typically exchanged electronically, rendering these limitations inapplicable.[35]

Inspection of Premises

A subpoena to inspect premises is performed at the premises to be inspected.

RULE 45(d)—PROTECTING A PERSON SUBJECT TO A SUBPOENA; ENFORCEMENT

CORE CONCEPT

An attorney has a duty not to issue a subpoena for improper purposes or to impose undue burden on the recipient of the subpoena. Rule 45(d) also provides mechanisms to challenge a subpoenas.

APPLICATIONS

Duty to Avoid Undue Burden

An attorney issuing a subpoena has a duty to avoid causing undue burden or expense on the recipient.[36] The court must enforce this duty and must impose an appropriate

---

[33] *Wultz v. Bank of China Ltd.,* 942 F.Supp.2d 452, n.103 (S.D.N.Y. 2014).

[34] The advisory committee note to the 2013 Amendments to Rule 45.

[35] The advisory committee note to the 2013 Amendments to Rule 45.

[36] *Northwestern Memorial Hosp. v. Ashcroft,* 362 F.3d 923, 938 (7th Cir. 2004).

sanction, which may include attorney's fees and lost wages, on a party or attorney who fails to comply with this duty.[37]

Attendance by Person Producing Documents

A person subpoenaed to produce documents or things or to permit an inspection need not actually appear at the designated time, as long as the person complies with the subpoena.

Objection to Subpoena to Produce Documents

A person subpoenaed to produce documents or things or to permit an inspection may serve an objection to all or part of the subpoena within 14 days after service of the subpoena (or before the time designated in the subpoena, if sooner).[38] Note that the objection procedure does not apply to testimonial subpoenas; those may only be challenged by a motion to quash or modify the subpoena.[39] Once an objection has been served on the party issuing the subpoena, the subpoena recipient is not obligated to comply with the subpoena.[40] Failure to serve timely objections may constitute a waiver of objections to the subpoena other than objections relating to service.[41] Only nonparties may serve objections; parties must contest a subpoena by a motion to quash or modify.[42]

Motion to Compel

If a subpoena recipient serves an objection to the subpoena, the serving party may file a motion to compel in the court for the district where compliance is required.[43] The motion must be served on the subpoena recipient. In ruling on such a motion, the court will protect nonparties from "significant" expense.[44] Some courts and local rules require counsel for the moving party to make a reasonable effort to confer with opposing counsel prior to filing a motion to compel.[45]

Compensation for Respondent

If the recipient of a subpoena to produce documents or permit inspection serves an objection and the issuing party files a motion to compel, the court must, if it grants the motion, protect the responding person from significant expense resulting from compliance, so long as the recipient is not a party or officer of a party.[46] The compensation may include wages lost because of the subpoena, and may also include attorney's fees.[47]

Motion to Quash or Modify

A subpoena recipient, or another person asserting privilege,[48] may move to quash a subpoena in the court for the district where compliance is required. The motion must be

---

[37] *See Legal Voice v. Stormans Inc.,* 738 F.3d 1178, 1185 (9th Cir. 2013).

[38] *In re C.R. Bard, Inc. Pelvic Repair Systems Products Liability Litigation,* 287 F.R.D. 377, 380–81 (S.D.W. Va. 2012).

[39] *Ceroni v. 4Front Engineered Solutions, Inc.,* 793 F.Supp.2d 1268 (D. Colo. 2011).

[40] *U.S. S.E.C. v. Hyatt,* 621 F.3d 687, 694 (7th Cir. 2010).

[41] *Judicial Watch, Inc. v. U.S. Dept. of Commerce,* 196 F.R.D. 1, 2 (D.D.C. 2000).

[42] *Moon v. SCP Pool Corp.,* 232 F.R.D. 633, 636 (C.D. Cal. 2005)

[43] *Martensen v. Koch,* 301 F.R.D. 562 (D. Colo. 2014).

[44] *See Klay v. All Defendants,* 425 F.3d 977, 984 (11th Cir. 2005).

[45] *See Boukadoum v. Hubanks,* 239 F.R.D. 427, 429–30 (D. Md. 2006).

[46] *See Legal Voice v. Stormans Inc.,* 738 F.3d 1178, 1184–85 (9th Cir. 2013).

[47] *Voice v. Stormans Inc.,* 757 F.3d 1015 (9th Cir. 2014).

[48] *Jee Family Holdings, LLC v. San Jorge Children's Healthcare, Inc.,* 297 F.R.D. 19, 20 (D. Puerto Rico 2014) (nonparty may move to quash to protect privileged information).

"timely" filed, and should certainly be filed before the subpoena's return date.[49] Failure to file a motion to quash may constitute a waiver of objections to the subpoena.[50] The courts vary as to who has the burden in a motion to quash.[51] Some courts and local rules require counsel for the moving party to make a reasonable effort to confer with opposing counsel prior to filing a motion to quash.[52] Rule 45(d)(3) lists situations in which a subpoena will be quashed or modified:[53]

(1) *Time to Comply:* Rule 45(d)(3)(A)(i) requires that the subpoena recipient be provided reasonable time to comply.[54]

(2) *Distance to Travel:* Rule 45(d)(3)(A)(ii) provides for the quashing of a subpoena requiring a person not a party or officer of a party[55] to travel beyond the limits specified in Rule 45(c) (generally, 100 miles from where the recipient resides, is employed, or regularly transacts business).

(3) *Privileged Matters:* Rule 45(d)(3)(A)(iii) provides that a subpoena must be quashed if it requires the disclosure of privileged or other protected matters.[56] Some courts require a subpoena recipient to provide the serving party with a privilege log when objecting on the basis of privilege.[57]

(4) *Undue Burden:* Rule 45(d)(3)(A)(iv) provides that a subpoena must be quashed if it subjects the recipient to undue burden.[58] This provision is sometimes used as justification for imposing the nonparty's expenses on the party issuing the subpoena to cure the undue burden on the nonparty.[59]

Substantial Need of Serving Party

Rule 45(d)(3)(B) lists circumstances in which a subpoena will be quashed unless the serving party shows a "substantial need" for the testimony, documents, or inspection.[60] In such cases, the court will condition compliance on the serving party compensating the recipient.[61] These circumstances are:

(1) *Trade Secrets:* Rule 45(c)(3)(B)(i) provides limited protection for trade secrets and other confidential research, development, and commercial information.[62]

---

[49]   *See Centrifugal Acquisition Corp., Inc. v. Moon*, 849 F.Supp.2d 814, 839 (E.D. Wis. 2012).

[50]   *In re Flat Glass Antitrust Litigation*, 288 F.3d 83, 90 (3d Cir. 2002) (failure to file motion to quash constitutes waiver of objections to manner of service of subpoena).

[51]   *See, e.g., In re Domestic Drywall Antitrust Litigation*, 300 F.R.D. 234 (E.D. Pa. 2014) (shifting burden).

[52]   *See Hill v. Wheatland Waters, Inc.*, 327 F.Supp.2d 1294, 1298 n.5 (D. Kan. 2004).

[53]   *See Texas Keystone, Inc. v. Prime Natural Resources, Inc.*, 694 F.3d 548, 554 (5th Cir. 2012).

[54]   *Ott v. City of Milwaukee*, 274 F.R.D. 238 (E.D. Wis. 2011) (remedy for unreasonable notice is to allow more time to respond).

[55]   *See Operation: Heroes, Ltd. v. Procter and Gamble Productions, Inc.*, 903 F.Supp.2d 1106, 1114–15 (D. Nev. 2012).

[56]   *Arista Records, LLC v. Doe 3*, 604 F.3d 110, 118 (2d Cir. 2010) (first amendment right to anonymous speech is a protectable interest).

[57]   *See, e.g., Williams v. Bridgeport Music, Inc.*, 300 F.R.D. 120 (S.D.N.Y. 2014).

[58]   *See AF Holdings, LLC v. Does 1–1058*, 752 F.3d 990, 993–95 (D.C. Cir. 2014) (a subpoena that seeks materials outside the scope of discovery automatically imposes an undue burden).

[59]   *See Alberts v. HCA Inc.*, 405 B.R. 498, 502 (D.D.C. 2009).

[60]   *In re Domestic Drywall Antitrust Litigation*, 300 F.R.D. 234 (E.D. Pa. 2014).

[61]   *In re Domestic Drywall Antitrust Litigation*, 300 F.R.D. 234 (E.D. Pa. 2014).

[62]   *Mattel, Inc. v. Walking Mountain Productions*, 353 F.3d 792, 814 (9th Cir. 2003).

(2) *Unretained Experts:* Rule 45(c)(3)(B)(ii) provides limited protection for experts who have not been retained, so that parties cannot obtain their testimony without paying their fees.[63]

Appeal

The courts are divided as to whether quashing or compelling compliance with subpoenas is interlocutory, not subject to immediate appeal, or may be appealed immediately as collateral orders.[64] Some courts require the recipient of the subpoena to refuse to comply, and then appeal the contempt and sanctions order.[65]

RULE 45(e)—DUTIES IN RESPONDING TO A SUBPOENA

CORE CONCEPT

Documents may be produced as they are normally kept or may be separated and organized. When privileges are asserted, the privilege must be expressly described.

APPLICATIONS

Production of Documents

The scope of production under a subpoena is the same as the scope for discovery generally under Rule 26.[66] The responding party has the option of allowing the serving party to inspect and copy the documents where they are normally kept *(e.g.,* "There is our file room").[67] The responding party may also collect the responsive documents and organize and label them to correspond to the categories requested.[68] The responding party may make copies for the requesting party, but is not obligated to do so.

Electronic Data

Rule 45 expressly allows for the party issuing the subpoena to request to inspect, copy, sample, or test electronic data.

- *Form of Electronic Data:* Rule 45(e)(1)(B) allows, but does not require, the requesting party to specify the form in which it is requesting electronic data (*i.e.,* hard copy or electronic, and if electronic, the precise manner of production). If the requesting party does not specify the form, then the responding person must produce it in the form in which it is ordinarily maintained or in a form that is reasonably usable. In any event, a person need not produce electronic data in more than one form.

- *Undue Burden or Cost:* If the responding person believes that the production of electronic data from certain sources will cause undue burden or cost, the person can, in lieu of producing the documents, identify those sources.[69] If a motion to compel or quash is filed, the responding person will have the burden of showing that production would cause undue burden or cost.[70] The burden would then shift

---

[63] *In re Domestic Drywall Antitrust Litigation,* 300 F.R.D. 234 (E.D. Pa. 2014) (protection does not apply when information sought is factual).

[64] *See, e.g., Legal Voice v. Stormans Inc.,* 738 F.3d 1178, 1183–84 (9th Cir. 2013) (ruling deemed appealable collateral order).

[65] *See, e.g., Ott v. City of Milwaukee,* 682 F.3d 552, 554–55 (7th Cir. 2012).

[66] *Chevron Corp. v. Salazar,* 275 F.R.D. 437, 447, n.8 (S.D.N.Y. 2011).

[67] *Kinetic Concepts, Inc. v. Convatec Inc.,* 268 F.R.D. 226 (M.D.N.C. 2010).

[68] *Kinetic Concepts, Inc. v. Convatec Inc.,* 268 F.R.D. 226 (M.D.N.C. 2010).

[69] *Guy Chemical Co., Inc. v. Romaco AG,* 243 F.R.D. 310 (N.D. Ind. 2007).

[70] *Guy Chemical Co., Inc. v. Romaco AG,* 243 F.R.D. 310 (N.D. Ind. 2007).

to the requesting party to show good cause why the data should be produced nonetheless.[71] In such cases, the court may specify conditions for the production, such as payment of the expenses of the production by the requesting party.[72]

Asserting a Privilege

When the subpoena recipient seeks to withhold information that is privileged, the recipient must expressly claim the privilege and describe the nature of the documents, communications, or things not produced in sufficient detail that the court and parties can assess the privilege.[73] The party asserting the privilege should provide a detailed privilege log at the time of asserting the privilege or within a reasonable time thereafter.[74]

Recalling Privileged Information

Rule 45(e)(2)(B) establishes a procedure to recall privileged information that has already been produced. Anyone believing that a person has produced privileged information in response to a subpoena may provide a notification to the parties who have received the information. After receiving such a notification, the receiving parties must return, sequester, or destroy the specified information and all copies (including taking reasonable steps to retrieve any information that the receiving party had already disclosed to other persons). If they do not agree with the privilege assertion, they can present the information to the court for the district where compliance is required under seal for a determination of the privilege claim. During the pendency of the court's review of the privilege claim, the receiving parties are prohibited from using the information and the producing party must preserve it.

RULE 45(f)—TRANSFERRING A SUBPOENA-RELATED MOTION

CORE CONCEPT

If a subpoena-related motion is filed in a court other than the one where the action is pending, that court can transfer the motion to the court where the action is pending. The court where the action is pending then transfers its order back to the original court for enforcement.

APPLICATIONS

Grounds for Transfer

A court will transfer a subpoena-related motion to the court where the action is pending if the person subject to the subpoena consents or the court finds "exceptional circumstances."[75] Such circumstances are rare, and the person seeking transfer bears the burden of establishing appropriate grounds.[76] Generally, a court will transfer a motion only when the potential for disrupting the underlying litigation outweighs the interests of the nonparty subpoena recipient in obtaining local resolution of the motion.[77]

Transfer of Resulting Order

The court ruling on the subpoena-related motion can transfer its order to the court for the district where compliance is required if such transfer is necessary to enforce the order.

---

[71] *Guy Chemical Co., Inc. v. Romaco AG*, 243 F.R.D. 310 (N.D. Ind. 2007) (good cause exists where no other source exists for the information).

[72] *Guy Chemical Co., Inc. v. Romaco AG,* 243 F.R.D. 310 (N.D. Ind. 2007).

[73] *Ott v. City of Milwaukee*, 682 F.3d 552, 558 (7th Cir. 2012) (failure to assert detailed objection constitutes waiver).

[74] *Perry v. Schwarzenegger*, 704 F.Supp.2d 921 (N.D. Cal. 2010) (court may waive log requirement to lessen burden on a nonparty).

[75] *Moon Mountain Farms, LLC v. Rural Community Insurance Company,* 301 F.R.D. 426 (N.D. Cal. 2014).

[76] The advisory committee note to the 2013 Amendments to Rule 45.

[77] *Wultz v. Bank of China Ltd.*, 32 F.Supp.3d 486 (S.D.N.Y. 2014).

Admission to the Court

In order to appear and file papers in the transferee court, the attorney for the subpoena recipient will need to be admitted to that court.

RULE 45(g)—CONTEMPT

CORE CONCEPT

Failure to obey a valid subpoena or subpoena-related order without adequate excuse is a contempt of the court for the district where compliance is required,[78] and also of the issuing court after transfer of a subpoena-related motion under Rule 45(f).[79]

APPLICATIONS

Challenge to Subpoena

If a party believes that a subpoena is not valid, the proper response is a motion to quash or a motion for a protective order.[80] If the motion is unsuccessful and the party disobeys the subpoena nonetheless, the party can also raise validity grounds again at the contempt proceedings.[81]

Standard for Holding Subpoena Recipient in Contempt

To prevail on a request for contempt finding, the moving party must establish by clear and convincing evidence that: (1) a subpoena set forth an unambiguous command; (2) the alleged contemnor violated that command; (3) the violation was significant, meaning the alleged contemnor did not substantially comply with the subpoena; and (4) the alleged contemnor failed to make a reasonable and diligent effort to comply.[82]

Due Process

Before sanctions may be imposed on a person charged with contempt under Rule 45, due process requires that the person receive notice and an opportunity to be heard and that the court have personal jurisdiction over the nonparty to be sanctioned.[83]

Adequate Excuse

Inability to comply is an adequate excuse.[84] The fact that the subpoena would require the recipient to travel greater distances than those listed in Rule 45(c) is also an adequate excuse.[85] Likewise, a timely objection to the subpoena is an adequate excuse.[86] Preferring to work instead of comply with the subpoena is not an adequate excuse.[87]

Appeal

Nonparty witnesses who are held in contempt may immediately appeal the contempt order.[88]

---

[78] *Blackmer v. United States,*284 U.S. 421, 52 S.Ct. 252, 76 L.Ed. 375 (1932).

[79] *Wultz v. Bank of China Ltd.,* 32 F.Supp.3d 486 (S.D.N.Y. 2014).

[80] *See United States ex rel. Ortiz v. Mount Sinai Hospital,* ___ F.Supp.3d ___, ___, 2016 WL 1319045, *4 (S.D.N.Y. 2016).

[81] *United States v. Ryan,* 402 U.S. 530, 533, 91 S.Ct. 1580, 1582, 29 L.Ed.2d 85 (1971).

[82] *Sprint Solutions, Inc. v. iCell Guru, Inc.,* 310 F.R.D. 563, 569 (N.D. Ill. 2015).

[83] *U.S. S.E.C. v. Hyatt,* 621 F.3d 687, 694 (7th Cir. 2010).

[84] *U.S. S.E.C. v. Hyatt,* 621 F.3d 687, 693, 697 (7th Cir. 2010).

[85] *See Hillard v. Guidant Corp.,* 76 F.Supp.2d 566, 570 (M.D. Pa. 1999).

[86] *Flatow v. The Islamic Republic of Iran,* 196 F.R.D. 203, 208 (D.D.C. 2000).

[87] *Higginbotham v. KCS Intern., Inc.,* 202 F.R.D. 444, 455 (D. Md. 2001).

[88] *Wallace v. Kmart Corp.,* 687 F.3d 86, 89 (3d Cir. 2012).

ADDITIONAL RESEARCH REFERENCES

Wright & Miller, *Federal Practice and Procedure* §§ 2451 to 2463

C.J.S., Federal Civil Procedure §§ 582 to 583 et seq., 644; Witnesses §§ 13 to 27 et seq.

West's Key Number Digest, Federal Civil Procedure ⊶1353 to 1354, 1456; Witnesses ⊶7 to 16, 21

RULE 46

OBJECTING TO A RULING OR ORDER

A formal exception to a ruling or order is unnecessary. When the ruling or order is requested or made, a party need only state the action that it wants the court to take or objects to, along with the grounds for the request or objection. Failing to object does not prejudice a party who had no opportunity to do so when the ruling or order was made.

[Amended effective August 1, 1987; April 30, 2007, effective December 1, 2007.]

AUTHORS' COMMENTARY ON RULE 46

PURPOSE AND SCOPE

In general, to preserve an issue for appeal, a party must object to the court's action or decision with particularity, but does not need to note an "exception" to the court's adverse ruling.

APPLICATIONS

Applies to All Stages

Rule 46 applies to all stages of a trial, from voir dire through jury instructions. The attorney must object even to questions asked by the judge, although the appeals court may be more lenient about the form and timing of such objections.

Form of Objection

In order to preserve an issue for appeal, an attorney must state the particular grounds upon which the objection rests.[1] It is not sufficient to state simply, "objection," or to make a general objection. The primary purpose of the specificity requirement is to apprise the court of the litigant's position so that the court can correct its ruling if appropriate.[2] Consequently, if the grounds are obvious to the trial judge, an appellate court may overlook a lack of specificity.[3] If the judge's ruling is ambiguous, a party cannot challenge it on appeal without first attempting to have the judge clarify the ruling.[4]

Formal Exceptions

It is not necessary to note an "exception" or take any other action to preserve a properly raised but overruled objection.[5]

Failure to Object

In general, failure to object to a ruling or issue constitutes a waiver of the ruling or issue.[6] An attorney need not object if there is no opportunity to do so.[7] Additionally, the appeals court may consider on appeal an issue to which no objection was asserted when the basis was so clear that no objection was necessary, such as when the attorney has already

---

[1] *Ramey v. District 141, Intern. Ass'n of Machinists and Aerospace Workers*, 378 F.3d 269, 281 (2d Cir. 2004).

[2] *In re Sealed Case*, 552 F.3d 841, 852 (D.C. Cir. 2009).

[3] *New England Newspaper Pub. Co. v. Bonner,* 68 F.2d 880 (1st Cir. 1934).

[4] *Kasper v. Saint Mary of Nazareth Hosp.,* 135 F.3d 1170, 1176 (7th Cir. 1998).

[5] *Jacques v. DiMarzio, Inc.,* 386 F.3d 192, 200–01 (2d Cir. 2004).

[6] *See S.E.C. v. Diversified Corporate Consulting Group,* 378 F.3d 1219, 1227 (11th Cir. 2004).

[7] *Ira Holtzman, C.P.A. v. Turza,* 728 F.3d 682, 688 (7th Cir. 2013).

objected to the same evidence.[8] Also, the appellate court may overlook the lack of an objection if the error was so fundamental that it caused a miscarriage of justice.[9]

Unsuccessful Motion *in Limine*

If a party files an unsuccessful motion *in limine* seeking the exclusion of certain evidence, that party does not have to formally object at trial when the evidence in question is introduced as long as two conditions are met: (1) the party filed a written pre-trial motion setting forth reasons in support of the request that the evidence be excluded;[10] and (2) the district court made a "definitive" ruling with no suggestion that it would reconsider the matter at trial.[11]

ADDITIONAL RESEARCH REFERENCES

Wright & Miller, *Federal Practice and Procedure* §§ 2471 to 2473

C.J.S., Federal Civil Procedure §§ 370 et seq., 941 to 942

West's Key Number Digest, Federal Civil Procedure ⊶2017 to 2019

---

[8]   *Beech Aircraft Corp. v. Rainey,* 488 U.S. 153, 109 S.Ct. 439, 102 L.Ed.2d 445 (1988).

[9]   *Sibbach v. Wilson & Co.,* 312 U.S. 1, 16, 312 U.S. 655, 61 S.Ct. 422, 427, 85 L.Ed. 479 (1941).

[10]   *Jimenez v. City of Chicago,* 732 F.3d 710 (2013) (issue not preserved where motion in limine asserted different grounds than those asserted on appeal).

[11]   *See Inter Medical Supplies, Ltd. v. EBI Medical Systems, Inc.,* 181 F.3d 446, 455 (3d Cir. 1999).

RULE 47

SELECTING JURORS

(a) Examining Jurors. The court may permit the parties or their attorneys to examine prospective jurors or may itself do so. If the court examines the jurors, it must permit the parties or their attorneys to make any further inquiry it considers proper, or must itself ask any of their additional questions it considers proper.

(b) Peremptory Challenges. The court must allow the number of peremptory challenges provided by 28 U.S.C. § 1870.

(c) Excusing a Juror. During trial or deliberation, the court may excuse a juror for good cause.

[Amended effective July 1, 1966; December 1, 1991; April 30, 2007, effective December 1, 2007.]

AUTHORS' COMMENTARY ON RULE 47

PURPOSE AND SCOPE

Rule 47 addresses the examination of prospective jurors (voir dire), peremptory challenges to prospective jurors, and excusing jurors for good cause.

RULE 47(a)—EXAMINING OF JURORS

CORE CONCEPT

The court and/or the parties may ask prospective jurors questions in order to determine bias and to enable the parties to exercise their peremptory challenges in a meaningful manner.

APPLICATIONS

Scope of Examinations

The court has broad discretion with respect to the scope of voir dire.[1] It may conduct the examination itself or allow the parties to do so.[2] If the court conducts the examination, the parties may submit proposed questions, which the court may ask if it deems them appropriate.[3] The court must allow sufficient questioning so that the selection process is meaningful.

Challenges for Cause

Challenges for cause are ruled on by the court. The party making the challenge has the burden of persuading the court. Partiality is the main grounds for such challenges.[4] Parties can challenge the individual jurors, the entire panel, or the selection process. Such challenges should be made at the time of jury selection, not in a motion for new trial.[5]

---

[1] *Smith v. Vicorp, Inc.*, 107 F.3d 816, 817 (10th Cir. 1997).
[2] *Csiszer v. Wren*, 614 F.3d 866, 875 (8th Cir. 2010).
[3] *Smith v. Tenet Healthsystem SL, Inc.*, 436 F.3d 879, 884 (8th Cir. 2006).
[4] *See Swain v. Alabama*, 380 U.S. 202, 220, 85 S.Ct. 824, 835, 13 L.Ed.2d 759 (1965).
[5] *Atlas Roofing Mfg. Co. v. Parnell*, 409 F.2d 1191 (5th Cir.1969).

Qualifications for Jurors

The qualifications for jurors is governed by the Jury Selection and Service Act of 1968, 28 U.S.C. § 1861 *et seq.* Essentially, jurors must be United States citizens, have resided in the district for at least one year, meet minimum literacy requirements and be fluent in English, be mentally and physically capable of service, and be free from pending charges or past convictions of crimes punishable by imprisonment for more than 2 years.

Excluded Groups

The Jury Selection and Service Act of 1968 provides for the establishment of certain groups who are precluded or excused from serving. Generally, these include: persons providing vital services (such as members of the armed services and policemen); persons for whom service would be a particular hardship (such as sole proprietors, mothers with young children, persons with gravely ill family members); and those excluded by the court for partiality or because they are likely to be disruptive.

RULE 47(b)—PEREMPTORY CHALLENGES

CORE CONCEPT

Peremptory challenges are governed by 28 U.S.C.A. § 1870, which provides that each party has three peremptory challenges, and generally need not give any explanation for using those challenges.[6] Peremptory challenges are not a constitutionally protected fundamental right, but are merely one means to the constitutional end of an impartial jury and a fair trial.[7] When there are multiple plaintiffs or defendants, the court may require them to exercise the challenges collectively or may allow additional challenges.[8]

APPLICATIONS

Improper Grounds

It is improper to use a peremptory challenge to exclude a juror on the basis of race[9] or gender.[10]

RULE 47(c)—EXCUSING A JUROR

CORE CONCEPT

The court may excuse a juror for reasons of sickness,[11] family emergency, juror misconduct, or for other "good cause shown."[12] A juror's refusal to join the majority is not grounds for excuse.[13]

APPLICATIONS

Considerations for Excuse

Characteristics of a juror to be scrutinized pursuant to Rule 47(c) include not only spoken words, but gestures and attitudes in order to ensure the jury's impartiality and competence.[14]

---

[6]   *Jimenez v. City of Chicago,* 732 F.3d 710, 715 (7th Cir. 2013).

[7]   *Alaska Rent-A-Car, Inc. v. Avis Budget Group, Inc.,* 709 F.3d 872, 880 (9th Cir. 2013).

[8]   *In re Air Crash Disaster,* 86 F.3d 498, 518–519 (6th Cir. 1996).

[9]   *Edmonson v. Leesville Concrete Co., Inc.,* 500 U.S. 614, 111 S.Ct. 2077, 114 L.Ed.2d 660 (1991).

[10] *J.E.B. v. Alabama ex rel. T.B.,* 511 U.S. 127, 129, 114 S.Ct. 1419, 1421 (1994).

[11] *Davis v. Velez,* 15 F.Supp.2d 234 (E.D.N.Y. 2014).

[12] *See Harris v. Folk Const. Co.,* 138 F.3d 365, 371 (8th Cir. 1998).

[13] *See Murray v. Laborers Union Local No. 324,* 55 F.3d 1445, 1450–51 (9th Cir. 1995).

[14] *Harris v. Folk Const. Co.,* 138 F.3d 365, 371 (8th Cir. 1998).

ADDITIONAL RESEARCH REFERENCES

Wright & Miller, *Federal Practice and Procedure* §§ 2481 to 2485. Bennett & Hirschhorn, Bennett's
  Guide to Jury Selection and Trial Dynamics in Civil and Criminal Litigation.

C.J.S., Juries §§ 208 to 250 et seq., 251 to 285 et seq.

West's Key Number Digest, Jury ☞83 to 142

RULE 48

NUMBER OF JURORS; VERDICT

(a) Number of Jurors. A jury must begin with at least 6 and no more than 12 members, and each juror must participate in the verdict unless excused under Rule 47(c).

(b) Verdict. Unless the parties stipulate otherwise, the verdict must be unanimous and must be returned by a jury of at least 6 members.

(c) Polling. After a verdict is returned but before the jury is discharged, the court must on a party's request, or may on its own, poll the jurors individually. If the poll reveals a lack of unanimity or lack of assent by the number of jurors that the parties stipulated to, the court may direct the jury to deliberate further or may order a new trial.

[Amended effective December 1, 1991; April 30, 2007, effective December 1, 2007; March 26, 2009, effective December 1, 2009.]

AUTHORS' COMMENTARY ON RULE 48

PURPOSE AND SCOPE

The court may select any number of jurors from 6 to 12, inclusive. Unless the parties stipulate otherwise, the verdict must be unanimous.

APPLICATIONS

Number of Jurors

The court may select any number of jurors from 6 to 12, inclusive.[1]

Verdicts Normally Unanimous

Absent a stipulation, verdicts must be unanimous.[2] However, verdicts are considered unanimous even if 1 or more jurors reluctantly joins just to reach a verdict.[3] If a jury reports being unable to reach a unanimous verdict, the majority of the courts allow an instruction to the jury to deliberate further to attempt to break the deadlock.[4]

Polling the Jury

After the verdict is read and before the jury is discharged, a party may demand that the jury be polled to verify that the verdict is unanimous and that no juror was coerced into signing the verdict.[5] The court may also poll the jury *sua sponte*. If 1 or more jurors dissents, the court may require the jury to deliberate further or may declare a mistrial. Polling must occur before the verdict is recorded and the jury is discharged.[6] The trial must be conducted in a manner that provides the parties an opportunity to exercise their right to have the jury

---

[1] *See Show v. Ford Motor Co.*, 659 F.3d 584, 586 (7th Cir. 2011).

[2] *Jazzabi v. Allstate Ins. Co.*, 278 F.3d 979, 985 (9th Cir. 2002) (jury must be unanimous as to affirmative defense as well as ultimate verdict).

[3] *See Verser v. Barfield,* 741 F.3d 734, 738 (7th Cir. 2013).

[4] *Cary v. Allegheny Technologies Inc.*, 267 F.Supp.2d 442, 446 (W.D. Pa. 2003).

[5] *See Wagner v. Jones*, 928 F.Supp.2d 1084 (S.D. Iowa 2013).

[6] *See Wagner v. Jones*, 928 F.Supp.2d 1084 (S.D. Iowa 2013).

polled.[7] The right to have the jury polled is not constitutional, however, and can be waived if not timely exercised.[8]

Excused Jurors

If a juror is excused for illness or other reason, a unanimous verdict among the remaining jurors will be valid if at least 6 jurors remain.[9] If fewer than 6 remain, the parties may consent to allow the trial or deliberations to continue and then will be bound by the verdict.[10]

Stipulations

By stipulation, the parties can agree that a unanimous decision is not necessary, and that the decision of a specified majority will be taken as the decision of the jury.[11] The parties may also stipulate to fewer than 6 jurors.[12]

Alternate Jurors

Alternate jurors are not used in civil trials in federal court.[13]

Advisory Jury

It does not appear that the provisions of Rule 48 regarding unanimity pertain to advisory juries.[14]

ADDITIONAL RESEARCH REFERENCES

Wright & Miller, *Federal Practice and Procedure* §§ 2491 to 2492. Bennett & Hirschhorn, Bennett's *Guide to Jury Selection and Trial Dynamics in Civil and Criminal Litigation.*

C.J.S., Federal Civil Procedure §§ 995 et seq.; Juries § 4

West's Key Number Digest, Federal Civil Procedure ⊶2191; Jury ⊶4

---

[7] *Verser v. Barfield*, 741 F.3d 734, 740–41 (7th Cir. 2013).

[8] *Ira Green, Inc. v. Military Sales & Service Co.*, 775 F.3d 12, 25 (1st Cir. 2014).

[9] *Weaver v. Blake*, 454 F.3d 1087 (10th Cir. 2006).

[10] *Meyers v. Wal-Mart Stores, East, Inc.*, 257 F.3d 625, 633 (6th Cir. 2001).

[11] *Baxter Healthcare Corp. v. Spectramed, Inc.*, 49 F.3d 1575 (Fed. Cir. 1995).

[12] *Meyers v. Wal-Mart Stores, East, Inc.*, 77 F.Supp.2d 826, 827 (E.D. Mich. 1999), aff'd, 257 F.3d 625 (6th Cir. 2001) (parties stipulated to 4 jurors).

[13] *Herbert v. Architect of Capitol*, 839 F.Supp.2d 284 (D.D.C. 2013).

[14] *N.A.A.C.P. v. Acusport Corp.*, 253 F.Supp.2d 459 (E.D.N.Y. 2003).

RULE 49

SPECIAL VERDICT; GENERAL VERDICT AND QUESTIONS

(a) Special Verdict.

(1) *In General.* The court may require a jury to return only a special verdict in the form of a special written finding on each issue of fact. The court may do so by:

    (A) submitting written questions susceptible of a categorical or other brief answer;

    (B) submitting written forms of the special findings that might properly be made under the pleadings and evidence; or

    (C) using any other method that the court considers appropriate.

(2) *Instructions.* The court must give the instructions and explanations necessary to enable the jury to make its findings on each submitted issue.

(3) *Issues Not Submitted.* A party waives the right to a jury trial on any issue of fact raised by the pleadings or evidence but not submitted to the jury unless, before the jury retires, the party demands its submission to the jury. If the party does not demand submission, the court may make a finding on the issue. If the court makes no finding, it is considered to have made a finding consistent with its judgment on the special verdict.

(b) General Verdict with Answers to Written Questions.

(1) *In General.* The court may submit to the jury forms for a general verdict, together with written questions on one or more issues of fact that the jury must decide. The court must give the instructions and explanations necessary to enable the jury to render a general verdict and answer the questions in writing, and must direct the jury to do both.

(2) *Verdict and Answers Consistent.* When the general verdict and the answers are consistent, the court must approve, for entry under Rule 58, an appropriate judgment on the verdict and answers.

(3) *Answers Inconsistent with the Verdict.* When the answers are consistent with each other but one or more is inconsistent with the general verdict, the court may:

    (A) approve, for entry under Rule 58, an appropriate judgment according to the answers, notwithstanding the general verdict;

    (B) direct the jury to further consider its answers and verdict; or

    (C) order a new trial.

(4) *Answers Inconsistent with Each Other and the Verdict.* When the answers are inconsistent with each other and one or more is also inconsistent with the general verdict, judgment must not be entered; instead, the court must direct the jury to further consider its answers and verdict, or must order a new trial.

[Amended effective July 1, 1963; August 1, 1987; April 30, 2007, effective December 1, 2007.]

AUTHORS' COMMENTARY ON RULE 49

PURPOSE AND SCOPE

Rule 49 provides mechanisms for directing specific questions to the jury. There are 2 alternative methods: special verdicts, which allow the jury to make findings as to each issue of fact; and written interrogatories, which, together with a general verdict, allow the parties and the court to verify that the jury is applying the law to the facts in the manner instructed by the court.

RULE 49(a)—SPECIAL VERDICT

CORE CONCEPT

The court may require the jury to return special verdicts as to each factual issue, instead of a general verdict in favor of one party.

APPLICATIONS

Comparison with General Verdict

A general verdict is a single statement disposing of the entire case (*e.g.,* "We find in favor of the defendant.").[1] Special verdicts ask the jury to decide specific factual questions (*e.g.,* "At the time of the accident, was the vehicle was proceeding at an excessive rate of speed?").[2]

Court's Discretion

The court has virtually absolute discretion as to the use of special verdicts.[3] This discretion extends to determining the content and layout of the verdict form, and any interrogatories submitted to the jury, provided the questions asked are reasonably capable of an interpretation that would allow the jury to address all factual issues essential to judgment.[4] Generally, special verdicts are more appropriate in complex cases.[5] Special verdicts are also valuable when the status of the law is uncertain, because if the trial court is reversed on the law, sufficient special verdicts may render a new trial unnecessary.

Scope of Questions

The special verdicts should fairly present the case, and should cover all factual issues.[6] In contrast to general verdicts, which entail application of law to the facts, special verdicts should be limited to factual findings.[7]

---

[1] *Mason v. Ford Motor Co., Inc.,* 307 F.3d 1271, 1274 (11th Cir. 2002).

[2] *See Kinetic Concepts, Inc. v. Smith & Nephew, Inc.,* 688 F.3d 1342, 1359 (Fed. Cir. 2012).

[3] *See Ling Nan Zheng v. Liberty Apparel Co. Inc.,* 617 F.3d 182, 186 (2d Cir. 2010).

[4] *E.E.O.C. v. Mgmt. Hospitality of Racine, Inc.,* 666 F.3d 422, 439–40 (7th Cir. 2012).

[5] *Dinco v. Dylex Ltd.,* 111 F.3d 964, 969 (1st Cir. 1997).

[6] *Sprinkle v. AMZ Mfg. Corp.,* 567 Fed.Appx. 163 (3d Cir. 2014).

[7] *Function Media, L.L.C. v. Google, Inc.,* 708 F.3d 1310, 1328–29 (Fed. Cir. 2013).

Form of Questions

Special verdicts may take different forms. Sometimes the questions will require the jury to write a brief answer (such as "yes" or "no"). Sometimes alternative special verdicts will be written out, and the jury need only choose one alternative.

Instructions to Jury

The court must give the jury sufficient instructions so that they can determine each issue before them.[8] When an issue before the jury involves mixed questions of fact and law, the court must give instructions as to the applicable law.[9]

Omission of Issues

If the court submits special verdicts to the jury and omits a question of fact raised by the pleadings or evidence, a party must object to the omission before the jury retires or that party waives the right to a jury trial on that issue.[10] As to issues not submitted to the jury and not objected to, the court may make the finding.[11] If the court merely issues a general verdict, the court will be deemed to have ruled in a consistent fashion on issues not submitted to the jury.[12]

Consistency of Special Verdicts

The jury's special verdicts must be certain, unequivocal, and consistent. If there is a construction of the special verdicts that renders them consistent, it will be adopted.[13] Otherwise, the court may require the jury to deliberate further[14] or may declare a mistrial. The court may not, however, enter judgment contrary to the jury's special verdicts.[15]

Failure to Find

If the jury fails to unanimously agree on some of the answers to special verdicts, the judge can: resubmit the special verdicts to the jury for further deliberations; ask the parties if they would be willing to accept the majority responses; enter judgment on the basis of the unanimous special verdicts if they are dispositive; declare the entire case a mistrial; or order a partial retrial of the issues not unanimously agreed upon.[16]

Objections

Objections to the special verdicts should be made before the jury retires.[17] Objections to the jury's responses or to the verdict to be entered based on the jury's responses should be made, if possible, before the jury is discharged. Courts disagree as to whether failure to do so results in a waiver of the objections.[18]

---

[8]   *Sprinkle v. AMZ Mfg. Corp.,* 567 Fed.Appx. 163 (3d Cir. 2014). *But see Aerotech Resources, Inc. v. Dodson Aviation, Inc.,* 191 F.Supp.2d 1209, 1220 (D. Kan. 2002), aff'd, 91 Fed. Appx. 37 (10th Cir. 2004) (with special interrogatories, the jury makes findings of fact as to each contested fact, then the court applies the law to those facts, so instructions of the law to the jury are unnecessary).

[9]   *Manufacturers Hanover Trust Co. v. Drysdale Securities Corp.,* 801 F.2d 13, 26 (2d Cir. 1986).

[10]   *See Vojdani v. Pharmsan Labs, Inc.,* 741 F.3d 777, 782 (7th Cir. 2013).

[11]   *Vojdani v. Pharmsan Labs, Inc.,* 741 F.3d 777, 782 (7th Cir. 2013).

[12]   *Ansin v. River Oaks Furniture, Inc.,* 105 F.3d 745, 756 (1st Cir. 1997).

[13]   *Technical Resource Services, Inc. v. Dornier Medical Systems, Inc.,* 134 F.3d 1458, 1464 (11th Cir. 1998).

[14]   *Selgas v. American Airlines, Inc.,* 858 F.Supp. 316 (D. Puerto Rico 1994).

[15]   *Kinetic Concepts, Inc. v. Smith & Nephew, Inc.,* 688 F.3d 1342, 1359 (Fed. Cir. 2012).

[16]   *Baxter Healthcare Corp. v. Spectramed, Inc.,* 49 F.3d 1575 (Fed. Cir. 1995).

[17]   *Cash v. Cnty. of Erie,* 654 F.3d 324, 340 (2d Cir. 2011).

[18]   *See Function Media, L.L.C. v. Google, Inc.,* 708 F.3d 1310, 1328 (Fed. Cir. 2013) (no waiver); *Trainor v. HEI Hospitality, LLC,* 699 F.3d 19, 34 (1st Cir. 2012) (waiver).

Law Governing

The form of verdict slip is a procedural issue governed by federal law, not by state law.[19]

RULE 49(b)—GENERAL VERDICT WITH ANSWERS TO WRITTEN QUESTIONS

CORE CONCEPT

The court may submit to the jury a general verdict and written questions or interrogatories about specific factual issues.[20]

APPLICATIONS

Purpose

Written interrogatories can serve 2 functions. First they focus the jury's attention on important factual issues and ensure that the general verdict is consistent with the factual findings. Second, if the court is subsequently reversed on a legal issue, a new trial may be avoided if the interrogatories contain sufficient findings.

Court's Discretion

As with special verdicts, the court has virtually absolute discretion with respect to the use of written interrogatories to the jury and with respect to the format of the questions.[21] The court also has broad discretion in evaluating the consistency of the interrogatories and the general verdict, and in selecting the remedy for any inconsistencies as described below.[22]

Content of Interrogatories

Because there is a general verdict, the content of the interrogatories is not as critical as with special verdicts—every issue need not be covered.[23]

Interrogatory Answers and Verdict Consistent

If the general verdict is consistent with the interrogatory answers, then the court will enter judgment accordingly. Any ambiguity will be resolved in favor of consistency.[24]

Interrogatory Answers and Verdict Not Consistent

If the interrogatory answers are internally consistent but not consistent with the general verdict,[25] the court has 3 options: it can order the jury to deliberate further;[26] it can enter judgment based on the interrogatories if they are sufficient;[27] or it can declare a mistrial.[28] The court may not enter judgment based on the general verdict in the face of inconsistent interrogatory answers (although judgment may be proper if the inconsistent

---

[19]   *Sprinkle v. AMZ Mfg. Corp.*, 567 Fed.Appx. 163 (3d Cir. 2014).

[20]   *Zhang v. American Gem Seafoods, Inc.*, 339 F.3d 1020 (9th Cir. 2003).

[21]   *Sprinkle v. AMZ Mfg. Corp.*, 567 Fed.Appx. 163 (3d Cir. 2014).

[22]   *Radvansky v. City of Olmsted Falls*, 496 F.3d 609, 618 (6th Cir. 2007).

[23]   *See Kinetic Concepts, Inc. v. Smith & Nephew, Inc.*, 688 F.3d 1342, 1359 (Fed. Cir. 2012).

[24]   *Hundley v. District of Columbia*, 494 F.3d 1097, 1102 (D.C. Cir. 2007) (the court has a duty to harmonize the jury's answers if it is possible under a fair reading of them).

[25]   *Wilbur v. Correctional Services Corp.*, 393 F.3d 1192, 1200 (11th Cir. 2004) (a verdict contains an inconsistency if answers given by the jury may not fairly be said to represent a logical and probable decision on the relevant issues as submitted).

[26]   *Kerman v. City of New York*, 261 F.3d 229, 244 (2d Cir. 2001).

[27]   *C.B. v. City of Sonora*, 730 F.3d 816, 824 (9th Cir. 2013).

[28]   *See Masters v. UHS of Delaware, Inc.*, 631 F.3d 464, 475 (8th Cir. 2011).

interrogatory response goes to a different issue or is not necessary for the judgment).[29] If the interrogatory answers are internally inconsistent and inconsistent with the general verdict, the court can order further deliberations or declare a mistrial, but cannot enter judgment.[30]

Inconsistent Interrogatories

When the interrogatory answers are internally inconsistent, the court may order the jury to deliberate further or may order a new trial.[31]

Inconsistent General Verdicts

When general verdicts on different claims are inconsistent, a court may not simply mold one of the two verdicts to be consistent with the other. Faced with inconsistent general verdicts, the court may take one of four approaches: (1) allow the verdicts to stand; (2) attempt to read the verdicts in a manner that will resolve the inconsistencies; (3) resubmit the question to the jury; or (4) order a new trial.[32]

Waiver of Objection to Inconsistency

Failure to object to an inconsistency prior to the jury being excused can result in waiver of the objection.[33]

ADDITIONAL RESEARCH REFERENCES

Wright & Miller, *Federal Practice and Procedure* §§ 2501 to 2513. Bennett & Hirschhorn, *Bennett's Guide to Jury Selection and Trial Dynamics in Civil and Criminal Litigation.*

C.J.S., Federal Civil Procedure §§ 1009 to 1027 et seq.

West's Key Number Digest, Federal Civil Procedure ⊷2211 to 2220, 2231 to 2242

---

[29] *Armstrong ex rel. Armstrong v. Brookdale University Hospital and Medical Center*, 425 F.3d 126, 135 (2d Cir. 2005).

[30] *King v. Ford Motor Co.*, 209 F.3d 886 (6th Cir. 2000) (court has broad discretion as to whether to send the jury out for further deliberations or order a new trial).

[31] *Wilbur v. Correctional Services Corp.*, 393 F.3d 1192, 1204 (11th Cir. 2004) (court has wide discretion as to which option to employ).

[32] *City of Los Angeles v. Heller*, 475 U.S. 796, 106 S.Ct. 1571, 89 L.Ed.2d 806 (1986)).

[33] *Function Media, L.L.C. v. Google, Inc.*, 708 F.3d 1310, 1328 (Fed. Cir. 2013).

RULE 50

JUDGMENT AS A MATTER OF LAW IN A JURY TRIAL; RELATED MOTION FOR A NEW TRIAL; CONDITIONAL RULING

(a) Judgment as a Matter of Law.

(1) *In General.* If a party has been fully heard on an issue during a jury trial and the court finds that a reasonable jury would not have a legally sufficient evidentiary basis to find for the party on that issue, the court may:

(A) resolve the issue against the party; and

(B) grant a motion for judgment as a matter of law against the party on a claim or defense that, under the controlling law, can be maintained or defeated only with a favorable finding on that issue.

(2) *Motion.* A motion for judgment as a matter of law may be made at any time before the case is submitted to the jury. The motion must specify the judgment sought and the law and facts that entitle the movant to the judgment.

(b) Renewing the Motion After Trial; Alternative Motion for a New Trial. If the court does not grant a motion for judgment as a matter of law made under Rule 50(a), the court is considered to have submitted the action to the jury subject to the court's later deciding the legal questions raised by the motion. No later than 28 days after the entry of judgment—or if the motion addresses a jury issue not decided by a verdict, no later than 28 days after the jury was discharged—the movant may file a renewed motion for judgment as a matter of law and may include an alternative or joint request for a new trial under Rule 59. In ruling on the renewed motion, the court may:

(1) allow judgment on the verdict, if the jury returned a verdict;

(2) order a new trial; or

(3) direct the entry of judgment as a matter of law.

(c) Granting the Renewed Motion; Conditional Ruling on a Motion for a New Trial.

(1) *In General.* If the court grants a renewed motion for judgment as a matter of law, it must also conditionally rule on any motion for a new trial by determining whether a new trial should be granted if the judgment is

later vacated or reversed. The court must state the grounds for conditionally granting or denying the motion for a new trial.

(2) *Effect of a Conditional Ruling.* Conditionally granting the motion for a new trial does not affect the judgment's finality; if the judgment is reversed, the new trial must proceed unless the appellate court orders otherwise. If the motion for a new trial is conditionally denied, the appellee may assert error in that denial; if the judgment is reversed, the case must proceed as the appellate court orders.

(d) Time for a Losing Party's New-Trial Motion. Any motion for a new trial under Rule 59 by a party against whom judgment as a matter of law is rendered must be filed no later than 28 days after the entry of the judgment.

(e) Denying the Motion for Judgment as a Matter of Law; Reversal on Appeal. If the court denies the motion for judgment as a matter of law, the prevailing party may, as appellee, assert grounds entitling it to a new trial should the appellate court conclude that the trial court erred in denying the motion. If the appellate court reverses the judgment, it may order a new trial, direct the trial court to determine whether a new trial should be granted, or direct the entry of judgment.

[Amended January 21, 1963, effective July 1, 1963; March 2, 1987, effective August 1, 1987; April 30, 1991, effective December 1, 1991; April 22, 1993, effective December 1, 1993; April 27, 1995, effective December 1, 1995; April 12, 2006, effective December 1, 2006; April 30, 2007, effective December 1, 2007; March 26, 2009, effective December 1, 2009.]

AUTHORS' COMMENTARY ON RULE 50

PURPOSE AND SCOPE

Rule 50 contains the provisions governing motions for judgment as a matter of law during and following jury trials. These remedies are generally available when the evidence in the record could not reasonably support a particular verdict.

♦ **NOTE:** A motion for judgment after trial must be filed within 28 days of entry of the judgment.

RULE 50(a)—JUDGMENT AS A MATTER OF LAW

CORE CONCEPT

Rule 50(a) allows the court to take a case away from the jury by entering a judgment if there is not sufficient evidence in the record to raise a genuine factual controversy.

APPLICATIONS

Content of Motion

A motion for judgment as a matter of law must state the judgment sought (*i.e.,* the counts or issues upon which judgment is sought[1]) and the law and facts supporting the judgment.[2]

---

[1]   *Laymon v. Lobby House, Inc.,* 613 F.Supp.2d 504, 512 (D.Del. 2009).
[2]   *Medisim Ltd. v. BestMed, LLC,* 758 F.3d 1352 (Fed. Cir. 2014).

Form and Timing of Motion

A motion for judgment as a matter of law may be made orally or in writing, but must be made on the record.[3] The motion may be made after the opposing party has been fully heard on an issue, at any time before submission of the case to the jury.[4] Such motions are typically made at the close of the plaintiff's case (by the defendant), at the close of the record, or both.

Subject of Motion

A motion for judgment as a matter of law may seek judgment on entire claims or defenses or on specific issues that are not wholly dispositive of a claim or defense.[5]

Opportunity to Cure

A major purpose of the motion is to call a deficiency in the evidence to the attention of the court so the opposing counsel may cure the defect.[6] The court then has a duty to apprise the non-moving party of the materiality of the dispositive fact and provide that party with an opportunity to present any available evidence.[7]

Standard

The standard for a motion for judgment as a matter of law is the same as for a motion for summary judgment (making that substantial body of case law applicable).[8] Judgment as a matter of law is appropriate when the evidence in the record could not properly support a particular verdict.[9] This determination is a matter of law for the court.[10] The court must view all evidence in the light most favorable to the party opposing the motion;[11] it may not make credibility determinations or weigh the evidence.[12] However, the court may disregard testimony that is opposed to undisputed physical facts.[13] Moreover, a "mere scintilla" of evidence is not sufficient.[14]

Inferences

The court must draw all reasonable inferences from the evidence that favor the party opposing the motion.[15] Thus, even if all the facts are undisputed, a motion for judgment as a matter of law will still be denied if the evidence is susceptible of conflicting inferences.[16] However, inferences created by statute or doctrine, such as *res ipsa loquitur*, may raise different issues requiring specific research.

---

[3]   *Ross v. Rhodes Furniture, Inc.*, 146 F.3d 1286, 1289 (11th Cir. 1998).

[4]   *Graham Const. Services v. Hammer & Steel Inc.*, 755 F.3d 611 (8th Cir. 2014).

[5]   *Ross v. Rhodes Furniture, Inc.*, 146 F.3d 1286, 1289–90 (11th Cir. 1998).

[6]   *See Hyundai Motor Finance Co. v. McKay Motors I, LLC*, 574 F.3d 637, 642 (8th Cir. 2009) (technical precision is not necessary so long as the court and opposing party are on notice of the issue).

[7]   *Waters v. Young*, 100 F.3d 1437, 1441 (9th Cir. 1996) (the court's duty is especially important when confronted with pro se litigants).

[8]   *See Linden v. CNH Am., LLC*, 673 F.3d 829, 834 (8th Cir. 2012).

[9]   *Anderson v. Liberty Lobby, Inc.*, 477 U.S. 242, 106 S.Ct. 2505, 91 L.Ed.2d 202 (1986).

[10] *See Brownstein v. Lindsay*, 742 F.3d 55, 63 (3d Cir. 2014).

[11] *Galloway v. United States*, 319 U.S. 372, 63 S.Ct. 1077, 87 L. Ed. 1458 (1943).

[12] *Reeves v. Sanderson Plumbing Prods., Inc.*, 530 U.S. 133, 150, 120 S.Ct. 2097, 147 L.Ed.2d 105 (2000).

[13] *See, e.g., O'Connor v. Pennsylvania R. Co.*, 308 F.2d 911 (2d Cir. 1962) (testimony about snowfall disregarded when contrary to the records of the Weather Bureau).

[14] *A.B. Small Co. v. Lamborn & Co.*, 267 U.S. 248, 254, 45 S.Ct. 300, 303, 69 L. Ed. 597 (1925).

[15] *Laxton v. Gap Inc.*, 333 F.3d 572, 577 (5th Cir. 2003).

[16] *Daniels v. Twin Oaks Nursing Home*, 692 F.2d 1321, 1325 (11th Cir. 1982).

Binding Jury Trials Only

Rule 50 applies only to binding jury cases.[17] The appropriate motion in non-jury trials and trials with an advisory jury is a motion for judgment on partial findings under Rule 52(c).[18]

Motion Held Under Consideration

The court is under no obligation to grant a motion for judgment as a matter of law even if the record supports the motion. Courts often allow the jury to reach a verdict in order to minimize the likelihood of needing a new trial. If the jury reaches the same conclusion as the judge, then the judge need take no action. If the jury reaches the opposite conclusion, the judge can enter judgment as a matter of law. Then, if the case is appealed and the appellate court disagrees with the judge, there is no need for a new trial as the court can simply reinstate the jury verdict.[19]

Motion Granted

If the court grants a motion for judgment as a matter of law, it will enter the appropriate verdict without involvement of the jury.

Motion Denied

If the motion for judgment as a matter of law is denied, the court is considered to have submitted the action to the jury subject to the court's later deciding the questions raised by the motion.[20] If it was the defendant's motion that the court denied, the defendant may put on evidence. However, if the plaintiffs case lacked evidence supporting a certain element and that evidence is brought out during the defendant's case, the deficiency will be cured.[21]

Who May Make Motion

Both defendants and plaintiffs may make motions for judgment as a matter of law. Thus, if the plaintiff enters evidence sufficient to support each element of the plaintiff's case and that evidence is not contradicted during the defendant's case, the plaintiff will be entitled to a judgment as a matter of law.[22] In addition, the judge may grant a judgment as a matter of law *sua sponte*.[23]

Prerequisite to Appeal

A motion for judgment as a matter of law before the close of the record is a prerequisite to challenging the sufficiency of the evidence on appeal.[24] The courts are divided as to whether appellate issues other than those relating to the sufficiency of the evidence are affected (see Summary Judgment Motions bullet below).[25] An exception to this principle occurs if the verdict constitutes plain error on the face of the record and a miscarriage of justice would result if the verdict remained in effect.[26]

---

[17] *Federal Ins. Co. v. HPSC, Inc.*, 480 F.3d 26, 32 (1st Cir. 2007).

[18] *Federal Ins. Co. v. HPSC, Inc.*, 480 F.3d 26, 32 (1st Cir. 2007).

[19] *Colonial Lincoln-Mercury, Inc. v. Musgrave*, 749 F.2d 1092, 1098 (4th Cir. 1984).

[20] *Holder v. Illinois Dept. of Corrections*, 751 F.3d 486, 490 (7th Cir. 2014).

[21] *Trustees of University of Pennsylvania v. Lexington Ins. Co.*, 815 F.2d 890, 903 (3d Cir. 1987).

[22] *Hurd v. American Hoist and Derrick Co.*, 734 F.2d 495, 499 (10th Cir. 1984).

[23] *American and Foreign Ins. Co. v. Bolt*, 106 F.3d 155, 160 (6th Cir. 1997).

[24] *Unitherm Food Systems, Inc. v. Swift-Eckrich, Inc.*, 546 U.S. 394, 126 S.Ct. 980, 987, 163 L.Ed.2d 974 (2006).

[25] *Feld v. Feld*, 688 F.3d 779, 782 (D.C.Cir. 2012).

[26] *Stephenson v. Doe*, 332 F.3d 68, 75–76 (2d Cir. 2003).

Summary Judgment Motions

The courts differ as to the extent to which a party must renew an unsuccessful motion for summary judgment as a motion for judgment as a matter of law during and following a jury trial. Some courts do not require presentation of pure legal issues in the form of a Rule 50 motion.[27] Others require all issues raised in a summary judgment motion to be presented in a Rule 50 motion in order to preserve the issues for appeal.[28] There are also gradations to these approaches.[29] If you are not sure which category your jurisdiction and/or motion falls into, it is good practice to raise summary judgment motions as Rule 50 motions at the end of the evidence, and again before submission to the jury if necessary.[30]

RULE 50(b)—RENEWING THE MOTION AFTER TRIAL; ALTERNATIVE MOTION FOR A NEW TRIAL

CORE CONCEPT

After trial, the court can enter a judgment that is inconsistent with the jury's verdict if it determines that the verdict was not supported by the evidence.

APPLICATIONS

Content of Motion

A motion for judgment after trial must state the grounds for relief,[31] and may include only those grounds raised in the original motion for judgment as a matter of law.[32]

Timing

The motion must be filed not later than 28 days after the *entry* of the judgment[33] (not the notice of entry of the judgment). If the jury does not return a verdict, such as with a mistrial, or if the subject of the motion for judgment as a matter of law was an issue not decided by the verdict, the parties have 28 days from the discharge of the jury. The courts are divided as to whether the time limit can be enlarged.[34]

Failure to File Is Waiver

Failure to file a postverdict motion under Rule 50(b) limits a party's right to appeal.[35] Some courts do not apply this restriction rigidly.[36]

---

[27] *See, e.g., HOK Sport, Inc., v. FC Des Moines, L.C.*, 495 F.3d 927, 942 (8th Cir. 2007).

[28] *See, e.g., Varghese v. Honeywell Intern., Inc.*, 424 F.3d 411, 420–23 (4th Cir. 2005).

[29] *See, e.g., Duban v. Waverly Sales Co.*, 760 F.3d 832 (8th Cir. 2014) (requiring a party to file a Rule 50(a) motion during trial but not a Rule 50(b) renewal in order to preserve a pure legal issue raised on summary judgment); *Becker v. Tidewater, Inc.*, 586 F.3d 358, 365, n.4 (5th Cir. 2009) (appeal permitted when the denial was based on a pure legal issue and the trial was non-jury).

[30] *Haberman v. The Hartford Insurance Group*, 443 F.3d 1257 (10th Cir. 2006).

[31] *Andreas v. Volkswagen of America, Inc.*, 336 F.3d 789 (8th Cir. 2003).

[32] *Wallace v. McGlothan*, 606 F.3d 410 (7th Cir. 2010) (responding to new issues raised in the Rule 50(b) motion waives the objection that they were not raised in the Rule 50(a) motion).

[33] *Hinz v. Neuroscience, Inc.*, 538 F.3d 979, 983 (8th Cir. 2008) (where motion filed timely but brief filed 1 day late, brief could not be considered).

[34] *Art Attacks Ink, LLC v. MGA Entertainment Inc.*, 581 F.3d 1138, 1142 (9th Cir. 2009).

[35] *Oritz v. Jordan*, 562 U.S. 180, 131 S.Ct. 884, 178 L.Ed.2d 703 (2011); *Unitherm Food Sys. v. Swift-Eckrich, Inc.*, 546 U.S. 394, 407, 126 S.Ct. 980, 163 L.Ed.2d 974 (2006).

[36] *See Holder v. Illinois Dept. of Corrections*, 751 F.3d 486, 491 (7th Cir. 2014).

Same Standard as Rule 50(a)

A renewed motion for judgment as a matter of law under Rule 50(b) is evaluated under the same standard as the initial motion under Rule 50(a) filed at the close of evidence;[37] the motion will be denied if the evidence in the record could properly support the verdict, viewing the evidence and all inferences in the light most favorable to the non-moving party.[38] This standard is discussed in more detail in the commentary to Rule 50(a) above.

Motion During Trial a Prerequisite

A party cannot make a motion for judgment after trial unless it filed a motion for judgment as a matter of law before the case was submitted to the jury,[39] and may not assert grounds that were not raised in the Rule 50(a) motion (unless the grounds were not available at that time).[40] If there was no motion for judgment as a matter of law but the evidence does not support the verdict, the court can order a new trial under Rule 59.[41]

Motion for a New Trial

A party may join a motion for a new trial with a motion for judgment after trial, or request a new trial in the alternative.[42] The motion will be granted if the verdict is contrary to the clear weight of the evidence.[43] A new trial is favored over a judgment contrary to the verdict when it appears that the party could present sufficient evidence to support the verdict at a future date.

Court's Options

If the jury returned a verdict, the court may allow the verdict to stand,[44] order a new trial, or direct entry of judgment as a matter of law.[45] If no verdict was returned, the court may order a new trial or direct the entry of judgment as a matter of law. When a motion for new trial is joined with a motion for judgment after trial, Rule 50 specifically requires that the court rule on both motions.[46]

Appeals

Rulings on motions for judgment after trial are final, appealable orders. In contrast, an order granting a new trial may not be a final, appealable order.[47]

---

[37] *Chaney v. City of Orlando*, 483 F.3d 1221, 1227 (11th Cir. 2007).

[38] *See Experience Hendrix L.L.C. v. Hendrixlicensing.com Ltd.*, 742 F.3d 377, 390 (9th Cir. 2014).

[39] *Medisim Ltd. v. BestMed, LLC*, 758 F.3d 1352 *(Fed. Cir. 2014); but see Minnesota Supply Co. v. Raymond Corp.*, 472 F.3d 524, 535–36 (8th Cir. 2006) (failure to renew the motion not a waiver when the court advised the party that there was no need to renew the motion).

[40] *Nassar v. Jackson*, 779 F.3d 547, 551 (8th Cir. 2015).

[41] *Johnson v. New York, N.H. & H.R. Co.*, 344 U.S. 48, 54, 73 S.Ct. 125, 128, 97 L. Ed. 77 (1952).

[42] *Pediatrix Screening, Inc. v. Telechem Intern., Inc.*, 602 F.3d 541, 546 (3d Cir. 2010).

[43] *Oritz v. Jordan*, 562 U.S. 180, 131 S.Ct. 884, 178 L.Ed.2d 703 (2011) (discussing the difference between insufficient evidence under Rule 50(b) and weight of the evidence under Rule 59).

[44] *Georges v. Novartis Pharmaceuticals Corp.*, 988 F.Supp.2d 1152, 1162 (C.D. Cal. 2013).

[45] *United States ex rel. Purcell v. MWI Corporation*, 15 F.Supp.3d 18 (D.D.C. 2014).

[46] *See Jennings v. Jones*, 587 F.3d 430, 432 (1st Cir. 2009).

[47] *Binder v. Long Island Lighting Co.*, 57 F.3d 193 (2d Cir.1995).

RULE 50(c)—GRANTING THE RENEWED MOTION; CONDITIONAL RULINGS ON A MOTION FOR A NEW TRIAL

CORE CONCEPT

If the court grants a motion for judgment as a matter of law after trial and a motion for a new trial was also filed, the court will make a conditional ruling on the motion for a new trial, setting forth the reasons for its conditional ruling.[48]

APPLICATIONS

Rulings Conditional on Reversal

The trial court's rulings on the motion for a new trial are applicable if the appeals court reverses the granting of the judgment after trial.[49] In that case, the appeals court will generally enter the original verdict or order a new trial, depending on the trial court's conditional ruling. However, the appeals court also may review the trial court's conditional ruling on the motion for a new trial.

Granting of Both Motions

If the trial court grants both a motion for judgment notwithstanding the verdict and a motion for a new trial, the ruling on the motion for a new trial is automatically deemed conditional.[50]

Failure to Issue a Conditional Ruling

If a court fails to issue a conditional ruling on the motion for a new trial, the appellate court has the authority to either remand to the trial court to decide the motion for a new trial or decide the motion itself.[51]

RULE 50(d)—TIME FOR A LOSING PARTY'S NEW-TRIAL MOTION

CORE CONCEPT

If the court grants a motion for judgment after trial, the party against whom judgment was entered may file a motion for a new trial no later than 28 days after the entry of judgment, pursuant to Rule 59.

RULE 50(e)—DENYING THE MOTION FOR JUDGMENT AS A MATTER OF LAW; REVERSAL ON APPEAL

CORE CONCEPT

If the losing party appeals the denial of a motion for judgment after trial, the prevailing party may on appeal assert grounds for a new trial in the event that the court reverses the denial of the motion for judgment after trial.[52] If the appellate court does reverse, it may order the entry of judgment, order a new trial, or remand to the trial court to determine whether a new trial is warranted.

---

[48] *Medisim Ltd. v. BestMed, LLC*, 758 F.3d 1352 (Fed. Cir. 2014).

[49] *Fioto v. Manhattan Woods Golf Enterprises, LLC*, 304 F.Supp.2d 541 (S.D. N.Y. 2004), aff'd, 123 Fed. Appx. 26 (2d Cir. 2005).

[50] *See Smart v. City of Miami Beach, Fla.*, 933 F.Supp.2d 1366 (S.D. Fla. 2013).

[51] *Acosta v. City and County of San Francisco*, 83 F.3d 1143, 1149 (9th Cir. 1996); *but see Christopher v. Florida*, 449 F.3d 1360, 1365 n.3 (11th Cir. 2006) (where the appellant fails to pursue a new trial on appeal, the court will consider the issue abandoned).

[52] *See Bunn v. Oldendorff Carriers GmbH & Co. KG*, 723 F.3d 454, 468 (4th Cir. 2013).

ADDITIONAL RESEARCH REFERENCES

Wright & Miller, *Federal Practice and Procedure* §§ 2521 to 2540

C.J.S., Federal Civil Procedure §§ 958 to 977 et seq.

C.J.S., Federal Civil Procedure § 1034, § 1089, § 1093, §§ 1219 to 1226 et seq.

West's Key Number Digest, Federal Civil Procedure ⊷2111 to 2156, 2601 to 2610

RULE 51

INSTRUCTIONS TO THE JURY; OBJECTIONS; PRESERVING A CLAIM OF ERROR

(a) Requests.

(1) *Before or at the Close of the Evidence.* At the close of the evidence or at any earlier reasonable time that the court orders, a party may file and furnish to every other party written requests for the jury instructions it wants the court to give.

(2) *After the Close of the Evidence.* After the close of the evidence, a party may:

   (A) file requests for instructions on issues that could not reasonably have been anticipated by an earlier time that the court set for requests; and

   (B) with the court's permission, file untimely requests for instructions on any issue.

(b) Instructions. The court:

(1) must inform the parties of its proposed instructions and proposed action on the requests before instructing the jury and before final jury arguments;

(2) must give the parties an opportunity to object on the record and out of the jury's hearing before the instructions and arguments are delivered; and

(3) may instruct the jury at any time before the jury is discharged.

(c) Objections.

(1) *How to Make.* A party who objects to an instruction or the failure to give an instruction must do so on the record, stating distinctly the matter objected to and the grounds for the objection.

(2) *When to Make.* An objection is timely if:

   (A) a party objects at the opportunity provided under Rule 51(b)(2); or

   (B) a party was not informed of an instruction or action on a request before that opportunity to object, and the party objects promptly after learning that the instruction or request will be, or has been, given or refused.

(d) Assigning Error; Plain Error.

(1) *Assigning Error.* A party may assign as error:

(A) an error in an instruction actually given, if that party properly objected; or

(B) a failure to give an instruction, if that party properly requested it and—unless the court rejected the request in a definitive ruling on the record—also properly objected.

(2) *Plain Error.* A court may consider a plain error in the instructions that has not been preserved as required by Rule 51(d)(1) if the error affects substantial rights.

[Amended effective August 1, 1987; March 27, 2003, effective December 1, 2003; April 30, 2007, effective December 1, 2007.]

AUTHORS' COMMENTARY ON RULE 51

PURPOSE AND SCOPE

Before the jury retires to deliberate, the judge must instruct the jury as to the law that they are to apply. The parties have an opportunity to request that certain instructions be given, and to object to the instructions given and to the instructions not given.

RULE 51(a)—REQUESTS

CORE CONCEPT

The parties may submit proposed jury instructions to the court. Proposed instructions are submitted at the close of the evidence or at such earlier time as directed by the court.

APPLICATIONS

Timing of Requests

Requests for jury instructions are normally made at the close of the evidence, or earlier if the court so directs.[1] If the court has set a time before the close of evidence for submission of requests for instructions, a party may submit additional requests for instructions after the close of evidence on issues that the party could not have anticipated when it first submitted its requests.[2] Local rules may set the time for making requests for jury instructions. The court, in its discretion, may consider untimely requests.[3]

Form and Content of Requests

Requests normally should be reasonably neutral statements of the law governing the case, and not overly argumentative. Requests are usually written, although they can be oral.

Service

Requests for instruction must be furnished to every other party.[4]

---

[1]   *Potthast v. Metro-North Railroad Co.*, 400 F.3d 143, 153 (2d Cir. 2005).

[2]   *Potthast v. Metro-North Railroad Co.*, 400 F.3d 143, 153 (2d Cir. 2005).

[3]   Rule 51(a)(2)(B).

[4]   Rule 51(a)(1).

RULE 51(b)—INSTRUCTIONS

CORE CONCEPT

The court must inform the parties of its proposed instructions before instructing the jury and before the parties' final arguments to the jury, and must give the parties an opportunity to object on the record and out of the jury's hearing.

APPLICATIONS

Rulings on Requests

The court is required to inform the parties of its rulings on the jury instruction requests before the closing arguments,[5] so that the counsel may adjust their closings accordingly. Failure to do so, however, will not be grounds for a new trial unless it is prejudicial.[6]

Form and Procedure for Instructions

Instructions are given to the jury in open court at any time after trial begins and before the jury is discharged.[7] The judge may repeat portions of the charge or give a supplemental charge at the jury's request, but must afford the parties notice and an opportunity to be present for such additional instructions. The judge may submit a written charge to the jury, although it is not commonly done.

Content of Instructions

The court should give an instruction on every material issue in the case.[8] The instruction should clearly and understandably convey the status of the applicable law.[9] There is no particular wording or order mandated,[10] and the judge need not use the language requested by the parties. Narrowly-tailored instructions are favored over broad statements of the law.

Deadlocked Jury

The judge may instruct a jury claiming to be deadlocked to make further attempts to reach a verdict. The judge may not, however, coerce reluctant jurors to join the majority.

Comments on Evidence

The court, in its discretion, may comment on the evidence and even focus the jury's attention on certain portions of the evidence. If the judge does so, the judge must make it clear to the jury that they, not the judge, are the ultimate fact finders.

Opportunity to Object

The court must give the parties an opportunity to raise objections to the instructions on the record and out of the hearing of the jury before the instructions and closing arguments are delivered.[11] If the court fails to give an opportunity to raise the objections, parties with

---

[5] *Johnson v. General Bd. of Pension & Health Benefits of the United Methodist Church*, 733 F.3d 722, 732 (7th Cir. 2013).

[6] *Johnson v. General Bd. of Pension & Health Benefits of the United Methodist Church*, 733 F.3d 722, 732 (7th Cir. 2013).

[7] *Heimlicher v. Steele*, 615 F.Supp.2d 884, 932 (N.D.Iowa 2009).

[8] *See Williams v. Dist. of Columbia*, 825 F.Supp.2d 88, 91 (D.D.C. 2011).

[9] *See Williams v. Dist. of Columbia*, 825 F.Supp.2d 88, 91 (D.D.C. 2011).

[10] *Williams v. Dist. of Columbia*, 825 F.Supp.2d 88, 91 (D.D.C. 2011).

[11] *Johnson v. General Bd. of Pension & Health Benefits of the United Methodist Church*, 733 F.3d 722, 732 (7th Cir. 2013).

objections should request an opportunity.[12] If instructions are reread or the jury is given additional instructions, an objection may be raised at that time.[13]

RULE 51(c)—OBJECTIONS

CORE CONCEPT

Objections to the instructions must be made on the record with a statement of the grounds.

APPLICATIONS

Content of Objection

Parties must state their objections with sufficient clarity and specificity that the judge can understand the nature of the objection and remedy the problem if the judge agrees.[14] Any appeal must be based upon issues so raised in an objection.[15]

Time of Objections

A party must object to the content of the instructions at the opportunity provided by the court before the instructions and closing arguments are delivered,[16] even if the party has previously raised and attempted to preserve the same objection.[17] If a party was not informed of an instruction or action on a request for an instruction prior to the opportunity to object provided by the court, the party may object promptly upon learning that the instruction was or would be given or refused.[18]

Objection on the Record

Objections to jury instructions must be on the record; objections made off the record in chambers are not effective.[19] It is not sufficient to have proposed an instruction that the court does not give.[20]

Failure to Object

If a party fails to object to an instruction before the jury begins deliberations and the court has not already made a definitive ruling on the record regarding the subject instruction,[21] the party loses the right to challenge the instruction on appeal.[22] Some courts will undertake appellate review in the absence of a timely objection if the party never had

---

[12] *See Johnson v. General Bd. of Pension & Health Benefits of the United Methodist Church*, 733 F.3d 722, 732 (7th Cir. 2013) (counsel objected promptly after the court gave the instructions when the court had not previously provided an opportunity to place objections on the record).

[13] *Barrett v. Orange County Human Rights Com'n*, 194 F.3d 341, 349 (2d Cir. 1999).

[14] *Lesende v. Borrero*, 752 F.3d 324, 335 (3d Cir. 2014); *Lopez v. Tyson Foods, Inc.*, 690 F.3d 869, 876 (8th Cir. 2012).

[15] *Lopez v. Tyson Foods, Inc.*, 690 F.3d 869, 876 (8th Cir. 2012).

[16] *Rosa-Rivera v. Dorado Health, Inc.*, 787 F.3d 614, 618 (1st Cir. 2015).

[17] *Torres-Rivera v. O'Neill-Cancel*, 406 F.3d 43, 49–50 (1st Cir. 2005) (party must object at the time of the instructions even if the party previously proposed the instruction that the court declined to give).

[18] *See Johnson v. General Bd. of Pension & Health Benefits of the United Methodist Church*, 733 F.3d 722, 732 (7th Cir. 2013).

[19] *See Colon-Millin v. Sears Roebuck De Puerto Rico, Inc.*, 455 F.3d 30, 41 (1st Cir. 2006) (judge's statement that the parties could rely on objections asserted earlier in chambers did not relieve them of the obligation to state the objections on the record).

[20] *Franklin Prescriptions, Inc. v. New York Times Co.*, 424 F.3d 336, 339 (3d Cir. 2005).

[21] *Obsidian Finance Group, LLC v. Cox*, 740 F.3d 1284, 1289 (9th Cir. 2014) (no need to object again if the court has already ruled on a motion *in limine* on the same point).

[22] *Fox v. Hayes*, 600 F.3d 819, 838 (7th Cir. 2010).

an opportunity to object,[23] but most courts strictly require a timely objection on the record.[24] Similarly, some courts will undertake appellate review in the absence of a timely objection if an objection would have been a pointless formality.[25] Thus, as a general matter, if a party does not make a timely objection, it is limited to objections of plain error under Rule 51(d).

RULE 51(d)—ASSIGNING ERROR; PLAIN ERROR

CORE CONCEPT

A party may base an appeal on an instruction if the party made a proper objection or upon plain error.

APPLICATIONS

Appeal of Issues Preserved by Objection

In general, a party may only raise on appeal issues regarding the instructions given that the party properly raised as objections before the trial court.[26] A party may only raise on appeal an issue regarding an instruction not given if the party made a proper request for the instruction[27] and either the court made a definitive ruling on the record rejecting the request[28] or the party made a proper objection regarding the omitted instruction.[29]

Appeal of Issues Not Preserved by Objection

The appeals court may, under extreme circumstances when justice demands, reverse even if no objections were made when an instruction contains plain error.[30] Additionally, the appeals court may consider an issue not preserved by objection where there has been a supervening change in the law.[31]

ADDITIONAL RESEARCH REFERENCES

Wright & Miller, *Federal Practice and Procedure* §§ 2551 to 2558. Devitt, Blackmar, Wolff & O'Malley, *Federal Jury Practice and Instructions.*

C.J.S., Federal Civil Procedure §§ 983 to 994 et seq.

West's Key Number Digest, Federal Civil Procedure ⊶2171 to 2185

---

[23] *Schmitz v. Canadian Pacific Ry. Co.*, 454 F.3d 678 (7th Cir.2006) (judge changed the instructions without notifying the parties).

[24] *See Shcherbakovskiy v. Da Capo Al Fine, Ltd.*, 490 F.3d 130, 141 n.2 (2d Cir. 2007) (judge's assurance that the movant would be deemed to have made "every motion available" did not preserve objections).

[25] *See Rosa-Rivera v. Dorado Health, Inc.*, 787 F.3d 614, 618 (1st Cir. 2015) (no need to object when the court has already made a definitive ruling on the record).

[26] *Connelly v. Hyundai Motor Co.*, 351 F.3d 535, 544 (1st Cir. 2003) (an objection on one ground does not preserve appellate review of a different ground).

[27] *Microsoft Corp. v. i4i Ltd. Partnership*, 504 U.S. 91, 111–12, 131 S.Ct. 2238, 180 L.Ed.2d 131 (2011).

[28] *Colon-Millin v. Sears Roebuck De Puerto Rico, Inc.*, 455 F.3d 30, 40 (1st Cir. 2006).

[29] *Lewis v. City of Chicago Police Dept.*, 590 F.3d 427, 434 (7th Cir. 2009) (plain error is one that probably changed the outcome of the trial).

[30] *Rasanen v. Doe,* 723 F.3d 325, 332 (2d Cir. 2013) (plain error exception should only be invoked with extreme caution).

[31] *See Cadena v. Pacesetter Corp.*, 224 F.3d 1203, 1212 (10th Cir. 2000).

RULE 52

FINDINGS AND CONCLUSIONS BY THE COURT; JUDGMENT ON PARTIAL FINDINGS

(a) Findings and Conclusions.

(1) *In General.* In an action tried on the facts without a jury or with an advisory jury, the court must find the facts specially and state its conclusions of law separately. The findings and conclusions may be stated on the record after the close of the evidence or may appear in an opinion or a memorandum of decision filed by the court. Judgment must be entered under Rule 58.

(2) *For an Interlocutory Injunction.* In granting or refusing an interlocutory injunction, the court must similarly state the findings and conclusions that support its action.

(3) *For a Motion.* The court is not required to state findings or conclusions when ruling on a motion under Rule 12 or 56 or, unless these rules provide otherwise, on any other motion.

(4) *Effect of a Master's Findings.* A master's findings, to the extent adopted by the court, must be considered the court's findings.

(5) *Questioning the Evidentiary Support.* A party may later question the sufficiency of the evidence supporting the findings, whether or not the party requested findings, objected to them, moved to amend them, or moved for partial findings.

(6) *Setting Aside the Findings.* Findings of fact, whether based on oral or other evidence, must not be set aside unless clearly erroneous, and the reviewing court must give due regard to the trial court's opportunity to judge the witnesses' credibility.

(b) Amended or Additional Findings. On a party's motion filed no later than 28 days after the entry of judgment, the court may amend its findings—or make additional findings—and may amend the judgment accordingly. The motion may accompany a motion for a new trial under Rule 59.

(c) Judgment on Partial Findings. If a party has been fully heard on an issue during a nonjury trial and the court finds against the party on that issue, the court may enter judgment against the party on a claim or defense that, under the controlling law, can be maintained or defeated only with a favorable finding on that issue. The court may, however, decline to render any judgment until the close of the evidence. A judgment on partial findings must

be supported by findings of fact and conclusions of law as required by Rule 52(a).

[Amended December 27, 1946, effective March 19, 1948; January 21, 1963, effective July 1, 1963; April 28, 1983, effective August 1, 1983; April 29, 1985, effective August 1, 1985; April 30, 1991, effective December 1, 1991; April 22, 1993, effective December 1, 1993; April 27, 1995, effective December 1, 1995; April 30, 2007, effective December 1, 2007; March 26, 2009, effective December 1, 2009.]

AUTHORS' COMMENTARY ON RULE 52

PURPOSE AND SCOPE

Following a non-jury trial, the trial judge make findings of fact and conclusions of law. Rule 52 sets the standard of review for such findings, and allows the judge to enter judgment during the trial if a party fails to carry its burden of proof.

RULE 52(a)—FINDINGS AND CONCLUSIONS

CORE CONCEPT

Following a non-jury trial, the trial judge must explicitly state findings of fact and conclusions of law upon which the judge bases the judgment.

APPLICATIONS

Findings and Conclusions Mandatory

The requirement that the judge make findings of fact and conclusions of law is mandatory.[1] The parties do not need to request findings.

Content of Findings and Conclusions

The findings must be sufficient to indicate the factual basis for the ultimate conclusion,[2] and permit meaningful appellate review,[3] but need not address all the evidence presented at trial.[4] The court need not make findings on uncontested or stipulated facts.[5] The court should make separate findings of fact and conclusions of law.[6]

Credibility Determinations and Inferences

When making findings of fact, the court may accept or reject the testimony of witnesses and draw any inferences it deems appropriate.[7]

---

[1]   *See In re Frescati Shipping Co., Ltd.*, 718 F.3d 184 (3d Cir. 2013).

[2]   *Valsamis v. Gonzalez-Romero*, 748 F.3d 61, 63 (1st Cir. 2014).

[3]   *United States v. Alabama Dept. of Mental Health and Mental Retardation*, 673 F.3d 1320, 1329 (11th Cir. 2012).

[4]   *See IPSCO Tubulars, Inc. v. Ajax TOCCO Magnathermic Corp.*, 779 F.3d 744, 751 (8th Cir. 2015).

[5]   *Simeonoff v. Hiner*, 249 F.3d 883, 891 (9th Cir. 2001) ("We will affirm the district court if . . . there can be no genuine dispute about omitted findings").

[6]   *U.S. Bank Nat. Ass'n v. Verizon Communications, Inc.*, 761 F.3d 409 (5th Cir. 2014).

[7]   *Diesel Props S.r.l. v. Greystone Business Credit II LLC*, 631 F.3d 42, 52 (2d Cir. 2011).

Proposed Findings and Conclusions

The court may require the parties to submit proposed findings of fact and conclusions of law,[8] although the court's wholesale adoption of the prevailing party's submission is discouraged.[9]

Proceedings Covered by Rule 52

The court must make findings of fact and conclusions of law in non-jury trials, trials with advisory juries,[10] proceedings for preliminary or permanent injunctions,[11] and when the court grants a motion for judgment after the plaintiff has presented evidence pursuant to Rule 52(c).[12] Rule 52 does not apply to motions for summary judgment under Rule 56,[13] motions to dismiss under Rule 12(b),[14] or motions for attorney's fees.[15] Likewise, findings are not required for actions before administrative agencies that submit reports and recommendations to the district court,[16] or in proceedings where the district court reviews rulings made by the bankruptcy court.

Findings in Jury Trials

In jury trials, Rule 52 applies to any issues decided by the court instead of the jury. The court must also make findings of fact and conclusions of law in a case tried before an advisory jury.[17]

Interlocutory Injunctions

Findings of fact and conclusions of law are required for interlocutory injunctions (*i.e.*, preliminary injunctions or TROs),[18] but not necessarily at the same level of detail as for other matters.[19] Findings are not required in ruling on a motion to dissolve an injunction.[20]

Form

The findings of fact may be a separate document or may be included in an opinion.[21] The court may also make its findings orally on the record.[22] If the court makes separate

---

[8]   *American River Transp. Co. v. Kavo Kaliakra SS*, 148 F.3d 446, 449 (5th Cir. 1998) (proposed findings adopted by the court are entitled to the same deference as findings crafted by the court).

[9]   *McLennan v. American Eurocopter Corp., Inc.*, 245 F.3d 403, 409 (5th Cir. 2001) ("the district court's decision to adopt one party's proposed findings and conclusions without change may cause us to approach such findings with greater caution, and as a consequence to apply the standard of review more rigorously").

[10]   *OCI Wyoming, L.P. v. Pacifi-Corp*, 479 F.3d 1199, 1203 (10th Cir. 2007).

[11]   *See Ali v. Quarterman*, 607 F.3d 1046 (5th Cir. 2010); *but see Dresser-Rand Co. v. Virtual Automation Inc.*, 361 F.3d 831, 847 (5th Cir. 2004) (findings not required when addressing a request for a permanent injunction at the conclusion of a jury trial).

[12]   *Nieto v. Kapoor*, 268 F.3d 1208, 1217 (10th Cir. 2001).

[13]   *Barry v. Moran*, 661 F.3d 696, 702, n.9 (1st Cir. 2011).

[14]   *Souza v. Pina*, 53 F.3d 423 (1st Cir.1995) (noting that, although not required, findings would be helpful).

[15]   *W.G. v. Senatore*, 18 F.3d 60, 4 A.D.D. 493 (2d Cir. 1994) (suggesting that findings regarding attorney fees would have been helpful, even though not required); *but see Kelly v. Golden*, 352 F.3d 344, 352 (8th Cir. 2003) (when awarding attorney's fees, the court must make findings).

[16]   *But see Muller v. First Unum Life Ins. Co.*, 341 F.3d 119, 124 (2d Cir. 2003) (findings are required in ruling on a motion for judgment on the administrative record).

[17]   *Kolstad v. American Dental Ass'n*, 108 F.3d 1431, 1440 (D.C. Cir. 1997).

[18]   *H-D Michigan, LLC v. Hellenic Duty Free Shops S.A.*, 694 F.3d 827, 845 (7th Cir. 2012).

[19]   *Osthus v. Whitesell Corp.*, 639 F.3d 841, 845 (8th Cir. 2011).

[20]   *Baltimore & O. R. Co. v. Chicago River & I. R. Co.*, 170 F.2d 654 (7th Cir. 1948).

[21]   *U.S. Bank Nat. Ass'n v. Verizon Communications, Inc.*, 761 F.3d 409 (5th Cir. 2014).

[22]   *Dexia Credit Local v. Rogan*, 602 F.3d 879, 884–85 (7th Cir. 2010).

findings, then on appeal those findings control over any contradictory factual statements in an opinion.[23]

Master's Findings

A master's findings are considered the court's findings if the court adopts them.[24]

Appeals of Findings

Rule 52(a)(6) sets the standard for appellate review of the trial court's findings, and provides that they will not be set aside unless clearly erroneous.[25] It also requires appellate courts to give "due regard" to the trial court's credibility determinations.[26] In contrast, the trial court's conclusions of law are reviewed *de novo*.[27]

RULE 52(b)—AMENDED OR ADDITIONAL FINDINGS

CORE CONCEPT

Upon motion, the court may amend its findings and/or judgment.

APPLICATIONS

Timing

Motions to amend the findings must be filed no later than 28 days after entry of judgment.[28] This time period is absolute, and cannot be enlarged by the court.[29] The motion may be filed before entry of judgment.

Grounds

Proper grounds for a motion to amend include newly discovered evidence,[30] a change in the law, or a manifest error of fact or law by the trial court.[31] A motion to amend should not merely relitigate old issues, reargue the merits of the case,[32] or to raise arguments that could have been raised prior to the issuance of judgment.[33] A party may move to amend the findings of fact even if the modified or additional findings in effect reverse the judgment.[34] Once a motion to amend has been filed, the court can amend any findings it deems appropriate, regardless of the issues raised in the motion.[35]

---

[23] *Snow Machines, Inc. v. Hedco, Inc.*, 838 F.2d 718, 727 (3d Cir. 1988).

[24] Rule 52(a)(4).

[25] *Teva Pharmaceuticals USA, Inc. v. Sandoz, Inc.*, ___ U.S. ___, 135 S.Ct. 831, 836–37 (2015) (rule applies to both subsidiary and ultimate facts).

[26] *Valenzuela v. Michel*, 736 F.3d 1173, 1176 (9th Cir. 2013).

[27] *U.S. Bank Nat. Ass'n v. Verizon Communications, Inc.*, 761 F.3d 409 (5th Cir. 2014).

[28] *Golden Blount, Inc. v. Robert H. Peterson Co.*, 438 F.3d 1354, 1358 (Fed. Cir. 2006).

[29] *Martin v. Monumental Life Ins. Co.*, 240 F.3d 223, 237–38 (3d Cir. 2001).

[30] *See Draim v. Virtual Geosatellite Holdings, Inc.*, 241 F.R.D. 48, 50 (D.D.C. 2007) (evidence that was merely not offered into evidence does not support a Rule 52(b) motion to amend).

[31] *In re Heritage Org., L.L.C.*, 466 B.R. 862, 868 (N.D. Tex 2012).

[32] *In re Busch*, 369 B.R. 614, 621 (B.A.P. 10th Cir. 2007).

[33] *Diocese of Winona v. Interstate Fire & Cas. Co.*, 89 F.3d 1386, 1397 (9th Cir. 1996).

[34] *Golden Blount, Inc. v. Robert H. Peterson Co.*, 438 F.3d 1354, 1358 (Fed. Cir. 2006) (if the trial court has entered an erroneous judgment, it should correct it).

[35] *Golden Blount, Inc. v. Robert H. Peterson Co.*, 438 F.3d 1354, 1358 (Fed. Cir. 2006).

Tolls Appeal Period

The filing of a motion to amend the findings tolls the running of the time to file an appeal.[36] The appeal clock starts over when the court enters an order granting or denying the motion to amend.

RULE 52(c)—JUDGMENT ON PARTIAL FINDINGS

CORE CONCEPT

At any time in a non-jury trial after a party has presented all its evidence with respect to a particular issue, the court may enter judgment against that party on that issue if the evidence failed to persuade the judge.

APPLICATIONS

Proceedings Applicable

Rule 52(c) applies only in non-jury trials.[37] The parallel for jury trials is a motion for judgment as a matter of law under Rule 50(a).[38]

Timing of Motion

A Rule 52(c) motion may be made at any time after all the evidence has been presented on a particular topic;[39] although motions for judgment on partial findings are typically made at the close of the opposing party's case,[40] the movant technically does not need to wait until the opposing party has rested.[41]

Standard for Granting

The trial judge rules on motions for judgment on partial findings as a final factfinder, reviewing all evidence presented thus far without presumptions in favor of either party.[42] The judge grants the motion if, upon the evidence already presented, the judge would find in favor of the moving party.[43]

Scope of Judgment

The judge will enter judgment on the claim or issue that is the subject of the motion and on any other claim, issue, counterclaim, crossclaim, or third-party claim that is determined by the outcome of the issue that is the subject of the motion.[44]

Findings of Fact

If the judge grants a motion for judgment on partial findings, the judge must make findings of fact pursuant to Rule 52(a).[45]

---

[36] *Weyant v. Okst,* 198 F.3d 311, 314–15 (2d Cir. 1999).

[37] *Fillmore v. Page,* 358 F.3d 496, 502–03 (7th Cir. 2004).

[38] *Federal Ins. Co. v. HPSC, Inc.,* 480 F.3d 26, 32 (1st Cir. 2007) (motion for judgment as a matter of law in a non-jury trial treated as a motion for judgment on partial findings under Rule 52(c)).

[39] *U.S. Bank Nat. Ass'n v. Verizon Communications, Inc.,* 761 F.3d 409 (5th Cir. 2014).

[40] *See, e.g., Pinkston v. Madry,* 440 F.3d 879, 885–86 (7th Cir. 2006).

[41] *Cajun Elec. Power Co-op., Inc. v. Gulf States Utilities Co.,* 848 F.Supp. 71 (M.D. La. 1994).

[42] *Lee v. West Coast Life Ins. Co.,* 688 F.3d 1004, 1009 (9th Cir. 2012).

[43] *See Connor B. ex rel. Vigurs v. Patrick,* 985 F.Supp.2d 129, 156 (D. Mass. 2013).

[44] *See Cantwell & Cantwell v. Vicario,* 464 B.R. 776, 783 (N.D. Ill. 2011).

[45] *Burger v. New York Institute of Technology,* 94 F.3d 830, 835 (2d Cir. 1996).

Deferred Ruling

The judge has discretion to defer ruling until all evidence has been presented.[46] If the judge defers ruling on a motion for judgment on partial findings and the nonmoving party enters additional evidence regarding the subject of the motion, the judge will consider all the evidence when ultimately ruling.[47]

ADDITIONAL RESEARCH REFERENCES

Wright & Miller, *Federal Practice and Procedure* §§ 2571 to 2591

C.J.S., Federal Civil Procedure §§ 1036 to 1056 et seq.

West's Key Number Digest, Federal Civil Procedure ⊷2261 to 2293

---

[46] *Cantwell & Cantwell v. Vicario*, 464 B.R. 776, 787 (N.D. Ill. 2011).
[47] *S.E.C. v. Razmilovic*, 822 F.Supp.2d 234, 257–58 (E.D.N.Y. 2011).

RULE 53

MASTERS

(a) Appointment.

(1) *Scope.* Unless a statute provides otherwise, a court may appoint a master only to:

(A) perform duties consented to by the parties;

(B) hold trial proceedings and make or recommend findings of fact on issues to be decided without a jury if appointment is warranted by:

(i) some exceptional condition; or

(ii) the need to perform an accounting or resolve a difficult computation of damages; or

(C) address pretrial and posttrial matters that cannot be effectively and timely addressed by an available district judge or magistrate judge of the district.

(2) *Disqualification.* A master must not have a relationship to the parties, attorneys, action, or court that would require disqualification of a judge under 28 U.S.C. § 455, unless the parties, with the court's approval, consent to the appointment after the master discloses any potential grounds for disqualification.

(3) *Possible Expense or Delay.* In appointing a master, the court must consider the fairness of imposing the likely expenses on the parties and must protect against unreasonable expense or delay.

(b) Order Appointing a Master.

(1) *Notice.* Before appointing a master, the court must give the parties notice and an opportunity to be heard. Any party may suggest candidates for appointment.

(2) *Contents.* The appointing order must direct the master to proceed with all reasonable diligence and must state:

(A) the master's duties, including any investigation or enforcement duties, and any limits on the master's authority under Rule 53(c);

(B) the circumstances, if any, in which the master may communicate ex parte with the court or a party;

(C) the nature of the materials to be preserved and filed as the record of the master's activities;

(D) the time limits, method of filing the record, other procedures, and standards for reviewing the master's orders, findings, and recommendations; and

(E) the basis, terms, and procedure for fixing the master's compensation under Rule 53(g).

(3) *Issuing.* The court may issue the order only after:

(A) the master files an affidavit disclosing whether there is any ground for disqualification under 28 U.S.C. § 455; and

(B) if a ground is disclosed, the parties, with the court's approval, waive the disqualification.

(4) *Amending.* The order may be amended at any time after notice to the parties and an opportunity to be heard.

(c) Master's Authority.

(1) *In General.* Unless the appointing order directs otherwise, a master may:

(A) regulate all proceedings;

(B) take all appropriate measures to perform the assigned duties fairly and efficiently; and

(C) if conducting an evidentiary hearing, exercise the appointing court's power to compel, take, and record evidence.

(2) *Sanctions.* The master may by order impose on a party any noncontempt sanction provided by Rule 37 or 45, and may recommend a contempt sanction against a party and sanctions against a nonparty.

(d) Master's Orders. A master who issues an order must file it and promptly serve a copy on each party. The clerk must enter the order on the docket.

(e) Master's Reports. A master must report to the court as required by the appointing order. The master must file the report and promptly serve a copy on each party, unless the court orders otherwise.

(f) Action on the Master's Order, Report, or Recommendations.

(1) *Opportunity for a Hearing; Action in General.* In acting on a master's order, report, or recommendations, the court must give the parties notice and an opportunity to be heard; may receive evidence; and may adopt or affirm, modify, wholly or partly reject or reverse, or resubmit to the master with instructions.

(2) *Time to Object or Move to Adopt or Modify.* A party may file objections to—or a motion to adopt or modify—the master's order, report, or

recommendations no later than 21 days after a copy is served, unless the court sets a different time.

(3) *Reviewing Factual Findings.* The court must decide de novo all objections to findings of fact made or recommended by a master, unless the parties, with the court's approval, stipulate that:

(A) the findings will be reviewed for clear error; or

(B) the findings of a master appointed under Rule 53(a)(1)(A) or (C) will be final.

(4) *Reviewing Legal Conclusions.* The court must decide de novo all objections to conclusions of law made or recommended by a master.

(5) *Reviewing Procedural Matters.* Unless the appointing order establishes a different standard of review, the court may set aside a master's ruling on a procedural matter only for an abuse of discretion.

(g) Compensation.

(1) *Fixing Compensation.* Before or after judgment, the court must fix the master's compensation on the basis and terms stated in the appointing order, but the court may set a new basis and terms after giving notice and an opportunity to be heard.

(2) *Payment.* The compensation must be paid either:

(A) by a party or parties; or

(B) from a fund or subject matter of the action within the court's control.

(3) *Allocating Payment.* The court must allocate payment among the parties after considering the nature and amount of the controversy, the parties' means, and the extent to which any party is more responsible than other parties for the reference to a master. An interim allocation may be amended to reflect a decision on the merits.

(h) Appointing a Magistrate Judge. A magistrate judge is subject to this rule only when the order referring a matter to the magistrate judge states that the reference is made under this rule.

[Amended February 28, 1966, effective July 1, 1966; April 28, 1983, effective August 1, 1983; March 2, 1987, effective August 1, 1987; April 30, 1991, effective December 1, 1991; April 22, 1993, effective December 1, 1993; March 27, 2003, effective December 1, 2003; April 30, 2007, effective December 1, 2007; March 26, 2009, effective December 1, 2009.]

AUTHORS' COMMENTARY ON RULE 53

PURPOSE AND SCOPE

Rule 53 provides the procedures governing the reference of designated aspects of an action to a master.

RULE 53(a)—APPOINTMENT

CORE CONCEPT

The court may appoint a special master to conduct trials in limited circumstances and to conduct certain pretrial and post-trial functions.

APPLICATIONS

Functions Performed by Master

Rule 53 defines three categories of functions that a master may perform:

- Perform duties consented to by the parties;[1]

- Hold trial proceedings and make recommended findings of fact on non-jury issues if the appointment is warranted by an exceptional condition or by the need to perform an accounting or resolve a difficult computation of damages;[2] or

- Address pretrial[3] or post-trial matters[4] if they cannot be addressed effectively and timely by the court.

Jury Trials

The court may not appoint a special master in matters to be tried to a jury unless the parties consent.[5]

Ineligible Persons

A person cannot be a master if related to the parties, the action, or the court under the same standards that govern disqualification of a judge set forth in 28 U.S.C. § 455.[6] The clerk of court and the clerk's deputies are also ineligible. The parties can waive this restriction with the court's approval.[7]

Court's Discretion—Fairness

In determining whether to appoint a master, the court must consider the fairness of imposing the cost of the master's compensation on the parties and the effects of delay.[8] The court has discretion as to whether to refer a matter to a master,[9] but reference should be the exception, not the rule.[10] The court also has discretion to refuse to appoint a master even if the parties have consented.[11]

---

[1]   *See Jones v. Tauber & Balser, P.C.*, 503 B.R. 510, 520 (N.D. Ga. 2013).

[2]   *See Beazer East, Inc. v. Mead Corp.*, 412 F.3d 429, 441 (3d Cir. 2005) (equitable allocation under CERCLA is not a computation of damages and thus may not be referred to a special master).

[3]   *Rohrbough v. Harris*, 549 F.3d 1313, 1318 (10th Cir. 2008) (master attended depositions to rule on objections).

[4]   *See United States v. Apple Inc.*, 787 F.3d 131, 134 (2d Cir. 2015) (approving a master to monitor compliance with the court's order).

[5]   The advisory committee note to the 2003 Amendments to Rule 53.

[6]   *United States v. Apple Inc.*, 787 F.3d 131, 138 (2d Cir. 2015).

[7]   *See Paycom Payroll, LLC v. Richison*, 758 F.3d 1198 (10th Cir. 2014).

[8]   *See Gaddis v. United States*, 381 F.3d 444, 462 (5th Cir. 2004).

[9]   *Middle Tennessee News Co., Inc. v. Charnel of Cincinnati, Inc.*, 250 F.3d 1077 (7th Cir.2001).

[10]   *United States v. State of Washington*, 135 F.3d 618, 646 (9th Cir. 1998).

[11]   The advisory committee note to the 2003 Amendments to Rule 53.

Magistrate Judges

The court may appoint a United States Magistrate Judge to serve as a special master.[12] The provisions regarding compensation do not apply when a United States Magistrate Judge is designated to serve as a special master.

Common References

References are most common in patent, trademark, and copyright actions.[13] They are also used occasionally to supervise discovery (and increasingly frequently with e-discovery), to determine damages following summary judgment on liability when the damages are difficult to calculate, and to oversee compliance with injunctions or other court orders.[14]

RULE 53(b)—ORDER APPOINTING A MASTER

CORE CONCEPT

A master is appointed by an order setting forth the duties and parameters of the reference.

APPLICATIONS

Notice and Opportunity to Be Heard

The court must give notice of the proposed appointment of a master to the parties and provide an opportunity to be heard before appointing the master.[15] Written submissions will provide an "opportunity to be heard" unless the circumstances require live testimony.[16]

Candidates for Appointment

A party may suggest candidates for appointment as master.[17]

Contents of Order

The order appointing a master must:

- Direct the master to proceed with all reasonable diligence;[18]

- State the master's duties and any limits on the master's authority;[19]

- State the circumstances, if any, in which the master may communicate *ex parte* with the court or a party;[20]

- State the nature of the materials to be preserved and filed as the record of the master's activities;[21]

- State the time limits, methods of filing the record, other procedures, and standards for reviewing the master's orders, findings, and recommendations;[22] and

---

[12] *S.E.C. v. AMX, Intern., Inc.*, 872 F.Supp. 1541 (N.D. Tex. 1994).

[13] *See Absolute Software, Inc. v. Stealth Signal, Inc.*, 659 F.3d 1121, 1131 (Fed. Cir. 2011).

[14] *See United States v. Microsoft Corp.*, 147 F.3d 935, 954 (D.C. Cir. 1998) (discussing the "well established tradition allowing use of special masters to oversee compliance.").

[15] *St. Jude Medical S.C., Inc. v. Janssen-Counotte*, 305 F.R.D. 630, 641 (D. Or. 2015).

[16] The advisory committee note to the 2003 Amendment to Rule 53.

[17] Rule 53(b)(1).

[18] Rule 53(b)(2).

[19] *See Sibley v. Sprint Nextel Corp.*, 298 F.R.D. 683, 685 (D. Kan. 2014).

[20] *United States v. Apple Inc.*, 787 F.3d 131, 138 (2d Cir. 2015).

[21] *Sibley v. Sprint Nextel Corp.*, 298 F.R.D. 683, 686–87 (D. Kan. 2014).

[22] *Sibley v. Sprint Nextel Corp.*, 298 F.R.D. 683, 687 (D. Kan. 2014).

- State the basis, terms, and procedures for determining the master's compensation under Rule 53(g).[23]

Affidavit re Grounds for Disqualification

Before the court can enter the order appointing the master, the master must file an affidavit disclosing whether there is any ground for disqualification under 28 U.S.C. § 455.[24] If a ground for disqualification is disclosed, the court may not enter the order unless the parties have consented to waive the disqualification.[25]

Amendment of Order

The order appointing the master may be amended at any time after notice to the parties and an opportunity to be heard.[26]

Challenging Reference

The proper method for contesting a reference is a motion to amend, vacate, or revoke the reference.[27] Failure to make such a motion may be deemed a consent or waiver.[28] If the motion to vacate is denied, the disgruntled party may attempt to compel the court to vacate by a writ of mandamus.[29] Orders of reference are interlocutory, and may not be appealed directly, but may be appealed at the conclusion of the district court proceedings.[30]

RULE 53(c)—MASTER'S AUTHORITY

CORE CONCEPT

Absent specific limitations in the order appointing the master, the master has all powers necessary to perform the referred matters, including the powers necessary to regulate the proceedings, rule on evidentiary issues, place witnesses under oath, and examine witnesses.[31] The master has discretion as to what procedures to employ, with the only requirement being that when the master determines that a hearing is necessary, the master must make a record of the evidence offered and excluded in the same manner and subject to the same limitations as provided in the Federal Rules of Evidence for a non-jury trial.[32] The court has the duty to oversee the special master's performance of the master's duties to ensure that they are appropriately discharged.[33]

APPLICATIONS

Authority to Impose Sanctions

The master may impose on a party any non-contempt sanction provided by Rule 37 or 45. The master may also recommend that the judge impose contempt sanctions against a party and sanctions against a nonparty.

Evidentiary Hearings

Unless otherwise limited by the order appointing the master, the master may exercise the powers of the court to compel (by subpoena under Rule 45), take, and record evidence.

---

[23] *Sibley v. Sprint Nextel Corp.*, 298 F.R.D. 683, 688 (D. Kan. 2014).

[24] Rule 53(b)(3).

[25] Rule 53(b)(3).

[26] Rule 53(b)(4).

[27] *Fajardo Shopping Center, S.E. v. Sun Alliance Ins. Co. of Puerto Rico, Inc.*, 167 F.3d 1, 6 (1st Cir. 1999).

[28] *See In re K-Dur Antitrust Litigation*, 686 F.3d 197, 207, n.5 (3d Cir. 2012).

[29] *La Buy v. Howes Leather Company*, 352 U.S. 249, 77 S.Ct. 309, 1 L.Ed.2d 290 (1957).

[30] *Sierra Club v. Clifford*, 257 F.3d 444 (5th Cir.2001).

[31] *United States v. Clifford Matley Family Trust*, 354 F.3d 1154, 1159 (9th Cir. 2004).

[32] *United States v. Clifford Matley Family Trust*, 354 F.3d 1154, 1159 (9th Cir. 2004).

[33] *Cordoza v. Pacific States Steel Corp.*, 320 F.3d 989, 999 (9th Cir. 2003).

RULE 53(d)—MASTER'S ORDERS

CORE CONCEPT

A master who makes an order must file the order with the clerk and promptly serve a copy on each party. The clerk must enter the order on the docket.

RULE 53(e)—MASTER'S REPORTS

CORE CONCEPT

A master must prepare reports as directed by the order of appointment. The master must file such reports with the clerk and promptly serve a copy upon each party unless the court directs otherwise.[34]

APPLICATIONS

Supporting Materials

The master should provide the court with all portions of the record that the master deems relevant to the report. The parties may seek to designate additional materials from the record, and may seek to supplement the record. The court may require that additional materials from the record be filed.[35]

Sealed Report

Sealing of the report from public access may be appropriate, particularly with respect to pretrial and post-trial matters. A report detailing a continuing or failed settlement effort is one example of a report that might be sealed.[36]

RULE 53(f)—ACTION ON THE MASTER'S ORDER, REPORT, OR RECOMMENDATIONS

CORE CONCEPT

Rule 53(f) sets forth the procedures for the court to act on the masters report and the standards by which the court should review the report.

APPLICATIONS

Actions by the Court

When considering an order, report, or recommendation from a master, the court may adopt or affirm, modify, reject or reverse in whole or in part, or resubmit to the master with instructions.[37]

Opportunity to Be Heard

Before taking action on an order, report, or recommendation from a master, the court must provide the parties with an opportunity to be heard.[38] Written submissions will provide an opportunity to be heard unless the circumstances require live testimony.[39]

---

[34]   *See Schaefer Fan Co., Inc. v. J & D Mfg.*, 265 F.3d 1282, 1289 (Fed. Cir. 2001).

[35]   The advisory committee note to the 2003 Amendment to Rule 53.

[36]   The advisory committee note to the 2003 Amendment to Rule 53.

[37]   *Consejo de Salud de la Comunidad de la Playa de Ponce, Inc. v. Gonzalez-Feliciano*, 695 F.3d 83, 99 (1st Cir. 2012).

[38]   *World Triathalon Corp. v. Dunbar*, 539 F.Supp.2d 1270, 1275 (D. Haw. 2008).

[39]   The advisory committee note to the 2003 Amendment to Rule 53.

Consideration of Additional Evidence

The court has discretion to consider additional evidence in connection with its review of the master's report, but is not required to do so.[40]

Time for Objections

A party may file objections to the master's order, report, or recommendations no later than 21 days from the time the order, report, or recommendations is served, unless the court sets a different time.[41] The parties may also file a motion to adopt or modify the order, report, or recommendations in the same timeframe.[42] This time period is not jurisdictional, and the court has the authority to consider a late objection or motion.[43]

Findings of Fact

Absent a stipulation otherwise,[44] the court must decide *de novo* all objections to findings of fact made or recommended by a master.[45] The court may also review *de novo* findings of fact made or recommended by a master in the absence of an objection.[46] The parties may stipulate, with the court's consent, that the master's findings of fact will only be reviewed for clear error.[47] The parties may also stipulate, with the court's consent, that the master's findings of fact will be final if the master was appointed by consent or was appointed to address pretrial or post-trial matters.[48] The court may withdraw its consent to a stipulation for clear error review or finality, and may reopen the opportunity for the parties to object.[49]

Conclusions of Law

The court must decide *de novo* all objections to conclusions of law made or recommended by a master.[50]

Procedural Matters

In the absence of a different standard set by the order of appointment, the court reviews a master's ruling on a procedural matter for abuse of discretion.[51]

Appeals

The report of the master is not appealable until adopted by the court. Only issues that are raised in objections to the special master's report are preserved for appeal.[52]

---

[40] *Commissariat à l'Energie Atomique v. Samsung Electronics Co.*, 245 F.R.D. 177, 179 (D. Del. 2007).

[41] *See Sibley v. Sprint Nextel Corp.*, 298 F.R.D. 683, 687, n.12 (D. Kan. 2014).

[42] Rule 53(f)(2).

[43] *See Wallace v. Skadden, Arps, Slate, Meagher & Flom, LLP*, 362 F.3d 810, 816 (D.C. Cir. 2004).

[44] *AgGrow Oils, L.L.C. v. National Union Fire Ins. Co. of Pittsburgh, PA*, 276 F.Supp.2d 999, 1005 (D.N.D. 2003), aff'd, 420 F.3d 751 (8th Cir. 2005) (when the parties stipulate that a master's findings of fact are final, the district court will only consider questions of law).

[45] *In re Refco Sec. Litig.*, 280 F.R.D. 102, 104 (S.D.N.Y. 2011).

[46] *Evans v. Bowser*, 87 F.Supp.3d 1, n.2 (D.D.C. 2015).

[47] Rule 53(f)(3)(A). *See also* The advisory committee note to the 2003 Amendment to Rule 53 (suggesting that clear error review is more likely to be appropriate with respect to findings that do not go to the merits of the claims or defenses, such as findings of fact going to a privilege issue).

[48] Rule 53(f)(3)(B).

[49] The advisory committee note to the 2003 Amendment to Rule 53.

[50] *In re: Cathode Ray Tube (CRT) Antitrust Litigation*, 911 F.Supp.2d 857 (N.D.Cal. 2012).

[51] *In re Cathode Ray Tube (CRT) Antitrust Litigation*, 301 F.R.D. 449, 451 (N.D. Cal. 2014).

[52] *Absolute Software, Inc. v. Stealth Signal, Inc.*, 659 F.3d 1121, 1131 (Fed. Cir. 2011).

RULE 53(g)—COMPENSATION

CORE CONCEPT

The court sets the compensation for a master. The master's compensation will be allocated among the parties or taken from the subject matter of the litigation.

APPLICATIONS

Amount of Compensation

The court fixes the compensation for a master.[53] The court may also require the posting of a bond to secure payment of the fee or require the payment of the fee into escrow.[54] The amount of compensation will be controlled by the order of appointment,[55] but the court may set a new basis and terms after notice to the parties and an opportunity to be heard.[56]

Source of Compensation

The court may impose the master's fee upon either party or may apportion it among the parties.[57] The court may also direct that the fee be paid from any fund or subject matter of the action in the custody of the court.[58]

Allocation Among Parties

If the compensation is to be paid by the parties, the court must allocate the compensation among the parties. The court should consider the nature and amount of the controversy, the parties' financial means, and the extent to which any party is more responsible for the reference to the master.[59] The court may make interim allocations and may adjust the interim allocation later to reflect the decision on the merits.[60]

Collection of Compensation

The master may obtain a writ of execution against a party not paying its share of the master's fee. The master may not withhold the report to obtain payment.

RULE 53(h)—APPOINTING A MAGISTRATE JUDGE

CORE CONCEPT

The provisions of Rule 53 do not pertain to matters referred to magistrate judges unless the order of reference specifically states that it is made pursuant to Rule 53.[61]

---

[53] *Cordoza v. Pacific States Steel Corp.*, 320 F.3d 989, 999 (9th Cir. 2003) (court has the duty to reduce special master's compensation if appropriate).

[54] *Allapattah Services, Inc. v. Exxon Corp.*, 157 F.Supp.2d 1291, 1325 (S.D. Fla. 2001), aff'd, 333 F.3d 1248 (11th Cir. 2003), aff'd, 545 U.S. 546, 125 S.Ct. 2611, 162 L.Ed.2d 502 (2005).

[55] *Gaddis v. United States,* 381 F.3d 444, 462 (5th Cir. 2004).

[56] Rule 53(g)(1).

[57] *See Netsphere, Inc. v. Baron*, 703 F.3d 296, 313 (5th Cir. 2012).

[58] *See Six L's Packing Co., Inc. v. Post & Taback, Inc.*, 132 F.Supp.2d 306, 309 (S.D. N.Y. 2001).

[59] *Zaki Kulaibee Establishment v. McFliker*, 771 F.3d 1301, 1315, n.26 (11th Cir. 2014).

[60] Rule 53(g)(3). *See also Kaplan v. First Hartford Corp.*, 716 F.Supp.2d 11 (D. Me. 2010).

[61] *See Wallace v. Skadden, Arps, Slate, Meagher & Flom, LLP*, 362 F.3d 810, 814–16 (D.C. Cir. 2004).

ADDITIONAL RESEARCH REFERENCES

Wright & Miller, *Federal Practice and Procedure* §§ 2601 to 2615

C.J.S., Federal Civil Procedure §§ 890 to 904; United States Commissioners § 3

West's Key Number Digest, Federal Civil Procedure ⊶1871 to 1908; United States Magistrates ⊶14

VII. JUDGMENT

RULE 54

JUDGMENT; COSTS

(a) Definition; Form. "Judgment" as used in these rules includes a decree and any order from which an appeal lies. A judgment should not include recitals of pleadings, a master's report, or a record of prior proceedings.

(b) Judgment on Multiple Claims or Involving Multiple Parties. When an action presents more than one claim for relief—whether as a claim, counterclaim, crossclaim, or third-party claim—or when multiple parties are involved, the court may direct entry of a final judgment as to one or more, but fewer than all, claims or parties only if the court expressly determines that there is no just reason for delay. Otherwise, any order or other decision, however designated, that adjudicates fewer than all the claims or the rights and liabilities of fewer than all the parties does not end the action as to any of the claims or parties and may be revised at any time before the entry of a judgment adjudicating all the claims and all the parties' rights and liabilities.

(c) Demand for Judgment; Relief to Be Granted. A default judgment must not differ in kind from, or exceed in amount, what is demanded in the pleadings. Every other final judgment should grant the relief to which each party is entitled, even if the party has not demanded that relief in its pleadings.

(d) Costs; Attorney's Fees.

(1) *Costs Other Than Attorney's Fees.* Unless a federal statute, these rules, or a court order provides otherwise, costs—other than attorney's fees—should be allowed to the prevailing party. But costs against the United States, its officers, and its agencies may be imposed only to the extent allowed by law. The clerk may tax costs on 14 days' notice. On motion served within the next 7 days, the court may review the clerk's action.

(2) *Attorney's Fees.*

(A) *Claim to Be by Motion.* A claim for attorney's fees and related nontaxable expenses must be made by motion unless the substantive law requires those fees to be proved at trial as an element of damages.

(B) *Timing and Contents of the Motion.* Unless a statute or a court order provides otherwise, the motion must:

(i) be filed no later than 14 days after the entry of judgment;

(ii) specify the judgment and the statute, rule, or other grounds entitling the movant to the award;

(iii) state the amount sought or provide a fair estimate of it; and

(iv) disclose, if the court so orders, the terms of any agreement about fees for the services for which the claim is made.

(C) *Proceedings.* Subject to Rule 23(h), the court must, on a party's request, give an opportunity for adversary submissions on the motion in accordance with Rule 43(c) or 78. The court may decide issues of liability for fees before receiving submissions on the value of services. The court must find the facts and state its conclusions of law as provided in Rule 52(a).

(D) *Special Procedures by Local Rule; Reference to a Master or a Magistrate Judge.* By local rule, the court may establish special procedures to resolve fee-related issues without extensive evidentiary hearings. Also, the court may refer issues concerning the value of services to a special master under Rule 53 without regard to the limitations of Rule 53(a)(1), and may refer a motion for attorney's fees to a magistrate judge under Rule 72(b) as if it were a dispositive pretrial matter.

(E) *Exceptions.* Subparagraphs (A)-(D) do not apply to claims for fees and expenses as sanctions for violating these rules or as sanctions under 28 U.S.C. § 1927.

[Amended December 27, 1946, effective March 19, 1948; April 17, 1961, effective July 19, 1961; March 2, 1987, effective August 1, 1987; April 22, 1993, effective December 1, 1993; amended April 29, 2002, effective December 1, 2002; March 27, 2003, effective December 1, 2003; April 30, 2007, effective December 1, 2007; March 26, 2009, effective December 1, 2009.]

AUTHORS' COMMENTARY ON RULE 54

PURPOSE AND SCOPE

Rule 54 defines the term "judgment", discusses the limits of recovery on a judgment, and allows the taxation of costs. The Rule also permits the federal court to enter judgment as to just one adjudicated claim or the adjudicated rights of just one party, and thus permit an immediate appeal from that otherwise incomplete judgment.

RULE 54(a)—DEFINITION AND FORM OF "JUDGMENT"

CORE CONCEPT

A judgment is any appealable decree or order.

APPLICATIONS

Definition

To be a "judgment" within the meaning of Rule 54(a), the court's order or decree must be a ruling from which an appeal can be taken.[1] Ordinarily, this requires "some clear and unequivocal manifestation" by the district court that, at least as far as that court is

---

[1]   *See In re Metropolitan Gov't of Nashville & Davidson County, Tenn.,* 606 F.3d 855, 860 (6th Cir. 2010).

concerned, the case is closed [2] (though preliminary injunctions, because they can be immediately appealed, qualify as "judgments" as well).[3] A ruling that partially adjudicates a claim or is an otherwise non-final order will not usually qualify as a judgment.[4]

Appears Alone

To avoid confusion and uncertainty about what is (and is not) a "judgment", it should appear alone. It should not include recitals of the pleadings, a report from a master, or a record of prior proceedings.[5] It should, instead, be set forth in its own document containing nothing of substance other than the judgment.[6]

RULE 54(b)—JUDGMENT ON MULTIPLE CLAIMS OR INVOLVING MULTIPLE PARTIES

CORE CONCEPT

A judgment entered as to fewer than all claims or all parties in a lawsuit is not immediately appealable. Instead, the appeal must generally await the entry of judgment as to all remaining claims and parties. However, the district court can make an adjudication of such claims or parties "final", and immediately appealable, by expressly determining that no just cause exists to delay the appeal and by directing the entry of judgment.

APPLICATIONS

Purpose

Separate, piecemeal appeals during a single litigation are often inefficient and uneconomical, and thus are contrary to the historic federal policy favoring one appeal on all issues at the conclusion of the lawsuit.[7] Rule 54(b) determinations allowing immediate appeal permit exceptions from this general policy for those infrequent instances where awaiting a final judgment would be unduly harsh or unjust.[8]

Prerequisites to Rule 54(b) Judgments

In evaluating whether to grant a Rule 54(b) determination, the district courts function somewhat like a "dispatcher".[9] They must decide whether three prerequisites for an immediately appealable partial judgment exist:

- **1:** *Multiple Claims or Parties Fully Resolved:* To be eligible for immediate appeal under Rule 54(b), an adjudication must *either* (a) finally resolve at least one claim or (b) finally resolve the rights and liabilities of at least one party. A claim or a party's interest *must* be adjudicated to finality, such that there is nothing more to do on that claim or for that party but await the conclusion of the remaining portions of the litigation.[10] This limitation is a pivotal one. Rule 54(b) does not alter the normal rules of appellate finality for individual claims, and no appeal

---

2   *See Diaz-Reyes v. Fuentes-Ortiz*, 471 F.3d 299, 301 (1st Cir. 2006).

3   *See People Against Police Violence v. City of Pittsburgh*, 520 F.3d 226, 233 n.5 (3d Cir. 2008).

4   *See Auto Servs. Co. v. KPMG, LLP*, 537 F.3d 853, 856 (8th Cir. 2008). *See also Alford v. Chevron U.S.A. Inc.*, 13 F.Supp.2d 581 (E.D. La. 2014) (order denying motion to dismiss is not a judgment). *But cf.* Rule 54(b); *infra* Authors' Commentary to Rule 54(b) (a judgment that fully adjudicates one distinct part of a lawsuit may qualify as an immediately-appealable judgment, even though the remainder of the lawsuit continues).

5   *See* Rule 54(a).

6   *See* Rule 58(a); *infra* Authors' Commentary to Rule 58(a).

7   *See Curtiss-Wright Corp. v. General Elec. Co.*, 446 U.S. 1, 8, 100 S.Ct. 1460, 1464–65, 64 L.Ed.2d 1 (1980).

8   *See Gelboim v. Bank of America Corp.*, ___ U.S. ___, 135 S.Ct. 897, 902–03, 190 L.Ed.2d 789 (2015).

9   *See Curtiss-Wright Corp. v. General Elec. Co.*, 446 U.S. 1, 8, 100 S.Ct. 1460, 1464, 64 L.Ed.2d 1 (1980).

10   *See Curtiss-Wright Corp. v. General Elec. Co.*, 446 U.S. 1, 7, 100 S.Ct. 1460, 1464, 64 L.Ed.2d 1 (1980).

may be taken from district court rulings on any particular claim until the court finally resolves that claim.[11] Rule 54(b) has no application where the lawsuit involves either a single claim only or multiple claims that have already been resolved to finality.[12] Thus, for example, where a portion of a claim is resolved, but the amount of damages, the question of insurance coverage, or affirmative defenses remain open and still to be decided, that claim has not been finally resolved (even if all other issues are completely adjudicated), and an immediate appeal is improper.[13]

o   *Multiple Claims:* An appeal from one dismissed claim (when other claims still remain) is possible only when that claim is resolved entirely and as to all parties.[14] Claims that have been severed or separated from the original claim, and which are thereafter proceeding independently, may themselves be eligible for an appeal once dismissed.[15]

o   *"Claim" Defined:* A "claim" has been defined to include all legal grounds based on closely related facts.[16] There are no bright-line rules for testing whether multiple claims are adequately "separate",[17] and this line-drawing can prove to be obscure.[18] A simple variation in legal theory alone will not suffice,[19] nor will the mere fact that the allegations were pleaded separately.[20] Rather, this assessment implicates practical concerns.[21] Multiple claims exist where each claim is factually separate and independent,[22] where each claim could be enforced separately,[23] where each claim seeks to vindicate a different legal right,[24] where there is more than one potential recovery, or where different types of relief are requested.[25] If, however, only one recovery is possible (even though several legal theories are offered to support that same recovery) or if alternative recoveries either substantially overlap or are mutually exclusive, the partial adjudication of such claims cannot be immediately appealed under Rule 54(b).[26] One test of a claim's separability asks whether that claim so

---

[11] *See Lee-Barnes v. Puerto Ven Quarry Corp.*, 513 F.3d 20, 25 (1st Cir. 2008). *See also N.W. Enterprises Inc. v. City of Houston*, 352 F.3d 162, 179 (5th Cir. 2003) (Rule 54(b) judgment improper where district court only authorized appeal of elements of claims, and not entire claims).

[12] *See Gelboim v. Bank of America Corp.*, ___ U.S. ___, 135 S.Ct. 897, 906, 190 L.Ed.2d 789 (2015).

[13] *See Kerr-McGee Chem. Corp. v. Lefton Iron & Metal Co.*, 570 F.3d 856, 857 (7th Cir. 2009). *See also Lowery v. Fed. Express Corp.*, 426 F.3d 817, 820–21 (6th Cir.2005) (discharged employee suing under Title VII and breach of contract has only one "claim").

[14] *See Tetra Techs., Inc. v. Continental Ins. Co.*, 755 F.3d 222, 228 (5th Cir. 2014).

[15] *See Brooks v. District Hosp. Partners, L.P.*, 606 F.3d 800, 805–06 (D.C. Cir. 2010).

[16] *See EJS Props., LLC v. City of Toledo*, 689 F.3d 535, 538 (6th Cir. 2012).

[17] *See Tetra Techs., Inc. v. Continental Ins. Co.*, 755 F.3d 222, 230 (5th Cir. 2014).

[18] *See Acumen Re Mgmt. Corp. v. General Sec. Nat. Ins. Co.*, 769 F.3d 135, 141 (2d Cir. 2014).

[19] *See Marseilles Hydro Power, LLC v. Marseilles Land and Water Co.*, 518 F.3d 459, 464 (7th Cir. 2008).

[20] *See EJS Props., LLC v. City of Toledo*, 689 F.3d 535, 538 (6th Cir. 2012).

[21] *See Waltman v. Georgia-Pacific, LLC*, 590 Fed.Appx. 799, 811 (10th Cir. 2014).

[22] *See Seatrain Shipbuilding Corp. v. Shell Oil Co.*, 444 U.S. 572, 100 S.Ct. 800, 63 L.Ed.2d 36 (1980). *See Lawyers Title Ins. Corp. v. Dearborn Title Corp.*, 118 F.3d 1157, 1162 (7th Cir.1997) (noting that test for "separate claims" is whether the claim at issue so overlaps the claims remaining that any appeal at the end of the case on the remaining claims would require the appellate court to cover the same ground addressed on the Rule 54(b) appeal).

[23] *See Acumen Re Mgmt. Corp. v. General Sec. Nat. Ins. Co.*, 769 F.3d 135, 141 (2d Cir. 2014). *Cf. General Acquisition, Inc. v. GenCorp, Inc.*, 23 F.3d 1022, 1028 (6th Cir. 1994) (if the action seeks to vindicate only one legal right, but merely alleges several elements of damage, only one claim is presented and Rule 54(b) does not apply).

[24] *See U.S. Citizens Ass'n v. Sebelius*, 705 F.3d 588, 594–96 (6th Cir. 2013).

[25] *See Marseilles Hydro Power, LLC v. Marseilles Land and Water Co.*, 518 F.3d 459, 464 (7th Cir. 2008).

[26] *See Acumen Re Mgmt. Corp. v. General Sec. Nat. Ins. Co.*, 769 F.3d 135, 143–44 (2d Cir. 2014).

overlaps the claims that remain for trial such that an appeal at the end of the case on the retained claims would compel the court to retrace the same ground it would have addressed had the first claim received a Rule 54(b) determination; if so, then the Rule 54(b) determination should be denied.[27] Counterclaims[28] and claims in consolidated cases[29] are assessed using this same inquiry.

o   *Multiple Parties:* An appeal by one dismissed party (when claims by other parties still remain) is possible only when that party's rights and interests are resolved entirely and the district court so signifies.[30] Rule 54(b) is not just limited to defendants. If the criteria for Rule 54(b) is satisfied, the dismissal of any party (plaintiff or defendant) may be appealed.[31] A named, but unserved, defendant will typically not be considered a "party" for the purpose of applying this Rule.[32]

- **2:   *No Just Cause for Delay:*** The district court must state, in clear and unmistakable language, that there is no just cause to delay the appeal of the adjudicated claim or the adjudicated rights and liabilities of a party. This determination requires a weighing of both the equities in the case and the judicial administrative interests (especially the interest in avoiding piecemeal appeals).[33] Ordinarily, this weighing will favor an immediate appeal only where delay in appealing presents some risk of hardship or injustice that would be avoided by an immediate review, where a plaintiff could be prejudiced by a delay in recovering a monetary judgment, or where an expensive, duplicative trial could be avoided by reviewing a dismissed claim promptly before the remaining claims reach trial.[34] Conversely, where multiple claims, even if separate, could again be subject to yet another review in a later appeal,[35] or where the claims—though discrete—are so interrelated as to form a single factual unit,[36] an immediate appeal would be improper. Whether "just cause" exists is a determination made on a case-by-case basis.[37] Certain nonexhaustive [38] criteria guide the court's consideration:

  o   The relationship between adjudicated and unadjudicated claims;

  o   The possibility that the need for appellate review might be mooted by future developments in the district court;

  o   The possibility that the district court might be obligated to consider the same issue on a later occasion;

  o   The presence (or absence) of a claim or counterclaim that could result in a set-off against the judgment now sought to be made final and appealed; and

---

[27]   *See Waltman v. Georgia-Pacific, LLC*, 590 Fed.Appx. 799, 811 & 811 n.10 (10th Cir. 2014).

[28]   *See Curtiss-Wright Corp. v. General Elec. Co.*, 446 U.S. 1, 9, 100 S.Ct. 1460, 64 L. Ed 2d 1 (1980).

[29]   *See Florida Wildlife Fed'n, Inc. v. Administrator, U.S. E.P.A.*, 737 F.3d 689, 692–93 (11th Cir. 2013).

[30]   *See Brooks v. District Hosp. Partners, L.P.*, 606 F.3d 800, 805 n.2 (D.C. Cir. 2010).

[31]   *See Brooks v. District Hosp. Partners, L.P.*, 606 F.3d 800, 805 n.2 (D.C. Cir. 2010).

[32]   *See Cambridge Holdings Group, Inc. v. Federal Ins. Co.*, 489 F.3d 1356, 1360–61 (D.C. Cir. 2007).

[33]   *See Adler v. Elk Glenn, LLC*, 758 F.3d 737, 738 (6th Cir. 2014).

[34]   *See Nystedt v. Nigro*, 700 F.3d 25, 30 (1st Cir. 2012).

[35]   *See Transport Workers Union of America, Local 100, AFL-CIO v. New York City Transit Authority*, 505 F.3d 226, 230 (2d Cir. 2007).

[36]   *See Novick v. AXA Network, LLC*, 642 F.3d 304, 311 (2d Cir. 2011).

[37]   *See Sears, Roebuck & Co. v. Mackey*, 351 U.S. 427, 76 S.Ct. 895, 100 L. Ed. 1297 (1956).

[38]   *See U.S. Citizens Ass'n v. Sebelius*, 705 F.3d 588, 596 (6th Cir. 2013).

o   Other factors, including delay, economic and solvency concerns, shortening of trial time, frivolity of competing claims, and expense.[39]

A Rule 54(b) determination is likely to be improper where the litigation itself, and the contested claim resolution, is routine and would inevitably return to the trial court on essentially the same set of facts.[40]

- ● *3: Entry of Judgment:* In clear and unmistakable language, the district court must also direct that judgment is entered as to that one claim or one party.[41]

Use of "Magic Language"

Immediate appealability hinges on the district court "expressly" determining that there is no just reason for delay and directing entry of the partial final judgment.[42] There is, however, some authority that the court's failure to incant this language may be overlooked, so long as the trial judge's intent to proceed under Rule 54(b) is otherwise unmistakably clear.[43] But not all courts follow this approach.[44] In any event, however it is communicated, the determination must always be made "expressly"[45] and the intent "unmistakable".[46]

- ● *Abandoned Claims:* A district court's judgment that resolves some open claims, but leaves others unaddressed, may still be deemed to be final (even without the inclusion of the "magic language"), if the court concluded that the unaddressed claims were abandoned[47] or otherwise terminated by subsequent events.[48]

- ● *Subsequent Determination:* An order lacking the Rule 54(b) specifics may be cured by a supplemental order,[49] even one issued upon remand from the courts of appeals.[50]

Explanation by the District Court

Detailed statements of reasons are not necessary.[51] But in its order entering a Rule 54(b) judgment, the district court must clearly and cogently explain why it has concluded that an immediate appellate review of the order is advisable,[52] or those reasons must be readily apparent from the record.[53] The district court should not simply reprint, in

---

[39] *See U.S. Citizens Ass'n v. Sebelius*, 705 F.3d 588, 596 (6th Cir. 2013).

[40] *See Wood v. GCC Bend, LLC*, 422 F.3d 873, 878 (9th Cir. 2005).

[41] *See Blackman v. District of Columbia*, 456 F.3d 167, 175–76 (D.C. Cir. 2006) (must be an express direction for entry of judgment); *Berckeley Inv. Group, Ltd. v. Colkitt*, 455 F.3d 195, 202 (3d Cir. 2006) (must be a final judgment on the merits); *Jordan v. Pugh*, 425 F.3d 820, 826 (10th Cir. 2005) (must be a final decision on at least one claim).

[42] *See* Rule 54(b). *See also HSBC Bank USA, N.A. v. Townsend*, 793 F.3d 771, 778 (7th Cir. 2015).

[43] *See Crostley v. Lamar County*, 717 F.3d 410, 420 (5th Cir. 2013). *See also Downie v. City of Middleburg Heights*, 301 F.3d 688, 693 (6th Cir. 2002) (district court need not enter partial final judgment in its certification, but it must recognize that such a partial final judgment has been entered).

[44] *See Schrock v. Wyeth, Inc.*, 727 F.3d 1273, 1278–79 (10th Cir. 2013).

[45] *See Nystedt v. Nigro*, 700 F.3d 25, 30 (1st Cir. 2012).

[46] *See Crostley v. Lamar County*, 717 F.3d 410, 420–21 (5th Cir. 2013).

[47] *See DIRECTV, Inc. v. Budden*, 420 F.3d 521, 525–26 (5th Cir. 2005).

[48] *See Schippers v. United States,*715 F.3d 879, 884–85 (11th Cir. 2013).

[49] *See Glover v. F.D.I.C.*, 698 F.3d 139, 144 n.5 (3d Cir. 2012).

[50] *See Rollins v. Mortgage Elec. Regis. Sys., Inc.*, 737 F.3d 1250, 1253–54 (9th Cir. 2013).

[51] *See Williams v. County of Dakota*, 687 F.3d 1064, 1068 (8th Cir. 2012).

[52] *See Boston Prop. Exchange Transfer Co. v. Iantosca*, 720 F.3d 1, 7–8 (1st Cir. 2013) ("some concise findings 'will likely be needed' "); *Novick v. AXA Network, LLC*, 642 F.3d 304, 310 (2d Cir. 2011) (reasoned, even if brief, explanation required).

[53] *See Brown v. Eli Lilly & Co.*, 654 F.3d 347, 355 (2d Cir. 2011).

boilerplate, the formula of the Rule[54] or autograph a defendant's Rule 54(b) request.[55] The court of appeals may, in the absence of such a written explanation, dismiss the appeal as inappropriately allowed under Rule 54(b),[56] or at the very least subject the determination to special scrutiny.[57] Although dismissal of the appeal is permitted (and perhaps even likely) without a corresponding explanation from the trial court, dismissal is not compulsory; the failure to offer a written explanation is *not* a jurisdictional defect that *compels* the appeal's dismissal.[58]

Duty of Counsel in Explanation Requirement

In moving for a Rule 54(b) determination, the courts expect counsel, as officers of the court and advocates for an immediate appeal, to assist the district court by making appropriate submissions that express the reasons for and basis of a Rule 54(b) determination.[59] In fact, if the trial judge fails to offer a detailed explanation for the Rule 54(b) determination, the reasons offered by counsel can assume special significance.[60] But counsel cannot, by agreement that they exist, create the Rule 54(b) prerequisites if they are absent.[61]

Burden of Proof

The moving party bears the burden of establishing that a partial judgment should be entered under Rule 54(b).[62]

Discretion of District Judge

The court is not *required* to enter a final judgment in an action involving multiple parties where the court resolves claims involving less than all parties or less than all claims.[63] To the contrary, whether to enter a judgment under Rule 54(b) is reserved for the sound discretion of the district judge.[64] Indeed, such judgments are contrary to the historic federal policy against piecemeal appeals, particularly during a period when the courts of appeals' caseload has grown faster than any other segment of the federal bench.[65] For this reason, Rule 54(b) orders are not granted routinely,[66] or merely with the hope of avoiding a

---

[54] *See iLOR, LLC v. Google, Inc.*, 550 F.3d 1067, 1072 (Fed.Cir. 2008).

[55] *See Boston Prop. Exchange Transfer Co. v. Iantosca*, 720 F.3d 1, 7–8 (1st Cir. 2013).

[56] *See Adler v. Elk Glenn, LLC*, 758 F.3d 737, 738 (6th Cir. 2014).

[57] *See Williams v. County of Dakota*, 687 F.3d 1064, 1068 (8th Cir. 2012).

[58] *See Brown v. Eli Lilly & Co.*, 654 F.3d 347, 355 (2d Cir. 2011) (order lacking supporting statement "is no less final"); *Carter v. City of Philadelphia*, 181 F.3d 339, 344 (3d Cir. 1999) (not jurisdictional). *See also McAdams v. McCord*, 533 F.3d 924, 928 (8th Cir. 2008) (although detailed statement not required, without it appeals court review is more speculative and less circumscribed); *Smith ex rel. Smith v. Half Hollow Hills Cent. School Dist.*, 298 F.3d 168, 171 (2d Cir. 2002) (noting that, under rare certain circumstances, the reason for certification may be sufficiently obvious that no explanation is required and the court of appeals is able to provide meaningful review without an explanation from the trial judge of why certification was deemed appropriate).

[59] *See Federal Home Loan Mortgage Corp. v. Scottsdale Ins. Co.*, 316 F.3d 431, 441–42 (3d Cir. 2003).

[60] *See Williams v. County of Dakota*, 687 F.3d 1064, 1067–68 (8th Cir. 2012).

[61] *See Williams v. County of Dakota*, 687 F.3d 1064, 1067 (8th Cir. 2012).

[62] *See Braswell Shipyards, Inc. v. Beazer East, Inc.*, 2 F.3d 1331, 1335 (4th Cir. 1993).

[63] *See generally Ruiz v. Blentech Corp.*, 89 F.3d 320, 323 (7th Cir. 1996) (court has two options in placing into final form individual orders in multiparty cases: Rule 54(b) finality order or final order disposing of all claims respecting all parties).

[64] *See Curtiss-Wright Corp. v. General Elec. Co.*, 446 U.S. 1, 100 S.Ct. 1460, 64 L.Ed.2d 1 (1980). *See generally Sears, Roebuck & Co. v. Mackey*, 351 U.S. 427, 437, 76 S.Ct. 895, 900, 100 L. Ed. 1297 (1956) (noting that discretion lies primarily with the district court "as the one most likely to be familiar with the case and with any justifiable reasons for delay").

[65] *See In re Southeast Banking Corp.*, 69 F.3d 1539, 1548 (11th Cir. 1995).

[66] *See Curtiss-Wright Corp. v. General Elec. Co.*, 446 U.S. 1, 10, 100 S.Ct. 1460, 1466, 64 L.Ed.2d 1 (1980) (writing that sound judicial administration does not require that Rule 54(b) requests be granted routinely).

trial,[67] or as an accommodation to counsel.[68] Instead, the district court must carefully balance the needs of the parties for an immediate appeal against the interest of efficient management of the litigation.[69] Rule 54(d) determinations are the exceptions, not the rule.[70]

Determination by Trial Judge Is *Not* Conclusive on Court of Appeals

That the district judge allowed a ruling for an immediate appeal under Rule 54(b) is not wholly dispositive. The courts of appeals will still review the matter to ensure that the trial judge allowed a ruling that was eligible for immediate review under the Rule.[71]

Procedure for Obtaining Rule 54(b) Determination

The Rule sets no defined procedure for obtaining a determination under Rule 54(b). The district court may grant such a determination *sua sponte* to accompany the order at issue. Alternatively, the parties may separately move the district court under Rule 54(b) to grant a determination. The time for making such a motion is not specified in the Rule. Prudent practitioners will seek a Rule 54(b) determination promptly, and within the 28-day period allotted for alterations or amendments to "judgments". Although Rule 54(b) motions are technically not motions seeking Rule 59 or Rule 60 relief (and, thus, might not fall within the ambit of the 28-day limit), this type of prompt action is consistent with the moving party's claim that the order qualifies as an immediate "judgment" under the Rule and comports with the Rule 54(b) objective of permitting some piecemeal appeals where delay would be unduly harsh or unjust.[72] If an appeal is taken prior to the district court's determination under Rule 54(b), most Circuits have ruled that the belated determination will "ripen" an otherwise improper appeal, so long as the determination issues prior to the date the court of appeals considers the appeal.[73]

WARNING: Effect of Rule 54(b) Judgments

Once a Rule 54(b) judgment is entered, the time for appeal on that judgment begins to run,[74] as does post-judgment interest.[75] Consequently, failing to file an appeal timely after entry of the Rule 54(b) judgment may forever forfeit the right of appeal.[76] Moreover, some courts have ruled that the time for appeal following a Rule 54(b) determination can begin to run even earlier, before entry on the docket—on the date the order granting Rule 54(b) relief was signed and mailed to the parties.[77]

---

[67]   *See Credit Francais Intern., S.A. v. Bio-Vita, Ltd.*, 78 F.3d 698, 706 (1st Cir. 1996) (possibility of avoiding a trial is "rarely, if ever, a self-sufficient basis for a Rule 54(b) certification").

[68]   *See Nystedt v. Nigro*, 700 F.3d 25, 29 (1st Cir. 2012); *Clark v. Baka*, 593 F.3d 712, 714–15 (8th Cir. 2010).

[69]   *See McAdams v. McCord*, 533 F.3d 924, 928 (8th Cir. 2008). *See also L.B. Foster Co. v. America Piles, Inc.*, 138 F.3d 81, 86 (2d Cir. 1998) (certification should be reserved for "the infrequent harsh case" where danger exists for hardship or injustice through delay, which could be alleviated by immediate appeal).

[70]   *See Elliott v. Archdiocese of New York*, 682 F.3d 213, 220 (3d Cir. 2012).

[71]   *See Noel v. Hall*, 568 F.3d 743, 747 (9th Cir. 2009).

[72]   There does not appear to be published case law resolving this issue, a factor that all the more urgently counsels in favor of prompt action by the moving party.

[73]   *See, e.g., Barrett ex rel. Estate of Barrett v. United States,* 462 F.3d 28, 34–35 (1st Cir. 2006).

[74]   *See Federal Deposit Ins. Corp. v. Tripati*, 769 F.2d 507, 508 (8th Cir. 1985). *See also Brown v. Eli Lilly & Co.*, 654 F.3d 347, 354 (2d Cir. 2011) (appeal time began and ended, while counsel relied on errant conclusion that appeal right had not yet ripened).

[75]   *See* 28 U.S.C.A. § 1961; *Hooks v. Washington Sheraton Corp.*, 642 F.2d 614, 616 (D.C. Cir. 1980).

[76]   *See Satkar Hospitality, Inc. v. Fox Television Holdings*, 767 F.3d 701, 706 (7th Cir. 2014).

[77]   *See Silivanch v. Celebrity Cruises, Inc.*, 333 F.3d 355, 364–65 (2d Cir. 2003) (commenting that "[t]here is no requirement that such a certification be docketed in order for it to become effective", and thus the order became effective, and the appeal period began to run, when the order "was signed and mailed to the parties"). *But cf. Brown v. Mississippi Valley State University*, 311 F.3d 328, 331–32 (5th Cir. 2002) (noting that, for purposes of Rule 4 of the Federal Rules of Appellate Procedure 4, judgment becomes final on the date Rule 54(b) determination is entered).

Effect of Dismissals Without Rule 54(b) Judgment

Unless the court enters a separate judgment under Rule 54(b), litigants in a multi-party case who are dismissed may technically remain in the case until the final resolution of all claims as to all parties. Dismissed litigants are, however, entitled to rely on the dismissal until notified that they have been rejoined as parties. Thus, until notified otherwise, dismissed litigants need not participate in discovery, in pretrial proceedings, or in the trial itself.[78]

No Counsel-Manipulated Rule 54(b) Dismissals

After the district court dismisses one claim or one party, the litigants might not be able to *create* appealability by voluntarily dismissing the remaining claims and parties in order to obtain immediate appellate review.[79]

No "Tag-Along" Partial Appeals

A decision to permit an immediate appeal of one part of a litigation is not, by itself, sufficient justification to grant Rule 54(b) relief for another part.[80]

"Certification" Nomenclature

Often in the case law, the Rule 54(b) determination procedure is described as a "certification", a "misnomer born of confusion".[81] The term "certification" is used accurately to describe the procedure for seeking immediate appellate review of interlocutory orders under 28 U.S.C. § 1292(b). Conversely, a Rule 54(b) determination, if granted, effectively severs what becomes a *final* judgment (albeit as to one or more but fewer than all claims or parties) from the remaining claims and parties in the case.[82]

Rule 54(b) and Tax Court Rulings

Although there is some division of authority on the point, recent case law supports the application of Rule 54(b) procedures to partial rulings by the United States Tax Court.[83]

Appealability of Denials of Rule 54(b) Requests

Allowing immediate appellate review of "partial" final judgments is a practice that departs from the federal courts' traditional opposition to piecemeal appeals. Rule 54(b), thus, represents an unusual exception to this settled policy. Predictably, the courts reject attempts to immediately challenge denials of Rule 54(b) determinations as premature and unappealable until a final ruling is entered on the merits.[84]

Appeals—Improper Rule 54(b) Determinations

If the appeals court finds that the district court's Rule 54(b) determination was given or prepared improperly, appellate jurisdiction is lost.[85] But counsel should be very careful

---

[78] *See Bennett v. Pippin*, 74 F.3d 578, 587 (5th Cir. 1996).

[79] *See Blue v. District of Columbia Pub. Schs.*, 764 F.3d 11, 18–19 (D.C.Cir. 2014) (voluntary, without-prejudice dismissals cannot be used to trigger Rule 54(b)).

[80] *See Edwards v. Prime, Inc.*, 602 F.3d 1276, 1288–89 (11th Cir. 2010); *O'Bert ex rel. Estate of O'Bert v. Vargo*, 331 F.3d 29, 43 (2d Cir. 2003).

[81] *See James v. Price Stern Sloan, Inc.*, 283 F.3d 1064, 1067–68 n.6 (9th Cir. 2002).

[82] *See James v. Price Stern Sloan, Inc.*, 283 F.3d 1064, 1067–68 n.6 (9th Cir. 2002) ("Referring to a Rule 54(b) severance order as a 'certification' misleadingly brings to mind the kind of rigorous judgment embodied in the section 1292(b) certification process. In reality, issuance of a Rule 54(b) order is a fairly routine act that is reversed only in the rarest instances").

[83] *See New York Football Giants, Inc. v. C.I.R.*, 349 F.3d 102, 106–07 (3d Cir. 2003) (so holding, and surveying division among Circuits).

[84] *See United Industries, Inc. v. Eimco Process Equipment Co.*, 61 F.3d 445, 448 (5th Cir. 1995).

[85] *See EJS Props., LLC v. City of Toledo*, 689 F.3d 535, 538 (6th Cir. 2012).

before relying on their own conclusions in this regard; if the court of appeals disagrees or, finding an impropriety, overlooks it, a litigant's failure to have filed the appeal could prove disastrous.[86] The court of appeals is not bound by counsel's views on the question of appellate jurisdiction. Even if the litigants do not themselves contest a Rule 54(b) determination, the court of appeals will consider its propriety *sua sponte* and, if the determination is found to be improper, will dismiss the appeal.[87]

Appeals—Prematurely Filed

If an appeal is taken prior to the district court issuing a Rule 54(b) determination, many Circuits have ruled that the belated determination "ripens" the otherwise premature appeal, so long as the determination issues prior to the date the court of appeals considers the appeal.[88]

Appeals—Scope of "Determination"

On appeal following a Rule 54(b) determination, the court of appeals will confine its review only to those specific claims or parties regarding which the determination was granted (including all merged interlocutory orders). Other aspects of the still-ongoing lawsuit will not be examined during the appeal.[89]

RULE 54(c)—DEMAND FOR JUDGMENT; RELIEF TO BE GRANTED

CORE CONCEPT

The district court generally must grant all the relief to which the prevailing party is entitled, whether or not such relief was requested in the pleadings. Pleadings serve as "guides" to the nature of the case, but the lawsuit is ultimately measured by what is pleaded and proven, not merely by what was demanded.[90] In default judgments, however, the district court may not award relief beyond that sought in the complaint.

APPLICATIONS

Default Judgments

Defendants don't always default by accident or neglect. Sometimes, defendants default deliberately, perhaps reasoning that the relief the claimant's pleading seeks is not worth the fight to resist. Consequently, because a litigant may be relying on the pleaded demand in choosing to default,[91] a claimant may not receive a default judgment that differs either in "kind" or in "amount" from what was sought in the pleadings.[92] Courts are also unlikely to construe closing, boilerplate language in a pleading to expand the available remedies in a default situation.[93] Among the sparse exceptions to this rule are where the defendant originally appeared in the action and was placed on proper notice of the possible expanded relief [94] and where the complaint fairly identified the nature of the claimed loss and placed

---

[86] *See Brown v. Eli Lilly & Co.*, 654 F.3d 347, 355 (2d Cir. 2011).

[87] *See Lowery v. Federal Exp. Corp.*, 426 F.3d 817, 820 (6th Cir. 2005).

[88] *See, e.g., Barrett ex rel. Estate of Barrett v. United States,* 462 F.3d 28, 34–35 (1st Cir. 2006).

[89] *See Meadaa v. K.A.P. Enters., L.L.C.*, 756 F.3d 875, 879 (5th Cir. 2014).

[90] *See Minyard Enterprises, Inc. v. Southeastern Chemical & Solvent Co.*, 184 F.3d 373, 386 (4th Cir. 1999.

[91] *See Hooper-Haas v. Ziegler Holdings, LLC*, 690 F.3d 34, 40 (1st Cir. 2012); *Silge v. Merz*, 510 F.3d 157, 160 (2d Cir.2007).

[92] *See Hooper-Haas v. Ziegler Holdings, LLC*, 690 F.3d 34, 39–40 (1st Cir. 2012); *Silge v. Merz*, 510 F.3d 157, 160 (2d Cir. 2007).

[93] *See Emory v. United Air Lines, Inc.*, 720 F.3d 915, 921 n.10 (D.C.Cir. 2013).

[94] *See Silge v. Merz*, 510 F.3d 157, 161 n.5 (2d Cir. 2007).

the defendant on notice that the value of that loss would continue to accrue during the litigation.[95]

- *"Defaulting" Party:* A party defaults within the meaning of Rule 54(b) by either failing to appear at all or defaulting following an appearance.[96]

- *Differing in "Kind":* Whether relief on default differs in "kind" hinges on whether the pleadings afforded adequate notice of that relief.[97]

- *Boilerplate Language:* In determining (for default purposes) what remedies have been pleaded, courts are disinclined to expand the available remedies on the basis of passing, boilerplate language in a pleading.[98]

- *Post-Restyling Impacts:* The post-restyled language of Rule 54(c) may have inadvertently broadened the scope of relief that a litigant can receive against a defaulting party, forbidding only relief that differs from the "pleadings" rather than the more restrictive differing from the "demand for judgment."[99]

Non-Default Judgments

Where the defendant has answered or otherwise appeared to defend the lawsuit, a plaintiff may receive a judgment for an amount greater or less than that sought in the complaint,[100] as well as types of relief not mentioned in the complaint's demand clause.[101] It is the court's duty to grant generally all appropriate relief.[102]

Limitations on Awarding Additional Relief

The courts' ability to award unpleaded relief is not unbounded. They are not licensed with untethered roaming authority, permitting them to provide remedies for all wrongs.[103] Rather, this Rule is simply designed to protect against clumsy drafting and to prevent technical missteps from depriving the pleader of a deserved recovery; it is not, however, meant to allow the pleader to recover on *claims* never alleged.[104]

It will not permit a recovery on issues that were not actually litigated, or revive a right to relief lost in the pleadings or through a failure of proof.[105] It will not allow relief against a defendant from whom no relief has been sought,[106] or force upon the litigants a remedy none of them desires.[107] Litigants will be held bound to representations made during a

---

[95] *See Boland v. Yoccabel Const. Co., Inc.*, 293 F.R.D. 13, 18–19 (D.D.C. 2013).

[96] *See Hooper-Haas v. Ziegler Holdings, LLC*, 690 F.3d 34, 40 n.4 (1st Cir. 2012).

[97] *See Belizaire v. RAV Investigative & Sec. Servs. Ltd.*, 61 F.Supp.3d 336, 345–46 (S.D.N.Y. 2014).

[98] *See Emory v. United Air Lines, Inc.*, 720 F.3d 915, 921 n.10 (D.C.Cir. 2013).

[99] *See Hooper-Haas v. Ziegler Holdings, LLC*, 690 F.3d 34, 40–41 (1st Cir. 2012) (discussing, without adopting, possible substantive impact).

[100] *See Avitia v. Metropolitan Club of Chicago, Inc.*, 49 F.3d 1219, 1229 (7th Cir. 1995) (holding that, except for "special damages" under Rule 9(g), plaintiffs are not obligated to itemize their damages in their complaints).

[101] *See Holt Civic Club v. City of Tuscaloosa*, 439 U.S. 60, 65–66, 99 S.Ct. 383, 387–388, 58 L.Ed.2d 292 (1978) (federal courts should not dismiss meritorious constitutional claims because pleadings specify one remedy, rather than another).

[102] *See Felce v. Fiedler*, 974 F.2d 1484, 1501 (7th Cir. 1992) (noting that Rule 54(c) is to be liberally construed so that there is no doubt but that the court must grant whatever relief is appropriate).

[103] *See Knight v. Alabama*, 476 F.3d 1219, 1229 n.19 (11th Cir. 2007).

[104] *See USX Corp. v. Barnhart*, 395 F.3d 161, 165 (3d Cir. 2004).

[105] *See Old Republic Ins. Co. v. Employers Reinsurance Corp.*, 144 F.3d 1077, 1080 (7th Cir. 1998) (trial court may not award relief upon theory not properly raised at trial); *Rodriguez v. Doral Mortg. Corp.*, 57 F.3d 1168, 1173 (1st Cir. 1995) (commenting that the thesis of Rule 54(c) is "hollow at its core", because the Rule creates no entitlement to any relief based on issues not presented to and tried before the factfinder).

[106] *See Powell v. National Bd. of Medical Examiners*, 364 F.3d 79, 86 (2d Cir. 2004).

[107] *See Minyard Enterprises, Inc. v. Southeastern Chemical & Solvent Co.*, 184 F.3d 373, 386 (4th Cir. 1999).

pretrial conference or in a pretrial order that outlined the claims and relief in the case.[108] In short, this Rule will not permit an additional award that would be unfairly prejudicial or unjust.[109] For example, pleaders may not manipulatively "cap" their claims to achieve some tactical advantage, and then receive under this Rule the very same relief they earlier shunned.[110]

- *Types of Unpleaded Relief Permitted:* Courts have permitted litigants to recover punitive damages,[111] nominal damages,[112] attorney's fees,[113] prejudgment interest,[114] accruing ERISA damages,[115] and even injunctive relief[116] where those remedies were not expressly sought in the complaints, in appropriate cases.

RULE 54(d)—COSTS AND ATTORNEY'S FEES

CORE CONCEPT

The district court should ordinarily award "costs" to the prevailing party in a lawsuit; the clerk may tax such "costs" on 14 days' notice. Taxable "costs" are limited to those items set by statute. An award of attorney's fees must be on motion (filed not later than 14 days from entry of judgment), unless those fees were established, at trial, as an element of compensable damages under the controlling substantive law.

APPLICATIONS

"Prevailing Party" Defined

A prevailing plaintiff is one who succeeds on some significant issue in the litigation and thereby achieves some of the benefit sought in filing the lawsuit.[117] A plaintiff, thus, "prevails" by obtaining a judgment on the merits or a court-order consent decree,[118] by obtaining an award of monetary damages (even nominal damages),[119] or by obtaining some other relief that materially alters the parties' legal relationship by modifying the behavior of the defendant in a way that directly benefits the plaintiff.[120] A party who loses the

---

[108] *See Walker v. Anderson Elec. Connectors,* 944 F.2d 841, 844 (11th Cir. 1991) (limiting plaintiff to the relief demanded at the pretrial conference, and finding no conflict between Rule 54(c) and requirement that plaintiff set forth, at the pretrial conference, all relief sought).

[109] *See Trim Fit, LLC v. Dickey,* 607 F.3d 528, 532 (8th Cir. 2010). *See also United Phosphorus, Ltd. v. Midland Fumigant, Inc.,* 205 F.3d 1219, 1235 (10th Cir. 2000) (although jury award exceeding relief requested does not invalidate jury's award, remittitur may be necessary to avoid a double recovery).

[110] *See Morgan v. Gay,* 471 F.3d 469, 476–77 (3d Cir. 2006), (construing Class Action Fairness Act of 2005(CAFA), Pub.L. No. 109–2, 119 Stat. 4 (2005) (codified in scattered sections of 28 U.S.C.)); *De Aguilar v. Boeing Co.,* 47 F.3d 1404, 1410 (5th Cir. 1995) (construing removal jurisdiction).

[111] *See Bowles v. Osmose Utilities Services, Inc.,* 443 F.3d 671, 675 (8th Cir. 2006).

[112] *See Jackson v. Hill,* 569 Fed.Appx. 697, 698 (11th Cir. 2014).

[113] *See Sea-Land Service, Inc. v. Murrey & Son's Co. Inc.,* 824 F.2d 740, 745 (9th Cir. 1987).

[114] *See, e.g., RK Co. v. See,* 622 F.3d 846, 853–54 (7th Cir. 2010). *But see Silge v. Merz,* 510 F.3d 157, 160 (2d Cir.2007) (award of prejudgment interest not permitted).

[115] *See Boland v. Yoccabel Const. Co., Inc.,* 293 F.R.D. 13, 18–19 (D.D.C. 2013).

[116] *See Vietnam Veterans of America v. C.I.A.,* 288 F.R.D. 192, 202–03 (N.D.Cal. 2012).

[117] *See Shum v. Intel Corp.,* 629 F.3d 1360, 1367 (Fed.Cir. 2010).

[118] *See SSL Servs., LLC v. Citrix Sys., Inc.,* 769 F.3d 1073, 1086–87 (Fed.Cir. 2014).

[119] *See Farrar v. Hobby,* 506 U.S. 103, 111–13, 113 S.Ct. 566, 573, 121 L.Ed.2d 494 (1992).

[120] *See Buckhannon Bd. and Care Home, Inc. v. West Virginia Dept. of Health and Human Resources,* 532 U.S. 598, 605, 121 S.Ct. 1835, 1840, 149 L.Ed.2d 855 (2001); *Farrar v. Hobby,* 506 U.S. 103, 111–13, 113 S.Ct. 566, 573, 121 L.Ed.2d 494 (1992).

judgment, but whose litigation nonetheless prompts the opponent to change its behavior in some way[121] or can otherwise cite to some "moral victory"[122] is likely *not* a prevailing party.

A prevailing defendant is one who defeats the litigation and obtains a denial of relief. Thus, a dismissal, with prejudice and on the merits, of all claims against a defendant will generally make that defendant a prevailing party.[123]

A litigant need not succeed on all issues to qualify as a prevailing party.[124] For example, a counterclaiming defendant may be deemed a prevailing party by defeating the larger primary claim even if losing on the smaller counterclaim.[125] Note, however, that at least one court has ruled that, for costs taxation purposes, there can be only one prevailing party, even in mixed judgment outcomes.[126]

Generally, there are no prevailing parties if the case is dismissed for lack of jurisdiction[127] or *forum non conveniens*.[128] Similarly, if certain parties prevail originally, but later lose under a subsequent ruling at the trial court or on appeal, their status has changed and their entitlement to costs is lost.[129]

A litigant who is deemed a "prevailing party" for purposes of awarding attorney's fees is likewise a "prevailing party" for purposes of taxing costs.[130]

Against Whom May Costs Be Taxed

Under Rule 54(d), costs may be taxed only against the nonprevailing party; costs may not be taxed under this Rule against counsel for a litigant.[131] When taxed in a multiple-lawsuit proceeding, costs should be allocated among the various cases.[132]

Types of Taxable Costs

The types of costs that can be taxed in favor of the prevailing party in a federal litigation are set by statute,[133] and are comparably modest—often only a fraction of the expenses of litigation.[134] Though limited, those costs can nevertheless still be substantial[135] and often

---

[121] *See Carter v. Incorporated Village of Ocean Beach*, 759 F.3d 159, 162 (2d Cir. 2014).

[122] *See Richardson v. City of Chicago*, 740 F.3d 1099, 1102 (7th Cir. 2014).

[123] *See Power Mosfet Technologies, L.L.C. v. Siemens AG*, 378 F.3d 1396 (Fed. Cir. 2004) (prevailing party is one who "wins completely on every claim at issue", and thus party who "had all claims against it dismissed with prejudice" so qualifies); *Weaver v. Toombs*, 948 F.2d 1004, 1009 (6th Cir.1991) (a dismissal, whether on the merits or not, makes defendant the prevailing party).

[124] *See Maker's Mark Distillery, Inc. v. Diageo North America, Inc.*, 679 F.3d 410, 425 (6th Cir. 2012). *See also Fireman's Fund Ins. Co. v. Tropical Shipping and Const. Co., Ltd.*, 254 F.3d 987, 1012–13 (11th Cir. 2001) (noting precedent supporting an award of costs where the prevailing party obtains a judgment "on even a fraction of the claims advanced").

[125] *See Ira Green, Inc. v. Military Sales & Serv. Co.*, 775 F.3d 12, 28 (1st Cir. 2014).

[126] *See Shum v. Intel Corp.*, 629 F.3d 1360, 1366–70 (Fed.Cir. 2010).

[127] *See Miles v. State of California*, 320 F.3d 986, 988 (9th Cir. 2003).

[128] *See Dattner v. Conagra Foods, Inc.*, 458 F.3d 98, 101 (2d Cir. 2006).

[129] *See E.E.O.C. v. AutoZone, Inc.*, 707 F.3d 824, 845 (7th Cir. 2013).

[130] *See Dattner v. Conagra Foods, Inc.*, 458 F.3d 98, 101 (2d Cir. 2006).

[131] *See In re Cardizem CD Antitrust Litigation*, 481 F.3d 355, 359–60 (6th Cir. 2007).

[132] *See Winter v. Novartis Pharms. Corp.*, 739 F.3d 405, 411–12 (8th Cir. 2014).

[133] *See* 28 U.S.C.A. § 1920. *See also* 28 U.S.C.A. §§ 1911 to 31 (defining costs provisions generally). In addition, the Rules allow costs to be taxed in other instances: when an attorney violates Rule 11, conducts discovery improperly in violation of Rule 37, or rejects unwisely an offer of settlement under Rule 68.

[134] *See Taniguchi v. Kan Pacific Saipan, Ltd.*, ___ U.S. ___, ___, 132 S.Ct. 1997, 2006, 182 L.Ed.2d 903 (2012).

[135] *See In re Online DVD-Rental Antitrust Litig.*, 779 F.3d 914, 925 (9th Cir. 2015) (reviewing award of $710,194 in costs against non-prevailing plaintiff); *In re Williams Secs. Litig.-WCG Subclass*, 558 F.3d 1144, 1147 (10th Cir. 2009) (affirming award of more than $600,000 in costs against non-prevailing plaintiff).

may constitute a substantial measure of discovery costs.[136] These statutorily permitted taxable costs are:

1. Clerk and U.S. Marshal fees,[137] which might even include *pro hac vice* admission fees;[138]

2. Transcript fees, for *both*[139] printed or electronically recorded transcripts, so long as they were "necessarily obtained for use in the case" (including transcripts received into evidence or otherwise "necessary" for trial preparation,[140] but not for transcripts taken solely for discovery purposes, as a mere convenience to counsel or the court, or of witnesses withdrawn or precluded);[141] court reporter attendance fees,[142] and, if allowed, costs can include videotape depositions [143] and perhaps even the stenographic transcription of those videotapes.[144]

3a. Printing fees;

3b. Witness fees and witnesses' travel and subsistence expenses, where the witnesses' testimony was material, relevant, and reasonably necessary to the case;[145]

4a. Fees to "exemplify" documents (which may include reimbursement for many methods of illustration, including models, charts, graphs, and sometimes even computerized presentation systems,[146] but likely not electronically-stored information processing expenses [147] or ancillary document gathering or other preparatory costs[148]);

4b. Fees to print copies of papers necessary for use in the case[149] (which likely will not include some, but not all, electronic data preparation costs (e.g., gathering, preserving, processing, searching, and culling ESI),[150] might not include copying documents for discovery,[151] but likely will include conversion from native files to

---

[136] *See Rundus v. City of Dallas*, 634 F.3d 309, 315–16 (5th Cir. 2011) (affirming taxation of substantial discovery costs against losing party); *Baisden v. I'm Ready Prods., Inc.*, 793 F.Supp.2d 970, 987 (S.D.Tex. 2011) (ordering reimbursement for costs of depositions of party's own witnesses and experts).

[137] *See Winniczek v. Nagelberg*, 400 F.3d 503, 504–05 (7th Cir. 2005) (allowing docketing fee to be taxed).

[138] *See Craftsmen Limousine, Inc. v. Ford Motor Co.*, 579 F.3d 894, 898 (8th Cir. 2009).

[139] *See Stanley v. Cottrell, Inc.*, 784 F.3d 454, 465–67 (8th Cir. 2015).

[140] *See In re Williams Secs. Litig.-WCG Subclass*, 558 F.3d 1144, 1147–48 (10th Cir. 2009). *See also Virginia Panel Corp. v. Mac Panel Co.*, 887 F.Supp. 880, 886 (W.D. Va. 1995), aff'd, 133 F.3d 860 (Fed. Cir. 1997) (cost of daily copies of trial transcripts is recoverable if daily copy is "indispensable", and not a convenience for counsel).

[141] *See In re Williams Secs. Litig.-WCG Subclass*, 558 F.3d 1144, 1147–48 (10th Cir. 2009).

[142] *See Harney v. City of Chicago*, 702 F.3d 916, 927–28 (7th Cir. 2012).

[143] *See Craftsmen Limousine, Inc. v. Ford Motor Co.*, 579 F.3d 894, 897–98 (8th Cir. 2009). *But cf. Cherry v. Champion Intern. Corp.*, 186 F.3d 442, 448–49 (4th Cir. 1999) (although costs of video depositions may be taxed, prevailing party must make a showing why *both* the transcript and the video deposition were "necessary").

[144] *See Little v. Mitsubishi Motors North America, Inc.*, 514 F.3d 699, 701–02 (7th Cir. 2008).

[145] *See Marmo v. Tyson Fresh Meats, Inc.*, 457 F.3d 748, 763 (8th Cir. 2006).

[146] *See Cefalu v. Village of Elk Grove*, 211 F.3d 416, 427–28 (7th Cir. 2000) (affirming reimbursement for cost of computerized, multi-media system used to present exhibits to jury). *But cf. Kohus v. Toys R Us, Inc.*, 282 F.3d 1355, 1357–61 (Fed. Cir. 2002) (reversing award of $12,950 for video model/animation as unauthorized under federal law); *Arcadian Fertilizer, L.P. v. MPW Indus. Services, Inc.*, 249 F.3d 1293, 1297 (11th Cir. 2001) (refusing reimbursement for videotape exhibits and computer animation).

[147] *See Country Vintner of North Carolina, LLC v. E. & J. Gallo Winery, Inc.*, 718 F.3d 249, 261–62 (4th Cir. 2013).

[148] *See CBT Flint Partners, LLC v. Return Path, Inc.*, 737 F.3d 1320, 1328 (Fed. Cir. 2013).

[149] *See Little v. Mitsubishi Motors North America, Inc.*, 514 F.3d 699, 701 (7th Cir. 2008).

[150] *See Colosi v. Jones Lang LaSalle Americas, Inc.*, 781 F.3d 293, 297–98 (6th Cir. 2015).

[151] *See In re Online DVD-Rental Antitrust Litig.*, 779 F.3d 914, 927 (9th Cir. 2015).

readable format,[152] and scanning and imaging of documents;[153] to recover costs, a copy-by-copy tracking might not be required, but a bill of costs showing a reasonably accurate calculation will be[154]);

5. Certain docket fees;[155] and

6. Fees for court-appointed experts (which often include guardians and special masters)[156] and interpreters (though limited to oral interpreters, not translators of written work).[157]

Types of Costs That Will Not Be Taxed

The district court may not tax costs under Rule 54(d) that are not authorized by statute or court rule.[158] Thus, in the absence of an express legal authority otherwise, courts generally may *not* tax as costs the fees and expenses of expert witnesses (beyond the modest travel and subsistence expenses noted above for witnesses generally);[159] computer-assisted legal research;[160] trial consultants who prepared computer animations, videos, powerpoint slides, and graphic illustrations;[161] postage, overnight courier, and similar messenger or delivery services;[162] telephone calls;[163] facsimile transmissions;[164] paralegals;[165] travel, lodging, transportation, and parking;[166] mediation;[167] or post-trial/pre-appeal costs (like supersedeas bond premiums).[168] Courts are divided on whether the costs of private process servers are taxable.[169]

---

[152] *See Race Tires America, Inc. v. Hoosier Racing Tire Corp.*, 674 F.3d 158, 166–68 (3d Cir. 2012).

[153] *See BDT Products, Inc. v. Lexmark Intern., Inc.*, 405 F.3d 415, 420 (6th Cir. 2005).

[154] *See In re Williams Secs. Litig.-WCG Subclass*, 558 F.3d 1144, 1148 (10th Cir. 2009).

[155] *See BDT Products, Inc. v. Lexmark Intern., Inc.*, 405 F.3d 415, 419–20 (6th Cir. 2005).

[156] *See Gaddis v. United States*, 381 F.3d 444, 451 (5th Cir. 2004).

[157] *See Taniguchi v. Kan Pacific Saipan, Ltd.*, ___ U.S. ___, ___, 132 S.Ct. 1997, 1999–2007, 182 L.Ed.2d 903 (2012).

[158] *See Arlington Cent. School Dist. Bd. of Educ. v. Murphy*, 548 U.S. 291, 301, 126 S.Ct. 2455, 2461–62, 165 L.Ed.2d 526 (2006).

[159] *See Arlington Cent. School Dist. Bd. of Educ. v. Murphy*, 548 U.S. 291, 301, 126 S.Ct. 2455, 165 L.Ed.2d 526 (2006); *West Virginia University Hospitals, Inc. v. Casey*, 499 U.S. 83, 102, 111 S.Ct. 1138, 113 L.Ed.2d 68 (1991); *Crawford Fitting Co. v. J. T. Gibbons, Inc.*, 482 U.S. 437, 439, 107 S.Ct. 2494, 96 L.Ed.2d 385 (1987).

[160] *See Jones v. Unisys Corp.*, 54 F.3d 624, 633 (10th Cir. 1995). *But see Little v. Mitsubishi Motors North America, Inc.*, 514 F.3d 699, 701 (7th Cir. 2008) (ruling such costs authorized by § 1920).

[161] *See Summit Technology, Inc. v. Nidek Co., Ltd.*, 435 F.3d 1371, 1374–75 (Fed. Cir. 2006). *But see Marmo v. Tyson Fresh Meats, Inc.*, 457 F.3d 748, 763 (8th Cir.2006) (taxing as "copying and exemplification" costs the expenses for graphic and visual aids, and other materials prepared for electronic display).

[162] *See Smith v. Tenet Healthsystem SL, Inc.*, 436 F.3d 879, 889–90 (8th Cir. 2006).

[163] *See O'Bryhim v. Reliance Standard Life Ins. Co.*, 997 F.Supp. 728, 737–38 (E.D. Va. 1998), *aff'd*, 188 F.3d 502 (4th Cir. 1999).

[164] *See O'Bryhim v. Reliance Standard Life Ins. Co.*, 997 F.Supp. 728, 737–38 (E.D. Va. 1998), *aff'd*, 188 F.3d 502 (4th Cir. 1999).

[165] *See Thomas v. Treasury Management Ass'n, Inc.*, 158 F.R.D. 364, 372 (D. Md. 1994).

[166] *See O'Bryhim v. Reliance Standard Life Ins. Co.*, 997 F.Supp. 728, 737–38 (E.D. Va. 1998), *aff'd*, 188 F.3d 502 (4th Cir. 1999).

[167] *See Brisco-Wade v. Carnahan*, 297 F.3d 781, 782 (8th Cir. 2002).

[168] *See Republic Tobacco Co. v. North Atlantic Trading Co., Inc.*, 481 F.3d 442, 447–48 (7th Cir. 2007).

[169] *See Francisco v. Verizon South, Inc.*, 272 F.R.D. 436, 441–42 (E.D.Va. 2011) (discussing divided case law).

Attorney's Fees as Costs

In the absence of a federal statute to the contrary, attorney's fees may not be taxed as costs beyond the modest provisions set forth in 28 U.S.C.A. § 1923.[170]

- *Exceptions:* Attorney's fees, however, may be taxed against a common fund generated in a class action or shareholders' derivative action,[171] and where a party instituted, defended, or conducted litigation in bad faith.[172]

Burden of Proof

The burden of proving the amount of compensable costs and expenses lies with the party seeking those costs.[173] Once the prevailing party demonstrates the amount of its costs and that they fall within an allowable category of taxable costs, the prevailing party enjoys the "strong presumption" that its costs will be awarded "in full measure".[174] The party opposing the award of costs bears the burden of demonstrating that the award would be improper.[175]

Diversity Jurisdiction Cases

Federal law governs the taxation of costs in the district courts, even where the district court's jurisdiction is premised on diversity of citizenship.[176]

Discretion of District Court

Rule 54(d) provides that costs "should" be taxed.[177] The courts have interpreted this mandate to create a presumption in favor of the award of costs in favor of the prevailing party,[178] but reserving for the district judge the discretion to deny costs in appropriate circumstances.[179] A "sound basis" is needed to overcome this presumption,[180] since denying costs is essentially a "penalty" that deprives a litigant of an entitlement.[181] If the court chooses not to award costs to a prevailing party, the court must explain its good reasons for not doing so[182] (although a formal written opinion is not required either when costs are

---

[170] *See Alyeska Pipeline Service Co. v. Wilderness Society*, 421 U.S. 240, 95 S.Ct. 1612, 44 L.Ed.2d 141 (1975). *See also Marx v. General Revenue Corp.*, ___ U.S. ___, ___, 133 S.Ct. 1166, 1175, 185 L.Ed.2d 242 (2013) (noting "bedrock principle" of "American Rule" where litigants each pay their own attorney's fees).

[171] *See Mills v. Electric Auto-Lite Co.*, 396 U.S. 375, 90 S.Ct. 616, 24 L.Ed.2d 593 (1970).

[172] *See Chambers v. NASCO, Inc.*, 501 U.S. 32, 111 S.Ct. 2123, 115 L.Ed.2d 27 (1991).

[173] *See In re Williams Secs. Litig.-WCG Subclass*, 558 F.3d 1144, 1148 (10th Cir. 2009).

[174] *See Shum v. Intel Corp.*, 629 F.3d 1360, 1370 (Fed.Cir. 2010).

[175] *See Stanley v. Cottrell, Inc.*, 784 F.3d 454, 464 (8th Cir. 2015).

[176] *See Humann v. KEM Elec. Co-op., Inc.*, 497 F.3d 810, 813 (8th Cir. 2007).

[177] *See Stafford Invs., LLC v. Vito*, 2009 WL 1362513, at *11 (E.D.Pa. May 14, 2009), *aff'd*, 375 Fed. Appx. 221 (3d Cir. 2010) (noting 2007 Restyling Amendments revision of syntax "as of course" to "should" retained pre-amendment meaning).

[178] *See Marx v. General Revenue Corp.*, U.S., 133 S.Ct. 1166, 1172, 185 L.Ed.2d 242 (2013); *Delta Air Lines, Inc. v. August*, 450 U.S. 346, 352, 101 S.Ct. 1146, 1150, 67 L.Ed.2d 287 (1981).

[179] *See Marx v. General Revenue Corp.*, U.S., 133 S.Ct. 1166, 1172–73, 185 L.Ed.2d 242 (2013); *Crawford Fitting Co. v. J. T. Gibbons, Inc.*, 482 U.S. 437, 107 S.Ct. 2494, 96 L.Ed.2d 385 (1987); *Farmer v. Arabian Am. Oil Co.*, 379 U.S. 227, 85 S.Ct. 411, 13 L.Ed.2d 248 (1964).

[180] *See Mathews v. Crosby*, 480 F.3d 1265, 1277 (11th Cir. 2007). *See also Goldberg v. Pacific Indem. Co.*, 627 F.3d 752, 755 n.4 (9th Cir. 2010) ("limited discretion" to refuse to tax costs).

[181] *See Debord v. Mercy Health System of Kansas, Inc.*, 737 F.3d 642, 659 (10th Cir. 2013).

[182] *See In re Online DVD-Rental Antitrust Litig.*, 779 F.3d 914, 932 (9th Cir. 2015).

awarded[183] or denied entirely).[184] An implicit justification will ordinarily be insufficient to sustain the denial on appeal,[185] at least unless the reasons for denying costs are clear.[186]

Mandatory Reasons for Denying Costs

The district court must deny costs if a federal statute, another Rule, or a court order so commands.[187] For example, although it need not displace Rule 54(d) expressly,[188] a statute may preclude a court from awarding costs or impose conditions on an award of costs.[189]

- *Effect of Rule 68 Settlement Offers:* When implicated, Rule 68 compels even a prevailing party to pay an opponent's costs if the victory is less favorable that an unaccepted offer of settlement.[190] The consensus view among the courts is that Rule 68 thus "reverses" Rule 54(d).[191]

Discretionary Reasons for Denying Costs

The proper exercise of a trial court's discretion to deny costs may hinge on whether the costs are of a type authorized by law and whether the costs pay for materials necessarily obtained for use in the case.[192] Costs may be denied, for example, where both parties partially prevail in the litigation,[193] where a prevailing plaintiff fails to prove that federal jurisdiction was proper (either because plaintiff fails to recover the $75,000 jurisdictional minimum in a diversity case or because plaintiff fails to win on the federal question counts),[194] where the prevailing party needlessly prolongs the litigation or otherwise acts in bad faith,[195] or, perhaps, where the losing party is unable to pay or would be rendered indigent by paying,[196] or is incarcerated,[197] or where the prevailing party's recovery was nominal or "substantially less" than what was sought,[198] where a voluntarily dismissal is entered but only after first obtaining some modicum of relief,[199] or where there would be some other "injustice" in approving an award of costs.[200] Generally, a district court may not deny costs simply upon a finding that the case was brought and litigated in "good faith" and

---

[183] *See In re Online DVD-Rental Antitrust Litig.*, 779 F.3d 914, 932 (9th Cir. 2015).

[184] *See Reger v. Nemours Found., Inc.*, 599 F.3d 285, 289 (3d Cir. 2010).

[185] *See Holton v. City of Thomasville School Dist.*, 425 F.3d 1325, 1355–56 (11th Cir. 2005).

[186] *See McLaughlin v. Hagel*, 767 F.3d 113, 120 (1st Cir. 2014).

[187] *See Marx v. General Revenue Corp.*, ___ U.S. ___, ___, 133 S.Ct. 1166, 1173, 185 L.Ed.2d 242 (2013).

[188] *See Marx v. General Revenue Corp.*, ___ U.S. ___, ___, 133 S.Ct. 1166, 1173, 185 L.Ed.2d 242 (2013). The absence of explicit language, however, can be considered in assessing Congress' intent. *See id.* at ___, 133 S.Ct. at 1177.

[189] *See Marx v. General Revenue Corp.*, ___ U.S. ___, ___, 133 S.Ct. 1166, 1173–74, 185 L.Ed.2d 242 (2013).

[190] *See* Rule 68. *See infra* Authors' Commentary to Rule 68.

[191] *See Stanczyk v. City of New York*, 752 F.3d 273, 280–82 (2d Cir. 2014) (discussing and then embracing consensus approach).

[192] *See Allison v. Bank One-Denver*, 289 F.3d 1223, 1248 (10th Cir. 2002).

[193] *See Farrar v. Hobby*, 506 U.S. 103, 115–16, 113 S.Ct. 566, 575, 121 L.Ed.2d 494 (1992) (having considered the amount and nature of the plaintiffs success on the merits, district courts may award modest fees or no fees at all). *See also Debord v. Mercy Health System of Kansas, Inc.*, 737 F.3d 642, 660 (10th Cir. 2013) (proper criteria to consider); *Estate of Hevia v. Portrio Corp.*, 602 F.3d 34, 46–47 (1st Cir. 2010) (courts commonly order such parties to bear their own costs).

[194] *See Miles v. State of California*, 320 F.3d 986, 988 (9th Cir. 2003).

[195] *See Debord v. Mercy Health System of Kansas, Inc.*, 737 F.3d 642, 660 (10th Cir. 2013).

[196] *See Marx v. General Revenue Corp.*, ___ U.S. ___, ___, 133 S.Ct. 1166, 1178 n.9, 185 L.Ed.2d 242 (2013). *But see Rodriguez v. Whiting Farms, Inc.*, 360 F.3d 1180, 1190–91 (10th Cir. 2004) (finding no error in district court's rejection of party's indigency as possible justification to deny costs).

[197] *See Lampkins v. Thompson*, 337 F.3d 1009, 1017 (8th Cir. 2003).

[198] *See Debord v. Mercy Health System of Kansas, Inc.*, 737 F.3d 642, 660 (10th Cir. 2013).

[199] *See Knology, Inc. v. Insight Communications Co., L.P.*, 460 F.3d 722, 727 (6th Cir. 2006).

[200] *See Debord v. Mercy Health System of Kansas, Inc.*, 737 F.3d 642, 660 (10th Cir. 2013) (costs unreasonably high or unnecessary).

without a vexatious motive,[201] because a significant disparity exists between the parties' financial resources,[202] because a heavy taxation would deter the poor from seeking redress,[203] because the case was "complex" or a "close call",[204] or because the case involved significant matters in the public interest.[205] In many cases, the district court will also be precluded from denying costs merely because the prevailing party failed to demand them in a pleading.[206]

Note, however, that the Circuits are not always uniform in their approaches to these various factors.[207]

Taxing Costs For or Against the United States

The United States may be awarded costs in the same manner as any prevailing party.[208] Costs may be taxed against the United States in accordance with the list set forth in 28 U.S.C.A. § 1920,[209] except that in non-tort actions, the district court may refuse to tax costs upon a finding that the United States' position was substantially justified or where special circumstances make an award of costs unjust.[210]

Taxing Costs Against States

Some courts have construed the Eleventh Amendment to the United States Constitution as prohibiting a district court's right to tax costs against a State.[211]

---

[201] *See Pacheco v. Mineta*, 448 F.3d 783, 794–95 (5th Cir. 2006) (surveying views from various circuits). *But see Champion Produce, Inc. v. Ruby Robinson Co., Inc.*, 342 F.3d 1016, 1022 (9th Cir. 2003) (whether losing party litigated in good faith could be considered).

[202] *See Moore v. CITGO Refining & Chems. Co.*, 735 F.3d 309, 319–20 (5th Cir. 2013) (rejecting "enormous" or "comparative" wealth as proper criteria); *Reger v. Nemours Found., Inc.*, 599 F.3d 285, 289 (3d Cir. 2010) (rejecting financial disparity as reason, holding this possibility should cause "pause" and calculation of risks of pressing marginal or meritless claims). *But see Escriba v. Foster Poultry Farms, Inc.*, 743 F.3d 1236, 1247–48 (9th Cir. 2014) (economic disparity between parties a proper consideration).

[203] *See Smith v. Tenet Healthsystem SL, Inc.*, 436 F.3d 879, 889–90 (8th Cir. 2006). *But see Escriba v. Foster Poultry Farms, Inc.*, 743 F.3d 1236, 1247–48 (9th Cir. 2014) (chilling effect on others a proper consideration).

[204] *See Rodriguez v. Whiting Farms, Inc.*, 360 F.3d 1180, 1190–91 (10th Cir. 2004). *But see Escriba v. Foster Poultry Farms, Inc.*, 743 F.3d 1236, 1247–48 (9th Cir. 2014) (close and difficult proper considerations).

[205] *See Mitchell v. City of Moore, Oklahoma*, 218 F.3d 1190, 1204 (10th Cir.2000) (presumption in favor of awarding costs applies even where prevailing party is defendant in civil rights case); *Cherry v. Champion Intern. Corp.*, 186 F.3d 442, 448 (4th Cir. 1999) (holding that presumptive award of costs cannot be defeated on the basis of the nature of the underlying litigation). *But see Escriba v. Foster Poultry Farms, Inc.*, 743 F.3d 1236, 1247–48 (9th Cir. 2014) (substantial public importance a proper consideration); *Stanley v. University of Southern California*, 178 F.3d 1069, 1079 (9th Cir. 1999) (directing courts, in civil rights cases, to consider plaintiffs financial resources and amount of cost so as to avoid unnecessarily chilling civil rights litigation; "Without civil rights litigants who are willing to test the boundaries of our laws, we would not have made much of the progress that has occurred in this nation since *Brown v. Board of Educ.*").

[206] *See Flynn v. AK Peters, Ltd.*, 377 F.3d 13, 26 (1st Cir. 2004) (right to attorney's fees not waived where prayer for fees not listed as "special damages" in complaint).

[207] *See Knology, Inc. v. Insight Communications Co., L.P.*, 460 F.3d 722, 726–27 (6th Cir. 2006) (factors that may justify denying costs include losing party's good faith, difficulty of case, winning party's behavior, and necessity of costs); *Rivera v. NIBCO*, 701 F.Supp.2d 1135, 1135–45 (E.D.Cal. 2010) (denying costs in language-based discrimination claim contesting English-only tests because, although unsuccessful, dispute involved: (1) issues of substantial public importance, (2) great economic disparity between plaintiffs and defendants, (3) close and difficult issues, (4) some merit, and (5) risk that award of costs would seriously chill future civil rights litigants).

[208] *See U.S. E.E.O.C. v. W&O, Inc.*, 213 F.3d 600, 620 (11th Cir. 2000).

[209] *See* 28 U.S.C.A. § 1920.

[210] *See* 28 U.S.C.A. § 2412.

[211] *See Alyeska Pipeline Service Co. v. Wilderness Society*, 421 U.S. 240, 269 n.44, 95 S.Ct. 1612, 1627 n.44, 44 L.Ed.2d 141 (1975).

Costs in Pauper Actions

The district court may, in its discretion, permit a civil litigant, criminal defendant, or appellant to proceed without the prepayment of costs upon receiving an affidavit showing an inability to pay costs.[212]

Procedure and Timing: Non-Attorney's Fee Costs

To obtain an award of costs, the prevailing party must file a "Bill of Costs" with the clerk (the district court may have a preprinted form for this purpose). The Bill of Costs must be verified by affidavit. The clerk may tax costs on 14-days' notice. Within 7 days thereafter, a disappointed party may seek court review of the clerk's assessment. Some courts have ruled that a failure to seek review within this period waives the losing party's right to challenge the award.[213] Other courts have noted that the time period is not jurisdictional and untimely objections may, in the trial court's discretion, be considered.[214] In any event, a party is not usually expected to file a bill of costs until that party has "prevailed".[215] The district court is authorized to conduct a *de novo* review of the clerk's assessments.[216] Costs may be taxed against multiple losing parties either in allocated amounts or jointly and severally.[217] The time for filing a Bill of Costs is typically regulated by local court rule, but usually is set after the court has rendered its decision in the case.[218]

Procedure and Timing: Attorney's Fees

Where an award of attorney's fees is appropriate, Rule 54(d)(2) fixes the procedure for obtaining an award of such fees and related non-taxable expenses.[219] This procedure does *not* apply to attorney's fees recoverable as an element of damages (*e.g.*, under terms of a contract) or to fees and expenses awarded as sanctions.[220] Courts are cautioned against permitting fees requests to spur a "second major litigation".[221] Typically, such motions are decided on affidavits alone, without additional discovery or evidentiary hearings.[222] The procedure follows:

1. *Motion Required:* The prevailing party must apply for such an award by motion. The motion must: (a) specify the judgment; (b) identify the legal source authorizing such an award of fees or expenses; and (c) state the amount, or a fair estimate of the amount, of the requested award.[223]

   - *Court-Implemented Settlements:* In cases where a settlement must be implemented by the court, the district court may also require that the motion disclose any fee agreement affecting the litigation.

---

[212] *See* 28 U.S.C.A. § 1915.

[213] *See Ahlberg v. Chrysler Corp.*, 481 F.3d 630, 638–39 (8th Cir. 2007).

[214] *See Debord v. Mercy Health System of Kansas, Inc.*, 737 F.3d 642, 659 (10th Cir. 2013).

[215] *See E.E.O.C. v. AutoZone, Inc.*, 707 F.3d 824, 845 (7th Cir. 2013).

[216] *See In re Paoli R.R. Yard PCB Litigation*, 221 F.3d 449, 453 (3d Cir. 2000).

[217] *In re Paoli R.R. Yard PCB Litigation*, 221 F.3d 449, 449 (3d Cir. 2000).

[218] *See S.A. Healy Co. v. Milwaukee Metropolitan Sewerage Dist.*, 60 F.3d 305, 307 (7th Cir. 1995) (commenting that because Rule 54(d) specifies no uniform national deadline for filing Bills of Costs, such timing is typically governed by local court rules).

[219] *See Riordan v. State Farm Mut. Auto. Ins. Co.*, 589 F.3d 999, 1005–06 (9th Cir. 2009) (ruling that such fees must be made by motion, and need not be pleaded).

[220] *See Taurus IP, LLC v. Daimler-Chrysler Corp.*, 726 F.3d 1306, 1342–43 (Fed.Cir. 2013). *See generally Richardson v. Wells Fargo Bank, N.A.*, 740 F.3d 1035, 1036–40 (5th Cir. 2014) (in appropriate cases, attorney's fees are recoverable under Rule 54(d) as collateral costs of litigation, even though authorized by contract term).

[221] *See Hensley v. Eckerhart*, 461 U.S. 424, 437, 103 S.Ct. 1933, 1941, 76 L.Ed.2d 40 (1983).

[222] *See Miller v. Dugan*, 764 F.3d 826, 830 (8th Cir. 2014).

[223] *See* Rule 54(d)(2)(A) to (2)(B). *See also In re Ferrell*, 539 F.3d 1186, 1192 (9th Cir. 2008).

2. *Time for Filing:* Unless provided otherwise by statute[224] or court order,[225] motions must be filed with the court "no later" than 14 days after entry of judgment.[226] This time trigger assumes a qualifying judgment (and may, therefore, be impacted by the separate document rule).[227] This deadline helps both to ensure that the opponent receives proper notice of the fees claim and to promote a prompt fees ruling from the district court, thus permitting simultaneous appellate review of both the merits and the fees award.[228] The deadline also forecloses the revival of disputes that adversaries long since thought were closed.[229] Failure to file within this allotted time constitutes a waiver of a party's right to recover such fees or expenses.[230] Nevertheless, because the 14-day time period is not jurisdictional, some courts have held that the district judge may exercise discretion to extend the time period.[231] Most courts also agree that this 14-day period does not begin to run until post-trial motions under Rules 50(b), 52(b), or 59 are resolved.[232]

- *Amended Judgments:* Amended judgments are "judgments" just the same, and the 14-day period will run from them as well.[233]

- *Local Rules and Standing Orders:* Practitioners must *carefully* consult the applicable local rules on Rule 54(d) attorneys fee motions. This 14-day period may be modified "by statute or order of the court".[234] Several courts have ruled that local rules which adopt longer periods for making attorney's fee motions qualify as "standing orders" and, thus, are authorized modifications of the 14-day period.[235]

3. *Time for Serving:* Originally, Rule 54(d) required that a motion for attorney's fees must be *both* served and filed within 14 days. This requirement was changed in the 2002 amendments to the Rule. Now, filing alone is the time trigger, although service remains required under Rule 5(a).[236]

4. *Opponent's Response:* Upon request, the court must provide the opponent with the opportunity to present evidence in opposition to the requested award.[237]

---

[224] Rule 54(b) has been interpreted to apply broadly. *See, e.g., Walker v. Astrue,* 593 F.3d 274, 274–80 (3d Cir. 2010) (noting Circuit split, but finding Rule 54(d) applies to certain fee petitions under Social Security Act).

[225] *See Heck v. Triche,* 775 F.3d 265, 276 (5th Cir. 2014).

[226] *See* Rule 54(d)(2)(B)(i). This Rule was amended in 2002 and 2007. The earlier 14-day time trigger was set to *service* of the motion as well, whereas the current trigger is set to *filing* of the motion alone. Because of the goal served by the time period, it is unlikely that this change will relax the period's mandatory nature.

[227] *See Cardinal Health 110, Inc. v. Cyrus Pharm., LLC,* 560 F.3d 894, 902 (8th Cir. 2009) (period does not begin to run until separate judgment entered).

[228] *See United Industries, Inc. v. Simon-Hartley, Ltd.,* 91 F.3d 762, 766 (5th Cir. 1996).

[229] *See Robinson v. City of Harvey,* 617 F.3d 915, 918–19 (7th Cir. 2010) ("Litigation must have its end.").

[230] *See Robinson v. City of Harvey,* 617 F.3d 915, 918–19 (7th Cir. 2010). *But cf. Johnson v. Lafayette Fire Fighters Ass'n Local 472, Intern. Ass'n of Fire Fighters, AFL-CIO-CLC,* 51 F.3d 726, 729 (7th Cir. 1995) (holding that local court rule, as a uniform "order of court", modified the 14-day period set forth in Rule 54(d)(2)(B)).

[231] *See Green v. Administrators of Tulane Educ. Fund,* 284 F.3d 642, 664 (5th Cir. 2002). *See also Tancredi v. Metropolitan Life Ins. Co.,* 378 F.3d 220, 227–28 (2d Cir. 2004) (before extension to 14-day deadline may be granted, trial court must find "excusable neglect").

[232] *See Bailey v. County of Riverside,* 414 F.3d 1023, 1024 (9th Cir. 2005).

[233] *See Quigley v. Rosenthal,* 427 F.3d 1232, 1236–37 (10th Cir. 2005).

[234] *See* Rule 54(d)(2)(B).

[235] *See Miltimore Sales, Inc. v. International Rectifier, Inc.,* 412 F.3d 685, 692 (6th Cir. 2005).

[236] *See* Rule 5(a). *See also* Rule 54(d)(2)(B) advisory committee note to 2002 amendments (noting deletion of 14-day service requirement "to establish a parallel with Rules 50, 52, and 59. Service continues to be required under Rule 5(a)").

[237] *See Sloane v. Equifax Information Services, LLC,* 510 F.3d 495, 507 (4th Cir. 2007).

5. *Court's Delegation:* The court may enlist the help of a Special Master for setting the proper value to be awarded for the attorney services provided. The court may also refer the entire motion to a magistrate judge for a Report & Recommendation.

6. *Court's Ruling:* In ruling on a Rule 54(d)(2) motion, the court must issue findings of fact and conclusions of law as required under Rule 52(a), and must issue a separate judgment as required under Rule 58. The court may, at its option, bifurcate its consideration of the motion to resolve liability issues first, before considering the amount of an appropriate award.

7. *Additional Procedures by Local Rule:* Rule 54(d)(2) permits the district courts to promulgate local rules to govern procedures for claims without the need for extensive evidentiary hearings.[238]

Procedure: Costs Bonds

Collateral to the authority to award costs, courts also have the authority to require litigants to post a bond to safeguard against dissipation of funds needed to reasonably cover anticipated taxable costs. But cost bonds are not sanctions, and may not be imposed upon indigent parties in a manner that functionally denies them access to the federal courts.[239]

Effect of an Attorney's Fees Motion on "Finality"

The filing of a Rule 54(d)(2) motion for an award of attorney's fees does not ordinarily affect the finality of the underlying judgment.[240] However, when a *timely* motion for fees is made, and so long as no notice of appeal has yet been filed (or become effective), the district court may enter an order directing that the fees motion be deemed to have the same effect as a timely Rule 59 motion and, thereby, toll the time for taking an appeal until after the motion is resolved.[241] This extension option applies only to fees motions, not to the taxation of costs.[242]

ADDITIONAL RESEARCH REFERENCES

Wright & Miller, *Federal Practice and Procedure* §§ 2651 to 79

C.J.S., Federal Civil Procedure §§ 1105 to 1120 et seq., 1236; Federal Courts § 293(17)

West's Key Number Digest, Federal Civil Procedure ⊶2391 to 2399, 2571 to 2587, 2721 to 2742.5; Federal Courts ⊶660

---

[238] Local rules *must* be consulted on this point. The advisory committee notes suggest that, by local rule, the district courts may even adopt schedules listing customary attorney's fees or factors that affect attorney's fees within a particular legal community. *See* Rule 54(d)(2)(D) advisory committee note.

[239] *See Gay v. Chandra*, 682 F.3d 590, 594–95 (7th Cir. 2012).

[240] *See* Rule 58(c)(1). *See also Moody Nat. Bank of Galveston v. GE Life and Annuity Assur. Co.*, 383 F.3d 249, 251 (5th Cir. 2004).

[241] *See* Rule 58(c)(2). *See also Moody Nat. Bank of Galveston v. GE Life and Annuity Assur. Co.*, 383 F.3d 249, 253 (5th Cir. 2004).

[242] *See Moody Nat. Bank of Galveston v. GE Life and Annuity Assur. Co.*, 383 F.3d 249, 253 (5th Cir. 2004).

RULE 55

DEFAULT; DEFAULT JUDGMENT

(a) **Entering a Default.** When a party against whom a judgment for affirmative relief is sought has failed to plead or otherwise defend, and that failure is shown by affidavit or otherwise, the clerk must enter the party's default.

(b) **Entering a Default Judgment.**

    (1) *By the Clerk.* If the plaintiff's claim is for a sum certain or a sum that can be made certain by computation, the clerk—on the plaintiff's request, with an affidavit showing the amount due—must enter judgment for that amount and costs against a defendant who has been defaulted for not appearing and who is neither a minor nor an incompetent person.

    (2) *By the Court.* In all other cases, the party must apply to the court for a default judgment. A default judgment may be entered against a minor or incompetent person only if represented by a general guardian, conservator, or other like fiduciary who has appeared. If the party against whom a default judgment is sought has appeared personally or by a representative, that party or its representative must be served with written notice of the application at least 7 days before the hearing. The court may conduct hearings or make referrals—preserving any federal statutory right to a jury trial—when, to enter or effectuate judgment, it needs to:

        (A) conduct an accounting;

        (B) determine the amount of damages;

        (C) establish the truth of any allegation by evidence; or

        (D) investigate any other matter.

(c) **Setting Aside a Default or a Default Judgment.** The court may set aside an entry of default for good cause, and it may set aside a final default judgment under Rule 60(b).

(d) **Judgment Against the United States.** A default judgment may be entered against the United States, its officers, or its agencies only if the claimant establishes a claim or right to relief by evidence that satisfies the court.

[Amended effective August 1, 1987; April 30, 2007, effective December 1, 2007; March 26, 2009, effective December 1, 2009; April 29, 2015, effective December 1, 2015.]

AUTHORS' COMMENTARY ON RULE 55

PURPOSE AND SCOPE

Rule 55 sets the procedure for defaults and default judgments in the federal courts. Because default judgments are not favored by the courts, Rule 55 also defines the procedure for setting aside defaults and default judgments.

RULE 55(a)—ENTERING A DEFAULT

CORE CONCEPT

Upon motion of a party, the clerk of court may enter a default against a party who has failed to plead or otherwise defend.

APPLICATIONS

Distinguished from Default Judgment

The clerk's entry of a party's default is the official recognition that a defending party is in default.[1] The entry of default is a prerequisite for the entry of judgment upon that default.[2] It is, in effect, akin to a finding of liability with the entry of final judgment yet to come.[3] Thus, there are two stages in a default proceeding-the establishment of the default itself, followed by the entry of a default judgment.[4]

Prerequisites

The party against whom the default is entered must have been properly served with process, and the district court must enjoy subject matter jurisdiction and either personal or quasi-in-rem/in-rem jurisdiction over the defaulting party.[5] The request for entry of default must be made promptly.[6] Additionally, the clerk must be satisfied, by the moving party's affidavit or otherwise, that the defaulting party has failed to plead or otherwise defend.[7] Courts have interpreted the phrase "otherwise defend" broadly, permitting entries of default for persistent lack of pretrial diligence or discovery misbehavior, failure to appear at an adjourned trial's resumption, dismissing counsel without an appointed replacement, and

---

[1] *See City of New York v. Mickalis Pawn Shop, LLC,* 645 F.3d 114, 128 (2d Cir. 2011).

[2] *See Heard v. Caruso,* 351 Fed. Appx. 1, 15–16 (6th Cir. 2009)

[3] *See Alameda v. Secretary of Health, Ed. and Welfare,* 622 F.2d 1044, 1048 (1st Cir. 1980).

[4] *See City of New York v. Mickalis Pawn Shop, LLC,* 645 F.3d 114, 128 (2d Cir. 2011). *See also Rowley v. Morant,* 276 F.R.D. 669, 670 (D.N.M. 2011) (both steps are required; default judgment cannot be granted absent prior entry of default).

[5] *See Meyers v. Pfizer, Inc.,* 581 Fed.Appx. 708, 711 (10th Cir. 2014) (default cannot be made when service is defective, even if defendant received actual notice); *Evans v. Larchmont Baptist Church Infant Care Ctr., Inc.,* 956 F.Supp.2d 695, 702 (E.D.Va. 2013) (subject-matter and personal jurisdiction are required before default can be entered).

[6] *See Harvey v. United States,* 685 F.3d 939, 946 (10th Cir. 2012) (actively litigating for more than two years before seeking default for a 1-day late filing forfeited the timeliness objection).

[7] *See New York Life Ins. Co. v. Brown,* 84 F.3d 137, 141 (5th Cir. 1996) (entry of default is made by clerk, once default established by affidavit or otherwise).

abandonment of an active defense.[8] Conversely, where a party has failed to properly plead but is unquestionably "otherwise" defending, a pleading failure might be excused.[9]

Entry of Default Is Mandatory

If a party is found to have failed to plead or otherwise defend, entry of default is mandatory, not discretionary.[10] Indeed, a delinquent party is considered already to be default, even if the formal entry of default has not yet been made.[11]

Entry of default is proper when a party fails to plead or to "otherwise defend." Courts have interpreted this phrase broadly, permitting entries of default for persistent lack of pretrial diligence or discovery misbehavior, failure to appear at an adjourned trial's resumption, dismissing counsel without an appointed replacement, and abandonment of an active defense.[12] But defaults are disfavored, and doubts should be resolved in the defaulting party's favor.[13] Thus, a failure to properly plead may be excused where the party is unquestionably "otherwise" defending.[14]

- *2007 "Restyling" Impact:* In 2007, the phrase "as provided by these rules" was stricken from Rule 55(a), confirming prior practice that an evinced "intent to defend" is sufficient to avoid a default even if it is manifested in a manner that does not comport strictly with the Rules.[15]

Entry by Clerk or Court

Although entry of default is typically a ministerial act undertaken by the clerk, the district judges themselves possess the power to enter default as well.[16]

Contested Motions for Entry of Default

Where a motion for entry of default is opposed by a party who has entered an appearance, the courts may, in considering the contested motion, apply the criteria guiding motions to set aside a default.[17]

Effect of Entry of Default

The entry of default provides formal notice to litigants that they are in default (that is, delinquent on the obligation to "plead or otherwise defend").[18] Upon entry, a defaulting party is deemed to have admitted all well-pleaded allegations of the complaint (except for the amount of damages);[19] allegations that are not well-pleaded, as well as conclusions of law,

---

[8]   *See City of New York v. Mickalis Pawn Shop, LLC,* 645 F.3d 114, 129–30 (2d Cir. 2011) (collecting cases).

[9]   *See Peters v. AstraZeneca LP,* 224 Fed. Appx. 503, 506 (7th Cir. 2007) (district judge had discretion—absent prejudice to plaintiff—to deny default judgment where defendants failed to file answer but were otherwise defending).

[10]   *See Bricklayers and Allied Craftworkers Local 2, Albany, N.Y. Pension Fund v. Moulton Masonry & Const., LLC,* 779 F.3d 182, 186 (2d Cir. 2015).

[11]   *See Perez v. Wells Fargo N.A.,* 774 F.3d 1329, 1337 (11th Cir. 2014).

[12]   *See City of New York v. Mickalis Pawn Shop, LLC,* 645 F.3d 114, 129–30 (2d Cir. 2011) (collecting cases). *See generally Curtis v. Illumination Arts, Inc.,* 33 F.Supp.3d 1200, 1210 (W.D. Wash. 2014) (describing circumstances).

[13]   *See Pacific M. Int'l Corp. v. Raman Int'l Gems, Ltd.,* 888 F.Supp.2d 385, 393 (S.D.N.Y. 2012).

[14]   *See Peters v. AstraZeneca LP,* 224 Fed. Appx. 503, 506 (7th Cir. 2007) (district judge had discretion—absent prejudice to plaintiff—to deny default judgment where defendants failed to file answer but were otherwise defending).

[15]   *See In re Clark,* 2010 WL 2639842, at *3 (W.D.Wash. June 28, 2010).

[16]   *See City of New York v. Mickalis Pawn Shop, LLC,* 645 F.3d 114, 128 (2d Cir. 2011).

[17]   *See* Rule 55(c). *See also Schmir v. Prudential Ins. Co. of America,* 220 F.R.D. 4, 5 (D. Me. 2004) (applying Rule 55(c) factors).

[18]   *See Tweedy v. RCAM Title Loans, LLC,* 611 F.Supp.2d 603, 605 (W.D.Va. 2009).

[19]   *See Bricklayers & Allied Craftworkers Local 2, Albany, N.Y. Pension Fund v. Moulton Masonry & Const., LLC,* 779 F.3d 182, 189 (2d Cir. 2015).

are not deemed admitted.[20] This greatly limits a defendant's ability to defend the lawsuit. A defendant in default is ordinarily foreclosed from raising any defenses other than a challenge to the legal sufficiency of the pleading to support a cognizable judgment, the adequacy of service of process, and the propriety of the court's jurisdiction.[21] Default is not, however, an absolute confession of liability and of the opponent's right to recover,[22] and the court may examine the pleaded allegations to confirm that they do, in fact, state a cognizable cause of action.[23]

Appealability

Entry of default is an interlocutory order, from which an immediate appeal ordinarily cannot be taken.[24] However, in an appeal from entry of a default judgment, the appeals court may review both the interlocutory entry of default as well as the ensuing entry of default judgment.[25]

RULE 55(b)—ENTERING A DEFAULT JUDGMENT

CORE CONCEPT

Where the defendant has defaulted for failing to appear and the moving party has submitted evidence by affidavit establishing damages in a sum certain or in a sum that can be made certain by computation, the clerk of court may enter a default judgment upon motion. In all other cases, the *court* (and *not* the clerk of court) may enter a default judgment.

APPLICATIONS

Effect of a Default Judgment

A default judgment transforms a defendant's admissions (which occur upon entry of the default) into a final judgment; it usually terminates the litigation by entering an enforceable, final award in favor of the pleader.[26]

Prerequisites

Before a default judgment may be granted, a "default" under Rule 55(a) must first have been entered.[27] The request for a default judgment must be made promptly.[28] The entering court must confirm that it has subject matter jurisdiction over the dispute,[29] and also may (some Circuits hold "must") confirm that it possesses personal jurisdiction over the defaulting defendant.[30] The court must then determine whether the now-admitted facts constitute a proper cause of action[31] and a legitimate basis for entry of a judgment.[32] (Although defaulting defendants are precluded from contesting facts now deemed admitted,

---

[20] *See Surtain v. Hamlin Terrace Found.*, 789 F.3d 1239, 1245 (11th Cir. 2015).

[21] *See Tyco Fire & Sec., LLC v. Alcocer*, 218 Fed.Appx. 860, 863–64 (11th Cir. 2007).

[22] *See Evans v. Larchmont Baptist Church Infant Care Ctr., Inc.*, 956 F.Supp.2d 695, 702–03 (E.D.Va. 2013).

[23] *See Gines v. D.R. Horton, Inc.*, 867 F.Supp.2d 824, 834 (M.D.La. 2012).

[24] *See City of New York v. Mickalis Pawn Shop, LLC*, 645 F.3d 114, 128 n.15 (2d Cir. 2011).

[25] *See City of New York v. Mickalis Pawn Shop, LLC*, 645 F.3d 114, 129 (2d Cir. 2011).

[26] *See City of New York v. Mickalis Pawn Shop, LLC*, 645 F.3d 114, 128 (2d Cir. 2011).

[27] *See Reed-Bey v. Pramstaller*, 607 Fed.Appx. 445, 449 (6th Cir. 2015).

[28] *See Harvey v. United States*, 685 F.3d 939, 946 (10th Cir. 2012) (actively litigating for more than two years before seeking a default judgment for a 1-day late filing forfeited the timeliness objection).

[29] *See Jennifer Matthew Nursing & Rehab. Ctr. v. U.S. Dep't of Health & Human Servs.*, 607 F.3d 951, 955 (2d Cir.2010).

[30] *See City of New York v. Mickalis Pawn Shop, LLC*, 645 F.3d 114, 133 (2d Cir. 2011) (surveying views on obligation to inquire).

[31] *See Joe Hand Promotions, Inc. v. Yakubets*, 3 F.Supp.3d 261, 270–71 (E.D. Pa. 2014).

[32] *See Purzel Video GmbH v. Martinez*, 13 F.Supp.3d 1140, 1148 (D. Colo. 2014).

they may always challenge whether those admitted facts establish a cognizable claim for relief.[33]) Some courts have characterized this inquiry as akin to a "reverse" motion to dismiss—confirming judicially that the pleaded allegations plausibly suggest an entitlement to the default remedy sought.[34] The court must respect the Due Process rights of the defaulting party,[35] which requires minimally the 7-day notice to appearing defendants (see below) and the opportunity to be heard on the details and nature of the resulting default judgment.[36]

The "Appearance" 7-Day Rule

If a default judgment is being sought against a party who has "appeared" (as that term is used in Rule 55(b)), that party must be served with *written* notice of the application for a default judgment at least 7 days before the hearing.[37] Such an appearance, obviously, must occur *before* the default judgment is entered in order to trigger the entitlement to written notice,[38] and that entitlement can be waived if an objection is not timely raised.[39]

Defining Defendant's "Appearance"

A defendant "appears" in the action by making some presentation or submission to the court (*e.g.*, serving a responsive pleading, filing an entry of appearance, serving a Rule 12 motion to dismiss, or having counsel attend a conference on the client's behalf).[40] Some courts have taken an even wider view,[41] ruling that "appearing" within the meaning of Rule 55(b) is not necessarily limited to a formal event in court.[42] In those courts, informal acts such as correspondence or telephone calls between counsel can constitute the requisite appearance,[43] as can engaging in settlement negotiations under certain circumstances.[44] Given the judicial philosophy disfavoring default judgments, the courts may search to find that an appearance has occurred.[45] Nevertheless, merely accepting or waiving service of process will not qualify as "appearing" within the meaning of this Rule.[46]

---

[33] *See Wooten v. McDonald Transit Assocs., Inc.*, 788 F.3d 490, 496 (5th Cir. 2015). *See also Ohio Cent. R. Co. v. Central Trust Co.*, 133 U.S. 83, 91, 10 S.Ct. 235, 33 L.Ed. 561 (1890) (defaulting defendant "is not precluded from contesting the sufficiency of the bill, or from insisting that the averments contained in it do not justify the decree").

[34] *See Surtain v. Hamlin Terrace Found.*, 789 F.3d 1239, 1245–48 (11th Cir. 2015). *Cf. Wooten v. McDonald Transit Assocs., Inc.*, 788 F.3d 490, 498 n.3 (5th Cir. 2015) (disavowing *Twombly*-like inquiry, then seemingly conducting one).

[35] *See City of New York v. Mickalis Pawn Shop, LLC*, 645 F.3d 114, 132–33 (2d Cir. 2011).

[36] *See City of New York v. Mickalis Pawn Shop, LLC*, 645 F.3d 114, 132 (2d Cir. 2011).

[37] *See* Rule 55(b)(2).

[38] *See Jenkens & Gilchrist v. Groia & Co.*, 542 F.3d 114, 118 n.2 (5th Cir. 2008).

[39] *See United States v. Varmado*, 342 Fed. Appx. 437, 439–40 (11th Cir. 2009) (unpublished opinion).

[40] *See Sun Bank of Ocala v. Pelican Homestead and Sav. Ass'n*, 874 F.2d 274, 276 (5th Cir. 1989) (filing motion to dismiss constitutes "appearing").

[41] *See New York v. Green*, 420 F.3d 99, 105 (2d Cir. 2005) (noting division among the Circuits on the issue).

[42] *See Silverman v. RTV Communications Group, Inc.*, 2002 WL 483421, at *3 (S.D. N.Y. 2002) (holding that appearance "is broadly defined and is not limited to a formal court filing"). *See also Rogers v. Hartford Life and Acc. Ins. Co.*, 167 F.3d 933, 936–37 (5th Cir. 1999) (noting that Fifth Circuit does not construe "appeared" as requiring the filing of responsive papers or actual in-court actions by the defendant). *But see Zuelzke Tool & Engineering Co., Inc. v. Anderson Die Castings, Inc.*, 925 F.2d 226, 230 (7th Cir. 1991) (rejecting informal contacts approach); *Town and Country Kids, Inc. v. Protected Venture Inv. Trust #1, Inc.*, 178 F.R.D. 453, 455 (E.D. Va. 1998) (holding that, for purposes of Rule 55(b), parties "appear" in action only where they make a presentation or submission to the court).

[43] *See Sun Bank of Ocala v. Pelican Homestead and Sav. Ass'n*, 874 F.2d 274, 276–77 (5th Cir. 1989). *See generally New York v. Green*, 420 F.3d 99, 106 (2d Cir.2005) (noting prevailing view, that informal contacts, like telephone calls, may suffice provided there is "clear intention to defend").

[44] *See S.E.C. v. Getanswers, Inc.*, 219 F.R.D. 698, 700 (S.D. Fla. 2004).

[45] *See Franchise Holding II, LLC. v. Huntington Restaurants Group, Inc.*, 375 F.3d 922, 927 (9th Cir. 2004).

[46] *See Rogers v. Hartford Life and Acc. Ins. Co.*, 167 F.3d 933, 936–37 (5th Cir. 1999).

hearing is mandatory in all cases,[5
award,[56] whether (and how) to c
Whether by hearing or otherwise,
of proving an entitlement to it.[58] A
right to contest most of the compla
the defendant may contest the an
complaint (except those relating t
moving party must prove damage
An evidentiary basis must suppor
all doubts[64] and reasonable infer
favor.[65]

- *Jury Right:* Most courts
defendants have no jury

Default in Multiple Defendant Cas

Where the plaintiff alleges jo
have closely related defenses, tl
judgment against another defend
to the other, non-defaulting def
plaintiff or judgment for defend
defendant as well.[67]

Defaulting Defendants in the Mili

The federal Soldiers' and S
federal or State judgment by de
first appoints counsel to represe
simply stay a lawsuit against the

♦ **NOTE:** In seeking a
averment or affidavit, attes

[55] *See Greathouse v. JHS Sec. Inc.*, 784 F.3d
[56] *See AngioDynamics, Inc. v. Biolitec AG*, 7
[57] *See Cement & Concrete Workers Dist. Co
Fund & Other Funds v. Metro Found. Contractors*
[58] *See Stephenson v. El-Batrawi*, 524 F.3d 9
[59] *See Ramos-Falcon v. Autoridad de Energi*
[60] *See Finkel v. Romanowicz*, 577 F.3d 79, 8
[61] *See Cement & Concrete Workers Dist. Co
Fund & Other Funds v. Metro Found. Contractor*
[62] *See Law Office G.A. Lambert & Assocs. v.*
[63] *See Cement & Concrete Workers Dist. C
Fund & Other Funds v. Metro Found. Contractor*
[64] *See Enron Oil Corp. v. Diakuhara*, 10 F.
[65] *See Finkel v. Romanowicz*, 577 F.3d 79, 8
[66] *See Olcott v. Del. Flood Co.*, 327 F.3d 111
[67] *See Frow v. De La Vega*, 82 U.S. 552, 21 I
1992) (construing *Frow* narrowly to hold that a d
set aside only where the liability is actually "joi
the defaulting defendant) liable if any one of the
[68] 50 U.S.C.A. App. § 501.

Entry of Default Judgment by C[...]

The clerk may only enter[...]
are met:

1. The defendant was d[...]

2. The defendant is not[...]

3. The moving party su[...]
   a sum certain or a su[...]

   - *"Sum Certain"*[...]
     there is no dou[...]
     due is beyond[...]
     instruments).[48]
     such as "reaso[...]
     determined.[49]

Entry of Default Judgment by [...]

In all other circumstance[...]

1. Where the defendar[...]
   be served with writ[...]
   days before any hea[...]

2. Where the defenda[...]
   judgment may be e[...]

3. Where the amount[...]
   of record (if approp[...]
   damages;[51] or

4. Where the defenda[...]
   appear.

   - *Default Judg*[...]
     judgment can[...]

Fashioning the Default Judgm[...]

When the damages amo[...]
hearing[53] or simply rely on[...]

---

[47] *See Franchise Holding II, LLC. v. Hu*[...]

[48] *See KPS & Associates, Inc. v. Designs*[...]

[49] *See Dailey v. R & J Comm'l Contractir*[...]
judgment involving punitive damages).

[50] *See Canal Ins. Co. v. Ashmore*, 61 I[...]
judgment where defendant never received no[...]

[51] *See Campbell v. Humphries*, 353 Fe[...]
Restaurant, 884 F.Supp. 663, 669 (E.D. N[...]
independent determination of sum to be awa[...]
whether material factual issues exist, whe[...]
judgment, likelihood that default would be s[...]

[52] *See Fanning v. Wegco, Inc.*, 5 F.Supp[...]

[53] *See Wooten v. McDonald Transit Ass*[...]

[54] *See Service Emps. Int'l Union Nat'l I*[...]
69 (D.D.C. 2014).

Limitation on Default Judgments

No judgment by default can be greater in amount or different in kind from the demand contained in the complaint.[69]

Discretion of District Court

Judgments by default are disfavored and are never granted as a matter of right.[70] Whether to enter a judgment by default is a decision entrusted to the sound discretion of the district court.[71] Thus, a defendant's default does not necessarily entitle the plaintiff to an automatic default judgment,[72] nor need the judge presume that the pleader's allegations constitute a valid cause of action.[73] Before exercising their discretion and entering a default judgment, courts may examine the standards for setting aside a default;[74] whether a responsive pleading has since (though belatedly) been received;[75] and a myriad of other factors, such as the federal policy favoring decisions on the merits, the presence of excusable neglect, the clarity of the grounds for default, the adequacy of notice, the size of the claim, the facts in dispute, and prejudice to either party.[76] Nevertheless, and notwithstanding the preference for decisions on the merits,[77] where the inquiry satisfies the court that a default judgment is proper, it will be entered.[78]

Appealability

The entry of a judgment by default is a final order, and is subject to immediate appeal.[79] Although often, upon the entry of a default judgment, the defaulted litigant will move the district court for relief from the default under Rule 55(c) and Rule 60(b), this is not required; because a default judgment is a final order, the defaulted litigant may appeal at once.[80]

RULE 55(c)—SETTING ASIDE DEFAULT OR A DEFAULT JUDGMENT

CORE CONCEPT

The court may set aside the entry of default for good cause, and may vacate a judgment by default in accordance with Rule 60(b) (which governs the grounds upon which a party may seek relief from a judgment).

APPLICATIONS

Policy and Liberality

Defaults and default judgments are disfavored, since they are inconsistent with the federal courts' preference for resolving disputes on their merits.[81] Accordingly, motions for

---

[69] *See* Rule 54(c).

[70] *See Surtain v. Hamlin Terrace Found.*, 789 F.3d 1239, 1244–45 (11th Cir. 2015).

[71] *See Belcourt Pub. Sch. Dist. v. Davis*, 786 F.3d 653, 661 (8th Cir. 2015).

[72] *See Bricklayers & Allied Craftworkers Local 2, Albany, N.Y. Pension Fund v. Moulton Masonry & Const., LLC*, 779 F.3d 182, 186 (2d Cir. 2015).

[73] *See Finkel v. Romanowicz*, 577 F.3d 79, 84 (2d Cir. 2009).

[74] *See Joe Hand Promotions, Inc. v. Yakubets*, 3 F.Supp.3d 261, 271 (E.D. Pa. 2014).

[75] *See Semler v. Klang*, 603 F.Supp.2d 1211, 1218–19 (D.Minn. 2009).

[76] *See, e.g., Belcourt Pub. Sch. Dist. v. Davis*, 786 F.3d 653, 661 (8th Cir. 2015) (listing various criteria).

[77] *See Belcourt Pub. Sch. Dist. v. Davis*, 786 F.3d 653, 661 (8th Cir. 2015).

[78] *See Swarna v. Al-Awadi*, 607 F.Supp.2d 509, 527–29 (S.D.N.Y. 2009).

[79] *See City of New York v. Mickalis Pawn Shop, LLC*, 645 F.3d 114, 129 (2d Cir. 2011).

[80] *See City of New York v. Mickalis Pawn Shop, LLC*, 645 F.3d 114, 127–28 (2d Cir. 2011).

[81] *See Harvey v. United States*, 685 F.3d 939, 946 (10th Cir. 2012). *But see O'Brien v. R.J. O'Brien & Assoc., Inc.*, 998 F.2d 1394, 1401 (7th Cir.1993) ("this circuit no longer follows the earlier doctrine disfavoring defaults").

Discre

de.
for
an
de.
di.
wh

Sua Sp

the

CORE CON

No defa
unless the pl

APPLICAT

Policy

Th
jud
cor
the
the
fre
go\

relief from both defaults and default judgments are considered liberally[82] and are often granted.[83] Where only a default has been entered (without an accompanying default judgment), the standard for lifting the default is especially generous.[84]

Setting Aside a Default

Rule 55(c) authorizes the district courts, "for good cause", to set aside the entry of a default.[85] Not susceptible to a precise definition, "good cause" has been labeled a liberal and "mutable" standard, one that varies from situation to situation.[86] It is a standard applied generously, and more liberally where only a default has been entered (with no accompanying default judgment).[87] Doubts in "close cases" will likely favor a finding of good cause.[88] Ergo, entries of default are often set aside.[89] The requisite "good cause", however, is not "good cause" for the defendant's mistake, but rather "good cause" justifying the court's decision to set the default aside.[90]

In testing for "good cause", the courts generally consider some or all of the following factors: (1) proof that the default was not willful or culpable[91] (which typically requires more than mere inaction or negligence);[92] (2) swiftness of the action to remedy the default;[93] (3) existence of a meritorious defense[94] (which usually is not a very heavy burden but requires only the alleging of sufficient facts that, if true, would constitute a defense);[95] and (4) whether the opponent would be prejudiced were the default lifted[96] (and prejudice means not merely delay or the chore of having to prove the merits,[97] but some loss of evidence, unavailability of witnesses, or other impairment of the ability to prove the merits).[98] In addition to these leading factors, courts have often considered other equitable criteria as well, including: (a) whether the default resulted from a good faith mistake in following a rule of procedure;[99] (b) the nature of the defendant's explanation for defaulting;[100] (c) any history

---

[82] *See Colleton Preparatory Academy, Inc. v. Hoover Universal, Inc.,* 616 F.3d 413, 417 (4th Cir. 2010).

[83] *See Indigo America, Inc. v. Big Impressions, LLC,* 597 F.3d 1, 6 (1st Cir. 2010).

[84] *See Colleton Preparatory Academy, Inc. v. Hoover Universal, Inc.,* 616 F.3d 413, 418 (4th Cir. 2010).

[85] *See Bricklayers & Allied Craftworkers Local 2, Albany, N.Y. Pension Fund v. Moulton Masonry & Const., LLC,* 779 F.3d 182, 186 (2d Cir. 2015).

[86] *See Perez v. Wells Fargo N.A.,* 774 F.3d 1329, 1338 n.7 (11th Cir. 2014).

[87] *See Colleton Preparatory Academy, Inc. v. Hoover Universal, Inc.,* 616 F.3d 413, 420 (4th Cir. 2010).

[88] *See Farnese v. Bagnasco,* 687 F.2d 761, 764 (3d Cir. 1982).

[89] *See California Trout v. F.E.R. C.,* 572 F.3d 1003, 1027 n.1 (9th Cir. 2009).

[90] *See Sims v. EGA Products, Inc.,* 475 F.3d 865, 868 (7th Cir. 2007).

[91] *See Bricklayers & Allied Craftworkers Local 2, Albany, N.Y. Pension Fund v. Moulton Masonry & Const., LLC,* 779 F.3d 182, 186 (2d Cir. 2015).

[92] *See Bricklayers & Allied Craftworkers Local 2, Albany, N.Y. Pension Fund v. Moulton Masonry & Const., LLC,* 779 F.3d 182, 186–87 (2d Cir. 2015).

[93] *See Perez v. Wells Fargo N.A.,* 774 F.3d 1329, 1338 n.7 (11th Cir. 2014).

[94] *See Bricklayers & Allied Craftworkers Local 2, Albany, N.Y. Pension Fund v. Moulton Masonry & Const., LLC,* 779 F.3d 182, 186 (2d Cir. 2015).

[95] *See United States v. Signed Personal Check No. 730 of Yurban S. Mesle,* 615 F.3d 1085, 1094 (9th Cir. 2010). *See also Mohamad v. Rajoub,* 634 F.3d 604, 606 (D.C.Cir. 2011) ("even a hint of a suggestion which, if proven, would constitute a complete defense" may suffice), *aff'd,* 132 S.Ct. 1702, 182 L.Ed.2d 720 (2012).

[96] *See Bricklayers & Allied Craftworkers Local 2, Albany, N.Y. Pension Fund v. Moulton Masonry & Const., LLC,* 779 F.3d 182, 186 (2d Cir. 2015).

[97] *See Colleton Preparatory Academy, Inc. v. Hoover Universal, Inc.,* 616 F.3d 413, 417 & 419 n.6 (4th Cir. 2010).

[98] *See East Coast Exp., Inc. v. Ruby, Inc.,* 162 F.R.D. 37, 39 (E.D. Pa. 1995).

[99] *See Indigo America, Inc. v. Big Impressions, LLC,* 597 F.3d 1, 3 (1st Cir. 2010).

[100] *See Indigo America, Inc. v. Big Impressions, LLC,* 597 F.3d 1, 3 (1st Cir. 2010).

[117] *See Un*
also Martin v. (

[118] *See Ma*

[119] *See Bu*

[120] *See In*

[121] *See Mo*

[122] *See Ju*
(approving *sua*

[123] *See Ha*

[124] *See Co*
Cir. 1996); *ABl*
U.S.C.A. § 160\
Commercial Ba
de Espana, 86\
judgment is pa
the burden to s

[125] *See Are*

[126] *See Pay*

[127] *See Un*

Applies Only to Default Judgments, Not Defaults

Although default judgments may not be entered summarily against the United States, the default itself may be.[128]

Plaintiff's High Burden

To obtain a default judgment against the United States or federal officers or agencies, plaintiffs must carry the heavy burden of establishing a claim or right-to-relief.[129] They must do so by evidence that is satisfactory to the court.[130] This inquiry does not necessarily require a hearing, or either more or different evidence than would otherwise be received.[131] (However, at least one court has ruled that the burden for default against the United States requires a demonstration of an evidentiary basis that is legally sufficient for a reasonable jury to find for the plaintiff.[132]) Instead, the courts assume a flexible approach in determining the procedures necessary to conduct this inquiry.[133] If uncontroverted, a plaintiff's *evidence* may be accepted as true,[134] but if the government comes forward with a meritorious defense and a willingness to litigate, the default judgment will likely be denied.[135]

Foreign Governments

By statute, Congress requires that this same "satisfies-the-court" standard be applied in actions against foreign governments, foreign political subdivisions, and foreign agencies and instrumentalities.[136]

ADDITIONAL RESEARCH REFERENCES

Wright & Miller, *Federal Practice and Procedure* §§ 2681 to 2702

C.J.S., Federal Civil Procedure §§ 1122 to 1134 et seq.

West's Key Number Digest, Federal Civil Procedure ⚷2411 to 2455

---

[128] *See Alameda v. Secretary of Health, Ed. and Welfare,* 622 F.2d 1044, 1048 (1st Cir. 1980) (noting that default may be entered, and commenting that the exemption from default judgments "heightens" the United States' obligation to cooperate with the court). *See also Washington v. Astrue,* 2009 WL 1916238, at *1 (S.D.Fla. June 30, 2009); *Flowers v. U.S. Postal Serv.,* 2009 WL 691291, at *2 (N.D.Ill. Mar. 16, 2009).

[129] *See Campbell v. United States,* 375 Fed. Appx. 254, 261 (3d Cir. 2010); *Willever v. United States,* 775 F.Supp.2d 771 (D.Md. 2011).

[130] *See Harvey v. United States,* 685 F.3d 939, 946–56 (10th Cir. 2012); *Campbell v. United States,* 375 Fed. Appx. 254, 261 (3d Cir. 2010).

[131] *See Commercial Bank of Kuwait v. Rafidain Bank,* 15 F.3d 238, 242 (2d Cir. 1994).

[132] *See Smith ex rel. Smith v. Islamic Emirate of Afghanistan,* 262 F.Supp.2d 217, 223–24 (S.D. N.Y. 2003).

[133] *See Jin v. Ministry of State Security,* 557 F.Supp.2d 131, 139–40 (D.D.C. 2008); *Gadoury v. United States,* 187 B.R. 816, 822 (D.R.I. 1995).

[134] *See Estate of Botvin ex rel. Ellis v. Islamic Republic of Iran,* 772 F.Supp.2d 218, 227 (D.D.C. 2011).

[135] *See Stewart v. Astrue,* 552 F.3d 26, 28–29 (1st Cir. 2009).

[136] *See* 28 U.S.C.A. § 1608(e). *See also Han Kim v. Democratic People's Republic of Korea,* 950 F.Supp.2d 29, 33–34 (D.D.C. 2013).

RULE 56

SUMMARY JUDGMENT

(a) Motion for Summary Judgment or Partial Summary Judgment. A party may move for summary judgment, identifying each claim or defense—or the part of each claim or defense—on which summary judgment is sought. The court shall grant summary judgment if the movant shows that there is no genuine dispute as to any material fact and the movant is entitled to judgment as a matter of law. The court should state on the record the reasons for granting or denying the motion.

(b) Time to File a Motion. Unless a different time is set by local rule or the court orders otherwise, a party may file a motion for summary judgment at any time until 30 days after the close of all discovery.

(c) Procedures.

(1) *Supporting Factual Positions.* A party asserting that a fact cannot be or is genuinely disputed must support the assertion by:

(A) citing to particular parts of materials in the record, including depositions, documents, electronically stored information, affidavits or declarations, stipulations (including those made for purposes of the motion only), admissions, interrogatory answers, or other materials; or

(B) showing that the materials cited do not establish the absence or presence of a genuine dispute, or that an adverse party cannot produce admissible evidence to support the fact.

(2) *Objection That a Fact Is Not Supported by Admissible Evidence.* A party may object that the material cited to support or dispute a fact cannot be presented in a form that would be admissible in evidence.

(3) *Materials Not Cited.* The court need consider only the cited materials, but it may consider other materials in the record.

(4) *Affidavits or Declarations.* An affidavit or declaration used to support or oppose a motion must be made on personal knowledge, set out facts that would be admissible in evidence, and show that the affiant or declarant is competent to testify on the matters stated.

(d) When Facts Are Unavailable to the Nonmovant. If a nonmovant shows by affidavit or declaration that, for specified reasons, it cannot present facts essential to justify its opposition, the court may:

(1) defer considering the motion or deny it;

(2) allow time to obtain affidavits or declarations or to take discovery; or

(3) issue any other appropriate order.

(e) Failing to Properly Support or Address a Fact. If a party fails to properly support an assertion of fact or fails to properly address another party's assertion of fact as required by Rule 56(c), the court may:

(1) give an opportunity to properly support or address the fact;

(2) consider the fact undisputed for purposes of the motion;

(3) grant summary judgment if the motion and supporting materials—including the facts considered undisputed—show that the movant is entitled to it; or

(4) issue any other appropriate order.

(f) Judgment Independent of the Motion. After giving notice and a reasonable time to respond, the court may:

(1) grant summary judgment for a nonmovant;

(2) grant the motion on grounds not raised by a party; or

(3) consider summary judgment on its own after identifying for the parties material facts that may not be genuinely in dispute.

(g) Failing to Grant All the Requested Relief. If the court does not grant all the relief requested by the motion, it may enter an order stating any material fact—including an item of damages or other relief—that is not genuinely in dispute and treating the fact as established in the case.

(h) Affidavit or Declaration Submitted in Bad Faith. If satisfied that an affidavit or declaration under this rule is submitted in bad faith or solely for delay, the court—after notice and a reasonable time to respond—may order the submitting party to pay the other party the reasonable expenses, including attorney's fees, it incurred as a result. An offending party or attorney may also be held in contempt or subjected to other appropriate sanctions.

[Amended effective March 19, 1948; July 1, 1963; August 1, 1987; April 30, 2007, effective December 1, 2007; March 26, 2009, effective December 1, 2009; April 28, 2010, effective December 1, 2010.]

The 2010 Summary Judgment Amendments

The federal summary judgment rule—Rule 56—was extensively revised effective December 2010. The current rule text is printed above. However, because earlier cases in your study of summary judgment may refer to the Rule's pre-amended text, that version is reprinted below for reference:

[Rule 56—Summary Judgment: Pre-Dec. 2010 Text]

(a) By a Claiming Party. A party claiming relief may move, with or without supporting affidavits, for summary judgment on all or part of the claim.

(b) By a Defending Party. A party against whom relief is sought may move, with or without supporting affidavits, for summary judgment on all or part of the claim.

(c) Time for a Motion, Response, and Reply; Proceedings.

(1) These times apply unless a different time is set by local rule or the court orders otherwise:

(A) a party may move for summary judgment at any time until 30 days after the close of all discovery;

(B) a party opposing the motion must file a response within 21 days after the motion is served or a responsive pleading is due, whichever is later; and

(C) the movant may file a reply within 14 days after the response is served.

(2) The judgment sought should be rendered if the pleadings, the discovery and disclosure materials on file, and any affidavits show that there is no genuine issue as to any material fact and that the movant is entitled to judgment as a matter of law.

(d) Case Not Fully Adjudicated on the Motion.

(1) *Establishing Facts.* If summary judgment is not rendered on the whole action, the court should, to the extent practicable, determine what material facts are not genuinely at issue. The court should so determine by examining the pleadings and evidence before it and by interrogating the attorneys. It should then issue an order specifying what facts—including items of damages or other relief—are not genuinely at issue. The facts so specified must be treated as established in the action.

(2) *Establishing Liability.* An interlocutory summary judgment may be rendered on liability alone, even if there is a genuine issue on the amount of damages.

(e) Affidavits; Further Testimony.

(1) *In General.* A supporting or opposing affidavit must be made on personal knowledge, set out facts that would be admissible in evidence, and show that the affiant is competent to testify on the matters stated. If a paper or part of a paper is referred to in an affidavit, a sworn or certified copy must be attached to or served with the affidavit. The court may permit an affidavit to be supplemented or opposed by depositions, answers to interrogatories, or additional affidavits.

(2) *Opposing Party's Obligation to Respond.* When a motion for summary judgment is properly made and supported, an opposing party may not rely merely on allegations or denials in its own pleading; rather, its response must—by affidavits or as otherwise provided in this rule—set out specific facts showing a genuine issue for trial. If the opposing party does not so respond, summary judgment should, if appropriate, be entered against that party.

(f) When Affidavits Are Unavailable. If a party opposing the motion shows by affidavit that, for specified reasons, it cannot present facts essential to justify its opposition, the court may:

(1) deny the motion;

(2) order a continuance to enable affidavits to be obtained, depositions to be taken, or other discovery to be undertaken; or

(3) issue any other just order.

(g) Affidavit Submitted in Bad Faith. If satisfied that an affidavit under this rule is submitted in bad faith or solely for delay, the court must order the submitting party to pay the other party the reasonable expenses, including attorney's fees, it incurred as a result. An offending party or attorney may also be held in contempt.

AUTHORS' COMMENTARY ON RULE 56

PURPOSE AND SCOPE

Rule 56 sets the procedure by which a party may request or oppose either full or partial summary judgment, and the standards the federal courts consider when ruling on motions for summary judgment.

COMPARISONS WITH OTHER RULES OF ADJUDICATION

Dismissals and Judgments on the Pleadings: Motions to dismiss (under Rule 12(b)(6)) and for judgment on the pleadings (under Rule 12(c)) are *as-alleged* challenges. They test whether a pleading's averments of law and fact, if proven true, would be legally sufficient to sustain a claim or defense.[1] In contrast, motions for summary judgment are *as-provable* challenges. They test whether, notwithstanding the allegations, evidence exists to establish a genuine factual dispute.

- *"Conversion":* If, in ruling on a Rule 12(b)(6) motion to dismiss, the court is invited to, and does, consider extrinsic materials beyond the pleadings, the court will convert the motion into a summary judgment challenge.[2]

Judgments as a Matter of Law (JMOL): Motions for judgments as a matter of law (under Rule 50) are *as-proven* challenges—the federal equivalent of directed verdict and JNOV motions. They test whether, irrespective of the allegations and solely in light of the evidence presented at trial, a reasonable jury could return a verdict for the non-moving party. In this respect, both summary judgment motions and JMOL motions alike use the lens of the reasonable factfinder to test a party's case or defense.[3] The difference is timing. Summary judgment assessments are made pre-trial, and are supported by pleadings, discovery, affidavits, and other "cold" evidence. JMOL assessments are made during or after trial, with the judge having listened to the actual, live testimony and evidentiary presentation. In other words, Rule 50 motions for JMOL ask whether there is any need for the trial—then underway—to continue on to the jury deliberation stage; Rule 56 motions for summary judgment ask whether there is any need to convene a trial in the first place.

RULE 56(a)—MOTION FOR SUMMARY JUDGMENT OR PARTIAL SUMMARY JUDGMENT

CORE CONCEPT

Parties may move to summarily terminate all or part of a claim, defense, or entire lawsuit. If the court determines that an actual trial before a factfinder is unnecessary to resolve all or part of those claims or defenses (because no true dispute as to any fact of consequence exists), the court shall grant summary judgment.

---

[1] *See Guidotti v. Legal Helpers Debt Resolution, L.L.C.,* 716 F.3d 764, 772 (3d Cir. 2013) (differences between dismissal and summary judgment motions).

[2] *See* Rule 12(d). *See also supra* Authors' Commentary to Rule 12(d).

[3] *See Anderson v. Liberty Lobby, Inc.,* 477 U.S. 242, 250–51, 106 S.Ct. 2505, 2511, 91 L.Ed.2d 202 (1986) (noting that summary judgment standard "mirrors the standard for a directed verdict under Federal Rule of Civil Procedure 50(a), which is that the trial judge must direct a verdict if, under the governing law, there can be but one reasonable conclusion as to the verdict").

APPLICATIONS

Motions by Claiming Parties

Summary judgment is not only a defensive tool; claimants can move for summary judgment on their own claims as well.[4]

Motions by Defending Parties

Defending parties may move for summary judgment.[5] Note, however, that the case law is unclear whether moving for summary judgment tolls the time for defending parties to answer a complaint.[6] The filing of an answer is clearly not, however, a prerequisite for filing a summary judgment motion.[7]

Motions by Both Parties (Cross-Motions)

Both parties may seek summary judgment in the same action, with "cross-motions" under Rule 56.[8]

Motions by Others

Summary judgment is available only when one party is formally asserting a claim against, or defending against a claim formally asserted by, another party. The rights of parties can only be resolved by summary judgment if claims or defenses are already pending.[9]

Motions Involving *Pro Se* Litigants

Courts construe a *pro se* litigant's submissions liberally and interpret them in a manner to raise the strongest arguments they suggest.[10]

Partial Motions

Motions may seek summary judgment as to the entire claim or defense, or just parts of a claim or defense.[11] This entitlement is made explicit in the current text of Rule 56(a).[12]

Purpose of Summary Judgment

The purpose of summary judgment is to isolate, and then terminate, claims and defenses that are factually unsupported.[13] It is not a disfavored technical shortcut, but rather an integral component of the Rules.[14] Summary judgment motions must be resolved not only with regard for the rights of those asserting claims and defenses to have their

---

[4]   *See Alexander v. CareSource,* 576 F.3d 551, 557–58 (6th Cir. 2009).

[5]   *See Jefferson v. Chattanooga Pub. Co.,* 375 F.3d 461, 463 (6th Cir. 2004).

[6]   *Compare Poe v. Cristina Copper Mines, Inc,* 15 F.R.D. 85, 87 (D. Del. 1953) (holding that summary judgment motion does not automatically toll the period for answering), *with Rashidi v. Albright,* 818 F.Supp. 1354, 1356 (D. Nev. 1993) (holding that summary judgment motion will toll the period for answering) *aff'd,* 39 F.3d 1188 (9th Cir. 1994) (table). *See generally* 10A Charles Alan Wright, Arthur R. Miller, Mary Kay Kane, *Federal Practice & Procedure § 2718,* at 303 to 04 (3d ed. 1998) (opining that Rule 12(a) tolling ought to apply to a pre-answer summary judgment motion).

[7]   *See HS Resources, Inc. v. Wingate,* 327 F.3d 432, 440 (5th Cir. 2003).

[8]   *See infra* Authors' Commentary to Rule 56(a) (**"Stipulated Facts and Cross Motions"**).

[9]   *See Scottsdale Ins. Co. v. Knox Park Const., Inc.,* 488 F.3d 680, 685 (5th Cir. 2007).

[10] *See Kirkland v. Cablevision Sys.,* 2014 WL 3686090, at *1 (2d Cir. 2014).

[11] *See Hotel 71 Mezz Lender LLC v. Nat'l Ret. Fund,* 778 F.3d 593, 606 (7th Cir. 2015).

[12] *See* Rule 56(a) (amended 2010). *See also* Rule 56(a) advisory committee note to 2010 amendments (revisions "make clear" that motions make seek summary judgment as to an entire claim or defense, or just part of one).

[13] *See Celotex Corp. v. Catrett,* 477 U.S. 317, 323–24, 106 S.Ct. 2548, 2552–53, 91 L.Ed.2d 265 (1986).

[14] *See Celotex Corp. v. Catrett,* 477 U.S. 317, 327, 106 S.Ct. 2548, 2554, 91 L.Ed.2d 265 (1986). *See generally Little v. Liquid Air Corp.,* 37 F.3d 1069, 1075 (5th Cir. 1994) (explaining prevailing pre-1986 view that summary judgment was disfavored).

positions heard by a factfinder, but also with due regard for the rights of persons opposing such claims and defenses to demonstrate, under this Rule and *before* trial, that the claims and defenses have no factual basis.[15] Thus, a party moving for summary judgment forces the opponent to come forward with at least one sworn averment of fact essential to that opponent's claims or defenses, before the time-consuming process of litigation will continue.[16] The non-moving party must do this by showing that there is a genuine dispute requiring a trial.[17] If that party is unable to make that showing, entry of a judgment in favor of the moving party "shall" be granted.[18] When an authentic dispute can be shown, the Rule imposes a "relatively lenient standard" to survive the motion and continue on to trial[19]—if, on the evidence presented, a fair-minded jury could return a verdict for the nonmoving party, summary judgment should be denied.[20]. Nonetheless, an authentic dispute must be shown, and the Rule brings with it "essentially 'put up or shut up' time for the non-moving party."[21]

Standards for Granting or Denying Summary Judgment

Summary judgment shall be granted if the summary judgment record shows that: (1) there is no genuine dispute, (2) as to any material fact, and (3) the moving party is entitled to judgment.[22]

- *Genuine Dispute:*[23] A "genuine dispute" exists (and, thus, summary judgment is improper) when a rational factfinder, considering the evidence in the summary judgment record, could find in favor of the non-moving party.[24] A genuine dispute is not created by a mere "scintilla" of favorable evidence, or evidence that is only "colorable" or insufficiently probative.[25] Nor will summary judgment be defeated if the claim or defense poses a factual scenario that is plainly contradicted by the summary judgment record.[26] When a claim or defense is factually improbable, a more persuasive record will be necessary to stave off summary judgment.[27] The court will test for a "genuine dispute" through the prism of whatever quantum and quality of proof will apply to the claims or defenses. Thus, if the claimant must

---

[15]   *See Celotex Corp. v. Catrett,* 477 U.S. 317, 327, 106 S.Ct. 2548, 2554, 91 L.Ed.2d 265 (1986).

[16]   *See Lujan v. National Wildlife Federation,* 497 U.S. 871, 888–89, 110 S.Ct. 3177, 3188–89, 111 L.Ed.2d 695 (1990).

[17]   *See Beard v. Banks,* 548 U.S. 521, 529, 126 S.Ct. 2572, 2578, 165 L.Ed.2d 697 (2006).

[18]   *See Beard v. Banks,* 548 U.S. 521, 529, 126 S.Ct. 2572, 2578, 165 L.Ed.2d 697 (2006).

[19]   *Amgen Inc. v. Connecticut Ret. Plans & Trust Funds,* ___ U.S. ___, ___, 133 S.Ct. 1184, 1203, 185 L.Ed.2d 308 (2013).

[20]   *See Anderson v. Liberty Lobby, Inc.,* 477 U.S. 242, 248, 106 S.Ct. 2505, 91 L.Ed.2d 202 (1986).

[21]   *See Harney v. Speedway Super-America, LLC,* 526 F.3d 1099, 1104 (7th Cir. 2008). *See generally Murray v. Kindred Nursing Ctrs. West LLC,* 789 F.3d 20, 24–25 (1st Cir. 2015) (avoids "full-dress trials in unwinnable cases").

[22]   *See Beard v. Banks,* 548 U.S. 521, 529, 126 S.Ct. 2572, 2578, 165 L.Ed.2d 697 (2006); *Department of Commerce v. U.S. House of Representatives,* 525 U.S. 316, 327, 119 S.Ct. 765, 772, 142 L.Ed.2d 797 (1999); *Nebraska v. Wyoming,* 507 U.S. 584, 589, 113 S.Ct. 1689, 1694, 123 L.Ed.2d 317 (1993); *Celotex Corp. v. Catrett,* 477 U.S. 317, 322, 106 S.Ct. 2548, 2552, 91 L.Ed.2d 265 (1986).

[23]   The 2010 Amendments to Rule 56 replaced the phrase "genuine issue" with "genuine dispute," reasoning that it better reflected the focus of the Rule 56 determination. *See* Rule 56(a) advisory committee note to 2010 amendments.

[24]   *See Ricci v. DeStefano,* 557 U.S. 557, 586, 129 S.Ct. 2658, 2677, 174 L.Ed.2d 490 (2009); *Scott v. Harris,* 550 U.S. 372, 380, 127 S.Ct. 1769, 167 L.Ed.2d 686 (2007); *Anderson v. Liberty Lobby, Inc.,* 477 U.S. 242, 247–252, 106 S.Ct. 2505, 91 L.Ed.2d 202 (1986); *Matsushita Elec. Indus. Co., Ltd. v. Zenith Radio Corp.,* 475 U.S. 574, 586–587, 106 S.Ct. 1348, 89 L.Ed.2d 538 (1986).

[25]   *See Anderson v. Liberty Lobby, Inc.,* 477 U.S. 242, 247–252, 106 S.Ct. 2505, 91 L.Ed.2d 202 (1986).

[26]   *See Scott v. Harris,* 550 U.S. 372, 380, 127 S.Ct. 1769, 167 L.Ed.2d 686 (2007) (court should not adopt plaintiff's version of high-speed auto chase that was "blatantly contradicted" by unchallenged videotape evidence). *See also Coble v. City of White House,* 634 F.3d 865, 868–69 (6th Cir. 2011) (the *Scott* principle—no need to credit "visible fiction"—applies not just to conflicting videotape but to all types of objective conflicting evidence).

[27]   *See Matsushita Elec. Indus. Co., Ltd. v. Zenith Radio Corp.,* 475 U.S. 574, 587, 106 S.Ct. 1348, 1356, 89 L.Ed.2d 538 (1986).

prove its case by clear and convincing evidence, the court will examine whether the summary judgment record would allow a rational factfinder to find that the claim has been established by clear and convincing evidence.[28]

- *Material Fact:* A fact is "material" if it might affect the outcome of the case.[29] Ergo, whether a fact qualifies as "material" hinges on the substantive law at issue. Disputes (even if "genuine") over irrelevant or unnecessary facts will not defeat a motion for summary judgment.[30]

- *Appropriate as a Matter of Law:* Judgment is appropriate "as a matter of law" when, in the absence of a genuine dispute of material fact, the moving party should prevail. Thus, the mere fact that the moving party's summary judgment record is uncontested,[31] or even unresponded to,[32] is not enough. But summary judgment is appropriate when the non-moving party fails to make an adequate showing on an essential element of its case, as to which that party has the burden of proof.[33]

District Court *"Shall"* Grant Summary Judgment

This choice of verb has proven controversial, as the drafters, courts, and practitioners debate the proper measure of discretion a district judge ought to retain in resolving a summary judgment motion.[34] The 2010 Amendments to Rule 56 did not settle this controversy, which remains guided only by case law. Ergo, a court *must* deny summary judgment when a genuine dispute of material fact remains to be tried, or where the moving party is not entitled to a judgment as a matter of law.[35] A court also may not decide the motion on the basis of clearly erroneous findings of fact, an improper application of the law, or an erroneous legal standard.[36] In all other contexts, a court enjoys some measure of discretion to grant or deny the motion.[37] Some case language suggests that this discretion might not be very broad.[38] Other precedent suggests differently. For example, summary judgment may be denied where the factual records are "disturbingly thin" or "contain gaps"

---

[28] *See Anderson v. Liberty Lobby, Inc.,* 477 U.S. 242, 254, 106 S.Ct. 2505, 2513, 91 L.Ed.2d 202 (1986).

[29] *See Anderson v. Liberty Lobby, Inc.,* 477 U.S. 242, 248, 106 S.Ct. 2505, 2510, 91 L.Ed.2d 202 (1986). *See also Wright ex rel. Trust Co. of Kansas v. Abbott Laboratories, Inc.,* 259 F.3d 1226, 1231–32 (10th Cir. 2001) ("material" if, under substantive law, fact is "essential to the proper disposition of the claim").

[30] *See Anderson v. Liberty Lobby, Inc.,* 477 U.S. 242, 248, 106 S.Ct. 2505, 2510, 91 L.Ed.2d 202 (1986). *See also Scott v. Harris,* 550 U.S. 372, 380, 127 S.Ct. 1769, 167 L.Ed.2d 686 (2007).

[31] *See Edwards v. Aguillard,* 482 U.S. 578, 595, 107 S.Ct. 2573, 96 L.Ed.2d 510 (1987).

[32] *See Torres-Rosado v. Rotger-Sabat,* 335 F.3d 1, 9 (1st Cir. 2003).

[33] *See Cleveland v. Policy Management Systems Corp.,* 526 U.S. 795, 804, 119 S.Ct. 1597, 1603, 143 L.Ed.2d 966 (1999); *Celotex Corp. v. Catrett,* 477 U.S. 317, 323, 106 S.Ct. 2548, 2552, 91 L.Ed.2d 265 (1986).

[34] After many decades as "shall", this verb was changed to "should" during the 2007 "restyling" amendments. *See* Rule 56(c) advisory committee note to 2007 amendments. The 2010 Amendments originally considered changing it again to "must" but decided instead to restore it back to the original "shall" in fear of inadvertently altering the prevailing summary judgment standard. *See* Rule 56(a) advisory committee note to 2010 amendments.

[35] *See Ortiz v. Jordan,* 562 U.S. 180, 188, 131 S.Ct. 884, 891, 178 L.Ed.2d 703 (2011). *See generally* Rule 56 advisory committee note to 2007 amendments.

[36] *See In re Brown,* 342 F.3d 620, 633 (6th Cir. 2003).

[37] *See* Rule 56 advisory committee note to 2007 amendments (citing *Kennedy v. Silas Mason Co.,* 334 U.S. 249, 256–57, 68 S.Ct. 1031, 92 L. Ed. 1347 (1948)). *But cf. Beard v. Banks,* 548 U.S. 521, 529, 126 S.Ct. 2572, 2578, 165 L.Ed.2d 697 (2006) (noting that, if the non-moving party is unable to demonstrate a genuine issue of material fact, the law "requires" entry of a judgment in favor of the moving party).

[38] *See Beard v. Banks,* 548 U.S. 521, 529, 126 S.Ct. 2572, 2578, 165 L.Ed.2d 697 (2006) (if non-moving party fails to show genuine issue of material fact, "the law requires entry of judgment"); *Celotex Corp. v. Catrett,* 477 U.S. 317, 322, 106 S.Ct. 2548, 2552, 91 L.Ed.2d 265 (1986) ("plain language of Rule 56(b) mandates the entry of summary judgment); *Everett v. Cook County,* 655 F.3d 723, 726 (7th Cir. 2011) (court "must" grant summary judgment if party fails to establishment essential element in party's case).

that could be resolved by readily obtainable evidence,[39] where the court concludes that a fuller factual development is necessary,[40] or where there is some particular reason to believe that the wiser course would be to proceed to trial.[41] In a non-jury/bench trial, the district judge may have more discretion still.[42] Nevertheless, a meritorious summary judgment motion should generally be granted.[43]

Doubts and Inferences

In ruling on a motion for summary judgment, the court will never weigh the evidence or find the facts.[44] Instead, the court's role under Rule 56 is narrowly limited to assessing the threshold issue of whether a genuine dispute exists as to material facts requiring a trial.[45] Thus, the evidence of the non-moving party will be believed as true, all doubts will be resolved against the moving party, all evidence will be construed in the light most favorable to the non-moving party, and all reasonable inferences will be drawn in the non-moving party's favor.[46] But the court may credit those portions of the moving party's evidence, from disinterested sources, that is uncontradicted and unimpeached.[47]

To be candid, the boundary dividing reasonable inferences from impermissible speculation is "often 'thin,'" though certainly consequential.[48] "Reasonable" inferences are those reasonably drawn from all the facts then before the court, after sifting through the universe of all possible inferences the facts could support. "Reasonable" inferences need not be necessarily more probable or likely than other inferences that might tilt in the moving party's favor. Instead, so long as more than one reasonable inference can be drawn, and one inference creates a genuine dispute of material fact, the trier of fact is entitled to decide which inference to believe and summary judgment on that ground is not appropriate.[49]

Ordinarily, an appropriately supported summary judgment motion cannot be defeated by inferences that are unreasonable or improbable, allegations that are conclusory, or mere speculation and imagination.[50] Nor will a motion be defeated by a posited factual scenario that is clearly contradicted by the summary judgment record,[51] or by the mere promise from

---

[39] *See Spratt v. Rhode Island Dept. Of Corrections,* 482 F.3d 33, 43 (1st Cir. 2007).

[40] *See Kennedy v. Silas Mason Co.,* 334 U.S. 249, 68 S.Ct. 1031, 92 L. Ed. 1347 (1948).

[41] *See Anderson v. Liberty Lobby, Inc.,* 477 U.S. 242, 255, 106 S.Ct. 2505, 2513, 91 L.Ed.2d 202 (1986).

[42] *See Johnson v. Diversicare Afton Oaks, LLC,* 597 F.3d 673, 676 (5th Cir. 2010) (has discretion to decide that evidence could not possibly persuade him or her to a different result).

[43] *See Weigel v. Broad,* 544 F.3d 1143, 1157 (10th Cir. 2008).

[44] *See Anderson v. Liberty Lobby, Inc.,* 477 U.S. 242, 255, 106 S.Ct. 2505, 91 L.Ed.2d 202 (1986).

[45] *See Anderson v. Liberty Lobby, Inc.,* 477 U.S. 242, 249, 106 S.Ct. 2505, 2510, 91 L.Ed.2d 202 (1986).

[46] *See Tolan v. Cotton,* ___ U.S. ___, 134 S.Ct. 1861, 1863 & 1866, 188 L.Ed.2d 895 (2014); *Crawford v. Metropolitan Gov't of Nashville & Davidson County,* 555 U.S. 271, 274 n.1, 129 S.Ct. 846, 849 n.1, 172 L.Ed.2d 650 (2009); *Beard v. Banks,* 548 U.S. 521, 530–31, 126 S.Ct. 2572, 2578, 165 L.Ed.2d 697 (2006); *Reeves v. Sanderson Plumbing Prods., Inc.,* 530 U.S. 133, 150–51, 120 S.Ct. 2097, 147 L.Ed.2d 105 (2000); *Hunt v. Cromartie,* 526 U.S. 541, 550–55, 119 S.Ct. 1545, 1551–52, 143 L.Ed.2d 731 (1999); *Eastman Kodak Co. v. Image Technical Services, Inc.,* 504 U.S. 451, 456, 112 S.Ct. 2072, 2076, 119 L.Ed.2d 265 (1992); *Anderson v. Liberty Lobby, Inc.,* 477 U.S. 242, 255, 106 S.Ct. 2505, 2513, 91 L.Ed.2d 202 (1986); *Adickes v. S. H. Kress & Co.,* 398 U.S. 144, 157–59, 90 S.Ct. 1598, 1608–09, 26 L.Ed.2d 142 (1970).

[47] *See Reeves v. Sanderson Plumbing Prods., Inc.,* 530 U.S. 133, 151, 120 S.Ct. 2097, 147 L.Ed.2d 105 (2000). *Cf. Little v. Liquid Air Corp.,* 37 F.3d 1069, 1075 (5th Cir. 1994) (resolving doubts in favor of non-moving party is triggered only when parties have submitted evidence of contradictory facts).

[48] *See Halsey v. Pfeiffer,* 750 F.3d 273, 287 (3d Cir. 2014).

[49] *See Hunt v. Cromartie,* 526 U.S. 541, 552, 119 S.Ct. 1545, 1552, 143 L.Ed.2d 731 (1999).

[50] *See Rosaura Bldg. Corp. v. Municipality of Mayaguez,* 778 F.3d 55, 61 (1st Cir. 2015) (not "conclusory allegations, empty rhetoric, unsupported speculation, or evidence which, in the aggregate, is less than significantly probative"); *Clay v. Credit Bureau Enters., Inc.,* 754 F.3d 535, 539 (8th Cir. 2014) (not "mere speculation, conjecture, or fantasy").

[51] *See Scott v. Harris,* 550 U.S. 372, 380, 127 S.Ct. 1769, 167 L.Ed.2d 686 (2007) (court should not adopt plaintiff's version of high-speed auto chase that was "blatantly contradicted" by unchallenged videotape evidence).

the non-moving party that he will later demonstrate the falsity of the moving party's facts.[52] "Evidence, not contentions, avoids summary judgment,"[53] and non-moving parties must arrive brandishing more than "a cardboard sword".[54] Alone, an "earnest hope" and "brash conjecture" are not enough.[55]

Credibility Questions

The court will not weigh the credibility of witnesses or other evidence in ruling on a motion for summary judgment.[56] Evaluating credibility, weighing evidence, and drawing factual inferences are all functions reserved for the jury.[57] However, simply lobbing broad, conclusory attacks on a witness's credibility is not enough to defeat summary judgment.[58]

State of Mind Questions

Summary judgment is not automatically foreclosed merely because a person's state of mind (such as motive, knowledge, intent, good faith or bad faith, malice, fraud, conspiracy, or consent) is at issue.[59] But such cases will seldom lend themselves to a summary disposition because questions of credibility will ordinarily abound.[60] Thus, summary judgment is used "sparingly" and "seldom granted" in cases involving peculiarly intensive state of mind questions such as employment discrimination actions,[61] antitrust cases,[62] and certain intellectual property disputes.[63]

Predominantly Legal Disputes

Summary judgment is often appropriate in cases where the remaining unresolved disputes are primarily legal, rather than factual in nature.[64]

---

[52]   *See Cutting Underwater Techs. USA, Inc. v. Eni U.S. Operating Co.,* 671 F.3d 512, 517 (5th Cir. 2012).

[53]   *See Al-Zubaidy v. TEK Industries, Inc.,* 406 F.3d 1030, 1036 (8th Cir. 2005).

[54]   *See Calvi v. Knox County,* 470 F.3d 422, 426 (1st Cir. 2006).

[55]   *See Balser v. Int'l Union of Elec., Elec., Salaried, Mach. & Furniture Workers (IUE) Local 201,* 661 F.3d 109, 118 (1st Cir. 2011).

[56]   *See Tolan v. Cotton,* ___ U.S. ___, 134 S.Ct. 1861, 1866, 188 L.Ed.2d 895 (2014); *Anderson v. Liberty Lobby, Inc.,* 477 U.S. 242, 255, 106 S.Ct. 2505, 91 L.Ed.2d 202 (1986).

[57]   *See Reeves v. Sanderson Plumbing Prods., Inc.,* 530 U.S. 133, 150–51, 120 S.Ct. 2097, 147 L.Ed.2d 105 (2000); *Anderson v. Liberty Lobby, Inc.,* 477 U.S. 242, 255, 106 S.Ct. 2505, 2513, 91 L.Ed.2d 202 (1986).

[58]   *See Deville v. Marcantel,* 567 F.3d 156, 165 (5th Cir. 2009).

[59]   *See Tolbert v. Smith,* 790 F.3d 427, 435 (2d Cir. 2015) (employment discrimination); *In re Online DVD-Rental Antitrust Litig.,* 779 F.3d 914, 921 (9th Cir. 2015) (antitrust). *See also Little v. Liquid Air Corp.,* 37 F.3d 1069, 1075 n.14 (5th Cir. 1994) (renouncing prior view that certain types of cases are inappropriate for Rule 56).

[60]   *See Hutchinson v. Proxmire,* 443 U.S. 111, 99 S.Ct. 2675, 61 L.Ed.2d 411 (1979). *See also Graham v. Long Island R.R.,* 230 F.3d 34, 38 (2d Cir. 2000) (commenting that summary judgment is used "sparingly" where intent and state of mind are implicated).

[61]   *See Tolbert v. Smith,* 790 F.3d 427, 434 (2d Cir. 2015) ("caution" needed in such cases); *Bagley v. Blagojevich,* 646 F.3d 378, 389 (7th Cir. 2011) (although no special rule exists for, and summary judgment can be proper in, discrimination cases, courts must not grant where intent is properly contested).

[62]   *See Smith Wholesale Co., Inc. v. R.J. Reynolds Tobacco Co.,* 477 F.3d 854, 862 (6th Cir. 2007) (disfavored, but not precluded, in antitrust litigation). *But cf. In re Wholesale Grocery Prods. Antitrust Litig.,* 752 F.3d 728, 732–33 & 733 n.4 (8th Cir. 2014) (neither favored nor disfavored in antitrust cases, but governed by same standard as all other cases); *In re Publ'n Paper Antitrust Litig.,* 690 F.3d 51, 61 (2d Cir. 2012) (favored in antitrust cases, serving (a "vital function" by avoiding a chilling effect on pro-competitive market forces).

[63]   *See Zobmondo Entm't, LLC v. Falls Media, LLC,* 602 F.3d 1108, 1113 (9th Cir. 2010) ("disfavored in the trademark arena").

[64]   *See Thomas v. Metropolitan Life Ins. Co.,* 631 F.3d 1153, 1160 (10th Cir. 2011).

Stipulated Facts and Cross-Motions

If the parties stipulate to the facts, obviously no genuine dispute as to material facts then exists for a factfinder to resolve.[65] Nevertheless, the summary judgment standard remains the same. The court must draw inferences from the stipulated facts, and resolve those inferences in favor of the non-moving party.[66] Cross-motions for summary judgment are also examined under the usual Rule 56 standards.[67] Each cross-motion must be evaluated on its own merits,[68] with the court viewing all facts and reasonable inferences in the light most favorable to the nonmoving party.[69] Thus, the mere fact that cross-motions have been filed does not, by itself, necessarily justify the entry of a summary judgment,[70] nor will the denial of one cross-motion compel the grant of the other cross-motion.[71]

Trial Court's Duty to Explain

Trial judges are directed to set forth, "on the record," the reasons for their disposition of summary judgment motions, although the particular form and content of that explanation is left to the court's discretion.[72] This requirement facilitates both subsequent trial-level proceedings and appeals.[73] But trial courts are ordinarily not expected to pen "elaborate essays using talismanic phrases," absent some reason to believe that material facts were overlooked or a wrong legal standard was applied.[74]

Supreme Court's Original Jurisdiction

These standards do not technically control summary judgment in cases where the Supreme Court is sitting in its original jurisdiction, but the Court has embraced them as a guide.[75]

Effect of Ruling—"Law of the Case"

The "law of the case" doctrine holds that when a court decides upon a rule of law, that decision should generally control the same issues throughout the subsequent stages in the same case.[76] It is based on the sound, salutary policy of judicial finality—that all litigation should come to an end.[77] This is a prudential doctrine; it guides and influences the court's exercise of discretion, but it does not limit the court's jurisdiction or power.[78] It may not

---

[65] *See Cincom Sys., Inc. v. Novelis Corp.*, 581 F.3d 431, 435 (6th Cir. 2009).

[66] *See Leebaert v. Harrington*, 332 F.3d 134, 138–39 (2d Cir. 2003); *Luden's Inc. v. Local Union No. 6 of Bakery, Confectionery and Tobacco Workers' Intern. Union of America*, 28 F.3d 347, 353 (3d Cir. 1994). *But see United Paperworkers Intern. Union Local 14, AFL-CIO-CLC v. International Paper Co.*, 64 F.3d 28, 31 (1st Cir. 1995) (noting that summary judgment standard may be modified where dispute arrives as a "case stated"; in that instance, trial judge is free to engage in certain factfinding, including the drawing of inferences).

[67] *See Sun Capital Partners III, LP v. New England Teamsters & Trucking Indus. Pension Fund*, 724 F.3d 129, 138 (1st Cir. 2013).

[68] *See Ins. Co. of Pa. v. Great Northern Ins. Co.*, 787 F.3d 632, 635 (1st Cir. 2015).

[69] *See Defenders of Wildlife v. v. North Carolina Dep't of Transp.*, 762 F.3d 374, 392–93 (4th Cir. 2014).

[70] *See Ultra Clean Holdings, Inc. v. TFG-Cal., L.P.*, 534 Fed. Appx. 776, 780 (10th Cir. 2013).

[71] *See Christian Heritage Academy v. Oklahoma Secondary School Activities Ass'n*, 483 F.3d 1025, 1030 (10th Cir. 2007).

[72] *See* Rule 56(a) advisory committee note to 2010 amendments.

[73] *See* Rule 56(a) advisory committee note to 2010 amendments.

[74] *See Jackson v. Federal Exp.*, 766 F.3d 189, 196–97 (2d Cir. 2014).

[75] *See* Sup. Ct. R. 17.2. *See also Alabama v. North Carolina*, 560 U.S. 330, 344, 130 S.Ct. 2295, 2308, 176 L.Ed.2d 1070 (2010).

[76] *See Arizona v. California*, 460 U.S. 605, 618, 103 S.Ct. 1382, 1391, 75 L.Ed.2d 318 (1983).

[77] *See Lyons v. Fisher*, 888 F.2d 1071, 1074 (5th Cir. 1989). *See also Gindes v. United States*, 740 F.2d 947, 949 (Fed. Cir. 1984) (commenting that doctrine rests upon important public policy litigants do not enjoy the right to cover the same ground twice, hoping that passage of time or changes in court's composition will alter outcome).

[78] *See Arizona v. California*, 460 U.S. 605, 618, 103 S.Ct. 1382, 1391, 75 L.Ed.2d 318 (1983).

apply where intervening controlling authority warrants a revisiting of an earlier decision.[79] Because *denials* of summary judgment generally do nothing more than acknowledge that a genuine issue of material fact remains for trial, such denials are typically not accorded any preclusive effect nor do they become "law of the case".[80] The same is true for other interlocutory rulings that preceded the entry of summary judgment.[81]

Constitutionality of Summary Judgment

Only once has the Supreme Court examined the constitutionality of summary judgment, on a claim that the procedure deprives defeated claimants of their Seventh Amendment rights to a trial by jury. The Court rejected this argument, reasoning that any time summary judgment is granted, it is only because there *is* no triable issue for the jury.[82] No lower federal court has ever declared summary judgment unconstitutional.

Appealability

The general rule is that an order granting summary judgment is appealable only when (1) it constitutes the "final order" in the case,[83] or (2) it constitutes a partial summary judgment that resolves one claim (among multiple claims) or one party (among multiple parties) and is accompanied by a proper Rule 54(b) determination from the trial court.[84] The appealability of an order denying summary judgment is less simple. If the denial is based on the presence of genuinely disputed facts, that order decides merely that the case must continue; it neither finally settles nor tentatively resolves anything else about the merits.[85] For this reason, it is ordinarily not immediately appealable[86] (unless the effect of the denial is to fully resolve all issues and cause entry of a final judgment).[87] In fact, several courts hold that, once a trial on the merits occurs, the order can never be reviewed, because the "prediction" that denial represented has been rendered moot by the actual introduction of evidence at trial.[88] Other courts recognize an exception to this general prohibition, and permit a summary judgment denial to be reviewed on appeal if the denial was based on the interpretation of a pure question of law.[89] Other courts narrow the exception still further, permitting review when the denial was based on a pure question of law and the judge was

---

[79] *See Marable v. Nitchman,* 511 F.3d 924, 930 n.11 (9th Cir. 2007).

[80] *See Switzerland Cheese Ass'n, Inc. v. E. Horne's Market, Inc.,* 385 U.S. 23, 25, 87 S.Ct. 193, 17 L.Ed.2d 23 (1966). *But see Federal Ins. Co. v. Scarsella Bros., Inc.,* 931 F.2d 599, 601 (9th Cir. 1991) (holding that doctrine is not amenable to such broad generalizations, and may apply to summary judgment denials when trial court intends to resolve definitively the legal questions in issue).

[81] *See Gander Mountain Co. v. Cabela's, Inc.,* 540 F.3d 827, 830–31 (8th Cir. 2008) (arguably inconsistent discovery rulings).

[82] *See Fidelity & Deposit Co. v. United States,*187 U.S. 315, 319–21, 23 S.Ct. 120, 47 L.Ed. 194 (1902). *See also J.R. Simplot v. Chevron Pipeline Co.,* 563 F.3d 1102, 1117 (10th Cir. 2009) (declaring Seventh Amendment question "well-settled"). *But see* Suja A. Thomas, *Why Summary Judgment is Unconstitutional,* 93 VA. L. REV. 139 (2007) (arguing why Rule 56 violates the Seventh Amendment).

[83] *See Santaella v. Metropolitan Life Ins. Co.,* 123 F.3d 456, 461 (7th Cir. 1997). *See also* 28 U.S.C.A. § 1291.

[84] *See* Rule 54(b). *See also Bonner v. Perry,* 564 F.3d 424, 427 (6th Cir. 2009). *Cf. Liberty Mut. Ins. Co. v. Wetzel,* 424 U.S. 737, 744, 96 S.Ct. 1202, 47 L.Ed.2d 435 (1976) (grant of partial summary judgment not an appealable final order).

[85] *See Switzerland Cheese Ass'n, Inc. v. E. Horne's Market, Inc.,* 385 U.S. 23, 25, 87 S.Ct. 193, 195, 17 L.Ed.2d 23 (1966).

[86] *See Plumhoff v. Rickard,* ___ U.S. ___, 134 S.Ct. 2012, 2018–19, 188 L.Ed.2d 1056 (2014); *Ortiz v. Jordan,* 562 U.S. 180, 188, 131 S.Ct. 884, 891, 178 L.Ed.2d 703 (2011).

[87] *See Karuk Tribe of Cal. v. U.S. Forest Serv.,* 640 F.3d 979, 987 (9th Cir. 2011).

[88] *See New York Marine & General Ins. Co. v. Continental Cement Co., LLC,* 761 F.3d 830, 2014 WL 3824226, at *5 (8th Cir. 2014). *Cf. Travelers Cas. & Sur. Co. v. Ins. Co. of N. America,* 609 F.3d 143, 167 n.32 (3d Cir. 2010) (court need not decide whether case presented "one of those rare instances" which permitted review of summary judgment denial following merits trial).

[89] *See New York Marine & General Ins. Co. v. Continental Cement Co., LLC,* 761 F.3d 830, 838 (8th Cir. 2014) (surveying divided case law, and permitting appeal).

the factfinder (non-jury, bench trial).[90] Other courts hold that, although such review is generally denied, an appeal might be tolerated were "extraordinary circumstances" to exist.[91] Still other courts permit appellate review of a denial of summary judgment when a companion ruling granting summary judgment is simultaneously appealed.[92] Mindful of the variety of these approaches and the uncertainty they introduce, prudent practitioners should always renew summary judgment motions with a Rule 50 motion for judgment as a matter of law at the close of the evidence (and, if rejected, again after the trial has concluded).[93]

- *Exceptions:* Exceptions to even these rules exist. For example, if the motion asserts questions of immunity from suit, a denial of summary judgment may be immediately appealable.[94] Similarly, a denial of a cross-motion for summary judgment may be immediately appealable along with a challenge to that portion of the cross-motion that was granted.[95]

RULE 56(b)—TIME TO FILE A MOTION

CORE CONCEPT

Parties may move for summary judgment at any time until 30 days after the close of all discovery, absent a local rule or court order directing otherwise. The time for responding to motions is left undefined, to be set by local rule or court order.

APPLICATIONS

Time for Filing

A national timing procedure governs summary judgment motions, permitting their filing at any time "until 30 days after the close of discovery".[96] This procedure is only a "default" provision, however, and can be modified freely by local rule or court order.[97] Indeed, noting that timing rules specially tailored to the needs of a particular case "are likely to work better," the drafters anticipate that this default rule is likely to be modified "in most cases" by case-specific scheduling orders, periods proposed by the parties, case staging regimes, or local rules.[98] Under a former version of the Rule, a claimant had to wait 20-days after commencing the action before becoming eligible to file for summary judgment; that restriction, deemed "outmoded" by the drafters, was deleted in 2009.[99] In current practice,

---

[90]   *See Robinson v. City of Harvey,* 489 F.3d 864, 868 (7th Cir. 2007) (finding it "clear that the time for appeal cannot be extended in anticipation of a fee petition").

[91]   *See Pahuta v. Massey-Ferguson, Inc.,* 170 F.3d 125, 132 (2d Cir. 1999).

[92]   *See McMullen v. Meijer, Inc.,* 355 F.3d 485, 489 (6th Cir.2004).

[93]   *See HOK Sport, Inc. v. FC Des Moines, L.C.,* 495 F.3d 927, 942 (8th Cir. 2007).

[94]   *See Plumhoff v. Rickard,* ___ U.S. ___, 134 S.Ct. 2012, 2018–19, 188 L.Ed.2d 1056 (2014); *Ortiz v. Jordan,* 562 U.S. 180, 188, 131 S.Ct. 884, 891, 178 L.Ed.2d 703 (2011).

[95]   *See Stilwell v. American Gen. Life Ins. Co.,* 555 F.3d 572, 576 (7th Cir. 2009).

[96]   *See* Rule 56(b) (amended 2010). *Note:* the syntax of this Rule includes a somewhat ambiguous use of the word "until". Because "until" could connote the last of the permitted days, or the first of the forbidden days, this word choice is not ideal. When read in conjunction with the 2009 amendments to Rule 6(a)(1)(C) and Rule 6(a) (4), however, the most reasonable reading seems to be that this "until" period runs to the close of the 30th day after the end of discovery.

[97]   *See Cioni v. Globe Specialty Metals, Inc.,* 618 Fed.Appx. 42, 45 n.2 (3d Cir. 2015). *See generally Hoffman v. Tonnemacher,* 593 F.3d 908, 911 (9th Cir. 2010) (case-specific, tailored scheduling orders "are likely to work better than default rules").

[98]   *See* Rule 56(c)(1) advisory committee notes to 2009 amendments. *See also Moss v. Wyeth, Inc.,* 872 F.Supp.2d 154, 160 (D.Conn. 2012) (motion timely if comports with scheduling order).

[99]   *See* Rule 56(c)(1) advisory committee notes to 2009 amendments. In current practice, unless local rules or scheduling orders provide otherwise, motions for summary judgment are timely even if filed before an answer or dismissal motion.

unless local rules or scheduling orders provide otherwise, motions for summary judgment are timely even if filed before an answer or dismissal motion.[100]

Quick Motions (Filed Before/During Discovery)

Early summary judgment motions (those filed at the time the lawsuit is commenced or otherwise before, or during, discovery) are clearly permitted, unless foreclosed by local rules or scheduling orders.[101] Such early filings, though consistent with some prior case law,[102] seemed at odds with the Supreme Court's admonition in 1986 that summary judgment should be granted only after the nonmoving party had an "adequate time for discovery".[103] Recent opinions, decided after the 2010 summary judgment amendments, continue to incant this assurance.[104] The drafters addressed this issue obliquely in 2009 and again in 2010, noting that motions filed at commencement, though permitted, may prove premature[105] and, if so, courts may readily extend the response time.[106] Seeking a deferral of a ruling pending further discovery also always remains an option for the nonmoving party.[107] In any event, in practice, pre-discovery summary judgment motions prove to be the exception, not the norm.[108]

Time for Responding

The Rules set no national time period for responding to summary judgment motions.[109] Following longstanding practice, this period is instead addressed by local rule in the applicable District or by chambers order.[110]

---

[100] *See Charvat v. ACO, Inc.,* 2012 WL 847328, at *4 (D.Neb. Mar. 13, 2012).

[101] *See* Rule 56(b) advisory committee note to 2010 amendments. *See also Scott v. State Farm Fire & Cas. Co.,* 86 F. Supp. 3d 727, 730 (E.D.Mich. 2015) (proper before discovery is complete); *Jernigan v. Crane,* 64 F.Supp.3d 1260, 1273 (E.D.Ark. 2014) (proper even at commencement); *Chevron Corp. v. Donziger,* 886 F.Supp.2d 235, 263 n.186 (S.D.N.Y. 2012) (proper while other dispositive motion is pending). *See generally Foley v. Wells Fargo Bank, N.A.,* 772 F.3d 63, 72 (1st Cir. 2014) (waiting until discovery ends sometimes is "an asinine exercise").

[102] *See, e.g., Alholm v. American Steamship Co.,* 144 F.3d 1172, 1177 (8th Cir. 1998) (noting that Rule 56 does not require that discovery be closed before motion can be heard).

[103] *Celotex Corp. v. Catrett,* 477 U.S. 317, 322, 106 S.Ct. 2548, 2552, 91 L.Ed.2d 265 (1986).

[104] *See, e.g., Ellis v. J.R.'s Country Stores, Inc.,* 779 F.3d 1184, 1205–06 (10th Cir. 2015) (should be refused, without opportunity for discovery); *Shelton v. Bledsoe,* 775 F.3d 554, 568 (3d Cir. 2015) ("rarely justified" if discovery is incomplete).

[105] *See* Rule 56(b) advisory committee note to 2010 amendments. *See also Jernigan v. Crane,* 64 F.Supp.3d 1260, 1273–74 (E.D.Ark. 2014) (proper even at commencement).

[106] *See* Rule 56(c)(1) advisory committee note to 2009 amendments.

[107] *See* Rule 56(d) (formerly Rule 56(f)).

[108] *See Miller v. Wolpoff & Abramson, L.L.P.,* 321 F.3d 292, 303–04 (2d Cir. 2003) (pre-discovery summary judgment granted in only rarest cases); *Vaughn v. U.S. Small Business Admin.,* 65 F.3d 1322, 1325 n.1 (6th Cir. 1995) (defendant's summary judgment motion cannot ordinarily be considered until the plaintiff has had the opportunity to conduct discovery).

[109] In 2009, the Rules drafters experimented with a national 21-day response period, but it was rescinded a year later in 2010. *See* Former Rule 56(c)(1)(B) (amended 2009; deleted 2010).

[110] *See* Rule 56(b) advisory committee note to 2010 amendments ("Scheduling orders or other pretrial orders can regulate timing to fit the needs of the case."). Historically, many courts, relying on the Rule's former language, had required at least a 10-day response period, although that requirement was subject to being lifted if a shortened period would cause no prejudice. *See* Former Rule 56(c) (rescinded 2007) ("The motion shall be served at least 10 days before the time fixed for the hearing."). *See also Celestine v. Petroleos de Venezuela SA,* 266 F.3d 343, 350 (5th Cir. 2001) (describing pre-amendment practice).

RULE 56(c)—PROCEDURES

CORE CONCEPT

Several summary judgment procedures are nationally defined: the manner for factually supporting motions and oppositions; the method for objecting to improper support for motions or oppositions; the content of the summary judgment record; and the proper content for supporting or opposing affidavits and declarations. Other summary judgment procedures developed through case law over time.

APPLICATIONS

Procedure #1: Supporting Factual Positions

Parties moving for summary judgment have the initial burden of "identifying" each claim, defense, or part thereof on which they seek summary judgment.[111] They thus isolate the battleground for the summary judgment contest (and, consequently, the nonmoving parties generally need not offer contesting evidence on issues and points not raised by the moving papers).[112] Once the contours of the contest are set, parties moving for, or resisting, summary judgment have the further burden to factually support their positions. They must discharge that obligation of factual support in either of two ways:

- *First,* they may cite the court to certain parts of the summary judgment record (which may contain depositions, documents, electronically stored information, affidavits or declarations, stipulations, admissions, interrogatory answers, and other materials). In doing so, their citation must be specific and to "particular parts" of the record materials.[113]

- *Second,* they may show either (a) that the materials cited by their opponent do not establish the absence or presence of a genuine dispute or (b) that the opponent cannot produce admissible evidence to support the claimed fact.[114]

This procedure seems to essentially codify the burden-shifting summary judgment procedure described by the Supreme Court in *Celotex Corp. v. Catrett.*[115] As the Court outlined it, the party moving for summary judgment always has the burden of persuasion on such a motion. The burden of going forward, however, shifts during the motion process.

The moving party must first make a prima facie showing that summary judgment is appropriate under Rule 56—that is, the movant must properly "put the ball in play".[116] This does not require the moving party to disprove the opponent's claims or defenses.[117] Instead, this prima facie burden may be discharged simply by pointing out for the court an absence of evidence in support of the non-moving party's claims or defenses.[118] However, where the

---

[111] *See* Rule 56(a).

[112] *See United States v. King-Vassel,* 728 F.3d 707, 711–12 (7th Cir. 2013). *But see infra* Authors' Commentary to Rule 56(f)(2) ("**Summary Judgment on Unrequested Grounds**").

[113] *See* Rule 56(c)(1)(A). *See also Clapper v. Amnesty Int'l USA,* ___ U.S. ___, ___, 133 S.Ct. 1138, 1148–49, 185 L.Ed.2d 264 (2013). *See generally* Rule 56(c)(1)(A) advisory committee note to 2010 amendments.

[114] *See* Rule 56(c)(1)(B). *See also Seng-Tiong Ho v. Taflove,* 648 F.3d 489, 496 (7th Cir. 2011). *See generally* Rule 56(c)(1)(A) advisory committee note to 2010 amendments.

[115] *Celotex Corp. v. Catrett,* 477 U.S. 317, 106 S.Ct. 2548, 91 L.Ed.2d 265 (1986). *See also* Rep. of Jud. Conf. Comm. on Rules of Practice & Procedure at 14 (Sept. 2009) ("The proposed amendments are not intended to change the summary-judgment standard or burdens.") (available at http://www.uscourts.gov/uscourts/RulesAndPolicies/rules/Reports/Combined_ST_Report_Sept_2009.pdf).

[116] *See Evans Cabinet Corp. v. Kitchen In'l, Inc.,* 593 F.3d 135, 140 (1st Cir. 2010).

[117] *See Edwards v. Aguillard,* 482 U.S. 578, 595, 107 S.Ct. 2573, 96 L.Ed.2d 510 (1987); *Celotex Corp. v. Catrett,* 477 U.S. 317, 323, 106 S.Ct. 2548, 2553, 91 L.Ed.2d 265 (1986).

[118] *See Celotex Corp. v. Catrett,* 477 U.S. 317, 106 S.Ct. 2548, 2553, 91 L.Ed.2d 265 (1986). *See also* Rule 56(c)(1)(B).

moving party is the party with the ultimate burden of proof at trial, the prima facie burden is often higher, requiring that party to show that it can, in fact, carry its burden of proving all essential elements of its claim or defense.[119]

If the moving party meets its prima facie burden,[120] then the burden of going forward shifts to the non-moving party to show, by affidavit or otherwise, that a genuine dispute of material fact remains for the factfinder to resolve.[121] The non-moving party must carry this burden as to each essential element on which it bears the burden of proof.[122] Thus, once this summary judgment stage arrives, the non-moving party is not saved by mere allegations or denials,[123] assertions in legal memoranda or argument,[124] speculation,[125] conclusory statements,[126] empty rhetoric,[127] characterizations of disputed facts,[128] or simply recounting the generous notice-pleading standards of the federal courts.[129] Nor will an "earnest hope" to discover evidence suffice,[130] or a promise to come forward later with proof[131] or a hope to discredit the opponent's evidence at trial.[132] Instead, the nonmoving party must "go beyond the pleadings,"[133] and show adequately probative evidence creating a triable controversy.[134] A party does not meet this burden by offering evidence which is merely colorable[135] or which implies some metaphysical factual doubt,[136] or by simply theorizing a "plausible scenario" in support of the party's claims, especially when that proffered scenario conflicts with direct, contrary evidence.[137]

Because summary judgment, when entered, obviates the need for a trial, facts forming the basis for such a ruling must be (1) material, (2) undisputed, and (3) admissible in evidence.[138] In addition to the parties' submissions, the court may, in an appropriate circumstance, also consider evidence of which it may take judicial notice,[139] and even court filings and discovery in another lawsuit, so long as those materials are made part of the summary judgment record.[140]

---

[119] See Hotel 71 Mezz Lender LLC v. Nat'l Ret. Fund, 778 F.3d 593, 601 (7th Cir. 2015).

[120] Cf. Hotel 71 Mezz Lender LLC v. Nat'l Ret. Fund, 778 F.3d 593, 601–02 (7th Cir. 2015) (if movant fails to carry this burden, court is obligated to deny motion).

[121] See Celotex Corp. v. Catrett, 477 U.S. 317, 106 S.Ct. 2548, 91 L.Ed.2d 265 (1986). See also Beard v. Banks, 548 U.S. 521, 529, 126 S.Ct. 2572, 2578, 165 L.Ed.2d 697 (2006).

[122] See Wheeler v. Aventis Pharmaceuticals, 360 F.3d 853, 857 (8th Cir. 2004).

[123] See Clapper v. Amnesty Int'l USA, ___ U.S. ___, ___, 133 S.Ct. 1138, 1148–49, 185 L.Ed.2d 264 (2013); First Nat. Bank of Ariz. v. Cities Service Co., 391 U.S. 253, 289, 88 S.Ct. 1575, 1592, 20 L.Ed.2d 569 (1968).

[124] See Berckeley Inv. Group, Ltd. v. Colkitt, 455 F.3d 195, 201 (3d Cir. 2006).

[125] See Design Resources, Inc. v. Leather Indus. of Am., 789 F.3d 495, 500 (4th Cir. 2015).

[126] See Design Resources, Inc. v. Leather Indus. of Am., 789 F.3d 495, 500 (4th Cir. 2015).

[127] See Rosaura Bldg. Corp. v. Municipality of Mayaguez, 778 F.3d 55, 61 (1st Cir. 2015).

[128] See Alman v. Reed, 703 F.3d 887, 895–96 (6th Cir. 2013); Carroll v. Lynch, 698 F.3d 561, 565 (7th Cir. 2012).

[129] See Tucker v. Union of Needletrades, Industrial and Textile Employees, 407 F.3d 784, 788 (6th Cir. 2005).

[130] See Balser v. Int'l Union of Elec., Elec., Salaried, Mach. & Furniture Workers (IUE) Local 201, 661 F.3d 109, 118 (1st Cir. 2011).

[131] See Cutting Underwater Techs. USA, Inc. v. Eni U.S. Operating Co., 671 F.3d 512, 517 (5th Cir. 2012).

[132] See Robbins v. Becker, 794 F.3d 988, 993 (8th Cir. 2015).

[133] See Celotex Corp. v. Catrett, 477 U.S. 317, 324, 106 S.Ct. 2548, 91 L.Ed.2d 265 (1986).

[134] See Robbins v. Becker, 794 F.3d 988, 993 (8th Cir. 2015).

[135] See Minnihan v. Mediacom Commc'ns Corp., 779 F.3d 803, 809 (8th Cir. 2015).

[136] See Ondo v. City of Cleveland, 795 F.3d 597, 603 (6th Cir. 2015).

[137] See Scott v. Harris, 550 U.S. 372, 380, 127 S.Ct. 1769, 1774–76, 167 L.Ed.2d 686 (2007).

[138] See Boyer-Liberto v. Fontainebleau Corp., 752 F.3d 350, 355 (4th Cir. 2014).

[139] See Spaine v. Community Contacts, Inc., 756 F.3d 542, 545 (7th Cir. 2014).

[140] See Alexander v. Casino Queen, Inc., 739 F.3d 972, 978–79 (7th Cir. 2014).

Procedure #2: Objecting to Improper Support

Materials offered to support or oppose a fact during summary judgment briefing must be capable of being offered at trial in an admissible form.[141] (Generally, this does not mean that the materials themselves must be presented in an admissible form during the summary judgment briefing, only that an admissible form exists by which those facts may be later introduced at trial).[142] A party may object that the opponent has supported a position (either seeking or opposing summary judgment) by material that cannot be presented at trial in a form that would be admissible as evidence.[143] The objections must specifically explain what particular exhibit is improper and why[144] (for example, demonstrating that the proffered evidence would be inadmissible as hearsay.)[145] Once made, the objection shifts the burden to the opponent to defend the contested material as admissible in its current form or to explain some other anticipated form by which it may be later admitted.[146] Failure to make an objection under this Rule does not forfeit a later objection to admissibility at time of trial,[147] though the absence of an objection invites the court to accept the evidence's admissibility as uncontested for the limited purpose of ruling on the summary judgment motion.[148] In considering objections under this Rule, the trial judge may rule explicitly, or implicitly so long as the record clearly supports the apparent determination.[149]

How this Rule harmonizes with certain elements of prior practice is as yet unclear. For example, formerly, a party objecting to summary judgment materials on other grounds *(e.g., that an affiant lacked personal knowledge or was incompetent)* was *compelled* to object in a timely fashion or risk forfeiting the objection entirely.[150] This procedure developed, examined one court, to avoid the objecting party playing the game of "dog-in-the-manger"— fighting the summary judgment motion on its merits and only later, if unsuccessful, unveiling technical objections as a hidden "ace".[151] Prior to the 2010 Amendments, the courts were also divided as to whether an improper affidavit could be challenged on a motion to strike.[152] Those that allowed the practice often compelled it on risk of waiver,[153] though courts were admonished in ruling on such motions to use "a scalpel, not a butcher knife"[154] so as to strike off only those offending portions.[155]

---

[141] *See* Rule 56(c)(2). *See also Southern California Darts Ass'n v. Zaffina*, 762 F.3d 921, 926 (9th Cir. 2014).

[142] *See Olson v. Morgan*, 750 F.3d 708, 714 (7th Cir. 2014). *See generally Celotex Corp. v. Catrett*, 477 U.S. 317, 324, 106 S.Ct. 2548, 2553, 91 L.Ed.2d 265 (1986) (commenting that party need not depose its own witnesses in order to defeat a summary judgment motion). Indeed, the most frequently submitted support on a summary judgment motion— affidavits—will rarely (if ever) be admissible at trial in the absence of the affiant.

[143] *See* Rule 56(c)(2).

[144] *See Halebian v. Berv*, 869 F.Supp.2d 420, 443 n.24 (S.D.N.Y. 2012).

[145] *See Spring Street Partners-IV, L.P. v. Lam*, 730 F.3d 427, 441–42 (5th Cir. 2013).

[146] *See* Rule 56(c)(2) advisory committee note to 2010 amendments. *See also Rodriguez v. Village Green Realty, Inc.*, 788 F.3d 31, 46 (2d Cir. 2015).

[147] *See* Rule 56(c)(2) advisory committee note to 2010 amendments.

[148] *See Lenox MacLaren Surgical Corp. v. Medtronic, Inc.*, 762 F.3d 1114, 1118 (10th Cir. 2014).

[149] *See Campbell v. Shinseki*, 546 Fed. Appx. 874, 878–79 (11th Cir. 2013).

[150] *See MSK EyEs Ltd. v. Wells Fargo Bank, Nat'l Ass'n*, 546 F.3d 533, 543 n.6 (8th Cir. 2008).

[151] *See Desrosiers v. Hartford Life and Acc. Co.*, 515 F.3d 87, 91–92 (1st Cir. 2008).

[152] *See Campbell v. Shinseki*, 546 Fed. Appx. 874, 879 (11th Cir. 2013) (describing pre-2010 practice and 2010 amendments' effect). *See also supra* Authors' Commentary to Rule 12(f) (**"Striking Documents Other Than Pleadings"**).

[153] *See Ruby v. Springfield R-12 Public School Dist.*, 76 F.3d 909, 912 (8th Cir. 1996) (absent motion to strike or other timely objection, district judge may consider a document which fails to conform to Rule 56's formal requirements); *In re Unisys Sav. Plan Litigation*, 74 F.3d 420, 437 (3d Cir. 1996), (party waived objection to form of affidavit by failing to move to strike or otherwise object).

[154] *See Perez v. Volvo Car Corp.*, 247 F.3d 303, 315–16 (1st Cir. 2001).

[155] *See Perez v. Volvo Car Corp.*, 247 F.3d 303, 315–16 (1st Cir. 2001).

Procedure #3: Content of Summary Judgment Record

In ruling on a summary judgment motion, the trial court is obliged to consider the materials cited by the parties in the motion papers,[156] but is merely permitted—not obligated—to conduct its own independent canvass of the record.[157] In both its respects, this codifies the prior majority practice.[158] The "record" for purposes of this Rule encompasses materials placed properly before the court through briefing and exhibits, and does not necessarily include materials that the court could itself gather by its own electronic initiative.[159] The fate of two earlier caveats to this practice remains unclear, however. Certain courts had commanded an independent record search in certain sensitive types of cases (like First Amendment disputes).[160] Other courts had cautioned that independent reviews of the record must be limited, and that trial judges remain vigilant to their limited, neutral roles and their duty to avoid partisan advocacy.[161]

Procedure #4: Content of Affidavits/Declarations

Affidavits or declarations may be used to support or oppose a motion for summary judgment, if they meet four prerequisites: (1) sworn or otherwise subscribed as true under a risk of perjury; (2) made on personal knowledge; (3) set out facts that would be admissible in evidence; and (4) show that the maker is competent to testify on the matters expressed.[162] A court generally will not consider affidavits and declarations failing these prerequisites,[163] though a submission may be received in part if a portion is inadmissible even if other portions are not.[164]

- *Sworn:* An affidavit must be sworn[165] and a declaration must be made under penalty of perjury[166] to qualify. Thus, verified complaints (ordinarily not required under the Rules) may suffice,[167] while an attorney's statements at oral argument generally will not.[168]

- *Personal Knowledge:* The affidavit or declaration must be made upon personal knowledge.[169] Statements based on "information and belief"—facts the maker

---

[156] *See* Rule 56(c)(3); *Phelps v. State Farm Mut. Auto. Ins. Co.*, 680 F.3d 725, 735 (6th Cir. 2012) (district court improperly failed to consider record evidence relied upon in motion briefing). *See generally* Rule 56(c)(3) advisory committee note to 2010 amendments.

[157] *See F.T.C. v. E.M.A. Nationwide, Inc.*, 767 F.3d 611, 630 n.11 (6th Cir. 2014).

[158] *See RSR Corp. v. Int'l Ins. Co.*, 612 F.3d 851, 857 (5th Cir. 2010).

[159] *See Alexander v. Casino Queen, Inc.*, 739 F.3d 972, 978–79 (7th Cir. 2014).

[160] *See Rohrbough v. Univ. of Colo. Hosp. Auth.*, 596 F.3d 741, 745 (10th Cir. 2010).

[161] *See Adler v. Wal-Mart Stores, Inc.*, 144 F.3d 664, 672 (10th Cir. 1998).

[162] *See* Rule 56(c)(4).

[163] *See Collins v. Seeman*, 462 F.3d 757, 760 n.1 (7th Cir. 2006). *But see Ruby v. Springfield R-12 Public School Dist.*, 76 F.3d 909, 912 (8th Cir. 1996) (absent motion to strike or other timely objection, district judge may consider a document which fails to conform to Rule 56's formal requirements).

[164] *See Ondo v. City of Cleveland*, 795 F.3d 597, 604 (6th Cir. 2015).

[165] *See Adickes v. S. H. Kress & Co.*, 398 U.S. 144, 158 n.17, 90 S.Ct. 1598, 1609 n.17, 26 L.Ed.2d 142 (1970); *Southern Grouts & Mortars, Inc. v. 3M Co.*, 575 F.3d 1235, 1248 n.8 (11th Cir. 2009). *Cf. Collins v. Seeman*, 462 F.3d 757, 760 n.1 (7th Cir. 2006) (rejecting unsworn written witness summaries); *Chaiken v. VV Pub. Corp.*, 119 F.3d 1018, 1033 (2d Cir. 1997) (same, for unsworn letters do not meet prerequisites); *Berwick Grain Co., Inc. v. Illinois Dept. of Agriculture*, 116 F.3d 231, 234 (7th Cir. 1997) (same, for unsworn transcript of witness interview).

[166] *See* Rule 56(c)(4) advisory committee note to 2010 amendments (noting that formal affidavits are "no longer required," and declarations under penalty of perjury pursuant to 28 U.S.C. § 1746 are sufficient).

[167] *See Stauffer v. Gearhart*, 741 F.3d 574, 581 (5th Cir. 2014). *But cf. Lantec, Inc. v. Novell, Inc.*, 306 F.3d 1003, 1019 (10th Cir. 2002) (district court properly refused to consider verified complaint as summary judgment affidavit where its allegations were merely conclusory).

[168] *See Lane v. Dep't of Interior*, 523 F.3d 1128, 1140 (9th Cir. 2008).

[169] *See Jain v. CVS Pharmacy, Inc.*, 779 F.3d 753, 758 (8th Cir. 2015).

believes are true, but does not *know* are true—are not proper.[170] Likewise, inferences and opinions must be premised on first-hand observations or personal experience.[171] A statement will not be rejected merely because it is a self-serving recitation by the party (indeed, it would make little sense for a party to submit one that was not self-serving).[172] But the self-serving affirmations must be more than mere conclusions or unsupported inferences; in other words, such statements must aver specific facts and otherwise satisfy the requirements of this Rule.[173]

- *Specific Admissible Facts:* The affidavit or declaration must also contain specific facts[174] which, in turn, must be admissible in evidence at time of trial.[175] For most courts, it is not necessary that the evidence be submitted in a *form* that would be admissible at trial (indeed, most summary judgment motions are supported and opposed by affidavit evidence), so long as the offered evidence may ultimately be presented at trial in an admissible form.[176] Thus, hearsay statements,[177] conclusory averments,[178] unfounded self-serving declarations,[179] ambiguous statements,[180] speculation or conjecture,[181] and inadmissible expert opinions[182] are generally improper in summary judgment affidavits and declarations. A party's promise that he or she has certain unidentified "additional evidence", which will be produced at trial, is insufficient to avoid summary judgment.[183]

- *Competence:* The affidavit or declaration must demonstrate that the maker is competent to testify as to the facts contained in the document.[184] Competence to testify may be inferred from the documents themselves.[185] Ordinarily, statements of counsel in a memorandum of law are not competent to support or oppose that litigant's own summary judgment position.[186]

---

[170] *See Automatic Radio Mfg. Co. v. Hazeltine Research,* 339 U.S. 827, 831, 70 S.Ct. 894, 896, 94 L. Ed. 1312 (1950).

[171] *See Briggs v. Potter,* 463 F.3d 507, 512 (6th Cir. 2006). *See also Payne v. Pauley,* 337 F.3d 767, 772 (7th Cir. 2003) (personal knowledge may include reasonable inferences grounded in observation or other first-hand experience; they may not be "flights of fancy, speculations, hunches, intuitions, or rumors about matters remote from that experience").

[172] *See Stewart v. Rise, Inc.,* 791 F.3d 849, 860–61 (8th Cir. 2015).

[173] *See Gonzalez v. Secretary of Dep't of Homeland Sec.,* 678 F.3d 254, 263 (3d Cir. 2012).

[174] *See Howard v. Kansas City Police Dep't,* 570 F.3d 984, 997 (8th Cir. 2009).

[175] *See Crews v. Monarch Fire Protection Dist.,* 771 F.3d 1085, 1092 (8th Cir. 2014).

[176] *See Alexander v. CareSource,* 576 F.3d 551, 558–59 (6th Cir. 2009).

[177] *See Crews v. Monarch Fire Protection Dist.,* 771 F.3d 1085, 1092 (8th Cir. 2014).

[178] *See SCR Joint Venture L.P. v. Warshawsky,* 559 F.3d 133, 138 (2d Cir. 2009). *See also Lujan v. National Wildlife Federation,* 497 U.S. 871, 888, 110 S.Ct. 3177, 3188, 111 L.Ed.2d 695 (1990) (noting that object of Rule 56 is not to replace conclusory averments in a pleading with conclusory allegations in an affidavit).

[179] *See Evans v. Technologies Applications & Service Co.,* 80 F.3d 954, 962 (4th Cir. 1996). *See also In re Kaypro,* 218 F.3d 1070, 1075 (9th Cir. 2000) ("self-serving" affidavit is not necessarily disqualified, so long as foundation was adequate).

[180] *See Archuleta v. Wal-Mart Stores, Inc.,* 543 F.3d 1226, 1234 (10th Cir. 2008).

[181] *See Stagman v. Ryan,* 176 F.3d 986, 995 (7th Cir. 1999).

[182] *See Felkins v. City of Lakewood,* 774 F.3d 647, 651–53 (10th Cir. 2014).

[183] *See Geske & Sons, Inc. v. N.L.R. B.,* 103 F.3d 1366, 1376 (7th Cir. 1997).

[184] *See Boyer-Liberto v. Fontainebleau Corp.,* 752 F.3d 350, 355 (4th Cir. 2014).

[185] *See Barthelemy v. Air Lines Pilots Ass'n,* 897 F.2d 999, 1018 (9th Cir. 1990) (noting that affiant's competence could be inferred from position with the company).

[186] *See Orson, Inc. v. Miramax Film Corp.,* 79 F.3d 1358, 1372 (3d Cir. 1996) (noting that legal memoranda and oral argument are not evidence and cannot independently create a genuine issue of disputed fact sufficient to preclude summary judgment).

- *"Acquired" Competence:* In appropriate circumstances, the makers of affidavits and declarations can "acquire" competence and personal knowledge they otherwise lack by research and a proper review of records.[187]

Affidavits and Declarations to Authenticate Summary Judgment Documents and Exhibits

Documents (even documents obtained through discovery) might not automatically become part of a summary judgment record merely because they are cited in a supporting memorandum.[188] Many courts have long required that every document used to support or oppose a summary judgment motion be authenticated through an affidavit or declaration, which must be made upon personal knowledge and must both identify and authenticate the offered document.[189] Documents that failed to satisfy this authentication requirement could be disregarded by the court in resolving the pending motion.[190] It remains unclear whether the 2010 Amendments to Rule 56 altered this practice.[191] The drafters had deleted earlier Rule language on which this authentication practice may have been based,[192] but did so for apparently unrelated reasons.[193] Moreover, the 2010 drafters had earlier emphasized that the Rule 56(c) amendments were not intended to dislodge prevailing local practices on submission form.[194]

"Vouching" Risk with Summary Judgment Affidavits

At least one court has ruled that a party offering a summary judgment affidavit or declaration effectively concedes that it qualifies for consideration (that is, that the statements made are sworn, made upon personal knowledge, factually specific and admissible, and competent). The court may properly deny a party's later, pretrial *in limine* motion to strike testimony that the same moving party had earlier itself offered in support of a summary judgment brief.[195]

Contradictory Sworn Evidence from Same Party

Most courts have embraced the "sham affidavit" rule, which ordinarily prevents a party from defeating summary judgment by simply denying, in an affidavit or declaration, a

---

[187] *See Nader v. Blair,* 549 F.3d 953, 963 (4th Cir. 2008) (affidavit from witness familiar with record-keeping practices). *But cf. Hernandez-Santiago v. Ecolab, Inc.,* 397 F.3d 30, 35 (1st Cir. 2005) (affidavit that represented merely the "review of relevant manufacturing and sales records" not sufficient, where affiant did not attest that he conducted or supervised review or had personal knowledge of results of review).

[188] *See Hoffman v. Applicators Sales and Serv., Inc.,* 439 F.3d 9, 15 (1st Cir. 2006).

[189] *See DG&G, Inc. v. FlexSol Packaging Corp. of Pompano Beach,* 576 F.3d 820, 825–26 (8th Cir. 2009).

[190] *See Scott v. Edinburg,* 346 F.3d 752, 759–60 n.7 (7th Cir. 2003).

[191] Some courts hold that the 2010 amendments changed this practice. *See Warner Bros. Entm't, Inc. v. X One X Prods.,* 644 F.3d 584, 592 n.4 (8th Cir. 2011) ("The current version of Rule 56 no longer requires attachment of a sworn or certified copy of each paper referenced in an affidavit," in preference to the objection procedure set out in Rule 56(c)(2)). Other courts seem to disagree. *See Smiley v. Columbia College Chicago,* 714 F.3d 998, 1005 (7th Cir. 2013) (documents must be authenticated by supporting affidavit).

[192] *See* Rule 56(e)(1) (rescinded 2010) ("If a paper or part of a paper is referred to in an affidavit, a sworn or certified copy must be attached to or served with the affidavit.").

[193] *See* Rule 56(c)(4) advisory committee notes to 2010 amendments ("The requirement that a sworn or certified copy of a paper referred to in an affidavit or declaration be attached to the affidavit or declaration is omitted as unnecessary given the requirement . . . that a statement or dispute of fact be supported by materials in the record.").

[194] *See* Rule 56(c)(1) advisory committee notes to 2010 amendments (noting that amended Rule 56(c)(1) "does not address the form for providing the required support," and that "[d]ifferent courts and judges have adopted different forms").

[195] *See Williams v. Trader Pub. Co.,* 218 F.3d 481, 485 (5th Cir. 2000) (in an employment case, party offered affidavits of certain male employees to support its summary judgment position, then later attempted to argue that the testimony of these same male employees was inadmissible because the male employees were not in situations "nearly identical" to the plaintiff; court ruled that the testimony was properly admitted because defendant, by introducing this same evidence at the summary judgment stage, contended that the evidence would be relevant and admissible at trial).

statement that the party had earlier admitted in a sworn statement.[196] To create a genuine dispute for trial sufficient to defeat summary judgment, such a party must, in addition to the denial itself, offer an explanation for the inconsistency that the district court finds adequate to allow a reasonable juror to *both* accept the current denial and yet still assume either the truth of, or the party's good faith belief in, the earlier sworn statement.[197] Where the original statement was truly ambiguous, and the later affidavit or declaration serves to clarify the testimony, the subsequent statement may be accepted.[198]

Form of Motion/Local Rule Requirements

Motions for summary judgment generally must be in writing.[199] Local rules may prescribe the briefing requirements for summary judgment motions, and such requirements have been enforced strictly.[200] These rules should always be consulted before briefing. In some judicial districts, for example, the local rules require the moving parties to compile a list of all material facts they believe are not in dispute, and require nonmoving parties to submit a counterstatement listing material facts they believe to be disputed.[201] A failure to contest the moving party's facts, in the manner prescribed by local rule, could constitute a concession accepting those facts as true.[202]

Miscellaneous Other Procedures

Over time, the federal courts have embraced various other local procedures for summary judgment practice, some local rule-based and some purely common law. Several of those are outlined below:

- *Party Admissions:* Admissions by a party-whether express (intentional acknowledgment) or through default (*e.g.,* where a party fails to deny Rule 36 requests for admission)-are considered conclusive as to the matters admitted, cannot be contradicted by affidavit or otherwise, and can support a grant of summary judgment.[203]

- *Transcribed Oral Testimony:* Deposition testimony may be used to support a motion for summary judgment, so long as the testimony meets the competence and admissibility requirements of Rule 56.[204]

- *Live Oral Testimony:* Entertaining live oral testimony in conjunction with a summary judgment motion is rare and problematic. Because the summary judgment procedure is intended to offer a speedy resolution when the material facts are undisputed, and because the trial court may not, under Rule 56, resolve

---

[196] *See In re Family Dollar FLSA Litig.,* 637 F.3d 508, 512–13 (4th Cir. 2011).

[197] *See Cleveland v. Policy Management Systems Corp.,* 526 U.S. 795, 804, 119 S.Ct. 1597, 1603, 143 L.Ed.2d 966 (1999).

[198] *See Stewart v. Rise, Inc.,* 791 F.3d 849, 861 (8th Cir. 2015).

[199] *See National Fire Ins. v. Bartolazo,* 27 F.3d 518, 520 (11th Cir. 1994).

[200] *See, e.g., Jackson v. Federal Exp.,* 766 F.3d 189, 194–95 (2d Cir. 2014).

[201] *See, e.g.,* M.D. Pa. Loc. R. 56.1 ("Upon any motion for summary judgment pursuant to Fed.R.Civ.P. 56, there shall be filed with the motion a separate, short and concise statement of the material facts, in numbered paragraphs, as to which the moving party contends there is no genuine issue to be tried. The papers opposing a motion for summary judgment shall include a separate, short and concise statement of the material facts, responding to the numbered paragraphs set forth in the statement required in the foregoing paragraph, as to which it is contended that there exists a genuine issue to be tried.").

[202] *See Jackson v. Federal Exp.,* 766 F.3d 189, 194–95 (2d Cir. 2014).

[203] *See In re Carney,* 258 F.3d 415, 420 (5th Cir. 2001).

[204] *See Baloco v. Drummond Co., Inc.,* 767 F.3d 1229, 1245 n.22 (11th Cir. 2014).

any facts that remain disputed, oral testimony in summary judgment proceedings will only be granted "sparingly" and "with great care".[205]

- *"Lodged" Not Filed Documents:* Documents attached to a submission that the court has refused to accept, although perhaps contained in the court clerk's official file, are not part of the summary judgment record.[206]

- *Briefs:* The court may consider concessions in a party's brief or during oral argument in gauging whether a genuine issue of material fact exists; otherwise, however, the parties' briefs are not evidence.[207]

Submitting New Evidence in the Reply

If the moving party introduces new evidence in a reply brief or memoranda, the trial court should not accept and consider the new evidence without first affording the non-moving party an opportunity to respond.[208]

Hearings and Oral Argument

Although the district court may, in its discretion, entertain a hearing or oral argument on the Rule 56 motion, hearings and oral argument are not obligatory.[209]

Multiple Summary Judgment Motions

The district court may permit a second motion for summary judgment,[210] especially where there has been an intervening change in the controlling law, where new evidence has become available or the factual record has otherwise expanded through discovery, or where a clear need arises to correct a manifest injustice.[211]

RULE 56(d)—WHEN FACTS ARE UNAVAILABLE TO THE NONMOVANT

CORE CONCEPT

Once a motion for summary judgment is filed, the non-moving party must show to the court that a genuine and material factual dispute exists to defeat summary judgment. If the non-moving party is still conducting productive discovery or for some other reason is not yet ready or able to make that showing, the party may file an affidavit or declaration explaining why a ruling on summary judgment should be postponed. The court, in its discretion, may then grant a temporary reprieve if the reasons offered are persuasive.

---

[205] *See Seamons v. Snow,* 206 F.3d 1021, 1025–26 (10th Cir. 2000).

[206] *See Nicholson v. Hyannis Air Serv., Inc.,* 580 F.3d 1116, 1127 & 1127 n.5 (9th Cir. 2009).

[207] *See Orson, Inc. v. Miramax Film Corp.,* 79 F.3d 1358, 1372 (3d Cir. 1996) (legal memoranda and oral argument are not evidence and cannot create a factual dispute that prevents summary judgment); *American Title Ins. Co. v. Lacelaw Corp.,* 861 F.2d 224, 226–27 (9th Cir. 1988) (noting that district court, in its discretion, may consider statements of fact contained in summary judgment briefing as party admissions for Rule 56 purposes).

[208] *See Mirando v. U.S. Dep't of Treasury,* 766 F.3d 540, 549 (6th Cir. 2014).

[209] *See* Rule 78(b) (authorizing determination of motions without oral argument). *See Jones v. Secord,* 684 F.3d 1, 6 (1st Cir. 2012).

[210] *See Hoffman v. Tonnemacher,* 593 F.3d 908, 910–12 (9th Cir. 2010).

[211] *See Lexicon, Inc. v. Safeco Ins. Co. of America, Inc.,* 436 F.3d 662, 670 n.6 (6th Cir. 2006) (where factual record has expanded); *Enlow v. Tishomingo County, Miss.,* 962 F.2d 501, 506 (5th Cir. 1992) (when new facts were presented by amended pleading).

APPLICATIONS

2010 Amendments—Amended Rule 56(d), Repositioned from Rule 56(f)

Current Rule 56(d) contains the content of former Rule 56(f)—without change in substance[212]—permitting the deferral or denial of summary judgment pending further discovery or for other reasons.

Purpose

The procedure created by Rule 56(d) serves a valuable purpose in summary judgment practice; it is the vehicle through which diligent litigants are assured a pre-ruling opportunity for fair discovery.[213] When properly invoked, Rule 56(d) serves as the "safety value" designed to abate a hasty swing of the "summary judgment axe".[214]

Affidavit Requirement for Motion

Some courts will not consider a Rule 56(d) request unless it is accompanied by a sworn affidavit or proper declaration.[215] Other courts accept representations of counsel (as officers of the court) as sufficient,[216] or, in appropriate circumstances, excuse the failure to submit a formal affidavit where all other necessary information has been supplied.[217]

Formal Request Requirement for Motion

A party seeking Rule 56(d) relief must make that request specifically, for example by plainly asking the trial court to deny the pending motion or to defer it until discovery is completed.[218] But the denial/deferral request need not necessarily be made by motion; indeed, the submission of affidavits or some other sworn declaration alone may be sufficient.[219] However, neglecting to seek relief at all,[220] or making passing mention in a footnote to a brief,[221] will not trigger the protection of this Rule.

Substantive Requirements for Motion

Although relief under this Rule is often and liberally granted,[222] it does not come automatically.[223] Before the courts will postpone a summary judgment ruling pending further discovery, the courts will generally require a Rule 56(d) movant to make three showings: (1) a description of the particular discovery the movant intends to seek; (2) an explanation showing how that discovery would preclude the entry of summary judgment; and (3) a statement justifying why this discovery had not been or could not have been obtained earlier.[224] Many courts require a further showing of a plausible basis for believing

---

[212] *See* Rule 56(d) advisory committee note to 2010 amendments.

[213] *See Toben v. Bridgestone Retail Operations, LLC*, 751 F.3d 888, 894 (8th Cir. 2014).

[214] *See Rivera-Torres v. Rey-Hernandez*, 502 F.3d 7, 10–11 (1st Cir. 2007).

[215] *See Sandusky Wellness Ctr., LLC v. Medco Health Solutions, Inc.*, 788 F.3d 218, 227 (6th Cir. 2015). *See also Pastore v. Bell Telephone Co. of Pennsylvania*, 24 F.3d 508, 511 (3d Cir. 1994) (noting that affidavit requirement ensures that the Rule's protection is being invoked in good faith and provides trial court with the showing necessary to assess the merits of the party's opposition to the motion).

[216] *See Baron Servs., Inc. v. Media Weather Innovations LLC*, 717 F.3d 907, 912 n.8 (Fed.Cir. 2013).

[217] *See Hicks v. Johnson*, 755 F.3d 738, 743 (1st Cir. 2014) (affidavit excused if statement received in "some other authoritative manner").

[218] *See Been v. O.K. Industries, Inc.*, 495 F.3d 1217, 1235 (10th Cir. 2007).

[219] *See Shelton v. Bledsoe*, 775 F.3d 554, 566–68 (3d Cir. 2015).

[220] *See Nieves-Romero v. United States,*715 F.3d 375, 381 (1st Cir. 2013).

[221] *See Allen v. Sybase, Inc.*, 468 F.3d 642, 662 (10th Cir. 2006).

[222] *See Shelton v. Bledsoe*, 775 F.3d 554, 568 (3d Cir. 2015).

[223] *See Hicks v. Johnson*, 755 F.3d 738, 743 (1st Cir. 2014).

[224] *See U.S. ex rel. Folliard v. Government Acquisitions, Inc.*, 764 F.3d 19, 25 (D.C.Cir. 2014).

that the sought-after facts likely exist.[225] Although the affidavit or declaration need not contain evidentiary facts,[226] the showings made must be specific[227]—vague or baldly conclusory statements will not suffice.[228] Nor will a vacant hope that discovery will yield helpful evidence,[229] or the mere assertion that critical evidence could lie in the opponent's possession.[230] Moreover, the affidavit or declaration containing these showings must be authoritative (that is, it must be taken by someone with first-hand knowledge of the statements made).[231] A fulsome showing of all requirements raises a strong presumption in favor of relief.[232] Conversely, a court is unlikely to grant relief where, for example, the moving party has not been diligent in beginning and pursuing discovery.[233] "Rule 56(d) is meant to minister to the vigilant, not to those who sleep upon perceptible rights."[234] If the moving party fails to adequately make any of these showings, the court may deny the requested postponement and rule upon the pending summary judgment motion.[235]

When Rule 56(d) Formalities May Not Be Required

Some courts have held that a postponement in entering summary judgment may still be appropriate, even in the absence of a Rule 56(d) affidavit or declaration, where the nonmoving party adequately notifies the trial court that summary judgment is premature and that additional discovery is necessary, and where the nonmoving party—through no fault—has had little or no opportunity for discovery.[236] *Pro se* litigants may, likewise, be forgiven some irregularities in the formality of their submissions.[237] Practitioners should be cautioned against relying on the hope of such liberal treatment; courts have "hasten[ed] to add that parties who ignore [the] affidavit requirement do so at their peril".[238]

Postponing Very Early Filed Motions for Summary Judgment

When a summary judgment motion is filed very early in the litigation, before a realistic opportunity for discovery, courts generally grant Rule 56(d) postponements freely.[239] In such cases, summary judgment should be refused as a matter of course,[240] with exceptions permitted in only rare cases.[241] With such early filed motions, the courts recognize that the

---

[225] *See Anzaldua v. Northeast Ambulance & Fire Protection Dist.*, 793 F.3d 822, 837 (8th Cir.2015).

[226] *See Price ex rel. Price v. Western Resources, Inc.*, 232 F.3d 779, 783–84 (10th Cir. 2000).

[227] *See Urquilla-Diaz v. Kaplan Univ.*, 780 F.3d 1039, 1063 (11th Cir. 2015).

[228] *See American Family Life Assur. Co. of Columbus v. Biles,* 714 F.3d 887, 894 (5th Cir. 2013).

[229] *See Anzaldua v. Northeast Ambulance & Fire Protection Dist.*, 793 F.3d 822, 836–37 (8th Cir.2015).

[230] *See Anzaldua v. Northeast Ambulance & Fire Protection Dist.*, 793 F.3d 822, 837 (8th Cir.2015).

[231] *See C.B. Trucking, Inc. v. Waste Management, Inc.*, 137 F.3d 41, 44 n.2 (1st Cir. 1998). *But cf. Simas v. First Citizens' Federal Credit Union,* 170 F.3d 37, 46 (1st Cir. 1999) (although movant must attest to personal knowledge of recited grounds, statement need not be presented in form admissible at trial, so long as it rises sufficiently above mere speculation; thus, reliance on hearsay is not necessarily a dispositive defect under this Rule).

[232] *See In re PHC, Inc. Shareholder Litig.*, 762 F.3d 138, 143 (1st Cir. 2014).

[233] *See Pina v. Children's Place,* 740 F.3d 785, 795 (1st Cir. 2014).

[234] *See Pina v. Children's Place,* 740 F.3d 785, 794–95 (1st Cir. 2014).

[235] *See Nitro Distrib., Inc. v. Alitcor, Inc.*, 565 F.3d 417, 430 (8th Cir. 2009). *See also Cervantes v. Jones,* 188 F.3d 805 (7th Cir. 1999) (affirming denial of motion where excuse for failing to conduct the deposition earlier was a desire to refrain from beginning discovery in order to "foster an atmosphere conducive to settlement").

[236] *See Nader v. Blair,* 549 F.3d 953, 961 (4th Cir. 2008).

[237] *See Dewitt v. Corizon, Inc.*, 760 F.3d 654, 659 (7th Cir. 2014). *But see Crowley v. Bannister,* 734 F.3d 967, 978–79 (9th Cir. 2013) (trial court has no obligation to specially notify *pro se* litigants of Rule 56(d) and its function).

[238] *See Harrods Ltd. v. Sixty Internet Domain Names,* 302 F.3d 214, 246 (4th Cir. 2002) (making comment, and "reiterat[ing]" that our court expects full compliance" with Rule). *See also Bradley v. United States,* 299 F.3d 197, 207 (3d Cir. 2002) (noting "strong presumption against a finding of constructive compliance" with Rule).

[239] *See Shelton v. Bledsoe,* 775 F.3d 554, 565 (3d Cir. 2015).

[240] *See Anderson v. Liberty Lobby, Inc.,* 477 U.S. 242, 250 n.5, 106 S.Ct. 2505, 91 L.Ed.2d 202 (1986).

[241] *See CenTra, Inc. v. Estrin,* 538 F.3d 402, 420–21 (6th Cir. 2008).

Rule 56(d) affiant or declarant may not be capable of framing a postponement request with great specificity.[242] Nevertheless, even with very early motions, Rule 56(d) relief may still be denied where the supporting affidavit or declaration is especially vague or conclusory or where additional discovery could not make a factual or legal difference to the outcome.[243]

Timing

A Rule 56(d) motion to postpone a summary judgment ruling must be made in a timely fashion, which at least generally means before the party files a response to the pending motion or, in any event, prior to any scheduled oral argument on the motion.[244] A party may not wait until after the court rules on the main Rule 56 motion. Thus, a party may not attempt to defeat the summary judgment motion on its merits and, only if an adverse ruling is entered, seek the Rule 56(d) extension for discovery in an effort to pursue reconsideration.[245]

Burden on the Movant

The party moving to postpone the summary judgment ruling bears the burden of demonstrating the requisite basis for relief under Rule 56(d).[246]

District Court's Discretion and Options

Whether to grant or deny a Rule 56(d) postponement is committed to the district court's discretion.[247] In ruling, the district court must balance the moving party's need for the requested discovery against the burden the discovery and delay will place on the opposing party.[248] Ordinarily, such requests are construed and granted liberally;[249] denying properly made and supported motions is "disfavored,"[250] especially following a showing that much of the sought-after information lies within the control of an adversary (particularly a recalcitrant one).[251] On the basis of a party's meritorious Rule 56(d) showings, the district court may: (1) deny the motion for summary judgment; (2) grant a continuance to allow affidavits to be prepared and submitted; (3) permit discovery; or (4) make any other order as is just.[252] If the court is presented with a Rule 56(d) motion, it generally may not proceed to decide the summary judgment motion without first considering and ruling upon the Rule 56(d) request.[253]

RULE 56(e)—FAILING TO PROPERLY SUPPORT OR ADDRESS A FACT

CORE CONCEPT

When a party fails to properly support or oppose a motion for summary judgment, the court has several options. It may grant summary judgment (but only when such an order is proper and never

---

[242] See *Burlington Northern Santa Fe R. Co. v. Assiniboine and Sioux Tribes of Fort Peck Reservation,* 323 F.3d 767, 773–74 (9th Cir. 2003) (noting that affiant cannot be expected to frame motion with great specificity as to nature of discovery likely to develop useful information because ground for such specificity has not yet been laid).

[243] See *CenTra, Inc. v. Estrin,* 538 F.3d 402, 420 (6th Cir. 2008).

[244] See *In re PHC, Inc. Shareholder Litig.,* 762 F.3d 138, 144 (1st Cir. 2014).

[245] See *Nieves-Romero v. United States,* 715 F.3d 375, 381 (1st Cir. 2013).

[246] See *Urquilla-Diaz v. Kaplan Univ.,* 780 F.3d 1039, 1063 (11th Cir. 2015).

[247] See *Pisano v. Strach,* 743 F.3d 927, 931 (4th Cir. 2014).

[248] See *Harbert Intern., Inc. v. James,* 157 F.3d 1271, 1280 (11th Cir. 1998).

[249] See *Shelton v. Bledsoe,* 775 F.3d 554, 568 (3d Cir. 2015).

[250] See *Ingle ex rel. Estate of Ingle v. Yelton,* 439 F.3d 191, 196 (4th Cir. 2006).

[251] See *In re PHC, Inc. Shareholder Litig.,* 762 F.3d 138, 144–45 (1st Cir. 2014).

[252] See *Ellis v. J.R.'s Country Stores, Inc.,* 779 F.3d 1184, 1206 (10th Cir. 2015).

[253] See *Doe v. Abington Friends School,* 480 F.3d 252, 257 (3d Cir. 2007).

merely because a party has procedurally defaulted on its burdens). It may grant the delinquent party a further opportunity to show its support or opposition. It may consider the unaddressed fact to be undisputed for the purpose of the motion. Or it may issue some other appropriate order.

APPLICATIONS

No Summary Judgments by "Default"

Summary judgment may not be entered automatically, upon the non-moving party's failure to respond at all or to respond properly.[254] Likewise, summary judgment may not be denied automatically, simply because the moving party failed to reply properly to the opponent's response.[255] The 2010 Amendments emphasize these points.[256] Instead, summary judgment may be granted only if it is appropriate to do so.[257] Consequently, although it is assuredly a dangerous practice to fail to oppose a summary judgment motion, even entirely uncontested motions must be examined carefully by the district court to determine whether no genuine dispute of material fact remains and whether judgment is appropriate as a matter of law.[258] Although the trial court may, under this Rule, properly consider facts to be undisputed for purposes of the motion,[259] it may not do so reflexively—merely because they were listed on the moving party's uncontested itemization of undisputed facts; instead, the court must consult the summary judgment record and satisfy itself that evidence supports the relief sought.[260] Of course, this does not compel the court to review all evidentiary materials on file, but it must at least review those materials supporting the motion itself.[261] Moreover, the district court's order should recount that it addressed the underlying motion on its merits.[262]

District Court's Options if Support Is Improper

When confronting an improperly supported motion or an improperly supported opposition, the court has several choices in how to respond:

- *Another Chance:* The court may (or may choose not to, in its discretion[263]) permit the delinquent party a further opportunity to file a proper motion or response, with Rule 56(c)-qualifying support.[264] The drafters presume that this choice is likely to be a court's "preferred first step".[265]

- *"Deemed" Undisputed:* A fact improperly contested by the opponent in its response, or a fact improperly contested by the movant its reply, may be considered by the

---

[254] *See Jackson v. Federal Exp.*, 766 F.3d 189, 194–95 (2d Cir. 2014).

[255] *See* Rule 56(e) advisory committee note to 2010 amendments.

[256] *See* Rule 56(e) advisory committee note to 2010 amendments ("summary judgment cannot be granted by default" upon either a complete failure to respond or a failure to respond properly).

[257] *See* Rule 56(a) (summary judgment entered only if no genuine dispute of material facts exists *and* movant is entitled to judgment).

[258] *See F.T.C. v. E.M.A. Nationwide, Inc.*, 767 F.3d 611, 629–30 (6th Cir. 2014).

[259] *See Vermont Teddy Bear Co., Inc. v. 1-800 Beargram Co.*, 373 F.3d 241, 244 (2d Cir. 2004).

[260] *See Jackson v. Federal Exp.*, 766 F.3d 189, 194–95 (2d Cir. 2014).

[261] *See* Rule 56(c)(3). *See also United States v. One Piece of Real Prop. Located at 5800 SW 74th Ave., Miami, Fla.,* 363 F.3d 1099, 1101–02 (11th Cir.2004).

[262] *See United States v. One Piece of Real Prop. Located at 5800 SW 74th Ave., Miami, Fla.,* 363 F.3d 1099, 1101–02 (11th Cir.2004).

[263] *See Martin v. Halifax Healthcare Systems, Inc.*, 621 Fed.Appx. 594, 600–01 (11th Cir. 2015) (no abuse of discretion in denying supplement where reason for delay not explained).

[264] *See* Rule 56(e)(1). *See also Cobalt Multifamily Investors I, LLC v. Shapiro*, 9 F.Supp.2d 399, 402 (S.D.N.Y. 2014) (granting additional response time).

[265] *See* Rule 56(e)(1) advisory committee note to 2010 amendments.

court to be undisputed.[266] The court is not compelled to do so, however,[267] especially if it is aware that the summary judgment record shows the fact to be genuinely disputed.[268] If the court does treat the fact as undisputed, that consequence is limited to the summary judgment motion only; if the delinquent party survives summary judgment, he or she is not barred from contesting the fact in later proceedings.[269]

- *Grant Summary Judgment:* Because a party's delinquent response cannot, alone, compel summary judgment,[270] summary judgment is properly granted following a delinquent response only if the standards for summary judgment are otherwise satisfied.[271] As to those standards, the court must conduct a full, normal inquiry.[272]

- *Other Appropriate Order:* The court may also enter some other appropriate order, when designed to prompt a proper presentation of the record.[273] Nudging *pro se* litigants forward,[274] striking a deficient submission and ordering its amendment,[275] striking off improper portions of affidavits,[276] and denying summary judgment but inviting a new motion later[277] are examples.

Pro Se Motions

In considering summary judgment motions involving *pro se* litigants, the courts construe liberally the *pro se* party's pleadings, but are not obligated to act as the party's advocate.[278]

Warning to Pro Se Litigants

Before summary judgment may be entered against unrepresented litigants, some courts have required that the unrepresented party first be expressly informed of the consequences of failing to come forward with contradicting evidence (*e.g.*, the party must be told he or she cannot rely merely on the allegations of the pleadings, and risks dismissal in doing so).[279] Other courts adopt this special warning duty only in the context of incarcerated

---

[266] *See* Rule 56(e)(2). *See also Ondo v. City of Cleveland*, 795 F.3d 597, 603 (6th Cir. 2015). *Compare Peck v. NAES Corp.*, 307 F.R.D. 43, 46 (D.D.C. 2014) (treating facts as undisputed), *with Dell's Maraschino Cherries Co. v. Shoreline Fruit Growers, Inc.*, 887 F.Supp.2d 459, 466 n.5 (E.D.N.Y. 2012) (declining to treat facts as undisputed).

[267] *See Warkentin v. Federated Life Ins. Co.*, 594 Fed.Appx. 900, 902–03 (9th Cir. 2014).

[268] *See* Rule 56(e)(2) advisory committee note to 2010 amendments.

[269] *See* Rule 56(e)(2) advisory committee note to 2010 amendments.

[270] *See supra* Authors' Commentary to Rule 56(e) (**"No Summary Judgment by 'Default' "**).

[271] *See* Rule 56(e)(3). *See also In re Nat'l Pool Constr., Inc.*, 598 Fed.Appx. 841, 845 (3d Cir. 2015).

[272] *See* Rule 56(e)(3) advisory committee note to 2010 amendments (noting that, even as to "deemed" undisputed facts, court "must determine the legal consequences of these facts and possible inferences from them").

[273] *See* Rule 56(e)(4). *See also Hammond v. City of Wilkes-Barre*, 600 Fed.Appx. 833, 837 n.7 (3d Cir. 2015).

[274] *See* Rule 56(e)(4) advisory committee note to 2010 amendments. *See also infra* Authors' Commentary to Rule 56(e) (**"Warning to Pro Se Litigants"**).

[275] *See Alcarmen v. J.P. Morgan Chase Bank*, 2014 WL 3368647, at *3 (N.D. Cal. July 8, 2014).

[276] *See Phat's Bar & Grill, Inc. v. Louisville-Jefferson County Metro Gov't*, 2013 WL 142481, at *3–*4 (W.D.Ky. Jan. 11, 2013).

[277] *See Johnson v. Railroad Controls, L.P.*, 2014 WL 3123659, at *5–*6 (W.D. La. July 7, 2014).

[278] *See Cardoso v. Calbone*, 490 F.3d 1194, 1197 (10th Cir. 2007). *See also supra* Authors' Commentary to Rule 8(e) (**"Pleadings Drafted by Laypersons"**).

[279] *See United States v. Ninety Three Firearms*, 330 F.3d 414, 427 (6th Cir. 2003) (collecting cases); *Rand v. Rowland*, 154 F.3d 952, 960–61 (9th Cir. 1998) (en banc).

unrepresented parties;[280] as to nonprisoner unrepresented parties, those courts would require no special warning.[281]

RULE 56(f)—JUDGMENT INDEPENDENT OF THE MOTION

CORE CONCEPT

Provided the court gives the parties notice and a reasonable time to respond, it may grant summary judgment in favor of a party who has not sought it, grant summary judgment on different grounds than those requested by the litigants, or grant summary judgment *sua sponte*.

APPLICATIONS

Summary Judgment for Non-Moving Parties

In resolving a pending motion for summary judgment, the court may grant summary judgment in favor of a party who has not requested it.[282] Before doing so, the court must give the parties notice and reasonable time to respond.[283] This might occur in at least two contexts. First, in a multi-defendant case where one co-defendant obtains summary judgment on motion, the court may enter a similar summary judgment *sua sponte* in favor of other similarly situated non-moving co-defendants.[284] Second, a court that denies a moving party's request for summary judgment may enter an unrequested summary judgment *against* that party and in favor of the non-moving party. Such judgments are generally only entered if the court is convinced that the factual record is fully developed, that the non-moving party is "clearly" entitled to judgment, and that entry of the judgment would not result in procedural prejudice to the moving party.[285] Before granting such relief, the court must find that entering summary judgment is both proper and is procedurally sound (that its entry does not offend fundamental fairness).[286]

Summary Judgment on Unrequested Grounds

In resolving a pending motion for summary judgment, the court may grant summary judgment on grounds not requested by the parties.[287] Before doing so, the court must give the parties notice and reasonable time to respond.[288] Even without proper notice, such summary judgments are permitted where that oversight proves to be harmless.[289] This is a change from prior practice, which had generally foreclosed such grants [290] or limited them to only situations that would suffice for *sua sponte* summary judgments.[291]

---

[280] *See United States v. Ninety Three Firearms,* 330 F.3d 414, 427–28 (6th Cir. 2003).

[281] *See United States v. Ninety Three Firearms,* 330 F.3d 414, 428 (6th Cir. 2003) (citing other precedent in concluding that this distinction "was only fair because parties choosing to have counsel 'must bear the risk of their attorney's mistakes,' and thus, 'a litigant who chooses himself as a legal representative should be treated no differently' ").

[282] *See* Rule 56(f)(1).

[283] *See* Rule 56(f)(1). *See also Albino v. Baca,* 747 F.3d 1162, 1176–77 (9th Cir. 2014).

[284] *See Judson Atkinson Candies, Inc. v. Latini-Hohberger Dhimantec,* 529 F.3d 371, 384–85 (7th Cir. 2008).

[285] *See Faustin v. City and County of Denver, Colo.,* 423 F.3d 1192, 1198–99 (10th Cir. 2005).

[286] *See Caswell v. City of Detroit Housing Com'n,* 418 F.3d 615, 617–18 (6th Cir.2005).

[287] *See* Rule 56(f)(2).

[288] *See* Rule 56(f)(2). *See also Jehovah v. Clarke,* 798 F.3d 169, 177 (4th Cir. 2015).

[289] *See Smith v. Perkins Bd. of Educ.,* 708 F.3d 821, 829 (6th Cir. 2013).

[290] *See Washburn v. Harvey,* 504 F.3d 505, 510 (5th Cir. 2007).

[291] *See Byars v. Coca-Cola Co.,* 517 F.3d 1256, 1264–65 (11th Cir. 2008).

Summary Judgment *Sua Sponte*

The court may enter summary judgment *sua sponte*.[292] In doing so, the court will apply the usual summary judgment standards, resolving all ambiguities and drawing all factual inferences in the target party's favor.[293] But the case law cautions great care in the grant of *sua sponte* summary judgments.[294] In practice, *sua sponte* summary judgments should be unnecessary because the trial court may always invite a party to file a summary judgment motion.[295]

Where the court considers entering a *sua sponte* judgment, it must first ensure that proper advance notice of this intention has been made.[296] A litigant must appreciate that he is the "target" of a summary judgment inquiry, and possess that motivation when preparing the response.[297] This notice must identify for the parties those material facts that the court believes might not be genuinely disputed.[298] The court must also confirm that the litigants have a full and fair opportunity to respond.[299] These notice-and-opportunity requirements apply even when the *sua sponte* summary judgment is entered against a party who, already, has moved for summary judgment.[300]

Prior to the 2010 Amendments, certain case law practices regarding *sua sponte* summary judgments had developed over time. Some courts had held that discovery must either be completed or clearly be of no further benefit, before *sua sponte* summary judgments could be granted.[301] Other courts had held that notice to the litigants need not be explicit, if the affected party is "fairly appraised" under the circumstances.[302] Previously, an order granting summary judgment *sua sponte* without notice was generally reversed unless the nonmoving party had waived this right or unless it was clear that the non-moving party suffered no prejudice (*e.g.*, because there was no additional evidence for the record or because none of the evidence would create a genuine issue of material fact).[303] Other courts had excused the notice and response requirement where three criteria were met: the summary judgment record was fully developed, there was no prejudice to the non-moving party, and the decision rested on a purely legal issue.[304]

RULE 56(g)—FAILING TO GRANT ALL OF THE REQUESTED RELIEF

CORE CONCEPT

After considering the standards for summary judgment, the court may conclude that such a judgment is not appropriate at all or not appropriate as to every claim or defense for which it was sought. Nevertheless, the inquiry might have revealed that certain material facts are not genuinely

---

[292] *See* Rule 56(f)(3). *See also Celotex Corp. v. Catrett*, 477 U.S. 317, 326, 106 S.Ct. 2548, 2554, 91 L.Ed.2d 265 (1986) (noting district court's right to enter *sua sponte* motions under Rule 56).

[293] *See NetJets Aviation, Inc. v. LHC Communications, LLC*, 537 F.3d 168, 178 (2d Cir. 2008).

[294] *See First American Kickapoo Operations, L.L.C. v. Multimedia Games, Inc.*, 412 F.3d 1166, 1170 (10th Cir. 2005) (practice is "not encourage[d]").

[295] *See Goldstein v. Fidelity and Guar. Ins. Underwriters, Inc.*, 86 F.3d 749, 751 (7th Cir. 1996).

[296] *See Georgia State Conf. of NAACP v. Fayette Cty. Bd. of Com'rs*, 775 F.3d 1336, 1344 (11th Cir. 2015).

[297] *See John G. Alden, Inc. of Mass. v. John G. Alden Ins. Agency of Fla., Inc.*, 389 F.3d 21, 25 (1st Cir. 2004).

[298] *See* Rule 56(f)(3).

[299] *See Hotel 71 Mezz Lender LLC v. Nat'l Ret. Fund*, 778 F.3d 593, 603 (7th Cir. 2015).

[300] *See Bridgeway Corp. v. Citibank*, 201 F.3d 134, 139–40 (2d Cir. 2000).

[301] *See Priestley v. Headminder, Inc.*, 647 F.3d 497, 504 (2d Cir. 2011).

[302] *See Priestley v. Headminder, Inc.*, 647 F.3d 497, 504 (2d Cir. 2011).

[303] *See Farouki v. Petra Int'l Banking Corp.*, 705 F.3d 515, 517 (D.C.Cir. 2013).

[304] *See DL Resources, Inc. v. First-Energy Solutions Corp.*, 506 F.3d 209, 223–24 (3d Cir. 2007).

disputed. The court may (but is not required to) declare those facts as established for purposes of the case.

APPLICATIONS

2010 Amendments—Amended Rule 56(g), Repositioned from Rules 56(c) and (d)

The current content of Rule 56(g) prescribes the trial court's ability to declare as undisputed those individual facts that the summary judgment inquiry showed to be not genuinely disputed. Former Rules 56(c) and (d) had set out this procedure previously, with one notable distinction. The prior language had seemed to urge the court to make such a ruling (using the verb "should"); the amended Rule is more permissive (with the verb "may").

Purpose of the "Declaring-as-Established" Procedure

The goal of this procedure is to allow trial courts to salvage some constructive result from their efforts in ruling upon otherwise denied (or partially denied) summary judgment motions.[305] Where the summary judgment inquiry demonstrates that certain material facts are not genuinely disputed, the court may declare them established for trial, even though summary judgment itself is being fully or partially denied.[306] Such declared-facts may accelerate litigations by winnowing down the number of issues that must be tried.[307]

Which Facts May Be Declared as Established

Provided the fact is a *material* one, any fact may be declared as undisputed by the court, including liability and damages facts (and even particular items of damages).[308]

Standard for Declaring Facts as Established

Because this procedure is in the nature of a collateral byproduct of the summary judgment inquiry itself, the standard for declaring facts to be established is the same standard used in granting summary judgment.[309] The parties need not *agree* on which material facts are undisputed (or that any of them are).[310] Rather, the burden of demonstrating that a material fact is genuinely undisputed lies with the moving party, employing the same burden-of-going-forward shift used with summary judgment motions generally.[311]

District Court's Discretion

The trial judge is not required to use this procedure to declare facts to be established for trial. Instead, the decision lies entirely within the trial judge's discretion.[312] Thus, for example, the court may decide that the exercise of declaring facts to be established will be more burdensome than addressing those facts through other means (like trial), or may

---

[305] *See D'Iorio v. Winebow, Inc.*, 68 F.Supp.3d 334, 356 (E.D.N.Y. 2014).

[306] *See F.D.I.C. v. Massingill*, 24 F.3d 768, 774 (5th Cir. 1994).

[307] *See Global Crossing Bandwidth, Inc. v. Locus Telecommc'n, Inc.*, 632 F.Supp.2d 224, 238 (W.D.N.Y. 2009).

[308] *See, e.g., Muir Enters. Inc. v. Deli Nation LLC*, 998 F.Supp.2d 1220, 1222 (D. Utah 2014) (establishing facts in an agricultural dispute); *United States v. Univ. of Neb. at Kearney*, 940 F.Supp.2d 974, 976–83 (D.Neb. 2013) (establishing that collegiate student housing are "dwellings" within the meaning of the Fair Housing Act).

[309] *See* Rule 56(g) advisory committee note to 2010 amendments. *See also California v. Campbell*, 138 F.3d 772, 780 (9th Cir. 1998).

[310] *See Global Crossing Bandwidth, Inc. v. Locus Telecommc'n, Inc.*, 632 F.Supp.2d 224, 238 (W.D.N.Y. 2009).

[311] *See Green v. Sun Life Assur. Co. of Canada*, 383 F.Supp.2d 1224, 1226 (C.D. Cal. 2005).

[312] *See* Rule 56(g) advisory committee note to 2010 amendments ("Even if the court believes that a fact is not genuinely in dispute it may refrain from ordering that the fact be treated as established."). *See also Triple H Debris Removal, Inc. v. Companion Prop. & Cas. Ins. Co.*, 647 F.3d 780, 785–86 (8th Cir. 2011).

conclude that a full trial may better illuminate those facts.[313] Nor is the court necessarily required, if it grants relief under this Rule, to set out the declared facts in a *separate* order.[314]

No Interference with Opposing Party's Strategy

Parties opposing summary judgment may choose strategically to concede (or to not affirmatively dispute) a certain fact, and to do so for summary judgment motion purposes only. The court must take care to ensure that such strategic, procedural concessions are not used to declare a fact as established when, at trial, it will be contested.[315]

Making a Motion to Declare-as-Established

Under the earlier version of this procedure, courts were divided whether parties could file an independent motion seeking to have certain facts declared as established.[316] The current language of the Rule has not resolved this uncertainty. Some courts held that litigants could only seek full (or partial) summary judgments and not "declared-as-established" facts,[317] or alternatively, that any such independent motion be made only "in the wake" of such an unsuccessful full motion.[318] Other courts rejected this reasoning, and permitted the filing of distinct motions seeking "declared-as-established" rulings.[319]

Effect of Declared-as-Established Rulings

If the court chooses to grant them, "declared-as-established" rulings are not "judgments" and do not become "final orders" until the district court enters a judgment disposing of the entire case.[320] Nevertheless, such declarations are still rulings on a "dispositive motion",[321] and will be accorded treatment as "law of the case".[322] Thus, the parties are entitled to rely on the conclusiveness of the declaration [323] and, absent good reason for doing so, the district court will not generally revisit or alter the issues adjudicated under Rule 56(g).[324] Nevertheless, such declarations are not immutable and have no *res judicata* effect; they may, under appropriate circumstances, be revisited.[325] If the court later decides that good reasons exist to alter a "declared-as-established" ruling, the court must so inform the parties and permit them an opportunity to present evidence concerning any of the revisited issues.[326]

---

[313] *See* Rule 56(g) advisory committee note to 2010 amendments. *See also Triple H Debris Removal, Inc. v. Companion Prop. & Cas. Ins. Co.*, 647 F.3d 780, 785–86 (8th Cir. 2011).

[314] *See U.S. Bank Nat'l Ass'n v. Verizon Commc'ns, Inc.*, 761 F.3d 409, 427 n.15 (5th Cir. 2014).

[315] *See also* Rule 56(g) advisory committee note to 2010 amendments. *See Triple H Debris Removal, Inc. v. Companion Prop. & Cas. Ins. Co.*, 647 F.3d 780, 785–86 (8th Cir. 2011).

[316] *See Beaty v. Republic of Iraq*, 480 F.Supp.2d 60, 100 (D.D.C. 2007) (discussing division), *rev'd on other grounds*, 556 U.S. 848, 129 S.Ct. 2183, 173 L.Ed.2d 1193 (2009).

[317] *See, e.g., Mullaney v. Hilton Hotels Corp.*, 634 F.Supp.2d 1130, 1161 (D.Haw. 2009).

[318] *See Kendall McGaw Labs., Inc. v. Community Mem. Hosp.*, 125 F.R.D. 420, 421 (D.N.J. 1989).

[319] *See, e.g., Zapata Hermanos Sucesores, S.A. v. Hearthside Baking Co., Inc.*, 313 F.3d 385, 391 (7th Cir. 2002).

[320] *See Alberty-Velez v. Corporacion de Puerto Rico Para La Difusion Publica*, 361 F.3d 1, 6 n.5 (1st Cir. 2004).

[321] *See Burkhart v. Washington Metropolitan Area Transit Auth.*, 112 F.3d 1207, 1215–16 (D.C. Cir. 1997).

[322] *See Burge v. Parish of St. Tammany*, 187 F.3d 452, 467 (5th Cir. 1999).

[323] *See Huss v. King Co., Inc.*, 338 F.3d 647, 650–51 (6th Cir. 2003).

[324] *See Carr v. O'Leary*, 167 F.3d 1124, 1126 (7th Cir. 1999).

[325] *See Latin American Music Co. v. Media Power Group, Inc.*, 705 F.3d 34, 40–41 (1st Cir. 2013).

[326] *See Alberty-Velez v. Corporacion de Puerto Rico Para La Difusion Publica*, 361 F.3d 1, 6 n.5 (1st Cir. 2004). *See also Joseph P. Caulfield & Assocs., Inc. v. Litho Prods., Inc.*, 155 F.3d 883, 888 (7th Cir. 1998) (holding that proper procedure to seek a revisitation of the adjudicated issues is to file a motion to vacate the ruling and request either that the issues be added to the trial or that they be resolved as a matter of law in favor of the moving party).

RULE 56(h)—AFFIDAVIT OR DECLARATION SUBMITTED IN BAD FAITH

CORE CONCEPT

If the district court concludes that an affidavit or declaration submitted in a summary judgment proceeding was presented in bad faith or solely for purposes of delay, the court may order the offending party to pay reasonable expenses incurred by the party's adversary (including attorney's fees) as a result of the improper affidavits or declarations.

APPLICATIONS

2010 Amendments—Repositioned as Rule 56(h)

Rule 56(h) sets forth the penalties for summary judgment affidavits and declarations made in bad faith. That content is repositioned here from its former location in Rule 56(g).

Purpose

The submission of bad faith affidavits and declarations derails, in an illegitimate way, the summary judgment process by creating the false impression of a genuine, material factual dispute that must await trial. Because the impression is not real, but dishonestly simulated, the maneuver forces the parties and the court to incur the time and costs of an unnecessary trial.[327] Rule 56(h) is intended to combat that abuse.

Express Requirements: Bad Faith or Delay

Less frequently invoked or granted,[328] this Rule permits the court to compensate a party who confronts summary judgment affidavits or declarations submitted either in bad faith or solely for purposes of delay.[329] One of those two situations must be proven [330] (or both may, because the bad faith motivation may be delay).[331] Thus, the mere disbelief by one party of the truth of an affidavit or declaration is not sufficient,[332] nor is the mere presence of a conflict between the affidavit or declaration and other testimony.[333] Instead, the circumstances must be "egregious"[334]—a "deliberate or knowing act for an improper purpose"[335]—such as perjurious or blatantly false allegations or facts,[336] a contradiction without a bona fide explanation,[337] or a statement made without color, with dishonesty of

---

[327] See United States v. Nguyen, 655 F.Supp.2d 1203, 1210 (S.D.Ala. 2009).

[328] See Fort Hill Builders, Inc. v. National Grange Mut. Ins. Co., 866 F.2d 11, 16 (1st Cir. 1989).

[329] See In re Gioioso, 979 F.2d 956, 961–62 (3d Cir.1992).

[330] See Klein v. Stahl GMBH & Co. Maschinefabrik, 185 F.3d 98, 110 (3d Cir. 1999). But cf. Hunt v. Tektronix, Inc., 952 F.Supp. 998, 1010 (W.D. N.Y. 1997) (denying sanctions where affiant's actions, though "unfortunate", were not deliberately taken in bad faith).

[331] See United States v. Nguyen, 655 F.Supp.2d 1203, 1210 (S.D.Ala. 2009).

[332] See Moorer v. Grumman Aerospace Corp., 964 F.Supp. 665, 676 (E.D. N.Y. 1997), aff'd, 162 F.3d 1148 (2d Cir. 1998).

[333] See Thoroughman v. Savittieri, 323 Fed. Appx. 548, 551 (9th Cir. 2009). See also OSA Healthcare, Inc. v. Mount Vernon Fire Ins. Co., 975 F.Supp.2d 1316, 1319 (N.D. Ga. 2013) (discerning when affidavit inconsistency crosses line into fabrication "is no easy matter"). See generally Cleveland v. Policy Mgmt. Sys. Corp., 526 U.S. 795, 804, 119 S.Ct. 1597, 1603, 143 L.Ed.2d 966 (1999) (party ordinarily cannot defeat summary judgment by simply denying, in an affidavit, a statement that the party had earlier admitted in a sworn statement unless an adequate explanation for the inconsistency is offered).

[334] See Fort Hill Builders, Inc. v. National Grange Mut. Ins. Co., 866 F.2d 11, 16 (1st Cir. 1989).

[335] See Rexroat v. Arizona Dep't of Educ., 2012 WL 5936672, at *4 (D.Ariz. Nov. 26, 2012).

[336] See Fort Hill Builders, Inc. v. National Grange Mut. Ins. Co., 866 F.2d 11, 16 (1st Cir. 1989).

[337] See Caron v. QuicKutz, Inc., 2012 WL 5497869, at *20 (D.Ariz. Nov. 13, 2012), aff'd, 528 Fed. Appx. 993 (Fed.Cir. 2013).

belief or motive, or asserted wantonly or to harass, delay, or for some other improper purpose.[338] The district courts have wide discretion in conducting this analysis.[339]

"Implied" Requirements: Prejudice and Causation

The Rule's language seems austere, yet some courts have implied additional prerequisites for relief under the Rule. Some courts require the moving party to show prejudice before sanctions are awarded,[340] and some courts will not award sanctions unless the offending document was actually considered by judge in resolving a summary judgment motion.[341]

District Court's Discretion

Sanctions for violating this Rule are now discretionary, not mandatory.[342] This is a change from prior practice.[343] But no sanctions may be imposed until the offending party is first afforded notice and a reasonable time to respond.[344]

Available Sanctions

The district court enjoys an array of choices to address bad faith affidavits or declarations in summary judgment practice. The courts may strike the offending affidavits,[345] compel the offenders to reimburse their adversaries for reasonable expenses (including attorney's fees) incurred by the submission,[346] hold the offenders or their counsel in contempt,[347] and impose "other appropriate sanctions."[348] Moreover, false swearing could also expose the offending party to criminal prosecution.[349]

Submissions from or to *Pro Se* Litigants

Some courts apply this sanctions Rule more gently in cases involving affidavits or declarations submitted by *pro se* litigants.[350] It is uncertain whether *pro se* litigants, if victimized by sanctionable conduct, are eligible to recover expenses or "fees" under this Rule.[351]

---

[338] *See Bowers v. University of Virginia,* 2008 WL 2346033, at *4 (W.D. Va. 2008). *See also Nuzzi v. St. George Cmty. Consol. Sch. Dist. No. 258,* 688 F.Supp.2d 815, 834 (C.D. Ill. 2010) (finding 100-page-long rambling, unsupported, "ranting" affidavits violate Rule).

[339] *See Turner v. Baylor Richardson Medical Center,* 476 F.3d 337, 349 (5th Cir. 2007).

[340] *See Trustees of Plumbers and Steamfitters Local Union No. 43 Health and Welfare Fund v. Crawford,* 573 F.Supp.2d 1023, 1039 (E.D. Tenn. 2008).

[341] *See, e.g., Sutton v. U.S. Small Bus. Admin.,* 92 Fed. Appx. 112, 117–18 (6th Cir.2003).

[342] *See* Rule 56(h) advisory committee note to 2010 amendments. *See also Denson v. BeavEx Inc.,* 2014 WL 3543718, at *11 (S.D. Tex. July 17, 2014) (noting change).

[343] *See Scott v. Metropolitan Health Corp.,* 234 Fed. Appx. 341, 345 (6th Cir. 2007). The curious explanation for this shift from mandatory to discretionary imposition was the drafters' observation that "courts seldom invoke the independent Rule 56 authority to impose sanctions." *See* Rule 56(h) advisory committee note to 2010 amendments.

[344] *See* Rule 56(h).

[345] *See Caron v. QuicKutz, Inc.,* 2012 WL 5497869, at *20 (D.Ariz. Nov. 13, 2012), *aff'd,* 528 Fed. Appx. 993 (Fed.Cir. 2013).

[346] *See Klein v. Stahl GMBH & Co. Maschinefabrik,* 185 F.3d 98, 110 (3d Cir. 1999).

[347] *See Klein v. Stahl GMBH & Co. Maschinefabrik,* 185 F.3d 98, 110 (3d Cir. 1999).

[348] *See* Rule 56(h).

[349] *See* 18 U.S.C.A. § 1623 (prescribing that person who makes a knowingly false material declaration to a court is subject to a $10,000 fine, five years in prison, or both).

[350] *See Boggs v. Die Fliedermaus, LLP,* 286 F.Supp.2d 291, 302 (S.D. N.Y. 2003) (finding sanctions inappropriate where litigant appeared *pro se,* no bad faith evidence existed, there had not been repeated unmeritorious filings, and no prior warnings to litigant had been given by the court).

[351] *See Coble v. Renfroe,* 2012 WL 4971997, at *2 (W.D.Wash. Oct. 17, 2012).

Submissions Made in Any Summary Judgment Setting

The Rule applies to all affidavits and declarations made in a summary judgment context, including those made by both the moving and non-moving parties under Rule 56(c), as well as affidavits and declarations under Rule 56(d) seeking to postpone a summary judgment ruling.[352]

Submissions Made in Non-Summary Judgment Settings

By its terms, this Rule applies only to affidavits and declarations presented in the summary judgment context. Affidavits and declarations submitted for other purposes, or in support of relief under other Rules, are not subject to Rule 56(h).[353]

ADDITIONAL RESEARCH REFERENCES

Wright & Miller, *Federal Practice and Procedure* §§ 2711 to 2742

C.J.S., Federal Civil Procedure §§ 1135 to 1187 et seq., §§ 1189 to 1216 et seq.

West's Key Number Digest, Federal Civil Procedure ⟜2461 to 2559

---

[352] *See Range v. Brubaker,* 2009 WL 161699, at *2 (N.D.Ind. Jan. 21, 2009) (applies to Rule 56(f) affidavits).

[353] *See Lownsberry v. Lees,* 2008 WL 4852791, at *5 (E.D.Mich. Nov. 7, 2008).

RULE 57

DECLARATORY JUDGMENT

These rules govern the procedure for obtaining a declaratory judgment under 28 U.S.C. § 2201. Rules 38 and 39 govern a demand for a jury trial. The existence of another adequate remedy does not preclude a declaratory judgment that is otherwise appropriate. The court may order a speedy hearing of a declaratory-judgment action.

[Amended effective October 20, 1949; April 30, 2007, effective December 1, 2007.]

AUTHORS' COMMENTARY ON RULE 57

PURPOSE AND SCOPE

Rule 57 permits parties to obtain a declaratory judgment to determine their rights and obligations in cases involving actual controversies. The Rule operates in conjunction with the federal Declaratory Judgment Act, 28 U.S.C.A. §§ 2201 to 02.

APPLICATIONS

Purpose

A declaratory judgment declares the rights and obligations of litigants. Its purpose is to afford litigants an early opportunity to resolve their federal disputes so as to avoid the threat of impending litigation,[1] and obtain both clarity in their legal relationships and the ability to make responsible decisions about their future.[2] Lacking an ultimately coercive effect capable of being remedied through contempt, it is considered a "milder" form of relief.[3] Nevertheless, it often provides very practical litigation solutions. It allows controversies to be settled before they mature into full-fledged violations of law or breaches of duty.[4] It enables probable-defendants to terminate a non-litigation standstill where the very delay in filing the lawsuit is a plaintiff's strategy.[5] It permits defendants who are confronting multiple claims to pursue an adequate, expedient, and comparably inexpensive declaration of rights that may avoid a multiplicity of actions.[6] In each of these ways, and others, declaratory judgments provide a prudent procedural vehicle for "clearing the air".[7]

Relationship Between Rule 57 and 28 U.S.C. § 2201

Courts have held that the federal Declaratory Judgment Act, 28 U.S.C.A. §§ 2201 to 02, is "mirrored by" and "functionally equivalent to" Rule 57.[8]

---

[1] *See Severe Records, LLC v. Rich,* 658 F.3d 571, 580 (6th Cir. 2011).

[2] *See Medtronic, Inc. v. Mirowski Family Ventures, LLC,* ___ U.S. ___, 134 S.Ct. 843, 850, 187 L.Ed.2d 703 (2014).

[3] *See Steffel v. Thompson,* 415 U.S. 452,471, 94 S.Ct. 1209, 39 L.Ed.2d 505 (1974).

[4] *See Maytag Corp. v. Int'l Union, United Auto., Aerospace & Agricultural Implement Workers of Am.,* 687 F.3d 1076, 1081–82 (8th Cir. 2012).

[5] *See Shell Gulf of Mexico Inc. v. Center for Biological Diversity, Inc.,* 771 F.3d 632, 635 (9th Cir. 2014). *See generally Medtronic, Inc. v. Mirowski Family Ventures, LLC,* ___ U.S. ___, 134 S.Ct. 843, 850, 187 L.Ed.2d 703 (2014) (procedure "rescues" a litigant from the dilemma of either abandoning rights or facing lawsuit).

[6] *See Biodiversity Legal Foundation v. Badgley,* 309 F.3d 1166, 1172 (9th Cir. 2002).

[7] *See Microchip Technology Inc. v. Chamberlain Group, Inc.,* 441 F.3d 936, 943 (Fed. Cir. 2006).

[8] *See Ernst & Young v. Depositors Economic Protection Corp.,* 45 F.3d 530, 534 n.8 (1st Cir. 1995).

The Constitutional Requirements: Subject Matter Jurisdiction, Actual Controversy, and Ripeness

Subject Matter Jurisdiction. A plaintiff seeking declaratory relief must establish an independent basis for the district court's subject matter jurisdiction (*e.g.,* diversity of citizenship or federal question).[9] Neither Rule 57 nor the Declaratory Judgment Act expands the court's jurisdiction; these provisions only provide a declaratory remedy in cases properly brought in federal court.[10]

♦ **NOTE:** In diversity cases, the amount in controversy is measured by the value of the object of the litigation.[11] In federal question cases, the district courts will apply the "well-pleaded complaint" rule to assess whether the plaintiff's action involves a federal question. Thus, where the federal nature of plaintiff's claim comes only from plaintiff's anticipation that the defendant will assert a federal defense, the court is likely to find that the plaintiff's claim lacks subject matter jurisdiction.[12] Likewise, where the declaratory judgment action is an "inverted" one (*i.e.,* the natural defendant filing against the natural plaintiff), it is the true claim, and not the defense, that vests subject matter jurisdiction.[13]

Actual Controversy. The district court may only enter a declaratory judgment where the dispute between the parties is definite and concrete, affecting the parties' adverse legal interests with sufficient immediacy as to justify relief.[14] No declaratory judgment may be entered where the parties' dispute is hypothetical, abstract, or academic.[15] Whether an actual controversy exists will be measured at the time the complaint was filed; post-filing events are not sufficient.[16]

♦ **NOTE:** The Supreme Court has confirmed that declaratory relief is available where the plaintiff is threatened by adverse government action, and has noted (without criticism) that the lower federal courts have long agreed that declaratory relief is available where the plaintiff is threatened by adverse action from a private party.[17]

Ripeness. The actual controversy requirement obligates the court to determine that the case is "ripe" for adjudication.[18] This "ripeness" must remain throughout the lawsuit. Thus, the district court must decide at the time it is about to enter judgment whether an

---

[9]   For further discussion on this point, *see* Part II of this text §§ 2.10 to 2.13 on subject matter jurisdiction.

[10]   *See Medtronic, Inc. v. Mirowski Family Ventures, LLC,* ___ U.S. ___, 134 S.Ct. 843, 848, 187 L.Ed.2d 703 (2014); *Vaden v. Discover Bank,* 556 U.S. 49, 70 n.19, 129 S.Ct. 1262, 1278 n.19, 173 L.Ed.2d 206 (2009); *Schilling v. Rogers,* 363 U.S. 666, 677, 80 S.Ct. 1288, 1295, 4 L.Ed.2d 1478 (1960); *Aetna Life Ins. Co. of Hartford, Conn. v. Haworth,* 300 U.S. 227, 240, 57 S.Ct. 461, 463, 81 L. Ed. 617 (1937).

[11]   *See Hunt v. Wash. State Apple Adver. Comm'n,* 432 U.S. 333, 347, 97 S.Ct. 2434, 53 L.Ed.2d 383 (1977).

[12]   *See Public Service Commission of Utah v. Wycoff Co., Inc.,* 344 U.S. 237, 73 S.Ct. 236, 97 L. Ed. 291 (1952). *See also Skelly Oil Co. v. Phillips Petroleum Co.,* 339 U.S. 667, 673, 70 S.Ct. 876, 880, 94 L. Ed. 1194 (1950) ("It would turn into the federal courts a vast amount of litigation indubitably arising under State law, in the sense that the right to be vindicated was State-created, if a suit for a declaration of rights could be brought into the federal courts merely because an anticipated defense derived from federal law").

[13]   *See Medtronic, Inc. v. Mirowski Family Ventures, LLC,* ___ U.S. ___, 134 S.Ct. 843, 848, 187 L.Ed.2d 703 (2014).

[14]   *See MedImmune, Inc. v. Genentech, Inc.,* 549 U.S. 118, 127, 127 S.Ct. 764, 771, 166 L.Ed.2d 604 (2007); *Maryland Cas. Co. v. Pacific Coal & Oil Co.,* 312 U.S. 270, 61 S.Ct. 510, 85 L. Ed. 826 (1941); *Aetna Life Ins. Co. of Hartford, Conn. v. Haworth,* 300 U.S. 227, 57 S.Ct. 461, 81 L. Ed. 617 (1937). *Cf. Calderon v. Ashmus,* 523 U.S. 740, 118 S.Ct. 1694, 140 L.Ed.2d 970 (1998) (holding that declaratory judgments cannot be sought merely for the purpose of testing the validity of a defense that a State may possibly raise in some future, as yet unfiled habeas proceeding).

[15]   *See MedImmune, Inc. v. Genentech, Inc.,* 549 U.S. 118, 127, 127 S.Ct. 764, 771, 166 L.Ed.2d 604 (2007).

[16]   *See Vantage Trailers, Inc. v. Beall Corp.,* 567 F.3d 745, 748 (5th Cir. 2009).

[17]   *See MedImmune, Inc. v. Genentech, Inc.,* 549 U.S. 118, 129–30, 127 S.Ct. 764, 772–73, 166 L.Ed.2d 604 (2007).

[18]   *See Pittsburgh Mack Sales & Service, Inc. v. Int'l Union of Operating Eng'rs, Local Union No. 66,* 580 F. 3d 185, 190 (3d Cir. 2009).

actual controversy still exists between the parties. Thus, even if an actual controversy existed at the time the lawsuit was filed, the court will not enter a declaratory judgment if later events ended the controversy and the dispute has become moot.[19]

◆ **NOTE:** The courts recognize an exception to this mootness limitation where the plaintiff is able to show a substantial likelihood that the dispute will re-occur in the future.[20]

The Prudential Concerns: Exercise of Discretion

Declaratory relief is never automatic or obligatory.[21] The courts have no "unflagging duty" to hear declaratory judgment cases.[22] Whether to grant or deny declaratory relief is vested in the sound discretion of the district court.[23] Likewise, the court has the discretion in fashioning the relief, and its extent.[24] This discretion, though wide, is not boundless; the district court may not refuse on "whim or personal disinclination" to hear a declaratory judgment action, but must instead base its refusal on good reason [25] (such as when the declaration would serve no useful purpose).[26] If the court decides not to entertain the declaratory proceeding, it may either stay or dismiss the federal action, and may enter such an order before trial or after all arguments come to a close.[27]

Factors for Court's Consideration

To decide whether to entertain a declaratory judgment action, courts generally assess three concerns: efficiency, fairness, and federalism.[28] To do so, courts may weigh various factors, including: (1) the likelihood that a federal declaration will resolve the uncertainty of obligation which gave rise to the controversy; (2) the parties' convenience; (3) the public interest in settling the uncertainty; (4) the availability and relative convenience of other remedies; (5) the restraint favored when the same issues are pending in a State court; (6) avoidance of duplicative litigation; (7) preventing the declaratory action's as a method of procedural fencing or a race for *res judicata;* and (8) (in insurance contexts), the inherent conflict of interest between an insurer's duty to defend and its attempt to characterize the federal action as falling within the scope of a policy exclusion.[29] (The fact that a declaratory judgment action was commenced before a later-filed coercive lawsuit is unlikely to carry dispositive weight.[30]) This list of factors in not exhaustive.[31]

---

[19] *See Preiser v. Newkirk,* 422 U.S. 395, 95 S.Ct. 2330, 45 L.Ed.2d 272 (1975); *Golden v. Zwickler,* 394 U.S. 103, 89 S.Ct. 956, 22 L.Ed.2d 113 (1969).

[20] *See Super Tire Engineering Co. v. McCorkle,* 416 U.S. 115, 94 S.Ct. 1694, 40 L.Ed.2d 1 (1974).

[21] *See Wilton v. Seven Falls Co.,* 515 U.S. 277, 288, 115 S.Ct. 2137, 132 L.Ed.2d 214 (1995).

[22] *See Diaz-Fonseca v. Puerto Rico,* 451 F.3d 13, 39 (1st Cir. 2006).

[23] *See MedImmune, Inc. v. Genentech, Inc.,* 549 U.S. 118, 136, 127 S.Ct. 764, 776, 166 L.Ed.2d 604 (2007); *Provident Tradesmens Bank & Trust Co. v. Patterson,* 390 U.S. 102, 88 S.Ct. 733, 19 L.Ed.2d 936 (1968). *See also Wilton v. Seven Falls Co.,* 515 U.S. 277, 281, 115 S.Ct. 2137, 2140, 132 L.Ed.2d 214 (1995) (noting that, even when subject matter jurisdiction prerequisites are otherwise satisfied, district courts enjoy discretion to determine whether, in what circumstances, to entertain declaratory judgment action).

[24] *See Strawberry Water Users Ass'n v. United States,* 576 F.3d 1133, 1142 (10th Cir. 2009).

[25] *See Public Affairs Associates, Inc. v. Rickover,* 369 U.S. 111, 112, 82 S.Ct. 580, 7 L.Ed.2d 604 (1962).

[26] *See Cincinnati Indem. Co. v. A & K Const. Co.,* 542 F.3d 623, 625 (8th Cir. 2008).

[27] *See Wilton v. Seven Falls Co.,* 515 U.S. 277, 287, 115 S.Ct. 2137, 2143, 132 L.Ed.2d 214 (1995).

[28] *See Western World Ins. Co. v. Hoey,* 773 F.3d 755, 759 (6th Cir. 2014).

[29] *See Morgan Drexen, Inc. v. Consumer Fin. Protection Bureau,* 785 F.3d 684, 696–97 (D.C.Cir. 2015) (listing certain factors).

[30] *See Morgan Drexen, Inc. v. Consumer Fin. Protection Bureau,* 785 F.3d 684, 697 (D.C.Cir. 2015) (proper question is not which was filed first, but which will best serve justice and the parties' needs).

[31] *See Morgan Drexen, Inc. v. Consumer Fin. Protection Bureau,* 785 F.3d 684, 696 (D.C.Cir. 2015).

- *Effect of Parallel Pending State Lawsuits:* When another lawsuit is pending in State court raising the same issues and involving the same parties, the federal court may choose to abstain from exercising jurisdiction to hear a related federal declaratory judgment action,[32] and is likely to do so unless, after rigorous examination, it is assured that other factors justify proceeding.[33] (Such abstention will, however, be rare if the federal action seeks both declaratory and nondeclaratory relief.[34]) Conversely, when no such parallel lawsuits are pending elsewhere, the federal court retains the discretion to decline to hear the federal case,[35] though the absence of parallel State proceedings militates heavily in favor of exercising federal jurisdiction.[36]

Statement of Circumstances Supporting Declaratory Jurisdiction

If a party contests the prudence of the district court's exercise of discretion to hear a declaratory judgment claim, the court must articulate the factual circumstances supporting the award of declaratory relief,[37] unless the claim would exist independently of the declaration request.[38]

Realignment of the Parties

In determining whether to grant a declaratory judgment, the courts may realign the parties in order to reflect the nature of the actual, underlying controversy.[39] In making this determination, the courts may consider the underlying purposes of declaratory relief, the parties' respective burdens of proof, and the best, clearest method for presenting evidence to the jury.[40] Where both sides will carry proof burdens at trial, realignment may properly be refused.[41]

Burden of Proof

A party seeking a declaratory judgment bears the burden of proving the existence of an actual case or controversy.[42] But the courts are divided on the question of the merits burden of proof in declaratory judgment actions. Because a declaratory judgment plaintiff often seeks a determination that the defendant lacks some type of right that, had defendant filed suit first, the defendant would bear the burden of proving, some courts permit a shift in the burden of proof.[43]

Type of Relief Available

The court may grant a successful plaintiff whatever relief is warranted by the evidence, regardless of the demand in the plaintiff's complaint. The Declaratory Judgment Act

---

[32] *See Morgan Drexen, Inc. v. Consumer Fin. Protection Bureau,* 785 F.3d 684, 694 (D.C.Cir. 2015). *See generally Wilton v. Seven Falls Co.,* 515 U.S. 277, 282, 115 S.Ct. 2137, 132 L.Ed.2d 214 (1995).

[33] *See Reifer v. Westport Ins. Corp.,* 751 F.3d 129, 144–45 (3d Cir. 2014).

[34] *See VonRosenberg v. Lawrence,* 781 F.3d 731, 735 (4th Cir. 2015).

[35] *See Reifer v. Westport Ins. Corp.,* 751 F.3d 129, 143–44 (3d Cir. 2014) (joining majority of other Circuits in so holding).

[36] *See Reifer v. Westport Ins. Corp.,* 751 F.3d 129, 144 (3d Cir. 2014).

[37] *See Reifer v. Westport Ins. Corp.,* 751 F.3d 129, 146–47 & 146 n.22 (3d Cir. 2014).

[38] *See Vasquez v. Rackauckas,* 734 F.3d 1025, 1039–40 (9th Cir. 2013).

[39] *See BASF Corp. v. Symington,* 50 F.3d 555, 557 (8th Cir. 1995).

[40] *See Fresenius Medical Care Holdings, Inc. v. Baxter Int'l, Inc.,* 2006 WL 1646110, at *1 (N.D. Cal. 2006).

[41] *See Anheuser-Busch, Inc. v. John Labatt Ltd.,* 89 F.3d 1339, 1344 (8th Cir. 1996).

[42] *See Cardinal Chemical Co. v. Morton Int'l Inc.,* 508 U.S. 83, 94, 113 S.Ct. 1967, 1974, 124 L.Ed.2d 1 (1993).

[43] *See Reliance Life Ins. Co. v. Burgess,* 112 F.2d 234, 238 (C.C.A. 8th Cir. 1940). *See also American Eagle Ins. Co. v. Thompson,* 85 F.3d 327, 331 (8th Cir. 1996) (burden remains on the party asserting the affirmative on an issue); *Utah Farm Bureau Ins. Co. v. Dairyland Ins. Co.,* 634 F.2d 1326, 1328 (10th Cir.1980) (noting divergent views on burden of proof in declaratory judgment actions).

provides that further relief can be awarded after reasonable notice and hearing. The courts, for example, possess "broad power" to make damages awards in declaratory judgment actions where appropriate.[44]

♦ **NOTE:** The Eleventh Amendment ordinarily does not preclude declaratory judgment proceedings instituted against State officials.[45]

Effect on Later Lawsuit for Different Remedy

Courts often recognize an exception to claim preclusion theory where the only relief sought in an original lawsuit is declaratory; in such cases, the plaintiff is often permitted to pursue a second claim for either injunctive relief or damages.[46]

The Existence of Other Possible Remedies

With one exception, declaratory relief is not foreclosed merely by showing that an adequate remedy other than a declaratory judgment exists.[47] A declaratory judgment may be entered whether or not further relief is sought or could have been awarded.[48] However, the existence of another, adequate remedy may convince the district court to exercise its discretion to deny declaratory relief in favor of some better or more effective remedy.[49] Moreover, where declaratory relief will not terminate the controversy, but further remedies will be sought in a different or subsequent proceeding, the declaratory judgment can be refused.[50]

Exception: Where a special statutory proceeding has been provided to adjudicate a special type of case, declaratory relief may not be awarded.[51]

Partial Remedy

If it exercises its discretion to hear a declaratory judgment case, the trial court is not obligated to rule on every issue presented. The court may, instead, properly choose to decide some of the issues raised and decline to decide others.[52]

Declaratory vs. Injunctive Remedies

As between a declaratory or injunctive remedy, the district court enjoys discretion. Although a declaratory judgment cannot be enforced in contempt, it is "a real judgment, not just a bit of friendly advice"; it fixes the litigants' legal rights.[53] Nevertheless, it is likely to be a more simple and less elaborate order than an injunction.[54]

---

[44] *See United Teacher Assocs. Ins. Co. v. Union Labor Life Ins. Co.,* 414 F.3d 558, 570 (5th Cir. 2005).

[45] *See Native Village of Noatak v. Blatchford,* 38 F.3d 1505, 1513–14 (9th Cir. 1994).

[46] *See Allan Block Corp. v. County Materials Corp.,* 512 F.3d 912, 916–17 (7th Cir. 2008).

[47] *See Reifer v. Westport Ins. Corp.,* 751 F.3d 129, 136 (3d Cir. 2014).

[48] *See Powell v. McCormack,* 395 U.S. 486, 89 S.Ct. 1944, 23 L.Ed.2d 491 (1969).

[49] *See National Private Truck Council, Inc. v. Oklahoma Tax Com'n,* 515 U.S. 582, 589, 115 S.Ct. 2351, 2356, 132 L.Ed.2d 509 (1995) (commenting that the availability of an adequate remedy at law may make declaratory relief unwarranted).

[50] *See* Rule 57 advisory committee note ("A declaratory judgment is appropriate when it will 'terminate the controversy' giving rise to the proceeding. . . . When declaratory relief will not be effective in settling the controversy, the court may decline to grant it.").

[51] *See Katzenbach v. McClung,* 379 U.S. 294, 296, 85 S.Ct. 377, 13 L.Ed.2d 290 (1964).

[52] *See Henglein v. Colt Industries Operating Corp.,* 260 F.3d 201, 210–11 (3d Cir. 2001).

[53] *See Badger Catholic, Inc. v. Walsh,* 620 F.3d 775, 782 (7th Cir. 2010).

[54] *See Badger Catholic, Inc. v. Walsh,* 620 F.3d 775, 782 (7th Cir. 2010).

Any Party May Seek a Declaratory Judgment

Any party who has an interest in an actual controversy has standing to seek a declaratory judgment.

Who Declaratory Judgments Benefit

Ordinarily, a declaratory judgment is effective only as to the plaintiffs who obtained it. Often, however, such relief has far broader ramifications (such as in cases declaring the invalidity of a statute or patent).

Rules of Procedure

All rules of procedure applicable generally to civil lawsuits apply in a declaratory judgment action.[55] Thus, for example, no declaratory relief request is properly before the court until it is pleaded in a complaint for declaratory judgment,[56] and the *Twombly* plausibility standard governs the adequacy of such a pleading.[57]

Expedited Treatment

The district court may order a speedy hearing in declaratory judgment cases, and may move such cases to the top of the court's calendar.

Jury Trial

The right to a jury trial is preserved in declaratory judgment actions. If the issues would have been triable by a jury had something other than declaratory relief been sought, a right to a jury trial exists.[58]

Common Uses

Classically, declaratory judgments are often useful in insurance cases, to resolve policy coverage and interpretation disputes,[59] and in intellectual property cases, to resolve questions of validity and infringement.[60] But declaratory judgments have a far broader range. For example, they may be useful in deciding the constitutionality of government laws,[61] immunity questions,[62] land title and property rights,[63] competition and trade claims,[64] scope of entitlements to beneficiaries,[65] and prisoner rights.[66]

Cautious Uses

The district court frequently will refrain from declaratory relief in cases involving important public issues, where the concreteness of a monetary or injunctive dispute is more

---

[55] *See Garanti Finansal Kiralama A.S. v. Aqua Marine & Trading Inc.,* 697 F.3d 59, 63 (2d Cir. 2012).

[56] *See Arizona v. City of Tucson,* 761 F.3d 1005, 1009–11 (9th Cir. 2014).

[57] *See Karnatcheva v. JPMorgan Chase Bank, N.A.,* 704 F.3d 545, 547 (8th Cir. 2013).

[58] *See Simler v. Conner,* 372 U.S. 221, 83 S.Ct. 609, 9 L.Ed.2d 691 (1963); *Beacon Theatres, Inc. v. Westover,* 359 U.S. 500, 79 S.Ct. 948, 3 L.Ed.2d 988 (1959). *See also Marseilles Hydro Power, LLC v. Marseilles Land and Water Co.,* 299 F.3d 643, 649 (7th Cir. 2002) (a claim by a litigant who, at common law, would have been a defendant, then a jury right exists; if, however, the action is the counterpart of an equity suit, no jury right exists).

[59] *See, e.g., Aetna Life Ins. Co. of Hartford, Conn. v. Haworth,* 300 U.S. 227, 57 S.Ct. 461, 81 L. Ed. 617 (1937).

[60] *See, e.g., CLS Bank Int'l v. Alice Corp. Pty. Ltd.,* 685 F.3d 1341, 1348 (Fed.Cir. 2012).

[61] *See, e.g., Greater Baltimore Ctr. for Pregnancy Concerns, Inc. v. Mayor of Baltimore,* 683 F.3d 539, 550 (4th Cir. 2012).

[62] *See, e.g., Aetna Life Ins. Co. of Hartford, Conn. v. Haworth,* 300 U.S. 227, 57 S.Ct. 461, 81 L. Ed. 617 (1937).

[63] *See, e.g., Nixon v. AgriBank, FCB,* 686 F.3d 912, 913 (8th Cir.2012).

[64] *See, e.g., Pensacola Motor Sales Inc. v. Eastern Shore Toyota, LLC,* 684 F.3d 1211, 1222 (11th Cir. 2012).

[65] *See, e.g., Fleisher v. Standard Ins. Co.,* 679 F.3d 116, 120 (3d Cir. 2012) (ERISA dispute).

[66] *See, e.g., McFaul v. Valenzuela,* 684 F.3d 564, 569 (5th Cir. 2012).

advisable.[67] The district judge will also often deny declaratory relief that would act to interfere with a State criminal prosecution.[68]

Improper Uses

Declaratory relief is generally not available to merely adjudicate past conduct or to proclaim that one litigant is liable to another.[69] It is also not available where a special statutory proceeding has been provided to adjudicate a special type of case.[70] And it is often not available in federal and State tax cases, particularly where State law provides for efficient tax challenges and remedies, and where the action contests the constitutionality of a State tax provision.

Appealability

Whether a declaratory judgment order is immediately appealable depends upon the nature of the court's ruling. Once the court disposes of all the issues presented in the declaratory judgment action (either by ruling upon them or by declining to rule upon them), the resulting declaratory judgment becomes complete, final, and appealable.[71] Conversely, if the court enters an order resolving certain of the issues presented, but expressly leaves open for later resolution other issues in the case, the order is merely interlocutory and, therefore, not immediately appealable under the final order doctrine.[72]

ADDITIONAL RESEARCH REFERENCES:

Wright & Miller, *Federal Practice and Procedure* §§ 2751 to 2771, §§ 2781 to 2787

C.J.S., Declaratory Judgments §§ 1 to 24 et seq., §§ 25 to 75, §§ 76 to 126, §§ 127 to 142 et seq., §§ 143 to 165; Federal Civil Procedure §§ 1227 to 1231 et seq.

West's Key Number Digest, Declaratory Judgment ⊷1 to 395

---

[67] *See Public Affairs Associates, Inc. v. Rickover,* 369 U.S. 111, 82 S.Ct. 580, 7 L.Ed.2d 604 (1962).

[68] *See Samuels v. Mackell,* 401 U.S. 66, 91 S.Ct. 764, 27 L.Ed.2d 688 (1971).

[69] *See Corliss v. O'Brien,* 200 Fed. Appx. 80, 84–85 (3d Cir. 2006).

[70] *See The New York Times Co. v. Gonzales,* 459 F.3d 160, 166 (2d Cir. 2006) (such proceedings include petitions for habeas corpus and motions to vacate criminal sentences, proceedings under the Civil Rights Act of 1964, and certain administrative proceedings).

[71] *See Henglein v. Colt Industries Operating Corp.,* 260 F.3d 201, 211 (3d Cir. 2001).

[72] *See Henglein v. Colt Industries Operating Corp.,* 260 F.3d 201, 211 (3d Cir. 2001).

RULE 58

ENTERING JUDGMENT

(a) Separate Document. Every judgment and amended judgment must be set out in a separate document, but a separate document is not required for an order disposing of a motion:

(1) for judgment under Rule 50(b);

(2) to amend or make additional findings under Rule 52(b);

(3) for attorney's fees under Rule 54;

(4) for a new trial, or to alter or amend the judgment, under Rule 59; or

(5) for relief under Rule 60.

(b) Entering Judgment.

(1) *Without the Court's Direction.* Subject to Rule 54(b) and unless the court orders otherwise, the clerk must, without awaiting the court's direction, promptly prepare, sign, and enter the judgment when:

(A) the jury returns a general verdict;

(B) the court awards only costs or a sum certain; or

(C) the court denies all relief.

(2) *Court's Approval Required.* Subject to Rule 54(b), the court must promptly approve the form of the judgment, which the clerk must promptly enter, when:

(A) the jury returns a special verdict or a general verdict with answers to written questions; or

(B) the court grants other relief not described in this subdivision (b).

(c) Time of Entry. For purposes of these rules, judgment is entered at the following times:

(1) if a separate document is not required, when the judgment is entered in the civil docket under Rule 79(a); or

(2) if a separate document is required, when the judgment is entered in the civil docket under Rule 79(a) and the earlier of these events occurs:

(A) it is set out in a separate document; or

(B) 150 days have run from the entry in the civil docket.

(d) Request for Entry. A party may request that judgment be set out in a separate document as required by Rule 58(a).

(e) Cost or Fee Awards. Ordinarily, the entry of judgment may not be delayed, nor the time for appeal extended, in order to tax costs or award fees. But if a timely motion for attorney's fees is made under Rule 54(d)(2), the court may act before a notice of appeal has been filed and become effective to order that the motion have the same effect under Federal Rule of Appellate Procedure 4(a)(4) as a timely motion under Rule 59.

[Amended December 27, 1946, effective March 19, 1948; January 21, 1963, effective July 1, 1963; April 22, 1993, effective December 1, 1993; April 29, 2002, effective December 1, 2002; April 30, 2007, effective December 1, 2007.]

AUTHORS' COMMENTARY ON RULE 58

PURPOSE AND SCOPE

Rule 58 sets the procedure by which the district court enters judgments on its docket records. The date a judgment is "entered" on the district court docket triggers the time for making post-trial motions, for taking an appeal, and for executing on the relief awarded.

RULE 58(a)—SEPARATE DOCUMENT

CORE CONCEPT

To avoid uncertainty about when the clock for taking an appeal begins to tick, the district courts are required to set forth most judgments (and amended judgments) in a "separate document".

APPLICATIONS

The "Old" Separate Document Rule

Prior to 2002, a judgment was required to be set forth in writing, in a "separate document", and entered on the docket. These requirements were intended to create a "bright line" for litigants and the courts in determining when finality attached and, thus, when the period for seeking an appeal began.[1] To abate any uncertainty as to when the appeal "clock" would start ticking, the courts generally applied these requirements mechanically.[2] Until each requirement was met, the judgment was not deemed to have been entered[3] and the time for filing an appeal would not begin to run.[4]

What resulted was a significant body of interpretative case law construing the "separate document" requirement, and deciding what, if any, effect it would have on the appeal period. Some cases explained how rulings orally announced from the bench[5] or included within the text of a minute-order, a memorandum, or a written opinion[6] could not qualify as "judgments" under Rule 58. Other cases explained how a little, but not too much, collateral discussion by the trial court might be overlooked when included on the "judgment" document.[7] Still other cases explained that the "separate document" requirement could be waived because it was not jurisdictional.[8] Some courts determined that waiver could occur

---

[1] *See Fogade v. ENB Revocable Trust,* 263 F.3d 1274, 1285–86 (11th Cir. 2001).

[2] *See Trotter v. Regents of University of New Mexico,* 219 F.3d 1179, 1183 (10th Cir. 2000).

[3] *See United States v. Indrelunas,* 411 U.S. 216, 93 S.Ct. 1562, 36 L.Ed.2d 202 (1973).

[4] *See Carter v. Hodge,* 726 F.3d 917, 919–20 (7th Cir. 2013) (under the prior Rule, "a losing party had forever to appeal if the district court never entered a Rule 58 judgment. Forever is too long.") (citations omitted).

[5] *See Atlantic Richfield Co. v. Monarch Leasing Co.,* 84 F.3d 204, 207 (6th Cir. 1996).

[6] *See United States v. Johnson,* 254 F.3d 279, 285 (D.C. Cir. 2001).

[7] *See Kidd v. District of Columbia,* 206 F.3d 35, 39 (D.C. Cir. 2000).

[8] *See Bankers Trust Co. v. Mallis,* 435 U.S. 381, 98 S.Ct. 1117, 55 L.Ed.2d 357 (1978).

by express agreement of the parties[9] or by failing to timely object.[10] In still other instances, the courts would simply excuse a "separate document" failure entirely where the circumstances made it plain that the court's decision was final.[11]

Ultimately, a split developed among the Circuits over how to address the nagging spectre of an appeal period being postponed indefinitely by the failure to meet the requirements of a "separate document" judgment.[12]

The Current Separate Document Rule

The underlying purpose of the current Rule 58 remains the same: the separate document requirement is designed to ensure that litigants are alerted to the entry of judgment and to the starting of the clock for post-verdict motions or an appeal.[13] The Rule is designed to resolve the long-haunting question of "when is a judgment a judgment".[14] As before, the Rule achieves this goal by insisting on a "clear line of demarcation" between a judgment and an opinion or memorandum.[15] The Rule mandates an extraordinarily austere approach to drafting judgments: the body of the proper judgment should state the relief granted and little else.[16] This austerity should make clear for the parties when the appeal time has begun.[17] In the cause of preserving appeal periods, the current version of the "separate document" rule is applied mechanically as well.[18] When extraneous text offends the separate document requirement, and when it does not, remains a question for the courts. But the postponement period for the appeals clock is now capped.[19] The "separate document" requirement applies to many categories of judgments, including summary judgments,[20] declaratory judgments,[21] and orders on habeas motions.[22]

When a "Separate Document" Is *Not* Required

A separate document is not required for an order "disposing" of a Rule 50(b) renewed motion for judgment after trial, a Rule 52(b) motion to amend or make additional findings of fact, a Rule 54(d) motion for attorney's fees, a Rule 59 motion for new trial or to alter or amend a judgment, or a Rule 60 motion for relief from a judgment or order.[23] These exceptions create grave risks for the unwary-because a "separate document" is not required for these dispositions, the time for taking an appeal *will begin to run immediately*.[24] Dispositions by Rule 41 dismissals also might not require a separate document.[25] Two nuances have arisen in the case law. First, it is unclear whether *amended* judgments require

---

[9]   *See Pohl v. United Airlines, Inc.,* 213 F.3d 336, 338 (7th Cir. 2000).

[10]   *See American Disability Ass'n, Inc. v. Chmielarz,* 289 F.3d 1315, 1318 (11th Cir. 2002).

[11]   *See Allison v. Bank One-Denver,* 289 F.3d 1223, 1232–33 (10th Cir. 2002).

[12]   *Compare White v. Fair,* 289 F.3d 1, 6 (1st Cir. 2002) (noting court rule that waiver will be inferred where a party fails to act within 3 months to resolve a separate document failure) *with Hammack v. Baroid Corp.,* 142 F.3d 266, 270 (5th Cir. 1998) (rejecting First Circuit's 3-month inferred waiver rule).

[13]   *See Bankers Trust Co. v. Mallis,* 435 U.S. 381, 384, 98 S.Ct. 1117, 55 L.Ed.2d 357 (1978) (per curiam).

[14]   *See United Auto. Workers Local 259 Social Sec. Dept. v. Metro Auto Center,* 501 F.3d 283, 287 n.1 (3d Cir. 2007).

[15]   *See Vaqueria Tres Monjitas, Inc. v. Comas-Pagan,* 772 F.3d 956, 959 (1st Cir. 2014).

[16]   *See In re Cendant Corp. Securities Litigation,* 454 F.3d 235, 245 (3d Cir. 2006).

[17]   *See In re Cendant Corp. Securities Litigation,* 454 F.3d 235, 245 (3d Cir. 2006).

[18]   *See Vaqueria Tres Monjitas, Inc. v. Comas-Pagan,* 772 F.3d 956, 959 (1st Cir. 2014).

[19]   *See infra* Authors' Commentary to Rule 58(c).

[20]   *See Perry v. Sheet Metal Workers' Local No. 73 Pension Fund,* 585 F.3d 358, 360–61 (7th Cir. 2009).

[21]   *See Specialized Seating, Inc. v. Greenwich Indus., LP,* 616 F.3d 722, 725–26 (7th Cir. 2010).

[22]   *See Jeffries v. United States,*721 F.3d 1008, 1012–13 (8th Cir. 2013) (joining majority of Circuits in so holding). *But see Williams v. United States,* 984 F.2d 28, 29–31 (2d Cir.1993) (rejecting majority view).

[23]   *See* Rule 58(a)(1).

[24]   *See S.L. ex rel. Loof v. Upland Unified Sch. Dist.,* 747 F.3d 1155, 1161 (9th Cir. 2014).

[25]   *See Federated Towing & Recovery, LLC v. Praetorian Ins. Co.,* 283 F.R.D. 644, 655 (D.N.M. 2012).

a "separate document" (the Rule's use of the phrase "disposing of" suggests possibly not).[26] Some courts navigate this uncertainty by requiring a "separate document" when an amended judgment is granted, but not when one is denied.[27] Second, it is unclear how to treat a ruling on a mis-labeled motion. One court chose to abide by the moving party's choice of labeling (even if errant); thus, a motion mislabeled as one filed under Rule 60 will be treated for Rule 58(a) purposes as a Rule 60 motion, and the "separate document" requirement will not apply.[28]

What Qualifies as a "Separate Document"?

Except for the five exempted instances set out in the Rule's text,[29] every judgment (as well as partial dispositions under Rule 54(b)[30]) must be labeled "judgment" and must be set forth on a separate document.[31] Neither a judicial memorandum or opinion,[32] nor marginal entry orders,[33] nor minute orders,[34] nor electronic docket notations [35] satisfy this requirement; indeed, even an otherwise qualifying judgment order that includes footnotes explaining its reasoning[36] or that is mistakenly stapled to the end of a memorandum opinion will fail this separateness requirement.[37] Likewise, a judgment that is encumbered with extraneous text, such as an "extensive" recitation of legal reasoning, analysis, facts, or procedural history, fails the separateness requirement.[38] (However, a very cursory explanation, devoid of any legal analysis, may survive this examination.[39]) Thus, to qualify as a "separate document", the judgment must (1) be a self-contained, separate document, (2) state the relief granted, and (3) omit the reasoning used by the district court to dispose of pending motions (which should, instead, be contained in the court's opinion).[40]

- *Two Documents?:* The majority view holds that the separate document requirement can, in appropriate circumstances, be met even if there is only one document (such as when the court's reasoning and analysis was conveyed orally, during oral argument or a hearing).[41]

- *Actual or Implied Clarity:* The fact that the litigants knew, or should have known, that the contested order was intended to serve as a final judgment will not excuse

---

26 *See Kunz v. DeFelice,* 538 F.3d 667, 673–74 (7th Cir. 2008).

27 *See Kunz v. DeFelice,* 538 F.3d 667, 673–74 (7th Cir. 2008).

28 *See Lawuary v. United States,* 669 F.3d 864, 865–67 (7th Cir. 2012).

29 *See* Rule 58(a)(1) to (a)(5). *See also supra* Authors' Commentary to Rule 58(a) (**"When a 'Separate Document' Is *Not* Required"**).

30 *See In re Cendant Corp. Securities Litigation,* 454 F.3d 235, 240 n.2 (3d Cir. 2006).

31 *See* Rule 58(a). *See also Arzuaga v. Quiros,* 781 F.3d 29, 33 (2d Cir. 2015). *But see LeBoon v. Lancaster Jewish Community Center Ass'n,* 503 F.3d 217, 224 (3d Cir. 2007) ("No magic words are necessary").

32 *See Constien v. United States,* 628 F.3d 1207, 1211–12 (10th Cir. 2010).

33 *See Inland Bulk Transfer Co. v. Cummins Engine Co.,* 332 F.3d 1007, 1015 n.7 (6th Cir. 2003).

34 *See Walters v. Wal-Mart Stores, Inc.,* 703 F.3d 1167, 1171 (10th Cir. 2013). *But see Carter v. Hodge,* 726 F.3d 917, 918–19 (7th Cir. 2013) (some minute-entries may qualify).

35 *See Barber v. Shinseki,* 660 F.3d 877, 879 (5th Cir. 2011).

36 *See Bazargani v. Radel,* 598 Fed.Appx. 829, 830 (3d Cir. 2015).

37 *See Alinsky v. United States,* 415 F.3d 639, 643 (7th Cir. 2005).

38 *See Jeffries v. United States,* 721 F.3d 1008, 1013–14 (8th Cir. 2013).

39 *See Vaqueria Tres Monjitas, Inc. v. Comas-Pagan,* 772 F.3d 956, 959–60 (1st Cir. 2014) (single explanatory sentence, without legal analysis, did not, under the circumstances, violate the "separate document" requirement).

40 *See LeBoon v. Lancaster Jewish Community Center Ass'n,* 503 F.3d 217, 224 (3d Cir. 2007). *See also Local Union No. 1992 of Intern. Broth. of Elec. Workers v. Okonite Co.,* 358 F.3d 278, 284–85 (3d Cir. 2004) (separate document requirement satisfied where order was self-contained and separate from opinion, had separate caption, was separately (not consecutively) paginated, was separately signed, was separately file-stamped, and was separately docketed).

41 *See In re Taumoepeau,* 523 F.3d 1213, 1217 (10th Cir. 2008).

a failure to meet the separateness requirement.[42] Debating over a "known-or-should-have-known" standard is precisely what Rule 58 is designed to avoid. As one court wrote: "Rule 58 is a touch-the-base requirement that lays perception aside".[43]

- *Using the "Order" Label:* The Circuits are divided as to whether a document marked "Order" can ever qualify under this Rule as a judgment, even if the "separate document" requirements are otherwise met.[44]

- *Using the "Judgment" Label:* Although Rule 58 ordinarily requires that a qualifying judgment be labeled "Judgment", the inverse is not necessarily true. If a court's order does not qualify as a judgment under Rule 58, labeling it that way will not rescue it.[45]

- *Using "Order and Judgment" Label:* At least one court has found that the use of this label did not contravene with the "separate document" requirement.[46]

- *Curing the Defect:* A purported judgment that violates the "separate document" requirement can be remedied by the court's entry of an amended judgment.[47]

- *R&R Adoptions:* An order adopting a report and recommendation may qualify as a "separate document".[48]

Waiving the "Separate Document" Requirement

The "separate document" requirement is designed to create protection, not traps.[49] An appellant can always waive the right to receive a judgment on a "separate document", and file an early appeal from a judgment that fails to meet this requirement.[50] Choosing not to wait until full compliance with the "separate document" requirement will not affect the validity of the appeal.[51] In other words, the "clock" for a timely appeal does not begin running until the judgment is placed in a "separate document" (unless, of course, the judgment is exempt from this requirement), or the capped outside time period set by the Rule expires.[52] During this time, the district court would never lose its jurisdiction over the case.[53] Nevertheless, while appellants are permitted to wait (until either the "separate document" requirement is met or the outside time period runs), they are not obligated to wait.[54]

- *Appellee Cannot Stop Appeal:* An appellee cannot oppose an appellant's early appeal in order to insist that the appellant first return to the district court to demand compliance with the ministerial act of preparing a "separate document"

---

[42] *See In re Cendant Corp. Secs. Litig.,* 454 F.3d 235, 241 n.4 (3d Cir. 2006).

[43] *See In re Cendant Corp. Secs. Litig.,* 454 F.3d 235, 241 n.4 (3d Cir. 2006).

[44] *See Local Union No. 1992 of Intern. Broth. of Elec. Workers v. Okonite Co.,* 358 F.3d 278, 285–86 (3d Cir. 2004) (finding "order" may qualify, and discussing case law). *See also* Rule 54(a) (defining "judgment" to include "a decree and any order from which an appeal lies").

[45] *See Riley v. Kennedy,* 553 U.S. 406, 419 128 S.Ct. 1970, 1981, 170 L.Ed.2d 837 (2008).

[46] *See Vaqueria Tres Monjitas, Inc. v. Comas-Pagan,* 772 F.3d 956, 960 (1st Cir. 2014).

[47] *See Jackman v. Fifth Judicial Dist. Dep't of Correctional Servs.,* 728 F.3d 800, 803–04 (8th Cir. 2013).

[48] *See Jeffries v. United States,* 721 F.3d 1008, 1013 (8th Cir. 2013).

[49] *See Bankers Trust Co. v. Mallis,* 435 U.S. 381, 386, 98 S.Ct. 1117, 55 L.Ed.2d 357 (1978) (per curiam) (requirement is to be "interpreted to prevent loss of the right of appeal, not to facilitate loss").

[50] *See Bankers Trust Co. v. Mallis,* 435 U.S. 381, 384, 98 S.Ct. 1117, 1119, 55 L.Ed.2d 357 (1978).

[51] *See Jeffries v. United States,* 721 F.3d 1008, 1014 (8th Cir. 2013).

[52] *See Shalala v. Schaefer,* 509 U.S. 292, 113 S.Ct. 2625, 125 L.Ed.2d 239 (1993) (decided under pre-2002 amendment, but noting that trial court's failure to enter judgment on a separate document kept the time for appeal open).

[53] *See Fogade v. ENB Revocable Trust,* 263 F.3d 1274, 1286 (11th Cir. 2001).

[54] *See* Rule 58(c); *see also infra* Authors' Commentary to Rule 58(c).

judgment.[55] If the appellant elects to waive the right to a "separate document" and immediately appeal, the appellee cannot stop it.

- *Waiver via Filing Post-Trial Motions:* Whether a party can waive a judgment's violation of the "separate document" requirement by filing post-trial motions to the improper judgment is unclear.[56]

- *Practitioners' Safe Harbor:* Because these early appeals are permitted, the effect grants the appellant a safe harbor. Consequently, when in doubt whether a "separate document" has been filed or not, the practitioner may always file an appeal.[57]

RULE 58(b)—ENTERING JUDGMENT

CORE CONCEPT

Judgments on a general verdict, for sums certain or costs, or that deny relief may be entered by the clerk. All other judgments must be entered by the court.

APPLICATIONS

Manner of Entering the Judgment

Unless it is a "partial" final judgment under Rule 54(b),[58] all federal judgments are entered either by the clerk or by the court:

- *By the Clerk:* Unless the court otherwise orders,[59] the clerk of court must, without awaiting any further direction from the court, promptly prepare, sign, and enter judgment when (i) the jury returns a general verdict, (ii) the court awards only costs or a sum certain, or (iii) the court denies all relief.[60]

- *By the Court:* The court must review and promptly approve the form of judgment (which the clerk then must promptly enter) when (i) the jury returns a special verdict or a general verdict accompanied by interrogatories, or (ii) the court grants other relief not described above.[61] The district court's obligation to personally "approve" the judgment may be critical. The text of judgments are often drafted by clerks and, while often satisfactory in form, they are likely to prove troublesome when the case's disposition is complicated and a non-attorney clerk is left "at sea" without judicial guidance.[62]

---

[55]   *See Bailey v. Potter,* 478 F.3d 409, 411 (D.C. Cir. 2007).

[56]   *Compare Casey v. Albertson's Inc,* 362 F.3d 1254, 1256–59 (9th Cir. 2004) (filing Rule 60(b) motion waived objection to "separate document" failure), *with Walters v. Wal-Mart Stores, Inc.,* 703 F.3d 1167, 1171–72 (10th Cir. 2013) (ling Rule 59 or 60 motion did not waive objection to "separate document" failure, or shorten appeal time).

[57]   *See In re Cendant Corp. Secs. Litig.,* 454 F.3d 235, 245 (3d Cir. 2006).

[58]   *See* Rule 54(b) (permitting court to direct the entry of final judgment "as to one or more but fewer than all of the claims or parties only upon an express determination that there is no just reason for delay and upon an express direction for the entry of judgment").

[59]   *See Passananti v. Cook County,* 689 F.3d 655, 660 (7th Cir. 2012).

[60]   *See* Rule 58(b)(1). *See also Otis v. City of Chicago,* 29 F.3d 1159, 1163 (7th Cir. 1994) (observing that Rule 58 places on clerk of court the onus of preparing the judgment). *See also Brown v. Fifth Third Bank,* 730 F.3d 698, 701 (7th Cir. 2013) (order unsigned by clerk does not satisfy Rule 58(b)).

[61]   *See* Rule 58(b)(2).

[62]   *See Rush University Medical Center v. Leavitt,* 535 F.3d 735, 737–38 (7th Cir. 2008).

Contents of Judgment

The judgment document must clearly state which parties are entitled to what relief.[63]

Transferring Judgments to Another Judicial District

A judgment for money or property entered by one federal district court may be transferred to, and executed upon in, another district court. Such transfers are accomplished by filing a certified copy of the judgment in the new district court *after* the judgment has become final after appeal, by the expiration of time for appeal, or when, still pending appeal, the court so orders for good cause.[64] The transferred judgment will have the same effect as any other judgment entered in the new district.[65]

RULE 58(c)—TIME OF ENTRY

CORE CONCEPT

Judgments are deemed to be entered when they are placed on the civil docket, unless a "separate document" is required. In those cases, the judgments are deemed entered *either* when the "separate document" requirement is met *or* 150-days after placement on the civil docket (whichever is earlier).

APPLICATIONS

Significance of Time of "Entry of Judgment"

The time for a civil litigant to take an appeal from an unsatisfying federal trial court judgment runs from the time of "entry" of that judgment.[66] Because that time period is jurisdictional, cannot often be extended, and is appeal-dooming if not honored,[67] knowing the date of a judgment's "entry" is critical in federal practice.

Triggering "Entry of Judgment" Date

The date the clerk enters the judgment "in the civil docket" is the trigger for calculating time under Rule 58(c). The clerk is obligated by Rule 79(a) to make this entry.[68] This ministerial, administrative duty is distinct from the Rule 58(b)(2) duty of the court to approve a "separate document" judgment before it is deemed a true Rule 58 judgment. Though ministerial, this docket "entering" event is still vulnerable to a surprising amount of confusion. *First,* there may be a flurry of docketing dates associated with any given order (*e.g.,* date of signing, date of filing, date of entry); only the date of entry controls for Rule 58(c) purposes.[69] *Second,* the clerk may, properly, record a "judgment" in the civil docket, even though the document so recorded fails the "separate document" requirement; in such cases, the time for appeal will usually not begin ticking until the 150-day cap expires.[70] *Third,* the syntax used by the clerk in making the entry may be ambiguous, such as a local clerk's office practice to omit the term "ENTERED" when the entry date is the same as the filed date; in those instances, the date of entry—albeit identified with uncertainty—

---

[63] *See United States v. Marrocco,* 578 F.3d 627, 631 n.3 (7th Cir. 2009) (document ineffectual if omits "who is entitled to what from whom") (citation omitted); *Citizens Elec. Corp. v. Bituminous Fire & Marine Ins. Co.,* 68 F.3d 1016, 1021 (7th Cir. 1995) (proper judgments say who is liable for how much, then stop).

[64] *See Stanford v. Utley,* 341 F.2d 265, 269–70 (8th Cir.1965).

[65] *See* 28 U.S.C.A. § 1963.

[66] *See* Fed. R. App. P. 4(a)(1)(A) (ordinarily, appeals must be filed within 30 days after entry of judgment). *See generally In re Deepwater Horizon,* 785 F.3d 986, 998 (5th Cir. 2015).

[67] *See infra* Authors' Commentary, Part VI, Appellate Procedure § 6.3 ("**Step Two: Time for Taking An Appeal**").

[68] *See* Rule 79(a)(1) (clerk must maintain the civil docket); Rule 79(a)(2) (C) (judgments must be entered chronologically in the civil docket).

[69] *See United States v. Fiorelli,* 337 F.3d 282, 287 (3d Cir.2003).

[70] *See Burnley v. City of San Antonio,* 470 F.3d 189, 194–96 (5th Cir. 2006).

controls.[71] *Fourth,* the clerk may defectively enter the judgment (by, for example, failing to sign the document); in which case, the time for appeal again tolls until the 150-day cap expires.[72] *Fifth,* the clerk may neglect to give notice of entry, or the notice given may fail to reach the litigants; because counsel are under an affirmative duty to monitor the official dockets, failure to discover such judgment entries may have calamitous consequences on post-trial motions and appeals.[73]

Computing "Entry of Judgment" Date

A judgment must always be entered on the docket.[74] To avoid the uncertainty created by the old "separate document" requirement (which could, theoretically, have allowed months or years to pass before the appeals clock might begin to run),[75] the current Rule now imposes an outside time limit for triggering the appeal period:

- *When Separate Document Required:* If a separate document is required, the judgment is deemed to be entered on the date when (1) it is actually entered in the civil docket, if it meet the separate document requirement *or* (2) 150 days elapses after entry in the civil docket, if it does not meet the separate document requirement.[76] Thus, the time for a civil appeal is either 30 days (the normal appeal period, assuming a Rule 58-qualifying judgment has been entered) or 180 days (the normal appeal period plus 150-days, if no Rule 58-qualifying judgment was entered).[77] Of course, at any point during the first 150 days, if the court were to discover that it had entered a deficient order, and then were the court to correct it with a proper Rule 58-qualifying judgment, presumably a normal 30-day appeal period would begin to run from that entry.

- *When Separate Document Not Required:* If a separate document is not required (*i.e.,* involving a qualifying Rule 50(b), 52(b), 54(d), 59, or 60 motion), the judgment is deemed to be entered when it is entered in the civil docket.[78]

Inapplicability of the 150-Day Cap

The 150-day outside time limit is only implicated when the order in question is a final one; absent a Rule 54(b) determination, an order disposing of less than all claims or less than all parties will not become a judgment merely because 150 days has passed since its entry.[79]

Disregarding the 150-Day Cap

The 150-day outside time limit should be disregarded where it serves no purpose to apply it.[80] Thus, for example, assessing the propriety of an appeal from a collateral order should *not* be complicated by the separate document requirement.[81] To the contrary, appeal

---

[71] *See Vargas Torres v. Toledo,* 672 F.Supp.2d 261, 262–65 (D.P.R. 2009).

[72] *See Brown v. Fifth Third Bank,* 730 F.3d 698, 701 (7th Cir. 2013).

[73] *See United States ex rel. McAllan v. New York,* 248 F.3d 48, 53 (2d Cir. 2001) (untimely notice of appeal not rescued by clerk's office docketing problems, "because parties have an obligation to monitor the docket sheet to inform themselves of the entry of orders they wish to appeal").

[74] *See* Rule 79 (providing for entries on the official court docket).

[75] *See Burnley v. City of San Antonio,* 470 F.3d 189, 195 (5th Cir. 2006) (noting that 2002 amendments to Rule 58 were designed to ensure that appeal time "does not linger on indefinitely").

[76] *See* Rule 58(c)(2). *See Taylor v. U.S.,* 792 F.3d 865, 867 n.1 (8th Cir. 2015).

[77] *See Arzuaga v. Quiros,* 781 F.3d 29, 33 (2d Cir. 2015).

[78] *See* Rule 58(c)(1). *See also Kunz v. DeFelice,* 538 F.3d 667, 673–74 (7th Cir. 2008).

[79] *See Boston Prop. Exchange Transfer Co. v. Iantosca,* 720 F.3d 1, 7–9 (1st Cir. 2013).

[80] *See* Rule 58 advisory committee notes to 2002 amendments.

[81] *See* Rule 58 advisory committee notes to 2002 amendments.

periods for collateral orders should start to run when the collateral order is entered, and should not await either the creation of a separate document or the passing of 150 days.[82]

RULE 58(d)—REQUEST FOR ENTRY

CORE CONCEPT

Because entry of judgment in a "separate document" has serious procedural consequences (for, among other things, the time for appealing), a party may request the court to prepare one.

APPLICATIONS

Former Prohibition on Attorney-Prepared Judgments

Before the 2002 amendments, Rule 58 prohibited attorneys from drafting and submitting proposed forms of judgment, unless directed to do so by the court.[83] This prohibition was designed to avoid delays encountered by such drafting and submission and to avoid occasionally inept drafting results.[84]

Party's Request to Prompt a "Separate Document"

A party may now request the district court to enter a "separate document" judgment.[85] Allowing such requests was intended to help protect a party's need to ensure that timing periods are promptly triggered for motions, appeals, and enforcement procedures.[86] Thus, a party may make such a request in order to cure a "separate document" problem with an existing judgment (and, thus, trigger the running of the appeals clock),[87] to seek a Rule 54(b) determination that would permit an immediate partial judgment appeal,[88] or to quicken the pace for enforcement.[89] Such a request can also be made by a party who suffers a dismissal *without prejudice,* and who wishes to appeal that dismissal rather than attempt to re-plead.[90]

RULE 58(e)—COST OR FEE AWARDS

CORE CONCEPT

To facilitate a single, consolidated appeal from both a merits ruling and a ruling on an award of attorney's fees, the district court may allow the pending (but yet undecided) attorney's fees motion to suspend the time for finality.

---

[82]   *See* Rule 58 advisory committee notes to 2002 amendments.

[83]   *See* Rule 58 (former language: "Attorneys shall not submit forms of judgment except upon direction of the court, and these directions shall not be given as a matter of course").

[84]   *See* Rule 58 advisory committee notes to 2002 amendment. *See also Matteson v. United States,* 240 F.2d 517, 519 (2d Cir. 1956) (commenting that earlier practice of having lawyers prepare form of judgment caused delay in the entry of judgment and forced the court to sift through "the normal excess of detail supplied by zealous advocates in their natural desire to press home all conceivable ad hoc advantages from the judgment").

[85]   *See Halcomb v. Black Mountain Resources, LLC,* 303 F.R.D. 496, 498–99 (E.D.Ky. 2014).

[86]   *See* Rule 58(d) advisory committee notes to 2002 amendment.

[87]   *See Perry v. Sheet Metal Workers' Local No. 73 Pension Fund,* 585 F.3d 358, 362 (7th Cir. 2009).

[88]   *See Jones v. Tidewater Inc.,* 2015 WL 222356, at *1 (E.D.La. Jan. 14, 2015).

[89]   *See Uhl v. Komatsu Forklift Co., Ltd.,* 466 F.Supp.2d 899, 911 (E.D. Mich. 2006), *aff'd,* 512 F.3d 294 (6th Cir. 2008).

[90]   *See Parker v. Google, Inc.,* 242 Fed. Appx. 833, 835–36 (3d Cir. 2007).

APPLICATIONS

Purpose

Generally, the entry of final judgment (and, thus, the triggering of the clock for taking an appeal) is neither delayed nor extended while the district court considers requests to tax costs or award attorney's fees.[91] A Rule 58(e) motion offers an exception to this practice, which enhances judicial efficiency by allowing the appeals court to review a fees award appeal at the same time as it reviews the merits.[92]

Effect of a Rule 58(e) Order

In order to allow a consolidated appeal of both its merits judgment and its ruling on attorney's fees, the district court may, in its discretion,[93] enter an order under Rule 58(e) that treats a pending motion for an award of attorney's fees as the equivalent of a Rule 59 motion.[94] If the court enters such an order, the time for appealing will not begin to run until the court decides the pending fees motion.[95] The court must, however, actually enter the Rule 58(e) order; the mere fact that a litigant has asked the court to enter such an order is not sufficient to toll.[96] Nor does tolling occur merely by the filing of some other (non-Rule 58) post-trial motion seeking an award of attorney's fees.[97] If the district court elects not to grant the order, it retains jurisdiction over the fee motion even while the merits appeal is pending,[98] which in turn deprives the appeals court of jurisdiction over that issue pending the district court's ruling.[99]

Prerequisites for a Rule 58(e) Order

The court may enter a Rule 58(e) order only if: (1) the motion for fees is pending and has been timely made (*i.e.,* within 14 days after entry of judgment, unless provided otherwise by statute or court order), (2) no effective notice of appeal has yet been made, and (3) a timely notice of appeal is still possible (*i.e.,* the time for appealing has not already expired).[100] An order under Rule 58(e) must satisfy the "separate document" requirement.[101]

Time for Entering a Rule 58(e) Order

While it is clear that the trial court may enter a Rule 58(e) order for a *pending* fees motion, courts are divided on whether such an order may be properly entered in anticipation of a *future* fees motion.[102]

When the Order Is *Not* Proper

The practical effect of a Rule 58(e) motion is to delay the arrival of finality and, with it, the time for taking an appeal from the court's order. The reason why district courts are

---

[91] *See* Rule 58(e). *See also Ray Haluch Gravel Co. v. Central Pension Fund of Int'l Union of Operating Eng'rs & Participating Employers,* ___ U.S. ___, 134 S.Ct. 773, 781, 187 L.Ed.2d 669 (2014).

[92] *See Hudson v. Pittsylvania Cty.,* 774 F.3d 231, 235 (4th Cir. 2014).

[93] *See Electronic Privacy Info. Ctr. v. U.S. Dep't of Homeland Sec.,* 811 F.Supp.2d 216, 225 n.2 (D.D.C. 2011).

[94] *See* Rule 58(e). *See also Burnley v. City of San Antonio,* 470 F.3d 189, 199 (5th Cir. 2006) (noting purpose).

[95] *See Ray Haluch Gravel Co. v. Central Pension Fund of Int'l Union of Operating Eng'rs & Participating Employers,* ___ U.S. ___, 134 S.Ct. 773, 781, 187 L.Ed.2d 669 (2014).

[96] *See Hudson v. Pittsylvania Cty.,* 774 F.3d 231, 235–36 (4th Cir. 2014);.

[97] *See House of Flavors, Inc. v. TFG-Mich., L.P.,* 700 F.3d 33, 38 (1st Cir. 2012).

[98] *See Kira, Inc. v. All Star Maint., Inc.,* 294 Fed. Appx. 139, 141 n.2 (5th Cir. 2008).

[99] *See McCarter v. Ret. Plan for Dist. Mngrs. of Am. Family Ins. Group,* 540 F.3d 649, 652–53 (7th Cir. 2008).

[100] *See Ray Haluch Gravel Co. v. Central Pension Fund of Int'l Union of Operating Eng'rs & Participating Employers,* ___ U.S. ___, 134 S.Ct. 773, 781, 187 L.Ed.2d 669 (2014).

[101] *See Deboard v. Sunshine Min. and Refining Co.,* 208 F.3d 1228, 1237 (10th Cir. 2000).

[102] *Compare Heck v. Triche,* 775 F.3d 265, 275–76 (5th Cir. 2014) (proper), *with Robinson v. City of Harvey,* 489 F.3d 864, 868 (7th Cir. 2007) (improper, but under earlier version of Rule).

authorized to grant this postponement is efficiency: to permit a simultaneous, joint appeal from both the trial court's judgment on the merits and its ruling on attorney's fees.[103] If that goal cannot be attained, no Rule 58(e) postponement order is proper. Thus, if an appeal has already been taken from the merits ruling, if the attorney's fees motion has already been ruled upon, or if the merits judgment has already become unappealable (*e.g.,* if the appeal time has already expired), the district court has no reason or authority to issue such a postponement order.[104]

Order Cannot Apply When Fees Are Part of Claim Itself

The district court may not grant a Rule 58(e) postponement when the fees are an integral part of the underlying substantive claim, such as where the fees are sought as an element of damages pursuant to a contract that authorizes fees.[105] Ordinarily, no final judgment is even possible in such a case until the fees issue (considered to be core damages) is resolved.[106]

Order Applies Only to Fees, Not Costs

A postponement of finality under Rule 58(e) is, by its terms, only applicable to attorney's fee awards; finality cannot be suspended while costs are being taxed.[107]

ADDITIONAL RESEARCH REFERENCES

Wright & Miller, *Federal Practice and Procedure §§* 2781 to 2787

C.J.S., Federal Civil Procedure §§ 1227 to 1231 et seq.

West's Key Number Digest, Federal Civil Procedure ⌫2621 to 2628

---

[103] *See Burnley v. City of San Antonio,* 470 F.3d 189, 199 (5th Cir. 2006).

[104] *See Burnley v. City of San Antonio,* 470 F.3d 189, 199 (5th Cir. 2006). *See also Robinson v. City of Harvey,* 489 F.3d 864, 868–69 (7th Cir. 2007) (appeal period must still be live at time of order; order may not "revive" an already-expired appeal period).

[105] *See House of Flavors, Inc. v. TFG-Mich., L.P.,* 700 F.3d 33, 37 (1st Cir. 2012).

[106] *See Carolina Power & Light Co. v. Dynegy Marketing and Trade,* 415 F.3d 354, 358–59 (4th Cir. 2005).

[107] *See Moody Nat. Bank of Galveston v. GE Life and Annuity Assur. Co.,* 383 F.3d 249, 253 (5th Cir. 2004). *See also Mahach-Watkins v. Depee,* 593 F.3d 1054, 1059 (9th Cir. 2010) (court's withholding of final decision on costs had no effect on resolution of attorney's fees motion).

RULE 59

NEW TRIAL; ALTERING OR AMENDING
A JUDGMENT

(a) In General.

(1) *Grounds for New Trial.* The court may, on motion, grant a new trial on all or some of the issues—and to any party—as follows:

(A) after a jury trial, for any reason for which a new trial has heretofore been granted in an action at law in federal court; or

(B) after a nonjury trial, for any reason for which a rehearing has heretofore been granted in a suit in equity in federal court.

(2) *Further Action After a Nonjury Trial.* After a nonjury trial, the court may, on motion for a new trial, open the judgment if one has been entered, take additional testimony, amend findings of fact and conclusions of law or make new ones, and direct the entry of a new judgment.

(b) Time to File a Motion for a New Trial. A motion for a new trial must be filed no later than 28 days after the entry of judgment.

(c) Time to Serve Affidavits. When a motion for a new trial is based on affidavits, they must be filed with the motion. The opposing party has 14 days after being served to file opposing affidavits. The court may permit reply affidavits.

(d) New Trial on the Court's Initiative or for Reasons Not in the Motion. No later than 28 days after the entry of judgment, the court, on its own, may order a new trial for any reason that would justify granting one on a party's motion. After giving the parties notice and an opportunity to be heard, the court may grant a timely motion for a new trial for a reason not stated in the motion. In either event, the court must specify the reasons in its order.

(e) Motion to Alter or Amend a Judgment. A motion to alter or amend a judgment must be filed no later than 28 days after the entry of the judgment.

[Amended effective March 19, 1948; July 1, 1966; April 27, 1995, effective December 1, 1995; April 30, 2007, effective December 1, 2007; March 26, 2009, effective December 1, 2009.]

AUTHORS' COMMENTARY ON RULE 59

PURPOSE AND SCOPE

When appropriate to prevent a miscarriage of justice, the district court may set aside a verdict and order a new trial or, alternatively, alter or amend a judgment. Effective December 1, 2009, a party moving for either a new trial or an order altering or amending a judgment must file such a motion no later than 28 days after the judgment is entered. The district court may *not* extend this period.

RULE 59(a)—NEW TRIALS, GENERALLY

CORE CONCEPT

In both jury and bench trials, the court may grant a new trial for any reason for which new trials (jury trials) or rehearings (bench trials) were formerly granted, such as where the verdict is against the weight of the evidence or is either excessive or inadequate, where probative evidence is newly discovered, or where conduct by the court, counsel, or the jury improperly influenced the deliberative process.

APPLICATIONS

Procedure

Motions for new trial are usually made in writing and must state with particularity the grounds for relief.

Discretion of District Court

Whether the circumstances justify the granting of a new trial is a decision left to the sound discretion of the trial judge,[1] and this discretion is far greater than the court's authority to grant a motion for judgment as a matter of law.[2] So broad is this discretion in certain contexts, that one court has described it as "virtually unassailable on appeal".[3] In exercising this discretion, the trial judge may reopen a judgment, hear additional testimony, and amend (or make new) findings of fact and conclusions of law.[4] Although there is some dispute on the point,[5] the majority view prescribes that a trial judge is not bound to view the evidence in the light most favorable to the verdict winner,[6] and may reweigh the evidence, accepting or rejecting evidence, witnesses, and other proof that the jury considered.[7] But the court must proceed carefully, and avoid merely substituting its judgment for the jury's without good reason.[8] (For this reason, some courts describe grants of new trials as "a rare occurrence"[9] and "disfavored."[10]). Nevertheless, in long, complicated trials involving topics beyond the ken of ordinary jurors, the judge ought to be especially vigilant in examining the

---

[1]   *See Gasperini v. Center for Humanities, Inc.,* 518 U.S. 415, 433, 116 S.Ct. 2211, 2222, 135 L.Ed.2d 659 (1996) ("the authority of trial judges to grant new trials . . . is large"); *Allied Chemical Corp. v. Daiflon, Inc.,* 449 U.S. 33, 101 S.Ct. 188, 66 L.Ed.2d 193 (1980) (noting that the authority to grant a new trial "is confided almost entirely to the exercise of discretion on the part of the trial court").

[2]   *See Jennings v. Jones,* 587 F.3d 430, 436 (1st Cir. 2009).

[3]   *See Michigan Millers Mut. Ins. Co. v. Asoyia, Inc.,* 793 F.3d 872, 878 (8th Cir. 2015). *See also Gasperini v. Center for Humanities, Inc.,* 518 U.S. 415, 433, 116 S.Ct. 2211, 2222, 135 L.Ed.2d 659 (1996) ("the authority of trial judges to grant new trials . . . is large").

[4]   *See Defenders of Wildlife v. Bernal,* 204 F.3d 920, 928–29 (9th Cir. 2000).

[5]   *See Robinson v. McNeil Consumer Healthcare,* 671 F.Supp.2d 975, 989 n.4 (N.D.Ill. 2009) (noting apparent division within panels of the Seventh Circuit); *Tatum v. Jackson,* 668 F.Supp.2d 584, 598 n.10 (S.D.N.Y. 2009) (same, within the Second Circuit). *But cf. Paradigm Alliance, Inc. v. Celeritas Techs., LLC,* 722 F.Supp.2d 1250, 1258 (D.Kan. 2010) (must view evidence most favorably to verdict winner).

[6]   *See Allied Chem. Corp. v. Daiflon, Inc.,* 449 U.S. 33, 36, 101 S.Ct. 188, 66 L.Ed.2d 193 (1980); *Jennings v. Jones,* 587 F.3d 430, 439 (1st Cir. 2009) (following "general rule in the circuits", and citing cases).

[7]   *See Jones ex rel. U.S. v. Massachusetts General Hosp.,* 780 F.3d 479, 492 (1st Cir. 2015).

[8]   *See Armisted v. State Farm Mut. Auto. Ins. Co.,* 675 F.3d 989, 995 (6th Cir. 2012). *See also Gerardi v. Conlin,* 938 F.Supp.2d 263, 264–65 & 265 n.2 (D.R.I. 2013) (judge does not sit as a "thirteenth juror").

[9]   *See Innovation Ventures, LLC v. N2G Distrib'g, Inc.,* 763 F.3d 524, 534 (6th Cir. 2014).

[10]   *See Guidance Endodontics, LLC v. Dentsply Int'l, Inc.,* 749 F.Supp.2d 1235, 1256 (D.N.M. 2010). *See generally Int'l Ore & Fertilizer Corp. v. SGS Control Servs., Inc.,* 38 F.3d 1279, 1287 (2d Cir.1994) (having fought once for the court's favor, the litigants should not—absent a corruption of the judicial process—be made to endure the fight anew).

verdict.[11] The task of assessing whether to grant a new trial is, obviously, a highly fact-dependent one.[12]

Grounds for New Trials

Rule 59(a) provides no list of proper reasons for which new trials may be granted, and relies instead upon historical practice.[13] What historically justified a new trial in an action at law in the federal courts, today warrants a new trial following a jury verdict; what historically justified a rehearing in a suit in equity in the federal courts, today warrants a new trial following a bench decision.[14] Understood broadly, new trials are proper when necessary to prevent a miscarriage of justice.[15] The courts have recognized that new trials may be properly granted in at least the following circumstances:

- *Verdict Against the Weight of Evidence:* when the district court concludes that the factfinder's verdict is against the "clear" or "great" weight of the evidence, and a new trial is therefore necessary to prevent a miscarriage of justice.[16] This ground-often premised entirely on a court's disagreement with a jury's credibility assessments-is a "rare occurrence,"[17] and ought to be considered with great restraint.[18]

- *Verdict Is Excessive or Inadequate:* when the district court determines that the amount of the verdict is so unreasonable that it shocks the conscience;[19]

  o *"Remittitur":* If the court decides that the verdict is excessive, the court may offer the verdict winner a reduction—called a "remittitur"—in exchange for the court's denial of a motion for a new trial.[20] If the verdict winner accepts the court's offer, the verdict winner waives the right of appeal.[21] If remitted, the jury's verdict will usually be reduced to the maximum amount the jury could have awarded without being excessive.[22] A trial court's decision on remittitur is accorded wide discretion, given that judge's ability to hear the testimony and assess the demeanor of the witnesses; a trial court's ruling that denies remittitur will be overturned on appeal only where the verdict is found

---

[11] *See Lind v. Schenley Indus. Inc.,* 278 F.2d 79, 90–91 (3d Cir.1960).

[12] *See Heimlicher v. Steele,* 615 F.Supp.2d 884, 899 (N.D.Iowa 2009).

[13] *See E.E.O.C. v. New Breed Logistics,* 783 F.3d 1057, 1065–66 (6th Cir. 2015).

[14] *See* Rule 59(a)(1). *See also United States v. Timms,* 537 Fed. Appx. 265, 267 (4th Cir. 2013).

[15] *See Michigan Millers Mut. Ins. Co. v. Asoyia, Inc.,* 793 F.3d 872, 878 (8th Cir. 2015).

[16] *See Byrd v. Blue Ridge Rural Elec. Co-op., Inc.,* 356 U.S. 525, 540, 78 S.Ct. 893, 902, 2 L.Ed.2d 953 (1958). *But cf. Latino v. Kaizer,* 58 F.3d 310, 314 (7th Cir. 1995) (ruling that jury's verdict should be accorded greater deference under Rule 59 in cases involving simple issues with highly disputed facts, than in cases involving complex issues with facts that are not as disputed).

[17] *See CFE Racing Prods., Inc. v. BMF Wheels, Inc.,* 793 F.3d 571, 591 (6th Cir. 2015).

[18] *See Raedle v. Credit Agricole Indosuez,* 670 F.3d 411, 418–19 (2d Cir. 2012).

[19] *See Mitchell v. Boelcke,* 440 F.3d 300, 303 (6th Cir. 2006). *See also Rivera Castillo v. Autokirey, Inc.,* 379 F.3d 4, 13 (1st Cir. 2004) (exceed "any rational appraisal or estimate of the damage that could be based on the evidence before the jury"). *But see Gasperini v. Center for Humanities, Inc.,* 518 U.S. 415, 116 S.Ct. 2211, 135 L.Ed.2d 659 (1996) (citing the *Erie* doctrine in applying New York's state law standard for judging "excessiveness", where state standard differed from federal "shocks the conscience" benchmark).

[20] *See Linn v. United Plant Guard Workers of America, Local 114,* 383 U.S. 53, 65–66, 86 S.Ct. 657, 664–65, 15 L.Ed.2d 582 (1966) (if damages award is excessive, trial judge has the "duty" to require a remittitur or grant a new trial). Note, however, that the court ordinarily may not reduce plaintiff's damages award without first offering plaintiff a new trial. *See Hetzel v. Prince William Cnty.,* 523 U.S. 208, 211, 118 S.Ct. 1210, 140 L.Ed.2d 336 (1998) (per curiam).

[21] *See Donovan v. Penn Shipping Co., Inc.,* 429 U.S. 648, 97 S.Ct. 835, 51 L.Ed.2d 112 (1977) (per curiam).

[22] *See Sloane v. Equifax Information Services, LLC,* 510 F.3d 495, 502–03 (4th Cir. 2007). *See also Earl v. Bouchard Transp. Co., Inc.,* 917 F.2d 1320, 1328–30 (2d Cir. 1990) (adopting same rule, but discussing the three views on remittitur and scholarly commentary's preferences).

to be so grossly excessive that the outcome is "monstrous or shocking".[23] Noneconomic damages (such as pain and suffering) are usually remitted in only extraordinary circumstances.[24] Properly done, remittitur will generally not offend the Seventh Amendment's entitlement to a jury trial,[25] and may serve the laudable ends of avoiding delay and expense and limiting judicial intrusion into the jury's domain.[26]

o   *"Additur":* If the court finds that the verdict is inadequate, the court may often *not* offer the verdict winner an increase in verdict size—called an "additur"—in exchange for the court's denial of a motion for new trial, due to Seventh Amendment concerns.[27] Where the verdict is inadequate, the court's only option is ordering a new trial.

- *Newly Discovered Evidence:* when the district court learns of a party's newly discovered evidence. To entitle the moving party to a new trial, the "newly discovered evidence" generally: (1) must have existed as of the time of trial; (2) must have been excusably overlooked by the moving party, notwithstanding the moving party's due diligence in attempting to discover it; (3) must be admissible; and (4) must be likely to alter the trial's outcome.[28]

- *Improper Conduct by Counsel or the Court:* when improper conduct by either an attorney [29] or the court [30] unfairly influenced the verdict.

- *Improper Conduct Affecting the Jury:* when the jury verdict was not unanimous or was facially inconsistent,[31] or when the jury was improperly influenced,[32] or when an erroneous jury instruction likely misled or confused the jury.[33] Note, however, that after the verdict is returned, jurors may not impeach or alter their verdict except to testify as to improper, extrinsic influences.[34]

Prejudice

Trial errors may only give rise to a new trial if they affect the substantive rights of the parties and are not cured by the trial judge's cautionary instructions to the jury.[35]

---

[23]   *See Hite v. Vermeer Mfg. Co.,* 446 F.3d 858, 869–70 (8th Cir. 2006).

[24]   *See Rodriguez v. Senor Frog's de la Isla, Inc.,* 642 F.3d 28, 39 (1st Cir. 2011).

[25]   *See Gasperini v. Center for Humanities, Inc.,* 518 U.S. 415, 433, 116 S.Ct. 2211, 135 L.Ed.2d 659 (1996); *Dimick v. Schiedt,* 293 U.S. 474, 486–87, 55 S.Ct. 296, 301, 79 L. Ed. 603 (1935). *See also Casey v. Long Island R. Co.,* 406 F.3d 142, 149 (2d Cir. 2005) (emphasizing that constitutionality of remittitur hinges on being given the choice between remittitur and new trial).

[26]   *See Dwyer v. Deutsche Lufthansa, AG,* 686 F.Supp.2d 216, 218 (E.D.N.Y. 2010).

[27]   *See Gasperini v. Center for Humanities, Inc.,* 518 U.S. 415, 433, 116 S.Ct. 2211, 135 L.Ed.2d 659 (1996); *Dimick v. Schiedt,* 293 U.S. 474, 486–87, 55 S.Ct. 296, 301, 79 L. Ed. 603 (1935). *But cf. Elm Ridge Exploration Co. v. Engle,* 721 F.3d 1199, 1221 n.13 (10th Cir. 2013) (suggesting *Erie* rule might permit some additurs).

[28]   *See Colon-Millin v. Sears Roebuck De Puerto Rico, Inc.,* 455 F.3d 30, 36 n.4 (1st Cir. 2006).

[29]   *See Tompkins v. Crown Corr, Inc.,* 726 F.3d 830, 835–36, 2013 WL 4038748, at *3–*4 (6th Cir. 2013) (denied, where no significant evidence of prejudice was shown from counsel's references to "south Florida litigation machine"); *Caudle v. District of Columbia,* 707 F.3d 354, 359–63 (D.C.Cir. 2013) (granted, for violating the "golden rule" by inviting personal juror sympathy).

[30]   *See Aggarwal v. Ponce School of Medicine,* 837 F.2d 17, 21–22 (1st Cir. 1988) (before conduct of judge will warrant a new trial, the moving party must be "so seriously prejudiced as to be deprived of a fair trial").

[31]   *See Monaco v. City of Camden,* 366 Fed. Appx. 330, 331–32 (3d Cir. 2010).

[32]   *Cf. Parker v. Gladden,* 385 U.S. 363, 87 S.Ct. 468, 17 L.Ed.2d 420 (1966) (per curiam) (statement by bailiff that defendant was a "wicked fellow" who was guilty, and that the higher courts would correct a guilty verdict if it was wrong).

[33]   *See Susan Wakeen Doll Co., Inc. v. Ashton Drake Galleries,* 272 F.3d 441, 452 (7th Cir. 2001).

[34]   *See Carson v. Polley,* 689 F.2d 562, 581 (5th Cir.1982).

[35]   *See* Rule 61 (directing that harmless errors are to be disregarded). *See also Trickey v. Kaman Indus. Techs. Corp.,* 705 F.3d 788, 807 (8th Cir. 2013).

(Consequently, appeals from new trial rulings should almost always be accompanied by the trial transcript.[36])

District Court Findings and Conclusions

In granting a new trial, the district court is ordinarily under no obligation to set out supporting findings of fact and conclusions of law.[37]

Burden of Proof

The burden of proving the necessity of a new trial lies with the party seeking it.[38]

Preservation and Waiver

A party may not seek a new trial on grounds not brought contemporaneously to the trial judge's attention.[39] The courts recognize a narrow exception to this waiver rule where a trial error is so fundamental that gross injustice would result were it not corrected. Beyond this obligation of general preservation, motions for new trials (unlike Rule 50 motions for judgment on the pleadings) do not require a further pre-verdict motion, nor is a new trial motion at the district court level essential to preserving a right of appeal[40] (although when the motion attacks sufficiency of the trial evidence, this point has been cast into some doubt).[41]

Bench Trials

If a new trial is awarded following a bench trial, the district court may, upon retrial, open a judgment already entered, hear additional testimony, revise or add findings of fact and conclusions of law, and direct the entry of a new judgment.[42] But such motions are usually not proper platforms for new evidence which could have been offered earlier, new theories, or a rehearing on the merits.[43] Moreover, trial courts may refuse a reopening upon examining the probative value of the evidence at issue, the justification for the failure to offer it earlier, and the likelihood that the reopening will inflict undue prejudice.[44]

Partial New Trials

The court may grant a partial new trial limited only to certain issues, provided the error justifying the new trial did not affect the determination of the remaining issues,[45] and provided that the singular issue for retrial is so clearly distinct and separate from all other issues that a retrial of it alone will not be unjust.[46] When a partial new trial is granted, those portions of the original judgment that were not set aside by the court become part of the single, ultimate judgment following the new trial. Most commonly, courts have granted partial new trials on damages, following an error-free trial on liability issues, but partial

---

[36] *See Rodriguez v. Senor Frog's de la Isla, Inc.,* 642 F.3d 28, 37–39 (1st Cir. 2011).

[37] *See Jennings v. Jones,* 587 F.3d 430, 441 n.11 (1st Cir. 2009).

[38] *See Battle v. District of Columbia,* 105 F. Supp. 3d 69, 70 (D.D.C. 2015). *See also Czekalski v. Secretary of Transp.,* 577 F.Supp.2d 120, 122–23 (D.D.C. 2008) (noting burden is "heavy").

[39] *See United States v. Walton,* 909 F.2d 915 (6th Cir. 1990). *But cf. Pulla v. Amoco Oil Co.,* 72 F.3d 648, 656 (8th Cir. 1995) (party may move for new trial under Rule 59 "based on the overwhelming evidence contrary to the verdict without ever previously raising such an objection").

[40] *See Pediatrix Screening, Inc. v. Telechem Int'l., Inc.,* 602 F.3d 541, 546–47 (3d Cir. 2010).

[41] *But see Pediatrix Screening, Inc. v. Telechem Int'l., Inc.,* 602 F.3d 541, 546–47 (3d Cir. 2010) (rejecting suggestion that Supreme Court's decision in *Unitherm Food Systems, Inc. v. Swift-Eckrich, Inc.,* 546 U.S. 394, 126 S.Ct. 980, 163 L.Ed.2d 974 (2006), demands further preservation).

[42] *See Rule 59(a)(2). See also Johnson v. Hix Wrecker Service, Inc.,* 528 Fed. Appx. 636, 639 (7th Cir. 2013).

[43] *See Chavez v. City of Albuquerque,* 640 F.Supp.2d 1340, 1343 (D.N.M. 2008).

[44] *See Precision Pine & Timber, Inc. v. United States,* 596 F.3d 817, 833–34 (Fed.Cir. 2010).

[45] *See Anderson v. Siemens Corp.,* 335 F.3d 466, 475–76 (5th Cir. 2003).

[46] *See Gasoline Products Co. v. Champlin Refining Co.,* 283 U.S. 494, 500, 51 S.Ct. 513, 515, 75 L. Ed. 1188 (1931).

new trials can be granted as to any "separable matter".[47] If, however, the trial court concludes that passion influenced the jury, a partial new trial on the issue of damages alone is ordinarily improper; the court must instead order a new trial on all issues.[48]

Comparing Rule 59 and Rule 60

Both Rule 59 and Rule 60 permit courts to grant relief from entered judgments. Beyond the timing differences between the two Rules,[49] the standards for granting relief also differ. The showing for relief under Rule 60 is considered greater than that needed for Rule 59.[50]

Appealability

An order granting a new trial is generally interlocutory and not immediately appealable, absent a showing that the court lacked authority to enter the order.[51] An order denying a new trial is also usually not immediately appealable,[52] or appealable at all;[53] rather, the party's proper appeal is typically an appeal from the final judgment itself, not from the mere denial of a new trial (at least absent new matters arising after entry of the judgment).[54] Note that even ultimate appellate review of denials of new trials may be further limited by Seventh Amendment constitutional concerns.[55]

RULE 59(b)—TIME TO FILE A MOTION FOR A NEW TRIAL

CORE CONCEPT

A party must file a motion for a new trial within 28 days after entry of the judgment.

APPLICATIONS

28-Day Period to *File* Motion for New Trial

This time period is for *filing,* not merely service.[56] Thus, a party seeking a new trial must *file* the Rule 59 motion within 28 days after the district court enters judgment on the docket.

Amended Judgments

Where an amended judgment is filed and alters the legal rights or obligations of the parties, a new time period for filing Rule 59 motions might be triggered.[57]

---

[47]   *See Rice v. Community Health Ass'n,* 203 F.3d 283, 290 (4th Cir. 2000).

[48]   *See Sanford v. Crittenden Memorial Hosp.,* 141 F.3d 882, 885 (8th Cir. 1998).

[49]   *Compare* Rule 59(b), (d), (e), *with* Rule 60(c).

[50]   *See Cincinnati Life Ins. Co. v. Beyrer,* 722 F.3d 939, 953 (7th Cir. 2013).

[51]   *See Allied Chemical Corp. v. Daiflon, Inc.,* 449 U.S. 33, 101 S.Ct. 188, 66 L.Ed.2d 193 (1980).

[52]   *See Clark By and Through Clark v. Heidrick,* 150 F.3d 912, 916 (8th Cir. 1998).

[53]   *See Youmans v. Simon,* 791 F.2d 341, 349 (5th Cir. 1986).

[54]   *See Johansen v. Combustion Eng'g, Inc.,* 170 F.3d 1320, 1329 n.12 (11th Cir. 1999). *But see Fiore v. Washington County Cmty. Mental Health Ctr.,* 960 F.2d 229, 232–33 & 233 n.8 (1st Cir. 1992) (noting conflict with other courts, but holding that denials of new trial motions are appealable independently from appeal of judgment itself).

[55]   *See Jocks v. Tavernier,* 316 F.3d 128, 137 (2d Cir. 2003) (commenting that district court's determination that jury's verdict was not against weight of evidence is not reviewable on appeal due to limitations imposed by Seventh Amendment).

[56]   *See Schudel v. General Elec. Co.,* 120 F.3d 991, 993–94 (9th Cir. 1997) (noting that Rule 59, as amended in 1995, requires that such motions be timely filed, not served).

[57]   *See Walker v. Bain,* 257 F.3d 660, 670 (6th Cir. 2001).

Early Motions

A party may move for a new trial before the formal entry of judgment and at any time during the 28 days following the entry of judgment.[58]

Each Party Seeking Relief Must File

In a multi-party case, a motion by one litigant under Rule 59 will not excuse the non-filing by another litigant; each party seeking relief under this Rule must move for it.[59] Likewise, a party whose post-trial motion period has run cannot belatedly "join" a co-party's pending motion to resuscitate his or her Rule 59 filing ability.[60]

No Extensions

This 28-day period may not be extended by court order.[61] Over the years, two common law exceptions were recognized to this prohibition, though only one persists.[62] If an out-of-time Rule 59 motion is filed, but not objected to, the court may, in its discretion, consider the untimely motion (though the ramifications for a later appeal remain uncertain).[63] In any event, courts may treat an untimely Rule 59 motion as one made under Rule 60 and assess it under that Rule.[64]

3-Day Service Extension Does *Not* Apply

Because Rule 59(b) requires *filing* (not service) no later than 28 days after entry of judgment, the 3-day extension after service by mail, by electronic means, or by certain other service methods does not apply.[65]

Timely Motion Tolls Appeal Period

A timely-filed motion for a new trial delays the finality of the underlying judgment and tolls the time for appeal until the district judge rules on the new trial motion.[66]

- *Tolling Applies to All Parties:* A timely filed Rule 59 motion tolls the time for appeal for all parties.[67]

Motion Filed After Notice of Appeal

The filing of a notice of appeal is jurisdictional; once filed, the district court is ordinarily divested of jurisdiction over those aspects of the case implicated in the appeal, and jurisdiction is conferred upon the court of appeals.[68] However, if a timely Rule 59 motion is filed, the earlier-filed notice of appeal lies dormant until the district court resolves the pending motion.[69]

---

[58]   *See Alam v. Miller Brewing Co.,* 709 F.3d 662, 665 & n.2 (7th Cir. 2013). *See generally infra* Authors' Commentary to Appellate Procedure § 6.3 (**"Premature Appeals"**). *See also supra* Authors' Commentary to Rule 58(a) (**"Waiving the 'Separate Document' Requirement"**).

[59]   *See Hertz Corp. v. Alamo Rent-A-Car, Inc.,* 16 F.3d 1126, 1128–29 (11th Cir. 1994).

[60]   *See Tarlton v. Exxon,* 688 F.2d 973, 977 n.4 (5th Cir. 1982).

[61]   *See* Rule 6(b)(2). *See also Blue v. Int'l Bhd. of Elec. Workers Local Union 159,* 676 F.3d 579, 584–85 (7th Cir. 2012).

[62]   *See supra* Authors' Commentary to Rule 6(b) (**"No Extensions"**).

[63]   *See Blue v. Int'l Bhd. of Elec. Workers Local Union 159,* 676 F.3d 579, 584–85 (7th Cir. 2012).

[64]   *See Banks v. Chicago Bd. of Educ.,* 750 F.3d 663, 665–67 (7th Cir. 2014).

[65]   *See* Rule 6(d); *Cavaliere v. Allstate Ins. Co.,* 996 F.2d 1111, 1112–14 (11th Cir. 1993).

[66]   *See* Fed. R. App. P. 4(a)(4)(A)(v). *See also York Group, Inc. v. Wuxi Taihu Tractor Co.,* 632 F.3d 399, 401 (7th Cir. 2011).

[67]   *See New Windsor Volunteer Ambulance Corps, Inc. v. Meyers,* 442 F.3d 101, 120 (2d Cir. 2006).

[68]   *See Griggs v. Provident Consumer Discount Co.,* 459 U.S. 56, 58, 103 S.Ct. 400, 402, 74 L.Ed.2d 225 (1982) (per curiam).

[69]   *See Warren v. American Bankers Ins.,* 507 F.3d 1239, 1244–45 (10th Cir. 2007).

Appeals Filed During Pendency of Motion

Formerly, a notice of appeal filed prematurely (before the trial court had ruled on a pending new trial motion) was considered a "nullity".[70] Under the current appellate rules, a prematurely filed appeal is now treated as filed as of the date the trial court ultimately disposes of the pending Rule 59 motion[71] (although the notice of appeal may well need to be amended to reflect the appealed-from order).[72]

RULE 59(c)—TIME TO SERVE AFFIDAVITS

CORE CONCEPT

A party may support a motion for new trial with affidavits. In such a case, the supporting affidavits must be filed with the motion. Opposing affidavits may be filed 14 days thereafter.

RULE 59(d)—NEW TRIAL ON THE COURT'S INITIATIVE OR FOR OTHER REASONS NOT IN THE MOTION

CORE CONCEPT

The court may grant a new trial entirely on its own initiative, or, upon reviewing a party's motion, may grant a new trial for a reason not stated in the moving papers.

APPLICATIONS

Grounds

The court may grant a new trial for any reason that a party could have permissibly requested by motion.[73]

Timing

A court that intends to grant a new trial on its own initiative must do so within 28 days after the entry of judgment. When a court receives a motion, but decides to grant a new trial for reasons not specified in the motion, the timing is less clear. One court has held that the timing requirement does not apply to such rulings;[74] another court has held the opposite.[75]

Granting on Different Grounds

When a court decides to grant a new trial for reasons different from those set forth in the moving party's papers, the court must give the parties notice of this intention and an opportunity to be heard.[76]

Specifying Grounds for New Trial

When the court grants a motion for a new trial on its own initiative or on grounds different from those stated in a party's motion papers, the order must specify the grounds for the court's decision.

---

[70] *See Griggs v. Provident Consumer Discount Co.,* 459 U.S. 56, 61, 103 S.Ct. 400, 403, 74 L.Ed.2d 225 (1982) (per curiam).

[71] *See Fed. R. App. P. 4(a)(4)(B). See also United States v. Holy Land Foundation for Relief & Dev't,* 722 F.3d 677, 684 (5th Cir. 2013).

[72] *See Weatherly v. Alabama State Univ.,* 728 F.3d 1263, 1270–71 (11th Cir. 2013).

[73] *See Experience Hendrix L.L.C. v. Hendrixlicensing.com Ltd.,* 762 F.3d 829, 840 (9th Cir. 2014).

[74] *See Kelly v. Moore,* 376 F.3d 481, 484 (5th Cir. 2004).

[75] *See Lesende v. Borrero,* 752 F.3d 324, 334 (3d Cir. 2014).

[76] *See Lesende v. Borrero,* 752 F.3d 324, 334–35 (3d Cir. 2014) (failure to give notice and opportunity is error).

Other *Sua Sponte* Revisions to Judgments

Although Rule 59(d) does not expressly contemplate it, one court has approved use of the Rule to substantively amend a judgment.[77]

RULE 59(e)—MOTION TO ALTER OR
AMEND A JUDGMENT

CORE CONCEPT

The court may alter or amend its judgment upon motion by a party.

APPLICATIONS

Purpose

The purpose of Rule 59(e) is to provide the district court with a means for correcting errors that may have "crept into the proceeding" while that court still holds jurisdiction over the case.[78] It thus gives the trial court the opportunity to cure its own mistakes (if it believes it made any).[79]

Grounds

No listing of proper grounds for altering or amending a judgment is included in the language of Rule 59(e), and federal case law has been left to fill in that void.[80] Broadly, a motion to alter or amend a judgment is appropriate where it seeks a re-examination of matters properly encompassed within the trial court's decision on the merits.[81] The case law acknowledges four grounds that justify altering or amending a judgment:

- *Intervening Change in the Law:* To qualify, the change must be to controlling law.[82]

- *Newly Discovered Evidence:* To qualify, such evidence must usually have been discovered only after trial, notwithstanding the party's diligence, be material and not merely cumulative or impeaching, and be likely to cause a new result.[83]

- *Correcting Legal Error:* To qualify, the error must be "clear".[84]

- *Prevent Manifest Injustice:* This is a "catch-all" factor, and implicit in any ruling that grants relief under the Rule.[85]

Thus, for example, a Rule 59(e) motion was appropriate where the court misunderstood the facts, a party's arguments, or the controlling law,[86] where the original judgment failed to provide that relief which the court found a party entitled to receive,[87] or where the party seeks a post-judgment award of prejudgment interest.[88] But the motion is improper if

---

[77] *See HyperQuest, Inc. v. N'Site Solutions, Inc.,* 632 F.3d 377, 386 (7th Cir. 2011).

[78] *See Sosebee v. Astrue,* 494 F.3d 583, 589 (7th Cir. 2007).

[79] *See Howard v. United States,* 533 F.3d 472, 475 (6th Cir. 2008).

[80] *See Sloas v. Ass'n of Am. R.R.s.,* 616 F.3d 380, 385 n.2 (4th Cir. 2010).

[81] *See White v. New Hampshire Dept. of Employment Sec.,* 455 U.S. 445, 451, 102 S.Ct. 1162, 1166, 71 L.Ed.2d 325 (1982).

[82] *See Parallel Networks, LLC v. Abercrombie & Fitch Co.,* 704 F.3d 958, 971 (Fed.Cir. 2013).

[83] *See Ferraro v. Liberty Mut. Fire Ins. Co.,* 796 F.3d 529, 534–35 (5th Cir. 2015).

[84] *See Carrero-Ojeda v. Autoridad de Energia Electrica,* 755 F.3d 711, 723 (1st Cir. 2014).

[85] *See Parallel Networks, LLC v. Abercrombie & Fitch Co.,* 704 F.3d 958, 971 (Fed.Cir. 2013).

[86] *See Barber ex rel. Barber v. Colorado Dep't of Revenue,* 562 F.3d 1222, 1228 (10th Cir. 2009).

[87] *See Continental Cas. Co. v. Howard,* 775 F.2d 876, 883–84 (7th Cir. 1985).

[88] *See Osterneck v. Ernst & Whinney,* 489 U.S. 169, 109 S.Ct. 987, 103 L.Ed.2d 146 (1989). *But see Buchanan v. Stanships, Inc.,* 485 U.S. 265, 108 S.Ct. 1130, 99 L.Ed.2d 289 (1988) (seeking an allowance of costs under Rule 54(d) is not appropriate for a Rule 59(e) motion, because such costs are collateral to the merits of the action); *White v. New*

grounded merely on a "rehashing" of previously considered and rejected arguments,[89] presenting long possessed "new" information,[90] or advancing positions that could have and should have been advanced prior to judgment.[91]

District Court's Discretion

The decision whether to alter or amend a judgment is generally committed to the discretion of the trial judge.[92] Exercising this discretion calls upon the court to balance two competing interests—the need to bring litigation to a close and the need to render just rulings based on all the facts.[93] Reconsideration of a judgment is an extraordinary remedy that is used only sparingly,[94] and a remedy "exceedingly difficult" for the moving party to obtain.[95]

Explanations for Rulings

Often, denials of Rule 59(e) motions are not accompanied by explanation, and none is usually required.[96]

28-Day Period to *File* Motion to Alter or Amend

The Rule 59(e) time period is for *filing,* not merely service.[97] Thus, a party seeking to alter or amend a judgment must *file* that Rule 59(e) motion with 28 days after the district court enters judgment on the docket.[98]

No Extensions

The court may not grant a party any extensions to this time period.[99] An untimely Rule 59(e) motion may be deemed a nullity,[100] or, in an appropriate case, treated as a Rule 60(b) motion for relief from a judgment.[101] However, a technical, electronic filing error may be excused, provided the clerk's office received the filing timely.[102] Moreover, there is developing case law that when an untimely Rule 59(e) motion is filed, but not objected to by the non-moving party, the timeliness objection may be deemed forfeited through waiver.[103] This is a

---

Hampshire Dept. of Employment Sec., 455 U.S. 445, 102 S.Ct. 1162, 71 L.Ed.2d 325 (1982) (seeking an award of attorney's fees is not appropriate for a Rule 59(e) motion).

[89]   *See Biltcliffe v. CitiMortgage, Inc.,* 772 F.3d 925, 930 (1st Cir. 2014).

[90]   *See Alcon Research Ltd. v. Barr Labs., Inc.,* 745 F.3d 1180, 1192 (Fed. Cir. 2014).

[91]   *See Perez v. Lorraine Enters., Inc.,* 769 F.3d 23, 28 (1st Cir. 2014).

[92]   *See Carrero-Ojeda v. Autoridad de Energia Electrica,* 755 F.3d 711, 723 (1st Cir. 2014).

[93]   *See Templet v. HydroChem Inc.,* 367 F.3d 473, 478–79 (5th Cir. 2004).

[94]   *See Mohammadi v. Islamic Republic of Iran,* 782 F.3d 9, 17 (D.C.Cir. 2015).

[95]   *See Soto-Padro v. Public Bldgs. Auth.,* 675 F.3d 1, 9 (1st Cir. 2012).

[96]   *See Parallel Networks, LLC v. Abercrombie & Fitch Co.,* 704 F.3d 958, 971 (Fed.Cir. 2013).

[97]   *See Schudel v. General Elec. Co.,* 120 F.3d 991, 994 (9th Cir. 1997), (noting that Rule 59, as amended in 1995, requires that such motions be filed, not served, within 10 days following entry of judgment). *See also Life Ins. Co. of North America v. Von Valtier,* 116 F.3d 279, 282–83 (7th Cir. 1997) (considering motion to be timely filed where it was delivered to district court, as required by standing chambers order, but trial judge delayed in transmitting motion to clerk's office for formal filing).

[98]   *See Keith v. Bobby,* 618 F.3d 594, 597–99 (6th Cir. 2010) (period runs from date order was entered, not date it became final).

[99]   *See* Rule 6(b). *See also Lexon Ins. Co. v. Naser,* 781 F.3d 335, 338 (6th Cir. 2015).

[100]   *See Fisher v. Kadant, Inc.,* 589 F.3d 505, 511 (1st Cir. 2009).

[101]   *See Lora v. O'Heaney,* 602 F.3d 106, 111 (2d Cir. 2010).

[102]   *See Shuler v. Garrett,* 715 F.3d 185, 185–87 (6th Cir. 2013) (although filed electronically under the wrong docket number, clerk received a timely filing and no prejudice was caused).

[103]   *See National Ecological Foundation v. Alexander,* 496 F.3d 466, 474–75 (6th Cir. 2007) (relying on two recent Supreme Court cases, *Eberhart v. United States,*546 U.S. 12, 126 S.Ct. 403, 163 L.Ed.2d 14 (2005) (per curiam) and *Kontrick v. Ryan,* 540 U.S. 443, 124 S.Ct. 906, 157 L.Ed.2d 867 (2004)).

dangerous gamble, though; if the trial court grants the motion, the aggrieved party may receive meaningful relief, but if the trial court denies the motion, the aggrieved party's time for taking an appeal may well be already long lost.[104]

3-Day Service Extension Does Not Apply

Because Rule 59(e) requires *filing* (not service) no later than 28 days after entry of judgment, the 3-day extension after service by mail, by electronic means, or by certain other service methods does not apply.[105]

Prisoner Plaintiffs

The prisoner "mailbox rule" has been adopted by some courts for Rule 59(e) motions. Consequently, a *pro se* prisoner's papers may be deemed filed when deposited with the post office.[106]

Motion Tolls Appeal Period

Like Rule 59 motions for new trial, a timely-filed Rule 59(e) motion to alter or amend the judgment tolls the time for appeal.[107] A prematurely filed appeal during the pendency of a Rule 59(e) motion is held in abeyance until the date the district court resolves the pending motion.[108] An untimely Rule 59(e) motion generally will not toll the time for appeal,[109] nor, generally, will a second or later Rule 59(e) motion.[110] However, the trial court's ruling on a Rule 59(e) motion may change "matters of substance" or resolve a "genuine ambiguity" in court's original order and, in those infrequent cases, a new judgment is recognized, from which a new Rule 59(e) motion (with appeal-period tolling effect) may be filed.[111]

"Particularity" Requirement for Motion

All Rule 59(e) motions must satisfy the "particularity" requirement of Rule 7(b)(1).[112] Failure to do so may have dire consequences, including a loss of appeal-period tolling. Thus, a "skeleton" motion that fails to alert the court or the other litigants of the grounds for which an alteration or amendment is sought may be deemed improper and, thus, ineffective in tolling the appeal period.[113] In any event, a motion that idly asks that an earlier judgment be reconsidered (without more) is almost certainly to be denied.[114]

- *Appeal Must Name Correct Order:* The filing of a timely, proper Rule 59(e) motion can toll the time for filing an appeal from the original underlying *merits* ruling,

---

[104] *See Lizardo v. United States,* 619 F.3d 273, 276–80 (3d Cir. 2010) (Rule 59(e) is "claim processing rule", and timeliness requirement may be forfeited, but for appeal purposes, untimely Rule 59(e) motions do not toll appeal period, which begins to run from judgment). *But see Nat'l Ecological Found. v. Alexander,* 496 F.3d 466, 476 (6th Cir. 2007) (discerning no reason why motion that was properly considered by trial court because timeliness objection was waived would fail to extend appeal period).

[105] *See Williams v. Illinois,* 737 F.3d 473, 475–76 (7th Cir. 2013).

[106] *See Long v. Atlantic City Police Dep't,* 670 F.3d 436, 440–45 (3d Cir. 2012).

[107] *Shuler v. Garrett,* 715 F.3d 185, 186 (6th Cir. 2013).

[108] *See* Fed. R. App. P. 4(a)(4) (as amended Dec. 1, 1993); *Stansell v. Revolutionary Armed Forces of Colombia,* 771 F.3d 713, 745–46 (11th Cir. 2014).

[109] *See Banks v. Chicago Bd. of Educ.,* 750 F.3d 663, 665 (7th Cir. 2014).

[110] *See Benson v. St. Joseph Reg'l Health Ctr.,* 575 F.3d 542, 546–47 (5th Cir. 2009).

[111] *See Andrews v. E.I. Du Pont De Nemours and Co.,* 447 F.3d 510, 516 (7th Cir. 2006) (noting exception, and stating that test is "whether the district court disturbed or revised legal rights settled in the original . . . order").

[112] *See Intera Corp. v. Henderson,* 428 F.3d 605, 611 (6th Cir. 2005).

[113] *See Talano v. Northwestern Medical Faculty Foundation, Inc.,* 273 F.3d 757, 760–61 (7th Cir. 2001) ("if a party could file a skeleton motion and later fill it in, the purpose of the time limitation would be defeated"). *But cf. Carlson v. CSX Transp., Inc.,* 758 F.3d 819, 826 (7th Cir. 2014) (constraining such holdings to only "extreme cases" with motions "*completely* devoid of substance").

[114] *See Wood v. Ryan,* 759 F.3d 1117, 1121 (9th Cir. 2014).

and not just from the court's disposition of the Rule 59(e) motion itself.[115] However, to benefit from that *merits* tolling effect, the litigant must list the *merits* ruling on the Notice of Appeal (in addition to any other orders from which the appeal is taken).[116] Although the appellate courts will liberally construe the Notice of Appeal to give effect to the parties' intentions if clearly obvious (and in the absence of prejudice to the adversary),[117] litigants have been cautioned by the courts "that such rescue missions are not automatic, and litigants will do well to draft notices of appeal with care".[118]

Motions for "Reconsideration"

The Rules do not expressly recognize motions for "reconsideration"[119] (although individual local Districts may).[120] When "reconsideration" is sought from an interlocutory order *(e.g.,* a denial of a motion to dismiss or for summary judgment), that motion is not properly considered under Rule 59(e) but, instead, as simply a request for the district court to revisit its earlier ruling.[121] When "reconsideration" is sought from a true judgment or other final order, such a motion will be treated *either* as one under Rule 59(e) *or* as one under Rule 60(b),[122] a classification typically dependent on the date the motion is filed. If filed within the 28-day period set for Rule 59(e) motions, the "reconsideration" will generally be treated under Rule 59(e).[123] Otherwise, the courts will ordinarily examine the motion under Rule 60(b).[124] In either case, however, the applicable legal analysis will depend on the grounds asserted for the relief requested.[125]

Motions for "reconsideration" will not be granted absent "highly unusual circumstances."[126] Such motions do not provide litigants with an opportunity for a "second bite at the apple"[127] or allow them, like Emperor Nero, to "fiddle as Rome burns",[128] or to "ante up and play a new hand,"[129] or license a litigation "game of hopscotch" in which parties switch from one legal theory to a new one "like a bee in search of honey",[130] or "to turn back the clock, erase the record, and try to reinvent [the] case."[131] In other words, motions for

---

[115] *See Andrews v. Columbia Gas Transmission Corp.,* 544 F.3d 618, 623 n.4 (6th Cir. 2008).

[116] *See Chamorro v. Puerto Rican Cars, Inc.,* 304 F.3d 1, 3 (1st Cir. 2002) (an appeal taken only from the order denying the Rule 59(e) motion will generally not be considered an appeal from the underlying merits judgment).

[117] *See Chamorro v. Puerto Rican Cars, Inc.,* 304 F.3d 1, 3 (1st Cir. 2002).

[118] *See Chamorro v. Puerto Rican Cars, Inc.,* 304 F.3d 1, 3 (1st Cir. 2002).

[119] *See Katyle v. Penn Nat'l Gaming, Inc.,* 637 F.3d 462, 470 n.4 (4th Cir. 2011).

[120] Local practice may set specific procedures. *See, e.g., In re Greektown Holdings, LLC,* 728 F.3d 567, 573–74 (6th Cir. 2013) (noting local Michigan procedure for "reconsideration", with accompanying "palpable defect" standard).

[121] *See Jones v. Bernanke,* 557 F.3d 670, 677–78 (D.C.Cir. 2009).

[122] *See Commonwealth Prop. Advocates, LLC v. Mortgage Elec. Registration Sys., Inc.,* 680 F.3d 1194, 1200 (10th Cir. 2011).

[123] *See Katyle v. Penn Nat'l Gaming, Inc.,* 637 F.3d 462, 470 n.4 (4th Cir. 2011).

[124] *See United States v. Comprehensive Drug Testing, Inc.,* 513 F.3d 1085, 1098 (9th Cir. 2008).

[125] *See Negron-Almeda v. Santiago,* 528 F.3d 15, 20 (1st Cir. 2008).

[126] *See McDowell v. Calderon,* 197 F.3d 1253, 1255 (9th Cir. 1999). *See also U.S. ex rel. Becker v. Westing-house Savannah River Co.,* 305 F.3d 284, 290 (4th Cir. 2002) (simple disagreement with the court's ruling will not support Rule 59(e) relief).

[127] *See Sequa Corp. v. GBJ Corp.,* 156 F.3d 136, 144 (2d Cir.1998).

[128] *Vasapolli v. Rostoff,* 39 F.3d 27, 36 (1st Cir. 1994) (Selya, J.)("Unlike the Emperor Nero, litigants cannot fiddle as Rome burns. A party who sits in silence, withholds potentially relevant information, allows his opponent to configure the summary judgment record, and acquiesces in a particular choice of law does so at his peril").

[129] *See Markel Am. Ins. Co. v. Diaz-Santiago,* 674 F.3d 21, 33 (1st Cir. 2012) (especially when the movant is "long past being a day late and well over a dollar short").

[130] *See Cochran v. Quest Software, Inc.,* 328 F.3d 1, 11 (1st Cir. 2003) (noting that litigants "frame the issues in a case before the trial court rules" and, once framed, should not be permitted to switch from theory to theory thereafter).

[131] *See Perez v. Lorraine Enters., Inc.,* 769 F.3d 23, 32 (1st Cir. 2014).

reconsideration are not vehicles for relitigating old issues.[132] But nor are they motions for "initial consideration".[133] Courts properly decline to consider new arguments or new evidence on reconsideration where those arguments or evidence were available earlier.[134]

Motions to Include Prejudgment Interest

Generally, motions to amend to include an award of either mandatory or discretionary prejudgment interest are treated under this Rule and, thus, must be sought within 28 days of entry of the judgment or be deemed waived.[135] However, for some courts, such a motion will be deemed untimely if the request for prejudgment interest is being raised for the first time on the Rule 59(e) motion.[136]

Mislabeled Motions

A motion made under Rule 59(e) but which is, in substance, a Rule 50(b) motion for judgment as a matter of law[137] or a Rule 58(e) motion for entry of a fees award, will be treated as such.[138]

ADDITIONAL RESEARCH REFERENCES

Wright & Miller, Federal Practice and Procedure §§ 2801 to 21

C.J.S., Federal Civil Procedure §§ 1061 to 1103 et seq., §§ 1233 to 1251 et seq.

West's Key Number Digest, Federal Civil Procedure ⊶2311 to 2377, ⊶2641 to 2663

---

[132] *See Prescott v. Higgins,* 538 F.3d 32, 45 (1st Cir. 2008).

[133] *See GSS Group Ltd v. Nat'l Port Auth.,* 680 F.3d 805, 812 (D.C.Cir. 2012).

[134] *See Holder v. United States,* 721 F.3d 979, 986 (8th Cir. 2013).

[135] *See Osterneck v. Ernst & Whinney,* 489 U.S. 169, 173–78, 109 S.Ct. 987, 989–92, 103 L.Ed.2d 146 (1989) (mandatory prejudgment interest).

[136] *See First State Bank of Monticello v. Ohio Cas. Ins. Co.,* 555 F.3d 564, 572 (7th Cir. 2009).

[137] *See Elm Ridge Exploration Co. v. Engle,* 721 F.3d 1199, 1220 (10th Cir. 2013).

[138] *See Trickey v. Kaman Indus. Techs. Corp.,* 705 F.3d 788, 808 (8th Cir. 2013).

RULE 60

RELIEF FROM A JUDGMENT OR ORDER

(a) Corrections Based on Clerical Mistakes; Oversights and Omissions. The court may correct a clerical mistake or a mistake arising from oversight or omission whenever one is found in a judgment, order, or other part of the record. The court may do so on motion or on its own, with or without notice. But after an appeal has been docketed in the appellate court and while it is pending, such a mistake may be corrected only with the appellate court's leave.

(b) Grounds for Relief from a Final Judgment, Order, or Proceeding. On motion and just terms, the court may relieve a party or its legal representative from a final judgment, order, or proceeding for the following reasons:

(1) mistake, inadvertence, surprise, or excusable neglect;

(2) newly discovered evidence that, with reasonable diligence, could not have been discovered in time to move for a new trial under Rule 59(b);

(3) fraud (whether previously called intrinsic or extrinsic), misrepresentation, or misconduct by an opposing party;

(4) the judgment is void;

(5) the judgment has been satisfied, released or discharged; it is based on an earlier judgment that has been reversed or vacated; or applying it prospectively is no longer equitable; or

(6) any other reason that justifies relief.

(c) Timing and Effect of the Motion.

(1) *Timing.* A motion under Rule 60(b) must be made within a reasonable time—and for reasons (1), (2), and (3) no more than a year after the entry of the judgment or order or the date of the proceeding.

(2) *Effect on Finality.* The motion does not affect the judgment's finality or suspend its operation.

(d) Other Powers to Grant Relief. This rule does not limit a court's power to:

(1) entertain an independent action to relieve a party from a judgment, order, or proceeding;

(2) grant relief under 28 U.S.C. § 1655 to a defendant who was not personally notified of the action; or

(3) set aside a judgment for fraud on the court.

(e) Bills and Writs Abolished. The following are abolished: bills of review, bills in the nature of bills of review, and writs of coram nobis, coram vobis, and audita querela.

[Amended effective March 19, 1948; October 20, 1949; August 1, 1987; April 30, 2007, effective December 1, 2007.]

AUTHORS' COMMENTARY ON RULE 60

PURPOSE AND SCOPE

The district judge may grant relief from a judgment or order to correct clerical errors or in circumstances justifying an alteration of the judgment or order. Motions to correct clerical errors may be made at any time. Motions for relief from judgment founded on other reasons must be made within a "reasonable" time after the judgment is entered and, in some cases, no later than 1 year after the judgment is entered. Motions for relief on the basis that the judgment is void may be made at any time.

RULE 60(a)—CORRECTION BASED ON CLERICAL MISTAKES; OVERSIGHTS AND OMISSIONS

CORE CONCEPT

The district court, on its own initiative or on motion of a party, may correct clerical errors in judgments, orders, or other parts of the record, as well as errors arising from oversight or omission.

APPLICATIONS

Procedure

Motions to correct clerical errors are made to the district court that rendered the judgment sought to be corrected (some early precedent questions the authority of a transferee court to enter clerical error relief).[1]

Sua Sponte Corrections

The court *sua sponte* may raise clerical errors for correction.[2] Before doing so, however, the court must provide the parties with fair notice of its intention, allow them the opportunity to present their positions, and assure itself that no significant prejudice would follow from correcting the errors.[3]

Types of Qualifying Errors

Rule 60(a) is reserved for correcting "blunders in execution," but not for "a change of mind."[4] Given the broad discretion the courts enjoy with Rule 60(a),[5] this distinction is pivotal. An error qualifying for correction under Rule 60(a) is quintessentially a minor and ministerial one, never a substantively factual or legal one.[6] The distinction lies with the

---

[1]   *See Tommills Brokerage Co. v. Thon,* 52 F.R.D. 200, 202 (D.P.R. 1971).

[2]   *See Matter of West Texas Marketing Corp.,* 12 F.3d 497, 503 (5th Cir. 1994).

[3]   *See Day v. McDonough,* 547 U.S. 198, 210, 126 S.Ct. 1675, 1684, 164 L.Ed.2d 376 (2006).

[4]   *See Harman v. Harper,* 7 F.3d 1455, 1457 (9th Cir. 1993). *See also Sartin v. McNair Law Firm PA,* 756 F.3d 259, 265 (4th Cir. 2014) (citing quotation with approval).

[5]   *See Diaz v. Jiten Hotel Mgmt., Inc.,* 741 F.3d 170, 174 (1st Cir. 2013).

[6]   *See Tattersalls, Ltd. v. DeHaven,* 745 F.3d 1294, 1297 (9th Cir. 2014). *See generally Matter of West Texas Mktg. Corp.,* 12 F.3d 497, 504–05 (5th Cir. 1994) ("As long as the intentions of the parties are clearly defined and all the court need do is employ the judicial eraser to obliterate a mechanical or mathematical mistake, the modification will be allowed. If, on the other hand, cerebration or research into the law or planetary excursions into facts is required, Rule 60(a) will

court's intent. Where the judgment, as entered, fails to reflect the original intention of the court (due to some inaccurate transcription, inadvertent omission, math error, or similar flaw in recitation),[7] the error can be corrected with Rule 60(a).[8] Conversely, where the judgment accurately captured an intention that the court is now rethinking, Rule 60(a) does not apply.[9] The "touchstone" is "fidelity to the intent" of the original judgment.[10] Nonetheless, Rule 60(a) is not always limited to mere typos. The Rule may be used to clarify the original order by inserting its "necessary implications" (to ensure full implementation and enforcement)[11] or by resolving an ambiguity to better reflect contemporaneous intent.[12]

Whose Errors

Relief under Rule 60(a) is not limited to clerical mistakes committed only by the clerk; the Rule applies to mistakes by the court, the parties, and the jury as well.[13]

Mislabeled "Substantive" Motions

An incorrectly labeled Rule 60(a) motion that actually seeks substantive alterations of a judgment may, in the court's discretion, be treated as a request seeking Rule 59(e) relief (and, then, would be tested under Rule 59(e)).[14]

Omission of Interest Award

Correction under Rule 60(a) might be available for omitted awards of interest, but only where the court had earlier announced the award and merely neglected to fix the amount.[15] If the court was previously silent on the question of an interest award, a motion under Rule 60(a) would likely be improper.[16]

Time for Correction

The district court may correct a Rule 60(a) error "whenever one is found."[17] Even after an appeal is taken, such mistakes can still be corrected by the district judge [18] (though, if the correction is not made pursuant to a Rule 60(a) motion filed within 28 days of judgment entry, the district court will need to seek leave from the appeals court to make the

---

not be available. . . . It is only mindless and mechanistic mistakes, minor shifting of facts, and no new additional legal perambulations which are reachable through Rule 60(a).").

  [7] *See Rivera v. PNS Stores, Inc.,* 647 F.3d 188, 193–94 (5th Cir. 2011). *See, e.g. Pfizer Inc. v. Uprichard,* 422 F.3d 124, 129–30 (3d Cir. 2005) (inclusion of prejudgment interest proper, but order to sign settlement agreement was not); *United States v. Mosbrucker,* 340 F.3d 664, 665–67 (8th Cir. 2003) (permitting correction to note true status of easement tract); *Rezzonico v. H & R Block, Inc.,* 182 F.3d 144, 151 (2d Cir. 1999) (used to correct district court's omission of word "not" from judgment); *Hale Container Line, Inc. v. Houston Sea Packing Co., Inc.,* 137 F.3d 1455, 1474 (11th Cir. 1998) (correcting damages award containing erroneous mathematical computation); *McNamara v. City of Chicago,* 138 F.3d 1219, 1221 (7th Cir. 1998) (replacing "Chicago Police Department" with "Chicago Fire Department" in one sentence of opinion).

  [8] *See Shuffle Tech Int'l, LLC v. Wolff Gaming, Inc.,* 757 F.3d 708, 709 (7th Cir. 2014).

  [9] *See Shuffle Tech Int'l, LLC v. Wolff Gaming, Inc.,* 757 F.3d 708, 709 (7th Cir. 2014).

  [10] *See Tattersalls, Ltd. v. DeHaven,* 745 F.3d 1294, 1298 (9th Cir. 2014).

  [11] *See Garamendi v. Henin,* 683 F.3d 1069, 1077–80 (9th Cir. 2012).

  [12] *See Sartin v. McNair Law Firm PA,* 756 F.3d 259, 265–66 (4th Cir. 2014) (sharpening the target of a sanctions order); *Tattersalls, Ltd. v. DeHaven,* 745 F.3d 1294, 1298 (9th Cir. 2014) (to implement the granting of full relief); *Diaz v. Jiten Hotel Mgmt., Inc.,* 741 F.3d 170, 174–75 (1st Cir. 2013) (to ensure proper fee reduction).

  [13] *See Day v. McDonough,* 547 U.S. 198, 210–11, 126 S.Ct. 1675, 1684, 164 L.Ed.2d 376 (2006).

  [14] *See Companion Health Serv., Inc. v. Kurtz,* 675 F.3d 75, 87 (1st Cir. 2012).

  [15] *See Stryker Corp. v. XL Ins. America Inc.,* 726 F.Supp.2d 754, 789 (W.D.Mich. 2010).

  [16] *See Osterneck v. Ernst & Whinney,* 489 U.S. 169, 109 S.Ct. 987, 103 L.Ed.2d 146 (1989) (ruling that Rule 59(e), not Rule 60(a), is implicated in such instances).

  [17] *See Shuffle Tech Int'l, LLC v. Wolff Gaming, Inc.,* 757 F.3d 708, 709 (7th Cir. 2014).

  [18] *See Rivera v. PNS Stores, Inc.,* 647 F.3d 188, 193 (5th Cir. 2011).

correction).[19] Corrections after the appeal is concluded may be made upon leave of the appeals court, or without leave if the corrections would not alter any appellate ruling.[20]

Implications for Appeal

A Rule 60(a) motion filed within 28 days of judgment entry tolls the time for taking an appeal.[21] An appeal from a Rule 60(a) motion filed beyond that period will likely be limited solely to correctness of the Rule 60(a) ruling and not to the underlying merits.[22]

RULE 60(b)—OTHER GROUNDS FOR RELIEF

CORE CONCEPT

In its discretion, the district court may grant relief from a final judgment, order, or proceeding for various enumerated reasons.

APPLICATIONS

Purpose

Tracing back to the original appearance of the federal civil rules, Rule 60(b) memorializes the courts' inherent, discretionary power—recognized for centuries in English practice—to set aside judgments where enforcement would produce an inequity.[23] The purpose of permitting substantive relief from a judgment or order is to allow the federal courts to strike the proper balance between two often conflicting principles—that litigation must be brought to a final close and that justice must be done.[24] Rule 60(b) is not a substitute for a timely appeal.[25] Because upsetting a settled judgment clashes with this finality objective,[26] the relief is considered "extraordinary" and generally reserved for only exceptional circumstances.[27] Broadly stated, relief under Rule 60(b) is not available for deliberate choices later shown to be unwise ones.[28]

Reasons for Granting Substantive Relief

Rule 60(b) provides five specified reasons for which substantive (non-clerical) relief may be granted, and adds a sixth catchall category for reasons not otherwise specifically listed. Ordinarily, proper post-judgment relief under Rule 60(b) will not be denied simply because the moving party failed to invoke the proper reason or Rule sub-part[29]—provided, of course, that the substantive argument for relief is apparent.[30]

---

[19]   *See* Rule 62.1. *See also Bancorp-South Bank v. Hazelwood Logistics Ctr., LLC,* 706 F.3d 888, 897 (8th Cir. 2013).

[20]   *See Hartis v. Chicago Title Ins. Co.,* 694 F.3d 935, 950 (8th Cir. 2012).

[21]   *See Catz v. Chalker,* 566 F.3d 839, 841–42 (9th Cir. 2009). *See also* Fed. R. App. P. 4(a)(4)(A)(vi) and advisory committee notes to 1993 amendment.

[22]   *See Garamendi v. Henin,* 683 F.3d 1069, 1077–81 (9th Cir. 2012).

[23]   *See Tanner v. Yukins,* 776 F.3d 434, 438 (6th Cir. 2015).

[24]   *See United Student Aid Funds, Inc. v. Espinosa,* 559 U.S. 260, 276, 130 S.Ct. 1367, 1380, 176 L.Ed.2d 158 (2010) (Rule 60(b) represents an "exception to finality"); *Gonzalez v. Crosby,* 545 U.S. 524, 529, 125 S.Ct. 2641, 2646, 162 L.Ed.2d 480 (2005) (Rule 60(b)'s "whole purpose is to make an exception to finality").

[25]   *See Lazare Kaplan Int'l, Inc. v. Photoscribe Techs., Inc.,* 714 F.3d 1289, 1297 (Fed.Cir. 2013). *See generally Banks v. Chicago Bd. of Educ.,* 750 F.3d 663, 667 (7th Cir. 2014) (generally must show that relief could not have been obtained in a direct appeal).

[26]   *See United Student Aid Funds, Inc. v. Espinosa,* 559 U.S. 260, 269–70, 130 S.Ct. 1367, 1376, 176 L.Ed.2d 158 (2010) (Rule 60(b) represents an "exception to finality").

[27]   *See Kathrein v. City of Evanston,* 752 F.3d 680, 690 (7th Cir. 2014).

[28]   *See Park West Galleries, Inc. v. Hochman,* 692 F.3d 539, 545 (6th Cir. 2012).

[29]   *See Mendez v. Republic Bank,* 725 F.3d 651, 658 (7th Cir. 2013).

[30]   *See Nelson v. Napolitano,* 657 F.3d 586, 589–90 (7th Cir. 2011) (noting mistaken belief that courts are "obliged to research and construct legal arguments for parties").

Reason 1—Mistake, Inadvertence, Surprise, or Excusable Neglect

Relief from a judgment or order may be granted for mistakes by any person, not just a party,[31] and even legal errors by the court.[32] This category may permit relief where the order or judgment results from such circumstances as an inability to consult with counsel,[33] a misunderstanding regarding the duty to appear,[34] a failure to receive service,[35] or, in some circumstances, an attorney's negligent failure to meet a deadline[36]or other professional misstep.[37] (Note, however, that not all courts recognize attorney negligence as capable of qualifying under this category, and those that do impose a heavy standard.[38]) This category also permits relief when the district court had made a substantive error of law or fact in its judgment or order.[39]

The standard for relief under this category is a demanding one.[40] Whether relief is appropriate is assessed on a case-by-case analysis: not every error or omission in the course of litigation will qualify as "excusable neglect",[41] nor will routine carelessness,[42] a lack of diligence,[43] a confusion concerning the Rules or the law,[44] or a party's misunderstanding of the consequences of her actions (even after advice of counsel) qualify for relief.[45] Relief cannot be invoked merely to evade consequences of legal positions and litigation strategies undertaken, when "unsuccessful, ill-advised, or even flatly erroneous."[46] Moreover, otherwise careful clients can be penalized for omissions of their careless attorneys.[47] As a threshold showing, the moving party must demonstrate that the error made did not result from his or her own culpable conduct,[48] and instead that the party has behaved with appropriate diligence.[49] To qualify as "excusable neglect", the conduct is tested against an equitable standard, one that weighs the totality of the circumstances;[50] among the factors [51] the courts consider in this analysis are: (1) prejudice to the opponent; (2) length of delay and impact on the proceedings; (3) reason for the delay; and (4) the moving party's good faith.[52]

---

[31]   *See Associates Discount Corp. v. Goldman,* 524 F.2d 1051, 1052 (3d Cir. 1975).

[32]   *See Mendez v. Republic Bank,* 725 F.3d 651, 658–59 (7th Cir. 2013).

[33]   *See Falk v. Allen,* 739 F.2d 461, 464 (9th Cir.1984).

[34]   *See Ellingsworth v. Chrysler,* 665 F.2d 180, 184 (7th Cir.1981).

[35]   *See Blois v. Friday,* 612 F.2d 938, 940 (5th Cir.1980).

[36]   *See Ahanchian v. Xenon Pictures, Inc.,* 624 F.3d 1253, 1261–62 (9th Cir. 2010).

[37]   *See Daniels v. Agin,* 736 F.3d 70, 86–87 (1st Cir. 2013).

[38]   *See Latshaw v. Trainer Wortham & Co., Inc.,* 452 F.3d 1097, 1101 (9th Cir. 2006) (surveying other Circuits, and ruling that Rule 60(b)(1) does not remedy erroneous legal advice (even innocent carelessness) of counsel, explaining that "[s]uch mistakes are more appropriately addressed through malpractice claims"); *Robb v. Norfolk & Western Ry. Co.,* 122 F.3d 354, 361–63 (7th Cir. 1997) (noting that Circuit discontinues its "hard-and-fast" rule barring application of Rule to attorney negligence, but sternly cautioning counsel against expecting such relief to be granted automatically).

[39]   *See Utah ex rel. Div. of Foresty, Fire & State Lands v. United States,*528 F.3d 712, 722–23 (10th Cir. 2008).

[40]   *See United States v. $23,000 in U.S. Currency,* 356 F.3d 157, 164 (1st Cir. 2004).

[41]   *See Rodgers v. Wyoming Atty. Gen.,* 205 F.3d 1201, 1206 (10th Cir. 2000) (party who simply misunderstands the legal consequences of his deliberate acts might not be deemed excusably neglectful).

[42]   *See U.S. Commodity Futures Trading Com'n v. Kratville,* 796 F.3d 873, 896 (8th 2015).

[43]   *See Aguiar-Carrasquillo v. Agosto-Alicea,* 445 F.3d 19, 28 (1st Cir. 2006).

[44]   *See United States v. Davenport,* 668 F.3d 1316, 1324–25 (11th Cir. 2012).

[45]   *See Cashner v. Freedom Stores, Inc.,* 98 F.3d 572, 577–78 (10th Cir. 1996).

[46]   *See U.S. Commodity Futures Trading Com'n v. Kratville,* 796 F.3d 873, 896 (8th Cir. 2015).

[47]   *See Daniels v. Agin,* 736 F.3d 70, 86–87 (1st Cir. 2013).

[48]   *See Yeschick v. Mineta,* 675 F.3d 622, 628–28 (6th Cir. 2012).

[49]   *See Robinson v. Wix Filtration Corp. LLC,* 599 F.3d 403, 413 (4th Cir. 2010).

[50]   *See Nansamba v. North Shore Med. Ctr., Inc.,* 727 F.3d 33, 38–39 (1st Cir. 2013).

[51]   Note that some courts require that each of these four factors *must* be considered and weighed before ruling. *See Ahanchian v. Xenon Pictures, Inc.,* 624 F.3d 1253, 1261–62 (9th Cir. 2010).

[52]   *See U.S. Commodity Futures Trading Com'n v. Kratville,* 796 F.3d 873, 896 (8th Cir. 2015).

The "reason-for-delay" factor is characterized as the "key" factor for this analysis,[53] although no *per se* rule, which elevates one factor to a singularly dispositive level, is usually proper.[54]

> ♦ **NOTE:** This provision has been applied for seeking relief under Rule 60(b) from default judgments, and, so applied, generally obligates the moving party to show good cause for defaulting, quick action in correcting the default, absence of prejudice to the non-movant, and the existence of a meritorious defense.[55] But the burden on the movant increases under Rule 60(b), since concerns of finality and repose are then implicated.[56] Courts may also consider whether the case implicates the public interest or would impose an especially significant financial loss on the defendant.[57]

Reason 2—Newly Discovered Evidence

Relief from an order or judgment may also be granted on the basis of new evidence where: (1) the evidence has been newly discovered since trial, (2) the moving party was diligent in discovering the new evidence, (3) the new evidence is not merely cumulative or impeaching, (4) the new evidence is material, and (5) in view of the new evidence, a new trial would probably produce a different result.[58] Implicit in these elements is the recognition that the evidence must be evidence of facts that were in existence at the time of trial, though not discovered until after trial.[59] Relief is not necessarily foreclosed, though, merely because the party was aware of the evidence earlier (if that evidence remained inaccessible),[60] nor merely because it relates to an issue that had been earlier litigated).[61] Moreover (and implicitly), the newly discovered evidence must be both admissible and credible.[62] These requirements are strictly enforced.[63] If the movant fails to meet *any* of these prerequisites, the Rule 60(b)(2) motion may be denied.[64]

Reason 3—Fraud, Misrepresentation, Other Adversary Misconduct

Relief from a judgment or order may be permitted on the basis of misconduct where: (1) the moving party possessed a meritorious claim at trial, (2) the adverse party engaged in fraud, misrepresentation, or other misconduct, and (3) the adverse party's conduct prevented the moving party from fully and fairly presenting its case during trial.[65] (Courts, though, are divided on whether the moving party must also show that the misconduct likely altered the case's outcome.[66]) This category is the "lineal descendant" of the rule in equity that a court, finding fraud or undue influence, may alter or negate a written instrument.[67] Relief is reserved for judgments that were unfairly obtained, not at those that are claimed to be just

---

[53]   *See Nansamba v. North Shore Med. Ctr., Inc.*, 727 F.3d 33, 39 (1st Cir. 2013).

[54]   *See Ahanchian v. Xenon Pictures, Inc.*, 624 F.3d 1253, 1261–62 (9th Cir. 2010).

[55]   *See supra* Authors' Commentary to Rule 55(c). *See also Architectural Ingenieria Siglo XXI, LLC v. Dominican Republic*, 788 F.3d 1329, 1343 (11th Cir. 2015).

[56]   *See Colleton Preparatory Academy, Inc. v. Hoover Universal, Inc.*, 616 F.3d 413, 420–21 (4th Cir. 2010).

[57]   *See In re OCA, Inc.*, 551 F.3d 359, 369 (5th Cir. 2008).

[58]   *See In re Global Energies, LLC*, 763 F.3d 1341, 1347 (11th Cir. 2014).

[59]   *See General Universal Systems, Inc. v. Lee*, 379 F.3d 131, 158 (5th Cir. 2004).

[60]   *See Bain v. MJJ Prods., Inc.*, 751 F.3d 642, 646–48 (D.C. Cir. 2014).

[61]   *See In re Global Energies, LLC*, 763 F.3d 1341, 1347 (11th Cir. 2014).

[62]   *See F.D.I.C. v. Arciero*, 741 F.3d 1111, 1118 (10th Cir. 2013).

[63]   *See Waddell v. Hendry County Sheriff's Office*, 329 F.3d 1300, 1309 (11th Cir. 2003).

[64]   *See Jones v. Lincoln Elec. Co.*, 188 F.3d 709, 735–36 (7th Cir. 1999) (commenting that if any of these prerequisites is not satisfied, Rule 60(b)(2) motion must fail).

[65]   *See In re Isbell Records, Inc.*, 774 F.3d 859, 869 (5th Cir. 2014).

[66]   *Compare United States v. City of New Orleans*, 731 F.3d 434, 442–43 (5th Cir. 2013) (not required), *with In re Levaquin Prods. Liab. Litig.*, 739 F.3d 401, 405 (8th Cir. 2014) (absent such showing, relief may be denied).

[67]   *See Ty Inc. v. Softbelly's, Inc.*, 517 F.3d 494, 498 (7th Cir. 2008).

factually in error.[68] Indeed, an actual factual error in the judgment may not even be required.[69] This provision is remedial, and is liberally construed.[70]

The rule does not define "fraud", and the definition is unlikely to be borrowed from State law, prompting one court to pronounce the "general common law understanding" of fraud to be: "the knowing misrepresentation of a material fact, or concealment of the same when there is a duty to disclose, done to induce another to act to his or her detriment."[71] In appropriate cases, relief under this category may be granted to remedy belatedly uncovered misconduct during discovery, but only where the challenged behavior substantially interfered with the moving party's ability to fully and fairly try the case.[72] Ordinarily, relief under this category is reserved for instances where the fraud was committed by the adversary (and not by the party's own counsel or other non-adversaries).[73] Further, the fraud must generally have been perpetrated in the course of litigation, and not, for example, during the course of an underlying commercial transaction.[74] A party's entitlement to relief must be proven by clear and convincing evidence.[75]

♦ **NOTE:** Some courts will presume or infer the third element (substantial interference with the ability to fully and fairly prepare) where the misconduct is proven to be knowing or deliberate.[76]

Reason 4—Void Judgment

Relief may also be granted where the judgment or order is void, whether because the court lacked jurisdiction over the subject matter, lacked personal jurisdiction over the parties, acted in some manner inconsistent with constitutional due process, or otherwise acted beyond the powers granted to it under the law.[77] When a motion challenges a judgment as void, the district court lacks discretion: either the judgment is void (in which case relief must be granted) or it is not.[78] As interpreted by the courts, however, the definition of a "void" judgment is a narrow one. A ruling alleged to be simply wrong is not "void",[79] nor is a judgment that is merely "voidable" (based on the existence of a particular defense or objection).[80]

Relief under Rule 60(b)(4) is not a substitute for a timely appeal.[81] Instead, a judgment is deemed "void" only when the judgment is a "legal nullity"[82]—premised on a fundamental

---

[68] *See General Universal Systems, Inc. v. Lee,* 379 F.3d 131, 156 (5th Cir. 2004).

[69] *See Hesling v. CSX Transp., Inc.,* 396 F.3d 632, 641 (5th Cir. 2005) (proof that withheld information would have altered outcome is not required, because Rule "is aimed at judgments which were unfairly obtained, not at those which are factually incorrect").

[70] *See Hesling v. CSX Transp., Inc.,* 396 F.3d 632, 641 (5th Cir. 2005).

[71] *See Info-Hold, Inc. v. Sound Merch., Inc.,* 538 F.3d 448, 455–56 (6th Cir. 2008).

[72] *See General Universal Systems, Inc. v. Lee,* 379 F.3d 131, 156–57 (5th Cir. 2004).

[73] *See Latshaw v. Trainer Wortham & Co., Inc.,* 452 F.3d 1097, 1102 (9th Cir. 2006).

[74] *See Roger Edwards, LLC v. Fiddes & Son Ltd.,* 427 F.3d 129, 134 (1st Cir. 2005).

[75] *See In re Isbell Records, Inc.,* 774 F.3d 859, 869 (5th Cir. 2014).

In re Levaquin Prods. Liab. Litig., 739 F.3d 401, 404–05 (8th Cir. 2014).

[76] *See Aguiar-Carrasquillo v. Agosto-Alicea,* 445 F.3d 19, 28 (1st Cir. 2006).

[77] *See United Student Aid Funds, Inc. v. Espinosa,* 559 U.S. 260, 270–71, 130 S.Ct. 1367, 1377, 176 L.Ed.2d 158 (2010).

[78] *See Thompson v. Deutsche Bank Nat. Trust Co.,* 775 F.3d 298, 306 (5th Cir. 2014).

[79] *See United Student Aid Funds, Inc. v. Espinosa,* 559 U.S. 260, 270, 130 S.Ct. 1367, 1377, 176 L.Ed.2d 158 (2010).

[80] *See Days Inns Worldwide, Inc. v. Patel,* 445 F.3d 899, 906–08 (6th Cir. 2006) (distinguishing between void ab initio and voidable).

[81] *See United Student Aid Funds, Inc. v. Espinosa,* 559 U.S. 260, 271, 130 S.Ct. 1367, 1377, 176 L.Ed.2d 158 (2010).

[82] *See Gillispie v. Warden, London Correctional Inst.,* 771 F.3d 323, 327 (6th Cir. 2014).

jurisdictional or due process error.[83] As other courts have restated it, a "void" judgment is one where the rendering court was powerless to enter it[84] or contravened due process by entering it,[85] or where the exercise of jurisdiction was otherwise "egregious" and a "clear usurpation of power" (with some cases going still further, requiring that the exercise of jurisdiction must have lacked even an arguable ground for support).[86] Courts are divided on which party bears the burden of proof in Rule 60(b)(4) challenges: some courts impose the burden on the party who invoked the court's jurisdiction originally,[87] while others vest the burden with the movant.[88]

Reason 5—Changed Circumstances

Relief from a judgment or order may also be granted where the circumstances justifying the ruling have changed, such as (1) when the judgment is satisfied, released, or discharged, (2) where a prior judgment on which the present judgment is based has been reversed or otherwise vacated, or (3) in any other circumstance where the continued enforcement of the judgment would be inequitable (*e.g.,* a change in legislative or decisional law, or a change in critical facts).[89] These three grounds are disjunctive; the presence of any one is sufficient to justify relief.[90] This encompasses the traditional power invested in a court of equity to modify its decree when appropriate in view of changed circumstances.[91]

In evaluating such motions, the courts consider whether a substantial change in circumstances or law has occurred since the contested order was entered, whether complying with the contested order would cause extreme and unexpected hardship, and whether a good reason for modification exists.[92] The party seeking relief bears the burden of proving changed circumstances warranting relief, but once that entitlement is shown, the court must modify the order.[93] The proposed modification must be "suitably tailored" to meet the new legal or factual circumstances.[94] Relief under the "changed circumstances" category is only available where there is a prospective effect to the challenged judgment;[95] the mere fact that the law has changed since the judgment was entered,[96] or that a ruling will have future collateral

---

[83]   *See United Student Aid Funds, Inc. v. Espinosa,* 559 U.S. 260, 271, 130 S.Ct. 1367, 1377, 176 L.Ed.2d 158 (2010).

[84]   *See Karsner v. Lothian,* 532 F.3d 876, 886 (D.C. Cir. 2008).

[85]   *See Baldwin v. Credit Based Asset Servicing and Securitization,* 516 F.3d 734, 737 (8th Cir. 2008).

[86]   *See Wendt v. Leonard,* 431 F.3d 410, 412–13 (4th Cir. 2005). *See also United Student Aid Funds, Inc. v. Espinosa,* 559 U.S. 260, 271, 130 S.Ct. 1367, 1377, 176 L.Ed.2d 158 (2010) (noting the no-arguable-ground prediction of lower courts, but finding no need to discuss it). *But see Bell Helicopter Textron, Inc. v. Islamic Republic of Iran,* 734 F.3d 1175, 1180–81 (D.C. Cir. 2013) (rejecting no-arguable-ground as constraint).

[87]   *See Craig v. Ontario Corp.,* 543 F.3d 872, 876 (7th Cir. 2008).

[88]   *See "R" Best Produce, Inc. v. DiSapio,* 540 F.3d 115, 126 (2d Cir. 2008) (in collateral challenge to personal jurisdiction, defendant bears burden if it had notice of original lawsuit).

[89]   *See Agostini v. Felton,* 521 U.S. 203, 117 S.Ct. 1997, 138 L.Ed.2d 391 (1997) (allowing relief under Rule 60(b)(5) to alter permanent injunction in light of Supreme Court's decision to overrule earlier constitutional precedent on which injunction was based); *Rufo v. Inmates of Suffolk County Jail,* 502 U.S. 367, 112 S.Ct. 748, 116 L.Ed.2d 867 (1992) (parties seeking a modification of an order entered by consent bear the burden of demonstrating a "significant change" in circumstances to warrant relief from the decree).

[90]   *See Horne v. Flores,* 557 U.S. 433, 454, 129 S.Ct. 2579, 2597, 174 L.Ed.2d 406 (2009).

[91]   *See Frew ex rel. Frew v. Hawkins,* 540 U.S. 431, 441–42, 124 S.Ct. 899, 905–06, 157 L.Ed.2d 855 (2004).

[92]   *See Horne v. Flores,* 557 U.S. 433, 447, 129 S.Ct. 2579, 174 L.Ed.2d 406 (2009); *Rufo v. Inmates of Suffolk County Jail,* 502 U.S. 367, 384, 112 S.Ct. 748, 116 L.Ed.2d 867 (1992).

[93]   *See Horne v. Flores,* 557 U.S. 433, 447, 129 S.Ct. 2579, 2593–95, 174 L.Ed.2d 406 (2009).

[94]   *See Reynolds v. McInnes,* 338 F.3d 1221, 1226 (11th Cir. 2003).

[95]   *See Baum v. Blue Moon Ventures, LLC,* 513 F.3d 181, 190 (5th Cir. 2008). *But cf. City of Duluth v. Fond du Lac Band of Lake Superior Chippewa,* 702 F.3d 1147, 1154 (8th Cir. 2013) (prospective relief under Rule 60(b)(5) could be coupled with retrospective relief under another Rule 60(b) subpart).

[96]   *See Kathrein v. City of Evanston,* 752 F.3d 680, 690 (7th Cir. 2014).

estoppel effect (something obviously common to many rulings)[97] or otherwise causes "some reverberations into the future"[98] does not provide the requisite "prospective" effect necessary for relief under this provision. Ordinarily, money judgments will not possess the required "prospective" effect because the set nature of the monetary outlay provides the finality.[99] However, the "satisfied, released, or discharged" clause is often invoked by parties seeking to have a judgment satisfied by the court, due to an ongoing dispute with the judgment holder over the judgment.[100] The "based-on-earlier-judgment" alternative usually requires that the prior judgment have a preclusionary (res judicata or collateral estoppel) effect, and not a mere precedential impact.[101] The courts are divided whether such relief may be granted *sua sponte.*[102]

♦ **NOTE:** The Supreme Court has confirmed that the lower courts should not apply Rule 60(b)(5) in *anticipation* of the Supreme Court's overruling of an earlier precedent. To the contrary, the Supreme Court instructs that where one of its precedents applies directly to the circumstances at hand, even though the precedent's reasoning has been undermined by other opinions, the lower courts should follow the precedent and leave to the Supreme Court the prerogative of overruling its own decisions.[103]

Reason 6—In the Interests of Justice

Finally, relief from a judgment or order may be permitted to further the interests of justice. This "catch-all" category is reserved for extraordinary circumstances[104] causing unexpected, extreme hardship.[105] Relief under this Rule is "exceedingly rare,"[106] and rests on a highly fact-intensive balancing of finality and doing justice.[107] It does not offer an unsuccessful litigant an opportunity "to take a mulligan,"[108] and is never a substitute for direct appeal.[109] Seeking relief under this Rule also generally requires a showing of actual injury and the presence of circumstances beyond the movant's control that prevented timely action to protect her interests.[110] There is also some authority for the conclusion that this Rule is limited to setting aside a judgment or order, and may not be used to grant affirmative relief.[111] Relief on the basis of a change in decisional law is unlikely.[112]

This "catch-all" category and the preceding five specific categories are mutually exclusive. If the reason for which relief is sought fits within one of the five specific categories (even though the facts fail to meet the prerequisites for that relief (*e.g.,* the neglect is not

---

[97] *See Coltec Industries, Inc. v. Hobgood,* 280 F.3d 262, 271–72 (3d Cir. 2002) ("If this [collateral estoppel argument] were enough to satisfy Rule 60(b)(5)'s threshold requirement, then the Rule's requirement of 'prospective application' would be meaningless").

[98] *See Kalamazoo River Study Group v. Rockwell Intern. Corp.,* 355 F.3d 574, 587–88 (6th Cir. 2004).

[99] *See Kalamazoo River Study Group v. Rockwell Intern. Corp.,* 355 F.3d 574, 587–88 (6th Cir. 2004).

[100] *See BUC Intern. Corp. v. International Yacht Council Ltd.,* 517 F.3d 1271, 1274–75 (11th Cir. 2008).

[101] *See Manzanares v. City of Albuquerque,* 628 F.3d 1237, 1240 (10th Cir. 2010).

[102] *See Baum v. Blue Moon Ventures, LLC,* 513 F.3d 181, 190 (5th Cir. 2008) *(sua sponte* grants permitted).

[103] *See Agostini v. Felton,* 521 U.S. 203, 117 S.Ct. 1997, 138 L.Ed.2d 391 (1997). *See also Cano v. Baker,* 435 F.3d 1337, 1341–43 (11th Cir. 2006) (rejecting, on similar grounds, Rule 60(b)(5)'s use by former abortion plaintiff who sought to revisit her earlier abortion rights decision as wrongly decided in light of intervening medical evidence).

[104] *See, e.g., Gonzalez v. Crosby,* 545 U.S. 524, 535, 125 S.Ct. 2641, 2649, 162 L.Ed.2d 480 (2005).

[105] *See Galbert v. West Caribbean Airways,* 715 F.3d 1290, 1294 (11th Cir. 2013).

[106] *See In re Guidant Corp. Implantable Defibrillators Products Liability Litigation,* 496 F.3d 863, 868 (8th Cir. 2007).

[107] *See West v. Carpenter,* 790 F.3d 693, 697 (6th Cir. 2015).

[108] *See Kramer v. Gates,* 481 F.3d 788, 792 (D.C. Cir. 2007).

[109] *See Banks v. Chicago Bd. of Educ.,* 750 F.3d 663, 668 (7th Cir. 2014).

[110] *See Gardner v. Martino,* 563 F.3d 981, 992 (9th Cir. 2009).

[111] *See Delay v. Gordon,* 475 F.3d 1039, 1044–45 (9th Cir. 2007).

[112] *See Arthur v. Thomas,* 739 F.3d 611, 631–32 (11th Cir. 2014).

truly excusable, the time period for seeking relief under that Rule provision has passed, etc.)), the catch-all category will not permit relief.[113] "Something more" is required, and, given the breadth of the reasons captured by Rule 60(b)(1) through (b)(5), there is an understandably thin volume of cases explaining when that "something more" will be present to warrant relief under Rule 60(b)(6).[114] Note, however, that some cases have ruled that Rule 60(b)(6) may be proper where a defaulted client seeks relief from judgment on the basis of extremely gross negligence of,[115] or abandonment by,[116] counsel.

Burden of Proof

The party seeking relief from a judgment or order bears the burden of demonstrating that the prerequisites for such relief are satisfied.[117] Because this relief is not intended to be a substitute for appeal, some courts have elevated the level of proof required for recovery.[118] Because the relief is fundamentally equitable, equitable defenses against the moving party (*e.g.,* unclean hands) may foreclose it.[119]

Discretion of District Judge

Whether to grant relief under Rule 60(b) is left to the broad discretion of the trial court.[120] In the case of "void" judgments attacked under Rule 60(b)(4), however, the district court's discretion is almost illusory, if it exists at all. True "void" judgments are "legal nullities", and the court's refusal to vacate such judgments is a *per se* abuse of discretion.[121]

Jurisdiction

No new independent basis for the court's jurisdiction is necessary to support a Rule 60(b) motion or ruling. Rather, such a proceeding is deemed to be a continuation of the original action, and jurisdiction to consider a later Rule 60(b) motion is not divested by subsequent events.[122]

Procedure

Motions under this Rule should be made to the court that rendered the judgment.[123] Absent a local rule dictating otherwise, the court is not required to convene a hearing on Rule 60(b) motions, but may choose to do so in its discretion.[124] The court generally does not need to enter findings of fact and conclusions of law to grant Rule 60(b) relief,[125] although a careful articulation of its analysis is advised as "helpful" and aiding appellate review.[126]

---

[113] *See Pioneer Inv. Servs. Co. v. Brunswick Assocs. Ltd. P'ship,* 507 U.S. 380, 393, 113 S.Ct. 1489, 123 L.Ed.2d 74 (1993); *Liljeberg v. Health Services Acquisition Corp.,* 486 U.S. 847, 108 S.Ct. 2194, 100 L.Ed.2d 855 (1988).

[114] *See East Brooks Books, Inc. v. City of Memphis,* 633 F.3d 459, 465 (6th Cir. 2011). *See generally Lopez v. Ryan,* 678 F.3d 1131, 1135–37 (9th Cir. 2012) (applying 6-factor test for habeas relief under Rule 60(b)(6)).

[115] *See Marino v. Drug Enforcement Admin.,* 685 F.3d 1076, 1080 (D.C.Cir. 2012).

[116] *See Moje v. Federal Hockey League, LLC,* 792 F.3d 756, 758 (7th Cir. 2015).

[117] *See Wooten v. McDonald Transit Assocs., Inc.,* 788 F.3d 490, 500–01 (5th Cir. 2015).

[118] *See Info-Hold, Inc. v. Sound Merch., Inc.,* 538 F.3d 448, 454 (6th Cir. 2008).

[119] *See Motorola Credit Corp. v. Uzan,* 561 F.3d 123, 127 (2d Cir. 2009).

[120] *See In re Levaquin Prods. Liab. Litig.,* 739 F.3d 401, 404 (8th Cir. 2014).

[121] *See, e.g., Bell Helicopter Textron, Inc. v. Islamic Republic of Iran,* 734 F.3d 1175, 1179 (D.C. Cir. 2013).

[122] *See D'Ambrosio v. Bagley,* 656 F.3d 379, 388 (6th Cir. 2011).

[123] *See Board of Trustees, Sheet Metal Workers' Nat. Pension Fund v. Elite Erectors, Inc.,* 212 F.3d 1031, 1034 (7th Cir. 2000).

[124] *See Atkinson v. Prudential Property Co., Inc.,* 43 F.3d 367, 374 (8th Cir. 1994).

[125] *See Atkinson v. Prudential Property Co., Inc.,* 43 F.3d 367, 374 (8th Cir. 1994).

[126] *See Lemoge v. United States,* 587 F.3d 1188, 1194 (9th Cir. 2009).

Who May Seek Relief

Relief under this Rule may be requested by a party, the party's legal representative,[127] or one in privity with a party.[128]

Relief Only from Final Judgments

Rule 60(b) relief is only available from final judgments, orders, and proceedings.[129] Rule 60(b) relief will likely be available able from voluntary dismissals [130] and consent decrees.[131]

Sua Sponte Motions

The Circuits are divided on whether a district court may, on its own initiative, grant relief from a judgment or order under Rule 60(b).[132] When such *sua sponte* relief is permitted, the courts generally demand that the parties receive notice and an opportunity to be heard before the relief is ordered.[133]

Vacating Judgments Entered by Other Courts

One court should attempt to vacate a judgment entered by a different court under Rule 60(b) only in extraordinary circumstances, but there is disputed case support for the proposition that courts may have the authority to do so in an appropriate case.[134]

Nature of Appellate Review

An appeal from a district court order denying relief under Rule 60(b) implicates only the propriety of that denial, and not the underlying judgment's merits (which ordinarily are reviewed only through a direct appeal of that judgment itself).[135]

RULE 60(c)—TIMING AND EFFECT OF MOTION

CORE CONCEPT

Relief under Rule 60(b) must be sought within a "reasonable" time after entry of the challenged judgment or order, except for three grounds which specify a 1-year time limit (from which no extensions may be granted).

APPLICATIONS

The "Void" Judgment Ground

Relief from a "void" judgment or order can be sought at any time.[136] Laches and similar finality principles generally have no effect on void judgments; the courts have held that the

---

[127] *See Matter of El Paso Refinery, LP,* 37 F.3d 230, 234 (5th Cir. 1994).

[128] *See Eyak Native Village v. Exxon Corp.,* 25 F.3d 773, 777 (9th Cir. 1994).

[129] *See Dassault Systemes, SA v. Childress,* 663 F.3d 832, 840 (6th Cir. 2011).

[130] *See Yesh Music v. Lakewood Church,* 727 F.3d 356, 361–63 (5th Cir. 2013) (surveying Circuits).

[131] *See Northeast Ohio Coalition for Homeless v. Husted,* 696 F.3d 580, 601–02 (6th Cir. 2012).

[132] *See Pierson v. Dormire,* 484 F.3d 486, 491–92 (8th Cir. 2007) (describing Circuit split). *Compare United States v. Pauley,* 321 F.3d 578, 581 (6th Cir. 2003) (no *sua sponte* relief), *with Baum v. Blue Moon Ventures, LLC,* 513 F.3d 181, 190 (5th Cir. 2008) *(sua sponte* relief permitted).

[133] *See Pierson v. Dormire,* 484 F.3d 486, 492 (8th Cir. 2007).

[134] *See Budget Blinds, Inc. v. White,* 536 F.3d 244, 251–55 (3d Cir. 2008). *But see Board of Trustees, Sheet Metal Workers' Nat. Pension Fund v. Elite Erectors, Inc.,* 212 F.3d 1031, 1034 (7th Cir. 2000) (ruling that courts do not have that authority).

[135] *See Browder v. Director, Dep't of Corrections of Illinois,* 434 U.S. 257, 263, 98 S.Ct. 556, 54 L.Ed.2d 521 (1978).

[136] *See Bell Helicopter Textron, Inc. v. Islamic Republic of Iran,* 734 F.3d 1175, 1179–80 (D.C. Cir. 2013). *But see Bridgeport Music, Inc. v. Smith,* 714 F.3d 932, 942 (6th Cir. 2013) (motions under Rule 60(b)(4) "must be brought 'within a reasonable time' ").

mere passage of time will not convert a void judgment into a proper one.[137] However, if a party attacks the court's jurisdiction and loses on that issue, the question of jurisdiction becomes *res judicata* and, accordingly, the judgment is not void; the party's only recourse in such a case is a proper, timely merits appeal, not relief under Rule 60(b).[138]

The Uncapped "Reasonable" Time Grounds

Relief from a judgment or order that is sought under either Reason 5 ("changed circumstances") or Reason 6 ("interests of justice") must be made "within a reasonable time" after entry of the judgment or order being challenged.[139] The courts determine whether the time of filing is "reasonable" on a case-by-case basis,[140] dependent on the circumstances.[141] It is not assessed merely by the length of time that passes between discovery and filing,[142] and the period is not necessarily *more* than a year (and might be less than one).[143] Rather, the courts consider the length of delay along with its explanation, any resulting prejudice, any circumstances favoring relief, the nature of the dispute, and whether the public interest is implicated.[144] For some courts, prejudice is a pivotal inquiry.[145] Moreover, to prevail under the catch-all category of Rule 60(b)(6), the moving party must also generally demonstrate faultlessness in the delay.[146]

The 1-Year Capped "Reasonable" Time Grounds

Seeking relief from a judgment or order under any one of the three remaining Rule 60(b) grounds for relief must be done within a reasonable time, but in no event later than 1 year from the entry of the challenged ruling.[147] Thus, this 1-year time limit applies to Reason 1 ("mistake, inadvertence, surprise"),[148] Reason 2 ("newly discovered evidence"),[149] and Reason 3 ("fraud, misrepresentation, other adversary misconduct").[150]

No Extensions

Where the 1-year time limit is specified in Rule 60(c), the period is "absolute" and the district court lacks the authority to extend the time for bringing a motion.[151] However, there is developing case law that when an untimely Rule 60(b) motion is filed, but not objected to by the non-moving party, the timeliness objection may be deemed forfeited through waiver.[152]

---

[137] *See Jackson v. FIE Corp.*, 302 F.3d 515, 523–24 (5th Cir. 2002).

[138] *See Durfee v. Duke,* 375 U.S. 106, 84 S.Ct. 242, 11 L.Ed.2d 186 (1963).

[139] *See* Rule 60(c)(1). *See also Lac Courte Oreilles Band of Lake Superior Chippewa Indians of Wisconsin v. Wisconsin,* 769 F.3d 543, 548 (7th Cir. 2014) (for Rule 60(b)(5) motions); *Bouret-Echevarria v. Caribbean Aviation Maintenance Corp.,* 784 F.3d 37, 43 (1st Cir. 2015) (for Rule 60(b)(6) motions).

[140] *See Bouret-Echevarria v. Caribbean Aviation Maintenance Corp.,* 784 F.3d 37, 43 (1st Cir. 2015).

[141] *See Bouret-Echevarria v. Caribbean Aviation Maintenance Corp.,* 784 F.3d 37, 43 (1st Cir. 2015).

[142] *See Doe v. Briley,* 562 F.3d 777, 781 (6th Cir. 2009).

[143] *See Massi v. Walgreen Co.,* 337 Fed. Appx. 542, 545 (6th Cir. 2009).

[144] *See Bridgeport Music, Inc. v. Smith,* 714 F.3d 932, 942–43 (6th Cir. 2013).

[145] *See Salazar ex rel. Salazar v. District of Columbia,* 633 F.3d 1110, 1118–19 (D.C.Cir. 2011).

[146] *See Amado v. Microsoft Corp.,* 517 F.3d 1353, 1363 (Fed. Cir. 2008).

[147] *See Pioneer Inv. Servs. Co. v. Brunswick Assocs. Ltd. P'ship,* 507 U.S. 380, 393, 113 S.Ct. 1489, 123 L.Ed.2d 74 (1993).

[148] *See The Tool Box, Inc. v. Ogden City Corp.,* 419 F.3d 1084, 1088 (10th Cir.2005).

[149] *See In re G.A.D., Inc.,* 340 F.3d 331, 334 (6th Cir. 2003).

[150] *See In re G.A.D., Inc.,* 340 F.3d 331, 334 (6th Cir. 2003).

[151] *See* Rule 60(c)(1). *See also Wilburn v. Robinson,* 480 F.3d 1140, 1147–48 (D.C. Cir. 2007) (noting that court may not extend).

[152] *See Wilburn v. Robinson,* 480 F.3d 1140, 1147–48 (D.C. Cir. 2007).

Effect on Finality or a Judgment's Operation

The filing of a motion for relief under Rule 60 does not affect the finality of the underlying judgment, nor does it suspend that judgment's operation.[153]

Effect on Appeals

A Rule 60 motion that is filed quickly—within the 28-day post-trial motions period—tolls the time for taking an appeal until the motion is resolved by the trial judge[154] (and, similarly, any appeal filed during such a motion's pendency lies dormant until the motion is resolved).[155] But only the first such motion has this tolling effect; second or later post-judgment motions will usually not toll.[156] Rule 60 motions filed outside the 28-day period do not suspend the appeal time,[157] and if the motion is filed while an appeal is then pending, the district judge is able to grant the motion only upon remand from the appeals court (although denials of the motion may be proper).[158]

RULE 60(d)—OTHER POWERS TO GRANT RELIEF

CORE CONCEPT

Although Rule 60(a) and Rule 60(b) give the district courts specific Rule-based authority to grant relief from judgments and orders, the courts also enjoy other vehicles for granting such relief as well.

APPLICATIONS

Relief by an Independent Action

Litigants may also seek relief from a judgment or order by filing an "independent action", a proceeding that sounds in equity.[159] Independent actions are completely distinct from a motion under Rule 60.[160] They are permitted in only exceptional cases to prevent grave miscarriages of justice.[161] An independent action may be maintained where:

(1)   the judgment should not, in good conscience, be enforced;

(2)   a good defense exists to the plaintiff's lawsuit;

(3)   fraud, accident, or mistake prevented the defendant from obtaining the benefit of the good defense;

(4)   the defendant is free of fault and negligence; *and*

(5)   there is no adequate remedy at law.[162]

The Rule 60(c) time limits do not apply to independent actions in equity[163] (although courts are wary—but not necessarily prohibitive—of litigants using independent actions to evade timeliness problems in what would otherwise be a Rule 60(b) motion).[164] If the independent action is filed in the same court that granted the judgment, supplemental

---

[153] *See* Rule 60(c)(2).

[154] *See* Fed. R. App. P. 4(a)(4)(A) (vi). *See also McKenna v. Wells Fargo Bank, N.A.,* 693 F.3d 207, 213 (1st Cir. 2012).

[155] *See* Fed. R. App. P. 4(a)(4)(B)(i).

[156] *See York Group, Inc. v. Wuxi Taihu Tractor Co.,* 632 F.3d 399, 401 (7th Cir. 2011).

[157] *See York Group, Inc. v. Wuxi Taihu Tractor Co.,* 632 F.3d 399, 401 (7th Cir. 2011).

[158] *See* Rule 62.1. *See also Home Prods. Int'l, Inc. v. United States,* 633 F.3d 1369, 1377 n.9 (Fed.Cir. 2011).

[159] *See United States v. Beggerly,* 524 U.S. 38, 118 S.Ct. 1862, 141 L.Ed.2d 32 (1998).

[160] *See Herring v. United States,* 424 F.3d 384, 389 (3d Cir. 2005).

[161] *See United States v. Beggerly,* 524 U.S. 38, 118 S.Ct. 1862, 141 L.Ed.2d 32 (1998).

[162] *See Aldana v. Del Monte Fresh Produce N.A., Inc.,* 741 F.3d 1349, 1359 (11th Cir. 2014).

[163] *See Park West Galleries, Inc. v. Hochman,* 692 F.3d 539, 545 (6th Cir. 2012).

[164] *See Turner v. Pleasant,* 663 F.3d 770, 775–76 (5th Cir. 2011).

jurisdiction exists—regardless of diversity or federal question jurisdiction.[165] Absent prejudice, a mislabeled independent action may be treated as a Rule 60(b) motion, and vice versa.[166]

Relief by Section 1655 of the Judiciary Code

Congress has, by statute, created a procedure for the enforcement and the removal of liens, incumbrances, and clouds upon the title to real or personal property. The statute provides a means for notifying the affected defendant of the pending proceeding. If, however, the defendant does not receive proper notification, he may act within 1 year to have the judgment lifted and appear to defend (provided he pays costs assessed by the court).[167]

Relief Due to Fraud on the Court

Finally, the district court also possesses the inherent power to grant relief where the judgment or order is obtained through a fraud on the court.[168] Since a ruling procured through fraud is not a true ruling at all,[169] no time limits apply,[170] provided relief is sought within a reasonable time.[171] The court may grant the relief on its own initiative or on motion. (Relief from this type of fraud may also be sought through an independent action or under Rule 60(b)(3)).[172] Movants bear the demanding burden of showing extraordinary circumstances.[173] Such fraud must be proven by clear and convincing evidence.[174] To constitute a fraud on the court, the alleged misconduct must be something more than fraud among the litigants.[175] Instead, the misconduct must be an assault on the integrity of the judicial process, which defiles the court itself or is perpetrated by officers of the court in such a manner that the impartial system of justice fails to function.[176] It must also have caused prejudice to the moving party,[177] such that it would be manifestly unconscionable to permit the judgment to remain.[178] Thus, the moving party must generally show (1) an officer of the court (2) committing an intentional fraud (3) directed against the court itself (4) which, in fact, succeeds in deceiving that court.[179] Fraud in the discovery process, to the extent it meets this standard, can support relief.[180]

---

[165] *See United States v. Beggerly,* 524 U.S. 38, 118 S.Ct. 1862, 141 L.Ed.2d 32 (1998).

[166] *See Mitchell v. Rees,* 651 F.3d 593, 595 (6th Cir. 2011).

[167] *See* 28 U.S.C.A. § 1655.

[168] *Universal Oil Products Co. v. Root Refining Co.,* 328 U.S. 575, 66 S.Ct. 1176, 90 L. Ed. 1447 (1946); *Hazel-Atlas Glass Co. v. Hartford-Empire Co.,* 322 U.S. 238, 64 S.Ct. 997, 88 L. Ed. 1250 (1944).

[169] *See U.S. v. Williams,* 790 F.3d 1059, 1071 (10th Cir. 2015).

[170] *See United States v. Chapman,* 642 F.3d 1236, 1240 n.3 (9th Cir. 2011).

[171] *See Apotex Corp. v. Merck & Co.,* 507 F.3d 1357, 1361 (Fed.Cir.2007).

[172] *See United States v. Baker,* 718 F.3d 1204, 1207 (10th Cir. 2013).

[173] *See Pizzuto v. Ramirez,* 783 F.3d 1171, 1180 (9th Cir. 2015).

[174] *See Pizzuto v. Ramirez,* 783 F.3d 1171, 1180 (9th Cir. 2015).

[175] *See Fox ex rel. Fox v. Elk Run Coal Co.,* 739 F.3d 131, 136 (4th Cir. 2014).

[176] *See Hazel–Atlas Glass Co. v. Hartford–Empire Co.,* 322 U.S. 238, 245–46, 64 S.Ct. 997, 88 L.Ed. 1250 (1944).

[177] *See Wickens v. Shell Oil Co.,* 620 F.3d 747, 759 (7th Cir. 2010).

[178] *See Superior Seafoods, Inc. v. Tyson Foods, Inc.,* 620 F.3d 873, 878 (8th Cir. 2010).

[179] *See Herring v. United States,* 424 F.3d 384, 386 (3d Cir.2005).

[180] *See Appling v. State Farm Mut. Auto. Ins. Co.,* 340 F.3d 769, 780 (9th Cir. 2003).

RULE 60(e)—BILLS AND WRITS ABOLISHED

CORE CONCEPT

The old common law writs of coram nobis, coram vobis, audita querela, and bills of review are abolished in civil proceedings.[181] Filings under these ancient writs may be treated by the courts as motions for relief under Rule 60(b).[182]

Many Such Writs Preserved in Criminal Cases

Although abolished by the Rules for civil cases, many such writs exist in criminal proceedings.[183]

ADDITIONAL RESEARCH REFERENCES

Wright & Miller, *Federal Practice and Procedure* §§ 2851 to 73

C.J.S., Federal Civil Procedure § 368, § 373, §§ 1233 to 1251 et seq.

West's Key Number Digest, Federal Civil Procedure ⬦613.1 to 613.20, ⬦2641 to 2663

---

[181] At the old common law, a writ of coram nobis (if sought at the King's Bench) or writ of coram vobis (if sought in the Courts of Common Pleas) were the procedural tools to correct errors of fact by petitioning to bring before the court certain facts which, if known earlier, would have prevented the entry of judgment. *Rawlins v. Kansas,* 714 F.3d 1189, 1193–95 (10th Cir. 2013). A person against whom execution has issued or was about to issue could seek a writ of audita querela to prevent execution where the execution would be contrary to justice. *See id.* at 1192–93. Finally, a bill of review was a new action, filed in equity, that sought the correction, reversal, alteration, or explanation of a decree issued in an earlier proceeding. *See* 27A Am. Jur. 2d Equity § 256 (1996). Each of these ancient writs—in civil actions only—have been abolished by the Federal Rules. *See* Rule 60(e).

[182] *See Green v. White,* 319 F.3d 560, 563 n.1 (3d Cir. 2003) (treating request for writ in the nature of a writ of coram nobis as motion under Rule 60(b)).

[183] *See Massey v. United States,*581 F.3d 172, 174 (3d Cir. 2009) (audita querela preserved in criminal cases); *Trenkler v. United States,*536 F.3d 85, 87 (1st Cir. 2008) (same, coram nobis).

RULE 61

HARMLESS ERROR

Unless justice requires otherwise, no error in admitting or excluding evidence—or any other error by the court or a party—is ground for granting a new trial, for setting aside a verdict, or for vacating, modifying, or otherwise disturbing a judgment or order. At every stage of the proceeding, the court must disregard all errors and defects that do not affect any party's substantial rights.

[Amended April 30, 2007, effective December 1, 2007.]

AUTHORS' COMMENTARY ON RULE 61

PURPOSE AND SCOPE

Rule 61 codifies the principle that "harmless" errors by the district court—those errors that do not affect the parties' substantial rights—will not justify a new trial, setting aside a verdict, or vacating, modifying, or otherwise disturbing the court's order.

APPLICATIONS

Standard for "Harmlessness"

Rule 61 defines a harmless error as one that does not affect the substantial rights of the parties or does not defeat substantial justice.[1] But an error will not be discounted as harmless if the court is left with a grave doubt as to whether the error had a substantial influence in the ultimate result.[2] A more exacting definition is probably impossible, just as it is impossible to ignore the subjectivity inherent in the inquiry itself.[3] Some baseline principles exist, however. In testing for harmlessness, the court considers the entire record, and applies the standard on a case-by-case basis.[4] Every reasonable possibility of prejudice need not be disproved,[5] but harmlessness cannot be founded merely on the court's belief that the trial ended in a correct result.[6] At its core, the harmless error inquiry asks whether the trial error could (or did) affect "the outcome of a case to the substantial disadvantage of the

---

[1] Rule 61. *See Brandt v. Vulcan, Inc.,* 30 F.3d 752, 760 (7th Cir.1994) (harmless error calls into question the fundamental fairness of the trial).

[2] *See Krulewitch v. United States,*336 U.S. 440, 444–45, 69 S.Ct. 716, 718–19, 93 L. Ed. 790 (1949) (defining harmlessness in criminal context); *Hearn v. McKay,* 603 F.3d 897, 904 n.11 (11th Cir. 2010) (not harmless if error had (or court has "grave doubt" whether it had) substantial influence on outcome); *Sims v. Great American Life Ins. Co.,* 469 F.3d 870, 886 (10th Cir. 2006) (reverse unless jury's verdict more probably than not was unaffected by error); *General Motors Corp. v. New A.C. Chevrolet, Inc.,* 263 F.3d 296, 329 (3d Cir. 2001) (non-constitutional legal errors harmless if it is "highly probable that the error did not affect the judgment").

[3] *See United States v. O'Keefe,* 169 F.3d 281, 287 n.5 (5th Cir. 1999) (citing formulations by Judge Traynor and Justice Rutledge as among the clearest formulations) (citing 11 Charles Alan Wright, Arthur R. Miller, & Mary Kay Kane, *Federal Practice & Procedure* § 2883, at 445 to 47 (2d ed. 1995)). *Cf.* Roger Traynor, *The Riddle of Harmless Error* 35 (1970) ("[U]nless the appellate court believes it highly probable that the error did not affect the judgment, it should reverse"); *Kotteakos v. United States,*328 U.S. 750, 760, 66 S.Ct. 1239, 1245, 90 L. Ed. 1557 (1946) (Rutledge, J.) ("Do not be technical, where technicality does not really hurt the party whose rights in the trial and in its outcome the technicality affects").

[4] *See Barber v. City of Chicago,* 725 F.3d 702, 715 (7th Cir. 2013).

[5] *See General Motors Corp. v. New A.C. Chevrolet, Inc.,* 263 F.3d 296, 329 (3d Cir. 2001).

[6] *See Matusick v. Erie County Water Auth.,* 757 F.3d 31, 50–51 (2d Cir. 2014).

losing party".[7] Unsurprisingly, this risk is considered greater in close cases, than in more one-sided cases.[8]

Burden of Proof

The party moving for relief bears the burden of establishing that a trial error affected that party's substantial rights and, thus, was not harmless.[9] (Note, however, that the standard for harmlessness (as articulated by some courts) seems to suppose that harm is presumed, rather than proved).[10]

Federal Law Controls

Under *Erie* principles,[11] the federal (not State) construction of the harmless error rule usually controls where the federal and State standards are inconsistent.[12]

Applies to All Errors

The harmless error rule applies to all types of errors, including most constitutional errors. The courts of appeals review rulings of the district courts under this standard as well.[13]

Errors in Rulings on Pleadings

Technical errors in pleadings will generally be discounted as harmless.[14] Likewise, errors in granting parties the right to intervene are not overturned unless they affected the substantial rights of the parties.[15]

Errors in Ruling on Motions

The same "substantial rights" standard applies to errors in ruling upon motions.[16] Thus, an improper striking of an amended complaint was harmless if the proposed amendment would not have prevented a dismissal,[17] an improper dismissal of a claim was harmless if, in light of later discovery, it would not have survived summary judgment,[18] an improper preclusion was harmless if similarly situated plaintiffs were also properly dismissed,[19] an improper dismissal of co-defendants was harmless if the plaintiffs were

---

[7]   *See United States v. O'Keefe,* 169 F.3d 281, 287 n.5 (5th Cir. 1999).

[8]   *See Sims v. Great American Life Ins. Co.,* 469 F.3d 870, 886 (10th Cir. 2006).

[9]   *See Palmer v. Hoffman,* 318 U.S. 109, 116, 63 S.Ct. 477, 481–82, 87 L. Ed. 645 (1943) (moving party bears the burden of showing resulting prejudice).

[10]   *Compare Sims v. Great American Life Ins. Co.,* 469 F.3d 870, 886 (10th Cir. 2006) (court must reverse unless it finds that jury's verdict was, more probably than not, unaffected by error) *with Barber v. City of Chicago,* 725 F.3d 702, 715 (7th Cir. 2013) (court will not grant new trial unless there was "significant chance" that error affected jury's verdict), *and Ball v. LeBlanc,* 792 F.3d 584, 591 (5th Cir. 2015) (court presumes errors are harmless).

[11]   *See Erie R. Co. v. Tompkins,* 304 U.S. 64, 58 S.Ct. 817, 82 L. Ed. 1188 (1938) (in diversity cases, the federal courts will apply federal rules of procedure but State substantive law). *See* discussion of the *Erie* Doctrine in Part II of this text.

[12]   *See Sokol Crystal Products, Inc. v. DSC Commc'ns Corp.,* 15 F.3d 1427, 1432–33 (7th Cir. 1994).

[13]   *See* 28 U.S.C.A. § 2111 (fixing harmlessness standard for appeals). *See also McDonough Power Equip., Inc. v. Greenwood,* 464 U.S. 548, 554, 104 S.Ct. 845, 849, 78 L.Ed.2d 663 (1984) (noting that appellate courts must act in accordance with the salutary policy embodied in Rule 61).

[14]   *See Toth v. Corning Glass Works,* 411 F.2d 912, 914 (6th Cir.1969) (refusal to strike a pleading's claim deemed harmless).

[15]   *See Prete v. Bradbury,* 438 F.3d 949, 959–60 (9th Cir. 2006).

[16]   *See, e.g., Hearing v. Minnesota Life Ins. Co.,* 793 F.3d 888, 893 (8th Cir. 2015) (motion for summary judgment); *Lore v. City of Syracuse,* 670 F.3d 127, 150 (2d Cir. 2012) (motions for judgment as a matter of law); *Henning v. Union Pacific R. Co.,* 530 F.3d 1206, 1216–17 (10th Cir. 2008) (motions for new trial).

[17]   *See Lopez v. Target Corp.,* 676 F.3d 1230, 1232 n.3 (11th Cir. 2012).

[18]   *See Quinn v. St. Louis County,* 653 F.3d 745, 750 (8th Cir. 2011).

[19]   *See Ellis v. CCA of Tennessee LLC,* 650 F.3d 640, 652 (7th Cir. 2011).

already barred from a recovery,[20] an improper dismissal of counterclaims was harmless when those claims could be asserted in another proceeding,[21] and an improper scope of a summary judgment ruling[22] or improper consideration (or exclusion) of summary judgment affidavits and exhibits was harmless where, in context, the effect could not have been prejudicial.[23]

Errors in Admitting or Excluding Evidence

The district court enjoys broad discretion to admit or exclude evidence,[24] including expert[25] and rebuttal[26] evidence. Errors in such rulings are harmless if the party raises no objection,[27] if the evidence wrongfully admitted or excluded was cumulative,[28] if adequate curative instructions are given,[29] or if the rulings are otherwise determined not to have caused substantial prejudice or to have substantially influenced the jury.[30] However, evidentiary rulings that affected the substantial rights of a party are *not* harmless, and the rulings must be reversed.[31] Thus, if the trial evidence is not sufficient to support the verdict without the wrongfully admitted evidence, the ruling is prejudicial.[32] Likewise, an improper decision to admit (or exclude) evidence of an invocation of Fifth Amendment rights can be prejudicial.[33] In making this "harmlessness" evaluation, the court views the error in light of the entire record.[34] The court considers the centrality of the evidence and the prejudicial effect of the inclusion or exclusion of the evidence.[35] The court also examines whether other evidence is "sufficiently strong" to support a conclusion that the evidentiary error had no effect on the outcome.[36] The courts often begin with a "presumption of prejudice"[37]—thus, only if the court can say with fair assurance that the judgment was not substantially affected by the wrongfully admitted or excluded evidence, will the error be considered harmless.[38] The courts are particularly careful in discounting an error as harmless in close cases,[39] or where it is substantively important, inflammatory, repeated, emphasized, or unfairly self-serving.[40]

---

[20] *See Bates v. City of Chicago,* 726 F.3d 951, 958 (7th Cir. 2013).

[21] *See Walter Kidde Portable Equip., Inc. v. Universal Sec. Instruments, Inc.,* 479 F.3d 1330, 1340 (Fed. Cir. 2007).

[22] *See Broadcast Music, Inc. v. Evie's Tavern Ellenton, Inc.,* 772 F.3d 1254, 1258 (11th Cir. 2014).

[23] *See S.E.C. v. Smart,* 678 F.3d 850, 856 (10th Cir. 2012).

[24] *See Jones v. Nat'l Am. Univ.,* 608 F.3d 1039, 1044 (8th Cir. 2010).

[25] *See Dresser-Rand Co. v. Virtual Automation Inc.,* 361 F.3d 831, 842 (5th Cir. 2004).

[26] *See Peals v. Terre Haute Police Dept.,* 535 F.3d 621, 630 (7th Cir. 2008).

[27] *See Abrams v. Lightolier Inc.,* 50 F.3d 1204, 1213 (3d Cir. 1995).

[28] *See Jensen v. Solvay Chems., Inc.,* 721 F.3d 1180, 1184 (10th Cir. 2013).

[29] *See Grizzle v. Travelers Health Network, Inc.,* 14 F.3d 261, 269 (5th Cir. 1994) (court must consider curative instructions when assessing harmlessness). In ruling on the effect of the curative instructions, a court will assume that the jury obeyed the court and followed its instructions. *See Trademark Research Corp. v. Maxwell Online, Inc.,* 995 F.2d 326, 340 (2d Cir. 1993). *Compare Davidson v. Smith,* 9 F.3d 4, 6 (2d Cir.1993) (improper testimony not cured by trial instructions) *with Trademark Research Corp. v. Maxwell Online, Inc.,* 995 F.2d 326, 331 (2d Cir.1993) (trial error deemed cured by court's instructions).

[30] *See CFE Racing Prods., Inc. v. BMF Wheels, Inc.,* 793 F.3d 571, 584 (6th Cir. 2015).

[31] *See Caudle v. District of Columbia,* 707 F.3d 354, 361–63 (D.C.Cir. 2013).

[32] *See S.E.C. v. Happ,* 392 F.3d 12, 28 (1st Cir. 2004).

[33] *See Hinojosa v. Butler,* 547 F.3d 285, 292–95 (5th Cir. 2008).

[34] *See Jordan v. Binns,* 712 F.3d 1123, 1137 (7th Cir. 2013).

[35] *See Standley v. Edmonds-Leach,* 783 F.3d 1276, 1284 (D.C.Cir. 2015).

[36] *See Jordan v. Binns,* 712 F.3d 1123, 1137 (7th Cir. 2013).

[37] *See Jerden v. Amstutz,* 430 F.3d 1231, 1240–41 (9th Cir. 2005).

[38] *See Barber v. City of Chicago,* 725 F.3d 702, 715 (7th Cir. 2013).

[39] *See Huthnance v. District of Columbia,* 722 F.3d 371, 381 (D.C.Cir. 2013).

[40] *See Doty v. Sewall,* 908 F.2d 1053, 1057 (1st Cir.1990).

- *Effect of Multiple Errors:* Although each individual evidentiary error might not, standing alone, have affected a party's substantial rights, the court may find that the collective effect of multiple evidentiary errors deprived the moving party of a fair trial.[41]

Errors in Seating Jurors

Errors in striking or refusing to strike prospective jurors are also measured under the harmless error standard.[42]

Errors in Jury Instructions

Jury instructions must be considered in their entirety.[43] If the charging errors would not have changed the trial result,[44] or if the parties waived the errors by failing to timely object,[45] challenges to jury instructions will be rejected as harmless.[46] Conversely, if the jury may have based their verdict on an erroneous instruction,[47] or if the instruction was otherwise prejudicially misleading, confusing, or legally incorrect,[48] or affected a party's substantial rights,[49] a new trial is warranted.

Errors in Jury Verdict Form Interrogatories

Whether mistakes in crafting jury interrogatories on the verdict form is deemed reversible error will also be measured under the harmless error standard.[50]

Errors During Jury Deliberations

Mistakes in permitting juror examination of exhibits (including those admitted for demonstrative purposes only) are tested under the harmless error standard.[51]

Errors in Ruling on Counsel's Conduct During Trial

Misconduct by counsel during trial will be deemed harmless unless the court determines that the misconduct affected the verdict,[52] as will errors in permitting inappropriate counsel invitations for jury participation in a trial demonstration.[53] In testing

---

[41]   *See Barber v. City of Chicago,* 725 F.3d 702, 715 (7th Cir. 2013).

[42]   *See Alaska Rent-A-Car, Inc. v. Avis Budget Group, Inc.,* 709 F.3d 872, 880 (9th Cir. 2013).

[43]   *See American Family Mut. Ins. Co. v. Hollander,* 705 F.3d 339, 355–56 (8th Cir. 2013).

[44]   *See Czekalski v. LaHood,* 589 F.3d 449, 453 (D.C.Cir. 2009) (must be prejudicial); *Richards v. Relentless, Inc.,* 341 F.3d 35, 48 (1st Cir. 2003) (new trial necessary only if instruction error could have affected jury's deliberation).

[45]   *See Tatum v. Moody,* 768 F.3d 806, 820 n.9 (9th Cir. 2014). *See generally Foley v. Commonwealth Elec. Co.,* 312 F.3d 517, 520 (1st Cir. 2002) (if party properly objects to jury instruction, harmless error Rule 61 applies; if proper objection not made, plain error rule applies which requires proof of: (1) error, (2) that error was plain, (3) that error likely altered outcome, and (4) that error was sufficiently fundamental to threaten fairness, integrity, or public reputation of judicial proceedings).

[46]   *See Terminate Control Corp. v. Horowitz,* 28 F.3d 1335, 1345 (2d Cir. 1994) (jury instructions warrant a new trial only if the court is persuaded, based on the record as a whole, that the error was prejudicial or the charge was highly confusing).

[47]   *See Ericsson, Inc. v. D-Link Sys., Inc.,* 773 F.3d 1201, 1235 (Fed.Cir. 2014); *Biegas v. Quickway Carriers, Inc.,* 573 F.3d 365, 377 (6th Cir. 2009).

[48]   *See Freudeman v. Landing of Canton,* 702 F.3d 318, 324–25 (6th Cir. 2012).

[49]   *See Kogut v. County of Nassau,* 789 F.3d 36, 47 (2d Cir. 2015).

[50]   *See Happel v. Walmart Stores, Inc.,* 602 F.3d 820, 826–28 (7th Cir. 2010).

[51]   *See Baugh ex rel. Baugh v. Cuprum S.A. de C.V.,* 730 F.3d 701, 710–11 (7th Cir. 2013).

[52]   *Cf.* Rule 39(c) (relating to advisory juries). *See Peterson v. Willie,* 81 F.3d 1033, 1036 (11th Cir. 1996) (noting that statements made during oral arguments will not constitute reversible error unless they are plainly unwarranted and clearly injurious); *Westfarm Associates Ltd. Partnership v. Washington Suburban Sanitary Com'n,* 66 F.3d 669, 685 (4th Cir. 1995) (inappropriate allusion made during closing argument, followed by proper instructions from the court, is not basis for reversal).

[53]   *See Noel v. Artson,* 641 F.3d 580, 592 (4th Cir. 2011).

errors occurring during argument by counsel, the court will assess (1) the argument's nature and seriousness, (2) if the opponent invited the argument, (3) if the argument could be rebutted effectively, (4) effective curative instructions, and (5) the weight of the evidence.[54]

Errors in Bench Judgments

In bench trials, errors are harmless if the record shows that the district judge would have reached the same judgment regardless of the error.[55] Thus, a judge's mistaken application of a certain method of damages valuation (one to which there was no testimony or other record basis) will be deemed harmless if the effect of the error caused no prejudice.[56]

Error in Granting or Denying Jury Trial

The court's mistaken decision to grant a jury trial is generally harmless error,[57] but an improper denial of a jury trial is usually grounds for reversal.[58]

ADDITIONAL RESEARCH REFERENCES

Wright & Miller, *Federal Practice and Procedure* §§ 2881 to 88

C.J.S., Federal Civil Procedure §§ 1062 to 1100 et seq., §§ 1241 to 1247 et seq.

West's Key Number Digest, Federal Civil Procedure ⊶2333 to 2353, ⊶2651 to 2663; Federal Courts ⊶891 to 914

---

[54] *See Stollings v. Ryobi Techs., Inc.,* 725 F.3d 753, 760 (7th Cir. 2013).

[55] *See Barber v. Ruth,* 7 F.3d 636, 641 (7th Cir. 1993).

[56] *See United States v. 191.07 Acres of Land,* 482 F.3d 1132, 1137 (9th Cir. 2007) (finding valuation error was harmless as to appellants because it resulted in a higher award than appellants (using other method) would otherwise have received).

[57] *See Mateyko v. Felix,* 924 F.2d 824, 828 (9th Cir. 1990). *See also Venture Properties, Inc. v. First Southern Bank,* 79 F.3d 90, 92 (8th Cir. 1996) (movant demonstrated no prejudice from court's decision to conduct a jury trial rather than a bench trial).

[58] *See Burns v. Lawther,* 53 F.3d 1237, 1241–42 (11th Cir. 1995) (harmless error rule may be applied to improper denials of trial by jury, but only if the issues could have been resolved by summary judgment or judgment as a matter of law); *King v. United Ben. Fire Ins. Co.,* 377 F.2d 728, 731 (10th Cir. 1967) (denial will be deemed harmless where only a question of law is involved or where a verdict for the movant would have been set aside).

RULE 62

STAY OF PROCEEDINGS TO ENFORCE
A JUDGMENT

(a) Automatic Stay; Exceptions for Injunctions, Receiverships, and Patent Accountings. Except as stated in this rule, no execution may issue on a judgment, nor may proceedings be taken to enforce it, until 14 days have passed after its entry. But unless the court orders otherwise, the following are not stayed after being entered, even if an appeal is taken:

(1) an interlocutory or final judgment in an action for an injunction or a receivership; or

(2) a judgment or order that directs an accounting in an action for patent infringement.

(b) Stay Pending the Disposition of a Motion. On appropriate terms for the opposing party's security, the court may stay the execution of a judgment—or any proceedings to enforce it—pending disposition of any of the following motions:

(1) under Rule 50, for judgment as a matter of law;

(2) under Rule 52(b), to amend the findings or for additional findings;

(3) under Rule 59, for a new trial or to alter or amend a judgment; or

(4) under Rule 60, for relief from a judgment or order.

(c) Injunction Pending an Appeal. While an appeal is pending from an interlocutory order or final judgment that grants, dissolves, or denies an injunction, the court may suspend, modify, restore, or grant an injunction on terms for bond or other terms that secure the opposing party's rights. If the judgment appealed from is rendered by a statutory three-judge district court, the order must be made either:

(1) by that court sitting in open session; or

(2) by the assent of all its judges, as evidenced by their signatures.

(d) Stay with Bond on Appeal. If an appeal is taken, the appellant may obtain a stay by supersedeas bond, except in an action described in Rule 62(a)(1) or (2). The bond may be given upon or after filing the notice of appeal or after obtaining the order allowing the appeal. The stay takes effect when the court approves the bond.

(e) Stay Without Bond on an Appeal by the United States, Its Officers, or Its Agencies. The court must not require a bond, obligation, or other security from the appellant when granting a stay on an appeal by the United

States, its officers, or its agencies or on an appeal directed by a department of the federal government.

(f) Stay in Favor of a Judgment Debtor Under State Law. If a judgment is a lien on the judgment debtor's property under the law of the state where the court is located, the judgment debtor is entitled to the same stay of execution the state court would give.

(g) Appellate Court's Power Not Limited. This rule does not limit the power of the appellate court or one of its judges or justices:

(1) to stay proceedings—or suspend, modify, restore, or grant an injunction—while an appeal is pending; or

(2) to issue an order to preserve the status quo or the effectiveness of the judgment to be entered.

(h) Stay with Multiple Claims or Parties. A court may stay the enforcement of a final judgment entered under Rule 54(b) until it enters a later judgment or judgments, and may prescribe terms necessary to secure the benefit of the stayed judgment for the party in whose favor it was entered.

[Amended effective March 19, 1948; October 20, 1949; July 19, 1961; August 1, 1987; April 30, 2007, effective December 1, 2007; March 26, 2009, effective December 1, 2009.]

AUTHORS' COMMENTARY ON RULE 62

PURPOSE AND SCOPE

Rule 62 provides for stays to prevent the enforcement of judgments pending post-trial motions and appeals.

RULE 62(a)—AUTOMATIC STAY; EXCEPTIONS FOR INJUNCTIONS, RECEIVERSHIPS, AND PATENT ACCOUNTINGS

CORE CONCEPT

Rule 62(a) establishes an automatic stay that postpones enforcement of a judgment for 14 days from the date of entry of the judgment.[1] However, Rule 62(a) provides no automatic stay in three circumstances: (1) an interlocutory or final judgment in an action for an injunction;[2] (2) an interlocutory or final judgment in a receivership action; and (3) a judgment or order directing an accounting in an action for infringement of patents.

---

[1]　*See, e.g., In re High Sulfur Content Gasoline Products Liab. Litig.,* 517 F.3d 220, 231 (5th Cir. 2008).

[2]　*See, e.g., Ogden Fire Co. No. 1 v. Upper Chichester TP.,* 504 F.3d 370, 377 n.3 (3d Cir. 2007).

APPLICATIONS

Effect

An automatic stay will prevent the enforcement of the judgment, but the stay will not affect the appealability of the judgment or the running of the appeal time.[3] Additionally, the judgment has *res judicata* effect during the pendency of the appeal.[4]

Judgments Covered

The automatic stay applies to any judgment defined in Rule 54(a). It does not apply to judgments granting interlocutory or final judgment in injunction or receivership actions or judgments or orders directing an accounting in actions for infringement of patents.

Expiration of Stay Period

Once the automatic stay period expires, a party may seek enforcement of the judgment unless the defendant posts security under Rule 62(d).[5]

Armed Services Personnel

The Soldiers and Sailors Civil Relief Act of 1940, 50 U.S.C.A. §§ 203–04, Appendix §§ 523 to 24, provides that a court may stay the execution of any judgment or vacate or stay an attachment or garnishment entered against a person in the military service.

Computation of Time

For purposes of 14-day stays under Rule 62(a), time is computed under the standards of Rule 6(a).[6]

RULE 62(b)—STAY PENDING THE DISPOSITION OF A MOTION

CORE CONCEPT

After judgment, a court has discretion to order a stay of execution or enforcement while it considers post-trial motions. The court also has discretion to establish conditions for the security of the adverse party during the pendency of the stay.

APPLICATIONS

Procedure

The filing of post-trial motions does not stay execution or enforcement of the judgment. Accordingly, a party seeking a stay should file a motion for stay before the end of the automatic stay period provided under Rule 62(a). Once the motion for stay is made, the court has discretion to stay execution or enforcement of the judgment pending disposition of the post-trial motions.

Motions Covered

The court is authorized to stay execution or enforcement of a judgment during the pendence of 4 specified post-trial motions—motions under: (1) Rule 50, for judgment as a matter of law; (2) Rule 52(b), to amend the findings or for additional findings; (3) Rule 59, for a new trial or to alter or amend a judgment; or (4) Rule 60, for relief from a judgment or order.

---

[3]   Fed.R.App.P. 4(a).

[4]   *See, e.g., Fish Market Nominee Corp. v. Pelofsky,* 72 F.3d 4, 7 (1st Cir. 1995) (noting distinction between bar to enforcing judgment and absence of bar to *res judicata*).

[5]   *See, e.g., Acevedo-Garcia v. Vera-Monroig,* 368 F.3d 49, 58 (1st Cir. 2004).

[6]   *See, e.g., KRW Sales, Inc. v. Kristel Corp.,* 154 F.R.D. 186, 188 (N.D. Ill. 1994).

Security

If the court orders a stay pending post-trial motions, it may order the movant to post security, including the amount of the judgment and interest, during the period of the stay. The court may also require the bond to include costs and damages for delay or any other loss that may result during the period of the stay. Additionally, the court may order the movant to provide written notice to the opposing parties of any material disposition of the movant's assets.

Effect of Denial

When the court denies a motion for a stay pending disposition of a post-trial motion, the judgment is binding (and may be enforced) until vacated by the court or reversed on appeal, unless the defendant posts security under Rule 62(d).

RULE 62(c)—INJUNCTION PENDING AN APPEAL

CORE CONCEPT

Rule 62(c) authorizes the district judge or a district court of three judges, having granted, dissolved, or denied a preliminary or final injunction, to stay its decision or grant other interim relief pending appeal.

♦ **NOTE:** The 14-day automatic stay in Rule 62(a) does not apply in injunction actions, nor does the ability to post security and automatically obtain a stay under Rule 62(d).

APPLICATIONS

Scope

Rule 62(c) covers interlocutory as well as final judgments in injunction cases and applies to cases where the court has denied an injunction as well as granted an injunction. However, the district court may not dissolve an injunction that has been appealed. Instead, the court may only modify the injunction while it is being appealed, with the purpose of maintaining the status quo.[7]

Time for Motion

A party may make a motion to stay an injunction immediately after the notice of appeal has been filed and at any time while the appeal is pending.[8]

Which Court

The movant should first assert the motion in the district court. If the district court denies relief or the district court provides inadequate relief, the movant may assert the motion in the court of appeals.[9] Where submission to a panel would prejudice the movant, the motion can be made to a single judge of the court of appeals.[10] In extraordinary circumstances, pending disposition of an application for writ of certiorari and during the pendency of an appeal to the court of appeals[11] or from a final judgment of the court of appeals,[12] a single justice of the Supreme Court, sitting as a single Circuit Justice, may take

---

[7]   *See, e.g., Armstrong v. Brown,* 732 F.3d 955, n6 (9th Cir. 2013).

[8]   *See, e.g., Credit Suisse First Boston Corp. v. Grunwald,* 400 F.3d 1119, 1124 (9th Cir. 2005) (motion may be made "at any time before entry of a final judgment").

[9]   Fed.R.App.P. 8(a). *See Rakovich v. Wade,* 834 F.2d 673, 675 (7th Cir. 1987).

[10]   Fed.R.App.P. 8(a).

[11]   *Atiyeh v. Capps,* 449 U.S. 1312, 101 S.Ct. 829, 66 L.Ed.2d 785 (1981).

[12]   *Graddick v. Newman,* 453 U.S. 928, 102 S.Ct. 4, 69 L.Ed.2d 1025 (1981); *Holtzman v. Schlesinger,* 414 U.S. 1304, 94 S.Ct. 1, 38 L.Ed.2d 18 (1973).

any action provided in Rule 62(g).[13] In addition, a judge of the court rendering the judgment may grant a stay on application for writ of certiorari to the Supreme Court.[14]

Requirements

When a party makes a motion under Rule 62(c), the courts will require the movant to show the following elements: (a) a strong likelihood of success on the merits of the appeal; (b) that unless the motion is granted the movant will suffer irreparable injury; (c) no substantial harm will come to other interested parties; and (d) a grant of the motion will not harm the public interest.[15] The courts have often balanced the irreparable injury to the movant if the court did not issue the stay against the harm the stay would cause to the other parties and to the public. The governing considerations are the same whether the party applies to the district court or to the appellate courts under Rule 62(g).

Requirements of Order

An order issued pursuant to Rule 62(c) must set forth the reasons for its issuance and be specific in its terms.

Security for Stay

The court will usually order the movant to post security during the period of the stay or the injunction.[16]

Three Judge District Court

When a district court of three judges, sitting by statute, renders judgment in an injunction case, a motion to stay that judgment should be addressed to all three judges. Such a court may only issue a stay pending an appeal in open court or by signature of all three judges.

RULE 62(d)—STAY WITH BOND UPON APPEAL

CORE CONCEPT

The act of appealing a judgment does not automatically create a stay of the judgment pending appeal.[17] However, a party may obtain a stay by filing a supersedeas bond with the court (*i.e.*, a bond posted as security against an appeal) that is approved by the court.[18]

APPLICATIONS

Stay as of Right

By posting a supersedeas bond with the court and upon approval of the bond by the court, a party obtains a stay as a matter of course.[19]

Amount of Bond

The amount of the bond will usually be an amount sufficient to satisfy the judgment plus interest.[20] The court may also require the bond to include costs,[21] plus any damages for

---

[13] 28 U.S.C.A. § 1651(a); U.S.Sup. Ct.R. 23.

[14] 28 U.S.C.A. 2101(f).

[15] *Hilton v. Braunskill*, 481 U.S. 770, 776, 107 S.Ct. 2113, 95 L.Ed.2d 724 (1987).

[16] *See, e.g., Roche Diagnostics Corp. v. Medical Automation Systems, Inc.*, 646 F.3d 424 (7th Cir. 2011).

[17] *See, e.g., Correa v. Cruisers, a Div. of KCS Intern., Inc.*, 298 F.3d 13, 29 (1st Cir. 2002).

[18] *See, e.g., Alphas Co. v. Dan Tudor & Sons Sales, Inc.*, 679 F.3d 35, 38 n.2 (1st Cir. 2012).

[19] *See, e.g., Exxon Valdez v. Exxon Mobil Corp.*, 568 F.3d 1077 (9th Cir. 2009).

[20] *See, e.g., Strong v. Laubach*, 443 F.3d 1297, 1299 (10th Cir. 2006).

[21] Fed.R.App.P. 7.

delay. The court has the discretion to provide a lesser amount or other types of security.[22] Local rule may provide the amount required.

Alternatives to Bond

Although Rule 62(d) speaks only of bonds, courts may permit "other forms of judgment guarantee."[23]

Deadline for Posting Bond

Rule 62(d) permits the bond to be posted at the time a party files a notice of appeal (or receives permission to appeal), or later.[24] However, because the stay does not become effective until the court approves the bond, it is wise to post the bond within the 14-day period of the automatic stay provided by Rule 62(a).

Actions Not Stayed

Rule 62(d) does not apply to: judgments in injunction actions;[25] judgments in receivership actions; and judgments requiring an accounting in patent infringement cases. In such cases an appealing party may not post a bond and obtain a stay of judgment under Rule 62(d).

Judgments for Damages and Injunctions

If a party seeks to use Rule 62(d) to stay a judgment by which the court ordered both money damages and equitable relief, the stay under Rule 62(d) is effective only to stop enforcement of the damage award.[26] Unless the appealing party can persuade the court to stay the injunction under Rule 62(c), the injunction portion of the judgment may be enforced pending appeal.

Failure to Post Bond

Failure to post bond under Rule 62(d) does not affect a party's right to appeal.[27] However, in the absence of a stay ordered pursuant to Rule 62(d), an adverse party may enforce a judgment while the appeal is pending,[28] which sometimes may render the appeal moot.[29]

Impact of Appeal by Prevailing Party

If the prevailing party also appeals some facet of a district court's judgment, there is some conflict in the cases as to whether the judgment debtor must post a bond to stay execution of judgment pending the judgment debtor's appeal.[30]

---

[22] *See, e.g., Olcott v. Delaware Flood Co.,* 76 F.3d 1538, 1559 (10th Cir. 1996).

[23] *See, e.g., Dale M. ex rel. Alice M. v. Board of Educ.,* 237 F.3d 813, 815 (7th Cir. 2001) (judgment debtor who pays judgment instead of posting bond is entitled to repayment of judgment if reversed).

[24] *See, E.E.O.C. v. Clear Lake Dodge,* 25 F.3d 265, 273 (5th Cir. 1994) (posting bond prior to appealing is inappropriate).

[25] *See, e.g., Solis v. Malkani,* 638 F.3d 269, 275 (4th Cir. 2011).

[26] *N.L.R.B. v. Westphal,* 859 F.2d 818 (9th Cir.1988) (Rule 62(d) cannot stay injunctions).

[27] *See, e.g., Porco v. Trustees of Indiana University,* 453 F.3d 390, 394 (7th Cir. 2006).

[28] *See, e.g., Eurasia Intern., Ltd. v. Holman Shipping, Inc.,* 411 F.3d 578, 585 (5th Cir. 2005).

[29] *But see Strong v. Laubach,* 443 F.3d 1297, 1299 (10th Cir. 2006).

[30] *Trustmark Ins. Co. v. Gallucci,* 193 F.3d 558, 559 (1st Cir. 1999).

RULE 62(e)—STAY WITHOUT BOND ON AN APPEAL BY THE UNITED STATES, ITS OFFICERS, OR ITS AGENCIES

CORE CONCEPT

The United States is not required to post a bond to obtain a stay of the enforcement of a judgment pending appeal. This exemption also extends to officers and agents of the United States government and any party acting under the direction of any department or agency of the government.[31]

RULE 62(f)—STAY IN FAVOR OF A JUDGMENT DEBTOR UNDER STATE LAW

CORE CONCEPT

When the judgment creates a lien upon the debtor's property and the judgment debtor is entitled to a stay under applicable state law, the district court shall stay the enforcement of the judgment to the same extent that state law directs a state court to enter a stay.[32] The court has no discretion to deny such a stay.[33]

RULE 62(g)—APPELLATE COURT'S POWER NOT LIMITED

CORE CONCEPT

The provisions of Rule 62 apply only to district courts, and do not limit appellate courts.

RULE 62(h)—STAY WITH MULTIPLE CLAIMS OR PARTIES

CORE CONCEPT

When a court issues a partial judgment under Rule 54(b), it may allow immediate enforcement of the partial judgment or it may stay enforcement of the partial judgment pending a further adjudication.

APPLICATIONS

Standards for Granting a Stay

The court has discretion to decide a motion for stay, balancing the equities of the parties and considering the administration of the case.[34]

Independent Actions

When a court consolidates independent actions and renders judgment on one of the independent actions, this is not a partial judgment under Rule 54(b), and a stay will not be granted under Rule 62(h).[35]

Posting of Security

When issuing a stay of a particular judgment, the court may require security to be posted to secure that part of the judgment.[36]

---

[31] 28 U.S.C.A. § 2408.

[32] *See, e.g., Hoban v. Washington Metropolitan Area Transit Auth.*, 841 F.2d 1157, 1159 (D.C. Cir. 1988).

[33] *Cf. Rodriguez-Vazquez v. Lopez-Martinez*, 345 F.3d 13, 14 (1st Cir. 2003).

[34] *See, e.g., North Penn Transfer, Inc. v. Maple Press Co.*, 176 B.R. 372, 375–77 (M.D. Pa. 1995).

[35] *In re Massachusetts Helicopter Airlines, Inc.*, 469 F.2d 439, 442 (1st Cir. 1972).

[36] *Curtiss-Wright Corp. v. General Elec. Co.*, 446 U.S. 1, 13, 100 S.Ct. 1460, 64 L.Ed.2d 1 (1980).

ADDITIONAL RESEARCH REFERENCES

Wright & Miller, Federal Practice and Procedure: Civil 2d §§ 2901 to 20

C.J.S., Federal Civil Procedure § 1263; Federal Courts § 294(1 to 5) et seq.

West's Key Number Digest, Federal Courts ⊶684 to 687

RULE 62.1

INDICATIVE RULING ON A MOTION
FOR RELIEF THAT IS BARRED
BY A PENDING APPEAL

(a) Relief Pending Appeal. If a timely motion is made for relief that the court lacks authority to grant because of an appeal that has been docketed and is pending, the court may:

(1) defer considering the motion;

(2) deny the motion; or

(3) state either that it would grant the motion if the court of appeals remands for that purpose or that the motion raises a substantial issue.

(b) Notice to the Court of Appeals. The movant must promptly notify the circuit clerk under Federal Rule of Appellate Procedure 12.1 if the district court states that it would grant the motion or that the motion raises a substantial issue.

(c) Remand. The district court may decide the motion if the court of appeals remands for that purpose.

[Added March 26, 2009, effective December 1, 2009.]

AUTHORS' COMMENTARY ON RULE 62.1

PURPOSE AND SCOPE

Rule 62.1 applies when a motion has been made to a district court in a case that has been appealed. If the district court lacks authority to grant the motion because the appeal is pending, the district court has several options to indicate the way in which it might act if the appellate court remands the case for the district court to adjudicate the motion.

RULE 62.1(a) RELIEF PENDING APPEAL

CORE CONCEPT

A district court may announce how it would rule on a pending motion that it cannot address because the case is subject to the jurisdiction of an appellate court. In that sense, a district court's decision to exercise its authority under Rule 62.1 is "indicative" only.

APPLICATIONS

Scope of District Court's Options

Rule 62.1 provides the court with the following options. First, the court may choose to defer consideration of the motion pending outcome of the appeal. Second the court may deny the motion. Thus, notwithstanding the existence of a pending appeal, a district court is normally free to deny any motion made during the pendency of the appeal even if the court might not have had authority to grant the motion. Third, the court may express its view that the motion would be granted if the appellate court chooses to remand the case for that

purpose. Fourth, the district court may state simply that the motion raises a substantial issue.

Requirement of Timeliness

Rule 62.1 only applies where the motion before the court was filed timely.[1]

Motions Which District Court May Grant Notwithstanding Appeal

Federal Rule of Appellate Procedure 4(a)(4) identifies six motions that, if timely filed with the district court, have the effect of stopping the appellate process (including the time limit for filing a notice of appeal) until the district court disposes of such motions.[2] These motions are generally motions to alter the court's judgment or for a new trial. In other words, notwithstanding that a party has already filed a notice of appeal, Appellate Rule 4 permits the district court to decide those motions. Because Rule 62.1 is expressly limited to circumstances in which a district court is prevented from granting a motion by an appeal, Rule 62.1 does not apply to motions that fall within the scope of Appellate Rule 4.

RULE 62.1(b) NOTICE TO THE COURT OF APPEALS

CORE CONCEPT

If the district court states that it would grant a motion filed while the case is on appeal or that the motion raises a substantial issue, the party that filed the motion must notify the appellate court.

APPLICATIONS

Notice

If a movant is obligated to notify an appellate court that the district court indicated it might grant the motion or that the motion raises a substantial issue, the manner of notification is governed by Federal Rule of Appellate Procedure 12.1[3] The movant's obligation to notify the appellate court does not apply if the district court either defers consideration of the motion or denies the motion.

RULE 62.1(c) REMAND

CORE CONCEPT

The district court may decide the motion if the court of appeals has remanded the case for that purpose.[4]

---

[1]   Cf. Binta B. ex rel. S.A. v. Gordon, 710 F.3d 608, 616 (6th Cir. 2013) (Rule 62.1 requires that issue be raised first in district court, not appellate court).

[2]   Fed.R.App.P 4(a)(4).

[3]   Fed.R.App.P. 12.1

[4]   See, e.g., Arlington Industries v. Bridgeport Fittings, Inc., 632 F.3d 1246 (Fed.Cir. 2011) (noting district court's authority to provide "indicative ruling).

RULE 63

JUDGE'S INABILITY TO PROCEED

If a judge conducting a hearing or trial is unable to proceed, any other judge may proceed upon certifying familiarity with the record and determining that the case may be completed without prejudice to the parties. In a hearing or a nonjury trial, the successor judge must, at a party's request, recall any witness whose testimony is material and disputed and who is available to testify again without undue burden. The successor judge may also recall any other witness.

[Amended effective August 1, 1987; December 1, 1991; April 30, 2007, effective December 1, 2007.]

AUTHORS' COMMENTARY ON RULE 63

PURPOSE AND SCOPE

When a judge withdraws after a trial or hearing begins, any other judge of the court may proceed with the case. The successor judge will read the pertinent portions of the record, certify familiarity with that record, and then decide whether he or she may proceed with the case without causing prejudice to the parties. In a non-jury hearing or trial format, if the successor judge proceeds with the case, he or she must recall any witnesses requested by the parties, if their testimony is material and disputed and where the witnesses are available to testify again without undue burden. In addition, the successor judge may recall any witnesses in order to become more familiar with the record.

APPLICATIONS

Caution in Relying on Pre-1992 Case Law

Rule 63 was substantially amended in late 1991 to expand the Rule's scope and to alter certain interpretations given to the Rule by the courts. Decisions that predate the 1991 amendment should be cited with due care.[1]

Conditions for Inability to Proceed

A judge's withdrawal must rest on compelling reasons, such as sickness, death, or other disability, including recusal and disqualification.[2] A judge may not withdraw for personal convenience.[3]

Statement of Grounds for Withdrawal

The withdrawing judge must state on the record the reasons for his or her withdrawal.[4]

---

[1]   *But see Zand v. C.I.R. Service,* 143 F.3d 1393, 1400 (11th Cir. 1998) (court may look to pre-1991 decisions for guidance given facts of particular case).

[2]   *See* Rule 63 advisory committee notes to 1991 amendment; 28 U.S.C. §§ 144 & 455 (providing for disqualification of judges). *See Cardiello v. Arbogast,* 533 Fed. Appx. 150, 154 (3d Cir. 2013) (death); *United States v. Nwoye,* 60 F.Supp.2d 225, 227 (D.D.C. 2014) (injury); *Redner's Markets, Inc. v. Joppatowne G.P. Ltd. P'ship,* 2013 WL 3678248, at *1 n.1 (D.Md. July 11, 2013) (retirement).

[3]   *See* Rule 63 advisory committee notes to 1991 amendment.

[4]   *See* Rule 63 advisory committee notes to 1991 amendment.

Only Applicable *After* Hearing or Trial Begins

The certification obligation of Rule 63 is only triggered if the substitution is made *after* a hearing or trial has begun; before that time, a substitution may be made without any requirement of certification by the substituting judge.[5]

Timing of Substitution

The original text of Rule 63 implied that, once a trial or hearing had begun, district judges could not be substituted unless the departing judge had already filed findings of fact and conclusions of law. The courts embraced this implication and, unless the parties stipulated otherwise, required new trials where the departing judge had not filed the findings and conclusions.[6]

This "negative inference" mandate ascribed to Rule 63 was abolished in 1991. Citing the increasing length of trials in federal court and the expected concomitant increase in the number of trials interrupted by a judge's disability,[7] the drafters provided that a substitution may be made after trial commences and even in the absence of filed findings and conclusions, if the replacement judge (1) can certify his or her familiarity with the proceedings in the case to date, and (2) can continue the proceedings without prejudicing the parties.

Certifying Familiarity with the Record

Once a trial or hearing has begun, no substitute judge can replace a departing judge without first "certifying familiarity with the record".[8] It is this certification procedure that ensures that Due Process is not violated when the case resumes.[9] Although an express "certification" is plainly preferred,[10] the court of appeals will likely not reverse in the absence of an express certification so long as the successor judge's statements confirm compliance with the record familiarity requirement.[11] Nor will the appeals court likely reverse for unfortunate, though nonprejudicial, misstatements in the certification.[12] This certification requirement obligates the substitute judge to read and consider all relevant portions of the record.[13] What portions of the record the successor judge is required to learn depends upon the nature of the successor judge's role in the case. For example, if the successor judge inherits a jury trial before the evidence has closed, the judge must become familiar with the entire record so as to properly rule upon relevance-based evidentiary objections; but if the successor judge inherits the case after the entry of verdict or judgment, the judge need only review those portions of the record relevant to the particular issues challenged by post-trial motions.[14]

---

[5]   *See Beck v. Dileo,* 2010 WL 4875685, at *1 (E.D.Cal. Nov. 23, 2010).

[6]   *See, e.g., In re Higginbotham,* 917 F.2d 1130, 1132 (8th Cir. 1990).

[7]   *See* Rule 63 advisory committee notes to 1991 amendment. *See also Mergentime Corp. v. Washington Metropolitan Area Transit Authority,* 166 F.3d 1257, 1262 (D.C. Cir. 1999) (noting motivation for Rule change, and commenting that successor judges may now take over at any point after the trial begins, subject to certain additional responsibilities imposed upon the successor judges).

[8]   *See Gaye v. Lynch,* 788 F.3d 519, 533–34 (6th Cir. 2015).

[9]   *See Patelco Credit Union v. Sahni,* 262 F.3d 897, 905 (9th Cir. 2001).

[10]   *See, e.g., Healey v. Murphy,* 2013 WL 1336786, at *2 (D.Mass. Mar. 29, 2013) (noting express certification).

[11]   *See Bisbal-Ramos v. City of Mayaguez,* 467 F.3d 16, 26 (1st Cir. 2006). *See also United States v. Washington,* 653 F.3d 1057, 1064 (9th Cir. 2011) ("ministerial" failure to certify "does not cast doubt on the proceeding's integrity").

[12]   *See In re Reale,* 584 F.3d 27, 32 n.2 (1st Cir. 2009) (finding certification's confirmation that successor judge had considered witnesses' demeanor "unfortunate" but, given the record evidence, not prejudicial).

[13]   *See Mergentime Corp. v. Washington Metropolitan Area Transit Authority,* 166 F.3d 1257, 1265 (D.C. Cir. 1999).

[14]   *See Mergentime Corp. v. Washington Metropolitan Area Transit Authority,* 166 F.3d 1257, 1265 (D.C. Cir. 1999).

Prerequisite for Substitution

In order for a judge to be substituted, there must be an available transcript or a videotape to permit the replacement judge to become familiar with the proceedings that occurred prior to the substitution. The Committee Notes encourage the prompt preparation of the trial or videotape transcript, so as to prevent delaying the jury longer than necessary.[15]

Jury Trials

In a jury trial, the parties do not have the right to insist that a witness be recalled.[16] Instead, if the successor judge can certify familiarity with the record and can determine that the proceedings are able to be completed without prejudice to the parties, nothing more is required.[17] Should the judge choose to do so, however, the successor judge has the discretion to recall a witness.[18]

Bench Trials

In a non-jury trial, the parties can insist that the successor judge recall a witness whose testimony is material and disputed *and* who is available to testify again:[19]

(1) *Testimony of Available Witness:* When a witness is available, the successor judge may decide to hear the witness' testimony if the testimony is material or disputed. It may be error for the new judge to decline to hear the testimony of a witness whose credibility is material to a finding of fact, particularly if a party so requests.[20]

(2) *Testimony of Unavailable Witness:* If a witness has become unavailable, such that a subpoena to compel testimony at trial is not possible, the successor judge can consider the testimony recorded at trial or, if the testimony was not material or not disputed, may choose not to hear the testimony at all.[21]

Previously Litigated Issues

Unless the controlling law has changed, the successor judge will not ordinarily revisit rulings made by the withdrawing judge. However, the successor judge is required to consider and rule upon allegations of trial error properly raised in post-trial motions.[22]

Option to Enter Summary Judgment

If, after reviewing the trial transcript, the successor judge decides that no credibility determinations are required and that one party is entitled to a judgment as a matter of law, summary judgment can be entered as an alternative to the successor judge "stepping into the shoes" of the unavailable trial judge.[23]

---

[15]   *See* Rule 63 advisory committee notes to 1991 amendment.

[16]   *See Jackson v. State of Alabama State Tenure Com'n,* 405 F.3d 1276, 1286–87 (11th Cir. 2005).

[17]   *See Jackson v. State of Alabama State Tenure Com'n,* 405 F.3d 1276, 1287 (11th Cir. 2005).

[18]   *See* Rule 63.

[19]   *See* Rule 63. *See also In re Reale,* 584 F.3d 27, 32 (1st Cir. 2009).

[20]   *See* Rule 63 advisory committee notes to 1991 amendment. *See also In re Karten,* 293 Fed. Appx. 734, 736 (11th Cir. 2008) (successor judge should not make credibility determinations, but should retry the case); *Canseco v. United States,* 97 F.3d 1224, 1227 (9th Cir. 1996) (as amended Dec. 18, 1996) (where credibility of witness is questioned, and where sufficiency of the evidence hinges on that witness's testimony and credibility cannot be determined from the record, substitute judge must recall the witness, if available without undue burden, and make own credibility determination).

[21]   *See* Rule 63 advisory committee notes to 1991 amendment.

[22]   *See Mergentime Corp. v. Washington Metropolitan Area Transit Authority,* 166 F.3d 1257, 1263 (D.C. Cir. 1999) (holding that successor judge may not refuse to consider post-trial motions out of deference to the original judge).

[23]   *See Patelco Credit Union v. Sahni,* 262 F.3d 897, 906 (9th Cir. 2001).

Waiver of Right to Object to New Judge

Following the departure of the original judge, the litigants may be deemed to have waived any objection to the case's reassignment to a new judge if the litigants fail either to timely seek a new trial or timely object to a reassignment,[24] or fail to timely insist upon the recall of witnesses.[25] Minimally, a failure to object will likely relegate the appellate court to the very forgiving "plain error" standard of review.[26]

ADDITIONAL RESEARCH REFERENCES

Wright & Miller, *Federal Practice and Procedure: Civil 2d* §§ 2921 to 30

C.J.S., Judges §§ 35 to 68

West's Key Number Digest, Judges ⊶21, ⊶32

---

[24] *See Littleton v. Pilot Travel Ctrs., LLC,* 568 F.3d 641, 648 (8th Cir. 2009) (party may not "sit back and await decision" before objecting); *Zand v. C.I.R. Service,* 143 F.3d 1393, 1400 (11th Cir. 1998) (ruling that parties had "cleverly tiptoe[d]" across a "procedural tightrope", refusing to consent to a reassignment while, simultaneously, failing to seek the added expense of a retrial; therefore, an unfavorable verdict by the successor judge could not be challenged under Rule 63).

[25] *See Marantz v. Permanente Med. Group, Inc. Long Term Disability Plan,* 687 F.3d 320, 327 (7th Cir. 2012); *In re Reale,* 584 F.3d 27, 32–33 (1st Cir. 2009).

[26] *See Bisbal-Ramos v. City of Mayaguez,* 467 F.3d 16, 26 (1st Cir. 2006).

VIII. PROVISIONAL AND FINAL REMEDIES

RULE 64

SEIZING A PERSON OR PROPERTY

(a) Remedies Under State Law—In General. At the commencement of and throughout an action, every remedy is available that, under the law of the state where the court is located, provides for seizing a person or property to secure satisfaction of the potential judgment. But a federal statute governs to the extent it applies.

(b) Specific Kinds of Remedies. The remedies available under this rule include the following—however designated and regardless of whether state procedure requires an independent action:

- arrest;
- attachment;
- garnishment;
- replevin;
- sequestration; and
- other corresponding or equivalent remedies.

[Amended April 30, 2007, effective December 1, 2007.]

AUTHORS' COMMENTARY ON RULE 64

PURPOSE AND SCOPE

After the commencement of an action and until the time of judgment, Rule 64 authorizes the use of state laws by which a claimant may seek an order of court to seize a person or property in order to secure satisfaction of the eventual judgment. Relief under Rule 64 is infrequently granted and should be infrequently sought.

RULE 64(a)—REMEDIES UNDER
STATE LAW—IN GENERAL

CORE CONCEPT

Federal courts may employ the remedies for seizing a person or property that are available to a state court in the state where the federal court is located.[1] However, if a federal statute is applicable, it governs in place of state law.[2]

---

[1] *See, e.g., Lee-Barnes v. Puerto Ven Quarry Corp.,* 513 F.3d 20, 23 n.1 (1st Cir. 2008).
[2] *See, e.g., United States v. Witham,* 648 F.3d 40, 44 (1st Cir. 2011).

APPLICATIONS

Time to Seek an Order

At any time after the commencement of an action and until the time of judgment, a party may assert an ancillary request to seize property under Rule 64.[3]

Comparison to Rule 70

Rule 64, where applicable, permits prejudgment relief. Rule 70, by contrast, is applicable to circumstances arising after a judgment is entered.[4]

Federal Statutory Remedies

If the remedy sought by the claimant exists under a federal statute, the provisions of the federal statute will apply rather than state law.[5] The Advisory Committee Notes to Rule 64 list some of the federal remedies. Otherwise, the movant may choose any provisional remedy available under applicable state law.[6]

RULE 64(b)—SPECIFIC KINDS OF REMEDIES

CORE CONCEPT

Rule 64(b) provides a non-exclusive list of remedies available to a federal court, without regard to how a state may designate those remedies. It also provides that a district court may use those remedies in the pending action, without regard to whether the state rules otherwise require an independent enforcement action.

APPLICATIONS

Method for Obtaining Relief

Where a federal remedy exists, the procedure for obtaining relief will be provided by the relevant statute and the Rules. When relief is sought under a state remedy, state law generally supplies the procedures, except to the extent that the Rules apply. The method for obtaining relief will vary from state to state and district to district. However, in all cases a U.S. Marshal rather than a state officer would seize the goods or property.

Subject Matter Jurisdiction

Procedures under Rule 64 whether asserted in a pending action or in an independent action do not require a separate basis of subject matter jurisdiction.[7]

Constitutional Limitations

The seizure of a person or property without notice or a prior hearing may often be a violation of constitutional due process.[8]

---

[3]   *See, e.g., Rosen v. Cascade Intern., Inc.,* 21 F.3d 1520, 1530 (11th Cir. 1994) (prejudgment attachment).

[4]   *See, e.g., Deegan v. Strategic Azimuth LLC,* 768 F.Supp.2d 107, 115 n.1 (D.D.C. 2011).

[5]   *See, e.g., Hoult v. Hoult,* 373 F.3d 47, 54 (1st Cir. 2004) ("federal statute governs to the extent applicable").

[6]   *See, e.g., Goya Foods, Inc. v. Wallack Management Co.,* 290 F.3d 63, 70 (1st Cir. 2002); *Stephens v. National Distillers and Chemical Corp.,* 69 F.3d 1226, 1228 n.2 (2d Cir. 1995).

[7]   *Cf. Skevofilax v. Quigley,* 810 F.2d 378, 385 (3d Cir. 1987).

[8]   *North Georgia Finishing, Inc. v. Di-Chem, Inc.,* 419 U.S. 601, 95 S.Ct. 719, 42 L.Ed.2d 751 (1975); *Mitchell v. W. T. Grant Co.,* 416 U.S. 600, 94 S.Ct. 1895, 40 L.Ed.2d 406 (1974); *Fuentes v. Shevin,* 407 U.S. 67, 92 S.Ct. 1983, 32 L.Ed.2d 556 (1972).

Armed Services Personnel

Relief under Rule 64 is subject to the Soldiers' and Sailors' Civil Relief Act of 1940, 50 U.S.C.A. §§ 203, 204, Appendix §§ 523, 524, which prohibits seizure of the assets of absent military personnel in many circumstances.

Execution

A plaintiff who recovers judgment is entitled to an execution sale of the previously seized property in satisfaction of the judgment.

ADDITIONAL RESEARCH REFERENCES

Wright & Miller, *Federal Practice and Procedure: Civil 2d* §§ 2931 to 40

C.J.S., Federal Civil Procedure §§ 233 to 241, § 1271

West's Key Number Digest, Attachment ⊶1 to 384; Garnishment ⊶1 to 251; Replevin ⊶1 to 135; Sequestration ⊶1 to 21

RULE 65

INJUNCTIONS AND RESTRAINING ORDERS

(a) Preliminary Injunction.

(1) *Notice.* The court may issue a preliminary injunction only on notice to the adverse party.

(2) *Consolidating the Hearing with the Trial on the Merits.* Before or after beginning the hearing on a motion for a preliminary injunction, the court may advance the trial on the merits and consolidate it with the hearing. Even when consolidation is not ordered, evidence that is received on the motion and that would be admissible at trial becomes part of the trial record and need not be repeated at trial. But the court must preserve any party's right to a jury trial.

(b) Temporary Restraining Order.

(1) *Issuing Without Notice.* The court may issue a temporary restraining order without written or oral notice to the adverse party or its attorney only if:

(A) specific facts in an affidavit or a verified complaint clearly show that immediate and irreparable injury, loss, or damage will result to the movant before the adverse party can be heard in opposition; and

(B) the movant's attorney certifies in writing any efforts made to give notice and the reasons why it should not be required.

(2) *Contents; Expiration.* Every temporary restraining order issued without notice must state the date and hour it was issued; describe the injury and state why it is irreparable; state why the order was issued without notice; and be promptly filed in the clerk's office and entered in the record. The order expires at the time after entry—not to exceed 14 days—that the court sets, unless before that time the court, for good cause, extends it for a like period or the adverse party consents to a longer extension. The reasons for an extension must be entered in the record.

(3) *Expediting the Preliminary-Injunction Hearing.* If the order is issued without notice, the motion for a preliminary injunction must be set for hearing at the earliest possible time, taking precedence over all other matters except hearings on older matters of the same character. At the hearing, the party who obtained the order must proceed with the motion; if the party does not, the court must dissolve the order.

(4) *Motion to Dissolve.* On 2 days' notice to the party who obtained the order without notice—or on shorter notice set by the court—the adverse party

may appear and move to dissolve or modify the order. The court must then hear and decide the motion as promptly as justice requires.

(c) Security. The court may issue a preliminary injunction or a temporary restraining order only if the movant gives security in an amount that the court considers proper to pay the costs and damages sustained by any party found to have been wrongfully enjoined or restrained. The United States, its officers, and its agencies are not required to give security.

(d) Contents and Scope of Every Injunction and Restraining Order.

(1) *Contents.* Every order granting an injunction and every restraining order must:

(A) state the reasons why it issued;

(B) state its terms specifically; and

(C) describe in reasonable detail-and not by referring to the complaint or other document— the act or acts restrained or required.

(2) *Persons Bound.* The order binds only the following who receive actual notice of it by personal service or otherwise:

(A) the parties;

(B) the parties' officers, agents, servants, employees, and attorneys; and

(C) other persons who are in active concert or participation with anyone described in Rule 65(d)(2)(A) or (B).

(e) Other Laws Not Modified. These rules do not modify the following:

(1) any federal statute relating to temporary restraining orders or preliminary injunctions in actions affecting employer and employee;

(2) 28 U.S.C. § 2361, which relates to preliminary injunctions in actions of interpleader or in the nature of interpleader; or

(3) 28 U.S.C. § 2284, which relates to actions that must be heard and decided by a three-judge district court.

(f) Copyright Impoundment. This rule applies to copyright-impoundment proceedings.

[Amended effective March 19, 1948; October 20, 1949; July 1, 1966; August 1, 1987; April 23, 2001, effective December 1, 2001; April 30, 2007, effective December 1, 2007; March 26, 2009, effective December 1, 2009.]

AUTHORS' COMMENTARY ON RULE 65

PURPOSE AND SCOPE

Rule 65 establishes the procedural requirements for obtaining a temporary restraining order or a preliminary injunction, and contains some provisions relating to permanent injunctions. Although a party must satisfy the procedures of Rule 65 before a court will grant such injunctive relief, the substantive requirements for an injunction are separate from and additional to Rule 65, and they must also be satisfied.[1]

The substantive requirements for injunctions are found predominantly in case law, as well as statutes authorizing injunctions in certain circumstances and limiting their applicability in others.[2] Although there can be substantial variations in the requirements from one jurisdiction to another, courts deciding whether to grant an injunction generally weigh some or all of the following factors: (1) whether the potential harm to the person seeking injunctive relief is irreparable,[3] *i.e.,* whether such harm could be cured through an award of money damages instead of an injunction;[4] (2) whether the person against whom an injunction would be entered would be harmed excessively by the injunction; (3) whether, and to what extent, the grant or denial of an injunction would affect interests of third persons,[5] including public interests; and (4) when a motion for a temporary restraining order or a preliminary injunction is before the court, whether the person seeking such relief is likely to succeed on the merits when the case comes to trial.[6]

◆   **NOTE:** Most of Rule 65 applies only to requests for preliminary relief. With the exception of Rule 65(d), Rule 65 has no application to grants or denials of permanent injunctions.[7]

RULE 65(a)—PRELIMINARY INJUNCTION

CORE CONCEPT

Rule 65(a) contains two distinct concepts. The first portion of the Rule ensures that courts will not issue preliminary injunctions until affected parties receive notice and an opportunity to be heard. The second part of Rule 65(a) provides that the court may consolidate an application for a preliminary injunction with a trial on the merits.

APPLICATIONS

Purpose of a Preliminary Injunction

The purpose of a preliminary injunction is usually to maintain the status quo until the merits of a case can be decided.[8] Courts grant preliminary injunctions ordering an alteration of the status quo only in unusual circumstances where the merits clearly favor one party over another.[9] A preliminary injunction can only apply during the pendency of the case, at the end of which the court will consider whether to enter a permanent injunction.

---

[1]   *See, e.g. Grupo Mexicano de Desarrollo S.A. v. Alliance Bond Fund, Inc.,* 527 U.S. 308, 319, 119 S.Ct. 1961, 144 L.Ed.2d 319 (1999).

[2]   *See, e.g., Muffley ex rel. N.L.R.B. v. Spartan Mining Co.,* 570 F.3d 534 (4th Cir. 2009).

[3]   *See, e.g., Rodriguez ex rel. Rodriguez v. DeBuono,* 175 F.3d 227, 235 (2d Cir. 1999).

[4]   *Cf. Grupo Mexicano de Desarrollo S.A. v. Alliance Bond Fund, Inc.,* 527 U.S. 308, 119 S.Ct. 1961, 144 L.Ed.2d 319 (1999).

[5]   *But cf., e.g., NML Capital, Ltd. v. Republic of Argentina,* 727 F.3d 230, 241–42 (2d Cir 2013).

[6]   *See, e.g., Prairie Band of Potawatomi Indians v. Pierce,* 253 F.3d 1234 (10th Cir.2001).

[7]   *See, e.g., United States v. Criminal Sheriff, Parish of Orleans,* 19 F.3d 238 (5th Cir. 1994).

[8]   *See, e.g., Resolution Trust Corp. v. Cruce,* 972 F.2d 1195, 1198 (10th Cir. 1992).

[9]   *See, e.g., Dominion Video Satellite, Inc. v. EchoStar Satellite Corp.,* 269 F.3d 1149, 1154–55 (10th Cir. 2001).

Notice

The court may not issue a preliminary injunction without notice to the opposing party.[10] However, there is little guidance as to which documents (if any) must be served.[11] A motion for a preliminary injunction should meet the timeliness requirements of Rule 6(d).[12]

Hearing

The court must hold a hearing before granting or refusing a preliminary injunction.[13] The scope of the hearing is subject to the discretion of the court.[14]

Consolidation with Trial on the Merits

The court has discretion to consolidate the preliminary injunction hearing with the trial on the merits.[15] Parties seeking a quick decision in the case may consent to consolidation because the schedule for the trial will be advanced to the date of the preliminary injunction hearing. If the case on the merits is not yet ripe for trial, as when discovery is not yet complete, courts will not consolidate the trial with the preliminary injunction hearing.[16]

Timing of Order to Consolidate

The court may order consolidation before or after commencement of the hearing on the preliminary injunction. Courts will not order consolidation unless all parties have adequate warning of the possibility of consolidation and a reasonable opportunity to prepare their positions on the merits.[17]

Preliminary Injunction Evidence

If the court does not consolidate the preliminary injunction hearing with trial on the merits, evidence presented at the preliminary hearing is preserved as part of the record. Thus, the evidence need not be repeated for trial.[18]

Trial by Jury

Consolidation and/or preservation of evidence for trial may not interfere with a party's right to a jury trial.[19] Thus, if the court decides a motion for a preliminary injunction by ruling on some issues of fact, evidence presented on those issues of fact is preserved for trial. However, a jury will not be bound by the previous findings of fact made by the judge in the preliminary injunction hearing.[20]

---

[10] *Cf. Western Water Management, Inc. v. Brown,* 40 F.3d 105, 109 (5th Cir. 1994) (prohibiting modification of injunction in absence of notice).

[11] *See, e.g., Wyandotte Nation v. Sebelius,* 443 F.3d 1247, 1253 (10th Cir. 2006) (rejecting need to give minimum 5 days' notice).

[12] *Cf., e.g., Gomperts v. Chase,* 404 U.S. 1237, 92 S.Ct. 16, 30 L.Ed.2d 30 (1971) (3 days insufficient notice).

[13] *See, e.g., Hunter v. Hamilton County Board of Elections,* 635 F.3d 219, 246 (6th Cir. 2011).

[14] *See, e.g., Schulz v. Williams,* 38 F.3d 657, 658 (2d Cir. 1994) (per curiam) (parties entitled only to "reasonable opportunity" to contest evidence).

[15] *See, e.g., American Train Dispatchers Dept. of Intern. Broth. of Locomotive Engineers v. Fort Smith R. Co.,* 121 F.3d 267, 270 (7th Cir. 1997).

[16] *Pughsley v. 3750 Lake Shore Drive Co-op. Bldg.,* 463 F.2d 1055, 1057 (7th Cir. 1972).

[17] *University of Texas v. Camenisch,* 451 U.S. 390, 101 S.Ct. 1830, 68 L.Ed.2d 175, 1 A.D.D. 76 (1981).

[18] *See, e.g., Attorney General of Oklahoma v. Tyson Foods, Inc.,* 565 F.3d 769, 776 (10th Cir. 2009).

[19] *See, e.g., New Windsor Volunteer Ambulance Corps v. Meyers,* 442 F.3d 101, 120 (2d Cir. 2006).

[20] *University of Texas v. Camenisch,* 451 U.S. 390, 395, 101 S.Ct. 1830, 1834, 68 L.Ed.2d 175 (1981).

Modifying or Dissolving a Preliminary Injunction

A preliminary injunction can be modified or dissolved on motion of a party who demonstrates that changed circumstances warrant a change to or end of the injunctive relief.[21]

Comparison with Temporary Restraining Order

The primary differences between a preliminary injunction and a TRO are duration and notice. A TRO may issue without notice, but only lasts for a short period of time. A preliminary injunction requires notice, but may last until the trial on the merits. Otherwise, the two orders have similar purposes and elements.

Relation to Rule 64

In cases involving only money damages on an unsecured claim, a party may not use Rule 65 to obtain a prejudgment injunction aimed at preventing dissipation of assets. Instead, such relief must be sought under other provisions, such as Rule 64's authorization to use state law prejudgment attachment provisions.[22] However, if the lawsuit also seeks equitable relief, the district court is not restricted by Rule 64 and may grant a prejudgment injunction that freezes specific assets that are the subject of a restitution or recission claim or that preserve the power of the court to grant final injunctive relief.[23]

Appeal

A court's decision to grant, deny, dissolve, continue, or modify a preliminary injunction is immediately appealable of right pursuant to 28 U.S.C.A. § 1292(a)(1).[24]

RULE 65(b)—TEMPORARY RESTRAINING ORDER

CORE CONCEPT

Rule 65(b) provides the procedure for obtaining a temporary restraining order or TRO. Although the Rule permits a party to obtain a TRO without first providing notice to opposing parties, it restricts such relief to circumstances where it is clear that notice was not feasible, and limits the duration of such restraining orders to a maximum of 28 days (including a single renewal).

APPLICATIONS

Purpose of a Temporary Restraining Order

The purpose of a TRO is generally to hold the status quo in place until the court has an opportunity to hear a request for fuller relief, such as a preliminary injunction.[25]

TRO Without Notice to Opposing Party

Although much of Rule 65(b) is devoted to the circumstances in which a party may obtain a TRO without first notifying opponents of the motion, such *ex parte* TROs are disfavored.[26] Before granting one, the court will search the record carefully to ascertain the need for *ex parte* relief, and will require that the party seeking relief satisfy all the

---

[21]   *United States v. United Shoe Machinery Corp.,* 391 U.S. 244, 88 S.Ct. 1496, 20 L.Ed.2d 562 (1968).

[22]   *Grupo Mexicano de Desarrollo S.A. v. Alliance Bond Fund, Inc.,* 527 U.S. 308, 330–31, 119 S.Ct. 1961, 1968–75, 144 L.Ed.2d 319 (1999).

[23]   *See, e.g., Deckert v. Independence Shares Corp.,* 311 U.S. 282, 289, 61 S.Ct. 229, 233, 85 L. Ed. 189 (1940).

[24]   *See, e.g., Nutrasweet Co. v. Vit-Mar Enterprises, Inc.,* 112 F.3d 689 (3d Cir.1997).

[25]   *See, e.g., Hospital Resource Personnel, Inc. v. United States,* 860 F.Supp. 1554, 1556 (S.D. Ga. 1994).

[26]   *See, e.g., Reno Air Racing Ass'n., Inc. v. McCord,* 452 F.3d 1126, 1131 (9th Cir. 2006).

requirements in Rule 65 for a TRO, as well as substantive prerequisites in case law governing such equitable remedies as restraining orders and injunctions.[27]

Oral Notice

The preferred method of notice for a motion for a TRO is formal service upon the opposing party. However, the court has substantial discretion to approve lesser notice.[28] If written notice is impractical, a party seeking a TRO should attempt to notify the adversary orally.

Prerequisites for TRO Without Prior Notice

In order to obtain a TRO without providing notice to opposing parties, a party must provide proof of irreparable injury and a statement of the efforts made to notify the opposing party.

Irreparable Injury

A party seeking a TRO must show by affidavit or verified complaint the irreparable injury that will occur if the TRO is not issued until the opposing parties are notified and have an opportunity to appear.[29]

(1) *Affidavit or Complaint:* The quality and detail required in an affidavit or complaint vary substantially, but the explanation should be sufficient for the court to understand the risk of irreparable injury, along with other relevant facts that will help the court understand the need for prompt action.

(2) *Irreparable Injury:* The concept of what constitutes irreparable injury is so flexible as to be elusive. However, a party can demonstrate that the loss likely to occur if an *ex parte* TRO is not issued is an irreparable loss when the damages will be of a nature as are difficult to calculate.[30] Thus, substantial risk of lost future profits or business reputation might constitute irreparable injury. Alternatively, if the loss will be of a nature that the courts normally consider beyond compensation by money, however calculated, the injury is likely to be irreparable. Thus, risk of damage to unique property, such as land, might also meet the standard of irreparable injury.

Efforts to Notify Adversary

An applicant for a TRO must explain in writing the efforts the applicant has made to notify the opposing party, and the reasons why the court should not require no further efforts at notification. The court may treat failure to make reasonable efforts as a ground for denying the motion for a TRO.[31]

Date and Time of Issuance

If a party is able to obtain a TRO without first providing notice to opposing parties, the order must be indorsed with the date and time it was issued. This indorsement is significant because it begins the running of the 14-day period for which the order is effective.

---

[27]   *See, e.g., Phillips v. Charles Schreiner Bank,* 894 F.2d 127, 131 (5th Cir. 1990).

[28]   *Cf. People of State of Ill. ex rel. Hartigan v. Peters,* 871 F.2d 1336, 1340 (7th Cir. 1989).

[29]   *See, e.g., American Can Co. v. Mansukhani,* 742 F.2d 314, 321–24 (7th Cir. 1984).

[30]   *Cf. In re Arthur Treacher's Franchisee Litigation,* 689 F.2d 1137, 1145 (3d Cir. 1982) ("we have never upheld an injunction where the claimed injury constituted a loss of money, a loss capable of recoupment in a proper action at law.").

[31]   *See, e.g., American Can Co. v. Mansukhani,* 742 F.2d 314, 321–24 (7th Cir. 1984).

Filing with Clerk

Once a TRO is issued without prior notice, it must be filed "forthwith" with the clerk of court and entered as part of the record of the case.[32]

Explanation of Injury and Lack of Notice

The TRO will explain the irreparable injury in detail sufficient to inform an appellate court,[33] and will also explain the reasons why the court found it necessary to issue the order without first hearing from opposing parties.

Duration of TRO

If a TRO issues without prior notice to opposing parties, the order will expire no later than 14 days after issuance.[34] The court may provide for expiration of the order in a lesser period. Additionally, even TROs issued with notice cannot continue indefinitely unless they meet the standards required for preliminary injunctions.[35]

Consent to Extension

If the opposing party consents to an extension of the temporary restraining order, the order may be extended for any length of time to which the parties agree.[36]

Judicial Extension of Time

TROs issued without prior notice may be extended by judicial order for an additional period not greater than the length of time in the original order, and in no event for more than 14 additional days.[37]

Obtaining a Judicial Extension

A party seeking judicial extension of a TRO must move for the extension within the time limitation of the original order, and must show good cause for the extension. Good cause might be a continuation of the circumstances of irreparable injury that justified the original order, or such new circumstances as the TRO produced. For example, if the court is considering issuance of a preliminary injunction, extension of a temporary restraining order might be appropriate to allow the court more time to decide the preliminary injunction question.[38]

Recording of Reasons for Extension

If a temporary restraining order is extended, the court must place its reasons for granting the extension on the record.[39]

Timing of Hearing on Preliminary Injunction

If the court grants a TRO without prior notice to opposing parties, the court must hold a hearing on a motion for a preliminary injunction "at the earliest possible time." The

---

[32] *See, e.g., Garcia v. Yonkers School District,* 561 F.3d 97, 106 (2d Cir. 2009).

[33] *See, e.g., Ben David v. Travisono,* 495 F.2d 562, 564–65 (1st Cir. 1974).

[34] *Cf. Sampson v. Murray,* 415 U.S. 61, 86, 94 S.Ct. 937, 39 L.Ed.2d 166 (1974) (temporary restraining order that is continued beyond time limits of Rule 65 must satisfy requirements of preliminary injunction).

[35] *See, e.g., In re Criminal Contempt Proceedings Against Gerald Crawford, Michael Warren,* 329 F.3d 131, 137 (2d Cir. 2003).

[36] *See, e.g., In re Arthur Treacher's Franchise Litigation,* 689 F.2d 1150 (3d Cir.1982); *Cf. Hudson v. Barr,* 3 F.3d 970, 973 (6th Cir. 1993).

[37] *See, e.g., Belbacha v. Bush,* 520 F.3d 452, 455 (D.C. Cir. 2008).

[38] *See, e.g., Joseph v. Hess Oil Virgin Islands Corp.,* 651 F.3d 348 (3d Cir. 2011) (good cause means a "legally sufficient reason").

[39] *But cf. Reliance Ins. Co. v. Mast Const. Co.,* 159 F.3d 1311, 1316 (10th Cir. 1998).

preliminary injunction hearing must move to the head of the court's docket, second only to preliminary injunction matters that are already pending.

Failure to Seek a Preliminary Injunction

If a party obtained a temporary restraining order without prior notice, and then fails to pursue a motion for a preliminary injunction, the court will terminate the temporary restraining order.

Motion to Modify or Dissolve TRO

Like preliminary injunctions, temporary restraining orders may be modified or dissolved on motion of a party.

Notice of Motion to Modify or Dissolve TRO

A party subject to a temporary restraining order issued without prior notice may move to dissolve or modify the order. The moving party must provide other parties at least 2 days' notice of a hearing on the motion to dissolve, unless the court permits less notice.

Timing of Hearing

Rule 65(b) establishes no specific time limit within which the court must hear a motion to dissolve or modify a temporary restraining order, instead requiring a hearing, "as expeditiously as the ends of justice require."

Comparison with Preliminary Injunction

The primary differences between a preliminary injunction and a TRO are duration and notice. A TRO may issue without notice, but only lasts for a short period of time. A preliminary injunction requires notice, but may last until the trial on the merits. Otherwise, the two orders have similar purposes and elements.

Appeal

Generally, a court's decision to grant, deny, modify, continue, or dissolve a temporary restraining order is not appealable.[40]

RULE 65(c)—SECURITY

CORE CONCEPT

As a condition of granting a preliminary injunction or temporary restraining order (TRO), the court must impose a bond or other security.[41] The party bound by the injunction or order is entitled to recover damages from the bond if the injunction or order is subsequently found to have been erroneously granted. The court has substantial discretion to determine the amount of the security.

APPLICATIONS

Mandatory Security

Although the language of Rule 65(c) directs a court to require a bond, many cases treat the decision to require a bond as a matter of discretion for the court.[42]

---

[40]   *See, e.g., In re Lorillard Tobacco Co.,* 370 F.3d 982, 986 (9th Cir. 2004).

[41]   *Cf. Mead Johnson & Co. v. Abbott Laboratories,* 209 F.3d 1032, 1033 (7th Cir. 2000).

[42]   *Snider v. Temple University,* 502 U.S. 1032, 112 S.Ct. 873, 116 L.Ed.2d 778 (1992) (sometimes a strict reading of bond requirement may be "inappropriate").

Timing

If a bond is required, it must be posted when the court grants a preliminary injunction or temporary restraining order.[43]

Amount of Security

The maximum amount of security that may be required is the court's estimate of the potential loss to a party proximately caused by erroneous issuance of the injunction or order.[44] The court has discretion to require posting of lesser amounts than the bound party's estimated potential loss.[45] In practice, that means in some cases the court may limit security to a nominal amount, if a small sum is in the interest of justice.[46]

Requests for Increase in Bond

If a party believes the amount designated for the bond is insufficient to cover damages, the party may seek an increase in the bond during the time when the preliminary relief is in effect—or when the preliminary remedy has been lifted, but might still be re-imposed. However, once an injunction or restraining order has been reversed and will not be replaced, the amount of the bond cannot be increased.[47]

Standard for "Wrongfully Enjoined"

A party has been wrongfully enjoined "if it is ultimately found that the enjoined party had at all times the right to do the enjoined act."[48]

Damages Recoverable

An injured party's maximum recovery is generally limited to the amount of the bond.[49] However, a party may pursue an independent action for malicious prosecution in the unusual cases where the elements of that tort are satisfied.[50]

Actions Involving the United States

The United States, its officers, and agencies do not need to post security.

Relation to Rule 65.1

Rule 65.1 governs the procedure by which a party may seek recovery against security posted pursuant to Rule 65(c).

---

[43] *But Compare Kos Pharmaceuticals, Inc. v. Andrx Corp.*, 369 F.3d 700, 728 (3d Cir. 2004).

[44] *See, e.g., Hoechst Diafoil Co. v. Nan Ya Plastics Corp.*, 174 F.3d 411, 421 (4th Cir. 1999).

[45] *See, e.g., GoTo.com, Inc. v. Walt Disney Co.*, 202 F.3d 1199, 1211 (9th Cir. 2000).

[46] *See, e.g., Davis v. Mineta*, 302 F.3d 1104 (10th Cir.2002) ("Ordinarily, where a party is seeking to vindicate the public interest served by [federal environmental law], a minimal bond amount should be considered.").

[47] *See, e.g., Mead Johnson & Co. v. Abbott Laboratories*, 209 F.3d 1032, 1033 (7th Cir. 2000).

[48] *Blumenthal v. Merrill Lynch, Pierce, Fenner & Smith, Inc.*, 910 F.2d 1049, 1054 (2d Cir. 1990).

[49] *W.R. Grace and Co. v. Local Union 759, Intern. Union of United Rubber, Cork, Linoleum and Plastic Workers of America*, 461 U.S. 757, 770, 103 S.Ct. 2177, 2185, 76 L.Ed.2d 298 (1983) ("A party injured by the issuance of an injunction later determined to be erroneous has no action for damages in the absence of a bond.").

[50] *Meyers v. Block*, 120 U.S. 206, 211, 7 S.Ct. 525, 528, 30 L. Ed. 642 (1887).

RULE 65(d)—CONTENTS AND SCOPE OF EVERY INJUNCTION AND RESTRAINING ORDER

CORE CONCEPT

Rule 65(d) governs the information that must be contained in injunctions and temporary restraining orders. The Rule also describes categories of persons who are bound by an injunction or order.

APPLICATIONS

Reasons for Issuance

The injunction or order must contain an explanation of the reasons for its issuance. However, a court's failure to provide an explanation does not, of itself, mandate reversal.[51] A sufficient explanation will state specifically the facts found by the court as well as the court's conclusions of law.[52]

Relation to Rule 52

Alongside the Rule 65(d) requirement of reasons for issuance of an injunction or restraining order, Rule 52(a) provides that district courts must make findings of fact and conclusions of law when granting or denying a request for an interlocutory injunction.[53]

Written Description of Acts Proscribed

The court's injunction order must be written, not oral.[54] The order must describe the prohibited acts with sufficient detail and clarity that a layperson bound by the order can distinguish between acts that are permitted and acts that are prohibited.[55] Thus, a court will ordinarily not use highly technical language unless there is no other way to describe the acts and the parties affected are likely to be capable of understanding such language.[56]

Incorporation by Reference

Prohibited acts may not be described only by reference to the complaint or other documents in the action.[57] However, some courts allow incorporation by reference to a document that is physically appended to the injunction order.[58]

Request for Clarification

If a party is uncertain as to the scope of an order, it may petition the court for clarification.[59] Such clarification is within the discretion of the court.[60]

---

[51] *See, e.g., Test Masters Educational Services, Inc. v. Singh*, 428 F.3d 559, 577 (5th Cir. 2005).

[52] *Schmidt v. Lessard*, 414 U.S. 473, 476, 94 S.Ct. 713, 715, 38 L.Ed.2d 661 (1974) ("The Rule was designed to prevent uncertainty and confusion on the part of those faced with injunction orders, and to avoid the possible founding of a contempt citation on a decree too vague to be understood.").

[53] *See, e.g., Prairie Band of Potawatomi Indians v. Pierce*, 253 F.3d 1234 (10th Cir.2001).

[54] *See, e.g., In re Rockford Products Corp.*, 741 F.3d 730, 734 (7th Cir. 2013).

[55] *See, e.g., Francisco Sanchez v. Esso Standard Oil Co.*, 572 F.3d 1 (1st Cir. 2009) (requirements of Rule 65(d)(1) applicable even to emergency situations).

[56] *See, e.g., Reno Air Racing Association, Inc. v. McCord*, 452 F.3d 1126, 1134 (9th Cir. 2006) ("The benchmark for clarity and fair notice is not lawyers and judges [but] the lay person, who is the target of the injunction.").

[57] *See, e.g., Advent Electronics, Inc. v. Buckman*, 112 F.3d 267 (7th Cir.1997).

[58] *LeBlanc-Sternberg v. Fletcher*, 143 F.3d 748 (2d Cir.1998).

[59] *Daniels Health Sciences, L.L.C. v. Vascular Health Sciences, L.L.C.*, 710 F.3d 579, 586 (5th Cir. 2013).

[60] *Regal Knitwear Co. v. NLRB*, 324 U.S. 9, 15, 65 S.Ct. 478, 89 L.Ed. 661 (1945) (if party is uncertain of its obligation under Rule 65 order, it would be surprising if district court withheld clarification).

Persons Bound

The categories of persons subject to an injunction or order are: (1) parties;[61] (2) their officers, agents, servants, employees, and attorneys;[62] and (3) other persons "in active concert or participation" with parties.[63]

"Persons in Active Concert or Participation"

Generally, assignees who take an interest from a party with actual or constructive notice of an injunction prohibiting that party from performing a certain act relating to the interest may also be barred from performing the act.[64] Similarly, an injunction can bind any unnamed member of a group that is subject to an injunction, provided that the group is sufficiently identified.[65]

Successors in Office: Relation to Rule 25

An injunction against a public official also binds successors in office.[66] This view is reinforced by Rule 25(d), which provides that in such circumstances, the successor in office automatically replaces the predecessor as the party to the action.[67]

Notice to Persons Bound

No one is bound by an injunction or order until that person receives fair notice of the judicial act.[68] However, formal notice in the form of service of process is not necessarily required to bind a party or those in privity with a party. A party or a person in a close relationship with a party may be bound if they simply have actual knowledge of the injunction or order.[69]

Personal Jurisdiction

Persons outside the jurisdiction of the court are not subject to its orders.[70]

Permanent Injunctions

Unlike other provisions of Rule 65, the provisions for a written explanation of the court's decision, an adequate description of prohibited acts, and the categories of persons bound by an injunction or order apply equally to permanent injunctions.[71]

Failure to Comply with Injunction or Order

Persons subject to an injunction or order and who do not comply are subject to the court's power of contempt.[72]

---

[61] *See, e.g., United States v. Vitek Supply Corp.,* 151 F.3d 580 (7th Cir. 1998) (Rule 65(d) extends scope of injunction to bind alter egos).

[62] *See, e.g., Whiting v. Marathon County Sheriff's Dept.,* 382 F.3d 700, 704 (7th Cir. 2004) (attorney bound by no-contact order issued against client).

[63] *Regal Knitwear Co. v. N.L.R.B.,* 324 U.S. 9, 65 S.Ct. 478, 89 L. Ed. 661 (1945). *See, e.g., Marshak v. Treadwell,* 595 F.3d 478 (3d Cir. 2009) (Rule 65(d)(2)(C) extends the binding effect of an injunction beyond "parties and their privies" to include nonparties who knowingly abet violation of injunction).

[64] *See, e.g., Golden State Bottling Co. v. NLRB,* 414 U.S. 168, 169, 94 S.Ct. 414, 38 L.Ed.2d 388 (1973) (bona fide successor in interest with knowledge of existing injunction is in privity with predecessor).

[65] *See, e.g., Zamecnik v. Indian Prairie School District No. 204,* 636 F.3d 874, 879 (7th Cir. 2011) (no requirement to name parties who may enforce injunction; students at school may enforce injunction against school).

[66] *See, e.g., Salt River Agricultural Improvement & Power District v. Lee,* 672 F.3d 1176, 1180 (9th Cir. 2012).

[67] Fed.R.Civ.P. 25(d).

[68] *See, e.g., ADT Security Services, Inc. v. Lisle-Woodridge Fire Protection District,* 724 F.3d 854, 873 (7th Cir. 2013).

[69] *Spallone v. United States,* 493 U.S. 265, 110 S.Ct. 625, 107 L.Ed.2d 644 (1990).

[70] *See, e.g., R.M.S. Titanic, Inc. v. Haver,* 171 F.3d 943, 957–58 (4th Cir. 1999).

[71] *See, e.g., Reich v. ABC/York-Estes Corp.,* 64 F.3d 316, 320 (7th Cir. 1995).

[72] *Gunn v. University Committee to End War in Viet Nam,* 399 U.S. 383, 90 S.Ct. 2013, 26 L.Ed.2d 684 (1970).

RULE 65(e)—OTHER LAWS NOT MODIFIED

CORE CONCEPT

Nothing in Rule 65 shall be construed to modify statutes relating to labor relations, interpleader actions, or actions subject to the jurisdiction of a three-judge court. In each of these three areas of law, federal statutes alter the typical power of courts to issue injunctions and restraining orders. When those statutes are applicable to a case and conflict with a provision of Rule 65, the statute governs.

RULE 65(f)—COPYRIGHT IMPOUNDMENT

CORE CONCEPT

Rule 65 applies to copyright impoundment proceedings.

ADDITIONAL RESEARCH REFERENCES

Wright & Miller, *Federal Practice and Procedure* §§ 2941 to 62

C.J.S., Injunctions §§ 4 to 54, §§ 60 to 110, §§ 111 to 158, §§ 160 to 206, §§ 213 to 263, §§ 264 to 314, §§ 320 to 341

West's Key Number Digest, Injunction ⟜1001 to 1835

RULE 65.1

PROCEEDINGS AGAINST A SURETY

Whenever these rules (including the Supplemental Rules for Admiralty or Maritime Claims and Asset Forfeiture Actions) require or allow a party to give security, and security is given through a bond or other undertaking with one or more sureties, each surety submits to the court's jurisdiction and irrevocably appoints the court clerk as its agent for receiving service of any papers that affect its liability on the bond or undertaking. The surety's liability may be enforced on motion without an independent action. The motion and any notice that the court orders may be served on the court clerk, who must promptly mail a copy of each to every surety whose address is known.

[Added effective July 1, 1966; amended effective August 1, 1987; April 12, 2006, effective December 1, 2006; April 30, 2007, effective December 1, 2007.]

AUTHORS' COMMENTARY ON RULE 65.1

PURPOSE AND SCOPE

Rule 65.1 provides a summary procedure by which parties can enforce their rights against a surety who has posted security.

APPLICATIONS

Scope

Rule 65.1 applies to proceedings to enforce a surety's liability on a supersedeas bond or an injunction bond posted pursuant to Rule 65(c). The Rule also applies when the Supplemental Rules for Certain Admiralty and Maritime Claims require the posting of bond. Finally, Rule 65.1 applies to the satisfaction of provisional remedies under Rule 64, when state law requires a bond.

Right to Collect Not Determined by Rule 65.1

Rule 65.1 does not determine the substantive right to collect against the surety—that right is determined under the Rule that creates the obligation to post security. Rule 65.1 simply sets the procedures when the right to collect exists.

Alternative Procedures

Rule 65.1 is not the only means by which a party can seek to collect on a bond. Instead of employing the Rule, a party may bring an independent action against the surety in a state or federal court.[1]

Motion for Judgment

The appropriate method for seeking to collect from a surety under Rule 65.1 is a motion for judgment on the bond.[2]

---

[1] *See, e.g., State of Ala. ex rel. Siegelman v. U.S. E.P.A.,* 925 F.2d 385, 388 (11th Cir. 1991).
[2] *See, e.g., Global Naps, Inc. v. Verizon New England, Inc.,* 489 F.3d 13, 20 (1st Cir. 2007).

Timing

Generally, a party may seek recovery under Rule 65.1 once the court has adjudicated or altered the relief that the bond secured. Thus, if a court determines that a preliminary injunction was improvidently granted or was of excessive scope, the party previously enjoined may then move against the bond for damages.[3]

Consent to Personal Jurisdiction

When a surety posts a bond or other security, the surety submits to the personal jurisdiction of the court for purposes of any litigation relating to liability on the bond.[4]

Service of Process

Upon posting bond, a surety appoints the clerk of court as the surety's agent to receive service of process in matters relating to liability on the bond. A party seeking to collect on a bond should serve the motion on the clerk of court, along with such other notice as the court may require. The clerk will "forthwith" mail copies of the documents to all affected sureties whose addresses are known.

Injunction Staying Enforcement

If a court enjoins proceedings against the bond, the injunction must be obeyed until it is modified or dissolved.[5]

Collecting from Principals

Although Rule 65.1 addresses the means by which a party may seek damages on a surety's bond or other undertaking, courts also permit the use of Rule 65.1 for similar relief against a surety's principal.[6]

Subject Matter Jurisdiction

If a party seeks in the original action to collect against a bond under Rule 65.1, the court will have supplemental jurisdiction over the claim.[7] If a party seeks to enforce a bond in an independent action, the court has subject matter jurisdiction under 28 U.S.C.A. § 1352, governing independent actions on bonds posted pursuant to federal law.[8]

ADDITIONAL RESEARCH REFERENCES

Wright & Miller, *Federal Practice and Procedure* §§B22971 to 74

C.J.S., Federal Civil Procedure §§ 1273 to 1295

West's Key Number Digest, Federal Civil Procedure ⊶2732 to 2733

---

[3] *See, e.g., American Bible Soc. v. Blount,* 446 F.2d 588, 595 n.12 (3d Cir. 1971) (liability on bond arises after defendant prevails on merits).

[4] *See, e.g., Instant Air Freight Co. v. C.F. Air Freight, Inc.,* 882 F.2d 797, 804 (3d Cir. 1989).

[5] *Celotex Corp. v. Edwards,* 514 U.S. 300, 115 S.Ct. 1493, 131 L.Ed.2d 403 (1995).

[6] *See, e.g., Willis v. Celotex Corp.,* 970 F.2d 1292 (4th Cir. 1992).

[7] *See, e.g., Buddy Systems, Inc. v. Exer-Genie, Inc.,* 545 F.2d 1164, 1166 (9th Cir. 1976) (jurisdiction over collection against bond exists until bond is discharged).

[8] *See, e.g., Milan Exp., Inc. v. Averitt Exp., Inc.,* 208 F.3d 975, 980 (11th Cir. 2000).

RULE 66

RECEIVERS

These rules govern an action in which the appointment of a receiver is sought or a receiver sues or is sued. But the practice in administering an estate by a receiver or a similar court-appointed officer must accord with the historical practice in federal courts or with a local rule. An action in which a receiver has been appointed may be dismissed only by court order.

[Amended effective March 19, 1948; October 20, 1949; April 30, 2007, effective December 1, 2007.]

AUTHORS' COMMENTARY ON RULE 66

PURPOSE AND SCOPE

Rule 66 provides that, when appointed by district courts, federal equity receivers shall administer estates in accordance with prior federal practice and local court rules. Once an equity receiver is appointed in a particular lawsuit, the action may not thereafter be dismissed without the court's prior approval.

APPLICATIONS

Role of Federal Equity Receiver

Receivership is an extraordinary equitable remedy, justified only in extreme circumstances.[1] It is not a substantive entitlement, but an ancillary remedy used to facilitate the primary relief sought in a lawsuit.[2] Federal courts appoint equity receivers to assume custody, control, and management of property that either is presently involved or is likely to become involved in litigation.[3] The receiver is charged to preserve the property, and any rents or profits the property earns, until a final disposition by the court.[4] Although typically appointed only to care for property, a federal equity receiver may be appointed where other, extraordinary circumstances compel intimate judicial supervision.[5]

- *Officer of the Court:* An equity receiver is not an agent of any of the parties to the litigation. Instead, the receiver is deemed to be an officer of the court.[6]

- *Auxiliary Remedy Only:* The appointment of a receiver is not permitted as an end in itself; receivers are only appointed as an auxiliary remedy necessary to some other, primary requested relief.[7]

---

[1] See *Netsphere, Inc. v. Baron,* 703 F.3d 296, 305 (5th Cir. 2012).

[2] See *U.S. Bank Nat'l Ass'n v. Nesbitt Bellevue Prop. LLC,* 866 F.Supp.2d 247, 254 (S.D.N.Y. 2012).

[3] See *Netsphere, Inc. v. Baron,* 703 F.3d 296, 305 (5th Cir. 2012).

[4] See *S.E.C. v. Vescor Capital Corp.,* 599 F.3d 1189, 1194 (10th Cir. 2010).

[5] See *Morgan v. McDonough,* 540 F.2d 527, 534 (1st Cir. 1976) (affirming appointment of federal receiver for public high school, to implement desegregation orders). *See also De Boer Structures (U.S.A.), Inc. v. Shaffer Tent and Awning Co.,* 187 F.Supp.2d 910, 925 (S.D. Ohio 2001) (noting that appointment of receiver is extraordinary remedy justified only in extreme situations).

[6] See *Liberte Capital Group, LLC v. Capwill,* 462 F.3d 543, 551 (6th Cir. 2006).

[7] See *Gordon v. Washington,* 295 U.S. 30, 37 n.4, 55 S.Ct. 584, 588 n.4, 79 L. Ed. 1282 (1935) ("A receivership is only a means to reach some legitimate end sought through the exercise of the power of a court of equity. It is not an end in itself").

Administration of Estates By Receivers

Traditional federal practice and, where promulgated, local court rules guide a federal equity receiver in administering the receivership property.[8]

- *State Law:* The substantive law of the State in which the receivership property is located dictates the manner in which the receiver must manage and operate the receivership property.[9]

Federal Rules Control

The Rules govern all actions in which a party seeks the appointment of a federal equity receiver, as well as all actions brought by or against the receiver once appointed.[10]

Appointment of Receivers

Rule 66 does not create a substantive right to the appointment of a receiver; a statute or general principle of equity must first justify the appointment. Federal law controls whether an equity receiver should be appointed, even in a diversity case.[11] But the Rule provides little guidance other than requiring that a receiver's appointment and work "accord with the historical practice in federal courts or with a local rule."[12] Absent explicit consent from the defendant, the plaintiff ordinarily bears the burden of making an adequate showing that a receiver should be appointed.[13]

- *Who May Seek An Appointment:* The appointment of a receiver may be requested by any person having a legally recognized right to the property—a mere interest or claim to the property will not be sufficient to justify the appointment of a receiver.[14] Receivers are appointed frequently at the request of secured creditors, mortgagees, judgment creditors, and plaintiffs in shareholder derivative actions.[15]

- *Prerequisites for Appointment:* The appointment of a receiver is an extraordinary remedy, available only upon a clear showing that no remedy at law is available or adequate,[16] and that a receivership is essential to protect the property from some threatened loss or injury pending a final disposition by the court.[17] Although no precise formula exists for assessing whether a receiver ought to be appointed,[18] the courts consider various factors, including:

  o the existence of a valid claim by the party seeking the appointment;

  o the imminent nature of any danger to the property, to its concealment or removal, or to its value;

  o the adequacy of other legal remedies;

---

[8]   *See S.E.C. v. Vescor Capital Corp.,* 599 F.3d 1189, 1193–94 (10th Cir. 2010).

[9]   *See* 28 U.S.C.A. § 959(b). *See also S.E.C. v. Vescor Capital Corp.,* 599 F.3d 1189, 1193–94 (10th Cir. 2010).

[10]   *See Canada Life Assur. Co. v. LaPeter,* 563 F.3d 837, 842–43 (9th Cir. 2009).

[11]   *See Canada Life Assur. Co. v. LaPeter,* 563 F.3d 837, 842–43 (9th Cir. 2009). *But see Office Depot Inc. v. Zuccarini,* 596 F.3d 696, 701 (9th Cir. 2010) (proper location for appointment of receiver in aid of execution of a judgment is assessed by looking to state law).

[12]   *See* Rule 66. *See also U.S. Bank Nat'l Ass'n v. Nesbitt Bellevue Prop. LLC,* 866 F.Supp.2d 247, 250 (S.D.N.Y. 2012).

[13]   *See U.S. Bank Nat'l Ass'n v. Nesbitt Bellevue Prop. LLC,* 866 F.Supp.2d 247, 255 (S.D.N.Y. 2012).

[14]   *See Netsphere, Inc. v. Baron,* 703 F.3d 296, 305–06 (5th Cir. 2012).

[15]   *See Santibanez v. Wier McMahon & Co.,* 105 F.3d 234, 241 (5th Cir. 1997) (appointments sought by judgment creditors).

[16]   *See United States v. Bradley,* 644 F.3d 1213, 1310 (11th Cir. 2011).

[17]   *See Gordon v. Washington,* 295 U.S. 30, 55 S.Ct. 584, 79 L. Ed. 1282 (1935).

[18]   *See Canada Life Assur. Co. v. LaPeter,* 563 F.3d 837, 844 (9th Cir. 2009).

- o   the lack of a less drastic equitable remedy;

- o   the plaintiff's probable success in the lawsuit and the risk of irreparable injury to the property;

- o   whether the defendant has engaged, or may engage, in any fraudulent actions with respect to the property;

- o   the likelihood that appointing the receiver will do more good than harm; *and*

- o   whether the potential harm to the plaintiff outweighs the injury to others.[19]

Each factor need not be satisfied, so long as the court determines that its review favors the receiver's appointment.[20] Courts have held that the existence of an express contractual right to the appointment of a receiver, along with adequate *prima facie* evidence of default, can suffice to justify appointment.[21]

Consent to Appointment

The court may appoint a receiver where the defendant both admits liability for the claim asserted in the litigation and consents to the appointment of a receiver—provided that there has been no improper attempt by the parties to collusively manufacture federal jurisdiction.[22]

Discretion of the District Court

Whether to appoint a receiver lies within the district judge's sound discretion.[23]

Who May Be Appointed

The court may appoint as the receiver any person deemed capable of serving in that capacity. Ordinarily, this requires the appointment of someone who is indifferent between the parties.[24] Federal law prevents the judge from appointing as a receiver any person related to the judge by consanguinity within the fourth degree,[25] a clerk or deputy of the court (absent special circumstances),[26] or a federal employee or person employed by the appointing judge.[27]

Place of Appointment

Because the appointment of a receiver is a type of *in rem* proceeding, the appointing court must enjoy a strong relationship to the contemplated receivership: a substantial portion of the defendant's business must be conducted in the host district, or a substantial portion of the anticipated receivership property must be located within the host district.

- • *Conflicting Claims to Jurisdiction:* If two courts of concurrent and coordinate jurisdiction (*e.g.,* two federal courts) attempt to assert a claim to the same property, the court where the legal papers are first filed assumes exclusive

---

[19] *See Canada Life Assur. Co. v. LaPeter,* 563 F.3d 837, 844 (9th Cir. 2009).

[20] *See Fleet Business Credit, L.L.C. v. Wings Restaurants, Inc.,* 291 B.R. 550, 556 (N.D. Okla. 2003) (appointing receiver where "several of the factors weigh in favor of the propriety of appointing a receiver").

[21] *See Pioneer Capital Corp. v. Environamics Corp.,* 2003 WL 345349, at *9 (D. Me. 2003), *aff'd,* 2003 WL 1923765 (D. Me. 2003).

[22] *See In re Reisenberg,* 208 U.S. 90, 28 S.Ct. 219, 52 L. Ed. 403 (1908).

[23] *See Netsphere, Inc. v. Baron,* 703 F.3d 296, 305 (5th Cir. 2012).

[24] *See Liberte Capital Group, LLC v. Capwill,* 462 F.3d 543, 551 n.2 (6th Cir. 2006).

[25] 28 U.S.C.A. § 458; 18 U.S.C.A. § 1910.

[26] 28 U.S.C.A. § 957.

[27] 28 U.S.C.A. § 958.

jurisdiction, irrespective of whether its receiver is the first to obtain physical possession of the property.

If the two courts are not of the same or concurrent jurisdiction (*e.g.,* one State and one federal court), and where the subject matter in the one litigation is not the same as in the other litigation, or where no constructive possession of the property is obtained through the filing, the court whose receiver first obtains actual possession of the property assumes exclusive jurisdiction.[28]

Notice of Appointment

Generally, the court gives notice to all parties before appointing an equity receiver. But where notice is impractical or self-defeating, or where the appointment must be made immediately, the court enjoys the power to appoint a receiver *ex parte*.[29]

Effect of Appointment

Once a receiver is appointed and gives the bond required by the court, the court and the receiver obtain exclusive jurisdiction of all of the defendant's property, no matter where it is kept.[30] To obtain such jurisdiction over property outside the appointing district, the receiver must first file a copy of the complaint and appointment order in that foreign district.[31] The fees and expenses of receivership are normally a charge against the administered property.[32]

Actions by Receivers

A federal equity receiver is authorized to commence and prosecute any action necessary to accomplish the objectives of the receivership.[33] The receiver may be directed to bring suit on specific instructions from the court, or the receiver may independently institute lawsuits pursuant to the receiver's general duties of receiving, controlling, and managing the receivership property.

- *May Sue in Any Jurisdiction:* The receiver may bring suit in any federal district, including those districts outside the court in which the receiver was formally appointed.[34]

- *Equitable Defenses:* Receivers are deemed to have stepped into the shoes of the persons or entities for whom they act. Thus, absent statutory provisions dictating otherwise, defenses that could be asserted against the original plaintiff are equally available against the plaintiff's equity receiver. However, equitable defenses (such as unclean hands) that could be asserted against the original plaintiff might not be effective against the receiver.[35]

---

[28]   *See Harkin v. Brundage,* 276 U.S. 36, 48 S.Ct. 268, 72 L. Ed. 457 (1928).

[29]   *See Arkansas Louisiana Gas Co. v. Kroeger,* 303 F.2d 129, 132 (5th Cir. 1962).

[30]   *See Liberte Capital Group, LLC v. Capwill,* 462 F.3d 543, 551 (6th Cir. 2006).

[31]   28 U.S.C.A. § 754.

[32]   *See Netsphere, Inc. v. Baron,* 703 F.3d 296, 311–13 (5th Cir. 2012) (noting general rule, and discussing how to assess such costs when receivership appointment was improper).

[33]   *See Gilchrist v. General Elec. Capital Corp.,* 262 F.3d 295, 302 (4th Cir. 2001) (noting that, when appointed, federal equity receivers may sue and be sued as provided by federal law).

[34]   28 U.S.C.A. § 754.

[35]   *See F.D.I.C. v. O'Melveny & Myers,* 61 F.3d 17, 19 (9th Cir. 1995) (commenting that while party may be denied right or defense due to its misdeeds, the same punishment should not be imposed upon innocent receiver who assumes control pursuant to court order or by operation of law).

Actions Against Receivers

A person may sue an equity receiver, without leave of court, for any of the receiver's actions taken after the receiver was appointed and during the receiver's management and operation of the receivership property.[36]

- *Leave of Court Needed:* Leave of court is required before the receiver may be sued for claims that arise from the property owner's actions or for claims that do not challenge the receiver's actions since appointment.[37] To protect the assets (and to avoid their diminution by the costs of defending lawsuits), the receivership court may issue a blanket injunction staying all litigation against the receiver and entities under the receiver's control.[38] Although claimants are entitled to have their claims heard, the court enjoys broad control over the time and manner of those proceedings.[39] Intentionally interfering with a receivership in violation of such an injunction is punishable as contempt.[40]

- *Subject to Court's General Equity Power:* Suits against receivers remain subject to the court's general equity powers, which the court may exercise to achieve the ends of justice.

Jurisdiction in Actions Involving Receivers

Receivers may only sue or be sued when the district court would enjoy subject matter jurisdiction over the dispute.

- *Diversity Cases:* In diversity jurisdiction cases, the citizenship of the appointed receiver is examined to determine whether complete diversity exists.[41]

- *Federal Question Cases:* The district court's act of appointing a federal receiver probably will suffice to vest that district court with subject matter jurisdiction over actions brought by or against the receiver in that district.[42] Thus, when instituted in the appointing district, suits by the receiver intended to accomplish the objectives of the receivership are deemed ancillary to the appointing court's subject matter jurisdiction.[43] Likewise, suits may be maintained against the receiver in the receiver's appointing district even though no independent basis for subject matter jurisdiction is present.[44]

- *Outside Appointing District:* Suits by or against receivers instituted outside the appointing district will generally require an independent basis for federal subject matter jurisdiction.[45]

---

[36] 28 U.S.C.A. § 959(a). *See Gilchrist v. General Elec. Capital Corp.,* 262 F.3d 295, 301 (4th Cir. 2001) (noting that, when appointed, federal equity receivers may sue and be sued as provided by federal law).

[37] *See Barton v. Barbour,* 104 U.S. 126, 128, 26 L.Ed. 672 (1881).

[38] *See Liberte Capital Group, LLC v. Capwill,* 462 F.3d 543, 551–52 (6th Cir. 2006).

[39] *See Liberte Capital Group, LLC v. Capwill,* 462 F.3d 543, 552 (6th Cir. 2006).

[40] *See Liberte Capital Group, LLC v. Capwill,* 462 F.3d 543, 552 (6th Cir. 2006).

[41] *See Barber v. Powell,* 135 F.2d 728, 729 (C.C.A. 4th Cir. 1943).

[42] *See Gay v. Ruff,* 292 U.S. 25, 54 S.Ct. 608, 78 L. Ed. 1099 (1934).

[43] *See Pope v. Louisville, N.A. & C. Ry. Co.,* 173 U.S. 573, 19 S.Ct. 500, 43 L. Ed. 814 (1899); *Haile v. Henderson Nat. Bank,* 657 F.2d 816, 825 (6th Cir. 1981).

[44] *See Rouse v. Hornsby,* 161 U.S. 588, 16 S.Ct. 610, 40 L. Ed. 817 (1896); *Robinson v. Michigan Consol. Gas Co. Inc.,* 918 F.2d 579, 584 (6th Cir. 1990).

[45] *See United States v. Franklin National Bank,* 512 F.2d 245, 251 (2d Cir. 1975).

Dismissal of Actions Involving Receivers

After the court appoints a receiver in a litigation, the parties may not thereafter dismiss the litigation without first obtaining the court's approval.[46] This requirement protects against a waste of the court's time in unnecessarily establishing a receivership.

Vacating or Terminating the Receivership

The district court may vacate the order appointing the receiver or terminate the receivership when the objectives of the receivership have been obtained or the need for the receiver has abated,[47] or when the receiver was found to be improper in the first place.[48]

Appeals

The district court's decision to appoint a receiver may be immediately appealed.[49] The court of appeals will review the appointment under the lenient abuse of discretion standard. If the appointment is found to have been improvident, the court of appeals may reverse and tax the costs and expenses incurred in the receivership on the persons who procured the receivership.[50]

Orders refusing to wind up the receivership or that otherwise have the effect of either ousting persons from their property or injuring the property may also be immediately appealed.[51]

All other orders involving receivers may only be appealed after entry of a final order.

ADDITIONAL RESEARCH REFERENCES

Wright & Miller, *Federal Practice and Procedure* §§ 2981 to 86

C.J.S., Mechanics Liens § 214; Receivers §§ 1 to 30 et seq., §§ 52 to 103 et seq., §§ 105 to 150 et seq., §§ 163 to 208 et seq., §§ 227 to 256 et seq., §§ 283 to 325 et seq., §§ 365 to 411 et seq., §§ 418 to 431 et seq.

West's Key Number Digest, Receivers 1 to 220

---

[46] *See* Rule 66.

[47] *See SEC v. An-Car Oil Co.,* 604 F.2d 114, 119–20 (1st Cir. 1979).

[48] *See Netsphere, Inc. v. Baron,* 703 F.3d 296, 305–11 (5th Cir. 2012).

[49] 28 U.S.C.A. § 1292(a)(2).

[50] *See Tucker v. Baker,* 214 F.2d 627, 631 (5th Cir.1954).

[51] 28 U.S.C.A. § 1292(a)(2).

RULE 67

DEPOSIT INTO COURT

(a) Depositing Property. If any part of the relief sought is a money judgment or the disposition of a sum of money or some other deliverable thing, a party—on notice to every other party and by leave of court—may deposit with the court all or part of the money or thing, whether or not that party claims any of it. The depositing party must deliver to the clerk a copy of the order permitting deposit.

(b) Investing and Withdrawing Funds. Money paid into court under this rule must be deposited and withdrawn in accordance with 28 U.S.C. §§ 2041 and 2042 and any like statute. The money must be deposited in an interest-bearing account or invested in a court-approved, interest-bearing instrument.

[Amended effective October 20, 1949; August 1, 1983; April 30, 2007, effective December 1, 2007.]

AUTHORS' COMMENTARY ON RULE 67

PURPOSE AND SCOPE

Rule 67 governs the circumstances in which a court may accept deposits of money and other personal property pending the outcome of a case.

RULE 67(a)—DEPOSITING PROPERTY

CORE CONCEPT

The court, in its discretion, may accept deposits of money or some other deliverable property in cases where such assets are genuinely at issue in the case.[1]

APPLICATIONS

Common Uses

Parties have used Rule 67 in cases concerning interpleader[2] and when Rule 62 provides for security as a condition of a stay pending appeal. If funds are actually deposited with the court, one effect may be to stop a party's liability for the accrual of interest on claims until the case is decided.[3]

Stakeholder's Decision

Rule 67 provides the holder of a disputed asset with an opportunity to seek relief from the burden of safeguarding the asset. However, it provides no authority for another party to demand surrender of the asset.

---

[1] *See, e.g., Alstom Caribe, Inc. v. Geo. P. Reintjes Co.,* 484 F.3d 106, 113 (1st Cir. 2007).

[2] *See, e.g., Gulf State Utilities Co. v. Alabama Power Co.,* 824 F.2d 1465, 1474 (5th Cir. 1987).

[3] *See, e.g., Cordero v. De Jesus-Mendez,* 922 F.2d 11, 18 (1st Cir. 1990); *Kotsopoulos v. Asturia Shipping Co.,* 467 F.2d 91, 94 (2d Cir. 1972).

Genuine Dispute: Sum Certain

Before a court will permit a party to make a deposit under Rule 67, the party must establish that there is a contested fund and that the amount of the disputed property is a sum certain.[4]

Leave of Court

Deposits may only be made with leave of court, on motion, and with notice to all other parties.[5]

Content of Motion

In the motion, the movant should state that opposing parties dispute the ownership of the property or money as well as the particular reasons for making the deposit, such as to avoid responsibility for the property or money.

Time for Motion

A party may move pursuant to Rule 67 at any time during an action.

Service of Order on the Clerk

If the court grants leave to make a deposit, the moving party must serve the order on the clerk of court at the time of making the deposit.

RULE 67(b)—INVESTING AND WITHDRAWING FUNDS

CORE CONCEPT

Rule 67(b) identifies the statutes governing deposits and withdrawals, and also provides that money paid into court under Rule 67 must be deposited in a court-approved interest-bearing account.

APPLICATIONS

Applicable Statutes

Sections 2041 (deposit) and 2042 (withdrawal) of Title 28 of the United State Code generally govern deposit and withdrawal of funds under Rule 67.

Interest-Bearing Account

The clerk of court must invest any money paid into the court in an interest-bearing account or in an interest-bearing instrument approved by the court in the name and to the credit of the court.

Withdrawal of Deposit

A person seeking the money deposited in court must make a motion asserting a judgment or any other document establishing that person's judicially defined interest in the deposit. The court may not disburse any deposit until it establishes ownership by court order, unless the parties have stipulated to the ownership of the property under the direction of the court.[6]

---

[4]   *See, e.g., CASCO, Inc. v. John Deere Construction Co. & Forestry Co.,* 293 F.R.D. 99, 100 (D.P.R. 2013) (rejecting use of Rule 67 because amount in dispute is unclear).

[5]   *See, e.g., Alstom Caribe, Inc. v. Geo. P. Reintjes Co., Inc.,* 484 F.3d 106, 113–14 (1st Cir. 2007) (noting court's discretion to accept deposit is limited to cases where there is genuine dispute as to entitlement to funds, and dispute is still alive at time of motion to make deposit).

[6]   *But cf. In re Craig's Stores of Texas, Inc.,* 402 F.3d 522, 524 (5th Cir. 2005) (where money was deposited in a proceeding in which court was lacking jurisdiction, court had to return funds to party who made deposit).

The Merits

Rule 67 provides a potential safe haven for an asset until a court determines rights in the asset. However, Rule 67 does not of itself establish a procedure for adjudicating such rights.[7]

Deposit Not Claimed

Once the right to withdraw the asset has been adjudicated or is no longer in dispute and the deposit has not been claimed for five years, the asset will be transferred to the U.S. Treasury in the name of and to the credit of the United States.[8]

ADDITIONAL RESEARCH REFERENCES

Wright & Miller, *Federal Practice and Procedure* §§ 2991 to 3000

C.J.S., Deposits in Court §§ 1 to 9

West's Key Number Digest, Deposits in Court ⊶1 to 12

---

[7] *See, e.g., LTV Corp. v. Gulf States Steel, Inc. of Alabama,* 969 F.2d 1050, 1063 (D.C. Cir. 1992) (Rule 67 "provides a place of safekeeping for disputed funds pending the resolution of a legal dispute, but it cannot be used as a means of altering the contractual relationships and legal duties of the parties.").

[8] 28 U.S.C.A. § 2042.

RULE 68

OFFER OF JUDGMENT

(a) Making an Offer; Judgment on an Accepted Offer. At least 14 days before the date set for trial, a party defending against a claim may serve on an opposing party an offer to allow judgment on specified terms, with the costs then accrued. If, within 14 days after being served, the opposing party serves written notice accepting the offer, either party may then file the offer and notice of acceptance, plus proof of service. The clerk must then enter judgment.

(b) Unaccepted Offer. An unaccepted offer is considered withdrawn, but it does not preclude a later offer. Evidence of an unaccepted offer is not admissible except in a proceeding to determine costs.

(c) Offer After Liability Is Determined. When one party's liability to another has been determined but the extent of liability remains to be determined by further proceedings, the party held liable may make an offer of judgment. It must be served within a reasonable time—but at least 14 days—before the date set for a hearing to determine the extent of liability.

(d) Paying Costs After an Unaccepted Offer. If the judgment that the offeree finally obtains is not more favorable than the unaccepted offer, the offeree must pay the costs incurred after the offer was made.

[Amended effective March 19, 1948; July 1, 1966; August 1, 1987; April 30, 2007, effective December 1, 2007; March 26, 2009, effective December 1, 2009.]

AUTHORS' COMMENTARY ON RULE 68

PURPOSE AND SCOPE

Rule 68 governs the circumstances in which a party defending against a claim for money damages or property may seek to resolve the claim by offering to allow judgment against that party for a specified amount of money or property. The Rule also establishes the consequences when a party does not accept an offer of judgment.

RULE 68(a)—MAKING AN OFFER; JUDGMENT ON AN ACCEPTED OFFER

CORE CONCEPT

A defendant may make an offer of judgment at least 14 days before the date set for trial. The plaintiff then has 14 days to accept the offer. The offer, acceptance, and proof of service will be filed with the court only if the opposing party accepts the offer. The clerk of court must then enter judgment.

APPLICATIONS

Scope

Rule 68 is generally applicable to any civil action in district court involving a claim for money or property.[1]

Contents of Offer

An offer of judgment must be for a specified dollar amount or specified property.[2] The offer must include costs accrued by the claiming party prior to receipt of the offer of judgment.[3] If the offer provides a specified amount for costs or provides that costs are included, the offer satisfies the requirements of the Rule.[4] If the offer is silent as to costs, the court may presume it included costs and add an amount for costs.[5]

Attorney's Fees

In general, Rule 68 does not include attorney's fees as costs that must be included in an offer of judgment. However, if the law underlying the cause of action includes attorney's fees as costs, then attorney's fees may be considered costs for purposes of an offer of judgment.[6]

Relation to Rule 54

Rule 54(d) provides that the party who prevails in a lawsuit is entitled to costs "as of course" unless some other provision of federal law or the federal rules intervenes.[7] When Rule 68 is applicable, it is a provision of the federal rules that overrides Rule 54(d) and can create a situation where a non-prevailing party may recover costs.[8]

Offering Judgment

The appropriate method of offering judgment is to serve a written offer upon the party whose claim is at issue.[9] However, until an offer is accepted by the claiming party, it is improper to file a copy of the offer with the clerk's office.[10]

Offer to Multiple Plaintiffs

If a defendant makes an offer of judgment to more than one plaintiff in the same case, the offer must itemize the proposed payment to each plaintiff. If the offer does not identify the proposed allocation of money among the plaintiffs, the defendant will not collect costs even if the plaintiffs' final judgment is for less than the offer.[11]

Joint Offer from Multiple Defendants

When more than one defendant makes an offer of judgment to a plaintiff, the defendants should be careful to make clear the proportion of the offer being made by each defendant. Failure to provide more than an unapportioned joint offer creates a significant possibility that, if one of the defendants is somehow excused but another is found liable, the

---

[1]   *See, e.g., Interfaith Community Organization v. Honeywell International, Inc.,* 726 F.3d 403, 408 (3d Cir. 2013).

[2]   *See, e.g., Basha v. Mitsubishi Motor Credit of America, Inc.,* 336 F.3d 451 (5th Cir.2003) (offer that proposed to settle all claims but did not quantify damages could not meet Rule 68 requirements).

[3]   *See, e.g., McCain v. Detroit II Auto Finance Center,* 378 F.3d 561 (6th Cir.2004).

[4]   *See, e.g., Utility Automation 2000, Inc. v. Choctawhatchee Elec. Co-op., Inc.,* 298 F.3d 1238, 1241 (11th Cir. 2002).

[5]   *Webb v. James,* 147 F.3d 617 (7th Cir.1998).

[6]   *Marek v. Chesny,* 473 U.S. 1, 8–9, 105 S.Ct. 3012, 87 L.Ed.2d 1 (1985).

[7]   Fed.R.Civ.P. 54(d).

[8]   *See, e.g., Payne v. Milwaukee County,* 288 F.3d 1021, 1027 (7th Cir. 2002).

[9]   *See, e.g., Driver Music Co., Inc. v. Commercial Union Ins. Companies,* 94 F.3d 1428, 1432 (10th Cir. 1996).

[10] *See, e.g., Kason v. Amphenol Corp.,* 132 F.R.D. 197 (N.D. Ill. 1990).

[11] *See, e.g., Gavoni v. Dobbs House, Inc.,* 164 F.3d 1071, 1075–77 (7th Cir. 1999).

offeror/defendants will not meet their burden of demonstrating that the offer was more favorable than the judgment the plaintiff later obtained.[12]

Settlement Offers

Settlement offers are not offers of judgment under Rule 68. Thus Rule 68 has no applicability to offers of settlement.[13]

Offers by Plaintiff

Unless a plaintiff is defending against a counterclaim or a crossclaim, as described in Rules 13 and 14, a plaintiff cannot make an offer of judgment.[14] Only parties defending against claims may use Rule 68 to make offers of judgment.[15]

Equitable Claims

Rule 68 generally applies to offers of specific sums or specific property. Typically the Rule is not used to resolve claims in equity where a party seeks only an injunction, but Rule 68 itself does not expressly prohibit such an application.[16]

Ambiguities: Ordinary Contract Analysis

In accordance with ordinary rules of contract law, ambiguities in Rule 68 offers are construed against the offeror.[17]

Timing of Offer

To be effective under Rule 68, an offer of judgment must be served on the party prosecuting a claim at least 14 days before the date set for the beginning of a trial.[18] However, if the trial is a bifurcated proceeding in which liability only is established in a first hearing, a timely offer of judgment may be served after a determination of liability but not less than 14 days before the date set for the damages hearing.[19]

Revocation

Except in exceptional circumstances a Rule 68 offer cannot be revoked during the 14 days for acceptance provided by the Rule.[20]

Time for Accepting an Offer

The defending party has 14 days to accept the offer, or it will be considered withdrawn pursuant to Rule 68(b).

Method of Accepting an Offer

The appropriate method for accepting an offer of judgment is by written notice of acceptance to the party who made the offer.

---

[12] *See, e.g., Harbor Motor Co., Inc. v. Arnell Chevrolet-Geo, Inc.,* 265 F.3d 638, 647–49 (7th Cir. 2001).

[13] *See, e.g., Menchise v. Senterfitt,* 532 F.3d 1146, 1152 (11th Cir. 2008).

[14] *Delta Air Lines, Inc. v. August,* 450 U.S. 346, 101 S.Ct. 1146, 67 L.Ed.2d 287 (1981).

[15] *See, e.g., Garcia v. Wal-Mart Stores, Inc.,* 209 F.3d 1170, 1176 (10th Cir. 2000).

[16] *See, e.g., Chathas v. Local 134 Intern. Broth. of Elec. Workers,* 233 F.3d 508, 511 (7th Cir. 2000).

[17] *See, e.g., Andretti v. Borla Performance Industries, Inc.,* 426 F.3d 824, 837 (6th Cir. 2005) (general contract principles apply).

[18] *See also Horowitch v. Diamond Aircraft Industries, Inc.,* 645 F.3d 1254 n.2 (11th Cir. 2011).

[19] *Delta Air Lines, Inc. v. August,* 450 U.S. 346, 101 S.Ct. 1146, 67 L.Ed.2d 287 (1981).

[20] *See, e.g., Richardson v. National R.R. Passenger Corp.,* 49 F.3d 760, 764 (D.C. Cir. 1995).

Terms of Acceptance

The offer must be accepted in its entirety, or it is deemed rejected.[21]

Entering Final Judgment

If the party prosecuting a claim accepts an offer of judgment, either party may file the offer and notice of acceptance, along with proof of service, with the clerk of court. The clerk then enters judgment consistent with the offer and acceptance.[22]

Relation to Rule 23

Rule 23 requires court approval for settlements, and parties cannot circumvent that requirement through the offer of judgment process.[23]

RULE 68(b)—UNACCEPTED OFFER

CORE CONCEPT

Unaccepted offers are deemed withdrawn, though the defending party may make a subsequent offer. Unaccepted offers are not admissible in court, except in a proceeding to determine costs or to challenge subject matter jurisdiction.[24]

APPLICATIONS

Timing of Acceptance

A party has 14 days after receipt of service of the written offer to accept the offer of judgment.[25] If the offer is not accepted within the 14-day period, Rule 68 treats the offer as withdrawn, and it cannot thereafter be accepted.

Offers Following Rejection or Withdrawal

Following rejection or withdrawal of an offer of judgment, the party that made the offer may renew the offer, or make a different offer, in which event the 14-day period for acceptance begins to run again.

Unaccepted Offer for Full Amount of Claim

The lower courts are divided as to whether an offer of judgment for the full amount of the claim ends the litigation even if the offer is not accepted,[26] and the Supreme Court has been unclear on the subject.[27]

Offer of Judgment as Evidence

If an offer of judgment is not accepted, the offer may not be used as evidence at trial. The only use to which a nonaccepted offer of judgment may be put is to establish the consequences, if any, to the nonaccepting party when final judgment is entered in the case, as set forth in Rule 68(d).

---

[21] *See, e.g., Whitcher v. Town of Matthews,* 136 F.R.D. 582, 585 (W.D.N.C. 1991).

[22] *See, e.g., Parental Guide of Texas, Inc. v. Thomson, Inc.,* 446 F.3d 1265, 1270 (Fed. Cir. 2006) (entry of judgment is a ministerial act).

[23] *See, e.g., Ramming v. Natural Gas Pipeline Co. of America,* 390 F.3d 366, 371 (5th Cir. 2004).

[24] *See, e.g., O'Brien v. Ed Donnelly Enterprises, Inc.,* 575 F.3d 567, 574 (6th Cir. 2009).

[25] *See, e.g., Perkins v. U.S. West Communications,* 138 F.3d 336 (8th Cir. 1998).

[26] *See Diaz v. First American Home Buyers Protection Corp.,* 732 F.3d 948, 951 (9th Cir. 2013) (collecting cases on both sides).

[27] *Genesis Healthcare Corp. v. Symczyk,* ___ U.S. ___, 133 S.Ct. 1523, 1528–29, 185 L.Ed.2d 636 (2013).

RULE 68(c)—OFFER AFTER LIABILITY IS DETERMINED

CORE CONCEPT

Rule 68(c) permits an offer after liability is determined, if the amount of liability has not been established. Such an offer must be served at least 14 days before the date set for a hearing on the extent of liability.

RULE 68(d)—PAYING COSTS AFTER AN UNACCEPTED OFFER

CORE CONCEPT

If an offer is not accepted and the offeree subsequently obtains a judgment that is not more favorable than the offer, the offeree must pay costs incurred by the offering party after the offer was made.

APPLICATIONS

Consequences of Nonacceptance

The consequences of nonacceptance of an offer under Rule 68 depend on the outcome of the litigation. Once final judgment is entered, if the party that did not accept the offer has won a judgment greater than the amount in the offer of judgment, the unaccepted offer has no consequence.[28] If, however, the nonaccepting party receives a favorable final judgment, but for less than the amount in the offer of judgment, the nonaccepting party must pay the offering party's costs incurred after it made the offer.[29] Rule 68 may thus permit a party that has made an offer of judgment, and then loses the case, to recover some costs from the prevailing party. To that extent, Rule 68 provides a possible exception to Rule 54(d), which provides that the prevailing party ordinarily will collect costs from the losing party.

Attorney's Fees

Some federal laws, such as federal civil rights laws, provide for prevailing parties (two-way cost shifting), or sometimes just prevailing plaintiffs (one-way cost shifting), to recover their attorney's fees as part of recoverable costs.[30] With two-way cost shifting statutes, the cost provisions for offers of judgment will apply in full to attorney's fees.[31] With one-way cost shifting statutes, the cost shifting provisions for offers of judgment do not entitle a defendant to recover its attorney's fees after an unaccepted offer, but they do end the plaintiff's rights to recover attorney's fees.[32]

Determining Whether Judgment Is "More Favorable"

In cases involving only money damages, it is usually not difficult to calculate whether the judgment a party won is more favorable than an earlier offer of judgment. However, where a party obtains an injunction as part of a favorable judgment, the value of an injunction should be included in the calculation in determining whether a judgment is more favorable than an earlier offer of judgment.[33]

---

[28] See, e.g., Brown v. Cox, 286 F.3d 1040, 1047 (8th Cir. 2002).

[29] See, e.g., Stanczyk v. City of New York, 752 F.3d 273, 280 (2d Cir. 2014).

[30] See, e.g., 42 U.S.C. § 1988.

[31] Marek v. Chesny, 473 U.S. 1, 8–9, 105 S.Ct. 3012, 87 L.Ed.2d 1 (1985).

[32] See, e.g., Hescott v. City of Saginaw, 757 F.3d 518, 528 (6th Cir. 2014).

[33] See, e.g., Reiter v. MTA New York City Transit Authority, 457 F.3d 224 (2d Cir. 2006).

When Defendant Prevails

If an opponent of a claim makes an offer of judgment that is not accepted, and if the offeror then wins the case, Rule 68 has *no* effect. Rule 68 is applied, if at all, only when an offer is not accepted, and then the offeree obtains judgment—but for less than the amount of the offer.[34]

ADDITIONAL RESEARCH REFERENCES

Wright & Miller, *Federal Practice and Procedure* §§ 3001 to 10. Lisnek, *Effective Negotiation and Mediation, A Lawyer's Guide.*

C.J.S., Federal Civil Procedure § 1276

West's Key Number Digest, Federal Civil Procedure ⊶2396.5, 2725

---

[34] *Delta Air Lines, Inc. v. August,* 450 U.S. 346, 352, 101 S.Ct. 1146, 1150, 67 L.Ed.2d 287 (1981).

RULE 69

EXECUTION

(a) In General.

    (1) *Money Judgment; Applicable Procedure.* A money judgment is enforced by a writ of execution, unless the court directs otherwise. The procedure on execution—and in proceedings supplementary to and in aid of judgment or execution—must accord with the procedure of the state where the court is located, but a federal statute governs to the extent it applies.

    (2) *Obtaining Discovery.* In aid of the judgment or execution, the judgment creditor or a successor in interest whose interest appears of record may obtain discovery from any person—including the judgment debtor—as provided in these rules or by the procedure of the state where the court is located.

(b) Against Certain Public Officers. When a judgment has been entered against a revenue officer in the circumstances stated in 28 U.S.C. § 2006, or against an officer of Congress in the circumstances stated in 2 U.S.C. § 118, the judgment must be satisfied as those statutes provide.

[Amended effective October 20, 1949; July 1, 1970; August 1, 1987; April 30, 2007, effective December 1, 2007.]

AUTHORS' COMMENTARY ON RULE 69

PURPOSE AND SCOPE

Rule 69 provides a mechanism for executing money judgments entered by a federal court. Rule 69 also provides for the execution of judgments entered against district directors of the Internal Revenue Service and officers of Congress.

RULE 69(a)—IN GENERAL

CORE CONCEPT

Rule 69(a) provides for the enforcement of money judgments generally through a writ of execution. If enforcement of a money judgment requires ancillary litigation, state law will usually control such litigation unless a federal statute otherwise provides.[1] However, discovery to enforce a money judgment may be conducted pursuant to either the federal discovery rules or the discovery rules of the forum state.

APPLICATIONS

Scope

    Rule 69 only applies to an execution of a money judgment entered by a federal court and has no application to state court judgments or other types of judgments.

---

[1] *See, e.g., United States v. Little,* 52 F.3d 495 (4th Cir. 1995).

Subject Matter Jurisdiction

Efforts to collect judgments under Rule 69 fall within the supplemental jurisdiction of district courts.[2]

Supplementing or Supplanting State Procedure

Although Rule 69(a) directs a district court to use state procedure[3] to enforce money judgments,[4] it also provides that the court may "direct otherwise." At the same time, federal courts have authority to supplement such procedure with federal practice when necessary.[5] Indeed, if state law is an obstacle to enforcement, federal courts may even be able to disregard state practice.[6] Finally, Rule 69(a) explicitly provides that any applicable federal statute supplants state law.[7]

Stay of Enforcement

Rule 62(a) directs that a federal money judgment may not be executed upon until 14 days after entry of judgment. The court may further stay execution of the final judgment when an appeal is properly taken or when the court reviews post-trial motions, as provided by Rule 62.[8]

Federal Statutes

In addition to the available state law remedies such as garnishment, arrest, mandamus, contempt, or the appointment of a receiver, a party seeking execution of a money judgment may use any applicable federal statute. Federal remedies for executions in aid of judgments are listed at 28 U.S.C.A. § 2001 *et seq.*

Registering a Judgment in District Outside Forum State

A judgment for money or property entered by any district court may be registered in any other district court by filing a certified copy of such judgment in the other district after the judgment has become final.[9] A judgment that has been registered has the same effect as the original judgment and may be enforced as would any other judgment. However, a potentially important result of registering a judgment in federal court that was previously awarded in a different federal court in a different state is that the law of the enforcing state—not the judgment state—will normally control.[10]

Writ of Execution

A writ of execution is a writ to enforce a judgment by the seizure and sale of property of the debtor in satisfaction of the judgment.

---

[2]   *See, e.g., Kokkonen v. Guardian Life Ins. Co. of America,* 511 U.S. 375, 379, 114 S.Ct. 1673, 1676, 128 L.Ed.2d 391 (1994).

[3]   *Peacock v. Thomas,* 516 U.S. 349, 359, 116 S.Ct. 862, 133 L.Ed.2d 817 (1996).

[4]   *See, e.g., Bergmann v. Michigan State Transportation Commission,* 665 F.3d 681, 684 (6th Cir. 2011).

[5]   *See, e.g., United States v. Harkins Builders, Inc.,* 45 F.3d 830, 833 (4th Cir. 1995) (Rule 69(a) permits use of federal procedure to further "the federal policy of affording judgment creditors the right to a writ of execution to enforce money judgments in federal courts.").

[6]   *See, e.g., Hankins v. Finnel,* 964 F.2d 853, 860 (8th Cir. 1992).

[7]   *See, e.g., Walters v. Industrial and Commercial Bank of China, Ltd.,* 651 F.3d 280 (2d Cir. 2011) (Foreign Sovereign Immunities Act may block application of Rule 69).

[8]   *Cf. Acevedo-Garcia v. Vera-Monroig,* 296 F.3d 13 (1st Cir. 2002).

[9]   28 U.S.C.A. § 1963.

[10]   *See, e.g., Condaire, Inc. v. Allied Piping, Inc.,* 286 F.3d 353, 357–58 (6th Cir. 2002).

Enforcement of Judgment

Upon obtaining a writ of execution, the judgment creditor may serve the writ on the U.S. Marshal or state officer, who will then execute, by attachment or otherwise, the property of the judgment debtor in the possession of third parties, and may have the judgment debtor's property sold at an execution sale. The specific procedures for obtaining a writ of execution and executing on the property of the judgment debtor will vary from state to state and district to district.

Comparison with Rule 70

In general, Rule 69 provides mechanisms for enforcement of money judgments. By contrast, Rule 70 authorizes the district court to issue orders to ensure that equitable relief is provided.[11]

Discovery

A party seeking to enforce a judgment may use either the federal or the state discovery rules to uncover information concerning assets of the debtor and to aid in execution of the judgment.[12] Rule 69(a) expressly provides that such discovery may be directed toward "any person," including persons not parties to the lawsuit.[13]

Property Subject to the Writ

State law will designate the property of the judgment debtor which may be levied upon in satisfaction of the judgment.

Foreign Sovereign Immunity

The Foreign Sovereign Immunities Act provides substantial immunity for foreign sovereigns from the jurisdiction of American courts.[14] The Act also immunizes the property of foreign states from attachment and execution on their property.[15] Rule 69 can be applied only to circumstances where the Act does not provide immunity against a foreign sovereign judgment creditor's attempt to execute against property.[16]

Eleventh Amendment Immunity

An attempt to use Rule 69 and state garnishment law to attach state property in satisfaction of a debt is generally barred by the Eleventh Amendment of the United States Constitution.[17]

Fees and Costs

Fees for writs, subpoenas, keeping attached property, seizing or levying on property, and for the sale of property may be taxed as costs.[18]

---

[11]   *See, e.g., Board of Com'rs of Stark County, OH v. Cape Stone Works, Inc.,* 206 F.Supp.2d 100, 102 (D. Mass. 2002).

[12]   *See, e.g., Natural Gas Pipeline Co. of America v. Energy Gathering, Inc.,* 2 F.3d 1397, 1403 (5th Cir. 1993).

[13]   *See, e.g., Credit Lyonnais, S.A. v. SGC Intern., Inc.,* 160 F.3d 428, 430 (8th Cir. 1998).

[14]   28 U.S.C. § 1604.

[15]   28 U.S.C. § 1609. *See, e.g., Walters v. Industrial & Commercial Bank of China, Ltd.,* 651 F.3d 280, 292 (2d Cir. 2011).

[16]   *See, e.g., Walters v. Industrial and Commercial Bank of China, Ltd.,* 651 F.3d 280 (2d Cir. 2011).

[17]   U.S. Const. Amend. 11. *See also Carpenters Pension Fund of Baltimore v. Maryland Department of Health and Mental Hygiene,* 721 F.3d 217 (4th Cir. 2013).

[18]   28 U.S.C.A. § 1921.

RULE 69(b)—AGAINST CERTAIN PUBLIC OFFICERS

CORE CONCEPT

If a district director of the Internal Revenue Service—a "collector" of revenue—or an officer of Congress has obtained a certificate of probable cause, a judgment entered against such district director[19] or officer[20] for damages resulting from any of the individual's official acts, or for the recovery of any money exacted by or paid to the individual and subsequently paid into the Treasury, may only be executed against the United States Treasury, and not against the individual's property.

APPLICATIONS

District Director

"District director" is defined as any district director of the Internal Revenue Service, former district director, or personal representative of a deceased district director.

Obtaining Certificate of Probable Cause

When a judgment creditor seeks to enforce a judgment, the district director or the officer of Congress may apply to the court for a certificate of probable cause. The court will determine whether the director or officer acted with probable and reasonable cause in performing their proper governmental duties. If the court so finds, the court will issue a certificate of probable cause.

Effect of Certificate

The certificate of probable cause converts the action to one against the United States, extinguishing the personal liability of the individual. Subsequently, the judgment creditor may serve the certificate of probable cause, along with the judgment, on the United States Treasury. The Treasury will pay the amount of the judgment.

ADDITIONAL RESEARCH REFERENCES

Wright & Miller, *Federal Practice and Procedure* §§ 3011 to 3020

C.J.S., Federal Civil Procedure §§ 1254 to 1272 et seq.

West's Key Number Digest, Execution ⊶1 to 474

---

[19] 28 U.S.C.A. § 2006 (Internal Revenue Officer).
[20] 2 U.S.C.A. § 118 (18 Stat. 401) (Officer of Congress).

RULE 70

ENFORCING A JUDGMENT FOR A SPECIFIC ACT

(a) Party's Failure to Act; Ordering Another to Act. If a judgment requires a party to convey land, to deliver a deed or other document, or to perform any other specific act and the party fails to comply within the time specified, the court may order the act to be done—at the disobedient party's expense—by another person appointed by the court. When done, the act has the same effect as if done by the party.

(b) Vesting Title. If the real or personal property is within the district, the court—instead of ordering a conveyance—may enter a judgment divesting any party's title and vesting it in others. That judgment has the effect of a legally executed conveyance.

(c) Obtaining a Writ of Attachment or Sequestration. On application by a party entitled to performance of an act, the clerk must issue a writ of attachment or sequestration against the disobedient party's property to compel obedience.

(d) Obtaining a Writ of Execution or Assistance. On application by a party who obtains a judgment or order for possession, the clerk must issue a writ of execution or assistance.

(e) Holding in Contempt. The court may also hold the disobedient party in contempt.

[April 30, 2007, effective December 1, 2007.]

AUTHORS' COMMENTARY ON RULE 70

PURPOSE AND SCOPE

Rule 70 provides that the court may convey property or perform any other specific act pursuant to a judgment when a party ordered to convey property or perform a specific act fails to comply.

RULE 70(a)—PARTY'S FAILURE TO ACT; ORDERING ANOTHER TO ACT

CORE CONCEPT

Rule 70(a) provides that if a judgment includes a requirement that a party transfer property or perform some other act, the court may appoint a person to do the act if the party fails to do so. Such appointment will be at the expense of the non-performing party and will carry the same legal result as if the party had performed the act.

APPLICATIONS

Judgment Required

Rule 70 "applies only to parties who have failed to perform specific acts pursuant to a judgment."[1] In the absence of a judgment, Rule 70 has no applicability.[2]

Comparison with Rule 69

In general, Rule 69 provides mechanisms for enforcement of money judgments.[3] By contrast, Rule 70 authorizes the district court to issue orders to ensure that equitable relief is provided,[4] but unlike Rule 69, Rule 70 does not require deference to state law.[5]

Application to Class Action Members

If other requirements of Rule 70 are satisfied, the Rule may also be enforced against members of Rule 23 classes.[6]

RULE 70(b)—VESTING TITLE

CORE CONCEPT

Rule 70(b) provides that if property to be transferred pursuant to judgment is located within the district where the court sits, the court may simply enter judgment transferring title, without going through the process of appointing a person to do the act.

APPLICATIONS

Property Within the District

If a party has failed to obey a court order pertaining to real or personal property physically located within the district in which the court sits, the court may order title transferred directly from the disobedient party to the prevailing party.

Property Outside the District

If the real or personal property is not physically located within the district in which the court sits, the court must appoint a person to convey the property. The act performed by the appointed party has the full effect as it if it were executed by the disobedient party.

Timing

Rule 70 applies to the enforcement of court orders after the entry of judgment and after the time for performing the ordered action has elapsed.[7]

Content of Motion

In a written motion, the movant should allege with specificity the disobedient party's noncompliance, as well as the relief sought to remedy noncompliance.

---

[1]   *See, e.g., Analytical Engineering, Inc. v. Baldwin Filters, Inc.,* 425 F.3d 443, 449 (7th Cir. 2005).

[2]   *See, e.g., Deegan v. Strategic Azimuth LLC,* 768 F.Supp.2d 107, 115 n.1 (D.D.C. 2011) (Rule 64, not Rule 70, applies to prejudgment relief).

[3]   *See, e.g., Bergmann v. Michigan State Transportation Commission,* 665 F.3d 681, 684 (6th Cir. 2011).

[4]   *See, e.g., Board of Com'rs of Stark County, OH v. Cape Stone Works, Inc.,* 206 F.Supp.2d 100, 102 (D. Mass. 2002).

[5]   *See, e.g., Bergmann v. Michigan State Transportation Commission,* 665 F.3d 681, 681 (6th Cir. 2011).

[6]   *See, e.g., Dick v. Sprint Communications Co., L.P.,* 297 F.R.D. 283, 292 (W.D. Ky. 2014).

[7]   *See, e.g., Barmat, Inc. v. United States,* 159 F.R.D. 578, 582 (N.D. Ga. 1994).

RULE 70(c)—OBTAINING A WRIT OF ATTACHMENT OR SEQUESTRATION

CORE CONCEPT

A party entitled to performance of an act may obtain a writ of sequestration or attachment to ensure performance.

APPLICATIONS

Writs of Attachment or Sequestration

Upon proper motion to the clerk of court, a prevailing party may obtain a writ of attachment or sequestration authorizing seizure of the disobedient party's property or money until that party complies with a judgment.

Costs Against Disobedient Party

A court may tax against the disobedient party the costs of transferring the property or performing the specific act.

RULE 70(d)—OBTAINING A WRIT OF EXECUTION OR ASSISTANCE

CORE CONCEPT

A party who has obtained a judgment or order for possession of property may apply for a writ of execution or assistance. Upon proper application, it is the duty of the clerk to issue such a writ.

RULE 70(e)—HOLDING IN CONTEMPT

CORE CONCEPT

Rule 70(e) provides that, in addition to other remedies available under Rule 70, the court has authority to hold disobedient parties in contempt.[8]

––––––––––

ADDITIONAL RESEARCH REFERENCES

Wright & Miller, *Federal Practice and Procedure* §§ 3021 to 3030

C.J.S., Assistance, Writ of § 3, § 4; Contempt § 12; Federal Civil Procedure §§ 1254 to 1260 et seq.

West's Key Number Digest, Assistance, Writ of ⊷2; Contempt ⊷20; Federal Civil Procedure ⊷2691, ⊷2695

––––––––––

[8]   *See, e.g., McMahan & Co. v. Po Folks, Inc.,* 206 F.3d 627, 634 (6th Cir. 2000).

RULE 71

ENFORCING RELIEF FOR
OR AGAINST A NONPARTY

When an order grants relief for a nonparty or may be enforced against a nonparty, the procedure for enforcing the order is the same as for a party.

[Amended effective August 1, 1987; April 30, 2007, effective December 1, 2007.]

AUTHORS' COMMENTARY ON RULE 71

PURPOSE AND SCOPE

Rule 71 provides for the enforcement of a court order by a nonparty in whose favor an order has been entered or against a nonparty.

APPLICATIONS

In Favor of a Nonparty

A court order may be enforced by a nonparty when that person shares an identity of interest with a prevailing party or is an intended beneficiary of the court order with the right to enforce it.[1]

Against a Nonparty

A court order may be enforced against a nonparty when that person's interests are so closely related to a losing party's interests that enforcement against that nonparty is not unfair.[2] When enforcing a judgment against nonparties, Rule 71 is restricted to circumstances where enforcement does not violate due process or is otherwise lawful.[3]

ADDITIONAL RESEARCH REFERENCES

Wright & Miller, *Federal Practice and Procedure* §§ 3031 to 3040

C.J.S., Federal Civil Procedure § 1107

West's Key Number Digest, Federal Civil Procedure ⊶ 2391

---

[1]   *See, e.g., Brennan v. Nassau County,* 352 F.3d 60, 65 (2d Cir. 2003).

[2]   *See, e.g., Irwin v. Mascott,* 370 F.3d 924, 931–32 (9th Cir. 2004) (Rule 71 permits use of contempt power of court to enforce order against nonparty who has notice of injunction).

[3]   *See, e.g., LiButti v. United States,*178 F.3d 114 (2d Cir. 1999) (enforcement of a judgment against a person who is a successor in interest to a party requires that the court first obtain personal jurisdiction over the successor in interest).

RULE 71.1

CONDEMNING REAL OR PERSONAL PROPERTY

(a) Applicability of Other Rules. These rules govern proceedings to condemn real and personal property by eminent domain, except as this rule provides otherwise.

(b) Joinder of Properties. The plaintiff may join separate pieces of property in a single action, no matter whether they are owned by the same persons or sought for the same use.

(c) Complaint.

    (1) *Caption.* The complaint must contain a caption as provided in Rule 10(a). The plaintiff must, however, name as defendants both the property—designated generally by kind, quantity, and location—and at least one owner of some part of or interest in the property.

    (2) *Contents.* The complaint must contain a short and plain statement of the following:

        (A) the authority for the taking;

        (B) the uses for which the property is to be taken;

        (C) a description sufficient to identify the property;

        (D) the interests to be acquired; and

        (E) for each piece of property, a designation of each defendant who has been joined as an owner or owner of an interest in it.

    (3) *Parties.* When the action commences, the plaintiff need join as defendants only those persons who have or claim an interest in the property and whose names are then known. But before any hearing on compensation, the plaintiff must add as defendants all those persons who have or claim an interest and whose names have become known or can be found by a reasonably diligent search of the records, considering both the property's character and value and the interests to be acquired. All others may be made defendants under the designation "Unknown Owners."

    (4) *Procedure.* Notice must be served on all defendants as provided in Rule 71.1(d), whether they were named as defendants when the action commenced or were added later. A defendant may answer as provided in

Rule 71.1(e). The court, meanwhile, may order any distribution of a deposit that the facts warrant.

(5) *Filing; Additional Copies.* In addition to filing the complaint, the plaintiff must give the clerk at least one copy for the defendants' use and additional copies at the request of the clerk or a defendant.

(d) Process.

(1) *Delivering Notice to the Clerk.* On filing a complaint, the plaintiff must promptly deliver to the clerk joint or several notices directed to the named defendants. When adding defendants, the plaintiff must deliver to the clerk additional notices directed to the new defendants.

(2) *Contents of the Notice.*

    (A) *Main Contents.* Each notice must name the court, the title of the action, and the defendant to whom it is directed. It must describe the property sufficiently to identify it, but need not describe any property other than that to be taken from the named defendant. The notice must also state:

        (i)   that the action is to condemn property;

        (ii)   the interest to be taken;

        (iii)   the authority for the taking;

        (iv)   the uses for which the property is to be taken;

        (v)   that the defendant may serve an answer on the plaintiff's attorney within 21 days after being served with the notice;

        (vi)   that the failure to so serve an answer constitutes consent to the taking and to the court's authority to proceed with the action and fix the compensation; and

        (vii)   that a defendant who does not serve an answer may file a notice of appearance.

    (B) *Conclusion.* The notice must conclude with the name, telephone number, and e-mail address of the plaintiff's attorney and an address within the district in which the action is brought where the attorney may be served.

(3) *Serving the Notice.*

    (A) *Personal Service.* When a defendant whose address is known resides within the United States or a territory subject to the administrative or judicial jurisdiction of the United States, personal service of the

notice (without a copy of the complaint) must be made in accordance with Rule 4.

(B) *Service by Publication.*

(i) A defendant may be served by publication only when the plaintiff's attorney files a certificate stating that the attorney believes the defendant cannot be personally served, because after diligent inquiry within the state where the complaint is filed, the defendant's place of residence is still unknown or, if known, that it is beyond the territorial limits of personal service. Service is then made by publishing the notice—once a week for at least three successive weeks—in a newspaper published in the county where the property is located or, if there is no such newspaper, in a newspaper with general circulation where the property is located. Before the last publication, a copy of the notice must also be mailed to every defendant who cannot be personally served but whose place of residence is then known. Unknown owners may be served by publication in the same manner by a notice addressed to "Unknown Owners."

(ii) Service by publication is complete on the date of the last publication. The plaintiff's attorney must prove publication and mailing by a certificate, attach a printed copy of the published notice, and mark on the copy the newspaper's name and the dates of publication.

(4) *Effect of Delivery and Service.* Delivering the notice to the clerk and serving it have the same effect as serving a summons under Rule 4.

(5) *Proof of Service; Amending the Proof or Notice.* Rule 4(1) governs proof of service. The court may permit the proof or the notice to be amended.

(e) Appearance or Answer.

(1) *Notice of Appearance.* A defendant that has no objection or defense to the taking of its property may serve a notice of appearance designating the property in which it claims an interest. The defendant must then be given notice of all later proceedings affecting the defendant.

(2) *Answer.* A defendant that has an objection or defense to the taking must serve an answer within 21 days after being served with the notice. The answer must:

(A) identify the property in which the defendant claims an interest;

(B) state the nature and extent of the interest; and

(C) state all the defendant's objections and defenses to the taking.

(3) *Waiver of Other Objections and Defenses; Evidence on Compensation.* A defendant waives all objections and defenses not stated in its answer. No other pleading or motion asserting an additional objection or defense is allowed. But at the trial on compensation, a defendant—whether or not it has previously appeared or answered—may present evidence on the amount of compensation to be paid and may share in the award.

(f) Amending Pleadings. Without leave of court, the plaintiff may—as often as it wants—amend the complaint at any time before the trial on compensation. But no amendment may be made if it would result in a dismissal inconsistent with Rule 71.1(i)(1) or (2). The plaintiff need not serve a copy of an amendment, but must serve notice of the filing, as provided in Rule 5(b), on every affected party who has appeared and, as provided in Rule 71.1(d), on every affected party who has not appeared. In addition, the plaintiff must give the clerk at least one copy of each amendment for the defendants' use, and additional copies at the request of the clerk or a defendant. A defendant may appear or answer in the time and manner and with the same effect as provided in Rule 71.1(e).

(g) Substituting Parties. If a defendant dies, becomes incompetent, or transfers an interest after being joined, the court may, on motion and notice of hearing, order that the proper party be substituted. Service of the motion and notice on a nonparty must be made as provided in Rule 71.1(d)(3).

(h) Trial of the Issues.

(1) *Issues Other Than Compensation; Compensation.* In an action involving eminent domain under federal law, the court tries all issues, including compensation, except when compensation must be determined:

   (A) by any tribunal specially constituted by a federal statute to determine compensation; or

   (B) if there is no such tribunal, by a jury when a party demands one within the time to answer or within any additional time the court sets, unless the court appoints a commission.

(2) *Appointing a Commission; Commission's Powers and Report.*

   (A) *Reasons for Appointing.* If a party has demanded a jury, the court may instead appoint a three-person commission to determine compensation because of the character, location, or quantity of the property to be condemned or for other just reasons.

   (B) *Alternate Commissioners.* The court may appoint up to two additional persons to serve as alternate commissioners to hear the case and replace commissioners who, before a decision is filed, the court finds

unable or disqualified to perform their duties. Once the commission renders its final decision, the court must discharge any alternate who has not replaced a commissioner.

(C) *Examining the Prospective Commissioners.* Before making its appointments, the court must advise the parties of the identity and qualifications of each prospective commissioner and alternate, and may permit the parties to examine them. The parties may not suggest appointees, but for good cause may object to a prospective commissioner or alternate.

(D) *Commission's Powers and Report.* A commission has the powers of a master under Rule 53(c). Its action and report are determined by a majority. Rule 53(d), (e), and (f) apply to its action and report.

(i) Dismissal of the Action or a Defendant.

(1) *Dismissing the Action.*

(A) *By the Plaintiff.* If no compensation hearing on a piece of property has begun, and if the plaintiff has not acquired title or a lesser interest or taken possession, the plaintiff may, without a court order, dismiss the action as to that property by filing a notice of dismissal briefly describing the property.

(B) *By Stipulation.* Before a judgment is entered vesting the plaintiff with title or a lesser interest in or possession of property, the plaintiff and affected defendants may, without a court order, dismiss the action in whole or in part by filing a stipulation of dismissal. And if the parties so stipulate, the court may vacate a judgment already entered.

(C) *By Court Order.* At any time before compensation has been determined and paid, the court may, after a motion and hearing, dismiss the action as to a piece of property. But if the plaintiff has already taken title, a lesser interest, or possession as to any part of it, the court must award compensation for the title, lesser interest, or possession taken.

(2) *Dismissing a Defendant.* The court may at any time dismiss a defendant who was unnecessarily or improperly joined.

(3) *Effect.* A dismissal is without prejudice unless otherwise stated in the notice, stipulation, or court order.

(j) Deposit and Its Distribution.

(1) *Deposit.* The plaintiff must deposit with the court any money required by law as a condition to the exercise of eminent domain and may make a deposit when allowed by statute.

(2) *Distribution; Adjusting Distribution.* After a deposit, the court and attorneys must expedite the proceedings so as to distribute the deposit and to determine and pay compensation. If the compensation finally awarded to a defendant exceeds the amount distributed to that defendant, the court must enter judgment against the plaintiff for the deficiency. If the compensation awarded to a defendant is less than the amount distributed to that defendant, the court must enter judgment against that defendant for the overpayment.

(k) Condemnation Under a State's Power of Eminent Domain. This rule governs an action involving eminent domain under state law. But if state law provides for trying an issue by jury—or for trying the issue of compensation by jury or commission or both—that law governs.

(l) Costs. Costs are not subject to Rule 54(d).

[Adopted April 30, 1951, effective August 1, 1951; amended January 21, 1963, effective July 1, 1963; April 29, 1985, effective August 1, 1985; March 2, 1987, effective August 1, 1987; April 25, 1988, effective August 1, 1988; amended by Pub.L. 100–690, Title VII, § 7050, November 18, 1988, 102 Stat. 4401 (although amendment by Pub.L. 100–690 could not be executed due to prior amendment by Court order which made the same change effective August 1, 1988); amended April 22, 1993, effective December 1, 1993; March 27, 2003, effective December 1, 2003; April 30, 2007, effective December 1, 2007; March 26, 2009, effective December 1, 2009.]

AUTHORS' COMMENTARY ON RULE 71.1

PURPOSE AND SCOPE

Rule 71.1 provides a uniform set of rules for the condemnation of real and personal property under the federal and state powers of eminent domain.

RULE 71.1(a)—APPLICABILITY OF OTHER RULES

CORE CONCEPT

Rule 71.1 establishes certain specific procedures for condemnation proceedings in federal courts under the power of eminent domain, then sets the general Federal Rules of Civil Procedure as the default procedures for issues not covered by Rule 71.1.

APPLICATIONS

Condemnation of Personal Property

Rule 71.1 applies to the condemnation of personal property.[1]

---

[1]   *See,* 42 U.S.C.A. §§ 1805, 1811, 1813 (Atomic Energy Act); 50 U.S.C.A. § 79 (nitrates); 50 U.S.C.A. §§ 161 to 166 (helium gas).

Inverse Condemnation Proceedings

Rule 71.1 does not apply to inverse condemnation proceedings. An inverse condemnation is a cause of action by which a landowner seeks just compensation from the government for a taking of his or her property when the government has not instituted condemnation proceedings.[2]

Choice of Law

Federal condemnation is strictly governed by federal law and precedent. State law only defines the nature of the real or personal property interest, such as the meaning of property, defining what is taken, or determining the ownership of land.

Condemnation Under State Law

A district court may entertain condemnation proceedings under state law, as provided by Rule 71.1(k).

Jurisdiction and Venue

The district courts have original jurisdiction over proceedings to condemn real property for the use of the United States, its agencies, or departments.[3] Venue will be in the district court of the district in which the real property is located or, if located in different districts in the same state, in any such districts.[4]

Other Rules Act as Default Procedures

In cases where Rule 71.1 does not provide a procedure concerning litigation, the court will apply other applicable Rules, such as the discovery Rules.[5]

RULE 71.1(b)—JOINDER OF PROPERTIES

CORE CONCEPT

Rule 71.1(b) permits condemnation of separate properties, including properties belonging to different owners, or properties for different public uses in the same court action.[6] Only in exceptional circumstances is the court required to conduct separate trials. To eliminate jury confusion over the relative value of properties, the court may separate the evidence concerning the damages sustained by each owner.

RULE 71.1(c)—COMPLAINT

CORE CONCEPT

The requirements for a complaint under Rule 71.1(c) are different from those in an ordinary civil action. In the complaint's caption, the plaintiff must name as defendants both the property and at least one of the owners. The plaintiff is not required to serve a summons and complaint on the defendants; rather the clerk of court arranges for notice to all defendants. However, prior to a hearing on compensation, the plaintiff must join all defendants who can be ascertained from a reasonably diligent search of the records.

---

[2]   *KLK, Inc. v. U.S. Dept. of Interior,* 35 F.3d 454, 455 n.1 (9th Cir. 1994).

[3]   28 U.S.C.A. § 1358.

[4]   28 U.S.C.A. § 1403.

[5]   *See East Tennessee Natural Gas Co. v. Sage,* 361 F.3d 808, 828–29 (4th Cir. 2004) (approving use of Rule 65 to obtain preliminary injunction enabling early occupation of land).

[6]   *See, e.g., McLaughlin v. Mississippi Power Co.,* 376 F.3d 344 (5th Cir.2004) (noting that joinder of properties under Rule 71.1 is "much broader" than joinder of parties under Rules 19 and 20).

APPLICATIONS

Caption

The complaint's caption must include the name of the court, the title of the action, the docket number, and the name of the type of pleading being presented.[7] The caption must name as defendants both the property and at least one of the owners. The plaintiff will name the property as the defendant by stating the kind, quantity, and location of the property.

Contents of Complaint

The complaint must contain a short and plain statement of:

(1)   the authority for the taking;

(2)   the use for which the property is to be taken;[8]

(3)   a description of the property sufficient for identification;[9]

(4)   the interests to be acquired; and

(5)   for each separate piece of property, the defendants who have been joined as owners or owners of an interest in the property.

Filing of Complaint and Notice

The plaintiff must file the complaint with the clerk and provide the clerk with at least one copy for the defendants. Upon the request of the clerk or the defendants, the plaintiff must furnish additional copies. This practice differs from the normal practice under Rule 4, which requires the plaintiff to serve a summons and a copy of the complaint on the defendants.

Joining Parties at Commencement

Although Rule 71.1(c)(1) provides that the caption must include at least one owner of the property, the condemnor must join as defendants all persons or entities of title record having or claiming an interest in the property whose names are then known. Thus, the plaintiff must join all known owners, but cannot commence the action unless the identity of at least one of the owners is known.

Joining of Parties Prior to Hearing on Compensation

Prior to a hearing involving compensation, the condemnor must add as defendants all persons who have an interest whose identities have been learned or can be ascertained by a reasonably diligent search of the records.[10] "Reasonably diligent" search means the type of search a title searcher would undertake, but the extent of the search required will depend upon the character and value of the property involved and the interests to be acquired. Property owners joined after the commencement of the action must be served with notice by the clerk and allowed to answer. If there are owners whose identity is not known, they may be designated as "Unknown Owners."

Failure to Join a Party

There are no indispensable parties in a condemnation action. Therefore, the failure to join a party will not defeat the condemnor's title to the land because a condemnation action

---

[7]   *See* Official Form 29.

[8]   *See, e.g., City of Arlington, Tex. v. Golddust Twins Realty Corp.,* 41 F.3d 960, 964 (5th Cir. 1994).

[9]   *See, e.g., Southern Natural Gas Co. v. Land, Cullman County,* 197 F.3d 1368, 1375 (11th Cir. 1999) (a legal description and plat map showing location of pipeline and related easements "easily" satisfies Rule 71A(c)(2)).

[10]   *See, e.g., Cadorette v. United States,* 988 F.2d 215, 224 (1st Cir. 1993) (Rule 71A(c) requires government to make an affirmative search for "lost" heirs).

is an action *in rem*.[11] If the condemnor fails to join a party, the omitted party may have the right to sue for compensation in the Claims Court after the condemnation is completed.[12]

RULE 71.1(d)—PROCESS

CORE CONCEPT

Rule 71.1(d) directs that the clerk will deliver a notice of the complaint to a marshal or specially appointed person who will make personal service on the defendants.

APPLICATIONS

Content of Notice

Each notice must state:

(1)   the court;

(2)   the title of the action;

(3)   the name of the defendant to whom it is directed;

(4)   the nature of the action (condemning property);

(5)   a description of the property sufficient for its identification;

(6)   the interest to be taken;

(7)   the authority for the taking;

(8)   the uses for which the property is being taken;

(9)   the time for answering the complaint (the defendant may serve an answer upon the plaintiff's attorney within 21 days after the service of the notice);

(10) the penalty for failing to answer (a consent to the taking, permitting the court to proceed to hear the action and fix compensation); and

(11) that any defendant who chooses not to file an answer may nevertheless file a notice of appearance.

The notice must, finally, include the name, telephone number, and e-mail address of the plaintiff's attorney as well as an address within the district in which the suit is brought where that attorney may be served.

Preparation of Notice

The plaintiff may prepare joint or separate notices. However, one notice must be delivered to each named defendant and need contain a description of only that property to be taken from the particular defendant to whom it is directed.

Filing of Notice

The plaintiff's attorney will prepare a notice and deliver it to the clerk with the complaint. Subsequently, the clerk will file and enter the complaint in the record and deliver the notice (but not a copy of the complaint itself) to the marshal or specially-appointed person for service.

---

[11] *Fulcher v. United States,* 632 F.2d 278, 282 (4th Cir. 1980) ("Persons not identified . . . can be impleaded as unknown.").

[12] *See, e.g., Cadorette v. United States,* 988 F.2d 215, 225 (1st Cir. 1993).

Persons Requiring Notice

At the commencement of the case, the clerk only provides notice to persons whose names are in the complaint. Property owners joined after the filing of the complaint must be served with notice and allowed to answer.

Personal Service on U.S. Residents

For defendants who reside within the United States or its territories or insular possessions and whose residence is known, personal service of the notice is made in accordance with Rule 4.

Service by Publication

(1) *Persons Served by Publication:* A plaintiff may make service by publication on three types of defendants:[13]

    (a) owners who do not reside in the United States, its territories, or insular possessions, and who, therefore, are beyond the territorial limits of personal service;

    (b) owners within the state in which the complaint is filed whose place of residence is unknown after a diligent search of the records; and

    (c) unknown owners.

(2) *Publication:* The plaintiff must publish the notice in a newspaper in the county where the land is located. When no newspaper exists in the county where the land is located, the plaintiff must publish the notice in a newspaper having a circulation in the area where the land is located. The plaintiff must publish the notice once a week for at least three successive weeks.

(3) *Proof of Publication:* When a plaintiff wishes to make proof of service by publication, the plaintiff's attorney must file with the court a certificate stating that the defendant cannot be served personally because the defendant's residence is beyond the personal service limits or after diligent inquiry defendant's residence is unknown. The plaintiff's attorney must attach to the certificate a printed copy of the published notice marked with the name of the newspaper and the dates of publication.

(4) *Defendants Who Cannot Be Served but Residence Known:* In addition to publication, the plaintiff must mail a copy of the notice to each defendant who cannot be personally served but whose place of residence is known prior to the date of the last publication. Service is complete on the date of the last publication.

RULE 71.1(e)—APPEARANCE OR ANSWER

CORE CONCEPT

A defendant may respond to a condemnation complaint in two ways. If the defendant intends to either contest the taking or make objections to the complaint, the defendant must file an answer. Alternatively, if the defendant has no defenses or objections to the taking, the defendant simply serves a notice of appearance designating the property in which the defendant has an interest. Filing a notice of appearance requires that the defendant be given notice of all subsequent proceedings that affect that defendant's interest.[14] However, regardless of whether the defendant files an answer or an

---

[13] *See, e.g., United States v. 499.472 Acres of Land More or Less in Brazoria County, Tex.,* 701 F.2d 545, 551 (5th Cir. 1983) (publication service permissible only in the explicit circumstances described in Rule 71.1(d)).

[14] *Cf. United States v. 14.02 Acres of Land,* 547 F.3d 943, 954 (9th Cir. 2008) (Rule 71.1(e) overrides requirement of Rule 5 that all post-complaint filings be served on all parties).

appearance, a defendant may present evidence at the hearing on compensation and share in the award.[15]

APPLICATIONS

Answer

The answer is the only document in which defenses or objections may be asserted.[16] Unlike most answers to complaints in ordinary civil actions, the defendant must make specific allegations. In the answer the defendant must identify the property, the defendant's interest in the property, and the defenses to the taking.

Counterclaims and Crossclaims

An answer may not contain a counterclaim or crossclaim.[17] A counterclaim must be brought in a separate action in the district court or the Court of Claims.

Timing of Answer

Within 21 days of service of the notice, the defendant must answer the complaint. This response period may be enlarged by motion, as provided by Rule 6(b).

Appearance

When the defendant has no defenses or objections to the taking or to the complaint, the defendant may serve a notice of appearance. The notice of appearance should designate the property in which the defendant claims an interest.

RULE 71.1(f)—AMENDING PLEADINGS

CORE CONCEPT

A plaintiff may amend the complaint multiple times without leave of court before the trial on the issue of just compensation. However, except as provided by Rule 71.1(i), the plaintiff may not amend the complaint to remove the names of defendants or claims. Within 21 days of the notice of each amended complaint, the defendant is entitled to file one amended answer as of right.

APPLICATIONS

Procedure for Amending Complaint

The plaintiff may amend the complaint by filing with the clerk the amended pleading and by serving notice of the amended pleading on each defendant. The plaintiff need not serve a copy of the amended pleading itself on defendants, a practice that differs from normal civil actions. Instead, if a defendant or the clerk requests copies of the amended complaint, the plaintiff must provide the clerk with additional copies.

RULE 71.1(g)—SUBSTITUTING PARTIES

CORE CONCEPT

Upon proper motion and notice of hearing, the court may order the substitution of parties when a defendant dies or becomes incompetent, or transfers an interest after the defendant's joinder. If a new party is substituted, the plaintiff must serve a copy of the motion and notice of hearing on the new party, as provided by Rule 71.1(d). Rule 25, governing substitution of parties in most civil actions, does not apply to condemnation actions.

---

[15]   *See, e.g., Bank One Texas v. United States,* 157 F.3d 397 (5th Cir. 1998).

[16]   *See, e.g., Washington Metropolitan Area Transit Authority v. Precision Small Engines,* 227 F.3d 224, 228 n.2 (4th Cir. 2000).

[17]   *See, e.g., United States v. Certain Land Situated in City of Detroit,* 361 F.3d 305, 308 (6th Cir. 2004).

RULE 71.1(h)—TRIAL OF THE ISSUES

CORE CONCEPT

All issues other than the issue of compensation will be decided by the court.[18] The issue of compensation will be decided by either a special tribunal, a commission, a jury, or the court, in condemnation actions instituted by the federal or state government under powers of eminent domain. Federal law may require the issue of compensation to be decided by a tribunal specially constituted by Congress. When any party demands a trial by jury, the court will decide whether to conduct a jury trial or to appoint a commission to decide the issue of compensation.

♦   **NOTE:** If a commission is appointed to decide the issue of compensation, the commission must issue a report. Within 21 days after service of the commission report, parties must make and serve on the other parties and the court their objections to the report.

APPLICATIONS

Trial by Jury

When any party demands a trial by jury, the court may conduct a jury trial or may appoint a commission to decide the issue of compensation. However, there is no constitutional right to a trial by jury in condemnation cases,[19] and the jury in such cases may decide only the issue of compensation.[20]

(1) *Time for Demand:* Within the time allowed for the answer to the condemnation complaint (21 days of service of the notice of the complaint) or a further time fixed by the court, any party may demand a trial by jury.

(2) *Procedure for Trial by Jury:* The trial of a condemnation action proceeds similarly to any other civil proceeding involving a trial by jury. However, the judge will determine all issues other than the amount of compensation.[21]

Trial by Commission

(1) *Appointment of Commission:* When a party demands a trial by jury, the court has discretion to appoint a commission to decide the issue of compensation rather than conducting a trial by jury.[22] Although the court is not required to make findings of fact to support its determination to appoint a commission, for purposes of appellate review the court will often state in writing its reasons for appointing a commission.

    (a) *Conditions for Reference to Commission:* Courts have appointed commissions for such reasons as: local preference or habit, the preference of the Justice Department, the distance of the property from the courthouse, the complexity of the issues, the character of the land, the nature of the interest or the number of tracts taken, the need for numerous jury trials, the desirability of uniform awards, or to prevent discrimination.

(2) *Number of Commissioners:* A commission is generally composed of three persons. The court may appoint two alternate commissioners to sit at the hearing with the other commissioners.

---

[18] *See, e.g., United States v. 480.00 Acres of Land,* 557 F.3d 1297, 1312 (11th Cir. 2009).

[19] *United States v. Reynolds,* 397 U.S. 14, 18, 90 S.Ct. 803, 806, 25 L.Ed.2d 12 (1970).

[20] *See, e.g., United States v. Certain Land Situated in the City of Detroit, Wayne County,* 450 F.3d 205, 208 (6th Cir. 2006).

[21] *See, e.g., United States v. 4.0 Acres of Land,* 175 F.3d 1133 (9th Cir. 1999).

[22] *But cf. United States v. 320.0 Acres of Land, More or Less in Monroe County, State of Fla.,* 605 F.2d 762, 828 (5th Cir. 1979) (acknowledging some contrary authority but holding that "a commission is to be used only for exceptional cases" such as large tracts of land held by many small landowners or tracts too distant for jury to view).

(3) *Appointment of Commissioners:* Usually, the court will appoint commissioners and alternate commissioners. Often, the court will appoint a lawyer or ex-judge as chair of the commission and one real estate person as a member. After appointing the commissioners, the court will advise the parties of the identity and qualifications of each prospective commissioner and alternate commissioner. The parties may examine the commissioners and may, for valid cause, object to the appointment of any commissioner.[23]

(4) *Reformation and Revocation of Commission:* When the court believes the judgment of the commission has been affected by bias, the court may reform the commission by replacing some or all of the commissioners.[24] When justice so requires, such as instances of undue delay, the court may vacate the reference to the commission.

(5) *Procedure for Trial by Commission:*

(a) *Powers:* The commission will only try the issue of compensation; all other issues will be decided by the court. The commission has the same powers as a master in a non-jury trial. Proceedings before the commission are governed by Rule 53(c). The commission may regulate its proceedings, require the production of documents, rule on the admissibility of evidence, call and examine witnesses, and permit witnesses to be examined by the parties. These powers will be regulated indirectly by the court through its instructions to the commission in the order of reference.

(b) *Instructions:* In its order of reference, the trial judge will instruct the commissioners as to such issues as: the qualifications of expert witnesses, the weight to be given to other opinions of evidence, competent evidence of value, the best evidence of value, the manner of the hearing and the method of conducting it, the right to view the property, the limited purpose of viewing, and the kind of evidence which is inadmissible and the manner of ruling on the admissibility of evidence.

(c) *Admission of Evidence:* Although the court will control the kind of evidence which is admissible, the commission will apply the Federal Rules of Evidence when ruling on the admissibility of the evidence.

(i) *View of Property:* When necessary or conducive to a proper determination of compensation and when not inconvenient or the cause of undue delay or expense, the commission may view the property.

(6) *Findings and Report of Commission:* A majority of the commissioners will decide the amount of compensation to award, and the commission will submit a report. The findings and the report of the commission will follow the provisions of Rule 53(e)(2). In its report, the commission must clearly show a factual basis for its finding, but need not make detailed findings. A suitable commission report will state what evidence and what measure of damages the commission accepted and why the commission reached its award.[25]

(7) *Objection to Commission Report:* Within 21 days after service of the commission's report, a party must make and file with the court and serve on all other parties

---

[23] *But cf. Guardian Pipeline, L.L.C. v. 950.80 Acres of Land,* 525 F.3d 554, 557–58 (7th Cir. 2008) (litigant who does not examine proposed commissioner at outset waives challenges).

[24] *But cf. City of Stilwell, Okl. v. Ozarks Rural Elec. Co-op. Corp.,* 166 F.3d 1064, 1069 (10th Cir. 1999) (commissioners need not have "complete and absolute impartiality").

[25] *See, United States v. Merz,* 376 U.S. 192, 198, 84 S.Ct. 639, 643, 11 L.Ed.2d 629 (1964).

objections to the report.[26] The party objecting to the report has the burden of demonstrating that the report is erroneous.

(8) *Trial Court Review of Commission Report:* The trial court must adopt the report of the commission unless it finds the report to be clearly erroneous.[27] A trial court may find the report clearly erroneous when there was a substantial error in the proceedings, when the report is unsupported by substantial evidence or is against the clear weight of the evidence,[28] or when the report involves a misapplication of law. Courts have also found commission reports clearly erroneous when the award was grossly inadequate. When the trial court finds the report clearly erroneous, the court may examine the testimony and make its own judgment or it may recommit the matter to the commission with instructions.[29]

(9) *Commissioners' Compensation:* Commissioners will be compensated in reasonable relation to the services rendered. The commissioners' compensation will be charged to the condemnor and may be included in the damage award, not taxed as costs against the award.

(10) *Appellate Court Review of Commission or Court Decision:* An appellate court reviews the judgment of a trial court under a clearly erroneous standard.[30]

RULE 71.1(i)—DISMISSAL OF THE ACTION OR A DEFENDANT

CORE CONCEPT

The procedures for dismissal depend on the posture of the proceedings. Prior to a hearing or declaration of taking, the action may be dismissed as of right. Where the government files a declaration of taking, acquires an interest, acquires title, or takes possession of the property before the entry of judgment, neither the plaintiff nor the court may dismiss an action, except by stipulation of the parties.[31]

APPLICATIONS

Dismissal

(1) *As of Right:* The plaintiff may dismiss the action by filing a notice of dismissal stating a brief description of the property at any time before a hearing on compensation has begun and before the plaintiff has either filed a declaration of taking as provided by statute, acquired title, acquired an interest, or taken possession of the property.

(2) *By Stipulation:* Before the entry of a judgment vesting plaintiff with title, an interest, or possession of the property, the parties may stipulate to a dismissal in whole or in part without an order of the court. After judgment, the parties may stipulate to a dismissal and the court may vacate the judgment and revest title in the defendant.

---

[26] *See,* Rule 53(f)(2).

[27] *United States v. Merz,* 376 U.S. 192, 198, 84 S.Ct. 639, 643, 11 L.Ed.2d 629 (1964).

[28] *Georgia Power Co. v. 138.30 Acres of Land,* 596 F.2d 644 (5th Cir. 1979).

[29] *See, e.g., Southern Natural Gas Co. v. Land, Cullman County,* 197 F.3d 1368, 1375 (11th Cir. 1999).

[30] *See, e.g., United States v. 179.26 Acres of Land in Douglas County, Kansas,* 644 F.2d 367, 373 (10th Cir. 1981).

[31] *Kirby Forest Industries, Inc. v. United States,* 467 U.S. 1, 12, n.18, 104 S.Ct. 2187, 2195 n.18 (1984).

(3) *By Court Order:* If compensation has not yet been determined and paid, the court will decide whether to grant a voluntary dismissal after motion and hearing.[32] However, if the plaintiff has taken title, acquired an interest, or taken possession of any part of the property, the court must award just compensation for the possession, title, or the interest taken.[33]

Dismissal of Improperly and Unnecessarily Joined Parties

At any time, upon a motion or *sua sponte,* the court may dismiss a defendant who has no interest but has been unnecessarily or improperly joined.

Dismissal Without Prejudice

Unless stated in the order or the stipulation, a dismissal of a condemnation proceeding is without prejudice.

RULE 71.1(j)—DEPOSIT AND ITS DISTRIBUTION

CORE CONCEPT

Rule 71.1(j) describes the procedure for the deposit of money with the court when required or permitted by statute. State substantive law will determine the amount to be deposited in state eminent domain actions, while federal substantive law will determine the amount to be deposited in federal eminent domain actions.

APPLICATIONS

The Declaration of Taking Act

The Declaration of Taking Act supplements the procedure under Rule 71.1(j), relating to the deposit and distribution in eminent domain cases. Under the Act, upon the filing of a declaration of taking and a deposit of the estimated compensation with the court, title immediately vests in the federal government.

(1) *Time for Filing:* A declaration of taking may be brought at the commencement of the condemnation action and at any time before a judgment.

(2) *Certification:* The chief of the government department or bureau acquiring the land will certify that the land is within the value prescribed by Congress.

(3) *Surrender of Possession; Encumbrances:* Upon the filing of a declaration of taking, the court will fix the time and the terms upon which the parties in possession will surrender possession of the property to the plaintiff. The court may also make orders concerning encumbrances, liens, rents, taxes, assessments, insurance, etc.

(4) *Amount of Award:* The judgment will include interest from the date of the taking to the date of the award, at the rate set by 40 U.S.C.A. § 3116. However, no interest will be ordered on money paid into the court. When the court or the jury awards an amount greater than the deposit, the court will enter judgment against the plaintiff and in favor of the defendant for the difference plus interest.[34] When the deposit exceeds the award, the plaintiff will obtain the excess deposit from the clerk or will obtain judgment against the landowner if the deposit was already distributed.[35]

---

[32] *See, e.g., United States v. 4,970 Acres of Land,* 130 F.3d 712, 714–15 (5th Cir. 1997).

[33] *See, e.g., Id. at* 715.

[34] *United States v. 9.20 Acres of Land, More or Less, Situated in Polk County, State of Iowa,* 638 F.2d 1123 (8th Cir. 1981) (deposit insufficient). *See also,* 40 U.S.C.A. § 258a.

[35] *United States v. Featherston,* 325 F.2d 539, 541 (10th Cir. 1963).

    (5)   *Deposit and Distribution:* At the time of the taking and the deposit into the court, the court may order distribution of the deposit to the known defendants.[36]

    (6)   *Appellate Review:* A transfer of title is not a final appealable judgment until a final judgment on compensation has been entered.[37]

Deposit and Distribution Under Other Statutes

Actions not proceeding under the Declaration of Taking Act proceed relatively similarly to actions proceeding under the Act. The plaintiff must deposit with the court any money required by law, and may deposit any money allowed by statute. After deposit, the court and parties expedite the proceedings so as to distribute the deposit and to determine compensation. At the conclusion, the funds are trued up so the plaintiff pays and the defendant receives the proper amount.

RULE 71.1(k)—CONDEMNATION UNDER A STATE'S POWER OF EMINENT DOMAIN

CORE CONCEPT

Although most federal court eminent domain cases will involve the federal power of eminent domain, a state may institute an eminent domain action in a federal district court when diversity jurisdiction exists. Similarly, a defendant (landowner) may remove a state eminent domain action to federal district court when the condemnor initiates the suit in state court and diversity jurisdiction exists.[38] These state eminent domain actions must be brought in the federal district court for the district in which the land is situated.

APPLICATIONS

Choice of Law

The federal court will apply the procedure described in Rule 71.1. The court will apply state substantive condemnation law.[39]

Trial by Jury

In state eminent domain cases, the court will follow state law provisions regarding the right to trial by jury or a commission.[40]

RULE 71.1(*l*)—COSTS

CORE CONCEPT

Rule 71.1(*l*) exempts condemnation proceedings from the cost provisions in Rule 54(d). Instead, the normal expenses of the proceeding will be charged to the condemnor. Expenses incurred in the distribution of the award are charged to the condemnee.

APPLICATIONS

Costs Paid by Condemnor

The condemnor pays the normal expenses such as the bills for publication of notice, commissioners' fees, the cost of transporting commissioners and jurors for a view, and witness fees. In addition, the condemnor shall pay for the expenses of a commissioner who

---

[36] *See,* Rule 71A(c)(2). *See also,* 40 U.S.C.A. § 258a.

[37] *Catlin v. United States,* 324 U.S. 229, 65 S.Ct. 631, 89 L. Ed. 911 (1945) (appeal must await final judgment).

[38] 28 U.S.C.A. § 1441(a), (b).

[39] *See, e.g., Donovan v. Town of Edgartown,* 568 F.Supp.2d 134, 135 (D. Mass. 2008).

[40] *West, Inc. v. United States,* 374 F.2d 218, 224 n.3 (5th Cir. 1967).

records the deed and executes the conveyance. These expenses will not be taxed against the award, except to the extent permitted by law.[41]

Expenses of Distribution

Expenses incurred in the distribution of the award, such as ascertaining the identity of the distributees and deciding between conflicting claimants, are chargeable against the award.[42]

ADDITIONAL RESEARCH REFERENCES

Wright & Miller, *Federal Practice and Procedure* §§ 3041 to 3056

C.J.S., Eminent Domain §§ 209 to 251 et seq., §§ 267 to 315 et seq., §§ 319 to 366 et seq., §§ 373 to 386 et seq.

West's Key Number Digest, Eminent Domain ⊶166 to 265(5)

---

[41] *See,* advisory committee note to Rule 71.1(l).
[42] *See,* advisory committee note to Rule 71.1(l).

RULE 72

MAGISTRATE JUDGES: PRETRIAL ORDER

(a) Nondispositive Matters. When a pretrial matter not dispositive of a party's claim or defense is referred to a magistrate judge to hear and decide, the magistrate judge must promptly conduct the required proceedings and, when appropriate, issue a written order stating the decision. A party may serve and file objections to the order within 14 days after being served with a copy. A party may not assign as error a defect in the order not timely objected to. The district judge in the case must consider timely objections and modify or set aside any part of the order that is clearly erroneous or is contrary to law.

(b) Dispositive Motions and Prisoner Petitions.

(1) *Findings and Recommendations.* A magistrate judge must promptly conduct the required proceedings when assigned, without the parties' consent, to hear a pretrial matter dispositive of a claim or defense or a prisoner petition challenging the conditions of confinement. A record must be made of all evidentiary proceedings and may, at the magistrate judge's discretion, be made of any other proceedings. The magistrate judge must enter a recommended disposition, including, if appropriate, proposed findings of fact. The clerk must promptly mail a copy to each party.

(2) *Objections.* Within 14 days after being served with a copy of the recommended disposition, a party may serve and file specific written objections to the proposed findings and recommendations. A party may respond to another party's objections within 14 days after being served with a copy. Unless the district judge orders otherwise, the objecting party must promptly arrange for transcribing the record, or whatever portions of it the parties agree to or the magistrate judge considers sufficient.

(3) *Resolving Objections.* The district judge must determine de novo any part of the magistrate judge's disposition that has been properly objected to. The district judge may accept, reject, or modify the recommended disposition; receive further evidence; or return the matter to the magistrate judge with instructions.

[Former Rule 72 abrogated December 4, 1967, effective July 1, 1968; new Rule 72 adopted April 28, 1983, effective August 1, 1983; amended April 30, 1991, effective December 1, 1991; April 22, 1993, effective December 1, 1993; April 30, 2007, effective December 1, 2007; March 26, 2009, effective December 1, 2009.]

AUTHORS' COMMENTARY ON RULE 72

PURPOSE AND SCOPE

Rule 72 provides that a district judge may refer pretrial and post-trial matters to a magistrate judge without the consent of the parties. A district judge may also refer prisoner petitions challenging conditions of confinement for consideration by a magistrate judge.

RULE 72(a)—NONDISPOSITIVE MATTERS

CORE CONCEPT

A district judge may refer, without the consent of the parties, pretrial matters nondispositive of a claim or a defense to a magistrate judge.[1] Decisions of the magistrate judge on such matters may be appealed to the district court for review.

APPLICATIONS

Nondispositive Pretrial Matters

A nondispositive pretrial matter is a matter which is collateral and nonessential to a full disposition of the plaintiff's claim and the defendant's liability, such as motions relating to discovery matters[2] and motions to add claims. It is unclear whether a magistrate judge may impose sanctions under Rule 72(a) for violations of Rule 11 (governing sanctions for inappropriate pleadings, motions and other papers) or may only recommend such sanctions to the district court pursuant to Rule 72(b).[3]

Dispositive Sanction Not Imposed

If a motion seeks a sanction that would be dispositive, but the magistrate judge denies the motion, the matter is not considered dispositive.[4]

Written Order

When appropriate, and to aid further proceedings, a magistrate judge may enter a written order on the record regarding nondispositive pretrial matters, subject to review on appeal by the district court. The order becomes effective when made, and requires no further action by the district judge.

Review of Nondispositive Pretrial Matter

A party must file written objections to the magistrate judge's order within 14 days after being served with a copy of the order. Failure to make a timely objection may constitute a waiver of appellate review of the magistrate judge's order.[5] Even if no objections are presented, the district judge may rehear or reconsider the matter *sua sponte*.

Review by Court of Appeals

A party may not appeal directly to the court of appeals from a magistrate judge's nondispositive pretrial order.[6]

---

[1] *Holder v. Holder*, 392 F.3d 1009, 1022 (9th Cir. 2004).

[2] *See, e.g., Hutchinson v. Pfeil*, 105 F.3d 562, 566 (10th Cir. 1997) (magistrate judge may impose sanctions in discovery as nondispositive matter).

[3] *See, e.g., Alpern v. Lieb*, 38 F.3d 933, 935 (7th Cir. 1994) (citing conflicting cases; holding that Rule 72(a) does not confer such authority on magistrate judges).

[4] *See, e.g., Gomez v. Martin Marietta Corp.*, 50 F.3d 1511 (10th Cir.1995).

[5] *See, e.g., Phinney v. Wentworth Douglas Hosp.*, 199 F.3d 1, 4 (1st Cir. 1999).

[6] *See, e.g., United States v. Gonzalez-Ramirez*, 350 F.3d 731, 733 (8th Cir. 2003).

RULE 72(b)—DISPOSITIVE MOTIONS AND PRISONER PETITIONS

CORE CONCEPT

When a district judge refers a dispositive matter to a magistrate judge, the magistrate judge will submit a report and recommendation to the district judge, conduct evidentiary hearings and submit proposed findings of fact as appropriate. If a party makes a timely written objection to the report and recommendation of the magistrate judge, the district judge must make a *de novo* review of the record.[7]

APPLICATIONS

Matters Considered Dispositive

The following matters are deemed dispositive by statute:[8] (1) a motion for injunctive relief; (2) a motion for judgment on the pleadings; (3) a motion for summary judgment; (4) a motion to dismiss or permit maintenance of a class action; (5) a motion to dismiss for failure to state a claim upon which relief may be granted; or (6) a motion for involuntary dismissal.[9] The following matters may also be considered dispositive, depending on the circumstances: (1) an application to proceed *in forma pauperis;*[10] (2) a motion to amend a pleading;[11] (3) a motion for attorney's fees;[12] and (4) an order remanding a removed case to state court.[13] It is unclear whether sanctions for violations of Rule 11 is within a magistrate judge's authority under Rule 72(a), or whether the magistrate judge may only make a recommendation to the district judge under Rule 72(b).[14]

Dispositive Sanction Not Imposed

If a motion seeks a sanction that would be dispositive, but the magistrate judge denies the motion, the matter is not considered dispositive. In such cases, the standard of review is provided by Rule 72(a) (clearly erroneous or contrary to law), rather than Rule 72(b) (de novo review upon the record).[15]

Habeas Corpus

Rule 72(b) does not extend to habeas corpus petitions. Habeas corpus petitions are governed by specific statutes.[16]

Procedure for Dispositive Pretrial Matters

A magistrate judge has substantial discretion to conduct hearings on dispositive matters. The magistrate judge shall make a record of all evidentiary proceedings, but has discretion whether to make a record of non-evidentiary proceedings. The magistrate judge shall submit a recommendation for disposition of the matter to the district judge who

---

[7]   28 U.S.C.A. § 636(b)(1)(C). *See also, Rajaratnam v. Moyer,* 47 F.3d 922, 925 n.8 (7th Cir. 1995) (de novo review does not require new trial; only a fresh look at issues to which objection has been raised).

[8]   28 U.S.C.A. § 636(b)(1)(A).

[9]   *See, e.g., Bennett v. General Caster Service of N. Gordon Co., Inc.,* 976 F.2d 995, 997 (6th Cir. 1992).

[10]   *See, e.g., Woods v. Dahlberg,* 894 F.2d 187, 187 (6th Cir. 1990) (motion to proceed *in forma pauperis* is dispositive, and therefore magistrate judge may only make recommendation).

[11]   *Lundy v. Adamar of New Jersey, Inc.,* 34 F.3d 1173, 1183 (3d Cir. 1994) (motion to amend is dispositive of statute of limitations defense).

[12]   *See, e.g., Massey v. City of Ferndale,* 7 F.3d 506 (6th Cir.1993).

[13]   *Vogel v. U.S. Office Products Co.,* 258 F.3d 509, 515 (6th Cir. 2001).

[14]   *See, e.g., Alpern v. Lieb,* 38 F.3d 933, 935 (7th Cir. 1994) (citing conflicting cases; holding that Rule 72(a) does not confer such authority on magistrate judges).

[15]   *See, e.g., Gomez v. Martin Marietta Corp.,* 50 F.3d 1511 (10th Cir.1995).

[16]   28 U.S.C.A. §§ 2254–2255.

assigned the case to the magistrate judge. When appropriate, the magistrate judge shall submit proposed findings of fact with the recommendation. The clerk of the court is required to mail copies of the magistrate judge's report and recommendation to all parties.

Obligation to Order Transcript

A party objecting to the magistrate judge's recommended disposition should promptly arrange for the transcription of the record or portions of the record agreed upon by the parties or as directed by the magistrate judge, unless directed otherwise by the district judge.

Objections

A party must file specific, written objections to the magistrate judge's report and recommendation within 14 days after being served with a copy of the report and recommendation. Failure to make timely objection constitutes a waiver of the right to review of the magistrate judge's report and recommendation.[17]

Response to Objections

A party may respond to another party's objections within 14 days after service of a copy of the objections.[18]

Failure to Object and Untimely Objections

The courts are split on whether and to what extent the district judge is obligated to review a magistrate judge's recommendation absent a timely objection.[19] Failure to file a timely objection to the district judge waives the party's right to appeal the issue to the court of appeals.[20]

De Novo Review of Dispositive Motions by District Judge

Upon proper objection, the district judge who assigned the motion to the magistrate judge shall make a *de novo* determination. After making a *de novo* review of the ruling, a district judge may accept, reject, or modify the recommended disposition or recommit the matter to the magistrate judge with instructions.[21]

A district judge, under the *de novo* review standard, is not required to conduct a new hearing, but is required to examine the issues upon which specific, written objections were based, either on the record or by receiving additional testimony.[22]

ADDITIONAL RESEARCH REFERENCES

Wright & Miller, *Federal Practice and Procedure* §§ 3076.1 to 3076.9

C.J.S., United States Commissioners § 3

West's Key Number Digest, United States Magistrates ⊷ 15 to 31

---

[17] *See Banco Del Atlantico, S.A. v. Woods Industries Inc.,* 519 F.3d 350, 354 (7th Cir. 2008).

[18] *See, e.g., United States v. Mora,* 135 F.3d 1351, 1357 (10th Cir. 1998).

[19] *See, e.g., Conetta v. National Hair Care Centers, Inc.,* 236 F.3d 67, 73 (1st Cir. 2001) (court must review even in absence of timely objection); *Diamond v. Colonial Life & Acc. Ins. Co.,* 416 F.3d 310 (4th Cir. 2005) (court need not review in the absence of timely objection, but must satisfy itself that there is no clear error).

[20] *See, e.g., Phillips ex rel. Estates of Byrd v. General Motors Corp.,* 307 F.3d 1206, 1210 (9th Cir. 2002).

[21] *See, e.g., Mendez v. Republic Bank,* 725 F.3d 651 (7th Cir. 2013).

[22] *See, e.g., Arista Records LLC v. Doe,* 604 F.3d 110, 116 (2d Cir. 2010).

RULE 73

MAGISTRATE JUDGES: TRIAL BY CONSENT; APPEAL

(a) Trial by Consent. When authorized under 28 U.S.C. § 636(c), a magistrate judge may, if all parties consent, conduct a civil action or proceeding, including a jury or nonjury trial. A record must be made in accordance with 28 U.S.C. § 636(c)(5).

(b) Consent Procedure.

(1) *In General.* When a magistrate judge has been designated to conduct civil actions or proceedings, the clerk must give the parties written notice of their opportunity to consent under 28 U.S.C. § 636(c). To signify their consent, the parties must jointly or separately file a statement consenting to the referral. A district judge or magistrate judge may be informed of a party's response to the clerk's notice only if all parties have consented to the referral.

(2) *Reminding the Parties About Consenting.* A district judge, magistrate judge, or other court official may remind the parties of the magistrate judge's availability, but must also advise them that they are free to withhold consent without adverse substantive consequences.

(3) *Vacating a Referral.* On its own for good cause—or when a party shows extraordinary circumstances—the district judge may vacate a referral to a magistrate judge under this rule.

(c) Appealing a Judgment. In accordance with 28 U.S.C. § 636(c)(3), an appeal from a judgment entered at a magistrate judge's direction may be taken to the court of appeals as would any other appeal from a district-court judgment.

[Former Rule 73 abrogated December 4, 1967, effective July 1, 1968; new Rule 73 adopted April 28, 1983, effective August 1, 1983; amended March 2, 1987, effective August 1, 1987; April 22, 1993, effective December 1, 1993, April 11, 1997, effective December 1, 1997; April 30, 2007, effective December 1, 2007.]

AUTHORS' COMMENTARY ON RULE 73

PURPOSE AND SCOPE

Upon consent of the parties, a district judge may refer cases to a magistrate judge for trial or final disposition. The district judge may also vacate the reference to the magistrate judge.

RULE 73(a)—TRIAL BY CONSENT

CORE CONCEPT

By local rule or by order of court, and with the consent of the parties, a magistrate judge may be designated with case-dispositive or final judgment authority to conduct any or all of the proceedings

in a jury or non-jury case. In such cases, the magistrate judge has all of the powers of a district judge except the power of contempt.

APPLICATIONS

Consent

All parties must make a free and voluntary consent to having a magistrate judge preside over their trial.[1]

Preserving the Record

The magistrate judge must decide by what means the record should be preserved, such as verbatim by a court reporter or by electronic sound recording.[2] When deciding the means of preservation of the record, the magistrate judge may consider the complexity of the case, the likelihood of appeal, the costs of recording, and time constraints.

Contempt

Magistrate judges may not hold contempt hearings. Instead, the magistrate judge will certify the facts of the contempt to the district judge and serve an order to show cause why the disobedient party should not be held in contempt. The district judge will then make the contempt determination and impose any sanction.[3]

RULE 73(b)—CONSENT PROCEDURE

CORE CONCEPT

The clerk of court handles the procedures for obtaining the parties' consent to trial before a magistrate judge, isolating the district judge from the consenting process.

APPLICATIONS

Consent Procedure

To prevent the district judge from exercising any influence over the decision by the parties and to prevent the district judge from knowing who may have opposed the reference, the clerk of court administers the complete consent procedure.

Notification

At the time the action is filed, the clerk of court notifies the parties in writing of their option to proceed before a magistrate judge.[4]

Time for Consent

The time for indicating a party's consent or lack of consent is set generally by local rule or court order.

Acceptance

Parties indicate their consent by submitting completed consent forms supplied by the clerk of court.

---

[1]   *See, e.g., Holt-Orsted v. City of Dickson,* 641 F.3d 230, 233 (6th Cir. 2011).

[2]   28 U.S.C.A. § 636(c)(5).

[3]   28 U.S.C.A. § 636(e).

[4]   28 U.S.C.A. § 636(c)(2).

Participation Without Objection

If a party participates in a trial before a magistrate judge without objection, the court may infer consent.[5]

Additional Parties and Consent

In general, local rules will control the time within which new parties must exercise their right to consent to trial before a magistrate judge. The clerk of court will notify new parties of their right to consent in the same manner as the original parties. When an additional party is joined who does not consent to the participation of the magistrate judge, the district judge must hear the case.[6]

Vacating the Reference to a Magistrate

The court may, for good cause shown on its own motion, or under extraordinary circumstances shown by any party, vacate its reference of a civil matter to a magistrate judge.[7] For example, it has been held that a district judge may vacate a proceeding from a magistrate judge when the magistrate judge is faced with extraordinary questions of law with potentially wide precedential effect.[8]

RULE 73(c)—APPEALING A JUDGMENT

CORE CONCEPT

A party makes a direct appeal of a magistrate judge's final judgment to the court of appeals in the same manner as a judgment from a district court judge.[9]

ADDITIONAL RESEARCH REFERENCES

Wright & Miller, *Federal Practice and Procedure* §§ 3077.1 to 3077.5

C.J.S., United States Commissioners § 3

West's Key Number Digest, United States Magistrates ⊶12 to 13, ⊶24 to 31

---

[5]   *Roell v. Withrow,* 538 U.S. 580, 581, 123 S.Ct. 1696, 1699, 155 L.Ed.2d 775 (2003).

[6]   *See, e.g., New York Chinese TV Programs, Inc. v. U.E. Enterprises, Inc.,* 996 F.2d 21, 24 (2d Cir. 1993) (intervenors must also consent, even when joined after magistrate judge begins to hear case).

[7]   28 U.S.C.A. § 636(c)(6).

[8]   *Gomez v. Harris,* 504 F.Supp. 1342, 1345 (D. Alaska 1981).

[9]   *See, e.g., Holt-Orsted v. City of Dickson,* 641 F.3d 230, 233 (6th Cir. 2011)

RULE 74[1]

[Abrogated (Apr. 11, 1997, eff. Dec. 1, 1997).]

---

[1] Rules 73(d) and 74 to 76 provided that when a magistrate judge hears a case, the parties could choose to appeal to either the district court or the court of appeals. However, in 1997 the so-called "optional appeal route" to the district court was abolished by Congress. Accordingly, the Supreme Court abrogated Rules 73(d) and 74 to 76 effective in December, 1997. Henceforth appeals from trials conducted by magistrate judges shall be made only to the appropriate court of appeals.

RULE 75[1]

[Abrogated (Apr. 11, 1997, eff. Dec. 1, 1997).]

---

[1] Rules 73(d) and 74 to 76 provided that when a magistrate judge hears a case, the parties could choose to appeal to either the district court or the court of appeals. However, in 1997 the so-called "optional appeal route" to the district court was abolished by Congress. Accordingly, the Supreme Court abrogated Rules 73(d) and 74 to 76 effective in December, 1997. Henceforth appeals from trials conducted by magistrate judges shall be made only to the appropriate court of appeals.

RULE 76[1]

[Abrogated (Apr. 11, 1997, eff. Dec. 1, 1997).]

---

[1] Rules 73(d) and 74 to 76 provided that when a magistrate judge hears a case, the parties could choose to appeal to either the district court or the court of appeals. However, in 1997 the so-called "optional appeal route" to the district court was abolished by Congress. Accordingly, the Supreme Court abrogated Rules 73(d) and 74 to 76 effective in December, 1997. Henceforth appeals from trials conducted by magistrate judges shall be made only to the appropriate court of appeals.

X. DISTRICT COURTS AND CLERKS

RULE 77

CONDUCTING BUSINESS; CLERK'S AUTHORITY; NOTICE OF AN ORDER OR JUDGMENT

(a) When Court Is Open. Every district court is considered always open for filing any paper, issuing and returning process, making a motion, or entering an order.

(b) Place for Trial and Other Proceedings. Every trial on the merits must be conducted in open court and, so far as convenient, in a regular courtroom. Any other act or proceeding may be done or conducted by a judge in chambers, without the attendance of the clerk or other court official, and anywhere inside or outside the district. But no hearing—other than one ex parte—may be conducted outside the district unless all the affected parties consent.

(c) Clerk's Office Hours; Clerk's Orders.

(1) *Hours.* The clerk's office—with a clerk or deputy on duty—must be open during business hours every day except Saturdays, Sundays, and legal holidays. But a court may, by local rule or order, require that the office be open for specified hours on Saturday or a particular legal holiday other than one listed in Rule 6(a)(4)(A).

(2) *Orders.* Subject to the court's power to suspend, alter, or rescind the clerk's action for good cause, the clerk may:

(A) issue process;

(B) enter a default;

(C) enter a default judgment under Rule 55(b)(1); and

(D) act on any other matter that does not require the court's action.

(d) Serving Notice of an Order or Judgment.

(1) *Service.* Immediately after entering an order or judgment, the clerk must serve notice of the entry, as provided in Rule 5(b), on each party who is not in default for failing to appear. The clerk must record the service on the docket. A party also may serve notice of the entry as provided in Rule 5(b).

(2) *Time to Appeal Not Affected by Lack of Notice.* Lack of notice of the entry does not affect the time for appeal or relieve—or authorize the court to

relieve—a party for failing to appeal within the time allowed, except as allowed by Federal Rule of Appellate Procedure (4)(a).

[Amended effective March 19, 1948; July 1, 1963; July 1, 1968; July 1, 1971; August 1, 1987; December 1, 1991; April 23, 2001, effective December 1, 2001; April 30, 2007, effective December 1, 2007.]

AUTHORS' COMMENTARY ON RULE 77

PURPOSE AND SCOPE

Rule 77 contains a variety of provisions pertaining to the operations of the district court and the clerk's office. It provides that the court is always "open," and requires that the clerk's physical office be open during "business hours." It also states that trials and hearings shall be conducted in the courtroom. Finally, Rule 77 controls notice of judgments and orders.

RULE 77(a)—WHEN COURT IS OPEN

CORE CONCEPT

The district courts are deemed open at all times for purposes like filing papers and issuing process.[1] This does not mean that the clerk's office will be manned and open at all times.[2] Rather, papers may be filed after hours by filing them on the court's electronic filing system, delivering them to the clerk or a deputy clerk, depositing them in a designated receptacle provided by the clerk and authorized by local rule,[3] or even leaving them with a judge under exceptional circumstances.[4] However, filing is not accomplished merely by delivery to the clerk's office without delivering the paper to a proper officer or otherwise using an established method of after-hours filing.[5]

RULE 77(b)—PLACE FOR TRIAL AND OTHER PROCEEDINGS

CORE CONCEPT

All trials must be conducted in open court, and in a regular courtroom to the extent practicable.[6] Other proceedings, such as pretrial conferences, may be conducted in chambers or some other location.[7] However, no hearing, other than one *ex parte,* may be held outside the district without consent of all parties.

RULE 77(c)—CLERK'S OFFICE HOURS; CLERK'S ORDERS

CORE CONCEPT

The clerk's office must be open at minimum during business hours on all days except weekends and holidays. The hours may be expanded by local rule. The clerk's office has the power to take certain

---

[1] *In re Bradshaw,* 283 B.R. 814, 817 (1st Cir. 2002) (the guiding principle is that clerks of court must be available in some fashion twenty-four hours a day).

[2] *Stone Street Capital, Inc. v. McDonald's Corp.,* 300 F.Supp.2d 345, 348 n.4 (D. Md. 2003).

[3] *Ticketmaster Corp. v. Tickets. Com, Inc.,* 2000 WL 525390, 2000 (C.D. Cal. 2000) (a drop box is one method to accommodate the fact that the court shall be deemed always open).

[4] *Turner v. City of Newport,* 887 F.Supp. 149 (E.D. Ky. 1995) (deposit in post office box of clerk deemed filing).

[5] *McIntosh v. Antonino,* 71 F.3d 29, 35 (1st Cir. 1995).

[6] *National Ass'n of Waterfront Employers v. Chao,* 587 F.Supp.2d 90, 98, n.5 (D.D.C. 2008).

[7] *B.H. v. McDonald,* 49 F.3d 294 (7th Cir. 1995).

acts, such as entering default judgments and process to execute judgments.[8] Such actions by the clerk's office are reviewable by the court and may be suspended, altered, or rescinded upon cause shown.[9]

RULE 77(d)—SERVING NOTICE OF AN ORDER OR JUDGMENT

CORE CONCEPT

The clerk's office must serve notice of the entry of judgment on all parties who have entered appearances.[10] However, the failure of the clerk to do so does not necessarily increase the time for appeal[11] (but note that the appellate courts may extend the time for appeal and may consider the failure of the clerk to send notice,[12] and that the district court may reopen and extend the time for appeal[13]). A party who wants to insure that all parties have notice of the judgment (and thus that the time for appeal has commenced running) may serve the notice.[14]

ADDITIONAL RESEARCH REFERENCES

Wright & Miller, *Federal Practice and Procedure* §§ 3081 to 3084

C.J.S., Courts § 236; Federal Civil Procedure §§ 915 et seq., § 1213; Federal Courts §§ 302 et seq.

West's Key Number Digest, Clerk of Courts ⊷1; Federal Courts ⊷971

---

[8]   *United States v. Laws,* 352 F.Supp.2d 707, 709 (E.D. Va. 2004) (writ of garnishment).

[9]   *Brady v. United States,*211 F.3d 499 (9th Cir. 2000) (clerk's entry of default may be set aside for cause shown).

[10]   *In re WorldCom, Inc.,* 708 F.3d 327, 329 (2d Cir. 2013).

[11]   *Maples v. Thomas,* ___ U.S. ___, 132 S.Ct. 912, 933, 181 L.Ed.2d 807 (2012).

[12]   *Maples v. Thomas,* ___ U.S. ___, 132 S.Ct. 912, 933, 181 L.Ed.2d 807 (2012) (but appellate Rule 4(a)(6) establishes an outside limit of 180 days after entry of judgment).

[13]   *Bowles v. Russell,* 551 U.S. 205, 127 S.Ct. 2360, 168 L.Ed.2d 96 (U.S. 2007).

[14]   *Resendiz v. Dretke,* 452 F.3d 356, 358 (5th Cir. 2006) (must be formal service pursuant to Rule 5(b)); *Ryan v. First Unum Life Ins. Co.,* 174 F.3d 302, 304–05 (2d Cir. 1999) (service must be by mail, not by hand delivery).

RULE 78

HEARING MOTIONS; SUBMISSION ON BRIEFS

(a) Providing a Regular Schedule for Oral Hearings. A court may establish regular times and places for oral hearings on motions.

(b) Providing for Submission on Briefs. By rule or order, the court may provide for submitting and determining motions on briefs, without oral hearings.

[Amended effective August 1, 1987; April 30, 2007, effective December 1, 2007.]

AUTHORS' COMMENTARY ON RULE 78

SCOPE AND PURPOSE

Rule 78 allows each district to enact local rules establishing regular motion days for the presentation of motions requiring a hearing. However, judges may conduct oral arguments on motions at other times. Furthermore, the districts or individual judges may also provide that motions are to be determined on briefs only, without oral argument.

RULE 78(a)—PROVIDING A REGULAR SCHEDULE FOR ORAL HEARINGS

CORE CONCEPT

The court may establish regular times for hearing arguments, but also may hear arguments at any time or place on notice that the court considers reasonable.

RULE 78(b)—PROVIDING FOR SUBMISSION ON BRIEFS

CORE CONCEPT

The court may decide motions on the papers, without oral argument.[1]

ADDITIONAL RESEARCH REFERENCES

Wright & Miller, *Federal Practice and Procedure* § 3091

C.J.S., Federal Civil Procedure § 933

West's Key Number Digest, Federal Civil Procedure ⊶1991

---

[1] *Ryan v. First Unum Life Ins. Co.*, 174 F.3d 302, 304–05 (2d Cir. 1999) (serv

RULE 79

RECORDS KEPT BY THE CLERK

(a) Civil Docket.

    (1) *In General.* The clerk must keep a record known as the "civil docket" in the form and manner prescribed by the Director of the Administrative Office of the United States Courts with the approval of the Judicial Conference of the United States. The clerk must enter each civil action in the docket. Actions must be assigned consecutive file numbers, which must be noted in the docket where the first entry of the action is made.

    (2) *Items to be Entered.* The following items must be marked with the file number and entered chronologically in the docket:

        (A) papers filed with the clerk;

        (B) process issued, and proofs of service or other returns showing execution; and

        (C) appearances, orders, verdicts, and judgments.

    (3) *Contents of Entries; Jury Trial Demanded.* Each entry must briefly show the nature of the paper filed or writ issued, the substance of each proof of service or other return, and the substance and date of entry of each order and judgment. When a jury trial has been properly demanded or ordered, the clerk must enter the word "jury" in the docket.

(b) Civil Judgments and Orders. The clerk must keep a copy of every final judgment and appealable order; of every order affecting title to or a lien on real or personal property; and of any other order that the court directs to be kept. The clerk must keep these in the form and manner prescribed by the Director of the Administrative Office of the United States Courts with the approval of the Judicial Conference of the United States.

(c) Indexes; Calendars. Under the court's direction, the clerk must:

    (1) keep indexes of the docket and of the judgments and orders described in Rule 79(b); and

    (2) prepare calendars of all actions ready for trial, distinguishing jury trials from nonjury trials.

(d) Other Records. The clerk must keep any other records required by the Director of the Administrative Office of the United States Courts with the approval of the Judicial Conference of the United States.

[Amended effective March 19, 1948; October 20, 1949; July 1, 1963; April 30, 2007, effective December 1, 2007.]

AUTHORS' COMMENTARY ON RULE 79

PURPOSE AND SCOPE

Rule 79 governs the record keeping duties of the district court clerk's office.

RULE 79(a)—CIVIL DOCKET

CORE CONCEPT

The clerk must keep a civil docket, which is a chronological listing of each pleading, motion, order, etc., filed in the case.[1] The docket may be maintained electronically.[2]

APPLICATIONS

Description

The docket should contain a brief description of each entry.[3] Entries should be entered chronologically[4] and should show the date on which each order and judgment is entered.[5]

Jury vs. Non-Jury

The docket should indicate if the case is to be tried before a jury.[6]

Judgments

Judgments are not effective until entered on the docket.[7] Under Rule 58, a judgment must be a separate document.[8]

Briefs

In general, briefs are not part of the record, so they are not filed and are not entered on the docket.

Time for Making Docket Entry

Rule 79 does not specify the time for making entries in the docket. However, the parties' rights will not be prejudiced by a delay in entry on the docket.

RULE 79(b)—CIVIL JUDGMENTS AND ORDERS

CORE CONCEPT

The clerk's office must retain a copy of every final judgment, appealable order, order creating a lien on property, and any other order as directed by the court.

RULE 79(c)—INDEXES; CALENDARS

CORE CONCEPT

The clerk's office must maintain an index of the civil docket and of every civil judgment, appealable order, order creating a lien on property, and other order as directed by the court. The clerk's

---

ice must be by mail, not by hand delivery).
[2] *Moncier v. Jones,* 803 F.Supp.2d 815 (M.D. Tenn. 2013) (electronic filing is sufficient).
[3] *Two-Way Media LLC v. AT & T, Inc.,* 782 F.3d 1311, 1316 (Fed. Cir. 2015).
[4] *Goode v. Winkler,* 252 F.3d 242 (2d Cir. 2001).
[5] *Connecticut ex rel. Blumenthal v. Crotty,* 346 F.3d 84, 92 (2d Cir. 2003).
[6] *Hentif v. Obama,* 733 F.3d 1243, 1246 (D.C. Cir. 2013).
[7] *In re Deepwater Horizon,* 785 F.3d 986, 998 (5th Cir. 2015).
[8] *S.L. ex rel. Loof v. Upland Unified School Dist.,* 747 F.3d 1155, 1161 (9th Cir. 2014).

office must also maintain a calendar of all actions ready for trial, distinguishing jury and non-jury trials.

RULE 79(D)—OTHER RECORDS

CORE CONCEPT

The Administrative Office of the United States may direct that the clerk's offices maintain other books and records.

ADDITIONAL RESEARCH REFERENCES

Wright & Miller, *Federal Practice and Procedure* §§ 3101 to 3107

C.J.S., Federal Civil Procedure § 933, §§ 1227 et seq.

West's Key Number Digest, Federal Civil Procedure ⊶1991, ⊶2621

RULE 80

STENOGRAPHIC TRANSCRIPT AS EVIDENCE

If stenographically reported testimony at a hearing or trial is admissible in evidence at a later trial, the testimony may be proved by a transcript certified by the person who reported it.

[Amended effective March 19, 1948; April 30, 2007, effective December 1, 2007.]

AUTHORS' COMMENTARY ON RULE 80

PURPOSE AND SCOPE

Rule 80 pertains to the use of testimony at one hearing or trial as evidence at a subsequent hearing or trial. The rule provides that a transcript certified by an official court reporter is proof of the prior testimony.[1]

ADDITIONAL RESEARCH REFERENCES

Wright & Miller, *Federal Practice and Procedure* §§ 3121 to 3122

C.J.S., Evidence §§ 629 to 633 et seq., §§ 652 et seq.

West's Key Number Digest, Evidence ⊶332(1), (4), ⊶340

---

[1] *Orr v. Bank of America, NT & SA,* 285 F.3d 764, 776 (9th Cir. 2002) (transcripts not properly certified not admitted).

RULE 81

APPLICABILITY OF THE RULES IN GENERAL; REMOVED ACTIONS

(a) Applicability to Particular Proceedings.

(1) *Prize Proceedings.* These rules do not apply to prize proceedings in admiralty governed by 10 U.S.C. §§ 7651 to 7681.

(2) *Bankruptcy.* These rules apply to bankruptcy proceedings to the extent provided by the Federal Rules of Bankruptcy Procedure.

(3) *Citizenship.* These rules apply to proceedings for admission to citizenship to the extent that the practice in those proceedings is not specified in federal statutes and has previously conformed to the practice in civil actions. The provisions of 8 U.S.C. § 1451 for service by publication and for answer apply in proceedings to cancel citizenship certificates.

(4) *Special Writs.* These rules apply to proceedings for habeas corpus and for quo warranto to the extent that the practice in those proceedings:

(A) is not specified in a federal statute, the Rules Governing Section 2254 Cases, or the Rules Governing Section 2255 Cases; and

(B) has previously conformed to the practice in civil actions.

(5) *Proceedings Involving a Subpoena.* These rules apply to proceedings to compel testimony or the production of documents through a subpoena issued by a United States officer or agency under a federal statute, except as otherwise provided by statute, by local rule, or by court order in the proceedings.

(6) *Other Proceedings.* These rules, to the extent applicable, govern proceedings under the following laws, except as these laws provide other procedures:

(A) 7 U.S.C. §§ 292, 499g(c), for reviewing an order of the Secretary of Agriculture;

(B) 9 U.S.C., relating to arbitration;

(C) 15 U.S.C. § 522, for reviewing an order of the Secretary of the Interior;

(D) 15 U.S.C. § 715d(c), for reviewing an order denying a certificate of clearance;

    (E) 29 U.S.C. §§ 159, 160, for enforcing an order of the National Labor Relations Board;

    (F) 33 U.S.C. §§ 918, 921, for enforcing or reviewing a compensation order under the Longshore and Harbor Workers' Compensation Act; and

    (G) 45 U.S.C. § 159, for reviewing an arbitration award in a railway-labor dispute.

(b) Scire Facias and Mandamus. The writs of scire facias and mandamus are abolished. Relief previously available through them may be obtained by appropriate action or motion under these rules.

(c) Removed Actions.

  (1) *Applicability.* These rules apply to a civil action after it is removed from a state court.

  (2) *Further Pleading.* After removal, repleading is unnecessary unless the court orders it. A defendant who did not answer before removal must answer or present other defenses or objections under these rules within the longest of these periods:

    (A) 21 days after receiving—through service or otherwise—a copy of the initial pleading stating the claim for relief;

    (B) 21 days after being served with the summons for an initial pleading on file at the time of service; or

    (C) 7 days after the notice of removal is filed.

  (3) *Demand for a Jury Trial.*

    (A) *As Affected by State Law.* A party who, before removal, expressly demanded a jury trial in accordance with state law need not renew the demand after removal. If the state law did not require an express demand for a jury trial, a party need not make one after removal unless the court orders the parties to do so within a specified time. The court must so order at a party's request and may so order on its own. A party who fails to make a demand when so ordered waives a jury trial.

    (B) *Under* Rule 38. If all necessary pleadings have been served at the time of removal, a party entitled to a jury trial under Rule 38 must be given one if the party serves a demand within 14 days after:

      (i) it files a notice of removal; or

      (ii) it is served with a notice of removal filed by another party.

(d) Law Applicable.

(1) *"State Law" Defined.* When these rules refer to state law, the term "law" includes the state's statutes and the state's judicial decisions.

(2) *"State" Defined.* The term "state" includes, where appropriate, the District of Columbia and any United States commonwealth or territory.

(3) *"Federal Statute" Defined in the District of Columbia.* In the United States District Court for the District of Columbia, the term "federal statute" includes any Act of Congress that applies locally to the District.

[Amended effective December 28, 1939; March 19, 1948; October 20, 1949; August 1, 1951; July 1, 1963; July 1, 1966; July 1, 1968; July 1, 1971; August 1, 1987; April 23, 2001, effective December 1, 2001; April 29, 2002, effective December 1, 2002; April 30, 2007, effective December 1, 2007; March 26, 2009, effective December 1, 2009.]

AUTHORS' COMMENTARY ON RULE 81

PURPOSE AND SCOPE

Rule 81 specifies whether the Federal Rules of Civil Procedure apply in various proceedings. It also abolishes the writs of Mandamus and Scire Facias, contains some provisions governing removed actions, defines "State" and "State Law," and specifies what "Federal Statute" means in the District of Columbia.

RULE 81(a)—APPLICABILITY TO PARTICULAR PROCEEDINGS APPLICABLE

CORE CONCEPT

Rule 81(a) lists specific proceedings to which the Rules apply and identifies specific proceedings to which the Rules do not apply.

APPLICATIONS

Not Applicable

The Rules do not apply to:

- Prize Proceedings in Admiralty;[1]

- Proceedings to Review Orders of the Secretary of Agriculture;[2]

- Proceedings to Review Orders of the Secretary of the Interior;[3]

- Proceedings to Review Orders of the Petroleum Control Boards;[4] and

- Proceedings to Enforce Orders of the National Labor Relations Board.[5]

---

[1]   Rule 81(a)(1).
[2]   *Riccelli's Produce, Inc. v. Horton Tomato Co., Inc.,* 155 F.R.D. 411 (N.D.N.Y. 1994).
[3]   Rule 81(a)(6)(C).
[4]   Rule 81(a)(6)(D).
[5]   Rule 81(a)(6)(E).

Applicable

The Rules supplement the statutory procedures for the following:

- Bankruptcy Proceedings, to the extent provided by the Bankruptcy Rules;[6]

- Admission to Citizenship Proceedings;[7]

- Habeas Corpus Proceedings;[8]

- Quo Warranto Proceedings;[9]

- Proceedings for Enforcement or Review of Compensation Orders under the Longshoremen's and Harbor Workers' Compensation Act;[10] and

- Proceedings to enforce subpoenas to testify or to produce documents issued by agencies of the United States.[11]

Arbitrations

In proceedings arbitrated under federal statute, the Rules generally act as default provisions, applying when no arbitration rule addresses a procedural issue.[12]

RULE 81(b)—SCIRE FACIAS AND MANDAMUS

CORE CONCEPT

Rule 81(b) abolishes the Writ of Scire Facias (a writ with a variety of functions such as reviving a judgment[13] or effecting execution) and the Writ of Mandamus (a writ compelling an official to take an action).[14]

APPLICATIONS

District Court Only

Rule 81(b) abolishes the writs in the district court only.[15] Thus, a court of appeals, under appropriate circumstances, may issue a Writ of Mandamus to a district judge.[16]

Relief Not Abolished

Only the writs themselves are abolished. The relief sought may be available through some other motion or proceeding.[17]

---

[6]   *Chrysler Financial Corp. v. Powe,* 312 F.3d 1241, 1243 n.1 (11th Cir. 2002).

[7]   *Kariuki v. Tarango,* 709 F.3d 495, 501 (5th Cir. 2013); *Chan v. Gantner,* 464 F.3d 289, 295 (2d Cir. 2006).

[8]   *Mayle v. Felix,* 545 U.S. 644, 125 S.Ct. 2562, 2569, 162 L.Ed.2d 582 (2005).

[9]   Rule 81(a)(4).

[10]   Rule 81(a)(6)(F); *Galle v. Director, Office of Workers' Compensation Programs,* 246 F.3d 440, 447 (5th Cir. 2001).

[11]   *F.T.C. v. Boehringer Ingelheim Pharmaceuticals, Inc.,* 778 F.3d 142, 149 (D.C. Cir. 2015).

[12]   *See Bacardi Intern. Ltd. v. V. Suarez & Co., Inc.,* 719 F.3d 1 (1st Cir. 2013).

[13]   *TDK Electronics Corp. v. Draiman,* 321 F.3d 677, 680 (7th Cir. 2003) (although the writ of *scire facias* is abolished, revival or reentry of a judgment is obtainable by a more modern motion).

[14]   *Competitive Enter. Inst. v. U.S. Envtl. Prot. Agency,* 67 F.Supp.3d 23, 35 (D.D.C. 2014).

[15]   *United States v. Choi,* 818 F.Supp.2d 79, 84–85 (D.D.C. 2011).

[16]   *In re Nagy,* 89 F.3d 115, 116–17 (2d Cir. 1996).

[17]   *In re Cheney,* 406 F.3d 723, 728–29 (D.C. Cir. 2005) (mandamus like relief can be obtained through a mandatory injunction).

RULE 81(c)—REMOVED ACTIONS

CORE CONCEPT

The Rules apply to actions commenced in state court and removed to federal court. Rule 81(c) contains procedures governing removed actions.

APPLICATIONS

Rules Apply After Removal

The Rules apply to pleadings or motions filed after the removal.[18] Thus, Rules governing the form or service of pleadings would not apply to pleadings filed and served in state court prior to removal.[19]

Time for Service of Complaint

The 90-day deadline for service of the complaint for defendants not served with the complaint prior to removal is calculated from the date of removal.[20]

Time to Answer

If the defendant has not yet answered at the time of removal, the defendant may file an answer or responsive motion either by 7 days from the date of removal,[21] or 21 days from service of the original pleading if the pleading has been filed, whichever is later.[22] Note, however, that the act of removal alone does not trigger an obligation to answer a complaint that has not yet been properly served.[23]

Repleading Unnecessary

Unless the court orders otherwise, pleadings filed while the action was in state court do not need to be repleaded after removal to federal court.[24]

Jury Demand

If a jury trial demand has been properly made in state court, no new demand is necessary.[25] If no jury trial demand was made in state court and if all pleadings were filed in state court, the parties may make a jury trial demand within 14 days of removal to federal court.[26] The 14 days are measured from filing the removal notice in the case of the plaintiff and from service of the notice for all other parties. If no express jury trial demand is required under state law, none will be required in the removed action unless the court so directs.[27] If a jury demand was made in the state court proceedings and the demand does not meet the state requirements but does satisfy federal requirements, it can be accepted by the federal court.[28] There remain some scenarios that are not covered by Rule 81(c). For example, in New York, jury demands may be made shortly before trial. In such cases, the court will have discretion to allow a late jury demand.[29]

---

[18] *Taylor v. Bailey Tool Mfg. Co.*, 744 F.3d 944, 946 (5th Cir. 2014).

[19] *See In re Amerijet Intern., Inc.*, 785 F.3d 967, 974 (5th Cir. 2015) (form).

[20] *Cardenas v. City of Chicago*, 646 F.3d 1001, 1004 (7th Cir. 2011).

[21] *D.H. Blair & Co., Inc. v. Gottdiener*, 462 F.3d 95, 102 (2d Cir. 2006).

[22] *Murphy Bros., Inc. v. Michetti Pipe Stringing, Inc.*, 526 U.S. 344, 346, 119 S.Ct. 1322, 1325 (1999).

[23] *Norsyn, Inc. v. Desai*, 351 F.3d 825, 829 (8th Cir. 2003).

[24] *Wasserman v. Rodacker*, 557 F.3d 635, 639 (D.C.Cir. 2009).

[25] *Lutz v. Glendale Union High School*, 403 F.3d 1061, 1063–64 (9th Cir. 2005).

[26] *Lutz v. Glendale Union High School*, 403 F.3d 1061, 1063–64 (9th Cir. 2005).

[27] *Bruns v. Amana*, 131 F.3d 761, 762 (8th Cir. 1997).

[28] *Wyatt v. Hunt Plywood Co., Inc.*, 297 F.3d 405, 415 (5th Cir. 2002).

[29] *See Felix-Hernandez v. American Airlines, Inc.*, 539 F.Supp.2d 511, 512 (D. Puerto Rico 2007).

RULE 81(d)—LAW APPLICABLE

CORE CONCEPT

Rule 81(d) provides that, in general, when the Rules refer to "states," they include the District of Columbia.[30] Thus, when the Rules refer to the law of the state in which the court sits, the United States District Court for the District of Columbia uses the law applied in the District of Columbia. Rule 81(d) also defines the phrase "law of a state" as including statutes and judicial decisions.

ADDITIONAL RESEARCH REFERENCES

Wright & Miller, *Federal Practice and Procedure* §§ 3131 to 3134

C.J.S., Federal Civil Procedure §§ 7 to 23 et seq.

West's Key Number Digest, Federal Civil Procedure ⊶31 to 44

---

[30]   *Wasserman v. Rodacker,* 557 F.3d 635, 639 (D.C. Cir. 2009).

RULE 82

JURISDICTION AND VENUE UNAFFECTED

These rules do not extend or limit the jurisdiction of the district courts or the venue of actions in those courts. An admiralty or maritime claim under Rule 9(h) is not a civil action for purposes of 28 U.S.C. §§ 1391–1392.

[Amended effective October 20, 1949; July 1, 1966; April 23, 2001, effective December 1, 2001; April 30, 2007, effective December 1, 2007.]

AUTHORS' COMMENTARY ON RULE 82

PURPOSE AND SCOPE

Federal subject matter jurisdiction and venue are not affected by the Rules.[1]

APPLICATIONS

Subject Matter Jurisdiction Only

As a general matter, the Rules do not extend the court's subject matter jurisdiction.[2] This principle is limited to *subject matter* jurisdiction (*i.e.,* the type of case a district court can hear), not *personal* jurisdiction (*i.e.,* which parties must appear and defend themselves).[3] Likewise, the Rules contain timing requirements that are often described as "jurisdictional" but do not affect the court's subject matter jurisdiction.[4]

Joinder

The Rules actually do affect subject matter jurisdiction in the sense that they govern the joinder of ancillary claims and parties.[5] However, intervention will not create subject matter jurisdiction where none existed before the intervention[6] or defeat diversity jurisdiction where it existed prior to the intervention.[7]

ADDITIONAL RESEARCH REFERENCES

Wright & Miller, *Federal Practice and Procedure* §§ 3141 to 3142

C.J.S., Federal Civil Procedure § 19

West's Key Number Digest, Federal Civil Procedure ⊷40

---

[1] *Henderson v. United States,* 517 U.S. 654, 116 S.Ct. 1638, 134 L.Ed.2d 880 (1996).

[2] *Neale v. Volvo Cars of North America, LLC,* 794 F.3d 353, 360 (3d Cir. 2015).

[3] *See Chambers Medical Foundation v. Chambers,* 236 F.R.D. 299 (W.D. La. 2006), *aff'd,* 221 Fed. Appx. 349 (5th Cir. 2007).

[4] *Kontrick v. Ryan,* 540 U.S. 443, 124 S.Ct. 906, 157 L.Ed.2d 867 (2004).

[5] *See Lunney v. United States,* 319 F.3d 550, 556–57 (2d Cir. 2003).

[6] *Disability Advocates, Inc. v. New York Coalition for Quality Assisted Living, Inc.,* 675 F.3d 149, 160 (2d Cir. 2012).

[7] *Freedom from Religion Found., Inc. v. Geithner,* 644 F.3d 836, 843 (9th Cir. 2011).

RULE 83

RULES BY DISTRICT COURTS; JUDGE'S DIRECTIVES

(a) Local Rules.

(1) *In General.* After giving public notice and an opportunity for comment, a district court, acting by a majority of its district judges, may adopt and amend rules governing its practice. A local rule must be consistent with—but not duplicate—federal statutes and rules adopted under 28 U.S.C. §§ 2072 and 2075, and must conform to any uniform numbering system prescribed by the Judicial Conference of the United States. A local rule takes effect on the date specified by the district court and remains in effect unless amended by the court or abrogated by the judicial council of the circuit. Copies of rules and amendments must, on their adoption, be furnished to the judicial council and the Administrative Office of the United States Courts and be made available to the public.

(2) *Requirement of Form.* A local rule imposing a requirement of form must not be enforced in a way that causes a party to lose any right because of a nonwillful failure to comply.

(b) Procedure When There Is No Controlling Law. A judge may regulate practice in any manner consistent with federal law, rules adopted under 28 U.S.C. §§ 2072 and 2075, and the district's local rules. No sanction or other disadvantage may be imposed for noncompliance with any requirement not in federal law, federal rules, or the local rules unless the alleged violator has been furnished in the particular case with actual notice of the requirement.

[Amended effective August 1, 1985; April 27, 1995, effective December 1, 1995; April 30, 2007, effective December 1, 2007.]

AUTHORS' COMMENTARY ON RULE 83

PURPOSE AND SCOPE

Rule 83 authorizes the districts to develop local rules that are "consistent" with the federal rules.

RULE 83(a)—LOCAL RULES

CORE CONCEPT

Each district court may develop local rules.[1] These local rules must be consistent with the federal rules, both in substance and in numbering. Local rules pertaining to matters of form cannot be enforced in a manner that prejudices the substantive rights of a party.

---

[1]   *Hollingsworth v. Perry,* 558 U.S. 183, 191, 130 S.Ct. 705, 710 (2010).

APPLICATIONS

Consistent with Federal Rules

Local rule must be consistent with, and not duplicative of,[2] Acts of Congress[3] and the federal rules.[4] Additionally, numbering must be consistent with the federal rules.

Typical Local Rules

Local rules can cover a wide variety of topics, and vary greatly in number and scope from district to district. Some typical local rules address:

- Admission to practice before the district courts;
- Admission *Pro Hac Vice;*
- Procedures for disbarment;
- Procedures for the recovery of court costs;
- Creation of divisions within the district;
- Form and number of copies of pleadings and briefs;
- Period of time for process;
- Manner for presentation of motions;
- Notice for constitutional challenges to acts of Congress;
- Continuances;
- Discovery procedures;
- Pretrial and status conferences, including pretrial statements;
- Impartial medical examinations;
- Courtroom rules and regulations, including the use of cameras and recording equipment;
- Size, selection, and instruction of the jury;
- Handling and marking of exhibits;
- Entry of judgment; and
- Motions for new trials.

Effect of Local Rule

A valid local rule has the effect of law,[5] and must be obeyed.[6] The court has authority to impose sanctions when a party violates the court's local rules.[7] However, a local rule imposing a requirement of form (as opposed to substance) may not be enforced in a manner that causes a party to lose rights for a "nonwillful" violation.[8] Thus, a party should not be

---

[2]   *United States v. Galiczynski,* 44 F.Supp.2d 707 (E.D. Pa. 1999), *aff'd,* 203 F.3d 818 (3d Cir. 1999).

[3]   *In re Ricoh Co., Ltd. Patent Litig.,* 661 F.3d 1361, 1370, n.5 (Fed. Cir. 2011) (local rule cannot render disallowable costs allowed under statute).

[4]   *Energy and Env't Legal Inst. v. Epel,* 793 F.3d 1169, 1176 (10th Cir. 2015).

[5]   *Hollingsworth v. Perry,* 558 U.S. 183, 191, 130 S.Ct. 705, 710 (2010).

[6]   *Weil v. Neary,* 278 U.S. 160, 169, 49 S.Ct. 144, 148, 73 L. Ed. 243 (1929).

[7]   *Carmona v. Wright,* 233 F.R.D. 270, 275 (N.D.N.Y. 2006).

[8]   *Farley v. Koepp,* 788 F.3d 681, 685 (7th Cir. 2015).

deprived of a right to a jury trial because it is unaware of or forgets a local rule requiring jury demands to be noted in the caption of pleadings.[9]

Promulgation of Local Rules

Local rules are adopted pursuant to the procedures in the Rules Enabling Act.[10]

Public Comment

Before a local rule may be enacted, it must be published for comment by the public.[11]

Obtaining Copies

Local rules are often available on the court's website. A copy of the local rules can also be obtained from the clerk's office for a nominal fee.

RULE 83(b)—PROCEDURE WHEN THERE IS NO CONTROLLING LAW

CORE CONCEPT

In the absence of a federal or local rule of procedure, judges may regulate proceedings before them as they see fit, so long the judge's procedures are consistent with federal law, the federal rules, and local rules.

APPLICATIONS

Standing Orders Consistent with Other Rules

Individual judges' standing orders or requirements must be consistent with Acts of Congress, the federal rules, and local rules.[12]

Parties Must Have Actual Notice of Court Requirements

The court may not sanction or disadvantage a party for noncompliance with a requirement not found in federal law, federal rules, or local rules unless that party has been furnished in the particular case with actual notice of the requirement.[13] Actual notice can be achieved by providing parties with a copy of the judge's requirements, by an order referencing the judge's standing order and indicating how copies can be obtained, or by oral notice at a Rule 16 conference.[14]

ADDITIONAL RESEARCH REFERENCES

Wright & Miller, *Federal Practice and Procedure* §§ 3151 to 3155

C.J.S., Federal Civil Procedure § 21

West's Key Number Digest, Federal Civil Procedure ⊷25

---

[9]   The advisory committee note to the 1995 amendment to Rule 83.

[10] 28 U.S.C. § 2071(b); *see also Hollingsworth v. Perry,* 558 U.S. 183, 191, 130 S.Ct. 705, 710 (2010).

[11] *In re Dorner,* 343 F.3d 910, 913 (7th Cir. 2003).

[12] *Carnes v. Zamani,* 488 F.3d 1057, 1059 (9th Cir. 2007).

[13] *Massachusetts Institute of Technology and Electronics For Imaging, Inc. v. Abacus Software,* 462 F.3d 1344, 1359 (Fed. Cir. 2006).

[14] *See Tyco Fire Products LP v. Victaulic Co.,* 777 F.Supp.2d 893 (E.D.Pa. 2011) (notice at status conference deemed sufficient).

RULE 84

FORMS

[ABROGATED (APR. ___, 2015, EFF. DECEMBER 1, 2015).]

[Amended effective March 19, 1948; April 30, 2007, effective December 1, 2007; April 29, 2015, effective December 1, 2015.]

RULE 85

TITLE

These rules may be cited as the Federal Rules of Civil Procedure.

[Amended April 30, 2007, effective December 1, 2007.]

AUTHORS' COMMENTARY ON RULE 85

PURPOSE AND SCOPE

The full title of the Rules is the "Federal Rules of Civil Procedure." The Rules should be cited as "Fed.R.Civ.P. ___."

ADDITIONAL RESEARCH REFERENCES

Wright & Miller, *Federal Practice and Procedure* § 3171

C.J.S., Federal Civil Procedure §§ 7 et seq.

West's Key Number Digest, Federal Civil Procedure ⊷31

RULE 86

EFFECTIVE DATES

(a) In General. These rules and any amendments take effect at the time specified by the Supreme Court, subject to 28 U.S.C. § 2074. They govern:

(1) proceedings in an action commenced after their effective date; and

(2) proceedings after that date in an action then pending unless:

(A) the Supreme Court specifies otherwise; or

(B) the court determines that applying them in a particular action would be infeasible or work an injustice.

(b) December 1, 2007 Amendments. If any provision in Rules 1–5.1, 6–73, or 77–86 conflicts with another law, priority in time for the purpose of 28 U.S.C. § 2072(b) is not affected by the amendments taking effect on December 1, 2007.

[Amended effective March 19, 1948; October 20, 1949; July 19, 1961; July 1, 1963; April 30, 2007, effective December 1, 2007.]

AUTHORS' COMMENTARY ON RULE 86

PURPOSE AND SCOPE

Rule 86 lists the effective dates of the Rules and certain of the amendments. Amendments typically become effective 90 days after transmittal to Congress.

RULE 86(a)—IN GENERAL

CORE CONCEPT

In general, amendments to the Rules will apply to all actions filed after the effective date of the amendments, and to proceedings in actions filed before the effective date unless the Supreme Court has specified otherwise or the court determines that application of an amended provision would not be feasible or would work an injustice.[1]

RULE 86(b)—DECEMBER 1, 2007 AMENDMENTS

CORE CONCEPT

Rule 86(b) addresses the interplay between the 2007 amendments to the Rules and the supersession clause in 28 U.S.C. § 2072(b). The supersession clause says that laws in conflict with one or more of the Rules shall have no further force and effect after such Rules have taken effect. In essence, the Rules are deemed to have superseded existing inconsistent laws. Because the supersession clause focuses on the sequence in time between the Rules and other laws, Rule 86(b) provides that the non-substantive changes to every Rule in the 2007 amendments do not affect the priority-in-time analysis.

---

[1]   *In re Harwell*, 628 F.3d 1312, 1317, n.4 (11th Cir. 2010).

ADDITIONAL RESEARCH REFERENCES

Wright & Miller, *Federal Practice and Procedure* §§ 3181 to 3182

C.J.S., Federal Civil Procedure §§ 7 et seq.

West's Key Number Digest, Federal Civil Procedure ⊶31

SUPPLEMENTAL RULES FOR ADMIRALTY OR MARITIME CLAIMS AND ASSET FORFEITURE ACTIONS

Adopted February 28, 1966, effective July 1, 1966

The former Rules of Practice in Admiralty and Maritime Cases, promulgated by the Supreme Court on December 6, 1920, effective March 7, 1921, as revised, amended and supplemented, were rescinded, effective July 1, 1966.

Including Amendments effective December 1, 2009

RULE A

SCOPE OF RULES

(1) These Supplemental Rules apply to:

   (A) the procedure in admiralty and maritime claims within the meaning of Rule 9(h) with respect to the following remedies:

   (i)   maritime attachment and garnishment,

   (ii) actions in rem,

   (iii) possessory, petitory, and partition actions, and

   (iv) actions for exoneration from or limitation of liability;

   (B) forfeiture actions in rem arising from a federal statute; and

   (C) the procedure in statutory condemnation proceedings analogous to maritime actions in rem, whether within the admiralty and maritime jurisdiction or not. Except as otherwise provided, references in these Supplemental Rules to actions in rem include such analogous statutory condemnation proceedings.

(2) The Federal Rules of Civil Procedure also apply to the foregoing proceedings except to the extent that they are inconsistent with these Supplemental Rules.

[Added Feb. 28, 1966, eff. July 1, 1966; April 12, 2006, effective December 1, 2006.]

RULE B

IN PERSONAM ACTIONS: ATTACHMENT AND GARNISHMENT

(1) **When Available; Complaint, Affidavit, Judicial Authorization, and Process.** In an in personam action:

   (a) If a defendant is not found within the district when a verified complaint praying for attachment and the affidavit required by Rule B(l)(b) are

filed, a verified complaint may contain a prayer for process to attach the defendant's tangible or intangible personal property—up to the amount sued for—in the hands of garnishees named in the process.

(b) The plaintiff or the plaintiff's attorney must sign and file with the complaint an affidavit stating that, to the affiant's knowledge, or on information and belief, the defendant cannot be found within the district. The court must review the complaint and affidavit and, if the conditions of this Rule B appear to exist, enter an order so stating and authorizing process of attachment and garnishment. The clerk may issue supplemental process enforcing the court's order upon application without further court order.

(c) If the plaintiff or the plaintiff's attorney certifies that exigent circumstances make court review impracticable, the clerk must issue the summons and process of attachment and garnishment. The plaintiff has the burden in any post-attachment hearing under Rule E(4)(f) to show that exigent circumstances existed.

(d) (i) If the property is a vessel or tangible property on board a vessel, the summons, process, and any supplemental process must be delivered to the marshal for service.

(ii) If the property is other tangible or intangible property, the summons, process, and any supplemental process must be delivered to a person or organization authorized to serve it, who may be (A) a marshal; (B) someone under contract with the United States; (C) someone specially appointed by the court for that purpose; or, (D) in an action brought by the United States, any officer or employee of the United States.

(e) The plaintiff may invoke state-law remedies under Rule 64 for seizure of person or property for the purpose of securing satisfaction of the judgment.

(2) Notice to Defendant. No default judgment may be entered except upon proof—which may be by affidavit—that:

(a) the complaint, summons, and process of attachment or garnishment have been served on the defendant in a manner authorized by Rule 4;

(b) the plaintiff or the garnishee has mailed to the defendant the complaint, summons, and process of attachment or garnishment, using any form of mail requiring a return receipt; or

(c) the plaintiff or the garnishee has tried diligently to give notice of the action to the defendant but could not do so.

(3) Answer.

    (a) By Garnishee. The garnishee shall serve an answer, together with answers to any interrogatories served with the complaint, within 21 days after service of process upon the garnishee. Interrogatories to the garnishee may be served with the complaint without leave of court. If the garnishee refuses or neglects to answer on oath as to the debts, credits, or effects of the defendant in the garnishee's hands, or any interrogatories concerning such debts, credits, and effects that may be propounded by the plaintiff, the court may award compulsory process against the garnishee. If the garnishee admits any debts, credits, or effects, they shall be held in the garnishee's hands or paid into the registry of the court, and shall be held in either case subject to the further order of the court.

    (b) By Defendant. The defendant shall serve an answer within 30 days after process has been executed, whether by attachment of property or service on the garnishee.

[Added Feb. 28, 1966, eff. July 1, 1966, and amended Apr. 29, 1985, effective Aug. 1, 1985; Mar. 2, 1987, effective Aug. 1, 1987; April 17, 2000, effective December 1, 2000; April 25, 2005, effective December 1, 2005; amended March 26, 2009, effective December 1, 2009.]

RULE C

IN REM ACTIONS: SPECIAL PROVISIONS

(1) When Available. An action in rem may be brought:

    (a) To enforce any maritime lien;

    (b) Whenever a statute of the United States provides for a maritime action in rem or a proceeding analogous thereto.

Except as otherwise provided by law a party who may proceed in rem may also, or in the alternative, proceed in personam against any person who may be liable.

Statutory provisions exempting vessels or other property owned or possessed by or operated by or for the United States from arrest or seizure are not affected by this rule. When a statute so provides, an action against the United States or an instrumentality thereof may proceed on in rem principles.

(2) Complaint. In an action in rem the complaint must:

    (a) be verified;

    (b) describe with reasonable particularity the property that is the subject of the action; and

(c) state that the property is within the district or will be within the district while the action is pending.

(3) Judicial Authorization and Process.

(a) Arrest Warrant.

(i) The court must review the complaint and any supporting papers. If the conditions for an in rem action appear to exist, the court must issue an order directing the clerk to issue a warrant for the arrest of the vessel or other property that is the subject of the action.

(ii) If the plaintiff or the plaintiff's attorney certifies that exigent circumstances make court review impracticable, the clerk must promptly issue a summons and a warrant for the arrest of the vessel or other property that is the subject of the action. The plaintiff has the burden in any post-arrest hearing under Rule E(4)(f) to show that exigent circumstances existed.

(b) Service.

(i) If the property that is the subject of the action is a vessel or tangible property on board a vessel, the warrant and any supplemental process must be delivered to the marshal for service.

(ii) If the property that is the subject of the action is other property, tangible or intangible, the warrant and any supplemental process must be delivered to a person or organization authorized to enforce it, who may be: (A) a marshal; (B) someone under contract with the United States; (C) someone specially appointed by the court for that purpose; or, (D) in an action brought by the United States, any officer or employee of the United States.

(c) Deposit in Court. If the property that is the subject of the action consists in whole or in part of freight, the proceeds of property sold, or other intangible property, the clerk must issue—in addition to the warrant—a summons directing any person controlling the property to show cause why it should not be deposited in court to abide the judgment.

(d) Supplemental Process. The clerk may upon application issue supplemental process to enforce the court's order without further court order.

(4) Notice. No notice other than execution of process is required when the property that is the subject of the action has been released under Rule E(5). If the property is not released within 14 days after execution, the plaintiff must promptly—or within the time that the court allows—give public notice of the action and arrest in a newspaper designated by court order and having general circulation in the district, but publication may be terminated if the

property is released before publication is completed. The notice must specify the time under Rule C(6) to file a statement of interest in or right against the seized property and to answer. This rule does not affect the notice requirements in an action to foreclose a preferred ship mortgage under 46 U.S.C. §§ 31301 et seq., as amended.

(5) Ancillary Process. In any action in rem in which process has been served as provided by this rule, if any part of the property that is the subject of the action has not been brought within the control of the court because it has been removed or sold, or because it is intangible property in the hands of a person who has not been served with process, the court may, on motion, order any person having possession or control of such property or its proceeds to show cause why it should not be delivered into the custody of the marshal or other person or organization having a warrant for the arrest of the property, or paid into court to abide the judgment; and, after hearing, the court may enter such judgment as law and justice may require.

(6) Responsive Pleading; Interrogatories.

    (a) Statement of Interest; answer. In an action in rem:

      (i)   a person who asserts a right of possession or any ownership interest in the property that is the subject of the action must file a verified statement of right or interest:

        (A) within 14 days after the execution of process, or

        (B) within the time that the court allows;

      (ii)   the statement of right or interest must describe the interest in the property that supports the person's demand for its restitution or right to defend the action;

      (iii) an agent, bailee, or attorney must state the authority to file a statement of right or interest on behalf of another; and

      (iv) a person who asserts a right of possession or any ownership interest must serve an answer within 21 days after filing the statement of interest or right.

    (b) Interrogatories. Interrogatories may be served with the complaint in an in rem action without leave of court. Answers to the interrogatories must be served with the answer to the complaint.

[Added Feb. 28, 1966, eff. Jul. 1, 1966, and amended Apr. 29, 1985, effective Aug. 1, 1985; Mar. 2, 1987, effective Aug. 1, 1987; Apr. 30, 1991, effective Dec. 1, 1991; April 17, 2000, effective December 1, 2000; April 29, 2002, effective December 1, 2002; April 25, 2005, effective December 1, 2005; April 12, 2006, effective December 1, 2006; amended March 26, 2009, effective December 1, 2009.]

RULE D

POSSESSORY, PETITORY, AND PARTITION ACTIONS

In all actions for possession, partition, and to try title maintainable according to the course of the admiralty practice with respect to a vessel, in all actions so maintainable with respect to the possession of cargo or other maritime property, and in all actions by one or more part owners against the others to obtain security for the return of the vessel from any voyage undertaken without their consent, or by one or more part owners against the others to obtain possession of the vessel for any voyage on giving security for its safe return, the process shall be by a warrant of arrest of the vessel, cargo, or other property, and by notice in the manner provided by Rule B(2) to the adverse party or parties.

[Added Feb. 28, 1966, eff. Jul. 1, 1966.]

RULE E

ACTIONS IN REM AND QUASI IN REM: GENERAL PROVISIONS

(1) **Applicability.** Except as otherwise provided, this rule applies to actions in personam with process of maritime attachment and garnishment, actions in rem, and petitory, possessory, and partition actions, supplementing Rules B, C, and D.

(2) **Complaint; Security.**

   (a) *Complaint.* In actions to which this rule is applicable the complaint shall state the circumstances from which the claim arises with such particularity that the defendant or claimant will be able, without moving for a more definite statement, to commence an investigation of the facts and to frame a responsive pleading.

   (b) *Security for Costs.* Subject to the provisions of Rule 54(d) and of relevant statutes, the court may, on the filing of the complaint or on the appearance of any defendant, claimant, or any other party, or at any later time, require the plaintiff, defendant, claimant, or other party to give security, or additional security, in such sum as the court shall direct to pay all costs and expenses that shall be awarded against the party by any interlocutory order or by the final judgment, or on appeal by any appellate court.

(3) Process.

    (a) In admiralty and maritime proceedings process in rem or of maritime attachment and garnishment may be served only within the district.

    (b) *Issuance and Delivery.* Issuance and delivery of process in rem, or of maritime attachment and garnishment, shall be held in abeyance if the plaintiff so requests.

(4) Execution of Process; Marshal's Return; Custody of Property; Procedures for Release.

    (a) *In General.* Upon issuance and delivery of the process, or, in the case of summons with process of attachment and garnishment, when it appears that the defendant cannot be found within the district, the marshal or other person or organization having a warrant shall forthwith execute the process in accordance with this subdivision (4), making due and prompt return.

    (b) *Tangible Property.* If tangible property is to be attached or arrested, the marshal or other person or organization having the warrant shall take it into the marshal's possession for safe custody. If the character or situation of the property is such that the taking of actual possession is impracticable, the marshal or other person executing the process shall affix a copy thereof to the property in a conspicuous place and leave a copy of the complaint and process with the person having possession or the person's agent. In furtherance of the marshal's custody of any vessel the marshal is authorized to make a written request to the collector of customs not to grant clearance to such vessel until notified by the marshal or deputy marshal or by the clerk that the vessel has been released in accordance with these rules.

    (c) *Intangible Property.* If intangible property is to be attached or arrested the marshal or other person or organization having the warrant shall execute the process by leaving with the garnishee or other obligor a copy of the complaint and process requiring the garnishee or other obligor to answer as provided in Rules B(3)(a) and C(6); or the marshal may accept for payment into the registry of the court the amount owed to the extent of the amount claimed by the plaintiff with interest and costs, in which event the garnishee or other obligor shall not be required to answer unless alias process shall be served.

    (d) *Directions With Respect to Property in Custody.* The marshal or other person or organization having the warrant may at any time apply to the court for directions with respect to property that has been attached or arrested, and shall give notice of such application to any or all of the parties as the court may direct.

(e) *Expenses of Seizing and Keeping Property; Deposit.* These rules do not alter the provisions of Title 28, U.S.C., § 1921, as amended, relative to the expenses of seizing and keeping property attached or arrested and to the requirement of deposits to cover such expenses.

(f) *Procedure for Release From Arrest or Attachment.* Whenever property is arrested or attached, any person claiming an interest in it shall be entitled to a prompt hearing at which the plaintiff shall be required to show why the arrest or attachment should not be vacated or other relief granted consistent with these rules. This subdivision shall have no application to suits for seamen's wages when process is issued upon a certification of sufficient cause filed pursuant to Title 46, U.S.C. §§ 603 and 604 or to actions by the United States for forfeitures for violation of any statute of the United States.

(5) **Release of Property.**

(a) *Special Bond.* Whenever process of maritime attachment and garnishment or process in rem is issued the execution of such process shall be stayed, or the property released, on the giving of security, to be approved by the court or clerk, or by stipulation of the parties, conditioned to answer the judgment of the court or of any appellate court. The parties may stipulate the amount and nature of such security. In the event of the inability or refusal of the parties so to stipulate the court shall fix the principal sum of the bond or stipulation at an amount sufficient to cover the amount of the plaintiff's claim fairly stated with accrued interest and costs; but the principal sum shall in no event exceed (i) twice the amount of the plaintiff's claim or (ii) the value of the property on due appraisement, whichever is smaller. The bond or stipulation shall be conditioned for the payment of the principal sum and interest thereon at 6 per cent per annum.

(b) *General Bond.* The owner of any vessel may file a general bond or stipulation, with sufficient surety, to be approved by the court, conditioned to answer the judgment of such court in all or any actions that may be brought thereafter in such court in which the vessel is attached or arrested. Thereupon the execution of all such process against such vessel shall be stayed so long as the amount secured by such bond or stipulation is at least double the aggregate amount claimed by plaintiffs in all actions begun and pending in which such vessel has been attached or arrested. Judgments and remedies may be had on such bond or stipulation as if a special bond or stipulation had been filed in each of such actions. The district court may make necessary orders to carry this rule into effect, particularly as to the giving of proper notice of any action against or attachment of a vessel for which a general

bond has been filed. Such bond or stipulation shall be indorsed by the clerk with a minute of the actions wherein process is so stayed. Further security may be required by the court at any time.

If a special bond or stipulation is given in a particular case, the liability on the general bond or stipulation shall cease as to that case.

(c) *Release by Consent or Stipulation; Order of Court or Clerk; Costs.* Any vessel, cargo, or other property in the custody of the marshal or other person or organization having the warrant may be released forthwith upon the marshal's acceptance and approval of a stipulation, bond, or other security, signed by the party on whose behalf the property is detained or the party's attorney and expressly authorizing such release, if all costs and charges of the court and its officers shall have first been paid. Otherwise no property in the custody of the marshal, other person or organization having the warrant, or other officer of the court shall be released without an order of the court; but such order may be entered as of course by the clerk, upon the giving of approved security as provided by law and these rules, or upon the dismissal or discontinuance of the action; but the marshal or other person or organization having the warrant shall not deliver any property so released until the costs and charges of the officers of the court shall first have been paid.

(d) *Possessory, Petitory, and Partition Actions.* The foregoing provisions of this subdivision (5) do not apply to petitory, possessory, and partition actions. In such cases the property arrested shall be released only by order of the court, on such terms and conditions and on the giving of such security as the court may require.

(6) **Reduction or Impairment of Security.** Whenever security is taken the court may, on motion and hearing, for good cause shown, reduce the amount of security given; and if the surety shall be or become insufficient, new or additional sureties may be required on motion and hearing.

(7) **Security on Counterclaim.**

(a) When a person who has given security for damages in the original action asserts a counterclaim that arises from the transaction or occurrence that is the subject of the original action, a plaintiff for whose benefit the security has been given must give security for damages demanded in the counterclaim unless the court for cause shown, directs otherwise. Proceedings on the original claim must be stayed until this security is given unless the court directs otherwise.

(b) The plaintiff is required to give security under Rule E(7)(a) when the United States or its corporate instrumentality counterclaims and would have been required to give security to respond in damages if a private party but is relieved by law from giving security.

(8) Restricted Appearance. An appearance to defend against an admiralty and maritime claim with respect to which there has issued process in rem, or process of attachment and garnishment, may be expressly restricted to the defense of such claim, and in that event is not an appearance for the purposes of any other claim with respect to which such process is not available or has not been served.

(9) Disposition of Property; Sales.

(a) Interlocutory Sales; Delivery.

    (i) On application of a party, the marshal, or other person having custody of the property, the court may order all or part of the property sold—with the sales proceeds, or as much of them as will satisfy the judgment, paid into court to await further orders of the court—if:

        (A) the attached or arrested property is perishable, or liable to deterioration, decay, or injury by being detained in custody pending the action;

        (B) the expense of keeping the property is excessive or disproportionate; or

        (C) there is an unreasonable delay in securing release of the property.

    (ii) In the circumstances described in Rule E(9)(a)(i), the court, on motion by a defendant or a person filing a statement of interest or right under Rule C(6), may order that the property, rather than being sold, be delivered to the movant upon giving security under these rules.

(b) *Sales; Proceeds.* All sales of property shall be made by the marshal or a deputy marshal, or by other person or organization having the warrant, or by any other person assigned by the court where the marshal or other person or organization having the warrant is a party in interest; and the proceeds of sale shall be forthwith paid into the registry of the court to be disposed of according to law.

(10) Preservation of Property. When the owner or another person remains in possession of property attached or arrested under the provisions of Rule E(4)(b) that permit execution of process without taking actual possession,

the court, on a party's motion or on its own, may enter any order necessary to preserve the property and to prevent its removal.

[Added Feb. 28, 1966, eff. Jul. 1, 1966, and amended Apr. 29, 1985, effective Aug. 1, 1985; Mar. 2, 1987, effective Aug. 1, 1987; Apr. 30, 1991, effective Dec. 1, 1991; April 17, 2000, effective December 1, 2000; April 12, 2006, effective December 1, 2006.]

RULE F

LIMITATION OF LIABILITY

(1) Time for Filing Complaint; Security. Not later than six months after receipt of a claim in writing, any vessel owner may file a complaint in the appropriate district court, as provided in subdivision (9) of this rule, for limitation of liability pursuant to statute. The owner (a) shall deposit with the court, for the benefit of claimants, a sum equal to the amount or value of the owner's interest in the vessel and pending freight, or approved security therefor, and in addition such sums, or approved security therefor, as the court may from time to time fix as necessary to carry out the provisions of the statutes as amended; or (b) at the owner's option shall transfer to a trustee to be appointed by the court, for the benefit of claimants, the owner's interest in the vessel and pending freight, together with such sums, or approved security therefor, as the court may from time to time fix as necessary to carry out the provisions of the statutes as amended. The plaintiff shall also give security for costs and, if the plaintiff elects to give security, for interest at the rate of 6 percent per annum from the date of the security.

(2) Complaint. The complaint shall set forth the facts on the basis of which the right to limit liability is asserted and all facts necessary to enable the court to determine the amount to which the owner's liability shall be limited. The complaint may demand exoneration from as well as limitation of liability. It shall state the voyage if any, on which the demands sought to be limited arose, with the date and place of its termination; the amount of all demands including all unsatisfied liens or claims of lien, in contract or in tort or otherwise, arising on that voyage, so far as known to the plaintiff, and what actions and proceedings, if any, are pending thereon; whether the vessel was damaged, lost, or abandoned, and, if so, when and where; the value of the vessel at the close of the voyage or, in case of wreck, the value of her wreckage, strippings, or proceeds, if any, and where and in whose possession they are; and the amount of any pending freight recovered or recoverable. If the plaintiff elects to transfer the plaintiff's interest in the vessel to a trustee, the complaint must further show any prior paramount liens thereon, and what voyages or trips, if any, she has made since the voyage or trip on which the claims sought to be limited arose, and any existing liens arising upon any such subsequent voyage or trip, with the amounts and causes thereof, and

the names and addresses of the lienors, so far as known; and whether the vessel sustained any injury upon or by reason of such subsequent voyage or trip.

(3) Claims Against Owner; Injunction. Upon compliance by the owner with the requirements of subdivision (1) of this rule all claims and proceedings against the owner or the owner's property with respect to the matter in question shall cease. On application of the plaintiff the court shall enjoin the further prosecution of any action or proceeding against the plaintiff or the plaintiff's property with respect to any claim subject to limitation in the action.

(4) Notice to Claimants. Upon the owner's compliance with subdivision (1) of this rule the court shall issue a notice to all persons asserting claims with respect to which the complaint seeks limitation, admonishing them to file their respective claims with the clerk of the court and to serve on the attorneys for the plaintiff a copy thereof on or before a date to be named in the notice. The date so fixed shall not be less than 30 days after issuance of the notice. For cause shown, the court may enlarge the time within which claims may be filed. The notice shall be published in such newspaper or newspapers as the court may direct once a week for four successive weeks prior to the date fixed for the filing of claims. The plaintiff not later than the day of second publication shall also mail a copy of the notice to every person known to have made any claim against the vessel or the plaintiff arising out of the voyage or trip on which the claims sought to be limited arose. In cases involving death a copy of such notice shall be mailed to the decedent at the decedent's last known address, and also to any person who shall be known to have made any claim on account of such death.

(5) Claims and Answer. Claims shall be filed and served on or before the date specified in the notice provided for in subdivision (4) of this rule. Each claim shall specify the facts upon which the claimant relies in support of the claim, the items thereof, and the dates on which the same accrued. If a claimant desires to contest either the right to exoneration from or the right to limitation of liability the claimant shall file and serve an answer to the complaint unless the claim has included an answer.

(6) Information to Be Given Claimants. Within 30 days after the date specified in the notice for filing claims, or within such time as the court thereafter may allow, the plaintiff shall mail to the attorney for each claimant (or if the claimant has no attorney to the claimant) a list setting forth (a) the name of each claimant, (b) the name and address of the claimant's attorney (if the claimant is known to have one), (c) the nature of the claim, i.e., whether property loss, property damage, death, personal injury etc., and (d) the amount thereof.

(7) Insufficiency of Fund or Security. Any claimant may by motion demand that the funds deposited in court or the security given by the plaintiff be increased on the ground that they are less than the value of the plaintiff's interest in the vessel and pending freight. Thereupon the court shall cause due appraisement to be made of the value of the plaintiff's interest in the vessel and pending freight; and if the court finds that the deposit or security is either insufficient or excessive it shall order its increase or reduction. In like manner any claimant may demand that the deposit or security be increased on the ground that it is insufficient to carry out the provisions of the statutes relating to claims in respect of loss of life or bodily injury; and, after notice and hearing, the court may similarly order that the deposit or security be increased or reduced.

(8) Objections to Claims: Distribution of Fund. Any interested party may question or controvert any claim without filing an objection thereto. Upon determination of liability the fund deposited or secured, or the proceeds of the vessel and pending freight, shall be divided pro rata, subject to all relevant provisions of law, among the several claimants in proportion to the amounts of their respective claims, duly proved, saving, however, to all parties any priority to which they may be legally entitled.

(9) Venue; Transfer. The complaint shall be filed in any district in which the vessel has been attached or arrested to answer for any claim with respect to which the plaintiff seeks to limit liability; or, if the vessel has not been attached or arrested, then in any district in which the owner has been sued with respect to any such claim. When the vessel has not been attached or arrested to answer the matters aforesaid, and suit has not been commenced against the owner, the proceedings may be had in the district in which the vessel may be, but if the vessel is not within any district and no suit has been commenced in any district, then the complaint may be filed in any district. For the convenience of parties and witnesses, in the interest of justice, the court may transfer the action to any district; if venue is wrongly laid the court shall dismiss or, if it be in the interest of justice, transfer the action to any district in which it could have been brought. If the vessel shall have been sold, the proceeds shall represent the vessel for the purposes of these rules.

[Added Feb. 28, 1966, eff. Jul. 1, 1966, and amended Mar. 2, 1987, effective Aug. 1, 1987.]

RULE G

FORFEITURE ACTIONS IN REM

(1) Scope. This rule governs a forfeiture action in rem arising from a federal statute. To the extent that this rule does not address an issue, Supplemental Rules C and E and the Federal Rules of Civil Procedure also apply.

(2) Complaint. The complaint must:

   (a) be verified;

   (b) state the grounds for subject—matter jurisdiction, in rem jurisdiction over the defendant property, and venue;

   (c) describe the property with reasonable particularity;

   (d) if the property is tangible, state its location when any seizure occurred and—if different—its location when the action is filed;

   (e) identify the statute under which the forfeiture action is brought; and

   (f) state sufficiently detailed facts to support a reasonable belief that the government will be able to meet its burden of proof at trial.

(3) Judicial Authorization and Process.

   (a) Real Property. If the defendant is real property, the government must proceed under 18 U.S.C. § 985.

   (b) Other Property; Arrest Warrant. If the defendant is not real property:

   (i) the clerk must issue a warrant to arrest the property if it is in the government's possession, custody, or control;

   (ii) the court—on finding probable cause—must issue a warrant to arrest the property if it is not in the government's possession, custody, or control and is not subject to a judicial restraining order; and

   (iii) a warrant is not necessary if the property is subject to a judicial restraining order.

   (c) Execution of Process.

   (i) The warrant and any supplemental process must be delivered to a person or organization authorized to execute it, who may be: (A) a marshal or any other United States officer or employee; (B) someone under contract with the United States; or (C) someone specially appointed by the court for that purpose.

   (ii) The authorized person or organization must execute the warrant and any supplemental process on property in the United States as soon as practicable unless:

   (A) the property is in the government's possession, custody, or control; or

   (B) the court orders a different time when the complaint is under seal, the action is stayed before the warrant and supplemental process are executed, or the court finds other good cause.

(iii) The warrant and any supplemental process may be executed within the district or, when authorized by statute, outside the district.

(iv) If executing a warrant on property outside the United States is required, the warrant may be transmitted to an appropriate authority for serving process where the property is located.

(4) Notice.

(a) Notice by Publication.

(i) When Publication Is Required. A judgment of forfeiture may be entered only if the government has published notice of the action within a reasonable time after filing the complaint or at a time the court orders. But notice need not be published if:

(A) the defendant property is worth less than $1,000 and direct notice is sent under Rule G(4)(b) to every person the government can reasonably identify as a potential claimant; or

(B) the court finds that the cost of publication exceeds the property's value and that other means of notice would satisfy due process.

(ii) Content of the Notice. Unless the court orders otherwise, the notice must:

(A) describe the property with reasonable particularity;

(B) state the times under Rule G(5) to file a claim and to answer; and

(C) name the government attorney to be served with the claim and answer.

(iii) Frequency of Publication. Published notice must appear:

(A) once a week for three consecutive weeks; or

(B) only once if, before the action was filed, notice of nonjudicial forfeiture of the same property was published on an official internet government forfeiture site for at least 30 consecutive days, or in a newspaper of general circulation for three consecutive weeks in a district where publication is authorized under Rule G(4)(a)(iv).

(iv) Means of Publication. The government should select from the following options a means of publication reasonably calculated to notify potential claimants of the action:

(A) if the property is in the United States, publication in a newspaper generally circulated in the district where the action is filed, where the property was seized, or where property that was not seized is located;

(B) if the property is outside the United States, publication in a newspaper generally circulated in a district where the action is filed, in a newspaper generally circulated in the country where the property is located, or in legal notices published and generally circulated in the country where the property is located; or

(C) instead of (A) or (B), posting a notice on an official internet government forfeiture site for at least 30 consecutive days.

(b) Notice to Known Potential Claimants.

(i) **Direct Notice Required.** The government must send notice of the action and a copy of the complaint to any person who reasonably appears to be a potential claimant on the facts known to the government before the end of the time for filing a claim under Rule G(5)(a)(ii)(B).

(ii) **Content of the Notice.** The notice must state:

(A) the date when the notice is sent;

(B) a deadline for filing a claim, at least 35 days after the notice is sent;

(C) that an answer or a motion under Rule 12 must be filed no later than 21 days after filing the claim; and

(D) the name of the government attorney to be served with the claim and answer.

(iii) **Sending Notice.**

(A) The notice must be sent by means reasonably calculated to reach the potential claimant.

(B) Notice may be sent to the potential claimant or to the attorney representing the potential claimant with respect to the seizure of the property or in a related investigation, administrative forfeiture proceeding, or criminal case.

(C) Notice sent to a potential claimant who is incarcerated must be sent to the place of incarceration.

(D) Notice to a person arrested in connection with an offense giving rise to the forfeiture who is not incarcerated when notice is sent may be sent to the address that person last gave to the agency that arrested or released the person.

(E) Notice to a person from whom the property was seized who is not incarcerated when notice is sent may be sent to the last address that person gave to the agency that seized the property.

(iv) When Notice Is Sent. Notice by the following means is sent on the date when it is placed in the mail, delivered to a commercial carrier, or sent by electronic mail.

(v) Actual Notice. A potential claimant who had actual notice of a forfeiture action may not oppose or seek relief from forfeiture because of the government's failure to send the required notice.

(5) Responsive Pleadings.

(a) Filing a Claim.

(i) A person who asserts an interest in the defendant property may contest the forfeiture by filing a claim in the court where the action is pending. The claim must:

(A) identify the specific property claimed;

(B) identify the claimant and state the claimant's interest in the property;

(C) be signed by the claimant under penalty of perjury; and

(D) be served on the government attorney designated under Rule G(4)(a)(ii)(C) or (b)(ii)(D).

(ii) Unless the court for good cause sets a different time, the claim must be filed:

(A) by the time stated in a direct notice sent under Rule G(4)(b);

(B) if notice was published but direct notice was not sent to the claimant or the claimant's attorney, no later than 30 days after final publication of newspaper notice or legal notice under Rule G(4)(a) or no later than 60 days after the first day of publication on an official internet government forfeiture site; or

(C) if notice was not published and direct notice was not sent to the claimant or the claimant's attorney:

(1) if the property was in the government's possession, custody, or control when the complaint was filed, no later than 60 days after the filing, not counting any time when the complaint was under seal or when the action was stayed before execution of a warrant issued under Rule G(3)(b); or

(2) if the property was not in the government's possession, custody, or control when the complaint was filed, no later than 60 days after the government complied with 18 U.S.C. § 985(c) as to real property, or 60 days after process was executed on the property under Rule G(3).

(iii) A claim filed by a person asserting an interest as a bailee must identify the bailor, and if filed on the bailor's behalf must state the authority to do so.

(b) Answer. A claimant must serve and file an answer to the complaint or a motion under Rule 12 within 21 days after filing the claim. A claimant waives an objection to in rem jurisdiction or to venue if the objection is not made by motion or stated in the answer.

(6) Special Interrogatories.

(a) Time and Scope. The government may serve special interrogatories limited to the claimant's identity and relationship to the defendant property without the court's leave at any time after the claim is filed and before discovery is closed. But if the claimant serves a motion to dismiss the action, the government must serve the interrogatories within 21 days after the motion is served.

(b) Answers or Objections. Answers or objections to these interrogatories must be served within 21 days after the interrogatories are served.

(c) Government's Response Deferred. The government need not respond to a claimant's motion to dismiss the action under Rule G(8)(b) until 21 days after the claimant has answered these interrogatories.

(7) Preserving, Preventing Criminal Use, and Disposing of Property; Sales.

(a) Preserving and Preventing Criminal Use of Property. When the government does not have actual possession of the defendant property the court, on motion or on its own, may enter any order necessary to preserve the property, to prevent its removal or encumbrance, or to prevent its use in a criminal offense.

(b) Interlocutory Sale or Delivery.

(i) Order to Sell. On motion by a party or a person having custody of the property, the court may order all or part of the property sold if:

(A) the property is perishable or at risk of deterioration, decay, or injury by being detained in custody pending the action;

(B) the expense of keeping the property is excessive or is disproportionate to its fair market value;

(C) the property is subject to a mortgage or to taxes on which the owner is in default; or

(D) the court finds other good cause.

   (ii) Who Makes the Sale. A sale must be made by a United States agency that has authority to sell the property, by the agency's contractor, or by any person the court designates.

   (iii) Sale Procedures. The sale is governed by 28 U.S.C. §§ 2001, 2002, and 2004, unless all parties, with the court's approval, agree to the sale, aspects of the sale, or different procedures.

   (iv) Sale Proceeds. Sale proceeds are a substitute res subject to forfeiture in place of the property that was sold. The proceeds must be held in an interest-bearing account maintained by the United States pending the conclusion of the forfeiture action.

   (v) Delivery on a Claimant's Motion. The court may order that the property be delivered to the claimant pending the conclusion of the action if the claimant shows circumstances that would permit sale under Rule G(7)(b)(i) and gives security under these rules.

(c) Disposing of Forfeited Property. Upon entry of a forfeiture judgment, the property or proceeds from selling the property must be disposed of as provided by law.

(8) Motions.

(a) Motion To Suppress Use of the Property as Evidence. If the defendant property was seized, a party with standing to contest the lawfulness of the seizure may move to suppress use of the property as evidence. Suppression does not affect forfeiture of the property based on independently derived evidence.

(b) Motion To Dismiss the Action.

   (i) A claimant who establishes standing to contest forfeiture may move to dismiss the action under Rule 12(b).

   (ii) In an action governed by 18 U.S.C. § 983(a)(3)(D) the complaint may not be dismissed on the ground that the government did not have adequate evidence at the time the complaint was filed to establish the forfeitability of the property. The sufficiency of the complaint is governed by Rule G(2).

(c) Motion To Strike a Claim or Answer.

   (i) At any time before trial, the government may move to strike a claim or answer:

   (A) for failing to comply with Rule G(5) or (6), or

   (B) because the claimant lacks standing.

(ii) The motion:

(A) must be decided before any motion by the claimant to dismiss the action; and

(B) may be presented as a motion for judgment on the pleadings or as a motion to determine after a hearing or by summary judgment whether the claimant can carry the burden of establishing standing by a preponderance of the evidence.

(d) Petition To Release Property.

(i) If a United States agency or an agency's contractor holds property for judicial or nonjudicial forfeiture under a statute governed by 18 U.S.C. § 983(f), a person who has filed a claim to the property may petition for its release under § 983(f).

(ii) If a petition for release is filed before a judicial forfeiture action is filed against the property, the petition may be filed either in the district where the property was seized or in the district where a warrant to seize the property issued. If a judicial forfeiture action against the property is later filed in another district—or if the government shows that the action will be filed in another district— the petition may be transferred to that district under 28 U.S.C. § 1404.

(e) Excessive Fines. A claimant may seek to mitigate a forfeiture under the Excessive Fines Clause of the Eighth Amendment by motion for summary judgment or by motion made after entry of a forfeiture judgment if:

(i) the claimant has pleaded the defense under Rule 8; and

(ii) the parties have had the opportunity to conduct civil discovery on the defense

(9) Trial. Trial is to the court unless any party demands trial by jury under Rule 38.

[Added Apr. 12, 2006, eff. Dec. 1, 2006; amended March 26, 2009, effective December 1, 2009.]

PART V

APPENDIX OF FORMS

ABROGATION OF THE ORIGINAL CIVIL FORMS

Since the day they first took effect in 1938, the Federal Rules of Civil Procedure have been accompanied by an "Appendix of Forms". They were unveiled with great pride by the lead crafter of the Rules, Dean Charles E. Clark, who pronounced them a "most important part of the rules" because, he explained, "when you can't define you can at least draw pictures to show your meaning."[1] Originally, there were 34 official federal forms, a number that grew by two in 1993, and nearly all of which were substantially reworked during the 2007 "restyling" project.

Those official forms were abrogated effective December 1, 2015. The Advisory Committee Notes accompanying the abrogation opined that the Forms' purpose in 1938, while useful then, had since "been fulfilled."[2] The Committee noted the availability of various alternative sources of federal civil forms (prepared by, among others, the Administrate Office of the United States Courts, the websites of various federal district courts, and private commercial suppliers), which it concluded rendered the official set "no longer necessary."[3] The Forms, however, have not left the scene without a fitting eulogy. *See* A. Benjamin Spencer, *The Forms Had A Function*, 15 NEV. L. REV. 1113 (2015).

NEW SOURCES OF FEDERAL CIVIL FORMS

Not all federal forms were abrogated. Two survived—for use in seeking and granting a waiver of formal service of process. This *Student's Guide* reprints both of these surviving official forms at the end of the text of Rule 4. In addition to various commercially-prepared form sources, the Administration Office of the United States Courts has compiled a small but handy set of downloadable forms available at: **http://www.uscourts.gov/forms/civil-forms**. This same source also facilitates the process of locating forms preferred for use in the various local federal courts.

---

[1]   *See* Charles E. Clark, *Pleading Under the Federal Rules*, 12 WYO. L.J. 177, 181 (1958).

[2]   *See* Rule 84 advisory committee note 2015.

[3]   *See id.* The abrogation may have been hastened by discomfort with the official pleading forms and their perceived misalignment with the U.S. Supreme Court's recent pleading decisions in *Bell Atlantic Corp. v. Twombly* and *Ashcroft v. Iqbal. See supra* Authors' Commentary to Rule 8(a) ("*'Plausible' Pleadings*"). The advisory committee note endeavored to sidestep any intimation that its abrogation of the Forms was intended to adjust those pleading standards. *See* Rule 84 advisory committee note 2015 ("The abrogation of Rule 84 does not alter existing pleading standards or otherwise change the requirements of Civil Rule 8.").

PART VI

MULTIDISTRICT LITIGATION

Table of Sections

§ 5.1   Introduction

Congress created the Judicial Panel on Multidistrict Litigation in the late 1960's in response to the challenge of efficiently and effectively managing related, protracted, and complex civil cases that were being filed in various federal courts throughout the Nation.[1] At that time, nearly 2,000 separate but related electrical equipment antitrust cases were pending in 36 different federal judicial districts.[2] To manage these numerous distinct but related antitrust cases, Chief Justice Earl Warren appointed an advisory "Coordinating Committee for Multiple Litigation" which invited counsel and district court judges to attend hearings on how to economically supervise these electrical equipment litigations.[3]

The Committee prepared and recommended more than 40 "national pretrial orders" for the cases, which were then entered voluntarily by the judges in most of the districts where these electrical equipment antitrust cases were pending.[4] The orders established a coordinated system of national pretrial discovery, including a central document depository available to all parties and the conduct of depositions on a coordinated, nationwide schedule.[5]

This voluntary, advisory procedure was so successful that Congress established a statutory, national multidistrict litigation court in 1968 with affirmative authority to direct the transfer of multidistrict civil cases that involve one or more common questions of fact to a single federal district for the purpose of consolidated or coordinated nationwide pretrial proceedings.[6] This specialized court, entitled the "Judicial Panel on Multidistrict Litigation", comprises 7 circuit and district court judges, designated from time to time by the Chief Justice, no 2 of whom may come from the same Circuit.[7]

The Judicial Panel is authorized to transfer cases for pretrial multidistrict litigation—or "MDL"-treatment upon three findings: (a) that civil cases, then pending in different federal judicial districts, involve one or more common questions of fact, and that coordinated or consolidated pretrial proceedings, centralized before a single district court, (b) will be for the convenience of parties and witnesses, and (c) will promote the just and efficient conduct of the lawsuits.[8] Once these prerequisite findings have been made, MDL transfer to a central judicial district is appropriate, even if federal diversity jurisdiction, personal jurisdiction, or venue would otherwise be improper there over the transferred cases.[9] The resulting post-transfer authority, of course, extends only to the parties and

---

[1] *See* 28 U.S.C. § 1407.

[2] *See* Robert A. Cahn, *A Look at the Judicial Panel on Multidistrict Litigation,* 72 F.R.D. 211, 211 (1976).

[3] *See* id. at 211–12.

[4] *See* id. at 212.

[5] *See* id.

[6] *See* 28 U.S.C. § 1407(a). *See generally Gelboim v. Bank of America Corp.,* ___ U.S. ___, 135 S.Ct. 897, 903, 190 L.Ed.2d 789 (2015).

[7] *See* 28 U.S.C. § 1407(d).

[8] *See* 28 U.S.C. § 1407(a). *See also Pinney v. Nokia, Inc.,* 402 F.3d 430, 451 (4th Cir.2005).

[9] *See Howard v. Sulzer Orthopedics, Inc.,* 382 Fed. Appx. 436, 441–42 (6th Cir. 2010).

disputes subject to the transfer; jurisdiction does not extend to those parties or disputes not brought before the transferee court.[10]

MDL treatment may be initiated by the Judicial Panel on its own initiative or upon motion by a party in any action believed to qualify for this type of coordination or consolidation.[11] A consolidation order by the Judicial Panel will ordinarily not be overturned unless it is "outlandish".[12]

If MDL treatment is granted by the Judicial Panel, the general procedure follows: a single judicial district and federal judge is selected by the Judicial Panel as the MDL court for all the cases; all qualifying federal lawsuits are then transferred to that federal judge for pretrial purposes;[13] the MDL judge presides over and manages a nationwide, coordinated discovery and pretrial procedures program; and, in the event the cases are not disposed of or settled by the MDL judge by the close of the pretrial stage, the lawsuits are each transferred back to their original districts for trial.[14] Though consolidated in the MDL, individual cases ordinarily do not lose their discrete, separate legal character or somehow fold into a new, single, monolithic "action".[15]

However, during consolidation, the MDL judge may rule on case-dispositive motions, and consequently may grant motions to dismiss both on substantive grounds[16] and for failures to abide by court scheduling orders and procedures.[17] Such orders—fully disposing of one or more cases, though leaving others still pending in the MDL—are usually final orders, subject to immediate appeal.[18] The MDL judge may also rule on motions to file amended complaints and superseding omnibus complaints, motions to otherwise amend or adjust pleadings, motions to enforce venue requirements, discovery motions, and other pretrial motions, and may order attendance at settlement conferences.[19] The MDL judge may supervise the use of "master" complaints either for substantive, consolidated treatment or as legally inert administrative summaries of pleadings.[20] The MDL judge may also impose litigation costs, but ought to allocate those costs ratably among the impacted cases.[21] The law the MDL judge will apply during diversity-based proceedings will, ordinarily, be the substantive law[22] and conflicts rules[23] of the various originating transferor jurisdictions.

Remands are made by the Judicial Panel (not by the transferee judge), although the transferee judge retains a vital role in the remand back to the original forum by notifying the Judicial Panel (typically through a *"Suggestion to Remand"*) that the coordinated or consolidated proceedings have been concluded.[24] The parties do not need to assert their intention to seek remand in order to preserve it; rather, a remand at the close of all pretrial proceedings is presumed.[25] The Judicial Panel *must*

---

[10]   *See In re Genetically Modified Rice Litig.*, 764 F.3d 864, 873 (8th Cir. 2014). Note, however, that attorneys who participate in the consolidated MDL litigations in the transferee district may, themselves, become subject to that court's personal jurisdiction for claims relating to their in-forum conduct.

[11]   *See* 28 U.S.C. § 1407(c). *See also D & S Marine Servs., L.L.C. v. Lyle Props., L.L.C.*, 586 Fed. Appx. 636, 639–40 (5th Cir. 2013) (only Judicial Panel, not individual district courts, have power to transfer into an MDL).

[12]   *See Bennett v. Bayer Healthcare Pharms., Inc.*, 577 Fed.Appx. 616, 617–18 (7th Cir. 2014).28 U.S.C. § 1407(c).

[13]   *See Boomer v. AT & T Corp.*, 309 F.3d 404, 413 (7th Cir.2002) (noting that multidistrict transfer order is effective only when filed in the office of the clerk in the transferee district).

[14]   *See* 28 U.S.C. § 1407(a). *See also Gelboim v. Bank of America Corp.*, ___ U.S. ___, 135 S.Ct. 897, 903, 190 L.Ed.2d 789 (2015). *Cf. In re Collins*, 233 F.3d 809 (3d Cir.2000) (refusing to disturb MDL practice of transferring back only compensatory damage asbestos claims to origination district, while retaining punitive damages claims in MDL).

[15]   *See Gelboim v. Bank of America Corp.*, ___ U.S. ___, 135 S.Ct. 897, 904, 190 L.Ed.2d 789 (2015).

[16]   *See In re African-American Slave Descendants Litig.*, 471 F.3d 754, 754–57 & 763 (7th Cir. 2006).

[17]   *See In re Guidant Corp. Implantable Defibrillators Prods. Liab. Litig.*, 496 F.3d 863, 867 (8th Cir. 2007).

[18]   *See Gelboim v. Bank of America Corp.*, ___ U.S. ___, 135 S.Ct. 897, 904–06, 190 L.Ed.2d 789 (2015).

[19]   *See In re Korean Air Lines Co.*, 642 F.3d 685, 699 (9th Cir. 2011) (collecting cases).

[20]   *See In re Refrigerant Compressors Antitrust Litig.*, 731 F.3d 586, 590–91 (6th Cir. 2013).

[21]   *See Winter v. Novartis Pharms. Corp.*, 739 F.3d 405, 411–12 (8th Cir. 2014).

[22]   *See Wahl v. General Elec. Co.*, 786 F.3d 491, 494–99 (6th Cir. 2015).

[23]   *See In re Volkswagen & Audi Warranty Extension Litig.*, 692 F.3d 4, 17–18 (1st Cir. 2012).

[24]   *See In re Wilson*, 451 F.3d 161, 165 & 165 n.5 (3d Cir.2006).

[25]   *See Armstrong v. LaSalle Bank Nat'l Ass'n*, 552 F.3d 613, 616 (7th Cir. 2009).

remand when the coordinated or consolidated proceedings have concluded,[26] but *may,* in its "unusually broad discretion", remand when all that remains to be accomplished is case-specific.[27] The transferee judge may not self-assign the case in lieu of remand,[28] at least absent a relinquishment by the parties to their entitlement to such a remand.[29] Thus, this MDL treatment is usually reserved as a vehicle for pretrial-and only pretrial-coordination and consolidation.[30]

The extent to which a transferor court, following remand, may overrule the MDL transferee judge remains unsettled; but because routine revisitations of the MDL judge's rulings would deal MDL litigants a "Return To Go" card[31] and thereby frustrate the intended goals of the MDL process,[32] the courts tend to affix law-of-the-case deference to the MDL judge's orders.[33]

The MDL procedure endeavors to achieve the economical use of the federal judiciary and the resolution of similar complex civil cases with the least cost and disruption to the parties and witnesses.[34] During the coordinated or consolidated pretrial MDL proceedings, the MDL judge will typically look to the Federal Judicial Center's *Manual for Complex Litigation* as a primary resource for guiding the nationwide proceedings.[35] With those guidelines in mind, documents are generally produced only once for hundreds or thousands of cases, with responsive documents made available to all parties at a centralized document depository. Interrogatories and requests for admissions are served on behalf of an entire series of related cases. Witnesses and parties, whose testimony is relevant to perhaps thousands of different cases, are deposed only once (or at least far less often than otherwise would be the case) by a select group of lead or liaison counsel. Throughout the MDL process, the transferee judge generally possesses the power to act not only on behalf of the transferee district, but also with the powers of a district judge in every district from which the consolidated cases have been transferred.[36]

The MDL judge's discretion is broad and commensurate with the enormous task of managing a large litigation involving numerous litigants from across the country and posing substantial legal questions implicating pleading, discovery, expert, timeliness, choice of law, cognizable claim, and causation issues.[37] This authority encompasses the power to dismiss claims for noncompliance with MDL procedures [38] and to rule on motions relating to subpoenas issued from other judicial districts, including motions to quash.[39] But, although broad, the MDL judge's discretion is not unbounded; the

---

[26] *See Lexecon Inc. v. Milberg Weiss Bershad Hynes & Lerach*, 523 U.S. 26, 41, 118 S.Ct. 956, 140 L.Ed.2d 62 (1998).

[27] *See In re Wilson,* 451 F.3d 161, 172–73 (3d Cir.2006).

[28] *See Lexecon Inc. v. Milberg Weiss Bershad Hynes & Lerach,* 523 U.S. 26, 32–41, 118 S.Ct. 956, 140 L.Ed.2d 62 (1998).

[29] *See Armstrong v. LaSalle Bank Nat'l Ass'n,* 552 F.3d 613, 616–17 (7th Cir. 2009).

[30] *See In re Patenaude,* 210 F.3d 135, 142 (3d Cir.2000) (noting that MDL statute limits transferee court to only proceedings that are (1) coordinated or consolidated and (2) pretrial). *See also id.* at 144 (commenting that "pretrial" is interpreted broadly to mean all judicial proceedings that occur before trial).

[31] *See In re Pharmacy Benefit Managers Antitrust Litig.,* 582 F.3d 432, 440 (3d Cir. 2009).

[32] *See McKay v. Novartis Pharm. Corp.,* 751 F.3d 694, 703 (5th Cir. 2014).

[33] *See McKay v. Novartis Pharm. Corp.,* 751 F.3d 694, 703–05 (5th Cir. 2014) (applying law of the case principles, advising that transferor courts should rarely reverse transferee court decisions).

[34] *See Gelboim v. Bank of America Corp.,* ___ U.S. ___, 135 S.Ct. 897, 903, 190 L.Ed.2d 789 (2015).

[35] For an excellent annotated and commentary-laden version of this essential MDL resource, *see* David Herr's *Annotated Manual for Complex Litigation Third* (Thomson West, revised annually). Multidistrict litigation under § 1407 is also discussed in detail in Wright, Miller & Cooper, *Federal Practice and Procedure* §§ 3861 to 68 (West Group).

[36] *See In re Korean Air Lines Co.,* 642 F.3d 685, 699 (9th Cir. 2011); *In re Flat Glass Antitrust Litig.,* 288 F.3d 83, 90 n.12 (3d Cir.2002).

[37] *See Freeman v. Wyeth,* 764 F.3d 806, 810 (8th Cir. 2014); *In re Asbestos Prods. Liab. Litig. (No. VI),* 718 F.3d 236, 243 & 247 (3d Cir. 2013).

[38] *See Freeman v. Wyeth,* 764 F.3d 806, 809–10 (8th Cir. 2014); *In re Asbestos Prods. Liab. Litig. (No. VI),* 718 F.3d 236, 249 (3d Cir. 2013).

[39] *See In re Clients & Former Clients of Baron & Budd, P.C.,* 478 F.3d 670 (5th Cir. 2007) (per curiam).

judge may not, in the cause of efficiency and docketing progress, engage in "assembly-line justice",[40] or retain post-pretrial authority over the case through self-reassignment.[41]

Appeals from the MDL judge's pretrial orders are often (but not always) heard by the Court of Appeals for the Circuit that encompasses the MDL judge's district.[42] Sometimes, for instance, the Judicial Panel on Multidistrict Litigation may, in its discretion, elect not to permit Rule 54(b) immediate appeals (to the MDL judge's Court of Appeals) but, instead, to remand back to the originating transferor courts (with appeals, if any, to be taken to those various Courts of Appeals).[43] Likewise, when the MDL judge's order implicates a ruling compelling or sanctioning a nonparty located outside the MDL judge's district, the appeal is generally taken to the Court of Appeals for the Circuit embracing the district of the foreign discovery event.[44] The preclusive effects of MDL litigation can be complicated. For example, the decision to appeal an MDL ruling as to some consolidated defendants (and not all) will likely be preclusive once a final judgment is entered on the appeal, but perhaps not before.[45]

Over the years, MDL pretrial treatment has been granted in many different types of lawsuits,[46] including national products liability cases,[47] personal injury cases,[48] airplane disaster[49] and other large calamity cases,[50] antitrust cases,[51] securities fraud cases,[52] trade practices and consumer fraud cases,[53] intellectual property cases,[54] and a variety of other cases.[55] In its first 27 years of use, the statutory multidistrict litigation procedure had been applied to more than 39,000 federal civil cases, of which more than 90% were resolved in the MDL and prior to trial.[56] All told, well over a thousand MDL's have occurred, involving some of the most challenging litigations in the history of the federal judiciary.[57] Today, a large percentage of the federal civil docket is conducted through MDL

---

[40]   *See In re Asbestos Prods. Liab. Litig. (No. VI)*, 718 F.3d 236, 247 (3d Cir. 2013) (commenting that "efficiency must not be achieved at the expense of preventing meritorious claims from going forward"); *In re Korean Air Lines Co.*, 642 F.3d 685, 700–01 (9th Cir. 2011) (although broad, discretion does not permit court to disregard normal standards for assessing critical motions).

[41]   *See Lexecon Inc. v. Milberg Weiss Bershad Hynes & Lerach*, 523 U.S. 26, 32–41, 118 S.Ct. 956, 140 L.Ed.2d 62 (1998).

[42]   *See United States ex rel. Pogue v. Diabetes Treatment Ctrs. of America, Inc.*, 444 F.3d 462, 467 (6th Cir.2006).

[43]   *See FedEx Ground Package Sys., Inc. v. U.S. Judicial Panel on Multidistrict Litig.*, 662 F.3d 887, 890–91 (7th Cir. 2011).

[44]   *See United States ex rel. Pogue v. Diabetes Treatment Ctrs. of America, Inc.*, 444 F.3d 462, 467–68 (6th Cir. 2006).

[45]   *See In re Cygnus Telecommc'ns Tech., LLC, Patent Litig.*, 536 F.3d 1343, 1349–51 & 1350 n.1 (Fed.Cir. 2008).

[46]   *See* Robert A. Cahn, *A Look at the Judicial Panel on Multidistrict Litigation*, 72 F.R.D. 211, 214 (1976).

[47]   *See, e.g., In re: Am. Med. Sys., Inc., Pelvic Repair Sys. Prods. Liab. Litig.*, 844 F.Supp.2d 1359 (J.P.M.L. 2012) (Nos. MDL 2325–27); *In re Diet Drugs (Phentermine, Fenfluramine, Dexfenfluramine) Prods. Liab. Litig.*, 990 F.Supp. 834 (J.P.M.L.1998) (MDL No. 1203).

[48]   *See, e.g., In re: Nat'l Football League Players' Concussion Injury Litig.*, 842 F.Supp.2d 1378 (J.P.M.L. 2012) (No. MDL 2323).

[49]   *See, e.g., In re Air Disaster at Lockerbie, Scotland, on Dec. 21, 1988*, 709 F.Supp. 231 (J.P.M.L.1989) (MDL No. 799), *aff'd*, 16 F.3d 513 (2d Cir. 1994).

[50]   *See, e.g., In re: Oil Spill by Oil Rig Deepwater Horizon in Gulf of Mexico, on Apr. 20, 2010*, 731 F.Supp.2d 1352 (J.P.M.L. 2010) (No. MDL 2179).

[51]   *See, e.g., In re Western States Wholesale Natural Gas Antitrust Litig.*, 290 F.Supp.2d 1376, (J.P.M.L. 2003) (MDL No. 1566).

[52]   *See, e.g., In re: Facebook, Inc., IPO Secs. & Derivative Litig.*, 899 F.Supp.2d 1374 (J.P.M.L. 2012) (No. MDL 2389).

[53]   *See In re: Mortgage Elec. Registration Sys. (MERS) Litig.*, 659 F.Supp.2d 1368 (J.P.M.L. 2009) (No. MDL 2119).

[54]   *See, e.g., In re Papst Licensing Digital Camera Patent Litig.*, 528 F.Supp.2d 1357 (J.P.M.L. 2007) (MDL No. 1880).

[55]   *See, e.g., In re South African Apartheid Litig.*, 238 F.Supp.2d 1379 (J.P.M.L. 2002) (MDL No. 1499).

[56]   *See Lexecon Inc. v. Milberg Weiss Bershad Hynes & Lerach*, 523 U.S. 26, 32, 118 S.Ct. 956, 961, 140 L.Ed.2d 62 (1998).

[57]   *See FedEx Ground Package Sys., Inc. v. U.S. Judicial Panel on Multidistrict Litig.*, 662 F.3d 887, 891 (7th Cir. 2011).

consolidations.[58] Indeed, some recent scholarship suggests MDL treatment has "supplemented and perhaps displaced the class action device as a procedural mechanism for large settlements."[59]

For a more extensive treatment of MDL practice, see David F. Herr, *Multidistrict Litigation Manual: Practice Before The Judicial Panel On Multidistrict Litigation* (Thompson-West, revised annually).

§ 5.2   The Federal Multidistrict Litigation Statute, 28 U.S.C.A. § 1407

1407.   Multidistrict Litigation

(a) When civil actions involving one or more common questions of fact are pending in different districts, such actions may be transferred to any district for coordinated or consolidated pretrial proceedings. Such transfers shall be made by the judicial panel on multidistrict litigation authorized by this section upon its determination that transfers for such proceedings will be for the convenience of parties and witnesses and will promote the just and efficient conduct of such actions. Each action so transferred shall be remanded by the panel at or before the conclusion of such pretrial proceedings to the district from which it was transferred unless it shall have been previously terminated: *Provided, however,* That the panel may separate any claim, crossclaim, counter-claim, or third-party claim and remand any of such claims before the remainder of the action is remanded.

(b) Such coordinated or consolidated pretrial proceedings shall be conducted by a judge or judges to whom such actions are assigned by the judicial panel on multidistrict litigation. For this purpose, upon request of the panel, a circuit judge or a district judge may be designated and assigned temporarily for service in the transferee district by the Chief Justice of the United States or the chief judge of the circuit, as may be required, in accordance with the provisions of chapter 13 of this title. With the consent of the transferee district court, such actions may be assigned by the panel to a judge or judges of such district. The judge or judges to whom such actions are assigned, the members of the judicial panel on multidistrict litigation, and other circuit and district judges designated when needed by the panel may exercise the powers of a district judge in any district for the purpose of conducting pretrial depositions in such coordinated or consolidated pretrial proceedings.

(c) Proceedings for the transfer of an action under this section may be initiated by—

(i) the judicial panel on multidistrict litigation upon its own initiative, or

(ii) motion filed with the panel by a party in any action in which transfer for coordinated or consolidated pretrial proceedings under this section may be appropriate. A copy of such motion shall be filed in the district court in which the moving party's action is pending.

The panel shall give notice to the parties in all actions in which transfers for coordinated or consolidated pretrial proceedings are contemplated, and such notice shall specify the time and place of any hearing to determine whether such transfer shall be made. Orders of the panel to set a hearing and other orders of the panel issued prior to the order either directing or denying transfer shall be filed in the office of the clerk of the district court in which a transfer hearing is to be or has been held. The panel's order of transfer shall be based upon a record of such hearing at which material evidence may be offered by any party to an action pending in any district that would be affected by the proceedings under this section, and shall be supported by findings of fact and conclusions of law based upon such record. Orders of transfer and such other orders as the panel may make thereafter shall be filed in the office of the clerk of the district court of the transferee district and shall be effective when thus filed. The clerk of the transferee district court shall forthwith transmit a certified copy of the panel's order to transfer to the clerk of the district court from which the action is being transferred.

---

[58]   *See In re Rolls Royce Corp.*, 775 F.3d 671, 681–82 (5th Cir. 2014).

[59]   *See Sullivan v. DB Invs., Inc.*, 667 F.3d 273, 334 (3d Cir. 2011) (Scirica, J., concurring) (citing Thomas E. Willging & Emery G. Lee III, *From Class Actions to Multidistrict Consolidations: Aggregate Mass-Tort Litigation after Ortiz*, 58 U. KAN. L. REV. 775, 801 (2010)).

An order denying transfer shall be filed in each district wherein there is a case pending in which the motion for transfer has been made.

(d) The judicial panel on multidistrict litigation shall consist of seven circuit and district judges designated from time to time by the Chief Justice of the United States, no two of whom shall be from the same circuit. The concurrence of four members shall be necessary to any action by the panel.

(e) No proceedings for review of any order of the panel may be permitted except by extraordinary writ pursuant to the provisions of title 28, section 1651, United States Code. Petitions for an extraordinary writ to review an order of the panel to set a transfer hearing and other orders of the panel issued prior to the order either directing or denying transfer shall be filed only in the court of appeals having jurisdiction over the district in which a hearing is to be or has been held. Petitions for an extraordinary writ to review an order to transfer or orders subsequent to transfer shall be filed only in the court of appeals having jurisdiction over the transferee district. There shall be no appeal or review of an order of the panel denying a motion to transfer for consolidated or coordinated proceedings.

(f) The panel may prescribe rules for the conduct of its business not inconsistent with Acts of Congress and the Federal Rules of Civil Procedure.

(g) Nothing in this section shall apply to any action in which the United States is a complainant arising under the antitrust laws. "Antitrust laws" as used herein include those acts referred to in the Act of October 15, 1914, as amended (38 Stat. 730; 15 U.S.C. 12), and also include the Act of June 19, 1936 (49 Stat. 1526; 15 U.S.C. 13, 13a, and 13b) and the Act of September 26, 1914, as added March 21, 1938 (52 Stat. 116, 117; 15 U.S.C. 56); but shall not include section 4A of the Act of October 15, 1914, as added July 7, 1955 (69 Stat. 282; 15 U.S.C. 15a).

(h) Notwithstanding the provisions of section 1404 or subsection (f) of this section, the judicial panel on multidistrict litigation may consolidate and transfer with or without the consent of the parties, for both pretrial purposes and for trial, any action brought under section 4C of the Clayton Act.

(Added Pub.L. 90–296, § 1, Apr. 29, 1968, 82 Stat. 109, and amended Pub.L. 94–435, Title III, § 303, Sept. 30, 1976, 90 Stat. 1396.)

PART VII

APPELLATE PROCEDURE

Table of Sections

§ 6.1   Introduction

The rules and procedures for appealing a district court's judgment or order are no longer included in the Federal Rules of Civil Procedure, as they once were. Since 1968, these rules and procedures have been set forth in the "Federal Rules of Appellate Procedure", as supplemented by local rules. In-depth, rule-by-rule commentary regarding the federal appeals rules is beyond the scope of this text. The following preview of federal appellate procedure is included only to orient the practitioner to the general procedures governing appeals in the federal courts.

§ 6.2   Step One: Appealability

CORE CONCEPT

Litigants are generally required to wait until a lawsuit is completed in the district court—until there is a "final order" in the case—before an appeal from any of the district court's rulings may be taken.[1] This "finality" doctrine was designed to limit the expense, delays, burdens, and inefficiencies of repeated, successive appeals in a single case,[2] as well as the resulting encroachments upon the special role played by federal trial judges in managing litigation.[3] Important exceptions to this finality or "final order" doctrine exist, however.

♦   **NOTE:** Practitioners must exercise great care in determining an order's finality. When an order becomes "final" it also usually becomes appealable, and a delay thereafter in taking the appeal may forever foreclose the right of appeal. When an order is not immediately appealable, the premature filing of an appeal may be dismissed summarily.

---

[1]   *See Digital Equip. Corp. v. Desktop Direct, Inc.,* 511 U.S. 863, 868, 114 S.Ct. 1992, 1996, 128 L.Ed.2d 842 (1994) (litigants are entitled to only a single appeal in their case, which is usually deferred until the district court enters its final judgment, and may include claims of trial error from every stage of the litigation).

[2]   *See generally Firestone Tire & Rubber Co. v. Risjord,* 449 U.S. 368, 374, 101 S.Ct. 669, 673, 66 L.Ed.2d 571 (1981). *See also Cobbledick v. United States,* 309 U.S. 323, 325, 60 S.Ct. 540, 541, 84 L.Ed. 783 (1940) (judicial administration's "momentum would be arrested by permitting separate reviews of the component elements in a unified cause").

[3]   *See Bullard v. Blue Hills Bank,* ___ U.S. ___, 135 S.Ct. 1686, 1691–92, 191 L.Ed.2d 621 (2015).

APPLICATIONS

Threshold Nature of Appellate Jurisdiction

The right to a federal appeal is a "creature of statute", and exists only to that extent granted by Congress.[4] Federal appellate jurisdiction is not assumed, nor can it be conferred by waiver or consent.[5] Instead, federal appellate courts have an independent obligation to confirm the presence of their jurisdiction, even where the parties to the appeal are prepared to concede it.[6] Moreover, if the appellate court determines that the trial court lacked subject matter jurisdiction over the dispute, the court of appeals has jurisdiction over the appeal for the limited purpose of correcting the jurisdictional error only.[7]

Final Orders

Congress has vested the courts of appeals with jurisdiction to hear appeals from "final orders" of the district courts.[8] Final orders are, thus, immediately appealable to the courts of appeals. A final order is a ruling that "ends the litigation on the merits and leaves nothing for the court to do but execute the judgment."[9] It is usually the order by which the trial court "disassociates" itself from the case.[10] The "final order" rule has been described as "pragmatic" not rigid,[11] and "practical" not "technical".[12] Thus, a district court's dismissal that is technically denominated as "without prejudice" may qualify as a "final order" if, in the particular circumstances, the trial judge is "finished" with the case.[13]

Partial Final Orders (Rule 54(b))

Ordinarily, a judgment as to less than all claims in a lawsuit, or as to less than all parties in a lawsuit, is not immediately appealable until all other claims affecting all other parties are finally resolved. However, the district court may, in the exercise of its discretion, convert such "partial" judgments into immediately appealable final orders by (a) finally resolving at least one claim or the rights and liabilities of at least one party, (b) expressly declaring that no just cause exists to delay the appeal from such a ruling, and (c) directing the entry of judgment on the ruling.[14] The purpose, prerequisites, and procedure for such immediately appealable "partial" judgments are discussed earlier in this text.[15]

Interlocutory Orders

Interlocutory orders are all other interim rulings by the district courts—rulings that do not end the litigation and that contemplate some type of further action by the trial judge.

---

4   *See Abney v. United States,* 431 U.S. 651, 656, 97 S.Ct. 2034, 52 L.Ed.2d 651 (1977).

5   *See New York ex rel. Bryant v. Zimmerman,* 278 U.S. 63, 66, 49 S.Ct. 61, 73 L.Ed. 184 (1928).

6   *See Bender v. Williamsport Area Sch. Dist.,* 475 U.S. 534, 541, 106 S.Ct. 1326, 1331, 89 L.Ed.2d 501 (1986).

7   *See Bender v. Williamsport Area Sch. Dist.,* 475 U.S. 534, 541, 106 S.Ct. 1326, 1331, 89 L.Ed.2d 501 (1986).

8   *See* 28 U.S.C.A. § 1291.

9   *See Van Cauwenberghe v. Biard,* 486 U.S. 517, 521–22, 108 S.Ct. 1945, 1949, 100 L.Ed.2d 517 (1988) (quoting *Catlin v. United States,* 324 U.S. 229, 233, 65 S.Ct. 631, 633, 89 L.Ed. 911 (1945)). *See also Riley v. Kennedy,* 553 U.S. 406, 419, 128 S.Ct. 1970, 1981, 170 L.Ed.2d 837 (2008) (holding that orders that resolve liability without addressing relief are not final); *Behrens v. Pelletier,* 516 U.S. 299, 304, 116 S.Ct. 834, 838, 133 L.Ed.2d 773 (1996) (commenting that finality prevents consideration of rulings that remain subject to revision).

10   *See Bullard v. Blue Hills Bank,* ___ U.S. ___, 135 S.Ct. 1686, 1691, 191 L.Ed.2d 621 (2015); *Mohawk Indus., Inc. v. Carpenter,* 558 U.S. 100, 130 S.Ct. 599, 604–05, 175 L.Ed.2d 458 (2009).

11   *See Mohawk Indus., Inc. v. Carpenter,* 558, U.S. 100, 130, S.Ct. 599, 605, 175 L.Ed.2d 458 (2009).

12   *See Gelboim v. Bank of America Corp.,* ___ U.S. ___, 135 S.Ct. 897, 902, 190 L.Ed.2d 789 (2015).

13   *See GO Computer, Inc. v. Microsoft Corp.,* 508 F.3d 170, 176 (4th Cir. 2007); *Hill v. Potter,* 352 F.3d 1142, 1144 (7th Cir.2003). *See also Frederico v. Home Depot,* 507 F.3d 188, 192 (3d Cir. 2007) (dismissals with leave to amend will be deemed "final orders" if plaintiff elects to stand on her original pleading).

14   *See* Rule 54(b).

15   *See supra* Authors' Commentary to Rule 54(b).

Interlocutory orders are generally not appealable immediately to the courts of appeals.[16] Review of interlocutory orders must ordinarily wait until the district court enters its final order on the merits of the litigation. Under well-settled appellate tenets, litigants may, in the course of appealing a final order, challenge many of the preceding interlocutory rulings previously entered by the trial court.[17]

Permitted Interlocutory Appeals (28 U.S.C. § 1292(a))

Certain rulings involving federal injunctions, receiverships, and admiralty orders are immediately appealable, notwithstanding that the rulings do not qualify as "final orders":

- *Injunctions:* Interlocutory orders that grant, continue, modify, refuse, or dissolve injunctions, or that refuse to dissolve or modify injunctions are appealable immediately.[18] This is considered a "narrowly tailored exception" to the general policy disfavoring piecemeal appeals,[19] and is construed strictly.[20] This means, at a threshold level, that the order must actually constitute an injunction, regardless of the specific nomenclature chosen by the district court to describe it.[21] Because of their brief duration, temporary restraining orders may not ordinarily be immediately appealed.[22] Rather, qualifying injunctive orders must generally possess three attributes: (1) a clearly defined, understandable directive that a party act or refrain from acting, (2) enforceable through contempt, and (3) gives some or all of the substantive relief sought in the complaint.[23] An order that has the "practical effect" of denying an injunction will not automatically trigger appellate review, unless its consequence is serious and only effectively challenged through immediate review.[24] Nor will an order "interpreting" or "clarifying" an injunction permit an immediate appeal.[25] An order "modifies" an injunction if it actually alters the parties' legal relationship.[26] If appellate jurisdiction exists over an injunctive ruling, that jurisdiction may extend to all matters inextricably bound up with that ruling.[27] During such an interlocutory appeal, the district court may be empowered to proceed further with the case.[28]

---

[16] *See Ortiz v. Jordan,* 562 U.S. 180, 188, 131 S.Ct. 884, 891, 178 L.Ed.2d 703 (2011) (summary judgment denial is interlocutory and, thus, usually not immediately appealable); *Ashcroft v. Iqbal,* 556 U.S. 662, 672, 129 S.Ct. 1937, 1946, 173 L.Ed.2d 868 (2009) (interlocutory appeals "are the exception, not the rule").

[17] *See Koch v. City of Del City,* 660 F.3d 1228, 1237 (10th Cir. 2011).

[18] 28 U.S.C.A. § 1292(a)(1). *See also Crowe & Dunlevy, P.C. v. Stidham,* 640 F.3d 1140, 1147 (10th Cir. 2011).

[19] *See Washington Metropolitan Area Transit Com'n v. Reliable Limousine Serv., LLC,* 776 F.3d 1, 8–9 (D.C.Cir. 2015).

[20] *See American River Transp Co. v. Ryan,* 579 F.3d 820, 824 (7th Cir. 2009).

[21] *See Turtle Island Restoration Network v. U.S. Dep't of Commerce,* 672 F.3d 1160, 1164–65 (9th Cir. 2012).

[22] *Service Employees Int'l Union v. Nat'l Union of Healthcare Workers,* 598 F.3d 1061, 1067 (9th Cir. 2010). *But see Grand Canyon Skywalk Dev't, LLC v. 'Sa' Nyu Wa Inc.,* 715 F.3d 1196, 1199–200 (9th Cir. 2013) (TROs that possess injunction qualities may be appealed).

[23] *See Alabama v. United States Army Corps of Eng'rs,* 424 F.3d 1117, 1128–29 (11th Cir.2005).

[24] *See Carson v. American Brands, Inc.,* 450 U.S. 79, 83–84, 101 S.Ct. 993, 67 L.Ed.2d 59 (1981).

[25] *See Gelboim v. Bank of America Corp.,* ___ U.S. ___, 135 S.Ct. 897, 906, 190 L.Ed.2d 789 (2015).

[26] *See Washington Metropolitan Area Transit Com'n v. Reliable Limousine Serv., LLC,* 776 F.3d 1, 9 (D.C.Cir. 2015).

[27] *Compare S.E.C. v. Smith,* 710 F.3d 87, 96–97 (2d Cir. 2013) (permitting appeal); *Tradesman Int'l, Inc. v. Black,* 724 F.3d 1004, 1010–11 (7th Cir. 2013) (refusing appeal).

[28] *See Free Speech v. Federal Election Com'n,* 720 F.3d 788, 791–92 (10th Cir. 2013).

- *Receivers:* Interlocutory orders that appoint receivers, or refuse orders to wind up receiverships or take steps to accomplish those purposes (*i.e.,* directing disposals of property) are appealable immediately,[29] although this exception, too, is construed narrowly.[30]

- *Admiralty:* Decrees that determine the rights and liabilities of parties to admiralty cases in which appeals from final decrees are allowed, are appealable immediately.[31] This exception is also construed narrowly.[32]

Discretionary Interlocutory Appeals (28 U.S.C. § 1292(b))

The district court may, in the exercise of its discretion,[33] choose to certify certain non-final, interlocutory orders as eligible for immediate appellate review.[34] Such certification by the district court does not require the court of appeals to hear the immediate appeal; rather, the courts of appeals also have discretion to reject interlocutory appeals,[35] and may do so for almost any reason (including docket congestion).[36]

Certification by the district judge is not routinely granted ("hen's teeth rare"[37]), and is reserved for "exceptional" cases.[38] Litigants seeking such certification bear a heavy burden.[39] Liberal grants of interlocutory appeals are "bad policy", and threaten the appropriate division of responsibility between federal trial and appellate courts.[40] The purpose of the procedure is to avoid protracted litigation, to assure the quick resolution of complicated legal issues, and to allow appellate review of ephemeral questions of law that could be lost in the context of a complete and final record.[41] The procedure was not intended to serve a mere error-correction function.[42]

To qualify for certification, the district court must state in writing:[43]

(1)   That the order in question involves a "controlling question of law" (which generally means a question of "pure law", which can be resolved "quickly and cleanly" without laboring over the record[44]—such as the meaning of a regulatory, statutory, or

---

[29]   28 U.S.C.A. § 1292(a)(2).

[30]   *See United States v. Antiques Ltd. P'ship,* 760 F.3d 668, 672 (7th Cir. 2014).

[31]   28 U.S.C.A. § 1292(a)(3). *See also Wajnstat v. Oceania Cruises, Inc.,* 684 F.3d 1153, 1155–57 (11th Cir. 2012).

[32]   *See Celtic Marine Corp. v. James C. Justice Cos., Inc.,* 760 F.3d 477, 480 (5th Cir. 2014). *But cf. Williamson v. Recovery Ltd. Partnership,* 731 F.3d 608, 617–20 (6th Cir. 2013) (though construed narrowly, construction may not conflict with statute's plain reading).

[33]   *See Swint v. Chambers County Comm'n,* 514 U.S. 35, 47, 115 S.Ct. 1203, 1210, 131 L.Ed.2d 60 (1995) (noting that Congress conferred upon district courts the "first line discretion to allow interlocutory appeals").

[34]   *See* 28 U.S.C.A. § 1292(b).

[35]   *See* 28 U.S.C.A. § 1292(b). *See also Van Cauwenberghe v. Biard,* 486 U.S. 517, 530, 108 S.Ct. 1945, 1953, 100 L.Ed.2d 517 (1988); *Coopers & Lybrand v. Livesay,* 437 U.S. 463, 475, 98 S.Ct. 2454, 2461, 57 L.Ed.2d 351 (1978).

[36]   *Coopers & Lybrand v. Livesay,* 437 U.S. 463, 475, 98 S.Ct. 2454, 2461, 57 L.Ed.2d 351 (1978).

[37]   *See Camacho v. Puerto Rico Ports Auth.,* 369 F.3d 570, 573 (1st Cir. 2004).

[38]   *See Caterpillar Inc. v. Lewis,* 519 U.S. 61, 74, 117 S.Ct. 467, 475, 136 L.Ed.2d 437 (1996) ("[r]outine resort to § 1292(b) requests would hardly comport with Congress' design to reserve interlocutory review for 'exceptional' cases while generally retaining for the federal courts a firm final judgment rule"); *Coopers & Lybrand v. Livesay,* 437 U.S. 463, 475, 98 S.Ct. 2454, 2461, 57 L.Ed.2d 351 (1978) ("exceptional circumstances" must exist).

[39]   *See OFS Fitel, LLC v. Epstein, Becker & Green, P.C.,* 549 F.3d 1344, 1358–59 (11th Cir. 2008).

[40]   *See Moorman v. UnumProvident Corp.,* 464 F.3d 1260, 1272 (11th Cir. 2006).

[41]   *See Weber v. United States,* 484 F.3d 154, 159 (2d Cir. 2007).

[42]   *See Weber v. United States,* 484 F.3d 154, 159 n.3 (2d Cir. 2007).

[43]   *See Metrou v. M.A. Mortenson Co.,* 781 F.3d 357, 359 (7th Cir. 2015).

[44]   *See McFarlin v. Conseco Servs., LLC,* 381 F.3d 1251, 1258 (11th Cir. 2004); *id.* at 1259 ("The legal question must be stated at a high enough level of abstraction to lift the question out of the details of the evidence or facts of a particular case and give it general relevance to other cases in the same area of law.").

constitutional provision or common law doctrine,[45] the resolution of which is *likely* (although not necessarily certain) to affect the future course of the litigation[46]); and

(2) There is "substantial ground for difference of opinion" on the legal issue the order resolves (which generally means either that there is conflicting legal authority on the disputed issue or that the issue is a particularly difficult or uncertain one of first impression);[47] and

(3) An immediate appeal from the interlocutory order may "materially advance" the ultimate termination of the litigation (which generally means that immediate appeal may avoid expensive and protracted litigation,[48] not that it must have a final, dispositive effect[49]).

The moving party must satisfy *all* of these criteria; unless each criterion is meet, the trial judge cannot grant the Rule 1292(b) certification.[50] If certification is granted, the trial judge generally should specify what question of law it finds to be "controlling"—although a failure to do so is not necessarily dispositive.[51] Certification is jurisdictional; if certification is not granted, the court of appeals lacks authority to hear the appeal under Section 1292(b).[52]

A party may move the district court for such a certification. There is no express time limit for seeking the trial judge to grant a Section 1292(b) certification, although unreasonably dilatory requests may be denied by the trial judge or refused by the courts of appeals.[53] If granted by the district judge, the party may petition the court of appeals within 10 days thereafter for permission to immediately appeal the certified question.[54] The scope of the appellate review is limited to the certified order. The court may not reach beyond that order to consider other, uncertified rulings

---

[45] *See Ahrenholz v. Board of Trustees of Univ. of Ill.,* 219 F.3d 674, 676 (7th Cir.2000).

[46] *See Sokaogon Gaming Enter. Corp. v. Tushie-Montgomery Assocs., Inc.,* 86 F.3d 656, 659 (7th Cir.1996) ("controlling" if issue's resolution is "quite likely" to affect further course of litigation); *In re Baker & Getty Fin. Servs., Inc.,* 954 F.2d 1169, 1172 n.8 (6th Cir.1992) ("controlling" if issue's resolution on appeal could materially affect outcome in trial court).

[47] *See Fortyune v. City of Lomita,* 766 F.3d 1098, 1101 n.2 (9th Cir. 2014) (shown if reasonable jurists might disagree); *McFarlin v. Conseco Servs., LLC,* 381 F.3d 1251, 1258 (11th Cir. 2004) (not shown when appeals court is in "complete and unequivocal" agreement with district court) *In re Baker & Getty Fin. Servs., Inc.,* 954 F.2d 1169, 1172 (6th Cir.1992) (shown by split among Circuits on issue); *Klinghoffer v. S.N. C. Achille Lauro Ed Altri-Gestione Motonave Achille Lauro in Amministrazione Straordinaria,* 921 F.2d 21, 25 (2d Cir.1990) (shown by difficult issues of first impression).

[48] *See McFarlin v. Conseco Servs., LLC,* 381 F.3d 1251, 1259 (11th Cir. 2004) (resolution would "avoid a trial or otherwise substantially shorten the litigation"). *See also White v. Nix,* 43 F.3d 374, 378–79 (8th Cir.1994) (when case will proceed in substantially similar manner regardless of decision on appeal, Court of Appeals' review will not "materially advance" termination of litigation).

[49] *See Sterk v. Redbox Automated Retail, LLC,* 672 F.3d 535, 536–37 (7th Cir. 2012).

[50] *See Couch v. Telescope Inc.,* 611 F.3d 629, 633 (9th Cir. 2010).

[51] *See McFarlin v. Conseco Servs., LLC,* 381 F.3d 1251, 1264 (11th Cir. 2004) ("Given our caseload, when the district court hands us an entire case to sort through for ourselves we are likely to hand it right back. If the district court is unsure about which of the questions, if any, that are answered by its order qualify for certification under § 1292(b), it should not certify the order for review. If convinced that a particular question does qualify, the district court should tell us which question it is.").

[52] *See In re Ford Motor Co., Bridgestone / Firestone North American Tire, LLC,* 344 F.3d 648, 654–55 (7th Cir. 2003) (noting jurisdictional nature, and how most courts hold that mandamus is not proper to compel district court to certify).

[53] *See Richardson Elecs., Ltd. v. Panache Broad. of Pa., Inc.,* 202 F.3d 957, 958 (7th Cir.2000). *See also Ahrenholz v. Board of Trustees of Univ. of Ill.,* 219 F.3d 674,675–76 (7th Cir.2000) (commenting that petitions for certification must be filed in the district court within a "reasonable time" after the contested order is entered).

[54] *See* 28 U.S.C.A. § 1292(b); Fed. R. App. P. 5. *See also Calderon v. GEICO General Ins. Co.,* 754 F.3d 201, 207 (4th Cir. 2014). The district court may, in certain circumstances, rescue a party's failure to petition timely by vacating and re-entering the certification order. Generally, this is permitted when the moving party is blameless and the delay is caused by the court itself or by a failure to timely receive the certification order. *See In re City of Memphis,* 293 F.3d 345, 348–50 (6th Cir.2002) (discussing process and National case law on point).

by the trial judge.[55] But the court of appeals may address any issue that is "fairly included" within the certified order itself; review is limited by the order that is certified,[56] not by the precise question found to be controlling.[57] Other issues that are "inextricably intertwined" with the certified issue may be reached as well.[58]

Collateral Order Doctrine

In addition to the Rule and statutory exceptions to the "final order" limitation, the Supreme Court has developed the common law "collateral order" doctrine, which recognizes that certain important legal rulings—collateral to the litigation's underlying merits—may nevertheless be deemed "final" and eligible for immediate appellate review. To qualify under the collateral order doctrine, the district court's order must:

(1)   Be conclusive on the issue sought to be immediately appealed; *and*

(2)   Resolve an "important question" that is completely separate from the underlying merits; *and*

(3)   Be effectively unreviewable if the appeal were to await a final order on the merits.[59]

A failure to satisfy even one of these three requirements defeats the use of the collateral order doctrine.[60]

The collateral order exception represents a narrow, common law construction of the final order doctrine.[61] It is applied stringently and is never permitted to "swallow" the general prohibition against piecemeal appeals.[62] Although collateral orders typically involve a claimed right to "avoid" trial (a right which would be lost and effectively unappealable later), the Supreme Court has rejected the notion that this characteristic alone justifies collateral order treatment.[63] Instead, the Court has ruled that true collateral orders are those that would imperil "a substantial public interest" or some high order value if not immediately reviewed.[64]

Other Exceptions

Various other exceptions to the general final order principle exist,[65] though an exhaustively comprehensive discussion of those nuances are beyond the scope of this text.

---

[55]   *See Yamaha Motor Corp., U.S.A. v. Calhoun,* 516 U.S. 199, 205, 116 S.Ct. 619, 623, 133 L.Ed.2d 578 (1996).

[56]   *See A.S. ex rel. Miller v. SmithKline Beecham Corp.,* 769 F.3d 204, 208 (3d Cir. 2014).

[57]   *See Yamaha Motor Corp. v. Calhoun,* 516 U.S. 199, 205, 116 S.Ct. 619, 623, 133 L.Ed.2d 578 (1996) ("it is the order that is appealable, and not the controlling question identified by the district court").

[58]   *See Murray v. Metropolitan Life Ins. Co.,* 583 F.3d 173, 176 (2d Cir. 2009).

[59]   *See Will v. Hallock,* 546 U.S. 345, 349, 126 S.Ct. 952, 956, 163 L.Ed.2d 836 (2006); *Coopers & Lybrand v. Livesay,* 437 U.S. 463, 468–69, 98 S.Ct. 2454, 2457–58, 57 L.Ed.2d 351 (1978).

[60]   *See Gulfstream Aerospace Corp. v. Mayacamas Corp.,* 485 U.S. 271, 276, 108 S.Ct. 1133, 99 L.Ed.2d 296 (1988).

[61]   *See Houston Cmty. Hosp. v. Blue Cross & Blue Shield of Tex., Inc.,* 481 F.3d 265, 268 (5th Cir. 2007).

[62]   *See Mohawk Indus., Inc. v. Carpenter,* 558 U.S. 100, 106, 130 S.Ct. 599, 605, 175 L.Ed.2d 458 (2009); *Digital Equip. Corp. v. Desktop Direct, Inc.,* 511 U.S. 863, 868, 114 S.Ct. 1992, 1996, 128 L.Ed.2d 842 (1994).

[63]   *See Will v. Hallock,* 546 U.S. 345, 350–51, 126 S.Ct. 952, 958, 163 L.Ed.2d 836 (2006).

[64]   *See Mohawk Indus., Inc. v. Carpenter,* 558 U.S. 100, 106–10, 130 S.Ct. 599, 605 & 606–07, 175 L.Ed.2d 458 (2009) (appealing denial of attorney-client privilege assertion does not qualify); *Will v. Hallock,* 546 U.S. 345, 352, 126 S.Ct. 952, 959, 163 L.Ed.2d 836 (2006) (offering, as examples, the need to respect the separation of powers, to preserve the efficiency of government and the initiative of its officials, to respect a State's dignitary interests, and to mitigate the government's advantage over the individual).

[65]   *See, e.g., Forgay v. Conrad,* 47 U.S. (6 How.) 201, 201, 12 L.Ed. 404 (1848) (allowing immediate appeal from order directing delivery of property to appellee); *Arc of California v. Douglas,* 757 F.3d 975, 992–93 (9th Cir. 2014) (using "pendent appellate jurisdiction" doctrine to permit review of ruling that is "inextricably intertwined" with, or necessary to meaningful review of, a properly appealable order).

ADDITIONAL RESEARCH REFERENCES

C.J.S. Federal Courts §§ 290(1) to 291(5) et seq.

West's Key Number Digest, Federal Courts ⊷551 to 600

§ 6.3   Step Two: Time for Taking an Appeal

CORE CONCEPT

In civil cases, an appeal generally must be taken within 30 days after the entry of the disputed judgment or order, although if the United States is a party this period is extended to 60 days. Except for a few narrow exceptions, this time period may not be waived or extended. A failure to file a timely appeal will forfeit that party's right of appeal.

APPLICATIONS

When United States Is a Party

When the United States or a federal officer, employee, or agency is a party to the litigation, the parties have 60 days after the entry of the disputed judgment or order in which to take an appeal.[66] This 60-day period applies to all parties in the case—the federal parties as well as all others. However, the federal entity must be an actual party (not a mere potential party) for the longer period to apply.[67]

When United States Is *Not* a Party

In all other cases, the parties have 30 days after the entry of the disputed judgment or order in which to take an appeal.[68]

When Opponent Appeals

After one party takes an appeal, all other parties to the litigation have at least 14 days thereafter in which to take their own appeals.[69] The parties receive the benefit of this 14-day "extension" period even if the original notice of appeal is defective or otherwise is dismissed.[70] But that benefit only follows from an appeal by *another* party (and cannot be used to bootstrap a second, corrective appeal by the same party).[71]

Some courts of appeals have ruled that this 14-day period is mandatory and jurisdictional—if the time period lapses, the right to cross-appeal is irretrievably lost.[72] Other courts of appeals view the 14-day period as "proper procedure", but not jurisdictional; if appellate jurisdiction was already properly invoked with the filing of the *original* notice of appeal (*i.e.,* the one to which the

---

[66]   Fed. R. App. P. 4(a)(1)(B).

[67]   *See U.S. ex rel. Eisenstein v. City of New York,* 556 U.S. 928, 931, 129 S.Ct. 2230, 2233, 173 L.Ed.2d 1255 (2009) (although aware of all Federal Claim Act lawsuits, United States is not a "party" (and 60-day period does not apply) unless it actually intervenes).

[68]   Fed. R. App. P.4(a)(1)(A).

[69]   Fed. R. App. P. 4(a)(3) (party may file notice of appeal within 14 days after first notice of appeal was filed or within the 30 or 60 day period prescribed in Rule 4(a), whichever period is longer).

[70]   *See In re Julien Co.,* 146 F.3d 420, 423 (6th Cir.1998) (applying 14-day extension rule even where first appeal was dismissed for lack of standing).

[71]   *See Cruz v. Int'l Collection Corp.,* 673 F.3d 991, 1002 (9th Cir. 2012).

[72]   *See Johnson v. Teamsters Local 559,* 102 F.3d 21, 29 (1st Cir.1996).

cross-notice would be filed) the court may permit the 14-day period to be excused in a proper circumstance.[73]

Appeal Time Is Mandatory and Jurisdictional

The applicable time period for taking an appeal is mandatory and jurisdictional.[74] It cannot be waived, even for good cause shown.[75] It also may not be extended, absent the few narrow exceptions discussed below.

Dated from "Entry" of Judgment or Order

For purposes of timeliness on appeal, the appeal period begins to run when the order is "entered" on the docket, after being filed by the district judge (and not when the court issues,[76] or the parties or their attorneys receive,[77] a copy).

♦ **NOTE:** When the "separate document" requirement of Rule 58 applies, the time for appeal will not begin to run until the "separate document" prerequisite is satisfied or the 150-day period expires.[78]

Computing Time for Taking Appeal

The period within which an appeal must be taken is calculated according to the counting method set in the federal appellate rules,[79] and those rules will apply unless a different method for computing time is specified.[80] In counting periods stated in units of time measured in days or longer (e.g., days, months, or years), the day that triggers the period is excluded and then every other day is included. If the period ends on a weekend, a legal holiday, or a day when the clerk's office is inaccessible, the period is extended to the end of the next day that is not a weekend, a legal holiday, or a clerk's-office-inaccessible day.[81] Unless otherwise specified, a day "ends" for electronic filing at midnight in the time zone of the court's principal office, and for most other filings when the clerk's office is scheduled to close.[82] Also now expressly addressed are time periods set in hours,[83] as well as the proper adjustments for federal and State holidays [84] and courthouse inaccessibility.[85]

Old "*Less-than-11-Day* Counting" Rule Is Abandoned

Under an earlier version of the federal appellate rules, time periods of less than 11 days were given a special computation method (*i.e.,* intervening weekends and legal holidays were excluded). To simplify time computation, this approach was abolished, effective December 1, 2009.[86]

---

[73] *See Mendocino Env'l Ctr. v. Mendocino County,* 192 F.3d 1283, 1297 (9th Cir.1999).

[74] *Bowles v. Russell,* 551 U.S. 205, 214, 127 S.Ct. 2360, 2366, 168 L.Ed.2d 96 (2007).

[75] *See Bowles v. Russell,* 551 U.S. 205, 214, 127 S.Ct. 2360, 2366, 168 L.Ed.2d 96 (2007).

[76] *See* Fed. R. App. P. 4(a)(7). *See also Lemos v. Holder,* 636 F.3d 365, 367 (7th Cir. 2011).

[77] *See Wheat v. Pfizer, Inc.,* 31 F.3d 340, 342 (5th Cir.1994).

[78] *See* Rule 58. *See also supra* Authors' Commentary to Rule 58. *See also Meilleur v. Strong,* 682 F.3d 56, 60–61 (2d Cir. 2012).

[79] *See* Fed. R. App. P. 26(a).

[80] *See* Fed. R. App. P. 26(a).

[81] *See* Fed. R. App. P. 26(a)(1). *See generally Chao Lin v. U.S. Atty. Gen.,* 677 F.3d 1043, 1044–46 (11th Cir. 2012) (clerk's office not inaccessible when inclement weather delayed opening until 10:30 a.m., and FedEx delivered appellate petition next day).

[82] *See* Fed. R. App. P. 26(a)(4).

[83] *See* Fed. R. App. P. 26(a)(2).

[84] *See* Fed. R. App. P. 26(a)(6).

[85] *See* Fed. R. App. P. 26(a)(3).

[86] *See* Fed. R. App. P. 26(a)(1) advisory committee note to 2009 amendment.

Extensions—By Filing Post-Trial Motions

The timely filing of certain post-trial motions will suspend the time for appeal.[87] The post-trial motions that qualify for this suspension effect are:

- Motions for judgment as a matter of law, under Federal Rule of Civil Procedure 50(b);

- Motions to alter or supplement findings of fact, under Federal Rule of Civil Procedure 52(b);

- Motions for attorney's fees, under Federal Rule of Civil Procedure 54(d), but only if the district court extends the time for appeal in accordance with Federal Rule of Civil Procedure 58; and

- Motions to alter or amend the judgment, under Federal Rule of Civil Procedure 59;

- Motions for a new trial, under Federal Rule of Civil Procedure 59; and

- Motions for relief from a judgment or order, under Federal Rule of Civil Procedure 60, but only if such motion is served within 28 days after entry of judgment.

These motions need not be successful in order to extend the appeal period.[88] But the motions must be filed timely; an untimely filed post-trial motion will *not* suspend the appeal time.[89] (Although the trial court may hear an untimely post-trial motion, if the non-moving party waives its timeliness objection, many courts of appeals consider the motion still untimely and, therefore, as having no tolling effect on the time for appeal.)[90] Once the district court grants or denies the last still-pending, timely post-trial motion,[91] the time for appeal begins to run.[92]

Triggering the Appeals Clock After Post-Trial Motions

The courts of appeals are divided on whether the district court must *expressly* rule on all pending post-trial motions before the appeal clock resumes ticking. The majority rule holds that the appeal time remains tolled until the trial court explicitly grants or denies the pending post-trial motions.[93] The minority view holds that the appeal period can begin to run as soon as the district court enters the judgment (interpreting the entry as an implicit denial of the post-trial motions).[94]

Successive Post-Trial Motions

Most courts of appeals have ruled that after the time for appeal has been *once* extended by the filing of a tolling post-trial motion, the appeal period cannot be suspended *again* by the filing of a *subsequent* post-trial motion.[95]

---

[87]   *See* Fed. R. App. P. 4(a)(4)(A).

[88]   *See Urso v. United States,* 72 F.3d 59, 61 (7th Cir. 1995).

[89]   *See Vaqueria Tres Monjitas, Inc. v. Comas-Pagan,* 772 F.3d 956, 958 (1st Cir. 2014).

[90]   *See Blue v. Int'l Bhd. of Elec. Workers Local Union 159,* 676 F.3d 579, 582–85 (7th Cir. 2012) (untimely post-trial motions forfeited right to appeal underlying judgment, though timely appeal from post-trial rulings permitted review limited to those rulings alone); *Lizardo v. United States,* 619 F.3d 273, 275–80 (3d Cir. 2010) (timeliness requirement may be forfeited, but for appeal purposes, untimely Rule 59(e) motions do not toll appeal period, which begins to run from judgment). *But see Obaydullah v. Obama,* 688 F.3d 784, 787–92 (D.C. Cir. 2012) (given opponent's waiver of timeliness objection, appeal was proper).

[91]   *See* Fed. R. App. P. 4(a)(4)(A). *See also Wallace v. FedEx Corp.,* 764 F.3d 571, 582 (6th Cir. 2014).

[92]   *See Slep-Tone Entm't Corp. v. Karaoke Kandy Store, Inc.,* 782 F.3d 712, 715 (6th Cir. 2015).

[93]   *See Havird Oil Co. v. Marathon Oil Co.,* 149 F.3d 283, 288 (4th Cir. 1998) (holding that district court must explicitly dispose of all outstanding post-trial motions before appeal period resumes).

[94]   *See Dunn v. Truck World, Inc.,* 929 F.2d 311, 313 (7th Cir. 1991) (holding that entry of judgment is implicitly the order denying a post-trial motion).

[95]   *See York Group, Inc. v. Wuxi Taihu Tractor Co.,* 632 F.3d 399, 401 (7th Cir. 2011).

Abandoned Post-Trial Motions

If a party files timely post-trial motions, but then abandons them, the filing of those motions can be ignored; if the appeal period lapsed while those now-withdrawn motions were pending, appellate jurisdiction will likely be deemed lost.[96]

Extensions—By District Court (Neglect or Good Cause)

Upon a showing of either excusable neglect or good cause, the district court may briefly extend the time for appeal.[97] To obtain such an extension, the movant *must* seek the extension within the original 30-day appeal period itself or within 30 days after the original appeal period expires.[98] The district court may only extend the time for appeal for 30 days after the original appeal period expires, or for 14 days after the order granting the motion for extension is granted, whichever time is later.[99] The moving party must prove *either* excusable neglect or good cause.[100]

- *Excusable Neglect Defined:* Excusable neglect applies in circumstances involving fault, and seeks an extension typically made necessary by something that should have been within the movant's control.[101] It is not a "toothless" standard nor a merciless one—equitable considerations drive the inquiry.[102] Whether the neglect is "excusable" is a determination vested to the district court's discretion.[103] In evaluating whether "excusable neglect" exists, the courts will assess the risk of prejudice to the non-moving party, the length of the delay, the delay's potential impact on the proceedings, the reason for the delay and (especially whether that reason was within the reasonable control of the moving party), and the moving party's good faith.[104] These factors (and others) are not mechanically given equal weight, and the actual balance may depend on the circumstances.[105] "Excusable neglect" generally requires something more than an attorney's busy caseload or an oversight in consulting or a misreading of the procedural rules,[106] or a clerk's failure to notify parties of a ruling they could have discovered by periodically checking the docket.[107]

---

[96] *See Vanderwerf v. SmithKline Beecham Corp.,* 603 F.3d 842, 845–46 (10th Cir.2010).

[97] *See* Fed. R. App. P. 4(a)(5).

[98] *See* Fed.R.App.P. 4(a)(5). *See also Cohen v. Empire Blue Cross & Blue Shield,* 142 F.3d 116, 118 (2d Cir.1998) (holding that district court lacks jurisdiction to grant extension that is not filed within 30-day grace period).

[99] Fed.R.App.P. 4(a)(5)(C).

[100] *See* Fed. R. App. P. 4(a)(5)(A). *See also id.* advisory committee notes to 2002 amendments. *See also Ragguette v. Premier Wines & Spirits,* 691 F.3d 315, 321 n.2 (3d Cir. 2012).

[101] *See* Fed. R. App. P. 4(a)(5)(A) advisory committee notes to 2002 amendments. *See also Sherman v. Quinn,* 668 F.3d 421, 425 (7th Cir. 2012).

[102] *See Abuelyaman v. Illinois State Univ.,* 667 F.3d 800, 808 (7th Cir. 2011).

[103] *See Sherman v. Quinn,* 668 F.3d 421, 425 (7th Cir. 2012).

[104] *See Pioneer Inv. Servs. Co. v. Brunswick Assocs. Ltd. P'ship,* 507 U.S. 380, 395, 113 S.Ct. 1489, 1498, 123 L.Ed.2d 74 (1993) (assessing "excusable neglect" in bankruptcy rules context). *See also Treasurer, Trustees of Drury Indus., Inc. Health Care Plan & Trust v. Goding,* 692 F.3d 888, 893 (8th Cir. 2012). *Cf. Ragguette v. Premier Wines & Spirits,* 691 F.3d 315, 325–26 (3d Cir. 2012) (listing five different nonexclusive factors).

[105] *See Treasurer, Trustees of Drury Indus., Inc. Health Care Plan & Trust v. Goding,* 692 F.3d 888, 893 (8th Cir. 2012); (excuse for delay given greatest weight); *Abuelyaman v. Illinois State Univ.,* 667 F.3d 800, 808 (7th Cir. 2011) (degree of prejudice to opponent and good faith of movant given greatest weight).

[106] *See Satkar Hospitality, Inc. v. Fox Television Holdings,* 767 F.3d 701, 706–09 (7th Cir. 2014) (denied, if inability or refusal to read/comprehend the Rules); *Ragguette v. Premier Wines & Spirits,* 691 F.3d 315, 321–33 (3d Cir. 2012) (denied, failure to properly task computer calendar); *Sherman v. Quinn,* 668 F.3d 421, 426–27 (7th Cir. 2012) (denied, overloaded with work); *Midwest Employers Cas. Co. v. Williams,* 161 F.3d 877, 879–80 (5th Cir. 1998) (denied, incorrect interpretation of the meaning of an unambiguous Rule). *Cf. Zipperer v. School Bd. of Seminole County,* 111 F.3d 847, 849–50 (11th Cir.1997) (finding excusable neglect where notice was filed one-day late, having been mailed to the Court, by in-State mailing, six days before filing, noting that normal mail delivery is three days).

[107] *See Two-Way Media LLC v. AT & T, Inc.,* 782 F.3d 1311, 1315–17 (Fed.Cir. 2015).

- *Good Cause Defined:* Good cause applies in circumstances where there is no fault (excusable or otherwise), and seeks an extension typically made necessary by something that was not within the movant's control.[108]

Extensions—By District Court (Non-Receipt)

If the district court determines that a party entitled to notice of the entry of a judgment or order did not timely receive that notice, the court may extend the time for appeal, but only under the following conditions:

- *Party's non-receipt within 21 days:* The court must first find that the party did not receive formal Rule 77(d) notice within 21 days after entry of the judgment or order[109] (note that some courts have construed "receipt" to be different than mere "service");[110] *and*

- *Party promptly moved to reopen the appeal period:* The non-noticed party must promptly move the district court to reopen the appeal period within 14 days after receiving or observing written notice of the entry from any source;[111] *and*

- *Party moved no later than 180 days after entry:* The maximum window for an appeal extension can never last longer than 180 days (thus obligating practitioners to routinely check the court dockets, even when no formal notice has been received);[112] *and*

- *No party is prejudiced by the extension:* The court must find that no party would be prejudiced by granting an appeal period extension;[113] *and*

- *Actual extension may last only 14 days:* If an extension is granted, it will compel the non-noticed party to file the appeal within 14 days.[114]

The burden of demonstrating non-receipt rests with the moving party.[115] Evidence that the order was properly mailed or transmitted over a court's official electronic filing system creates a presumption of receipt; if contested, the district court will, as factfinder, assess the evidence and determine the question of receipt or non-receipt.[116] This Rule is triggered only by non-receipt; receiving but not opening or reading the notice does not qualify for relief.[117] Motions for extensions

---

[108] *See* Fed. R. App. P. 4(a)(5)(A) advisory committee notes to 2002 amendments. *See also Bishop v. Corsentino,* 371 F.3d 1203, 1207 (10th Cir.2004).

[109] *See* Fed. R. App. P. 4(a)(6)(A). This 21-day trigger requires actual, formal notice under Rule 77(d). Thus, if no formal Rule 77(d) notice was served within 21 days, but the party nevertheless receives informal notice of the entry, an extension of the appeal time may still be sought. *See* Fed. R. App. P. 4(a)(6)(A) advisory committee note (2005).

[110] *See* Fed. R. App. P. 4(a)(6)(A). *See also In re WorldCom, Inc.,* 708 F.3d 327, 332–35 (2d Cir. 2013) (transmission to outdated email was not "receipt"); *Khor Chin Lim v. Courtcall Inc.,* 683 F.3d 378, 381 (7th Cir. 2012) ("receipt" occurred when letter arrived at litigant's home, even though envelope had not yet been opened).

[111] *See* Fed. R. App. P. 4(a)(6)(B) (This 14-day period became effective on December 1, 2009; until that time, the period was 7-days). The extension window will start to run on the day the party receives or observes "written" notice from "any source" *(e.g.,* by fax, e-mail, viewing a website entry, etc.), and will last for only 14 days. *See* Fed. R. App. P. 4(a)(6)(B) advisory committee note (2005) (as revised in 2009). Oral notice, "no matter how specific, reliable, or unequivocal", will not start the period running. *Id.*

[112] *See* Fed. R. App. P. 4(a)(6)(B).

[113] *See* Fed. R. App. P. 4(a)(6)(C).

[114] *See* Fed. R. App. P. 4(a)(6).

[115] *See Nunley v. City of Los Angeles,* 52 F.3d 792, 795 (9th Cir.1995).

[116] *See American Boat Co., Inc. v. Unknown Sunken Barge,* 567 F.3d 348, 352–53 (8th Cir. 2009) (official email notices of a court's CM/ECF system are *presumed* received; absent evidence to disprove it, court may rely on presumption). *But see Nunley v. City of Los Angeles,* 52 F.3d 792, 796 (9th Cir.1995) (once specific factual denial of receipt is made, district court can give no further weight to presumption of receipt).

[117] *See Two-Way Media LLC v. AT & T, Inc.,* 782 F.3d 1311, 1317–18 (Fed.Cir. 2015).

due to non-receipt are committed to the district court's discretion.[118] In exercising that discretion, the district court may deny this extension even where the litigant otherwise satisfies the technical elements of the extension rule[119] (provided, of course, that the basis for the court's denial is something other than the district court's own assessment of the merits of the appeal[120] or that the party failed to learn of the entry of judgment independently through its own means.)[121] The moving party is ordinarily not required to demonstrate "excusable neglect" in order to justify such relief.[122]

♦ **NOTE:** Seeking relief from orders under other rules, such as Rule 60(b), cannot be used to circumvent this 180-day limitation.[123] Although this inflexible 180-day time boundary sometimes "may work misfortune," it is designed to finality the interests of finality in judgments against inequity to parties.[124]

Extensions—By District Court (Fee Motions)

When a party makes a timely attorneys' fees motion under Rule 54(d), the district court may suspend the time for taking an appeal until the fees motion is resolved.[125]

Extensions—By Court of Appeals

The courts of appeals may not grant litigants an extension of the time for appeal under any circumstances.[126]

Premature Appeals

A notice of appeal is *not* necessarily fatally defective merely because it is filed too quickly. If the notice is filed after the district court announces its decision, but before the judgment or order is formally entered, the notice of appeal will be deemed "filed" on the day the district court formally enters the judgment or order (at least as to orders that would be immediately appealable upon entry).[127] This rule, however, will not apply to orders that are clearly interlocutory and, thus, would not be immediately appealable upon entry[128]—unless the otherwise interlocutory order is thereafter given a Rule 54(b) determination.[129]

If the notice of appeal is filed after the district court formally enters the judgment or order, but before the district court rules upon those types of post-trial motions that suspend the time for appeal, the notice is deemed to lie dormant. The notice will become effective on the date the trial

---

[118] *See* Fed. R. App. P. 4(a)(6) ("The district court . . . *may* extend the time for filing a notice of appeal . . . ") (emphasis added).

[119] *See In re WorldCom, Inc.,* 708 F.3d 327, 335–42 (2d Cir. 2013) (extension denied when non-receipt was caused by attorney's failure to update clerk's office's electronic filing system with his new email address).

[120] *See Kuhn v. Sulzer Orthopedics, Inc.,* 498 F.3d 365, 369–70 (6th Cir. 2007).

[121] *See United States v. Withers,* 618 F.3d 1008, 1014–15 (9th Cir. 2010).

[122] *See In re WorldCom, Inc.,* 708 F.3d 327, 337 (2d Cir. 2013).

[123] *See U.S. v. Winkles,* 795 F.3d 1134, 1143–44 (9th Cir. 2015). *But see Tanner v. Yukins,* 776 F.3d 434, 441–44 (6th Cir. 2015) (permitting Rule 60(b)(6) relief in exceptional circumstances to persons who missed deadline).

[124] *See Tanner v. Yukins,* 776 F.3d 434, 440–41 (6th Cir. 2015).

[125] *See* Rule 58(e). *See also supra* Authors' Commentary to Rule 58(e).

[126] Fed. R. App. P. 26(b)(1). *See In re Fischer,* 554 F.3d 656, 657 (7th Cir. 2009).

[127] Fed. R. App. P. 4(a)(2). *See FirsTier Mortg. Co. v. Investors Mortg. Ins. Co.,* 498 U.S. 269, 276, 111 S.Ct. 648, 112 L.Ed.2d 743 (1991).

[128] *See FirsTier Mortg. Co. v. Investors Mortg. Ins. Co.,* 498 U.S. 269, 276, 111 S.Ct. 648, 652, 112 L.Ed.2d 743 (1991). *But cf. Bonner v. Perry,* 564 F.3d 424, 427–29 (6th Cir. 2009) (notice of appeal filed after a partial disposition (that might have qualified for Rule 54(b) determination) may properly be treated as filed upon final disposition of all remaining claims).

[129] *See Brown v. Columbia Sussex Corp.,* 664 F.3d 182, 189–90 (7th Cir. 2011). *But cf. Bielskis v. Louisville Ladder, Inc.,* 663 F.3d 887, 893 (7th Cir. 2011) (entry of Rule 58 judgment "obviates" unfiled Rule 54(b) determination).

court rules on the outstanding post-trial motions,[130] although a new or amended notice (identifying the newly entered ruling) may be necessary.[131]

ADDITIONAL RESEARCH REFERENCES

C.J.S., Federal Courts §§ 293(5 to 17) et seq.

West's Key Number Digest, Federal Courts ⊶652 to 660.40

§ 6.4 Step Three: Procedure for Taking an Appeal

CORE CONCEPT

A federal appeal is taken by filing a notice of appeal with the district court. Thus, there are essentially two "modest tasks" that must be completed before an appeal is properly taken: the appellants must give proper "notice" of their intent to appeal and they must deliver that notice "in time".[132]

APPLICATIONS

Contents of Notice of Appeal

A notice of appeal is typically a simple, one-page form. Its essential contents are: (1) naming the party or parties taking the appeal; (2) naming the court to which the appeal is taken; and (3) naming the order that is being appealed.[133] It need not name the appellees,[134] nor should it contain the appellant's legal arguments.

- *Naming All Parties:* The parties to the appeal should each be individually named.[135] Appeals are permitted only by those parties whose names appear on the notice of appeal itself (or whose intent to appeal is otherwise "objectively clear" from the notice).[136] Although the phrase "et al."[137] and other shorthand expressions[138] may, in some limited

---

[130] *See* Fed. R. App. P. 4(a)(4)(B). *See also Slep-Tone Entm't Corp. v. Karaoke Kandy Store, Inc.*, 782 F.3d 712, 715 (6th Cir. 2015). This Rule represents a change in earlier practice, which before 1993 held that a notice of appeal was a "nullity" if prematurely filed while post-trial motions remained pending. *See Leader Nat'l Ins. Co. v. Industrial Indem. Ins. Co.*, 19 F.3d 444, 445 (9th Cir.1994) (noting 1993 amendment's change to practice).

[131] *See* Fed. R. App. P. 4(a)(4)(B)(ii). *See also Weatherly v. Alabama State Univ.*, 728 F.3d 1263, 1271–72 (11th Cir. 2013).

[132] *See Isert v. Ford Motor Co.*, 461 F.3d 756, 758 (6th Cir.2006).

[133] *See* Fed. R. App. P. 3(c)(1). *See also Bennett v. Gaetz*, 592 F.3d 786, 790 (7th Cir. 2010).

[134] *See MIF Realty L.P. v. Rochester Assocs.*, 92 F.3d 752, 758 (8th Cir. 1996).

[135] *See* Fed. R. App. P. 3(c)(1)(A). *See also M.E.S., Inc. v. Snell*, 712 F.3d 666, 668 (2d Cir. 2013).

[136] *See* Fed. R. App. P. 3(c)(4) & advisory committee note to 1993 amendment. *See also 1756 W. Lake St. LLC v. Am. Chartered Bank*, 787 F.3d 383, 385 (7th Cir. 2015) ("bobble" in notice overlooked where appealing intent was clear); *S.E.C. v. Wealth Mgmt. LLC,* 628 F.3d 323, 331 (7th Cir. 2010) (holders of trust entitled to appeal where no confusion existed as to their identity).

[137] *See Massie v. U.S. Dep't of Housing & Urban Dev't,* 620 F.3d 340, 348–49 (3d Cir. 2010) (though discouraged, use of "et al." preserved appeal by class members). *But cf. Murphy v. Keystone Steel & Wire Co.,* 61 F.3d 560 (7th Cir. 1995) (only named class members could appeal, because intent of unnamed class members was unclear). Note, this rule reversed prior practice, which held that the failure to specifically name all appealing parties forfeited their right of appeal. *Cf. Torres v. Oakland Scavenger Co.,* 487 U.S. 312, 108 S.Ct. 2405, 101 L.Ed.2d 285 (1988).

[138] *See Air Line Pilots Ass'n v. Continental Airlines,* 125 F.3d 120 (3d Cir.1997) (finding term "the LPP Claimants" sufficient to adequately identify appellants).

contexts, be sufficient, an express designation is always the safer course.[139] Where that clarity is missing, the appeal may be lost.[140]

- *Naming All Parts of Order Appealed from:* Each part of a separable judgment or separable order appealed from must be named.[141] Ordinarily, an appeal taken from the final judgment itself will support appellate review of most earlier interlocutory orders in the case,[142] so long as the intent to appeal from each particular interlocutory order is clear.[143] However, if a party chooses to name in the notice of appeal a particular order or ruling *(e.g.,* appealing from the order of November 10 granting summary judgment), the court of appeals may rule that the party has *not* also appealed from other rulings in the same case.[144] Some courts of appeals, however, will allow added information supplied in the party's other filings to supplement (and, perhaps, rescue) an otherwise insufficiently detailed notice of appeal.[145] An order not listed in the notice of appeals may, nevertheless, be reviewed if it has a connection with the listed orders, the intention to appeal from it is clear, and the opponent has not been prejudiced.[146]

- *Naming Court of Appeals:* The notice of appeal must identify the specific court to which the appeal is being taken[147] (unless only one proper court is possible).[148]

Errors in Notice of Appeal

Although jurisdictional in nature,[149] the rules prescribing the proper contents of a notice of appeal are construed liberally,[150] and not hyper-technically.[151] A "technical variance" from the rules may be excused, if the rule requirements are "functionally" satisfied.[152] That function is notice, both to the court and the adversaries, of the appealing parties and the rulings to be reviewed.[153] If the appellant's intent is clear (or fairly inferred) and the appellee is not prejudiced by a technical error (generally, through ensuring a full opportunity to brief the issue), such mistakes may be overlooked.[154] This liberality may even permit a party's brief to substitute for an unfiled notice of appeal, where it provides all the requisite notice.[155] *Pro se* appeals will be assessed with special liberality.[156] Nevertheless, an appellant's subjective intentions are not

---

[139] *See Olenhouse v. Commodity Credit Corp.,* 42 F.3d 1560, 1572 n.19 (10th Cir.1994).

[140] *See Valadez-Lopez v. Chertoff,* 656 F.3d 851, 859 n.2 (9th Cir. 2011).

[141] *See* Fed. R. App. P. 3(c)(1)(B).

[142] *See Hall v. City of Los Angeles,* 697 F.3d 1059, 1070–71 (9th Cir. 2012).

[143] *See Ramsey v. Penn Mut. Life Ins. Co.,* 787 F.3d 813, 818–19 (6th Cir. 2015) (appellant presumed to appeal from entering judgment, not just magistrate judge's order recommending entry); *Lolli v. County of Orange,* 351 F.3d 410, 414–15 (9th Cir. 2003) (appellant presumed to appeal from merits of summary judgment motion, and not just denial of reconsideration).

[144] *See Schell v. Bluebird Media, LLC,* 787 F.3d 1179, 1184 (8th Cir. 2015).

[145] *See Hallquist v. United Home Loans, Inc.,* 715 F.3d 1040, 1044–46 (8th Cir. 2013) (appeal information form clarified scope of intended appeal) *One Indus., LLC v. Jim O'Neal Distrib., Inc.,* 578 F.3d 1154, 1159 (9th Cir. 2009) (opening briefs extensive discussion sufficed to preserve issue missing from notice of appeal).

[146] *See Harvey v. Town of Merrillville,* 649 F.3d 526, 528 (7th Cir. 2011).

[147] *See* Fed. R. App. P. 3(c)(1)(C). *See also Bradley v. Work,* 154 F.3d 704 (7th Cir.1998).

[148] *See Jackson v. Lightsey,* 775 F.3d 170, 175–76 (4th Cir. 2014).

[149] *See Smith v. Barry,* 502 U.S. 244, 248, 112 S.Ct. 678, 681, 116 L.Ed.2d 678 (1992).

[150] *See Sayger v. Riceland Foods, Inc.,* 735 F.3d 1025, 1033 (8th Cir. 2013).

[151] *See Sines v. Wilner,* 609 F.3d 1070, 1074–75 (10th Cir. 2010).

[152] *See Smith v. Barry,* 502 U.S. 244, 248, 112 S.Ct. 678, 681, 116 L.Ed.2d 678 (1992).

[153] *See Smith v. Barry,* 502 U.S. 244, 248, 112 S.Ct. 678, 682, 116 L.Ed.2d 678 (1992).

[154] *See Harvey v. Town of Merrillville,* 649 F.3d 526, 528 (7th Cir. 2011).

[155] *See Taylor v. Johnson,* 257 F.3d 470, 474 (5th Cir.2001).

[156] *See Sines v. Wilner,* 609 F.3d 1070, 1074–75 (10th Cir. 2010).

enough,[157] and if the notice demanded by the rules is not satisfied either literally or functionally, the appeal will fail.[158]

Privacy Protection for Personal Data Identifiers

The vulnerability of electronically-accessible court files to privacy and security mischief prompted the adoption of special redaction and sealing privileges for certain civil cases.[159] In cases where these privileges applied at the district court level, the privileges will extend to the appeal as well.[160]

Notice Must Be *Filed* Timely

The notice of appeal must be actually *filed* with the clerk of court within the time allotted for taking an appeal.[161] Mailing the notice to the court or serving the notice on other parties is not sufficient. For *pro se* prisoners, however, a notice of appeal is deemed to be "filed" when the prisoner deposits the notice into the prison's internal mail system.[162]

Place of Filing

A notice of appeal is filed with the clerk of the district court from which the appeal is taken.[163] However, mistakenly filing the notice with the court of appeals will *not* defeat the appeal. If the notice is filed timely, albeit with the court of appeals, the appeals court clerk will note the date of filing and send the notice to the clerk of the district court.[164]

Electronic Filing

Each individual court of appeals may (but is not obligated to) permit the electronic filing of appeal papers.[165] In fact, the Appellate Rules now authorize a court of appeals to *require* electronic filing, so long as reasonable exceptions are allowed for litigants for whom such electronic filing would impose a hardship.[166]

Service Not Required

The appealing party need not serve the notice of appeal on all other parties; this service is made by the clerk of court.[167] The clerk's failure to serve the notice, however, does not defeat the appeal.[168]

- *Service Copies to the Court:* Although the appellant does not actually serve the notice of appeal on the other parties, the appellant is required to provide the clerk's office with sufficient copies of the notice for service.[169]

---

[157] *See Smith v. Barry,* 502 U.S. 244, 248, 112 S.Ct. 678, 682, 116 L.Ed.2d 678 (1992).

[158] *See Smith v. Barry,* 502 U.S. 244, 248, 112 S.Ct. 678, 682, 116 L.Ed.2d 678 (1992).

[159] *See* Rule 5.2. *See also supra* Authors' Commentary to Rule 5.2.

[160] *See* Fed. R. App. P. 25(a)(5).

[161] *See* Fed. R. App. P. 3(a)(1) & 4(a)(1).

[162] Fed. R. App. P. 4(c) (requiring accompanying notarized statement or declaration).

[163] Fed. R. App. P. 3(a).

[164] Fed. R. App. P. 4(d).

[165] *See* Fed. R. App. P. 25(a)(2)(D).

[166] *See* Fed. R. App. P. 25(a)(2)(D) and advisory committee note to 2006 amendments.

[167] Fed. R. App. P. 3(d)(1).

[168] Fed. R. App. P. 3(d)(3).

[169] Fed. R. App. P. 3(a)(1).

Joint Appeals

Joint appeals may be taken by two or more parties whose similar interests make such joinder practicable.[170] Each plaintiff, however, must file a timely notice of appeal. The fact that some similarly situated plaintiff's timely appealed is immaterial; the appeal of each plaintiff must be appropriately noticed to the court.[171]

Consolidated Appeals

Upon its own motion or by motion of a party, the court of appeals may consolidate the appeals of different parties.[172]

Fees

The appealing party must pay to the district court both the district court fee for appeal and the court of appeals' docket fee.[173]

ADDITIONAL RESEARCH REFERENCES

C.J.S. Federal Courts §§ 282 to 301(48) et seq.

West's Key Number Digest, Federal Courts ⊶521 to 956

§ 6.5 Step Four: Stays Pending Appeal

CORE CONCEPT

A party may seek a stay of judgment by filing such an application with the district court. In applications *not* involving stays of injunctions, receiverships, or accountings in patent infringement actions, a party may request a stay pending appeal by filing a supersedeas bond. Stay applications must be filed timely and, generally, initially in the district court.

APPLICATIONS

14-Day "Automatic" Stay

For a period of 14 days after a judgment is entered, the parties are barred from executing upon the judgment or pursuing further proceedings for its enforcement.[174] This automatic stay does *not* apply to judgments involving injunctions, judgments in receivership actions, or judgments or orders directing accountings in patent infringement actions.

Time to Apply for Stay

Applications for stay generally should be filed at the earliest possible opportunity. Because the automatic stay does not apply in certain injunction, receivership, and patent infringement circumstances, appellants in those cases do not enjoy the automatic 14-day stay period and the time for execution and enforcement will immediately arrive. Even in automatic stay cases, supersedeas bonds must first be approved by the court before any stay is effective.[175] Consequently, a delay in seeking a stay will expose the defeated party to execution and enforcement of the judgment.

---

[170] Fed. R. App. P. 3(b)(1)

[171] *See Wooden v. Board of Regents of Univ. Sys. of Ga.,* 247 F.3d 1262, 1273 (11th Cir.2001).

[172] Fed. R. App. P. 3(b)(2).

[173] Fed. R. App. P. 3(e).

[174] *See* Rule 62(a).

[175] *See* Rule 62(d).

Where to Apply for Stay

Ordinarily, stays pending appeal must be filed first with the district court.[176] Only in circumstances where applying in the district court is not practicable, or where the district court has denied the request or failed to grant all the relief requested, may a party request a stay in the court of appeals.[177]

Procedure for Stay Applications in the District Court

In cases that do not involve injunctions, receivers, or accountings in patent infringement cases, the posting of a supersedeas bond-after it has been approved by the court-will stay execution and enforcement of the judgment.[178]

In cases involving injunctions, the district court may, in its discretion, grant a stay of the injunction pending appeal.[179] To obtain such a stay, the moving party must generally make the traditional showing required for any injunction: strong likelihood of success on the merits, irreparable injury, no substantial harm to others, and no damage to the public interest.[180] The court may condition such a stay upon the posting of a bond or other appropriate security.[181]

Procedure for Stay Applications in the Court of Appeals

In applying for a stay in the court of appeals, the moving party must make several showings in the motion papers:[182]

a. *Proceedings Before Trial Court:* The motion must show why a stay application cannot be practicably directed to the district judge, or that the district judge has denied a stay or failed to grant all the relief requested (the district court's reasons must be set forth); *and*

b. *Reasons for Relief:* The motion must show the reasons for the relief requested, and set forth the facts relied upon in support of that showing. Relevant parts of the record shall be included and, where the facts relied upon are subject to dispute, supporting affidavits or other sworn statements shall also be included; *and*

c. *Reasonable Notice:* Reasonable notice of the motion shall be given to the non-moving party; *and*

d. *Disposition:* The motion will ordinarily be resolved by a panel or division of the court, unless exceptional circumstances justify submitting the motion to a single judge; *and*

e. *Bond or Security:* If the motion is granted, the court of appeals can condition the stay upon the filing in the district court of a bond or other appropriate security.[183]

§ 6.6   Step Five: The Appeal Process

CORE CONCEPT

Once the appeal is timely filed, the court of appeals will mail to each party a briefing notice that will schedule the filing of an Appellant's Brief, an Appellee's Brief, and an Appellant's Reply Brief.

---

[176] *See* Fed. R. App. P. 8(a)(1).

[177] *See* Fed. R. App. P. 8(a)(2).

[178] *See* Rule 62(d).

[179] *See* Rule 62(c).

[180] *See supra* Author's Commentary to Rule 62(c).

[181] *See* Rule 62(c).

[182] *See* Fed. R. App. P. 8(a)(2)(A) to (2)(D).

[183] *See* Fed. R. App. P. 8(a)(2)(E).

Thereafter, the court of appeals may schedule oral argument, the case will be submitted, and a written disposition on appeal will be filed.

APPLICATIONS

Effect of Appeal

Once the appeal is taken, jurisdiction over the case generally passes from the district court to the court of appeals.[184] The district court thereafter usually enjoys only the narrow power to preform ministerial functions, issues stays, and injunctions pending appeal, and, in certain instances, award counsel fees. However, under the new "indicative ruling" procedure, if the district court (after being divested of jurisdiction by an appeal) states that it would grant a trial-level motion or considers such a motion to raise a "substantial issue", the court of appeals may[185] remand back to the district judge for further proceedings.[186]

Compliance with Schedule and Procedures

Failure to comply with the court of appeals' schedule and procedures is ground for such action as the court of appeals deems appropriate, including denial of right to participate in oral argument or even dismissal of the appeal itself.[187]

Designation of the Record and Statement of Issues

The "record" on appeal consists of (1) the original papers and exhibits filed in the trial court, (2) the transcript, and (3) a certified copy of docket entries.[188] The "record" encompasses not just those exhibits admitted into evidence, but may include items presented for admission and denied by the district court.[189] Within 14 days after filing the notice of appeal, the appealing party must order those portions of the transcript that are necessary for the appeal. Unless the appellant orders the entire transcript, the appellant must, during this same 14-day period, file a statement of the issues for appeal and a list of the intended contents of the Appendix. The appellee may thereafter serve a counter-designation of additional portions of the transcript to be included.[190]

♦ **NOTE:** Some districts have promulgated Local Rules requiring the appellant to transcribe the entire proceedings.[191] Practitioners should be diligent in consulting their local rules for guidance on this point.

Briefing Procedures

Briefing procedures are generally set in the Federal Rules of Appellate Procedure,[192] but additional provisions vary by Local Rules among the different courts of appeals. The practitioner should always consult the Local Rules for these additional procedures.

---

[184] *See Griggs v. Provident Consumer Discount Co.*, 459 U.S. 56, 58, 103 S.Ct. 400, 402, 74 L.Ed.2d 225 (1982) (noting that notice of appeal is an event of jurisdictional significance, conferring jurisdiction on the Court of Appeals and divesting the district court of control over those aspects of the litigation involved in the appeal).

[185] *See In re Checking Account Overdraft Litig.*, 754 F.3d 1290, 1297 (11th Cir. 2014) (appeals court retains discretion, even if indicative ruling is issued).

[186] *See* Fed. R. App. P. 12.1 (effective Dec. 1, 2009); *see also* Rule 62.1 (effective Dec. 1 2009) (parallel district court provision).

[187] *See* Fed. R. App. P. 3(a)(2). *See also Lehman Bros. Holdings, Inc. v. Gateway Funding Diversified Mortg. Servs., L.P.*, 785 F.3d 96, 101 (3d Cir. 2015) (failure to compile record warranted forfeiture of first argument on appeal).

[188] *See Morton Int'l, Inc. v. A.E. Staley Mfg. Co.*, 343 F.3d 669, 682 (3d Cir.2003).

[189] *See Morton Int'l, Inc. v. A.E. Staley Mfg. Co.*, 343 F.3d 669, 682 (3d Cir.2003).

[190] *See* Fed. R. App. P. 10, 11, & 30.

[191] *See* E.D.Pa. Loc. R. 7.1(e) (requiring moving party to order "a transcript of the trial"); *Bongard v. Korn,* 1993 WL 39267 (E.D.Pa.1993) ("the whole transcript is to be ordered rather than a mere portion of the trial transcript as the particular party requesting post-trial relief unilaterally deems necessary").

[192] *See* Fed. R. App. P. 25, 28, 28,1, 30, 31, 32.

Briefing Privacy

Special redaction and sealing privileges may be applied to certain civil cases in the district court *(e.g.,* social security numbers, taxpayer identification numbers, financial account numbers, birth years, and full names of minors may be presented in an abbreviated form).[193] In cases where these privileges applied at the district court level, the privileges will extend to the appeal as well.[194]

Briefing Reminders

The "Do's" and "Don't's" of effective appellate briefing could fill volumes. Several common oversights, however, are worth special mention:

- *Corporate Disclosure Statement:* The Appellate Rules require each non-governmental corporate party in every civil case to file a statement identifying each of its parent corporations and all publicly-held companies that own 10% or more of the party's stock, and to supplement that statement whenever the necessary information changes.[195] The Rules require that this Statement be reprinted in front of the Table of Contents in that party's opening brief, even if the Statement has already been filed with the Court of Appeals.[196]

- *Footnote Restrictions:* Some courts of appeals have adopted local rules that severely limit the use of footnotes in appellate briefs.[197] Practitioners should be careful to consult their court of appeals' local rules to be certain their briefs comply with these restrictions.

- *Citing "Unpublished" Decisions:* For years, many courts of appeals forbade the citation of "unpublished", "nonprecedential", "not-for-publication", or similarly labeled decisions. Effective January 1, 2007, the Appellate Rules invalidated this local practice. Courts of appeals may no longer prohibit or discourage the citation of such decisions[198] (although litigants citing such opinions that are not publicly accessible through a commercial, legal research service, or court database must file and serve copies).[199] The amendment, however, is a narrow one; it does not restrict a court of appeals from *issuing* decisions bearing those labels, nor does it prescribe what effect the court must give (or not give) to such decisions.[200] The amendment merely addresses the question of citation.

Oral Argument

Oral argument is permitted generally unless the appeal is frivolous, the dispositive issues were authoritatively decided, or the decisional process would not be significantly aided by argument because the facts and legal arguments are adequately set forth in the briefs.[201] The length, scheduling, and location of argument is set by the particular court of appeals.

♦ **NOTE:** The parties cannot postpone oral argument by stipulation; postponement can occur only upon court order.

---

[193] *See* Rule 5.2. *See also supra* Authors' Commentary to Rule 5.2.

[194] *See* Fed. R. App. P. 25(a)(5).

[195] Fed. R. App. P. 26.1(a).

[196] Fed. R. App. P. 26.1(b).

[197] *See* 3d Cir. Loc. App. R. 32.2(a) ("Excessive footnotes in briefs are discouraged. Footnotes must be printed in the same size type utilized in the text.").

[198] Fed. R. App. P. 32.1(a). *See also id.* advisory committee note to 2006 amendment.

[199] Fed. R. App. P. 32.1(b). *See also id.* advisory committee note to 2006 amendment.

[200] Fed. R. App. P. 32.1. *See also id.* advisory committee note to 2006 amendment.

[201] Fed. R. App. P. 34(a)(2).

§ 6.7   Step Six: Appeals to the United States Supreme Court

CORE CONCEPT

A party enjoys an appeal as of right to the United States Supreme Court in only very few circumstances. In all other cases, the Supreme Court has the discretion whether to permit or refuse appeals to the Court. In practice, only a small handful of the many thousands of requests for Supreme Court review are granted each year.

APPLICATIONS

Appeals as of Right; Time to File

Whenever a specially convened three-judge district court panel declares any Act of Congress to be unconstitutional, a direct appeal may be taken to the Supreme Court.[202] Such appeals must be filed within 30 days of the date the district court's order is entered.[203] Congress may permit other direct appeals from the district courts, and such appeals must also be filed within 30 days of the district court's action.[204]

Discretionary Appeals; Time to File

The Supreme Court may, in its discretion, grant a party appellate review from other federal and State court rulings. Supreme Court review of federal appellate court decisions may be sought by petitioning for a Writ of Certiorari [205] or by seeking a certification from the court of appeals.[206] The Supreme Court may, in its discretion, also grant a Writ of Certiorari to review of decisions from the highest court of any State, but only where (a) a federal treaty or statute is drawn into question, (b) a State statute is drawn into question on federal grounds, or (c) any title, right, privilege, or immunity is specially set up or claimed under federal law.[207]

Petitions for Writs of Certiorari from federal court of appeals rulings must be filed with the Supreme Court within 90 days after the entry of the disputed judgment or decree.[208] Petitions for Writs from qualifying State court rulings must also be filed with the Supreme Court within 90 days after the entry of the disputed judgment or decree.[209]

Considerations in Granting Writs of Certiorari

The Supreme Court Rules provide a non-controlling, non-exhaustive list of the types of "compelling reasons" that may prompt the Supreme Court to grant a Writ of Certiorari:

(1)   A conflict among the federal Circuits on an "important matter";

(2)   A conflict between a federal court of appeals and the highest court of a State on an "important federal question";

(3)   A ruling by a court of appeals that "so far departed from the accepted and usual course of judicial proceedings" (or that sanctions such a departure by a lower court) that the Supreme Court's "supervisory power" is called for;

---

[202] *See* 28 U.S.C.A. § 1253.

[203] *See* 28 U.S.C.A. § 2102(a).

[204] *See* 28 U.S.C.A. § 2102(b).

[205] *See* 28 U.S.C.A. § 1254(1). In Latin, "certiorari" means "to be informed of"; such writs of certiorari are of common law origin, and were (and are) issued by a higher court to a lower court requiring that the certified record in a case be delivered for review. *See Black's Law Dictionary* 207 (5th ed. 1979).

[206] *See* 28 U.S.C.A. § 1254(2).

[207] *See* 28 U.S.C.A. § 1257.

[208] *See* 28 U.S.C.A. § 2101(c); U.S. S.Ct. R. 13(1), (3). *See also id.* (permitting Supreme Court, for good cause shown, to extend this 90-day period for another 60 days); U.S. S.Ct. R. 13(5) (same).

[209] *See* 28 U.S.C. § 2101(d); U.S. S.Ct. R. 13(1), (3).

(4) A ruling by the highest court of a State that conflicts with the decision of another State's highest court or a federal court of appeals on an "important federal question"; or

(5) A ruling by a State court or a federal court of appeals that decides "an important question of federal law that has not been, but should be," settled by the Supreme Court, or that decides "an important federal question in a way that conflicts with relevant decisions" of the Supreme Court.[210]

§ 6.8   *Federal Rules of Appellate Procedure* (Effective July 1, 1968; with amendments through December 1, 2016)

---

[210] *See* U.S. S.Ct. R. 10(a) to (c).

TITLE I.   APPLICABILITY OF RULES

RULE 1. SCOPE OF RULES; DEFINITION; TITLE

(a)   Scope of Rules.

(1)   These rules govern procedure in the United States courts of appeals.

(2)   When these rules provide for filing a motion or other document in the district court, the procedure must comply with the practice of the district court.

(b)   Definition. In these rules, "state" includes the District of Columbia and any United States commonwealth or territory.

(c)   Title. These rules are to be known as the Federal Rules of Appellate Procedure.

RULE 2. SUSPENSION OF RULES

On its own or a party's motion, a court of appeals may—to expedite its decision or for other good cause—suspend any provision of these rules in a particular case and order proceedings as it directs, except as otherwise provided in Rule 26(b).

TITLE II.   APPEAL FROM A JUDGMENT OR ORDER OF A DISTRICT COURT

RULE 3. APPEAL AS OF RIGHT—HOW TAKEN

(a)   Filing the Notice of Appeal.

(1)   An appeal permitted by law as of right from a district court to a court of appeals may be taken only by filing a notice of appeal with the district clerk within the time allowed by Rule 4. At the time of filing, the appellant must furnish the clerk with enough copies of the notice to enable the clerk to comply with Rule 3(d).

(2)   An appellant's failure to take any step other than the timely filing of a notice of appeal does not affect the validity of the appeal, but is ground only for the court of appeals to act as it considers appropriate, including dismissing the appeal.

(3)   An appeal from a judgment by a magistrate judge in a civil case is taken in the same way as an appeal from any other district court judgment.

(4)   An appeal by permission under 28 U.S.C. § 1292(b) or an appeal in a bankruptcy case may be taken only in the manner prescribed by Rules 5 and 6, respectively.

(b)   Joint or Consolidated Appeals.

(1)   When two or more parties are entitled to appeal from a district-court judgment or order, and their interests make joinder practicable, they may file a joint notice of appeal. They may then proceed on appeal as a single appellant.

(2)   When the parties have filed separate timely notices of appeal, the appeals may be joined or consolidated by the court of appeals.

(c)   Contents of the Notice of Appeal.

(1)   The notice of appeal must:

(A)   specify the party or parties taking the appeal by naming each one in the caption or body of the notice, but an attorney representing more than one party may describe those parties with such terms as "all plaintiffs," "the defendants," "the plaintiffs A, B, et al.," or "all defendants except X";

(B)   designate the judgment, order, or part thereof being appealed; and

(C)   name the court to which the appeal is taken.

(2)   A pro se notice of appeal is considered filed on behalf of the signer and the signer's spouse and minor children (if they are parties), unless the notice clearly indicates otherwise.

(3)   In a class action, whether or not the class has been certified, the notice of appeal is sufficient if it names one person qualified to bring the appeal as representative of the class.

(4)   An appeal must not be dismissed for informality of form or title of the notice of appeal, or for failure to name a party whose intent to appeal is otherwise clear from the notice.

(5)   Form 1 in the Appendix of Forms is a suggested form of a notice of appeal.

(d)   Serving the Notice of Appeal.

(1)   The district clerk must serve notice of the filing of a notice of appeal by mailing a copy to each party's counsel of record—excluding the appellant's—or, if a party is proceeding pro se, to the party's last known address. When a defendant in a criminal case appeals, the clerk must also serve a copy of the notice of appeal on the defendant, either by personal service or by mail addressed to the defendant. The clerk must promptly send a copy of the notice of appeal and of the docket entries—and any later docket entries—to the clerk of the court of appeals named in the notice. The district clerk must note, on each copy, the date when the notice of appeal was filed.

(2)   If an inmate confined in an institution files a notice of appeal in the manner provided by Rule 4(c), the district clerk must also note the date when the clerk docketed the notice.

(3)   The district clerk's failure to serve notice does not affect the validity of the appeal. The clerk must note on the docket the names of the parties to whom the clerk mails copies, with the date of mailing. Service is sufficient despite the death of a party or the party's counsel.

(e)   Payment of Fees. Upon filing a notice of appeal, the appellant must pay the district clerk all required fees. The district clerk receives the appellate docket fee on behalf of the court of appeals.

RULE 3.1.   APPEAL FROM A JUDGMENT OF A MAGISTRATE JUDGE IN A CIVIL CASE [ABROGATED]

RULE 4. APPEAL AS OF RIGHT—WHEN TAKEN

(a) Appeal in a Civil Case.

    (1) Time for Filing a Notice of Appeal.

        (A) In a civil case, except as provided in Rules 4(a)(1)(B), 4(a)(4), and 4(c), the notice of appeal required by Rule 3 must be filed with the district clerk within 30 days after entry of the judgment or order appealed from.

        (B) The notice of appeal may be filed by any party within 60 days after entry of the judgment or order appealed from if one of the parties is:

        (i)   the United States;

        (ii)   a United States agency;

        (iii) a United States officer or employee sued in an official capacity; or

        (iv) a current or former United States officer or employee sued in an individual capacity for an act or omission occurring in connection with duties performed on the United States' behalf—including all instances in which the United States represents that person when the judgment or order is entered or files the appeal for that person.

        (C) An appeal from an order granting or denying an application for a writ of error *coram nobis* is an appeal in a civil case for purposes of Rule 4(a).

    (2) Filing Before Entry of Judgment. A notice of appeal filed after the court announces a decision or order—but before the entry of the judgment or order—is treated as filed on the date of and after the entry.

    (3) Multiple Appeals. If one party timely files a notice of appeal, any other party may file a notice of appeal within 14 days after the date when the first notice was filed, or within the time otherwise prescribed by this Rule 4(a), whichever period ends later.

    (4) Effect of a Motion on a Notice of Appeal.

        (A) If a party files in the district court any of the following motions under the Federal Rules of Civil Procedure—and does so within the time allowed by those rules—the time to file an appeal runs for all parties from the entry of the order disposing of the last such remaining motion:

        (i)   for judgment under Rule 50(b);

        (ii)   to amend or make additional factual findings under Rule 52(b), whether or not granting the motion would alter the judgment;

        (iii) for attorney's fees under Rule 54 if the district court extends the time to appeal under Rule 58;

        (iv) to alter or amend the judgment under Rule 59;

        (v)   for a new trial under Rule 59; or

        (vi) for relief under Rule 60 if the motion is filed no later than 28 days after the judgment is entered.

        (B) (i)   If a party files a notice of appeal after the court announces or enters a judgment—but before it disposes of any motion listed in Rule 4(a)(4)(A) —the notice becomes effective to appeal a judgment or order, in whole or in part, when the order disposing of the last such remaining motion is entered.

(ii) A party intending to challenge an order disposing of any motion listed in Rule 4(a)(4)(A), or a judgment's alteration or amendment upon such a motion, must file a notice of appeal, or an amended notice of appeal-in compliance with Rule 3(c) —within the time prescribed by this Rule measured from the entry of the order disposing of the last such remaining motion.

(iii) No additional fee is required to file an amended notice.

(5) Motion for Extension of Time.

(A) The district court may extend the time to file a notice of appeal if:

(i) a party so moves no later than 30 days after the time prescribed by this Rule 4(a) expires; and

(ii) regardless of whether its motion is filed before or during the 30 days after the time prescribed by this Rule 4(a) expires, that party shows excusable neglect or good cause.

(B) A motion filed before the expiration of the time prescribed in Rule 4(a)(1) or (3) may be ex parte unless the court requires otherwise. If the motion is filed after the expiration of the prescribed time, notice must be given to the other parties in accordance with local rules.

(C) No extension under this Rule 4(a)(5) may exceed 30 days after the prescribed time or 14 days after the date when the order granting the motion is entered, whichever is later.

(6) Reopening the Time to File an Appeal. The district court may reopen the time to file an appeal for a period of 14 days after the date when its order to reopen is entered, but only if all the following conditions are satisfied:

(A) the court finds that the moving party did not receive notice under Federal Rule of Civil Procedure 77(d) of the entry of the judgment or order sought to be appealed within 21 days after entry;

(B) the motion is filed within 180 days after the judgment or order is entered or within 14 days after the moving party receives notice under Federal Rule of Civil Procedure 77(d) of the entry, whichever is earlier; and

(C) the court finds that no party would be prejudiced.

(7) Entry Defined.

(A) A judgment or order is entered for purposes of this Rule 4(a):

(i) if Federal Rule of Civil Procedure 58(a) does not require a separate document, when the judgment or order is entered in the civil docket under Federal Rules of Civil Procedure 79(a); or

(ii) if Federal Rule of Civil Procedure 58(a) requires a separate document, when the judgment or order is entered in the civil docket under Federal Rule of Civil Procedure 79(a) and when the earlier of these events occurs:

• the judgment or order is set forth on a separate document, or

• 150 days have run from entry of the judgment or order in the civil docket under Federal Rule of Civil Procedure 79(a).

(B) A failure to set forth a judgment or order on a separate document when required by Federal Rule of Civil Procedure 58(a) does not affect the validity of an appeal from that judgment or order.

(b)   Appeal in a Criminal Case.

    (1)   Time for Filing a Notice of Appeal.

        (A)   In a criminal case, a defendant's notice of appeal must be filed in the district court within 14 days after the later of:

           (i)   the entry of either the judgment or the order being appealed; or

           (ii)   the filing of the government's notice of appeal.

        (B)   When the government is entitled to appeal, its notice of appeal must be filed in the district court within 30 days after the later of:

           (i)   the entry of the judgment or order being appealed; or

           (ii)   the filing of a notice of appeal by any defendant.

    (2)   Filing Before Entry of Judgment. A notice of appeal filed after the court announces a decision, sentence, or order—but before the entry of the judgment or order—is treated as filed on the date of and after the entry.

    (3)   Effect of a Motion on a Notice of Appeal.

        (A)   If a defendant timely makes any of the following motions under the Federal Rules of Criminal Procedure, the notice of appeal from a judgment of conviction must be filed within 14 days after the entry of the order disposing of the last such remaining motion, or within 14 days after the entry of the judgment of conviction, whichever period ends later. This provision applies to a timely motion:

           (i)   for judgment of acquittal under Rule 29;

           (ii)   for a new trial under Rule 33, but if based on newly discovered evidence, only if the motion is made no later than 14 days after the entry of the judgment; or

           (iii)   for arrest of judgment under Rule 34.

        (B)   A notice of appeal filed after the court announces a decision, sentence, or order—but before it disposes of any of the motions referred to in Rule 4(b)(3)(A)—becomes effective upon the later of the following:

           (i)   the entry of the order disposing of the last such remaining motion; or

           (ii)   the entry of the judgment of conviction.

        (C)   A valid notice of appeal is effective—without amendment—to appeal from an order disposing of any of the motions referred to in Rule 4(b)(3)(A).

    (4)   Motion for Extension of Time. Upon a finding of excusable neglect or good cause, the district court may—before or after the time has expired, with or without motion and notice—extend the time to file a notice of appeal for a period not to exceed 30 days from the expiration of the time otherwise prescribed by this Rule 4(b).

    (5)   Jurisdiction. The filing of a notice of appeal under this Rule 4(b) does not divest a district court of jurisdiction to correct a sentence under Federal Rule of Criminal Procedure 35(c), nor does the filing of a motion under 35(c) affect the validity of a notice of appeal filed before entry of the order disposing of the motion. The filing of a motion under Federal Rule of Criminal Procedure 35(a) does not suspend the time for filing a notice of appeal from a judgment of conviction.

    (6)   Entry Defined. A judgment or order is entered for purposes of this Rule 4(b) when it is entered on the criminal docket.

(c) Appeal by an Inmate Confined in an Institution.

(1)   If an institution has a system designed for legal mail, an inmate confined there must use that system to receive the benefit of this Rule 4(c)(1). If an inmate files a notice of appeal in either a civil or a criminal case, the notice is timely if it is deposited in the institution's internal mail system on or before the last day for filing and:

> (A)   it is accompanied by:
>
>> (i)   a declaration in compliance with 28 U.S.C. § 1746—or a notarized statement—setting out the date of deposit and stating that first-class postage is being prepaid; or
>>
>> (ii)   evidence (such as a postmark or date stamp) showing that the notice was so deposited and that postage was prepaid; or
>
> (B)   the court of appeals exercises its discretion to permit the later filing of a declaration or notarized statement that satisfies Rule 4(c)(1)(A)(i).

(d)   Mistaken Filing in the Court of Appeals. If a notice of appeal in either a civil or a criminal case is mistakenly filed in the court of appeals, the clerk of that court must note on the notice the date when it was received and send it to the district clerk. The notice is then considered filed in the district court on the date so noted.

RULE 5. APPEAL BY PERMISSION

(a)   Petition for Permission to Appeal.

(1)   To request permission to appeal when an appeal is within the court of appeals' discretion, a party must file a petition for permission to appeal. The petition must be filed with the circuit clerk with proof of service on all other parties to the district-court action.

(2)   The petition must be filed within the time specified by the statute or rule authorizing the appeal or, if no such time is specified, within the time provided by Rule 4(a) for filing a notice of appeal.

(3)   If a party cannot petition for appeal unless the district court first enters an order granting permission to do so or stating that the necessary conditions are met, the district court may amend its order, either on its own or in response to a party's motion, to include the required permission or statement. In that event, the time to petition runs from entry of the amended order.

(b)   Contents of the Petition; Answer or Cross-Petition; Oral Argument.

(1)   The petition must include the following:

> (A)   the facts necessary to understand the question presented;
>
> (B)   the question itself;
>
> (C)   the relief sought;
>
> (D)   the reasons why the appeal should be allowed and is authorized by a statute or rule; and
>
> (E)   an attached copy of:
>
>> (i)   the order, decree, or judgment complained of and any related opinion or memorandum, and
>>
>> (ii)   any order stating the district court's permission to appeal or finding that the necessary conditions are met.

(2)   A party may file an answer in opposition or a cross-petition within 10 days after the petition is served.

(3)   The petition and answer will be submitted without oral argument unless the court of appeals orders otherwise.

(c) **Form of Papers; Number of Copies; Length Limits.** All papers must conform to Rule 32(c)(2). An original and 3 copies must be filed unless the court requires a different number by local rule or by order in a particular case. Except by the court's permission, and excluding the accompanying documents required by Rule 5(b)(1)(E):

(1)   a paper produced using a computer must not exceed 5,200 words; and

(2)   a handwritten or typewritten paper must not exceed 20 pages.

(d) **Grant of Permission; Fees; Cost Bond; Filing the Record.**

(1)   Within 14 days after the entry of the order granting permission to appeal, the appellant must:

     (A)   pay the district clerk all required fees; and

     (B)   file a cost bond if required under Rule 7.

(2)   A notice of appeal need not be filed. The date when the order granting permission to appeal is entered serves as the date of the notice of appeal for calculating time under these rules.

(3)   The district clerk must notify the circuit clerk once the petitioner has paid the fees. Upon receiving this notice, the circuit clerk must enter the appeal on the docket. The record must be forwarded and filed in accordance with Rules 11 and 12(c).

RULE 5.1.   APPEAL BY LEAVE UNDER 28 U.S.C. § 636(c)(5) [ABROGATED]

RULE 6. APPEAL IN A BANKRUPTCY CASE

(a) **Appeal From a Judgment, Order, or Decree of a District Court Exercising Original Jurisdiction in a Bankruptcy Case.** An appeal to a court of appeals from a final judgment, order, or decree of a district court exercising jurisdiction under 28 U.S.C. § 1334 is taken as any other civil appeal under these rules.

(b) **Appeal From a Judgment, Order, or Decree of a District Court or Bankruptcy Appellate Panel Exercising Appellate Jurisdiction in a Bankruptcy Case.**

(1) **Applicability of Other Rules.** These rules apply to an appeal to a court of appeals under 28 U.S.C. § 158(d)(1) from a final judgment, order, or decree of a district court or bankruptcy appellate panel exercising appellate jurisdiction under 28 U.S.C. § 158(a) or (b), but with these qualifications:

     (A)   Rules 4(a)(4), 4(b), 9, 10, 11, 12(c), 13–20, 22–23, and 24(b) do not apply;

     (B)   the reference in Rule 3(c) to "Form 1 in the Appendix of Forms" must be read as a reference to Form 5;

     (C)   when the appeal is from a bankruptcy appellate panel, "district court," as used in any applicable rule, means "appellate panel"; and

     (D)   in Rule 12.1, "district court" includes a bankruptcy court or bankruptcy appellate panel.

(2) **Additional Rules.** In addition to the rules made applicable by Rule 6(b)(1), the following rules apply:

     (A) **Motion for Rehearing.**

         (i)   If a timely motion for rehearing under Bankruptcy Rule 8022 is filed, the time to appeal for all parties runs from the entry of the order disposing of the motion. A notice of appeal filed after the district court or bankruptcy appellate panel announces or enters a judgment, order, or decree—but before disposition of the motion for rehearing—becomes effective when the order disposing of the motion for rehearing is entered.

(ii)   If a party intends to challenge the order disposing of the motion—or the alteration or amendment of a judgment, order, or decree upon the motion—then the party, in compliance with Rules 3(c) and 6(b)(1)(B), must file a notice of appeal or amended notice of appeal. The notice or amended notice must be filed within the time prescribed by Rule 4—excluding Rules 4(a)(4) and 4(b)—measured from the entry of the order disposing of the motion.

(iii)   No additional fee is required to file an amended notice.

(B)   **The Record on Appeal.**

(i)   Within 14 days after filing the notice of appeal, the appellant must file with the clerk possessing the record assembled in accordance with Bankruptcy Rule 8009—and serve on the appellee—a statement of the issues to be presented on appeal and a designation of the record to be certified and made available to the circuit clerk.

(ii)   An appellee who believes that other parts of the record are necessary must, within 14 days after being served with the appellant's designation, file with the clerk and serve on the appellant a designation of additional parts to be included.

(iii)   The record on appeal consists of:

- the redesignated record as provided above;
- the proceedings in the district court or bankruptcy appellate panel; and
- a certified copy of the docket entries prepared by the clerk under Rule 3(d).

(C)   **Making the Record Available.**

(i)   When the record is complete, the district clerk or bankruptcy-appellate-panel clerk must number the documents constituting the record and promptly make it available to the circuit clerk. If the clerk makes the record available in paper form, the clerk will not send documents of unusual bulk or weight, physical exhibits other than documents, or other parts of the record designated for omission by local rule of the court of appeals, unless directed to do so by a party or the circuit clerk. If unusually bulky or heavy exhibits are to be made available in paper form, a party must arrange with the clerks in advance for their transportation and receipt.

(ii)   All parties must do whatever else is necessary to enable the clerk to assemble the record and make it available. When the record is made available in paper form, the court of appeals may provide by rule or order that a certified copy of the docket entries be made available in place of the redesignated record. But any party may request at any time during the pendency of the appeal that the redesignated record be made available.

(D)   **Filing the Record.** When the district clerk or bankruptcy-appellate-panel clerk has made the record available, the circuit clerk must note that fact on the docket. The date noted on the docket serves as the filing date of the record. The circuit clerk must immediately notify all parties of the filing date.

(c)   **Direct Review by Permission Under 28 U.S.C. § 158(d)(2).**

(1)   **Applicability of Other Rules.** These rules apply to a direct appeal by permission under 28 U.S.C. § 158(d)(2), but with these qualifications:

(A)   Rules 3–4, 5(a)(3), 6(a), 6(b), 8(a), 8(c), 9–12, 13–20, 22–23, and 24(b) do not apply;

(B)   as used in any applicable rule, "district court" or "district clerk" includes—to the extent appropriate—a bankruptcy court or bankruptcy appellate panel or its clerk; and

(C)   the reference to "Rules 11 and 12(c)" in Rule 5(d)(3) must be read as a reference to Rules 6(c)(2)(B) and (C).

(2) **Additional Rules.** In addition, the following rules apply:

    (A) **The Record on Appeal.** Bankruptcy Rule 8009 governs the record on appeal.

    (B) **Making the Record Available.** Bankruptcy Rule 8010 governs completing the record and making it available.

    (C) **Stays Pending Appeal.** Bankruptcy Rule 8007 applies to stays pending appeal.

    (D) **Duties of the Circuit Clerk.** When the bankruptcy clerk has made the record available, the circuit clerk must note that fact on the docket. The date noted on the docket serves as the filing date of the record. The circuit clerk must immediately notify all parties of the filing date.

    (E) **Filing a Representation Statement.** Unless the court of appeals designates another time, within 14 days after entry of the order granting permission to appeal, the attorney who sought permission must file a statement with the circuit clerk naming the parties that the attorney represents on appeal.

RULE 7. BOND FOR COSTS ON APPEAL IN A CIVIL CASE

In a civil case, the district court may require an appellant to file a bond or provide other security in any form and amount necessary to ensure payment of costs on appeal. Rule 8(b) applies to a surety on a bond given under this rule.

RULE 8. STAY OR INJUNCTION PENDING APPEAL

(a) Motion for Stay.

(1) Initial Motion in the District Court. A party must ordinarily move first in the district court for the following relief:

    (A) a stay of the judgment or order of a district court pending appeal;

    (B) approval of a supersedeas bond; or

    (C) an order suspending, modifying, restoring, or granting an injunction while an appeal is pending.

(2) Motion in the Court of Appeals; Conditions on Relief. A motion for the relief mentioned in Rule 8(a)(1) may be made to the court of appeals or to one of its judges.

    (A) The motion must:

        (i) show that moving first in the district court would be impracticable; or

        (ii) state that, a motion having been made, the district court denied the motion or failed to afford the relief requested and state any reasons given by the district court for its action.

    (B) The motion must also include:

        (i) the reasons for granting the relief requested and the facts relied on;

        (ii) originals or copies of affidavits or other sworn statements supporting facts subject to dispute; and

        (iii) relevant parts of the record.

    (C) The moving party must give reasonable notice of the motion to all parties.

    (D) A motion under this Rule 8(a)(2) must be filed with the circuit clerk and normally will be considered by a panel of the court. But in an exceptional case in which time requirements make that procedure impracticable, the motion may be made to and considered by a single judge.

(E)   The court may condition relief on a party's filing a bond or other appropriate security in the district court.

(b)   Proceeding Against a Surety. If a party gives security in the form of a bond or stipulation or other undertaking with one or more sureties, each surety submits to the jurisdiction of the district court and irrevocably appoints the district clerk as the surety's agent on whom any papers affecting the surety's liability on the bond or undertaking may be served. On motion, a surety's liability may be enforced in the district court without the necessity of an independent action. The motion and any notice that the district court prescribes may be served on the district clerk, who must promptly mail a copy to each surety whose address is known.

(c)   Stay in a Criminal Case. Rule 38 of the Federal Rules of Criminal Procedure governs a stay in a criminal case.

RULE 9. RELEASE IN A CRIMINAL CASE

(a)   Release Before Judgment of Conviction.

(1)   The district court must state in writing, or orally on the record, the reasons for an order regarding the release or detention of a defendant in a criminal case. A party appealing from the order must file with the court of appeals a copy of the district court's order and the court's statement of reasons as soon as practicable after filing the notice of appeal. An appellant who questions the factual basis for the district court's order must file a transcript of the release proceedings or an explanation of why a transcript was not obtained.

(2)   After reasonable notice to the appellee, the court of appeals must promptly determine the appeal on the basis of the papers, affidavits, and parts of the record that the parties present or the court requires. Unless the court so orders, briefs need not be filed.

(3)   The court of appeals or one of its judges may order the defendant's release pending the disposition of the appeal.

(b)   Release After Judgment of Conviction. A party entitled to do so may obtain review of a district-court order regarding release after a judgment of conviction by filing a notice of appeal from that order in the district court, or by filing a motion in the court of appeals if the party has already filed a notice of appeal from the judgment of conviction. Both the order and the review are subject to Rule 9(a). The papers filed by the party seeking review must include a copy of the judgment of conviction.

(c)   Criteria for Release. The court must make its decision regarding release in accordance with the applicable provisions of 18 U.S.C. §§ 3142, 3143, and 3145(c).

RULE 10. THE RECORD ON APPEAL

(a)   Composition of the Record on Appeal. The following items constitute the record on appeal:

(1)   the original papers and exhibits filed in the district court;

(2)   the transcript of proceedings, if any; and

(3)   a certified copy of the docket entries prepared by the district clerk.

(b)   The Transcript of Proceedings.

(1)   **Appellant's Duty to Order.** Within 14 days after filing the notice of appeal or entry of an order disposing of the last timely remaining motion of a type specified in Rule 4(a)(4)(A), whichever is later, the appellant must do either of the following:

(A)   order from the reporter a transcript of such parts of the proceedings not already on file as the appellant considers necessary, subject to a local rule of the court of appeals and with the following qualifications:

(i)   the order must be in writing;

(ii)   if the cost of the transcript is to be paid by the United States under the Criminal Justice Act, the order must so state; and

(iii) the appellant must, within the same period, file a copy of the order with the district clerk; or

(B)   file a certificate stating that no transcript will be ordered.

(2) Unsupported Finding or Conclusion. If the appellant intends to urge on appeal that a finding or conclusion is unsupported by the evidence or is contrary to the evidence, the appellant must include in the record a transcript of all evidence relevant to that finding or conclusion.

(3) Partial Transcript. Unless the entire transcript is ordered:

(A)   the appellant must—within the 14 days provided in Rule 10(b)(l)—file a statement of the issues that the appellant intends to present on the appeal and must serve on the appellee a copy of both the order or certificate and the statement;

(B)   if the appellee considers it necessary to have a transcript of other parts of the proceedings, the appellee must, within 14 days after the service of the order or certificate and the statement of the issues, file and serve on the appellant a designation of additional parts to be ordered; and

(C)   unless within 14 days after service of that designation the appellant has ordered all such parts, and has so notified the appellee, the appellee may within the following 14 days either order the parts or move in the district court for an order requiring the appellant to do so.

(4) Payment. At the time of ordering, a party must make satisfactory arrangements with the reporter for paying the cost of the transcript.

(c) Statement of the Evidence When the Proceedings Were Not Recorded or When a Transcript Is Unavailable. If the transcript of a hearing or trial is unavailable, the appellant may prepare a statement of the evidence or proceedings from the best available means, including the appellant's recollection. The statement must be served on the appellee, who may serve objections or proposed amendments within 14 days after being served. The statement and any objections or proposed amendments must then be submitted to the district court for settlement and approval. As settled and approved, the statement must be included by the district clerk in the record on appeal.

(d) Agreed Statement as the Record on Appeal. In place of the record on appeal as defined in Rule 10(a), the parties may prepare, sign, and submit to the district court a statement of the case showing how the issues presented by the appeal arose and were decided in the district court. The statement must set forth only those facts averred and proved or sought to be proved that are essential to the court's resolution of the issues. If the statement is truthful, it-together with any additions that the district court may consider necessary to a full presentation of the issues on appeal-must be approved by the district court and must then be certified to the court of appeals as the record on appeal. The district clerk must then send it to the circuit clerk within the time provided by Rule 11. A copy of the agreed statement may be filed in place of the appendix required by Rule 30.

(e) Correction or Modification of the Record.

(1)   If any difference arises about whether the record truly discloses what occurred in the district court, the difference must be submitted to and settled by that court and the record conformed accordingly.

(2)   If anything material to either party is omitted from or misstated in the record by error or accident, the omission or misstatement may be corrected and a supplemental record may be certified and forwarded:

(A)   on stipulation of the parties;

(B)   by the district court before or after the record has been forwarded; or

(C)   by the court of appeals.

(3)   All other questions as to the form and content of the record must be presented to the court of appeals.

RULE 11.   FORWARDING THE RECORD

(a)   Appellant's Duty. An appellant filing a notice of appeal must comply with Rule 10(b) and must do whatever else is necessary to enable the clerk to assemble and forward the record. If there are multiple appeals from a judgment or order, the clerk must forward a single record.

(b)   Duties of Reporter and District Clerk.

(1)   Reporter's Duty to Prepare and File a Transcript. The reporter must prepare and file a transcript as follows:

(A)   Upon receiving an order for a transcript, the reporter must enter at the foot of the order the date of its receipt and the expected completion date and send a copy, so endorsed, to the circuit clerk.

(B)   If the transcript cannot be completed within 30 days of the reporter's receipt of the order, the reporter may request the circuit clerk to grant additional time to complete it. The clerk must note on the docket the action taken and notify the parties.

(C)   When a transcript is complete, the reporter must file it with the district clerk and notify the circuit clerk of the filing.

(D)   If the reporter fails to file the transcript on time, the circuit clerk must notify the district judge and do whatever else the court of appeals directs.

(2)   District Clerk's Duty to Forward. When the record is complete, the district clerk must number the documents constituting the record and send them promptly to the circuit clerk together with a list of the documents correspondingly numbered and reasonably identified. Unless directed to do so by a party or the circuit clerk, the district clerk will not send to the court of appeals documents of unusual bulk or weight, physical exhibits other than documents, or other parts of the record designated for omission by local rule of the court of appeals. If the exhibits are unusually bulky or heavy, a party must arrange with the clerks in advance for their transportation and receipt.

(c)   Retaining the Record Temporarily in the District Court for Use in Preparing the Appeal. The parties may stipulate, or the district court on motion may order, that the district clerk retain the record temporarily for the parties to use in preparing the papers on appeal. In that event the district clerk must certify to the circuit clerk that the record on appeal is complete. Upon receipt of the appellee's brief, or earlier if the court orders or the parties agree, the appellant must request the district clerk to forward the record.

(d)   [Abrogated.]

(e)   Retaining the Record by Court Order.

(1)   The court of appeals may, by order or local rule, provide that a certified copy of the docket entries be forwarded instead of the entire record. But a party may at any time during the appeal request that designated parts of the record be forwarded.

(2)   The district court may order the record or some part of it retained if the court needs it while the appeal is pending, subject, however, to call by the court of appeals.

(3)   If part or all of the record is ordered retained, the district clerk must send to the court of appeals a copy of the order and the docket entries together with the parts of the original record allowed by the district court and copies of any parts of the record designated by the parties.

(f)   Retaining Parts of the Record in the District Court by Stipulation of the Parties. The parties may agree by written stipulation filed in the district court that designated parts of the record be retained in the district court subject to call by the court of appeals or request by a party. The parts of the record so designated remain a part of the record on appeal.

(g)   Record for a Preliminary Motion in the Court of Appeals. If, before the record is forwarded, a party makes any of the following motions in the court of appeals:

- for dismissal;

- for release;

- for a stay pending appeal;

- for additional security on the bond on appeal or on a supersedeas bond; or

- for any other intermediate order—

the district clerk must send the court of appeals any parts of the record designated by any party.

RULE 12.   DOCKETING THE APPEAL; FILING A REPRESENTATION STATEMENT; FILING THE RECORD

(a)   Docketing the Appeal. Upon receiving the copy of the notice of appeal and the docket entries from the district clerk under Rule 3(d), the circuit clerk must docket the appeal under the title of the district-court action and must identify the appellant, adding the appellant's name if necessary.

(b)   Filing a Representation Statement. Unless the court of appeals designates another time, the attorney who filed the notice of appeal must, within 14 days after filing the notice, file a statement with the circuit clerk naming the parties that the attorney represents on appeal.

(c)   Filing the Record, Partial Record, or Certificate. Upon receiving the record, partial record, or district clerk's certificate as provided in Rule 11, the circuit clerk must file it and immediately notify all parties of the filing date.

RULE 12.1.   REMAND AFTER AN INDICATIVE RULING BY THE DISTRICT COURT ON A MOTION FOR RELIEF THAT IS BARRED BY A PENDING APPEAL

(a)   Notice to the Court of Appeals. If a timely motion is made in the district court for relief that it lacks authority to grant because of an appeal that has been docketed and is pending, the movant must promptly notify the circuit clerk if the district court states either that it would grant the motion or that the motion raises a substantial issue.

(b)   Remand After an Indicative Ruling. If the district court states that it would grant the motion or that the motion raises a substantial issue, the court of appeals may remand for further proceedings but retains jurisdiction unless it expressly dismisses the appeal. If the court of appeals remands but retains jurisdiction, the parties must promptly notify the circuit clerk when the district court has decided the motion on remand.

TITLE III. APPEALS FROM THE UNITED STATES TAX COURT

RULE 13.   APPEALS FROM THE TAX COURT

(a) Appeal as of Right.

(1) How Obtained; Time for Filing a Notice of Appeal.

(A)   An appeal as of right from the United States Tax Court is commenced by filing a notice of appeal with the Tax Court clerk within 90 days after the entry of the Tax Court's decision. At the time of filing, the appellant must furnish the clerk with enough copies of the notice to enable the clerk to comply with Rule 3(d). If one party files a timely notice of appeal, any other party may file a notice of appeal within 120 days after the Tax Court's decision is entered.

(B)   If, under Tax Court rules, a party makes a timely motion to vacate or revise the Tax Court's decision, the time to file a notice of appeal runs from the entry of the order disposing of the motion or from the entry of a new decision, whichever is later.

(2) Notice of Appeal; How Filed. The notice of appeal may be filed either at the Tax Court clerk's office in the District of Columbia or by mail addressed to the clerk. If sent by mail the notice is considered filed on the postmark date, subject to § 7502 of the Internal Revenue Code, as amended, and the applicable regulations.

(3) Contents of the Notice of Appeal; Service; Effect of Filing and Service. Rule 3 prescribes the contents of a notice of appeal, the manner of service, and the effect of its filing and service. Form 2 in the Appendix of Forms is a suggested form of a notice of appeal.

(4) The Record on Appeal; Forwarding; Filing.

(A)   Except as otherwise provided under Tax Court rules for the transcript of proceedings, the appeal is governed by the parts of Rules 10, 11, and 12 regarding the record on appeal from a district court, the time and manner of forwarding and filing, and the docketing in the court of appeals.

(B)   If an appeal is taken to more than one court of appeals, the original record must be sent to the court named in the first notice of appeal filed. In an appeal to any other court of appeals, the appellant must apply to that other court to make provision for the record.

(b) Appeal by Permission. An appeal by permission is governed by Rule 5.

RULE 14.   APPLICABILITY OF OTHER RULES TO THE REVIEW OF A TAX COURT DECISION

All provisions of these rules, except Rules 4, 6–9, 15–20, and 22–23, apply to appeals from the Tax Court. References in any applicable rule (other than Rule 24(a)) to the district court and district clerk are to be read as referring to the Tax Court and its clerk.

TITLE IV. REVIEW OR ENFORCEMENT OF AN ORDER OF AN ADMINISTRATIVE AGENCY, BOARD, COMMISSION, OR OFFICER

RULE 15.   REVIEW OR ENFORCEMENT OF AN AGENCY ORDER— HOW OBTAINED; INTERVENTION

(a) Petition for Review; Joint Petition.

(1)   Review of an agency order is commenced by filing, within the time prescribed by law, a petition for review with the clerk of a court of appeals authorized to review the agency order. If

their interests make joinder practicable, two or more persons may join in a petition to the same court to review the same order.

(2)   The petition must:

(A)   name each party seeking review either in the caption or the body of the petition—using such terms as "et al.," "petitioners," or "respondents" does not effectively name the parties;

(B)   name the agency as a respondent (even though not named in the petition, the United States is a respondent if required by statute); and

(C)   specify the order or part thereof to be reviewed.

(3)   Form 3 in the Appendix of Forms is a suggested form of a petition for review.

(4)   In this rule "agency" includes an agency, board, commission, or officer; "petition for review" includes a petition to enjoin, suspend, modify, or otherwise review, or a notice of appeal, whichever form is indicated by the applicable statute.

(b)   Application or Cross-Application to Enforce an Order; Answer; Default.

(1)   An application to enforce an agency order must be filed with the clerk of a court of appeals authorized to enforce the order. If a petition is filed to review an agency order that the court may enforce, a party opposing the petition may file a cross-application for enforcement.

(2)   Within 21 days after the application for enforcement is filed, the respondent must serve on the applicant an answer to the application and file it with the clerk. If the respondent fails to answer in time, the court will enter judgment for the relief requested.

(3)   The application must contain a concise statement of the proceedings in which the order was entered, the facts upon which venue is based, and the relief requested.

(c)   Service of the Petition or Application. The circuit clerk must serve a copy of the petition for review, or an application or cross-application to enforce an agency order, on each respondent as prescribed by Rule 3(d), unless a different manner of service is prescribed by statute. At the time of filing, the petitioner must:

(1)   serve, or have served, a copy on each party admitted to participate in the agency proceedings, except for the respondents;

(2)   file with the clerk a list of those so served; and

(3)   give the clerk enough copies of the petition or application to serve each respondent.

(d)   Intervention. Unless a statute provides another method, a person who wants to intervene in a proceeding under this rule must file a motion for leave to intervene with the circuit clerk and serve a copy on all parties. The motion—or other notice of intervention authorized by statute-must be filed within 30 days after the petition for review is filed and must contain a concise statement of the interest of the moving party and the grounds for intervention.

(e)   Payment of Fees. When filing any separate or joint petition for review in a court of appeals, the petitioner must pay the circuit clerk all required fees.

RULE 15.1.   BRIEFS AND ORAL ARGUMENT IN A NATIONAL LABOR RELATIONS BOARD PROCEEDING

In either an enforcement or a review proceeding, a party adverse to the National Labor Relations Board proceeds first on briefing and at oral argument, unless the court orders otherwise.

RULE 16. THE RECORD ON REVIEW OR ENFORCEMENT

(a) Composition of the Record. The record on review or enforcement of an agency order consists of:

    (1)   the order involved;

    (2)   any findings or report on which it is based; and

    (3)   the pleadings, evidence, and other parts of the proceedings before the agency.

(b) Omissions From or Misstatements in the Record. The parties may at any time, by stipulation, supply any omission from the record or correct a misstatement, or the court may so direct. If necessary, the court may direct that a supplemental record be prepared and filed.

RULE 17. FILING THE RECORD

(a) Agency to File; Time for Filing; Notice of Filing. The agency must file the record with the circuit clerk within 40 days after being served with a petition for review, unless the statute authorizing review provides otherwise, or within 40 days after it files an application for enforcement unless the respondent fails to answer or the court orders otherwise. The court may shorten or extend the time to file the record. The clerk must notify all parties of the date when the record is filed.

(b) Filing—What Constitutes.

    (1)   The agency must file:

        (A)   the original or a certified copy of the entire record or parts designated by the parties; or

        (B)   a certified list adequately describing all documents, transcripts of testimony, exhibits, and other material constituting the record, or describing those parts designated by the parties.

    (2)   The parties may stipulate in writing that no record or certified list be filed. The date when the stipulation is filed with the circuit clerk is treated as the date when the record is filed.

    (3)   The agency must retain any portion of the record not filed with the clerk. All parts of the record retained by the agency are a part of the record on review for all purposes and, if the court or a party so requests, must be sent to the court regardless of any prior stipulation.

RULE 18. STAY PENDING REVIEW

(a) Motion for a Stay.

    (1) Initial Motion Before the Agency. A petitioner must ordinarily move first before the agency for a stay pending review of its decision or order.

    (2) Motion in the Court of Appeals. A motion for a stay may be made to the court of appeals or one of its judges.

        (A)   The motion must:

            (i)   show that moving first before the agency would be impracticable; or

            (ii)   state that, a motion having been made, the agency denied the motion or failed to afford the relief requested and state any reasons given by the agency for its action.

        (B)   The motion must also include:

            (i)   the reasons for granting the relief requested and the facts relied on;

            (ii)   originals or copies of affidavits or other sworn statements supporting facts subject to dispute; and

            (iii)   relevant parts of the record.

(C)   The moving party must give reasonable notice of the motion to all parties.

(D)   The motion must be filed with the circuit clerk and normally will be considered by a panel of the court. But in an exceptional case in which time requirements make that procedure impracticable, the motion may be made to and considered by a single judge.

(b)   Bond. The court may condition relief on the filing of a bond or other appropriate security.

RULE 19.   SETTLEMENT OF A JUDGMENT ENFORCING AN AGENCY ORDER IN PART

When the court files an opinion directing entry of judgment enforcing the agency's order in part, the agency must within 14 days file with the clerk and serve on each other party a proposed judgment conforming to the opinion. A party who disagrees with the agency's proposed judgment must within 10 days file with the clerk and serve the agency with a proposed judgment that the party believes conforms to the opinion. The court will settle the judgment and direct entry without further hearing or argument.

RULE 20.   APPLICABILITY OF RULES TO THE REVIEW OR ENFORCEMENT OF AN AGENCY ORDER

All provisions of these rules, except Rules 3–14 and 22–23, apply to the review or enforcement of an agency order. In these rules, "appellant" includes a petitioner or applicant, and "appellee" includes a respondent.

TITLE V.   EXTRAORDINARY WRITS

RULE 21.   WRITS OF MANDAMUS AND PROHIBITION, AND OTHER EXTRAORDINARY WRITS

(a)   Mandamus or Prohibition to a Court: Petition, Filing, Service, and Docketing.

(1)   A party petitioning for a writ of mandamus or prohibition directed to a court must file a petition with the circuit clerk with proof of service on all parties to the proceeding in the trial court. The party must also provide a copy to the trial-court judge. All parties to the proceeding in the trial court other than the petitioner are respondents for all purposes.

(2)   (A)   The petition must be titled "In re [name of petitioner]."

(B)   The petition must state:

(i)   the relief sought;

(ii)   the issues presented;

(iii) the facts necessary to understand the issue presented by the petition; and

(iv) the reasons why the writ should issue.

(C)   The petition must include a copy of any order or opinion or parts of the record that may be essential to understand the matters set forth in the petition.

(3)   Upon receiving the prescribed docket fee, the clerk must docket the petition and submit it to the court.

(b)   Denial; Order Directing Answer; Briefs; Precedence.

(1)   The court may deny the petition without an answer. Otherwise, it must order the respondent, if any, to answer within a fixed time.

(2)   The clerk must serve the order to respond on all persons directed to respond.

(3)   Two or more respondents may answer jointly.

(4)　The court of appeals may invite or order the trial-court judge to address the petition or may invite an amicus curiae to do so. The trial-court judge may request permission to address the petition but may not do so unless invited or ordered to do so by the court of appeals.

(5)　If briefing or oral argument is required, the clerk must advise the parties, and when appropriate, the trial-court judge or amicus curiae.

(6)　The proceeding must be given preference over ordinary civil cases.

(7)　The circuit clerk must send a copy of the final disposition to the trial-court judge.

(c)　Other Extraordinary Writs. An application for an extraordinary writ other than one provided for in Rule 21(a) must be made by filing a petition with the circuit clerk with proof of service on the respondents. Proceedings on the application must conform, so far as is practicable, to the procedures prescribed in Rule 21(a) and (b).

(d)　Form of Papers; Number of Copies; Length Limits. All papers must conform to Rule 32(c)(2). An original and 3 copies must be filed unless the court requires the filing of a different number by local rule or by order in a particular case. Except by the court's permission, and excluding the accompanying documents required by Rule 21(a)(2)(C):

(1)　a paper produced using a computer must not exceed 7,800 words; and

(2)　a handwritten or typewritten paper must not exceed 30 pages.

TITLE VI. HABEAS CORPUS; PROCEEDINGS IN FORMA PAUPERIS

RULE 22.　HABEAS CORPUS AND SECTION 2255 PROCEEDINGS

(a)　Application for the Original Writ. An application for a writ of habeas corpus must be made to the appropriate district court. If made to a circuit judge, the application must be transferred to the appropriate district court. If a district court denies an application made or transferred to it, renewal of the application before a circuit judge is not permitted. The applicant may, under 28 U.S.C. § 2253, appeal to the court of appeals from the district court's order denying the application.

(b)　Certificate of Appealability.

(1)　In a habeas corpus proceeding in which the detention complained of arises from process issued by a state court, or in a 28 U.S.C. § 2255 proceeding, the applicant cannot take an appeal unless a circuit justice or a circuit or district judge issues a certificate of appealability under 28 U.S.C. § 2253(c). If an applicant files a notice of appeal, the district clerk must send to the court of appeals the certificate (if any) and the statement described in Rule 11(a) of the Rules Governing Proceedings Under 28 U.S.C. § 2254 or § 2255 (if any), along with the notice of appeal and the file of the district-court proceedings. If the district judge has denied the certificate, the applicant may request a circuit judge to issue it.

(2)　A request addressed to the court of appeals may be considered by a circuit judge or judges, as the court prescribes. If no express request for a certificate is filed, the notice of appeal constitutes a request addressed to the judges of the court of appeals.

(3)　A certificate of appealability is not required when a state or its representative or the United States or its representative appeals.

RULE 23.　CUSTODY OR RELEASE OF A PRISONER IN A HABEAS CORPUS PROCEEDING

(a)　Transfer of Custody Pending Review. Pending review of a decision in a habeas corpus proceeding commenced before a court, justice, or judge of the United States for the release of a prisoner, the person having custody of the prisoner must not transfer custody to another unless a transfer is directed in accordance with this rule. When, upon application, a custodian shows the need for a

transfer, the court, justice, or judge rendering the decision under review may authorize the transfer and substitute the successor custodian as a party.

(b) Detention or Release Pending Review of Decision Not to Release. While a decision not to release a prisoner is under review, the court or judge rendering the decision, or the court of appeals, or the Supreme Court, or a judge or justice of either court, may order that the prisoner be:

(1) detained in the custody from which release is sought;

(2) detained in other appropriate custody; or

(3) released on personal recognizance, with or without surety.

(c) Release Pending Review of Decision Ordering Release. While a decision ordering the release of a prisoner is under review, the prisoner must—unless the court or judge rendering the decision, or the court of appeals, or the Supreme Court, or a judge or justice of either court orders otherwise—be released on personal recognizance, with or without surety.

(d) Modification of the Initial Order on Custody. An initial order governing the prisoner's custody or release, including any recognizance or surety, continues in effect pending review unless for special reasons shown to the court of appeals or the Supreme Court, or to a judge or justice of either court, the order is modified or an independent order regarding custody, release, or surety is issued.

RULE 24.   PROCEEDING IN FORMA PAUPERIS

(a) Leave to Proceed in Forma Pauperis.

(1) Motion in the District Court. Except as stated in Rule 24(a)(3), a party to a district-court action who desires to appeal in forma pauperis must file a motion in the district court. The party must attach an affidavit that:

(A) shows in the detail prescribed by Form 4 of the Appendix of Forms, the party's inability to pay or to give security for fees and costs;

(B) claims an entitlement to redress; and

(C) states the issues that the party intends to present on appeal.

(2) Action on the Motion. If the district court grants the motion, the party may proceed on appeal without prepaying or giving security for fees and costs, unless a statute provides otherwise. If the district court denies the motion, it must state its reasons in writing.

(3) Prior Approval. A party who was permitted to proceed in forma pauperis in the district-court action, or who was determined to be financially unable to obtain an adequate defense in a criminal case, may proceed on appeal in forma pauperis without further authorization, unless:

(A) the district court—before or after the notice of appeal is filed-certifies that the appeal is not taken in good faith or finds that the party is not otherwise entitled to proceed in forma pauperis and states in writing its reasons for the certification or finding; or

(B) a statute provides otherwise.

(4) Notice of District Court's Denial. The district clerk must immediately notify the parties and the court of appeals when the district court does any of the following:

(A) denies a motion to proceed on appeal in forma pauperis;

(B) certifies that the appeal is not taken in good faith; or

(C) finds that the party is not otherwise entitled to proceed in forma pauperis.

(5) Motion in the Court of Appeals. A party may file a motion to proceed on appeal in forma pauperis in the court of appeals within 30 days after service of the notice prescribed in Rule 24(a)(4). The motion must include a copy of the affidavit filed in the district court and the district

court's statement of reasons for its action. If no affidavit was filed in the district court, the party must include the affidavit prescribed by Rule 24(a)(1).

(b) Leave to Proceed In Forma Pauperis on Appeal from the United States Tax Court or on Appeal or Review of an Administrative-Agency Proceeding. A party may file in the court of appeals a motion for leave to proceed on appeal in forma pauperis with an affidavit prescribed by Rule 24(a)(1):

(1) in an appeal from the United States Tax Court; and

(2) when an appeal or review of a proceeding before an administrative agency, board, commission, or officer proceeds directly in the court of appeals.

(c) Leave to Use Original Record. A party allowed to proceed on appeal in forma pauperis may request that the appeal be heard on the original record without reproducing any part.

TITLE VII.   GENERAL PROVISIONS

RULE 25.   FILING AND SERVICE

(a) Filing.

(1) Filing with the Clerk. A paper required or permitted to be filed in a court of appeals must be filed with the clerk.

(2) Filing: Method and Timeliness.

(A) In general. Filing may be accomplished by mail addressed to the clerk, but filing is not timely unless the clerk receives the papers within the time fixed for filing.

(B) A brief or appendix. A brief or appendix is timely filed, however, if on or before the last day for filing, it is:

(i) mailed to the clerk by First-Class Mail, or other class of mail that is at least as expeditious, postage prepaid; or

(ii) dispatched to a third-party commercial carrier for delivery to the clerk within 3 days.

(C) Inmate Filing. If an institution has a system designed for legal mail, an inmate confined there must use that system to receive the benefit of this Rule 25(a)(2)(C). A paper filed by an inmate is timely if it is deposited in the institution's internal mail system on or before the last day for filing and:

(i) it is accompanied by:

- a declaration in compliance with 28 U.S.C. § 1746—or a notarized statement—setting out the date of deposit and stating that first-class postage is being prepaid; or

- evidence (such as a postmark or date stamp) showing that the paper was so deposited and that postage was prepaid; or

(ii) the court of appeals exercises its discretion to permit the later filing of a declaration or notarized statement that satisfies Rule 25(a)(2)(C)(i).

(D) Electronic filing. A court of appeals may by local rule permit or require papers to be filed, signed, or verified by electronic means that are consistent with technical standards, if any, that the Judicial Conference of the United States establishes. A local rule may require filing by electronic means only if reasonable exceptions are allowed. A paper filed by electronic means in compliance with a local rule constitutes a written paper for the purpose of applying these rules.

(3)   Filing a Motion with a Judge. If a motion requests relief that may be granted by a single judge, the judge may permit the motion to be filed with the judge; the judge must note the filing date on the motion and give it to the clerk.

(4)   Clerk's Refusal of Documents. The clerk must not refuse to accept for filing any paper presented for that purpose solely because it is not presented in proper form as required by these rules or by any local rule or practice.

(5)   Privacy Protection. An appeal in a case whose privacy protection was governed by Federal Rule of Bankruptcy Procedure 9037, Federal Rule of Civil Procedure 5.2, or Federal Rule of Criminal Procedure 49.1 is governed by the same rule on appeal. In all other proceedings, privacy protection is governed by Federal Rule of Civil Procedure 5.2, except that Federal Rule of Criminal Procedure 49.1 governs when an extraordinary writ is sought in a criminal case.

(b)   Service of All Papers Required. Unless a rule requires service by the clerk, a party must, at or before the time of filing a paper, serve a copy on the other parties to the appeal or review. Service on a party represented by counsel must be made on the party's counsel.

(c)   Manner of Service.

(1)   Service may be any of the following:

(A)   personal, including delivery to a responsible person at the office of counsel;

(B)   by mail;

(C)   by third-party commercial carrier for delivery within 3 days; or

(D)   by electronic means, if the party being served consents in writing.

(2)   If authorized by local rule, a party may use the court's transmission equipment to make electronic service under Rule 25(c)(1)(D).

(3)   When reasonable considering such factors as the immediacy of the relief sought, distance, and cost, service on a party must be by a manner at least as expeditious as the manner used to file the paper with the court.

(4)   Service by mail or by commercial carrier is complete on mailing or delivery to the carrier. Service by electronic means is complete on transmission, unless the party making service is notified that the paper was not received by the party served.

(d)   Proof of Service.

(1)   A paper presented for filing must contain either of the following:

(A)   an acknowledgment of service by the person served; or

(B)   proof of service consisting of a statement by the person who made service certifying:

(i)   the date and manner of service;

(ii)   the names of the persons served; and

(iii) their mail or electronic addresses, facsimile numbers, or the addresses of the places of delivery, as appropriate for the manner of service.

(2)   When a brief or appendix is filed by mailing or dispatch in accordance with Rule 25(a)(2)(B), the proof of service must also state the date and manner by which the document was mailed or dispatched to the clerk.

(3)   Proof of service may appear on or be affixed to the papers filed.

(e)   Number of Copies. When these rules require the filing or furnishing of a number of copies, a court may require a different number by local rule or by order in a particular case.

RULE 26.   COMPUTING AND EXTENDING TIME

(a) Computing Time. The following rules apply in computing any time period specified in these rules, in any local rule or court order, or in any statute that does not specify a method of computing time.

(1) **Period Stated in Days or a Longer Unit.** When the period is stated in days or a longer unit of time:

(A) exclude the day of the event that triggers the period;

(B) count every day, including intermediate Saturdays, Sundays, and legal holidays; and

(C) include the last day of the period, but if the last day is a Saturday, Sunday, or legal holiday, the period continues to run until the end of the next day that is not a Saturday, Sunday, or legal holiday.

(2) **Period Stated in Hours.** When the period is stated in hours:

(A) begin counting immediately on the occurrence of the event that triggers the period;

(B) count every hour, including hours during intermediate Saturdays, Sundays, and legal holidays; and

(C) if the period would end on a Saturday, Sunday, or legal holiday, the period continues to run until the same time on the next day that is not a Saturday, Sunday, or legal holiday.

(3) **Inaccessibility of the Clerk's Office.** Unless the court orders otherwise, if the clerk's office is inaccessible:

(A) on the last day for filing under Rule 26(a)(1), then the time for filing is extended to the first accessible day that is not a Saturday, Sunday, or legal holiday; or

(B) during the last hour for filing under Rule 26(a)(2), then the time for filing is extended to the same time on the first accessible day that is not a Saturday, Sunday, or legal holiday.

(4) **"Last Day" Defined.** Unless a different time is set by a statute, local rule, or court order, the last day ends:

(A) for electronic filing in the district court, at midnight in the court's time zone;

(B) for electronic filing in the court of appeals, at midnight in the time zone of the circuit clerk's principal office;

(C) for filing under Rules 4(c)(1), 25(a)(2)(B), and 25(a)(2)(C)—and filing by mail under Rule 13(a)(2)—at the latest time for the method chosen for delivery to the post office, third-party commercial carrier, or prison mailing system; and

(D) for filing by other means, when the clerk's office is scheduled to close.

(5) **"Next Day" Defined.** The "next day" is determined by continuing to count forward when the period is measured after an event and backward when measured before an event.

(6) **"Legal Holiday" Defined.** "Legal holiday" means:

(A) the day set aside by statute for observing New Year's Day, Martin Luther King Jr.'s Birthday, Washington's Birthday, Memorial Day, Independence Day, Labor Day, Columbus Day, Veterans' Day, Thanksgiving Day, or Christmas Day;

(B) any day declared a holiday by the President or Congress; and

(C)   for periods that are measured after an event, any other day declared a holiday by the state where either of the following is located: the district court that rendered the challenged judgment or order, or the circuit clerk's principal office.

(b)   Extending Time. For good cause, the court may extend the time prescribed by these rules or by its order to perform any act, or may permit an act to be done after that time expires. But the court may not extend the time to file:

(1)   a notice of appeal (except as authorized in Rule 4) or a petition for permission to appeal; or

(2)   a notice of appeal from or a petition to enjoin, set aside, suspend, modify, enforce, or otherwise review an order of an administrative agency, board, commission, or officer of the United States, unless specifically authorized by law.

(c)   Additional Time after Certain Kinds of Service. When a party may or must act within a specified time after being served, 3 days are added after the period would otherwise expire under Rule 26(a), unless the paper is delivered on the date of service stated in the proof of service. For purposes of this Rule 26(c), a paper that is served electronically is treated as delivered on the date of service stated in the proof of service.

RULE 26.1.   CORPORATE DISCLOSURE STATEMENT

(a)   Who Must File. Any nongovernmental corporate party to a proceeding in a court of appeals must file a statement that identifies any parent corporation and any publicly held corporation that owns 10% or more of its stock or states that there is no such corporation.

(b)   Time for Filing; Supplemental Filing. A party must file the Rule 26.1(a) statement with the principal brief or upon filing a motion, response, petition, or answer in the court of appeals, whichever occurs first, unless a local rule requires earlier filing. Even if the statement has already been filed, the party's principal brief must include the statement before the table of contents. A party must supplement its statement whenever the information that must be disclosed under Rule 26.1(a) changes.

(c)   Number of Copies. If the Rule 26.1(a) statement is filed before the principal brief, or if a supplemental statement is filed, the party must file an original and 3 copies unless the court requires a different number by local rule or by order in a particular case.

RULE 27.   MOTIONS

(a)   In General.

(1)   Application for Relief. An application for an order or other relief is made by motion unless these rules prescribe another form. A motion must be in writing unless the court permits otherwise.

(2)   Contents of a Motion.

(A)   Grounds and relief sought. A motion must state with particularity the grounds for the motion, the relief sought, and the legal argument necessary to support it.

(B)   Accompanying documents.

(i)   Any affidavit or other paper necessary to support a motion must be served and filed with the motion.

(ii)   An affidavit must contain only factual information, not legal argument.

(iii) A motion seeking substantive relief must include a copy of the trial court's opinion or agency's decision as a separate exhibit.

(C)   Documents barred or not required.

(i)   A separate brief supporting or responding to a motion must not be filed.

(ii)   A notice of motion is not required.

(iii)   A proposed order is not required.

(3)   Response.

(A)   Time to file. Any party may file a response to a motion; Rule 27(a)(2) governs its contents. The response must be filed within 10 days after service of the motion unless the court shortens or extends the time. A motion authorized by Rules 8, 9, 18, or 41 may be granted before the 10-day period runs only if the court gives reasonable notice to the parties that it intends to act sooner.

(B)   Request for affirmative relief. A response may include a motion for affirmative relief. The time to respond to the new motion, and to reply to that response, are governed by Rule 27(a)(3)(A) and (a)(4). The title of the response must alert the court to the request for relief.

(4)   Reply to Response. Any reply to a response must be filed within 7 days after service of the response. A reply must not present matters that do not relate to the response.

(b)   Disposition of a Motion for a Procedural Order. The court may act on a motion for a procedural order-including a motion under Rule 26(b)-at any time without awaiting a response, and may, by rule or by order in a particular case, authorize its clerk to act on specified types of procedural motions. A party adversely affected by the court's, or the clerk's, action may file a motion to reconsider, vacate, or modify that action. Timely opposition filed after the motion is granted in whole or in part does not constitute a request to reconsider, vacate, or modify the disposition; a motion requesting that relief must be filed.

(c)   Power of a Single Judge to Entertain a Motion. A circuit judge may act alone on any motion, but may not dismiss or otherwise determine an appeal or other proceeding. A court of appeals may provide by rule or by order in a particular case that only the court may act on any motion or class of motions. The court may review the action of a single judge.

(d)   Form of Papers; Length Limits; and Number of Copies.

(1)   Format.

(A)   Reproduction. A motion, response, or reply may be reproduced by any process that yields a clear black image on light paper. The paper must be opaque and unglazed. Only one side of the paper may be used.

(B)   Cover. A cover is not required but there must be a caption that includes the case number, the name of the court, the title of the case, and a brief descriptive title indicating the purpose of the motion and identifying the party or parties for whom it is filed. If a cover is used, it must be white.

(C)   Binding. The document must be bound in any manner that is secure, does not obscure the text, and permits the document to lie reasonably flat when open.

(D)   Paper size, line spacing, and margins. The document must be on $8^{1}/_{2}$ by 11 inch paper. The text must be double-spaced, but quotations more than two lines long may be indented and single-spaced. Headings and footnotes may be single-spaced. Margins must be at least one inch on all four sides. Page numbers may be placed in the margins, but no text may appear there.

(E)   Typeface and type styles. The document must comply with the typeface requirements of Rule 32(a)(5) and the type-style requirements of Rule 32(a)(6).

(2)   Length Limits. Except by the court's permission, and excluding the accompanying documents authorized by Rule 27(a)(2)(B):

(A)   a motion or response to a motion produced using a computer must not exceed 5,200 words;

(B)   a handwritten or typewritten motion or response to a motion must not exceed 20 pages;

(C)   a reply produced using a computer must not exceed 2,600 words; and

(D)   a handwritten or typewritten reply to a response must not exceed 10 pages.

(3)   Number of Copies. An original and 3 copies must be filed unless the court requires a different number by local rule or by order in a particular case.

(e)   Oral Argument. A motion will be decided without oral argument unless the court orders otherwise.

RULE 28.   BRIEFS

(a)   Appellant's Brief. The appellant's brief must contain, under appropriate headings and in the order indicated:

(1)   a corporate disclosure statement if required by Rule 26.1;

(2)   a table of contents, with page references;

(3)   a table of authorities—cases (alphabetically arranged), statutes, and other authorities— with references to the pages of the brief where they are cited;

(4)   a jurisdictional statement, including:

(A)   the basis for the district court's or agency's subject-matter jurisdiction, with citations to applicable statutory provisions and stating relevant facts establishing jurisdiction;

(B)   the basis for the court of appeals' jurisdiction, with citations to applicable statutory provisions and stating relevant facts establishing jurisdiction;

(C)   the filing dates establishing the timeliness of the appeal or petition for review; and

(D)   an assertion that the appeal is from a final order or judgment that disposes of all parties' claims, or information establishing the court of appeals' jurisdiction on some other basis;

(5)   a statement of the issues presented for review;

(6)   a concise statement of the case setting out the facts relevant to the issues submitted for review, describing the relevant procedural history, and identifying the rulings presented for review, with appropriate references to the record (see Rule 28(e));

(7)   a summary of the argument, which must contain a succinct, clear, and accurate statement of the arguments made in the body of the brief, and which must not merely repeat the argument headings;

(8)   the argument, which must contain:

(A)   appellant's contentions and the reasons for them, with citations to the authorities and parts of the record on which the appellant relies; and

(B)   for each issue, a concise statement of the applicable standard of review (which may appear in the discussion of the issue or under a separate heading placed before the discussion of the issues);

(9)   a short conclusion stating the precise relief sought; and

(10) the certificate of compliance, if required by Rule 32(g)(1).

(b) Appellee's Brief. The appellee's brief must conform to the requirements of Rule 28(a)(1)-(8) and (10), except that none of the following need appear unless the appellee is dissatisfied with the appellant's statement:

    (1)   the jurisdictional statement;

    (2)   the statement of the issues;

    (3)   the statement of the case; and

    (4)   the statement of the standard of review.

(c) Reply Brief. The appellant may file a brief in reply to the appellee's brief. Unless the court permits, no further briefs may be filed. A reply brief must contain a table of contents, with page references, and a table of authorities—cases (alphabetically arranged), statutes, and other authorities—with references to the pages of the reply brief where they are cited.

(d) References to Parties. In briefs and at oral argument, counsel should minimize use of the terms "appellant" and "appellee." To make briefs clear, counsel should use the parties' actual names or the designations used in the lower court or agency proceeding, or such descriptive terms as "the employee," "the injured person," "the taxpayer," "the ship," "the stevedore."

(e) References to the Record. References to the parts of the record contained in the appendix filed with the appellant's brief must be to the pages of the appendix. If the appendix is prepared after the briefs are filed, a party referring to the record must follow one of the methods detailed in Rule 30(c). If the original record is used under Rule 30(f) and is not consecutively paginated, or if the brief refers to an unreproduced part of the record, any reference must be to the page of the original document. For example:

- Answer p. 7;
- Motion for Judgment p. 2;
- Transcript p. 231.

Only clear abbreviations may be used. A party referring to evidence whose admissibility is in controversy must cite the pages of the appendix or of the transcript at which the evidence was identified, offered, and received or rejected.

(f) Reproduction of Statutes, Rules, Regulations, etc. If the court's determination of the issues presented requires the study of statutes, rules, regulations, etc., the relevant parts must be set out in the brief or in an addendum at the end, or may be supplied to the court in pamphlet form.

(g) [Reserved]

(h) [Reserved]

(i) Briefs in a Case Involving Multiple Appellants or Appellees. In a case involving more than one appellant or appellee, including consolidated cases, any number of appellants or appellees may join in a brief, and any party may adopt by reference a part of another's brief. Parties may also join in reply briefs.

(j) Citation of Supplemental Authorities. If pertinent and significant authorities come to a party's attention after the party's brief has been filed—or after oral argument but before decision—a party may promptly advise the circuit clerk by letter, with a copy to all other parties, setting forth the citations. The letter must state the reasons for the supplemental citations, referring either to the page of the brief or to a point argued orally. The body of the letter must not exceed 350 words. Any response must be made promptly and must be similarly limited.

RULE 28.1.   CROSS-APPEALS

(a) Applicability. This rule applies to a case in which a cross-appeal is filed. Rules 28(a)–(c), 31(a)(1), 32(a)(2), and 32(a)(7)(A)–(B) do not apply to such a case, except as otherwise provided in this rule.

(b) Designation of Appellant. The party who files a notice of appeal first is the appellant for the purposes of this rule and Rules 30 and 34. If notices are filed on the same day, the plaintiff in the proceeding below is the appellant. These designations may be modified by the parties' agreement or by court order.

(c) Briefs. In a case involving a cross-appeal:

(1) Appellant's Principal Brief. The appellant must file a principal brief in the appeal. That brief must comply with Rule 28(a).

(2) Appellee's Principal and Response Brief. The appellee must file a principal brief in the cross-appeal and must, in the same brief, respond to the principal brief in the appeal. That appellee's brief must comply with Rule 28(a), except that the brief need not include a statement of the case unless the appellee is dissatisfied with the appellant's statement.

(3) Appellant's Response and Reply Brief. The appellant must file a brief that responds to the principal brief in the cross-appeal and may, in the same brief, reply to the response in the appeal. That brief must comply with Rule 28(a)(2)-(8) and (10), except that none of the following need appear unless the appellant is dissatisfied with the appellee's statement in the cross-appeal:

(A)   the jurisdictional statement;

(B)   the statement of the issues;

(C)   the statement of the case; and

(D)   the statement of the standard of review.

(4) Appellee's Reply Brief. The appellee may file a brief in reply to the response in the cross-appeal. That brief must comply with Rule 28(a)(2)–(3) and (10) and must be limited to the issues presented by the cross-appeal.

(5) No Further Briefs. Unless the court permits, no further briefs may be filed in a case involving a cross-appeal.

(d) Cover. Except for filings by unrepresented parties, the cover of the appellant's principal brief must be blue; the appellee's principal and response brief, red; the appellant's response and reply brief, yellow; the appellee's reply brief, gray; an intervenor's or amicus curiae's brief, green; and any supplemental brief, tan. The front cover of a brief must contain the information required by Rule 32(a)(2).

(e) Length.

(1) Page Limitation. Unless it complies with Rule 28.1(e)(2), the appellant's principal brief must not exceed 30 pages; the appellee's principal and response brief, 35 pages; the appellant's response and reply brief, 30 pages; and the appellee's reply brief, 15 pages.

(2) Type-Volume Limitation.

(A)   The appellant's principal brief or the appellant's response and reply brief is acceptable if it:

(i)   contains no more than 13,000 words; or

(ii)   uses a monospaced face and contains no more than 1,300 lines of text.

(B)   The appellee's principal and response brief is acceptable if it:

(i)   contains no more than 15,300 words; or

  (ii) uses a monospaced face and contains no more than 1,500 lines of text.

  (C) The appellee's reply brief is acceptable if it contains no more than half of the type volume specified in Rule 28.1(e)(2)(A).

(3) Certificate of Compliance. A brief submitted under Rule 28.1(e)(2) must comply with Rule 32(a)(7)(C).

(f) Time to Serve and File a Brief. Briefs must be served and filed as follows:

(1) the appellant's principal brief, within 40 days after the record is filed;

(2) the appellee's principal and response brief, within 30 days after the appellant's principal brief is served;

(3) the appellant's response and reply brief, within 30 days after the appellee's principal and response brief is served; and

(4) the appellee's reply brief, within 14 days after the appellant's response and reply brief is served, but at least 7 days before argument unless the court, for good cause, allows a later filing.

RULE 29. BRIEF OF AN AMICUS CURIAE

(a) During Initial Consideration of a Case on the Merits.

(1) Applicability. This Rule 29(a) governs amicus filings during a court's initial consideration of a case on the merits.

(2) When Permitted. The United States or its officer or agency or a state may file an amicus-curiae brief without the consent of the parties or leave of court. Any other amicus curiae may file a brief only by leave of court or if the brief states that all parties have consented to its filing.

(3) Motion for Leave to File. The motion must be accompanied by the proposed brief and state:

  (A) the movant's interest; and

  (B) the reason why an amicus brief is desirable and why the matters asserted are relevant to the disposition of the case.

(4) Contents and Form. An amicus brief must comply with Rule 32. In addition to the requirements of Rule 32, the cover must identify the party or parties supported and indicate whether the brief supports affirmance or reversal. An amicus brief need not comply with Rule 28, but must include the following:

  (A) if the amicus curiae is a corporation, a disclosure statement like that required of parties by Rule 26.1;

  (B) a table of contents, with page references;

  (C) a table of authorities—cases (alphabetically arranged), statutes, and other authorities—with references to the pages of the brief where they are cited;

  (D) a concise statement of the identity of the amicus curiae, its interest in the case, and the source of its authority to file;

  (E) unless the amicus curiae is one listed in the first sentence of Rule 29(a)(2), a statement that indicates whether:

    (i) a party's counsel authored the brief in whole or in part;

    (ii) a party or a party's counsel contributed money that was intended to fund preparing or submitting the brief; and

(iii) a person—other than the amicus curiae, its members, or its counsel—contributed money that was intended to fund preparing or submitting the brief and, if so, identifies each such person;

(F)   an argument, which may be preceded by a summary and which need not include a statement of the applicable standard of review; and

(G)   a certificate of compliance under Rule 32(g)(1), if length is computed using a word or line limit.

(5)   Length. Except by the court's permission, an amicus brief may be no more than one-half the maximum length authorized by these rules for a party's principal brief. If the court grants a party permission to file a longer brief, that extension does not affect the length of an amicus brief.

(6)   Time for Filing. An amicus curiae must file its brief, accompanied by a motion for filing when necessary, no later than 7 days after the principal brief of the party being supported is filed. An amicus curiae that does not support either party must file its brief no later than 7 days after the appellant's or petitioner's principal brief is filed. A court may grant leave for later filing, specifying the time within which an opposing party may answer.

(7)   Reply Brief. Except by the court's permission, an amicus curiae may not file a reply brief.

(8)   Oral Argument. An amicus curiae may participate in oral argument only with the court's permission.

(b)   During Consideration of Whether to Grant Rehearing.

(1)   Applicability. This Rule 29(b) governs amicus filings during a court's consideration of whether to grant panel rehearing or rehearing en banc, unless a local rule or order in a case provides otherwise.

(2)   When Permitted. The United States or its officer or agency or a state may file an amicus curiae brief without the consent of the parties or leave of court. Any other amicus curiae may file a brief only by leave of court.

(3)   Motion for Leave to File. Rule 29(a)(3) applies to a motion for leave.

(4)   Contents, Form, and Length. Rule 29(a)(4) applies to the amicus brief. The brief must not exceed 2,600 words.

(5)   Time for Filing. An amicus curiae supporting the petition for rehearing or supporting neither party must file its brief, accompanied by a motion for filing when necessary, no later than 7 days after the petition is filed. An amicus curiae opposing the petition must file its brief, accompanied by a motion for filing when necessary, no later than the date set by the court for the response.

RULE 30.   APPENDIX TO THE BRIEFS

(a)   Appellant's Responsibility.

(1)   Contents of the Appendix. The appellant must prepare and file an appendix to the briefs containing:

(A)   the relevant docket entries in the proceeding below;

(B)   the relevant portions of the pleadings, charge, findings, or opinion;

(C)   the judgment, order, or decision in question; and

(D)   other parts of the record to which the parties wish to direct the court's attention.

(2)   Excluded Material. Memoranda of law in the district court should not be included in the appendix unless they have independent relevance. Parts of the record may be relied on by the court or the parties even though not included in the appendix.

(3) Time to File; Number of Copies. Unless filing is deferred under Rule 30(c), the appellant must file 10 copies of the appendix with the brief and must serve one copy on counsel for each party separately represented. An unrepresented party proceeding in forma pauperis must file 4 legible copies with the clerk, and one copy must be served on counsel for each separately represented party. The court may by local rule or by order in a particular case require the filing or service of a different number.

(b) All Parties' Responsibilities.

(1) Determining the Contents of the Appendix. The parties are encouraged to agree on the contents of the appendix. In the absence of an agreement, the appellant must, within 14 days after the record is filed, serve on the appellee a designation of the parts of the record the appellant intends to include in the appendix and a statement of the issues the appellant intends to present for review. The appellee may, within 14 days after receiving the designation, serve on the appellant a designation of additional parts to which it wishes to direct the court's attention. The appellant must include the designated parts in the appendix. The parties must not engage in unnecessary designation of parts of the record, because the entire record is available to the court. This paragraph applies also to a cross-appellant and a cross-appellee.

(2) Costs of Appendix. Unless the parties agree otherwise, the appellant must pay the cost of the appendix. If the appellant considers parts of the record designated by the appellee to be unnecessary, the appellant may advise the appellee, who must then advance the cost of including those parts. The cost of the appendix is a taxable cost. But if any party causes unnecessary parts of the record to be included in the appendix, the court may impose the cost of those parts on that party. Each circuit must, by local rule, provide for sanctions against attorneys who unreasonably and vexatiously increase litigation costs by including unnecessary material in the appendix.

(c) Deferred Appendix.

(1) Deferral Until After Briefs Are Filed. The court may provide by rule for classes of cases or by order in a particular case that preparation of the appendix may be deferred until after the briefs have been filed and that the appendix may be filed 21 days after the appellee's brief is served. Even though the filing of the appendix may be deferred, Rule 30(b) applies; except that a party must designate the parts of the record it wants included in the appendix when it serves its brief, and need not include a statement of the issues presented.

(2) References to the Record.

(A) If the deferred appendix is used, the parties may cite in their briefs the pertinent pages of the record. When the appendix is prepared, the record pages cited in the briefs must be indicated by inserting record page numbers, in brackets, at places in the appendix where those pages of the record appear.

(B) A party who wants to refer directly to pages of the appendix may serve and file copies of the brief within the time required by Rule 31(a), containing appropriate references to pertinent pages of the record. In that event, within 14 days after the appendix is filed, the party must serve and file copies of the brief, containing references to the pages of the appendix in place of or in addition to the references to the pertinent pages of the record. Except for the correction of typographical errors, no other changes may be made to the brief.

(d) Format of the Appendix. The appendix must begin with a table of contents identifying the page at which each part begins. The relevant docket entries must follow the table of contents. Other parts of the record must follow chronologically. When pages from the transcript of proceedings are placed in the appendix, the transcript page numbers must be shown in brackets immediately before the included pages. Omissions in the text of papers or of the transcript must be indicated by asterisks. Immaterial formal matters (captions, subscriptions, acknowledgments, etc.) should be omitted.

(e) Reproduction of Exhibits. Exhibits designated for inclusion in the appendix may be reproduced in a separate volume, or volumes, suitably indexed. Four copies must be filed with the

appendix, and one copy must be served on counsel for each separately represented party. If a transcript of a proceeding before an administrative agency, board, commission, or officer was used in a district-court action and has been designated for inclusion in the appendix, the transcript must be placed in the appendix as an exhibit.

(f)   Appeal on the Original Record Without an Appendix. The court may, either by rule for all cases or classes of cases or by order in a particular case, dispense with the appendix and permit an appeal to proceed on the original record with any copies of the record, or relevant parts, that the court may order the parties to file.

RULE 31.   SERVING AND FILING BRIEFS

(a)   Time to Serve and File a Brief.

(1)   The appellant must serve and file a brief within 40 days after the record is filed. The appellee must serve and file a brief within 30 days after the appellant's brief is served. The appellant may serve and file a reply brief within 14 days after service of the appellee's brief but a reply brief must be filed at least 7 days before argument, unless the court, for good cause, allows a later filing.

(2)   A court of appeals that routinely considers cases on the merits promptly after the briefs are filed may shorten the time to serve and file briefs, either by local rule or by order in a particular case.

(b)   Number of Copies. Twenty-five copies of each brief must be filed with the clerk and 2 copies must be served on each unrepresented party and on counsel for each separately represented party. An unrepresented party proceeding in forma pauperis must file 4 legible copies with the clerk, and one copy must be served on each unrepresented party and on counsel for each separately represented party. The court may by local rule or by order in a particular case require the filing or service of a different number.

(c)   Consequence of Failure to File. If an appellant fails to file a brief within the time provided by this rule, or within an extended time, an appellee may move to dismiss the appeal. An appellee who fails to file a brief will not be heard at oral argument unless the court grants permission.

RULE 32.   FORM OF BRIEFS, APPENDICES, AND OTHER PAPERS

(a)   Form of a Brief.

(1)   Reproduction.

(A)   A brief may be reproduced by any process that yields a clear black image on light paper. The paper must be opaque and unglazed. Only one side of the paper may be used.

(B)   Text must be reproduced with a clarity that equals or exceeds the output of a laser printer.

(C)   Photographs, illustrations, and tables may be reproduced by any method that results in a good copy of the original; a glossy finish is acceptable if the original is glossy.

(2)   Cover. Except for filings by unrepresented parties, the cover of the appellant's brief must be blue; the appellee's, red; an intervenor's or amicus curiae's, green; any reply brief, gray; and any supplemental brief, tan. The front cover of a brief must contain:

(A)   the number of the case centered at the top;

(B)   the name of the court;

(C)   the title of the case (see Rule 12(a));

(D)   the nature of the proceeding (e.g., Appeal, Petition for Review) and the name of the court, agency, or board below;

(E)   the title of the brief, identifying the party or parties for whom the brief is filed; and

(F)   the name, office address, and telephone number of counsel representing the party for whom the brief is filed.

(3)   Binding. The brief must be bound in any manner that is secure, does not obscure the text, and permits the brief to lie reasonably flat when open.

(4)   Paper Size, Line Spacing, and Margins. The brief must be on 8½ by 11 inch paper. The text must be double-spaced, but quotations more than two lines long may be indented and single-spaced. Headings and footnotes may be single-spaced. Margins must be at least one inch on all four sides. Page numbers may be placed in the margins, but no text may appear there.

(5)   Typeface. Either a proportionally spaced or a monospaced face may be used.

(A)   A proportionally spaced face must include serifs, but sans-serif type may be used in headings and captions. A proportionally spaced face must be 14-point or larger.

(B)   A monospaced face may not contain more than 10½ characters per inch.

(6)   Type Styles. A brief must be set in a plain, roman style, although italics or boldface may be used for emphasis. Case names must be italicized or underlined.

(7)   Length.

(A)   **Page Limitation.** A principal brief may not exceed 30 pages, or a reply brief 15 pages, unless it complies with Rule 32(a)(7)(B).

(B)   **Type-Volume Limitation.**

(i)   A principal brief is acceptable if it:

- contains no more than 13,000 words; or

- uses a monospaced face and contains no more than 1,300 lines of text.

(ii)   A reply brief is acceptable if it contains no more than half of the type volume specified in Rule 32(a)(7)(B)(i).

(iii)   Headings, footnotes, and quotations count toward the word and line limitations. The corporate disclosure statement, table of contents, table of citations, statement with respect to oral argument, any addendum containing statutes, rules or regulations, and any certificates of counsel do not count toward the limitation.

(C)   **Certificate of compliance.**

(i)   A brief submitted under Rules 28.1(e)(2) or 32(a)(7)(B) must include a certificate by the attorney, or an unrepresented party, that the brief complies with the type-volume limitation. The person preparing the certificate may rely on the word or line count of the word-processing system used to prepare the brief. The certificate must state either:

- the number of words in the brief; or

- the number of lines of monospaced type in the brief.

(ii)   Form 6 in the Appendix of Forms is a suggested form of a certificate of compliance. Use of Form 6 must be regarded as sufficient to meet the requirements of Rules 28.1(e)(3) and 32(a)(7)(C)(i).

(b)   Form of an Appendix. An appendix must comply with Rule 32(a)(1), (2), (3), and (4), with the following exceptions:

(1)   The cover of a separately bound appendix must be white.

(2)   An appendix may include a legible photocopy of any document found in the record or of a printed judicial or agency decision.

(3)   When necessary to facilitate inclusion of odd-sized documents such as technical drawings, an appendix may be a size other than $8^{1}/_{2}$ by 11 inches, and need not lie reasonably flat when opened.

(c)   Form of Other Papers.

(1)   Motion. The form of a motion is governed by Rule 27(d).

(2)   Other Papers. Any other paper, including a petition for panel rehearing and a petition for hearing or rehearing en banc, and any response to such a petition, must be reproduced in the manner prescribed by Rule 32(a), with the following exceptions:

(A)   A cover is not necessary if the caption and signature page of the paper together contain the information required by Rule 32(a)(2). If a cover is used, it must be white.

(B)   Rule 32(a)(7) does not apply.

(d)   Signature. Every brief, motion, or other paper filed with the court must be signed by the party filing the paper or, if the party is represented, by one of the party's attorneys.

(e)   Local Variation. Every court of appeals must accept documents that comply with the form requirements of this rule and the length limits set by these rules. By local rule or order in a particular case, a court of appeals may accept documents that do not meet all the form requirements of this rule or the length limits set by these rules.

(f)   Items Excluded from Length. In computing any length limit, headings, footnotes, and quotations count toward the limit but the following items do not:

- the cover page;
- a corporate disclosure statement;
- a table of contents;
- a table of citations;
- a statement regarding oral argument;
- an addendum containing statutes, rules, or regulations;
- certificates of counsel;
- the signature block;
- the proof of service; and
- any item specifically excluded by these rules or by local rule.

(g)   Certificate of Compliance.

(1)   Briefs and Papers That Require a Certificate. A brief submitted under Rules 28.1(e)(2), 29(b)(4), or 32(a)(7)(B)—and a paper submitted under Rules 5(c)(1), 21(d)(1), 27(d)(2)(A), 27(d)(2)(C), 35(b)(2)(A), or 40(b)(1)—must include a certificate by the attorney, or an unrepresented party, that the document complies with the type-volume limitation. The person preparing the certificate may rely on the word or line count of the word-processing system used to prepare the document. The certificate must state the number of words—or the number of lines of monospaced type—in the document.

(2)   Acceptable Form. Form 6 in the Appendix of Forms meets the requirements for a certificate of compliance.

RULE 32.1. CITING JUDICIAL DISPOSITIONS

(a) Citation Permitted. A court may not prohibit or restrict the citation of federal judicial opinions, orders, judgments, or other written dispositions that have been:

(i) designed as "unpublished," "not for publication," "non-precedential," "not precedent," or the like; and

(ii) issued on or after January 1, 2007.

(b) Copies Required. If a party cites a federal judicial opinion, order, judgment, or other written disposition that is not available in a publicly accessible electronic database, the party must file and serve a copy of that opinion, order, judgment, or disposition with the brief or other paper in which it is cited.

RULE 33. APPEAL CONFERENCES

The court may direct the attorneys—and, when appropriate, the parties—to participate in one or more conferences to address any matter that may aid in disposing of the proceedings, including simplifying the issues and discussing settlement. A judge or other person designated by the court may preside over the conference, which may be conducted in person or by telephone. Before a settlement conference, the attorneys must consult with their clients and obtain as much authority as feasible to settle the case. The court may, as a result of the conference, enter an order controlling the course of the proceedings or implementing any settlement agreement.

RULE 34. ORAL ARGUMENT

(a) In General.

(1) Party's Statement. Any party may file, or a court may require by local rule, a statement explaining why oral argument should, or need not, be permitted.

(2) Standards. Oral argument must be allowed in every case unless a panel of three judges who have examined the briefs and record unanimously agrees that oral argument is unnecessary for any of the following reasons:

(A) the appeal is frivolous;

(B) the dispositive issue or issues have been authoritatively decided; or

(C) the facts and legal arguments are adequately presented in the briefs and record, and the decisional process would not be significantly aided by oral argument.

(b) Notice of Argument; Postponement. The clerk must advise all parties whether oral argument will be scheduled, and, if so, the date, time, and place for it, and the time allowed for each side. A motion to postpone the argument or to allow longer argument must be filed reasonably in advance of the hearing date.

(c) Order and Contents of Argument. The appellant opens and concludes the argument. Counsel must not read at length from briefs, records, or authorities.

(d) Cross-Appeals and Separate Appeals. If there is a cross-appeal, Rule 28.1(b) determines which party is the appellant and which is the appellee for purposes of oral argument. Unless the court directs otherwise, a cross-appeal or separate appeal must be argued when the initial appeal is argued. Separate parties should avoid duplicative argument.

(e) Nonappearance of a Party. If the appellee fails to appear for argument, the court must hear appellant's argument. If the appellant fails to appear for argument, the court may hear the appellee's argument. If neither party appears, the case will be decided on the briefs, unless the court orders otherwise.

(f) Submission on Briefs. The parties may agree to submit a case for decision on the briefs, but the court may direct that the case be argued.

(g) Use of Physical Exhibits at Argument; Removal. Counsel intending to use physical exhibits other than documents at the argument must arrange to place them in the courtroom on the day of the argument before the court convenes. After the argument, counsel must remove the exhibits from the courtroom, unless the court directs otherwise. The clerk may destroy or dispose of the exhibits if counsel does not reclaim them within a reasonable time after the clerk gives notice to remove them.

RULE 35.   EN BANC DETERMINATION

(a) When Hearing or Rehearing En Banc May Be Ordered. A majority of the circuit judges who are in regular active service and who are not disqualified may order that an appeal or other proceeding be heard or reheard by the court of appeals en banc. An en banc hearing or rehearing is not favored and ordinarily will not be ordered unless:

(1)   en banc consideration is necessary to secure or maintain uniformity of the court's decisions; or

(2)   the proceeding involves a question of exceptional importance.

(b) Petition for Hearing or Rehearing En Banc. A party may petition for a hearing or rehearing en banc.

(1)   The petition must begin with a statement that either:

(A)   the panel decision conflicts with a decision of the United States Supreme Court or of the court to which the petition is addressed (with citation to the conflicting case or cases) and consideration by the full court is therefore necessary to secure and maintain uniformity of the court's decisions; or

(B)   the proceeding involves one or more questions of exceptional importance, each of which must be concisely stated; for example, a petition may assert that a proceeding presents a question of exceptional importance if it involves an issue on which the panel decision conflicts with the authoritative decisions of every other United States Court of Appeals that has addressed the issue.

(2)   Except by the court's permission:

(A)   a petition for an en banc hearing or rehearing produced using a computer must not exceed 3,900 words; and

(B)   a handwritten or typewritten petition for an en banc hearing or rehearing must not exceed 15 pages.

(3)   For purposes of the limits in Rule 35(b)(2), if a party files both a petition for panel rehearing and a petition for rehearing en banc, they are considered a single document even if they are filed separately, unless separate filing is required by local rule.

(c) Time for Petition for Hearing or Rehearing En Banc. A petition that an appeal be heard initially en banc must be filed by the date when the appellee's brief is due. A petition for a rehearing en banc must be filed within the time prescribed by Rule 40 for filing a petition for rehearing.

(d) Number of Copies. The number of copies to be filed must be prescribed by local rule and may be altered by order in a particular case.

(e) Response. No response may be filed to a petition for an en banc consideration unless the court orders a response.

(f) Call for a Vote. A vote need not be taken to determine whether the case will be heard or reheard en banc unless a judge calls for a vote.

RULE 36.   ENTRY OF JUDGMENT; NOTICE

(a) Entry. A judgment is entered when it is noted on the docket. The clerk must prepare, sign, and enter the judgment:

(1)   after receiving the court's opinion—but if settlement of the judgment's form is required, after final settlement; or

(2)   if a judgment is rendered without an opinion, as the court instructs.

(b) Notice. On the date when judgment is entered, the clerk must serve on all parties a copy of the opinion—or the judgment, if no opinion was written—and a notice of the date when the judgment was entered.

RULE 37.   INTEREST ON JUDGMENT

(a) When the Court Affirms. Unless the law provides otherwise, if a money judgment in a civil case is affirmed, whatever interest is allowed by law is payable from the date when the district court's judgment was entered.

(b) When the Court Reverses. If the court modifies or reverses a judgment with a direction that a money judgment be entered in the district court, the mandate must contain instructions about the allowance of interest.

RULE 38.   FRIVOLOUS APPEAL—DAMAGES AND COSTS

If a court of appeals determines that an appeal is frivolous, it may, after a separately filed motion or notice from the court and reasonable opportunity to respond, award just damages and single or double costs to the appellee.

RULE 39.   COSTS

(a) Against Whom Assessed. The following rules apply unless the law provides or the court orders otherwise:

(1)   if an appeal is dismissed, costs are taxed against the appellant, unless the parties agree otherwise;

(2)   if a judgment is affirmed, costs are taxed against the appellant;

(3)   if a judgment is reversed, costs are taxed against the appellee;

(4)   if a judgment is affirmed in part, reversed in part, modified, or vacated, costs are taxed only as the court orders.

(b) Costs For and Against the United States. Costs for or against the United States, its agency, or officer will be assessed under Rule 39(a) only if authorized by law.

(c) Costs of Copies. Each court of appeals must, by local rule, fix the maximum rate for taxing the cost of producing necessary copies of a brief or appendix, or copies of records authorized by Rule 30(f). The rate must not exceed that generally charged for such work in the area where the clerk's office is located and should encourage economical methods of copying.

(d) Bill of Costs: Objections; Insertion in Mandate.

(1)   A party who wants costs taxed must—within 14 days after entry of judgment—file with the circuit clerk, with proof of service, an itemized and verified bill of costs.

(2)   Objections must be filed within 14 days after service of the bill of costs, unless the court extends the time.

(3)   The clerk must prepare and certify an itemized statement of costs for insertion in the mandate, but issuance of the mandate must not be delayed for taxing costs. If the mandate issues before costs are finally determined, the district clerk must—upon the circuit clerk's request—add the statement of costs, or any amendment of it, to the mandate.

(e) Costs on Appeal Taxable in the District Court. The following costs on appeal are taxable in the district court for the benefit of the party entitled to costs under this rule:

(1) the preparation and transmission of the record;

(2) the reporter's transcript, if needed to determine the appeal;

(3) premiums paid for a supersedeas bond or other bond to preserve rights pending appeal; and

(4) the fee for filing the notice of appeal.

RULE 40.   PETITION FOR PANEL REHEARING

(a) Time to File; Contents; Answer; Action by the Court if Granted.

(1) Time. Unless the time is shortened or extended by order or local rule, a petition for panel rehearing may be filed within 14 days after entry of judgment. But in a civil case, unless an order shortens or extends the time, the petition may be filed by any party within 45 days after entry of judgment if one of the parties is:

(A) the United States;

(B) a United States agency;

(C) a United States officer or employee sued in an official capacity; or

(D) a current or former United States officer or employee sued in an individual capacity for an act or omission occurring in connection with duties performed on the United States' behalf—including all instances in which the United States represents that person when the court of appeals' judgment is entered or files the petition for that person.

(2) Contents. The petition must state with particularity each point of law or fact that the petitioner believes the court has overlooked or misapprehended and must argue in support of the petition. Oral argument is not permitted.

(3) Answer. Unless the court requests, no answer to a petition for panel rehearing is permitted. But ordinarily rehearing will not be granted in the absence of such a request.

(4) Action by the Court. If a petition for panel rehearing is granted, the court may do any of the following:

(A) make a final disposition of the case without reargument;

(B) restore the case to the calendar for reargument or resubmission; or

(C) issue any other appropriate order.

(b) Form of Petition; Length. The petition must comply in form with Rule 32. Copies must be served and filed as Rule 31 prescribes. Except by the court's permission:

(1) a petition for panel rehearing produced using a computer must not exceed 3,900 words; and

(2) a handwritten or typewritten petition for panel rehearing must not exceed 15 pages.

RULE 41.   MANDATE: CONTENTS; ISSUANCE AND EFFECTIVE DATE; STAY

(a) Contents. Unless the court directs that a formal mandate issue, the mandate consists of a certified copy of the judgment, a copy of the court's opinion, if any, and any direction about costs.

(b) When Issued. The court's mandate must issue 7 days after the time to file a petition for rehearing expires, or 7 days after entry of an order denying a timely petition for panel rehearing, petition for rehearing en banc, or motion for stay of mandate, whichever is later. The court may shorten or extend the time.

(c) Effective Date. The mandate is effective when issued.

(d) Staying the Mandate.

(1) On Petition for Rehearing or Motion. The timely filing of a petition for panel rehearing, petition for rehearing en banc, or motion for stay of mandate, stays the mandate until disposition of the petition or motion, unless the court orders otherwise.

(2) Pending Petition for Certiorari.

(A) A party may move to stay the mandate pending the filing of a petition for a writ of certiorari in the Supreme Court. The motion must be served on all parties and must show that the certiorari petition would present a substantial question and that there is good cause for a stay.

(B) The stay must not exceed 90 days, unless the period is extended for good cause or unless the party who obtained the stay files a petition for the writ and so notifies the circuit clerk in writing within the period of the stay. In that case, the stay continues until the Supreme Court's final disposition.

(C) The court may require a bond or other security as a condition to granting or continuing a stay of the mandate.

(D) The court of appeals must issue the mandate immediately when a copy of a Supreme Court order denying the petition for writ of certiorari is filed.

RULE 42. VOLUNTARY DISMISSAL

(a) Dismissal in the District Court. Before an appeal has been docketed by the circuit clerk, the district court may dismiss the appeal on the filing of a stipulation signed by all parties or on the appellant's motion with notice to all parties.

(b) Dismissal in the Court of Appeals. The circuit clerk may dismiss a docketed appeal if the parties file a signed dismissal agreement specifying how costs are to be paid and pay any fees that are due. But no mandate or other process may issue without a court order. An appeal may be dismissed on the appellant's motion on terms agreed to by the parties or fixed by the court.

RULE 43. SUBSTITUTION OF PARTIES

(a) Death of a Party.

(1) After Notice of Appeal Is Filed. If a party dies after a notice of appeal has been filed or while a proceeding is pending in the court of appeals, the decedent's personal representative may be substituted as a party on motion filed with the circuit clerk by the representative or by any party. A party's motion must be served on the representative in accordance with Rule 25. If the decedent has no representative, any party may suggest the death on the record, and the court of appeals may then direct appropriate proceedings.

(2) Before Notice of Appeal Is Filed—Potential Appellant. If a party entitled to appeal dies before filing a notice of appeal, the decedent's personal representative—or, if there is no personal representative, the decedent's attorney of record—may file a notice of appeal within the time prescribed by these rules. After the notice of appeal is filed, substitution must be in accordance with Rule 43(a)(1).

(3) Before Notice of Appeal Is Filed—Potential Appellee. If a party against whom an appeal may be taken dies after entry of a judgment or order in the district court, but before a notice of appeal is filed, an appellant may proceed as if the death had not occurred. After the notice of appeal is filed, substitution must be in accordance with Rule 43(a)(1).

(b) Substitution for a Reason Other Than Death. If a party needs to be substituted for any reason other than death, the procedure prescribed in Rule 43(a) applies.

(c) **Public Officer: Identification; Substitution.**

(1) **Identification of Party.** A public officer who is a party to an appeal or other proceeding in an official capacity may be described as a party by the public officer's official title rather than by name. But the court may require the public officer's name to be added.

(2) **Automatic Substitution of Officeholder.** When a public officer who is a party to an appeal or other proceeding in an official capacity dies, resigns, or otherwise ceases to hold office, the action does not abate. The public officer's successor is automatically substituted as a party. Proceedings following the substitution are to be in the name of the substituted party, but any misnomer that does not affect the substantial rights of the parties may be disregarded. An order of substitution may be entered at any time, but failure to enter an order does not affect the substitution.

RULE 44.   CASE INVOLVING A CONSTITUTIONAL QUESTION WHEN THE UNITED STATES OR THE RELEVANT STATE IS NOT A PARTY

(a) **Constitutional Challenge to Federal Statute.** If a party questions the constitutionality of an Act of Congress in a proceeding in which the United States or its agency, officer, or employee is not a party in an official capacity, the questioning party must give written notice to the circuit clerk immediately upon the filing of the record or as soon as the question is raised in the court of appeals. The clerk must then certify that fact to the Attorney General.

(b) **Constitutional Challenge to State Statute.** If a party questions the constitutionality of a statute of a State in a proceeding in which that State or its agency, officer, or employee is not a party in an official capacity, the questioning party must give written notice to the circuit clerk immediately upon the filing of the record or as soon as the question is raised in the court of appeals. The clerk must then certify that fact to the attorney general of the State.

RULE 45.   CLERK'S DUTIES

(a) **General Provisions.**

(1) **Qualifications.** The circuit clerk must take the oath and post any bond required by law. Neither the clerk nor any deputy clerk may practice as an attorney or counselor in any court while in office.

(2) **When Court Is Open.** The court of appeals is always open for filing any paper, issuing and returning process, making a motion, and entering an order. The clerk's office with the clerk or a deputy in attendance must be open during business hours on all days except Saturdays, Sundays, and legal holidays. A court may provide by local rule or by order that the clerk's office be open for specified hours on Saturdays or on legal holidays other than New Year's Day, Martin Luther King, Jr.'s Birthday, Washington's Birthday, Memorial Day, Independence Day, Labor Day, Columbus Day, Veterans' Day, Thanksgiving Day, and Christmas Day.

(b) **Records.**

(1) **The Docket.** The circuit clerk must maintain a docket and an index of all docketed cases in the manner prescribed by the Director of the Administrative Office of the United States Courts. The clerk must record all papers filed with the clerk and all process, orders, and judgments.

(2) **Calendar.** Under the court's direction, the clerk must prepare a calendar of cases awaiting argument. In placing cases on the calendar for argument, the clerk must give preference to appeals in criminal cases and to other proceedings and appeals entitled to preference by law.

(3) **Other Records.** The clerk must keep other books and records required by the Director of the Administrative Office of the United States Courts, with the approval of the Judicial Conference of the United States, or by the court.

(c) Notice of an Order or Judgment. Upon the entry of an order or judgment, the circuit clerk must immediately serve a notice of entry on each party, with a copy of any opinion, and must note the date of service on the docket. Service on a party represented by counsel must be made on counsel.

(d) Custody of Records and Papers. The circuit clerk has custody of the court's records and papers. Unless the court orders or instructs otherwise, the clerk must not permit an original record or paper to be taken from the clerk's office. Upon disposition of the case, original papers constituting the record on appeal or review must be returned to the court or agency from which they were received. The clerk must preserve a copy of any brief, appendix, or other paper that has been filed.

RULE 46.   ATTORNEYS

(a) Admission to the Bar.

(1) **Eligibility.** An attorney is eligible for admission to the bar of a court of appeals if that attorney is of good moral and professional character and is admitted to practice before the Supreme Court of the United States, the highest court of a state, another United States court of appeals, or a United States district court (including the district courts for Guam, the Northern Mariana Islands, and the Virgin Islands).

(2) **Application.** An applicant must file an application for admission, on a form approved by the court that contains the applicant's personal statement showing eligibility for membership. The applicant must subscribe to the following oath or affirmation: "I, _____, do solemnly swear [or affirm] that I will conduct myself as an attorney and counselor of this court, uprightly and according to law; and that I will support the Constitution of the United States."

(3) **Admission Procedures.** On written or oral motion of a member of the court's bar, the court will act on the application. An applicant may be admitted by oral motion in open court. But, unless the court orders otherwise, an applicant need not appear before the court to be admitted. Upon admission, an applicant must pay the clerk the fee prescribed by local rule or court order.

(b) Suspension or Disbarment.

(1) **Standard.** A member of the court's bar is subject to suspension or disbarment by the court if the member:

(A) has been suspended or disbarred from practice in any other court; or

(B) is guilty of conduct unbecoming a member of the court's bar.

(2) **Procedure.** The member must be given an opportunity to show good cause, within the time prescribed by the court, why the member should not be suspended or disbarred.

(3) **Order.** The court must enter an appropriate order after the member responds and a hearing is held, if requested, or after the time prescribed for a response expires, if no response is made.

(c) Discipline. A court of appeals may discipline an attorney who practices before it for conduct unbecoming a member of the bar or for failure to comply with any court rule. First, however, the court must afford the attorney reasonable notice, an opportunity to show cause to the contrary, and, if requested, a hearing.

RULE 47.   LOCAL RULES BY COURTS OF APPEALS

(a) Local Rules.

(1) Each court of appeals acting by a majority of its judges in regular active service may, after giving appropriate public notice and opportunity for comment, make and amend rules governing its practice. A generally applicable direction to parties or lawyers regarding practice before a court must be in a local rule rather than an internal operating procedure or standing order. A local rule must be consistent with—but not duplicative of—Acts of Congress and rules adopted under 28 U.S.C. § 2072 and must conform to any uniform numbering system prescribed by the Judicial Conference of the United States. Each circuit clerk must send the Administrative Office

of the United States Courts a copy of each local rule and internal operating procedure when it is promulgated or amended.

(2)   A local rule imposing a requirement of form must not be enforced in a manner that causes a party to lose rights because of a nonwillful failure to comply with the requirement.

(b) Procedure When There Is No Controlling Law. A court of appeals may regulate practice in a particular case in any manner consistent with federal law, these rules, and local rules of the circuit. No sanction or other disadvantage may be imposed for noncompliance with any requirement not in federal law, federal rules, or the local circuit rules unless the alleged violator has been furnished in the particular case with actual notice of the requirement.

RULE 48.   MASTERS

(a) Appointment; Powers. A court of appeals may appoint a special master to hold hearings, if necessary, and to recommend factual findings and disposition in matters ancillary to proceedings in the court. Unless the order referring a matter to a master specifies or limits the master's powers, those powers include, but are not limited to, the following:

(1)   regulating all aspects of a hearing;

(2)   taking all appropriate action for the efficient performance of the master's duties under the order;

(3)   requiring the production of evidence on all matters embraced in the reference; and

(4)   administering oaths and examining witnesses and parties.

(b) Compensation. If the master is not a judge or court employee, the court must determine the master's compensation and whether the cost is to be charged to any party.

§ 6.9   Appendix of Forms to the *Federal Rules of Appellate Procedure*

1.   Notice of Appeal to a Court of Appeals from a Judgment or Order of a District Court
2.   Notice of Appeal to a Court of Appeals from a Decision of the United States Tax Court
3.   Petition for Review of Order of an Agency, Board, Commission or Officer
4.   Affidavit Accompanying Motion for Permission to Appeal in Forma Pauperis
5.   Notice of Appeal to a Court of Appeals from a Judgment or Order of a District Court or a Bankruptcy Appellate Panel
6.   Certificate of Compliance With Type-Volume Limit
7.   Declaration of Inmate Filing

Appendix. Length Limits Stated in the Federal Rules of Appellate Procedure

Form 1. Notice of Appeal to a Court of Appeals from a Judgment or Order of a District Court

United States District Court for the _____

District of _____

File Number _____

A.B., Plaintiff
v.
C.D., Defendant

Notice of Appeal

Notice is hereby given that _____(here name all parties taking the appeal), (plaintiffs) (defendants) in the above named case,* hereby appeal to the United States Court of Appeals for the _____ Circuit (from the final judgment) (from an order (describing it)) entered in this action on the _____ day of _____, 20___.

(s) _____

Attorney for _____

Address:_____

[**Note to inmate filers:** *If you are an inmate confined in an institution and you seek the timing benefit of Fed. R. App. P. 4(c)(1), complete Form 7 (Declaration of Inmate Filing) and file that declaration along with this Notice of Appeal.*]

---

* *See* Rule 3(c) for permissible ways of identifying appellants.

Form 2. Notice of Appeal to a Court of Appeals from a Decision of the United States Tax Court

UNITED STATES TAX COURT Washington, D.C.

A.B., Plaintiff

v.   Docket No. _____

Commissioner of
Internal Revenue,
Respondent

Notice of Appeal

Notice is hereby given that *[here name all parties taking the appeal* [211]*]*, hereby appeals to the United States Court of Appeals for the _____ Circuit from (that part of) the decision of this court entered in the above captioned proceeding on the _____ day of _____, 20_____ (relating to _____).

(s) _____

Counsel for [_____]

Address: [_____]

---

[211] *See* Rule 3(c) for permissible ways of identifying appellants.

Form 3. Petition for Review of Order of an Agency, Board, Commission or Officer

United States Court of Appeals

for the _____ Circuit

A.B., Petitioner v. XYZ Commission, Respondent	Petition for Review

[*(here name all parties bringing the petition* [212]*)*] hereby petitions the court for review of the Order of the XYZ Commission (describe the order) entered on _____, 20_____.

[(s)] _____

Attorney for Petitioners _____

Address:_____

---

[212] *See* Rule 15.

Form 4. Affidavit Accompanying Motion for Permission to Appeal in Forma Pauperis

United States District Court for the

_____ District of _____

<Name(s) of Plaintiff(s)>, Plaintiff(s) v. <Name(s) of Defendant(s)>, Defendant(s)	**Case No.** <Number>

Affidavit in Support of Instructions Motion

I swear or affirm under penalty of perjury that, because of my poverty, I cannot prepay the docket fees of my appeal or post a bond for them. I believe I am entitled to redress. I swear or affirm under penalty of perjury under United States laws that my answers on this form are true and correct. (28 U.S.C. § 1746; 18 U.S.C. § 1621.)

Signed: _____

Complete all questions in this application and then sign it. Do not leave any blanks: if the answer to a question is "0," "none," or "not applicable (N/A)," write in that response. If you need more space to answer a question or to explain your answer, attach a separate sheet of paper identified with your name, your case's docket number, and the question number.

Dated: _____

My issues on appeal are:

1. For both you and your spouse estimate the average amount of money received from each of the following sources during the past 12 months. Adjust any amount that was received weekly, biweekly, quarterly, semiannually, or annually to show the monthly rate. Use gross amounts, that is, amounts before any deductions for taxes or otherwise.

Income source	Average monthly amount during the past 12 months		Amount expected next month	
	You	Spouse	You	Spouse
Employment	$ _____	$ _____	$ _____	$ _____
Self-employment	$ _____	$ _____	$ _____	$ _____
Income from real property (such as rental income)	$ _____	$ _____	$ _____	$ _____
Interest and dividends	$ _____	$ _____	$ _____	$ _____
Gifts	$ _____	$ _____	$ _____	$ _____
Alimony	$ _____	$ _____	$ _____	$ _____
Child support	$ _____	$ _____	$ _____	$ _____
Retirement (such as social security, pensions, annuities, insurance	$ _____	$ _____	$ _____	$ _____
Disability (such as social security, insurance payments)	$ _____	$ _____	$ _____	$ _____
Unemployment payments	$ _____	$ _____	$ _____	$ _____
Public assistance (such as welfare)	$ _____	$ _____	$ _____	$ _____
Other (specify):	$ _____	$ _____	$ _____	$ _____
Total monthly income:	$ _____	$ _____	$ _____	$ _____

2. List your employment history for the past two years, most recent employer first. (Gross monthly pay is before taxes or other deductions.)

Employer	Address	Dates of employment	Gross monthly pay
_____	_____	_____	_____
_____	_____	_____	_____
_____	_____	_____	_____

3. List your spouse's employment history for the past two years, most recent employer first. (Gross monthly pay is before taxes or other deductions.)

Employer	Address	Dates of employment	Gross monthly pay
_____	_____	_____	_____
_____	_____	_____	_____
_____	_____	_____	_____

4.   *How much cash do you and your spouse have?* $_____

Below, state any money you or your spouse have in bank accounts or in any other financial institution.

Financial Institution	Type of account	Amount you have	Amount your spouse has
_____	_____	$_____	$_____
_____	_____	$_____	$_____
_____	_____	$_____	$_____

If you are a prisoner seeking to appeal a judgment in a civil action or proceeding, you must attach a statement certified by the appropriate institutional officer showing all receipts, expenditures, and balances during the last six months in your institutional accounts. If you have multiple accounts, perhaps because you have been in multiple institutions, attach one certified statement of each account.

5.   *List the assets, and their values, which you own or your spouse owns. Do not list clothing and ordinary household furnishings.*

Home (Value)	**Other real estate** (Value)	**Motor vehicle #1** (Value)
_____	_____	Make & year: _____
_____	_____	Model: _____
_____	_____	Registration #: _____

Motor vehicle #2 (Value)	**Other assets** (Value)	**Other assets** (Value)
Make & year: _____	_____	_____
Model: _____	_____	_____
Registration #: _____	_____	_____

6.   *State every person, business, or organization owing you or your spouse money, and the amount owed.*

Person owing you or your spouse money	Amount owed to you	Amount owed to your spouse
_____	_____	_____
_____	_____	_____
_____	_____	_____

7.   *State the persons who rely on you or your spouse for support.*

Name [or, if under 18, initials only]	Relationship	Age
_____	_____	_____
_____	_____	_____
_____	_____	_____

8.   *Estimate the average monthly expenses of you and your family. Show separately the amounts paid by your spouse. Adjust any payments that are made weekly, biweekly, quarterly, semiannually, or annually to show the monthly rate.*

	You	**Your Spouse**
Rent or home-mortgage payment (include lot rented for mobile home)	$ _____	$ _____
Are real-estate taxes included? __ Yes __ No		
Is property insurance included? __ Yes __ No		
Utilities (electricity, heating fuel, water, sewer, and Telephone)	$ _____	$ _____
Home maintenance (repairs and upkeep)	$ _____	$ _____
Food	$ _____	$ _____
Clothing	$ _____	$ _____
Laundry and dry-cleaning	$ _____	$ _____
Medical and dental expenses	$ _____	$ _____
Transportation (not including motor vehicle payments)	$ _____	$ _____
Recreation, entertainment, newspapers, magazines, etc.	$ _____	$ _____
Insurance (not deducted from wages or included in Mortgage payments)	$ _____	$ _____
Homeowner's or renter's	$ _____	$ _____
Life	$ _____	$ _____
Health	$ _____	$ _____
Motor Vehicle	$ _____	$ _____
Other: _____	$ _____	$ _____
Taxes (not deducted from wages or included in Mortgage payments) (specify): _____	$ _____	$ _____
Installment payments	$ _____	$ _____
Motor Vehicle	$ _____	$ _____
Credit card (name): _____	$ _____	$ _____
Department store (name): _____	$ _____	$ _____
Other: _____	$ _____	$ _____

Alimony, maintenance, and support
    paid to others $ _____ $ _____

Regular expenses for operation of business,
    profession, or farm (attach detailed
    statement) $ _____ $ _____

Other (specify):

_____ $ _____ $ _____

Total monthly expenses: $ _____ $ _____

     9.   *Do you expect any major changes to your monthly income or expenses or in your assets or liabilities during the next 12 months?*

        _____ Yes _____ No If yes, describe on an attached sheet.

     10.   *Have you spent—or will you be spending—any money for expenses or attorney fees in connection with this lawsuit?* _____ Yes ____ No

        If yes, how much? $_____

     11.   *Provide any other information that will help explain why you cannot pay the docket fees for your appeal.*

        _____

        _____

        _____

     12.   *Provide any other information that will help explain why you cannot pay the docket fees for your appeal.*

     13.   *State the city and state of your legal residence.*

        _____

        _____

        Your daytime phone number: (_____) _____

        Your age: _____ Your years of schooling: _____

        Last four digits of your social-security number: _____

Form 5. Notice of Appeal to a Court of Appeals from a Judgment or Order of a District Court or a Bankruptcy Appellate Panel

United States District Court for the _____

District of _____

In re

_____,

Debtor

_____,

Plaintiff   File No. _____

v.

_____,

Defendant

Notice of Appeal to United States Court of Appeals for the

_____ Circuit

_____, the plaintiff [or defendant or other party] appeals to the United States Court of Appeals for the _____ Circuit from the final judgment [or order or decree] of the district court for the district of _____ [or bankruptcy appellate panel of the _____ circuit], entered in this case on _____, 20___ [here describe the judgment, order, or decree]

_____ .

The parties to the judgment [or order or decree] appealed from and the names and addresses of their respective attorneys are as follows:

Dated _____

Signed _____

Attorney for Appellant

Address _____

_____

[*Note to inmate filers:* *If you are an inmate confined in an institution and you seek the timing benefit of Fed. R. App. P. 4(c)(1), complete Form 7 (Declaration of Inmate Filing) and file that declaration along with this Notice of Appeal.*]

Form 6. Certificate of Compliance With Type-Volume Limit

Certificate of Compliance With Type-Volume Limit,
Typeface Requirements, and Type-Style Requirements

1.   This document complies with [the type-volume limit of Fed. R. App. P. [*insert Rule citation; e.g., 32(a)(7)(B)*] [the word limit of Fed. R. App. P. [*insert Rule citation; e.g., 5(c)(1)*] because, excluding the parts of the document exempted by Fed. R. App. P. 32(f) [and [*insert applicable Rule citation, if any*]]:

☐   this document contains [*state the number of*] words, **or**

☐   this brief uses a monospaced typeface and contains [*state the number of*] lines of text.

2.   This document complies with the typeface requirements of Fed. R. App. P. 32(a)(5) and the type-style requirements of Fed. R. App. P. 32(a)(6) because:

☐   this document has been prepared in a proportionally spaced typeface using [*state name and version of word-processing program*] in [*state font size and name of type style*], or

☐   this document has been prepared in a monospaced typeface using [*state name and version of word-processing program*] with [*state number of characters per inch and name of type style*].

(s)_____

Attorney for _____

Dated: _____

Form 7. Declaration of Inmate Filing

_____

[insert name of court; for example,
United States District Court for the District of Minnesota]

A.B., Plaintiff	
v.	Case No. _____
C.D., Defendant	

      I am an inmate confined in an institution. Today, _____ *[insert date]*, I am depositing the _____ *[insert title of document; for example, "notice of appeal"]* in this case in the institution's internal mail system. First-class postage is being prepaid either by me or by the institution on my behalf.

      I declare under penalty of perjury that the foregoing is true and correct (see 28 U.S.C. § 1746; 18 U.S.C. § 1621).

Sign your name here_____

Signed on _____ *[insert date]*

*[**Note to inmate filers:** If your institution has a system designed for legal mail, you must use that system in order to receive the timing benefit of Fed. R. App. P. 4(c)(1) or Fed. R. App. P. 25(a)(2)(C).]*

Appendix.   **Length Limits Stated in the Federal Rules of Appellate Procedure**

This chart summarizes the length limits stated in the Federal Rules of Appellate Procedure. Please refer to the rules for precise requirements, and bear in mind the following:

- In computing these limits, you can exclude the items listed in Rule 32(f).
- If you use a word limit or a line limit (other than the word limit in Rule 28(j)), you must file the certificate required by Rule 32(g).
- For the limits in Rules 5, 21, 27, 35, and 40:
  — You must use the word limit if you produce your document on a computer; and
  — You must use the page limit if you handwrite your document or type it on a typewriter.
- For the limits in Rules 28.1, 29(a)(5), and 32:
  — You may use the word limit or page limit, regardless of how you produce the document; or
  — You may use the line limit if you type or print your document with a monospaced typeface. A typeface is monospaced when each character occupies the same amount of horizontal space.

	Rule	Document type	Word limit	Page limit	Line limit
Permission to appeal	5(c)	• Petition for permission to appeal • Answer in opposition • Cross-petition	5,200	20	Not applicable
Extraordinary writs	21(d)	• Petition for writ of mandamus or prohibition or other extraordinary writ • Answer	7,800	30	Not applicable
Motions	27(d)(2)	• Motion • Response to a motion	5,200	20	Not applicable
	27(d)(2)	• Reply to a response to a motion	2,600	10	Not applicable
Parties' briefs (where no cross-appeal)	32(a)(7)	• Principal brief	13,000	30	1,300
	32(a)(7)	• Reply brief	6,500	15	650
Parties' briefs (where cross appeal)	28.1(e)	• Appellant's principal brief • Appellant's response and reply brief	13,000	30	1,300
	28.1(e)	• Appellee's principal and response brief	15,300	35	1,500
	28.1(e)	• Appellee's reply brief	6,500	15	650
Party's supplemental letter	28(j)	• Letter citing supplemental authorities	350	Not applicable	Not applicable

	Rule	Document type	Word limit	Page limit	Line limit
Amicus briefs	29(a)(5)	• Amicus brief during initial consideration of case on merits	One-half the length set by the Appellate Rules for a party's principal brief	One-half the length set by the Appellate Rules for a party's principal brief	One-half the length set by the Appellate Rules for a party's principal brief
	29(b)(4)	• Amicus brief during consideration of whether to grant rehearing	2,600	Not applicable	Not applicable
Rehearing and en banc filings	35(b)(2) & 40(b)	• Petition for hearing en banc • Petition for panel rehearing; petition for rehearing en banc	3,900	15	Not applicable

---

ADDITIONAL RESEARCH REFERENCES

David G. Knibb, *Federal Court of Appeals Manual: A Manual on Practice in the United States Court of Appeals*

Charles A. Wright, Arthur R. Miller, & Edward H. Cooper, *Federal Practice and Procedure* §§ 3945 to 4000

C.J.S. Federal Courts §§ 291(1) to 301(48) et seq.

West's Key Number Digest, Federal Courts ⊷741 to 956

PART VIII

TITLE 28, JUDICIARY AND JUDICIAL PROCEDURE—SELECTED PROVISIONS

Including Amendments Current as of July 1, 2016

Table of Sections

§ 144.   Bias or Prejudice of Judge

Whenever a party to any proceeding in a district court makes and files a timely and sufficient affidavit that the judge before whom the matter is pending has a personal bias or prejudice either against him or in favor of any adverse party, such judge shall proceed no further therein, but another judge shall be assigned to hear such proceeding.

The affidavit shall state the facts and the reasons for the belief that bias or prejudice exists, and shall be filed not less than ten days before the beginning of the term at which the proceeding is to be heard, or good cause shall be shown for failure to file it within such time. A party may file only one such affidavit in any case. It shall be accompanied by a certificate of counsel of record stating that it is made in good faith.

§ 451.   Definitions

As used in this title:

The term "court of the United States" includes the Supreme Court of the United States, courts of appeals, district courts constituted by chapter 5 of this title, including the Court of International Trade and any court created by Act of Congress the judges of which are entitled to hold office during good behavior.

The terms "district court" and "district court of the United States" mean the courts constituted by chapter 5 of this title.

The term "judge of the United States" includes judges of the courts of appeals, district courts, Court of International Trade and any court created by Act of Congress, the judges of which are entitled to hold office during good behavior.

The term "justice of the United States" includes the Chief Justice of the United States and the associate justices of the Supreme Court.

The term "district" and "judicial district" mean the districts enumerated in Chapter 5 of this title.

The term "department" means one of the executive departments enumerated in section 1 of Title 5, unless the context shows that such term was intended to describe the executive, legislative, or judicial branches of the government.

The term "agency" includes any department, independent establishment, commission, administration, authority, board or bureau of the United States or any corporation in which the United States has a proprietary interest, unless the context shows that such term was intended to be used in a more limited sense.

§ 452.   Courts Always Open; Powers Unrestricted by Expiration of Sessions

All courts of the United States shall be deemed always open for the purpose of filing proper papers, issuing and returning process, and making motions and orders.

The continued existence or expiration of a session of court in no way affects the power of the court to do any act or take any proceeding.

§ 455.   Disqualification of Justice, Judge, or Magistrate

(a) Any justice, judge, or magistrate of the United States shall disqualify himself in any proceeding in which his impartiality might reasonably be questioned.

(b) He shall also disqualify himself in the following circumstances:

   (1) Where he has a personal bias or prejudice concerning a party, or personal knowledge of disputed evidentiary facts concerning the proceeding;

   (2) Where in private practice he served as lawyer in the matter in controversy, or a lawyer with whom he previously practiced law served during such association as a lawyer concerning the matter, or the judge or such lawyer has been a material witness concerning it;

   (3) Where he has served in governmental employment and in such capacity participated as counsel, adviser or material witness concerning the proceeding or expressed an opinion concerning the merits of the particular case in controversy;

   (4) He knows that he, individually or as a fiduciary, or his spouse or minor child residing in his household, has a financial interest in the subject matter in controversy or in a party to the proceeding, or any other interest that could be substantially affected by the outcome of the proceeding;

   (5) He or his spouse, or a person within the third degree of relationship to either of them, or the spouse of such a person:

      (i) Is a party to the proceeding, or an officer, director, or trustee of a party;

      (ii) Is acting as a lawyer in the proceeding;

      (iii) Is known by the judge to have an interest that could be substantially affected by the outcome of the proceeding;

      (iv) Is to the judge's knowledge likely to be a material witness in the proceeding.

(c) A judge should inform himself about his personal and fiduciary financial interests, and make a reasonable effort to inform himself about the personal financial interests of his spouse and minor children residing in his household.

(d) For the purposes of this section the following words or phrases shall have the meaning indicated:

   (1) "proceeding" includes pretrial, trial, appellate review, or other stages of litigation;

   (2) the degree of relationship is calculated according to the civil law system;

   (3) "fiduciary" includes such relationships as executor, administrator, trustee, and guardian;

   (4) "financial interest" means ownership of a legal or equitable interest, however small, or a relationship as director, adviser, or other active participant in the affairs of a party, except that:

    (i) Ownership in a mutual or common investment fund that holds securities is not a "financial interest" in such securities unless the judge participates in the management of the fund;

    (ii) An office in an educational, religious, charitable, fraternal, or civic organization is not a "financial interest" in securities held by the organization;

    (iii) The proprietary interest of a policyholder in a mutual insurance company, of a depositor in a mutual savings association, or a similar proprietary interest, is a "financial interest" in the organization only if the outcome of the proceeding could substantially affect the value of the interest;

    (iv) Ownership of government securities is a "financial interest" in the issuer only if the outcome of the proceeding could substantially affect the value of the securities.

(e) No justice, judge, or magistrate shall accept from the parties to the proceeding a waiver of any ground for disqualification enumerated in subsection (b). Where the ground for disqualification arises only under subsection (a), waiver may be accepted provided it is preceded by a full disclosure on the record of the basis for disqualification.

(f) Notwithstanding the preceding provisions of this section, if any justice, judge, magistrate, or bankruptcy judge to whom a matter has been assigned would be disqualified, after substantial judicial time has been devoted to the matter, because of the appearance or discovery, after the matter was assigned to him or her, that he or she individually or as a fiduciary, or his or her spouse or minor child residing in his or her household, has a financial interest in a party (other than an interest that could be substantially affected by the outcome), disqualification is not required if the justice, judge, magistrate judge, bankruptcy judge, spouse or minor child, as the case may be, divests himself or herself of the interest that provides the grounds for the disqualification.

§ 636.   Jurisdiction, Powers, and Temporary Assignment

(a) Each United States magistrate judge serving under this chapter shall have within the district in which sessions are held by the court that appointed the magistrate judge, at other places where that court may function, and elsewhere as authorized by law—

    (1) all powers and duties conferred or imposed upon United States commissioners by law or by the Rules of Criminal Procedure for the United States District Courts;

    (2) the power to administer oaths and affirmations, issue orders pursuant to section 3142 of title 18 concerning release or detention of persons pending trial, and take acknowledgements, affidavits, and depositions;

    (3) the power to conduct trials under section 3401, title 18, United States Code, in conformity with and subject to the limitations of that section;

    (4) the power to enter a sentence for a petty offense; and

    (5) the power to enter a sentence for a class A misdemeanor in a case in which the parties have consented.

(b)   **(1)** Notwithstanding any provision of law to the contrary—

    (A) a judge may designate a magistrate judge to hear and determine any pretrial matter pending before the court, except a motion for injunctive relief, for judgment on the pleadings, for summary judgment, to dismiss or quash an indictment or information made by the defendant, to suppress evidence in a criminal case, to dismiss or to permit maintenance of a class action, to dismiss for failure to state a claim upon which relief can be granted, and to involuntarily dismiss an action. A judge of the court may reconsider any pretrial matter under this subparagraph (A) where it has been shown that the magistrate judge's order is clearly erroneous or contrary to law.

(B) a judge may also designate a magistrate judge to conduct hearings, including evidentiary hearings, and to submit to a judge of the court proposed findings of fact and recommendations for the disposition, by a judge of the court, of any motion excepted in subparagraph (A), of applications for posttrial [1] relief made by individuals convicted of criminal offenses and of prisoner petitions challenging conditions of confinement.

(C) the magistrate judge shall file his proposed findings and recommendations under subparagraph (B) with the court and a copy shall forthwith be mailed to all parties.

Within fourteen days after being served with a copy, any party may serve and file written objections to such proposed findings and recommendations as provided by rules of court. A judge of the court shall make a de novo determination of those portions of the report or specified proposed findings or recommendations to which objection is made. A judge of the court may accept, reject, or modify, in whole or in part, the findings or recommendations made by the magistrate judge. The judge may also receive further evidence or recommit the matter to the magistrate judge with instructions.

(2) A judge may designate a magistrate judge to serve as a special master pursuant to the applicable provisions of this title and the Federal Rules of Civil Procedure for the United States district courts. A judge may designate a magistrate judge to serve as a special master in any civil case, upon consent of the parties, without regard to the provisions of rule 53(b) of the Federal Rules of Civil Procedure for the United States district courts.

(3) A magistrate judge may be assigned such additional duties as are not inconsistent with the Constitution and laws of the United States.

(4) Each district court shall establish rules pursuant to which the magistrate judges shall discharge their duties.

(c) Notwithstanding any provision of law to the contrary—

(1) Upon the consent of the parties, a full-time United States magistrate judge or a part-time United States magistrate judge who serves as a full-time judicial officer may conduct any or all proceedings in a jury or nonjury civil matter and order the entry of judgment in the case, when specially designated to exercise such jurisdiction by the district court or courts he serves. Upon the consent of the parties, pursuant to their specific written request, any other part-time magistrate judge may exercise such jurisdiction, if such magistrate judge meets the bar membership requirements set forth in section 631(b)(1) and the chief judge of the district court certifies that a full-time magistrate judge is not reasonably available in accordance with guidelines established by the judicial council of the circuit. When there is more than one judge of a district court, designation under this paragraph shall be by the concurrence of a majority of all the judges of such district court, and when there is no such concurrence, then by the chief judge.

(2) If a magistrate judge is designated to exercise civil jurisdiction under paragraph (1) of this subsection, the clerk of court shall, at the time the action is filed, notify the parties of the availability of a magistrate judge to exercise such jurisdiction. The decision of the parties shall be communicated to the clerk of court. Thereafter, either the district court judge or the magistrate judge may again advise the parties of the availability of the magistrate judge, but in so doing, shall also advise the parties that they are free to withhold consent without adverse substantive consequences. Rules of court for the reference of civil matters to magistrate judges shall include procedures to protect the voluntariness of the parties' consent.

(3) Upon entry of judgment in any case referred under paragraph (1) of this subsection, an aggrieved party may appeal directly to the appropriate United States court of appeals from the judgment of the magistrate judge in the same manner as an appeal from any other judgment of a district court. The consent of the parties allows a magistrate judge designated to exercise civil

---

[1]   So in original. Probably should be "post-trial".

jurisdiction under paragraph (1) of this subsection to direct the entry of a judgment of the district court in accordance with the Federal Rules of Civil Procedure. Nothing in this paragraph shall be construed as a limitation of any party's right to seek review by the Supreme Court of the United States.

(4) The court may, for good cause shown on its own motion, or under extraordinary circumstances shown by any party, vacate a reference of a civil matter to a magistrate judge under this subsection.

(5) The magistrate judge shall, subject to guidelines of the Judicial Conference, determine whether the record taken pursuant to this section shall be taken by electronic sound recording, by a court reporter, or by other means.

(d) The practice and procedure for the trial of cases before officers serving under this chapter shall conform to rules promulgated by the Supreme Court pursuant to section 2072 of this title.

(e) Contempt authority.—

(1) In general.—A United States magistrate judge serving under this chapter shall have within the territorial jurisdiction prescribed by the appointment of such magistrate judge the power to exercise contempt authority as set forth in this subsection.

(2) Summary criminal contempt authority.—A magistrate judge shall have the power to punish summarily by fine or imprisonment, or both, such contempt of the authority of such magistrate judge constituting misbehavior of any person in the magistrate judge's presence so as to obstruct the administration of justice. The order of contempt shall be issued under the Federal Rules of Criminal Procedure.

(3) Additional criminal contempt authority in civil consent and misdemeanor cases.—In any case in which a United States magistrate judge presides with the consent of the parties under subsection (c) of this section, and in any misdemeanor case proceeding before a magistrate judge under section 3401 of title 18, the magistrate judge shall have the power to punish, by fine or imprisonment, or both, criminal contempt constituting disobedience or resistance to the magistrate judge's lawful writ, process, order, rule, decree, or command. Disposition of such contempt shall be conducted upon notice and hearing under the Federal Rules of Criminal Procedure.

(4) Civil contempt authority in civil consent and misdemeanor cases.—In any case in which a United States magistrate judge presides with the consent of the parties under subsection (c) of this section, and in any misdemeanor case proceeding before a magistrate judge under section 3401 of title 18, the magistrate judge may exercise the civil contempt authority of the district court. This paragraph shall not be construed to limit the authority of a magistrate judge to order sanctions under any other statute, the Federal Rules of Civil Procedure, or the Federal Rules of Criminal Procedure.

(5) Criminal contempt penalties.—The sentence imposed by a magistrate judge for any criminal contempt provided for in paragraphs (2) and (3) shall not exceed the penalties for a Class C misdemeanor as set forth in sections 3581(b)(8) and 3571(b)(6) of title 18.

(6) Certification of other contempts to the district court. Upon the commission of any such act—

(A) in any case in which a United States magistrate judge presides with the consent of the parties under subsection (c) of this section, or in any misdemeanor case proceeding before a magistrate judge under section 3401 of title 18, that may, in the opinion of the magistrate judge, constitute a serious criminal contempt punishable by penalties exceeding those set forth in paragraph (5) of this subsection, or

(B) in any other case or proceeding under subsection (a) or (b) of this section, or any other statute, where—

      (i)   the act committed in the magistrate judge's presence may, in the opinion of the magistrate judge, constitute a serious criminal contempt punishable by penalties exceeding those set forth in paragraph (5) of this subsection,

      (ii)   the act that constitutes a criminal contempt occurs outside the presence of the magistrate judge, or

      (iii)   the act constitutes a civil contempt,

the magistrate judge shall forthwith certify the facts to a district judge and may serve or cause to be served, upon any person whose behavior is brought into question under this paragraph, an order requiring such person to appear before a district judge upon a day certain to show cause why that person should not be adjudged in contempt by reason of the facts so certified. The district judge shall thereupon hear the evidence as to the act or conduct complained of and, if it is such as to warrant punishment, punish such person in the same manner and to the same extent as for a contempt committed before a district judge.

(7) Appeals of magistrate judge contempt orders.—The appeal of an order of contempt under this subsection shall be made to the court of appeals in cases proceeding under subsection (c) of this section. The appeal of any other order of contempt issued under this section shall be made to the district court.

(f) In an emergency and upon the concurrence of the chief judges of the districts involved, a United States magistrate judge may be temporarily assigned to perform any of the duties specified in subsection (a), (b), or (c) of this section in a judicial district other than the judicial district for which he has been appointed. No magistrate judge shall perform any of such duties in a district to which he has been temporarily assigned until an order has been issued by the chief judge of such district specifying (1) the emergency by reason of which he has been transferred, (2) the duration of his assignment, and (3) the duties which he is authorized to perform. A magistrate judge so assigned shall not be entitled to additional compensation but shall be reimbursed for actual and necessary expenses incurred in the performance of his duties in accordance with section 635.

(g) A United States magistrate judge may perform the verification function required by section 4107 of title 18, United States Code. A magistrate judge may be assigned by a judge of any United States district court to perform the verification required by section 4108 and the appointment of counsel authorized by section 4109 of title 18, United States Code, and may perform such functions beyond the territorial limits of the United States. A magistrate judge assigned such functions shall have no authority to perform any other function within the territory of a foreign country.

(h) A United States magistrate judge who has retired may, upon the consent of the chief judge of the district involved, be recalled to serve as a magistrate judge in any judicial district by the judicial council of the circuit within which such district is located. Upon recall, a magistrate judge may receive a salary for such service in accordance with regulations promulgated by the Judicial Conference, subject to the restrictions on the payment of an annuity set forth in section 377 of this title or in subchapter III of chapter 83, and chapter 84, of title 5 which are applicable to such magistrate judge. The requirements set forth in subsections (a), (b)(3), and (d) of section 631, and paragraph (1) of subsection (b) of such section to the extent such paragraph requires membership of the bar of the location in which an individual is to serve as a magistrate judge, shall not apply to the recall of a retired magistrate judge under this subsection or section 375 of this title. Any other requirement set forth in section 631(b) shall apply to the recall of a retired magistrate judge under this subsection or section 375 of this title unless such retired magistrate judge met such requirement upon appointment or reappointment as a magistrate judge under section 361.

§ 1251.   Original Jurisdiction

(a)   The Supreme Court shall have original and exclusive jurisdiction of all controversies between two or more States.

(b)   The Supreme Court shall have original but not exclusive jurisdiction of:

(1)   All actions or proceedings to which ambassadors, other public ministers, consuls, or vice consuls of foreign states are parties;

(2)   All controversies between the United States and a State;

(3)   All actions or proceedings by a State against the citizens of another State or against aliens.

§ 1253.   Direct Appeals from Decisions of Three-Judge Courts

Except as otherwise provided by law, any party may appeal to the Supreme Court from an order granting or denying, after notice and hearing, an interlocutory or permanent injunction in any civil action, suit or proceeding required by any Act of Congress to be heard and determined by a district court of three judges.

§ 1254.   Courts of Appeals; Certiorari; Certified Questions

Cases in the courts of appeals may be reviewed by the Supreme Court by the following methods:

(1)   By writ of certiorari granted upon the petition of any party to any civil or criminal case, before or after rendition of judgment or decree;

(2)   By certification at any time by a court of appeals of any question of law in any civil or criminal case as to which instructions are desired, and upon such certification the Supreme Court may give binding instructions or require the entire record to be sent up for decision of the entire matter in controversy.

§ 1257.   State Courts; Certiorari

(a)   Final judgments or decrees rendered by the highest court of a State in which a decision could be had, may be reviewed by the Supreme Court by writ of certiorari where the validity of a treaty or statute of the United States is drawn in question or where the validity of a statute of any State is drawn in question on the ground of its being repugnant to the Constitution, treaties, or laws of the United States, or where any title, right, privilege, or immunity is specially set up or claimed under the Constitution or the treaties or statutes of, or any commission held or authority exercised under, the United States.

(b)   For the purposes of this section, the term "highest court of a State" includes the District of Columbia Court of Appeals.

§ 1291.   Final Decisions of District Courts

The courts of appeals (other than the United States Court of Appeals for the Federal Circuit) shall have jurisdiction of appeals from all final decisions of the district courts of the United States, the United States District Court for the District of the Canal Zone, the District Court of Guam, and the District Court of the Virgin Islands, except where a direct review may be had in the Supreme Court. The jurisdiction of the United States Court of Appeals for the Federal Circuit shall be limited to the jurisdiction described in sections 1292(c) and (d) and 1295 of this title.

§ 1292.   Interlocutory Decisions

(a) Except as provided in subsections (c) and (d) of this section, the courts of appeals shall have jurisdiction of appeals from:

(1) Interlocutory orders of the district courts of the United States, the United States District Court for the District of the Canal Zone, the District Court of Guam, and the District Court of the Virgin Islands, or of the judges thereof, granting, continuing, modifying, refusing or dissolving injunctions, or refusing to dissolve or modify injunctions, except where a direct review may be had in the Supreme Court;

(2) Interlocutory orders appointing receivers, or refusing orders to wind up receiverships or to take steps to accomplish the purposes thereof, such as directing sales or other disposals of property;

(3) Interlocutory decrees of such district courts or the judges thereof determining the rights and liabilities of the parties to admiralty cases in which appeals from final decrees are allowed.

(b) When a district judge, in making in a civil action an order not otherwise appealable under this section, shall be of the opinion that such order involves a controlling question of law as to which there is substantial ground for difference of opinion and that an immediate appeal from the order may materially advance the ultimate termination of the litigation, he shall so state in writing in such order. The Court of Appeals which would have jurisdiction of an appeal of such action may thereupon, in its discretion, permit an appeal to be taken from such order, if application is made to it within ten days after the entry of the order: *Provided, however,* that application for an appeal hereunder shall not stay proceedings in the district court unless the district judge or the Court of Appeals or a judge thereof shall so order.

(c) The United States Court of Appeals for the Federal Circuit shall have exclusive jurisdiction—

(1) of an appeal from an interlocutory order or decree described in subsection (a) or (b) of this section in any case over which the court would have jurisdiction of an appeal under section 1295 of this title; and

(2) of an appeal from a judgment in a civil action for patent infringement which would otherwise be appealable to the United States Court of Appeals for the Federal Circuit and is final except for an accounting.

(d) (1) When the chief judge of the Court of International Trade issues an order under the provisions of section 256(b) of this title, or when any judge of the Court of International Trade, in issuing any other interlocutory order, includes in the order a statement that a controlling question of law is involved with respect to which there is a substantial ground for difference of opinion and that an immediate appeal from that order may materially advance the ultimate termination of the litigation, the United States Court of Appeals for the Federal Circuit may, in its discretion, permit an appeal to be taken from such order, if application is made to that Court within ten days after the entry of such order.

(2) When the chief judge of the United States Court of Federal Claims issues an order under section 798(b) of this title, or when any judge of the United States Court of Federal Claims, in issuing an interlocutory order, includes in the order a statement that a controlling question of law is involved with respect to which there is a substantial ground for difference of opinion and that an immediate appeal from that order may materially advance the ultimate termination of the litigation, the United States Court of Appeals for the Federal Circuit may, in its discretion, permit an appeal to be taken from such order, if application is made to that Court within ten days after the entry of such order.

(3) Neither the application for nor the granting of an appeal under this subsection shall stay proceedings in the Court of International Trade or in the Court of Federal Claims, as the case may be, unless a stay is ordered by a judge of the Court of International Trade or of the Court of

Federal Claims or by the United States Court of Appeals for the Federal Circuit or a judge of that court.

(4) **(A)** The United States Court of Appeals for the Federal Circuit shall have exclusive jurisdiction of an appeal from an interlocutory order of a district court of the United States, the District Court of Guam, the District Court of the Virgin Islands, or the District Court for the Northern Mariana Islands, granting or denying, in whole or in part, a motion to transfer an action to the United States Court of Federal Claims under section 1631 of this title.

(B) When a motion to transfer an action to the Court of Federal Claims is filed in a district court, no further proceedings shall be taken in the district court until 60 days after the court has ruled upon the motion. If an appeal is taken from the district court's grant or denial of the motion, proceedings shall be further stayed until the appeal has been decided by the Court of Appeals for the Federal Circuit. The stay of proceedings in the district court shall not bar the granting of preliminary or injunctive relief, where appropriate and where expedition is reasonably necessary. However, during the period in which proceedings are stayed as provided in this subparagraph, no transfer to the Court of Federal Claims pursuant to the motion shall be carried out.

(e) The Supreme Court may prescribe rules, in accordance with section 2072 of this title, to provide for an appeal of an interlocutory decision to the courts of appeals that is not otherwise provided for under subsection (a), (b), (c), or (d).

§ 1331.   Federal Question

The district courts shall have original jurisdiction of all civil actions arising under the Constitution, laws, or treaties of the United States.

§ 1332.   Diversity of Citizenship; Amount in Controversy; Costs

(a) The district courts shall have original jurisdiction of all civil actions where the matter in controversy exceeds the sum or value of $75,000, exclusive of interest and costs, and is between—

(1) citizens of different States;

(2) citizens of a State and citizens or subjects of a foreign state, except that the district courts shall not have original jurisdiction under this subsection of an action between citizens of a State and citizens or subjects of a foreign state who are lawfully admitted for permanent residence in the United States and are domiciled in the same State;

(3) citizens of different States and in which citizens or subjects of a foreign state are additional parties; and

(4) a foreign state, defined in section 1603(a) of this title, as plaintiff and citizens of a State or of different States.

(b) Except when express provision therefor is otherwise made in a statute of the United States, where the plaintiff who files the case originally in the Federal courts is finally adjudged to be entitled to recover less than the sum or value of $75,000, computed without regard to any setoff or counterclaim to which the defendant may be adjudged to be entitled, and exclusive of interest and costs, the district court may deny costs to the plaintiff and, in addition, may impose costs on the plaintiff.

(c) For the purposes of this section and section 1441 of this title—

(1) a corporation shall be deemed to be a citizen of every State and foreign state by which it has been incorporated and of the State or foreign state where it has its principal place of business, except that in any direct action against the insurer of a policy or contract of liability insurance, whether incorporated or unincorporated, to which action the insured is not joined as a party-defendant, such insurer shall be deemed a citizen of—

    (A) every State and foreign state of which the insured is a citizen;

    (B) every State and foreign state by which the insurer has been incorporated; and

    (C) the State or foreign state where the insurer has its principal place of business; and

(2) the legal representative of the estate of a decedent shall be deemed to be a citizen only of the same State as the decedent, and the legal representative of an infant or incompetent shall be deemed to be a citizen only of the same State as the infant or incompetent.

(d) (1) In this subsection—

    (A) the term "class" means all of the class members in a class action;

    (B) the term "class action" means any civil action filed under rule 23 of the Federal Rules of Civil Procedure or similar State statute or rule of judicial procedure authorizing an action to be brought by 1 or more representative persons as a class action;

    (C) the term "class certification order" means an order issued by a court approving the treatment of some or all aspects of a civil action as a class action; and

    (D) the term "class members" means the persons (named or unnamed) who fall within the definition of the proposed or certified class in a class action.

(2) The district courts shall have original jurisdiction of any civil action in which the matter in controversy exceeds the sum or value of $5,000,000, exclusive of interest and costs, and is a class action in which—

    (A) any member of a class of plaintiffs is a citizen of a State different from any defendant;

    (B) any member of a class of plaintiffs is a foreign state or a citizen or subject of a foreign state and any defendant is a citizen of a State; or

    (C) any member of a class of plaintiffs is a citizen of a State and any defendant is a foreign state or a citizen or subject of a foreign state.

(3) A district court may, in the interests of justice and looking at the totality of the circumstances, decline to exercise jurisdiction under paragraph (2) over a class action in which greater than one-third but less than two-thirds of the members of all proposed plaintiff classes in the aggregate and the primary defendants are citizens of the State in which the action was originally filed based on consideration of—

    (A) whether the claims asserted involve matters of national or interstate interest;

    (B) whether the claims asserted will be governed by laws of the State in which the action was originally filed or by the laws of other States;

    (C) whether the class action has been pleaded in a manner that seeks to avoid Federal jurisdiction;

    (D) whether the action was brought in a forum with a distinct nexus with the class members, the alleged harm, or the defendants;

    (E) whether the number of citizens of the State in which the action was originally filed in all proposed plaintiff classes in the aggregate is substantially larger than the number of citizens from any other State, and the citizenship of the other members of the proposed class is dispersed among a substantial number of States; and

    (F) whether, during the 3-year period preceding the filing of that class action, 1 or more other class actions asserting the same or similar claims on behalf of the same or other persons have been filed.

(4) A district court shall decline to exercise jurisdiction under paragraph (2)—

    (A) **(i)** over a class action in which—

        (I) greater than two-thirds of the members of all proposed plaintiff classes in the aggregate are citizens of the State in which the action was originally filed;

        (II) at least 1 defendant is a defendant—

            (aa) from whom significant relief is sought by members of the plaintiff class;

            (bb) whose alleged conduct forms a significant basis for the claims asserted by the proposed plaintiff class; and

            (cc) who is a citizen of the State in which the action was originally filed; and

        (III) principal injuries resulting from the alleged conduct or any related conduct of each defendant were incurred in the State in which the action was originally filed; and

        (ii) during the 3-year period preceding the filing of that class action, no other class action has been filed asserting the same or similar factual allegations against any of the defendants on behalf of the same or other persons; or

    (B) two-thirds or more of the members of all proposed plaintiff classes in the aggregate, and the primary defendants, are citizens of the State in which the action was originally filed.

(5) Paragraphs (2) through (4) shall not apply to any class action in which—

    (A) the primary defendants are States, State officials, or other governmental entities against whom the district court may be foreclosed from ordering relief; or

    (B) the number of members of all proposed plaintiff classes in the aggregate is less than 100.

(6) In any class action, the claims of the individual class members shall be aggregated to determine whether the matter in controversy exceeds the sum or value of $5,000,000, exclusive of interest and costs.

(7) Citizenship of the members of the proposed plaintiff classes shall be determined for purposes of paragraphs (2) through (6) as of the date of filing of the complaint or amended complaint, or, if the case stated by the initial pleading is not subject to Federal jurisdiction, as of the date of service by plaintiffs of an amended pleading, motion, or other paper, indicating the existence of Federal jurisdiction.

(8) This subsection shall apply to any class action before or after the entry of a class certification order by the court with respect to that action.

(9) Paragraph (2) shall not apply to any class action that solely involves a claim

    (A) concerning a covered security as defined under 16(f)(3)[2] of the Securities Act of 1933 (15 U.S.C. 78p(f)(3)) and section 28(f)(5)(E) of the Securities Exchange Act of 1934 (15 U.S.C. 78bb(f)(5)(E));

    (B) that relates to the internal affairs or governance of a corporation or other form of business enterprise and that arises under or by virtue of the laws of the State in which such corporation or business enterprise is incorporated or organized; or

---

[2] So in original. Reference to "16(f)(3)" probably should be preceded by "section".

(C) that relates to the rights, duties (including fiduciary duties), and obligations relating to or created by or pursuant to any security (as defined under section 2(a)(1) of the Securities Act of 1933 (15 U.S.C. 77b(a)(1)) and the regulations issued thereunder).

(10) For purposes of this subsection and section 1453, an unincorporated association shall be deemed to be a citizen of the State where it has its principal place of business and the State under whose laws it is organized.

(11) (A) For purposes of this subsection and section 1453, a mass action shall be deemed to be a class action removable under paragraphs (2) through (10) if it otherwise meets the provisions of those paragraphs.

(B) (i) As used in subparagraph (A), the term "mass action" means any civil action (except a civil action within the scope of section 1711(2)) in which monetary relief claims of 100 or more persons are proposed to be tried jointly on the ground that the plaintiffs' claims involve common questions of law or fact, except that jurisdiction shall exist only over those plaintiffs whose claims in a mass action satisfy the jurisdictional amount requirements under subsection (a).

(ii) As used in subparagraph (A), the term "mass action" shall not include any civil action in which—

(I) all of the claims in the action arise from an event or occurrence in the State in which the action was filed, and that allegedly resulted in injuries in that State or in States contiguous to that State;

(II) the claims are joined upon motion of a defendant;

(III) all of the claims in the action are asserted on behalf of the general public (and not on behalf of individual claimants or members of a purported class) pursuant to a State statute specifically authorizing such action; or

(IV) the claims have been consolidated or coordinated solely for pretrial proceedings.

(C) (i) Any action(s) removed to Federal court pursuant to this subsection shall not thereafter be transferred to any other court pursuant to section 1407, or the rules promulgated thereunder, unless a majority of the plaintiffs in the action request transfer pursuant to section 1407.

(ii) This subparagraph will not apply—

(I) to cases certified pursuant to rule 23 of the Federal Rules of Civil Procedure; or

(II) if plaintiffs propose that the action proceed as a class action pursuant to rule 23 of the Federal Rules of Civil Procedure.

(D) The limitations periods on any claims asserted in a mass action that is removed to Federal court pursuant to this subsection shall be deemed tolled during the period that the action is pending in Federal court.

(e) The word "States", as used in this section, includes the Territories, the District of Columbia, and the Commonwealth of Puerto Rico.

§ 1333.   Admiralty, Maritime and Prize Cases

The district courts shall have original jurisdiction, exclusive of the courts of the States, of:

(1) Any civil case of admiralty or maritime jurisdiction, saving to suitors in all cases all other remedies to which they are otherwise entitled.

(2) Any prize brought into the United States and all proceedings for the condemnation of property taken as prize.

§ 1334.   Bankruptcy Cases and Proceedings

(a) Except as provided in subsection (b) of this section, the district courts shall have original and exclusive jurisdiction of all cases under title 11.

(b) Except as provided in subsection (e)(2), and notwithstanding any Act of Congress that confers exclusive jurisdiction on a court or courts other than the district courts, the district courts shall have original but not exclusive jurisdiction of all civil proceedings arising under title 11, or arising in or related to cases under title 11.

(c) (1) Except with respect to a case under chapter 15 of title 11, nothing in this section prevents a district court in the interest of justice, or in the interest of comity with State courts or respect for State law, from abstaining from hearing a particular proceeding arising under title 11 or arising in or related to a case under title 11.

(2) Upon timely motion of a party in a proceeding based upon a State law claim or State law cause of action, related to a case under title 11 but not arising under title 11 or arising in a case under title 11, with respect to which an action could not have been commenced in a court of the United States absent jurisdiction under this section, the district court shall abstain from hearing such proceeding if an action is commenced, and can be timely adjudicated, in a State forum of appropriate jurisdiction.

(d) Any decision to abstain or not to abstain made under subsection (c) (other than a decision not to abstain in a proceeding described in subsection (c)(2)) is not reviewable by appeal or otherwise by the court of appeals under section 158(d), 1291, or 1292 of this title or by the Supreme Court of the United States under section 1254 of this title. Subsection (c) and this subsection shall not be construed to limit the applicability of the stay provided for by section 362 of title 11, United States Code, as such section applies to an action affecting the property of the estate in bankruptcy.

(e) The district court in which a case under title 11 is commenced or is pending shall have exclusive jurisdiction—

(1) of all the property, wherever located, of the debtor as of the commencement of such case, and of property of the estate; and

(2) over all claims or causes of action that involve construction of section 327 of title 11, United States Code, or rules relating to disclosure requirements under section 327.

§ 1335.   Interpleader

(a) The district courts shall have original jurisdiction of any civil action of interpleader or in the nature of interpleader filed by any person, firm, or corporation, association, or society having in his or its custody or possession money or property of the value of $500 or more, or having issued a note, bond, certificate, policy of insurance, or other instrument of value or amount of $500 or more, or providing for the delivery or payment or the loan of money or property of such amount or value, or being under any obligation written or unwritten to the amount of $500 or more, if

(1) Two or more adverse claimants, of diverse citizenship as defined in subsection (a) or (d) of section 1332 of this title, are claiming or may claim to be entitled to such money or property, or to any one or more of the benefits arising by virtue of any note, bond, certificate, policy or other instrument, or arising by virtue of any such obligation; and if (2) the plaintiff has deposited such money or property or has paid the amount of or the loan or other value of such instrument or the amount due under such obligation into the registry of the court, there to abide the judgment of the court, or has given bond payable to the clerk of the court in such amount and with such surety as the court or judge may deem proper, conditioned upon the compliance by the plaintiff with the future order or judgment of the court with respect to the subject matter of the controversy.

(b) Such an action may be entertained although the titles or claims of the conflicting claimants do not have a common origin, or are not identical, but are adverse to and independent of one another.

§ 1337. Commerce and Antitrust Regulations; Amount in Controversy, Costs

(a) The district courts shall have original jurisdiction of any civil action or proceeding arising under any Act of Congress regulating commerce or protecting trade and commerce against restraints and monopolies: Provided, however, That the district courts shall have original jurisdiction of an action brought under section 11706 or 14706 of title 49, only if the matter in controversy for each receipt or bill of lading exceeds $10,000, exclusive of interest and costs.

(b) Except when express provision therefor is otherwise made in a statute of the United States, where a plaintiff who files the case under section 11706 or 14706 of title 49, originally in the Federal courts is finally adjudged to be entitled to recover less than the sum or value of $10,000, computed without regard to any setoff or counterclaim to which the defendant may be adjudged to be entitled, and exclusive of any interest and costs, the district court may deny costs to the plaintiff and, in addition, may impose costs on the plaintiff.

(c) The district courts shall not have jurisdiction under this section of any matter within the exclusive jurisdiction of the Court of International Trade under chapter 95 of this title.

§ 1338. Patents, Plant Variety Protection, Copyrights, Mask Works, Designs, Trademarks, and Unfair Competition

(a) The district courts shall have original jurisdiction of any civil action arising under any Act of Congress relating to patents, plant variety protection, copyrights and trademarks. No State court shall have jurisdiction over any claim for relief arising under any Act of Congress relating to patents, plant variety protection, or copyrights. For purposes of this subsection, the term "State" includes any State of the United States, the District of Columbia, the Commonwealth of Puerto Rico, the United States Virgin Islands, American Samoa, Guam, and the Northern Mariana Islands.

(b) The district courts shall have original jurisdiction of any civil action asserting a claim of unfair competition when joined with a substantial and related claim under the copyright, patent, plant variety protection or trademark laws.

(c) Subsections (a) and (b) apply to exclusive rights in mask works under chapter 9 of title 17, and to exclusive rights in designs under chapter 13 of title 17, to the same extent as such subsections apply to copyrights.

§ 1339. Postal Matters

The district courts shall have original jurisdiction of any civil action arising under any Act of Congress relating to the postal service.

§ 1340. Internal Revenue; Customs Duties

The district courts shall have original jurisdiction of any civil action arising under any Act of Congress providing for internal revenue, or revenue from imports or tonnage except matters within the jurisdiction of the Court of International Trade.

§ 1343. Civil Rights and Elective Franchise

(a) The district courts shall have original jurisdiction of any civil action authorized by law to be commenced by any person:

(1) To recover damages for injury to his person or property, or because of the deprivation of any right or privilege of a citizen of the United States, by any act done in furtherance of any conspiracy mentioned in section 1985 of Title 42;

(2) To recover damages from any person who fails to prevent or to aid in preventing any wrongs mentioned in section 1985 of Title 42 which he had knowledge were about to occur and power to prevent;

(3) To redress the deprivation, under color of any State law, statute, ordinance, regulation, custom or usage, of any right, privilege or immunity secured by the Constitution of the United States or by any Act of Congress providing for equal rights of citizens or of all persons within the jurisdiction of the United States;

(4) To recover damages or to secure equitable or other relief under any Act of Congress providing for the protection of civil rights, including the right to vote.

(b) For purposes of this section—

(1) the District of Columbia shall be considered to be a State; and

(2) any Act of Congress applicable exclusively to the District of Columbia shall be considered to be a statute of the District of Columbia.

§ 1345. United States As Plaintiff

Except as otherwise provided by Act of Congress, the district courts shall have original jurisdiction of all civil actions, suits or proceedings commenced by the United States, or by any agency or officer thereof expressly authorized to sue by Act of Congress.

§ 1346. United States As Defendant

(a) The district courts shall have original jurisdiction, concurrent with the United States Court of Federal Claims, of:

(1) Any civil action against the United States for the recovery of any internal-revenue tax alleged to have been erroneously or illegally assessed or collected, or any penalty claimed to have been collected without authority or any sum alleged to have been excessive or in any manner wrongfully collected under the internal-revenue laws;

(2) Any other civil action or claim against the United States, not exceeding $10,000 in amount, founded either upon the Constitution, or any Act of Congress, or any regulation of an executive department, or upon any express or implied contract with the United States, or for liquidated or unliquidated damages in cases not sounding in tort, except that the district courts shall not have jurisdiction of any civil action or claim against the United States founded upon any express or implied contract with the United States or for liquidated or unliquidated damages in cases not sounding in tort which are subject to sections 7104(b)(1) and 7107(a)(1) of title 41. For the purpose of this paragraph, an express or implied contract with the Army and Air Force Exchange Service, Navy Exchanges, Marine Corps Exchanges, Coast Guard Exchanges, or Exchange Councils of the

National Aeronautics and Space Administration shall be considered an express or implied contract with the United States.

(b) **(1)** Subject to the provisions of chapter 171 of this title, the district courts, together with the United States District Court for the District of the Canal Zone and the District Court of the Virgin Islands, shall have exclusive jurisdiction of civil actions on claims against the United States, for money damages, accruing on and after January 1, 1945, for injury or loss of property, or personal injury or death caused by the negligent or wrongful act or omission of any employee of the Government while acting within the scope of his office or employment, under circumstances where the United States, if a private person, would be liable to the claimant in accordance with the law of the place where the act or omission occurred.

    (2) No person convicted of a felony who is incarcerated while awaiting sentencing or while serving a sentence may bring a civil action against the United States or an agency, officer, or employee of the Government, for mental or emotional injury suffered while in custody without a prior showing of physical injury or the commission of a sexual act (as defined in section 2246 of Title 18).

(c) The jurisdiction conferred by this section includes jurisdiction of any set-off, counterclaim, or other claim or demand whatever on the part of the United States against any plaintiff commencing an action under this section.

(d) The district courts shall not have jurisdiction under this section of any civil action or claim for a pension.

(e) The district courts shall have original jurisdiction of any civil action against the United States provided in section 6226, 6228(a), 7426, or 7428 (in the case of the United States district court for the District of Columbia) or section 7429 of the Internal Revenue Code of 1986.

(f) The district courts shall have exclusive original jurisdiction of civil actions under section 2409a to quiet title to an estate or interest in real property in which an interest is claimed by the United States.

(g) Subject to the provisions of chapter 179, the district courts of the United States shall have exclusive jurisdiction over any civil action commenced under section 453(2) of title 3, by a covered employee under chapter 5 of such title.

§ 1349.   Corporation Organized under Federal Law As Party

The district courts shall not have jurisdiction of any civil action by or against any corporation upon the ground that it was incorporated by or under an Act of Congress, unless the United States is the owner of more than one-half of its capital stock.

§ 1357.   Injuries under Federal Laws

The district courts shall have original jurisdiction of any civil action commenced by any person to recover damages for any injury to his person or property on account of any act done by him, under any Act of Congress, for the protection or collection of any of the revenues, or to enforce the right of citizens of the United States to vote in any State.

§ 1359.   Parties Collusively Joined or Made

A district court shall not have jurisdiction of a civil action in which any party, by assignment or otherwise, has been improperly or collusively made or joined to invoke the jurisdiction of such court.

§ 1361. Action to Compel an Officer of the United States to Perform His Duty

The district courts shall have original jurisdiction of any action in the nature of mandamus to compel an officer or employee of the United States or any agency thereof to perform a duty owed to the plaintiff.

§ 1367. Supplemental Jurisdiction

(a) Except as provided in subsections (b) and (c) or as expressly provided otherwise by Federal statute, in any civil action of which the district courts have original jurisdiction, the district courts shall have supplemental jurisdiction over all other claims that are so related to claims in the action within such original jurisdiction that they form part of the same case or controversy under Article III of the United States Constitution. Such supplemental jurisdiction shall include claims that involve the joinder or intervention of additional parties.

(b) In any civil action of which the district courts have original jurisdiction founded solely on section 1332 of this title, the district courts shall not have supplemental jurisdiction under subsection (a) over claims by plaintiffs against persons made parties under Rule 14, 19, 20, or 24 of the Federal Rules of Civil Procedure, or over claims by persons proposed to be joined as plaintiffs under Rule 19 of such rules, or seeking to intervene as plaintiffs under Rule 24 of such rules, when exercising supplemental jurisdiction over such claims would be inconsistent with the jurisdictional requirements of section 1332.

(c) The district courts may decline to exercise supplemental jurisdiction over a claim under subsection (a) if—

(1) the claim raises a novel or complex issue of State law,

(2) the claim substantially predominates over the claim or claims over which the district court has original jurisdiction,

(3) the district court has dismissed all claims over which it has original jurisdiction, or

(4) in exceptional circumstances, there are other compelling reasons for declining jurisdiction.

(d) The period of limitations for any claim asserted under subsection (a), and for any other claim in the same action that is voluntarily dismissed at the same time as or after the dismissal of the claim under subsection (a), shall be tolled while the claim is pending and for a period of 30 days after it is dismissed unless State law provides for a longer tolling period.

(e) As used in this section, the term "State" includes the District of Columbia, the Commonwealth of Puerto Rico, and any territory or possession of the United States.

§ 1369. Multiparty, Multiforum Jurisdiction

(a) In general.—The district courts shall have original jurisdiction of any civil action involving minimal diversity between adverse parties that arises from a single accident, where at least 75 natural persons have died in the accident at a discrete location, if—

(1) a defendant resides in a State and a substantial part of the accident took place in another State or other location, regardless of whether that defendant is also a resident of the State where a substantial part of the accident took place;

(2) any two defendants reside in different States, regardless of whether such defendants are also residents of the same State or States; or

(3) substantial parts of the accident took place in different States.

(b) Limitation of jurisdiction of district courts.—The district court shall abstain from hearing any civil action described in subsection (a) in which—

(1) the substantial majority of all plaintiffs are citizens of a single State of which the primary defendants are also citizens; and

(2) the claims asserted will be governed primarily by the laws of that State.

(c) Special rules and definitions.—For purposes of this section—

(1) minimal diversity exists between adverse parties if any party is a citizen of a State and any adverse party is a citizen of another State, a citizen or subject of a foreign state, or a foreign state as defined in section 1603(a) of this title;

(2) a corporation is deemed to be a citizen of any State, and a citizen or subject of any foreign state, in which it is incorporated or has its principal place of business, and is deemed to be a resident of any State in which it is incorporated or licensed to do business or is doing business;

(3) the term "injury" means—

   (A) physical harm to a natural person; and

   (B) physical damage to or destruction of tangible property, but only if physical harm described in subparagraph (A) exists;

(4) the term "accident" means a sudden accident, or a natural event culminating in an accident, that results in death incurred at a discrete location by at least 75 natural persons; and

(5) the term "State" includes the District of Columbia, the Commonwealth of Puerto Rico, and any territory or possession of the United States.

(d) Intervening parties.—In any action in a district court which is or could have been brought, in whole or in part, under this section, any person with a claim arising from the accident described in subsection (a) shall be permitted to intervene as a party plaintiff in the action, even if that person could not have brought an action in a district court as an original matter.

(e) Notification of judicial panel on multidistrict litigation.—A district court in which an action under this section is pending shall promptly notify the judicial panel on multidistrict litigation of the pendency of the action.

§ 1390. Scope

(a) Venue defined.—As used in this chapter, the term "venue" refers to the geographic specification of the proper court or courts for the litigation of a civil action that is within the subject-matter jurisdiction of the district courts in general, and does not refer to any grant or restriction of subject-matter jurisdiction providing for a civil action to be adjudicated only by the district court for a particular district or districts.

(b) Exclusion of certain cases.—Except as otherwise provided by law, this chapter shall not govern the venue of a civil action in which the district court exercises the jurisdiction conferred by section 1333, except that such civil actions may be transferred between district courts as provided in this chapter.

(c) Clarification regarding cases removed from state courts.—This chapter shall not determine the district court to which a civil action pending in a State court may be removed, but shall govern the transfer of an action so removed as between districts and divisions of the United States district courts.

§1391.   Venue Generally

(a) Applicability of section.—Except as otherwise provided by law—

(1)   this section shall govern the venue of all civil actions brought in district courts of the United States; and

(2)   the proper venue for a civil action shall be determined without regard to whether the action is local or transitory in nature.

(b) Venue in general.—A civil action may be brought in—

(1)   a judicial district in which any defendant resides, if all defendants are residents of the State in which the district is located;

(2)   a judicial district in which a substantial part of the events or omissions giving rise to the claim occurred, or a substantial part of property that is the subject of the action is situated; or

(3)   if there is no district in which an action may otherwise be brought as provided in this section, any judicial district in which any defendant is subject to the court's personal jurisdiction with respect to such action.

(c) Residency.—For all venue purposes—

(1)   a natural person, including an alien lawfully admitted for permanent residence in the United States, shall be deemed to reside in the judicial district in which that person is domiciled;

(2)   an entity with the capacity to sue and be sued in its common name under applicable law, whether or not incorporated, shall be deemed to reside, if a defendant, in any judicial district in which such defendant is subject to the court's personal jurisdiction with respect to the civil action in question and, if a plaintiff, only in the judicial district in which it maintains its principal place of business; and

(3)   a defendant not resident in the United States may be sued in any judicial district, and the joinder of such a defendant shall be disregarded in determining where the action may be brought with respect to other defendants.

(d) Residency of corporations in states with multiple districts.—For purposes of venue under this chapter, in a State which has more than one judicial district and in which a defendant that is a corporation is subject to personal jurisdiction at the time an action is commenced, such corporation shall be deemed to reside in any district in that State within which its contacts would be sufficient to subject it to personal jurisdiction if that district were a separate State, and, if there is no such district, the corporation shall be deemed to reside in the district within which it has the most significant contacts.

(e) Actions where defendant is officer or employee of the united states.—(1) In general.— A civil action in which a defendant is an officer or employee of the United States or any agency thereof acting in his official capacity or under color of legal authority, or an agency of the United States, or the United States, may, except as otherwise provided by law, be brought in any judicial district in which (A) a defendant in the action resides, (B) a substantial part of the events or omissions giving rise to the claim occurred, or a substantial part of property that is the subject of the action is situated, or (C) the plaintiff resides if no real property is involved in the action. Additional persons may be joined as parties to any such action in accordance with the Federal Rules of Civil Procedure and with such other venue requirements as would be applicable if the United States or one of its officers, employees, or agencies were not a party.

(2) Service.—The summons and complaint in such an action shall be served as provided by the Federal Rules of Civil Procedure except that the delivery of the summons and complaint to the officer or agency as required by the rules may be made by certified mail beyond the territorial limits of the district in which the action is brought.

(f) Civil actions against a foreign state.—A civil action against a foreign state as defined in section 1603(a) of this title may be brought—

(1) in any judicial district in which a substantial part of the events or omissions giving rise to the claim occurred, or a substantial part of property that is the subject of the action is situated;

(2) in any judicial district in which the vessel or cargo of a foreign state is situated, if the claim is asserted under section 1605(b) of this title;

(3) in any judicial district in which the agency or instrumentality is licensed to do business or is doing business, if the action is brought against an agency or instrumentality of a foreign state as defined in section 1603(b) of this title; or

(4) in the United States District Court for the District of Columbia if the action is brought against a foreign state or political subdivision thereof.

(g) Multiparty, multiforum litigation.—A civil action in which jurisdiction of the district court is based upon section 1369 of this title may be brought in any district in which any defendant resides or in which a substantial part of the accident giving rise to the action took place.

§ 1397.   Interpleader

Any civil action of interpleader or in the nature of interpleader under section 1335 of this title may be brought in the judicial district in which one or more of the claimants reside.

§ 1400.   Patents and Copyrights, Mask Works, and Designs

(a) Civil actions, suits, or proceedings arising under any Act of Congress relating to copyrights or exclusive rights in mask works or designs may be instituted in the district in which the defendant or his agent resides or may be found.

(b) Any civil action for patent infringement may be brought in the judicial district where the defendant resides, or where the defendant has committed acts of infringement and has a regular and established place of business.

§ 1401.   Stockholder's Derivative Action

Any civil action by a stockholder on behalf of his corporation may be prosecuted in any judicial district where the corporation might have sued the same defendants.

§ 1402.   United States As Defendant

(a) Any civil action in a district court against the United States under subsection (a) of section 1346 of this title may be prosecuted only:

(1) Except as provided in paragraph (2), in the judicial district where the plaintiff resides;

(2) In the case of a civil action in a district court by a corporation under paragraph (1) of subsection (a) of section 1346, in the judicial district in which is located the principal place of business or principal office or agency of the corporation; or if it has no principal place of business or principal office or agency in any judicial district (A) in the judicial district in which is located the office to which was made the return of the tax in respect of which the claim is made, or (B) if no return was made, in the judicial district in which lies the District of Columbia. Notwithstanding the foregoing provisions of this paragraph a district court, for the convenience of the parties and witnesses, in the interest of justice, may transfer any such action to any other district or division.

(b) Any civil action on a tort claim against the United States under subsection (b) of section 1346 of this title may be prosecuted only in the judicial district where the plaintiff resides or wherein the act or omission complained of occurred.

(c) Any civil action against the United States under subsection of section 1346 of this title may be prosecuted only in the judicial district where the property is situated at the time of levy, or if no levy is made, in the judicial district in which the event occurred which gave rise to the cause of action.

(d) Any civil action under section 2409a to quiet title to an estate or interest in real property in which an interest is claimed by the United States shall be brought in the district court of the district where the property is located or, if located in different districts, in any of such districts.

§ 1404.   Change of Venue

(a) For the convenience of parties and witnesses, in the interest of justice, a district court may transfer any civil action to any other district or division where it might have been brought or to any district or division to which all parties have consented.

(b) Upon motion, consent or stipulation of all parties, any action, suit or proceeding of a civil nature or any motion or hearing thereof, may be transferred, in the discretion of the court, from the division in which pending to any other division in the same district. Transfer of proceedings in rem brought by or on behalf of the United States may be transferred under this section without the consent of the United States where all other parties request transfer.

(c) A district court may order any civil action to be tried at any place within the division in which it is pending.

(d) Transfers from a district court of the United States to the District Court of Guam, the District Court for the Northern Mariana Islands, or the District Court of the Virgin Islands shall not be permitted under this section. As otherwise used in this section, "district court" includes the District Court of Guam, the District Court for the Northern Mariana Islands, and the District Court of the Virgin Islands, and the term "district" includes the territorial jurisdiction of that court.

§ 1406.   Cure or Waiver of Defects

(a) The district court of a district in which is filed a case laying venue in the wrong division or district shall dismiss, or if it be in the interest of justice, transfer such case to any district or division in which it could have been brought.

(b) Nothing in this chapter shall impair the jurisdiction of a district court of any matter involving a party who does not interpose timely and sufficient objection to the venue.

(c) As used in this section, "district court" includes the District Court of Guam, the District Court for the Northern Mariana Islands, and the District Court of the Virgin Islands, and the term "district" includes the territorial jurisdiction of that court.

§ 1407.   Multidistrict Litigation

[Note to Reader: See Part V of this text.]

§ 1412.   Change of Venue

A district court may transfer a case or proceeding under title 11 to a district court for another district, in the interest of justice or for the convenience of the parties.

§ 1441.   Removal of Civil Actions

(a) Generally.—Except as otherwise expressly provided by Act of Congress, any civil action brought in a State court of which the district courts of the United States have original jurisdiction, may be removed by the defendant or the defendants, to the district court of the United States for the district and division embracing the place where such action is pending.

(b) Removal based on diversity of citizenship.—(1) In determining whether a civil action is removable on the basis of the jurisdiction under section 1332(a) of this title, the citizenship of defendants sued under fictitious names shall be disregarded.

(2) A civil action otherwise removable solely on the basis of the jurisdiction under section 1332(a) of this title may not be removed if any of the parties in interest properly joined and served as defendants is a citizen of the State in which such action is brought.

(c) Joinder of federal law claims and state law claims.—(1) If a civil action includes

    (A) a claim arising under the Constitution, laws, or treaties of the United States (within the meaning of section 1331 of this title), and

    (B) a claim not within the original or supplemental jurisdiction of the district court or a claim that has been made nonremovable by statute,

the entire action may be removed if the action would be removable without the inclusion of the claim described in subparagraph (B).

(2) Upon removal of an action described in paragraph (1), the district court shall sever from the action all claims described in paragraph (1)(B) and shall remand the severed claims to the State court from which the action was removed. Only defendants against whom a claim described in paragraph (1)(A) has been asserted are required to join in or consent to the removal under paragraph (1).

(d) Actions against foreign states.—**Any** civil action brought in a State court against a foreign state as defined in section 1603(a) of this title may be removed by the foreign state to the district court of the United States for the district and division embracing the place where such action is pending. Upon removal the action shall be tried by the court without jury. Where removal is based upon this subsection, the time limitations of section 1446(b) of this chapter may be enlarged at any time for cause shown.

(e) Multiparty, multiforum jurisdiction.—(1) Notwithstanding the provisions of subsection (b) of this section, a defendant in a civil action in a State court may remove the action to the district court of the United States for the district and division embracing the place where the action is pending if—

    (A) the action could have been brought in a United States district court under section 1369 of this title; or

    (B) the defendant is a party to an action which is or could have been brought, in whole or in part, under section 1369 in a United States district court and arises from the same accident as the action in State court, even if the action to be removed could not have been brought in a district court as an original matter.

The removal of an action under this subsection shall be made in accordance with section 1446 of this title, except that a notice of removal may also be filed before trial of the action in State court within 30 days after the date on which the defendant first becomes a party to an action under section 1369 in a United States district court that arises from the same accident as the action in State court, or at a later time with leave of the district court.

(2) Whenever an action is removed under this subsection and the district court to which it is removed or transferred under section 1407(j) has made a liability determination requiring further proceedings as to damages, the district court shall remand the action to the State court from

which it had been removed for the determination of damages, unless the court finds that, for the convenience of parties and witnesses and in the interest of justice, the action should be retained for the determination of damages.

(3) Any remand under paragraph (2) shall not be effective until 60 days after the district court has issued an order determining liability and has certified its intention to remand the removed action for the determination of damages. An appeal with respect to the liability determination of the district court may be taken during that 60-day period to the court of appeals with appellate jurisdiction over the district court. In the event a party files such an appeal, the remand shall not be effective until the appeal has been finally disposed of. Once the remand has become effective, the liability determination shall not be subject to further review by appeal or otherwise.

(4) Any decision under this subsection concerning remand for the determination of damages shall not be reviewable by appeal or otherwise.

(5) An action removed under this subsection shall be deemed to be an action under section 1369 and an action in which jurisdiction is based on section 1369 of this title for purposes of this section and sections 1407, 1697, and 1785 of this title.

(6) Nothing in this subsection shall restrict the authority of the district court to transfer or dismiss an action on the ground of inconvenient forum.

(f) Derivative removal jurisdiction.—The court to which a civil action is removed under this section is not precluded from hearing and determining any claim in such civil action because the State court from which such civil action is removed did not have jurisdiction over that claim.

§ 1442. Federal Officers or Agencies Sued or Prosecuted

(a) A civil action or criminal prosecution that is commenced in a State court and that is against or directed to any of the following may be removed by them to the district court of the United States for the district and division embracing the place wherein it is pending:

(1) The United States or any agency thereof or any officer (or any person acting under that officer) of the United States or of any agency thereof, in an official or individual capacity, for or relating to any act under color of such office or on account of any right, title or authority claimed under any Act of Congress for the apprehension or punishment of criminals or the collection of the revenue.

(2) A property holder whose title is derived from any such officer, where such action or prosecution affects the validity of any law of the United States.

(3) Any officer of the courts of the United States, for or relating to any act under color of office or in the performance of his duties;

(4) Any officer of either House of Congress, for or relating to any act in the discharge of his official duty under an order of such House.

(b) A personal action commenced in any State court by an alien against any citizen of a State who is, or at the time the alleged action accrued was, a civil officer of the United States and is a nonresident of such State, wherein jurisdiction is obtained by the State court by personal service of process, may be removed by the defendant to the district court of the United States for the district and division in which the defendant was served with process.

(c) Solely for purposes of determining the propriety of removal under subsection (a), a law enforcement officer, who is the defendant in a criminal prosecution, shall be deemed to have been acting under the color of his office if the officer—

(1) protected an individual in the presence of the officer from a crime of violence;

(2)   provided immediate assistance to an individual who suffered, or who was threatened with, bodily harm; or

(3)   prevented the escape of any individual who the officer reasonably believed to have committed, or was about to commit, in the presence of the officer, a crime of violence that resulted in, or was likely to result in, death or serious bodily injury.

(d)   In this section, the following definitions apply:

(1)   The terms "civil action" and "criminal prosecution" include any proceeding (whether or not ancillary to another proceeding) to the extent that in such proceeding a judicial order, including a subpoena for testimony or documents, is sought or issued. If removal is sought for a proceeding described in the previous sentence, and there is no other basis for removal, only that proceeding may be removed to the district court.

(2)   The term "crime of violence" has the meaning given that term in section 16 of title 18.

(3)   The term "law enforcement officer" means any employee described in subparagraph (A), (B), or (C) of section 8401(17) of title 5 and any special agent in the Diplomatic Security Service of the Department of State.

(4)   The term "serious bodily injury" has the meaning given that term in section 1365 of title 18.

(5)   The term "State" includes the District of Columbia, United States territories and insular possessions, and Indian country (as defined in section 1151 of title 18).

(6)   The term "State court" includes the Superior Court of the District of Columbia, a court of a United States territory or insular possession, and a tribal court.

§ 1442a.   Members of Armed Forces Sued or Prosecuted

A civil or criminal prosecution in a court of a State of the United States against a member of the armed forces of the United States on account of an act done under color of his office or status, or in respect to which he claims any right, title, or authority under a law of the United States respecting the armed forces thereof, or under the law of war, may at any time before the trial or final hearing thereof be removed for trial into the district court of the United States for the district where it is pending in the manner prescribed by law, and it shall thereupon be entered on the docket of the district court, which shall proceed as if the cause had been originally commenced therein and shall have full power to hear and determine the cause.

§ 1443.   Civil Rights Cases

Any of the following civil actions or criminal prosecutions, commenced in a State court may be removed by the defendant to the district court of the United States for the district and division embracing the place wherein it is pending:

(1)   Against any person who is denied or cannot enforce in the courts of such State a right under any law providing for the equal civil rights of citizens of the United States, or of all persons within the jurisdiction thereof;

(2)   For any act under color of authority derived from any law providing for equal rights, or for refusing to do any act on the ground that it would be inconsistent with such law.

§ 1445.   Nonremovable Actions

(a)   A civil action in any State court against a railroad or its receivers or trustees, arising under sections 1–4 and 5–10 of the Act of April 22, 1908 (45 U.S.C. 51 to 54, 55 to 60), may not be removed to any district court of the United States.

(b) A civil action in any State court against a carrier or its receivers or trustees to recover damages for delay, loss, or injury of shipments, arising under section 11706 or 14706 of title 49, may not be removed to any district court of the United States unless the matter in controversy exceeds $10,000, exclusive of interest and costs.

(c) A civil action in any State court arising under the workmen's compensation laws of such State may not be removed to any district court of the United States.

(d) A civil action in any State court arising under section 40302 of the Violence Against Women Act of 1994 may not be removed to any district court of the United States.

§ 1446.   Procedure for Removal of Civil Actions

(a) Generally.—A defendant or defendants desiring to remove any civil action from a State court shall file in the district court of the United States for the district and division within which such action is pending a notice of removal signed pursuant to Rule 11 of the Federal Rules of Civil Procedure and containing a short and plain statement of the grounds for removal, together with a copy of all process, pleadings, and orders served upon such defendant or defendants in such action.

(b) Requirements; generally.—**(1)** The notice of removal of a civil action or proceeding shall be filed within 30 days after the receipt by the defendant, through service or otherwise, of a copy of the initial pleading setting forth the claim for relief upon which such action or proceeding is based, or within 30 days after the service of summons upon the defendant if such initial pleading has then been filed in court and is not required to be served on the defendant, whichever period is shorter.

(2) (A) When a civil action is removed solely under section 1441(a), all defendants who have been properly joined and served must join in or consent to the removal of the action.

(B) Each defendant shall have 30 days after receipt by or service on that defendant of the initial pleading or summons described in paragraph (1) to file the notice of removal.

(C) If defendants are served at different times, and a later served defendant files a notice of removal, any earlier-served defendant may consent to the removal even though that earlier-served defendant did not previously initiate or consent to removal.

(3) Except as provided in subsection (c), if the case stated by the initial pleading is not removable, a notice of removal may be filed within thirty days after receipt by the defendant, through service or otherwise, of a copy of an amended pleading, motion, order or other paper from which it may first be ascertained that the case is one which is or has become removable.

(c) Requirements; removal based on diversity of citizenship.—**(1)** A case may not be removed under subsection (b)(3) on the basis of jurisdiction conferred by section 1332 more than 1 year after commencement of the action, unless the district court finds that the plaintiff has acted in bad faith in order to prevent a defendant from removing the action.(2) If removal of a civil action is sought on the basis of the jurisdiction conferred by section 1332(a), the sum demanded in good faith in the initial pleading shall be deemed to be the amount in controversy, except that—

(A) the notice of removal may assert the amount in controversy if the initial pleading seeks—

(i) nonmonetary relief; or

(ii) a money judgment, but the State practice either does not permit demand for a specific sum or permits recovery of damages in excess of the amount demanded; and

(B) removal of the action is proper on the basis of an amount in controversy asserted under subparagraph (A) if the district court finds, by the preponderance of the evidence, that the amount in controversy exceeds the amount specified in section 1332(a).

(3) **(A)** If the case stated by the initial pleading is not removable solely because the amount in controversy does not exceed the amount specified in section 1332(a), information relating to the amount in controversy in the record of the State proceeding, or in responses to discovery, shall be treated as an "other paper" under subsection (b)(3).

(B) If the notice of removal is filed more than 1 year after commencement of the action and the district court finds that the plaintiff deliberately failed to disclose the actual amount in controversy to prevent removal, that finding shall be deemed bad faith under paragraph (1).

(d) Notice to adverse parties and state court.—Promptly after the filing of such notice of removal of a civil action the defendant or defendants shall give written notice thereof to all adverse parties and shall file a copy of the notice with the clerk of such State court, which shall effect the removal and the State court shall proceed no further unless and until the case is remanded.

(e) Counterclaim in 337 proceeding.—With respect to any counterclaim removed to a district court pursuant to section 337(c) of the Tariff Act of 1930, the district court shall resolve such counterclaim in the same manner as an original complaint under the Federal Rules of Civil Procedure, except that the payment of a filing fee shall not be required in such cases and the counterclaim shall relate back to the date of the original complaint in the proceeding before the International Trade Commission under section 337 of that Act.

(g)[3] **(1)** Where the civil action or criminal prosecution that is removable under section 1442(a) is a proceeding in which a judicial order for testimony or documents is sought or issued or sought to be enforced, the 30-day requirement of subsection (b) of this section and paragraph (1) of section 1455(b) is satisfied if the person or entity desiring to remove the proceeding files the notice of removal not later than 30 days after receiving, through service, notice of any such proceeding.

§ 1447.   Procedure after Removal Generally

(a) In any case removed from a State court, the district court may issue all necessary orders and process to bring before it all proper parties whether served by process issued by the State court or otherwise.

(b) It may require the removing party to file with its clerk copies of all records and proceedings in such State court or may cause the same to be brought before it by writ of certiorari issued to such State court.

(c) A motion to remand the case on the basis of any defect other than lack of subject matter jurisdiction must be made within 30 days after the filing of the notice of removal under section 1446(a). If at any time before final judgment it appears that the district court lacks subject matter jurisdiction, the case shall be remanded. An order remanding the case may require payment of just costs and any actual expenses, including attorney fees, incurred as a result of the removal. A certified copy of the order of remand shall be mailed by the clerk to the clerk of the State court. The State court may thereupon proceed with such case.

(d) An order remanding a case to the State court from which it was removed is not reviewable on appeal or otherwise, except that an order remanding a case to the State court from which it was removed pursuant to section 1442 or 1443 of this title shall be reviewable by appeal or otherwise.

(e) If after removal the plaintiff seeks to join additional defendants whose joinder would destroy subject matter jurisdiction, the court may deny joinder, or permit joinder and remand the action to the State court.

---

[3]   ED Note: In 2012, revisions to Section 1446 repositioned subpart 1446(f), leaving that subpart empty in the current statute.

§ 1448.   Process after Removal

In all cases removed from any State court to any district court of the United States in which any one or more of the defendants has not been served with process or in which the service has not been perfected prior to removal, or in which process served proves to be defective, such process or service may be completed or new process issued in the same manner as in cases originally filed in such district court.

This section shall not deprive any defendant upon whom process is served after removal of his right to move to remand the case.

§ 1449.   State Court Record Supplied

Where a party is entitled to copies of the records and proceedings in any suit or prosecution in a State court, to be used in any district court of the United States, and the clerk of such State court, upon demand, and the payment or tender of the legal fees, fails to deliver certified copies, the district court may, on affidavit reciting such facts, direct such record to be supplied by affidavit or otherwise. Thereupon such proceedings, trial, and judgment may be had in such district court, and all such process awarded, as if certified copies had been filed in the district court.

§ 1451.   Definitions

For purposes of this chapter—

(1) The term "State court" includes the Superior Court of the District of Columbia.

(2) The term "State" includes the District of Columbia.

§ 1453.   Removal of Class Actions

(a) **Definitions.**—In this section, the terms "class", "class action", "class certification order", and "class member" shall have the meanings given such terms under section 1332(d)(1).

(b) **In general.**—A class action may be removed to a district court of the United States in accordance with section 1446 (except that the 1-year limitation under section 1446(c)(1) shall not apply), without regard to whether any defendant is a citizen of the State in which the action is brought, except that such action may be removed by any defendant without the consent of all defendants.

(c) **Review of remand orders.**—

(1) **In general.**—Section 1447 shall apply to any removal of a case under this section, except that notwithstanding section 1447(d), a court of appeals may accept an appeal from an order of a district court granting or denying a motion to remand a class action to the State court from which it was removed if application is made to the court of appeals not more than 10 days after entry of the order.

(2) **Time period for judgment.**—If the court of appeals accepts an appeal under paragraph (1), the court shall complete all action on such appeal, including rendering judgment, not later than 60 days after the date on which such appeal was filed, unless an extension is granted under paragraph (3).

(3) **Extension of time period.**—The court of appeals may grant an extension of the 60-day period described in paragraph (2) if—

(A) all parties to the proceeding agree to such extension, for any period of time; or

(B) such extension is for good cause shown and in the interests of justice, for a period not to exceed 10 days.

(4) Denial of appeal.—If a final judgment on the appeal under paragraph (1) is not issued before the end of the period described in paragraph (2), including any extension under paragraph (3), the appeal shall be denied.

(d) Exception.—This section shall not apply to any class action that solely involves—

(1) a claim concerning a covered security as defined under section 16(f) (3) of the Securities Act of 1933 (15 U.S.C. 78p(f) (3)) and section 28(f)(5)(E) of the Securities Exchange Act of 1934 (15 U.S.C. 78bb(f)(5)(E));

(2) a claim that relates to the internal affairs or governance of a corporation or other form of business enterprise and arises under or by virtue of the laws of the State in which such corporation or business enterprise is incorporated or organized; or

(3) a claim that relates to the rights, duties (including fiduciary duties), and obligations relating to or created by or pursuant to any security (as defined under section 2(a)(1) of the Securities Act of 1933 (15 U.S.C. 77b(a)(1)) and the regulations issued thereunder).

§ 1631.   Transfer to Cure Want of Jurisdiction

Whenever a civil action is filed in a court as defined in section 610 of this title or an appeal, including a petition for review of administrative action, is noticed for or filed with such a court and that court finds that there is a want of jurisdiction, the court shall, if it is in the interest of justice, transfer such action or appeal to any other such court in which the action or appeal could have been brought at the time it was filed or noticed, and the action or appeal shall proceed as if it had been filed in or noticed for the court to which it is transferred on the date upon which it was actually filed in or noticed for the court from which it is transferred.

§ 1651.   Writs

(a) The Supreme Court and all courts established by Act of Congress may issue all writs necessary or appropriate in aid of their respective jurisdictions and agreeable to the usages and principles of law.

(b) An alternative writ or rule nisi may be issued by a justice or judge of a court which has jurisdiction.

§ 1652.   State Laws As Rules of Decision

The laws of the several states, except where the Constitution or treaties of the United States or Acts of Congress otherwise require or provide, shall be regarded as rules of decision in civil actions in the courts of the United States, in cases where they apply.

§ 1653.   Amendment of Pleadings to Show Jurisdiction

Defective allegations of jurisdiction may be amended, upon terms, in the trial or appellate courts.

§ 1654.   Appearance Personally or by Counsel

In all courts of the United States the parties may plead and conduct their own cases personally or by counsel as, by the rules of such courts, respectively, are permitted to manage and conduct causes therein.

§ 1657.   Priority of Civil Actions

(a) Notwithstanding any other provision of law, each court of the United States shall determine the order in which civil actions are heard and determined, except that the court shall expedite the consideration of any action brought under chapter 153 or section 1826 of this title, any action for

temporary or preliminary injunctive relief, or any other action if good cause therefor is shown. For purposes of this subsection, "good cause" is shown if a right under the Constitution of the United States or a Federal Statute (including rights under section 552 of title 5) would be maintained in a factual context that indicates that a request for expedited consideration has merit.

(b) The Judicial Conference of the United States may modify the rules adopted by the courts to determine the order in which civil actions are heard and determined, in order to establish consistency among the judicial circuits.

§1658. Time Limitations on the Commencement of Civil Actions Arising under Acts of Congress

(a) Except as otherwise provided by law, a civil action arising under an Act of Congress enacted after the date of the enactment of this section may not be commenced later than 4 years after the cause of action accrues.

(b) Notwithstanding subsection (a), a private right of action that involves a claim of fraud, deceit, manipulation, or contrivance in contravention of a regulatory requirement concerning the securities laws, as defined in section 3(a)(47) of the Securities Exchange Act of 1934 (15 U.S.C. 78c(a)(47)), may be brought not later than the earlier of—

    (1) 2 years after the discovery of the facts constituting the violation; or

    (2) 5 years after such violation.

§1691. Seal and Teste of Process

All writs and process issuing from a court of the United States shall be under the seal of the court and signed by the clerk thereof.

§1692. Process and Orders Affecting Property in Different Districts

In proceedings in a district court where a receiver is appointed for property, real, personal, or mixed, situated in different districts, process may issue and be executed in any such district as if the property lay wholly within one district, but orders affecting the property shall be entered of record in each of such districts.

§1695. Stockholder's Derivative Action

Process in a stockholder's action in behalf of his corporation may be served upon such corporation in any district where it is organized or licensed to do business or is doing business.

§1696. Service in Foreign and International Litigation

(a) The district court of the district in which a person resides or is found may order service upon him of any document issued in connection with a proceeding in a foreign or international tribunal. The order may be made pursuant to a letter rogatory issued, or request made, by a foreign or international tribunal or upon application of any interested person and shall direct the manner of service. Service pursuant to this subsection does not, of itself, require the recognition or enforcement in the United States of a judgment, decree, or order rendered by a foreign or international tribunal.

(b) This section does not preclude service of such a document without an order of court.

§ 1697.   Service in Multiparty, Multiforum Actions

When the jurisdiction of the district court is based in whole or in part upon section 1369 of this title, process, other than subpoenas, may be served at any place within the United States, or anywhere outside the United States if otherwise permitted by law.

§ 1731.   Handwriting

The admitted or proved handwriting of any person shall be admissible, for purposes of comparison, to determine genuineness of other handwriting attributed to such person.

§ 1732.   Record Made in Regular Course of Business; Photographic Copies

If any business, institution, member of a profession or calling, or any department or agency of government, in the regular course of business or activity has kept or recorded any memorandum, writing, entry, print, representation or combination thereof, of any act, transaction, occurrence, or event, and in the regular course of business has caused any or all of the same to be recorded, copied, or reproduced by any photographic, photostatic, microfilm, micro-card, miniature photographic, or other process which accurately reproduces or forms a durable medium for so reproducing the original, the original may be destroyed in the regular course of business unless its preservation is required by law. Such reproduction, when satisfactorily identified, is as admissible in evidence as the original itself in any judicial or administrative proceeding whether the original is in existence or not and an enlargement or facsimile of such reproduction is likewise admissible in evidence if the original reproduction is in existence and available for inspection under direction of court. The introduction of a reproduced record, enlargement, or facsimile does not preclude admission of the original. This subsection shall not be construed to exclude from evidence any document or copy thereof which is otherwise admissible under the rules of evidence.

§ 1733.   Government Records and Papers; Copies

(a) Books or records of account or minutes of proceedings of any department or agency of the United States shall be admissible to prove the act, transaction or occurrence as a memorandum of which the same were made or kept.

(b) Properly authenticated copies or transcripts of any books, records, papers or documents of any department or agency of the United States shall be admitted in evidence equally with the originals thereof.

(c) This section does not apply to cases, actions, and proceedings to which the Federal Rules of Evidence apply.

§ 1734.   Court Record Lost or Destroyed, Generally

(a) A lost or destroyed record of any proceeding in any court of the United States may be supplied on application of any interested party not at fault, by substituting a copy certified by the clerk of any court in which an authentic copy is lodged.

(b) Where a certified copy is not available, any interested person not at fault may file in such court a verified application for an order establishing the lost or destroyed record. Every other interested person shall be served personally with a copy of the application and with notice of hearing on a day stated, not less than sixty days after service. Service may be made on any nonresident of the district anywhere within the jurisdiction of the United States or in any foreign country.

Proof of service in a foreign country shall be certified by a minister or consul of the United States in such country, under his official seal.

If, after the hearing, the court is satisfied that the statements contained in the application are true, it shall enter an order reciting the substance and effect of the lost or destroyed record. Such order, subject to intervening rights of third persons, shall have the same effect as the original record.

§ 1735.   Court Record Lost or Destroyed Where United States Interested

(a) When the record of any case or matter in any court of the United States to which the United States is a party, is lost or destroyed, a certified copy of any official paper of a United States attorney, United States marshal or clerk or other certifying or recording officer of any such court, made pursuant to law, on file in any department or agency of the United States and relating to such case or matter, shall, on being filed in the court to which it relates, have the same effect as an original paper filed in such court. If the copy so filed discloses the date and amount of a judgment or decree and the names of the parties thereto, the court may enforce the judgment or decree as though the original record had not been lost or destroyed.

(b) Whenever the United States is interested in any lost or destroyed records or files of a court of the United States, the clerk of such court and the United States attorney for the district shall take the steps necessary to restore such records or files, under the direction of the judges of such court.

§ 1738.   State and Territorial Statutes and Judicial Proceedings; Full Faith and Credit

The Acts of the legislature of any State, Territory, or Possession of the United States, or copies thereof, shall be authenticated by affixing the seal of such State, Territory or Possession thereto.

The records and judicial proceedings of any court of any such State, Territory or Possession, or copies thereof, shall be proved or admitted in other courts within the United States and its Territories and Possessions by the attestation of the clerk and seal of the court annexed, if a seal exists, together with a certificate of a judge of the court that the said attestation is in proper form.

Such Acts, records and judicial proceedings or copies thereof, so authenticated, shall have the same full faith and credit in every court within the United States and its Territories and Possessions as they have by law or usage in the courts of such State, Territory or Possession from which they are taken.

§ 1739.   State and Territorial Nonjudicial Records; Full Faith and Credit

All nonjudicial records or books kept in any public office of any State, Territory, or Possession of the United States, or copies thereof, shall be proved or admitted in any court or office in any other State, Territory, or Possession by the attestation of the custodian of such records or books, and the seal of his office annexed, if there be a seal, together with a certificate of a judge of a court of record of the county, parish, or district in which such office may be kept, or of the Governor, or secretary of state, the chancellor or keeper of the great seal, of the State, Territory, or Possession that the said attestation is in due form and by the proper officers.

If the certificate is given by a judge, it shall be further authenticated by the clerk or prothonotary of the court, who shall certify, under his hand and the seal of his office, that such judge is duly commissioned and qualified; or, if given by such Governor, secretary, chancellor, or keeper of the great seal, it shall be under the great seal of the State, Territory, or Possession in which it is made.

Such records or books, or copies thereof, so authenticated, shall have the same full faith and credit in every court and office within the United States and its Territories and Possessions as they have by law or usage in the courts or offices of the State, Territory, or Possession from which they are taken.

§ 1746.   Unsworn Declarations under Penalty of Perjury

Wherever, under any law of the United States or under any rule, regulation, order, or requirement made pursuant to law, any matter is required or permitted to be supported, evidenced, established, or proved by the sworn declaration, verification, certificate, statement, oath, or affidavit, in writing of the person making the same (other than a deposition, or an oath of office, or an oath required to be taken before a specified official other than a notary public), such matter may, with like force and effect, be supported, evidenced, established, or proved by the unsworn declaration, certificate, verification, or statement, in writing of such person which is subscribed by him, as true under penalty of perjury, and dated, in substantially the following form:

   (1)   If executed without the United States: "I declare *(or certify, verify, or state)* under penalty of perjury under the laws of the United States of America that the foregoing is true and correct. Executed on *(date)*.

(Signature)".

   (2)   If executed within the United States, its territories, possessions, or commonwealths: "I declare *(or certify, verify, or state)* under penalty of perjury that the foregoing is true and correct. Executed on *(date)*.

(Signature)".

§ 1781.   Transmittal of Letter Rogatory or Request

(a)   The Department of State has power, directly, or through suitable channels—

   (1)   to receive a letter rogatory issued, or request made, by a foreign or international tribunal, to transmit it to the tribunal, officer, or agency in the United States to whom it is addressed, and to receive and return it after execution; and

   (2)   to receive a letter rogatory issued, or request made, by a tribunal in the United States, to transmit it to the foreign or international tribunal, officer, or agency to whom it is addressed, and to receive and return it after execution.

(b)   This section does not preclude—

   (1)   the transmittal of a letter rogatory or request directly from a foreign or international tribunal to the tribunal, officer, or agency in the United States to whom it is addressed and its return in the same manner; or

   (2)   the transmittal of a letter rogatory or request directly from a tribunal in the United States to the foreign or international tribunal, officer, or agency to whom it is addressed and its return in the same manner.

§ 1782.   Assistance to Foreign and International Tribunals and to Litigants before Such Tribunals

(a)   The district court of the district in which a person resides or is found may order him to give his testimony or statement or to produce a document or other thing for use in a proceeding in a foreign or international tribunal, including criminal investigations conducted before formal accusation. The order may be made pursuant to a letter rogatory issued, or request made, by a foreign or international tribunal or upon the application of any interested person and may direct that the testimony or statement be given, or the document or other thing be produced, before a person appointed by the court. By virtue of his appointment, the person appointed has power to administer any necessary oath and take the testimony or statement. The order may prescribe the practice and procedure, which may be in whole or part the practice and procedure of the foreign country or the international tribunal, for taking the testimony or statement or producing the document or other thing. To the extent that the

order does not prescribe otherwise, the testimony or statement shall be taken, and the document or other thing produced, in accordance with the Federal Rules of Civil Procedure.

A person may not be compelled to give his testimony or statement or to produce a document or other thing in violation of any legally applicable privilege.

(b) This chapter does not preclude a person within the United States from voluntarily giving his testimony or statement, or producing a document or other thing, for use in a proceeding in a foreign or international tribunal before any person and in any manner acceptable to him.

§ 1783.   Subpoena of Person in Foreign Country

(a) A court of the United States may order the issuance of a subpoena requiring the appearance as a witness before it, or before a person or body designated by it, of a national or resident of the United States who is in a foreign country, or requiring the production of a specified document or other thing by him, if the court finds that particular testimony or the production of the document or other thing by him is necessary in the interest of justice, and, in other than a criminal action or proceeding, if the court finds, in addition, that it is not possible to obtain his testimony in admissible form without his personal appearance or to obtain the production of the document or other thing in any other manner.

(b) The subpoena shall designate the time and place for the appearance or for the production of the document or other thing. Service of the subpoena and any order to show cause, rule, judgment, or decree authorized by this section or by section 1784 of this title shall be effected in accordance with the provisions of the Federal Rules of Civil Procedure relating to service of process on a person in a foreign country. The person serving the subpoena shall tender to the person to whom the subpoena is addressed his estimated necessary travel and attendance expenses, the amount of which shall be determined by the court and stated in the order directing the issuance of the subpoena.

§ 1784.   Contempt

(a) The court of the United States which has issued a subpoena served in a foreign country may order the person who has failed to appear or who has failed to produce a document or other thing as directed therein to show cause before it at a designated time why he should not be punished for contempt.

(b) The court, in the order to show cause, may direct that any of the person's property within the United States be levied upon or seized, in the manner provided by law or court rules governing levy or seizure under execution, and held to satisfy any judgment that may be rendered against him pursuant to subsection (d) of this section if adequate security, in such amount as the court may direct in the order, be given for any damage that he might suffer should he not be found in contempt. Security under this subsection may not be required of the United States.

(c) A copy of the order to show cause shall be served on the person in accordance with section 1783(b) of this title.

(d) On the return day of the order to show cause or any later day to which the hearing may be continued, proof shall be taken. If the person is found in contempt, the court, notwithstanding any limitation upon its power generally to punish for contempt, may fine him not more than $100,000 and direct that the fine and costs of the proceedings be satisfied by a sale of the property levied upon or seized, conducted upon the notice required and in the manner provided for sales upon execution.

§ 1785.   Subpoenas in Multiparty, Multiforum Actions

When the jurisdiction of the district court is based in whole or in part upon section 1369 of this title, a subpoena for attendance at a hearing or trial may, if authorized by the court upon motion for good cause shown, and upon such terms and conditions as the court may impose, be served at any place within the United States, or anywhere outside the United States if otherwise permitted by law.

§ 1821.   Per Diem and Mileage Generally; Subsistence

(a) **(1)** Except as otherwise provided by law, a witness in attendance at any court of the United States, or before a United States Magistrate, or before any person authorized to take his deposition pursuant to any rule or order of a court of the United States, shall be paid the fees and allowances provided by this section.

(2) As used in this section, the term "court of the United States" includes, in addition to the courts listed in section 451 of this title, any court created by Act of Congress in a territory which is invested with any jurisdiction of a district court of the United States.

(b) A witness shall be paid an attendance fee of $40 per day for each day's attendance. A witness shall also be paid the attendance fee for the time necessarily occupied in going to and returning from the place of attendance at the beginning and end of such attendance or at any time during such attendance.

(c) **(1)** A witness who travels by common carrier shall be paid for the actual expenses of travel on the basis of the means of transportation reasonably utilized and the distance necessarily traveled to and from such witness's residence by the shortest practical route in going to and returning from the place of attendance. Such a witness shall utilize a common carrier at the most economical rate reasonably available. A receipt or other evidence of actual cost shall be furnished.

(2) A travel allowance equal to the mileage allowance which the Administrator of General Services has prescribed, pursuant to section 5704 of title 5, for official travel of employees of the Federal Government shall be paid to each witness who travels by privately owned vehicle. Computation of mileage under this paragraph shall be made on the basis of a uniformed table of distances adopted by the Administrator of General Services.

(3) Toll charges for toll roads, bridges, tunnels, and ferries, taxicab fares between places of lodging and carrier terminals, and parking fees (upon presentation of a valid parking receipt), shall be paid in full to a witness incurring such expenses.

(4) All normal travel expenses within and outside the judicial district shall be taxable as costs pursuant to section 1920 of this title.

(d) **(1)** A subsistence allowance shall be paid to a witness when an overnight stay is required at the place of attendance because such place is so far removed from the residence of such witness as to prohibit return thereto from day to day.

(2) A subsistence allowance for a witness shall be paid in an amount not to exceed the maximum per diem allowance prescribed by the Administrator of General Services, pursuant to section 5702(a) of title 5, for official travel in the area of attendance by employees of the Federal Government.

(3) A subsistence allowance for a witness attending in an area designated by the Administrator of General Services as a high-cost area shall be paid in an amount not to exceed the maximum actual subsistence allowance prescribed by the Administrator, pursuant to section 5702(c)(B) of title 5, for official travel in such area by employees of the Federal Government.

(4) When a witness is detained pursuant to section 3144 of title 18 for want of security for his appearance, he shall be entitled for each day of detention when not in attendance at court, in addition to his subsistence, to the daily attendance fee provided by subsection (b) of this section.

(e) An alien who has been paroled into the United States for prosecution, pursuant to section 212(d)(5) of the Immigration and Nationality Act (8 U.S.C. 1182(d)(5)), or an alien who either has admitted belonging to a class of aliens who are deportable or has been determined pursuant to section 240 of such Act (8 U.S.C. 1252(b)) to be deportable, shall be ineligible to receive the fees or allowances provided by this section.

(f) Any witness who is incarcerated at the time that his or her testimony is given (except for a witness to whom the provisions of section 3144 of title 18 apply) may not receive fees or allowances under this section, regardless of whether such a witness is incarcerated at the time he or she makes a claim for fees or allowances under this section.

§ 1826.   Recalcitrant Witnesses

(a) Whenever a witness in any proceeding before or ancillary to any court or grand jury of the United States refuses without just cause shown to comply with an order of the court to testify or provide other information, including any book, paper, document, record, recording or other material, the court, upon such refusal, or when such refusal is duly brought to its attention, may summarily order his confinement at a suitable place until such time as the witness is willing to give such testimony or provide such information. No period of such confinement shall exceed the life of—

    (1) the court proceeding, or

    (2) the term of the grand jury, including extensions, before which such refusal to comply with the court order occurred, but in no event shall such confinement exceed eighteen months.

(b) No person confined pursuant to subsection (a) of this section shall be admitted to bail pending the determination of an appeal taken by him from the order for his confinement if it appears that the appeal is frivolous or taken for delay. Any appeal from an order of confinement under this section shall be disposed of as soon as practicable, but not later than thirty days from the filing of such appeal.

(c) Whoever escapes or attempts to escape from the custody of any facility or from any place in which or to which he is confined pursuant to this section or section 4243 of title 18, or whoever rescues or attempts to rescue or instigates, aids, or assists the escape or attempt to escape of such a person, shall be subject to imprisonment for not more than three years, or a fine of not more than $10,000, or both.

§ 1914.   District Court; Filing and Miscellaneous Fees; Rules of Court

(a) The clerk of each district court shall require the parties instituting any civil action, suit or proceeding in such court, whether by original process, removal or otherwise, to pay a filing fee of $350, except that on application for a writ of habeas corpus the filing fee shall be $5.

(b) The clerk shall collect from the parties such additional fees only as are prescribed by the Judicial Conference of the United States.

(c) Each district court by rule or standing order may require advance payment of fees.

§ 1915.   Proceedings in Forma Pauperis

(a) (1) Subject to subsection (b), any court of the United States may authorize the commencement, prosecution or defense of any suit, action or proceeding, civil or criminal, or appeal therein, without prepayment of fees or security therefor, by a person who submits an affidavit that includes a statement of all assets such prisoner possesses that the person is unable to pay such fees or give security therefor. Such affidavit shall state the nature of the action, defense or appeal and affiant's belief that the person is entitled to redress.

    (2) A prisoner seeking to bring a civil action or appeal a judgment in a civil action or proceeding without prepayment of fees or security therefor, in addition to filing the affidavit filed under paragraph (1), shall submit a certified copy of the trust fund account statement (or institutional equivalent) for the prisoner for the 6-month period immediately preceding the filing of the complaint or notice of appeal, obtained from the appropriate official of each prison at which the prisoner is or was confined.

    (3) An appeal may not be taken in forma pauperis if the trial court certifies in writing that it is not taken in good faith.

(b) **(1)** Notwithstanding subsection (a), if a prisoner brings a civil action or files an appeal in forma pauperis, the prisoner shall be required to pay the full amount of a filing fee. The court shall assess and, when funds exist, collect, as a partial payment of any court fees required by law, an initial partial filing fee of 20 percent of the greater of—

(A) the average monthly deposits to the prisoner's account; or

(B) the average monthly balance in the prisoner's account for the 6-month period immediately preceding the filing of the complaint or notice of appeal.

(2) After payment of the initial partial filing fee, the prisoner shall be required to make monthly payments of 20 percent of the preceding month's income credited to the prisoner's account. The agency having custody of the prisoner shall forward payments from the prisoner's account to the clerk of the court each time the amount in the account exceeds $10 until the filing fees are paid.

(3) In no event shall the filing fee collected exceed the amount of fees permitted by statute for the commencement of a civil action or an appeal of a civil action or criminal judgment.

(4) In no event shall a prisoner be prohibited from bringing a civil action or appealing a civil or criminal judgment for the reason that the prisoner has no assets and no means by which to pay the initial partial filing fee.

(c) Upon the filing of an affidavit in accordance with subsections (a) and (b) and the prepayment of any partial filing fee as may be required under subsection (b), the court may direct payment by the United States of the expenses of (1) printing the record on appeal in any civil or criminal case, if such printing is required by the appellate court; (2) preparing a transcript of proceedings before a United States magistrate in any civil or criminal case, if such transcript is required by the district court, in the case of proceedings conducted under section 636(b) of this title or under section 3401(b) of title 18, United States Code; and (3) printing the record on appeal if such printing is required by the appellate court, in the case of proceedings conducted pursuant to section 636(c) of this title. Such expenses shall be paid when authorized by the Director of the Administrative Office of the United States Courts.

(d) The officers of the court shall issue and serve all process, and perform all duties in such cases. Witnesses shall attend as in other cases, and the same remedies shall be available as are provided for by law in other cases.

(e) **(1)** The court may request an attorney to represent any person unable to afford counsel.

(2) Notwithstanding any filing fee, or any portion thereof, that may have been paid, the court shall dismiss the case at any time if the court determines that—

(A) the allegation of poverty is untrue; or

(B) the action or appeal—

(i) is frivolous or malicious;

(ii) fails to state a claim on which relief may be granted; or

(iii) seeks monetary relief against a defendant who is immune from such relief.

(f) **(1)** Judgment may be rendered for costs at the conclusion of the suit or action as in other proceedings, but the United States shall not be liable for any of the costs thus incurred. If the United States has paid the cost of a stenographic transcript or printed record for the prevailing party, the same shall be taxed in favor of the United States.

(2) **(A)** If the judgment against a prisoner includes the payment of costs under this subsection, the prisoner shall be required to pay the full amount of the costs ordered.

(B) The prisoner shall be required to make payments for costs under this subsection in the same manner as is provided for filing fees under subsection (a)(2).

(C) In no event shall the costs collected exceed the amount of the costs ordered by the court.

(g) In no event shall a prisoner bring a civil action or appeal a judgment in a civil action or proceeding under this section if the prisoner has, on 3 or more prior occasions, while incarcerated or detained in any facility, brought an action or appeal in a court of the United States that was dismissed on the grounds that it is frivolous, malicious, or fails to state a claim upon which relief may be granted, unless the prisoner is under imminent danger of serious physical injury.

(h) As used in this section, the term 'prisoner' means any person incarcerated or detained in any facility who is accused of, convicted of, sentenced for, or adjudicated delinquent for, violations of criminal law or the terms and conditions of parole, probation, pretrial release, or diversionary program.

§ 1917.   District Courts; Fee on Filing Notice of or Petition for Appeal

Upon the filing of any separate or joint notice of appeal or application for appeal or upon the receipt of any order allowing, or notice of the allowance of, an appeal or of a writ of certiorari $5 shall be paid to the clerk of the district court, by the appellant or petitioner.

§ 1920.   Taxation of Costs

A judge or clerk of any court of the United States may tax as costs the following:

(1) Fees of the clerk and marshal;

(2) Fees for printed or electronically recorded manuscripts necessarily obtained for use in the case;

(3) Fees and disbursements for printing and witnesses;

(4) Fees for exemplification and the costs of making copies of any materials where copies are necessarily obtained for use in the case;

(5) Docket fees under section 1923 of this title;

(6) Compensation of court appointed experts, compensation of interpreters, and salaries, fees, expenses, and costs of special interpretation services under section 1828 of this title.

A bill of costs shall be filed in the case and, upon allowance, included in the judgment or decree.

§ 1924.   Verification of Bill of Costs

Before any bill of costs is taxed, the party claiming any item of cost or disbursement shall attach thereto an affidavit, made by himself or by his duly authorized attorney or agent having knowledge of the facts, that such item is correct and has been necessarily incurred in the case and that the services for which fees have been charged were actually and necessarily performed.

§ 1927.   Counsel's Liability for Excessive Costs

Any attorney or other person admitted to conduct cases in any court of the United States or any Territory thereof who so multiplies the proceedings in any case unreasonably and vexatiously may be required by the court to satisfy personally the excess costs, expenses, and attorneys' fees reasonably incurred because of such conduct.

§ 1961.   Interest

(a) Interest shall be allowed on any money judgment in a civil case recovered in a district court. Execution therefor may be levied by the marshal, in any case where, by the law of the State in which such court is held, execution may be levied for interest on judgments recovered in the courts of the State. Such interest shall be calculated from the date of the entry of the judgment, at a rate equal to the weekly average 1-year constant maturity Treasury yield, as published by the Board of Governors

of the Federal Reserve System, for the calendar week preceding the date of the judgment. The Director of the Administrative Office of the United States Courts shall distribute notice of that rate and any changes in it to all Federal judges.

(b) Interest shall be computed daily to the date of payment except as provided in section 2516(b) of this title and section 1304(b) of title 31, and shall be compounded annually.

(c) **(1)** This section shall not apply in any judgment of any court with respect to any internal revenue tax case. Interest shall be allowed in such cases at the underpayment rate or overpayment rate (whichever is appropriate) established under section 6621 of the Internal Revenue Code of 1986.

(2) Except as otherwise provided in paragraph (1) of this subsection, interest shall be allowed on all final judgments against the United States in the United States Court of Appeals for the Federal circuit,[4] at the rate provided in subsection (a) and as provided in subsection (b).

(3) Interest shall be allowed, computed, and paid on judgments of the United States Court of Federal Claims only as provided in paragraph (1) of this subsection or in any other provision of law.

(4) This section shall not be construed to affect the interest on any judgment of any court not specified in this section.

§ 1963. Registration of Judgments for Enforcement in Other Districts

A judgment in an action for the recovery of money or property entered in any court of appeals, district court, bankruptcy court, or in the Court of International Trade may be registered by filing a certified copy of the judgment in any other district or, with respect to the Court of International Trade, in any judicial district, when the judgment has become final by appeal or expiration of the time for appeal or when ordered by the court that entered the judgment for good cause shown. Such a judgment entered in favor of the United States may be so registered any time after judgment is entered. A judgment so registered shall have the same effect as a judgment of the district court of the district where registered and may be enforced in like manner.

A certified copy of the satisfaction of any judgment in whole or in part may be registered in like manner in any district in which the judgment is a lien.

The procedure prescribed under this section is in addition to other procedures provided by law for the enforcement of judgments.

§ 1964. Constructive Notice of Pending Actions

Where the law of a State requires a notice of an action concerning real property pending in a court of the State to be registered, recorded, docketed, or indexed in a particular manner, or in a certain office or county or parish in order to give constructive notice of the action as it relates to the real property, and such law authorizes a notice of an action concerning real property pending in a United States district court to be registered, recorded, docketed, or indexed in the same manner, or in the same place, those requirements of the State law must be complied with in order to give constructive notice of such an action pending in a United States district court as it relates to real property in such State.

---

[4]   So in original. Probably should be "Circuit,".

§ 2071.   Rule-Making Power Generally

(a) The Supreme Court and all courts established by Act of Congress may from time to time prescribe rules for the conduct of their business. Such rules shall be consistent with Acts of Congress and rules of practice and procedure prescribed under section 2072 of this title.

(b) Any rule prescribed by a court, other than the Supreme Court, under subsection (a) shall be prescribed only after giving appropriate public notice and an opportunity for comment. Such rule shall take effect upon the date specified by the prescribing court and shall have such effect on pending proceedings as the prescribing court may order.

(c) **(1)** A rule of a district court prescribed under subsection (a) shall remain in effect unless modified or abrogated by the judicial council of the relevant circuit.

(2) Any other rule prescribed by a court other than the Supreme Court under subsection (a) shall remain in effect unless modified or abrogated by the Judicial Conference.

(d) Copies of rules prescribed under subsection (a) by a district court shall be furnished to the judicial council, and copies of all rules prescribed by a court other than the Supreme Court under subsection (a) shall be furnished to the Director of the Administrative Office of the United States Courts and made available to the public.

(e) If the prescribing court determines that there is an immediate need for a rule, such court may proceed under this section without public notice and opportunity for comment, but such court shall promptly thereafter afford such notice and opportunity for comment.

(f) No rule may be prescribed by a district court other than under this section.

§ 2072.   Rules of Procedure and Evidence; Power to Prescribe

(a) The Supreme Court shall have the power to prescribe general rules of practice and procedure and rules of evidence for cases in the United States district courts (including proceedings before magistrates thereof) and courts of appeals.

(b) Such rules shall not abridge, enlarge or modify any substantive right. All laws in conflict with such rules shall be of no further force or effect after such rules have taken effect.

(c) Such rules may define when a ruling of a district court is final for the purposes of appeal under section 1291 of this title.

§ 2101.   Supreme Court; Time for Appeal or Certiorari; Docketing; Stay

(a) A direct appeal to the Supreme Court from any decision under section 1253 of this title, holding unconstitutional in whole or in part, any Act of Congress, shall be taken within thirty days after the entry of the interlocutory or final order, judgment or decree. The record shall be made up and the case docketed within sixty days from the time such appeal is taken under rules prescribed by the Supreme Court.

(b) Any other direct appeal to the Supreme Court which is authorized by law, from a decision of a district court in any civil action, suit or proceeding, shall be taken within thirty days from the judgment, order or decree, appealed from, if interlocutory, and within sixty days if final.

(c) Any other appeal or any writ of certiorari intended to bring any judgment or decree in a civil action, suit or proceeding before the Supreme Court for review shall be taken or applied for within ninety days after the entry of such judgment or decree. A justice of the Supreme Court, for good cause shown, may extend the time for applying for a writ of certiorari for a period not exceeding sixty days.

(d) The time for appeal or application for a writ of certiorari to review the judgment of a State court in a criminal case shall be as prescribed by rules of the Supreme Court.

(e) An application to the Supreme Court for a writ of certiorari to review a case before judgment has been rendered in the court of appeals may be made at any time before judgment.

(f) In any case in which the final judgment or decree of any court is subject to review by the Supreme Court on writ of certiorari, the execution and enforcement of such judgment or decree may be stayed for a reasonable time to enable the party aggrieved to obtain a writ of certiorari from the Supreme Court. The stay may be granted by a judge of the court rendering the judgment or decree or by a justice of the Supreme Court, and may be conditioned on the giving of security, approved by such judge or justice, that if the aggrieved party fails to make application for such writ within the period allotted therefor, or fails to obtain an order granting his application, or fails to make his plea good in the Supreme Court, he shall answer for all damages and costs which the other party may sustain by reason of the stay.

(g) The time for application for a writ of certiorari to review a decision of the United States Court of Appeals for the Armed Forces shall be as prescribed by rules of the Supreme Court.

§ 2104.   Reviews of State Court Decisions

A review by the Supreme Court of a judgment or decree of a State court shall be conducted in the same manner and under the same regulations, and shall have the same effect, as if the judgment or decree reviewed had been rendered in a court of the United States.

§ 2106.   Determination

The Supreme Court or any other court of appellate jurisdiction may affirm, modify, vacate, set aside or reverse any judgment, decree, or order of a court lawfully brought before it for review, and may remand the cause and direct the entry of such appropriate judgment, decree, or order, or require such further proceedings to be had as may be just under the circumstances.

§ 2107.   Time for Appeal to Court of Appeals

(a) Except as otherwise provided in this section, no appeal shall bring any judgment, order or decree in an action, suit or proceeding of a civil nature before a court of appeals for review unless notice of appeal is filed, within thirty days after the entry of such judgment, order or decree.

(b) In any such action, suit, or proceeding, the time as to all parties shall be 60 days from such entry if one of the parties is—

    (1) the United States;

    (2) a United States agency;

    (3) a United States officer or employee sued in an official capacity; or

    (4) a current or former United States officer or employee sued in an individual capacity for an act or omission occurring in connection with duties performed on behalf of the United States, including all instances in which the United States represents that officer or employee when the judgment, order, or decree is entered or files the appeal for that officer or employee.

(c) The district court may, upon motion filed not later than 30 days after the expiration of the time otherwise set for bringing appeal, extend the time for appeal upon a showing of excusable neglect or good cause. In addition, if the district court finds—

    (1) that a party entitled to notice of the entry of a judgment or order did not receive such notice from the clerk or any party within 21 days of its entry, and

    (2) that no party would be prejudiced,

the district court may, upon motion filed within 180 days after entry of the judgment or order or within 14 days after receipt of such notice, whichever is earlier, reopen the time for appeal for a period of 14 days from the date of entry of the order reopening the time for appeal.

(d) This section shall not apply to bankruptcy matters or other proceedings under Title 11.

§ 2111. Harmless Error

On the hearing of any appeal or writ of certiorari in any case, the court shall give judgment after an examination of the record without regard to errors or defects which do not affect the substantial rights of the parties.

§ 2201. Creation of Remedy

(a) In a case of actual controversy within its jurisdiction, except with respect to Federal taxes other than actions brought under section 7428 of the Internal Revenue Code of 1986, a proceeding under section 505 or 1146 of title 11, or in any civil action involving an antidumping or countervailing duty proceeding regarding a class or kind of merchandise of a free trade area country (as defined in section 516A(f)(10) of the Tariff Act of 1930), as determined by the administering authority, any court of the United States, upon the filing of an appropriate pleading, may declare the rights and other legal relations of any interested party seeking such declaration, whether or not further relief is or could be sought. Any such declaration shall have the force and effect of a final judgment or decree and shall be reviewable as such.

(b) For limitations on actions brought with respect to drug patents see section 505 or 512 of the Federal Food, Drug, and Cosmetic Act, or section 351 of the Public Health Service Act.

§ 2202. Further Relief

Further necessary or proper relief based on a declaratory judgment or decree may be granted, after reasonable notice and hearing, against any adverse party whose rights have been determined by such judgment.

§ 2283. Stay of State Court Proceedings

A court of the United States may not grant an injunction to stay proceedings in a State court except as expressly authorized by Act of Congress, or where necessary in aid of its jurisdiction, or to protect or effectuate its judgments.

§ 2284. Three-Judge Court; When Required; Composition; Procedure

(a) A district court of three judges shall be convened when otherwise required by Act of Congress, or when an action is filed challenging the constitutionality of the apportionment of congressional districts or the apportionment of any statewide legislative body.

(b) In any action required to be heard and determined by a district court of three judges under subsection (a) of this section, the composition and procedure of the court shall be as follows:

    (1) Upon the filing of a request for three judges, the judge to whom the request is presented shall, unless he determines that three judges are not required, immediately notify the chief judge of the circuit, who shall designate two other judges, at least one of whom shall be a circuit judge. The judges so designated, and the judge to whom the request was presented, shall serve as members of the court to hear and determine the action or proceeding.

    (2) If the action is against a State, or officer or agency thereof, at least five days' notice of hearing of the action shall be given by registered or certified mail to the Governor and attorney general of the State.

(3) A single judge may conduct all proceedings except the trial, and enter all orders permitted by the rules of civil procedure except as provided in this subsection. He may grant a temporary restraining order on a specific finding, based on evidence submitted, that specified irreparable damage will result if the order is not granted, which order, unless previously revoked by the district judge, shall remain in force only until the hearing and determination by the district court of three judges of an application for a preliminary injunction. A single judge shall not appoint a master, or order a reference, or hear and determine any application for a preliminary or permanent injunction or motion to vacate such an injunction, or enter judgment on the merits. Any action of a single judge may be reviewed by the full court at any time before final judgment.

§ 2361.   Process and Procedure

In any civil action of interpleader or in the nature of interpleader under section 1335 of this title, a district court may issue its process for all claimants and enter its order restraining them from instituting or prosecuting any proceeding in any State or United States court affecting the property, instrument or obligation involved in the interpleader action until further order of the court. Such process and order shall be returnable at such time as the court or judge thereof directs, and shall be addressed to and served by the United States marshals for the respective districts where the claimants reside or may be found.

Such district court shall hear and determine the case, and may discharge the plaintiff from further liability, make the injunction permanent, and make all appropriate orders to enforce its judgment.

§ 2401.   Time for Commencing Action Against United States

(a) Except as provided by chapter 71 of title 41, every civil action commenced against the United States shall be barred unless the complaint is filed within six years after the right of action first accrues. The action of any person under legal disability or beyond the seas at the time the claim accrues may be commenced within three years after the disability ceases.

(b) A tort claim against the United States shall be forever barred unless it is presented in writing to the appropriate Federal agency within two years after such claim accrues or unless action is begun within six months after the date of mailing, by certified or registered mail, of notice of final denial of the claim by the agency to which it was presented.

§ 2402.   Jury Trial in Actions Against United States

Subject to chapter 179 of this title, any action against the United States under section 1346 shall be tried by the court without a jury, except that any action against the United States under section 1346(a)(1) shall, at the request of either party to such action, be tried by the court with a jury.

§ 2403.   Intervention by United States or a State; Constitutional Question

(a) In any action, suit or proceeding in a court of the United States to which the United States or any agency, officer or employee thereof is not a party, wherein the constitutionality of any Act of Congress affecting the public interest is drawn in question, the court shall certify such fact to the Attorney General, and shall permit the United States to intervene for presentation of evidence, if evidence is otherwise admissible in the case, and for argument on the question of constitutionality. The United States shall, subject to the applicable provisions of law, have all the rights of a party and be subject to all liabilities of a party as to court costs to the extent necessary for a proper presentation of the facts and law relating to the question of constitutionality.

(b) In any action, suit, or proceeding in a court of the United States to which a State or any agency, officer, or employee thereof is not a party, wherein the constitutionality of any statute of that State

affecting the public interest is drawn in question, the court shall certify such fact to the attorney general of the State, and shall permit the State to intervene for presentation of evidence, if evidence is otherwise admissible in the case, and for argument on the question of constitutionality. The State shall, subject to the applicable provisions of law, have all the rights of a party and be subject to all liabilities of a party as to court costs to the extent necessary for a proper presentation of the facts and law relating to the question of constitutionality.

§ 2404. Death of Defendant in Damage Action

A civil action for damages commenced by or on behalf of the United States or in which it is interested shall not abate on the death of a defendant but shall survive and be enforceable against his estate as well as against surviving defendants.

§ 2408. Security Not Required of United States

Security for damages or costs shall not be required of the United States, any department or agency thereof or any party acting under the direction of any such department or agency on the issuance of process or the institution or prosecution of any proceeding.

Costs taxable, under other Acts of Congress, against the United States or any such department, agency or party shall be paid out of the contingent fund of the department or agency which directed the proceedings to be instituted.

§ 2411. Interest

In any judgment of any court rendered (whether against the United States, a collector or deputy collector of internal revenue, a former collector or deputy collector, or the personal representative in case of death) for any overpayment in respect of any internal-revenue tax, interest shall be allowed at the overpayment rate established under section 6621 of the Internal Revenue Code of 1986 upon the amount of the overpayment, from the date of the payment or collection thereof to a date preceding the date of the refund check by not more than thirty days, such date to be determined by the Commissioner of Internal Revenue. The Commissioner is authorized to tender by check payment of any such judgment, with interest as herein provided, at any time after such judgment becomes final, whether or not a claim for such payment has been duly filed, and such tender shall stop the running of interest, whether or not such refund check is accepted by the judgment creditor.

§ 2412. Costs and Fees

(a) (1) Except as otherwise specifically provided by statute, a judgment for costs, as enumerated in section 1920 of this title, but not including the fees and expenses of attorneys, may be awarded to the prevailing party in any civil action brought by or against the United States or any agency or any official of the United States acting in his or her official capacity in any court having jurisdiction of such action. A judgment for costs when taxed against the United States shall, in an amount established by statute, court rule, or order, be limited to reimbursing in whole or in part the prevailing party for the costs incurred by such party in the litigation.

(2) A judgment for costs, when awarded in favor of the United States in an action brought by the United States, may include an amount equal to the filing fee prescribed under section 1914(a) of this title. The preceding sentence shall not be construed as requiring the United States to pay any filing fee.

(b) Unless expressly prohibited by statute, a court may award reasonable fees and expenses of attorneys, in addition to the costs which may be awarded pursuant to subsection (a), to the prevailing party in any civil action brought by or against the United States or any agency or any official of the United States acting in his or her official capacity in any court having jurisdiction of such action. The United States shall be liable for such fees and expenses to the same extent that any other party would

be liable under the common law or under the terms of any statute which specifically provides for such an award.

(c) (1) Any judgment against the United States or any agency and any official of the United States acting in his or her official capacity for costs pursuant to subsection (a) shall be paid as provided in sections 2414 and 2517 of this title and shall be in addition to any relief provided in the judgment.

(2) Any judgment against the United States or any agency and any official of the United States acting in his or her official capacity for fees and expenses of attorneys pursuant to subsection (b) shall be paid as provided in sections 2414 and 2517 of this title, except that if the basis for the award is a finding that the United States acted in bad faith, then the award shall be paid by any agency found to have acted in bad faith and shall be in addition to any relief provided in the judgment.

(d) (1) (A) Except as otherwise specifically provided by statute, a court shall award to a prevailing party other than the United States fees and other expenses, in addition to any costs awarded pursuant to subsection (a), incurred by that party in any civil action (other than cases sounding in tort), including proceedings for judicial review of agency action, brought by or against the United States in any court having jurisdiction of that action, unless the court finds that the position of the United States was substantially justified or that special circumstances make an award unjust.

(B) A party seeking an award of fees and other expenses shall, within thirty days of final judgment in the action, submit to the court an application for fees and other expenses which shows that the party is a prevailing party and is eligible to receive an award under this subsection, and the amount sought, including an itemized statement from any attorney or expert witness representing or appearing in behalf of the party stating the actual time expended and the rate at which fees and other expenses were computed. The party shall also allege that the position of the United States was not substantially justified. Whether or not the position of the United States was substantially justified shall be determined on the basis of the record (including the record with respect to the action or failure to act by the agency upon which the civil action is based) which is made in the civil action for which fees and other expenses are sought.

(C) The court, in its discretion, may reduce the amount to be awarded pursuant to this subsection, or deny an award, to the extent that the prevailing party during the course of the proceedings engaged in conduct which unduly and unreasonably protracted the final resolution of the matter in controversy.

(D) If, in a civil action brought by the United States or a proceeding for judicial review of an adversary adjudication described in section 504(a)(4) of title 5, the demand by the United States is substantially in excess of the judgment finally obtained by the United States and is unreasonable when compared with such judgment, under the facts and circumstances of the case, the court shall award to the party the fees and other expenses related to defending against the excessive demand, unless the party has committed a willful violation of law or otherwise acted in bad faith, or special circumstances make an award unjust. Fees and expenses awarded under this subparagraph shall be paid only as a consequence of appropriations provided in advance.

(2) For the purposes of this subsection—

(A) "fees and other expenses" includes the reasonable expenses of expert witnesses, the reasonable cost of any study, analysis, engineering report, test, or project which is found by the court to be necessary for the preparation of the party's case, and reasonable attorney fees (The amount of fees awarded under this subsection shall be based upon prevailing market rates for the kind and quality of the services furnished, except that (i) no expert

witness shall be compensated at a rate in excess of the highest rate of compensation for expert witnesses paid by the United States; and (ii) attorney fees shall not be awarded in excess of $125 per hour unless the court determines that an increase in the cost of living or a special factor, such as the limited availability of qualified attorneys for the proceedings involved, justifies a higher fee.);

(B) "party" means (i) an individual whose net worth did not exceed $2,000,000 at the time the civil action was filed, or (ii) any owner of an unincorporated business, or any partnership, corporation, association, unit of local government, or organization, the net worth of which did not exceed $7,000,000 at the time the civil action was filed, and which had not more than 500 employees at the time the civil action was filed; except that an organization described in section 501(c)(3) of the Internal Revenue Code of 1986 (26 U.S.C. 501(c)(3)) exempt from taxation under section 501(a) of such Code, or a cooperative association as defined in section 15(a) of the Agricultural Marketing Act (12 U.S.C. 1141j(a)), may be a party regardless of the net worth of such organization or cooperative association or for purposes of subsection (d)(l)(D), a small entity as defined in section 601 of Title 5;

(C) "United States" includes any agency and any official of the United States acting in his or her official capacity;

(D) "position of the United States" means, in addition to the position taken by the United States in the civil action, the action or failure to act by the agency upon which the civil action is based; except that fees and expenses may not be awarded to a party for any portion of the litigation in which the party has unreasonably protracted the proceedings;

(E) "civil action brought by or against the United States" includes an appeal by a party, other than the United States, from a decision of a contracting officer rendered pursuant to a disputes clause in a contract with the Government or pursuant to chapter 71 of title 41;

(F) "court" includes the United States Court of Federal Claims and the United States Court of Appeals for Veterans Claims;

(G) "final judgment" means a judgment that is final and not appealable, and includes an order of settlement;

(H) "prevailing party", in the case of eminent domain proceedings, means a party who obtains a final judgment (other than by settlement), exclusive of interest, the amount of which is at least as close to the highest valuation of the property involved that is attested to at trial on behalf of the property owner as it is to the highest valuation of the property involved that is attested to at trial on behalf of the Government; and

(I) "demand" means the express demand of the United States which led to the adversary adjudication, but shall not include a recitation of the maximum statutory penalty (i) in the complaint, or (ii) elsewhere when accompanied by an express demand for a lesser amount.

(3) In awarding fees and other expenses under this subsection to a prevailing party in any action for judicial review of an adversary adjudication, as defined in subsection (b)(l)(C) of section 504 of title 5, United States Code, or an adversary adjudication subject to chapter 71 of title 41, the court shall include in that award fees and other expenses to the same extent authorized in subsection (a) of such section, unless the court finds that during such adversary adjudication the position of the United States was substantially justified, or that special circumstances make an award unjust.

(4) Fees and other expenses awarded under this subsection to a party shall be paid by any agency over which the party prevails from any funds made available to the agency by appropriation or otherwise.

[(5) Repealed. Pub.L. 104–66, Title I, § 1091(b), Dec. 21, 1995, 109 Stat. 722]

(e) The provisions of this section shall not apply to any costs, fees, and other expenses in connection with any proceeding to which section 7430 of the Internal Revenue Code of 1986 applies (determined without regard to subsections (b) and (f) of such section). Nothing in the preceding sentence shall prevent the awarding under subsection (a) of section 2412 of title 28, United States Code, of costs enumerated in section 1920 of such title (as in effect on October 1, 1981).

(f) If the United States appeals an award of costs or fees and other expenses made against the United States under this section and the award is affirmed in whole or in part, interest shall be paid on the amount of the award as affirmed. Such interest shall be computed at the rate determined under section 1961(a) of this title, and shall run from the date of the award through the day before the date of the mandate of affirmance.

§ 2413.   Executions in Favor of United States

A writ of execution on a judgment obtained for the use of the United States in any court thereof shall be issued from and made returnable to the court which rendered the judgment, but may be executed in any other State, in any Territory, or in the District of Columbia.

§ 2414.   Payment of Judgments and Compromise Settlements

Except as provided by chapter 71 of title 41, payment of final judgments rendered by a district court or the Court of International Trade against the United States shall be made on settlements by the Secretary of the Treasury. Payment of final judgments rendered by a State or foreign court or tribunal against the United States, or against its agencies or officials upon obligations or liabilities of the United States, shall be made on settlements by the Secretary of the Treasury after certification by the Attorney General that it is in the interest of the United States to pay the same.

Whenever the Attorney General determines that no appeal shall be taken from a judgment or that no further review will be sought from a decision affirming the same, he shall so certify and the judgment shall be deemed final.

Except as otherwise provided by law, compromise settlements of claims referred to the Attorney General for defense of imminent litigation or suits against the United States, or against its agencies or officials upon obligations or liabilities of the United States, made by the Attorney General or any person authorized by him, shall be settled and paid in a manner similar to judgments in like causes and appropriations or funds available for the payment of such judgments are hereby made available for the payment of such compromise settlements.

§ 2415.   Time for Commencing Actions Brought by the United States

(a) Subject to the provisions of section 2416 of this title, and except as otherwise provided by Congress, every action for money damages brought by the United States or an officer or agency thereof which is founded upon any contract express or implied in law or fact, shall be barred unless the complaint is filed within six years after the right of action accrues or within one year after final decisions have been rendered in applicable administrative proceedings required by contract or by law, whichever is later: *Provided,* That in the event of later partial payment or written acknowledgment of debt, the right of action shall be deemed to accrue again at the time of each such payment or acknowledgment: *Provided further,* That an action for money damages brought by the United States for or on behalf of a recognized tribe, band or group of American Indians shall not be barred unless the complaint is filed more than six years and ninety days after the right of action accrued: *Provided further,* That an action for money damages which accrued on the date of enactment of this Act in accordance with subsection (g) brought by the United States for or on behalf of a recognized tribe, band, or group of American Indians, or on behalf of an individual Indian whose land is held in trust or restricted status, shall not be barred unless the complaint is filed sixty days after the date of

publication of the list required by section 4(c) of the Indian Claims Limitation Act of 1982: *Provided,* That, for those claims that are on either of the two lists published pursuant to the Indian Claims Limitation Act of 1982, any right of action shall be barred unless the complaint is filed within (1) one year after the Secretary of the Interior has published in the Federal Register a notice rejecting such claim or (2) three years after the date the Secretary of the Interior has submitted legislation or legislative report to Congress to resolve such claim or more than two years after a final decision has been rendered in applicable administrative proceedings required by contract or by law, whichever is later.

(b) Subject to the provisions of section 2416 of this title, and except as otherwise provided by Congress, every action for money damages brought by the United States or an officer or agency thereof which is founded upon a tort shall be barred unless the complaint is filed within three years after the right of action first accrues: *Provided,* That an action to recover damages resulting from a trespass on lands of the United States; an action to recover damages resulting from fire to such lands; an action to recover for diversion of money paid under a grant program; and an action for conversion of property of the United States may be brought within six years after the right of action accrues, except that such actions for or on behalf of a recognized tribe, band or group of American Indians, including actions relating to allotted trust or restricted Indian lands, may be brought within six years and ninety days after the right of action accrues, except that such actions for or on behalf of a recognized tribe, band or group of American Indians, including actions relating to allotted trust or restricted Indian lands, or on behalf of an individual Indian whose land is held in trust or restricted status which accrued on the date of enactment of this Act in accordance with subsection (g) may be brought on or before sixty days after the date of the publication of the list required by section 4(c) of the Indian Claims Limitation Act of 1982: *Provided,* That, for those claims that are on either of the two lists published pursuant to the Indian Claims Limitation Act of 1982, any right of action shall be barred unless the complaint is filed within (1) one year after the Secretary of the Interior has published in the Federal Register a notice rejecting such claim or (2) three years after the Secretary of the Interior has submitted legislation or legislative report to Congress to resolve such claim.

(c) Nothing herein shall be deemed to limit the time for bringing an action to establish the title to, or right of possession of, real or personal property.

(d) Subject to the provisions of section 2416 of this title and except as otherwise provided by Congress, every action for the recovery of money erroneously paid to or on behalf of any civilian employee of any agency of the United States or to or on behalf of any member or dependent of any member of the uniformed services of the United States, incident to the employment or services of such employee or member, shall be barred unless the complaint is filed within six years after the right of action accrues: *Provided,* That in the event of later partial payment or written acknowledgment of debt, the right of action shall be deemed to accrue again at the time of each such payment or acknowledgment.

(e) In the event that any action to which this section applies is timely brought and is thereafter dismissed without prejudice, the action may be recommenced within one year after such dismissal, regardless of whether the action would otherwise then be barred by this section. In any action so recommenced the defendant shall not be barred from interposing any claim which would not have been barred in the original action.

(f) The provisions of this section shall not prevent the assertion, in an action against the United States or an officer or agency thereof, of any claim of the United States or an officer or agency thereof against an opposing party, a co-party, or a third party that arises out of the transaction or occurrence that is the subject matter of the opposing party's claim. A claim of the United States or an officer or agency thereof that does not arise out of the transaction or occurrence that is the subject matter of the opposing party's claim may, if time-barred, be asserted only by way of offset and may be allowed in an amount not to exceed the amount of the opposing party's recovery.

(g) Any right of action subject to the provisions of this section which accrued prior to the date of enactment of this Act shall, for purposes of this section, be deemed to have accrued on the date of enactment of this Act.

(h) Nothing in this Act shall apply to actions brought under the Internal Revenue Code or incidental to the collection of taxes imposed by the United States.

(i) The provisions of this section shall not prevent the United States or an officer or agency thereof from collecting any claim of the United States by means of administrative offset, in accordance with section 3716 of title 31.

§ 2416.   Time for Commencing Actions Brought by the United States—Exclusions

For the purpose of computing the limitations periods established in section 2415, there shall be excluded all periods during which—

(a) the defendant or the res is outside the United States, its territories and possessions, the District of Columbia, or the Commonwealth of Puerto Rico; or

(b) the defendant is exempt from legal process because of infancy, mental incompetence, diplomatic immunity, or for any other reason; or

(c) facts material to the right of action are not known and reasonably could not be known by an official of the United States charged with the responsibility to act in the circumstances; or

(d) the United States is in a state of war declared pursuant to article I, section 8, of the Constitution of the United States.

PART IX

THE CONSTITUTION OF THE UNITED STATES[1]

1787[2]

Preamble

We the People of the United States, in Order to form a more perfect Union, establish Justice, insure domestic Tranquility, provide for the common defence, promote the general Welfare, and secure the Blessings of Liberty to ourselves and our Posterity, do ordain and establish this Constitution for the United States of America.

Article I

Section 1. All legislative Powers herein granted shall be vested in a Congress of the United States, which shall consist of a Senate and House of Representatives.

Section 2. [1] The House of Representatives shall be composed of Members chosen every second Year by the People of the several States, and the Electors in each State shall have the Qualifications requisite for Electors of the most numerous Branch of the State Legislature.

[2]   No Person shall be a Representative who shall not have attained to the Age of twenty five Years, and been seven Years a Citizen of the United States, and who shall not, when elected, be an Inhabitant of that State in which he shall be chosen.

[3]   [Representatives and direct Taxes shall be apportioned among the several States which may be included within this Union, according to their respective Numbers, which shall be determined by adding to the whole Number of free Persons, including those bound to Service for a Term of Years, and excluding Indians not taxed, three fifths of all other Persons.] The actual Enumeration shall be made within three Years after the first Meeting of the Congress of the United States, and within every subsequent Term of ten Years, in such Manner as they shall by Law direct. The Number of Representatives shall not exceed one for every thirty Thousand, but each State shall have at Least one Representative; and until such enumeration shall be made, the State of New Hampshire shall be entitled to chuse three, Massachusetts eight, Rhode Island and Providence Plantations one, Connecticut five, New York six, New Jersey four, Pennsylvania eight, Delaware one, Maryland six, Virginia ten, North Carolina five, South Carolina five, and Georgia three.

---

[1]   Adapted, with permission, from United States Code Annotated, Constitution of the United States, Annotated (West Publishing Co. 1968).

[2]   In May, 1785, a committee of Congress made a report recommending an alteration in the Articles of Confederation, but no action was taken on it, and it was left to the State Legislatures to proceed in the matter. In January, 1786, the Legislature of Virginia passed a resolution providing for the appointment of five commissioners, who, or any three of them, should meet such commissioners as might be appointed in the other States of the Union, at a time and place to be agreed upon, to take into consideration the trade of the United States; to consider how far a uniform system in their commercial regulations may be necessary to their common interest and their permanent harmony; and to report to the several States such an act, relative to this great object, as, when ratified by them, will enable the United States in Congress effectually to provide for the same. The Virginia commissioners, after some correspondence, fixed the first Monday in September as the time, and the city of Annapolis as the place for the meeting, but only four other States were represented, viz.: Delaware, New York, New Jersey, and Pennsylvania; the commissioners appointed by Massachusetts, New Hampshire, North Carolina, and Rhode Island failed to attend. Under the circumstances of so partial a representation, the commissioners present agreed upon a report, (drawn by Mr. Hamilton of New York,) expressing their unanimous conviction that it might essentially tend to advance the interests of the Union if the States by which they were respectively delegated would concur, and use their endeavors to procure the concurrence of the other States, in the appointment of commissioners to meet at Philadelphia on the second Monday of May following, to take into consideration the situation of the United States; to devise such further provisions as should appear to them necessary to render the Constitution of the Federal Government adequate to the exigencies of the Union; and to report such an act for that purpose to the United States in Congress assembled as, when agreed to by them, and afterwards confirmed by the Legislatures of every State, would effectually provide for the same.

The clause of this paragraph inclosed in brackets was amended, as to the mode of apportionment of representatives among the several states, by the Fourteenth Amendment, § 2, and as to taxes on incomes without apportionment, by the Sixteenth Amendment.

[4]   When vacancies happen in the Representation from any State, the Executive Authority thereof shall issue Writs of Election to fill such Vacancies.

[5]   The House of Representatives shall chuse their Speaker and other Officers; and shall have the sole Power of Impeachment.

Section 3. [1] [The Senate of the United States shall be composed of two Senators from each State, chosen by the Legislature thereof, for six Years; and each Senator shall have one Vote.]

This paragraph and the clause of following paragraph inclosed in brackets were superseded by the Seventeenth Amendment.

[2]   Immediately after they shall be assembled in Consequence of the first Election, they shall be divided as equally as may be into three Classes. The Seats of the Senators of the first Class shall be vacated at the Expiration of the Second Year, of the second Class at the Expiration of the fourth Year, and of the third Class at the Expiration of the sixth Year, so that one third may be chosen every second Year; [and if Vacancies happen by Resignation, or otherwise, during the Recess of the Legislature of any State, the Executive thereof may make temporary Appointments until the next Meeting of the Legislature, which shall then fill such Vacancies.]

See note to preceding paragraph of this section.

[3]   No Person shall be a Senator who shall not have attained to the Age of thirty Years, and been nine Years a Citizen of the United States, and who shall not, when elected, be an Inhabitant of that State for which he shall be chosen.

[4]   The Vice President of the United States shall be President of the Senate, but shall have no Vote, unless they be equally divided.

[5]   The Senate shall chuse their other Officers, and also a President pro tempore, in the Absence of the Vice President, or when he shall exercise the Office of President of the United States.

[6]   The Senate shall have the sole Power to try all Impeachments. When sitting for that Purpose, they shall be on Oath or Affirmation. When the President of the United States is tried, the Chief Justice shall preside: And no Person shall be convicted without the Concurrence of two thirds of the Members present.

[7]   Judgment in Cases of Impeachment shall not extend further than to removal from Office, and disqualification to hold and enjoy any Office of honor, Trust, or Profit under the United States: but the Party convicted shall nevertheless be liable and subject to Indictment, Trial, Judgment, and Punishment, according to Law.

Section 4. [1] The Times, Places and Manner of holding Elections for Senators and Representatives, shall be prescribed in each State by the Legislature thereof; but the Congress may at any time by Law make or alter such Regulations, except as to the Places of chusing Senators.

[2]   The Congress shall assemble at least once in every Year, and such Meeting shall be on the first Monday in December, unless they shall by Law appoint a different Day.

Section 5. [1] Each House shall be the Judge of the Elections, Returns, and Qualifications of its own Members, and a Majority of each shall constitute a Quorum to do Business; but a smaller Number may adjourn from day to day, and may be authorized to compel the Attendance of absent Members, in such Manner, and under such Penalties as each House may provide.

[2]   Each House may determine the Rules of its Proceedings, punish its Members for disorderly Behaviour, and, with the Concurrence of two thirds, expel a Member.

[3] Each House shall keep a Journal of its Proceedings, and from time to time publish the same, excepting such Parts as may in their Judgment require Secrecy; and the Yeas and Nays of the Members of either House on any question shall, at the Desire of one fifth of those Present, be entered on the Journal.

[4] Neither House, during the Session of Congress, shall, without the Consent of the other, adjourn for more than three days, nor to any other Place than that in which the two Houses shall be sitting.

Section 6. [1] The Senators and Representatives shall receive a Compensation for their Services, to be ascertained by Law, and paid out of the Treasury of the United States. They shall in all Cases, except Treason, Felony and Breach of the Peace, be privileged from Arrest during their Attendance at the Session of their respective Houses, and in going to and returning from the same; and for any Speech or Debate in either House, they shall not be questioned in any other Place.

[2] No Senator or Representative shall, during the Time for which he was elected, be appointed to any civil Office under the Authority of the United States, which shall have been created, or the Emoluments whereof shall have been increased during such time; and no Person holding any Office under the United States, shall be a Member of either House during his Continuance in Office.

Section 7. [1] All Bills for raising Revenue shall originate in the House of Representatives; but the Senate may propose or concur with Amendments as on other Bills.

[2] Every Bill which shall have passed the House of Representatives and the Senate, shall, before it become a Law, be presented to the President of the United States; If he approve he shall sign it, but if not he shall return it, with his Objections to the House in which it shall have originated, who shall enter the Objections at large on their Journal, and proceed to reconsider it. If after such Reconsideration two thirds of that House shall agree to pass the Bill, it shall be sent together with the Objections, to the other House, by which it shall likewise be reconsidered, and if approved by two thirds of that House, it shall become a Law. But in all such Cases the Votes of both Houses shall be determined by Yeas and Nays, and the Names of the Persons voting for and against the Bill shall be entered on the Journal of each House respectively. If any Bill shall not be returned by the President within ten Days (Sundays excepted) after it shall have been presented to him, the Same shall be a Law, in like Manner as if he had signed it, unless the Congress by their Adjournment prevent its Return in which Case it shall not be a Law.

[3] Every Order, Resolution, or Vote, to Which the Concurrence of the Senate and House of Representatives may be necessary (except on a question of Adjournment) shall be presented to the President of the United States; and before the Same shall take Effect, shall be approved by him, or being disapproved by him, shall be repassed by two thirds of the Senate and House of Representatives, according to the Rules and Limitations prescribed in the Case of a Bill.

Section 8. [1] The Congress shall have Power to lay and collect Taxes, Duties, Imposts and Excises, to pay the Debts and provide for the common Defence and general Welfare of the United States; but all Duties, Imposts and Excises shall be uniform throughout the United States;

[2] To borrow money on the credit of the United States;

[3] To regulate Commerce with foreign Nations, and among the several States, and with the Indian Tribes;

[4] To establish an uniform Rule of Naturalization, and uniform Laws on the subject of Bankruptcies throughout the United States;

[5] To coin Money, regulate the Value thereof, and of foreign Coin, and fix the Standard of Weights and Measures;

[6] To provide for the Punishment of counterfeiting the Securities and current Coin of the United States;

[7]   To Establish Post Offices and Post Roads;

[8]   To promote the Progress of Science and useful Arts, by securing for limited Times to Authors and Inventors the exclusive Right to their respective Writings and Discoveries;

[9]   To constitute Tribunals inferior to the supreme Court;

[10] To define and punish Piracies and Felonies committed on the high Seas, and Offenses against the Law of Nations;

[11] To declare War, grant Letters of Marque and Reprisal, and make Rules concerning Captures on Land and Water;

[12] To raise and support Armies, but no Appropriation of Money to that Use shall be for a longer Term than two Years;

[13] To provide and maintain a Navy;

[14] To make Rules for the Government and Regulation of the land and naval Forces;

[15] To provide for calling forth the Militia to execute the Laws of the Union, suppress Insurrections and repel Invasions;

[16] To provide for organizing, arming, and disciplining, the Militia, and for governing such Part of them as may be employed in the Service of the United States, reserving to the States respectively, the Appointment of the Officers, and the Authority of training the Militia according to the discipline prescribed by Congress;

[17] To exercise exclusive Legislation in all Cases whatsoever, over such District (not exceeding ten Miles square) as may, by Cession of particular States and the Acceptance of Congress, become the Seat of the Government of the United States, and to exercise like Authority over all Places purchased by the Consent of the Legislature of the State in which the Same shall be, for the Erection of Forts, Magazines, Arsenals, dock-Yards, and other needful Buildings;—And

[18] To make all Laws which shall be necessary and proper for carrying into Execution the foregoing Powers, and all other Powers vested by this Constitution in the Government of the United States, or in any Department or Officer thereof.

Section 9. [1] The Migration or Importation of Such Persons as any of the States now existing shall think proper to admit, shall not be prohibited by the Congress prior to the Year one thousand eight hundred and eight, but a Tax or duty may be imposed on such Importation, not exceeding ten dollars for each Person.

[2]   The privilege of the Writ of Habeas Corpus shall not be suspended, unless when in Cases of Rebellion or Invasion the public Safety may require it.

[3]   No Bill of Attainder or ex post facto Law shall be passed.

[4]   No Capitation, or other direct, Tax shall be laid, unless in Proportion to the Census or Enumeration herein before directed to be taken.

[5]   No Tax or Duty shall be laid on Articles exported from any State.

[6]   No Preference shall be given by any Regulation of Commerce or Revenue to the Ports of one State over those of another: nor shall Vessels bound to, or from, one State be obliged to enter, clear, or pay Duties in another.

[7]   No money shall be drawn from the Treasury, but in Consequence of Appropriations made by Law; and a regular Statement and Account of the Receipts and Expenditures of all public Money shall be published from time to time.

[8]   No Title of Nobility shall be granted by the United States: And no Person holding any Office of Profit or Trust under them, shall, without the Consent of the Congress, accept of any present, Emolument, Office, or Title, of any kind whatever, from any King, Prince, or foreign State.

Section 10. [1] No State shall enter into any Treaty, Alliance, or Confederation; grant Letters of Marque and Reprisal; coin Money; emit Bills of Credit; make any Thing but gold and silver Coin a Tender in Payment of Debts; pass any Bill of Attainder, ex post facto Law, or Law impairing the Obligation of Contracts, or grant any Title of Nobility.

[2]   No State shall, without the Consent of the Congress, lay any Imposts or Duties on Imports or Exports, except what may be absolutely necessary for executing it's inspection Laws: and the net Produce of all Duties and Imposts, laid by any State on Imports or Exports, shall be for the Use of the Treasury of the United States; and all such Laws shall be subject to the Revision and Controul of the Congress.

[3]   No State shall, without the Consent of Congress, lay any Duty of Tonnage, keep Troops, or Ships of War in time of Peace, enter into any Agreement or Compact with another State, or with a foreign Power or engage in War, unless actually invaded, or in such imminent Danger as will not admit of delay.

Article II

Section 1. [1] The executive Power shall be vested in a President of the United States of America. He shall hold his Office during the Term of four Years, and, together with the Vice President, chosen for the same Term, be elected, as follows:

[2]   Each State shall appoint, in such Manner as the Legislature thereof may direct, a Number of Electors, equal to the whole Number of Senators and Representatives to which the State may be entitled in the Congress; but no Senator or Representative, or Person holding an Office of Trust or Profit under the United States, shall be appointed an Elector.

[3]   [The Electors shall meet in their respective States, and vote by Ballot for two Persons, of whom one at least shall not be an Inhabitant of the same State with themselves. And they shall make a List of all the Persons voted for, and of the Number of Votes for each; which List they shall sign and certify, and transmit sealed to the Seat of the Government of the United States, directed to the President of the Senate. The President of the Senate shall, in the Presence of the Senate and House of Representatives, open all the Certificates, and the Votes shall then be counted. The Person having the greatest Number of Votes shall be the President, if such Number be a Majority of the whole Number of Electors appointed; and if there be more than one who have such Majority, and have an equal Number of Votes, then the House of Representatives shall immediately chuse by Ballot one of them for President; and if no Person have a Majority, then from the five highest on the List the said House shall in like Manner chuse the President. But in chusing the President, the Votes shall be taken by States, the Representation from each State having one Vote; A quorum for this Purpose shall consist of a Member or Members from two thirds of the States, and a Majority of all the States shall be necessary to a Choice. In every Case, after the Choice of the President, the Person having the greater Number of Votes of the Electors shall be the Vice President. But if there should remain two or more who have equal Votes, the Senate shall chuse from them by Ballot the Vice President.]

This paragraph, inclosed in brackets, was superseded by the Twelfth Amendment, post.

[4]   The Congress may determine the Time of chusing the Electors, and the Day on which they shall give their Votes; which Day shall be the same throughout the United States.

[5]   No person except a natural born Citizen, or a Citizen of the United States, at the time of the Adoption of this Constitution, shall be eligible to the Office of President; neither shall any Person be eligible to that Office who shall not have attained to the Age of thirty five Years, and been fourteen Years a Resident within the United States.

[6]   In case of the removal of the President from Office, or of his Death, Resignation or Inability to discharge the Powers and Duties of the said Office, the Same shall devolve on the Vice President and the Congress may by Law provide for the Case of Removal, Death, Resignation or Inability, both of the President and Vice President, declaring what Officer shall then act as President, and such Officer shall act accordingly, until the Disability be removed, or a President shall be elected.

[7]   The President shall, at stated Times, receive for his Services, a Compensation, which shall neither be increased nor diminished during the Period for which he shall have been elected, and he shall not receive within that Period any other Emolument from the United States, or any of them.

[8]   Before he enter on the Execution of his Office, he shall take the following Oath or Affirmation: "I do solemnly swear (or affirm) that I will faithfully execute the Office of President of the United States, and will to the best of my Ability, preserve, protect and defend the Constitution of the United States."

Section 2. [1] The President shall be Commander in Chief of the Army and Navy of the United States, and of the militia of the several States, when called into the actual Service of the United States; he may require the Opinion, in writing, of the principal Officer in each of the Executive Departments, upon any Subject relating to the Duties of their respective Offices and he shall have Power to grant Reprieves and Pardons for Offenses against the United States, except in Cases of Impeachment.

[2]   He shall have Power, by and with the Advice and Consent of the Senate, to make Treaties, provided two thirds of the Senators present concur; and he shall nominate, and by and with the Advice and Consent of the Senate, shall appoint Ambassadors, other public Ministers and Consuls, Judges of the supreme Court, and all other Officers of the United States, whose Appointments are not herein otherwise provided for, and which shall be established by Law; but the Congress may by Law vest the Appointment of such inferior Officers, as they think proper, in the President alone, in the Courts of Law, or in the Heads of Departments.

[3]   The President shall have Power to fill up all Vacancies that may happen during the Recess of the Senate, by granting Commissions which shall expire at the End of their next Session.

Section 3. He shall from time to time give to the Congress Information of the State of the Union, and recommend to their Consideration such Measures as he shall judge necessary and expedient; he may, on extraordinary Occasions, convene both Houses, or either of them, and in Case of Disagreement between them, with Respect to the Time of Adjournment, he may adjourn them to such Time as he shall think proper; he shall receive Ambassadors and other public Ministers; he shall take Care that the Laws be faithfully executed, and shall Commission all the Officers of the United States.

Section 4. The President, Vice President and all civil Officers of the United States, shall be removed from Office on Impeachment for, and Conviction of, Treason, Bribery, or other high Crimes and Misdemeanors.

Article III

Section 1. The judicial Power of the United States, shall be vested in one supreme Court, and in such inferior Courts as the Congress may from time to time ordain and establish. The Judges, both of the supreme and inferior Courts, shall hold their Offices during good Behaviour, and shall, at stated Times, receive for their Services a Compensation, which shall not be diminished during their Continuance in Office.

Section 2. [1] The judicial Power shall extend to all Cases, in Law and Equity, arising under this Constitution, the Laws of the United States, and Treaties made, or which shall be made, under their Authority;—to all Cases affecting Ambassadors, other public Ministers and Consuls;—to all Cases of admiralty and maritime Jurisdiction;—to Controversies to which the United States shall be a Party;—to Controversies between two or more States;—between a State and Citizens of another State;—between Citizens of different States;—between Citizens of the same State claiming Lands under the Grants of different States, and between a State, or the Citizens thereof, and foreign States, Citizens or Subjects.

[2]   In all Cases affecting Ambassadors, other public Ministers and Consuls, and those in which a State shall be a Party, the supreme Court shall have original Jurisdiction. In all the other Cases before mentioned, the supreme Court shall have appellate Jurisdiction, both as to Law and Fact, with such Exceptions, and under such Regulations as the Congress shall make.

[3]   The trial of all Crimes, except in Cases of Impeachment, shall be by Jury; and such Trial shall be held in the State where the said Crimes shall have been committed; but when not committed within any State, the Trial shall be at such Place or Places as the Congress may by Law have directed.

Section 3. [1] Treason against the United States, shall consist only in levying War against them, or, in adhering to their Enemies, giving them Aid and Comfort. No Person shall be convicted of Treason unless on the Testimony of two Witnesses to the same overt Act, or on Confession in open Court.

[2]   The Congress shall have Power to declare the Punishment of Treason, but no Attainder of Treason shall work Corruption of Blood, or Forfeiture except during the Life of the Person attainted.

Article IV

Section 1. Full Faith and Credit shall be given in each State to the public Acts, Records, and judicial Proceedings of every other State. And the Congress may by general Laws prescribe the Manner in which such Acts, Records and Proceedings shall be proved, and the Effect thereof.

Section 2. [1] The Citizens of each State shall be entitled to all Privileges and Immunities of Citizens in the several States.

[2]   A Person charged in any State with Treason, Felony, or other Crime, who shall flee from Justice, and be found in another State, shall on demand of the executive Authority of the State from which he fled, be delivered up, to be removed to the State having Jurisdiction of the Crime.

[3]   No Person held to Service or Labour in one State, under the Laws thereof, escaping into another, shall, in Consequence of any Law or Regulation therein, be discharged from such Service or Labour, but shall be delivered up on Claim of the Party to whom such Service or Labour may be due.

Section 3. [1] New States may be admitted by the Congress into this Union; but no new State shall be formed or erected within the Jurisdiction of any other State; nor any State be formed by the Junction of two or more States, or Parts of States, without the Consent of the Legislatures of the States concerned as well as of the Congress.

[2]   The Congress shall have Power to dispose of and make all needful Rules and Regulations respecting the Territory or other Property belonging to the United States; and nothing in this Constitution shall be so construed as to Prejudice any Claims of the United States, or of any particular State.

Section 4. The United States shall guarantee to every State in this Union a Republican Form of Government, and shall protect each of them against Invasion; and on Application of the Legislature, or of the Executive (when the Legislature cannot be convened) against domestic Violence.

Article V

The Congress, whenever two thirds of both Houses shall deem it necessary, shall propose Amendments to this Constitution, or, on the Application of the Legislatures of two thirds of the several States, shall call a Convention for proposing Amendments, which, in either Case, shall be valid to all Intents and Purposes, as part of this Constitution, when ratified by the Legislatures of three fourths of the several States, or by Conventions in three fourths thereof, as the one or the other Mode of Ratification may be proposed by the Congress; Provided that no Amendment which may be made prior to the Year One thousand eight hundred and eight shall in any Manner affect the first and fourth Clauses in the Ninth Section of the first Article; and that no State, without its Consent, shall be deprived of its equal Suffrage in the Senate.

Article VI

[1]   All Debts contracted and Engagements entered into, before the Adoption of this Constitution, shall be as valid against the United States under this Constitution, as under the Confederation.

[2]   This Constitution, and the Laws of the United States which shall be made in Pursuance thereof; and all Treaties made, or which shall be made, under the Authority of the United States, shall be the supreme Law of the Land; and the Judges in every State shall be bound thereby, any Thing in the Constitution or Laws of any State to the Contrary notwithstanding.

[3]   The Senators and Representatives before mentioned, and the Members of the several State Legislatures, and all executive and judicial Officers, both of the United States and of the several States, shall be bound by Oath or Affirmation, to support this Constitution; but no religious Test shall ever be required as a Qualification to any Office or public Trust under the United States.

Article VII

The Ratification of the Conventions of nine States shall be sufficient for the Establishment of this Constitution between the States so ratifying the Same.

DONE in Convention by the Unanimous Consent of the States present the Seventeenth Day of September in the Year of Our Lord one thousand seven hundred and Eighty seven and of the Independence of the United States of America the Twelfth. IN WITNESS whereof We have hereunto subscribed our Names,

Go. WASHINGTON—
Presidt.
and deputy from
Virginia

New Hampshire

JOHN LANGDON   NICHOLAS GILMAN

Massachusetts

NATHANIEL GORHAM   RUFUS KING

Connecticut

WM. SAML. JOHNSON   ROGER SHERMAN

New York

ALEXANDER HAMILTON

New Jersey

WIL: LIVINGSTON   WM. PATERSON
DAVID BREARLEY   JONA: DAYTON

Pennsylvania

B. FRANKLIN   THOS. FITZSIMONS
THOMAS MIFFLIN   JARED INGERSOLL
ROBT. MORRIS   JAMES WILSON
GEO. CLYMER   GOUV MORRIS

Delaware

GEO: READ   RICHARD BASSETT
GUNNING BEDFORD JUN   JACO: BROOM
JOHN DICKINSON

Maryland

JAMES MCHENRY
DAN OF ST THOS. JENIFER

DANL. CARROLL

Virginia

JOHN BLAIR

JAMES MADISON, JR.

North Carolina

WM. BLOUNT
RICHD. DOBBS SPAIGHT

HU WILLIAMSON

South Carolina

J. RUTLEDGE
CHARLES COTESWORTH PINCKNEY

CHARLES PINCKNEY
PIERCE BUTLER

Georgia

WILLIAM FEW
Attest

ABR BALDWIN
WILLIAM JACKSON
Secretary

ARTICLES IN ADDITION TO, AND AMENDMENT OF, THE CONSTITUTION OF THE UNITED STATES OF AMERICA, PROPOSED BY CONGRESS, AND RATIFIED BY THE LEGISLATURES OF THE SEVERAL STATES PURSUANT TO THE FIFTH ARTICLE OF THE ORIGINAL CONSTITUTION.[3]

Amendment [I] [1791][4]

Congress shall make no law respecting an establishment of religion, or prohibiting the free exercise thereof; or abridging the freedom of speech, or of the press; or the right of the people peaceably to assemble, and to petition the Government for a redress of grievances.

Amendment [II] [1791]

A well regulated Militia, being necessary to the security of a free State, the right of the people to keep and bear Arms, shall not be infringed.

Amendment [III] [1791]

No Soldier shall, in time of peace be quartered in any house, without the consent of the Owner, nor in time of war, but in a manner to be prescribed by law.

Amendment [IV] [1791]

The right of the people to be secure in their persons, houses, papers, and effects, against unreasonable searches and seizures, shall not be violated, and no Warrants shall issue, but upon probable cause, supported by Oath or affirmation, and particularly describing the place to be searched, and the persons or things to be seized.

---

[3] All of the Amendments except the 13th, 14th, 15th, and 16th, were not specifically assigned a number in the resolution proposing the Amendment. Brackets enclose the number for such Amendments. The 13th, 14th, 15th, and 16th Amendments were ratified by number and thus no brackets enclose such Amendment numbers.

[4] The first ten amendments to the Constitution of the United States were proposed to the legislatures of the several States by the First Congress, on the 25th of September 1789. They were ratified by the following States, and the notifications of ratification by the governors thereof were successively communicated by the President to Congress: New Jersey, November 20, 1789; Maryland, December 19, 1789; North Carolina, December 22, 1789; South Carolina, January 19, 1790; New Hampshire, January 25, 1790; Delaware, January 28, 1790; Pennsylvania, March 10, 1790; New York, March 27, 1790; Rhode Island, June 15, 1790; Vermont, November 3, 1791, and Virginia, December 15, 1791. The legislatures of Connecticut, Georgia, and Massachusetts ratified them on April 19, 1939, March 24, 1939, and March 2, 1939, respectively.

Note: other amendments have also been ratified by states after the amendment has been announced as ratified; these other, after-the-fact ratifications are not usually noted in this appendix.

Amendment [V] [1791]

No person shall be held to answer for a capital, or otherwise infamous crime, unless on a presentment or indictment of a Grand Jury, except in cases arising in the land or naval forces, or in the Militia, when in actual service in time of War or public danger; nor shall any person be subject for the same offence to be twice put in jeopardy of life or limb; nor shall be compelled in any criminal case to be a witness against himself, nor be deprived of life, liberty, or property, without due process of law; nor shall private property be taken for public use, without just compensation.

Amendment [VI] [1791]

In all criminal prosecutions, the accused shall enjoy the right to a speedy and public trial, by an impartial jury of the State and district wherein the crime shall have been committed, which district shall have been previously ascertained by law, and to be informed of the nature and cause of the accusation; to be confronted with the witnesses against him; to have compulsory process for obtaining witnesses in his favor, and to have the Assistance of Counsel for his defence.

Amendment [VII] [1791]

In Suits at common law, where the value in controversy shall exceed twenty dollars, the right of trial by jury shall be preserved, and no fact tried by jury, shall be otherwise re-examined in any Court of the United States, than according to the rules of the common law.

Amendment [VIII] [1791]

Excessive bail shall not be required, nor excessive fines imposed, nor cruel and unusual punishments inflicted.

Amendment [IX] [1791]

The enumeration in the Constitution, of certain rights, shall not be construed to deny or disparage others retained by the people.

Amendment [X] [1791]

The powers not delegated to the United States by the Constitution, nor prohibited by it to the States, are reserved to the States respectively, or to the people.

Amendment [XI] [1798]

The Judicial power of the United States shall not be construed to extend to any suit in law or equity, commenced or prosecuted against one of the United States by Citizens of another State, or by Citizens or Subjects of any Foreign State.

Historical Note

This amendment was proposed to the legislatures of the several States by the Third Congress, on the 5th September, 1794, and was declared in a message from the President to Congress, dated the 8th of January, 1798, to have been ratified by the legislatures of three-fourths of the States.

Amendment [XII] [1804]

The Electors shall meet in their respective states and vote by ballot for President and Vice–President, one of whom, at least, shall not be an inhabitant of the same state with themselves; they shall name in their ballots the person voted for as President, and in distinct ballots the person voted for as Vice–President, and they shall make distinct lists of all persons voted for as President, and of all persons voted for as Vice–President, and of the number of votes for each, which lists they shall sign and certify, and transmit sealed to the seat of the government of the United States, directed to the President of the Senate;—The President of the Senate shall, in the presence of the Senate and House of Representatives, open all the certificates and the votes shall then be counted;—The person having the greatest number of votes for President, shall be the President, if such number be a majority of the whole number of Electors appointed; and if no person have such majority, then from the persons having

the highest numbers not exceeding three on the list of those voted for as President, the House of Representatives shall choose immediately, by ballot, the President. But in choosing the President, the votes shall be taken by states, the representation from each state having one vote; a quorum for this purpose shall consist of a member or members from two-thirds of the states, and a majority of all the states shall be necessary to a choice. And if the House of Representatives shall not choose a President whenever the right of choice shall devolve upon them before the fourth day of March next following, then the Vice–President shall act as President, as in the case of the death or other constitutional disability of the President.—The person having the greatest number of votes as Vice–President, shall be the Vice–President, if such number be a majority of the whole number of Electors appointed, and if no person have a majority, then from the two highest numbers on the list, the Senate shall choose the Vice–President; a quorum for the purpose shall consist of two-thirds of the whole number of Senators, and a majority of the whole number shall be necessary to a choice. But no person constitutionally ineligible to the office of President shall be eligible to that of Vice–President of the United States.

Historical Note

This amendment was proposed to the legislatures of the several States by the Eighth Congress, on the 12th of December, 1803, in lieu of the original third paragraph of the first section of the second article, and was declared in a proclamation of the Secretary of State, dated the 25th of September, 1804, to have been ratified by the legislatures of three-fourths of the States.

Amendment XIII [1865]

Section 1. Neither slavery nor involuntary servitude, except as a punishment for crime whereof the party shall have been duly convicted, shall exist within the United States, or any place subject to their jurisdiction.

Section 2. Congress shall have power to enforce this article by appropriate legislation.

Historical Note

This amendment was proposed to the legislatures of the several States by the Thirty-eighth Congress, on the 1st of February, 1865, and was declared, in a proclamation of the Secretary of State, dated the 18th of December, 1865, to have been ratified by the legislatures of twenty-seven of the thirty-six States, viz: Illinois, Rhode Island, Michigan, Maryland, New York, West Virginia, Maine, Kansas, Massachusetts, Pennsylvania, Virginia, Ohio, Missouri, Nevada, Indiana, Louisiana, Minnesota, Wisconsin, Vermont, Tennessee, Arkansas, Connecticut, New Hampshire, South Carolina, Alabama, North Carolina, and Georgia.

Amendment XIV [1868]

Section 1. All persons born or naturalized in the United States, and subject to the jurisdiction thereof, are citizens of the United States and of the State wherein they reside. No State shall make or enforce any law which shall abridge the privileges or immunities of citizens of the United States; nor shall any State deprive any person of life, liberty, or property, without due process of law; nor deny to any person within its jurisdiction the equal protection of the laws.

Section 2. Representatives shall be apportioned among the several States according to their respective numbers, counting the whole number of persons in each State, excluding Indians not taxed. But when the right to vote at any election for the choice of electors for President and Vice President of the United States, Representatives in Congress, the Executive and Judicial officers of a State, or the members of the Legislature thereof, is denied to any of the male inhabitants of such State, being twenty-one years of age, and citizens of the United States, or in any way abridged, except for participation in rebellion, or other crime, the basis of representation therein shall be reduced in the proportion which the number of such male citizens shall bear to the whole number of male citizens twenty-one years of age in such State.

Section 3. No person shall be a Senator or Representative in Congress, or elector of President and Vice President, or hold any office, civil or military, under the United States, or under any State, who having previously taken an oath, as a member of Congress, or as an officer of the United States, or as a member of any State legislature, or as an executive or judicial officer of any State, to support the Constitution of the United States, shall have engaged in insurrection or rebellion against the same, or given aid or comfort to the enemies thereof. But Congress may by a vote of two-thirds of each House, remove such disability.

Section 4. The validity of the public debt of the United States, authorized by law, including debts incurred for payment of pensions and bounties for services in suppressing insurrection or rebellion, shall not be questioned. But neither the United States nor any State shall assume or pay any debt or obligation incurred in aid of insurrection or rebellion against the United States, or any claim for the loss or emancipation of any slave; but all such debts, obligations and claims shall be held illegal and void.

Section 5. The Congress shall have power to enforce, by appropriate legislation, the provisions of this article.

Historical Note

This amendment was proposed to the legislatures of the several States by the Thirty-ninth Congress, on the 16th of June, 1866. On the 21st of July, 1868, Congress adopted and transmitted to the Department of State a concurrent resolution, declaring that "the legislatures of the States of Connecticut, Tennessee, New Jersey, Oregon, Vermont, New York, Ohio, Illinois, West Virginia, Kansas, Maine, Nevada, Missouri, Indiana, Minnesota, New Hampshire, Massachusetts, Nebraska, Iowa, Arkansas, Florida, North Carolina, Alabama, South Carolina, and Louisiana, being three-fourths and more of the several States of the Union, have ratified the fourteenth article of amendment to the Constitution of the United States, duly proposed by two-thirds of each House of the Thirty-ninth Congress: Therefore, Resolved, That said fourteenth article is hereby declared to be a part of the Constitution of the United States, and it shall be duly promulgated as such by the Secretary of State." The Secretary of State accordingly issued a proclamation, dated the 28th of July, 1868, declaring that the proposed fourteenth amendment had been ratified, in the manner hereafter mentioned by the legislatures of thirty of the thirty-six States, viz: Connecticut, June 30, 1866; New Hampshire, July 7, 1866; Tennessee, July 19, 1866; New Jersey, September 11, 1866, (and the legislature of the same State passed a resolution in April, 1868, to withdraw its consent to it); Oregon, September 19, 1866; Vermont, November 9, 1866; Georgia rejected it November 13, 1866, and ratified it July 21, 1868; North Carolina rejected it December 4, 1866, and ratified it July 4, 1868; South Carolina rejected it December 20, 1866, and ratified it July 9, 1868; New York ratified it January 10, 1867; Ohio ratified it January 11, 1867, (and the legislature of the same State passed a resolution in January, 1868, to withdraw its consent to it); Illinois ratified it January 15, 1867; West Virginia, January 16, 1867; Kansas, January 18, 1867; Maine, January 19, 1867; Nevada, January 22, 1867; Missouri, January 26, 1867; Indiana, January 29, 1867; Minnesota, February 1, 1867; Rhode Island, February 7, 1867; Wisconsin, February 13, 1867; Pennsylvania, February 13, 1867; Michigan, February 15, 1867; Massachusetts, March 20, 1867; Nebraska, June 15, 1867; Iowa, April 3, 1868; Arkansas, April 6, 1868; Florida, June 9, 1868; Louisiana, July 9, 1868; and Alabama, July 13, 1868. Georgia again ratified the amendment February 2, 1870. Texas rejected it November 1, 1866, and ratified it February 18, 1870. Virginia rejected it January 19, 1867, and ratified October 8, 1869. The amendment was rejected by Kentucky January 10, 1867; by Delaware February 8, 1867; by Maryland March 23, 1867.

Amendment XV [1870]

Section 1. The right of citizens of the United States to vote shall not be denied or abridged by the United States or by any State on account of race, color, or previous condition of servitude.

Section 2. The Congress shall have power to enforce this article by appropriate legislation.

Historical Note

This amendment was proposed to the legislatures of the several States by the Fortieth Congress, on the 27th of February, 1869, and was declared, in a proclamation of the Secretary of State, dated March 30, 1870, to have been ratified by the legislatures of twenty-nine of the thirty-seven States. The dates of these ratifications (arranged in the order of their reception at the Department of State) were: from North Carolina, March 5, 1869; West Virginia, March 3, 1869; Massachusetts, March 12, 1869; Wisconsin, March 9, 1869; Maine, March 12, 1869; Louisiana, March 5, 1869; Michigan, March 8, 1869; South Carolina, March 16, 1869; Pennsylvania, March 26, 1869; Arkansas, March 30, 1869; Connecticut, May 19, 1869; Florida, June 15, 1869; Illinois, March 5, 1869; Indiana, May 14, 1869; New York, April 14, 1869, (and the legislature of the same State passed a resolution January 5, 1870, to withdraw its consent to it); New Hampshire, July 7, 1869; Nevada, March 1, 1869; Vermont, October 21, 1869; Virginia, October 8, 1869; Missouri, January 10, 1870; Mississippi, January 17, 1870; Ohio, January 27, 1870; Iowa, February 3, 1870; Kansas, January 19, 1870; Minnesota, February 19, 1870; Rhode Island, January 18, 1870; Nebraska, February 17, 1870; Texas, February 18, 1870. The State of Georgia also ratified the amendment February 2, 1870.

Amendment XVI [1913]

The Congress shall have power to lay and collect taxes on incomes, from whatever source derived, without apportionment among the several States, and without regard to any census or enumeration.

Historical Note

This Amendment was proposed to the legislatures of the several states by the Sixty–First Congress, on the 31st of July, 1909, and was declared, in a proclamation by the Secretary of State, dated the 25th of February, 1913, to have been ratified by the legislatures of the states of Alabama, Kentucky, South Carolina, Illinois, Mississippi, Oklahoma, Maryland, Georgia, Texas, Ohio, Idaho, Oregon, Washington, California, Montana, Indiana, Nevada, North Carolina, Nebraska, Kansas, Colorado, North Dakota, Michigan, Iowa, Missouri, Maine, Tennessee, Arkansas, Wisconsin, New York, South Dakota, Arizona, Minnesota, Louisiana, Delaware, and Wyoming, in all, thirty-six. The legislatures of New Jersey and New Mexico also passed resolutions ratifying the said proposed amendment.

Amendment [XVII] [1913]

[1]   The Senate of the United States shall be composed of two Senators from each State, elected by the people thereof, for six years; and each Senator shall have one vote. The electors in each State shall have the qualifications requisite for electors of the most numerous branch of the State legislatures.

[2]   When vacancies happen in the representation of any State in the Senate, the executive authority of such State shall issue writs of election to fill such vacancies: *Provided, that the legislature of any State may empower the executive thereof to make temporary appointments until the people fill the vacancies by election as the legislature may direct.*

[3]   This amendment shall not be so construed as to affect the election or term of any Senator chosen before it becomes valid as part of the Constitution.

Historical Note

This amendment was proposed to the legislatures of the several states by the Sixty–Second Congress, on the 16th of May, 1912, in lieu of the original first paragraph of section 3 of article I, and in lieu of so much of paragraph 2 of the same section as related to the filling of vacancies, and was declared, in a proclamation by the Secretary of State, dated the 31st of May, 1913, to have been ratified by the legislatures of the

states of Massachusetts, Arizona, Minnesota, New York, Kansas, Oregon, North Carolina, California, Michigan, Idaho, West Virginia, Nebraska, Iowa, Montana, Texas, Washington, Wyoming, Colorado, Illinois, North Dakota, Nevada, Vermont, Maine, New Hampshire, Oklahoma, Ohio, South Dakota, Indiana, Missouri, New Mexico, New Jersey, Tennessee, Arkansas, Connecticut, Pennsylvania, and Wisconsin, said states constituting three-fourths of the whole number of states.

Amendment [XVIII] [1919]

Section 1. After one year from the ratification of this article the manufacture, sale, or transportation of intoxicating liquors within, the importation thereof into, or the exportation thereof from the United States and all territory subject to the jurisdiction thereof for beverage purposes is hereby prohibited.

Section 2. The Congress and the several States shall have concurrent power to enforce this article by appropriate legislation.

Section 3. This article shall be inoperative unless it shall have been ratified as an amendment to the Constitution by the legislatures of the several States, as provided in the Constitution, within seven years from the date of the submission hereof to the States by the Congress.

Historical Note

This amendment was proposed to the legislatures of the several states by the Sixty–Fifth Congress, on the 19th day of December, 1917, and was declared, in a proclamation by the Acting Secretary of State, dated on the 29th day of January, 1919, to have been ratified by the legislatures of the states of Alabama, Arizona, California, Colorado, Delaware, Florida, Georgia, Idaho, Illinois, Indiana, Kansas, Kentucky, Louisiana, Maine, Maryland, Massachusetts, Michigan, Minnesota, Mississippi, Montana, Nebraska, New Hampshire, North Carolina, North Dakota, Ohio, Oklahoma, Oregon, South Dakota, South Carolina, Texas, Utah, Virginia, Washington, West Virginia, Wisconsin, and Wyoming.

Amendment [XIX] [1920]

[1]   The right of citizens of the United States to vote shall not be denied or abridged by the United States or by any State on account of sex.

[2]   Congress shall have power to enforce this article by appropriate legislation.

Historical Note

This amendment was proposed to the legislatures of the several states by the Sixty–Sixth Congress, on the 5th day of June, 1919, and was declared, in a proclamation by the Secretary of State, dated on the 26th day of August, 1920, to have been ratified by the legislatures of the states of Arizona, Arkansas, California, Colorado, Idaho, Illinois, Indiana, Iowa, Kansas, Kentucky, Maine, Massachusetts, Michigan, Minnesota, Missouri, Montana, Nebraska, Nevada, New Hampshire, New Jersey, New Mexico, North Dakota, New York, Ohio, Oklahoma, Oregon, Pennsylvania, Rhode Island, South Dakota, Tennessee, Texas, Utah, Washington, West Virginia, Wisconsin and Wyoming.

Amendment [XX] [1933]

Section 1. The terms of the President and Vice President shall end at noon on the 20th day of January, and the terms of Senators and Representatives at noon on the 3d day of January, of the years in which such terms would have ended if this article had not been ratified; and the terms of their successors shall then begin.

Section 2. The Congress shall assemble at least once in every year, and such meeting shall begin at noon on the 3d day of January, unless they shall by law appoint a different day.

Section 3. If, at the time fixed for the beginning of the term of the President, the President elect shall have died, the Vice President elect shall become President. If the President shall not have been chosen before the time fixed for the beginning of his term, or if the President elect shall have failed to qualify, then the Vice President elect shall act as President until a President shall have qualified; and the Congress may by law provide for the case wherein neither a President elect nor a Vice President elect shall have qualified, declaring who shall then act as President, or the manner in which one who is to act shall be selected, and such person shall act accordingly until a President or Vice President shall have qualified.

Section 4. The Congress may by law provide for the case of the death of any of the persons from whom the House of Representatives may choose a President whenever the right of choice shall have devolved upon them, and for the case of the death of any of the persons from whom the Senate may choose a Vice President whenever the right of choice shall have devolved upon them.

Section 5. Sections 1 and 2 shall take effect on the 15th day of October following the ratification of this article.

Section 6. This article shall be inoperative unless it shall have been ratified as an amendment to the Constitution by the legislatures of three-fourths of the several States within seven years from the date of its submission.

Historical Note

This amendment was proposed to the legislatures of the several states by the Seventy–Second Congress, on March 3, 1932, and was declared, in a proclamation by the Secretary of State, dated Feb. 6, 1933, to have been ratified by the legislatures of the states of Alabama, Arizona, Arkansas, California, Colorado, Connecticut, Delaware, Georgia, Idaho, Illinois, Indiana, Kansas, Kentucky, Louisiana, Maine, Massachusetts, Michigan, Minnesota, Mississippi, Missouri, Montana, Nebraska, New Jersey, New York, North Carolina, North Dakota, Ohio, Oklahoma, Pennsylvania, Rhode Island, South Carolina, South Dakota, Texas, Utah, Virginia, Washington, West Virginia, Wisconsin, and Wyoming.

Amendment [XXI] [1933]

Section 1. The eighteenth article of amendment to the Constitution of the United States is hereby repealed.

Section 2. The transportation or importation into any State, Territory, or possession of the United States for delivery or use therein of intoxicating liquors, in violation of the laws thereof, is hereby prohibited.

Section 3. This article shall be inoperative unless it shall have been ratified as an amendment to the Constitution by conventions in the several States, as provided in the Constitution, within seven years from the date of the submission hereof to the States by the Congress.

Historical Note

This amendment was proposed to the several states by the Seventy–Second Congress, on Feb. 20, 1933, and was declared, in a proclamation by the Secretary of State, dated Dec. 5, 1933, to have been ratified by conventions in the States of Arizona, Alabama, Arkansas, California, Colorado, Connecticut, Delaware, Florida, Idaho, Illinois, Indiana, Iowa, Kentucky, Maryland, Massachusetts, Michigan, Minnesota, Missouri, Nevada, New Hampshire, New Jersey, New Mexico, New York, Ohio, Oregon, Pennsylvania, Rhode Island, Tennessee, Texas, Utah, Vermont, Virginia, Washington, West Virginia, Wisconsin and Wyoming.

Amendment [XXII] [1951]

Section 1. No person shall be elected to the office of the President more than twice, and no person who has held the office of President, or acted as President, for more than two years of a term to which

some other person was elected President shall be elected to the office of President more than once. But this Article shall not apply to any person holding the office of President when this Article was proposed by the Congress, and shall not prevent any person who may be holding the office of President, or acting as President, during the term within which this Article becomes operative from holding the office of President or acting as President during the remainder of such term.

Section 2. This article shall be inoperative unless it shall have been ratified as an amendment to the Constitution by the legislatures of three-fourths of the several States within seven years from the date of its submission to the States by the Congress.

Historical Note

Proposal and Ratification. This amendment was proposed to the legislatures of the several States by the Eightieth Congress on Mar. 24, 1947 by House Joint Res. No. 27, and was declared by the Administrator of General Services on Mar. 1, 1951, to have been ratified. The legislatures ratified this Amendment on the following dates: Maine, Mar. 31, 1947; Michigan, Mar. 31, 1947; Iowa, Apr. 1, 1947; Kansas, Apr. 1, 1947; New Hampshire, Apr. 1, 1947; Delaware, Apr. 2, 1947; Illinois, Apr. 3, 1947; Oregon, Apr. 3, 1947; Colorado, Apr. 12, 1947; California, Apr. 15, 1947; New Jersey, Apr. 15, 1947; Vermont, Apr. 15, 1947; Ohio, Apr. 16, 1947; Wisconsin, Apr. 16, 1947; Pennsylvania, Apr. 29, 1947; Connecticut, May 21, 1947; Missouri, May 22, 1947; Nebraska, May 23, 1947; Virginia, Jan. 28, 1948; Mississippi, Feb. 12, 1948; New York, Mar. 9, 1948; South Dakota, Jan. 21, 1949; North Dakota, Feb. 25, 1949; Louisiana, May 17, 1950; Montana, Jan. 25, 1951; Indiana, Jan. 29, 1951; Idaho, Jan. 30, 1951; New Mexico, Feb. 12, 1951; Wyoming, Feb. 12, 1951; Arkansas, Feb. 15, 1951; Georgia, Feb. 17, 1951; Tennessee, Feb. 20, 1951; Texas, Feb. 22, 1951; Utah, Feb. 26, 1951; Nevada, Feb. 26, 1951; Minnesota, Feb. 27, 1951, and North Carolina, Feb. 28, 1951.

Subsequent to the proclamation, Amendment XXII was ratified by South Carolina on Mar. 13, 1951; Maryland, Mar. 14, 1951; Florida, Apr. 16, 1951, and Alabama, May 4, 1951.

Certification of Validity. Publication of the certifying statement of the Administrator of General Services that the Amendment had become valid was made on Mar. 1, 1951, F.R.Doc. 51–2940, 16 F.R. 2019.

Amendment [XXIII] [1961]

Section 1. The District constituting the seat of Government of the United States shall appoint in such manner as the Congress may direct:

A number of electors of President and Vice President equal to the whole number of Senators and Representatives in Congress to which the District would be entitled if it were a State, but in no event more than the least populous state; they shall be in addition to those appointed by the states, but they shall be considered, for the purposes of the election of President and Vice President, to be electors appointed by a state; and they shall meet in the District and perform such duties as provided by the twelfth article of amendment.

Section 2. The Congress shall have power to enforce this article by appropriate legislation.

Historical Note

Proposal and Ratification. This amendment was proposed by the Eighty-sixth Congress on June 16, 1960 and was declared by the Administrator of General Services on Apr. 3, 1961, to have been ratified.

The amendment was ratified by the following States: Hawaii, June 23, 1960; Massachusetts, Aug. 22, 1960; New Jersey, Dec. 19, 1960; New York, Jan. 17, 1961; California, Jan. 19, 1961; Oregon, Jan. 27, 1961; Maryland, Jan. 30, 1961; Idaho, Jan. 31, 1961; Maine, Jan. 31, 1961; Minnesota, Jan. 31, 1961; New Mexico, Feb. 1, 1961; Nevada, Feb. 2, 1961; Montana, Feb. 6, 1961; Colorado, Feb. 8, 1961; Washington, Feb. 9, 1961;

West Virginia, Feb. 9, 1961; Alaska, Feb. 10, 1961; Wyoming, Feb. 13, 1961; South Dakota, Feb. 14, 1961; Delaware, Feb. 20, 1961; Utah, Feb. 21, 1961; Wisconsin, Feb. 21, 1961; Pennsylvania, Feb. 28, 1961; Indiana, Mar. 3, 1961; North Dakota, Mar. 3, 1961; Tennessee, Mar. 6, 1961; Michigan, Mar. 8, 1961; Connecticut, Mar. 9, 1961; Arizona, Mar. 10, 1961; Illinois, Mar. 14, 1961; Nebraska, Mar. 15, 1961; Vermont, Mar. 15, 1961; Iowa, Mar. 16, 1961; Missouri, Mar. 20, 1961; Oklahoma, Mar. 21, 1961; Rhode Island, Mar. 22, 1961; Kansas, Mar. 29, 1961; Ohio, Mar. 29, 1961, and New Hampshire, Mar. 30, 1961.

Certification of Validity. Publication of the certifying statement of the Administrator of General Services that the Amendment had become valid was made on Apr. 3, 1961, F.R.Doc. 61–3017, 26 F.R. 2808.

Amendment [XXIV] [1964]

Section 1. The right of citizens of the United States to vote in any primary or other election for President or Vice President, for electors for President or Vice President, or for Senator or Representative in Congress, shall not be denied or abridged by the United States or any State by reason of failure to pay any poll tax or other tax.

Section 2. The Congress shall have power to enforce this article by appropriate legislation.

Historical Note

Proposal and Ratification. This amendment was proposed by the Eighty-seventh Congress by Senate Joint Resolution No. 29, which was approved by the Senate on Mar. 27, 1962, and by the House of Representatives on Aug. 27, 1962. It was declared by the Administrator of General Services on Feb. 4, 1964, to have been ratified.

This amendment was ratified by the following States: Illinois, Nov. 14, 1962; New Jersey, Dec. 3, 1962; Oregon, Jan. 25, 1963; Montana, Jan. 28, 1963; West Virginia, Feb. 1, 1963; New York, Feb. 4, 1963; Maryland, Feb. 6, 1963; California, Feb. 7, 1963; Alaska, Feb. 11, 1963; Rhode Island, Feb. 14, 1963; Indiana, Feb. 19, 1963; Utah, Feb. 20, 1963; Michigan, Feb. 20, 1963; Colorado, Feb. 21, 1963; Ohio, Feb. 27, 1963; Minnesota, Feb. 27, 1963; New Mexico, Mar. 5, 1963; Hawaii, Mar. 6, 1963; North Dakota, Mar. 7, 1963; Idaho, Mar. 8, 1963; Washington, Mar. 14, 1963; Vermont, Mar. 15, 1963; Nevada, Mar. 19, 1963; Connecticut, Mar. 20, 1963; Tennessee, Mar. 21, 1963; Pennsylvania, Mar. 25, 1963; Wisconsin, Mar. 26, 1963; Kansas, Mar. 28, 1963; Massachusetts, Mar. 28, 1963; Nebraska, Apr. 4, 1963; Florida, Apr. 18, 1963; Iowa, Apr. 24, 1963; Delaware, May 1, 1963; Missouri, May 13, 1963; New Hampshire, June 12, 1963; Kentucky, June 27, 1963; Maine, Jan. 16, 1964; South Dakota, Jan. 23, 1964.

Certification of Validity. Publication of the certifying statement of the Administrator of General Services that the Amendment had become valid was made on Feb. 5, 1964, F.R.Doc. 64–1229, 29 F.R. 1715. President Johnson and the Administrator signed this certificate on Feb. 4, 1964.

Amendment [XXV] [1967]

Section 1. In the case of the removal of the President from office or of his death or resignation, the Vice President shall become President.

Section 2. Whenever there is a vacancy in the office of the Vice President, the President shall nominate a Vice President who shall take office upon confirmation by a majority vote of both Houses of Congress.

Section 3. Whenever the President transmits to the President pro tempore of the Senate and the Speaker of the House of Representatives his written declaration that he is unable to discharge the powers and duties of his office, and until he transmits to them a written declaration to the contrary, such powers and duties shall be discharged by the Vice President as Acting President.

Section 4. Whenever the Vice President and a majority of either the principal officers of the executive departments or of such other body as Congress may by law provide, transmit to the President

pro tempore of the Senate and the Speaker of the House of Representatives, their written declaration that the President is unable to discharge the powers and duties of his office, the Vice President shall immediately assume the powers and duties of the office as Acting President.

Thereafter, when the President transmits to the President pro tempore of the Senate and the Speaker of the House of Representatives his written declaration that no inability exists, he shall resume the powers and duties of his office unless the Vice President and a majority of either the principal officers of the executive department or of such other body as Congress may by law provide, transmit within four days to the President pro tempore of the Senate and the Speaker of the House of Representatives their written declaration that the President is unable to discharge the powers and duties of his office. Thereupon Congress shall decide the issue, assembling within forty-eight hours for that purpose if not in session. If the Congress, within twenty-one days after receipt of the latter written declaration, or, if Congress is not in session, within twenty-one days after Congress is required to assemble, determines by two-thirds vote of both Houses that the President is unable to discharge the powers and duties of his office, the Vice President shall continue to discharge the same as Acting President; otherwise, the President shall resume the powers and duties of his office.

Historical Note

Proposal and Ratification. This amendment was proposed by the Eighty-ninth Congress by Senate Joint Resolution No. 1, which was approved by the Senate on Feb. 19, 1965, and by the House of Representatives, in amended form, on Apr. 13, 1965. The House of Representatives agreed to a Conference Report on June 30, 1965, and the Senate agreed to the Conference Report on July 6, 1965. It was declared by the Administrator of General Services, on Feb. 23, 1967, to have been ratified.

This amendment was ratified by the following States: Nebraska, July 12, 1965; Wisconsin, July 13, 1965; Oklahoma, July 16, 1965; Massachusetts, Aug. 9, 1965; Pennsylvania, Aug. 18, 1965; Kentucky, Sept. 15, 1965; Arizona, Sept. 22, 1965; Michigan, Oct. 5, 1965; Indiana, Oct. 20, 1965; California, Oct. 21, 1965; Arkansas, Nov. 4, 1965; New Jersey, Nov. 29, 1965; Delaware, Dec. 7, 1965; Utah, Jan. 17, 1966; West Virginia, Jan. 20, 1966; Maine, Jan. 24, 1966; Rhode Island, Jan. 28, 1966; Colorado, Feb. 3, 1966; New Mexico, Feb. 3, 1966; Kansas, Feb. 8, 1966; Vermont, Feb. 10, 1966; Alaska, Feb. 18, 1966; Idaho, Mar. 2, 1966; Hawaii, Mar. 3, 1966; Virginia, Mar. 8, 1966; Mississippi, Mar. 10, 1966; New York, Mar. 14, 1966; Maryland, Mar. 23, 1966; Missouri, Mar. 30, 1966; New Hampshire, June 13, 1966; Louisiana, July 5, 1966; Tennessee, Jan. 12, 1967; Wyoming, Jan. 25, 1967; Washington, Jan. 26, 1967; Iowa, Jan. 26, 1967; Oregon, Feb. 2, 1967; Minnesota, Feb. 10, 1967; Nevada, Feb. 10, 1967; Connecticut, Feb. 14, 1967; Montana, Feb. 15, 1967; South Dakota, Mar. 6, 1967; Ohio, Mar. 7, 1967; Alabama, Mar. 14, 1967; North Carolina, Mar. 22, 1967; Illinois, Mar. 22, 1967; Texas, Apr. 25, 1967; Florida, May 25, 1967.

Certification of Validity. Publication of the certifying statement of the Administrator of General Services that the Amendment had become valid was made on Feb. 25, 1967, F.R.Doc. 67–2208, 32 F.R. 3287, and signed on July 23, 1967.

Amendment [XXVI] [1971]

Section 1. The right of citizens of the United States, who are eighteen years of age or older, to vote shall not be denied or abridged by the United States or by any State on account of age.

Section 2. The Congress shall have power to enforce this article by appropriate legislation.

Historical Note

Proposal and Ratification. This amendment was proposed by the Ninety-second Congress by Senate Joint Resolution No. 7, which was approved by the Senate on Mar. 10, 1971, and by the House of Representatives on Mar. 23, 1971. It was declared by the Administrator of General Services on July 5, 1971, to have been ratified.

This amendment was ratified by the following States: Connecticut, Mar. 23, 1971; Delaware, Mar. 23, 1971; Minnesota, Mar. 23, 1971; Tennessee, Mar. 23, 1971; Washington, Mar. 23, 1971; Hawaii, Mar. 24, 1971; Massachusetts, Mar. 24, 1971; Idaho, Mar. 30, 1971; Montana, Mar. 31, 1971; Arkansas, Apr. 1, 1971; Iowa, Apr. 1, 1971; Nebraska, Apr. 2, 1971; Kansas, Apr. 7, 1971; Michigan, Apr. 7, 1971; Indiana, Apr. 8, 1971; Maine, Apr. 9, 1971; Vermont, Apr. 16, 1971; California, Apr. 19, 1971; South Carolina, Apr. 28, 1971; West Virginia, Apr. 28, 1971; Pennsylvania, May 3, 1971; New Jersey, May 4, 1971; Texas, May 5, 1971; Maryland, May 6, 1971; New Hampshire, May 13, 1971; Arizona, May 17, 1971; Colorado, May 24, 1971; Louisiana, May 27, 1971; Rhode Island, May 27, 1971; New York, June 2, 1971; Oregon, June 5, 1971; Missouri, June 14, 1971; Wisconsin, June 18, 1971; Illinois, June 29, 1971; Alabama, June 30, 1971; Ohio, June 30, 1971; North Carolina, July 1, 1971; Oklahoma, July 1, 1971.

Certification of Validity. Publication of the certifying statement of the Administrator of General Services that the Amendment had become valid was made on July 7, 1971, F.R.Doc. 71–9691, 36 F.R. 12725, and signed on July 5, 1971.

Amendment [XXVII] [1992]

No law, varying the compensation for the services of the Senators and Representatives, shall take effect, until an election of Representatives shall have intervened.

Historical Note

Proposal and Ratification. This amendment was one of twelve that the first Congress proposed on September 25, 1789. Ten of these twelve became the first ten amendments, often called the Bill of Rights. A sufficient number of states did not ratify until 203 years later.

This amendment was ratified by the following States: Maryland, Dec. 19, 1789; North Carolina, Dec. 22, 1789; South Carolina, Jan. 19, 1790; Delaware, Jan. 28, 1790; Vermont, Nov. 3, 1791; Virginia, Dec. 15, 1791; Ohio, May 6, 1873; Wyoming, Mar. 3, 1978; Maine, Apr. 2, 1983; Colorado, Apr. 18, 1984; South Dakota, Feb. 21, 1985; New Hampshire, Mar. 7, 1985; Arizona, Apr. 3, 1985; Tennessee, May 23, 1985; Oklahoma, July 10, 1985; New Mexico, Feb. 14, 1986; Indiana, Feb. 24, 1986; Utah, Feb. 26, 1986; Arkansas, Mar. 5, 1987; Montana, Mar. 17, 1987; Connecticut, May 13, 1987; Wisconsin, June 30, 1987; Georgia, Feb. 2, 1988; West Virginia, Mar. 10, 1988; Louisiana, July 6, 1988; Iowa, Feb. 7, 1989; Idaho, Mar. 23, 1989; Nevada, Apr. 26, 1989; Alaska, May 5, 1989; Oregon, May 19, 1989; Minnesota, May 22, 1989; Texas, May 25, 1989; Kansas, Apr. 4, 1990; Florida, May 31, 1990; North Dakota, Mar. 25, 1991; Missouri, May 5, 1992; Alabama, May 5, 1992; Michigan, May 7, 1992; New Jersey, May 7, 1992; Illinois, May 12, 1992.

Certification of Validity. On May 13, 1992, the Archivist of the United States announced that he would accept this amendment as valid once he received formal notice pursuant to 1 U.S.C.A. § 106b.